ACCOUNTING INFORMATION SYSTEMS

Seventh Edition

MARSHALL B. ROMNEY
Brigham Young University

PAUL JOHN STEINBART
Saint Louis University

BARRY E. CUSHING
University of Utah

An imprint of Addison Wesley Longman, Inc.

Reading, Massachusetts • Menlo Park, California • New York
Harlow, England • Don Mills, Ontario • Sydney
Mexico City • Madrid • Amsterdam

Executive Editor: *Michael Payne*
Senior Project Manager: *Mary Clare McEwing*
Assistant Editor: *Kate Morgan*
Development Editor: *Janice Jutras*
Production Supervisor: *Patricia A. Oduor*
Production Services: *Barbara Gracia*
Copy Editor: *Joyce Grandy*
Text Designer: *Rebecca Lemna*
Cover Designer: *Eileen R. Hoff*
Marketing Manager: *Mark Childs*
Manufacturing Supervisor: *Hugh Crawford*

Library of Congress Cataloging-in-Publication Data
Romney, Marshall B.
Accounting information systems.—7th ed. / Marshall B. Romney
Paul J. Steinbart, Barry E. Cushing.
p. cm.
Rev. ed. of: Accounting information systems / Barry E. Cushing.
6th ed. c1994.
Includes bibliographical references and index.
ISBN 0-201-80972-9
1. Accounting—Data processing. 2. Information storage and retrieval systems—Accounting. I. Steinbart, Paul John.
II. Cushing, Barry E. III. Cushing, Barry E. Accounting
HF5679.A34 1996
657'.0285—dc20 96-33701
CIP

Reprinted with corrections January, 1997

5 6 7 8 9 10-MA-00 99 98

To
Our Wives and Families
for
Their Support and Encouragement

Preface

The seventh edition of *Accounting Information Systems* has been revised extensively to provide students with the knowledge and skills they need to pursue successful careers in accounting. The text reflects how information technology (IT) is altering the nature of accounting. Specifically, we discuss how such developments as the Internet, EDI, data bases, and artificial intelligence are fundamentally transforming the way that organizations perform their business activities. We also explain how these IT developments are changing the way that businesses account for the results of those activities.

In addition to technology-driven changes, companies are responding to the increasingly competitive business environment by reexamining every internal activity in an effort to reap the most value at the least cost. As a result, accountants are being asked to do more than just report the results of past activities. As such, they must take a more proactive role in both providing and interpreting financial and nonfinancial information about the organization's activities. Therefore, throughout this text we discuss how accountants can improve the design and functioning of the accounting information system so that it truly adds value to the organization. For example, each cycle chapter uses data modeling to illustrate how accounting information systems can effectively integrate internally generated financial and nonfinancial data about organizational activities with other, externally generated data (e.g., customer credit ratings and satisfaction).

In summary, every chapter in this seventh edition has been rewritten to help students better understand the following key concepts:

- The business activities performed in the five major business cycles
- The collection and processing of data about those business activities
- The use of the latest IT developments to improve the efficiency and effectiveness of business activities
- The development, implementation, and maintenance of accounting information systems (AIS)
- Internal control objectives and the effects of IT on these objectives
- Fundamental concepts of data base technology and its effect on AIS
- The design of an AIS to provide the information needed to make key decisions in each business cycle

MAJOR CHANGES IN THE SEVENTH EDITION

A new co-author, Paul John Steinbart, Ernst & Young Distinguished Professor of Accounting at Saint Louis University, has been added to the seventh edition of this book. Every chapter has been extensively rewritten, and students will find the text easier to read. The whole text has been reexamined with a view to tightening the exposition and presenting every concept in as clear and straightforward a manner as possible. As a result, this edition is leaner and shorter than the previous edition. Many new real-world examples using familiar companies such as Levi Strauss, Harley-Davidson, and JC Penney have been added to each chapter to stimulate student interest. As with previous revisions, numerous changes have been made to reflect recent developments in the practice and teaching of accounting information systems. At the same time, successful features introduced in previous editions, such as the focus boxes, have been retained.

New Features

Two new chapters have been added to the seventh edition. Chapter 2 presents an overview of AIS topics, illustrated in the context of a simple manual system. This coverage is especially useful if the curriculum has been changed so that the AIS course is now the first class accounting majors take after Principles. Chapter 6 discusses data modeling and the design of data base AIS. This chapter illustrates how data base technology (covered in Chapter 5) can be used to design an AIS that more fully meets the information needs of managers.

Nine other chapters have been substantially revised. Chapter 5, which covers data base technology, now includes detailed coverage of how to use query languages to extract financial information from a data base AIS. The material on the systems development process, which was previously spread out over four chapters, has been reorganized into three chapters that group related topics together. Chapter 10 introduces the systems development life cycle and discusses systems analysis and business process reengineering. Chapter 11 covers the remaining steps in the systems development life cycle, assuming that any new programs will be developed in-house. Chapter 12 then discusses alternatives to in-house development of software. The five cycle chapters (17–21) have been completely rewritten to include a discussion of the effects of data bases on the design and functioning of AIS.

The remaining 10 chapters have also been rewritten and updated to reflect current developments in information technology and accounting applications. For example, Chapter 9 on data communication systems has been updated to include coverage of the Internet and the World Wide Web. Numerous real-world examples, featuring both large and small companies in a variety of industries, have been added to each chapter to highlight and reinforce key concepts. In addition, questions have been added to each focus box so that these real-world applications can also be used as in-class discussion cases. Each chapter now also includes a short multiple-choice quiz, with corresponding answers provided at the end of the chapter. Students can use the quiz to test their understanding of the main topics in the chapter.

A fifth comprehensive case has been added to the appendix. As in the previous edition, each case contains a list of requirements that correspond to specific chapters. This organization allows the instructor to tailor the case requirements to his or her choice of course objectives and topical coverage.

Continuing Features

Each chapter begins with an integrative case, based on one of three fictional companies, that introduces the chapter's key concepts and topics. This case is integrated throughout the chapter, and a description of how the issues are resolved is provided in the summary and case conclusion.

We continue to include one to three focus boxes in each chapter. The focus boxes are summaries of articles describing how specific companies are using the latest IT developments to improve their AIS.

Each chapter continues to have at least two end-of-chapter cases. One is a stand-alone case. The other is the AnyCompany case, which provides students with the opportunity to apply their knowledge to the specific problems and challenges faced by a business in their local area. The AnyCompany case also gives students the chance to practice their written and oral communication skills in a realistic setting. The requirements for each AnyCompany case are tailored to the topics covered in each particular chapter. These suggested requirements are too extensive to permit assignment of multiple AnyCompany cases in one semester. Instead, we encourage instructors to select the case(s) with requirements that most closely match their course objectives. Alternatively, instructors can choose selected requirements from several chapters to create a customized term project that reflects the topics they stress in their course.

The end-of-chapter material is designed to help students develop and test their knowledge. It includes both new and revised discussion questions, problems, and cases that integrate material from various parts of the chapter. Many problems were developed from reports in current periodicals and reflect the challenges faced by actual companies. In addition, we continue to include a number of problems selected from the various professional examinations, including the CPA, CMA, CIA, and SMAC exams.

The text contains hundreds of figures, diagrams, flowcharts, tables, and photographs that are new or have been revised specifically for this edition. At the end of the book is an extensive bibliography, organized by chapter. This list contains references to the real-world examples used in each chapter and provides students with a starting point for further research on topics of interest. Finally, the comprehensive glossary at the back of the book has been extensively revised.

AN OVERVIEW OF THE SEVENTH EDITION

The Introductory Chapters

Part One, "Conceptual Foundations of Accounting Information Systems," consists of six chapters that present the underlying concepts fundamental to an understanding of AIS. Chapter 1 introduces basic terminology and discusses how AIS can add value to an organization. Chapter 2 provides an overview of AIS in a manual setting. This information helps students to understand what an accounting information system does; as they read the remainder of the book, they see how advances in information technology affect the manner in which those functions are performed. Chapter 3 covers systems development and documentation techniques, focusing primarily on data flow diagrams and flowcharts. Chapter 4 discusses transaction processing in automated systems, presenting basic information processing and data storage concepts. Chapter 5 introduces students to data bases, with a particular emphasis on the relational data model and query languages. Chapter 6 is new, covering data modeling and demonstrating how traditional financial statements and managerial reports can be derived from a data base AIS.

Information Technology

The objective of Part Two, "The Technology of Accounting Information Systems," is to provide students with the knowledge they need to understand and appreciate how changes in IT affect the design and operation of AIS. The three chapters in this section focus on the technology used to design and operate computer-based AIS. Chapter 7 reviews hardware and software. Chapter 8 covers personal computers from an end-user focus. Chapter 9 discusses the role of telecommunications in AIS. All of these chapters reflect the latest developments in IT. The multitude of real-world examples in this section will help students see how IT affects the design and operation of an AIS.

The Systems Development Process

The material in Part Three, "The Systems Development Process," has been reorganized into three chapters. Chapter 10 introduces the systems development life cycle and discusses the introductory steps of this process (feasibility analysis and planning, systems analysis, and business process reengineering). Particular emphasis is placed on the behavioral ramifications of change. Chapter 11 covers the remaining stages of the systems development life cycle (design, implementation, and operation) and emphasizes the interrelationships among each phase. Chapter 12 discusses alternative approaches (e.g., prototyping, outsourcing, and purchasing software) to developing new AIS. Many new real-world examples are included in all three of these chapters to enable students to understand the accountant's role in the systems development process.

Control and Audit of Accounting Information Systems

Part Four, "Control and Audit of Accounting Information Systems," consists of four chapters. Chapter 13 provides a conceptual overview of controls and control theory. The material has been rewritten to reflect the terminology used in the COSO report. Chapter 14 discusses specific computer controls. Chapter 15 focuses on fraud, explaining how and why fraud occurs and the methods for preventing and detecting it. Chapter 16 reviews principles and techniques for audit evaluation of internal control in computer-based AIS and introduces the topic of computer-assisted auditing.

Accounting Information Systems Applications

Part Five, "Accounting Information Systems Applications," consists of five chapters that integrate the material presented in the first four parts of the book. Each of the five chapters focuses on one business cycle. Some material previously presented in separate chapters in the sixth edition has been consolidated in one chapter so that students can more clearly see the interrelationships between various business activities. Chapter 17 covers the revenue cycle, including sales, billing, accounts receivable, and cash receipts (thus combining material that was presented in Chapters 16 and 20 in the sixth edition). Chapter 18 covers the expenditure cycle, including purchases, receiving, accounts payable, and cash disbursements (thus combining material that had been presented in Chapters 17 and 20 in the sixth edition). Chapter 19 covers the production cycle, with a special focus on the implications of recent cost accounting developments, such as activity-based costing, for the design of the production cycle information system. Chapter 20 discusses the human resources management (HRM)/payroll cycle and explores the ways in which these two systems can be integrated. Chapter 21 focuses on the general ledger and reporting cycle.

All five chapters have been rewritten to reflect the three basic functions performed by the AIS: (1) efficient transaction processing, (2) provision of adequate internal controls to safeguard assets (including data), and (3) preparation of information useful for effective decision making. Both batch and on-line processing systems are presented. In addition, a data model for each cycle is described. As in the sixth edition, the role of information technology in providing a competitive advantage is stressed and numerous real-world examples are incorporated throughout these five chapters.

INSTRUCTIONAL SUPPLEMENTS

Our objective in preparing this textbook has been to simplify the teaching of AIS by enabling instructors to concentrate on classroom presentation and discussion, rather than on locating, assembling, and distributing teaching materials. As further support, a number of supplementary materials are also available free of charge to adopters of the text.

An *Instructor's Manual / Test Bank / Transparency Masters* is available to instructors who adopt this textbook. The first of its four sections presents sample syllabi that represent various approaches to teaching AIS as either a one-semester or a one-quarter course. The second section consists of outlines and lecture notes for each of the 21 text chapters. There is a one-page outline of each chapter, suitable for reproduction as a transparency. The teaching notes include references that link key figures and problems to chapter topics and, where appropriate, suggestions for alternative lecture topics and readings. The third section consists of a test bank (also available on a 3.5-inch diskette in IBM format) containing approximately 1500 objective questions, along with suggested answers. The final section of the *Instructor's Manual* contains more than 100 transparency masters of key tables and figures that appear in the textbook.

A separate *Solutions Manual* is also available to those instructors who adopt this book. It provides suggested solutions to the discussion questions, problems, and cases that appear at the end of each chapter. These guidelines facilitate the process of choosing which end-of-chapter exercises to assign as homework. Suggested solutions to the five cases that appear in the text appendix are also presented.

ACKNOWLEDGMENTS

We wish to express our appreciation to Professor Bill Cummings of Northern Illinois University for preparing the *Instructor's Manual* and *Test Bank* to accompany this edition. We also thank Dr. Martha M. Eining of the University of Utah and Dr. Carol F. Venable of San Diego State University for preparing the comprehensive cases included in this edition.

We appreciate the help of Linda Veteto of Brigham Young University in typing and preparing the various drafts of the book and the *Solutions Manual.* Finally, we are grateful to Iris Vessey for her contributions to the problem material.

We are indebted to numerous faculty members throughout the world who have adopted the earlier editions of this book and who have been generous with their suggestions for improvement. We are especially grateful to those who participated in reviewing the seventh edition throughout various stages of the revision process:

Ron Abraham, University of Northern Iowa
Gary Ames, Illinois State University
Alan Blankley, Western Michigan University
Bill Cummings, Northern Illinois University
Martha Eining, University of Utah
Amy Gatian, University of Tennessee–Knoxville
Severin Grabski, Michigan State University
Steven C. Hunt, University of North Texas
Marcus Odom, University of Southwestern Louisiana
Buck K. W. Pei, Arizona State University
Jerry D. Siebel, University of South Florida
Carol F. Venable, San Diego State University
Wallace Wood, University of Cincinnati

We are grateful for permission received from four professional accounting organizations to use problems and unofficial solutions from their past professional examinations in this book. Thanks are extended to the American Institute of Certified Public Accountants for use of CPA Examination materials, to the Institute of Certified Management Accountants for use of CMA Examination materials, to the Institute of Internal Auditors for use of CIA Examination materials, and to the Society of Management Accountants of Canada for use of SMAC Examination materials.

In addition, we would like to thank Janice Jutras, development editor; Barbara Gracia, production packager; Joyce Grandy, copy editor; and others on the staff at Addison-Wesley Publishing Company for their efforts in helping us make this a better book.

Of course, any errors in this book remain our responsibility. We welcome your comments and suggestions for further improvement.

Finally, we want to thank our wives and families for their love, support, and encouragement. We also want to thank God for giving us the ability to start and complete this book.

Marshall B. Romney
Provo, Utah

Paul John Steinbart
St. Louis, Missouri

Barry E. Cushing
Salt Lake City, Utah

Contents

Chapter 6 DATA MODELING AND DATA BASE DESIGN 165

Part Two THE TECHNOLOGY OF ACCOUNTING INFORMATION SYSTEMS

Chapter 7 A Review of Computer Hardware and Software 199

Chapter 11 SYSTEMS DESIGN, IMPLEMENTATION, AND OPERATION 359

Chapter 12 SYSTEMS ACQUISITION, OUTSOURCING, AND PROTOTYPING 392

PART FOUR CONTROL AND AUDIT OF ACCOUNTING INFORMATION SYSTEMS

Chapter 13 CONTROL AND ACCOUNTING INFORMATION SYSTEMS 425

P A R T   O N E

Chapter 1

Accounting Information Systems: An Overview

LEARNING OBJECTIVES

After studying this chapter, you should be able to:

- Explain what an accounting information system (AIS) is.
- Explain why studying AIS is an important part of your educational program.
- Explain how an AIS adds value to businesses.
- Explain why the AIS is the principal information system in an organization.

Integrative Case: S&S, Inc.

After working for several years as a regional manager for a national retailing organization, Scott Parry decided to open his own business. Susan Gonzalez, one of his district managers, had also expressed a desire to go into business for herself. Together they formed S&S, Inc., to sell home appliance products to the public. Their product line will range from large kitchen and laundry appliances to small appliances such as toasters and radios. They have rented a large and attractive building in a heavy–traffic pattern area of town. They figure that they have adequate capital to see them through the first six months of business.

Scott and Susan have arranged for all of the major manufacturers to supply them with appliances. Because of limited funds, they will initially sell only a few models of each appliance in their showroom. The manufacturers will also supply parts, since S&S wants to provide full service for everything it sells. Scott and Susan estimate they will need 10 to 15 employees—2 or 3 as office personnel, 2 or 3 in delivery, 2 in service and repair, and 4 to 6 in sales. They plan to begin hiring these employees within the next two weeks.

The grand opening of S&S is in five weeks. Although many arrangements for their opening are complete, Scott and Susan have not yet made a number of important decisions:

1. How to organize their accounting records so that the financial statements required by their banker can be easily produced.
2. How to meet all of their government obligations, such as sales, income, and payroll taxes as well as employee withholdings.
3. How to price their products to be competitive yet make a profit, and whether to extend credit, and in what amounts, to potential customers.

If credit is granted, how should S&S bill customers and collect their payments?

4. How to hire, train, and supervise their employees, what compensation and benefits packages to offer them, and how to process their payroll.
5. How to keep track of cash inflows and outflows so they are not caught in a cash squeeze. They also need to determine how best to meet their capital acquisition needs when their initial cash reserves are used up.
6. The appropriate product mix and quantities for their limited showroom space.

How should Scott and Susan address these problems? They can make many of these decisions by using educated guesses or by going with their gut-level feelings. They can make much better decisions, however, if they have the proper information. How can they get the information they need to make these decisions? What they need is an accounting information system (AIS).

INTRODUCTION

This chapter begins by defining an AIS and discussing why it is important for you to study an AIS. Then it discusses how an AIS adds value to businesses. The chapter concludes by discussing information, information systems (ISs), and why the AIS should be the principal IS in an organization.

WHAT IS AN AIS?

An **accounting information system (AIS)** processes data and transactions to provide users with the information they need to plan, control, and operate their businesses. To produce the information decision makers need, the AIS must perform the following tasks:

- *Collect* transaction and other data and *enter* it into the AIS.
- *Process* the data.
- *Store* the data for future use.
- *Provide* users with the information they need by producing a *report,* or allow users to *query* the data stored in the AIS.
- *Control* the whole process so that the information produced is accurate and reliable.

An AIS can be a very simple paper-and-pen-based manual system, a very complex system using the very latest in computers and information technology (IT), or somewhere between these two extremes. Regardless of the approach used, the process is the same. The AIS and the people who use it must still collect, enter, process, store, and report data and information. The paper and pencil or the computer hardware and software are merely the tools used to produce the information. Chapter 2 briefly discusses a manual system; the rest of the text assumes a computer-based AIS.

Most organizations engage in many similar and repetitive transactions. For example:

- Buy and pay for raw materials, goods for resale, or services.
- Hire and pay employees.
- Convert raw materials and labor into finished products. (*Note:* Not all organizations manufacture goods; for example, retail stores such as S&S simply buy finished goods for resale to others.)
- Sell goods or services and collect cash. Many also extend credit and manage accounts receivable.
- Summarize and report the results to management, shareholders, and creditors.

These five activity cycles constitute the five main subsystems of an AIS, as shown in Fig. 1.1. The smaller circles represent the subsystems, and the arrows show the interrelationships between the subsystems. These subsystems are discussed more fully in Chapter 2 as well as in Chapters 17–21.

Traditionally, the AIS was concerned only with financial data and accounting transactions. No other information about the sale was captured. For example, when a sale took place, an entry showing the date of the sale, a debit to cash, and a credit to sales was made in the sales journal. The entry was posted to the appropriate general ledger accounts, and the amount of the entry eventually showed up in the cash account on the balance sheet and in the sales account on the income statement. As a result, the AIS traditionally was referred to as a transaction processing system. As explained at the end of the chapter, the authors believe that the traditional definition and role of an AIS must be expanded so it captures all relevant company information, not just traditional accounting data.

Figure 1.1

An AIS and Its Subsystems

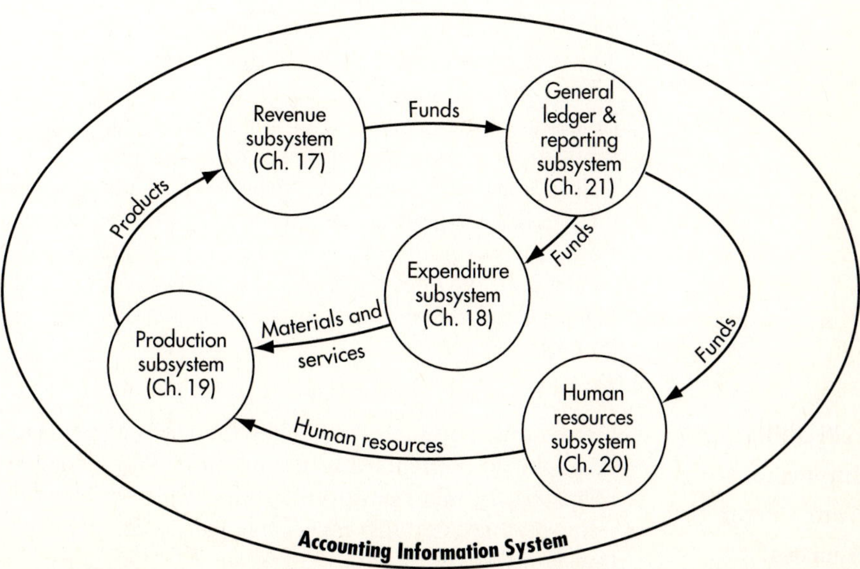

WHY STUDY ACCOUNTING INFORMATION SYSTEMS?

Some accounting students wonder why they have to take an AIS class and they question its importance. AIS instructors sometimes hear comments such as the following:

> *I don't need to study AIS, since it is not "real" accounting (presumably meaning debits, credits, and FASB statements).*
>
> *The AIS course will have little relevance to my career once I graduate and get a job. If I wanted to learn about computers I would have studied information systems or computer science.*

There are several reasons why a student's knowledge of accounting is not complete without an understanding of an AIS. Each will be explained in the following sections. Unfamiliar terms may be used, but don't worry, they will be explained later in the text. The important thing now is to realize why it is important to study AIS.

The AIS Is a Fundamental Part of Your Accounting Education

Recently there have been a number of calls for significant changes in accounting education. A reoccurring theme is the crucial need for information systems to be a fundamental part of accounting education. The Accounting Education Change Commission stated that accounting courses need to teach students that accounting is an information identification, development, measurement, and communication process. Students should come away from their accounting courses with a solid understanding of three essential concepts: (1) the use of information in decision making; (2) the nature, design, use, and implementation of an AIS; and (3) financial information reporting. To reach these goals, accounting students need to understand how an AIS is used to gather, process, store, and disclose information.

Historically, accounting has been taught in separate functional courses such as auditing, financial accounting, law, managerial accounting, accounting information systems, and tax. This approach sometimes makes it difficult for you as a student to integrate concepts from the individual classes and to see why AIS concepts are such an important part of accounting education. Most accounting courses place you in the role of an information producer or user (making journal entries, preparing or reading financial statements or other reports). They assume you have access to certain data and can address questions about how to account for, report, or audit information. For example, a managerial accounting class may discuss how to use information to make decisions but never discuss how the information is collected, stored, or made available to the decision maker. The question of where the information comes from is usually never asked in these classes. The answer is that it is provided by an AIS.

AIS Skills Are Important to Your Career Success

Graduating accountants typically take jobs as management, government, tax, or public accountants; internal auditors; and management consultants. Many recruiters for these positions specifically look for accountants with AIS skills. Almost all accountants must have sufficient AIS skills to accomplish the following tasks:

- Access and analyze company data, prepare reports, and make decisions. To do so, accountants use the AIS as well as spreadsheets, word processors, data bases, graphics packages, decision support software, expert systems, and other software packages.
- Help develop and design a new AIS as well as evaluate and improve existing ones.
- Access public and private data bases to research accounting or auditing standards and tax regulations as well as locate information needed to make managerial decisions.
- Communicate with others using the latest in technology, such as electronic mail (E-mail) and electronic data interchange (EDI). In addition, accountants in different locations use groupware to simultaneously work on joint projects.

More accounting students take jobs as management accountants (or end up there after time in public accounting) than any other career choice. As the primary custodians of company data, management accountants enter, process, retrieve, and use AIS data. Examples include entering sales information, producing invoices and monthly billings, and accessing company data bases to analyze inventory quantities and prices. In addition, accountants are often directly responsible for managing the AIS.

Many CPA firms now derive less than half their revenue from traditional auditing and tax services; the majority comes from consulting services. One of the fastest growing consulting services is helping organizations design, select, evaluate, and manage their AIS. Several partners of Big 6 CPA firms have commented publicly that they compete fiercely for $50,000 audit jobs but pass on $50 million consulting jobs because they do not have enough people with the necessary AIS skills. The president of a leading consulting firm said that, if all college students changed their majors to information systems or computer science, there still would not be enough talent to satisfy the demand for people in the IS services market. As a result, one of the fastest growing areas for hiring students is within AIS. The implication is that fewer accounting graduates will be involved in auditing and tax and more will be in less traditional areas of accounting such as AISs.

Tax accountants help individuals and business entities comply with tax laws and file income tax returns. They also perform tax planning so that clients can legally avoid as much tax as possible. Virtually all tax accountants use personal computers (PCs) and tax planning and preparation software.

Internal and external auditors evaluate the accuracy and reliability of information produced by the AIS. This service requires that they understand how a system is developed, how it operates, and how it can be properly controlled. They must be able to evaluate and understand the strengths and weaknesses of an AIS and its programs. They must have the skills to access company data, download it into their software tools, and analyze it. They use the computer as a tool to audit data stored in the system as well as the programs that process the data. Many CPA firms have teams of computer audit specialists that audit complex AISs.

An AIS Will Be a Key Component in Your Decision Making

An AIS course helps you understand the central role an AIS plays in decision making. You and others in your company will make three levels of decisions:

1. **Structured decisions** are repetitive, routine, and understood well enough to be delegated to clerks or automated on a computer. They are decisions for which a decision model is already built.
2. **Semistructured decisions** may be partially but not fully automated. They require subjective assessments and judgments in conjunction with formal data analysis and model building.
3. **Unstructured decisions** are nonrecurring and nonroutine—no framework or model exists for solving them. You must rely on judgment and intuition. Such unstructured decisions are often supported by a decision support system.

You will also make decisions about three types of activities:

1. **Operational control** ensures the effective and efficient execution of specific tasks. Examples include scheduling production, controlling inventory, and extending credit.
2. **Management control** ensures the effective and efficient use of resources in accomplishing organizational objectives. Examples include formulating budgets and working capital plans, developing human resource practices, and deciding on research projects and product improvements.
3. **Strategic planning** determines a company's objectives and the policies that govern the acquisition, use, and disposition of resources used to attain them. Examples include setting financial and accounting policies, choosing a new product line, and acquiring a new division.

The two-dimensional decision taxonomy in Table 1.1 shows how these two types of decisions interrelate. A correspondence exists between a manager's level in the organization and her or his decision-making responsibilities. Top management faces unstructured or semistructured decisions involving strategic planning issues. Middle-level managers deal with semistructured decisions concerning management control. Supervisors and employees face semistructured or structured decisions involving operational control.

What underlies all these decisions? All require information. Where does that information come from? It comes from an AIS, which must provide employees with the information they need to plan, control, and operate their organizations. You need to understand AIS concepts so you can help prepare or use this decision-making information.

An AIS Will Meet Your Information Needs

Business organizations are complex, with operations ranging from the engineering and development of new products to the recording and summation of accounting transactions. How can an organization plan, coordinate, and control all the activities it undertakes? How can it supply valuable information about these activities? The AIS plays a vital role in accomplishing these tasks.

The AIS serves two categories of users: external and internal. Financial accounting focuses on external users and their various information needs. For example, investors and creditors need general-purpose financial statements.

Table 1.1 **Managerial Activities and Decision-Making Taxonomy**

	Management Activity			
Type of Decision	**Operational Control**	**Management Control**	**Strategic Planning**	**Support Needed**
Structured	Inventory reordering	Linear programming for manufacturing	Plant location	Clerical, EDP, or management science models
Semistructured	Bond trading	Setting market budgets for consumer projects	Capital acquisition analysis	Decision support systems
Unstructured	Selecting a cover for *Time* magazine	Hiring managers	R & D portfolio management	Human intuition

Source: Peter G. W. Keen and Michael S. Scott Morton, *Decision Support Systems: An Organizational Perspective* (Reading, Mass.: Addison-Wesley, 1978), 87. Reprinted by permission.

Customers need to know what is available for purchase, what they have purchased, and their account status, including amount owed and payment due date. Suppliers need to know the items and quantities to be purchased. Stockholders need information concerning stock transactions and dividend payments. Employees need information about total pay and deductions, such as income and Social Security taxes and insurance premiums. Lenders are interested in the business's ability to meet its financial obligations and its potential for future success. Federal, state, and local governments require information about earnings, withholdings, and taxes.

Management accounting focuses on internal information needs, with a common objective being the maximization of the organization's economic well-being. Examples of internal information needs include cost and inventory status reports, accounts receivable aging, budgets, cash flow projections, and profitability analyses.

Accounting information plays two major roles in managerial decision making. First, it identifies situations requiring management action. For example, a cost report with a large variance might stimulate management to investigate and, if necessary, take corrective action. Second, by reducing uncertainty, accounting information provides a basis for choosing among alternative actions. For example, accounting information is often used as a basis for setting prices and determining credit policies.

Internal users, such as the five functional management areas that follow, need AIS information to answer the given types of questions. These information needs correspond with the five accounting cycles introduced earlier in the chapter.

- *Marketing management.* How much should the company charge for each item it sells? What should the company's discount, credit terms, and warranty policies be? Which items are the most and least profitable? How much should the company spend on advertising and promotion campaigns as well as market research?

- *Purchasing and inventory control.* How much inventory should be purchased and when? Which vendors should the company use? What combination of price, reliability, product styling, brand, and quality should be purchased?
- *Production management.* When and how much of each product item should the company produce? What production method and which materials should it use? How should common costs be allocated to the different products?
- *Human resource management.* How many hours did employees work, and how much should they be paid? What deductions should be made from employees' paychecks? What are each employee's skills and experience? What are the trends in hours worked, efficiency, turnover, and absenteeism?
- *Financial management.* What are the current cash inflows and outflows? What are the sources and uses of capital funds? How should the company plan for capital expenditures? What is adequate insurance coverage? What should the credit and collection procedures be?

You Will Be Affected by the Information Technology Revolution

Many accounting students and even some accounting professors erroneously refer to the AIS course as "the computer course." In actuality, the AIS course teaches students about collecting, storing, and providing information for decision making. To do this in the most efficient and effective manner, we must use all the tools at our disposal. Currently, one of the best tools is the computer, but if a better tool came along, we would use it instead. This is not a computer course therefore but one that uses the computer as a tool to achieve our information processing objectives.

The ongoing revolution in information technology (IT) has had a profound effect on AIS, and the driving force behind this revolution is the computer. Virtually all organizations use the computer to process transactions and prepare reports. Most accountants, in fact, use computers on a daily basis.

As computers become smaller, faster, easier to use, and less expensive, the computerization of accounting work will continue. Networks now link 40% of all computers, and transmission of data over phone wires grows 30% yearly. InterDesign, an Ohio-based company, is a good example of that growth. The company sells $10 million annually in very low tech household goods to hundreds of stores. As a result of improvements in its AIS, errors in order entry and shipping have almost completely disappeared. In the 1970s InterDesign used the post office to send invoices and receive sales orders. In the early 1980s the company installed an 800 number and in the late 1980s a fax. It now receives more than half of its orders directly from customers' computers through electronic data interchange. That number is expected to increase over time.

In a world rapidly moving toward networked computers, accountants must understand networking, electronic data interchange, and other computer technologies if they want to survive. Representatives of IBM, Boeing, General Electric, and many other companies have commented that recent business and accounting graduates have not mastered these essential computer technologies. They contend that all accounting graduates need a strategic understanding of technology as a source of competitive advantage. Schools with integrated accounting, business, and IS training programs have been quite successful. For example, MBAs at the University of Texas that graduated with an information systems management specialty received significantly more job offers than other graduates.

Most undergraduate accounting and business curricula have incorporated computer education for many years. Although general course work dealing with computers and electronic data processing is important and useful, accounting students also need to know how modern IT is applied to provide useful information to accountants and other information users. This book builds a solid foundation of knowledge for accounting graduates who will participate in the evaluation, design, use, audit, control, and management of an AIS.

A final reason to study the AIS is to understand how it can add value to business organizations.

HOW AN AIS ADDS VALUE TO BUSINESSES

According to authors Michael Porter and Victor Millar (1985), the ultimate goal of any business is to provide value to its customers. A business will be profitable if the value it creates is greater than the cost of its products or services. The next section discusses how value-adding activities are part of a company's value chain.

The Value Chain

Each company has nine distinct **value activities** that are linked in a **value chain** (see Fig. 1.2). The following five **primary activities** create, market, and deliver a product to buyers and then service and support it.

Figure 1.2

The Value Chain

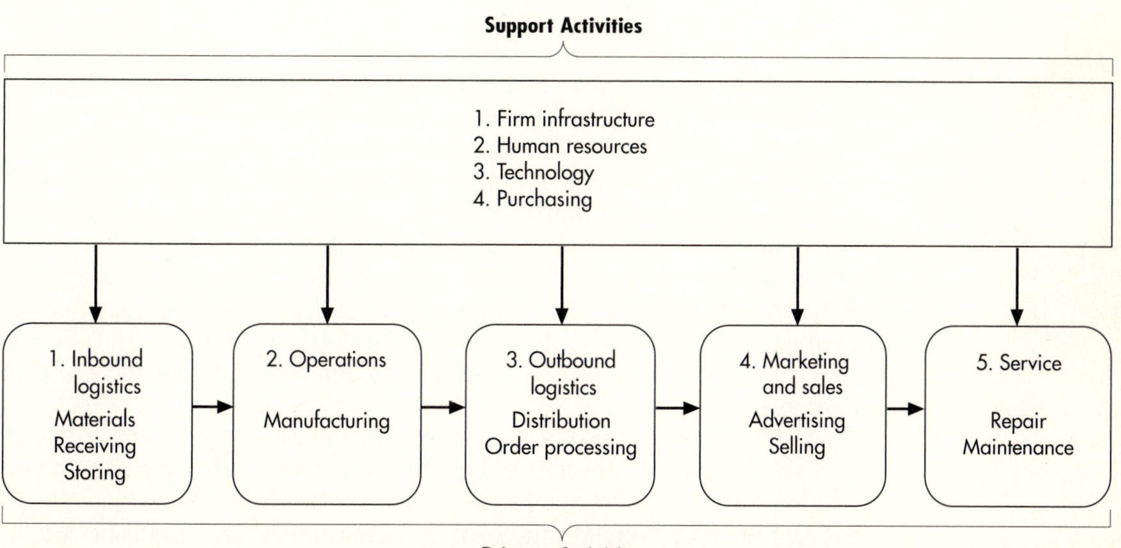

Adapted from "How Information Gives You Competitive Advantage," by Michael E. Porter and Victor E. Millar, *Harvard Business Review*, Vol. 63, No. 4, July/August 1985.

1. **Inbound logistics** consists of receiving, storing, and distributing materials that are inputs to the products or services of the organization. An example is the receipt and handling of the steel, rubber, and glass materials that an automobile manufacturing plant uses to produce a car.
2. **Operations activities** transform inputs into final products or services. For example, the assembly line in an automobile plant converts raw materials into a finished car.
3. **Outbound logistics** facilitates the distribution of finished products or services to buyers. Shipping automobiles to dealers is an outbound activity.
4. **Marketing and sales activities** facilitate the purchase of products or services. Television ads and promotions for new cars are marketing and sales activities.
5. **Service activities** provide repair and maintenance functions. Assembly line employees who repair machines are performing a service activity.

The following four **support activities** make it possible for the primary activities to take place:

1. **Firm infrastructure** is the organizational support activities and functions that support the value chain. They include an AIS, accounting, finance, the legal department, and general management.
2. **Human resources** refers to activities such as recruiting, hiring, training, and providing employee compensation and benefits.
3. **Technology** activities improve a product or service. This area encompasses research and development, computer technology, and product design.
4. **Purchasing** refers to procuring the materials, supplies, machinery, and buildings needed for the primary activities.

Each activity adds value as a product or service is created. For instance, value is added as raw materials are turned into a final product. To be competitive, a business must be able to perform its value activities at a lower cost or a higher quality than can its competitors.

Business organizations are composed of business processes or activities, such as taking orders, manufacturing products, and purchasing raw materials. A business process that a customer is willing to pay for, such as turning raw lumber into furniture, is referred to as a **customer-value-added** activity. A business process that is essential to managing an organization, such as producing an aged accounts receivable trial balance, is referred to as a **business-value-added** activity. Business processes that customers will not pay for and that do not result in an increased value to the business are referred to as **non-value-added** activities.

In the past, many organizations merely automated existing manual accounting systems when they developed their computer-based AIS. They did not use IT to improve and streamline processes. The result is many non-value-added processes in modern organizations. Many organizations are now using recent IT advances to reengineer their business processes to (1) maximize customer-value-added activities, (2) minimize the cost and maximize the effectiveness of business-value-added activities, and (3) eliminate non-value-added activities.

Figure 1.3

The Value System

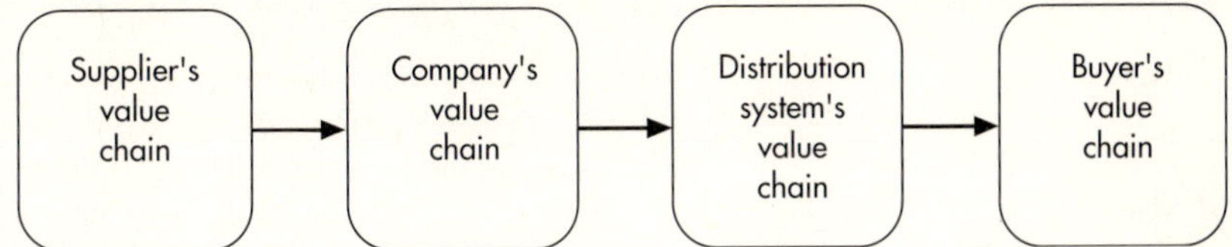

Adapted from "How Information Gives You Competitive Advantage," by Michael E. Porter and Victor E. Millar, *Harvard Business Review,* Vol. 63, No. 4, July/August 1985.

An organization's value chain is a part of a **value system** that, as shown in Fig. 1.3, is composed of the value chains of a company, its suppliers, its distributors, and its customers. By paying attention to the intercompany linkages in the value system, a company can add value not only to itself but to those in the value system. In our opening case, for example, a just-in-time inventory system that links S&S with its suppliers can reduce the firm's handling and storage costs. The suppliers also benefit, through increased information about S&S sales and orders that allows them to plan production and reduce inventories.

Using an AIS to Add Value to Businesses

An AIS is an important support activity that can be used to perform primary activities more effectively and efficiently. Accountants should use the value chain to determine where and how an AIS can add value to an organization. To do so, they should identify the activities in the chain, determine the cost and the value of each activity, and analyze where and how the AIS can add value. This process also helps users understand the business and the relationships between the activities. An AIS can provide value in the following ways:

1. *An AIS can improve products or services by increasing quality, reducing costs, or adding desirable features.* For example, an AIS can monitor machinery so that if defects occur, an operator is instantaneously notified. The result is a higher-quality product with less wasted materials.
2. *An AIS increases efficiency.* To illustrate, suppose a company is experiencing delays on an assembly line because the manufacturing department is running out of raw materials, even though sufficient quantities are available in the warehouse. An AIS could add value by tracking raw materials on hand in the manufacturing area and automatically sending an order to the warehouse when they are needed.
3. *An AIS provides timely and reliable information to improve decision making.* The sales force of 10,000 at Frito-Lay enters order data on a hand-held terminal for some 100 products sold at 400,000 stores. Each night the data from the terminals are combined and analyzed. In studying the sales in Texas, management noted a decline in the sales of Tostitos tortilla chips. An investigation found that a small competitor had introduced a new white corn tortilla chip. Within three months Frito-Lay had introduced a competing product and won back its lost market share.
4. *An AIS provides a company with a competitive advantage.* Price Waterhouse (PW) developed a system that facilitates sharing of expertise with

FOCUS 1.1

Wal-Mart's Successful Use of IT

Wal-Mart is the most successful and fastest-growing retail store in history. In part, this success is due to the way it uses its AIS to add value in distribution, inventory control, communications, purchasing, and management. In 1974 the company started using computers to control inventory on an item-by-item basis. Then in 1983 it began using point-of-sale (POS) scanners, which reduced the time customers waited at the checkout by 25% to 30%. When a product is sold, a POS terminal records the sale and automatically reduces the inventory level. Because the system is integrated throughout the Wal-Mart network, the inventory level for each product is always up-to-date for each of its stores.

Between 1985 and 1987 Wal-Mart installed the nation's largest satellite communication network. Since then it has invested over a billion dollars to improve information quality and transmission. The Wal-Mart network allows two-way voice and data communication and one-way video communication between headquarters, distribution centers, suppliers, and stores. The overall cost of this communication network is less than that of the previous telephone network.

The IT network is used in a variety of ways. First, the video system allows management to speak with all employees at once or to hold meetings with the managers from each store. Second, the system transfers data between stores, headquarters, distribution, and suppliers. Third, Wal-Mart is linked to about seventeen hundred vendors who supply about 80% of the goods that Wal-Mart sells. Electronic purchase orders and instant data exchange simplify the ordering process. Fourth, credit card authorizations, which take only five seconds, are handled through the network. Fifth, management receives detailed figures on nearly every aspect of Wal-Mart's operations.

Wal-Mart established a just-in-time ordering and delivery system with one of its major suppliers, Procter & Gamble (P&G). When the stock of a P&G product reaches a reorder point, a computer automatically sends an electronic purchase order by satellite to the nearest P&G factory. P&G's

clients, giving PW a significant competitive advantage. The new system allows PW personnel to search a companywide data base for employees with whatever expertise is required for a particular client. Personnel can search the data base for the results of similar engagements. They can also make use of an interactive system that allows individuals from widely separated offices to work together. The interactive system results in significant cost and time savings, since travel is not required.

5. *An AIS improves communication.* PW employees use laptop computers to access the PW network from almost anywhere to send and receive messages, search company data files, research a problem, prepare presentations, and make travel plans. The system also facilitates communication with clients. For example, newly enacted tax legislation is immediately scanned into the system, and a summary of the legislation, along with an analysis by PW tax experts, is sent to clients within a matter of hours. Clients can also be notified electronically of conference calls to discuss the tax changes.

6. *An AIS improves the use of knowledge.* To help its tax staff profit from the expertise of its leading tax experts, Coopers and Lybrand (C&L) developed an expert system. The firm interviewed a number of its leading tax experts and reduced their thought processes to some 3000 rules. These rules now make up the ExperTax system used to help small- to medium-sized clients execute tax planning. The system guides the staff as they gather information from clients

information system checks its inventory, notifies its distribution system of the order, and then automatically ships the product directly to the store. The purchase and payment procedures are all done electronically. This system saves days or even weeks over the time it would otherwise take to order and receive products. The system is a win–win situation because it provides both Wal-Mart and P&G with lower costs.

For products that are not shipped directly to the stores, Wal-Mart uses a centralized distribution system. Boxes of merchandise, placed on a conveyor system, travel to a central location where a computer sorts them. A laser scanner reads a bar code on the box and tells the automatic sorter where they should go. The boxes are diverted to the appropriate shipping doors. Because an information system controls the distribution system, more products can be shipped and distribution costs are lower.

Wal-Mart's distribution system provides a significant cost advantage over its competitors.

Wal-Mart also uses its information system to control the climate in every store. The lighting, heating, and air-conditioning controls in all Wal-Mart stores are connected via computer to Wal-Mart's headquarters. This system reduces costs by centrally managing the use of energy and freeing store management from having to control the utility costs.

Wal-Mart's use of technology and information systems has given it a technological and a competitive advantage over most other discounters. Through the use of information systems technology, Wal-Mart has increased productivity and profitability, helped fuel its explosive growth, and driven down costs.

Focus Questions

1. How has Wal-Mart's use of information systems and modern technology helped the company grow into the largest and most successful retail marketer in history?
2. How does Wal-Mart use its satellite communication network?
3. How does Wal-Mart's network add value to the organization? to Wal-Mart customers?
4. What are the benefits and risks of Wal-Mart's relationship with Procter & Gamble?

Source: Arthur A. Thompson, Jr.,and A. J. Strickland III, *Strategic Management—Concepts and Cases,* 6th ed. (Boston: Irwin, 1992), 955–987.

about the many complex tax planning problems they face. A C&L tax expert then reviews that information and makes specific recommendations to the client. The expert system replaces the 200-page questionnaire that C&L clients filled out in the past.

Focus 1.1 describes some of the ways in which Wal-Mart uses IT to add value. The next section of the chapter explains what information is, how its value is derived, and how too much information can produce information overload.

WHAT IS INFORMATION?

Data are facts that are entered, stored, and processed by an AIS. **Information** is organized, meaningful, and useful data. Data are processed into information so that decision makers can make better decisions. As a general rule, the greater the quality of information available to a decision maker, the better the odds for a sound decision. To be useful, information must possess the characteristics described in Table 1.2.

Information can be provided to both external and internal users. The information supplied to external users is either **mandatory information** (required by a governmental entity) or **essential information** (required to conduct business with external parties). An example of mandatory information is a report to the government on taxable income and tax withholdings. Examples of essential

Table 1.2 **Characteristics of Useful Information**

Relevant	Adds knowledge or value to decision makers by reducing uncertainty, increasing their ability to predict, or confirming or correcting earlier expectations.
Reliable	Is free from error or bias and accurately represents the events or activities of the organization.
Complete	Does not omit important data users expect it to contain.
Timely	Is provided in time to affect the decision-making process.
Understandable	Appears in a useful and intelligible format.
Verifiable	Allows two knowledgeable people to produce the same information independently.

information include purchase orders and customer billings. The primary consideration in producing mandatory and essential information is to minimize costs while meeting minimum standards of reliability and usefulness and meeting regulatory requirements.

Most internal information is **discretionary information,** since choices must be made regarding what information should be made available, to whom, and how frequently. The primary consideration in producing it is that its benefits exceed its costs. Internal reporting is more difficult than external reporting because (1) most managerial decisions demand more detailed information than does external reporting and (2) there are more ways to report information to internal users than to external users.

Value of Information

An AIS transforms data into information of value to decision makers. The **value of information** is the benefit produced by the information minus the cost of producing it. The major benefits of information are a reduction of uncertainty, improved decisions, and a better ability to plan and schedule activities. The costs are the time and resources expended in capturing the data and processing, storing, and reporting the information.

Unfortunately, determining the value of information is not as easy as it sounds. First, the costs, and especially the benefits, of information are difficult to quantify. Second, it is difficult to determine the value of information before it has been produced and utilized. Nevertheless, the expected value of information should be calculated as effectively as possible so that the costs associated with the information do not exceed its benefits.

To illustrate the value of information, consider the case of 7-Eleven. A Japanese company licensed the 7-Eleven name in 1973 from Southland Corp., after the 7-Eleven convenience store was already a big success. Believing that information about its customers and products had value, 7-Eleven Japan invested heavily in information technology. The U.S. stores did not perceive that customer and product information had as much value and so did not make the same IT investment.

Each 7-Eleven store in Japan uses a computer to execute the following functions:

- Track the 3000 items sold in each store and determine which products are moving, at what time of day, and under what weather conditions.
- Track the best customers and what and when they buy. If the best customers are single men, for example, the store makes sure it has sufficient quantities of the fresh rice dishes they purchase on their lunch hour and at the end of the workday.
- Automatically order sandwiches and rice dishes from suppliers. Orders are placed and filled three times a day so that stores always have fresh food. Since food orders take as many as 12 hours to prepare, 7-Eleven allows its suppliers to access sales data in their computers so they can forecast demand.
- Coordinate deliveries with suppliers. This task allows stores to reduce the number of deliveries from 34 to 12 a day, resulting in less clerical receiving time.
- Prepare a color graphic display that indicates which store areas contribute the most to sales and profits.

The information produced by this system is invaluable. Average daily sales of 7-Eleven Japan are 30% higher and its operating margins are almost double those of its closest competitor.

And what of Southland and its 7-Eleven stores in the United States? Profits declined and Southland eventually had to file for bankruptcy. Who came to their rescue? 7-Eleven Japan and its parent company, which now own 64% of Southland. 7-Eleven Japan obviously made the wise choice in assessing the value of information about its stores, products, and customers.

Information Overload and Information Literacy

Many people believe that, if more information is good, then a whole lot more information is even better. This is true only to a point, since humans can absorb only so much information. At some point they reach a state of **information overload,** where additional information cannot be used efficiently and has no marginal value. Information overload is costly, in that decision-making performance decreases while the costs associated with providing the information increase. As a result, producing information beyond information overload decreases the value of information.

Decision models can be developed to structure problems and help employees organize and process larger quantities of information. These systems have their limits, however, and can also reach a point of information overload. For example, electronic mail systems, which significantly increase productivity because workers can conveniently communicate with many people simultaneously, also make it so easy to communicate that some people flood others in their organizations with too many E-mail messages. As a result, some people now have to sort their junk E-mail from important E-mail.

WHAT IS AN INFORMATION SYSTEM?

A **system** is two or more interrelated components that interact to achieve a goal. Systems are almost always composed of smaller **subsystems,** each performing a specific function important to and supportive of the system of which it is a part. For example, a college bookstore is a system composed of various departments (texts, supplies), or subsystems. Yet the bookstore itself is often a subsystem of the university or of a company that controls other bookstores.

Any system must evaluate alternative courses of action from the standpoint of the system as a whole, rather than from one or more subsystems. This is referred to as the **systems concept.** Each subsystem is designed to achieve one or more organizational goals. Because all subsystems are related, changes in subsystems cannot be made without considering the effects of those changes on the other subsystems. **Goal conflict** occurs when a decision or action consistent with one subgoal or subsystem is inconsistent with another subgoal or subsystem. **Goal congruence** is achieved when employees can achieve their assigned subgoals while contributing to the achievement of their organization's overall goal. The ultimate objective of all subsystems should be to maximize the organizational goals, even if the goals of a subsystem are not maximized. The larger the organization and the more complicated the system, the more difficult is goal congruence to achieve.

The systems concept also encourages **integration,** or the combining of subsystems. Integration has made data processing more efficient by eliminating duplication of recording, storage, reporting, and other processing activities within an organization. For example, companies that formerly used separate programs to prepare customer statements, collect cash, and maintain accounts receivable records now combine these functions into a single application.

An **information system** is an organized means of collecting, entering, and processing data and of storing, managing, controlling, and reporting information so that an organization can achieve its objectives and goals. The importance of having a quality information system is illustrated in Focus 1.2.

A **formal information system** has an explicit responsibility to produce information. An **informal information system** arises out of a need not satisfied by a formal channel. Unfortunately, many informal systems are created because formal ones such as the AIS do not provide users with the information they need. Such duplication creates a number of problems. As time passes it becomes increasingly difficult to reconcile the information in the informal systems with that in the formal system. This can put accountants in a bad light when management begins to question which system houses the correct information. In addition, the informal systems are often of inferior quality because they are not well thought out and are poorly maintained and documented. The implication is that the AIS will not be a fully value-added service until it is able to provide all the information users need when and in the form they need it.

In a **manual information system** people are the primary information processors. People can think, reason, and adapt to unfamiliar situations but are slow and make mistakes. A **computer-based information system** uses a computer to process data. Computer-based systems can perform processing functions without human intervention and operate at incredibly fast speeds with great accu-

FOCUS 1.2

So Where Has All the Money Gone?

For years the Red Lake Band of the Chippewa Indians in northern Minnesota prospered from timber, mineral, and fishing resources. Revenues as great as $500,000 a year poured into a government trust fund managed by the Bureau of Indian Affairs (BIA). A 1982 audit discovered, however, that years of sloppy bookkeeping by the BIA has actually left the tribe more than $800,000 short. Two years ago the BIA deducted an additional $1.2 million from the fund to correct alleged accounting errors. At that point the Chippewa had had enough and filed suit against the federal government for mismanagement of funds. The Chippewa are not the only tribe with problems. Millions of dollars in grazing fee profits are missing from BIA accounts. Some American Indians have not seen a statement on their account balances for more than 70 years. Apparently, the BIA problems are only the tip of an enormous iceberg of faulty accounting systems in the federal government.

In the 1950s the federal government was on the cutting edge of accounting information systems. But years of underinvestment and budget-slashing have gutted back-office spending for most government agencies. The result: Most federal agencies lack adequate systems and technology to monitor revenues, expenditures, and cash resources. For example, the air force currently has over 130 separate accounting information systems, many of them antiquated. Auditor attempts to balance air force books are a good lesson in futility.

As a result of poor training and inadequate information systems, the books of many agencies, including the BIA, haven't been balanced in half a century. The BIA has two computer systems to monitor fund accounts, yet most staffers still record entries by hand. As a result, payments often go to incorrect accounts and to the wrong people. To balance the books, financial clerks routinely plug in fake accounting entries. According to a General Accounting Office (GAO) investigator, the BIA is like a bank that doesn't know how much money it has.

Government inefficiency is costing taxpayers dearly, perhaps masking the true scope of the annual budget deficit. According to GAO audits, most government agencies pay their bills too early or too late, costing taxpayers millions in unearned interest and late fees. Other taxpayer costs of poor information systems include poor tax collection procedures, limited inventory controls, and inadequate monitoring of government loans to individuals.

Focus Questions

1. Why are government agencies having problems?
2. How did the federal government and the Bureau of Indian Affairs get in such a mess?
3. What would you do if you were the leader of the Chippewa Indians? the BIA? an accountant hired to advise the Indians?
4. What should the federal government do at this point to solve the problem? How should it go about doing it?

Source: Dean Foust, "Uncle Sam Can't Keep Track of His Trillions," *Business Week* (September 2, 1991): 72–73.

racy. However, they are less flexible and adaptable than manual systems, and they are costly to design and develop. Large-scale computer-based systems employ a mainframe computer, are centrally organized, and are fast and powerful. They are operated and managed by computer specialists and are easier to control. Small-scale systems use personal computers (PC) dispersed throughout an organization. They are operated and managed by end users, are flexible and easy to use, but are difficult to control. They are often connected to another computer, called a **server,** that allows users to share information and software. These small systems are referred to as **client/server systems.**

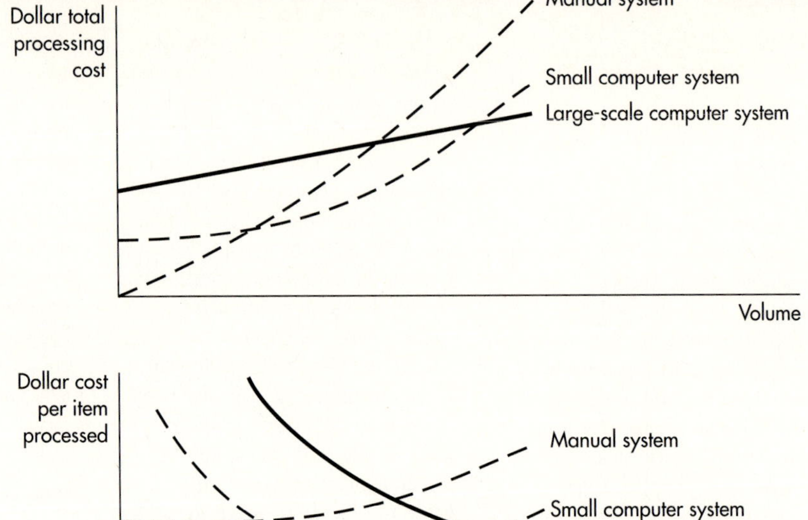

Figure 1.4

Relationship of Processing Costs to Processing Volume in Manual and Automated Data Processing Systems

Figure 1.4 illustrates that manual systems are suited to very low volume operations, small computer systems to low- to moderate-volume operations, and large computer systems to high-volume operations. The curves represent relative values rather than actual figures.

Components of an Information System

As shown in Fig. 1.5, an AIS has eight components.

Goals and Objectives. Each AIS is designed to accomplish one or more goals or objectives, which reflect the driving force behind the system and its purpose. For example, when customers called GTE for help in the past, they were bumped from person to person. Then GTE developed a system to improve customer service and generate new sales. The company's new system links phone operators with corporate data bases containing the information most frequently needed by customers. Operators now can solve 35% of customer problems on the initial phone call, compared to .5% before the system was installed.

Inputs. Data must be gathered and entered as **input** into the system. The most common inputs to an AIS are transaction data and journal entries. However, the role of many AIS is expanding to include nontraditional accounting data. For example, Phillips Petroleum designed a system to gather, in each of its markets, daily information on sales volume, current Phillips prices, competitors' prices, and market spot prices. This information helps local Phillips managers make better pricing decisions.

Figure 1.5

Components of an Information System

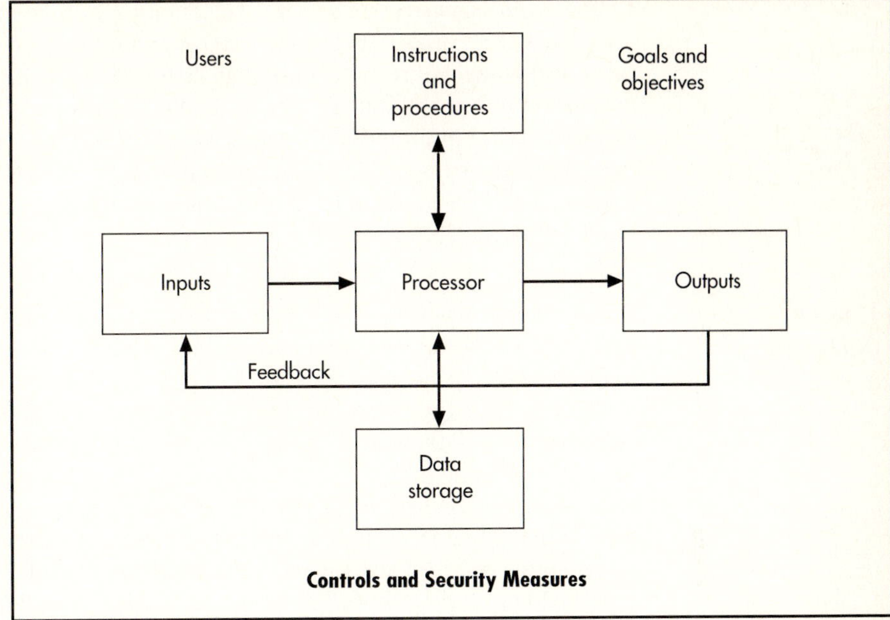

Outputs. Information produced by a system is called **output.** Output from the system that is reentered into the system as input is referred to as **feedback.** The most common AIS output is financial statements and internal reports such as accounts receivable listings, budgets, and cash flow projections. But many AIS also produce nontraditional accounting output as well. For example, each regional vice president at Consolidated Freightways used an extensive support staff to prepare graphs and charts to analyze revenue, number of tons shipped, and other operational data. Their new system allows the vice presidents not only to receive many more reports and statistics than before but to receive them in a much more understandable graphics mode. All this output is available with just the click of a button.

Data Storage. Data are often stored in the AIS for later use. Stored data must be updated frequently to keep it current.

Processor. Data must be processed to produce information. Most businesses process their data using computers.

Instructions and Procedures. Information systems cannot process data to produce information without detailed instructions and procedures. Software is written to instruct computers how to process data. Instructions and procedures for users are typically placed in procedures manuals.

Users. People who interact with a system and use the information it produces are referred to as **users.** In a business, users include those who execute and record transactions and those who manage and control the system.

Controls and Security Measures. Information produced by a system must be accurate, free of errors, and protected from unauthorized access. **Security measures and controls** are built into an AIS to ensure accurate information and proper system operation. To illustrate, the chief teller at Union Dime Bank embezzled $1.5 million dollars over several years. When apprehended, he said that simple controls such as requiring him to take an annual vacation and having someone else perform his duties while he was gone would have prevented him from perpetrating his scheme.

Types of Information Systems

When computers were first employed to process data for businesses in the 1950s and 1960s, the first computer-based IS developed was the AIS. These systems had a fairly narrow focus: They supported day-to-day operations by collecting and storing accounting transactions and helped to ensure that organizational data were processed consistently. The information produced by the AIS was made available to all levels of management for use in planning and controlling an organization's activities. However, managers needed more information than the AIS provided. This led to the development of the **management information system (MIS),** whose purpose was to collect and process all the data needed to plan, operate, monitor, evaluate, and control organizational activities.

Although the MIS and the AIS provided a great deal of information, they did not meet the needs of all information users nor did they make the information available in a way certain users needed it. These shortcomings have led to the development of various other types of systems:

- **Executive information systems (EIS)** were developed to provide executives and managers with easy-to-understand access to the information they need to make strategic plans, monitor business and economic conditions, identify business problems and opportunities, and make decisions. An EIS accepts data from many sources; combines, integrates, and summarizes the data; and makes the data available in a highly interactive format. It is graphically oriented and makes use of pointing devices and touch screens. Ernst & Young estimates that 25% of all banks currently have an EIS and that 40% are in the process of installing one.
- **Decision support systems (DSS)** were developed to help users make decisions in unstructured environments where there is a high degree of uncertainty and ill-defined reporting requirements. It allows the user to explore alternatives, ask what-if questions, deal with changing business problems, and make decisions in unanticipated situations. The DSS is discussed in Chapter 8.
- **Expert systems (ES)** contain the knowledge and expertise of one or more specialists in a well-defined area. Others make use of the knowledge stored in the system to solve problems and make decisions. An expert system guides decision processes, produces more consistent decisions, and ensures that important decision criteria are considered. Expert systems are discussed in Chapter 8.
- **End-user systems (EUS)** are developed by users to meet their own information retrieval, personal productivity, and application development needs. It

usually consists of a microcomputer workstation and DSS tools. The EUS is discussed in Chapter 8.

All of these systems are currently being used in the business world. Unfortunately, multiple-system use causes a number of problems and inefficiencies. Often, the same data must be captured by more than one system, leading to data redundancies and discrepancies if the data are changed in one system but not in the others. Another challenge is that it is often difficult for the systems to communicate effectively with one another or to share information. Gathering information from the various systems can be a difficult and time-consuming process.

For example, the IBM PC Company used to be managed with 223 incompatible computer systems. The absence of a coordinated information system was one reason why other PC companies were able to overtake and pass IBM as the world leader in PC sales. When a new manager was hired at IBM PC, he quickly identified the information system as one of his major priorities. He hired a chief information officer to put "headlights" on the company, saying he was tired of managing using "taillights"—outdated information. To solve the immediate problem, a new system was developed that collects data from all the individual systems. IBM PC managers now get one report that shows, by product line, how many computers are on hand and how many were built the previous day. Managers are now able to tell what products are and are not moving so that they can alter production as needed to avoid obsolescence and stockouts. The longer-term solution is to combine the various information systems into a single, comprehensive one.

Because of problems like those at IBM PC, organizations realize they need a single IS that serves the needs of all users and provides them with instantaneous access to all corporate information. For that to happen the accounting and IS functions must be combined. Integration can occur in one of two ways: IS can expand and take over the accounting function and blend it into the MIS, or the AIS can be expanded and gather more than just traditional accounting data. As explained later, the authors feel that the role of the AIS must be expanded. Because of this perspective, we do not try to distinguish between an AIS and an MIS. This text assumes that the AIS is the system that provides all users with the information they need.

The Future Role of the AIS

Deloitte and Touche (1995) surveyed accounting executives and found that only 1% of 221 respondents felt they operated a "world-class" AIS. The main reason the executives disliked their AIS was that it did not give them the information they needed. Over 80% of the executives that had installed a new AIS recently indicated that they were plagued by poor performance and had poor analysis tools.

Business managers often complain that to make decisions they must pick the brains of their staff, analyze the information they receive, and then rely on their own knowledge and instincts. They say they cannot tap into the vast amount of information that already exists in their companies because it has not been made easily available. Because of global competition, they are finding it increasingly hard to steer their businesses by looking into the rearview mirror of historical performance. What they need is real-time knowledge of what is happening and a best-estimate of what will be, rather than a recounting of what was.

An April 1995 workshop sponsored by the American Institute of CPAs brought together 40 senior financial executives, educators, consultants, and CPAs to discuss the future role of accounting and finance.[1] The participants came to a number of important conclusions with respect to the accounting profession and accounting information systems:

- Many people who manage and operate organizations are losing confidence in their AIS.
- Traditional financial reports will never be the sole basis for business decisions, because they are not effective performance indicators.
- No single financial report can hope to meet everyone's information needs.
- Accountants will become information specialists and will provide others in the organization with a detailed analysis of all data stored by the company.
- The controller must be a more active business partner. She can no longer confine her role to processing accounting transactions in the backroom.

Accountants can do several things to overcome these problems:

- The accounting profession cannot continue to narrowly define accounting data. Nor can it continue to limit its role in the organization. The role of the accountant must change from one of collecting and processing only accounting data to one of collecting and processing all information needed by the company.
- Corporate accountants and controllers must change their role from corporate cops to business advocates. Accountants must learn to add value to the company or they will cease to exist in their present role.
- Accountants must not limit the amount of information in the AIS. The AIS must be cross functional and must gather, process, and store the data needed by all users regardless of their department or function. In essence, the AIS must become *the* information system for business organizations.
- Accountants must define all accounting and information processing functions as their domain and integrate the two into one discipline.

SUMMARY AND CASE CONCLUSION

A properly designed AIS can provide Scott and Susan with the information to successfully plan, control, and manage their business. The most significant accounting transactions S&S will engage in are cash, credit, installment, trade-in, and parts and service sales; cash receipts; payroll; expenses, including utilities, advertising, supplies, insurance, and taxes; purchases of inventory; and cash disbursements. S&S needs to determine how to input, process, store, and output the information for these transactions. Most small retail businesses use a computer-based system designed specially for the retail industry.

S&S must maintain inventory data such as cost, list price, and quantities for each inventory item. Inventory records must be updated when sales occur or shipments are received. The accounts receivable records should contain data

[1]Stanley Zarowin, "The Future of Finance," *Journal of Accountancy* (August 1995): 47–49.

on each credit customer, including the amount due, credit terms, and addresses. Other significant accounting files needed include accounts payable, payroll, and general ledger.

Scott and Susan will need information to make management decisions such as what to purchase and when, how to determine pricing policy, what trade-in allowances to provide, and what the relative profitability of each product line will be. The system should provide this information on a regular basis, perhaps in the form of a daily or weekly report. Scott and Susan should be able to access the system to answer specific questions when the information they need is not found on their periodic reports.

A significant part of any accounting system is the control procedures followed in processing accounting data. On a daily basis the cash in the registers should be compared with the cash register totals. A similar comparison should be made between service work orders and cash received for parts and services. To ensure control over company assets, either Scott or Susan should open the mail, total the checks received, sign outgoing checks, and prepare a monthly bank reconciliation. Accounts receivable records should be reviewed periodically to identify late-paying customers so follow-up letters can be sent. Inventory stocks should be reviewed periodically to determine what items to order. At the end of each month various accounting tasks should be performed: adjusting entries, a trial balance, and a balance sheet and an income statement.

You will examine further examples of accounting information systems throughout the book, all containing the same basic set of components: people, equipment, transactions, input, stored data, output, documents, and procedures.

KEY TERMS

accounting information system (AIS)
structured decisions
semistructured decisions
unstructured decisions
operational control
management control
strategic planning
value activities
value chain
primary activities
inbound logistics
operations activities
outbound logistics
marketing and sales activities
service activities
support activities
firm infrastructure
human resources
technology activities
purchasing activities
customer-value-added
business-value-added
non-value-added
value system
data
information
mandatory information
essential information
discretionary information
value of information
information overload
system
subsystems
systems concept
goal conflict
goal congruence
integration
information system
formal information system
informal information system
manual information system
computer-based information system
server
client/server systems
input
output
feedback
users
security measures and controls
management information system (MIS)
executive information systems (EIS)
decision support systems (DSS)
expert system (ES)
end-user system (EUS)

CHAPTER QUIZ

1. Data differ from information in that
   a. data are the output of an AIS; information is the input.
   b. information is the output of an AIS; data are the input.
   c. data are meaningful for decision making; information is not.
   d. there is no difference between data and information.

2. All of the following are characteristics of information except
   a. reliable.
   b. timely.
   c. inexpensive.
   d. relevant.

3. Which of the following statements is *false?*
   a. The value of information is the cost of producing information minus the benefit produced by the information.
   b. A major benefit of information is a reduction of uncertainty, improved decisions, and a better ability to plan and schedule activities.
   c. Determining the value of information is not easy.
   d. At some point people reach a state of information overload, where additional information cannot be used efficiently and has little or no marginal value.

4. Supervisors and employees are most likely to face
   a. semistructured decisions involving operational control.
   b. structured decisions involving strategic planning.
   c. unstructured decisions involving management control.
   d. semistructured decisions involving strategic planning.

5. The systems concept is
   a. the set of equipment, programs, data, procedures, and people used to process information.
   b. transforming a manual information system into an automated system.
   c. combining previously separated subsystems.
   d. evaluating alternative courses of action from the standpoint of the system as a whole, rather than from that of any single subsystem.

6. All of the following are support activities in the value chain except
   a. technology.
   b. firm infrastructure.
   c. service activities.
   d. purchasing activities.

7. Which of the following statements is *true?*
   a. A decision support system is the main data processing system for financial and transaction data.
   b. An executive information system contains expert knowledge to support clerical users who need expertise in a well-defined area.
   c. A management information system is developed by users to meet their own information retrieval, personal productivity, and application development needs.
   d. An accounting information system processes data and transactions to provide users with the necessary information for planning, controlling, and operating their organizations.

8. Information for internal users is usually
   a. mandatory.
   b. discretionary.
   c. essential.
   d. mandatory or essential.

9. It is important that you study accounting information systems because
   a. you will personally be affected by the IT revolution.
   b. you will most likely use an AIS in your job.
   c. AIS is a fundamental part of accounting education.
   d. All of the above.

10. All of the following are examples of how an AIS adds value *except*
   a. improves products or services.
   b. eliminates all organizational errors.
   c. increases efficiency.
   d. improves the management process by providing timely and reliable information.

DISCUSSION QUESTIONS

1.1 Should an accounting information system be structured to meet the needs of external users or of internal users? To what extent are these user needs different and similar?

1.2 The IRS has always had an abundance of data that its executives have never been able to use effectively. To analyze tax data, agency executives hired scores of people to wade through stacks of paper-based records and to crunch numbers. The IRS recently developed an EIS (executive management support system) that is one of the most innovative in use today. It uses multidimensional modeling software to help executives compare and contrast tax data. Agency executives now can quickly review national and regional tax data and identify tax return trends, such as geographical pockets of nonfilers. The IRS used $2.5 million dollars of taxpayer funds to develop the system. Do you believe that the system adds value to the taxpayers? Do you believe it was a wise use of taxpayer money?

1.3 Would you ever produce information if you believed its costs would outweigh its benefit? If so, give several examples of when and why you would produce this information.

1.4 This chapter introduced the concept of information overload. When is more information not always better? Provide two examples.

1.5 Accountants have significant involvement with an AIS, both as users and designers. Accounting graduates become auditors, management accountants, consultants, business managers, and business owners. Compare and contrast these professions in terms of their use and involvement in the design of an AIS.

1.6 A well-designed computer-based accounting information system must be able to ensure that the data and information are accurate. How could you ensure that the data input into an AIS are accurate? How could you ensure that the data entered into the system are processed properly? How could you ensure that the output is accurate?

1.7 You are the new controller at the Management Training Center (MTC). MTC specializes in executive training courses that run from three to eight weeks. You are struggling to learn your job and are looking for helpful information. You find that you can get information on MTC's computer from three sources: a microcomputer that sits on your desk, a daily printout of the prior day's activities, and a monthly report. Compare and contrast each report based on the six characteristics of information discussed in the chapter.

1.8 The chapter discussed eight information system components. Give an example of each for the following companies:

a. An automobile dealership
b. A small manufacturer of plastics
c. A developer of software products for microcomputers
d. A CPA firm
e. A major league sports franchise

1.9 Financial statements are a key output of an accounting information system. Describe how the balance sheet and income statement for a midsized manufacturing firm can be helpful to each of the following users:

a. Customers
b. Suppliers
c. Stockholders
d. Managers
e. A bank that has lent them money
f. The Securities and Exchange Commission

1.10 Ricky Hatch is the president of a company that manufactures footwear. Because of rapid growth over the past five years, the sales department has been complaining that orders are not being filled correctly, shoes are being returned because of defects, pricing is not competitive, and stockouts have been common. Ricky is considering installing an accounting information system to solve these problems. How can an AIS add value to Ricky's company?

PROBLEMS

1.1 Joan Anderson manages the accounting department of a small company. She regularly uses the formal communication system (e.g., memoranda from her and other company managers) to inform employees of changes in company policy and other pertinent matters. She also uses the informal communications network that exists in the company to update her employees.

REQUIRED

a. Discuss the differences between formal and informal communication systems with respect to each of the following features of a communication system:

1. The accuracy of communication.
2. The speed of communication.
3. The influence the communication has on the employee.

b. Can an informal communication system be beneficial to the management process? Explain your answer. (CMA Examination, adapted)

1.2 United Services Automotive Association (USAA) grew to become the fourth-largest insurer of homes and the fifth-largest insurer of automobiles during its first fifteen years. One major reason for its success is the use of technology to lower costs and improve customer service. USAA has spent almost $150 million on computer and imaging technologies in the last 25 years. Its system is so advanced that it is able to keep track of minute details, such as which auto parts are getting fixed most frequently.

USAA also uses its extensive data base of information to spot ways to reduce the costs of claims. For example, USAA discovered that repair shops would rather charge up to $300 to replace a windshield with punctures than to charge $40 to repair it. When the problem was identified, USAA began offering to waive the deductible if owners would have their windshields repaired rather than replaced. Unfortunately, the repair shops convinced 95% of owners to replace their damaged windshields instead of repairing them.

USAA has spent extensively to develop an image-processing system that takes electronic, or digitized, pictures of all paper documents sent in by claimants (some 25 million a year). These pictures are stored on optical disks the size of phonograph records. It takes only a few keystrokes for a policy service representative to retrieve pictures of all the documents in a customer's file. The system can sort and prioritize documents so that employees are always working on the most important and urgent tasks.

REQUIRED

a. Why should USAA collect information on which auto parts are getting fixed most frequently? What could it do with the data?

b. Even though USAA offered to waive the deductible, the repair shops still managed to convince 95% of owners to replace rather than repair their damaged windshields. How could USAA use its information system to persuade more shop owners to repair damaged windshields?

c. How does the image-processing system at USAA add value to the organization?

1.3 The annual report is considered by some to be the single most important printed document that companies produce. In recent years company annual reports have become large documents. They now include such sections as letters to the stockholders, descriptions of the business, operating highlights, financial review, management discussion and analysis, segment reporting, and inflation data as well as the basic financial statements. The expansion has been due in part to a general increase in the degree of sophistication and complexity in accounting standards and disclosure requirements for financial reporting.

The expansion also is reflective of the change in the composition and level of sophistication of its users. Current users include not only stockholders, but financial and securities analysts, potential investors, lending institutions, stockbrokers, customers, employees, and, whether the reporting company likes it or not, competitors. Thus a report that was designed as a device for communicating basic financial information has increased its scope either to meet the needs of an expanding audience or to meet the need to expand the audience.

Users hold conflicting views on the value of annual reports, ranging from failure to provide adequate data to meet the intent of the report, to provision of an unfathomable information overload. The future of most companies depends on acceptance by the investing public and by its customers; therefore companies should take this opportunity to communicate well-defined corporate strategies.

REQUIRED

a. The goal of preparing an annual report is to communicate information from the corporation to its targeted users.

1. Identify and discuss the basic factors of communication that must be considered in the presentation of this information.
2. Discuss the communication problems a corporation faces in preparing the annual report that

result from the diversity of the users being addressed.

b. Select two types of information found in an annual report, other than the financial statements and accompanying footnotes, and describe how they are useful to the users of annual reports.

c. Discuss at least two advantages and two disadvantages of stating well-defined corporate strategies in the annual report.

d. Evaluate the effectiveness of annual reports in fulfilling the information needs of the following current and potential users:

1. Shareholders
2. Creditors
3. Employees
4. Customers
5. Financial analysts

e. Discuss the effect on the communication of information to all users as a consequence of knowing that competitors will read and analyze the annual report. (CMA Examination, adapted)

1.4 Many management accountants are included among an expanding group of middle managers who are experiencing changes in their job definition and in their role in the organization. The management accountant's primary function of monitoring and controlling operations began to diminish with the computerization of data. The initial thrust of computerization was to displace or replace some clerical functions. Middle management's role and function remained unchanged due to the remoteness of the computer. The only changes were the amount, quantity, and speed with which information was generated. Middle management still monitored activities, interpreted data, and controlled operations. Thus middle management was the link between information generation and top management.

Top management now has direct access to the generated data through improved computer output and desktop computers that allow not only passive monitoring but also immediate, on-line interactive capacity.

REQUIRED

a. Discuss the effect that these changes in computer technology and computerized information systems have on the following:

1. The role and work of middle managers
2. Line and staff structures

b. The refining of computerized information systems and its effects have been termed a technological revolution. Compare this technological revolution to the Industrial Revolution with respect to the impact on the human element of the business organization. (CMA Examination, adapted)

CASE 1.1: ANYCOMPANY, INC.—AN ONGOING COMPREHENSIVE CASE

This case allows you to apply immediately what you have just studied. You will select a local company that you can work with. The first case at the end of each chapter is an assignment that allows you to apply key chapter concepts to the company you have selected as a reference. This case, then, may become an ongoing case study that you work on throughout the term.

Visit a small- to medium-sized business in your community and explain that you have been assigned to study a local business. Ask for permission to study the company and explain that you will need to meet with company employees several times during the term to get pertinent information. However, you will not need a great deal of their time or disrupt their business. Offer to share your findings and to make suggestions as a way of motivating the firm to allow you to study them.

Once you have lined up a company, answer the following questions.

1. What types of information systems does the company have? What subsystems does it have? Describe each information system and explain its purpose.
2. Who are the major external users of company information? the major internal users? What information is produced for each set of users?
3. For two system outputs, identify the decision(s) that is made, the data entered to produce the information, how data are stored and processed to produce the information, and how instructions and procedures are given to the system and its users. Use the characteristics of information (reliable, timely, etc.) to evaluate the usefulness of the information provided.
4. What information does the company lack that it would like to have?
5. How does the company's information system add value to the organization?

CASE 1.2: THE USE AND MISUSE OF INFORMATION

An AIS can provide users with important benefits, such as better and faster communication. An AIS can also create ethical dilemmas if not managed properly. Consider the following two uses of information systems.

Case 1

An anonymous letter arrived at the main office of a large engineering firm, claiming that many of the employees and even some of the managers were using illegal drugs. The company immediately began an internal investigation. The person in charge of the investigation obtained the passwords of all employees and began to read their E-mail, which suggested that some of the company's employees were indeed using illegal drugs. The investigation also uncovered evidence of an illicit affair between a manager and a lower-level employee, which, based on company guidelines, was considered sexual harassment.

Senior management found themselves in an ethical dilemma. They did not know whether they could or should use the E-mail messages as evidence. Some believed the evidence should not be used in any way, and some believed all the evidence should be used. Others believed it should be used only in the drug case because that was the only situation for which they had probable cause for a search. Still others did not know what to do and wished they had never heard of E-mail.

Evaluate this case, and answer these questions:

1. What could the company do with the information about illegal drug use? about the illicit affair? What should it do with the information? Do the ends (stopping illegal drug use and illicit affairs) justify the means (secretly monitoring E-mail messages)? Explain.
2. Should management have the right to read employee's E-mail messages regardless of the situation? Why or why not? if there are special circumstances?
3. Should E-mail messages belong to an employee or to the company? Why?
4. What effect do you think it would have on employees if they knew management was secretly monitoring their E-mail messages?

Case 2

A data entry clerk at a direct marketing firm began experiencing anxiety and sought medical treatment. Her nervous condition was diagnosed as an adverse behavioral reaction to the new computer system at work. This new system measured the efficiency of each data entry clerk and displayed motivational messages to those whose performance did not meet certain standards. For example, if the number of keystrokes in a given time period fell below a set number, a message stating that the employee should work faster was displayed on the computer screen. As a further motivational tool, management posted employee efficiency ratings and ranking on company bulletin boards. When threatened with a lawsuit, management began to wonder whether they had not taken the attempts to motivate their employees too far.

Evaluate this case, and answer the following questions:

1. Is it appropriate for management to monitor the efficiency of data entry clerks? Why or why not?
2. What is your opinion and reaction to the motivational tactics used by the marketing firm? Would they serve to improve or worsen your performance?
3. Is it appropriate for management to display the motivational messages? to post the efficiency rankings? Explain.

CASE 1.3: PANCANADIAN PETROLEUM

PanCanadian Petroleum used to be referred to as a sleeping giant. That was before David O'Brien took over as CEO. Within a few short years oil production had doubled, the number of wells drilled had tripled, and revenues and profits had skyrocketed even though the price of oil had decreased. O'Brien credits the turnaround to the pipeline that the company built—not an oil or gas pipeline, but an information pipeline. O'Brien considers the oil business to be a knowledge business and the information pipeline the company developed to have given PanCanadian a competitive advantage.

Virtually all aspects of PanCanadian's operations have been computerized in the last few years.

O'Brien quadrupled the IT budget to $60 million. Almost all employees have at least one personal computer on their desks, compared to only 20% a few years ago. O'Brien transferred dozens of managers and employees from their operational positions into IT. They spent two years learning about IT and performing IT-related tasks. In the process the barriers that existed between IT and other areas of the company were broken down.

PanCanadian used its new information system to solve a number of problems. For instance, the company was not having much success drilling wells even though it used state-of-the-art drilling technology and computerized seismic data. PanCanadian had good decision-making data but was unable to see the whole picture when considering a drilling site. This "big-picture" information was stored in many locations: some on paper, some in libraries, and some in company data bases that were not linked together.

A second problem was the amount of time it took to make drilling decisions. When all the data on a site were assembled, the information was forwarded to top management along with a report. Management would often ask for additional information or delay the decision for some time while trying to decide whether to drill.

A third problem was that PanCanadian was one of the higher-cost producers of oil. Maintaining well and pipeline pumps is an important key to reducing costs. PanCanadian has 400 service professionals working out of seven regional offices throughout western Canada. Every morning these service professionals show up at the regional offices, receive working assignments, drive to their assigned locations, read the pump-monitoring equipment, make any needed repairs, and drive back to the offices to write up four reports. Between travel and report preparation time, service professionals were spending an average of only two hours a day working on pumps. Most of the two hours were spent fixing malfunctioning pumps rather than performing preventative maintenance, which is far more cost-effective. The reports were mailed to the main office for review by management.

Evaluate PanCanadian's operations, and answer the following questions:

1. What could PanCanadian do to make all the information about a particular drilling site available to its employees faster and more efficiently?
2. How could PanCanadian streamline the drilling decision?
3. How could PanCanadian use both an AIS and an IT to make its service professionals more effective and to get their reports to management faster and more efficiently?

CASE 1.4: ACKOFF'S MANAGEMENT MISINFORMATION SYSTEMS

This case is adapted from a classic article entitled "Management Misinformation Systems." It was written by Russell L. Ackoff and appeared in *Management Science.* In the article Ackoff identified five common assumptions about information systems and then explained why he disagreed with them.

Read the five assumptions, contentions, and Ackoff's explanation. For each of the five, decide whether you agree or disagree with Ackoff's contentions. Defend the stand you take by preparing a report that explains why you believe the way you do. Be prepared to defend your beliefs in class.

Assumption 1: Management Needs More Information

Assumption 1. Most MISs are designed based on the assumption that the critical deficiency under which most managers operate is the lack of relevant information.

Contention 1. I do not deny that most managers lack a good deal of information that they should have, but I do deny that this is the most important informational deficiency from which they suffer. It seems to me that they suffer more from an overabundance of irrelevant information.

This is not a play on words. The consequences of changing the emphasis of an MIS from supplying relevant information to eliminating irrelevant information is considerable. If one is preoccupied with supplying relevant information, attention is almost exclusively given to the generation, storage, and retrieval of information: Hence emphasis is placed on constructing data banks, coding, indexing, updating files, using access languages, and so on. The ideal that has emerged from this orientation is an infinite pool of data into which managers can reach to pull out any information they want. If, on the other hand, one sees the manager's information problem primarily, but not exclusively, as one that arises out of an overabundance of irrelevant information, most of which was not asked for, then the two most important functions of an information system become filtration (or evaluation) and condensation. The literature on the MIS seldom refers to these functions, let alone considers how to carry them out.

My experience indicates that most managers receive much more data (if not information) than they can possibly absorb even if they spend all of their time trying to do so. Hence they already suffer from an information overload. They must spend a great deal of time separating the relevant documents. For example, I have found that I receive an average of 43 hours of unsolicited reading material each week. The solicited material is usually half again this amount.

I have seen a daily stock status report that consists of approximately six hundred pages of computer printout. The report is circulated daily across managers' desks. I've also seen requests for major capital expenditures that come in book size, several of which are distributed to managers each week. It is not uncommon for many managers to receive an average of one journal a day or more. One could go on and on.

Unless the information overload to which managers are subjected is reduced, any additional information made available by an MIS cannot be expected to be used effectively.

Even relevant documents have too much redundancy. Most documents can be considerably condensed without loss of content. My point here is best made, perhaps, by describing briefly an experiment that a few of my colleagues and I conducted on the operations research (OR) literature several years ago. By using a panel of well-known experts, we identified four OR articles that all members of the panel considered to be "above average" and four articles that were considered to be "below average." The authors of the eight articles were asked to prepare "objective" examinations (duration 30 minutes) plus answers for graduate students who were to be assigned the articles for reading. (The authors were not informed about the experiment.) Then several experienced writers were asked to reduce each article to two-thirds and one-third of its original length only by eliminating words. They also prepared a brief abstract of each article. Those who did the condensing did not see the examinations to be given to the students.

A group of graduate students who had not previously read the articles were then selected. Each one was given four articles randomly selected, each of which was in one of its four versions: 100%, 67%, 33%, or abstract. Each version of each article was read by two students. All were given the same examinations. The average scores on the examinations were compared.

For the above-average articles there was no significant difference between average test scores for the 100%, 67%, and 33% versions, but there was a significant decrease in average test scores for those who had read only the abstract. For the below-average articles there was no difference in average test scores among those who had read the 100%, 67%, and 33% versions, but there was a significant increase in average test scores of those who had read only the abstract.

The sample used was obviously too small for general conclusions, but the results strongly indicate the extent to which even good writing can be condensed without loss of information. I refrain from drawing the obvious conclusions about bad writing.

It seems clear that condensation as well as filtration, performed mechanically or otherwise, should be an essential part of an MIS, and that such a system should be capable of handling much, if not all, of the unsolicited as well as solicited information that a manager receives.

Assumption 2: Managers Need the Information They Want

Assumption 2. Most MIS designers "determine" what information is needed by asking managers what information they would like to have. This is based on the assumption that managers know what information they need and want.

Contention 2. For a manager to know what information he needs, he must be aware of each type of decision he should (as well as does) make and he must have an adequate model of each. These conditions are seldom satisfied.

Most managers have some conception of at least some of the types of decisions they must make. Their conceptions, however, are likely to be deficient in a very critical way, a way that follows from an important principle of scientific economy: The less we understand a phenomenon, the more variables we require to explain it. Hence managers who do not understand the phenomena they control play it "safe" and, with respect to information, want "everything." The MIS designer, who has even less understanding of the relevant phenomena than the manager, tries to provide even more than everything.

She thereby increases what is already an overload of irrelevant information.

For example, market researchers in a major oil company once asked their marketing managers what variables they thought were relevant in estimating the sales volume of future service stations. Almost 70 variables were identified. The market researchers then added about half again this many variables and performed a large multiple linear regression analysis of sales of existing stations against these variables and found about 35 to be statistically significant. A forecasting equation was based on this analysis. An OR team subsequently constructed a model based on only one of these variables, traffic flow, which predicted sales better than the 35-variable regression equation. The team went on to explain sales at service stations in terms of the customers' perception of the amount of time lost by stopping for service. The relevance of all but a few of the variables used by the market researchers could be explained by their effect on such a perception.

The moral is simple: One cannot specify what information is required for decision making until an explanatory model of the decision process and the system involved has been constructed and tested. Information systems are subsystems of control systems. They cannot be designed adequately without taking control into account. Furthermore, whatever else regression analyses can yield, they cannot yield understanding and explanation of phenomena. They describe and, at best, predict.

Assumption 3: Giving Managers the Information They Need Improves Their Decision Making

Assumption 3. It is frequently assumed that if managers are provided with the information they need, they will then have no problem in using it effectively.

Contention 3. Operation research (an academic subject area dealing with the application of mathematical models and techniques to business decisions) stands to the contrary.

Give most managers an initial tableau of a typical "real" mathematical programming, sequencing, or network problem and see how close they come to an optimal solution. If their experience and judgment have any value, they may not do badly, but they will seldom do very well. In most management problems there are too many possibilities to expect experience, judgment, or intuition to provide good guesses, even with perfect information.

Furthermore, when several probabilities are involved in a problem, the unguided mind of even a manager has difficulty in aggregating them in a valid way. We all know many simple problems in probability in which untutored intuition usually does very badly (e.g., What are the correct odds that 2 of 25 people selected at random will have their birthdays on the same day of the year?). For example, very few of the results obtained by queuing theory, when arrivals and service are probabilistic, are obvious to managers; nor are the results of risk analysis where the managers' own subjective estimates of probabilities are used.

The moral: It is necessary to determine how well managers can use needed information. When, because of the complexity of the decision process, they can't use it well, they should be provided with either decision rules or performance feedback so that they can identify and learn from their mistakes.

Assumption 4: More Communication Means Better Performance

Assumption 4. One characteristic of most MISs is that they provide managers with better current information about what other managers and their departments are doing. Underlying this provision is the belief that better interdepartmental communication enables managers to coordinate their decisions more effectively and hence improves the organization's overall performance.

Contention 4. Not only is this not necessarily so, but it seldom is so. One would hardly expect two competing companies to become more cooperative because the information each acquires about the other is improved.

For example, consider the following very much simplified version of a situation I once ran into. The simplification of the case does not affect any of its essential characteristics. A department store has two "line" operations: buying and selling. Each function is performed by a separate department. The Purchasing Department primarily controls one variable: how much of each item is bought. The Merchandising Department controls the price at which it is sold. Typically, the measure of performance applied to the Purchasing Department was the turnover rate of inventory. The measure applied to the Merchandising Department was gross sales; this department sought to maximize the number of items sold times their price.

Now by examining a single item, let us consider what happens in this system. The merchandising manager, using his knowledge of competition and consumption, set a price that he judged would maximize gross sales. In doing so, he utilized price–demand curves for each type of item. For each price the curves show the expected sales and values on an upper and lower confidence band as well. (See Fig. 1.6.) When instructing the Purchasing Department about how many items to make available, the merchandising manager quite naturally used the value on the upper confidence curve. This minimized the chances of his running short, which, if it occurred, would hurt his performance. It also maximized the chances of being overstocked, but this was not his concern, only the purchasing manager's. Say, therefore, that the merchandising manager initially selected price P_1 and requested that amount Q_1 be made available by the Purchasing Department.

In this company the purchasing manager also had access to the price–demand curves. She knew that the merchandising manager always ordered optimistically. Therefore, using the same curve, she read over from Q_1 to the upper limit and down to the expected value, from which she obtained Q_2, the quantity she actually intended to make available. She did not intend to pay for the merchandising manager's optimism. If merchandising ran out of stock, it was not her worry. Now the merchandising manager was informed about what the purchasing manager had done, so he adjusted his price to P_2. The purchasing manager in turn was told that the merchandising manager had made this readjustment, so she planned to make only Q_3 available. If this process (made possible only by perfect communication between departments) had been allowed to continue, nothing would have been bought and nothing would have been sold. This outcome was avoided by prohibiting communication between the two departments and forcing each to guess what the other was doing.

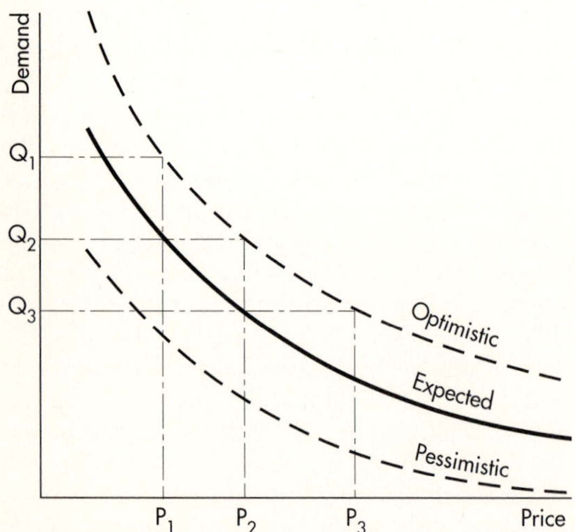

Figure 1.6

Price–Demand Curve

I have obviously caricatured the situation in order to make the point clear: When organizational units have inappropriate measures of performance that put them in conflict with each other, as is often the case, communication between them may hurt organizational performance, not help it. Organizational structure and performance measurement must be taken into account before opening the floodgates and permitting the free flow of information between parts of the organization.

Assumption 5: Managers Need Only to Understand How to Use an Information System

Assumption 5. A manager does not have to understand how an information system works, only how to use it.

Contention 5. Managers must understand their MIS or they are handicapped and cannot properly operate and control their company.

Most MIS designers seek to make their systems as innocuous and unobtrusive as possible to managers, lest they become frightened. The designers try to provide managers with very easy access to the system and assure them that they need to know nothing more about it. The designers usually succeed in keeping managers ignorant in this regard. This leaves managers unable to evaluate the MIS as a whole. It often makes them afraid to even try to do so, lest they display their ignorance publicly. In failing to evaluate their MIS, managers delegate much of the control of the organization to the system's designers and operators—who may have many virtues, but managerial competence is seldom among them.

Let me cite a case in point. A chairman of the board of a medium-size company asked for help on the following problem. One of his larger (decentralized) divisions had installed a computerized production inventory control and manufacturing manager information system about a year earlier. It had acquired about \$2 million worth of equipment to do so. The board chairman had just received a request from the division for permission to replace the original equipment with newly announced equipment that would cost several times the original amount. An extensive "justification" for so doing was provided with the request. The chairman wanted to know whether the request was justified. He admitted to complete incompetence in this connection.

A meeting was arranged at the division, at which I was subjected to an extended and detailed briefing. The system was large but relatively simple. At the heart of it was a reorder point for each item and a maximum allowable stock level. Reorder quantities took lead time as well as the allowable maximum into account. The computer kept track of stock, ordered items when required, and generated numerous reports on both the state of the system it controlled and its own "actions."

When the briefing was over, I was asked if I had any questions. I did. First I asked if, when the system had been installed, there had been many parts whose stock level exceeded the maximum amount possible under the new system. I was told there were many. I asked for a list of about 30 and for some graph paper. Both were provided. With the help of the system designer and volumes of old daily reports I began to plot the stock level of the first listed item over time. When this item reached the maximum "allowable" stock level, it had been reordered. The system designer was surprised and said that by sheer "luck" I had found one of the few errors made by the system. Continued plotting showed that because of repeated premature reordering the item had never gone much below the maximum stock level. Clearly, the program was confusing the maximum allowable stock level and the reorder point. This turned out to be the case in more than half of the items on the list.

Next I asked if they had many paired parts, ones that were only used with each other, for example, matched nuts and bolts. They had many. A list was produced and we began checking the previous day's withdrawals. For more than half of the pairs the differences in the numbers recorded as withdrawn were very large. No explanation was provided.

Before the day was out it was possible to show by some quick and dirty calculations that the new computerized system was costing the company almost $150,000 per month more than the hand system that it had replaced, most of this in excess inventories.

The recommendation was that the system be redesigned as quickly as possible and that the new equipment not be authorized for the time being.

The questions asked of the system had been obvious and simple ones. Managers should have been able to ask them, but—and this is the point—they felt themselves incompetent to do so. They would not have allowed a hand-operated system to get so far out of their control.

No MIS should ever be installed unless the managers for whom it is intended are trained to evaluate and hence control it rather than be controlled by it.

Source: Reprinted by permission of Russell Ackoff, "Management Misinformation Systems," *Management Sciences* Vol. 14, No. 4, December 1967, The Institute of Management Sciences, 290 Westminster Street, Providence, RI 02903.

ANSWERS TO CHAPTER QUIZ

1. b	**3.** a	**5.** d	**7.** d	**9.** d
2. c	**4.** a	**6.** c	**8.** b	**10.** b

Chapter 2

Elements and Procedures of Accounting Information Systems

LEARNING OBJECTIVES

After studying this chapter, you should be able to:

- Explain the three basic functions performed by an accounting information system (AIS).
- Describe the documents and procedures used in an AIS to collect and process transaction data.
- Discuss the types of information that can be provided by an AIS.
- Describe the basic internal control objectives of an AIS and explain how they are accomplished.

Integrative Case: S&S, Inc.

The grand opening of S&S, Inc. is two weeks away. Scott Parry and Susan Gonzalez are working long hours to make the final arrangements for the store opening. They are hiring salespeople, both to work in the store and to call on outside businesses such as builders, apartment complex owners, and others who may need large volumes of appliances. The training for both sets of salespeople is scheduled to begin next week. Several people experienced in appliance repair are also being hired.

Susan has ordered what she thinks will be an adequate amount of inventory for the first month. The store is being remodeled and will have a bright, cheery decor. All seems to be in order. All, that is, except the accounting records.

Like many entrepreneurs, Scott and Susan have not given as much thought to their accounting records as they have to other parts of their business. They recognize that they need qualified accounting help and have hired a full-time accountant, Ashton Fleming. Scott and Susan think Ashton is perfect for the job because of his two years' experience with a national CPA firm. Ashton is looking forward to working for S&S because he has always wanted to be involved in building a company from the ground up.

On Ashton's first day on the job, Susan shows him where all the invoices for the inventory that she purchased are located. Scott explains that the sales staff are paid a fixed salary plus commissions and that all other employees are paid hourly rates. Employees are paid every two weeks, with their first paychecks due next week. Susan then pulls out several folders and hands them to Ashton. One contains the documentation on their bank loan, with the first payment due several days after the grand opening. The other folders contain information on rental payments, utilities, and other expenses. Susan tells Ashton that she and Scott do not know much about accounting and are relying on him to help them decide how to run the accounting end of S&S. She adds that the only thing they have done so far is to open a checking account for S&S and that they have kept the check register up-to-date so that they can monitor their cash flow.

Ashton asks Scott to show him where the computer is, because he wants to see what type of system he will have to assist him in his responsibilities. Scott replies that with all the challenges they have had in opening up S&S, he and Susan have not had time to tackle that aspect yet. Scott adds that they will get a computer as soon as the store opens and business stabilizes. That could take several months, however, so for now Ashton will have to keep the books by hand. Scott wants Ashton to design the manual accounting system, however, so that it can be easily automated when S&S acquires a computer.

After Scott leaves, Ashton feels both excited and a little nervous about his responsibility for creating an accounting information system (AIS) for S&S. Although Ashton has audited many companies, he has never organized a company's books and is unsure how to go about it. Nor does he really understand how to plan for a computer-based AIS. A million questions run through his head. Here are just a few of them:

1. How am I going to organize things? Where do I start? What information do Scott and Susan need to run S&S effectively? How can that information be provided?
2. How am I going to collect and process data about all the types of transactions that S&S will engage in?
3. How do I organize all the data that will be collected?
4. How should I design the AIS so that the information provided is reliable and accurate?

INTRODUCTION

The introductory story indicates that Ashton needs to design an accounting information system for S&S. We have chosen to begin with a manual AIS so that you can clearly see all the components of the system and how they interact with one another. Moreover, many commercially available accounting packages work in basically the same way as a manual AIS. Thus, when we discuss automated systems in later chapters, you will already understand the basic functions and objectives of an AIS and can concentrate on learning how developments in information technology provide opportunities to improve system efficiency and effectiveness.

This chapter addresses the three basic functions performed by an AIS:

1. To collect and process data about the organization's business activities efficiently and effectively.

2. To provide information useful for decision making.
3. To provide adequate controls to ensure that data about business activities are recorded and processed accurately and to safeguard those data and other organizational assets.

Notice how closely these three functions relate to one another. Data about business activities are summarized in financial statements and managerial reports. These reports are then used to make decisions about those business activities. As explained in Chapter 1, however, to be useful for decision making, information must be reliable.

This chapter provides an overview of how an AIS fulfills the three functions just outlined. We begin by discussing the basic types of business activities an organization engages in, the key decisions that must be considered when managing those activities, and the information needed to make those decisions. In doing so, we show that the nature and objectives of an organization affect the design of its AIS. The next section then describes the documents and procedures that are needed to capture and process data about the typical business activities engaged in by an organization. Then we discuss the types of information reports that can be produced by the AIS for use in decision making. We conclude the chapter with a brief discussion of internal controls in a manual AIS.

BUSINESS ACTIVITIES AND INFORMATION NEEDS

Ashton decides that before designing an AIS for S&S, he must first understand how the company functions. This insight will enable him to identify the kinds of information Scott and Susan will need to manage S&S effectively. Then Ashton can determine the types of data and procedures that will be needed to collect that information.

Ashton creates a three-column table to summarize the results of his analysis. In the left column he lists some of the basic business activities that S&S will engage in. Next, in the middle column, he writes down some of the key decisions that will need to be made for each of these activities. Finally, in the right column, he lists some of the information that Scott and Susan will need to make these decisions. Table 2.1 shows the results of this effort.

Ashton realizes that his list is not exhaustive, but he is satisfied that it provides a good overview of S&S. He also recognizes that not all the information needs listed in the right-hand column will be produced internally by S&S's AIS. Information about payment terms for merchandise purchases, for example, will be provided by vendors. Thus the AIS must be designed for effective integration of such external data with internally generated data so that Scott and Susan can use both types of information to run S&S.

Next, Ashton reorganizes the business activities listed in Table 2.1 into groups of related transactions. For example, the sale of merchandise is related to the collection of payments from customers. Similarly, the acquisition of merchandise is related to the payment of vendors. These groups of related business activities form what are called **transaction cycles.** Each transaction cycle typically processes a large number of individual transactions. Most of these transactions, however, can be categorized into a relatively small

Table 2.1 **Overview of S & S's Business Activities, Key Decisions, and Information Needs**

Business Activities	Key Decisions	Information Needs
Acquire capital	How much? Invest or borrow? If borrow, best terms?	Cash flow projections Pro-forma financial statements Loan amortization schedule
Acquire building and equipment	Size of building? Amount of equipment? Rent or buy? Location? How to depreciate?	Capacity needs Prices Market study Tax tables and regulations
Hire and train employees	Experience requirements? How to assess integrity and competence of applicants? How to train?	Job description Applicant job history and skills
Acquire inventory	What models to carry? How much to purchase? Which vendors? How to manage inventory (store, control, etc.)	Market analyses Inventory status reports Vendor performance and payment terms
Engage in advertising and marketing	Which media? Content?	Cost analyses Market coverage
Sell merchandise	Markup percentage? Offer in-house credit? Which credit cards to accept?	Pro-forma income statement Credit card costs Customer credit status
Collect payments from customers	If offer credit, what terms? How to handle cash receipts?	Customer account status Accounts receivable aging report
Pay employees	Amount to pay? Deductions and withholdings? Process payroll in-house or use outside service?	Sales (for commissions) Time worked (for hourly employees) W4 forms Costs of external payroll service
Pay taxes	Payroll tax requirements Sales tax requirements	Government regulations Total wage expense Total sales
Pay vendors	Whom to pay? When to pay? How much to pay?	Vendor invoices Accounts payable

number of distinct types. For example, the majority of the individual transactions processed in the revenue cycle relate either to the sale of goods or services to customers or to the collection of cash from customers in payment for those sales.

Ashton draws Fig. 2.1 to simplify further and organize what he knows about S&S. This figure groups business activities into transaction cycles and identifies

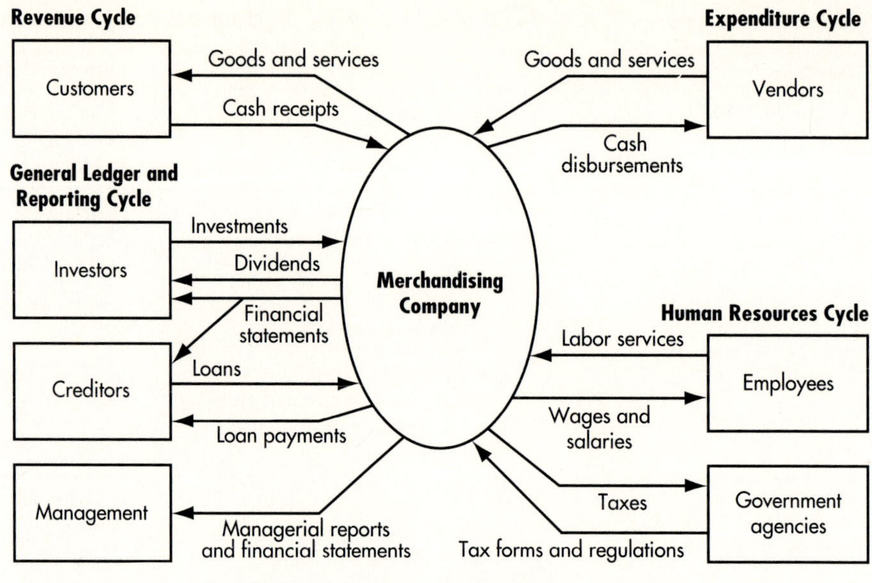

Transaction Cycle	Transactions (Business Activities)
Revenue	Customer orders, sales, shipping/delivery, cash receipts, sales discounts, sales returns and allowances, bad debts.
Expenditure	Purchase requisitions, purchases, receipt of inventory, cash disbursements, purchase returns and allowances, purchase discounts.
Human resources	Hiring, training, promotion, firing, payroll, and taxes.
General ledger and reporting	Nonroutine transactions, adjusting entries, closing entries, managerial reports and financial statements.

Figure 2.1

Typical Transaction Cycles and External Relationships for a Retail Company.

the most common external relationships for each cycle. The figure also lists the basic types of transactions in each cycle.

The four transaction cycles shown in Fig. 2.1 (revenue, expenditure, general ledger and reporting, and human resources) are found in most organizations, not just retail merchandising companies like S&S. Other types of organizations, however, may have additional transaction cycles. Manufacturing companies, for example, have a production cycle consisting of all transactions involved in the manufacture of products. Financial institutions have demand-deposit and installment-loan cycles that relate to the transactions involving customer accounts and loans, respectively. In addition, the nature of a given transaction cycle differs across types of organizations. For example, the expenditure cycle of a service company, such as a public accounting or a law firm, does not involve processing transactions related to the purchase, receipt, and payment for merchandise that will be resold to customers.

After preparing Table 2.1 and Fig. 2.1, Ashton believed that he understood S&S well enough to begin designing its AIS. In the next three sections we examine the components of the manual system he developed. Although this discussion is set in the context of S&S, the components of the system represent the features typically found in any manual AIS.

TRANSACTION PROCESSING: DOCUMENTS AND PROCEDURES

One basic function of the AIS is the efficient and effective processing of data about a company's transactions. Transaction processing consists of three basic steps, performed in the following sequence:

1. Capture transaction data on source documents.
2. Record transaction data in journals, which present a chronological record of what occurred.
3. Post data from journals to ledgers, which sort data by account type. Let us now examine the specific documents and procedures used to perform each of these steps.

Capture Transaction Data on Source Documents

Although data about business activities could be recorded on blank pieces of paper, in notepads, or even on blackboards, better control and accuracy is provided by using special forms called **source documents.** An example of a source document used in the expenditure cycle is the purchase order (see Fig. 2.2), which is used to request merchandise from suppliers. Table 2.2 lists other common source documents used in each transaction cycle and describes their function.

Control over data collection is improved by prenumbering each source document (note the upper right corner of the purchase order). Prenumbering simplifies verifying that all transactions have been recorded and that none of the documents have been misplaced. Accuracy is improved because source documents specify which information to collect, preprint standard information, such as addresses, and provide directions for completing the form.

Accuracy and efficiency in recording transaction data can be further improved if source documents are properly designed. Ashton recalled learning about forms design in his college AIS course. He scanned his old AIS textbook and found a checklist of principles for forms design that applied to both paper documents and computer input screens (see Table 2.3, on page 42).

Refer back now to Fig. 2.2 to see how the principles listed in Table 2.3 are reflected in the sample purchase order Ashton developed. Notice that the top of the form clearly indicates that this document is a purchase order from S&S. The heading also specifies where the merchandise should be shipped and where the invoice should be sent. Also note that the purchase order is prenumbered to facilitate tracking its status and that the vendor is instructed to reference this purchase order number in all correspondence.

Notice how the main body of the purchase order uses lines and boxes to group logically related information together. This design not only facilitates completing the form correctly, but it also helps the recipient correctly read it. Thus adequate space is provided to record the date of the order, the date the merchandise is needed, and the terms desired. Below that, column headings indicate all the important data that needs to be entered. For example, each row in the purchase order has a space for the product number, description, quantity, and quoted unit price of the ordered item, plus a column for an extension (quantity times price) of each line item. There is also a box for the total amount of the order.

The bottom of the purchase order provides a space to check off the desired shipping option so that the purchasing agent needn't write out the desired

Figure 2.2

Sample Purchase Order for S&S (bold items are preprinted)

PURCHASE ORDER **No. 101**

S&S, Inc.
Phone: (314) 555-2238
Fax: (314) 555-9863

Reference this number on all correspondence

Ship To:
S&S, Inc.
2533 Farthington Dr.
St. Louis, MO 63104-2345

Bill To:
S&S, Inc.
P.O. Box 457
St. Louis, Mo 63104-0457

To: Appliance Wholesalers
4533 Telegraph Rd.
St. Louis, MO 63129-2290

Date:	**Date Needed By:**	**Terms:**
11/23/97	12/05/97	2/10, net 30

Item Number	**Description**	**Quantity**	**Unit Price**	**Extension**
1344	Maytag Dishwasher Model 907	10	399.95	3,999.50
2455	Maytag Freezer Model 211	5	799.95	3,999.75
			Total	$7,999.25

Shipping Instructions

____ UPS
____ Federal Express
____ U.S. Postal Service
_x_ Other: *Acme Freight*

Distribution of Copies:

white — vendor
yellow — accounts payable
blue — receiving
green — purchasing

Heather Finney

Purchasing Agent

delivery method. Also, note that the distribution list for each copy of the completed form is clearly indicated. Finally, there is a space at the bottom of the purchase order for the signature of the person placing the order. This indicates that the order has been reviewed and approved.

Record Transaction Data in Journals

After transaction data have been captured on source documents, the next step is to record the data in a journal. A journal entry is made for each transaction showing the accounts and amounts to be debited and credited. Ashton decided that S&S will follow the practice of most companies and use both a general journal and a set of specialized journals. The **general journal** records infrequent or nonroutine transactions, such as loan payments and end-of-period adjusting and closing entries. **Specialized journals** simplify the process of recording large numbers of repetitive transactions. S&S, like most organizations, will use spe-

Table 2.2 **Common Source Documents and Functions**

Source Document	Function
Revenue Cycle	
Sales order	Record customer order.
Delivery ticket	Record delivery of merchandise to customer.
Credit memo	Support adjustments to customer accounts for sales returns and allowances, sales discounts, and write-off of uncollectible accounts.
Expenditure Cycle	
Purchase order	Request merchandise from vendors.
Receiving report	Record receipt of merchandise from vendors.
Human Resources Cycle	
Time cards	Record time worked by employees.
W4 forms	Collect employee withholding data.
General Ledger & Reporting Cycle	
Journal voucher	Record entry posted to general ledger.

cialized journals to record the four most common types of transactions: credit sales, cash receipts, purchases on account, and cash disbursements. To see how these specialized journals can save time, let us examine Table 2.4, which shows an example of a sales journal.

Notice that the sales journal has only one column to record the transaction amount. The reason is that the sales journal is used only for recording credit sales of inventory or services; consequently, every entry represents a debit to accounts receivable and a credit, for the same amount, to sales revenue. This also means that there is no need to write an explanation of each entry, as would be the case if credit sales were recorded in the general journal. Instead, all the information about the transaction is recorded in one line: the date, invoice number, name and account number of the customer, and the amount of the sale. When we consider the number of sales transactions likely to occur every day, the time saved by recording these transactions in a sales journal, rather than in the general journal, is considerable.

The remaining column in the sales journal, titled Post Ref, indicates completion of the next step in transaction processing: posting from the journals to the appropriate ledgers.

Post Transactions to Ledgers

Ledgers are used to summarize the financial status, including the current balance, of individual accounts. In a manual system, ledgers are actually books; hence the phrase "keeping the books" refers to the process of maintaining the ledgers.

Ashton decided that S&S, like most companies, should have both a general ledger and a set of subsidiary ledgers. The **general ledger** contains summary-level data for every asset, liability, equity, revenue, and expense account of the organization. A **subsidiary ledger** records all the detailed data for any general

Table 2.3 **Principles of Good Forms Design**

General Considerations
- Are preprinted data used to the maximum extent possible?
- Are the weight and grade of the paper appropriate for the planned use?
- Are bold type, double-thick lines, and shading used appropriately to highlight different parts of the form?
- Is the form a standard size?
- Is the size of the form consistent with requirements for filing, binding, or mailing?
- If the form is intended to be mailed to external parties, is the address positioned so that the form can be used in a window envelope?
- Are copies of the form printed in different colors to facilitate proper distribution?
- Are their clear instructions on how to fill out the form?

Introductory Section of Form
- Does the name of the form appear at the top, in bold type?
- Is the form prenumbered consecutively?
- If the form is to be distributed to external parties, is the company's name and address preprinted on the form?

Main Body of Form
- Is logically related information (e.g., customer name, address) grouped together?
- Is there sufficient room to record each data item?
- Is the ordering of data items consistent with the sequence in which those items are most likely to be acquired?
- Are standardized explanations preprinted so that codes or checkoffs can be used instead of requiring written user entries?

Conclusion Section of Form
- Is space provided to record the final disposition of the form?
- Is space provided for a signature or signatures to indicate final approval of the transaction?
- Is space provided to record the date of final disposition or approval?
- Is space provided for a dollar or other numeric total?
- Is the distribution of each copy of the form clearly indicated?

Table 2.4 **Sample Sales Journal**

Sales Journal					Page 5
Date	**Invoice Number**	**Account Debited**	**Account Number**	**Post Ref.**	**Amount**
Oct. 15	151	Brown Hospital Supply	120-035	✓	798.00
15	152	Greenshadows Hotel Suites	120-122	✓	1,267.00
15	153	Heathrow Apartments	120-057	✓	5,967.00
15	154	LMS Construction	120-173	✓	2,312.50
15	155	Gardenview Apartments	120-084	✓	3,290.00
15	156	KDR Builders	120-135	✓	1,876.50
		TOTAL			15,511.00
				120/502	

ledger account that has many individual subaccounts. Subsidiary ledgers are commonly used for accounts receivable, inventory, fixed assets, and accounts payable.

The general ledger account corresponding to a subsidiary ledger, called a **control account,** contains the total amount for all individual accounts in the subsidiary ledger. Thus the accounts payable control account in the general ledger represents the total amount owed to all vendors. The balances in the subsidiary accounts payable ledger indicate the amount owed to each specific vendor.

The relationship between the general ledger control account and the individual account balances in the subsidiary ledger plays an important role in maintaining the accuracy of the data stored in the AIS. Specifically, the sum of all entries in the subsidiary ledger should equal the amount in the corresponding general ledger control account. For example, the inventory subsidiary ledger would contain dollar balances and quantities for each inventory item carried by S&S. The sum of all the dollar balances in the inventory subsidiary ledger should equal the total dollar balance in the inventory control account in the general ledger. Any discrepancy between the total of the subsidiary ledger and the balance in the corresponding general ledger control account indicates that an error in recording and posting process has occurred.

The Posting Process. Ashton drew Fig. 2.3 to show Scott and Susan how the process of journalizing and posting sales transactions works. As shown in the top portion of the figure, each credit sale is first recorded in the sales journal. Each individual entry in the sales journal is then posted to the appropriate customer's account in the accounts receivable subsidiary ledger (note the arrow at the top of Fig. 2.3 linking the $1876.50 sale to KDR Builders in the sales journal to the debit for $1876.50 in the accounts receivable subsidiary ledger at the bottom of the figure). The same process is followed for credit sales to all other customers. Periodically, the total of all entries recorded in the sales journal is then posted to the general ledger (note the debit of $15,511, representing total sales on October 15, linked by the arrow to the accounts receivable general ledger account in the middle of Fig. 2.3 and to the corresponding credit to the general ledger sales account for the same amount).

The Audit Trail. Figure 2.3 also shows how the posting references and document numbers provide what is known as an audit trail. An **audit trail** provides a means to check the accuracy and validity of ledger postings. To illustrate this process, observe that the posting reference for the $15,511 credit to the sales account in the general ledger, SJ5, refers back to page 5 of the sales journal. By checking page 5 of the sales journal, it is possible to verify that $15,511 represents the total credit sales recorded on October 15. Similarly, the posting reference for the $1876.50 debit to the KDR Builders account in the subsidiary accounts receivable ledger also refers to page 5 of the sales journal as the source of that entry. Furthermore, note that the sales journal lists the invoice numbers for each individual entry. Invoice numbers provide the means for locating and examining the appropriate source documents in order to verify that the transaction did occur and was recorded accurately.

Figure 2.3

Recording and Posting a Credit Sale

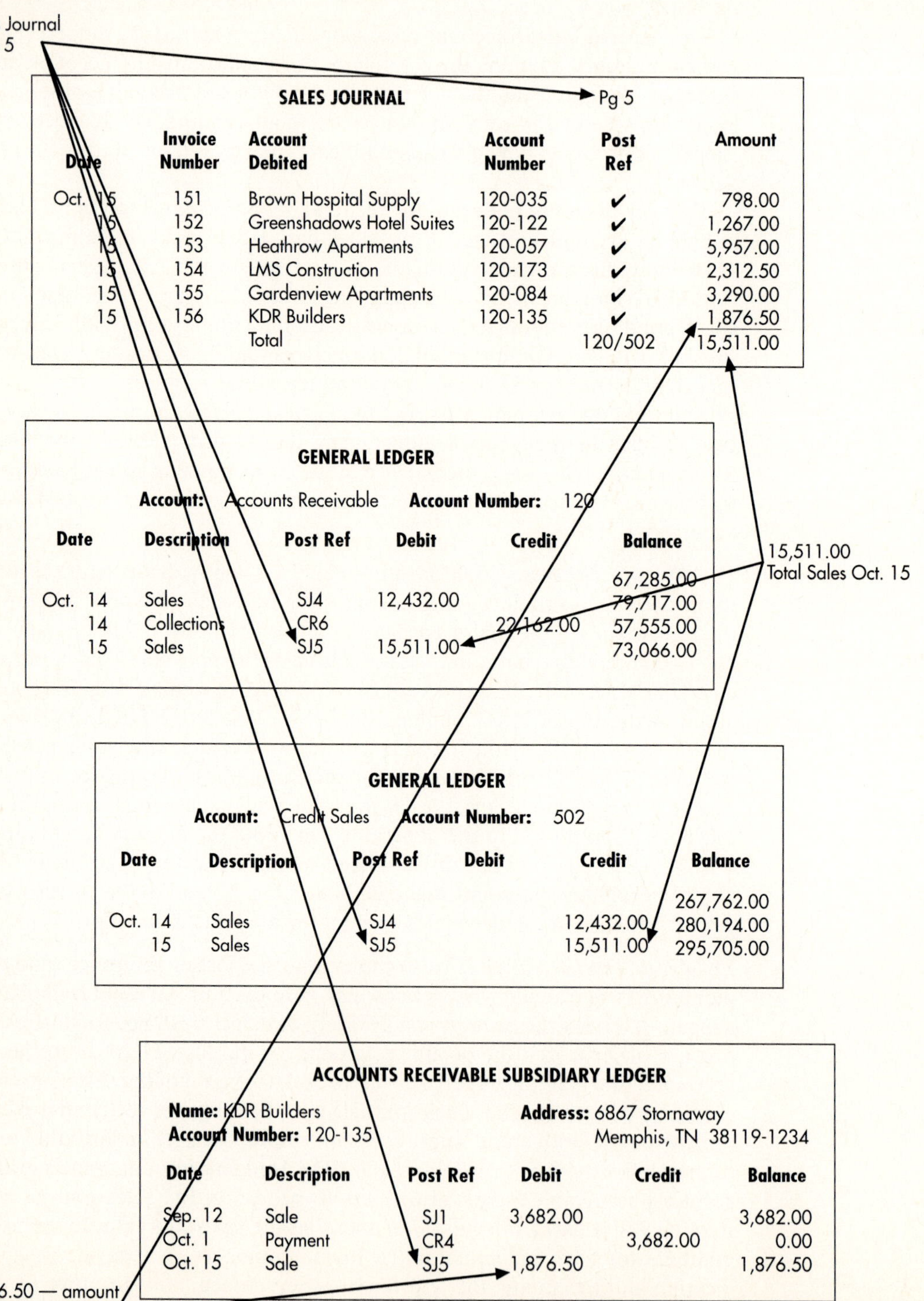

SALES JOURNAL Pg 5

Date	Invoice Number	Account Debited	Account Number	Post Ref	Amount
Oct. 15	151	Brown Hospital Supply	120-035	✔	798.00
15	152	Greenshadows Hotel Suites	120-122	✔	1,267.00
15	153	Heathrow Apartments	120-057	✔	5,957.00
15	154	LMS Construction	120-173	✔	2,312.50
15	155	Gardenview Apartments	120-084	✔	3,290.00
15	156	KDR Builders	120-135	✔	1,876.50
		Total		120/502	15,511.00

GENERAL LEDGER

Account: Accounts Receivable **Account Number:** 120

Date	Description	Post Ref	Debit	Credit	Balance
					67,285.00
Oct. 14	Sales	SJ4	12,432.00		79,717.00
14	Collections	CR6		22,162.00	57,555.00
15	Sales	SJ5	15,511.00		73,066.00

GENERAL LEDGER

Account: Credit Sales **Account Number:** 502

Date	Description	Post Ref	Debit	Credit	Balance
					267,762.00
Oct. 14	Sales	SJ4		12,432.00	280,194.00
15	Sales	SJ5		15,511.00	295,705.00

ACCOUNTS RECEIVABLE SUBSIDIARY LEDGER

Name: KDR Builders **Address:** 6867 Stornaway
Account Number: 120-135 Memphis, TN 38119-1234

Date	Description	Post Ref	Debit	Credit	Balance
Sep. 12	Sale	SJ1	3,682.00		3,682.00
Oct. 1	Payment	CR4		3,682.00	0.00
Oct. 15	Sale	SJ5	1,876.50		1,876.50

The Chart of Accounts. Figure 2.3 also shows that each general ledger account has its own number. The **chart of accounts** is a list of all general ledger accounts used by an organization. The structure of the chart of accounts is one of the most important aspects of an AIS, because it affects the preparation of financial statements and reports. Data stored in individual accounts can easily be summed for presentation in reports, but data stored in summary accounts cannot be easily broken down and reported in more detail. Consequently, it is important that the chart of accounts contain sufficient detail to meet the information needs of the organization.

To illustrate, consider the consequences if S&S were to use only one general ledger account for all sales transactions. It would be easy to produce reports showing the total amount of sales for a given time period, but it would be very difficult to prepare reports separating cash and credit sales. Indeed, the only way to produce these latter reports would be to trace the audit trail back to the journals and source documents to identify the nature of each sales transaction. Clearly, this approach would not be very practical. If, however, S&S used separate general ledger accounts for cash and credit sales, then reports showing both types of sales could be easily produced. Total sales could also be easily reported by summing each type of sale.

Table 2.5 shows the chart of accounts Ashton developed for S&S. Let us examine its structure. Each account number is three digits long, with each digit serving a specific purpose. The first digit represents the major account categories as they appear on S&S's financial statements: current assets, noncurrent assets, liabilities, equity accounts, revenues, expenses, and summary accounts. Notice that each major category is assigned a separate block of numbers, which corresponds with the sequence in which it appears in the financial statements. Thus all current assets are numbered in the 100s, noncurrent assets are numbered in the 200s, and so on.

The second digit in each account code represents the primary financial subaccounts within each category. Again, the accounts are assigned numbers to match the order of their appearance in financial statements (in order of decreasing liquidity). Thus account 120 represents accounts receivable and account 150 represents inventory.

Finally, the third digit identifies the specific account to which the transaction data will be posted. For example, account 501 represents Cash Sales of appliances, account 502 represents Credit Sales of appliances, and account 503 represents revenues from service calls. Similarly, accounts 101 through 103 represent the various Cash accounts used by S&S.

It is important to realize that the chart of accounts will differ, depending on the nature and purpose of the organization it represents. For example, the sample chart of accounts for S&S reflects the fact that the company is a partnership. Corporations would not have separate capital and drawing accounts but instead, accounts for common stock and retained earnings. Likewise, since S&S is a retail organization, it has only one type of general ledger inventory account. A manufacturing company, in contrast, would have separate general ledger accounts for raw materials, work in process, and finished goods inventories.

A chart of accounts should also provide room for growth. Notice that Ashton left a number of gaps in S&S's chart of accounts to allow for later

Table 2.5 **Sample Chart of Accounts for S&S**

Account Code	Account Name
100-199	Current Assets
101	Checking Account
102	Saving Account
103	Petty Cash
120	Accounts Receivable
125	Allowance for Doubtful Accounts
130	Notes Receivable
150	Inventory
160	Supplies
170	Prepaid Rent
180	Prepaid Insurance
200-299	Noncurrent Assets
200	Land
210	Buildings
215	Accumulated Depreciation —Buildings
230	Equipment
235	Accumulated Depreciation —Equipment
240	Furniture and Fixtures
245	Accumulated Depreciation —Furniture & Fixtures
250	Other Assets
300-399	Liabilities
300	Accounts Payable
310	Wages Payable
321	Employee Income Tax Payable
322	FICA Tax Payable
323	Federal Unemployment Tax Payable
324	State Unemployment Tax Payable
330	Accrued Interest Payable
360	Other Liabilities

Account Code	Account Name
400-499	Equity Accounts
400	Parry, Capital
410	Gonzalez, Capital
500-599	Revenues
501	Cash Sales
502	Credit Sales
503	Service Revenues
510	Sales Returns & Allowances
511	Sales Discounts
520	Interest Revenue
530	Miscellaneous Revenue
600-799	Expenses
600	Cost of Goods Sold
611	Wages Expense
612	Commissions Expense
613	Payroll Tax Expense
620	Rent Expense
630	Insurance Expense
640	Supplies Expense
650	Bad Debt Expense
701	Depreciation Expense— Buildings
702	Depreciation Expense— Equipment
703	Depreciation Expense— Furniture & Fixtures
710	Income Tax Expense
900-999	Summary Accounts
901	Drawing, Parry
902	Drawing, Gonzalez
910	Income Summary

insertion of additional accounts. For example, S&S does not currently have enough excess cash to invest in marketable securities. Later, when it can do so, a new general ledger account for marketable securities can be created and assigned the number 110. Ashton also knows that Scott and Susan hope to open additional stores in the future. When this occurs, he plans to add two more digits to the chart of accounts to represent each store in the chain, so that S&S can track sales, expenses, inventory, and other items in each individual store.

Finally, accounts in the subsidiary ledgers often have longer account codes than those used in the general ledger. For example, notice in Fig. 2.3 that each individual account receivable has a six-digit code. The first three digits are 120, the code for accounts receivable in the general ledger. The additional three digits provide a means for identifying up to 1000 individual customers. The accounts payable and inventory subsidiary ledgers would be organized in a similar manner.

This concludes our description of the documents and procedures that Ashton developed for S&S's AIS. In a small company like S&S, it will be Ashton's responsibility not only to design and manage the AIS but also to perform most of the procedures we have just described. These tasks are only part of Ashton's responsibilities, however. As Focus 2.1 explains, controllers in small businesses must play a number of roles. Similarly, we pointed out earlier that transaction processing is only one of three key functions of the AIS.

PROVIDING INFORMATION FOR DECISION MAKING

A second function of the AIS is to provide management with information useful for decision making. In manual systems, this information is provided in the form of reports that fall into two main categories: financial statements and managerial reports.

Financial Statements

The preparation of financial statements consists of a sequence of activities. First, all the accounts in the general ledger and their balances are listed in a report called a **trial balance.** It is so named because one of its purposes is to allow the accountant to verify that the total debit balances in various accounts equal the total credit balances in other accounts. Once the trial balance has been prepared and checked, any necessary adjusting entries are made. Then another trial balance, called the **adjusted trial balance** because it reflects the effects of all adjusting entries, is prepared. The adjusted trial balance is examined to verify the equality of debits and credits and the accuracy of all adjusting entries. The income statement can then be produced from the adjusted trial balance. Next, closing entries are made to zero out all revenue and expense accounts and transfer the amount of net income (or loss) to the appropriate equity account. The balance sheet is then produced. Finally, the statement of cash flows is prepared, using information from the income statement and balance sheet.

Managerial Reports[1]

In addition to preparing financial statements, the AIS must be able to provide managers with detailed operational information about the organization's performance. For example, Scott and Susan need reports about inventory status, relative profitability of products, relative performance of each salesperson, cash collections and pending obligations, and S&S's performance in meeting its delivery and service commitments.

Often, both traditional financial measures and operational data are required for proper and complete evaluation of performance. To illustrate, consider the

---

[1]The material in this section is drawn largely from two articles by Robert S. Kaplan and David P. Norton: "The Balanced Scorecard—Measures That Drive Performance," *Harvard Business Review* (January–February 1992): 71–79; and "Putting the Balanced Scorecard to Work," *Harvard Business Review* (September–October 1993): 134–147.

FOCUS 2.1

What *Does* a Small Business Controller Do?

Controllers in small businesses play at least four distinct roles. The first role can be characterized as a technician. In this role, the controller is responsible for collecting and processing the data needed to prepare not only financial statements but also a wide variety of managerial reports. Moreover, just turning out those reports is not enough. The controller must understand the business issues behind the numbers well enough to be able to help management interpret those numbers correctly. He or she must also work with various managers to learn exactly what information they really need to do their jobs effectively, and then devise the means for providing that information.

A second role of the controller is to act as "company cop." This entails ensuring that the company is in compliance with all applicable regulations and that assets, including data, are adequately safeguarded. It also involves establishing procedures to ensure that business activities are performed correctly and efficiently and that data about them are recorded accurately.

A third role played by the controller in a small business is that of booster and trainer. This entails helping managers and staff to understand how their individual duties fit into the company's overall goals and objectives. It also involves overseeing sufficient cross training of staff so that in the event of an employee's absence, due to vacations or illness, the business can continue to function smoothly. It may even include providing advice to young employees about career development, such as encouraging them to go back to school for further training. Moreover, in a small business, the controller may get involved in the kinds of employee counseling that in larger companies would be the province of a separate human resource management department.

A fourth role played by the small business controller is that of technology and accounting expert. The controller must keep abreast of technology and accounting developments and how they affect both business operations and employee responsibilities. Developing and maintaining a good personal "network" is essential to meeting this role, because no one individual can keep abreast of all the accounting and technological changes that occur each year. One way to develop such a network is to get involved in the local Institute of Management Accountants (IMA) chapter.

In summary, the small business controller is responsible for more than just "keeping the books."

Focus Questions

1. Which do you think is more important for the small business controller: technical accounting knowledge or good interpersonal skills? Why?
2. How can a controller develop a good understanding of the business so that he or she can explain to management the implications underlying the accounting numbers?
3. What can you do now, as a student, to better prepare yourself for the various roles you may be asked to play as a management accountant?

Source: Bonnie D. Labrack, "Small Business Controller," *Management Accounting* (November 1994): 38–41.

evaluation of sales staff. Dividing sales revenue by the number of sales staff provides one measure of productivity. Dividing the number of sales by the same denominator provides another way to look at productivity. Dividing sales revenue by the number of hours worked by sales staff provides yet another measure of productivity. Additional perspective is gained by calculating the average sale amount and the cost of sales staff salaries as percentages of sales revenue. All these measures are valid, and all five together provide a better overall evaluation of performance than any one alone.

Most source documents capture both financial and operational data about business transactions. The key is to design the AIS so that both kinds of data are stored in a manner that facilitates their integration in reports. Traditionally, most AIS systems have failed in this regard because they were designed primarily to support the preparation of financial statements, rather than the decision needs of internal management.

Corporate accountants must also know how to reorganize existing internally generated data and present it in a manner that sheds new light on operational results. For example, innovation is one vital requirement for continued long-run growth. One way that companies like Rockwater, a subsidiary of Brown & Root/Halliburton and a worldwide leader in underwater engineering and construction projects, measure innovation success is to track and report the percentage of sales revenues that are generated by new products.

Some important data must be collected from external sources, however. Data about customer satisfaction is one good example. It is not sufficient simply to measure and track how long it takes to fill and deliver customer orders. That merely provides information about how well a company is meeting its *own* goals for customer service. Information about whether the company is meeting its customers' requirements and expectations is also needed. The only way to find out the "real story" is to ask customers directly. Consequently, companies like Apple Computer regularly survey their customers. Other firms, such as the Big 3 U.S. automobile manufacturers, hire market research firms like J.D. Powers to collect that data. Once again, it is important to design the AIS so that such externally generated data are integrated with internally generated measures in a manner that facilitates the preparation of reports based on both kinds of data.

Budgets and Performance Reports. Two important types of managerial reports are budgets and performance reports. A **budget** is the formal expression of goals in financial terms. One of the most common and important types of budgets is the cash budget. A **cash budget** shows projected cash inflows and outflows (see Table 2.6). This information is especially important to a small business because cash flow problems are one of the principal causes of small-business failures. A cash budget can provide advance warning of cash flow problems in time to permit corrective action to be taken.

Another commonly used budget is the operating budget. An **operating budget** projects an organization's revenues and expenses for a given time period, usually a month or a year. Typically, operating budgets are structured along the lines of financial statements.

Budgets are financial planning tools. Performance reports, in contrast, are used for financial control. A **performance report** lists the budgeted and actual amounts of revenues and expenses and also shows the variances, or differences, between these two amounts (see Table 2.7).

Budgeted amounts, however, are estimates; consequently, there are almost certain to be variances for each item in the performance report. Therefore the principle of **management by exception** should be used to interpret those variances. If the performance report shows actual performance to be at or near

Table 2.6 **Sample Cash Budget**

	January	February	March	April
Beginning Balance	10,000	11,000	8,000	8,000
Projected Cash Receipts:				
Cash Sales	7,000	8,500	8,000	9,000
Collections on Account	26,000	29,000	28,000	30,000
Total Cash Available (A)	43,000	48,500	44,000	47,000
Projected Cash Disbursements (B)	(32,000)	(41,000)	(39,000)	(36,000)
Projected Ending Cash Balance (C = A – B)	11,000	7,500	5,000	11,000
Desired Minimum Balance (D)	8,000	8,000	8,000	8,000
Amount Needed to Borrow (D – C)	0	500	3,000	0
Ending Balance	11,000	8,000	8,000	11,000

Table 2.7 **Sample Performance Report**

L & P, Inc.: Monthly Performance Report						
	Current Month			Year-to-Date		
	Budget	Actual	Variance	Budget	Actual	Variance
Sales	$55,000	$56,500	1,500	$500,000	$512,000	12,000
Cost of Goods	39,000	39,400	400	350,000	354,000	4,000
Gross Margin	$16,000	$17,100	1,000	$150,000	$158,000	8,000
Selling Expenses	8,000	8,500	500	75,000	81,000	6,000
Other Operating Expenses	5,000	6,000	1,000	45,000	46,000	1,000
Income Before Taxes	$ 3,000	$ 2,600	(400)	$ 30,000	$ 31,000	1,000

budgeted figures, a manager can assume that the item is under control and that no action needs to be taken. On the other hand, significant deviations from budgeted amounts, in *either* direction, signal the need to investigate the cause of the discrepancy and take whatever action is appropriate to correct the problem.

Behavioral Implications of Managerial Reports. There is an old saying that measurement affects behavior. As applied to business, this means that employees tend to focus their efforts primarily on those tasks that are measured and evaluated. This can be either good or bad, depending on the nature of the relationship between the behavior being measured and the organization's overall goals. To illustrate, consider the task of customer complaint resolution. The organization wants to satisfy its customers to the greatest extent possible at the lowest possible cost. If customer service representatives are evaluated solely in terms of the number of complaints "resolved" per unit of time, however, two types of problems may arise. The customer service representatives may be so focused on quickly resolving each complaint in the store's favor that they alienate some customers in the process. Or customer service representatives may "give away the store" just to appease and please every customer with a complaint.

Budgets can often result in dysfunctional behavior. For example, the managers at a company that did not budget funds to purchase all the equipment needed to meet performance goals rented the equipment. This allowed them to meet their performance targets and remain within budget, although a subsequent review by the company's internal auditors disclosed that renting the equipment cost the organization, over a period of years, $684,000 more than if the equipment had been purchased outright![2]

Indeed, the budgeting process itself can be dysfunctional. Management may expend a great deal of effort in "number crunching," trying to get the budget numbers to turn out as desired, rather than focusing on how to accomplish the organization's mission and goals. Focus 2.2 discusses how to avoid this potential problem and turn the budgeting process into a value-added activity.

We have presented several examples of how reports produced by the AIS can unintentionally result in dysfunctional behavior. The key point to remember is that the AIS does not just "neutrally" report on employee performance. Rather, it directly affects behavior. In the next section, we look at how the AIS can be designed to encourage employees to behave in ways congruent with the organizational goals of providing accurate, reliable information and safeguarding assets.

INTERNAL CONTROL CONSIDERATIONS

The third function of an AIS is to provide adequate internal controls to accomplish three basic objectives:

1. Ensure that the information produced by the system is reliable.
2. Ensure that business activities are performed efficiently and in accordance with management's objectives while also conforming to any applicable regulatory policies.
3. Safeguard organizational assets, including its data.

Two important methods for accomplishing these objectives are to provide for adequate documentation of all business activities and to design the AIS for effective segregation of duties. Additional aspects of internal control are covered in Chapters 13 and 14.

Adequate Documentation

Adequate documentation of all business transactions is the key to accountability. Documentation allows management to verify that assigned responsibilities were completed correctly. Ashton recalls an example he encountered while working as an auditor that gave him a firsthand glimpse of the types of problems that can arise from inadequate documentation. One of his audit clients sold and serviced computers, providing free repairs during the warranty period. Service personnel were instructed to treat repairs as being under

[2] "Budget-busting Leases," reported in the column "Rountable," edited by E. Theodore Keys, Jr., in the *Internal Auditor* (June 1995): 66.

FOCUS 2.2

Avoiding Dysfunctional Budgeting Behavior

To fly an airplane safely, you need to concentrate on where you are going, not on the instrument panel. Similarly, the key to running a business effectively is to focus on attaining the organization's goals, not on the budget process. This does not mean that budgeting has no value. Just as the instrument panel in a plane alerts the pilot about potential problems, budgets provide warning signs about organizational performance. The key to success in flying a plane or running a business, however, is not to spend too much time examining the instrument panel or budget. Accountants can use the following five-step process to help managers develop the proper perspective toward budgeting.

First, explain that the purpose of the budget is to identify and allocate the resources needed to accomplish the organization's goals. Moreover, stress that the objective is not only to accomplish those goals, but to do so as efficiently as possible.

Second, begin the budget process by identifying measurable goals. Each department manager needs to specify the unit's goals and how they relate to those of the entire organization.

Third, have each department manager develop several alternative strategies for accomplishing these goals. No cost data should be involved at this time, however. Instead, the focus should be solely on identifying alternative methods for accomplishing objectives.

Fourth, the accounting department, rather than the department managers, should assign costs to each alternative strategy. This keeps the department managers focused on how their unit's goals and strategies relate to those of the entire organization, not on "playing games" to get the budget numbers "right."

Fifth, the department manager reviews the budget figures prepared by the accounting department. Each manager should be encouraged to develop alternative strategies that may more efficiently achieve their unit's goals. Any such changes are then returned to the accounting department for assignment of costs. Steps four and five are repeated until the manager is satisfied with the final budget.

The key to this process is a division of responsibilities between the accounting department and unit managers. Managers focus on setting goals and developing strategies to meet those goals; accountants do the "number crunching" to translate those goals and strategies into a budget. The result is that managers focus on running the organization, not on budgeting. The accountant becomes a "flight instructor," teaching managers to "fly the plane instead of watching the instrument panel."

Focus Questions

1. What are the benefits and drawbacks if accountants follow this approach to budgeting?
2. If the focus should be on running the organization rather than preparing budgets, why develop a budget at all?

Source: Stephen M. Rehnberg, "Keep Your Head Out of the Cockpit," *Management Accounting* (July 1995): 34–37.

warranty unless explicitly informed otherwise. The client had no procedures, however, for tracking warranty periods. Consequently, the company was completing a great deal of "free" repair work that should have been charged to customers. Indeed, the results of the audit estimated that the client had failed to bill almost $1 million worth of repair work! The client has since hired a new employee whose primary responsibility is to track warranty records for all computer sales.

Well-designed documents and records can also enhance the accuracy and efficiency of transaction processing. That is why Ashton took such care in designing S&S's source documents. Prenumbering source documents is especially important because it facilitates accounting for them. Any gaps in the sequence of completed source documents should be promptly investigated. Missing documents may have been misplaced, in which case some transactions may have not been recorded. They may also, however, be a sign of a more serious problem. For example, a missing check may have been written for fraudulent purposes. The use of posting references in journals and ledgers is also important because it facilitates checking the accuracy of all entries posted to the ledgers. Finally, the use of specialized journals can improve the efficiency of recording business transactions.

Adequate documents and records can also ensure that an organization does not make commitments it cannot keep. For example, Ashton wants S&S to avoid promises to sell and deliver appliances that it does not currently have in stock. Consequently, he wants S&S to use a perpetual inventory system. To maintain the accuracy of those records, he will periodically reconcile recorded amounts with physical counts of inventory on hand.

Adequately written descriptions of task procedures are also important. Ashton recalls another audit problem he encountered that related to a weakness in this area. The clerk responsible for processing customer payments had not been instructed how to handle checks for which no match could be found in the accounts receivable records. Consequently, the clerk had decided that the "proper thing to do" was to return such checks to customers along with a note requesting additional information about why the check had been sent. This added more than a week to the time it took to turn accounts receivable into cash. After this situation was uncovered, the clerk was instructed to endorse restrictively and deposit all such checks and then to initiate correspondence with the customer for resolution of the matter. The company also put this policy in writing in the procedures manual, to avoid similar problems in the future.

Segregation of Duties

Segregation of duties refers to dividing responsibility for different portions of a transaction among several people. The objective is to prevent one person from having total control over all aspects of a business transaction. Specifically, the functions of authorizing transactions, recording transactions, and maintaining custody of assets should be performed by different people. Segregation of these three duties helps to safeguard assets and improve accuracy because each person can look at and thereby limit the others' actions. Effective segregation of duties should make it difficult for an individual employee to steal cash or other assets successfully.

Segregation of duties is especially important in business activities that involve the receipt or disbursement of cash, because it can be stolen so easily. For example, in processing cash receipts from customers, one person should be responsible for handling and depositing those receipts (the custody function) and another person should be responsible for updating the accounts receivable records (the recording function). Otherwise, a person who performed both functions could divert customer payments for personal use and conceal the theft by falsifying the accounts. Similarly, in the realm of cash disbursements,

FOCUS 2.3

Stealing the Entire Company

The case of Thomas Brimberry and Stix & Co. illustrates how severe the problem of employee fraud can become. Brimberry began working at Stix & Co. as a clerk earning $20,000 a year. He had greater ambitions, however, and with other family members he borrowed heavily to buy into a nightclub. It failed, saddling him with $3000 monthly debt payments. To make ends meet, he started to steal from his employer, Stix & Co.

He began by opening a margin account in his wife's maiden name. He increased the account's borrowing power by inflating stockholdings or erasing debt. The documents authorizing these transactions were added to batches of similar transactions, all of which were processed by an unsuspecting clerk who did not always carefully examine each transaction.

At first, Brimberry succeeded in his illegal stock trades and was able to cover his debt payments. A run of bad trades, however, eventually left him $1 million in debt to Stix & Co. To cover this shortage, he began to counterfeit stock certificates. He carefully selected firms that did not pay dividends, so that no one at Stix would notice the failure to receive a dividend check. Stix's policy requiring two people to be present whenever stock certificates were put into or removed from the bank vault was not a problem. Brimberry says he simply chose clerks to accompany him who were "too busy or too dumb" to ask any questions about what he was doing!

Eventually, the illusion of rapid growth created by Brimberry's fake accounts made Stix & Co. a takeover target. Brimberry then contacted James Massa, a lawyer, and introduced him to the Stix & Co. board of directors as a big investor. Massa eventually bought a controlling interest in the firm, using $1 million that he and Brimberry had embezzled from Stix & Co.! They then proceeded to steal at will, using their position as owners to fool the external auditors.

The scheme finally fell apart several years later when Brimberry and Massa began to argue about their relative share of the profits. Both were eventually convicted of embezzlement and sentenced to prison.

Focus Questions

1. How was Brimberry able to bypass Stix & Co.'s internal controls to start his embezzlement scheme?
2. The story says that once Brimberry and Massa became owners, they could steal at will. What does this imply about the limits of internal controls?

Source: John Curley, "How a Clerk Built Up a Brokerage Business by Hook or by Crook," *The Wall Street Journal* (February 7, 1985): A1, A22.

one person should be responsible for preparing and approving checks for payment (the authorization function), and another person should be responsible for signing and subsequently mailing those checks (the custody function). Indeed, Ashton recalls a fraud that occurred at one of his former audit clients because these cash disbursement functions were not adequately segregated. In that case, the treasurer signed all checks prepared by accounts payable, but instead of mailing them out himself, he returned them to accounts payable. After receiving the signed checks, however, the accounts payable manager would change the payee name by using the erase feature on the typewriter that had been used to prepare those checks! After the fraud was detected, the treasurer was instructed to mail all checks after signing them.

As this example shows, inadequate segregation of duties can create opportunities for the theft of organizational assets. Focus 2.3 provides an example of how bad this situation can get.

Small organizations like S&S, however, do not always have enough staff to segregate duties effectively. In such cases, effective control can still be achieved through close supervision and owner-performance of some key business activities. For example, Ashton intends to recommend that Scott and Susan be the only ones authorized to write checks on the company's account. In addition, only Scott and Susan should have the authority to approve the granting of credit to new customers or the extension of additional credit to existing ones.

SUMMARY AND CASE CONCLUSION

An AIS plays three key roles in any organization: (1) providing information useful for decision making, (2) efficiently and effectively processing data about the transactions an organization engages in, and (3) including adequate internal control procedures to ensure the reliability of information produced and to safeguard the organization's assets. Ashton was confident that the AIS he had designed for S&S would fulfill those three functions. Table 2.8 lists the documents, journals, and ledgers that would comprise that system. Further details about these items will be provided in Chapters 17–21.

Ashton reflected on the steps he had followed to build the system. He had begun by obtaining an understanding of the basic business activities engaged in by S&S and of the key decisions that Scott and Susan would need to make to run the business effectively. Since S&S is a retail merchandising company, its operations could be described in terms of four basic transaction cycles:

1. The *revenue cycle* encompasses all transactions involving the sales of goods and services to customers and the collection of cash receipts in payment for those sales.
2. The *expenditure cycle* encompasses all transactions involving the purchase of and payment for the merchandise sold and other services consumed by S&S, such as rent and utilities.
3. The *human resources cycle* encompasses all the transactions involving the hiring, training, and payment of employees.
4. The *general ledger and reporting cycle* includes all activities related to the preparation of financial statements and other managerial reports, as well as nonroutine transactions such as the repayment of bank loans and various adjusting entries.

Ashton had then used this knowledge to identify the types of data that needed to be collected for each transaction. He then followed general principles of forms design to create source documents that would be easy to complete for capturing transaction data. He also designed a set of journals and ledgers in which to record and organize the data.

An important step had been designing the chart of accounts. Ashton had coded the general ledger accounts so that they would support not only the preparation of financial statements but also a variety of other managerial reports for S&S. In addition, although the chart of accounts reflected the current structure of S&S, it could be easily expanded as the organization grew.

***Table 2.8* Documents, Journals, and Ledgers for S&S**

Title	Purpose
Documents	
Sales Invoice	Record cash and credit sales of appliances and parts
Service Invoice	Record sales of repair services
Delivery Ticket	Record delivery of appliances to customers
Monthly Statement	Inform customers of outstanding account balances
Credit Memo	Support adjustments to customer accounts for sales returns & allowances and sales discounts; also support write-off of uncollectible accounts
Purchase Order	Order merchandise from vendors
Receiving Report	Record receipt of merchandise from vendors, indicating both quantity and condition of items received
Time Card	Record time worked by employees
Specialized Journals	
Sales	Record all credit sales
Cash Receipts	Record cash sales, payments from customers, and other cash receipts
Purchases	Record all purchases from vendors
Cash Disbursements	Record all cash disbursements
General Journal	Record infrequent, nonroutine transactions; also record adjusting and closing entries.
Subsidiary Ledgers	
Accounts Receivable	Maintain details about each individual customer
Accounts Payable	Maintain details about each individual vendor
Inventory	Maintain details about each inventory item
Fixed Assets	Maintain details about each piece of equipment and other fixed assets
General Ledger	Maintain details about all major asset, liability, equity, revenue, and expense accounts

In the end, Ashton felt satisfied with the system's fundamental controls. Scott and Susan would perform certain key functions, such as approving credit and signing checks. The posting references in the various journals and ledgers, together with prenumbering all source documents, would provide an adequate audit trail. The use of specialized journals would facilitate the recording process. Finally, the periodic reconciliation of subsidiary ledger totals with their respective general ledger control accounts would provide a check on the accuracy of transaction processing.

Nevertheless, Ashton realized that the manual AIS he designed would not be adequate in the long run. As S&S grew and the volume of transactions increased, the system would have to be automated. Thus he began to gather information about how to make that transition. Although he is not yet sure exactly what computer equipment and programs S&S will need, Ashton is confident that with a little more study (see Chapters 3–9) he will be able to handle this transition.

KEY TERMS

- transaction cycles
- source documents
- general journal
- specialized journals
- general ledger
- subsidiary ledger
- control account
- audit trail
- chart of accounts
- trial balance
- adjusted trial balance
- budget
- cash budget
- operating budget
- performance report
- management by exception
- segregation of duties

CHAPTER QUIZ

1. The set of transactions involving interactions between an organization and its suppliers is the
  a. revenue cycle.
  b. expenditure cycle.
  c. human resources cycle.
  d. general ledger and reporting cycle.

2. Transaction data are first captured and recorded on
  a. specialized journals.
  b. subsidiary ledgers.
  c. journal vouchers.
  d. source documents.

3. Adjusting entries are recorded first in
  a. specialized journals.
  b. the general journal.
  c. the general ledger.
  d. a subsidiary ledger.

4. Which of the following is most likely to be a general ledger control account?
  a. Accounts Receivable
  b. Petty Cash
  c. Prepaid Rent
  d. Retained Earnings

5. Which of the following is useful for projecting the need for short-term borrowing?
  a. Operating budget
  b. Performance report
  c. Cash budget
  d. Statement of cash flows

6. A report that expresses goals in financial terms is called a
  a. performance report.
  b. financial statement.
  c. budget.
  d. chart of accounts.

7. The chart of accounts lists general ledger accounts in
  a. alphabetical order.
  b. chronological order.
  c. order by size.
  d. the order in which they appear in financial statements.

8. Which of the following is the best way to compensate for inadequate segregation of duties?
  a. Maintaining a complete audit trail
  b. Preparing a trial balance
  c. Directly involving ownership in key functions
  d. Maintaining sound hiring practices

9. Which of the following is one of the three key functions of the AIS?
  a. Processing transactions efficiently
  b. Providing adequate segregation of duties
  c. Ensuring that business activities are performed in a manner consistent with management's desires and regulatory rules
  d. Developing a chart of accounts

10. Which of the following is the most important step in developing an AIS?
  a. Developing well-designed source documents
  b. Developing a sound chart of accounts
  c. Developing subsidiary ledgers
  d. Developing specialized journals

DISCUSSION QUESTIONS

2.1 Examine Table 2.1 and discuss how the various information items would be collected and reported by a company's AIS.

2.2 Many restaurants use customer checks with prenumbered sequence codes. Each food server is given a packet of these checks on which to write up customer orders. Food servers are told not to destroy any customer checks; if a mistake is made, they are to void that check and write a new one. All voided checks are to be turned in to the manager daily. How does this policy help the restaurant control cash receipts?

2.3 Look at the principles of forms design listed in Table 2.3. Which apply only to paper documents? Which apply to both paper documents and information presented on computer screens? What modifications, if any, do you think are needed to adapt those principles to the design of computer input screens?

2.4 How does an organization's line of business affect the design of its AIS? Give several examples of how differences among organizations are reflected in their AIS.

2.5 At most movie theaters, one employee is usually responsible for issuing tickets and collecting cash and another person collects those tickets when patrons enter the theater. What is the reason for this practice?

2.6 Some individuals argue that accountants should focus on producing financial statements and leave the design and production of managerial reports to information systems specialists. What are the advantages and disadvantages of following this advice? To what extent *should* accountants be involved in producing reports that include more than just financial measures of performance? Why?

PROBLEMS

2.1 The chart of accounts must be tailored to the specific needs of an organization. Discuss how the chart of accounts for each of the following organizations would differ from the one presented for S&S in Table 2.5:

a. A university
b. A bank
c. A government unit (city or state)
d. A manufacturing company
e. The expansion of S&S to a chain of 23 stores

2.2 Specialized journals should include columns for accounts commonly debited or credited. Refer to Table 2.4, which depicts an example of a sales journal, and use your knowledge of basic journal entries to design the following specialized journals:

a. Cash receipts journal (to include cash sales)
b. Purchases journal
c. Cash disbursements journal

2.3 Ollie Mace has recently been appointed controller of S. Dilley & Company, a family-owned manufacturing firm founded 28 years ago. The firm manufactures automotive parts. Its four major operating divisions are Heat Treating, Extruding, Small Parts Stamping, and Machining. Last year's sales from each division ranged from $150,000 to over $3 million. Each division is physically and managerially independent, except for the constant surveillance of S. Dilley, the firm's founder.

The accounting system for each division has evolved according to its needs and the abilities of its accounting staff. Mace is the first controller in the firm's history to have responsibility for overall financial management. Dilley expects to retire in a few years and wants Mace to improve the AIS before he retires so that it will be easier to monitor performance in each division.

Mace decides that the financial reporting system should be redesigned to include the following features:

- It should give managers uniform, timely, and accurate reports of business activity. Monthly reports should be uniform across divisions and be completed by the fifth of the following month, to provide enough time to take corrective actions to affect the next month's performance. Companywide financial reports should be available at the same time.
- Reports should provide a basis for measuring the return on investment for each division. Thus, in addition to revenue and expense accounts, reports should show assets assigned to each division.
- The system should generate meaningful budget data for planning and decision-making purposes. Budgets should reflect managerial responsibility and show costs for major product groups.

Mace believes that a new chart of accounts is required to accomplish these goals. He wants to divide asset accounts into six major categories, such as current assets and plant and equipment. He does not foresee a need for more than 10 control accounts within each of these categories. From his observations to date, 100 subsidiary accounts are more than adequate for each control account.

No division now has more than five major product groups. Mace foresees a maximum of six cost centers within any product group, including both the operating and nonoperating groups. He views general divisional costs as a non-revenue-producing product group. Altogether, Mace estimates that about 44 natural expense accounts plus about 12 specific variance accounts would be adequate.

REQUIRED

Design a chart of accounts for S. Dilley & Company. Explain how you structured the chart of accounts to meet the company's needs and operating characteristics. Keep total account code length to a minimum, while still satisfying all of Mace's desires.
(CMA Examination, adapted)

2.4 Washington County Hospital is located in a well-known summer resort area. The county population doubles during the summer months, and hospital activity increases correspondingly. A new administrator has decided to implement a responsibility accounting system. This program was announced when the quarterly cost reports were presented to department heads. Previously, cost data were infrequently supplied to department heads. Excerpts from the announcement of the new program follow:

> *The hospital has adopted a responsibility accounting system. From now on you will receive quarterly reports comparing actual with budgeted costs for your department. The reports will highlight the variances so that you can zero in on departures from budget (this is called management by exception). Responsibility accounting means that you are accountable for keeping your department's costs within budget. Variations from budget will help you identify which costs are out of line, and the size of the variance will indicate the relative importance of the deviations. Your first report accompanies this announcement. [See Table 2.9]*

The new administrator constructed the annual budget for 1997 and set quarterly budgets at one-fourth the annual budget. The administrator compiled the budget by analyzing costs for the past three years. The analysis showed that all costs increased each year, with a dramatic increase this past year. The administrator considered setting the budget at the average amount for the past three years, hoping that the new system would help to control cost increases. He finally decided, however, to set the budget at 3%

Table 2.9 **Washington County Hospital: Performance Report, Laundry Department, July–September 1997**

	Budget	**Actual**	**(Over) Under Budget**	**Percent (Over) Under Budget**
Patient Days	9,500	11,900	(2,400)	(25)
Pounds Processed—laundry	125,000	156,000	(31,000)	(25)
Costs:				
Laundry labor	$9,000	$12,500	$(3,500)	(39)
Supplies	1,100	1,875	(775)	(70)
Water, heating, & softening	1,700	2,500	(800)	(47)
Maintenance	1,400	2,200	(800)	(57)
Supervisor's salary	3,150	3,750	(600)	(19)
Allocated administrative costs	4,000	5,000	(1,000)	(25)
Equipment depreciation	1,200	1,250	(50)	(4)
Totals	$21,550	$29,075	$(7,525)	(35)

Administrator's Comments: Costs are significantly above budget for the quarter. Particular attention needs to be paid to labor, supplies, and maintenance.

below last year's actual costs. The activity level measured by patient days and pounds of laundry was set at last year's level too, because these numbers had remained basically constant over the past three years.

REQUIRED

a. Comment on the method used to set the budget.
b. What do budget variances mean? Is the administrator interpreting this information correctly? Explain.
c. Does the report presented in Table 2.9 accurately represent the department's performance efficiency? Why or why not?
(CMA Examination, adapted)

2.5 Denny Daniels is production manager for the jazz division of QRS, Inc., which manufactures audio CDs. Daniels is dissatisfied with the reports provided by the accounting department, because they are virtually useless for helping him manage the production process. He also feels that the reports do not accurately reflect how hard or how effectively he works as a production manager. Daniels tried to discuss these perceptions and concerns with June Smith, the controller for the jazz division. He told her, "I think the cost report is misleading. I know I've had better production over a number of periods, but the cost report still says I have excessive costs. Look, I'm not an accountant, I'm a production manager. I know how to get a good-quality product out. Over a number of years, I've even cut the amount of raw materials used to do it. But the cost report doesn't show any of this. Basically, it's always negative, no matter what I do. There's no way you can win with accounting or the people at corporate who use these reports."

Smith gave Daniels little consolation. She stated that the accounting system and cost reports are designed by headquarters and cannot be changed. She added, "Although these accounting reports are pretty much the basis for evaluating the efficiency of your division and the means that corporate uses to determine whether you have done a good job, you shouldn't worry too much. You haven't been fired yet! Besides, these reports have been used for the last 25 years."

After talking with the production manager at the country division of QRS, Daniels concluded that most of what June Smith said was probably true. However, the country division was able to get corporate to agree to some minor cost reporting changes. Daniels also knew from the trade grapevine that turnover of production managers at QRS was considered high, even though relatively few were ever fired. Most seemed to end up quitting, usually in disgust, because they believed they were being evaluated unfairly. The following comment sums up the general feeling of production managers who had left QRS:

> *Corporate headquarters doesn't really listen to us. All they consider are those misleading cost reports. They don't want them changed, and they don't want any supplemental information. The accountants may be quick with numbers, but they don't know anything about production. As it was, I either had to ignore the cost reports entirely or pretend they were important, even though they didn't reflect how well I had done my job. No matter what they say about not firing people, negative reports mean negative evaluations. I'm better off working for another company.*

Table 2.10 is an example of the cost report that has Daniels in such an agitated state.

Table 2.10 **Sample Cost Report for Problem 2.5**

QRS, Inc. Jazz Division Cost Report April 1997 (000 omitted)			
	Master Budget	**Actual Cost**	**Excess Cost**
Materials	$ 400	$ 437	$37
Labor	560	540	(20)
Overhead	100	134	34
Total	$1060	$1111	$51

REQUIRED

a. Comment on how Denny's perceptions of the following elements are likely to affect his behavior and performance: June Smith, the controller; corporate headquarters, the cost report, himself, and the AIS.
b. Identify and explain three changes that should be made in the cost report to make the information more meaningful and useful to production managers like Daniels.
(CMA Examination, adapted)

2.6 You have recently hired a full-time employee to assist you in the opening of Katie's Flower Shop. Because you anticipate that the majority of sales will be made over the phone, collection of accounts is likely to be a challenge for your business. To help solve this problem, you have asked your newly hired assistant to design a form that can be used to record sales transactions. Your assistant has just completed the form shown in Fig. 2.4.

REQUIRED

a. Which principles of form design are followed by this form?
b. Suggest at least three changes to the form that would make it more useful in collecting accounts.

2.7 An audit trail is a set of references that enables a person to trace a source document to its ultimate effect on the financial statements or vice versa. Describe in detail the audit trail for the following:

a. Purchases of inventory
b. Sale of inventory
c. Employee payroll

2.8 Check a recent newspaper or magazine for an article about employee fraud. Write a two-page

Figure 2.4

Sample Form for Katie's Flower Shop

KATIE'S FLOWER SHOP **No. 1234**
123 Elm St. 456-7890

Order Date ____________

Sold To:

Terms:
_____ **Paid**
_____ **30 Day Account**
_____ **C.O.D.**

Deliver To:

Delivery Date ____________

Delivered By ____________

Quantity	Description	Amount

Goods Received By ____________

Tax	
Total	

report summarizing how the fraud occurred and what control procedures could have prevented it.

2.9 Search popular business magazines (*Business Week, Fortune, Forbes*) for an article that describes some dysfunctional behavior that resulted from a poorly designed managerial reporting and performance evaluation system. Write a two-page report summarizing the problem and explaining how the managerial report led to the unplanned (and undesired) behavior.

2.10 Shauna Washington started a business to sell art supplies and related curricula to home school families. The business grew quickly, with sales doubling three times during a five-year period. At that point, she sold the business because it had grown too large to manage from her home. Under the new owners, sales doubled again during the next two years. Profits, however, did not keep pace with sales. In addition, the firm had borrowed heavily to open a warehouse. Inventory costs and operating expenses at the warehouse were higher than anticipated and the monthly payments on the loan were proving to be burdensome. Recently, the number and amount of past due accounts had risen dramatically. Together, these problems created a severe cash flow problem. If the cash flow situation does not improve quickly, the firm may have to declare bankruptcy, even though sales are continuing to increase.

REQUIRED

Describe some of the information that a good AIS could have provided for this firm and that, if provided in a timely manner, could have helped it avoid some of its problems.

CASE 2.1: ANYCOMPANY, INC.—AN ONGOING COMPREHENSIVE CASE

Identify a local company (you may use the same company that you identified to complete Case 1.1) and answer the following questions:

1. How many transaction cycles does the company have? Does it have any additional ones that were not discussed in this chapter? If so, identify and describe them.
2. Select any two transaction cycles and list the major transactions that occur in each. Trace how those transactions are processed by explaining what happens at each step in the cycle. Evaluate the adequacy of the audit trail related to those transactions.
3. What source documents does the company use to capture the relevant data for the transactions you identified in step 2? Comment on the adequacy of their design, using the criteria listed in Table 2.3.
4. What reports are produced in the two business cycles that you identified in step 2? What decisions are influenced by these reports? Comment on the adequacy of the reports for their intended purpose.
5. Examine the company's chart of accounts. How is it structured? How well does that structure meet the information needs of decision makers? How flexible is it in terms of providing for future growth?

CASE 2.2: S&S, INC.

You have been hired to assist Ashton Fleming in designing a manual accounting system for S&S. Ashton has developed a list of all the reports and documents that he thinks S&S needs (see Table 2.8). He asks you to complete the following tasks:

1. Prepare a preliminary design of the following documents, specifying which data elements should be captured on each:
   a. Sales invoice
   b. Repair services invoice
   c. Receiving report
   d. Employee time card
2. Design a report to manage appliance inventory.
3. Design a report to assist in managing credit sales and cash collections.
4. Design a report to track machines requiring service and warranty repairs.
5. Visit a local office supply store and identify what types of journals, ledgers, and blank forms are available. Describe how easily they could be adapted to meet S&S's needs.

ANSWERS TO CHAPTER QUIZ

1. b	**3.** b	**5.** c	**7.** d	**9.** a
2. d	**4.** a	**6.** c	**8.** c	**10.** b

Chapter 3

Systems Development and Documentation Techniques

LEARNING OBJECTIVES

After studying this chapter, you should be able to:

- Prepare and utilize data flow diagrams to understand, evaluate, and design information systems.
- Prepare and utilize flowcharts to understand, evaluate, and design information systems.
- Prepare and utilize decision tables.

Integrative Case: S&S, Inc.

What a hectic few months it has been for Ashton Fleming! He was very busy beginning his new job and preparing for the week-long grand opening of S&S. Then he was swamped processing all the transactions from the highly successful opening. To top it all off, he became confused and discouraged after an impromptu visit to Computer Applications (CA), a local computer company.

Ashton spoke with Kimberly Serra, CA's manager. She explained that CA developed systems ranging from simple general ledger operations to highly integrated software. The company handles a wide variety of accounting applications, including accounts receivable and payable, inventory, payroll, cost accounting, fixed assets, and cash receipts and disbursements.

Although Kimberly asked about S&S's system requirements and management's expectations, Ashton couldn't answer her specifically. He had not yet thought through these issues. When she asked how S&S's system worked, Ashton plunged into a discussion about how the various company documents were utilized. However, Kimberly seemed unable to follow his explanation. Ashton felt that part of his discussion was helpful, but overall it was irrelevant to the issue at hand.

Ashton came away impressed by CA and Kimberly. She offered to begin studying how S&S worked so she could assist him in finalizing the company's system needs. Unfortunately, he doesn't have the official go-ahead from Susan to begin work on a new system. Besides, Ashton had the distinct impression that S&S was not quite ready to develop or acquire a system. Ashton's first priority is to understand S&S's information needs more clearly.

From his days as an auditor, Ashton knows the value of good system documentation in assisting unfamiliar users with both understanding and evaluating a system. Good system documentation would be a big help to him and Kimberly as well as Scott and Susan as they evaluate the current and proposed system.

After sharing his conclusions with Susan and Scott, Ashton's plan to document the current and proposed systems was well received. They support his taking a leadership role in moving toward a new system and were especially interested in diagrams or charts that would help them quickly grasp how the system worked. Ashton was given the following assignment:

1. What types of tools and techniques should S&S use to document its existing system so it is easy to understand and evaluate?
2. What development tools and techniques should S&S use to design its new computer-based information system?

INTRODUCTION

Documentation is the narratives, flowcharts, diagrams, and other written material that explain how a system works. This information covers the who, what, when, where, why, and how of data entry, processing, storage, information output, and system controls. Since "a picture is worth a thousand words," one popular means of documenting a system is to develop diagrams, flowcharts, tables, and other graphical representations of information. They are then supplemented by a **narrative description** of the system, a written step-by-step explanation of system components and interactions. In this chapter we explain the most common systems documentation tools and techniques. They include data flow diagrams, flowcharts, and decision tables. These tools save both time and money, adding value to an organization.

Depending on your job function, you will need to understand documentation tools on one or more of the following levels:

1. At a minimum, you must be able to *read* documentation so that you can determine how the system works.
2. You may be required to *evaluate* the documentation. You may have to evaluate internal control system documentation to identify control strengths and weaknesses and recommend improvements. Alternatively, you may have to evaluate the documentation for a proposed system to determine whether the system meets your needs.
3. The greatest amount of skill is needed to *prepare* documentation. If you are a member of a team that is developing a new system you will have to prepare documentation to show how the existing as well as the proposed new system operates. You also may be required to document your understanding of a company's system of internal controls for others to review.

An understanding of documentation tools is required no matter what accounting career you choose. For example, Statement on Auditing Standards (SAS)55 *Consideration of the Internal Control Structure in a Financial Statement Audit,* requires that independent auditors understand a client's system of internal controls before conducting an audit. SAS 55 recommends that auditors use flowcharts and decision tables to document large, complex systems. Auditors can spot internal control weaknesses and strengths more easily from such graphic portrayals.

The documentation tools explained in this chapter are used throughout the book. Data flow diagrams and systems flowcharts, for example, are used extensively to show how systems work and how data and information flow. They are also tested on professional examinations—as you can see by noting the number of questions in the book that are adapted from these exams. Learning about these tools will better prepare you for these examinations.

DATA FLOW DIAGRAMS[1]

A **data flow diagram (DFD)** graphically describes the flow of data within an organization. It is used to document existing systems and to plan and design new ones. There is no ideal way to develop a DFD; different problems call for different methods. One good approach, recommended by DeMarco, one of the pioneers of the DFD approach, is highlighted in Focus 3.1.

Elements in a Data Flow Diagram

A DFD is composed of four basic elements: data sources and destinations, data flows, transformation processes, and data stores. Each is represented on a DFD by one of the symbols shown in Fig. 3.1.

Figure 3.1
Data Flow Diagram Symbols

Symbol	Name	Explanation
□	Data sources and destinations	The people and organizations that send data to and receive data from the system are represented by square boxes. Data destinations are also referred to as data sinks.
 ↗	Data flows	The flow of data into or out of a process is represented by curved or straight lines with arrows.
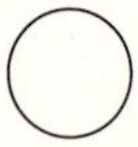 ○	Transformation processes	The processes that transform data from inputs to outputs are represented by circles. They are often referred to as bubbles.
=	Data stores	The storage of data is represented by two horizontal lines.

[1]Parts of this discussion were based on Tom DeMarco, *Structured Analysis and System Specification* (Englewood Cliffs, N.J.: Prentice-Hall, 1979). DeMarco has been at the forefront of structural analysis and design techniques and is a well-respected authority on the subject.

FOCUS 3.1

Guidelines for Drawing a DFD

Determine System Boundaries

The main objective in determining a system's boundaries is to include all relevant data elements. Since anything excluded will not be considered during system development, data elements should be included until a definitive decision can be made to discard them. Once the system boundary has been determined, all data flows entering or leaving the boundary should be identified.

Determine System Data Flows and Relationships

This step emphasizes *actual* versus expected data flows and relationships. An understanding of how the system works can be obtained by observing the flow of information through an organization and by interviewing the individuals who use and process the data. It is usually best to construct a DFD by concentrating first on data flows, rather than on processes or data stores. Any significant movement of information is usually a data flow and should be entered on the diagram. Where the data originates and its final destination should be identified.

Circles should be placed wherever work is required to transform one data flow into another. Each of these circles should be examined to determine whether there are any internal data flows that might be used within the process. If so, replace it with two or more processes and indicate the data flows between them. Files should be entered to represent all data repositories and the data flowing into and out of the file should be identified.

Determining how the system starts and stops is usually deferred to a later stage in the DFD development process, as are the details of unimportant error paths. Important error paths, such as those that require previous entries to be reversed, should be included in the DFD. A final guideline is to diagram flows of data, not control processes or control actions.

Label DFD Elements

The names given to DFD elements significantly impact the quality and readability of the diagram. An improperly or incompletely named element will result in an ineffective diagram. The reader will end up with either an incomplete or an improper understanding of the system.

Since the main emphasis of a DFD is the flow of information through a system, all the data flows should be named first. This approach forces the developer to concentrate on data flows, rather than on the processes or stores. Once the data flows have been labeled, naming the processes should be relatively easy, since the flow of data through the system is already understood and processes typically take their names from the data inflows or outflows.

Several guidelines should be followed in naming data elements. First, name all DFD elements. Second, make sure the names describe all the data or the entire process. If a name cannot completely describe the data or process, then decompose the flow or process further. Third, avoid names that are not fully descriptive, like *input data* or *update process.* Instead, choose active and descriptive names, like *daily inventory update* and *validate transaction.* Fourth, never combine unrelated items into a single data flow or process. If data do not flow together naturally or are not processed together, separate them.

Repeat the Process

DFD developers must work through organization data flows several times. Each subsequent pass helps refine the diagram and identify the fine points.

These four symbols are combined to show how data are processed. For example, the DFD in Fig. 3.2 shows that the input to process C is data flow B, which comes from data source A. The outputs of process C are data flows D and E. Data flow E is sent to data destination J. Process F uses data flows D and G as input and produces data flow I and G as output. Data flow G comes from and returns to data store H. Data flow I is sent to data destination K.

Figure 3.2

Basic Data Flow Diagram Elements

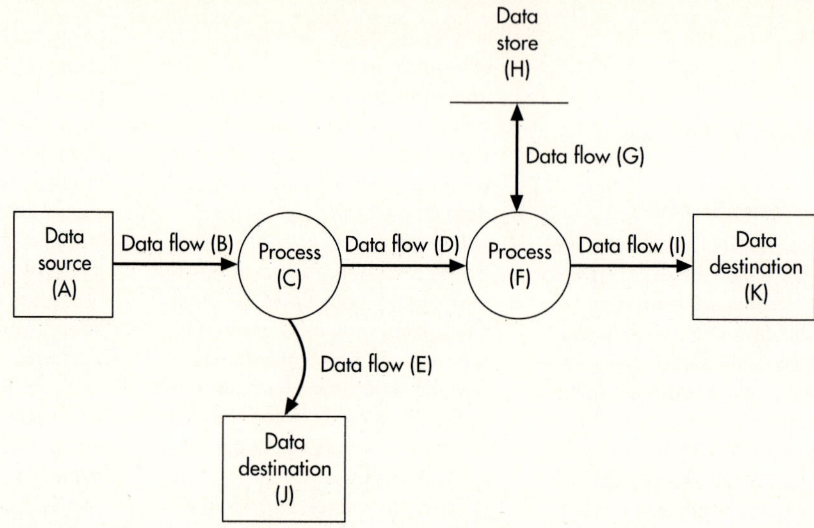

Figure 3.3 assigns specific titles to each of the processes depicted in Fig. 3.2. Figures 3.2 and 3.3 will be used to examine the four basic elements of a DFD in more detail.

Data Sources and Destinations. A source or destination symbol on the DFD represents an organization or individual that sends or receives data used or produced by the system. An entity can be both a source and a destination. **Data sources** and **data destinations** are represented by squares, as illustrated by items A (customer), J (bank), and K (credit manager) in Fig. 3.3.

Figure 3.3

Data Flow Diagram of Customer Payment Process

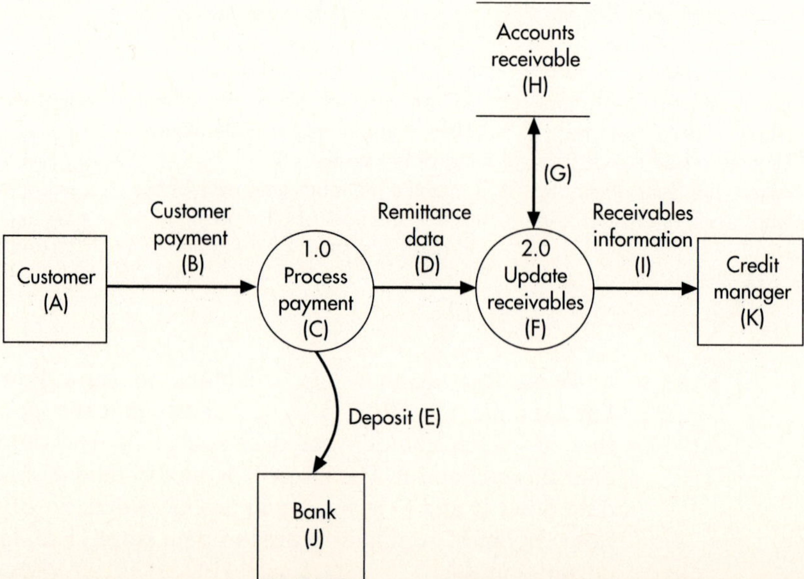

Data Flows. A **data flow** represents the flow of data between processes, data stores, and data sources and destinations. Data that pass between data stores and either a data source or a destination must go through some form of data processing—that is, through a transformation process. Data flow arrows are labeled to indicate the type of data being passed. Thus the reader knows exactly what information is flowing; no inferences are required. Data flows are represented in Fig. 3.3 by items B (customer payment), D (remittance data), E (deposit), G (unlabeled; represents information entered into or retrieved from an accounts receivable data file), and I (receivables information).

A data flow can consist of one or more pieces of datum. For example, data flow B (customer payment) consists of two parts: a payment and remittance data. Process 1.0 (process payment) splits these two data elements and sends them in different directions. The remittance data (D) flows to another process, where it is used to update accounts receivable records, and the payment (E) is sent to the bank with a deposit slip.

Because data flows may be composed of more than one data element, it must be determined whether to show one or more lines. The determining factor is whether the data elements always flow together. For example, if customers sometimes send inquiries about the processing of their payments, the DFD could be revised as shown in Fig. 3.4. The figure shows two lines because customer inquiries, although interacting with the same elements of the DFD, do not always accompany a payment. The two data elements have different purposes, and customer inquiries occur less frequently. If represented by the same data flow, the separate elements would be obscured, and the DFD would be more difficult to interpret.

A number of DFD guidelines have been developed over the years. First, different data flows cannot have the same name, and those chosen should represent and reflect what is known about the data. Second, data flows that move into and out of data stores (such as item G in Fig. 3.3) do not require names; the data store name is sufficient for identification. All other data flows should be named. Third, a DFD does not indicate why a process begins, such as inventory falling below a certain value (a purchase order is then issued) or a receivable becoming overdue (an overdue notice is drafted). Finally, data flows can move in two directions, as shown in item G of Fig. 3.3. In this example data flow out of the file, to facilitate an update and to produce a receivables report, and back to the file in the form of updated receivables balances.

Processes. **Processes** represent the transformation of data. Figure 3.3 shows that process payment (C) takes the customer payment and splits it into the

Figure 3.4

Splitting Customer Payments and Inquiries

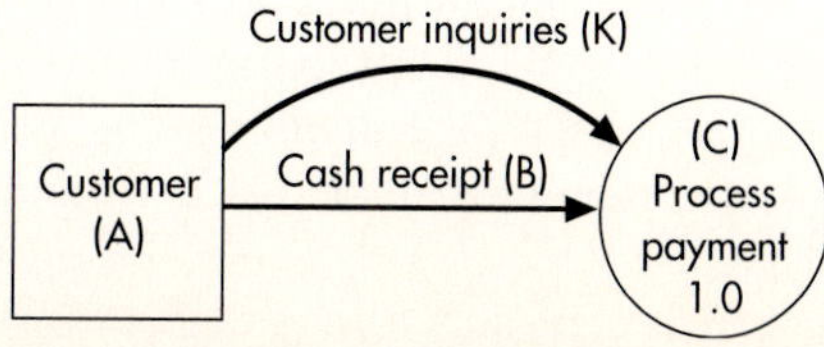

remittance data and the deposit (which includes the checks and deposit slip created within process payment). The updating process (F) takes the remittance data and the accounts receivables data and produces an updated receivables record and sends receivables information to the credit manager.

The name of each process should be as descriptive as possible to provide the reader with key information. Process names should include action verbs such as *update, edit, prepare, reconcile,* and *record.* Most processes are characterized by the data flows that move in and out of them (hence the names *process payment* and *update receivables*). In a completed DFD, as shown in Fig. 3.3, each process is given a number that helps readers move back and forth between the different levels of DFDs. (These levels and numbers are explained in more depth later in the chapter.)

Data Stores. A **data store** is a temporary or permanent repository of data. DFDs do not show the physical storage medium (disks, paper, and the like) used to store the data. As with the other DFD elements, data store names should be descriptive. As shown in Fig. 3.3, item H, data stores are represented by horizontal lines, with the data store's name listed inside.

Data Dictionary. Data flows and stores are typically collections of data elements. For example, a data flow labeled Employee Information might contain elements such as name, address, job title, and birth date. A **data dictionary** contains a description of all the data elements, stores, and flows in a system, including the storage and processing of data, the documents, and physical items such as inventory. Typically, a master copy of the data dictionary is maintained to ensure consistency and accuracy throughout the development process.

Subdividing the DFD

DFDs are subdivided into successively lower levels in order to provide ever increasing amounts of detail, since few systems can be fully diagramed on one sheet of paper. Since users have differing needs, a variety of levels can better satisfy these requirements.

The highest-level DFD is referred to as a context diagram. A **context diagram** provides the reader with a summary-level view of a system. It depicts a data processing system as well as the external entities that are the sources and destinations of the system's inputs and outputs.

Figure 3.5 is the context diagram that Ashton Fleming drew as he was analyzing the payroll processing procedures at S&S. It shows that the payroll processing system receives time cards from different departments and employee data from the human resources department. When these data are processed, the system produces (1) tax reports and payments for governmental agencies, (2) employee paychecks, (3) a check to deposit in the payroll account at the bank, and (4) management payroll reports.

Ashton also wants to diagram the details of the system. To do so, he decides to decompose the context diagram into successively lower levels, each with an increasing amount of detail. In preparation for this task he wrote the narrative description of S&S's payroll processing procedures contained in Table 3.1. Take a few minutes to read this description and determine the following:

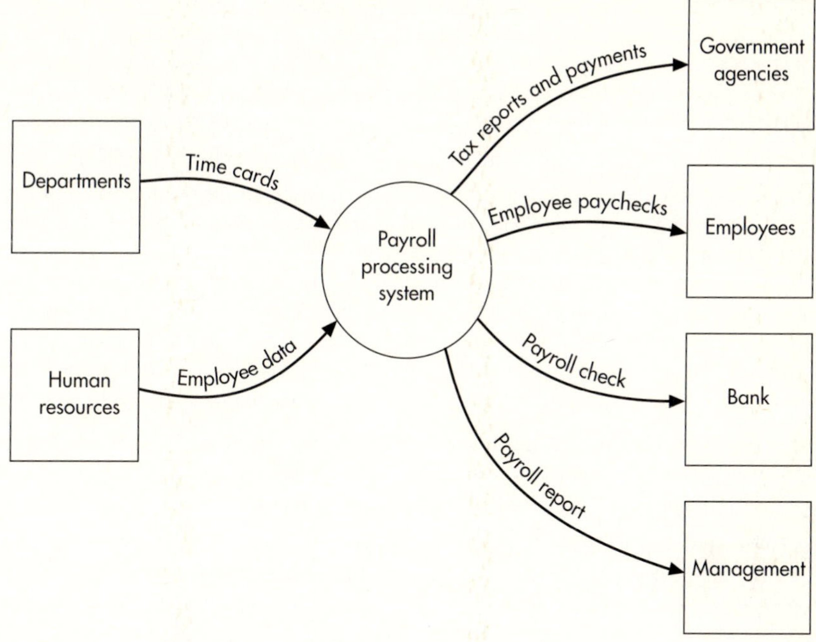

Figure 3.5

Context Diagram for S&S Payroll Processing

- The number of major data processing activities involved.
- The data inputs and outputs of each activity (ignoring all references to people, departments, and document destinations).

Based on Ashton's description, you should have identified approximately five data processing activities. You may have noted more or less, depending on how you identified the activities. The first is updating the employee/payroll master file (first paragraph of the narrative). The second is employee compensation (second, fifth, and sixth paragraphs). Later in the chapter you will see that this activity is broken out into smaller parts in a lower-level DFD. A third is the generation of management reports (third paragraph). A fourth is the payment of taxes (fourth paragraph). A fifth is posting entries to the general ledger (last paragraph). All the data inflows and outflows, as well as the five activities, form the basis of the DFD and are summarized in Table 3.2.

Using this information, Ashton exploded his context diagram and created the DFD shown in Fig. 3.6 (on page 74). The data coming from the human resources department were grouped together and called Employee Data. Notice that some data inputs and outputs have been excluded from this DFD. For example, in process 2.0 the data inflows and outflows that are not related to an external entity or to another process are not depicted (tax tables and payroll register in this case). These data flows are internal to the "pay employees" activity and are shown on the next DFD level.

Not fully satisfied with the level of detail he had captured, Ashton exploded process 2.0 (pay employees). Figure 3.7 (on page 75) provides more detail

Table 3.1 **Narrative Description of Payroll Processing at S&S**

When employees are hired, they fill out a new employee form. When a change to an employee's payroll status occurs, such as a raise or a change in the number of exemptions, human resources fills out an employee change form. A copy of these forms is sent to payroll. These forms are used to create or update the records in the employee/payroll file and are then stored in the file. Employee records are stored alphabetically.

Some S&S employees are paid a salary, but most are hourly workers who record the times they work on time cards. At the end of each pay period department managers send the time cards to the payroll department. The payroll clerk uses the time card data, data from the employee file (such as pay rate and annual salary), and the appropriate tax tables to prepare a two-part check for each employee. The clerk also prepares a two-part payroll register showing gross pay, deductions, and net pay for each employee. The clerk updates the employee file to reflect each employee's current earnings. The original copy of the employee paychecks are forwarded to Susan. The payroll register is forwarded to the accounts payable clerk. The time cards and the duplicate copies of the payroll register and paychecks are stored by date in the payroll file.

Every pay period the payroll clerk uses the data in the employee/payroll file to prepare a payroll summary report for Susan so that she can control and monitor labor expenses. This report is forwarded to Susan along with the original copies of the employee paychecks.

Every month the payroll clerk uses the data in the employee/payroll file to prepare a two-part tax report. The original is forwarded to the accounts payable clerk, and the duplicate is added to the tax records in the payroll file. The accounts payable clerk uses the tax report to prepare a two-part check for taxes and a two-part cash disbursements voucher. The tax report and the original copy of each document are forwarded to Susan. The duplicates are stored by date in the accounts payable file.

The accounts payable clerk uses the payroll register to prepare a two-part check for the total amount of the employee payroll and a two-part disbursements voucher. The original copy of each document is forwarded to Susan, and the payroll register and the duplicates are stored by date in the accounts payable file.

Susan reviews each packet of information she receives and approves and signs the checks. She forwards the cash disbursements vouchers to Ashton, the tax reports and payments to the appropriate governmental agency, the payroll check to the bank, and the employee checks to the employees. She files the payroll report chronologically.

Ashton uses the payroll tax and the payroll check cash disbursement vouchers to update the general ledger. He then cancels the journal voucher by marking it "posted" and files it numerically.

about the data processes involved in paying employees, and it includes the tax tables and the payroll register data flow left out of Fig. 3.6. In a similar fashion, each of the processes shown in Fig. 3.6 could be exploded to show a greater level of detail.

FLOWCHARTS

A **flowchart** is an analytical technique used to describe some aspect of an information system in a clear, concise, and logical manner. Flowcharts use a standard set of symbols to describe pictorially the transaction processing procedures used by a company and the flow of data through a system. General guidelines for preparing flowcharts so that they are readable, clear, concise, consistent, and understandable are presented in Focus 3.2.

Flowchart Symbols

The symbols used to create flowcharts are shown in Fig. 3.8 (on page 77). Each symbol has a special meaning that is easily conveyed by its shape. The shape

Table 3.2 **Activities and Data Flows in Payroll Processing at S&S**

Activities	Data Inputs	Data Outputs
Update employee/ payroll file	New employee form Employee change form Employee/payroll file	Updated employee/ payroll file
Pay employees	Time cards Employee/payroll file Tax tables	Employee checks Payroll register Updated employee/payroll file Payroll check Payroll cash disbursements voucher
Prepare reports	Employee/payroll file	Payroll report
Pay taxes	Employee/payroll file	Tax report Tax payment Payroll tax cash disbursements voucher Updated employee/ payroll file
Update general ledger	Payroll tax cash disbursements voucher Payroll cash disbursements voucher	Updated general ledger

indicates and describes the operations performed and the input, output, processing, and storage media employed. The symbols are drawn by a software program or with a **flowcharting template,** a piece of hard, flexible plastic on which the shapes of symbols have been cut out.

Flowcharting symbols can be divided into the following four categories, as shown in Fig. 3.8:

1. *Input/output* symbols represent devices or media that provide input to or record output from processing operations.
2. *Processing* symbols either show what type of device is used to process data or indicate when processing is completed manually.
3. *Storage* symbols represent the devices used to store data that the system is not currently using.
4. *Flow and miscellaneous* symbols indicate the flow of data and goods. They also represent such operations as where flowcharts begin or end, where decisions are made, and when to add explanatory notes to flowcharts.

Document Flowcharts

A **document flowchart** illustrates the flow of documents and information between areas of responsibility within an organization. Document flowcharts trace a document from its cradle to its grave. It shows where each document originates, its distribution, the purposes for which it is used, its ultimate disposition, and everything that happens as it flows through the system.

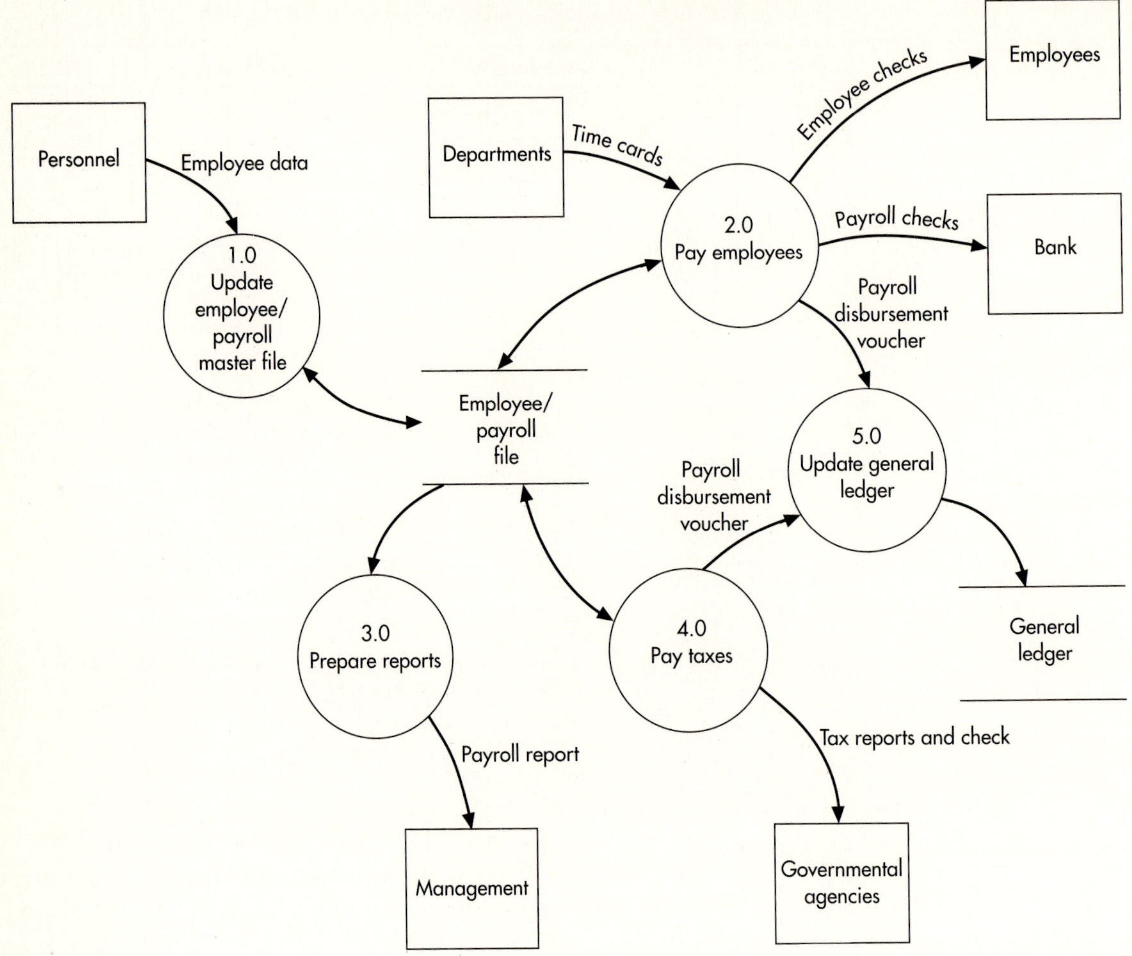

Figure 3.6

DFD for S&S Payroll Processing

A document flowchart is particularly useful in analyzing the adequacy of control procedures in a system, such as internal checks and separation of functions. Flowcharts that describe and evaluate internal controls are often referred to as **internal control flowcharts.** The document flowchart can reveal weaknesses or inefficiencies in a system, such as inadequate communication flows, unnecessary complexity in document flows, or procedures responsible for causing wasteful delays. Document flowcharts can also be prepared as part of the systems design process and should be included in the documentation of an information system.

The document flowchart that Ashton developed for the payroll process at S&S, as described in Table 3.2, is shown in Fig. 3.9 (on pages 80–81).

Figure 3.7

DFD for Process 2.0 in S&S Payroll Processing

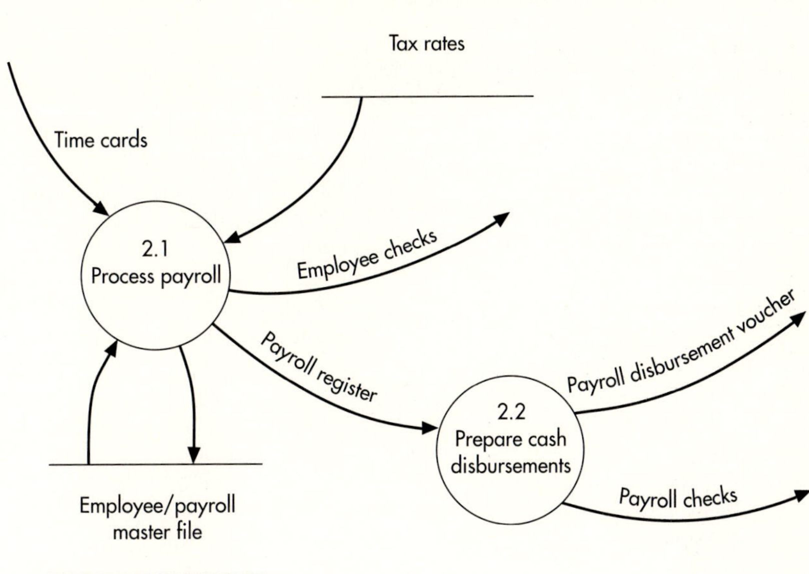

Computer System Flowcharts

System flowcharts depict the relationship among the input, processing, and output of an AIS. A system flowchart begins by identifying both the inputs that enter the system and their origins. The input can be new data entering the system, data stored for future use, or both. The input is followed by the processing portion of the flowchart, the steps performed on the data. The logic used by the computer to perform the processing task is shown on a program flowchart (explained in the following section). The resulting new information is the output component, which can be stored for later use, displayed on a screen, or printed on paper. In many instances, the output from one process is an input to another.

The sales processing system flowchart in Fig. 3.10 (on page 82) represents Ashton's proposal to capture sales data using state-of-the-art sales terminals. These terminals will edit the sales data (e.g., ensuring that all necessary sales data are collected) and print out a customer receipt. All sales data will be stored in a sales data file on a disk. At the end of each day, the data will be forwarded to S&S's computers, where it will be summarized and batch totals will be printed. The summary data will then be processed, and batch totals will again be generated and printed. These amounts will be compared with the batch totals generated prior to processing, and all errors and exceptions will be reconciled. The accounts receivable, inventory, and sales marketing master files and the general ledger will be updated. Users can access the files at any time by using an inquiry processing system. This system will produce standard reports and allow the user to access the data needed for special analyses.

FOCUS 3.2

General Guidelines for Preparing Flowcharts

1. Understand a system before flowcharting it. Interview users, developers, auditors, and management, or have them fill out a questionnaire; read through a narrative description of the system; or walk through system transactions.
2. Identify the entities to be flowcharted, such as departments, job functions, or external parties. Identify documents and information flows in the system as well as the activities or processes performed on the data. (For example, when reading a description of the system, the preparer could draw a box around the entities, a circle around the documents, and a line under the activities.)
3. When several entities, such as departments or functions, need to be shown on a flowchart, divide the flowchart into columns with a label for each. Flowchart the activities of each entity in its respective column.
4. Flowchart only the normal flow of operations, making sure that all procedures and processes are in the right order. Identify exception procedures by using the annotation symbol.
5. Design the flowchart so that flow proceeds from top to bottom and from left to right.
6. Give the flowchart a clear beginning and ending. Designate where each document originated, and show the final disposition of all documents so there are no loose ends that leave the reader dangling.
7. Use the standard flowcharting symbols; draw them with a template or a computer.
8. Clearly label all symbols. Write a description of the input, process, or output inside the symbol. If the description will not fit, use the annotation symbol. Print neatly, rather than writing in freehand.
9. When using multiple copies of a document, place document numbers in the top right-hand corner of the symbol. The document number should accompany the symbol as it moves through the system.
10. Each manual processing symbol should have an input and an output. Do not directly connect two documents, except when moving from one column to another. When a document is moved to another column, show the document in both.
11. Use on-page connectors to avoid flow lines that go all over the page and make it look cluttered. Use off-page connectors to move from one flowchart page to another. Clearly label all connectors to avoid confusion.
12. Use arrowheads on all flow lines. Do not assume that the reader will know the direction of the flow.
13. If a flowchart cannot fit on a single page, clearly label the pages 1 of 3, 2 of 3, and so on.
14. Show documents or reports first in the column in which they are created. They can then be shown moving to another column for further processing. A manual process is not needed to show documents being forwarded.
15. Show all data entered into or retrieved from a computer file as passing through a processing operation (a computer program) first.
16. Use a line from the document to a file to indicate that it is being filed. A manual process is not needed to show a document entering a file.
17. Draw a rough sketch of the flowchart as a first effort. You should be more concerned with capturing content than a perfect drawing. Few systems can be flowcharted in a single draft.
18. Redesign the flowchart to avoid clutter and a large number of crossed lines.
19. Verify the flowchart's accuracy by reviewing it with those familiar with the system. Be sure all uses of flowcharting conventions are consistent.
20. Draw a final copy of the flowchart. Place the name of the flowchart, the date, and the preparer's name on each page.

Figure 3.8

Common Flowcharting Symbols

Symbol	Name	Explanation
Input/Output Symbols		
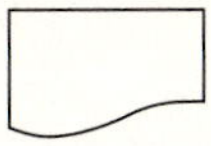	Document	A document or report; the document may be prepared by hand or printed by a computer
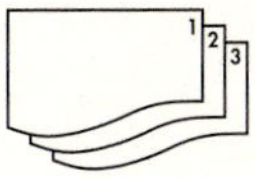	Multiple copies of one document	Illustrated by overlapping the document symbol and printing the document number on the face of the document in the upper right corner
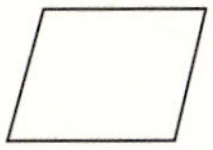	Input/output; Journal/ledger	Any function of input and output on a program flowchart Represents accounting journals and ledgers on document flowchart
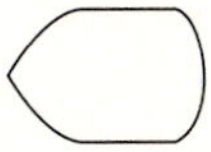	Display	Information displayed by an on-line output device such as a CRT terminal or personal computer monitor
	On-line keying	Data entry by on-line devices such as a CRT terminal or personal computer
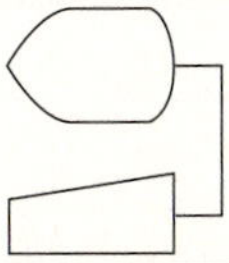	CRT terminal, personal computer	The display and on-line keying symbols are used together to represent CRT terminals and personal computers
	Transmittal tape	Manually prepared control totals; used for control purposes to compare to computer-generated totals
Processing Symbols		
	Computer processing	A computer-performed processing function; usually results in a change in data or information
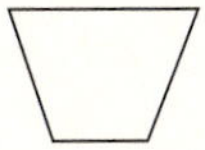	Manual operation	A processing operation performed manually
	Auxiliary operation	A processing function done by a device that is not a computer
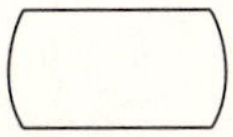	Off-line keying operation	An operation utilizing an off-line keying device (e.g., key to disk, cash register)

continued

Figure 3.8
Continued

Symbol	Name	Explanation
Storage Symbols		
	Magnetic disk	Data stored permanently on a magnetic disk; used for master files
	Magnetic tape	Data stored on a magnetic tape
	Magnetic diskette	Data stored on a diskette
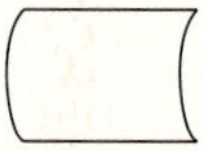	On-line storage	Data stored in a temporary on-line file in a direct-access medium such as a disk
 N	File	File of documents manually stored and retrieved; inscribed letter indicates file-ordering sequence: N = numerically A = alphabetically D = by date
Flow and Miscellaneous Symbols		
	Document or processing flow	Direction of processing or document flow; normal flow is down and to the right
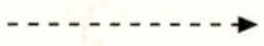	Data/information flow	Direction of data/information flow; often used to show data copied from one document to another
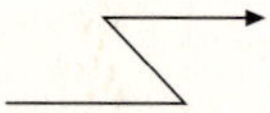	Communications link	Transmission of data from one location to another via communication lines
	On-page connector	Connects the processing flow on the same page; its usage avoids connecting lines crisscrossing a page
	Off-page connector	An entry from, or an exit to, another page
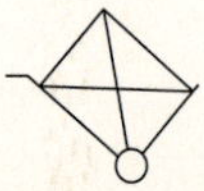	Flow of goods	Physical movement of goods; used primarily with document flowcharts

Figure 3.8
Continued

Symbol	Name	Explanation
Flow and Miscellaneous Symbols (continued)		
	Terminal	A beginning, end, or point of interruption in a process or program; also used to indicate an external party
	Decision	A decision-making step; used in a computer program flowchart to show branching to alternative paths
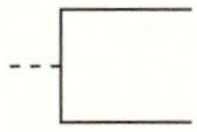	Annotation	Addition of descriptive comments or explanatory notes as clarification

System flowcharts are an important tool of systems analysis, design, and evaluation. They are universally employed in systems work and provide an immediate form of communication among workers. The systems flowchart is an excellent vehicle for describing information flows and procedures within an AIS.

Program Flowcharts

A **program flowchart** illustrates the sequence of logical operations performed by a computer in executing a program. The relationship between systems and program flowcharts is shown in Fig. 3.11 (on page 83).

Program flowcharts employ a subset of the symbols shown in Fig. 3.8. As shown in Fig. 3.12 (on page 84), a flow line connects the symbols and indicates the sequence of operations. The processing symbol represents a data movement or arithmetic calculation. The input/output symbol represents either the reading of input or the writing of output. The decision symbol represents a comparison of one or more variables and the transfer of flow to alternative logic paths. All points where the flow begins or ends are represented by the terminal symbol. Connectors, labeled with a digit or a capital letter, represent the continuation of the logic flow at a different location. Several exit connectors may have the same label, but labels can have only one entry connector. Once designed and approved, the program flowchart serves as the blueprint for coding the computer program.

The flowchart in Fig. 3.12 shows a simple example of the logic S&S's computer could use to process credit orders. After entering a sales order, customer credit approval is determined. If credit has not been approved, the order is rejected. Otherwise, the system determines whether present inventory can fill the order. If not, the order is held until sufficient inventory arrives. If there is enough inventory, the system checks the quantity. An order for 500 units or less is filled; an order greater than 500 units receives a 20% discount and is filled.

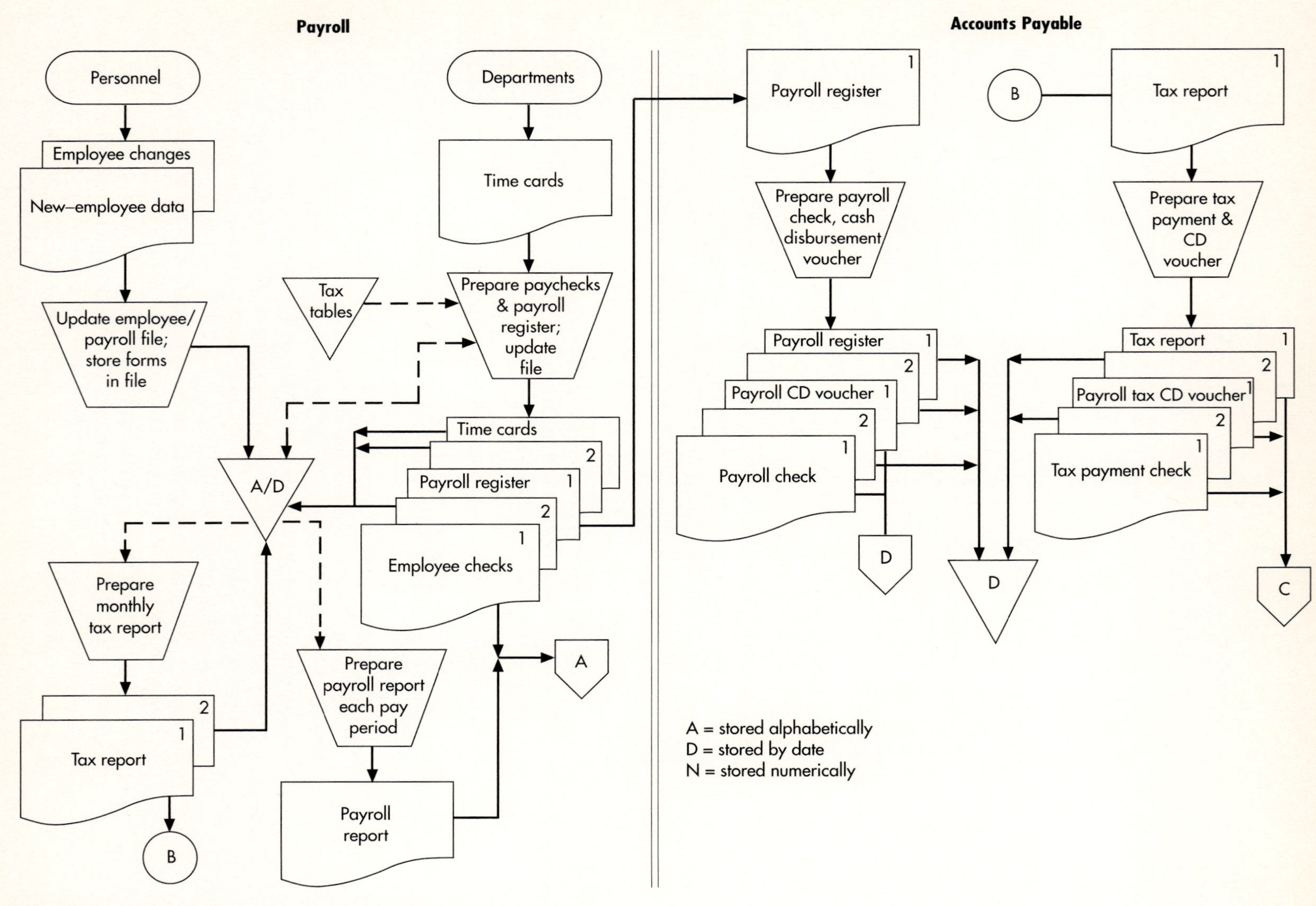

Figure 3.9 *Document Flowchart of Payroll Processing at S&S*

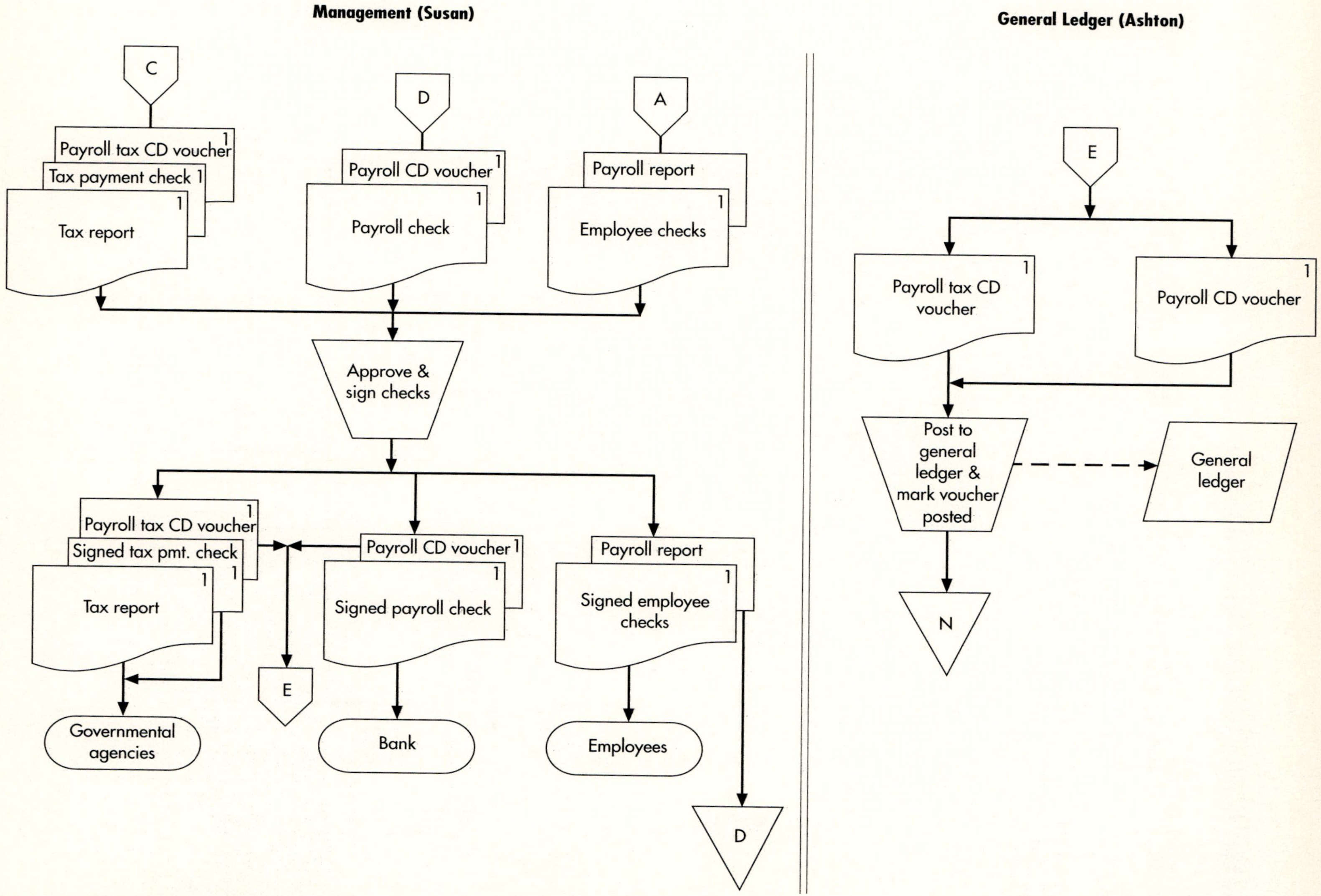

Management (Susan)

C

Payroll tax CD voucher 1

Tax payment check 1

Tax report 1

D

Payroll CD voucher 1

Payroll check 1

A

Payroll report

Employee checks 1

Approve & sign checks

Payroll tax CD voucher 1

Signed tax pmt. check 1

Tax report 1

Governmental agencies

E

Payroll CD voucher 1

Signed payroll check 1

Bank

Payroll report

Signed employee checks 1

Employees

D

General Ledger (Ashton)

E

Payroll tax CD voucher 1

Payroll CD voucher 1

Post to general ledger & mark voucher posted

General ledger

N

Figure 3.9 *(Continued)*

Figure 3.10 *Systems Flowchart of Sales Processing System at S&S*

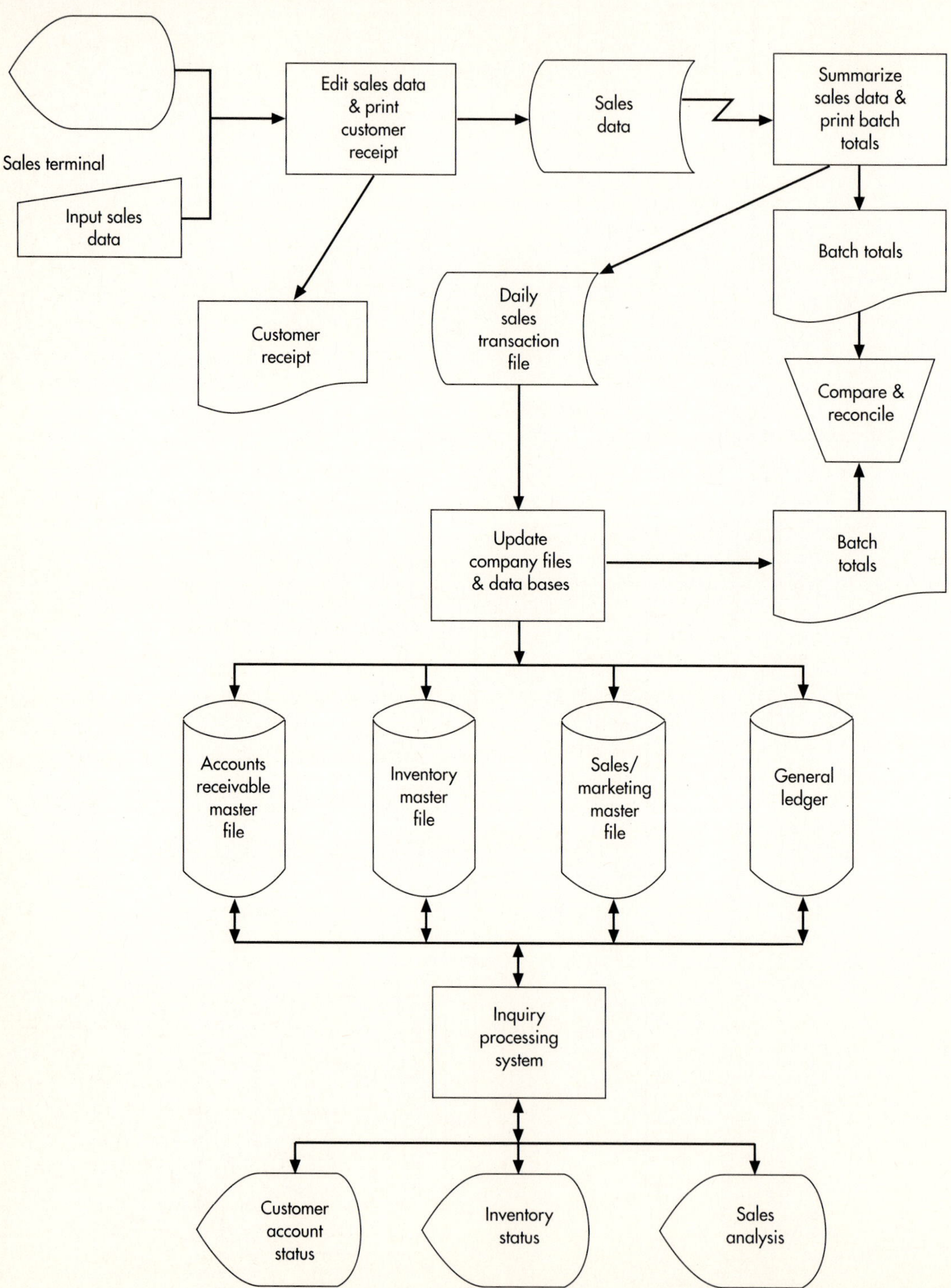

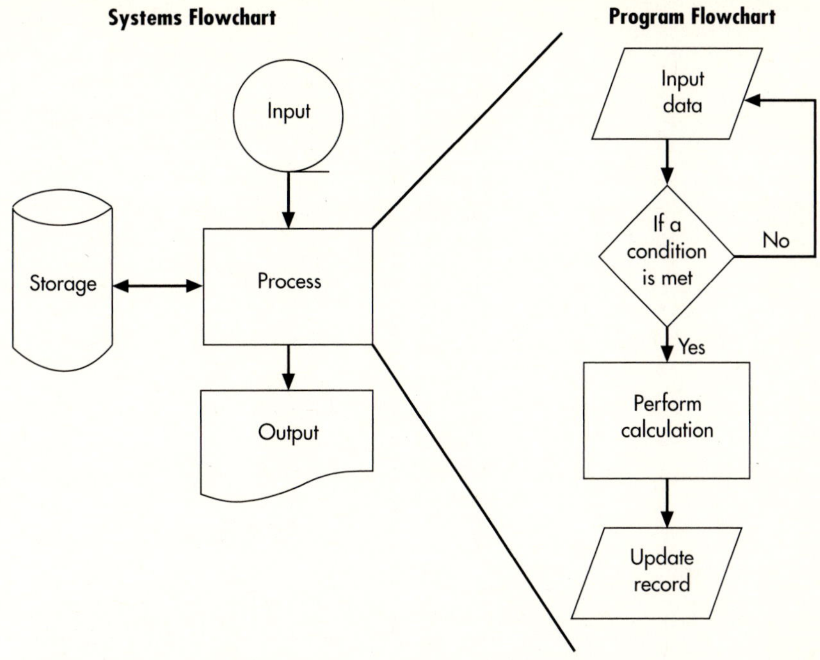

Figure 3.11

Relationship Between Systems and Program Flowcharts. A program flowchart describes the specific logic to perform a process shown on a systems flowchart.

Computer Configuration Chart

Flowcharting symbols can also be used to prepare a **computer configuration chart.** For example, Fig. 3.13 illustrates a configuration that Ashton might consider recommending to Susan and Scott if they set up an administrative office away from the store. It consists of a minicomputer, a magnetic disk (an external hard disk), a printer, and a personal computer (PC) that would be located in the accounting department. It also includes a sales terminal in the store. Although the chart shows only one of each device, it could easily be expanded to show multiple terminals and PCs.

Notice in Fig. 3.13 that the communications link symbol is used to indicate that the sales terminal is geographically remote from the central processor. In contrast, the straight line connecting the printer and the PC to the central processor indicates all three are located at the same site. Also note this illustration uses combinations of symbols to represent the terminal and the PC. There is no single symbol for representing a PC or a terminal. However, because they have both a monitor and a keyboard, they can be represented by a combination of on-line keyboard and the information display symbols. Note that a printer is represented by the document symbol.

A more sophisticated computer configuration chart appears in Fig. 3.14 (on page 86). This figure shows a computer system that includes two tape drives, three disk drives, a PC, a terminal, an optical character reader, a printer, and a central processing unit (CPU) with an on-line console keyboard.

Differences Between DFDs and Flowcharts

According to a study by Kievit and Martin (1989), data flow diagrams and flowcharts are the two most frequently used development and documentation tools. Their study shows that 62.5% of information professionals use DFDs and that 97.6% use flowcharts. Over 92% of users were satisfied with the use of both DFDs and flowcharts.

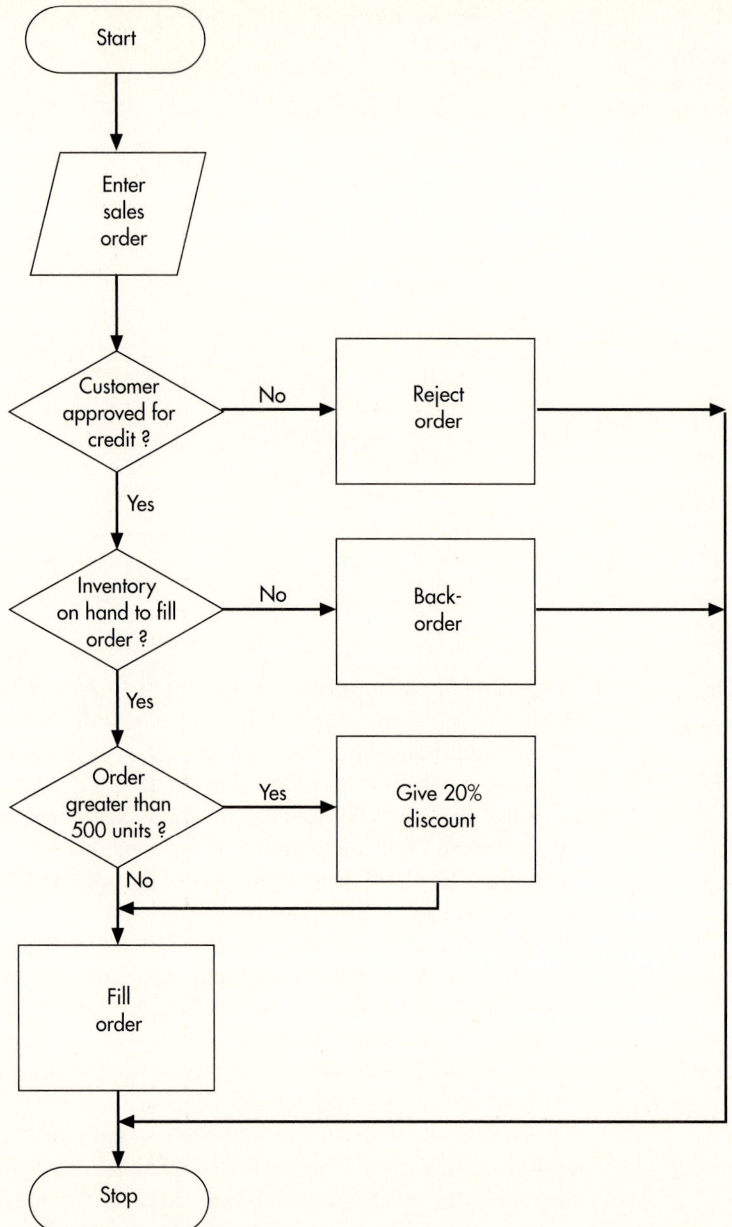

Figure 3.12

A Simple Program Flowchart for Processing Credit Orders

A number of differences separate DFDs and systems flowcharts. First, a DFD emphasizes the flow of data and what is happening in a system, whereas a flowchart emphasizes the flow of documents or records containing data. A DFD represents the logical flow of data, whereas a flowchart represents the physical flow of data. The **logical view** of data is the way users conceptually organize and understand the relationships between data items. It shows what

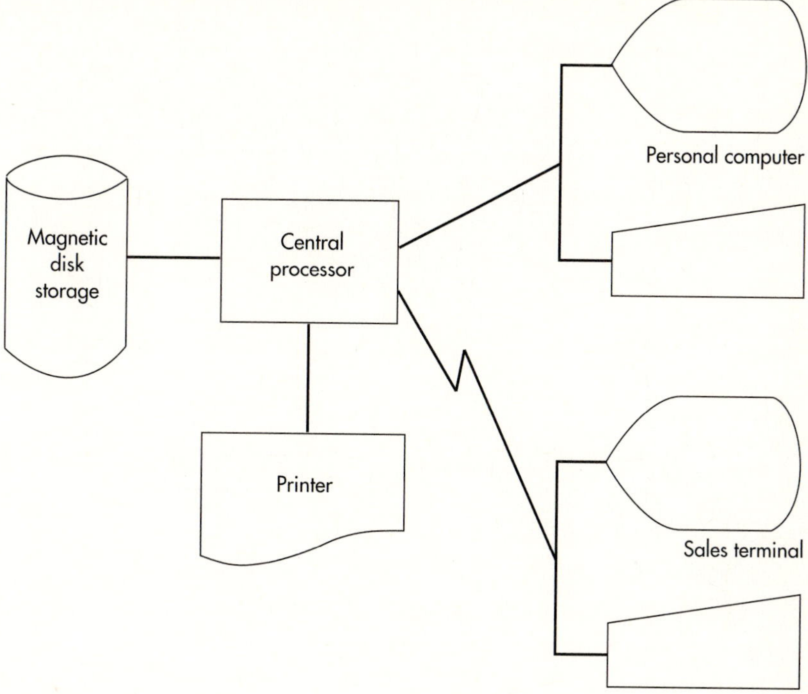

Figure 3.13

Simple Computer System Configuration

the system does with data—where data originate and are subsequently stored, the processes data undergo, and what ultimately happens to the processed data. The **physical view** refers to how, where, and by whom data are physically arranged and stored on disks or tapes. It is concerned with the physical aspects of the system, such as hardware, software, data structure, and file organization.

Second, flowcharts are used primarily to document existing systems, since they emphasize how data are processed and stored. DFDs, in contrast, are primarily used in the design of new systems and do not concern themselves with the physical devices used to process, store, and transform data. Using a flowchart during the design of a new system could result in a premature physical design; that is, physical implementation decisions (such as *how* something should be done) would be made when only conceptual design issues (such as *what* should be done) should be discussed.

Third, DFDs make use of only four symbols. Flowcharts, on the other hand, use many symbols and thus can show more pictorially than can DFDs. Consequently, it is imperative that DFD labels and accompanying descriptions effectively communicate what is happening. Finally, a flowchart shows the sequence of processes and data flows; DFDs do not. Nor do DFDs convey the timing of events, as a flowchart can.

Both DFDs and flowcharts are easy to prepare and revise when one of the recently developed DFD or flowcharting software packages is used. These packages are easier to use, in fact, than most word processors. Once a few basic

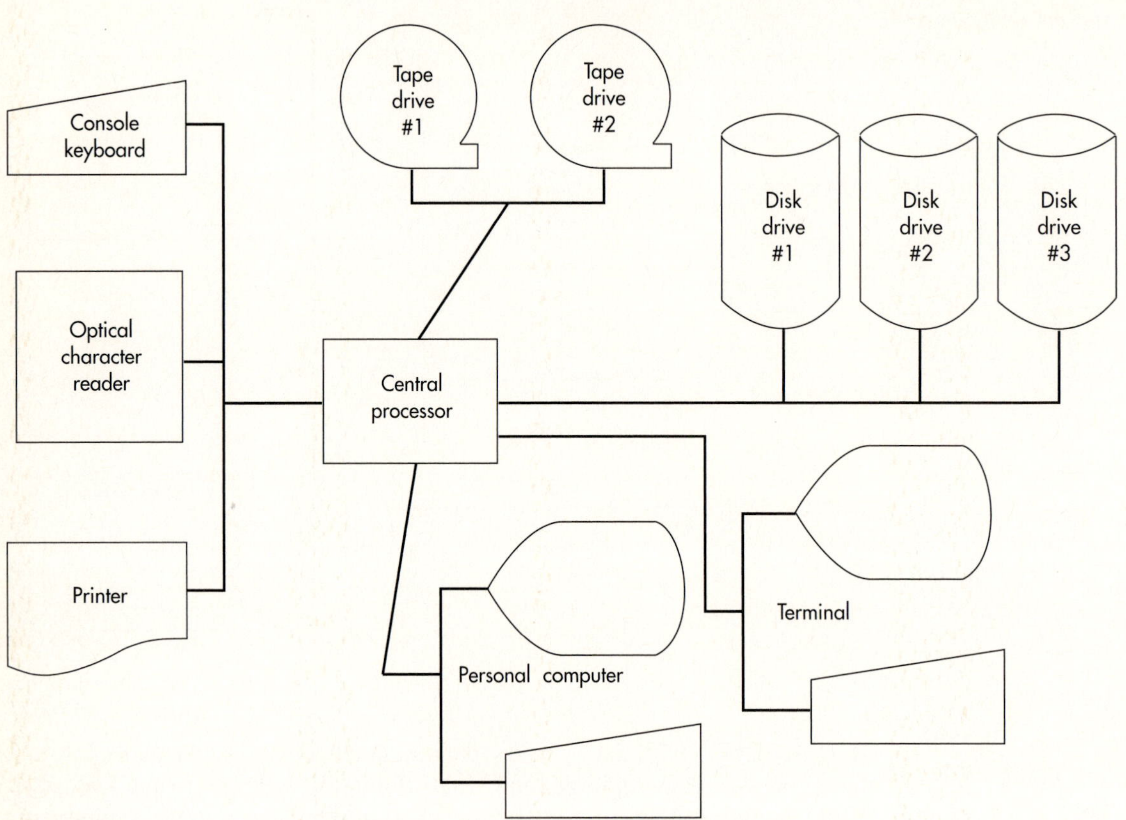

Figure 3.14

Business-Oriented Computer System

commands are mastered, users can quickly and easily prepare, store, revise, and print presentation-quality DFDs or flowcharts. To create a flowchart, the user selects the appropriate symbol, indicates where it should be placed, enters the appropriate text, and moves to the next symbol. Editing a flowchart is easy; users merely click on the appropriate symbol and add, delete, or move it.

DECISION TABLES

A **decision table** is a tabular representation of decision logic. For any given situation a decision table lists all the conditions (the *ifs*) that are possible in making a decision. It also lists the alternative actions (the *thens*) as well. Each unique relationship (*if* this condition exists, *then* take this action) is referred to as a **decision rule.** The general form of the decision table is illustrated in Table 3.3. The decision table in Table 3.4 outlines potential decisions and

Table 3.3
General Form of a Decision Table

Stub	**Entry**								
	Condition Rule								
Condition	**1**	**2**	**3**	**4**	**5**	**6**	**7**	**8**	**9**
(Specific conditions)									
	Action Rule								
Action	**1**	**2**	**3**	**4**	**5**	**6**	**7**	**8**	**9**
(Specific actions)									

actions by S&S when filling credit orders. It corresponds with the program flowchart in Fig. 3.12.

A decision table has four parts: the condition and action stubs and the condition and action entries. The condition stub contains the various logic conditions for which the input data are tested. For example, there are three entries in the condition stub in Table 3.4. Note that they correspond to the three decision symbols in the program flowchart in Fig. 3.12.

The condition entry consists of a set of vertical columns, each representing a decision rule in which the entries must be either yes (Y), no (N), or a dash (—). The dash indicates an indifferent result of the condition test. For example, when credit is not approved, the quantity or inventory on hand is not relevant.

Table 3.4
Simple Decision Table for Processing Credit Orders

	a	**b**	**c**	**d**
Credit approved	N	Y	Y	Y
Order ≤ inventory on hand	—	N	Y	Y
Order > 500 units	—	—	N	Y
Reject order	X			
Back-order		X		
Fill order			X	X
Give 20% discount				X

The action stub contains the actions the program should take. Table 3.4 indicates that four actions can be undertaken: reject the order, back-order, fill the order, or give a discount. The action entry columns indicate when an action is to occur. They display an X if the action is performed (if the input data meet the condition tests). A blank indicates the action is not performed.

Systems personnel use decision tables to illustrate the set of conditions present in most data processing programs and the corresponding courses of action for each condition. The advantage of decision tables is they indicate clearly all possible logical relationships among the input data. As a result a program can be prepared to recognize and respond properly to each decision rule. Decision tables, however, do not reflect the sequence of operations within a program and may become unmanageably large for complex programs. Program flowcharts and decision tables are often used together to help design and code computer programs.

Auditors can use decision tables to evaluate a client's application programs. If a decision table already exists, it can be reviewed for completeness and accuracy. If not, an auditor can create a decision table and then review it for weaknesses or errors in the computer program. Some studies have shown that up to 70% of application programs contain logic or syntax errors. For example, one savings and loan computer program failed to recognize that there were not 31 days in each month, resulting in over $100,000 in excess interest payments. Using a decision table, an auditor can create transaction data that can be processed by the system on a test basis. One or more transactions can be developed to test each separate decision rule, in this way assuring the auditor that the program actually meets its objectives. These concepts are discussed in more depth in Chapter 16.

SUMMARY AND CASE CONCLUSION

Ashton prepared the DFDs and flowcharts of S&S's payroll processing system (Figs. 3.6–3.10) to document and explain the operation of the existing system. He was pleased to see that Scott and Susan were able to grasp the essence of the system from this documentation. The DFDs indicated the logical flow of data, and the flowcharts illustrated the physical dimensions of the system—the origin and final disposition as well as what happened to the documents in each department were clear.

Susan and Scott agreed to have Ashton document the remainder of the system. The documentation would help all three not only understand but improve the current system. In fact, the payroll documentation had already helped them identify a few minor changes they wanted to make in their system. Using the information from Fig. 3.9, Susan now understood why the payroll clerk sometimes had to borrow the only copy of the payroll report that was prepared. She thus recommended that a second copy be made and kept in the payroll department. Susan also questioned the practice of keeping all the payroll records in one employee/payroll file. To keep the file from becoming unwieldy, she recommended that it be broken up into three files: personal employee data, pay period documentation, and payroll tax data. A discussion with the payroll clerk verified that this approach would make payroll processing easier and more efficient.

Over the next few weeks Ashton was able to document the rest of the accounting cycles. This process helped him identify inefficiencies and unneeded reports. He also found that some system documents were inadequately controlled. In addition, he got several ideas about how an automated system could help him reengineer the business processes at S&S. Outdated processes and procedures could be eliminated to make the system more effective by substituting technology for manpower.

When Ashton completed his analysis and documentation of the current system, Susan and Scott asked him to take the lead in moving the company from a manual to a computerized system. To do that, Ashton will need to gain a thorough understanding of the information needs of the various employees in the company. He will then need to design a new system using the tools, such as DFDs and flowcharts, that were explained in this chapter (systems development is discussed in Chapters 10–12 and data bases and data modeling are discussed in Chapters 5 and 6). He will also need to begin investigating the hardware and software options that are available to S&S (information technology is discussed in Chapters 7–9).

KEY TERMS

documentation
narrative description
data flow diagram (DFD)
data sources
data destinations
data flow
processes
data store
data dictionary
context diagram
flowchart
flowcharting template
document flowchart
internal control flowcharts
system flowchart
program flowchart
computer configuration chart
logical view
physical view
decision table
decision rule

CHAPTER QUIZ

1. A DFD is a representation of
   a. the physical view of data.
   b. the logical view of data.
   c. the decision rules in a computer program.
   d. a computer hardware configuration.

2. Documentation methods such as DFDs and flowcharts save both time and money, adding value to an organization.
   a. True
   b. False

3. Which of the following statements is false?
   a. DFDs make use of only four symbols; flowcharts make use of many symbols.
   b. A DFD emphasizes the flow of data and what is happening in a system, whereas a flowchart emphasizes the flow of documents or records containing data.
   c. DFDs can convey the timing of events; flowcharts cannot.
   d. A flowchart shows the sequence of processes and data flows; DFDs do not.

4. A DFD is composed of the following four basic elements: data sources and destinations, data flows, transformation processes, and data stores. Each is represented on a DFD by a different symbol.
   a. True
   b. False

5. Which of the following is *not* one of the guidelines that should be followed in naming DFD data elements?
   a. If a name cannot completely describe the data or process, then decompose the flow or process further.

b. Make sure the names describe all the data or the entire process.
c. Name only the most important DFD elements.
d. Choose active and descriptive names.

6. The understanding of documentation skills that accountants need varies with their job function. However they should at least be able to
a. read documentation to determine how the system works.
b. critique documentation prepared by others.
c. prepare documentation for a newly developed information system.
d. teach others how to prepare documentation.

7. Which of the following statements is *false?*
a. A flowchart is an analytical technique used to describe some aspect of an information system in a clear, concise, and logical manner.
b. Flowcharts use a standard set of symbols to describe pictorially the flow of data through a system.
c. Flowcharts are easy to prepare and revise when prepared with a flowcharting software package.
d. A systems flowchart is a narrative representation of an information system.
e. A program flowchart shows the logic used in computer programs.

8. Which of the following flowcharts illustrates the flow of information between areas of responsibility in an organization?
a. Program flowchart
b. Computer configuration chart
c. Systems flowchart
d. Document flowchart

9. Which of the following is *not* one of the recommended guidelines for making flowcharts more readable, clear, concise, consistent, and understandable?
a. Divide the flowchart into columns with labels.
b. Flowchart all information flows, especially exception procedures and error routines.
c. Design the flowchart so that flow proceeds from top to bottom and from left to right.
d. Show the final disposition of all documents so that there are no loose ends that leave the reader dangling.
e. Each manual processing symbol should have an input and an output.

10. Which of the following is a *false* statement with respect to decision tables?
a. Auditors can use decision tables to evaluate a client's application programs.
b. A decision table lists the conditions (the *ifs*) and the alternatives (the *thens*) that are possible in making a decision.
c. Decision tables do not indicate logical relationships among the input data, but they do reflect the sequence in which the operations shown are to be performed.
d. A decision table has four parts: the condition and action stubs and the condition and action entries.
e. Decision tables may become unmanageably large if a program is complex.

DISCUSSION QUESTIONS

3.1 Prepare arguments for and against the use of flowcharts and DFDs and explain when it is most appropriate to use each documentation technique.

3.2 Identify the DFD elements in the following narrative: A customer purchases a few items from a local grocery store. Jill, a salesclerk, enters the transaction in the cash register and takes the customer's money. At closing, Jill gives both the cash and the register tape to her manager.

3.3 Do you agree with the following statement: "Any one of the systems documentation procedures, such as a DFD, can adequately document a given system"? Explain.

3.4 Compare the guidelines for preparing flowcharts and DFDs. What general design principles and limitations are common to both documentation techniques?

3.5 Your classmate asks you to explain flowcharting conventions using real-world examples. Draw each of the major ANSI flowchart symbols from memory, placing them into one of five categories: input, output, processing, storage, data flow, and miscellaneous. For each symbol, suggest several uses.

PROBLEMS

3.1 Prepare systems flowcharting segments for each of the following operations:

a. Processing transactions stored on magnetic tape to update a master file stored on magnetic tape
b. Processing transactions stored on magnetic tape to update a master file stored on a disk
c. Converting source documents off-line to magnetic tape using an optical character reader (OCR)
d. Processing OCR documents on-line to update a master file on magnetic disk
e. Reading data from a disk file into the computer to be listed on a printed report
f. Keying data from source documents to magnetic tape using an off-line, key-to-tape encoder
g. Manually sorting and filing invoices
h. Processing source data on-line using a terminal from a remote location to a central computer system for updating and recording source data on a magnetic disk master file

3.2 The Happy Valley Utility Company uses turnaround documents in its computerized customer accounting system. Meter readers are provided with preprinted computer forms, each containing the account number, name, address, and previous meter readings. Each form also contains a formatted area in which the customer's current meter reading can be marked in pencil. After making their rounds, meter readers turn in batches of these documents to the Computer Data Preparation Department, where they are processed by a mark-sense document reader that transfers their contents to magnetic tape.

This magnetic tape file is then sent to the computer center, where it is used as input for two computer runs. The first run sorts the transaction records on the tape into sequential order by customer account number. On the second run, the sorted transaction tape is processed against the customer master file, which is stored on a magnetic disk. Second-run outputs are (1) a printed report listing summary information and any erroneous transactions detected by the computer and (2) customer bills printed in a special OCR-readable font. Bills are mailed and customers are requested to return the stub portion along with payment.

Customer payments are received in the mail room and checked for consistency against the returned stubs. Checks are then sent to the cashier's office. The mail room provides the Computer Data Preparation Department with three sets of records: (1) stubs with agreeing amounts, (2) stubs with differing amounts, and (3) a list of amounts received from customers without stubs. For the latter two types of records, data preparation personnel use a special typewriter to prepare corrected stubs. An OCR document reader then processes all the stubs and transfers their contents onto magnetic tape.

The magnetic tape containing the payment records is then sent to the computer center, where it is sorted on the computer into sequential order by customer account number and processed against the customer master file to post the payment amounts. Two printed outputs from this second process are reports listing erroneous transactions and summary information and past-due customer balances.

REQUIRED

a. Draw a systems flowchart of the billing operations, commencing with the computer preparation of the meter reading forms and ending with the mailing of customer bills.
b. Draw a systems flowchart depicting customer payments processing, starting with the mail room operations and ending with the computer run that posts the payment amounts to the customer master file.
c. Draw a computer configuration flowchart showing the hardware required to accomplish all the operations described.

3.3 Prepare a program flowchart and a decision table for the following operation: Input to the program consists of an accounts receivable file containing (among other things) the amount due, date due, and customer credit limit. The program checks the due date of each customer record against the current date and prepares an aging schedule. Each customer's record is listed on a separate line of the aging schedule, with the amount due printed in one of three columns: (1) less than 60 days past due; (2) 61–180 days past due, and (3) over 180 days past due.

The program compares the amount due with the customer's credit limit. Customer records that are over 180 days past due and have an amount due in excess of the credit limit are printed on a Bad Debts Report for possible write-off by the credit manager. Other accounts that have an amount due in excess of the credit limit are printed on a Credit Review

Report that goes to the treasurer. After the last record in the accounts receivable file is processed, the program is halted.

3.4 The Andy Dandy Company is a retailer that purchases goods from wholesalers and resells them to the public. The company wishes to purchase from the most reliable wholesaler. The following information was compiled and stored in the computer:

- A quality rating from 1 to 4 for each wholesaler (1 is considered the highest)
- Percentage of times each wholesaler has been late in delivering an Andy Dandy Company order
- Whether each wholesaler's prices have been stable or unstable
- Whether each wholesaler is in an economically rich or depressed area
- Whether each vendor has periodically suggested new products

The purchasing department has established the following criteria to be used in wholesaler selection:

- If the quality rating is 1, award the wholesaler 20% of the business.
- If the quality rating is 2 and the wholesaler is late less than 10% of the time, award that vendor 15% of the business.
- If the quality rating is 2 and the wholesaler is late less than 25% of the time, reject the vendor.
- If the quality rating is 2 and the wholesaler is late between 10% and 25% of the time, award that vendor 10% of the business, but only if prices have been stable.
- If the quality rating is 3 and the wholesaler is late less than 5% of the time, award that vendor 10% of the business, but only if the vendor is in a depressed area and has consistently suggested new products.
- If the quality rating is 4, reject the wholesaler.

REQUIRED

Prepare a decision table to show the computer logic that is needed to write a program for vendor selection. (SMAC Examination, adapted)

3.5 The Dewey Construction Company processes its payroll transactions to update both its payroll master file and its work-in-process master file in the same computer run. Both the payroll master file and the work-in-process master file are maintained on disk and accessed randomly.

Data to be input to this system are keyed onto a disk using a key-to-tape encoder. The tape is then processed to update the files. This processing run also produces a payroll register on magnetic tape, employee paychecks and earnings statements, and a printed report listing error transactions and summary information.

REQUIRED

Prepare a systems flowchart of the process described.

3.6 Prepare a document flowchart to reflect how ANGIC insurance company processes its casualty claims. The process begins when the Claims Department receives a notice of loss from a claimant. Claims prepares and sends the claimant four copies of a proof-of-loss form on which the claimant must detail the cause, amount, and other aspects of the loss. Claims also initiates a record of the claim, which is sent with the notice of loss to Data Processing, where it is filed by claim number.

The claimant must fill out the proof-of-loss forms with the assistance of an adjustor, who must concur with the claimant on the estimated amount of loss. The claimant and adjustor each keep one copy of the proof-of-loss form. The claimant sends the two remaining copies to the Claims Department. Separately, the adjustor submits a report to the Claims Department confirming the estimates on the claimant's proof-of-loss form.

The Claims Department authorizes a payment to the claimant, forwards a copy of the proof-of-loss form to Data Processing, and files the original proof-of-loss form and the adjustor's report alphabetically. The Data Processing Department prepares payment checks and mails them to the customers, files the proof-of-loss with the claim record, and prepares a list of disbursements, which it transmits to the Accounting Department.

3.7 Beccan Company is a discount tire dealer operating 25 retail stores in the metropolitan area. Beccan sells both private-brand and name-brand tires. The company operates a centralized purchasing and warehousing facility and employs a perpetual inventory system. All purchases of tires and related supplies are placed through the company's central Purchasing Department to take advantage of quantity discounts. The tires and supplies are received at the central warehouse and distributed to the retail stores as needed. The perpetual inventory system at the central facility maintains current inventory records, designated reorder points, and optimum order quantities for each type and size of tire and other related supplies. Beccan uses five documents in its inventory control system.

Retail stores requisition. The retail stores submit this document to the central warehouse whenever they need tires or supplies. The shipping clerks in the

Warehouse Department fill the orders from inventory and authorize delivery to the stores.

Purchase requisition. The inventory control clerk in the Inventory Control Department prepares this document when the quantity on hand for an item falls below the designated reorder point. It is then forwarded to the Purchasing Department.

Purchase order. The Purchasing Department prepares this document when items need to be ordered. It is then submitted to an authorized vendor.

Receiving report. The Warehouse Department prepares this document when ordered items are received from vendors. The receiving clerk completes the document by indicating the vendor's name and the date and quantity of the shipment received.

Invoice. An invoice is received from vendors, specifying the amounts owed by Beccan.

The following departments are involved in Beccan's inventory control system:

Inventory Control Department. Responsible for the maintenance of all perpetual inventory records for all stock items. This inventory includes current quantity on hand, reorder point, optimum order quantity, and quantity on order for each item carried.

Warehouse Department. Maintains the physical inventory of all items carried in stock. All orders from vendors are received (receiving clerk) and all distributions to retail stores are filled (shipping clerks) in this department.

Purchasing Department. Places all orders for items needed by the company.

Accounts Payable Department. Maintains all open accounts with vendors and other creditors, in addition to processing payments.

REQUIRED

Prepare a document flowchart that indicates the interaction and use of these documents among all departments at the central facility of Beccan Company. It should provide adequate internal control over the receipt, issuance, replenishment, and payment of tires and supplies. You may assume that there are a sufficient number of document copies to ensure that the perpetual inventory system has the necessary basic internal controls. (CMA Examination, adapted)

3.8 For cases 1–4, perform these two steps.

a. Determine what type of hardware the company will need.
b. Draw a computer systems flowchart of the system described. See Figs. 3.13 and 3.14 for examples of computer systems flowcharts.

Case 1. U-Bag-M Groceries maintains an electronic inventory system and has computerized the receipt, sales, and ordering of merchandise. When a shipment arrives, cases run along specialized conveyer belts. A scanner, connected to the store's central computer and located on each side of the conveyer, reads the universal product code on each package and updates the inventory records for the items received. When merchandise is sold, the customer's purchase is scanned as it passes through the checkout stand and the appropriate inventory levels are credited. When the on-hand quantity of a stock item falls below the reorder point, the computer system prints a copy of the order form. All receiving and sales transactions that cannot be handled by the scanners are entered manually.

Case 2. Higher Education University has a computerized registration system. Prior to the start of classes, students can register 24 hours a day from anywhere in the country using a Touch-Tone phone. Once classes begin, telephone registration terminates and the add/drop process begins, handled by registration employees who process registration queries and requests through an on-line terminal. Prior to the beginning of class the computer generates a class confirmation form that is mailed to the student. A report for each class section is also prepared and distributed to the professors who are teaching the class.

Case 3. Quick Snack Incorporated distributes its snack food items through grocery stores and vending machines. Routers deliver items, stock the shelves, and collect out-of-date products from client stores. They use small laptop computers to help them record the sales and the removal of out-of-date products at each store. Routers also provide store managers with printed bills and receipts. At the end of the day, the data stored in each laptop are transferred to the company's centralized computer. To stock vending machines, the company's computer prepares a card on each machine to be serviced on a given day. The vendor then services the machine and records the stock information on the card. The vendor returns the card to the main office, where the cards are processed nightly by computer. Management can access the corporate data through on-line queries and through the use of the periodic, scheduled reports prepared by the computer.

Case 4. U-Dial Phone Company maintains branch offices as well as a corporate office. U-Dial staggers both monthly billing and payment deadline dates to handle its large volume of customers. When a customer billing date arrives, an itemized bill (including a payment form) is prepared by computer and mailed to the customer. A customer can either mail the payment and the payment form to the corporate office or personally pay the bill at a branch office. Each day the preprinted forms are read and transferred onto a tape that is used to update the customer master file stored on disk. If a customer pays in person, a teller updates the customer's files on-line.

3.9 As the internal auditor for No-Wear Products of Hibbing, Minnesota, you've been asked by your supervisor to document the company's current payroll processing system. Based on your documentation, No-Wear hopes to develop a plan for revising the current information system to eliminate unnecessary delays in the processing of paychecks. Your best explanation of the system came from an interview with the head payroll clerk:

The payroll processing system at No-Wear Products is fairly simple. Time data are recorded in each department using time cards and clocks. It is annoying, however, when people forget to punch out at night and we have to record their time information by hand. At the end of the period our payroll clerks enter the time card data into a payroll file for processing. Our clerks are pretty good—though I've had to make my share of corrections when they mess up the data entry.

Before the payroll file is processed for the current period, human resources sends us data on personnel changes, such as increases in pay rates and new employees. Our clerks enter this information into the payroll file so it is available for processing. Usually, when mistakes get back to us, it's because human resources is recording the wrong pay rate or an employee has left and they forget to remove the record.

The data are then processed and individual employee paychecks are generated. Several important reports are also generated for management—though I don't know exactly what they do with them. In addition, the government requires regular federal and state withholding reports for tax purposes. Currently, the system generates these reports automatically, which is nice.

REQUIRED

a. Prepare a context diagram for the current payroll processing system at No-Wear Products.

b. Develop a DFD to document the payroll processing system at No-Wear Products.

3.10 Ashton Fleming has decided to analyze the accounts payable process at S&S. His intent is to document how the present system works so the transition to a computerized system will be easier. He also hopes to improve on any weaknesses he discovers in the system. He has written the following narrative to explain what happens at S&S.

Before a vendor invoice is paid by S&S, it must be matched against the purchase order used to request the goods and the receiving report prepared by the Receiving Department. Since all three of these documents enter the Accounts Payable Department at different times, a separate alphabetical file is kept for each type of document. The purchase orders that are forwarded from purchasing are stored in a purchase order file. The receiving reports are stored in a receiving report file. When vendor invoices are received, the accounts payable clerk records the amount due in the accounts payable ledger and then files the invoices in the vendor invoice file.

The policy at S&S is to make sure all accounts are paid within 30 days to take advantage of the early-payment discounts that suppliers offer. When it comes time to pay a particular bill, the accounts payable clerk retrieves the vendor invoice and attaches the purchase order and the receiving report. These matched documents are forwarded to Ashton Fleming.

Ashton reviews the documents to ensure they are complete and prepares a two-part check. The checks as well as the other three documents are forwarded to Susan for her approval and signature. Ashton records the check amount in the cash disbursements journal.

Susan reviews the documents to ensure they are valid payables and then signs the checks. She forwards the check to the vendor and returns the documents as well as the second copy of the check to the accounts payable clerk. The clerk files the documents alphabetically in a paid invoice file.

At the end of every month the accounts payable clerk uses information from the accounts payable ledger to prepare an accounts payable report. This report is forwarded to Susan for her review. After she is finished with the report, Susan files it chronologically.

REQUIRED

a. Prepare a DFD to document accounts payable processing at S&S.

b. Prepare a document flowchart to document accounts payable processing at S&S.

3.11 Since opening its doors in Hawaii two years ago, Oriental Trading has enjoyed tremendous success. As a wholesaler, Oriental Trading purchases textiles from Asian markets and resells the textiles to local retail shops. To keep up with the strong demand for textiles in the Hawaiian Islands, Oriental Trading is expanding its local operations. At the heart of the expansion is the introduction of a new information system to handle the tremendous increase in purchases.

You have conducted several interviews with supervisors in the departments that interact with the acquisition/payment system. The following is a summary of your discussions.

> *A purchase requisition is sent from the inventory system and is received by Sky Ishibashi, a clerk in the Purchasing Department. Sky prepares a purchase order from information in the vendor and inventory files and mails it to the vendor. The vendor returns a vendor acknowledgment to Sky indicating receipt of the purchase order. Sky then sends a purchase order notification to Elei Mateaki, a clerk in the Accounts Payable Department.*
>
> *When the Receiving Department accepts vendor goods, the inventory system notifies Elei by sending him a receiving report. Elei also receives the invoices that are mailed by the various vendors. Elei matches the invoices with the purchase order notification and the receiving report and updates the accounts payable master file.*
>
> *Elei then sends a payment authorization to the Accounting Department. In the Accounting Department Andeloo Nonu prepares and mails a check to the vendor. When the check is issued, the system automatically updates the accounts payable master file and the general ledger.*

REQUIRED

Develop a context diagram and a DFD of the acquisition/payment system at Oriental Trading.

3.12 Ashton Fleming has worked furiously for the past month trying to completely document the major business information flows at S&S. Upon completing his personal interviews with cash receipts clerks Ashton asks you to develop a comprehensive DFD for the cash receipts system. Ashton's narrative of the system follows:

> *Customer payments include cash received at the time of purchase as well as account payments received in the mail. At the end of the day all checks are endorsed by the treasurer, and a deposit slip is prepared for the checks and the cash. The checks, cash, and deposit slip are then deposited daily at the local bank by a clerk.*
>
> *When checks are received as payment for accounts due, a remittance slip is included with the payment. The remittance slips are used to update the accounts receivable file at the end of the day. The remittance slips are stored in a file drawer by date.*
>
> *Every week a cash receipts report and an aged trial balance are generated from the data in the accounts receivable ledger. The cash receipts report is sent to Scott and Susan. A copy of the aged trial balance by customer account is sent to the Credit and Collections Department.*

REQUIRED

Develop a context diagram and a DFD for the cash receipts system at S&S.

3.13 A mail-order skin and body care company advertises in magazines. Most orders are initiated by magazine subscribers who fill in and send coupons directly to the company. The firm also takes orders over the phone, answers inquiries about products, and handles payments and cancellations of orders. Products that have been ordered are sent either directly to the customer or to regional offices of the company that handle the required distribution. The mail-order company has three basic data files that retain customer mailing information, product inventory information, and billing information based on invoice number. During the next few years, the company expects to become a multimillion-dollar operation. Recognizing the need to computerize much of the mail order business, the company has begun the process by calling you.

REQUIRED

Draw a context diagram and at least two levels of logical DFDs for the preceding operations.

3.14 The local community college requires that each student complete a registration request form and mail or deliver it to the registrar's office. A clerk enters the request into the system. First, the accounts receivable subsystem is checked to ensure that no fees are owed from the previous quarter. Next, for each course, the student transcript is checked to ensure that the course prerequisites are completed. Then class position availability is checked and the student's Social Security number is added to the class list.

The report back to the student shows the result of registration processing: If fees are owed, the student is sent a bill and the registration is rejected. If prerequisites for a course are not fulfilled, the student is notified and that course is not registered. If the class is full, the student request is annotated with "course closed." If a student is accepted into a class, the day, time, and room are printed next to the course number. Student fees and total tuition are computed and printed on the form. Student fee information is interfaced to the accounts receivable subsystem. Course enrollment reports are prepared for the instructors.

REQUIRED

Prepare a context diagram and at least two levels of logical DFDs for this operation.

CASE 3.1: ANYCOMPANY, INC.—AN ONGOING COMPREHENSIVE CASE

Identify a local company (you may use the same company you identified in Case 1.1) and perform the following steps:

1. Select one of the company's business cycles for study. Examine all available documentation of the cycle's information system.
2. Prepare a report as follows:
   a. Describe who is involved in processing the data in the system. Include in your report a partial organization chart showing the relationships between employees.
   b. Describe the information flowing through the organization. Include in your report a context diagram and as many levels of DFDs as necessary to show the flow of information in the cycle.
   c. Describe what documents are used in the system. Include in your report a document flowchart showing the main documents used in processing transactions in the cycle, from origination to final destination. Also include a sample of the system documents.
   d. Identify the master files the company uses and describe how and when they are updated. Include in your report a systems flowchart that shows the following: (1) all inputs to the computerized system, (2) all processing performed, and (3) all system output.
   e. Describe any other development tools used to create and document the system.
3. Select one of the software programs or applications the company uses. Do not choose anything too complex or difficult to understand. You may want to select only a portion of a program. As directed by your instructor, do one or more of the following steps.
   a. Draw a program flowchart showing the logic used in the program.
   b. Create a decision table that shows the conditions tested in the program and the actions to be taken when each unique condition is met.
4. In assignments 2 and 3 you used techniques and tools with a system that already existed. As an alternative to those assignments, analyze a system that is currently being developed.

CASE 3.2: DUB 5

You are the systems analyst for the Wee Willie Williams Widget Works (also known as Dub 5, which is a shortened version of 5 W's). Dub 5 produces computer keyboard components. It has been producing keyboards for IBM, its biggest customer, for over 20 years and has recently signed an exclusive 10-year contract to provide the keyboards for all IBM personal computers.

As the systems analyst, you have been assigned the task of developing a DFD for Dub 5's order processing system. You have finished gathering all the information you need to develop the first-pass DFD and have just sat down to complete the diagram.

Customer orders, which are all credit sales, arrive via mail and by phone. When an order is processed, a number of other documents are prepared. You have diagramed the overall process and the documents produced, as shown in Fig. 3.15.

The following documents are created.

- A packing slip is prepared by the Order Processing Department and then used by the Warehouse Department to fill the order. The packing slip accompanies the goods shipped from the warehouse.
- A customer invoice is prepared and mailed once the goods have been shipped.
- A monthly customer statement is mailed to the customer.
- An order rejection is sent to the customer explaining why the goods cannot be shipped.
- A receivables notice, which is a copy of the customer invoice, is sent to the Accounting Department so accounts receivable records can be updated.

After reviewing your notes, you write the following narrative summary.

When an order comes in, the order processing clerk checks the customer's credit file to confirm credit approval and ensure the amount falls within the credit limit. If either of these conditions is valid, the order is sent to the Credit Department. When an order has been approved for credit, it is entered into the system on a standard order form. The information on the form is used to update the company's customer file (in which the name, address, and other information is stored), and the form is then placed in the company's order file.

When a rejected order is received by the Credit Department, the clerk first determines why the order has been rejected. If the customer has exceeded its credit limit, it is sent a personalized copy of a standard letter explaining that its credit limit has been exceeded and that the merchandise will be shipped as soon as Dub 5 receives payment. If the company has not been approved for credit, a credit application is sent to the company along with a letter stating that the order will be shipped as soon as credit approval is granted.

Before preparing a packing slip, the order processing employee checks the inventory records to determine whether the company has the products ordered on hand. If the items are in stock, a packing slip is prepared for every order form that is completed.

Figure 3.15

Overall Process for Dub 5

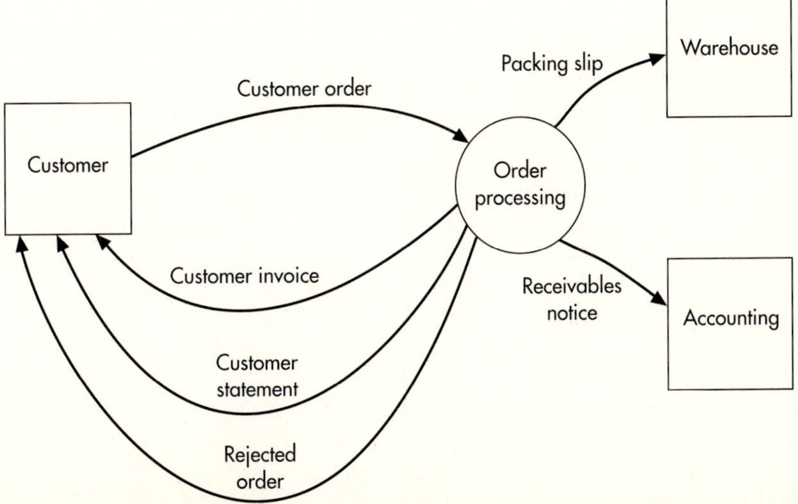

Once notification of shipped goods has been received, a customer invoice is prepared. One copy of the customer invoice is kept by the Order Processing Department, one is sent to the customer, and one is sent to the Accounting Department so that the receivables file can be updated. The receivables file contains all account information except name and address. A note is made in the customer file that the invoice has been sent. Every month customer statements are sent by Dub 5.

From the information just discussed, complete a DFD for Dub 5.

ANSWERS TO CHAPTER QUIZ

1. b	**3.** c	**5.** c	**7.** d	**9.** b
2. a	**4.** a	**6.** a	**8.** d	**10.** c

Chapter 4

The Data Processing Cycle

LEARNING OBJECTIVES

After completing this chapter, you should be able to:

- Describe and give examples of the basic activities that take place in the data processing cycle.
- Explain how data are captured and entered into a data processing system.
- Explain fundamental data storage concepts and describe files and data bases and their uses.
- Explain how data files are maintained and the approaches used to maintain them.
- Explain how information can be organized and presented to help users fulfill their job responsibilities.

Integrative Case: S&S, Inc.

Susan Gonzalez is frustrated. Over the past few months she has spent a great deal of time managing the store. She has just received the sales figures for October and sales are down for the second month in a row. She is trying to figure out what is wrong and what she can do to reverse the trend by increasing sales ore decreasing costs or decreasing costs.

For example, the special television promotion S&S ran in October was not as successful as past promotions. Susan believes that if she is able to compare the TV promotion with prior ones, she can find some answers. The problem is that the data she needs just aren't available in a usable form. The store still processes its accounting data using a manual system. This doesn't provide much of the information she needs to make strategic decisions—data such as individual customer tastes and preferences, special discounts and promotions run by S&S's numerous suppliers, and national economic trends that affect purchasing patterns.

Susan's thoughts are interrupted by a telephone call. It's an old friend, Denise Ainge, who has made several recent purchases. She is having problems with one of the appliances and has a question about her account. Denise doesn't have the invoice number of the sale, but she does recall buying the appliance in October. Susan knows it will take time to track down the appropriate invoice. Since she has a meeting in just a few minutes with Scott and Ashton, she tells Denise she will have one of her staff call her back after they have found the information needed to answer her question.

During the meeting, Susan expresses her frustrations and wants to know how S&S can gather and store the necessary data. Susan explains her experience with trying to compare the monthly promotions and her call from Denise Ainge. She argues that this type of information should be available at her fingertips. For example, searching for information and then returning phone calls wastes valuable time. In addition, there will be other information needs in the future, and Susan wants quick access to the information to meet those needs. Ashton thinks many of Susan's needs can be met with a computer system. Susan asks him to investigate computerized systems and find answers to the following questions:

1. How are transactions processed using a computer?
2. What is the best way to enter data into the system? How are reports generated from a computerized system, and what reports are needed?
3. How can S&S store the data it needs and make it readily available to those who need it?

INTRODUCTION

An AIS produces information for record keeping, planning and evaluation, and decision making. A computer-based AIS translates transaction data into machine-readable form and enters it into a computer. After processing, the data are stored in computer-readable form and converted into human-readable form for users. The operations performed on data in computer-based systems to produce information are referred to as the **data processing cycle.** Figure 4.1 shows the four stages of the data processing cycle: data input, data storage, data processing, and information output. The next four sections discuss these stages in more detail.

Accountants play a significant role in the data processing cycle. They must interact with systems analysts to help answer questions such as: What data should be entered and stored by the organization, and who should have access to the data? Which data storage approach should be used: manual, file-based, or data base? How should the data be organized, updated, stored, accessed, and retrieved? How can both scheduled and unanticipated information needs be met? To answer these and related questions, accountants must understand the data processing cycle concepts explained in this chapter. Focus 4.1 describes how an efficient system can save a great deal of money.

DATA INPUT

During the data input stage, transaction data are captured and converted to machine-processable form. To facilitate subsequent processing, data input may also require the following preparation:

Figure 4.1

Four Stages of the Data Processing Cycle

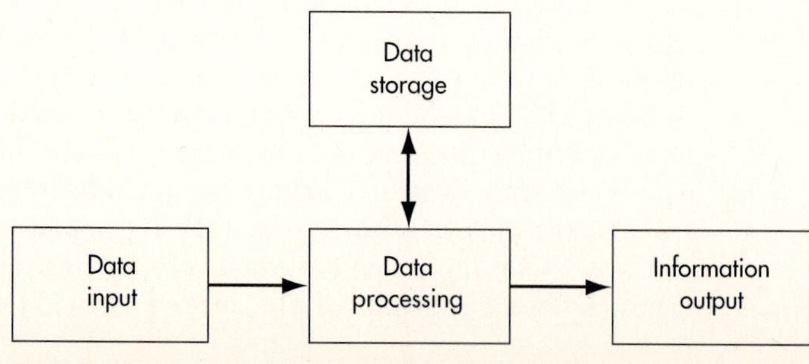

FOCUS 4.1

Information Systems Can Reduce Health Care Costs

At the Lake Charles Memorial Hospital more than twelve thousand claims errors occurred when claims were misplaced, mailed to the wrong office, or returned by Medicare or insurance companies due to inaccurate information on payment forms. Two years later more than 90% of the billing errors at the hospital had been eliminated by a new medical claims system. At Miami's Baptist Hospital a more efficient system cut in half the 30 to 35 days it took to receive reimbursements for medical services from government agencies.

Most of the country's six thousand hospitals have a hospital information system (HIS) that collects and processes information internally. However, the way hospitals move patient information from their HIS to the billing department and then to the insurance companies differs greatly. Many insurance company systems print billing data and drop it in the mail. The hospitals key the data into their HIS and process the claim. The printing, mailing, and rekeying process takes a great deal of time, slows the payment cycle, and introduces errors into the process. Less than 5% of the estimated 3.5 billion health care claims are filed electronically each year.

Due to their current billing and collection systems, hospitals face a number of problems. Often they must use different methods of billing, depending on the payer's billing preference. The result is a great deal of confusion and a high rate of errors. A second problem is that the interface between hospitals and insurance companies is still in the Dark Ages. A third problem is that systems developers at hospitals have so much to do in terms of running the hospital and providing patients with adequate health care that the billing and collection areas of the hospital system take a backseat.

So what can be done? Hospitals and insurance companies are hammering out electronic billing and payment standards that can be applied consistently across the industry. Thus hospitals will have to place a high priority on improving their billing and collection systems. The hospitals mentioned here have already proven that such efforts can yield a high payback.

Focus Questions

1. Which processes delay efficient processing of claims?
2. What are the advantages and disadvantages of automating hospital billing systems? Would you recommend automation? Why or why not?
3. Why are hospitals slow to implement automated billing systems?
4. What needs to be done before hospitals can successfully automate their billing systems?

- *Classification* by assigning identification codes (account number, department number, etc.) to data records based on a predetermined system, such as a chart of accounts.
- *Verification* to ensure data accuracy. It is less costly and more efficient to prevent data entry errors than to detect and correct them at the time of entry or once they are in the system.
- *Transmittal* from one location to another. For example, most bank ATMs capture and forward transaction data to their main office for processing.

One way to capture data is to use a source document, a preprinted form on which an initial record of transaction data is entered. Examples of internal source documents include sales orders, purchase requisitions, receiving reports, and employee time cards. External source documents include invoices from suppliers and checks and remittance advices from customers. Source documents are accumulated in batches before they are scanned or keyed into the system. Devices that perform these scanning activities are described in Chapter 7.

FOCUS 4.2

Insurance Company Is Eliminating Paperwork

Insurance underwriters at Central Life Assurance Company (CLA) were drowning in paper. For 96 years CLA handwrote insurance applications and associated documentation and forwarded them to data processing for entry into the system. Documents were frequently misplaced, misfiled, or mixed with outdated documents. The filing cabinets took up valuable floor space, and finding a document that was being processed was difficult.

CLA is solving its paper glut by moving to a paperless system that captures data as it is received in the office. When documents are received, they are scanned in the mail room and their images are stored on magnetic disks. Each document is indexed and checked for accuracy as it is scanned. After documents are scanned, they are routed to the proper department based on an assigned index number.

Scanned underwriting files contain all the information about a specific account: applications, financial reports, medical information, photographs, and so on. Because each scanned image (document) is indexed, the system organizes images by case. Agents can quickly access this information at any time using their PCs. After a case is closed, the images are archived on an optical disk instead of in a filing cabinet.

The new system has benefited CLA in several ways. Customer service has improved, because applications are processed faster and more accurately. In the past, when a customer would call an agent about a claim, the agent would have to look up the necessary information and call the person back. Now agents can access the information instantly while the customer is on the phone. The voluminous amounts of paperwork have been eliminated, and the new system is much more organized and easier to use. The result is better service and more efficient processing at significant cost savings.

Focus Questions

1. Identify the data processing elements in the advanced system adopted by CLA.
2. What problems was CLA having with its older automated system? In what ways is imaging technology improving the quality of data processed at CLA?
3. How does the customer benefit from the new system? What effect will the system have on CLA's biggest competitors?
4. As a systems consultant, would you recommend an imaging system to a client? Why or why not?

Data can also be input using a **turnaround document,** a record of company data sent to an external party and then returned to the system as input. Turnaround documents are prepared in machine-readable form to facilitate their subsequent processing as input records. An example is a utility bill that is read by a special scanning device when it is returned with its payment.

Data can also be keyed into an on-line terminal or a microcomputer. For example, bank tellers key in a customer's account code when money is deposited or withdrawn. One way to increase the accuracy, completeness, and speed of data entry using keying devices is to use preformatted computer screens. These screens often resemble source documents, such as sales invoices and purchase orders.

Another keying aid is a series of prompts that ask questions until the system has all the necessary data. Often the nature of a succeeding question depends on the answer to a previous one. For example, consider a system built to help automobile insurance agents update their client's insurance policies. A yes response to the question "Is the insured adding a new driver?" will result in a series of questions to capture the needed data about the new driver. A no response will cause a cessation in further questions about a new driver.

Source data automation devices capture transaction data in machine-readable form at the time and place of their origin. Examples include ATMs used by banks and scanners used in retail stores. Focus 4.2 describes how one insurance company has successfully implemented scanning technology.

DATA STORAGE

A company's data is one of its most important resources. However, the mere existence of relevant data does not guarantee its usefulness. An organization must have ready and easy access to its data in order to function properly. Therefore, accountants need to understand how data are organized and stored in an AIS and how it can be accessed. In essence, they need to know how to manage data for maximum corporate use.

Fundamental Data Storage Concepts and Definitions

Imagine how difficult a textbook would be to read if it were not organized into chapters, sections, paragraphs, and sentences. Now imagine how hard it would be for S&S to find a particular invoice if all of its key documents were randomly dumped into file cabinets. Fortunately, most textbooks and company files are organized for easy retrieval. Likewise, information in an AIS can be organized for easy and efficient access. This section explains basic data storage concepts and definitions using accounts receivable information as an example.

An **entity** is something about which information is stored. Examples of an entity include employees, inventory items, and customer accounts. Each entity has **attributes,** or characteristics of interest, that need to be stored. An employee pay rate and a customer address are examples of attributes.

Figure 4.2

Hierarchy of Data Storage Elements

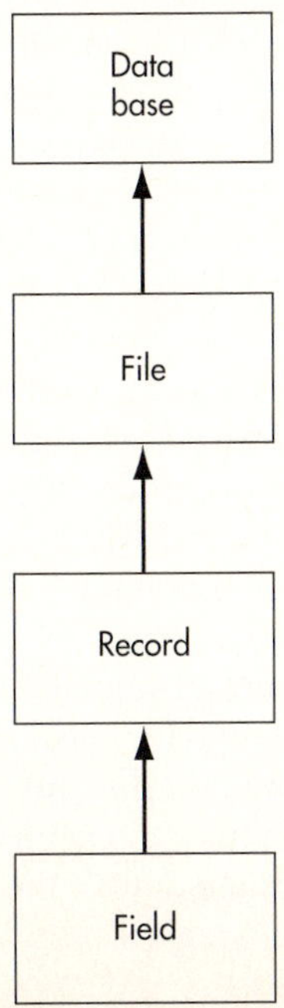

Characters, which are numbers or letters, are combined in a meaningful way to form a **data value.** For example, P.O. Box 7 (the data value) is the address (an attribute) of XYZ Company (the entity). Generally, each type of entity possesses the same set of attributes. For example, all employees possess an employee number, pay rate, and home address. The specific data values for those attributes, however, will differ among entities. For example, one employee's pay rate might be $8.00, whereas another's might be $8.25.

Electronic data processing (EDP) systems store data by organizing smaller units of data into larger, more meaningful ones. This data storage hierarchy, beginning with fields (the smallest element) and ending with data bases (the largest), is shown in Fig. 4.2. Data values are stored in a physical space called a **field.** A number of fields are grouped together to form a **record,** a collection of data values that describe specific attributes of an entity. In Fig. 4.3 each row represents a different record and each column represents an attribute. Each intersecting row and column is a field that contains characters (a data value) that describe the particular attribute and the record to which it pertains.

Related records are grouped together to form a **file.** For example, all customer receivable records are stored in an accounts receivable file. Files containing related data are combined to form a **data base.** A set of interrelated, centrally coordinated data files facilitate both updating of the data and user access to the data. For example, the accounts receivable file might be combined with customer, sales analysis, and related files to form a customer data base.

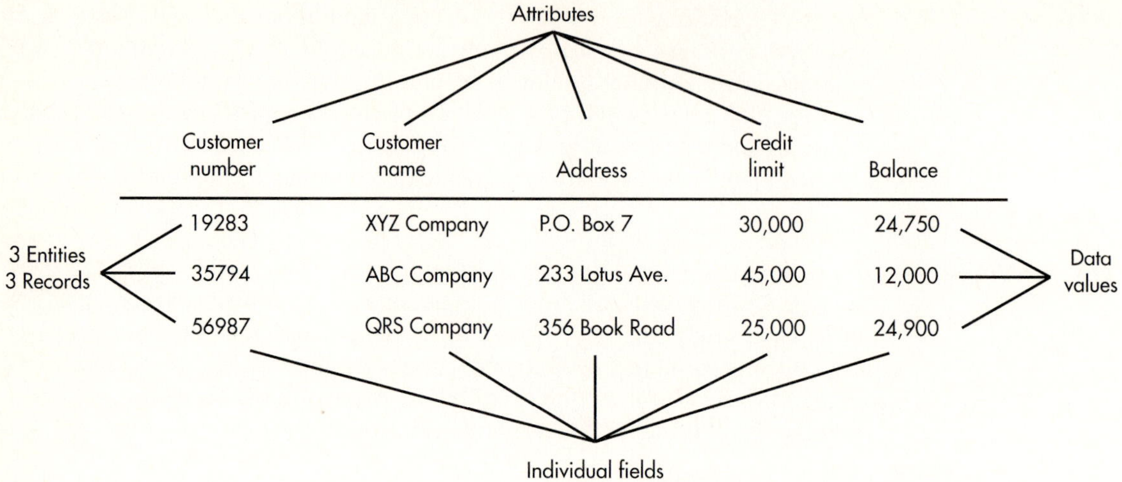

This accounts receivable file stores information about three separate entities: XYZ Company, ABC Company, and QRS Company. As a result, there are three records in the file. Five separate attributes are used to describe each customer: customer number, customer name, address, credit limit, and balance. There are therefore five separate fields in each record. Each field contains a data value that describes an attribute of a particular entity (customer). For example, the data value 19283 is the customer number for the XYZ Company.

Figure 4.3

Accounts Receivable File

Types of Files

Companies use seven types of files to store their data. The first, a **master file,** is similar in concept to a subsidiary ledger and contains all the data that a company needs about an item of interest. For example, records in an accounts receivable file include such information as customer name, address, balance due, and terms. Master files are continually updated as transactions occur and the current status of items, such as the balance due, changes as sales are made and receivables are collected. Examples include a payroll master file, an accounts receivable master file, and a fixed assets master file.

Master files are frequently queried by users for current balances or to extract information for analysis. Most company reports are prepared by printing out information contained on one or more master files. A master file is permanent in that it will exist indefinitely, even though individual records within it may frequently be inserted, deleted, or changed. It is the most common type of file maintained in an AIS.

A **transaction file,** which is comparable in concept to a journal, groups similar transactions for processing purposes. Since they are used to update master files, transaction files must contain all the transaction data needed for that purpose. For example, a sales transaction file that updates the accounts receivable master file would contain the customer number and the amount and date of the sale. Examples of transaction files include inventory issue and receipt transactions, purchase transactions, and employee timekeeping records.

A **table file** contains reference data retrieved during data processing to facilitate calculations or other tasks. Examples are payroll tax withholding, sales tax, and freight rate tables.

A **history file** contains transactions that have already been processed. They are retained for reference purposes and are often a source of useful management information. For example, a sales history file may be analyzed to provide summary and trend information on total sales by region, salesperson, customer, or product.

A **backup file** is a duplicate copy of a current file. It protects against the partial or complete loss of a file.

A **suspense file** contains records that have been temporarily removed from regular processing so that they can be investigated and corrected. An example is a credit sale transaction without a corresponding accounts receivable record.

A **report file** is a temporary file containing information that is to be printed at a later date.

Data Bases

For many years companies created new files and programs each time an information need arose. The result was a significant increase in the number of master files required to support new applications. For example, Bank America at one time had 36 million customer accounts in 23 separate systems. One governmental agency identified data that were entered into 22 separate systems.

The **data base approach** views data as an organizational resource that should be used by and managed for the entire organization, not just the originating department or function. Its focus is data integration and data sharing with all authorized users. Integration is achieved by combining master files into larger "pools" of data that can be accessed by many application programs. An example is an employee data base that consolidates data formerly contained in payroll, human resources, and job skills master files. Figure 4.4 illustrates the differences between a file-oriented and a data base approach.

The program that manages and controls the data and interfaces between the data and the application programs is the **data base management system (DBMS).** The combination of the data base, the DBMS, and the application programs that access the data base through the DBMS is the **data base system.** The person responsible for the data base is the **data base administrator (DBA).**

As technology improves many companies are developing very large data bases called **data warehouses.** For example, Bank of America recently created a customer information data base to provide customer service, marketing analysis, and managerial information. Believed to be the largest in the banking industry, it has 600 billion characters of data. It contains copies of all the bank's data on checking and savings accounts; real estate, consumer, and commercial loans; ATMs; and bank cards. Although it costs the bank $14 million a year, it is well worth the price. Queries that used to average two hours now average five minutes. Minutes after Los Angeles suffered an earthquake, the bank sorted its $28 billion mortgage loan portfolio by zip code, identified the real estate loans in the earthquake area, and calculated their potential loan loss. Data warehousing is explained in graphic form in Focus 4.3.

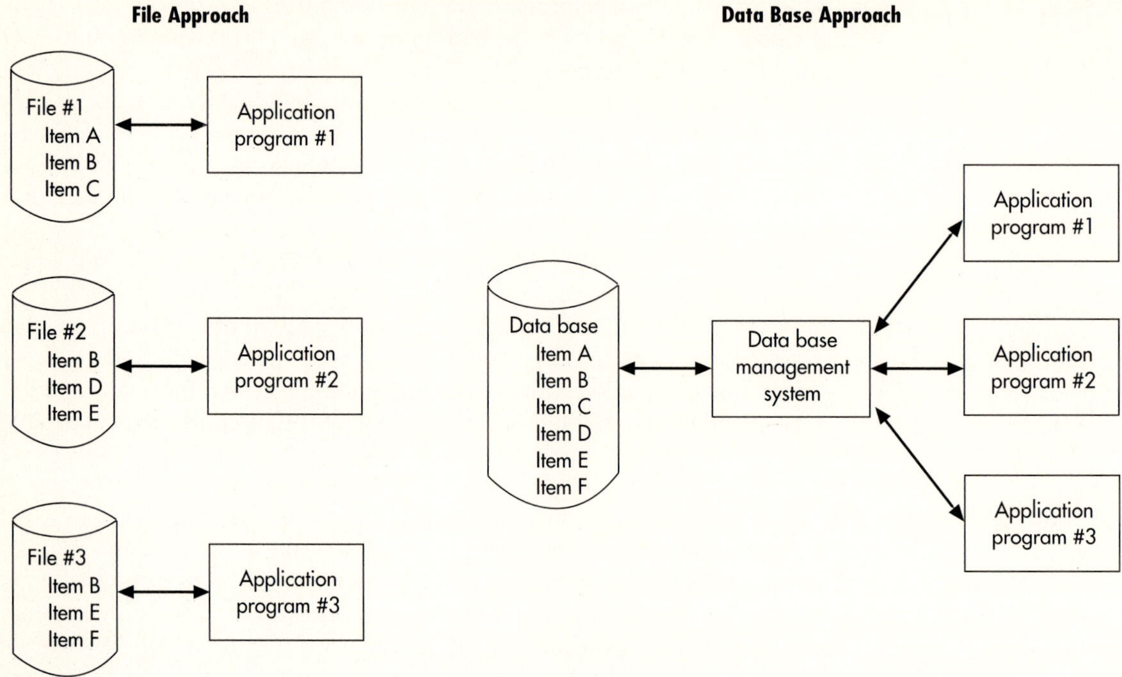

Figure 4.4

File-Oriented Approach Versus Data Base Approach

Logical and Physical View of Data

In file-oriented systems, programmers must know the physical location and layout of records used in an application program. Figure 4.5 shows a **record layout** of an accounts receivable file. Suppose a programmer wants a credit report showing the customer number, credit limit, and current balance. To write the program, she must understand the location and length of the fields needed (record positions 1 through 10 for customer number, for example) and the format of each field (alphanumeric or numeric). The process becomes more complex if data are needed from several files.

Data base systems overcome this problem by separating the storage and use of data elements. The data base approach provides two separate views of data: the logical view and the physical view. The **logical view** is concerned with how users conceptually organize, view, and understand data relationships. The

Figure 4.5

Accounts Receivable File Record Layout

Customer number A	Customer name A	Address A	Credit limit N	Balance N
1 – 10	11 – 30	31 – 60	61 – 68	69 – 76

A = alphanumeric field
N = numeric field

FOCUS 4.3

Data Warehousing: The Dynamics of Data Flow

Inflow

Application data and data from E-mail, wire services, and external databases, are edited and entered into the data warehouse.

Upflow

Highly detailed data are aggregated, summarized, classified, and processed so users can get quick responses to their queries.

Outflow

Users run prewritten and ad hoc queries to obtain needed business information. If the warehouse is structured correctly, a high percentage of queries will use highly summarized data, and a small number of ad hoc queries will use highly detailed data.

Downflow

Data are constantly added to the warehouse through inflow. To prevent the warehouse from becoming clogged with marginally useful data, older data are sent to an archive to be accessed as needed.

Metaflow

Users and IS need to know about warehouse data; its location, what it represents, where it came from. That information comes from several flows of metadata—data about the data.

Source: Richard Hackathorn, "Data Warehousing Energizes Your Enterprise," *Datamation,* February 1, 1995, p. 39. Reprinted with permission.

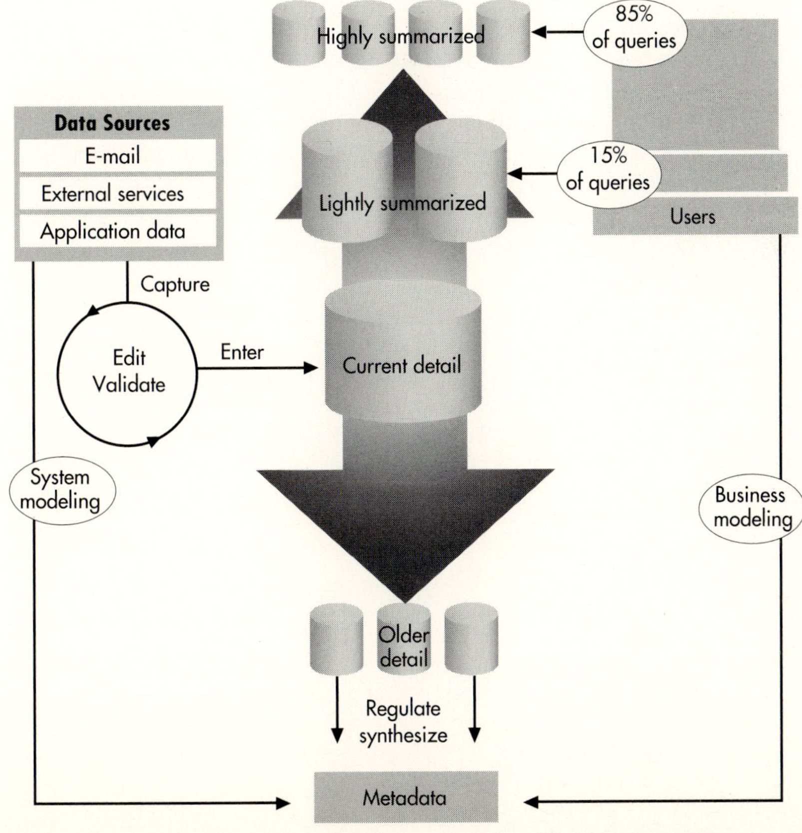

physical view refers to how and where data are physically arranged and stored on disks, tapes, and other media. Figure 4.6 illustrates these two views using accounts receivable data.

Data base management system software provides the link between the way data are physically stored on disks and each user's logical view of that data. DBMS controls the data base such that users can access, query, or update it without reference to how or where the data are physically stored. The user is responsible only for defining the logical data requirements of the application.

Separating how data are used from how they are stored and accessed means that users can change their logical view (the data items needed) without making changes in the physical view (the physical storage of the data). Likewise, the data base administrator can change the physical storage of the data even if users have not changed the related application programs.

EDP personnel use the physical view to make efficient use of storage and processing resources. The data base administrator is responsible for physically storing the data so that logical requirements can be met. Programmers and users, however, generally do not need to understand the physical view since they are primarily interested in using the data, regardless of how it is stored.

Advantages of Data Base Systems

Data base systems offer the following advantages:

- *Data integration.* Information can be combined in unlimited ways. For example, S&S can answer questions like "Which appliances are supplied by GE Corporation?" and "Which sales employees speak Spanish?"
- *Report flexibility.* Reports can be revised easily and generated as needed rather than on a fixed (weekly or monthly) schedule. The data base can be browsed to research a problem or obtain detailed information underlying a summary report.
- *Minimal data redundancy and data inconsistencies.* Because data items are usually stored only once, data redundancy and data inconsistencies are minimized.
- *Data independence.* Because data and the programs that use them are independent of each other, each can be changed without having to change the other. This feature simplifies both programming and data management.

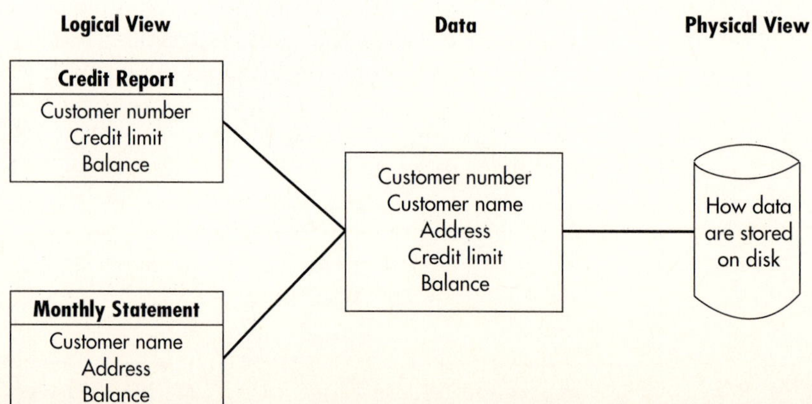

Figure 4.6

Logical and Physical Views of Data in a Customer Data Base

- *Central management of data.* Data management is more efficient because a data base administrator is responsible for coordinating, controlling, and managing data.
- *Security.* DBMS software has built-in controls, such as passwords, that help ensure data integrity.
- *Cross-functional analysis.* In a data base system, relationships such as the association between selling costs and promotional campaigns can be defined explicitly and used in the preparation of management reports.

How Businesses Use Data Base Technology

Data base technology is a fact of life and everyone is or will be affected by it. Most new AIS implementations use a data base approach. In fact, over 90% of all mainframe computer sites were estimated to be using data base technology in the late 1990s, and data base use in personal computers is also growing rapidly. Most accounting students will work for a company that uses data base technology to store, process, and report accounting transactions. Many accountants work directly with data bases, since they are directly involved in entering, processing, and querying the data in data bases. They are also responsible for developing and evaluating the internal controls necessary to ensure data base integrity. Some will become involved as designers and managers of data bases.

Internal Data Bases. Many functional areas other than accounting are building internal data bases to gain a competitive advantage. For example, a recent survey showed that 60% of manufacturers and retailers are now building a marketing data base, 10% plan to do so, and 90% believe they will need data base marketing to remain competitive at the turn of the century. Data bases developed by other functional areas include the following examples:

- *Sports Illustrated (SI)* uses sophisticated data bases to house subscriber information, and custom publishing to provide individual readers with specialized magazines. Based on customer preferences stored in the data base, *SI* customizes its editorial pages and inserts a four-page weekly section on the subscriber's favorite football team and its divisional rivals. Such selective binding technology allows *Newsweek* to juggle its ad mix to create as many as 160 different versions of its magazine, depending on factors such as a subscriber's address and income level.
- Freida's, a specialty produce wholesaler, sells specialty produce in all 50 states. Each piece of fruit it sells carries a label that helps shoppers know how to prepare the item. The label also encourages them to write the company for recipes and additional product information and to express their opinions on the produce. Almost 20,000 people a year respond and all are logged into Freida's data base, which currently has information on over 120,000 customers nationwide. Freida's can analyze the data base by product type, zip code, location of store, date of correspondence, and type of response (positive, negative, request for recipes, etc.). Because it knows so much about supermarket customers, Freida's is able to use the data to convince supermarkets that may not think there is a market for their produce to otherwise carry it.
- The Travelers Corp. has saved $100 per automobile repair estimate and cut the turnaround time for estimates by half using a graphical data base system.

The system consists of a personal computer and a data base, stored on the system's hard disk and two CD-ROMs, that contains labor and parts costs on every vehicle on the road. Adjusters use a portable version of the system, and repair shops use a desktop version. Adjustors use a modem to access a mainframe in Michigan and to gather data from public data bases. A miniprinter allows adjustors to produce a repair estimate virtually anywhere. With both sides having access to the same repair information data base, disputes and haggling over costs are significantly reduced.

The trend in business today is away from specialized functional data bases and toward a data warehouse that is, in essence, a single data base serving the needs of all users. The result is that traditionally separate data bases will be integrated. Instead of having marketing, accounting, and production data bases there will be just one data base. The data base developed by Vons Supermarkets is an example of one that serves more than one functional area. Over a million customers in Vons Club purchase groceries with a magnetic card that works like a magnetic check. Each time a card is used, transaction data are captured and stored in the data base. In addition, electronic funds from the card are deposited into Von's bank, which collects the amount due from the customer's bank. This system greatly simplifies transaction processing and eliminates problems with bad checks. In addition, analyzing the buying habits of its customers improves Vons marketing efforts and helps the company reach today's intensely price- and promotion-sensitive customers.

External Data Bases. A number of organizations are in the business of gathering and storing useful information in "external" data bases. These information service companies charge users an hourly fee or sell the information on a compact disk. A few of the areas that accountants may need to access include the following:

- Tax services containing federal and state tax codes; regulations; tax guides with code citations, explanations, and examples; tax forms and instructions; and IRS revenue and private letter rulings.
- Accounting and auditing pronouncements such as the FASB opinions and the Statements on Auditing Standards.
- Complete company annual reports, including footnotes and auditor reports.
- Related SEC documents as well as a listing of the officers and directors of companies and partnerships.
- Economic forecasts, stock quotes, and other financial information.
- Federal and state case laws and rulings.
- Business directories containing information on over 9 million businesses.
- Literature citations and full text of hundreds of current periodicals.

DATA PROCESSING

The most common data processing activity is data maintenance, which is the periodic processing of transactions to update stored data. Four types of data maintenance are commonly used. *Additions* insert new records into the file. *Deletions* extract records from the file. *Updates* revise current balances, generally by adding or subtracting an amount from a transaction record. *Changes* modify fields that may need an occasional update such as credit ratings and addresses.

Figure 4.7 depicts the data maintenance steps required to update an accounts receivable record with a sales transaction. The two records are matched using the account number. The sale amount ($360) is added to the account balance ($1500) to obtain a new current balance ($1860).

Data processing can also include other activities:

- *Calculating,* by any form of mathematical manipulation.
- *Comparing,* by examining two or more data items, such as inventory on hand and a reorder point, to determine whether one is equal to, less than, or greater than the others.
- *Summarizing,* by combining data into meaningful totals.
- *Filtration,* or screening extraneous data from subsequent processing.
- *Retrieval,* or fetching data items from storage for processing or output purposes.

Primary and Secondary Keys

Records are typically updated, stored, and retrieved using an identifier called a **key.** The basic purpose of the **primary key** is to uniquely identify each record. Table 4.1 lists some common data records in a business organization and identifies a primary key and two or more secondary keys for each one.

Figure 4.7

File Update Example

TRANSACTION DATA

Account Number	Transaction Type	Transaction Date	Document Number	Transaction Amount
0123	Sale	02/19/87	9876	$360.00

ACCOUNTS RECEIVABLE RECORD

Account Number	Credit Limit	Previous Balance	Current Balance
0123	$2000.00	$1000.00	$1500.00

FILE UPDATE PROCESS

- Verify data accuracy
- Match primary key (account number)
- Add transaction amount to current balance
- Compare new balance to credit limit
- Repeat for all transactions
- Print summary reports

UPDATED ACCOUNTS RECEIVABLE RECORD

Account Number	Credit Limit	Previous Balance	Current Balance
0123	$2000.00	$1500.00	$1860.00

Table 4.1 **Examples of Record Keys for Typical Business Records**

Record Type	Primary Key	Secondary Keys
Payroll	Employee number	Employee name, payroll date, department
Customer	Account number	Customer name, balance, credit limit
Parts inventory	Stock number	Location, description, vendor number
Work in process	Job number	Location, start date
Finished goods	Product number	Location, sales price
General ledger	Account code	Department number, current balance
Fixed assets	Asset number	Location, date of acquisition, vendor number
Accounts payable	Vendor number	Payment due date, vendor number

A **secondary key** is another field used to identify a record, although it is not unique. Secondary keys can be used to sort records. For example, to record grades in computerized grade rolls, the file may need to be in alphabetical order. When determining final grades, the professor may want the file in descending order, based on total points earned. In this example the unique identifier, the last name, is the primary key and the total points earned is the secondary key.

The appropriate primary key for each record is generally obvious. For example, customer number for the customer file and invoice number for the invoice file. The selection of secondary keys is significant, because it can enhance data base processing efficiency and facilitate information retrieval. The most appropriate secondary keys are those data elements that identify certain properties held in common by groups of records. Examples include invoice due date, employee department number, and inventory location code.

All computer systems must have some formalized means of organizing and accessing data so that it can be accessed easily and efficiently. The following section describes several ways of organizing and accessing files.

File Organization and Access

File organization is the way data are stored on the physical storage media. **File access** refers to the way a computer locates stored records. Two methods are used to organize and access data, referred to as sequential and direct (or random). Records in sequential files are stored in order according to their primary key (e.g., customer numbers from 00001 to 99999), and records in direct-access files are not stored in any particular order. With **sequential access,** the system starts at the beginning and reads each record until the one desired is located. Because the search process is so inefficient, it is impractical for applications that require immediate access to records. With **direct access,** the computer locates records without reading each record in the file. The direct-access approaches used to locate records are explained later in the chapter.

Accountants need not understand the technical details of the storage and access process. However, they must know how files are organized and accessed in order to (1) recognize the constraints imposed on data by organization and access methods and (2) select the approach that best meets their needs. Sequential and direct-access file processing are now explained.

Sequential File Processing

Sequential file processing organizes and processes the master and transaction files in the same order. For example, the updating process maintains accounts receivable and sales transaction files in customer number order. To illustrate sequential file processing, Table 4.2 presents a master, transaction, and updated master file. The only fields shown are the primary key (customer account number), account balance, and transaction amount. A positive transaction amount indicates a sale; a negative amount a payment. For clarification, each step in the update process is numbered.

During sequential file processing the computer reads a master (step 1) and transaction record (step 2). Since the account numbers match, the master file

Table 4.2 **Example of Sequential File Updating**

Files Before Update

Master File		Transaction File	
Account #	**Balance**	**Account #**	**Amount**
101	1000	101	+700
102	600	101	–1000
104	1900	103	+500
		104	+1600

Update Process

		Master File		Transaction File	
Step	**Action**	**Acct #**	**Balance**	**Acct #**	**Amount**
1	Read master file record	101	1000		
2	Read transaction file record			101	700
3	Match and update	101	1700		
4	Read transaction file record			101	–1000
5	Match and update	101	700		
6	Read transaction file record			103	500
7	No match; write 101 to new master file	—	—		
8	Read master file record	102	600		
9	No match; write 102 to new master file	—			
10	Read master file record	104	1900		
11	No match; write 103 to error file	—			
12	Read transaction file record			104	1600
13	Match and update	104	3500		

Files After Update

Master File		Error File	
Account #	**Balance**	**Account #**	**Amount**
101	700	103	500
102	600		
104	3500		

record is updated (step 3); the balance for customer 101 is now $1700. Since a master record may have more than one update, a new transaction record is read (step 4). The account numbers are again compared; since they match, customer 101's master record is updated again (step 5) and the balance is now $700. A new transaction record is read (step 6). Since the account number of the master record is smaller than that of the transaction record (step 7), there are no further updates to the master record. The master file record is stored on the new master file.

A new master file record is read (step 8). The match (step 9) shows there is no update to master file record 102, so it is written to the new master file. Another master file record is read (step 10). A match (step 11) shows that the key of the transaction record is now smaller than the master record. Thus either an error has occurred (record 103 has been lost from the master file) or transaction record 103 is an addition to the master file. Assuming the former, record 103 is written to a special error file. A new transaction record is read (step 12), and customer 104's master record is updated (step 13). The system continues to alternate the reading of the master and transaction files as needed until all the master records have been updated.

Sequential file organization is fast and efficient when a large volume and a high percentage of records are processed periodically in a file that doesn't require frequent updates. It is very efficient for batch processing operations. For example, a company that pays all employees weekly or monthly could easily process its file sequentially.

Direct-Access File Processing

In **direct-access processing,** transactions are processed as they occur. Unlike sequential processing, the master and transaction files can be in any order. When a transaction occurs, the computer uses the primary key of the transaction file (such as account number) to search the master file for the desired record. The record is then retrieved, updated, and written back to the master file.

Direct-access processing is appropriate if files are constantly accessed, queried, or updated. For example, airline reservation systems are updated using direct-access processing, since information such as airfares and departure and arrival times are constantly changing. Direct-access methods are used when it is impossible to anticipate the sequence in which records will be processed or queried.

A program flowchart illustrating a generalized, direct-access file update appears in Fig. 4.8. To update a record, users notify the system (step 1) of their intentions. The system prompts the user to enter transaction data (step 2). Once entered (step 3), the system searches for the corresponding master record (step 4). If it cannot be found (step 5), the user is sent an error message (step 6) and asked to correct the error or abort the update until the transaction is corrected.

If the master record is found (step 5), the transaction data are used to update the master record (step 7). The updated record is written back out (step 8) to the direct-access storage medium. Since the updated record is written over the old record, the original data are lost unless first written to a separate file. The system asks whether there are any more updates (step 9). If so, the program returns to step 2 and begins again. Otherwise, processing is terminated.

Figure 4.8

Generalized Direct-Access File Processing Program Flowchart

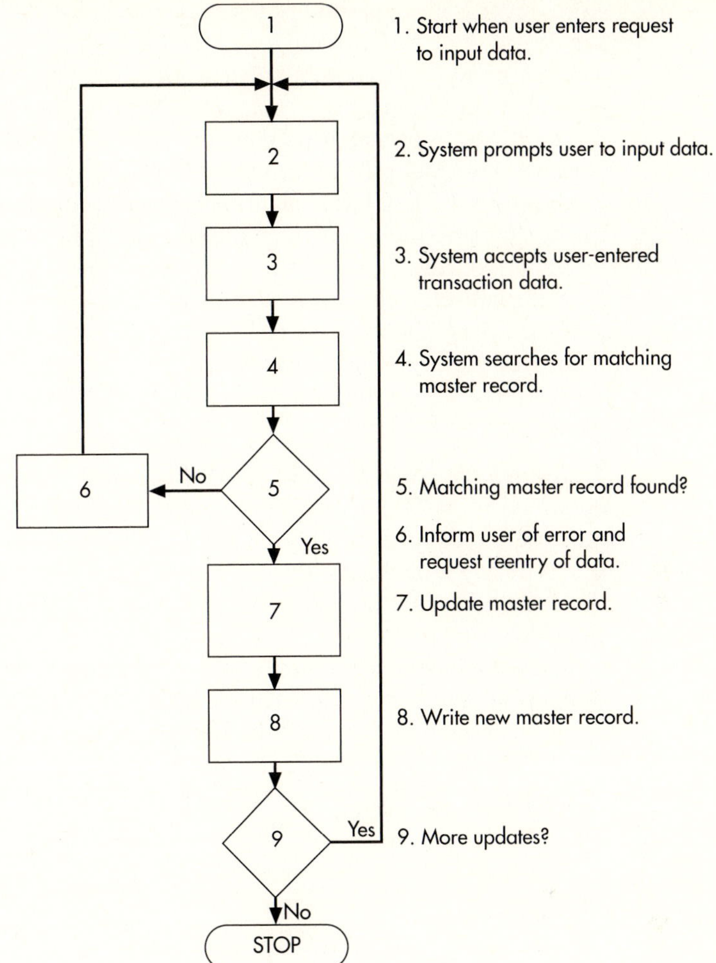
1
2
3
4
5
6
No
Yes
7
8
9
Yes
No
STOP
1. Start when user enters request to input data.
2. System prompts user to input data.
3. System accepts user-entered transaction data.
4. System searches for matching master record.
5. Matching master record found?
6. Inform user of error and request reentry of data.
7. Update master record.
8. Write new master record.
9. More updates?

Determining where to store records and how to find them once they have been stored (step 4) is complicated. Several methods of record storage and access that are used to achieve direct-access capabilities are briefly discussed next.

Indexed File Organization. An **index file** contains the primary key and physical address of each record. It is similar to a card catalog in a library. To find a library book, a user searches the card catalog, determines the approximate physical location, proceeds to the proper shelf, and searches that shelf for the book. In a similar fashion, an index file can be used to find a record in a data file. The user requests a record by specifying its key, the key is looked up in the index, and the computer uses the address in the index file to find and retrieve the desired record.

Indexed-Sequential-Access Method (ISAM). The most popular indexing approach is the **indexed-sequential-access method (ISAM).** An ISAM file stores records in sequential order by their primary key on a direct-access storage device. It also creates an index file for the master file. This means the file can be accessed both sequentially and directly. The advantages of both sequential and direct file organization that ISAM provides accounts for its popularity.

The ISAM approach does have drawbacks. It requires more storage space because of the index. In addition, creating, storing, and maintaining the indexes can be costly. Finally, large quantities of new records cannot be added easily to the file. To solve the problem of additions and deletions, the file can be reorganized periodically.

In the indexed-sequential file example in Fig. 4.9, 25 customer records numbered 1478 to 1502 are stored in blocks of five in five storage addresses numbered 4061 to 4065. The index contains five entries, one for each address. Each index entry contains the key of the block's last customer record as well as the address of that block.

Multiattribute Search File Organization. The file organizations just described allow the file to be accessed by the primary key, but they do not facilitate the access of data records based on one or more secondary keys. When access through secondary keys is desired, a multiattribute search file organization is used. Two methods are discussed here: linked lists and inverted lists (also called inverted files).

In a **linked list,** each data record has a **pointer field** containing the address of the next record in the list. Thus all related records are linked by pointers. A group of records "connected" by pointers is referred to as a **chain.** Table 4.3

Figure 4.9 *An Indexed-Sequential File*

Index

Key	*Address*
1482	4061
1487	4062
1492	4063
1497	4064
1502	4065

Data Storage Area

Address No. 4061	Customer No. 1478	Customer No. 1479	Customer No. 1480	Customer No. 1481	Customer No. 1482
Address No. 4062	Customer No. 1483	Customer No. 1484	Customer No. 1485	Customer No. 1486	Customer No. 1487
Address No. 4063	Customer No. 1488	Customer No. 1489	Customer No. 1490	Customer No. 1491	Customer No. 1492
Address No. 4064	Customer No. 1493	Customer No. 1494	Customer No. 1495	Customer No. 1496	Customer No. 1497
Address No. 4065	Customer No. 1498	Customer No. 1499	Customer No. 1500	Customer No. 1501	Customer No. 1502

Table 4.3 **Use of Secondary Keys to Link Embedded Pointers**

Address	Part #	Supplier	Next S	Product Line	Next PL
11	125	ABC Co.	16	Widget	17
12	164	XYZ Inc.	14	Doodad	16
13	189	GHI Corp.	18	Clavet	15
14	205	XYZ Inc.	24	Lodix	18
15	271	RST Mfg.	19	Clavet	22
16	293	ABC Co.	17	Doodad	20
17	316	ABC Co.	21	Widget	23
18	348	GHI Corp.	20	Lodix	19
19	377	RST Mfg.	22	Lodix	21
20	383	GHI Corp.	23	Doodad	24
21	451	ABC Co.	30	Lodix	25
22	465	RST Mfg.	25	Clavet	27
23	498	GHI Corp.	26	Widget	*
24	521	XYZ Inc.	28	Doodad	26
25	572	RST Mfg.	*	Lodix	28
26	586	GHI Corp.	27	Doodad	29
27	603	GHI Corp.	29	Clavet	*
28	647	XYZ Inc.	*	Lodix	30
29	653	GHI Corp.	*	Doodad	*
30	719	ABC Co.	*	Lodix	*

*End of chain.

illustrates the use of embedded pointers to chain together parts records having the same secondary keys. The links in each chain are pointers contained in the fields labeled Next S and Next PL. Each of these fields "points to" the storage address of the next record having the same value for supplier and product line, respectively. For example, the chain for all parts supplied by ABC Co. contains the records at machine addresses 11, 16, 17, 21, and 30.

Linked lists and pointers are commonly used in AIS to connect a set of detail records to a master record. For example, an accounts receivable record may have associated with it a number of transaction records, which could be connected to it by means of linked lists. Similarly, an invoice or purchase order record could have line-item records connected to it using pointers. Chains may also be used to link all records in a file that have the same secondary key, such as all employees who work in the same department.

Whereas linked lists use pointers embedded within the records, **inverted lists** use pointers stored in an index. An **inverted file** maintains inverted lists for some of the attributes. Table 4.4 shows inverted lists for the secondary keys supplier and product line, created from the sample data records in Table 4.3. There is one list for each value of each attribute, and each list contains the machine addresses of all records having that value. Using these inverted lists, any or all records containing a particular supplier or product line can be easily and quickly accessed.

Table 4.4 **Inverted Lists for the Secondary Keys of Table 4.3**

Supplier	Addresses	Product Line	Addresses
ABC Co.	11, 16, 17, 21, 30	Clavet	13, 15, 22, 27
GHI Corp.	13, 18, 20, 23, 26, 27, 29	Doodad	12, 16, 20, 24, 26, 29
RST Mfg.	15, 19, 22, 25	Lodix	14, 18, 19, 21, 25, 28, 30
XYZ Inc.	12, 14, 24, 28	Widget	11, 17, 23

Files also differ depending on when transactions are processed. Transactions can be used to update files as they occur or they can be stored temporarily and processed in groups. These two approaches are now explained.

Batch Processing

Processing similar transactions in groups is called **batch processing.** Processing occurs at given times (such as hourly or daily) or whenever a manageable number (50 to 100, for example) of source documents are gathered. It is most appropriate for processing common transactions that occur in large numbers, such as payroll and accounts payable. Batch processing requires that the master file be organized as either a sequential or ISAM file. **Remote batch processing** occurs when transaction records are recorded in machine-readable form at geographically dispersed locations and electronically transmitted to a central processing site. Batch processing is illustrated in Fig. 4.10.

In batch processing the inputs to the file maintenance process are the old master file and the transactions. Before transactions can be processed they must be captured electronically, sorted into the same order as the master file (if processed sequentially), and edited for errors and incomplete data; then control totals must be generated for each batch. Examples of **control totals** are the number of transactions processed and the dollar amount of all updates. These totals are calculated during subsequent processing steps and compared to the original totals to ensure that all data are processed.

Batch processing output includes a new master file and reports for external and internal users. For example, a payroll processing program would produce checks and a transaction report that lists each transaction that was processed as well as summary totals. In addition, an exception report would list errors detected by the system during processing.

On-Line Processing

In **on-line batch processing,** the computer captures the data electronically and stores it so that it can be processed later. For example, a bank may capture data using on-line terminals but choose to process the transactions after it has closed for the day. In **on-line, real-time processing,** the computer captures data electronically, edits it for accuracy and completeness, and immediately processes it. In addition, the computer processes information requests from users by locating the desired information in the data files and displaying it in the specified format. Examples of on-line, real-time systems are airline reservation systems and the New York stock exchange quotation system. Both on-line batch and on-line, real-time processing are illustrated in Fig. 4.10.

Many companies are using real-time systems because of the competitive advantages they offer. For example, a few years ago Federal Express updated

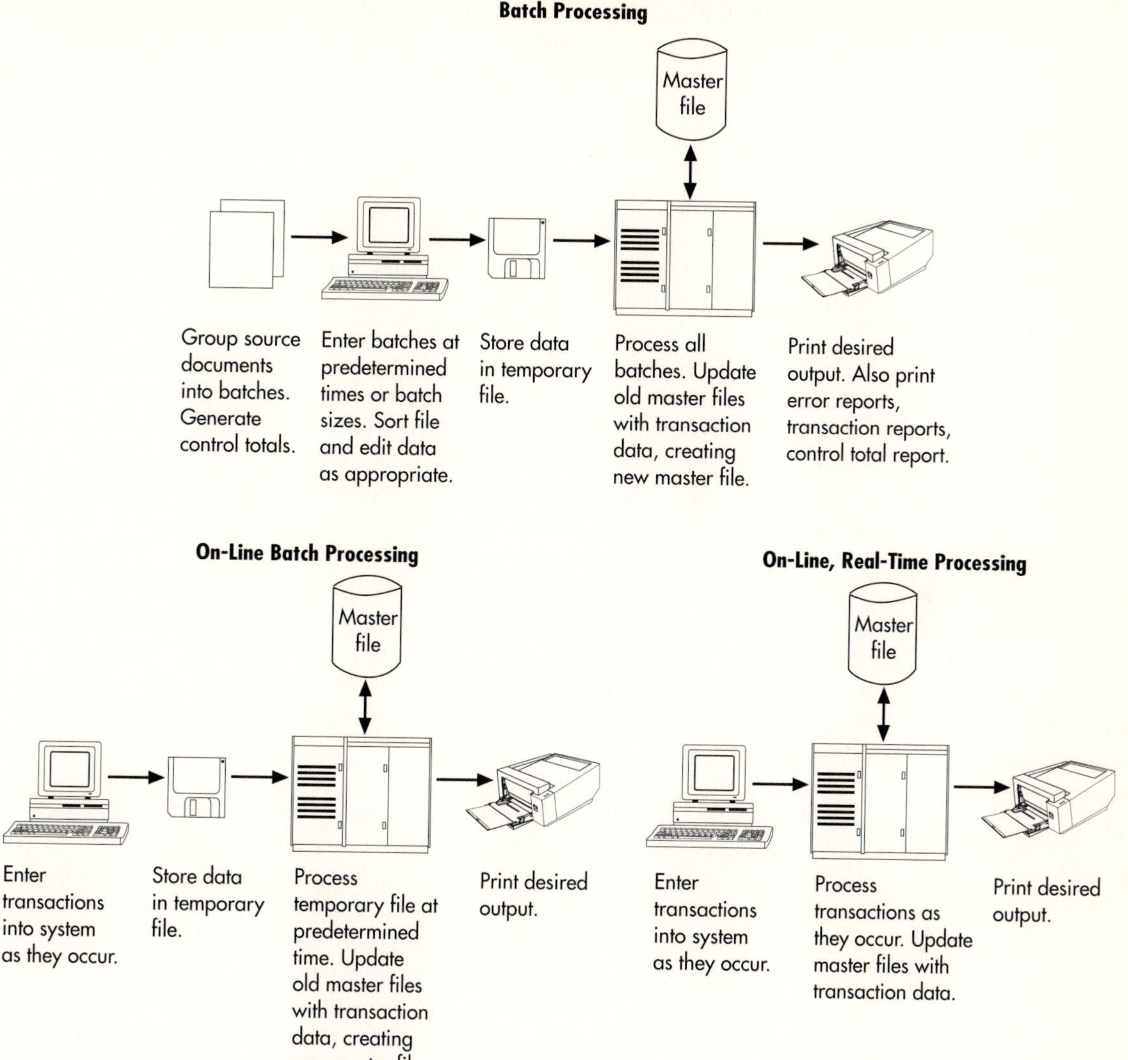

Figure 4.10 *Batch and On-Line Processing*

its mission statement to include the phrase "positive control of each package will be maintained by utilizing real-time electronic tracking and tracing systems." The company now has a real-time system that tells the exact location of each package and estimates its arrival time. Federal Express also provides customers with personal computer software that allows them to track their own parcels.

Efficiency is the main advantage of batch processing, since many similar transactions are processed simultaneously rather than intermittently as they occur. However, since transactions are captured as they occur, on-line entry is more timely. It is also more accurate, because the system can refuse incomplete or erroneous transactions. With on-line updating, records are current and users can obtain up-to-date information in response to a query. With batch processing, files are current only immediately after they are updated, which may be as infrequently as once a day or once a week.

INFORMATION OUTPUT

The final step in the data processing cycle is information output. In the following section you will learn about the format, purpose, and user responsibilities associated with output.

Forms of Information Output

Information is presented in three forms: a document, a report, or a response to a query. **Documents** are records of transaction or other company data. Some, such as checks and invoices, are transmitted to external parties. Others, such as receiving reports and purchase requisitions, are used internally. Documents generated at the end of transaction processing activities are called **operational documents** to distinguish them from source documents, which are used at the beginning of a process.

Documents can be printed out or they can be stored as electronic images in a computer. For example, Toys 'R' Us uses electronic data interchange to communicate with its suppliers. Every year it processes over half a million invoices electronically, thereby eliminating paper documents and dramatically reducing costs and errors. This has resulted in higher profits and more accurate information.

Reports are prepared for both internal and external users. They are used by employees to control operational activities and by managers to make decisions and design strategies for the business. External users need reports for a wide variety of reasons, such as to evaluate company profitability, to judge creditworthiness, or to comply with regulatory requirements. For example, Eli Lilly, a large drug manufacturer, has applications that automatically gather, process, and display data in any form, such as text, spreadsheets, or easy-to-understand graphs or charts. When the Food and Drug Administration (FDA) mandated that it receive certain information electronically, Eli Lilly programmed its system to gather the needed data from its different systems, organize it, and submit it electronically to the FDA.

Some reports, such as financial statements and sales analyses, are produced on a regular basis. Others are produced on an exception basis to call attention to unusual conditions. For example, S&S could have its system produce a report to indicate when product returns exceed a certain percentage of sales. Finally, reports can be produced on demand. For example, Susan could produce a report to identify the S&S salesperson who sold the most items during a specific promotional period.

Increasingly, information needs cannot be satisfied strictly by documents or periodic reports. Instead, problems and questions that need rapid action or answers constantly arise. To respond to this problem, PCs or terminals are used to **query** the system. A user enters a request for a specific piece of information, and the system uses the indices, lists, and pointers to find the information. Once found, the information is retrieved, displayed, or analyzed as requested. Since many queries are repetitive, most users will have a predetermined set of queries available to them. To shorten the time required to develop the queries and to improve their efficiency, these repetitive queries are often developed by IS specialists. Any unusual or one-time queries are usually developed by the users themselves. When displayed on a monitor, output is referred to as *soft copy.* When printed on paper, it is referred to as *hard copy.*

Some companies have even made it possible for their suppliers to query their own data bases. For example, KMart allows Black and Decker to access any information in its data bases—excluding any data about Black and Decker's competitors—that will help it better serve KMart's needs. Thus Black and Decker can gauge how well a product, such as a new electric drill, is selling in every KMart store in the world. KMart and Black and Decker can both maximize sales by stocking and promoting those items that are selling well. Customers are satisfied because the items they want are always available.

Goal of the Information

For external users, financial statements are produced to meet stewardship requirements. In addition, income tax returns and 10-K filings with the Securities and Exchange Commission are produced to comply with legal requirements. For internal users, budgets, sales forecasts, projected cash flow statements, and new product revenue and cost estimates are prepared for planning purposes. In addition, reports such as production and delivery schedules, open purchase orders, and inventory stock status reports are prepared to help effectively manage day-to-day operations.

Companies should periodically reassess the need for each report produced. All too often reports continue to be prepared long after their need disappears, wasting time, money, and computer resources. For example, a team at Ameritech, a regional Bell telephone company, interviewed the preparers and users of every report. They found many duplicate and unnecessary reports, including a 25-page report that took five days to prepare and sat unread. In the end 6 million pages of reports were eliminated, a stack four times higher than Ameritech's 41-story headquarters in Chicago.

For control purposes, an organization must constantly monitor its progress so that problems that arise can be corrected as soon as possible. Often, monitoring consists of comparing standards or expected performances with actual performance. When variances get too far out of line, management takes corrective action to bring them back within an acceptable range. Examples of control reports include comparisons of standard and actual production rates, materials use, labor efficiency, profitability, and sales.

SUMMARY AND CASE CONCLUSION

The immediate need at S&S is to develop a computerized AIS. Ashton decided to enter and process transaction data in several ways. Crucial sales data will be captured in electronic form, using source data automation, and processed as they occur so inventory files are always up to date. Other data such as inventory receipts, accounts payable, accounts receivable collections, and purchasing can be keyed into the computer as they occur for either immediate processing or nightly batch processing. Ashton will defer the decision on implementing either on-line batch or on-line, real-time processing until S&S

selects software and designs the system for each cycle. Other data files, such as payroll, can be handled with time cards as the source document and can be processed sequentially in batch mode.

Because Ashton wants quick and easy access to company data, he plans to investigate the various data base packages on the market. The software must allow S&S to produce the output Ashton will need to handle his accounting duties as well as the information that Scott and Susan will need to manage the company. Scott, Susan, and Ashton hope to have just one corporate data base. That way, data will be captured only once and will not have to be entered into different data bases, and all systems will be able to communicate with one another.

Every employee with a regular need for information will have a set of one or more queries tailored to his or her specific needs. Employees will use these on-line queries and their microcomputers to retrieve from the data base the information they need to perform their jobs. For example, Susan wants to check the sales figures and the inventory levels at each store every morning. She also wants to produce an income statement for S&S for any time period she specifies. Finally, each morning she wants to run a query to produce an exception report that flags any unusual activity at any of the stores.

Developing the system at S&S will not be easy. Ashton needs to learn more about how data bases work and how to develop data base systems (see Chapters 5 and 6). Ashton is not yet sure just what computer equipment and programs he will need, but he is sure that with a little more study (see Chapters 7–9) he will be able to handle this aspect of the system. It will require a great deal of time and effort to determine the needs of users and to ensure that the system meets those needs (see Chapters 10–12). He will also need to ensure that the system is adequately controlled and secure (see Chapters 13–15). Chapters 17–21 discuss the different business cycles and the information a data base must contain for each of these cycles.

KEY TERMS

data processing cycle
turnaround document
source data automation
entity
attributes
characters
data value
field
record
file
data base
master file
transaction file
table file
history file
backup file
suspense file
report file
data base approach
data base management system (DBMS)
data base system
data base administrator (DBA)
data warehouses
record layout
logical view
physical view
data maintenance
key
primary key
secondary key
file organization
file access
sequential access
direct access
sequential file processing
direct-access processing
index file
indexed-sequential-access method (ISAM)
linked lists
pointer field
chain
inverted lists
inverted file
batch processing
remote batch processing
control totals
on-line batch processing
on-line, real-time processing
documents
operational documents
reports
query

CHAPTER QUIZ

1. Which of the following is *not* a method of collecting transaction data for entry into a computer system?
   a. Source document
   b. Turnaround document
   c. Source data automation
   d. Inquiry processing
2. The hierarchy of data elements, from largest to smallest, is
   a. field, record, file, data base.
   b. record, file, data base, field.
   c. record, file, field, data base.
   d. data base, file, record, field.
   e. data base, record, file, field.
3. A permanent file that contains all the data a company needs about an item of interest is called
   a. transaction file.
   b. master file.
   c. history file.
   d. table file.
   e. suspense file.
4. A data base provides users with all of the following advantages *except*
   a. minimal data redundancy.
   b. minimal data inquiry capabilities.
   c. central management of data.
   d. data independence.
   e. cross-functional analysis.
5. The manner in which data are actually arranged and stored on disks, tapes, or other storage medium is referred to as the
   a. physical view of data.
   b. logical view of data.
   c. primary key.
   d. secondary key.
   e. index file.
6. Which of the following attributes in a professor's class file is *most* likely to serve as the primary key?
   a. Student ID number
   b. Major
   c. Last name
   d. Point total for the course
   e. Test scores
7. The way that a computer locates records that have been stored on a disk is referred to as
   a. file organization.
   b. file access.
   c. batch processing.
   d. conceptual data modeling.
   e. source data automation.
8. Which of the following statements is true?
   a. The indexed-sequential-access method (ISAM) approach permits both sequential and direct-access processing.
   b. A sequential file organization permits both sequential and direct-access processing.
   c. The random file organization must store records in order of their primary key.
   d. None of the above statements are true.
9. Capturing sales transactions electronically as they occur and immediately processing them is called
   a. remote batch processing.
   b. on-line real-time processing.
   c. on-line batch processing.
   d. query processing.
   e. direct-access updating.
10. Sales invoices, purchase requisitions, and employee time cards are examples of
    a. turnaround documents.
    b. source documents.
    c. journal vouchers.
    d. source data automation.

DISCUSSION QUESTIONS

4.1 The following data items comprise an accounts receivable record that is to be incorporated into a data base system. Identify the data items within this record that are good candidates for secondary keys. Explain each of your choices.

Customer account number (primary key)
Customer name
Customer address
Location code
Credit rating code
Credit limit
Beginning account balance
Current transactions
Transaction type
Document number
Transaction date

Amount
Current balance

4.2 Identify some of the master files you would be likely to encounter in the following organizations:

a. A university
b. A hospital
c. A bank
d. An insurance company
e. A stockbrokerage
f. An advertising agency

4.3 Computer data processing is based on the logical organization of data into files, records, and fields. State whether each of the following is a file, a record, or a field.

a. All data on one customer
b. Accounts receivable subsidiary ledger
c. Employee number
d. Amount owed to a particular vendor
e. General ledger
f. Accounts payable subsidiary ledger
g. Data on a particular vendor
h. The name of one vendor
i. All data on one inventory item

4.4 Indicate whether the following data would appear on a master file, a transaction file, or both:

a. Date
b. Account balance
c. Account number
d. Amount of payment
e. Customer name
f. Location of a sale
g. Phone number
h. Product number
i. Product description
j. Customer address
k. Invoice number
l. Credit limit
m. Vendor name
n. Quantity on hand
o. Amount of sale
p. Vendor number
q. Quantity received

4.5 For each of the following data processing applications, indicate which is more appropriate: batch or on-line, real-time processing. Explain your answers.

a. Weekly processing of employee time cards to prepare paychecks
b. Processing of customer reservation requests by a motel chain
c. Processing of credit checks by a retail credit bureau
d. Preparation of monthly customer bills by a utility company
e. Processing of customer transactions at a bank teller window
f. Scheduling of material and labor activity in an automated factory
g. Preparation of monthly financial statements
h. Processing of cash receipts on account from customers
i. Reordering of merchandise inventory in a high-volume retail store

4.6 Suppose you were designing a computer-based transaction processing system and needed to identify all the data, information, and other items that would make up the system. Where would you begin? On which stage of the data processing cycle would you concentrate—data input, data processing, data storage, or information output? Why?

4.7 A data base allows two distinct views of data—a logical view and a physical view. Contrast the two views, and discuss why separate views are necessary in data base applications. Describe which perspective is most useful for each of the following employees: a programmer, a manager, and an internal auditor. How will understanding logical data structures assist accountants in designing and using data base systems?

4.8 A new data base designed and operated by Equifax is revolutionizing the auto insurance industry. To combat fraudulent applications for auto insurance, over three hundred insurance companies use the Comprehensive Loss Underwriting Exchange data base to share information about potential customers. The data base contains all auto insurance claims made by customers against any insurance company in the past three to five years. It also contains the current status of claims and their cost. The availability of this information at low cost has improved the effectiveness of the traditional applicant-screening process and has helped insurance companies to keep insurance premiums down.

The way the system works is simple. Companies pay an annual fee to subscribe to the data base service and a fee of $2.25 for each application check. Data base searches turn up prior claims in 20% of the cases, 90% of which were unreported by the insurance applicant. Any new information discovered during this check that was omitted from the application can cause a company to raise premiums or even to cancel a policy. To ensure fairness, customers can gain access to a copy of their report and can challenge the accuracy of findings.

What advantages does this data base technology provide insurance companies and auto insurance applicants? What are the possible risks of this data base system?

4.9 Referring to the inverted lists in Table 4.4, describe the process the system would follow to answer the question, "Which parts supplied by RST Mfg. are used in the Lodix product line?" Retrieve the appropriate part numbers from Table 4.3.

PROBLEMS

4.1 This problem involves tracing the operations performed on a hypothetical set of master and transaction records through the sequential updating process shown in Table 4.2. Assume that a new master file is created to replace the old one and that any unmatched transaction records represent errors. Assume that the master file and the transaction file are composed of the following record numbers in the sequence given:

Master File		Transaction File	
Account #	**Balance**	**Account #**	**Balance**
011	1400	011	+570
013	700	012	+700
014	250	014	+1400
015	2950	014	–250
016	1725	016	+275
017	885	018	–350
018	1150	EOF (End of File)	
019	2780		
EOF (End of File)			

REQUIRED

a. Construct a table similar to Table 4.2 to show how the transactions would be processed. Alternate between reading master file records, reading transaction file records, updating master file records, and writing records to the new master file, as necessary. Number the steps as shown in Table 4.2. Continue until you have traced all records through the program.

b. Suppose that there was a transaction record with the account number 020 and a +625 balance after record number 018 and in front of the end-of-file record. Beginning at the point at which this change would first make a difference, trace the records through the program to the finish, recording the actions in your table as described in part (a).

4.2 The first few days of sales at S&S were excellent. Consumer demand for appliances exceeded all initial expectations. However, Scott arrived at the accounting office in a state of alarm. Apparently, the strong demand has rapidly diminished the inventory of S&S's most popular items. In fact, this afternoon a customer left the store quite upset that S&S would have to place a special order for an advertised appliance that wouldn't be delivered for several weeks.

Scott is concerned with his inability as a manager to monitor the level of inventory on hand as sales are transacted. Scott encourages you to focus on the inventory problem and draft a potential solution aimed at integrating an inventory processing system into the future information system.

REQUIRED

a. What are the underlying causes of S&S's inventory problem?

b. What information does Scott need to facilitate the flow of inventory? What impact does timeliness have on the value of information?

c. How effective would a manual system be in helping solve the inventory problem?

d. As you design a computerized information system, what data input and data processing methods should be used to deal with the inventory problem? Justify your selection.

4.3 On a day-to-day basis, students are involved with a number of transaction processing systems. On a college campus transactions occur in the administration office, in the bookstore, and at the local pizza place.

REQUIRED

Identify three transaction processing systems that you were involved in over the past month.

a. What are the outputs of the system? How are they used?

b. Identify the inputs and input methods used in each system. What role do source documents play in the data collection and input process for the information system?
c. What data processing and storage techniques are being used in each example?
d. Based on current technology, recommend two or more improvements to each existing information system. What types of benefits would these suggestions provide?

4.4 Ron Black, controller of Kessler Corporation, has been working with the Systems Department to revise and implement a data entry and data retention system. The departments involved and details of their data processing activities follow.

General Accounting

- Daily processing of journal entries submitted by various departments.
- Weekly updating of file balances with subsystem data from areas such as payroll, accounts receivable, and accounts payable.
- Sporadic requests for account activity and balances during the month, with increased activity at month-end.

Accounts Receivable

- Daily processing of accounts receivable receipts.
- Daily processing of customer sales.
- Customer credit limit checks.
- Daily identification of orders exceeding $20,000 per customer.
- Daily requests for customer credit status.
- Weekly reporting to the general accounting file.

Accounts Payable

- Processing of payments to vendors three times per week.
- Weekly expense distribution update to the general accounting file.

Budget Planning and Control

- Updating of flexible budgets on a monthly basis.
- Quarterly budget revisions based on sales forecast and production schedule changes.
- Monthly inquiries for budget balances.

Mary Crandall, manager of the Systems Department, has explained to Black and his staff the concepts of batch processing versus on-line, real-time processing, as well as off-line versus on-line file retention. Crandall has indicated that batch processing, along with off-line file retention, is the least expensive combination of techniques. A rough cost estimate reflecting alternative combinations has also been prepared:

Data Entry/File Retention Techniques	Cost in Relation to Batch/Off-line Processing
Batch/on-line	1.5 times
Real-time/on-line	2.5 times

REQUIRED

a. Define and discuss the major differences between batch processing and real-time processing.
b. Define and discuss the major differences between off-line and on-line file retention.
c. For each of the four departments that report to Black, identify and explain (1) the type of data entry technique and (2) the type of file retention that should be used. Assume that the volume of transactions is not a key variable in the decision.
d. From a managerial perspective, Black feels that the Budget Planning and Control Department should be more effective in assisting operations with controlling costs. Of the data entry techniques identified in part (a), which technique will best help Black achieve this objective. Explain your answer. (CMA Examination adapted)

4.5 The MASI Corporation has decided to store its records using the indexing approach known as ISAM. Assume that 50 records with key values numbered sequentially from 500 to 549 are stored in blocks of five at 10 machine addresses numbered sequentially from 200 to 209. Each entry in the index contains the key of the last record in a block, as well as the address of that block.

REQUIRED

a. Prepare an index for this file segment.
b. Assuming an indexed-sequential file organization, explain how the system would access record number 522.

4.6 Assume that the hypothetical inventory records in Table 5.5 (p. 138) are stored sequentially at machine addresses numbered from 1 to 9 and that we wish to use embedded pointers to chain together all items having the same color.

REQUIRED

a. Prepare a table with the column headings Machine Address, Part number, Color, and Next C (for the pointer to the next item of the same color). Fill in this table according to the specifications just described.
b. Using an index, invert this file on the secondary key "color."

Table 4.5 **Records of Independent Insurance Brokers**

Address	Policy No.	Insured	Company	Agent
50	999	Joseph	ABCDE	Kathy
51	888	Elizabeth	FGHIJ	Kevin
52	777	Peter	KLMNO	Jeri
53	666	Heidi	ABCDE	Dee
54	555	Paul	QRSTU	Kevin
55	444	Julie	KLMNO	Kathy
56	333	James	FGHIJ	Jeri
57	222	Teresa	QRSTU	Kevin
58	111	John	ABCDE	Jeri
59	100	Carolyn	KLMNO	Dee
60	90	Mark	FGHIJ	Kathy
61	80	Anna	QRSTU	Dee

4.7 Using "company" and "agent" as secondary keys, chain together the independent insurance broker records shown in Table 4.5. Set up a pointer field for each secondary key that contains the address of the next logical record in the list. (*Hint:* See Table 4.3.) Independent of your preceding answer, prepare an inverted list for the secondary keys. (*Hint:* See Table 4.4.)

CASE 4.1: ANYCOMPANY, INC.—AN ONGOING COMPREHENSIVE CASE

Identify a local company (you may use the same company that you identified to complete Case 1.1) and answer the following questions:

1. Describe the data input processes of the company. How are data entered into the system? Does the company use batch input or on-line data entry? If it uses a combination, specify which data are entered using each process. Explain the company's use of any of the following: source or turnaround documents, batch totals, and source data automation.
2. Describe the company's data storage procedures. How large are the company's data bases or files? How many records are in each file or data base? Which of the various files described in this chapter does the company use? How often are files updated?
3. Describe the company's data processing procedures. Does it use batch or on-line processing? sequential or direct-access processing? If it uses on-line processing, describe its updating and inquiry processing procedures.
4. What are the major information outputs of each transaction cycle? What are the main outputs for planning, control, and operation? For each output, explain what output format is used.
5. If your company uses a data base, prepare a brief report that explains the following.
   a. The name of the data base
   b. The way the data base is used

c. How the data base is controlled
d. Resources needed to implement, operate, and maintain the data base
e. Any problems encountered in using the data base
f. Advantages of using the data base

CASE 4.2: S&S, INC.

You are a student accountant that S&S has hired to help with its accounting system. Although Ashton has not yet purchased a computerized system, he feels the need to do some advance planning and design work. At the present time he is trying to analyze the input, storage, and output needs of S&S. Ashton would like you to prepare the following for your next meeting with him.

1. A list of the reports and documents S&S needs to ensure its business is properly managed. Specify how the data should be stored and organized. Make a list of the following:
   a. Relevant reports, documents, and other informational output (hard or soft copy) that you feel S&S will need to properly manage its business
   b. Input "forms" that S&S will need to collect transaction and other input data; these inputs may take the form of source documents, preformatted screens, or user prompts
   c. Files or data bases that S&S needs to store all the data it will process
2. Ashton would also like your input on what data and information should be collected, processed, and reported. A complete list of all data elements for every single output, input, and file would be too much information for Ashton to assimilate, so you have decided to provide him with some representative examples. You will list all of the data items (specific items of information such as company name, date, amounts) that should appear on the following output reports and documents to make them fully functioning system output:
   a. Purchase order
   b. Sales invoice (for sales on credit)
   c. Stock status report (a report of inventory on hand)

   You will also list the data that should be captured on each of the following documents (whether it be a source document, preformatted screen, or user prompt):
   d. Receiving report
   e. Employee time card for hourly employees

   Finally, you will list the data that should be stored in the following data base.
   f. Sales/accounts receivable
3. Scott would like to see what some of these system inputs and outputs will look like. He has asked you to design the following items:
   a. Sales invoice
   b. Receiving report

(*Hint:* You may find it helpful to refer to Chapters 17–21 for ideas.)

CASE 4.3: WEKENDER CORPORATION

Wekender Corporation owns and operates 15 large retail hardware stores. Each store carries a wide variety of merchandise, mostly geared toward the weekend do-it-yourselfer. The company has been successful in this field, almost doubling the number of stores in the chain since 1980.

The company wishes to maintain its competitive position with similar stores. However, Wekender has been having some difficulties with its purchasing and inventory procedures. Each retail store currently acquires its merchandise from the company's centrally located warehouse. The warehouse must maintain an up-to-date and well-stocked inventory so that stores can meet customer demands.

The number of stores, the number of inventory items carried, and the volume of business are creating pressure on the company to change from a manual to a computerized system. Recently, the company has been investigating two approaches to computerization—batch processing and on-line, real-time processing. No decision has been reached on which approach to use.

The current warehousing and purchasing procedures are as follows:

• Stock is stored in bins and is located by inventory number. The numbers are supposed to be listed sequentially on the bins, but this system is not always followed. As a result, some items are difficult to locate.

• Whenever a store needs merchandise, a three-part request form is completed—one copy is kept by the store and two copies are mailed to the warehouse. If the merchandise is on hand, the goods are delivered to the store along with the third copy of the request. The second copy is filed at the warehouse. If goods are not in stock, the warehouse ships whatever quantity is available and notes the quantity shipped on the request form. Then a purchase memorandum for the shortage is prepared by the warehouse. At the end of each day, all the memos are sent to the purchasing department.

• When ordered goods are received, they are checked at the receiving area and a receiving report is prepared. One copy of the receiving report is retained at the receiving area, one is forwarded to Accounts Payable, and one is filed at the warehouse with the purchase memorandum.

• When the purchase memoranda are received from the warehouse, purchase orders are prepared. Vendor catalogs are used to select the best source for the requested goods, and the purchase order is filled out and mailed. Copies of the order are sent to Accounts Payable and the receiving area; one copy is retained in the Purchasing Department.

• When the receiving report arrives in the Purchasing Department, it is compared with the purchase order on file. Both documents are compared with the invoice before it is forwarded to Accounts Payable for payment.

• The Purchasing Department is supposed to evaluate vendors periodically for financial soundness, reliability, and trade relationships. However, because the volume of requests received from the warehouse is so high, this activity is given a low priority.

• Each week a report of the open purchase orders is prepared to determine whether any action should be taken on overdue deliveries. This report is prepared manually by scanning the file of outstanding purchase orders.

Top management wants the new system to improve these four areas:

1. Rapid ordering to replenish warehouse inventory stocks with as little delay as possible. (Wekender buys from over 1500 vendors.)
2. Quick filling and shipping of merchandise to the stores. (This process involves determining whether sufficient stock exists.)
3. Some indication of inventory activity. (Over 800 purchase orders are prepared each week.)
4. Perpetual records that permit management to determine inventory levels by item number quickly. (Wekender sells over 7500 separate items.)

Given the current operations procedures and the goals of top management, answer the following questions:

1. Would a batch processing or an on-line, real-time computer system better meet the needs of Wekender Corporation? Explain.
2. Identify the data files Wekender would need for its new system, and briefly indicate the type of information that would be contained in each.
3. How should the files identified in part (b) be organized and accessed?
4. How might Wekender benefit from using a data base system?

ANSWERS TO CHAPTER QUIZ

1. d	**3.** b	**5.** a	**7.** b	**9.** b
2. d	**4.** b	**6.** a	**8.** a	**10.** b

Chapter 5

Data Base Systems

LEARNING OBJECTIVES

After studying this chapter, you should be able to:

- Explain what a data base management system (DBMS) is, its function, and its components.
- Explain how a relational DBMS operates.
- Use a query language to retrieve data from a relational DBMS.
- Discuss the potential effects of DBMS on accounting and financial reporting.

Integrative Case: S&S, Inc.

Ashton Fleming believes that if Scott Parry and Susan Gonzalez want easy access to the information they need to run their business, S&S's new AIS should be a data base system. Ashton has read that almost all new data base systems are relational, although he is not quite sure what a relational data base is and whether it is really appropriate for S&S. He knows that Scott and Susan are likely to have similar questions. Ashton therefore decides to prepare a brief report for them explaining why S&S's new automated AIS should be a data base system. He completes his report by addressing the following questions:

1. What are the components of a data base system?
2. What is a relational data base system, and how does it work?
3. How easily can Ashton, Scott, Susan, and other employees retrieve data from a relational data base?
4. How will acquisition of a data base system affect S&S's AIS?

INTRODUCTION

An organization's data are one of its most valuable assets. Consequently, the effective management and storage of that data is one of the most crucial functions of an accounting information system. As explained in Chapter 4, most organizations now use data base systems (a data base, a data base management system, hardware, and personnel) to organize and manage information about their operations. Accountants must therefore understand the basic data base management and storage concepts explained in this chapter.

We begin Chapter 5 by examining the data base management system, which is the software that manipulates and accesses the data base. Next we discuss the structure and mechanics of relational data bases. Then we show how easily users can retrieve data from a relational data base. After that we discuss the newest development in data base systems: object-oriented data bases. We conclude the chapter with an examination of the potential effects of data bases on accounting and financial reporting.

DATA BASE MANAGEMENT SYSTEMS

In Chapter 4 we introduced the distinction between the logical and physical views of data. The way the user or programmer conceptually organizes and understands the relationships among data items represents the logical view of the data; the way that those data items are actually stored represents the physical view of the data. For example, a sales manager may conceptualize all information about customers as being stored in the form of a table (the logical view), although that data may actually be stored in an indexed sequential file (the physical view). As shown in Fig. 5.1, the data base management system (DBMS) translates the user's logical view of the data into the underlying physical view so the desired data can be retrieved and presented to the user.

Although users' logical views of the data base may differ, the system stores data in only one way. In some cases, however, the physical organization of data can be quite different from the user's perception of how those data are stored. For example, data items such as customer account balance, name, address, and credit history may be stored in separate locations, or even on separate disks, even though users perceive a close logical relationship between those items. The DBMS hides these details about physical storage from users, so that they can concentrate on the logical relationships among data items. Ideally, the

Figure 5.1
Function of the DBMS

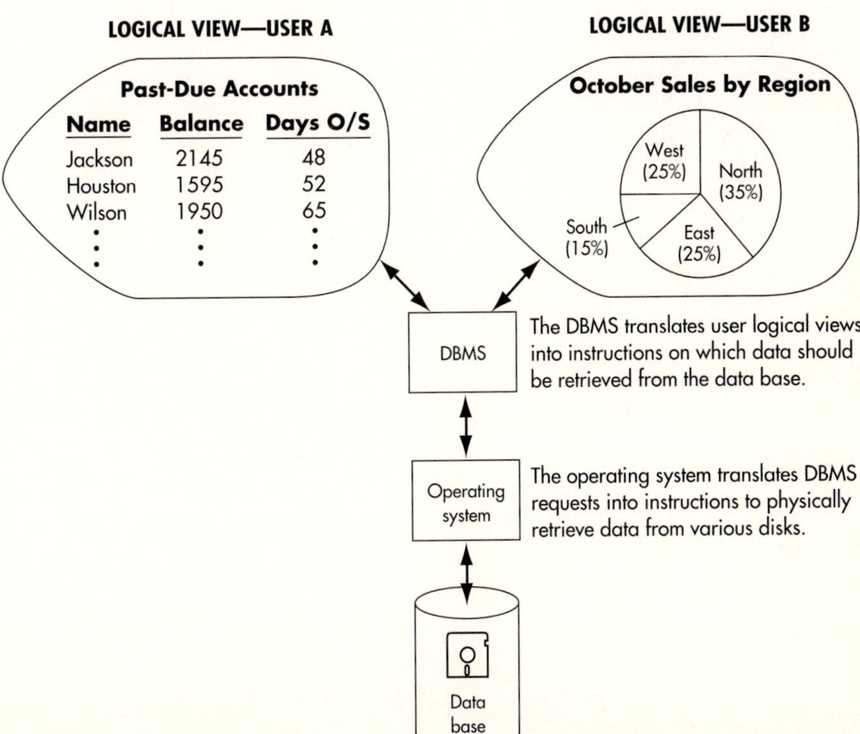

DBMS governs the behavior of the system so that each user thinks that the data are actually stored in exactly the way she logically views them. It accomplishes this by maintaining a set of schemas and mappings between them.

Schemas

A **schema** describes the logical structure of a data base. There are three levels of schemas: the conceptual, the external, and the internal. Figure 5.2 shows the relationships between these three levels.

The **conceptual level schema** is an organization wide view of the entire data base. It lists all data elements and the relationships between them. The **external level schema** consists of a set of individual user views of portions of the data base, each of which views is also referred to as a **subschema.** The **internal level schema** provides a low-level view of the data base. It describes how the data are actually stored and accessed, including information about pointers, indexes, record lengths, and so forth.

Figure 5.2

Three Levels of Schemas

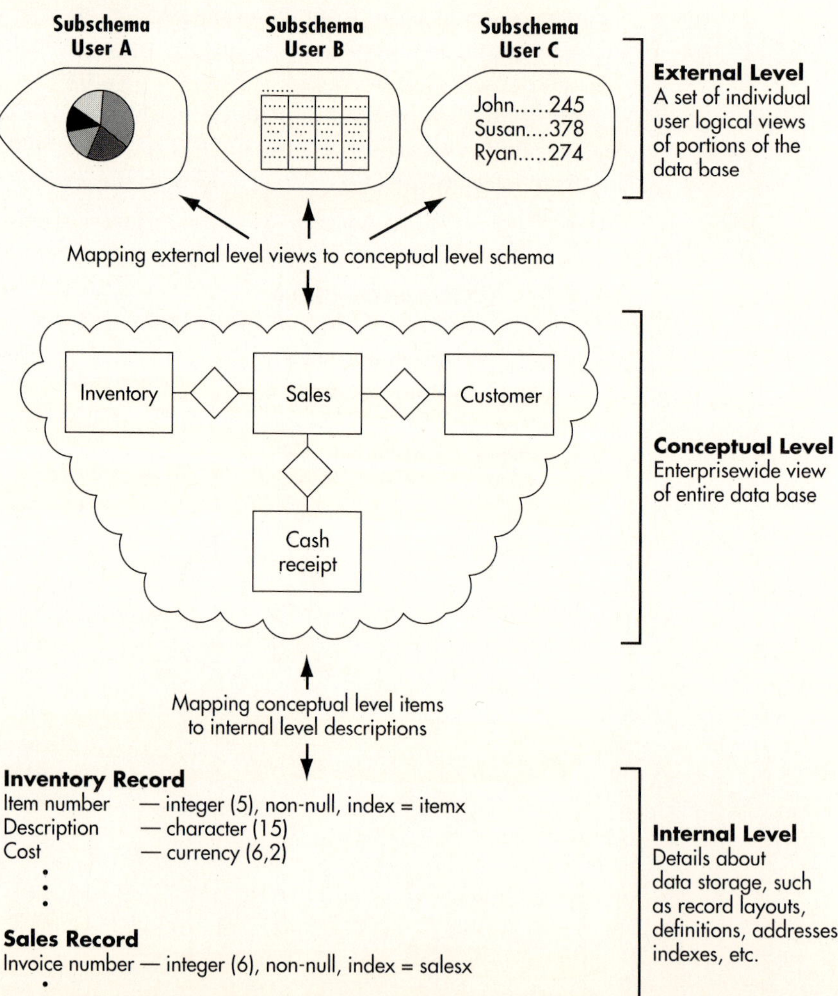

Figure 5.2 connects each of these levels with bidirectional arrows, which represent the mappings between the schemas. The DBMS uses these mappings to translate a user's or an application program's request for data, expressed in terms of logical names and relationships, into the corresponding pointers, indexes, and addresses needed to physically access the data. The mapping arrows are bidirectional because the DBMS must also be able to translate user requests, which are expressed at the logical level, into their corresponding physical actions.

Accountants are involved in developing the conceptual and external level schemas, but they seldom participate in developing the internal level schema. Thus it is important to understand the difference between the conceptual and external level schemas. To illustrate this difference, consider the revenue cycle for S&S. The conceptual schema for the revenue cycle data base would contain information about customers, sales, cash receipts, sales staff, cash, and inventory. At the external level, a number of subschema could be derived from this schema, each tailored to the needs of different users or application programs. Each subschema would also be designed to prevent access to those portions of the data base irrelevant to a user's job. For example, the external level subschema for sales order entry staff would include information about customer credit limits and current balances, inventory quantities and prices but would probably not include information about the costs of inventory or current company bank account balances. The external level subschema for the delivery staff would include information about the customer's address, but would probably not include information about each customer's credit limit or employee pay rates. Similarly, additional subschema would define the relevant portions of the data base that other employees need to access to perform their jobs.

The Data Dictionary

One of the key components of a DBMS is a special file called the data dictionary. The **data dictionary** contains information about the structure of the data base. For each data element stored in the data base, such as the customer number, there is a corresponding record in the data dictionary describing it. Table 5.1 shows examples of the kind of information the data dictionary contains about each data element.

Accountants have a very good understanding of the data elements that exist in a business organization, where they originate, and where they are used. This knowledge is a result of the accountant's role in the design of information systems and in the processing of financial data. For this reason, accountants should participate in the development of the data dictionary.

The data dictionary is usually maintained automatically by the DBMS. In fact, this is often one of the first applications of a newly implemented data base system. Inputs to the data dictionary include records of any new or deleted data elements, as well as changes in names, descriptions, or uses of existing data elements. Outputs include a variety of reports useful to programmers, data base designers, and users of the information system. Sample reports include (1) a list of all programs in which a data item is used, (2) a list of all synonyms for the data elements in a particular file, (3) a list of all data elements used by a particular user, and (4) a list of all output reports in which a data element is used.

Table 5.1 **Example of a Data Dictionary**

Data Element Name	Description	Records in Which Contained	Source	Field Length	Field Type	Programs in Which Used	Outputs in Which Contained	Authorized Users	Other Data Names
Customer number	Unique identifier of each customer	A/R record, customer record, sales analysis record	Customer number listing	10	Alphanumeric	A/R update, customer file update, sales analysis update, credit analysis	A/R aging report, customer status report, sales analysis report, credit report	No restrictions	None
Customer name	Complete name of customer	Customer record	Initial customer order	20	Alphanumeric	Customer file update, statement processing	Customer status report, monthly statement	No restrictions	None
Address	Street, city, state, and zip code	Customer record	Credit application	30	Alphanumeric	Customer file update, statement processing	Customer status report, monthly statement	No restrictions	None
Credit limit	Maximum credit that can be extended to customer	Customer record, A/R record	Credit application	8	Numeric	Customer file update, A/R update, credit analysis	Customer status report, A/R aging report, credit report	R. Drummond W. Francom H. Heaton	CR_limit
Balance	Balance due from customer on credit purchases	A/R record, sales analysis record	Various sales and payment transactions	8	Numeric	A/R update, sales analysis update, statement processing, credit analysis	A/R aging report, sales analysis report, monthly statement, credit report	O. Cherrington J. Hansen K. Stocks	Cust_bal

Reports of this type are extremely useful in the design and implementation of a data base system, as documentation of the system, and as an audit trail.

DBMS Languages

Every DBMS must provide a means of performing the three basic functions of creating, changing, and querying the data base. The set of commands used to perform these functions are referred to as the data definition, data manipulation, and data query languages, respectively.

The **data definition language (DDL)** is used to (1) build the data dictionary, (2) initialize or create the data base, (3) describe the logical views for each individual user or programmer, and (4) specify any limitations or constraints on security imposed on data base records or fields. Table 5.2 shows an example of a DDL command used to create a table to store information about vendors.

The **data manipulation language (DML)** is used for data maintenance, which includes such operations as updating, inserting, and deleting portions of the data base. The DML simplifies the writing of programs to accomplish these tasks by requiring references only to the names of data items, rather than to their physical storage locations. Table 5.3 shows examples of the three basic types of DML commands.

The **data query language (DQL)** is used to interrogate the data base. Whereas the DML is used to change the contents of the data base, the DQL merely retrieves, sorts, orders, and presents subsets of the data base in response

***Table 5.2* Example of Data Definition Language (DDL) Command**

The following command creates a table to store information about vendors:

```
CREATE TABLE          Vendor
     (Vendor#            INTEGER (5) NOT NULL,
     Name                CHARACTER(15),
     Street_Address      CHARACTER(20),
     City                CHARACTER(12),
     State               CHARACTER(2),
     Zipcode             CHARACTER(10),
     Balance             FLOATING(10)   )
```

This command creates a vendor table with seven columns. The vendor number and balance columns must contain only numeric values; vendor# will take integer values, whereas balance can be any numeric value, including decimal format. The remaining columns may contain either numbers or letters. The number in parentheses indicates the maximum number of characters that can be stored in that column. Finally, the constraint NOT NULL indicates that vendor# cannot be left blank.

Result of the command:

Vendor

Vendor#	**Name**	**Street_ Address**	**City**	**State**	**Zipcode**	**Balance**

Note: This command creates an empty table. Filling the table requires the use of data manipulation language commands.

Table 5.3 **Example of Data Manipulation Language (DML) Operations**

This command inserts a new row, containing information about St. Louis Appliances, into the vendor table:

```
INSERT
INTO      Vendor (Vendor#, name, street_address, city, state, zipcode, balance)
VALUES    (10004, 'St. Louis Appliances', '2455 Chippewa', 'St. Louis', 'MO',
          '63109-2643', 0)
```

This command updates the address of St. Louis Appliances:

```
UPDATE    Vendor
SET       Street_address = '3542 Chippewa',
          Zipcode = '63110-2214'
WHERE     Vendor# = 10004
```

This command deletes from the vendor table the row containing information about St. Louis Appliances:

```
DELETE
FROM      Vendor
WHERE     Vendor# = 10004
```

to user queries. Most DQLs contain a fairly powerful, but easy to use, set of commands that enable users to satisfy many of their own information needs, without the assistance of a programmer. Table 5.4 presents a sample query command.

Many DBMSs also include a **report writer,** which is a language that simplifies report creation. Typically, users need only specify which data elements they want printed and how the report should be formatted. The report writer then searches the data base, extracts the specified data items, and prints them out according to the user-specified format.

DBMS Functions and Users

All users generally have access to both the DQL and the report writer. Access to the DDL and DML, however, should be restricted to those employees with administrative and programming responsibilities. This helps to limit the number of people who have the capability to make changes to the data base. Let us now briefly discuss the principal administrative and programming functions in a data base system.

Data Administrator. The **data administrator (DA)** is responsible for developing general policies and procedures governing all organizational data, not just what is stored in the data base. The DA is ultimately responsible for understanding the information needs of the organization in order to decide what should be included in the data base.

Data Base Administrator. The **data base administrator (DBA)** is responsible for coordinating, controlling, and managing the data base. In a way, the

Table 5.4 **Example of Data Query Language (DQL) Command**

Query:

```
SELECT     Name, Balance
FROM       Vendor
ORDER BY   Balance, Descending
```

Result:

Name	*Balance*
South Side Electronics	3,987.00
St. Louis Electronics Supply	3,250.67
St. Louis Computer Warehouse	2,311.85
Oakville Electronics	954.95

This query specifies that the name and balance columns (the SELECT command) in the vendor table (the FROM command) be displayed. The result is arranged in descending order (the ORDER BY and the DESCENDING commands) by the amount owed.

DBA can be thought of as the human equivalent of the DBMS. That is, the DBA must be aware not only of users and their data requirements but also of how the DBMS operates and how data are stored and processed. Specifically, the DBA has the following major responsibilities:

- Create logical models of the data base.
- Establish data standards and specifications.
- Approve changes to the data base structure.
- Develop retrieval methods as required by data base users.
- Specify and maintain the physical structure of the data base.
- Maintain the data dictionary.
- Design and implement controls to ensure the accuracy and security of the data base.

The DBA uses the DDL to specify the structure of the data base, implement and maintain the data dictionary, and specify controls.

Application Programmers. The programs that interact with the DBMS to process data are written by **application programmers.** Billing and payroll are two common examples of application programs. These application programs use the DML to access and change the contents of the data base. The DML improves the productivity of application programmers by allowing them to concentrate solely on correctly specifying the logical description of the task to be performed, without concern about how to access the data or about the structure of that data. To see how this simplifies programming, refer back to Table 5.3 and examine the DML command to update the vendor table. Notice the absence of information about field lengths, locations, and so forth, all of which would have to be included in traditional programming languages.

RELATIONAL DBMS

A DBMS is characterized by the type of logical data model on which it is based. A **data model** is an abstract representation of the contents of a data base. The overwhelming majority of new DBMS are called relational data bases because they use the relational data model developed by Dr. E. F. Codd in 1970. The **relational data model** *represents* everything in the data base as being stored in the form of tables (see Table 5.5). Technically, these tables are called **relations** (hence the name relational data model), but we will use the two words interchangeably. Moreover, keep in mind that the relational data model only describes how the data appear in the conceptual and external level schemas. The data are not actually stored in tables, but rather in the manner described in the internal level schema.

Each row in a relation, called a **tuple** (rhymes with the *couple*), contains data about a specific occurrence of the type of entity represented by that table. Thus each row in Table 5.5 contains all the pertinent data about a particular inventory item. Each column in the table contains information about one specific attribute of the represented object. Thus the columns in the inventory table in Table 5.5 represent specific characteristics about each inventory item carried by S&S.

Basic Requirements of the Relational Data Model

The relational data model imposes certain constraints on the structure of tables. We discuss six of the most important constraints here. The first two ensure the integrity, or accuracy, of the data base:

1. *Primary keys must be unique.* The primary key is the attribute, or combination of attributes, that uniquely identifies a specific row in a table. For example, the primary key in Table 5.5 is item number. Each different merchandise item sold by S&S can be uniquely identified by its item number. For this to be true, however, the primary key of any row in a relation cannot be null, for there would never be a way to uniquely identify that row and retrieve the data stored there. A non-null value for the primary key indicates that a specific object exists and can be identified by reference to its primary key value. Consequently, this constraint is referred to as the **entity integrity rule,** because it ensures that every row in every relation must represent data about some specific object in the real world.

Table 5.5 **Sample Inventory Table for S&S**

Item Number	Description	Color	Vendor Number	Quantity on Hand	Price
1036	Refrigerator	White	10023	12	1199
1038	Refrigerator	Almond	10023	07	1299
1039	Refrigerator	Hunter Green	10023	05	1499
2061	Range	White	10011	06	799
2063	Range	Black	10011	05	999
3541	Washer	White	10008	15	499
3544	Washer	Black	10008	10	699
3785	Dryer	White	10008	12	399
3787	Dryer	Almond	10019	08	499

2. *Every foreign key must either be null or have a value corresponding to the value of a primary key in another relation.* A **foreign key** is an attribute in one table that is the primary key of another table. In Table 5.5 vendor number is a foreign key. It is the primary key of the vendor table (not shown), uniquely identifying each vendor. Foreign keys are used to link tables together; in this example, the vendor number is used to identify the primary source for that particular inventory item. Additional information about that vendor, such as its address, can be obtained from the vendor table. This is possible only if the value in the vendor number column in the inventory table equals the value of the vendor number column in some row in the vendor table. Otherwise, the data base would be inconsistent. Consequently, this constraint is referred to as the **referential integrity rule.** Note, however, that the foreign key can be null if there is no existing relationship between the two tables. For example, a null value for vendor number in any row in Table 5.5 would indicate that there is no primary preferred vendor for that inventory item.

Four additional constraints contribute to the simplicity of a relational DBMS and enhance its efficiency and effectiveness for transaction processing:

3. *Each column in a table must describe a characteristic of the object identified by the primary key.* Look again at Table 5.5 and notice that every column in that table describes some property of the various inventory items carried by S&S. Facts about the vendors who supply those products and the customers who purchase them, however, are not included in the inventory table.

4. *Each column in a row must be single-valued.* Again, referring back to Table 5.5, notice that every column has one, and only one, value recorded in each row.

5. *The values in every row of a specific column must be of the same data type.* In Table 5.5, the item number column has integer values in every row.

6. *Neither column order nor row order is significant.* Rearranging the sequence of rows or columns does not alter the information presented in Table 5.5.

In the next section we apply these constraints to designing a relational data base for S&S. In doing so, we illustrate their value by showing examples of the types of problems that can arise when these constraints are violated.

Case Study: Designing a Relational Data Base for S&S, Inc.

In its existing manual accounting system, S&S captures sales information on a sales invoice. This hard copy document provides both a logical and physical view of the data collected. Physical storage of sales invoice data is simple: S&S retains one or more copies of the invoice in a file cabinet. For example, one copy may be stored by invoice number to provide a chronological record of all sales and another is filed by customer name to facilitate analysis of specific customer accounts.

The procedure for storing the same data on computer is a little more complex. Suppose, for example, that S&S had five sales invoices (numbered from 101 to 105) that it wanted to store electronically. On several of these invoices,

Table 5.6 **Example of Storing all Sales Data for S&S in One Table**

Sales Invoice #	Date	Salesperson	Customer #	Invoice Total	Customer Name	Street
101	10/15/96	J. Buck	151	1447	D. Ainge	123 Lotus Lane
101	10/15/96	J. Buck	151	1447	D. Ainge	123 Lotus Lane
102	10/15/96	S. Knight	152	4394	G. Kite	40 Quatro Road
102	10/15/96	S. Knight	152	4394	G. Kite	40 Quatro Road
102	10/15/96	S. Knight	152	4394	G. Kite	40 Quatro Road
103	10/28/96	S. Knight	151	898	D. Ainge	123 Lotus Lane
104	10/31/96	J. Buck	152	789	G. Kite	40 Quatro Road
105	11/14/96	J. Buck	153	3994	F. Roberts	401 Excel Way
105	11/14/96	J. Buck	153	3994	F. Roberts	401 Excel Way
105	11/14/96	J. Buck	153	3994	F. Roberts	401 Excel Way

S&S records that the customer purchased more than one item (a television and a refrigerator, for example). Let us look at the effects of several potential ways of storing this information.

Option 1: Store All Data in One Uniform Table. S&S could store its sales data in one table, as illustrated in Table 5.6, but this approach has two disadvantages. First, it creates redundancy in terms of stored data. For example, examine sales invoice number 102 in Table 5.6. Since there are three separate inventory items sold, the invoice and customer data (columns 1–9) are recorded three times. Likewise, inventory descriptions and unit prices are repeated each time an item is sold. Because sales volume can be fairly high in a retail store (remember, this table represents only five invoices), such redundancy can make file maintenance unnecessarily time-consuming and error-prone. For example, recording a customer's address change requires searching the entire table and changing every occurrence of that customer's address. A similar process would be required to update the unit price of inventory items. In either case, it would be easy to overlook some occurrence and thereby create an inconsistency in the data base.

The second weakness of Table 5.6 is that customer and inventory data are not maintained independently of sales invoice data. Consequently, there is no

Table 5.7 **Example of Modifying a Table's Structure in Order to Store S&S Sales Data by Adding Columns for Each Additional Item Sold**

Sales Invoice #	Columns 2–9	Item #	Quantity	Description	Unit Price	Extended Amount	Item #
101		10	2	Television	499	998	50
102		10	1	Television	499	499	20
103		50	2	Microwave	449	898	
104		40	1	Range	789	789	
105		10	3	Television	499	1497	20

City	State	Item #	Quantity	Description	Unit Price	Extended Amount
Phoenix	AZ	10	2	Television	499	998
Phoenix	AZ	50	1	Microwave	449	449
Mesa	AZ	10	1	Television	499	499
Mesa	AZ	20	3	Freezer	699	2097
Mesa	AZ	30	2	Refrigerator	899	1798
Phoenix	AZ	50	2	Microwave	449	898
Mesa	AZ	40	1	Range	789	789
Chandler	AZ	10	3	Television	499	1497
Chandler	AZ	20	1	Freezer	699	699
Chandler	AZ	30	2	Refrigerator	899	1798

way to store information about prospective customers until they actually make a purchase. Conversely, if a customer made only one purchase, consisting of a single item, deleting that row from the table would result in the loss of all information about that customer.

Option 2: Vary the Number of Columns. An alternative to the data storage scheme depicted in Table 5.6 is to record the sales invoice and customer information just once within the first nine columns and then add additional columns to record each item sold. This strategy is illustrated in Table 5.7.

Although this approach does reduce some of the data redundancy associated with the data storage scheme illustrated in Table 5.6, it still has its drawbacks. S&S would have to decide in advance how many item numbers to leave room for in each row. If room is left for only a few items, how would information about a sale involving many items be stored? If room is left for many items, however, there will be a great deal of wasted space, as is the case for sales invoices 103 and 104.

The Solution: A Set of Tables. The problems associated with the data storage schemes from Tables 5.6 and 5.7 are a direct result of violating the six

Quantity	Description	Unit Price	Extended Amount	Item #	Quantity	Description	Unit Price	Extended Amount
1	Microwave	449	449					
3	Freezer	699	2097	30	2	Refrigerator	899	1798
1	Freezer	699	699	30	2	Refrigerator	899	1798

Table 5.8 **Set of Relational Tables for Storing S&S Sales Data**

Invoice

Sales Invoice #	Date	Salesperson	Customer #	Invoice Total
101	10/15/96	J. Buck	151	1447.00
102	10/15/96	S. Knight	152	4394.00
103	10/28/96	S. Knight	151	898.00
104	10/31/96	J. Buck	152	789.00
105	11/14/96	J. Buck	153	3994.00

Line Item

Sales Invoice #	Item #	Quantity	Extended Amount
101	10	2	998.00
101	50	1	449.00
102	10	1	499.00
102	20	3	2097.00
102	30	2	1798.00
103	50	2	898.00
104	40	1	789.00
105	10	3	1497.00
105	20	1	699.00
105	30	2	1798.00

Customer

Customer #	Customer Name	Street	City	State
151	D. Ainge	123 Lotus Lane	Phoenix	AZ
152	G. Kite	40 Quatro Road	Mesa	AZ
153	F. Roberts	401 Excel Way	Chandler	AZ

Inventory

Item #	Unit Price	Description
10	499.00	Television
20	699.00	Freezer
30	899.00	Refrigerator
40	789.00	Range
50	449.00	Microwave

constraints presented earlier for designing relational tables. Table 5.8 shows the results of applying those six constraints to S&S's sales invoice data.

Notice how the data storage scheme illustrated in Table 5.8 avoids the problems we discussed earlier. First, redundancy is greatly reduced. For example, in the schema shown in Table 5.8, customer addresses and inventory item unit prices are stored just once. This avoids any potential inconsistencies that may arise as a result of not changing every occurrence of a data item. This type of problem is referred to as an **update anomaly.**

Second, data about various items of interest (customers, inventory, and sales) are stored in separate tables. This makes it easier to add new data to the system. For example, the schema represented in Table 5.8 allows information about prospective customers to be stored, simply by adding another row in the customer table. In the schemas represented by Tables 5.6 and 5.7, however, information about new customers could not be added until they had actually made a purchase. Otherwise, the sales invoice number column would be empty. The sales invoice number, however, is part of the primary key of Tables 5.6 and 5.7. Consequently, it cannot be null, for that would violate the entity integrity rule of a relational data base. This problem of not being able to insert new information without violating the basic integrity rules of a relational data base is referred to as an **insert anomaly.**

The schema shown in Table 5.8 also simplifies the deletion of information. For example, deleting sales invoice 105, representing the only sale to customer 153 (F. Roberts), would not result in the loss of all information about that customer. In contrast, deleting sales invoice 105 from Table 5.7 would have the unintended side effect of removing all information about customer 153 from the data base. This type of problem is referred to as a **delete anomaly.**

The third benefit of Table 5.8 is that space is used efficiently. The line item table contains a row for each item sold on each invoice. There are no blank rows, yet all data about each sale is recorded. In contrast, the schema depicted in Table 5.7 results in much wasted space.

The process of following the guidelines for designing relational tables that follow the data storage scheme illustrated in Table 5.8 is called **normalization.** Normalization has two benefits. First, as you have just seen, normalization produces a well-structured data base that is easy to maintain and free from update, insert, and delete anomalies. In the next section, we examine the second benefit of normalization: the ability of a relational DBMS to provide a simple, yet powerful, data query language.

QUERYING A RELATIONAL DATA BASE

The relational data model allows three fundamental types of operations to be performed on tables:

1. PROJECT creates a new table (or relation) by selecting specified columns from the original table.
2. RESTRICT creates a new table by selecting from the original table those rows that meet specified conditions.
3. JOIN creates a new table by selecting the designated columns from two or more tables and then choosing the rows that meet specified conditions. The JOIN operation is used frequently, since a single relation often does not contain all the data necessary to satisfy a user inquiry.

The key property of the relational data model is that each of these three basic operations always results in the creation of a new table. This means that the result of a query using these operations can itself be the object of additional queries. It is this possibility for nesting queries that makes relational data query languages so powerful.

Relational query languages can be classified into two broad categories: text-based query languages and graphical query languages. Let us examine how each type works.

Structured Query Language: A Text-Based Query Language

The standard text-based query language provided by most, but not all, relational DBMSs is called **structured query language (SQL).** Many popular microcomputer accounting packages also provide SQL access to the general ledger. SQL is powerful, yet simple to use. Its power and simplicity enable easy generation of special-purpose reports so corporate accountants can meet management's information requests. Similarly, SQL permits auditors easy retrieval of information from client data bases. Consequently, it is important to gain a basic understanding of how SQL works. In the remainder of this section we introduce the principal SQL commands; additional information about SQL can be found in the reference manuals that accompany relational DBMS products.

SQL Syntax. Five basic keywords are used to construct most SQL queries:

1. *SELECT.* Used to list the columns that should be displayed in answering the query. This keyword implements the PROJECT operation.
2. *FROM.* Used to list the names of the tables that are referenced in answering the query. If two or more table names are listed, the JOIN operation is applied to them.
3. *WHERE.* Used to specify which rows to retrieve when answering the query. This keyword implements the RESTRICT operation.
4. *ORDER BY.* Used to specify how to format the answer. The column that serves as the basis for ordering is listed, along with the desired sequence (ascending or descending).
5. *GROUP BY.* Used to specify which rows in a table should be subject to basic mathematical operations (such as SUM, MINIMUM, and MAXIMUM). For example, applying GROUP BY to the salesperson column in the invoice table in Table 5.8 calculates total sales made by each salesperson. Alternatively, applying GROUP BY to the customer number column calculates total sales by customer.

Sample SQL Queries. Let us now see how these five keywords can be used to retrieve information from the data base shown in Table 5.8.

Table 5.9 **Query 1**

Show the dates and invoice totals for all sales in October, arranged in descending order by amount of the sale

Invoice				
Sales Invoice #	**Date**	**Salesperson**	**Customer #**	**Invoice Total**
101	10/15/96	J. Buck	151	1447.00
102	10/15/96	S. Knight	152	4394.00
103	10/28/96	S. Knight	151	898.00
104	10/31/96	J. Buck	152	789.00
105	11/14/96	J. Buck	153	3994.00

The SELECT clause in the query invokes the relational PROJECT operation to display only the date and invoice total columns. The FROM clause specifies that these columns are to be found in the Invoice table. The WHERE clause then invokes the relational RESTRICT operation to display only those rows representating sales made during October. The ORDER BY clause specifies that the answer should be displayed in descending order by the amount in the invoice total column.

Query Response	
Date	**Invoice Total**
10/15/96	4394.00
10/15/96	1447.00
10/28/96	898.00
10/31/96	789.00

Query 1: Show the dates and invoice totals for all sales in October, arranged in descending order by amount of the sale.

This query would be written in SQL as follows:

```
SELECT      Date, Invoice Total
FROM        Invoice
WHERE       Date BETWEEN 10/01/96 and 10/31/96
ORDER BY    Invoice Total, DESCENDING
```

Table 5.9 shows the original Invoice table and the response to this query.

Query 2: What are the invoice numbers of all sales made to D. Ainge, and who completed these sales?

This query would be written in SQL as follows:

```
SELECT   Sales Invoice #, Salesperson, Customer Name
FROM     Invoice, Customer
WHERE    Invoice.Customer # = Customer.Customer # AND Customer
         Name = 'D. Ainge'
```

Table 5.10 shows the original tables and the result of the query.

Query 3: How many televisions were sold in October?

This query would be written in SQL as follows:

```
SELECT   Sum (quantity)
FROM     Line Item, Invoice, Inventory
WHERE    Line Item.Item # = Inventory.Item # AND Description = 'Television'
         AND Line Item.Sales Invoice # = Invoice.Sales Invoice # AND Date
         BETWEEN 10/01/96 and 10/31/96
```

This query shows that basic mathematical operators can be included in the SQL SELECT clause. In this case the query is asking for the sum of the quantity sold column in the line item table. Table 5.11 shows the result of this query.

Query 4: Display the names and addresses of all customers buying televisions in October.

This query would be written in SQL as follows:

```
SELECT   Customer Name, Street, City, State
FROM     Customer, Invoice, Line Item, Inventory
WHERE    Date BETWEEN 10/01/96 and 10/31/96 AND
         Description = 'Television' AND
         Invoice.Customer # = Customer.Customer # AND
         Invoice.Sales Invoice # = Line Item.Sales Invoice # AND
         Line Item.Item # = Inventory.Item #
```

The answer to this query is shown in Table 5.12 (p. 148). Although only two lines long, the relational DBMS had to use all four tables to answer the query.

Query 5: How much did each salesperson sell so far this year?

Table 5.10 **Query 2**

What are the invoice numbers of all sales made to D. Ainge, and who completed these sales?

Invoice				
Sales Invoice #	**Date**	**Salesperson**	**Customer #**	**Invoice Total**
101	10/15/96	J. Buck	151	1447.00
102	10/15/96	S. Knight	152	4394.00
103	10/28/96	S. Knight	151	898.00
104	10/31/96	J. Buck	152	789.00
105	11/14/96	J. Buck	153	3994.00

The SELECT clause in the query invokes the relational PROJECT operation to select the shaded columns in the invoice and customer tables. The FROM clause instructs the DBMS to apply the JOIN operator to the invoice and customer tables. The first WHERE clause specifies that customer #, the common column in both tables, is used to join them.

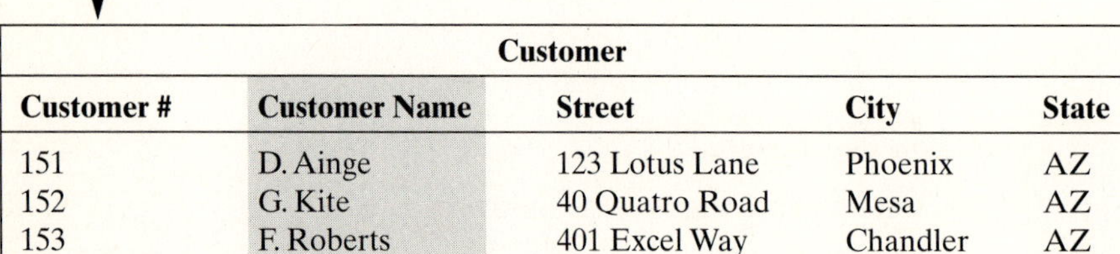

Customer				
Customer #	**Customer Name**	**Street**	**City**	**State**
151	D. Ainge	123 Lotus Lane	Phoenix	AZ
152	G. Kite	40 Quatro Road	Mesa	AZ
153	F. Roberts	401 Excel Way	Chandler	AZ

Temporary Table After PROJECT and JOIN Commands		
Sales Invoice #	**Salesperson**	**Customer Name**
101	J. Buck	D. Ainge
102	S. Knight	G. Kite
103	S. Knight	D. Ainge
104	J. Buck	G. Kite
105	J. Buck	F. Roberts

This temporary table is the result of executing the relational PROJECT and JOIN operations specified in the query. This temporary table would *not* appear on the screen; it is presented for illustrative purposes only. The second WHERE clause then invokes the relational RESTRICT operation to select only the shaded rows for display.

Query Response		
Sales Invoice #	**Salesperson**	**Customer Name**
101	J. Buck	D. Ainge
103	S. Knight	D. Ainge

The completed query looks like this. The customer name column can be deleted, if desired.

This query would be written in SQL as follows:

```
SELECT      Sum (invoice total), Salesperson
FROM        INVOICE
GROUP BY    Salesperson
```

This query uses the GROUP BY keyword to instruct the DBMS to sum the invoice totals separately for each distinct value in the salesperson column. Table 5.13 (p. 149) shows the result of this query.

Table 5.11 **Query 3**
How many televisions were sold in October?

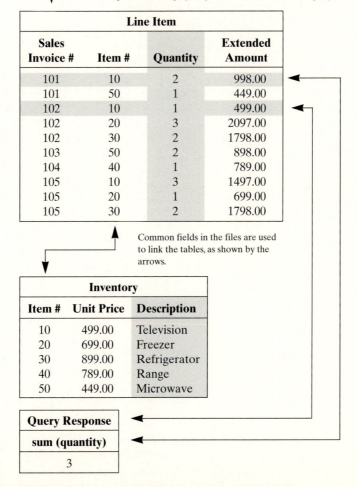

Invoice				
Sales Invoice #	**Date**	**Salesperson**	**Customer #**	**Invoice Total**
101	10/15/96	J. Buck	151	1447.00
102	10/15/96	S. Knight	152	4394.00
103	10/28/96	S. Knight	151	898.00
104	10/31/96	J. Buck	152	789.00
105	11/14/96	J. Buck	153	3994.00

This query needs information from the invoice, line item, and inventory tables. The SELECT clause in the query invokes the relational PROJECT operation to select the shaded columns in all three tables. Those columns are joined to form a temporary table (not shown). The WHERE clause specifies the basis for linking the tables using columns common to each table (see arrows). It also invokes the relational RESTRICT operation to display only those rows that meet the query criteria.

Line Item			
Sales Invoice #	**Item #**	**Quantity**	**Extended Amount**
101	10	2	998.00
101	50	1	449.00
102	10	1	499.00
102	20	3	2097.00
102	30	2	1798.00
103	50	2	898.00
104	40	1	789.00
105	10	3	1497.00
105	20	1	699.00
105	30	2	1798.00

Common fields in the files are used to link the tables, as shown by the arrows.

Inventory		
Item #	**Unit Price**	**Description**
10	499.00	Television
20	699.00	Freezer
30	899.00	Refrigerator
40	789.00	Range
50	449.00	Microwave

Query Response
sum (quantity)
3

Table 5.12 **Query 4**
Display the names and addresses of all customers buying televisions in October

Invoice

Sales Invoice #	Date	Salesperson	Customer #	Invoice Total
101	10/15/96	J. Buck	151	1447.00
102	10/15/96	S. Knight	152	4394.00
103	10/28/96	S. Knight	151	898.00
104	10/31/96	J. Buck	152	789.00
105	11/14/96	J. Buck	153	3994.00

This query only displays data taken from the customer table. However, data from all four tables are used to answer the query. The data used in each table are shaded. The description column in the inventory table is used to decide what item number relates to televisions (10). The item number column in the line item table is used to identify on which invoice numbers televisions were sold (101, 102, and 105). The date column in the invoice table is used to narrow talevision sales to October sales (invoices 101, 102).

Customer

Customer #	Customer Name	Street	City	State
151	D. Ainge	123 Lotus Lane	Phoenix	AZ
152	G. Kite	40 Quatro Road	Mesa	AZ
153	F. Roberts	401 Excel Way	Chandler	AZ

Sales invoices 101 and 102 correspond to customers 151 and 152. Those names and addresses are retrieved from the customer table and displayed as shown here.

Line Item

Sales Invoice #	Item #	Quantity	Extended Amount
101	10	2	998.00
101	50	1	449.00
102	10	1	499.00
102	20	3	2097.00
102	30	2	1798.00
103	50	2	898.00
104	40	1	789.00
105	10	3	1497.00
105	20	1	699.00
105	30	2	1798.00

Inventory

Item #	Unit Price	Description
10	499.00	Television
20	699.00	Freezer
30	899.00	Refrigerator
40	789.00	Range
50	449.00	Microwave

Query Response

Customer Name	Street	City	State
D. Ainge	123 Lotus Lane	Phoenix	AZ
G. Kite	40 Quatro Road	Mesa	AZ

Analysis of SQL. As seen from these five examples, SQL is simple to use yet quite powerful. SQL's simplicity allows users to specify the desired result without having to specify *how* the data are to be retrieved. All five example queries specified only the conditions to be met in providing the answer; no looping or

Table 5.13 **Query 5**
How much did each salesperson sell?

Invoice				
Sales Invoice #	**Date**	**Salesperson**	**Customer #**	**Invoice Total**
101	10/15/96	J. Buck	151	1447.00
102	10/15/96	S. Knight	152	4394.00
103	10/28/96	S. Knight	151	898.00
104	10/31/96	J. Buck	152	789.00
105	11/14/96	J. Buck	153	3994.00

The GROUP BY clause in the query directs that the invoice total column be summed for all rows in the invoice table having the same value in the salesperson column (as indicated by the arrows).

Query Response	
Sum (Invoice Total)	**Salesperson**
6230.00	J. Buck
5292.00	S. Knight

procedural commands were required to tell the system how to search for the desired records.

The simplicity of SQL reflects the properties of the relational data model, especially the nonimportance of row and column order (constraint number 6). In contrast, the location of a data item in a nonrelational DBMS does provide important information. Consequently, users and application programmers working with nonrelational DBMS must know how to navigate through the data base to find the answer to their queries. For example, a DBMS based on the hierarchical (or tree) data model (e.g., IBM's IMS) represents data as being stored in hierarchies. Users of a hierarchical DBMS must navigate up and down the hierarchy to retrieve the desired data. Although providing such specific navigational instructions may, in some cases, result in faster retrieval times, it poses an extra burden on the end user to be aware of at least some aspects of the data base structure. It also requires that special operators be included in the query language for using pointers or otherwise navigating from one record to another. This makes it harder for users to write ad hoc queries, which in turn increases the demands placed on application programmers to write those queries for users.

SQL is powerful because it is set-based; every query inherently returns a subset of the tables referenced. In contrast, traditional programming languages such as COBOL, FORTRAN, and BASIC operate on just one record (row in a table) at a time. Consequently, using one of those languages to write these queries would have been much more complicated.

***Table 5.14* QBE Query**

Show the dates and invoice totals for all sales in October

Stored Relational Table . . .

Invoice				
Sales Invoice #	**Date**	**Salesperson**	**Customer #**	**Invoice Total**
101	10/15/96	J. Buck	151	1447.00
102	10/15/96	S. Knight	152	4394.00
103	10/28/96	S. Knight	151	898.00
104	10/31/96	J. Buck	152	789.00
105	11/14/96	J. Buck	153	3994.00

QBE Query Table . . .

Invoice				
Sales Invoice #	**Date**	**Salesperson**	**Customer #**	**Invoice Total**
	P. _Month			P.
CONDITIONS				
Month BETWEEN 10/01/96 AND 10/31/96				

The P. character specifies which columns should be displayed in the answer. The _Month example element is used in the CONDITIONS box to specify that the sale must have occurred in October.

Result of the query . . .

Query Response	
Date	**Invoice Total**
10/15/96	1447.00
10/15/96	4394.00
10/28/96	898.00
10/31/96	789.00

Query by Example: A Graphical Query Language

In addition to SQL, some relational DBMSs also provide users with a graphical query language. In fact, some PC relational DBMS products do not provide users with direct access to SQL, but only with a graphical query language. These graphical query languages are often referred to as **query-by-example (QBE)** languages.

QBE languages are compatible with SQL; indeed, many systems translate QBE queries into SQL in order to retrieve the desired data. Tables 5.14 and 5.15 show examples of using a QBE language to write two of the SQL queries against the data base contained in Table 5.8. These examples show that QBE languages are so named because queries use example markers in a pictorial

Table 5.15 **QBE Query**

Display the names and addresses of all customers buying televisions in October

QBE Query Tables . . .

Invoice				
Sales Invoice #	**Date**	**Salesperson**	**Customer #**	**Invoice Total**
_sale	_Month		_cust	

Customer				
Customer #	**Customer Name**	**Street**	**City**	**State**
_cust	P.	P.	P.	P.

Line Item			
Sales Invoice #	**Item #**	**Quantity**	**Extended Amount**
_sale	_tv		

Inventory		
Item #	**Unit Price**	**Description**
_tv		Television

CONDITIONS
_Month BETWEEN 10/01/96 AND 10/31/96

The P. character specifies which columns should be displayed in the answer. The _Month example element is used in the CONDITIONS box to specify that the sale must have occurred in October. The example elements _sale, _cust, and _tv specify the conditions for linking (the relational JOIN operation) the tables. Finally, the value of *Television* in the Description column specifies which rows from that table should be selected (the relational RESTRICT operation).

Result of the query:

Query Response			
Customer Name	**Street**	**City**	**State**
D. Ainge	123 Lotus Lane	Phoenix	AZ
G. Kite	40 Quatro Road	Mesa	AZ

representation of data base tables to indicate which columns and rows should be displayed.

Query: Show the dates and invoice totals for all sales in October.

Table 5.14 shows how query 1 would be written in QBE. The system begins by displaying a blank table. After the user enters the name of the stored table to be queried, the column titles for that table are then displayed. Thus typing the name of the invoice table corresponds to naming that table in the FROM clause in SQL. The user then places *P.* in the columns that are to be displayed; this corresponds to listing those columns in the SELECT clause in an SQL. An example element is used to link columns to conditions that specify which rows should be displayed. This corresponds to the WHERE clause in SQL.

Query: Display the names and addresses of all customers buying televisions in October.

Table 5.15 shows how query 4 would be written in QBE. Example elements are used to indicate the basis for joining tables. For example, *_cust* appears in the customer number column in both the invoice and customer tables; this is equivalent to writing *customer.customer # = invoice.customer #* in the WHERE clause in SQL. Entering a value in a column specifies which rows should be displayed. Thus typing *Television* in the description column of the inventory table is equivalent to writing *Description = Television* in the WHERE clause in SQL.

Advantages and Limitations of Relational DBMS

A relational DBMS can significantly increase the speed and ease of accessing data. For example, it used to take up to 30 minutes for managers of the Coca-Cola Bottling Company of New York to retrieve details about individual journal entries from Coke's old file-based system. That dropped to about 10 seconds, after Coke moved its general ledger data to a relational DBMS. The new system also lets managers create ad hoc reports whenever needed. As Focus 5.1 explains, such improved access to information can have strategic implications.

Relational DBMS also make it easy to tailor accounting and other information systems to the needs of individual subunits of the organization. For example, R.P. Scherer, a Troy, Michigan, manufacturer of drug-delivery systems, has used a relational DBMS to integrate its regulatory, financial, and production systems. SQL enabled Scherer to define tables and user views that could be shared across applications. This made it easy to adapt the basic system to each of its manufacturing plants. Moreover, by integrating data across systems, Scherer can better manage the scheduling and production of customer orders. As a result, work-in-process inventories are greatly reduced.

Notwithstanding these benefits, a relational DBMS does have some limitations. It is generally less efficient for transaction processing and requires more memory than a file-based or nonrelational DBMS. These problems, however, are becoming less important as computers continue to increase in power and decrease in cost.

The most serious limitation of a relational DBMS is that current implementations of the relational data model do not easily accommodate the integration of complex data types, such as graphs, maps, sounds, and images, with the text and numeric data commonly associated with transaction processing. Proponents of the relational data model note that theoretically, a relational DBMS can accommodate these complex data types. They argue that current difficulties in doing so merely reflect shortcomings in existing relational DBMS products, not in the underlying model. Nevertheless, the

FOCUS 5.1

Using Relational Data Bases to Market Credit Cards

Competition is stiff in the credit card business, with estimates of close to 1 billion credit cards in circulation in the United States alone. Consequently, card issuers are looking for creative ways to entice people to use their cards.

Many banks are discovering that a relational DBMS can help accomplish this goal by enabling them to develop and more effectively monitor the results of innovative promotional schemes. For example, FCC National Bank in Elgin, Illinois, which issues First Card, is using IBM's DB2 relational data base to build its new credit-processing system. The new system will allow FCC to segment its cardholders more easily by various demographic and spending characteristics, thereby enabling them to tailor promotions to the specific needs and interests of various cardholders.

Chase BankCard Services, a division of Chase Manhattan Bank in New York, is another card issuer turning to a relational DBMS. It is migrating to the Sybase DBMS, which will run on an NCR 3600, a massively parallel processing computer. The new system will allow Chase to efficiently track how many of its cardholders respond to periodic offers, such as lower interest rates during the holidays. This capability will enable Chase to better evaluate the worth of such promotions. Banc One Services, a division of Banc One Corporation in Columbus, Ohio, is also migrating to a relational DBMS. Its new system, called Triumph, was developed by Andersen Consulting. Banc One anticipates that the new system will make it easier to access a customer's credit history, thereby reducing the time it takes to decide whether to increase credit limits, and by how much.

The common theme to all these efforts is the use of a relational DBMS. All three banks note that their existing file-based and nonrelational data base systems, although adequate for processing credit card transactions, do not provide the flexibility for effectively and efficiently tailoring their marketing strategies to the needs of specific subsets of cardholders. All three banks are convinced that switching to a relational DBMS will better support their innovative marketing strategies.

Focus Questions

1. As more credit card issuers adopt a relational DBMS, will there continue to be any competitive advantage to having such systems? Why or why not?
2. In which other industries can relational DBMS be used to support innovative marketing strategies?

Source: Linda Wilson, "Bank Systems Earn Credit," *Information Week* (May 30, 1994): 70–72.

---

difficulties of representing such data in a relational DBMS are causing some companies to look at using an object-oriented DBMS for storing and processing such data.

OBJECT-ORIENTED DATA BASES

In the **object-oriented data model** the basic conceptual building blocks are objects, rather than tables. An **object** is a reusable segment of program code that not only describes a data element but also contains instructions on how to manipulate that data. For example, the sales invoice object would not only store information about a particular sales transaction, but would also include instructions on how to (1) calculate extensions for each line item, (2) add sales tax to arrive at the total, and (3) update the appropriate customer account. This bundling together of data and instructions is called **encapsulation.**

Object-oriented data bases are hierarchical, as shown in Fig. 5.3. All levels in the hierarchy, except the bottom one, represent object classes. Thus, in Fig. 5.3,

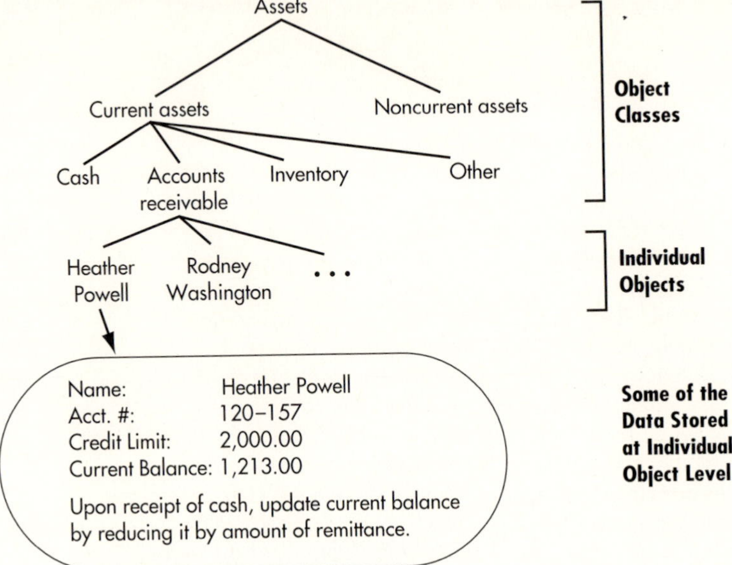

Figure 5.3

Partial Schema for Object-Oriented Data Base

assets, current assets, and accounts receivable are all object classes. Entries at the bottom level of the hierarchy represent individual objects. For example, the accounts for Heather Powell and Rodney Washington represent individual objects. Each individual object is assigned a unique object identifier that serves the same function as the primary key in the relational data model. Pointers are used and explicitly included in the data model as a way to link objects and object classes. These pointers are then referred to in queries in order to navigate through the hierarchy to find the desired objects.

Each object class can be assigned its own properties or defining characteristics. An important feature of the hierarchical nature of the object-oriented data model is that each subclass inherits all the general properties of the classes above it in the hierarchy. Thus, referring to Fig. 5.3, the accounts receivable subclass automatically possesses all the characteristics assigned to current assets. In turn, the current assets subclass possesses all the properties defined for the class called assets. Consequently, at each level only those properties or rules that are unique to that subclass need to be specified. This characteristic of inheriting the properties associated with nodes higher up in the hierarchy facilitates the quick design of new subschema in the object-oriented data model.

Advantages and Criticisms of Object-Oriented DBMS

One important property of object-oriented data bases is their ability to handle complex data types such as graphs, maps, sounds, and images, in addition to the words and numbers that are manipulated and stored by the relational data model. Object-oriented DBMS are especially useful for projects in which spatial relationships must be represented. For example, Ameritech, a Regional Bell Operating Company, uses an object-oriented DBMS to model the telecommunications network. This makes it easy to locate the source of problems. Florida Power & Light uses an object-oriented DBMS to help it design and lay out utility requirements in subdivisions.

Another important property of object-oriented DBMS is that the reusability of object code speeds the development of new data base systems. Reusability is particularly important in fast-changing environments, such as financial services. Thus Fidelity Investments has used an object-oriented DBMS to model some of its new product offerings. Chemical Bank of New York used an object-oriented DBMS to build a data base system to track trading in derivatives when those new instruments began to appear.

There are some criticisms of the object-oriented data model, however. One criticism relates to the principle of encapsulation. Encapsulation permits object code to be reused in new applications, thereby improving programmer efficiency. If taken to the extreme, however, the principle of encapsulation can eliminate the ability to do ad hoc queries, because it limits the methods for accessing and manipulating an object to those that are predefined by the system designer when creating the object.

A second criticism concerns the explicit use of pointers in object-oriented DBMS. This forces users to explicitly navigate through the data base to retrieve information. Proponents of the relational data model argue that this represents a step backward to a data base built to accommodate the programmer's, rather than the end user's, view of the world. Finally, perhaps the most serious limitation of object-oriented DBMS is the lack of a standard, easy-to-use query language like SQL.

The Future of Relational and Object-Oriented Data Bases

It is likely that businesses will continue to use both object-oriented and relational data bases. Some organizations currently use object-oriented DBMS as the front-end to integrate all organizational data, whether stored in a DBMS or in traditional files. For example, both the Federal Reserve and the Municipality of Metropolitan Toronto use an object-oriented DBMS to retrieve data currently stored in a variety of ISAM files, nonrelational DBMS, and a number of different relational DBMS products. Using an object-oriented DBMS as an intelligent front-end is simpler and cheaper than trying to merge all those separate data stores into one unified data base.

It is also likely that the relational and object-oriented data models will merge. Indeed, software that merges the characteristics of both the relational and object-oriented data model is already beginning to appear. This product, called an object-oriented relational DBMS (ORDBMS), uses objects to support the storage and manipulation of complex data types while also maintaining the simplicity, flexibility, and easy-to-use query languages provided by the relational model. For example, Renaissance Technologies Corporation, in Stony Brook, New York, uses an ORDBMS for its stock trading data base. It chose an ORDBMS because a pure object-oriented DBMS would not have been compatible with its existing historical data base of stock price data, and a pure relational DBMS would have been too slow.

Thus businesses will likely use both object-oriented and relational DBMS for the foreseeable future. Object-oriented DBMS will be used to store and manipulate complex data types such as sound and images in tasks requiring such multimedia capabilities. Much routine business transaction data, however, consist of just words and numbers. Relational DBMS have already proved to be ideal for handling such data and therefore will likely continue to be used for such applications.

The Effect of Data Base Systems on the Future of Accounting

Data base systems may profoundly affect the fundamental nature of accounting. Indeed, data base systems could lead to the abandonment of the double-entry accounting model. The basic rationale for the double-entry model is that the redundancy of recording the amount of a transaction twice provides a check on the accuracy of data processing. Every transaction generates equal debit and credit entries, and the equality of debits and credits is checked and rechecked at numerous points in the accounting process. Data redundancy, however, is the antithesis of the data base concept. If the amounts associated with a transaction are entered into a data base system correctly, it is necessary to store them only once, not twice. Computer data processing is sufficiently accurate to make the elaborate system of checks and double checks, which characterizes the double-entry accounting model, unnecessary.

Data base systems also have the potential to alter the nature of external reporting significantly. Considerable time and effort is currently invested in defining how companies should summarize and report accounting information to external users. Why not simply make a copy of the company's financial data base and make it available to external users in lieu of the traditional financial statements? Users would then be free to manipulate and analyze the raw data in whatever manner they see fit. Focus 5.2 discusses this possibility in more detail.

Perhaps the most significant effect of data base systems will be in the way that accounting information is used in decision making. The difficulty of formulating ad hoc queries in accounting systems based on traditional files or nonrelational DBMS meant that accountants acted, in effect, as information gatekeepers. Financial information was readily available only in predefined formats and at specified times. The accountants specified the format of those reports and the times when they would be produced (usually monthly, quarterly, and annually).

As we have seen in this chapter, however, relational DBMS provide users with powerful yet easy-to-use query languages. These query languages make financial information available to managers whenever they want it. Financial statements can be easily prepared to cover whatever time periods managers want to examine, not just the time frames traditionally used by accountants. Relational DBMS can also easily accommodate multiple views of the same underlying phenomenon. For example, tables storing information about assets can include columns not only for historical cost, but also for current replacement costs and market values. Thus managers will no longer be forced to look at data in ways predefined by accountants. Finally, relational DBMS provide the capability of integrating financial and operational data. For example, data about customer satisfaction, collected by surveys or interviews, could be stored in the same table used to store information about current account balances and credit limits. Managers would thus have access to a richer set of data for making tactical and strategic decisions.

FOCUS 5.2

Data Bases or Financial Statements?

Although information technology has dramatically changed the way that business is conducted, it has had relatively little effect on external reporting. Companies still produce periodic (quarterly and annual) financial reports of past activities based on historical costs. Moreover, they present that information at a highly aggregated level. It is estimated that the average financial data base of a typical large company is on the order of 100 gigabytes. Yet annual reports contain, on average, only about 100KB of data! Consequently, users of annual reports see only a small portion of the data about the organization. On top of that, the information is presented in a predefined format (the financial statements).

Why not replace the annual report with a copy of the company's financial data base? Many companies already give their suppliers and customers limited access to their internal data bases. Suppliers, for example, may be given access to inventory data so that they can plan production and deliveries to replenish shortages. They are not, however, given access to human resource or payroll data. Companies could similarly define a view of their data base that excluded data too sensitive to be allowed to fall into the hands of competitors. This view of the data base could be placed on CD-ROMs or made available over the Internet to investors, creditors, and other external users.

The technical capability for providing such data base access exists. The computing power of current PCs makes processing such a data base feasible for a wide range of users. External users would get a fuller picture of the organization's performance, and the information would also be more timely.

In such a system, the company's primary financial reporting function would involve the definition of data elements and data base structure. Users would then be free to aggregate and classify that information using whatever decision model they believed to be appropriate.

Focus Questions

1. What are some of the advantages and disadvantages of providing external users with a disaggregated view of a company's financial data base?
2. If companies provide suppliers and customers with limited access to internal data bases, why not provide similar services to investors and creditors?

Source: Robert K. Elliott, "Confronting the Future: Choices for the Attest Function," *Accounting Horizons* (September 1994): 106–124.

In all these ways, relational DBMS have the potential to increase the use and value of accounting information for making the tactical and strategic decisions involved in running an organization. Accountants, however, must become knowledgeable about data base systems so that they can participate in designing the accounting information systems of the future. Such participation is important for ensuring that adequate controls are included in those systems to safeguard the data and assure the reliability of the information produced.

SUMMARY AND CASE CONCLUSION

Ashton prepared a report highlighting what he had learned about data base systems in general, and the relational data model in particular. His report contained four key points:

1. A data base management system is the software program that makes a data base system work. The DBMS functions as an intermediary between

the users and the data base. As such, it maintains a complex addressing scheme using pointers, indexes, and other methods to link individual data elements to one another. Although these methods are used to retrieve and update information stored in the data base, users are not aware of them.

2. The logical data model underlying a DBMS determines how the user perceives the data as being stored. The relational model represents data as being stored in the form of tables, which are called relations. Every row in a column in a table has only one value and each entry is of the same data type (integer, date, etc.). Neither row order nor column position is significant. Consequently, all interaction with a relational DBMS is based on references to specific data values, rather than by specifying how the desired data are to be retrieved.

3. Relational DBMS supports both text-based and graphical query languages. SQL is the standard text-based relational data query language; QBE represents the typical graphical relational data query language. Both languages provide an easy way for users to retrieve information from a relational database.

4. Almost all new DBMS, whether implemented on mainframes, networks, or personal computers, are based on the relational data model because of its flexibility and its support of easy-to-use query languages. Current relational DBMS products, however, have difficulty in handling complex data types such as sound and graphics. Consequently, a new type of DBMS, based on the object-oriented data model, has been developed to handle such data. Use of the relational DBMS will likely continue, however, to store and manipulate text and numerical data.

After completing his research, Ashton examined a number of DBMS models at a local computer store. He invited Scott and Susan to a demonstration of the relational DBMS that he liked best. Ashton built a sample data base for the sales cycle (refer to Fig. 5.3) and showed Susan and Scott how easy it was to use SQL to query the data base. Scott and Susan were impressed with the demonstration and agreed with Ashton's recommendation to purchase a relational DBMS for S&S. They then asked Ashton to begin work on designing S&S's new data base AIS.

KEY TERMS

schema
conceptual level schema
external level schema
subschema
internal level schema
data dictionary
data definition language (DDL)
data manipulation language (DML)
data query language (DQL)
report writer
data administrator (DA)
application programmer
data model
relational data model
relations
tuple
entity integrity rule
foreign key
referential integrity rule
update anomaly
insert anomaly
delete anomaly
normalization
structured query language (SQL)
query-by-example (QBE)
object-oriented data model
object
encapsulation

CHAPTER QUIZ

1. The relational data model portrays data as being stored in
   a. hierarchies.
   b. tables.
   c. objects.
   d. files.

2. Users will most likely have access to the
   a. data manipulation language.
   b. data query language.
   c. data definition language.
   d. data dictionary.

3. Which SQL command selects only certain rows from a table?
   a. SELECT
   b. FROM
   c. WHERE
   d. GROUP BY

4. Which SQL command is used to link two or more tables?
   a. SELECT
   b. FROM
   c. WHERE
   d. GROUP BY

5. Which of the following is an advantage of the relational data model?
   a. Optimal efficiency in storing and retrieving data
   b. Minimal memory requirements
   c. Ability to handle complex data types like sounds and images
   d. Simplicity

6. Which of the following is *not* a basic requirement (constraint) of the relational data model?
   a. All rows must be unique.
   b. There can be only one value in every row in a column.
   c. All rows in a column must be of the same data type.
   d. The order of columns (their position) conveys important information.

7. Which of the following is *not* an advantage of the relational data model?
   a. Easy-to-use query language
   b. Ability for users to specify how to navigate the data base to retrieve data
   c. Ability to do ad hoc queries
   d. Easily understood data model

8. An individual user's view of the data base is called the
   a. Conceptual level schema.
   b. External level schema.
   c. Internal level schema.
   d. Logical level schema.

9. Which language is used by the DBA to create and maintain the data dictionary?
   a. QBE
   b. DQL
   c. DML
   d. DDL

10. Who is responsible for developing general policies regarding the storage and maintenance of all organizational data?
   a. The data administrator (DA)
   b. The data base administrator (DBA)
   c. Application programmers
   d. The controller

DISCUSSION QUESTIONS

5.1 To what extent should accountants be involved in developing the data dictionary? In which functional business areas do accountants possess much of the knowledge needed to build the data dictionary? In which areas are they most likely to need the assistance of other experts?

5.2 The relational data model represents data as being stored in tables. Spreadsheets are another tool that accountants use that employs a tabular representation of data. What are some similarities and differences in the way that both of these tools use tables? How might an accountant's familiarity with the tabular representation of spreadsheets facilitate or hinder learning how to use a relational DBMS?

5.3 SQL commands can be embedded within application programs that are written in traditional programming languages, like COBOL, whereas QBE commands cannot. How significant is this difference? Why?

5.4 Which language do you think the average accountant would find easier to learn: SQL or QBE? Why?

5.5 Data base systems can help companies fight fraud. For example, over 300 insurance companies are using the Comprehensive Loss Underwriting Exchange data base to share information about potential customers. The data base contains all auto insurance claims made by a customer against any insurance company in the past three to five years. It also contains the current status and cost of each claim to the insurer. Any information that a check turns up that is not on the application can cause a company to raise premiums or even to cancel a policy. To ensure fairness, customers can gain access to a copy of their report and can challenge the accuracy of findings.

What advantages does this data base system provide over traditional file systems for insurance companies and auto insurance applicants? What risks to individual privacy and freedom, if any, are created by these types of data base systems?

5.6 The text explained how data base technology may eliminate the need for double-entry accounting. This creates three possibilities: (1) the double-entry model will be abandoned, (2) the double-entry model will not be used directly, but an external level schema based on the double-entry model will be defined for use by accountants, or (3) the double-entry model will be retained in data base systems. Which alternative do you think is most likely to occur? Why?

PROBLEMS

5.1 The following data elements comprise the conceptual level schema for a data base:

Item number	Customer number
Cost	Customer name
Description	Shipping address
Quantity on hand	Billing address
Invoice number	Credit limit
Date	Account balance
Quantity sold	
Price	
Terms	

REQUIRED

Identify three potential users and design a subschema for each. Justify your design by explaining why each user needs access to that data element.

5.2 The Paradise Hotel is a 1000-room, 50-story resort hotel in San Diego, California. The hotel is very popular with tourists and is also the site of many business conventions. A convention center was built next to the hotel to meet the needs of the business clientele.

The number of rooms rented at the Paradise fluctuates because of seasonal cycles, business convention schedules, and special promotions offered by the competition. Business is heaviest during the tourist season, when reservations must be booked several months in advance to ensure room preferences and availability. Even though most business conventions are held during the off season, advance notice of nearly a year must be made for business conventions in order to have a large enough block of rooms available. In the off season, reservations are not as important for nonconvention guests.

If the Paradise Hotel charged the same room rate over the entire year, the hotel would be empty during the off season and overcrowded during the tourist season. To control demand, low rates are charged during the off season, premium rates are charged during the peak tourist season, and regular rates are charged the rest of the year. When people making reservations identify themselves as members of an approved convention, they are extended a special rate. A group reserving a large block of rooms is extended an even lower rate. In addition to varying by season, convention, and group, room prices vary according to floor and size.

Staffing and managing a complex as large as the Paradise Hotel and convention center is a formidable task. The work force must be kept low in the off season, and additional help must be hired during peak time. Employees must be assigned to departments and scheduled so that adequate help is always on hand. Meal planning and preparation vary according to how many guests are anticipated; smaller conventions need to be planned around the larger ones. Throughout the entire process, adequate information must be kept for the accounting function.

Since most of the hotel's clientele come through travel agencies, the hotel works closely with them. Travel agencies make their reservations by using the hotel's toll-free number to call service representatives, who record the reservations.

REQUIRED

How could Paradise use a relational data base to improve the effectiveness and efficiency of its operation?

5.3 Mariposa Products, a textile and apparel manufacturer, has always developed its own application programs in-house. The first application to be developed and implemented was production and inventory control. Other applications that were added in succession were payroll, accounts receivable, and accounts payable.

These applications were not integrated due to the piecemeal manner in which they were developed and implemented. Nevertheless, the system proved satisfactory for several years. Generally, reports were prepared on time, and information was readily accessible.

Mariposa operates in a very competitive industry. A combination of increased operating costs and the competitive nature of the industry have had an adverse effect on profit margins and operating profits. Ed Wilde, Mariposa's president, suggested that some special analyses be prepared in an attempt to provide information that would help management improve operations. Unfortunately, some of the data were not consistent among the reports. In addition, there were no data by product line or by department. These problems were attributable to the fact that Mariposa's applications were developed piecemeal and, as a consequence, duplicate data that were not necessarily consistent existed on Mariposa's computer system.

Wilde was concerned that Mariposa's computer system was not able to generate the information his managers needed to make decisions. He called a meeting with top management and certain data processing employees to discuss potential solutions to Mariposa's problems. The consensus of the meeting was that a new information system that would integrate Mariposa's applications was needed. Mariposa's controller suggested that the company consider a data base system that all departments would use. As a first step, the controller proposed hiring a data base administrator on a consulting basis to determine the feasibility of converting to a data base system.

REQUIRED

a. Identify the components that comprise a data base system.
b. Discuss the advantages and disadvantages of a data base system for Mariposa.
c. Describe the duties of a data base administrator. (CMA adapted)

5.4 Most DBMS packages contain a data definition language, a data manipulation language, and a data query language. For each of the following examples, indicate which language would be used and why.

a. A data base administrator defines the logical structure of the data base.
b. The controller requests a cost accounting report containing a list of all employees being paid for more than ten hours overtime in a given week.
c. A programmer develops a program to update the fixed assets records stored in the data base.
d. The human resources manager requests a report noting all employees that are retiring within five years.
e. The inventory serial number field is extended in the inventory records to allow for

recognition of additional inventory items with serial numbers containing more than ten digits.

f. A user develops a program to print out all purchases made during the past two weeks.

g. An additional field is added to the fixed asset records to record the estimated salvage value of each asset.

5.5 Refer to Table 5.8 to determine the answers to each of the following SQL queries. Describe the answer that would be displayed.

```
a. SELECT   ALL
   FROM     Invoice
b. SELECT   ALL
   FROM     Invoice
   WHERE    Salesperson = 'S. Knight'
c. SELECT   ALL
   FROM     Invoice
   WHERE    Salesperson = 'J. Buck' AND
            Date <= 10/31/96
d. SELECT   Item #
   FROM     Line Item
   WHERE    quantity > 1
e. SELECT   Description
   FROM     Inventory, Line Item
   WHERE    Inventory.Item # = Line
            Item.Item # AND Quantity = 1
f. SELECT   Customer Name
   FROM     Customer, Invoice
   WHERE    Customer.Customer # =
            Invoice.Customer # AND
            Salesperson = 'J. Buck'
```

5.6 SQL can use various mathematical commands in the SELECT clause. For example, the chapter introduced the use of the SUM operation, to calculate a total for a numerical column. Other operations include MAX, MIN, and AVERAGE, which respectively return the maximum, minimum, and average value of a numerical column. In addition, the COUNT operation returns the number of rows in the table that meet the specified criteria.

REQUIRED

Use these mathematical operators to write SQL queries (or QBE versions of those queries if you have access to a DBMS that provides QBE) to answer the following questions (refer again to the data base in Table 5.8):

a. How many different inventory items does S&S sell?

b. How many sales were made during October?

c. What is the average amount of sales?

d. What was the invoice number, date, salesperson, customer number, and amount of the largest sale?

e. What is the lowest selling price of any inventory item?

f. What quantity of each inventory item was sold?

5.7 Refer to Table 5.16 to determine the answers to the following SQL queries. Describe what would be displayed in response to each query.

```
a. SELECT     Sum (amount)
   FROM       Sales
   WHERE      Date < 11/01/96
b. SELECT     Item_number, Sum
              (quantity)
   FROM       Sales-Inventory
   GROUP BY   Item _Number
c. SELECT     Customer_number, Name,
              Credit_Limit, Balance
   FROM       Customer
   WHERE      (Credit_Limit-Balance) > 1000
d. SELECT     All
   FROM       Inventory
   WHERE      QOH > 100
e. SELECT     Description
   FROM       Inventory, Sales–Inventory
   WHERE      Inventory.Item_Number =
              Sales-Inventory.Item_Number
              AND Quantity > 1
f. SELECT     COUNT (Item_ Number)
   FROM       Inventory
```

5.8 Refer to Table 5.16 to write SQL or QBE queries when answering the following questions:

a. Which customers (show their names) made purchases from Martinez?
b. Who has the largest credit limit?
c. How many sales were made in October?
d. What were the item numbers, price, and quantity sold of each item on invoice number 103?
e. How much did each salesperson sell?
f. How many customers live in Arizona?
g. How much credit does each customer still have available?
h. How much of each item was sold (show item number, description, and quantity sold)?

Table 5.16 **Sample Relational Tables for Problems 5.7 and 5.8**

Inventory

Item_Number	Description	Unit Cost	Unit Price	QOH
1010	Blender	14.00	29.95	200
1015	Toaster	12.00	19.95	300
1020	Mixer	23.00	33.95	250
1025	Television	499.00	699.95	74
1030	Freezer	799.00	999.95	32
1035	Refrigerator	699.00	849.95	25
1040	Radio	45.00	79.95	100
1045	Clock	79.00	99.95	300

Customer

Customer_Number	Name	City	State	Credit_Limit	Balance
1000	Smith	Phoenix	AZ	2500	1200
1001	Jones	St. Louis	MO	1500	1235
1002	Jeffries	Atlanta	GA	4000	3000
1003	Gilkey	Phoenix	AZ	5000	300
1004	Lankford	Phoenix	AZ	2000	1800
1005	Zeile	Chicago	IL	2000	1900
1006	Pagnozzi	Salt Lake	UT	3000	2400
1007	Arocha	Chicago	IL	1000	750

Sales

Invoice_Number	Date	Salesperson	Customer_Number	Amount
101	10/03/96	Wilson	1000	1549.90
102	10/05/96	Mahomet	1003	299.85
103	10/05/96	Jackson	1002	1449.80
104	10/15/96	Drezen	1000	799.90
105	10/15/96	Martinez	1005	849.95
106	10/16/96	Martinez	1007	99.95
107	10/29/96	Mahomet	1002	2209.70
108	11/03/96	Martinez	1000	779.90

Sales-Inventory

Invoice_Number	Item_Number	Quantity	Extension
101	1025	1	699.95
101	1035	1	849.95
102	1045	3	299.85
103	1010	1	29.95
103	1015	1	19.95
103	1025	2	1399.90
104	1025	1	699.95
104	1045	1	99.95
105	1035	1	849.95
106	1045	1	99.95
107	1030	1	999.95
107	1035	1	849.95
107	1040	2	159.90
107	1045	2	199.90
108	1025	1	699.95
108	1045	1	99.95

CASE 5.1: ANYCOMPANY, INC.—AN ONGOING COMPREHENSIVE CASE

Identify a local company (you may use the same company that you identified to complete Case 1.1) that uses a data base system and write a report that includes the following information:

1. The type of DBMS (relational, object-oriented, etc.) used.
2. The reason(s) why that particular DBMS and data model were chosen.
3. How the company transferred its data to the data base system.
4. Advantages the DBMS provides to the company.
5. Any problems or disadvantages encountered as a result of using the DBMS.
6. The involvement of the accounting staff in choosing the DBMS, designing the schemas, and implementing and maintaining the system.

CASE 5.2: RESEARCH PROJECTS

Research how businesses are using DBMS models. Write a report that addresses the following issues:

1. The most popular relational DBMS packages used on mainframes and on microcomputers.
2. How companies use relational DBMS.
3. Limitations of relational DBMS.
4. The nature of object-oriented DBMS.
5. The relative advantages and disadvantages of relational and object-oriented DBMS models.

Note: Many articles are currently extolling the benefits of object-oriented DBMS. One of the best defenses of the relational model is found in the Summer 1993 issue (Volume 3, Number 2) of *Interface,* entitled "The Relational World of Chris Date."

ANSWERS TO CHAPTER QUIZ

1. b	**3.** c	**5.** d	**7.** b	**9.** d
2. b	**4.** b	**6.** d	**8.** b	**10.** a

Chapter 6

Data Modeling and Data Base Design

LEARNING OBJECTIVES

After studying this chapter, you should be able to:

- Explain the steps involved in designing a data base.
- Describe the data modeling process and explain the elements of the REA accounting data model.
- Analyze an E–R diagram and explain what it reveals about the organization being modeled.
- Draw an Entity–Relationship (E–R) diagram as a means of documenting the contents of an accounting information system data base.
- Build a set of tables to implement an E–R diagram in a relational data base.
- Explain how a data base AIS affects internal controls.

Integrative Case: S&S, Inc.

Ashton Fleming is frustrated. When S&S, Inc. purchased a relational DBMS, it was with the intention that Ashton would design the data base, since Scott and Susan could not afford to hire an external consultant. Ashton had originally supported this plan. He had found it easy, with the help of the computer store salesperson, to build the sample data base that had convinced Scott and Susan to buy the package in the first place. Now, however, Ashton is learning that designing a relational data base for S&S is not as easy as the salesperson made it seem. The software manuals did indeed provide "step-by-step" instructions for designing a relational data base, but they assumed a lot of background knowledge that Ashton did not possess. He wished that the instructor of his accounting information systems class in college had spent more time on the topic of data bases.

While mulling over his situation, Ashton began to sort through his stack of mail from the AICPA and his state CPA society. Suddenly, he saw something that attracted his attention: a flyer announcing a two-day seminar on data modeling and data base design to be held the following week at a downtown hotel. The seminar's objective was to teach accountants the basics on how to design a relational data base—for small businesses! Ashton immediately called and learned that registration was still open. He then went to Susan and admitted he was having some difficulty in designing S&S's data base. Ashton explained the benefits he thought the seminar could provide and Susan agreed to send him.

Ashton hopes to have answers for the following questions by the end of the seminar:

1. What are the basic steps to follow when designing a data base?
2. When creating a relational data base, how exactly do you decide which attributes belong in which tables?

3. How can you document a relational data base?
4. What effect does a relational DBMS have on internal controls?

INTRODUCTION

Like many companies, S&S is converting to the data base approach for storing its accounting data. In this chapter you will learn how to design and document a relational data base for an accounting information system. These topics are important to study for two reasons. First, building a data base involves much more than simply learning the syntax of how to use a particular DBMS. As is the case for building reliable spreadsheet templates, building accurate data bases requires a great deal of careful planning and design *before* even sitting down at the computer.

Second, data base systems are increasingly likely to affect the day-to-day activities of accountants as we enter the twenty-first century. Consider the following predictions about the future of corporate accounting that were generated by a group of 40 senior financial executives, accounting educators, and consultants at an AICPA workshop:[1]

- Data will be stored in a central data base, accessible to everyone in the company, rather than in separate departmental files and data bases.
- The title of the chief financial position may change from CFO (chief financial officer) to CAO (chief analytical officer) as accountants become information specialists whose primary duty is not just to produce but also to analyze the organization's data.
- The CAO will be involved in modeling the organization's data base.
- Nonfinancial performance measures will increase in popularity because traditional financial reports do not provide all the information needed to make important business decisions. The corporate data base must therefore integrate financial and nonfinancial data.

Although these predictions deal with the future of corporate accounting, an understanding of the principles of data base design is also important for future entrants to the public accounting profession. Consultants will likely be involved in helping corporations adopt these new data base AIS models. Auditors will need to understand the structure and mechanics of data base AIS, and how to document that understanding, to effectively perform audits.

The remainder of this chapter is divided into five sections. We first describe the basic steps in designing and operating a data base system, then focus on one of the aspects of data base design with which accountants should be involved: data modeling. We introduce the REA accounting model and Entity-Relationship (E–R) diagrams and show how to use those tools to build a data model of an AIS. The third section then describes how to implement the resulting data model in a relational data base. In the next section we demonstrate how the traditional elements (journals and ledgers) and outputs (managerial

---

[1] Stanley Zarowin, "The Future of Finance," *Journal of Accountancy* (August 1995): 47–49.

reports and financial statements) are stored and produced by a data base AIS. We conclude the chapter by discussing internal control considerations in a data base environment.

DATA BASE DESIGN

Ashton learned in his seminar that the design and operation of a data base system consists of the six stages shown in Fig. 6.1. These six stages are repetitive. There will eventually come a time during the operation and maintenance stage when the need to redesign the data base, and possibly acquire a new DBMS, becomes apparent. At that point, the entire process starts over, beginning with a planning study to determine the feasibility of developing a new data base system. Let us now examine what occurs during each of these six stages of data base design.

Planning

The first stage in data base design consists of initial planning to determine the need for and feasibility of developing a new system. The objective is to determine whether the proposed system is technologically and economically feasible. If it is, then the project should proceed to the next stage: requirements definition.

Requirements Definition

Requirements definition involves defining the scope of the proposed data base system, determining general hardware and software requirements, and identifying user information needs. The scope of the project is defined in consultation with management and reflects the organization's information needs, strategic goals, and objectives. Once the scope of the system has been defined, information about factors such as the number of users and the expected

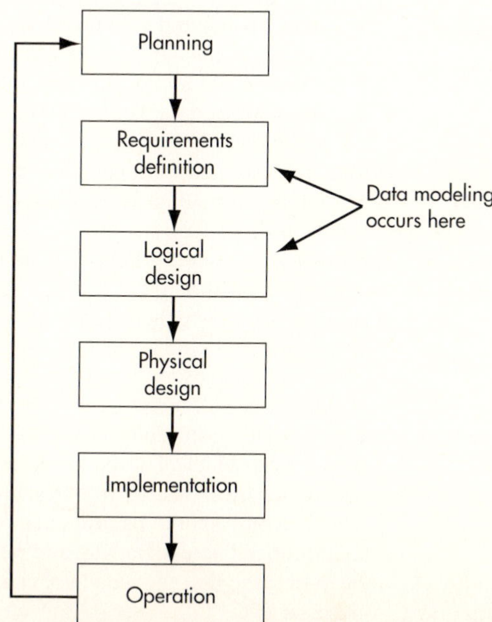

Figure 6.1

Six Stages in Data Base Design

transaction volume is used to determine the general hardware and software requirements of the new system. Data about user needs are collected by a variety of methods, including interviews and questionnaires. The data are used to develop preliminary individual user views (external level schemas) that reflect both transaction processing requirements and decision-making needs.

Data base design must take into account a number of objectives (see Table 6.1). Unfortunately, it is not always possible to maximize every objective; thus, as in all areas of systems design, trade-offs are required. For example, cost-effectiveness is often at odds with flexibility and accessibility. The data base designer's key task is therefore to try to achieve the best possible balance among these objectives.

Logical Design

The third stage in the data base design process, **logical design,** involves completing the external level schemas and translating the data requirements of different users and application programs into the conceptual level schema. It is often easier to create the conceptual schema by subdividing it into major functional areas. This can be accomplished by identifying "clusters" of files and programs that are closely linked to one another in terms of processing and usage. For example, the different accounting cycles (revenue, expenditure, production, payroll, and general ledger) can be classified as clusters that occur "naturally" in an accounting data base. The revenue cycle schema would then include all data related to sales order processing, shipping, billing and accounts receivable, and cash collections.

Table 6.1 **Data Base Design Objectives**

Completeness	The data base should contain all the data (and the relationships between the data) needed by its various users. There should be proper integration and coordination of all users and suppliers of data. The data contained in the data base should be recorded in the data dictionary.
Relevance	Only relevant and useful data should be captured and stored.
Accessibility	Stored data should be accessible to all authorized users on a timely basis.
Up-to-dateness	Stored data should be kept current and up to date.
Flexibility	The data base should be flexible enough that a wide variety of users can satisfy their information needs.
Efficiency	Data storage should be accomplished as efficiently as possible, using the least amount of resources necessary. Data base update, retrieval, and maintenance time should be minimized.
Cost-effectiveness	Data should be stored in such a way that desired system benefits can be achieved at the lowest possible cost.
Integrity	The data base should be free from errors and irregularities.
Security	The data base should be protected from loss, destruction, and unauthorized access. Backup and recovery procedures should be in place so that the data base can be reconstructed if necessary.

In addition to specifying the relationships that exist among data elements, logical design also involves designating both primary and secondary keys. The appropriate primary key for each record is generally obvious—for example, customer number for the customer file and invoice number for the invoice file. Identifying secondary keys is not as simple. Indeed, as explained in Chapter 4, secondary keys should be selected carefully because their use affects data base processing efficiency and information retrieval. The most appropriate secondary keys generally are those data elements that identify groups of records likely to be of interest to management. Examples of attributes commonly used as secondary keys include invoice due date, employee department number, and inventory location code.

The data dictionary is also developed during the logical design stage. In addition controls over access to and allowable operations on the data base are specified.

Physical Design

The fourth stage of the data base design process, **physical design,** consists of taking the conceptual design and converting it into physical storage structures. First, the conceptual level schema is translated into an internal level schema. Second, the data dictionary is created. Third, the manner in which the data are to be physically stored and accessed is specified. This involves decisions about such matters as the use of pointers and indexes for linking records.

Implementation and Operation

The final two stages of the data base design process are implementation and operation. The implementation stage consists of all the activities associated with getting the new data base system up and running. These include transferring data from existing files to the new data base, developing new application programs and modifying existing ones, and training users on how to use the new system. The operation stage includes all the activities associated with running and maintaining the new system. This includes careful monitoring of system performance and user satisfaction with the system to determine the need for enhancements and modifications.

Role of the Accountant

Accountants are usually involved in all stages of the data base design process except physical design. In the planning stage, accountants both provide some of the information used to evaluate the feasibility of the proposed project and participate in making that decision. In the requirements definition and logical design stages, accountants participate in identifying user information needs, in developing schemas and the data dictionary, and specifying controls. During the implementation stage, accountants are involved in testing the accuracy of the new data base and the application programs that will use that data. Finally, accountants use the data base system to process transactions and sometimes help manage it.

Part III of this book (Chapters 10–12) discusses in more detail the planning and implementation stages of systems design. Part V (Chapters 17–21) provides detailed information about the use of AIS to process transactions and the design of internal controls for each of the major accounting cycles. Therefore we devote the remainder of this chapter to the requirements definition and logical design stages of the data base design process.

DATA MODELING

Data modeling is the process of defining a data base such that it faithfully represents all key components of an organization's environment. The objective is to explicitly capture and store data about each and every business activity that the organization wishes to plan, control, or evaluate. As shown in Fig. 6.1, data modeling occurs during both the requirements analysis and logical design stages of data base design. Two data modeling tools are used by accountants: the REA data model and Entity–Relationship diagrams.

The REA Data Model[2]

The **REA data model** was developed explicitly for use in designing AIS data bases. REA is an acronym signifying that the data model contains information about three fundamental types of objects: the *R*esources acquired and used by an organization, the *E*vents engaged in by the organization, and the *A*gents participating in these events.

The term **resources** refers to identifiable objects that have economic value to the organization. Most of the objects accountants traditionally classify as assets (cash, inventory, equipment, supplies, warehouses, factories, stores, and so forth) are considered resources.

The term **events** is defined broadly to include all of an organization's business activities. Thus events in the REA model are not limited to those transactions for which accounting journal entries are traditionally made (sales, cash receipts, purchases, cash disbursements). Instead, events in the REA data model also encompass other business activities that are not normally recorded in journal entries, such as customer orders, but about which the organization wants to collect data. Events, however, must represent business activities that in some way directly affect the organization's resources; they cannot merely be information processing activities. For example, the posting of data from a journal to a ledger would *not* be considered an "event" in the REA data model. This activity only affects the *recording* of data about economic resources; it does not directly alter any resource.

The term **agents** refers to the groups of people an organization collects data about to help it better plan, control, and evaluate the performance of its basic business activities. Examples of agents include employees, vendors, and customers.

The REA data model supports the expansion of the AIS to include not only traditional financial data, but also the nonfinancial operational performance measures that managers need to run an organization effectively. For example, information about the time a sales transaction occurred, not just the date, can be stored along with the financial characteristics of the transaction. This information is then readily available for use in analyzing peak sales periods and determining staffing needs.

In contrast, the traditional approach to designing an AIS uses the chart of accounts to store and organize data based on the structure of financial state-

---

[2]The material in this section is based on William E. McCarthy, "An Entity–Relationship View of Accounting Models," *The Accounting Review* (October 1979): 667–686; William E. McCarthy, "The REA Accounting Model: A Generalized Framework for Accounting Systems in a Shared Data Environment," *The Accounting Review* (July 1982): 554–578.

ments. In terms of the previous example, the traditional AIS contains data only about the financial aspects of a sales transaction; data useful for evaluating operational performance would be stored in a separate data base or information system.

It is vitally important that an organization's AIS be capable of storing both traditional financial measures and other operational performance measures. As Robert Elliott explains:[3]

> *Information technology (IT) is changing everything. It represents a new, post-industrial paradigm of wealth creation that is replacing the industrial paradigm and is profoundly changing the way business is done. Because of these changes in business, the decisions that management must make are very different from former decisions.* If the purpose of accounting information is to support business decision-making, and management's decision types are changing, then it is natural to expect accounting to change—both internal and external accounting. [*Emphasis added.*]

The REA data model can be used to build a data base that allows the AIS to change in response to management's changing information requirements.

Entity–Relationship Diagrams[4]

An **Entity–Relationship (E–R) diagram** graphically depicts a data base's contents. It shows the various entities being modeled and the important relationships among them. An entity is any class of objects about which data are collected. Thus the resources, events, and agents that comprise the REA data model are all entities. An E–R diagram represents entities as rectangles and relationships between entities as lines and diamonds (see Fig. 6.2).

Figure 6.2 is a partial E–R diagram of the REA data model for S&S's revenue cycle. To simplify the discussion, we have included only two business events: the sale of merchandise to customers and the collection of cash from customers. More complex E–R diagrams of each accounting cycle are presented in Chapters 17–21. Also, to further enhance the readability of Fig. 6.2, we have included column headings to identify whether an entity is a resource, an event, or an agent. These column headings normally would not appear in an E–R diagram.

Reading an E–R Diagram. An E–R diagram based on the REA data model must link every event entity to at least one resource and two agent entities. Consequently, the easiest way to read an E–R diagram like that depicted in Fig. 6.2 is to begin with the event entities (shown in the middle column) and examine how they are related to resources, agents, and other events. Since Fig. 6.2 is modeling only retail sales, the sales event entity is linked to the inventory resource entity. The relationship between them is called *line items* and represents the fact that each sale consists of one or more items of merchandise, each of which appears as a line item on the sales invoice. Figure 6.2 also shows that two agents participate in the sales event: a salesperson and a customer. Finally,

[3]Robert K. Elliott, "The Third Wave Breaks on the Shores of Accounting," *Accounting Horizons* (June 1992): 61.

[4]The material in this section is based on P. Chen, "The Entity Relationship Model—Toward a Unified View of Data," *Transactions on Database Systems* (March 1976, 1:1): 9–36.

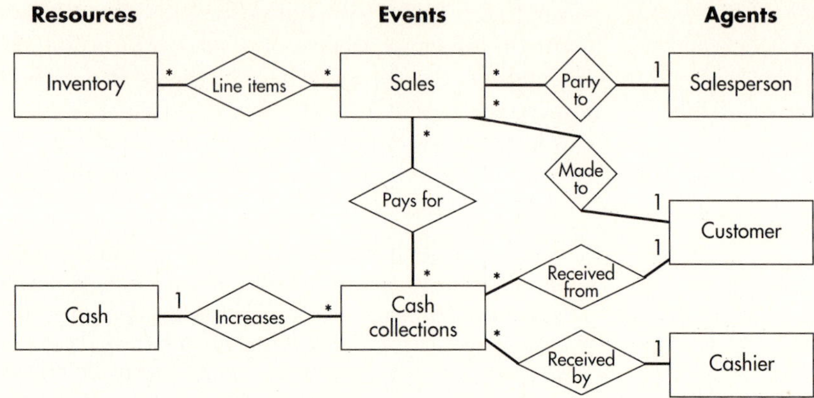

Figure 6.2

Simplified E–R Diagram of S&S's Revenue Cycle: Retail Sales

the sales event is linked to the cash collection event by the *pays for* relationship. These two events may occur simultaneously, in the case of in-store sales, or on separate days, in the case of credit sales.

Figure 6.2 also includes symbols (either a "1" or a "*") next to each entity. These symbols provide information about the cardinality, or nature, of the relationship between entities. The **cardinality** of a relationship describes the number of occurrences of one entity that may be associated with a single occurrence of the other entity. The symbols in Figure 6.2 indicate the maximum cardinality of the relationship, which can be either one (1) or many (*). In terms of maximum cardinality, three types of relationships between entities are possible:

1. One-to-one (1:1).
2. One-to-many (1:* and *:1).
3. Many-to-many (*:*).

Figure 6.3 shows examples of each of type of relationship in the context of linking the sales and cash collections events.

The cardinalities in an E–R diagram are read by looking at the symbol (1 or *) at the other end of the relationship. For example, consider the relationship between the sales event entity and the salesperson agent entity in Fig. 6.2. The * next to the sales event entity indicates that many sales can be associated with a particular salesperson. The 1 next to the salesperson entity, however, indicates that each sale can be associated with at most one salesperson.

Now examine the relationship between the sales and cash receipt events. The * next to cash receipts indicates that a particular sale can be linked to many cash receipts, each of which represents a partial or installment payment. Conversely, the * next to the sales event indicates that each cash receipt can be associated with many sales events, all of which are paid for in one remittance.

Thus far we have focused on maximum cardinalities. Relationships also have minimum cardinalities. The minimum cardinality of a relationship can be either zero or one, depending on whether an occurrence of that entity must exist in a relationship. Later, we will show how depicting minimum

Figure 6.3

Possible Cardinalities of the Sales–Cash Collections Relationship

A. One-to-One (1:1) Relationship

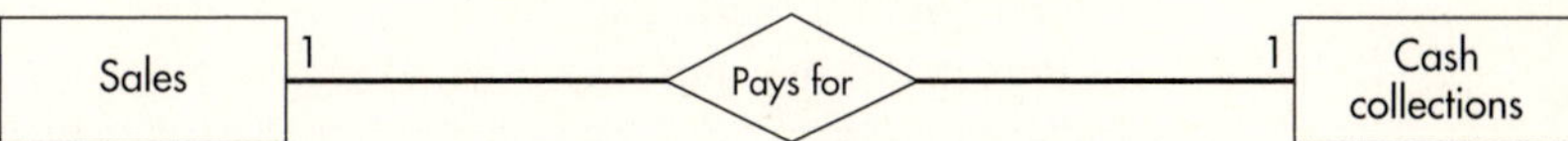

Each instance of a sales event (each sales transaction) is linked to *at most one* instance of a cash collections event (remittance from a customer). Conversely, each instance of a cash collection event is linked to *one and only one* instance of a sales event.

Example: cash sales.

B. One-to-Many (1:*) Relationship

Each sales event is linked to *many* cash collection events; each cash collection event is linked to *one and only one* sales event.

Example: installment payments.

C. Many-to-One (*:1) Relationship

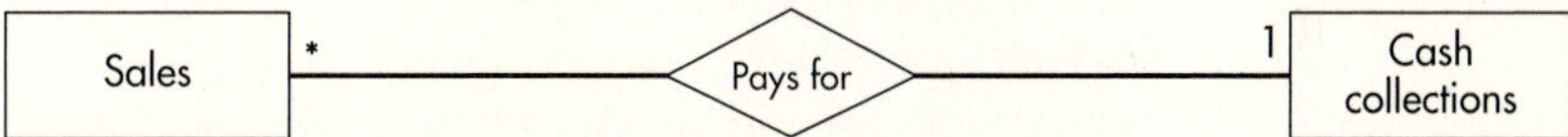

Each cash collection event (remittance from a customer) is linked to *one or more* sales events; each sales event is linked to *at most one* cash collections event.

Example: paying monthly store charge in full.

D. Many-to-Many (*:*) Relationship

Each sales event is linked to *many* cash collection events; each cash collection event is linked to *one or more* sales events.

Example: credit card, with partial payments in some months.

cardinalities in an E–R diagram provides some useful information about an organization's internal control policies.

E–R Diagrams and Other Forms of Documentation. E–R diagrams complement the other forms of documentation discussed in Chapter 3. They are especially useful, however, for documenting an advanced AIS built using data bases. E–R diagrams provide two important types of information about a data base AIS. First, they explicitly depict the relationships among the various data items that are stored in the accounting data base. In contrast, flowcharts show only which files exist and describe their basic characteristics, such as how they are organized (alphabetical, numerical, etc.) and stored (paper files, magnetic disk, etc.). Similarly, data flow diagrams describe the contents of each file in the system, but they do not show explicitly how those files relate to one another. As Fig. 6.2 shows, however, E–R diagrams show explicitly how the various items stored in the data base relate to one another.

Second, the maximum cardinalities in E–R diagrams provide useful information about the nature of the company being modeled and the business policies that it follows. For example, close examination of Fig. 6.2 reveals much information about S&S. First, note that the relationship between the sales and cash collections events is modeled as being *:* (read as many-to-many). The fact that each cash collection event can be linked to many sales events indicates that S&S extends credit to its customers, who may then pay for a number of sales with one remittance. Conversely, the fact that each sale can be linked to many cash collections indicates that S&S also allows its customers to make installment payments on major purchases. Keep in mind, however, that a many-to-many relationship only refers to maximum cardinalities; thus S&S may also make cash sales that are paid for at the time of purchase.

Next, notice that the relationship between the inventory and sales entities is also modeled as being *:*. This indicates that S&S sells mass-produced goods because each type of inventory item (each instance of the inventory entity) can appear in many different sales events. For example, many different sales invoices can record the sale of the same refrigerator model. At the same time, each individual sale event can involve several types of inventory items. For example, a customer may purchase a refrigerator and a freezer at the same time. Finally, remember that *:* indicates only the maximum cardinality of the relationship. Thus a specific sale may be linked to only one inventory item (example: a customer who purchases only a television set). Conversely, it is also possible that a particular inventory item (such as a washer model) may be sold only once. Of course, Scott and Susan hope to avoid carrying such unpopular models.

Figure 6.2 also shows that the relationships between customers and both the sales and cash collections events are modeled as being 1:*. This reflects the fact that (hopefully) customers make repeat purchases and therefore multiple remittances over time. The maximum cardinality of 1 attached to the customer entity indicates the general business rule that a sale must be made to some specific customer and that a remittance, whether in the form of cash, check, or credit card, must come from a specific customer as well. Similarly, each sale must involve one and only one salesperson and each cash collection event is processed by one particular cashier. Finally, the relationship between the cash and cash collection entities is modeled as being 1:*, which indicates that all of S&S's cash collections are deposited into only one bank account.

Thus E–R diagrams provide detailed information about how a business functions that neither flowcharts nor DFDs can provide. In addition, as the next section shows, E–R diagrams are a useful data modeling tool for *designing* the structure of a data base.

Using E–R Diagrams for Data Modeling

Drawing an E–R diagram as part of the data base design process consists of four steps: (1) identify the entities (resources, events, and agents) of interest, (2) draw rectangles for each entity, (3) add diamonds to represent important relationships between entities, and (4) specify the cardinality of these relationships. We will now follow these four steps to produce the model of S&S's revenue cycle depicted in Fig. 6.2.

Step 1: Identify the Entities of Interest. An E–R diagram must include the three basic types of entities: events, resources, and agents. Begin by listing the business activities that management wants to plan, control, and evaluate (the events of the REA data model). A level 0 DFD, if one exists, provides a good foundation for this list. It is extremely important, however, that the data model reflect the needs and desires of those who will use the system. Thus the level 0 DFD should be supplemented with data about user information needs.

To keep our example simple, suppose that Ashton interviews Scott and Susan and learns that the two main events they are concerned with in S&S's revenue cycle are (1) the sale of merchandise to customers and (2) collecting cash from customers as payment for those sales. Therefore, those two event entities will appear in the E–R diagram for S&S's revenue cycle.

Next, identify the resources that are required, used, or disposed of in each event. To continue our example, Ashton observes that the sales event involves the disposal of inventory and that the cash collections event involves the acquisition of cash. Thus the E–R diagram will include two resource entities: inventory and cash.

What about accounts receivable? It is not included because accounts receivable does not meet the REA data model's definition of a resource. Accounts receivable is not an independent object, but simply represents the difference between two events: sales and cash collections. Consequently, if data about both sales and cash collections are already stored in the data base, there is no need to store, redundantly, information about accounts receivable. Later, we will show how to extract information about accounts receivable from an AIS data base built using the REA data model.

Finally, identify the agents who participate in each event. There will always be at least one internal agent (employee) and, in most cases, an external agent (customer or vendor) involved in each event. In the case of S&S's revenue cycle, customers and salespersons participate in the sales event; customers and the cashier participate in the cash collection event. Thus three agent entities will be included in the E–R diagram of S&S's revenue cycle: salespersons, customers, and cashiers.

It is important to understand that the agents in an REA data model represent *functions,* not specific people. Thus Fig. 6.2 models the salesperson and cashier agents as separate entities. It is possible, however, that the same person may fill both roles. For example, in a cash sale, the salesperson may also act as the cashier and collect payment from the customer. We would still use two agents to model this situation, however.

Step 2: Draw Rectangles to Represent Each Entity. Now that we have identified all the entities of interest, we are ready to draw the E–R diagram. (Remember that to keep our example simple, we have focused on only a part of the revenue cycle; a complete data model would include many additional entities, such as deliveries, repairs, delivery staff, and banks).

Divide a piece of paper into three columns, one for each type of entity (resources, events, and agents). Use the middle column for events, since they are linked to both resources and agents. Draw a rectangle to represent each event you are including in the model. List the events from top to bottom in the order they occur; this will make the list easy to read and check later on.

Next, draw rectangles for each resource in the left column and for each agent in the right column. Place these opposite the events to which they are related. To reduce clutter and improve readability, each entity should appear only once on an E–R diagram. Therefore Ashton draws only one rectangle for the customer entity, even though customers participate in two events. At this point, the E–R diagram for S&S's revenue cycle should look like Fig. 6.4.

Step 3: Add Diamonds to Represent Important Relationships. Next, the data modeler should interview management to determine which relationships should be included in the E–R diagram. The three most common relationships are those linking the following:

1. Two events that are causally or temporarily related (such as sales and cash collections).
2. An event with the resource that is acquired, used, or disposed of during performance of that event.
3. An event and the agents who participate in it.

Once these relationships have been identified, they are included by drawing a diamond between the two entities. Each diamond should include a label describing the nature of the relationship. The diamond is then connected to each entity (rectangle) by a line. After applying these steps to Fig. 6.4 the E–R diagram for S&S's revenue cycle should look like Fig. 6.5.

Step 4: Specify Relationship Cardinalities. The final step is to add information about relationship cardinalities to the diagram. Determining the cardinality of a relationship is not an arbitrary decision made by the person drawing the E–R diagram, but rather reflects two key sources of information:

1. *The business policies followed by the company being modeled.* Figure 6.3 depicted the various ways the relationship between the sales and cash collection event could be described. To model this relationship for a given company

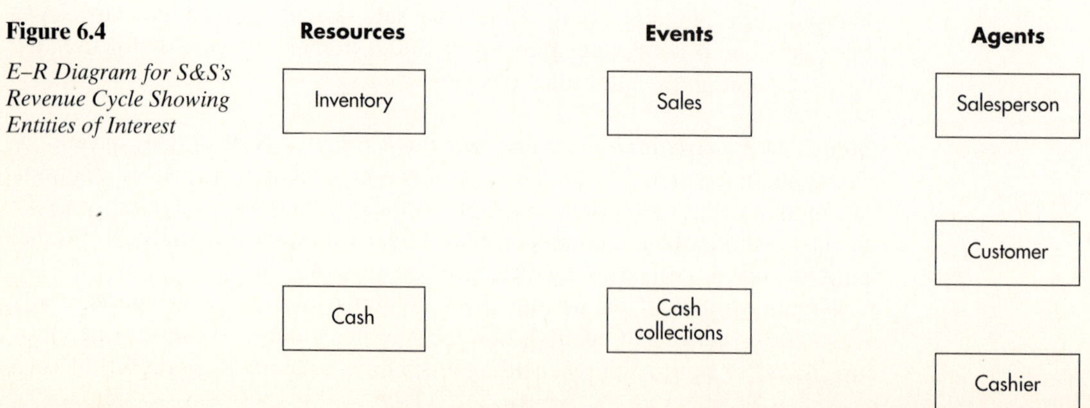

Figure 6.4

E–R Diagram for S&S's Revenue Cycle Showing Entities of Interest

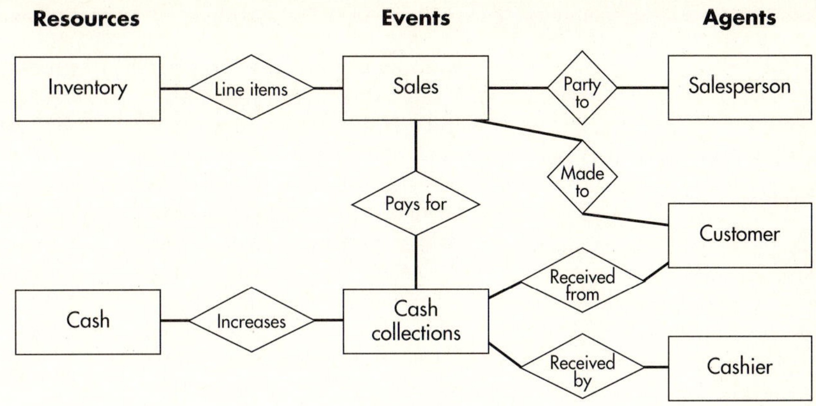

Figure 6.5

E–R Diagram for S&S's Revenue Cycle Showing Relationships Between Entities

accurately, the data modeler must study how that company conducts its business. For example, if the company makes only installment sales, then the relationship between sales and cash collections should be modeled as being 1:* (each sale can be linked to many cash collection events). If the company extends credit but does not make installment sales, however, then the relationship between sales and cash collections should be modeled as being *:1 (many sales may be linked to one specific cash collection event). Relationship cardinalities should reflect the way the business functions, not the opinions of the data modeler.

2. *General business knowledge.* Some cardinalities reflect general business policies common to most organizations. For example, Fig. 6.2 models the relationship between sales and customers as being *:1 (many sales can be linked to one customer). This reflects the fact that a sale can be made only to a *particular* customer or company, who then pays for that sale; a *set* of customers cannot be billed for one sale. A specific customer may, however, participate in many sales events. Similarly, the relationship between cash collections and customers is modeled as being *:1 (many cash collections can be linked to one customer). A remittance must come from some specific customer; a specific customer, however, can make many remittances.

Ashton used both of these sources of information about relationship cardinalities to develop an E–R diagram for S&S's revenue cycle. Refer back to Fig. 6.2 to see what the final E–R diagram looked like.

Organizational Specificity of E–R Diagrams

Although the development of the E–R diagram for S&S's revenue cycle was relatively straightforward and intuitive, data modeling can be a complex and repetitive process. One common source of difficulty is the use of different terminology by various users. Therefore, Focus 6.1 highlights the importance of involving the eventual users of the system in the data modeling process.

In addition, keep in mind that an E–R diagram is unique to the organization being modeled. S&S, for example, is a retail store. Consequently, it need not model the customer order and sales events separately, because they occur simultaneously. A manufacturing company, in contrast, would usually model

FOCUS 6.1

Why Involve Users in Data Modeling?

Data modeling is not an easy task, as Hewlett-Packard learned when it began designing a new data base for its accounting and finance function. A major problem was that the same term meant different things to different people. For example, accounting used the term *orders* to refer to the total dollar amount of orders per time period, whereas the sales department used the term *orders* to refer to individual customer orders. Moreover, such confusions existed even within the accounting and finance function. For example, the reporting group used the term *product* to refer to any good currently sold to customers. Thus the primary key for this entity was product-number. In contrast, the forecasting group used the term *product* to refer to goods that were often still in the planning stage and therefore did not yet have a product number assigned.

To overcome these problems, Hewlett-Packard had to get the various user groups to participate in the data modeling process. The first step was to convince all users of the need for and benefits of creating a data model for their function. Then it was necessary to define carefully the scope of the modeling effort. Hewlett-Packard found that the time invested in these early steps was well worth the effort, because they facilitated the activities of clarifying definitions and developing attribute lists that took place later in the process. The latter activity was an iterative affair involving many revisions. Documentation was crucial to this process. Each member of the modeling team and user groups had copies of the proposed lists, making it easy to spot inconsistencies in definitions.

Hewlett-Packard credits the data modeling approach as contributing significantly to the overall success of the project. Data modeling allowed the participants to concentrate first on understanding the essential business characteristics of the new system, instead of getting bogged down in specifying the contents of relational tables. This helped them to identify and resolve conflicting viewpoints early in the process, and paved the way for eventual acceptance of the resulting system. The key step, however, was in getting the various user groups to participate in the data modeling process. Otherwise, it is likely that the resulting data model would not have been accurate or widely accepted.

Focus Questions

1. Do you think that inconsistent and contradictory terminology is common across business functions? Why or why not? Do you think these differences create problems outside of implementing a new data base? Why or why not?
2. How might the use of a data modeling tool like E–R diagrams help identify inconsistencies in data models?
3. How could the data modeling process encourage accountants and other users to get more involved in data base design?

Source: C. Randall Byers and Lysa Beltz, "Financial Data Modeling at Hewlett-Packard," *Journal of Systems Management* (January 1994): 28–33.

---

these two events separately because they may often occur at different times. Similarly, whereas a retail store like S&S needs to model only one type of inventory, a manufacturing company would need to track raw materials, work-in-process, and finished goods inventories separately. Finally, most organizations model the relationship between sales and inventory as *:* to reflect the sale of mass produced goods. For a rare art dealer, however, each instance of the inventory entity is a unique original. Consequently, the relationship between sales and inventory would be modeled as 1:* because, although several different items could be sold in one transaction, each inventory item can be sold only once.

IMPLEMENTING A DATA MODEL IN A RELATIONAL DATA BASE

One benefit of using E–R diagrams and the REA model as the basis for data modeling is that the resulting data model can be easily implemented in a relational data base. We now describe the four steps involved in translating an E–R diagram into a relational data base.

Step 1: Create Tables for Each Entity and *:* Relationship

In the case of S&S's revenue cycle, nine tables would be created from the E–R diagram shown in Fig. 6.2: one for each of the seven entities (inventory, sales, salesperson, customer, cashier, cash collections, and cash) and one for each of the *:* relationships (sales–inventory, and sales–cash collections). Creating tables for each entity and for each *:* relationship ensures that the data base satisfies the requirements of normalization and therefore will not be subject to update, insert, and delete anomalies.

The title of each table should be the same as the name of the entity it represents. Tables representing *:* relationships, however, should be titled by hyphenating the names of the two linked entities. Thus, in terms of Fig. 6.2, we would create tables titled Sales–Inventory and Sales–Cash Collections to represent the *:* relationship between sales and inventory and sales and cash collections, respectively. A table should not bear the name of the relationship as it appears in the E–R diagram because several different relationships may have the same name. For example, Fig. 6.2 labels the relationship between inventory and sales to customers as *line items.* When Fig. 6.2 is expanded to include the expenditure cycle, however, the relationship between purchases from vendors and inventory would also be labeled as *line items.* Although this duplication of names would not cause a problem when reading the E–R diagram, it would make it difficult to retrieve the correct data from the system.

Step 2: Identify Attributes for Each Table

The next step is to identify attributes for inclusion in each table. Attributes, identified from interviews with management to determine what information they need, fall into two categories: primary keys and nonkey attributes. Table 6.2 shows the tables for the data model depicted in Fig. 6.2 and the attributes assigned to each table.

Assigning Primary Keys to Tables. Every table must have a primary key. Companies usually create numeric identifiers that uniquely identify specific resources, events, and agents; these numeric identifiers are good candidates for primary keys. Usually, the primary key of a table representing an entity is a single attribute. The primary key for *:* relationship tables, however, always consists of two attributes, representing the primary keys of each entity linked in that relationship. For example, the primary key of the sales–inventory table would consist of both the invoice number (the primary key of the sales entity) and item number (the primary key of the inventory entity). Such multiple-attribute primary keys are called **concatenated keys.**

Assigning Nonkey Attributes to Tables. Table 6.2 also shows the nonkey attributes associated with each table in the S&S revenue cycle data base. Some attributes, such as the date and amount of each sale, are necessary for complete and accurate transaction processing and the production of financial statements

Table 6.2 **Relational Tables for S&S's Revenue Cycle: Retail Sales (primary key in bold type, *foreign keys* in italics)**

Inventory			
Item #	Description	Cost	Price
10	Television	399	499
20	Freezer	999	1299
30	Refrigerator	899	999
40	Refrigerator	1099	1299
50	Range	599	799
60	Washer	499	599
70	Washer	599	799

Sales–Inventory				
Invoice #	**Item #**	Quantity Sold	Replacement	Age
101	10	3	Yes	6
101	30	1	Yes	7
102	60	1	No	0
103	20	1	Yes	12
103	30	2	Yes	7
103	60	1	Yes	10
104	40	3	No	0
105	30	1	Yes	6
105	60	1	No	0

Sales					
Invoice #	Date	*Salesperson #*	*Customer #*	Amount	Time
101	10/09/97	101	10001	2655	0930
102	10/10/97	102	10002	625	1045
103	10/10/97	101	10004	4295	1535
104	10/12/97	101	10001	4295	1230
105	10/13/97	102	10003	1735	1415

Salesperson			
Employee #	Name	Date hired	Salary
101	J. Buck	09/23/82	33000
102	M. Shannon	09/25/87	30000

Cashier			
Employee #	Name	Date hired	Salary
121	O. Smith	09/10/85	26000
122	T. Pagnozzi	05/18/75	32000

continued

***Table 6.2* (Continued)**

Sales – Cash Collections		
Invoice #	**Remittance #**	Amount
101	122	2655
103	123	4295
104	122	4295

Cash		
Account #	Type	Location
101	Checking	First Bank
102	Savings	First Bank

Cash_Collections					
Remittance #	Date	*Customer #*	*Cashier #*	Amount	*Account #*
122	10/28/97	10001	121	6950	101
123	10/31/97	10004	122	4295	101

Customer					
Customer #	Name	Street	City	State	Credit limit
10001	E. Banks	14 First	Chicago	IL	10000
10002	R. Santo	10 Third	St. Louis	MO	6000
10003	B. Williams	33 Left	Chicago	IL	7500
10004	G. Beckert	12 Second	Chicago	IL	3500

and managerial reports. Other nonkey attributes are stored because they facilitate the effective management of an organization's resources, events, and agents. For example, collecting a salesperson's employee number provides a means not only for calculating sales commissions but also for evaluating sales staff performance.

Chapter 5 discussed several rules that must be followed for placing attributes in tables (refer to pages 138–139). That discussion can be summarized in the following two principles:

1. Every attribute in the table must describe a characteristic about the primary key (or be foreign keys).
2. Every attribute in a table must be single-valued.

The assignment of attributes to the relational tables shown in Table 6.2 follows these two principles. Each of the seven entity tables contains only information about the object identified by the primary key. Similarly, the attributes assigned to the two *:* relationship tables also represent facts about the concatenated primary key of that table. Indeed, those attributes cannot be placed in any other table.

Consider the sales–inventory table. Each row in this table contains information about a line item in an invoice. Consequently, the Quantity Sold attribute is included here because it is a characteristic of an invoice line item. Although most of S&S's sales will involve the purchase of just one of each appliance, some customers, such as apartment owners or builders, may buy in larger quantities.

The Quantity Sold attribute cannot be included in either the sales or inventory tables because to do so would violate the rules of relational data base design and result in the types of update, insert, and delete anomaly problems that were illustrated in Figs. 5.6 and 5.7 in Chapter 5 (see pages 139–143). First, the quantity sold is not a characteristic either of the invoice number alone (the primary key of the sales table) or of just the item number of the merchandise being sold (the primary key of the inventory table), but depends on both attributes. Second, S&S, like most companies, allows customers to purchase more than one item. Consequently, even if columns for item number and quantity sold were added to the sales table, there could, and often would, be more than one value entered in those columns for a given row (invoice).

The same line of reasoning that led to placing the quantity sold attribute in the sales–inventory table underlies the placement of the attribute Amount applied in the sales–cash collections table. As explained earlier, the *:* relationship depicted in Fig. 6.2 between the sales and cash collections events indicates that S&S not only extends credit to its customers but also makes installment sales. Thus a remittance can apply to several invoices or can represent partial payment of just one invoice. The attribute Amount applied in the sales–cash collections table provides a method of tracking which portion of a remittance applies to each outstanding invoice.

Notice that price is an attribute of the inventory table. The reason is that S&S, like most retail businesses, charges the same price to all customers. Thus, if price were included in the sales–inventory table, the same value would be stored many times. But what about quantity discounts? In our example, we are assuming that S&S does not offer quantity discounts. If it did, however, the discounted price would still be a characteristic of that specific inventory item. Consequently, it would be stored as an additional attribute in the inventory table.

The prices of items, however, do change over time. The price stored in the inventory table is the *current* selling price. Storing information about price trends across time would require creating another table in addition to those shown in Table 6.2. This table would have at least four columns: inventory item#, beginning date, ending date, and price. The first three attributes would form a concatenated primary key identifying the period of time that a particular price applied to a specific item.

What about cumulative data like quantity on hand or cash account balances? These items do not need to be stored separately in the data base because the system can readily compute them whenever necessary. For example, information about the quantity sold for each item is stored in the sales–inventory table. Information about quantities purchased would be stored in a similar table linking purchases and inventory. To determine quantity on hand, the AIS would simply calculate the difference between the quantity sold and the quantity purchased. In a similar manner, the cash receipts and cash disbursements tables would contain information about cash inflows and outflows. The AIS can calculate the difference to display the current balance in the cash account.

This does not mean, however, that users would have to write queries to display quantity on hand or account balances. Individual user views (external schema) can be defined that show quantity on hand as an attribute of the inventory table and current balance as an attribute of the cash table. Those views would define those columns to be the result of executing the appropriate queries. Thus the user would see the data in the desired format, but the system would not store the redundant information. This is another example of the benefits of separating the logical and physical views of data.

Step 3: Implement 1:1 Relationships

Up to this point, only *:* relationships have been explicitly modeled in the relational data base. Relationships that are 1:1 need not be represented by separate tables, but can be implemented by means of foreign keys. Recall from Chapter 5 that a foreign key is an attribute of one entity that is itself the primary key of another entity. For example, if the attribute Customer#, which is the primary key of the customer table, is also included as an attribute in the sales table, it would be a foreign key in the sales table.

In a relational data base, 1:1 relationships between entities can be implemented by including the primary key of one entity as a foreign key in the table representing the other entity. As long as the relationship does not involve two event entities, the foreign key can be placed in either table. If the 1:1 relationship is between two event entities, however, the primary key of the event that normally occurs first should be used as a foreign key in the table for the event occurring later. For example, if the relationship between sales and cash collections were 1:1, Invoice# (the primary key of the sales table) would appear as a foreign key in the cash collections table. This modeling provides better control over changes made to the data base, because the person authorized to update the table pertaining to the subsequent event (cash collections, in this example) is not allowed to update the table storing data about the prior event (sales).

Step 4: Implement 1:* Relationships

As a general rule, 1:* relationships are also implemented in relational data bases by means of foreign keys. To do this, the primary key of the entity participating once in the relationship appears as a foreign key in the table of the entity that participates many times in that relationship. For example, in Table 6.2's depiction of S&S's revenue cycle, the primary keys of the salesperson and customer tables are included as foreign keys in the sales table. Similarly, the primary keys of the cash, customer, and cashier tables are included as primary keys in the cash collections table.

There is one exception to this general rule for implementing 1:* relationships: If the 1:* relationship involves two event entities *and* the event that normally occurs first is also the one that can participate many times in that relationship, then better internal control is provided by creating a separate table. This table will contain only two columns, each of which represents the primary key of one of the related events.

At this point the design of S&S's revenue cycle data base is almost complete. All that remains is to document the structure of the data base in the data dictionary. In the next section, we demonstrate how accounting information can be produced from an AIS based on the REA data model.

PRODUCING ACCOUNTING INFORMATION FROM THE REA DATA MODEL

Table 6.2 and Fig. 6.2 depict a data base AIS for S&S's revenue cycle that is built using the REA data model. At first glance, it may appear that a number of elements found in a traditional AIS, such as accounts receivable, journals, and ledgers, are missing. In reality, all that information is present but is stored in a different format.

Deriving Accounts Receivable

Earlier, we explained that accounts receivable is not considered a resource in the REA data model. Consequently, it does not appear in Table 6.2 or in the E–R diagram for S&S's revenue cycle (see Fig. 6.2). Now we will illustrate how to derive accounts receivable from an AIS built according to the REA data model. Keep in mind, however, the distinction between the logical and physical views of data. Users would not have to write the following queries every time they wanted to look at accounts receivable. Instead, these queries could be stored as the definition of the accounts receivable subschema. Accounts receivable data would then *appear* to be stored in a table, although no such table would physically exist.

The following two SQL queries are needed to retrieve the total amount of accounts receivable that would appear in the financial statement:

Query 1

```
SELECT   Sum (amount)
FROM     Sales
```

Query 2

```
SELECT   Sum (amount)
FROM     Sales–Cash_Collections
```

Query 1 retrieves the total amount of all sales; query 2 retrieves the total amount of all cash collections on sales. Subtracting the latter from the former yields total accounts receivable.

Retrieving the outstanding balance for a specific customer is a little more complex. The previous two SQL queries need to be modified as follows:

Query 3

```
SELECT   Sum (amount)
FROM     Sales, Customer
WHERE    Customer.Customer# = Sales.Customer# AND Name = "Moody"
```

Query 4

```
SELECT   Sum (amount)
FROM     Sales–Cash_Collections, Customer, Cash_Collections
```

```
WHERE   Customer.Customer# = Cash_Collections.Customer# AND
        Cash_Collections.Remittance# = Sales–Cash_Collections.Remittance#
        AND Name = "Moody"
```

Finally, Table 6.3 shows how to produce an aged listing of unpaid invoices.

The same principles underlying the treatment of accounts receivable apply to other accounting concepts that represent imbalances between two events. Thus a data model for S&S's expenditure cycle would not explicitly need to include a table for accounts payable. Instead, the system could be programmed to derive accounts payable by comparing the purchases and cash disbursements events. The queries would be similar to the accounts receivable examples shown in queries 1 and 2.

Journals and Ledgers

SQL queries can also be used to generate journals and ledgers from a relational data base built on the REA model. Let us consider journals first. The information normally found in a journal is stored in the tables used to record data about events. For example, Table 6.4 shows the SQL query to produce a sales journal.

Similar queries can be written to generate cash collections, purchases, or cash disbursements journals. Moreover, since these journals are no longer used to simplify the recording process, but rather to provide information about past activity, they can be modified. For example, the following SQL query would generate a "journal" of all sales, both cash and credit:

```
SELECT  Date, Name, Invoice#, Customer#, Amount
FROM    Customer, Sales
WHERE   Customer.Customer# = Sales.Customer#
```

The information traditionally contained in ledgers is often stored in a relational data base in a combination of resource, event, and agent tables. Table 6.5 (on page 188) shows various approaches to retrieving the information typically found in an accounts receivable subsidiary ledger.

Query 1 takes the approach of listing the current account balance for each customer. Queries 2–4, in contrast, retrieve the information needed to create a complete subsidiary ledger for customer number 10001, returning the details of all sales, remittances, and permanent customer data. The responses to these three queries could be saved and the DBMS report writer could then be used to present the data in the format of a traditional subsidiary ledger.

Preparing Financial Statements and Managerial Reports

SQL queries can also be written to generate the numbers that would be included in financial statements and managerial reports. We have already presented queries for calculating accounts receivable. The following queries would retrieve sales and cost of goods sold figures from Table 6.2:

To retrieve Sales

```
SELECT  Sum (amount)
FROM    Sales
```

Table 6.3 **SQL Query to Produce Aged Listing of All Unpaid Invoices**

Sales

Invoice #	Date	*Salesperson #*	*Customer #*	Amount	Time
101	10/09/97	101	10001	2655	0930
102	10/10/97	102	10002	625	1045
103	10/10/97	101	10004	4295	1535
104	10/12/97	101	10001	4295	1230
105	10/13/97	102	10003	1735	1415

Sales–Cash_Collections

Invoice #	**Remittance #**	Amount
101	122	2655
103	123	4295
104	122	4295

Customer

Customer #	Name	Street	City	State	Credit Limit
10001	E. Banks	14 First	Chicago	IL	10000
10002	R. Santo	10 Third	St. Louis	MO	6000
10003	B. Williams	33 Left	Chicago	IL	7500
10004	G. Beckert	12 Second	Chicago	IL	3500

Query: (on November 10, 1997)

```
SELECT   Name, Invoice#, Amount, Current_Date — Date
  FROM   Sales, Customer
 WHERE   Sales.Customer# = Customer.Customer# AND
         Invoice#  NOT IN
   (SELECT    Invoice#
     FROM     Sales–Cash_Collections)
```

Query Response

Name	Invoice#	Amount	Current date – date
R. Santo	102	625	31
B. Williams	105	1735	28

The nested query is executed first. This query returns a list of all sales invoices in the sales–cash_collections table (invoice numbers 101, 103, and 104). Then, the main query is executed. The sales and customer tables are linked by values in their common column (customer#), as indicated by the arrows. The WHERE clause specifies that only those rows in the sales table with invoice numbers that do *not* appear in the list retrieved by the nested query should be displayed in the answer.

***Table 6.4* SQL Query to Produce Sales Journal**

Sales					
Invoice #	Date	*Salesperson#*	*Customer#*	Amount	Time
101	10/09/97	101	10001	2655	0930
102	10/10/97	102	10002	625	1045
103	10/10/97	101	10004	4295	1535
104	10/12/97	101	10001	4295	1230
105	10/13/97	102	10003	1735	1415

Sales–Cash_Collections		
Invoice#	**Remittance#**	Amount
101	122	2655
103	123	4295
104	122	4295

Cash_Collections					
Remittance#	Date	*Customer#*	*Cashier#*	Amount	*Account#*
122	10/28/97	10001	121	6950	101
123	10/31/97	10004	122	4295	101

Customer					
Customer#	Name	Street	City	State	Credit Limit
10001	E. Banks	14 First	Chicago	IL	10000
10002	R. Santo	10 Third	St. Louis	MO	6000
10003	B. Williams	33 Left	Chicago	IL	7500
10004	G. Beckert	12 Second	Chicago	IL	3500

Query:

```
SELECT    Date, Name, Invoice#, Customer#, Amount
  FROM    Sales, Customer
WHERE     Customer.Customer# = Sales.Customer# AND   Invoice# NOT IN
    (SELECT    Invoice#
      FROM     Sale, Cash_Collections, Sales–Cash_Collections)
     WHERE     Sales.Invoice# = Sales–Cash_Collections.Invoice# AND
             Sales–Cash_Collections.Remittance# = Cash_Collections.Remittance#
             AND Sales.Date = Cash_Collections.Date)
```

The nested query returns a list of all invoices for which a remittance was received the same day. These represent cash sales (there are none in this sample data base). The main query then retrieves data from the sales and customer tables for only those invoices that do not represent cash sales. The order of column names in the SELECT clause specifies how to format the answer:

Query Response				
Date	Name	Invoice#	Customer#	Amount
10/09/97	E. Banks	101	10001	2655
10/10/97	R. Santo	102	10002	625
10/10/97	G. Beckert	103	10004	4295
10/12/97	E. Banks	104	10001	4295
10/13/97	B. Williams	105	10003	1735

Table 6.5 SQL Queries to Create Accounts Receivable Subsidiary Ledger

Query 1

```
SELECT   Customer#, Sum (amount)
FROM     Sales
WHERE    Invoice# NOT IN
             (SELECT Invoice#
              FROM   Sales–Cash_Collections)
```

Response to Query 1	
Customer#	**sum (amount)**
10002	625
10003	1735

Query 2

```
SELECT   Date, Invoice#, Amount
FROM     Sales
WHERE    Customer# = 10001
```

Response to Query 2		
Date	**Invoice#**	**Amount**
10/09/97	101	2655
10/12/97	104	4295

Query 3

```
SELECT   Date, Remittance#, Amount
FROM     Cash_Collections
WHERE    Customer# = 10001
```

Response to Query 3		
Date	**Invoice#**	**Amount**
10/28/97	122	6950

Query 4

```
SELECT   All
FROM     Customer
WHERE    Customer# = 10001
```

Response to Query 4					
Customer#	**Name**	**Street**	**City**	**State**	**Credit limit**
10001	E. Banks	14 First	Chicago	IL	10000

To retrieve Cost of Goods Sold

```
SELECT   Sum (cost*quantity sold)
FROM     Inventory, Sales–Inventory
WHERE    Inventory.Item# = Sales–Inventory.Item#
```

Notice that the data model shown in Table 6.2 integrates nonfinancial and financial data in the AIS and makes both types of data easily accessible for use in managerial decision making. For example, one of the attributes in the sales table is the time that the sale occurred. Scott and Susan can use this data element to track sales activity during different times of the day, in order to better plan staffing needs. The sales–inventory table also includes two useful nonfinancial attributes: whether the purchase is a replacement or the first-time acquisition of a product, and the age of the appliance being replaced. Scott and Susan can use these data elements to improve their marketing efforts. For example, Scott and Susan can calculate the average frequency with which their customers replace appliances and then mail customized advertisements describing the models and prices currently available at S&S to those customers approaching replacement decisions regarding appliances.

Finally, the S&S revenue cycle data base shown in Table 6.2 can also be easily expanded to integrate data from external sources. For example, to better evaluate customer credit status, Scott and Susan may decide to collect information from a credit rating agency, such as Dun & Bradstreet. This information could be added to the data base by creating additional columns in the customer table to store the customer's credit rating. A similar process could be used to append information to the vendor table that could be used in the vendor selection process.

Effect of the REA Data Model on Accounting

The SQL queries presented earlier in this section demonstrate that accounting is not limited to the traditional double-entry model with its journals, ledgers, and chart of accounts. Instead, accounting is a process or system for collecting and disseminating information about the business transactions engaged in by an organization. The means by which those objectives are accomplished, however, may change with new developments in information processing technology. Indeed, Focus 6.2 suggests that there may be some significant changes in store for *how* accounting is accomplished in many organizations. Nevertheless, although the *mechanics* of accounting may change, the need for the results (managerial reports and financial statements) of accounting remains.

INTERNAL CONTROL CONSIDERATIONS

The use of a data base AIS does not change the need for a sound internal control structure. The organization still needs to ensure the following:

1. That transaction data are processed accurately and that the information produced from the data base is reliable.
2. That business activities are performed efficiently and in accordance with management policies and regulatory requirements.
3. That the data base, and other organizational assets, are safeguarded.

The use of a data base does, however, affect the risks of internal control problems. For example, since the data base is used by many people in the organization, the effects of errors are more widespread. In addition, the availability of easy-to-use query languages increases the risk of unauthorized access to data. On the other hand, data base systems also provide the capability for dealing with such internal control threats more effectively than is possible in traditional manual or file-based AIS.

FOCUS 6.2

The Changing Nature of Accounting at IBM

In 1979 IBM used 315 separate worldwide accounting systems to support six accounting applications: general ledger, fixed assets, intracompany and intercompany transactions, accounts receivable, and accounts payable. During the 1980s IBM worked to consolidate these systems and, by the end of 1991, had reduced the number of separate accounting systems to 36. The remaining systems, however, still were not flexible enough to support the kind of companywide decision making that IBM desired. Consequently, IBM set out to completely overhaul its accounting processes.

IBM began by rethinking and redesigning the way business processes are performed from the ground up, instead of merely applying new technology to existing processes. A major component of this change involved expanding the transaction-driven orientation of existing accounting systems to incorporate nonfinancial measures of business activities. The objective was to fully integrate financial and nonfinancial information so that both could be used in decision making. IBM also integrated information technology within the business processes so that data are recorded in real time, as the events unfolded. The final part of the solution involved realigning ownership of the data, so that the company will now be responsible for developing the corporate data model, specifying which data need to be recorded for each event, and providing the appropriate information retrieval tools to users. Relieved of these duties, functional managers will now be responsible for ensuring that the appropriate data about each event are recorded and that adequate controls are in place. Individual users are then responsible for using the company-provided tools to retrieve the information they need.

The Relational Data Model and Data Base Accuracy

The design constraints of a relational data base that were discussed in Chapter 5 (pp. 138–139) help to ensure the accuracy and reliability of the information contained therein. For example, following the principles of normalization results in well-structured tables that are free from update, insert, and delete anomalies. The entity integrity rule, which requires that every primary key be non-null, ensures that all data entered in the system can later be retrieved.

The referential integrity rule, which requires that every non-null foreign key must represent the value of a primary key in another table, is especially helpful for ensuring accurate transaction processing. To see how, consider the sales table in Table 6.2. If both the salesperson and customer number attributes are defined to be foreign keys, then the referential integrity rule ensures that the following types of errors cannot occur:

- *Recording a sale to a customer who is not listed in the customer table.* The system would not accept entry of a sales invoice that contains a customer number that is not one of the primary keys in the customer table. Notice that this control prevents making a credit sale and not collecting the information needed to bill that customer.
- *Recording a sale made by a nonexistent salesperson.* As was the case with customer number, the system would not accept entry of a sales invoice that contains a salesperson number that is not one of the primary keys of the salesperson table. This restriction ensures that all salespeople receive proper credit for their work efforts.

IBM has used this procedure to merge four previously separate fund disbursement processes (payroll, travel expense, miscellaneous expense reimbursement, and time and attendance recording) into one integrated process. IBM estimates that the project will save more than $300 million over 10 years, while reducing the time required to process claims by 65% to 70%!

These changes dramatically affect the roles of the accounting staff and the controller. Most of the projected cost savings in the reimbursement project come from eliminating clerical jobs and redundant systems. Indeed, an internal study at IBM suggests that almost 60% of the work done by the accounting staff is clerical in nature and can therefore be eliminated. The controller becomes a key player in redesigning the AIS by identifying redundant processes and suggesting ways to use information technology to perform tasks more efficiently, while maintaining adequate controls. At the same time, the controller's responsibility expands to include nonfinancial as well as financial data. Consequently, the controller and the accounting staff become more involved in the company's strategic decision-making process.

Focus Questions

1. If the type of changes made by IBM reduce the size of the accounting staff, how will the controller retain and expand his or her influence?
2. If the manager of each business process is now responsible for both recording appropriate data and ensuring that adequate controls exist, how does this affect the role of the controller? How does it affect the role of the internal audit function?

Source: From David P. Andros, J. Owen Cherrington, and Eric L. Denna, "Reengineering Your Accounting, The IBM Way," *Financial Executive* (July/August 1992): 28–31.

These are just two of the control procedures that need to be included in a data base AIS. In Chapter 14 we discuss in more detail many additional types of control procedures that must be included in an AIS to ensure that the information produced is both accurate and reliable.

Minimum Cardinalities and Internal Control

Figure 6.2 depicted only the maximum relationship cardinalities for S&S's revenue cycle. Although information about maximum cardinalities is sufficient for designing a well-structured data base, including information about minimum cardinalities can help ensure that the design includes adequate internal controls. Information about minimum cardinalities helps focus the DBA's attention on implementing the organization's rules concerning how business activities should be performed. Moreover, an E–R diagram that contains both maximum and minimum relationship cardinalities helps auditors to assess the quality of internal controls in a data base AIS.

Figure 6.6 shows an enhanced E–R diagram for S&S's revenue cycle that includes both maximum and minimum relationship cardinalities. Next to each entity is a pair of symbols: (minimum cardinality, maximum cardinality). Let us see what this information reveals about S&S's business policies and internal control procedures by examining the three basic types of relationships: (1) event–event, (2) event–agent, and (3) event–resource.

Event–Event Relationships. Figure 6.6 depicts only one event–event relationship, that between sales and cash collections. The minimum cardinality of

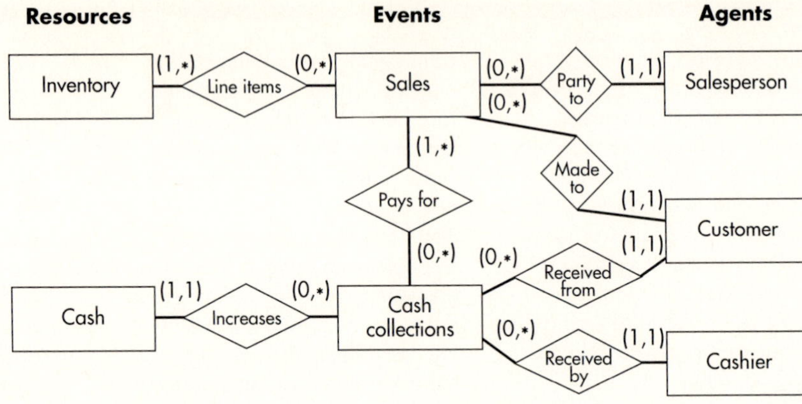

Figure 6.6

E–R Diagram for S&S's Revenue Cycle Including Minimum Cardinalities

the sales event is 1, indicating that every cash collection event must be linked to at least one sales event. This ensures that any payments mistakenly sent to S&S will be returned to the customer. The minimum cardinality of the cash collections event, however, is zero. This represents the fact that at any point in time, customers may not yet have paid for all their credit sales.

Indeed, for purposes of sound internal control, the following rule should be followed when modeling the minimum cardinalities of any event–event relationship:

> *The minimum cardinality of the first event is 1; the minimum cardinality of the subsequent event is zero.*

This rule helps ensure the legitimacy of subsequent events. To see this, consider the sequence of events related to the purchase of and payment for merchandise inventory. Clearly, the organization does not want to authorize payment for goods that it has not purchased and received, so each cash disbursement event must be linked to at least one receipt of inventory. Thus the minimum cardinality of the preceding event must be 1. On the other hand, the organization may not wish to pay for all deliveries immediately, to better control its cash flow. Consequently, at any point in time, not all inventory receipts are paid for. Thus the minimum cardinality of the subsequent event is zero.

Event–Agent Relationships. Figure 6.6 depicts four event–agent relationships. Notice that in each case, the minimum cardinality associated with the agent entity is 1. This reflects the fact that every event must involve either or both internal and external agents. Indeed, there is another important internal control principle:

> *In modeling event–agent relationships, the minimum cardinality of the agent entity is 1.*

This rule ensures that all events are legitimate. To see this, consider what could happen if the minimum cardinality associated with customers is zero in the sales–customer relationship. It would mean that a sale could be recorded, even though it was not made to any specific customer! Clearly, allowing this would seriously compromise the accuracy and reliability of the data base.

In contrast, the minimum cardinality associated with the event entities in event–agent relationships can be either zero or 1, depending on the wishes of management and the nature of the event. For example, in Fig. 6.6, the minimum cardinality associated with the sales event entity in the sales–customer relationship is zero. This reflects S&S's policy of collecting and maintaining data about both actual and potential customers. If, however, S&S decided to keep information only about actual customers, then the minimum cardinality associated with the sales event in the sales–customer relationship would be 1. On the other hand, the minimum cardinality associated with the cash collections event must be zero, because some, but hopefully not very many, customers may not pay for their purchases. Finally, the minimum cardinality associated with the event entities in the relationships with internal agents (salesperson and cashier) is zero, because it is possible that an employee may not have participated in any events. Of course, if such a situation continued for long, Scott and Susan might be forced to reevaluate the need for that employee.

Event–Resource Relationships. Figure 6.6 depicts two event–resource relationships. In both cases, the minimum cardinality associated with the resource entity is 1. Indeed, there is a third general rule for modeling minimum cardinalities:

> *In an event–resource relationship, the minimum cardinality of the resource relationship is 1.*

This rule reflects the fact that every event must involve the acquisition, use, or disposal of some resource. For example, a sale must involve at least one inventory item. On the other hand, the minimum cardinality associated with the event entity in event–resource relationships may be zero. This reflects the possibility that a particular resource object may not be involved in any events. For example, S&S could be stuck with some types of appliances that it cannot sell to any customer.

Other Control Information

Auditors can also use E–R diagrams to obtain other information about controls included in a data base AIS. For example, they can use E–R diagrams to write queries to identify all actions performed by an employee (internal agent). This information can then be analyzed to assess whether there is adequate segregation of duties. In addition, examination of E–R diagrams can help identify whether any individual external schemas create problems concerning access to sensitive data.

We have only touched on some of the basic concepts of internal control. Additional details about internal control are provided in Chapters 13 and 14.

SUMMARY AND CASE CONCLUSION

Designing a data base involves six steps: planning, requirements definition, logical design, physical design, implementation, and operation. Accountants should participate in the data modeling activities that occur during steps two and three, because of their extensive knowledge of transaction processing requirements, internal controls, and general business functions.

One way to perform the activities of requirements definition and conceptual design is to build a data model of the AIS. The REA accounting data model is developed specifically for building a data base AIS. The REA model classifies data into three basic categories: resources, events, and agents. The REA model can be documented in the form of an E–R diagram, which shows the entities about which data are collected and highlights the important relationships among them. The cardinalities of the relationships depicted in E–R diagrams also provide information about the basic business policies followed by the company.

A data model documented in an E–R diagram can be readily implemented in a relational DBMS. This involves four steps. First, tables are created for all entities and *:* relationships in the E–R diagram. Second, primary keys and nonkey attributes are assigned to each table. Third, 1:1 relationships are implemented by means of foreign keys. Fourth, 1:* relationships are implemented by means of foreign keys and separate tables.

Ashton Fleming followed these steps to implement a data base AIS for S&S's revenue cycle. He drew Fig. 6.2 to represent his understanding of the in-store sales and cash collections procedures followed at S&S. After validating this E–R diagram with Scott and Susan, Ashton created the relational tables shown in Table 6.2. He then demonstrated how SQL queries could be written to retrieve a variety of managerial reports, as well as financial statements, from the relational DBMS. Scott and Susan were quite impressed and eagerly anticipated Ashton extending the data base to encompass all of S&S's business activities.

KEY TERMS

requirements definition
logical design
physical design
data modeling
REA data model
resources
events
agents
Entity–Relationship (E–R) diagram
cardinality
concatenated keys

CHAPTER QUIZ

1. Which documentation tool provides information about a company's business policies?
a. The REA model
b. An E–R diagram
c. A DFD
d. SQL

2. Which of the following is not a resource in an REA data model?
a. Cash
b. Accounts receivable
c. Inventory
d. Equipment

3. Which of the following is not considered an entity in an E–R diagram?
a. Sales
b. Sales line items
c. Customers
d. Inventory

4. Which type of relationship *must* be implemented as a separate table in a relational data base?
a. 1:1
b. *:1
c. 1:*
d. *:*

5. Which of the following is least likely to be modeled as an event in an REA data model?
a. Customer orders
b. Customer payments
c. Receipt of vendor invoices
d. Shipping merchandise to customers

6. If a company pays for each of its purchases by invoice and does not make installment payments, the relationship between cash disbursements and purchases would be modeled as
a. 1:1.
b. 1:*.
c. *:1.
d. *:*.

7. An E–R diagram shows a relationship between the sales approval and shipment events. The company's policy is to ship merchandise to customers only after the sale has been approved. To describe this policy in the E–R diagram, the minimum cardinality associated with the sales approval event in that relationship should be
a. 1.
b. 0.
c. *.
d. not determinable.

8. If vendor number appears as an attribute in the purchases table, it is an example of a
a. primary key.
b. secondary key.
c. foreign key.
d. record key.

9. Which activities are performed as part of data modeling?
a. Requirements definition and physical design
b. Physical design and logical design
c. Physical design, implementation, and operation
d. Requirements definition and logical design

10. A company wants to maintain information about alternative vendors, even though it has not purchased anything from them yet. To document this policy in an E–R diagram, the minimum cardinality associated with the purchases event in the purchases–vendors relationship would be
a. 0.
b. 1.
c. *.
d. not determinable.

DISCUSSION QUESTIONS

6.1 It has been argued that advances in information technology, especially the development of DBMS, have made the double-entry model of accounting obsolete. Specifically, the ability of the computer to sort and summarize transaction data quickly and accurately has made the practice of maintaining ledgers in order to produce periodic reports unnecessary. Indeed, financial reports can now be produced at any time. What are the likely effects of these types of changes on the nature of accounting jobs in the future?

6.2 Traditional accounting systems are based on the chart of accounts, which establishes one predetermined basis for organizing and summarizing transaction data. How does the REA data model provide more flexibility in meeting the information needs of various decision makers?

6.3 The data base developed for S&S's revenue cycle did not explicitly include a table for accounts receivable because that information could be derived from the sales and cash collections tables. Although this approach minimizes data redundancy, can you think of any reasons that a separate table should be created solely for storing information about accounts receivable?

6.4 A criticism of traditional accounting systems is that data are stored at too high a level of aggregation (summarization). That is, transaction data are recorded at the individual event level in journals but once posted to ledgers the data are kept in summarized form. Thus users can easily obtain information at only three levels of aggregation: (1) individual transactions (from the journals or transaction files), (2) totals for a particular account for a particular time period (by summarizing transaction activity), or (3) the cumulative balance in the ledger accounts. In contrast, one objective of the REA model and the events-based approach is to store accounting data at a less aggregated level. How important is this objective in meeting user needs? Are the three levels of aggregation provided by the traditional AIS sufficient to support all of an organization's information needs? Why or why not?

6.5 The traditional chart of accounts stores only financial information about transactions. One objective of the REA accounting model is to facilitate the integration of financial and nonfinancial information. Is it necessary to abandon the chart of accounts to accomplish this objective? Why or why not? (*Hint:* Think about how operational data, such as average time to fill and ship customer orders, can be stored in an AIS that uses the chart of accounts.)

6.6 Relational DBMS query languages provide easy access to information about the organization's activities. Does this mean that on-line real-time processing should be used for all transactions? Are real-time financial reports needed by an organization? Why or why not?

PROBLEMS

6.1 Revise the E–R diagram in Fig. 6.6 to include the following:

a. Sales calls on corporate customers. Assume that not every call results in a sale, but that Scott and Susan want to record data about each call in order to evaluate sales staff effectiveness.

b. Delivery of merchandise to customers. Assume that deliveries are scheduled weekly so that one delivery to a customer could include merchandise from several sales transactions. Also assume that deliveries occur independently of the cash collections event. For example, sometimes products are delivered after the customer has paid for the merchandise, but other times deliveries occur before payment is collected.

6.2 Develop an REA data model for S&S's payroll and human resource management needs and express that model in the form of an E–R diagram. Then create a set of relational tables, complete with attributes, to implement your model. Put yourself in Scott and Susan's place: What information about your employees do you need to collect and analyze?

6.3 The following information describes S&S's expenditure cycle in terms of purchasing inventory. The three principal events are: (1) ordering of merchandise from vendors, (2) receipt of merchandise from vendors, and (3) payment of vendors for merchandise ordered and received. For the first two events, Scott and Susan wish to track the performance of their purchasing agents and receiving dock workers. Scott and Susan sign all checks. Vendor invoices are received for each delivery of inventory and are paid when due.

REQUIRED

a. Develop an REA model for S&S's expenditure cycle and draw a corresponding E–R diagram for this model.

b. Develop a set of relational tables to implement your data model. Specify each table's primary key and list several other nonkey attributes that should be included as well.

6.4 Develop a data model of S&S's expenditure cycle activities related to the acquisition of office equipment and other fixed assets. Assume that S&S makes installment payments for most fixed asset acquisitions but occasionally pays for some equipment in full at the time of purchase.

REQUIRED

a. Draw an E–R diagram of your data model.

b. Develop a set of relational tables that implements your data model. Specify each table's primary key and list several other nonkey attributes that should also be included in each table.

6.5 S&S has incorporated and issued shares of common stock.

REQUIRED

a. Modify Fig. 6.6 to reflect this change in structure. Be sure to include both the inflow of funds from the initial sale of S&S's stock and the outflow of funds in the form of dividends to those shareholders.

b. Develop a set of relational tables to implement these modifications. Specify the primary key for each table and list several other nonkey attributes that should also be included. Use your own judgment in selecting which attributes of common stock transactions should be collected and stored.

6.6 Provide an example (in terms of companies with which you are familiar) for each of the business situations described by the following relationship cardinalities:

a. Sales (1, *) to cash collections (0, *)

b. Sales (0, 1) to inventory (1, 1)

c. Purchases (1, *) to cash disbursements (0, *)
d. Purchases (1, *) to cash disbursements (0, 1)
e. Purchases (1, 1) to cash disbursements (0, *)
f. Employees (1, *) to departments (1, 1)
g. Purchases (1, *) to inventory_receipts (0, 1)

6.7 Model the cardinalities of the following business policies:

a. The sales–cash collection relationship for installment sales
b. The sales–cash collection relationship at most self-service gasoline stations
c. The customer order-sales relationship in a situation where sometimes several shipments are required to fill an order because some items were out of stock
d. The sales–inventory relationship for a custom home builder

6.8 The following tables and attributes exist in a relational data base. Assume that all purchases are paid for in full by one check.

Table	**Attributes**
Vendor	Vendor#, Name, Street_Address, City, State, Rating
Purchases	P.O.#, Date, Amount, Vendor#, Purchasing_Agent
Cash_Disbursed	Check#, Date, Amount
Purchases–Cash_Disbursed	Check#, P.O.#

REQUIRED

Write SQL queries to retrieve the following information. (*Hint:* You may need to write more than one query to arrive at the answer to some of these questions.)

a. Total accounts payable
b. Accounts payable owed to Micro-Electronics, Incorporated
c. The number of purchases made from Easy-Way
d. A list of all vendors rated "Superior"
e. The total dollar amounts purchased from each vendor
f. The largest purchase order completed by Frank Tolliver (a purchasing agent)
g. A list of all unpaid purchase orders

6.9 Refer to Table 6.2 to answer the following questions.

REQUIRED

a. What would the following SQL queries display?

```
1. SELECT      Sum (amount), Customer#
   FROM        Sales
   GROUP BY    Customer#
2. SELECT      Description, Customer.Name
   FROM        Inventory, Customer, Sales,
               Sales–Inventory
   WHERE       Customer.Customer# =
               Sales_Customer# AND
               Sales_Invoice# =
               Sales–Inventory.Invoice#
               AND Inventory_Item# =
               Sales–Inventory.Item# AND
               Customer.Name = 'R. Santo'
```

b. Write an SQL query to determine the number of televisions sold.

c. Write an SQL query to determine the quantity sold of each inventory item.

CASE 6.1: ANYCOMPANY, INC.—AN ONGOING COMPREHENSIVE CASE

Identify a local company (you may use the same company that you identified in Case 1.1) and study its revenue and expenditure cycles.

1. Develop an REA model for both cycles, using an E–R diagram for documentation.
2. Develop a set of relational tables to implement your data model. Interview management and employees to determine which attributes should be included in your model.

CASE 6.2: PRACTICAL DATA BASE DESIGN

Hands-on practice in data base design is important. Implement either the basic data model for S&S's revenue cycle that was presented in this chapter, or one of the enhanced data models from homework problems 1–5, or some combination thereof, using a relational DBMS. Then, perform the following tasks:

1. Create a user view of accounts receivable that is based on data stored in other tables.
2. Create a user view for sales order entry that includes information about quantity on hand of inventory items.
3. Write queries to develop an income statement and a balance sheet from your data base (or at least those portions of each statement that are included in your data model).

ANSWERS TO CHAPTER QUIZ

1. b **3.** b **5.** c **7.** a **9.** d
2. b **4.** d **6.** a **8.** c **10.** a

P A R T   T W O

Chapter 7

A Review of Computer Hardware and Software

LEARNING OBJECTIVES

After studying this chapter, you should be able to:

- Explain why accountants must understand computer concepts.
- Differentiate among supercomputers, mainframes, minicomputers, and microcomputers.
- Explain how the three components of a CPU function and how data are represented in a computer.
- Compare and contrast the secondary storage devices used in computer systems.
- Compare and contrast the input and output devices used in computer systems.
- Compare and contrast the different levels of hardware and computer languages.
- Identify the functions and purposes of the different types of systems and application software.

Integrative Case: S&S, Inc.

Scott is delighted that S&S is progressing toward a computerized system. His reaction was evident at a meeting with Ashton and Kimberly Serra, the manager of a local computer firm. Ashton set up the meeting after he was asked to begin investigating a computerized AIS.

It is evident to Scott that Ashton has a good grasp of how S&S operates. For several weeks Ashton has used every spare minute to analyze S&S's information needs and document its current system. In the meeting Ashton explained S&S's system and identified what he wants the system to do. Kimberly pointed out several additional capabilities. Scott and Ashton left the meeting with a list of ideas and things to investigate.

The next day Scott calls Ashton into his office to tell him he wants to be more involved in the system acquisition process. Scott confides that his initial reluctance had to do with his lack of knowledge about computers. His only exposure to them was a college class a number of years ago. Scott comments he understood much of what went on in the meeting, but when Ashton and Kimberly began talking about computers, it was like they had switched to a foreign language. Scott asks Ashton to bring him some material that will help him get up to speed on computer technology so that he is better able to understand basic computer concepts. Scott also has the following questions:

1. Which size computer system does S&S need: a mainframe, minicomputer, or personal computer?
2. Which storage medium should S&S use: hard disks, optical disks, tapes, or floppy disks? Which input and output devices?
3. What do all the acronyms stand for that he and Kimberly used—terms like CPU, ROM, RAM, MIPS, POS, UPC, 4GL, and DBMS? How much is a megabyte? How fast is a nanosecond?

4. What is the difference between systems and application software?
5. Which software does S&S need? What exactly do software programs do?

INTRODUCTION

Many accountants are like Scott Parry. They think people are speaking a foreign language when they begin to talk about computers. Accountants who do not understand the terminology of computers, or the "computer language," may encounter difficulty when it comes to understanding an AIS. Although they need not be technical experts, most accountants need to understand what computers are, what they are composed of, how they operate, and how they store and process data. This understanding helps them use, develop, evaluate, and manage an AIS.

Accountants need to understand computer concepts for five key reasons. First, they are system users. Most employers expect accounting students to have a high degree of personal computer (PC) proficiency before they come to work. Most new hires receive a PC and are expected to know how to use it to access and analyze corporate data. Accountants also need to know how to use the computer as a stand-alone system to satisfy their own information needs on a timely basis, without having to wait for the assistance of their programming staff. This allows programmers to concentrate on the complex, multiuser AIS needed by large organizations. It has also made computer power available to those without programming staffs. "Taking computer power to the people" has resulted in an explosive growth in microcomputers and personal productivity tools such as word processors, spreadsheets, graphics, and data bases.

Second, information technology is a very powerful agent of change and is transforming the way business is conducted and companies operate. Companies that take advantage of new advancements and participate in the technological revolution are getting smarter, leaner, and closer to the customer, and they are capturing important competitive advantages. Companies that lag behind will be unable to compete; they will have to scramble to catch up or they will go out of business. Accountants must be major players in this technological revolution or they too will be unable to compete. They must play a major role in systems development as members of AIS design and acquisition teams. An understanding of hardware and software concepts is essential in determining system requirements.

Third, accountants are AIS evaluators. Both internal and external auditors assess the strengths and weaknesses of an AIS. In doing so, they evaluate systems on the basis of criteria such as the adequacy of their internal controls and the effectiveness and usefulness of the overall system. It is difficult to assess systems effectively without an understanding of hardware and software concepts.

Fourth, accountants often manage computer resources. They may oversee the purchase of the systems, supervise those who use them, and evaluate the use of computer resources.

Finally, accountants will earn more if they are computer literate. A recent survey showed that college graduates in 1991 earned over 50% more than high school graduates. Princeton economist Alan Kruegar found that over 40% of the increase was due to their knowledge of computers.

The three chapters in Section II will provide you with an understanding of systems terminology and technology. This chapter is divided into two main sections: hardware and software. It emphasizes *what* computers are and *how* they work. The intent is to help you learn to speak "computerese." Chapter 8 explains end-user computing and discusses its impact on an AIS, and Chapter 9 discusses data communications and advanced systems.

SECTION A: COMPUTER HARDWARE

Computer hardware is the physical equipment that performs the electronic data processing (EDP) tasks of a computer system. It includes the central processing unit (CPU) and the **peripherals,** the input, output, storage, and telecommunications devices. Figure 7.1 shows the various data preparation, input, processing, storage, data communications, and output devices.

The speed, power, and storage capacities of computers have increased dramatically while their size and cost have decreased. For example, the first computers were capable of processing hundreds of instructions per second; current computers can process hundreds of millions of instructions per second. Storage capacity has expanded from thousands to billions of characters. The cost of executing a million instructions has fallen from $10 to less than a tenth of a cent. Early computers filled a whole room; modern computers can fit in the palm of your hand.

The features of the modern computer were first proposed in 1834, by Charles Babbage. However, in 1842 the British prime minister labeled the calculating machine "worthless" and the government refused further support of Babbage's invention. More than one hundred years later the British realized what a powerful tool they had passed on, and in 1991 they spent $600,000 to build the engine from Babbage's original design. That "computer" is 6 feet high and 10 feet long, contains 4000 parts, and weighs 3 tons.

COMPUTER CLASSIFICATIONS: FROM SUPERCOMPUTERS TO MICROCOMPUTERS

Computers have been classified into four main categories based on their size and power: supercomputers, mainframes, minicomputers, and microcomputers. Power is measured by speed, memory capacity, computational power, and the number of users and peripherals the computer can support.

Supercomputer. **Supercomputers** are used for high-speed, number-crunching military and scientific tasks. They have enormous storage capacities and are up to 10 times faster than mainframes. Recently, smaller supercomputers have been developed using powerful microprocessor chips. These supercomputers are small enough to sit by a desk, although they are only half as fast as their larger "cousins."

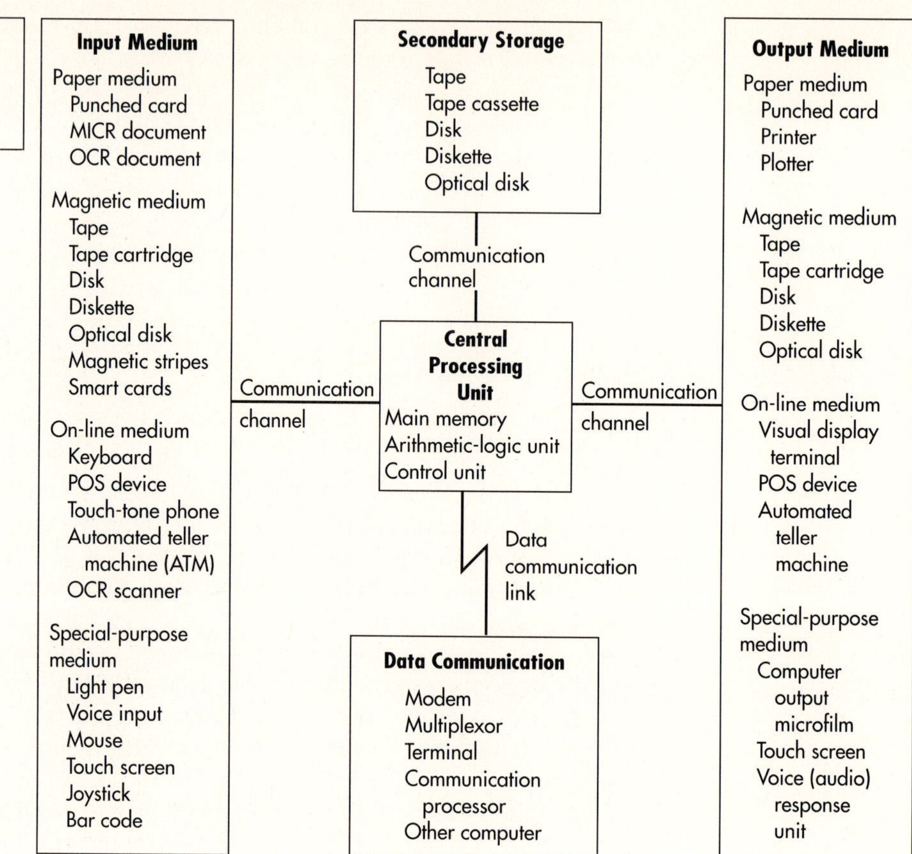

Figure 7.1

Computer Hardware

Mainframe Computer. **Mainframe computers** are used extensively in business because they provide the speed and power needed to handle large and complex tasks. They can process millions of transactions a day in hundreds of different programs and respond to and coordinate hundreds of peripherals simultaneously. In addition to their higher performance and throughput, mainframe hardware and software is more reliable than that found in networks of PCs. Mainframes are so complex, in fact, that they require professional programmers, operators, and analysts. Mainframes and peripherals are housed in a controlled room called the **data processing center.**

Minicomputer. **Minicomputers** are larger and more powerful than microcomputers and smaller and less powerful than mainframes. Minicomputers and mainframes often come in a family of compatible computers that differ mainly in size and capacity. Such cross-usage allows a company to start off small and then upgrade within the family as its needs increase. Moreover, minicomputers function in an ordinary office environment and do not need air-conditioning, special wiring, or a staff of computer experts, as do mainframes. Many organizations use them to handle all their data processing tasks. Other minicomputers are connected to mainframes to assist with time-consuming input and output tasks and telecommunications networks.

Many organizations are **downsizing** their AIS (shifting data processing from larger to smaller computers). Their old systems, which use dated technologies, do not provide adequate access to managerial information, are unresponsive to new business directions, and are difficult to maintain and enhance. Downsizing also saves money and allows users to become more involved in processing. The trend toward smaller systems has accelerated such that some accountants predict that as much as 75% of accounting data will be processed by desktop computers in the next few years. As downsizing continues, the use of mainframes and minicomputers to coordinate and facilitate the interchange of data within a network of powerful microcomputers will increase. For example, Texas Instruments has downsized from 37 large data centers scattered around the world to a single data center and smaller, distributed systems in most departments. The company's 62,000 employees now use over 50,000 personal computers and minicomputers at 344 sites around the world. This change allowed the company to realize annual savings of over $23 million.

Microcomputer. **Microcomputers** range in size from a "computer on a chip" to a typewriter-sized, desktop unit. The first microcomputer, the Altair 8800, was introduced in 1975 and sold for $650. In 1977 the Apple II, Commodore Pet, and Tandy TRS-80 computers were introduced. In 1979 three major software products significantly increased the attractiveness of the micro: Visicalc, a spreadsheet; dBASE II, a data base; and WordStar, a word processor. Users now had a desktop computer and software that processed columns of numbers and written text and stored and retrieved data in an organized fashion. IBM introduced its **personal computer (PC)** in 1981 and it soon became the industry standard. IBM estimated sales of 250,000 over a five-year period; by 1983 they were selling 250,000 a month. Suddenly, microcomputers were no longer toys for hobbyists but powerful business tools.

If the automobile and airline industries had progressed as fast as the computer industry, a Mercedes-Benz would now cost $2.00, travel 10,000 miles per hour, and get three million miles per gallon. A Boeing 767 would cost $400 and could circle the globe in 150 minutes on 4 gallons of fuel. These figures reflect reductions in cost, increases in speed, and decreases in energy consumption analogous to those undergone by computers. As a result, today's PCs have as much processing speed as a 1980s mainframe costing millions of dollars. In fact, home video cameras have more processing power than the IBM 360 that initiated the mainframe era. The Sega Saturn game system uses a processor with higher performance capabilities than the original Cray supercomputer built 20 years ago.

Microcomputers are classified according to use: pocket, hand-held, pen-based, notebook, subnotebook, laptop, portable, transportable, desktop, and floor standing. Movable microcomputers (from pocket to portable) are appealing because they can be used almost anywhere. PCs have been classified according to where and how they are used: home, personal, professional, workstation, and multiuser, the latter being powerful microcomputers designed to

FOCUS 7.1

Future Fashion in Personal Computing Is Intimate "Hardwear"

If a one-pound laptop sounds like the last word in computing style, I have news for you. The next wave is intimate computing; and the ultrahip won't carry their computers, they will wear them. A coming "hardwear" revolution will deliver everything from goggle/display combinations to chips embedded in our clothes. These devices will delight consumers and become important business tools.

So why would anyone wear a screen on his face? Imagine you are an aircraft mechanic working in the wheel well of a 747, and you need to refer to your manual for a wiring sequence. Instead of getting in your jeep and driving to your office to look it up, you flip a small head-mounted display over one eye and, talking into a small boom microphone, you call up an image from an optical disk spinning in a Walkman-size computer on your belt. Thanks to peculiarities in our binocular vision, you can still see your work even as the image hangs in space the size of a normal screen viewed from reading distance.

Everything in this vision can be done today with off-the-shelf hardware. One start-up, Reddy Systems, has already mocked up the CD ROM unit just described. Wearable computers will appear first on the belts of field maintenance professionals and then spread into other deskless, information-intensive jobs. For example, Long Island Lighting technicians strap a 7-pound 487 computer with a 270-MB hard drive to their belts. They wear a headset with a display unit that fits over the eyes and a microphone that carries verbal commands by digital wireless communication to a remote computer. The device contains all of the printed manuals they need to install or repair equipment.

Wearing a computer may sound like a strange thing to do, but we already do it today with electronic watches and tiny pagers. A decade from now executives may feel naked without their electronic "information exoskeletons," and softwear goggles may be de rigueur accessories for fashion-conscious teens.

Focus Questions

1. Use your imagination and creative skills to look into the future. What new and exciting ways do you see computer technology being used?
2. How can accountants make use of this type of technology?
3. How could students and educational institutions make use of this technology?

Source: "The Latest in Fashion," *Information Week* (April 25, 1994): 20; Alison L. Sprout, "Reality Boost," *Fortune* (March 21, 1994): 93; Paul Saffo, "Future Tense," *InfoWorld* (December 9, 1991): 77.

---

support several users at a time. Focus 7.1 discusses another classification, referred to as "wearable" computers.

Avis and Hertz use hand-held computers to print customer receipts and to speed car returns. Otis Elevator uses hand-held computers to communicate with repair personnel. Now, when workers are paged, they do not have to climb out of an elevator shaft and find a telephone to call the office. Instead, the computer displays instructions on its two-line screen.

A new type of hand-held computer, called a **personal digital assistant (PDA),** is expected to have a big impact. For example, Prudential Insurance bought 10,000 of Sharp's Wizard for its agents. Holiday Inn is having its frequent guests test Herbie, a PDA that helps customers make travel plans. Travelers tell Herbie where they want to go and the PDA uses a cellular phone to dial into a computer reservation system to find the lowest cost airfare and car rentals. Herbie also books travelers into the nearest Holiday Inn.

Another recent advancement is a pen-based computer that allows users to interface with the computer without using a keyboard or a mouse. Instead, data are entered by writing directly on the screen with a penlike device called a **stylus.** The Alabama State Auditors office uses hand-held, pen-based computers to inventory over 315,000 items. Southwestern Gas uses them to upload and download orders on a local area network, record data, transmit work-site information to dispatch offices, read meters, and record sales and marketing operations.

Another recent advancement is personal communicators with built-in modems that allow for two-way wireless data communications. These personal communicators are used to send electronic mail messages and to transmit and retrieve data. Some police officers use them to record license plate numbers and fingerprints and to take photos. These communicators send data to a patrol car via radio waves and then forward it to the police station. The data are then sent to a national computer network where federal officials make a quick identification and send pertinent data back to the officer. In a several-month period police in Newark, New Jersey, booted or towed over 1600 cars and assessed more than half a million dollars in fines using the system.

In the future you will have a **software agent,** a computer program that learns how to do often-performed, tedious, time-consuming, or complex tasks. For example, you could send your agent out on the various computer networks to find and filter information about your company or your clients or about accounting or tax changes that will affect them. The agents will also be able to perform such tasks as scheduling meetings, screening and prioritizing your E-mail, tracking stock investments and the weather, or finding the least expensive price on goods and services and purchasing them. With agents, users no longer need to remember long lists of computer commands; instead, they can talk to the computer or write a message on a touch-sensitive screen. For example, if you say, "Send a fax to Janice," it would know who Janice is and her fax number and would proceed to send the fax as requested. If you ask your agent how other companies handle a problem in their financial statements, the agent would search the appropriate data bases and report which companies have a similar problem and how they handle it.

Microcomputers are used as stand-alone computers and as a part of a network. As a stand-alone, they allow users to maintain and use their own data and software for tasks such as word processing, spreadsheets, graphics presentations, and accounting. As part of a network, they allow documents, mail, and data to be transmitted electronically to other network users. Peripherals and computer files can be shared. For example, when users need data stored on a mainframe data base, they can access the appropriate computer files and **download** the data to their PC. They can also **upload** data or send it to someone else in the network.

The Microcomputer Revolution

Microcomputers are one of the more important technological developments in the last hundred years. Some people claim that microcomputers will have a greater impact than the Industrial Revolution. They have spawned a revolution in the way we do business; an estimated 80% of workers use PCs. Well over 100 million are in use worldwide and sales are growing 10%–15% per year. American businesses spend more on computers, software, and services (over $35 billion a year) than on all other capital equipment combined. Today, well over 100 microcomputer manufacturers and thousands of companies develop software, manufacture peripheral devices, sell system components, and provide training, service, maintenance, consulting, and other products and services.

Enormous sums are spent on research and development, and new products with improved technology are announced regularly. The industry reinvents itself approximately every 18 months. Microcomputers purchased today will be technologically (but not functionally) obsolete in 6–12 months. Each new generation of computers seems to be smaller, faster, more powerful, more functional, and less expensive; to have greater storage capacity; and to be more user-friendly. Many are more portable and more easily linked to other computer systems. It is astounding to think about what the next 15 years hold, considering that technology has come so far in the past 15 years. Truly, the microcomputer revolution has just begun.

The Use of Microcomputers by Accountants

The tools that successful accountants need have changed. They must now use powerful networked micros instead of calculators, pencils, and paper. Many employers expect accounting graduates to have at least a working knowledge of operating systems, networking, spreadsheets, data base management systems, word processing, and methods of transferring data between programs. They also want some familiarity with general ledger programs, graphics software, and downloading from a mainframe. Many make computer literacy a requirement for promotion. As time passes, microcomputer competence as a condition for employment and advancement will increase.

Microcomputers are revolutionizing accounting by significantly increasing productivity. Accountants widely use micros for the following tasks: to run an entire accounting system, download data from mainframes to PCs for analysis and decision making, and develop their own information and office automation systems. Auditors regularly use micros to automate time and expense worksheets and audit workpapers; conduct audit planning, risk analysis, engagement management, statistical sampling, and audit tests; access mainframe data; prepare audit reports and opinions; and conduct research using online data bases. Finally, tax accountants use PCs to research tax issues; view the consequences of different tax-planning strategies; and enter, process, and prepare tax returns.

Management consultants use micros for decision support, such as helping clients decide whether to buy or lease a building; manufacture a product; acquire another company; or divest themselves of a line of business. Because they travel so much, consultants actually use their PCs as offices; they also use them for sending and receiving messages and data files, word processing, and working with spreadsheets and data bases. Most organizations need experienced PC consultants who can determine business needs, communicate with management, and apply existing application software to the particular business's problems. To do so, CPA firms have special consulting groups and organizations with PC support staffs. The need for PC consultants will increase as the market continues to grow, thereby offering a career path to students familiar with accounting and PCs. No matter which career path you choose, a key to your success will be understanding how to use PC hardware and software.

Regardless of how computers are classified or used, they all have common ingredients. One of those, the central processing unit, is discussed next.

CENTRAL PROCESSING UNIT

Computer processing functions are performed by the **central processing unit (CPU).** It has three main components: the arithmetic-logic unit, the control unit, and primary memory. The **arithmetic-logic unit** performs all math calculations and logical comparisons. The **control unit** interprets program instructions and coordinates all input, output, and storage devices. Data and program instructions are stored in the **primary memory.** The relationships of these components to each other and to computer input, output, and storage are illustrated in Fig. 7.2.

There are two types of primary memory: read-only and random-access. **Read-only memory (ROM)** can be read but not altered by other program instructions. ROM contains information that is stored permanently in the computer, such as all or part of the operating system. Computers temporarily store programs, data, and instructions in **random-access memory (RAM).** The amount of RAM a PC can hold determines how much data and how many programs it can handle at any one time. In today's world, a minimum of 16 MB of RAM is required. A **semiconductor**—a tiny silicon chip inscribed with a number of miniature circuits—is the most common form of RAM.

In contrast to conventional primary memory, a **flash memory chip** does not lose its contents when the power is shut off. Flash memory chips are used to replace hard disks in hand-held computers and to store operating systems and application software. They eliminate the time it takes for software to load when a computer is turned on. These chips are easily erased and reprogrammed and do not require moving mechanical parts, which makes them more reliable, faster, lighter, smaller, more durable, and more power efficient than hard or floppy disks. However, they wear out after 100,000 cycles of data input, compared to billions for conventional RAM.

Peripheral devices connected to the CPU by cables or telephone lines are called **on-line devices** because they directly access the CPU. **Off-line devices** are not connected directly to the CPU and are used to prepare data input or output.

Storage Measurements

Computers execute and store data in **bits** (short for "binary digit"), and a group of 8 bits is called a **byte.** A bit can assume one of two possible states, commonly referred to as "on" or "off," or "0" or "1". Each unique combination of bits represents a different character, such as a number or letter of the alphabet. As shown in Table 7.1, memory capacity is expressed in terms of a **kilobyte** (K or KB), **megabyte** (MB), **gigabyte** (GB), and **terabyte** (TB).

Back at S&S, Ashton is convinced that big advancements in storage capacities are forthcoming. For example, he read that Peter Rentzepis, a chemistry professor at the University of California at Irvine, has patented a

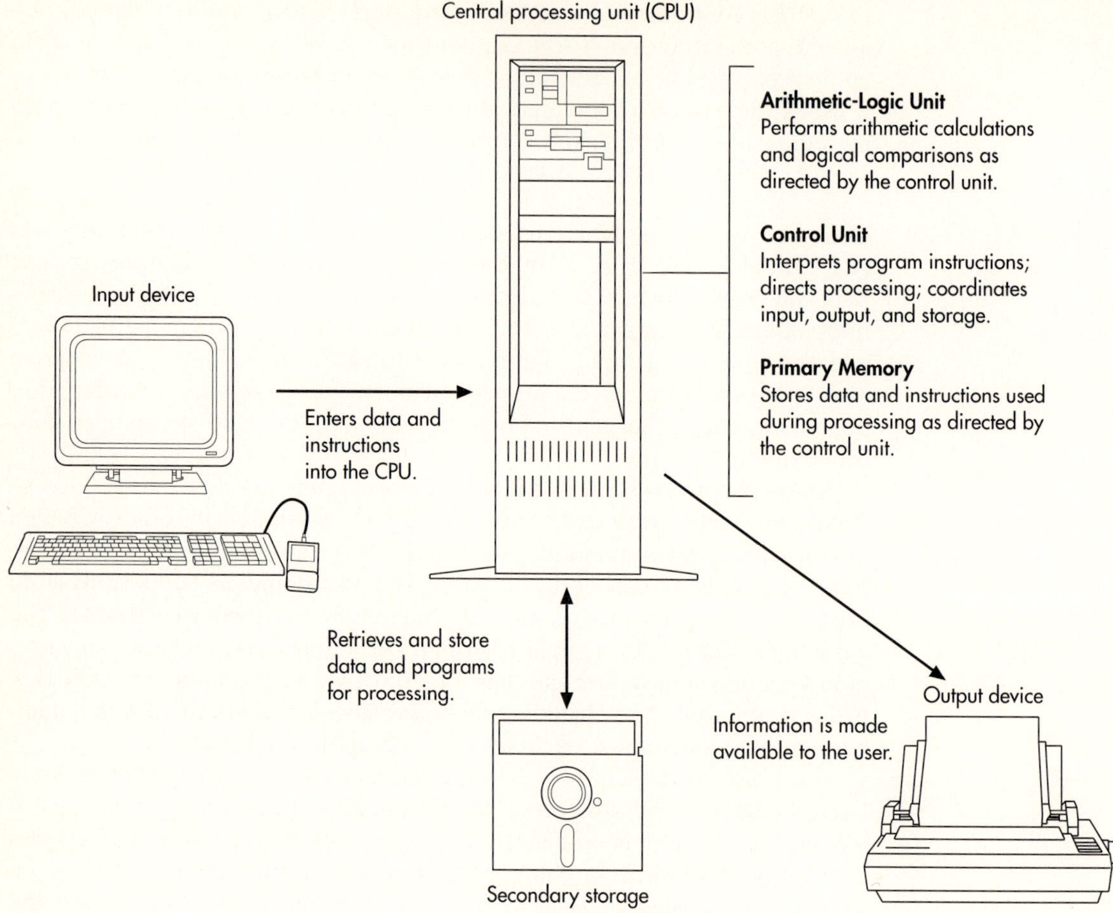

Figure 7.2 *Interaction of the Main Components of a Computer System*

three-dimensional storage medium the size of a sugar cube that is capable of storing as much as 7.5 TB of data. The device is still a number of years away from commercial applications.

Speed Measurements

The processing speed of a CPU is measured in terms of **MIPS, BIPS,** and **TIPS** (millions, billions, and trillions of instructions per second, respectively). First Bank in Minneapolis, for example, uses two IBM mainframes with a combined speed of 525 MIPS for processing checking account data, customer service, and other core business processing tasks. **Access time** is the time required to retrieve data from memory. **Execution time** is the time required to perform a computer instruction, such as add or compare. As shown in Table 7.1, these times are measured in fractions of a second: **millisecond** (thousandth), **microsecond** (millionth), **nanosecond** (billionth), and **picosecond** (trillionth). How fast are these speeds? If you took one step per nanosecond, you could circle the earth 20 times in one second.

Table 7.1 **Measuring Computer Speeds and Capacities**

Time Measures	Storage Measures
Millisecond = 1,000th of a second Microsecond = 1,000,000th of a second Nanosecond = 1,000,000,000th of a second Picosecond = 1,000,000,000,000th of a second Megahertz = millions of cycles per second (measurement of processing speed of microcomputers) MIPS = million of instructions per second (measurement of speed of computers)	Bit = storage location that is on or off Byte = 8 bits that represent 1 character Kilobyte = 1,000 characters Megabyte = 1,000,000 characters Gigabyte = 1,000,000,000 characters Terabyte = 1,000,000,000,000 characters

Microcomputer Hardware

The central processing unit in a PC, called a **microprocessor,** is a large-scale integrated circuit on a silicon chip. It is about the size of a thumbnail. Other silicon chips constitute the computer's primary memory, where both instructions and data are stored. Still other chips govern the input and output of data and carry out control operations. Many PCs contain several processors. For example, an arithmetic processor can complete calculations up to two hundred times faster than the main processor.

Microprocessor chips are identified by a number. The 80486 chip from Intel contains 1.2 million transistors and operates at 50 MIPS. The Pentium (586 chip) has 3.3 million transistors and operates at over 100 MIPS. The Pentium Pro (686) chip operates at 300 MIPS and has 5.5 million transistors. The Pentium Pro chip is 1000 times more powerful than the 8088 chip used in the original IBM PC. The Pentium Pro looks forward in the software, predicts which instruction will be processed and in what order, and spreads the instructions out to keep the chip's four parallel processing units busy. This dynamic execution enables four instructions to be processed with each of the chips' 130 million ticks per second. Intel has already started work on the 786 and the 886 chips. By the year 2000 Intel hopes to have a chip that will have 100 million transistors and execute at a speed of 2 BIPS.

In addition to the chip number, chips use suffixes to describe their features. A DX chip is the standard configuration, SX is less powerful, DX2 more powerful, and DX4 even more powerful. An SL chip is used in laptops.

Apple, IBM, and Motorola have recently developed a new chip that competes with Intel's Pentium. Most Apple computers are based on these new PowerPC chips. The PowerPC is a RISC (reduced instruction set computing) chip and is faster than other chips because it needs fewer instructions to complete a given task.

The chips are mounted on the main circuit board, or **motherboard.** Most PCs have expansion slots on the motherboard so that additional capabilities (such as increased memory or modems) and communication ports can be added. Communications between the computer's electrical components are in the form of digital electronic pulses that travel along a **data bus,** which connects the various components of the microcomputer.

There are three measures of the speed and computational power of microprocessors. The first is the number of bits processed at a time. The first generation of microcomputers had 4- or 8-bit microprocessors. Now 64-bit microprocessor chips are widely available and a number of companies are working on 128-bit chips. The second is the frequency of the processor's electronic clock—how many steps a computer can execute per second. Microcomputer clock frequency speeds have increased from 1 **megahertz** (1 million cycles per second) to over 166 megahertz. The third is the bus size, or the number of bits transmitted at one time from one computer location to another. The trend is toward larger word and bus sizes and higher frequency.

The microprocessor is fast becoming the vital ingredient of the information age, just as the internal combustion engine was the main ingredient in worldwide advances in the mid-1900s. If technological advancements in microprocessors continue at their current rate, within 15 years chips will be 30 to 50 times faster than they are today and will perform tasks we can barely dream of. They will be an integral part of computer networks that will make global transactions as easy and convenient as those made at the local mall.

Computer manufacturers have linked the microprocessors used in PCs to create **massively parallel processing (MPP)** computers. MPP is explained in more depth in Focus 7.2.

SECONDARY STORAGE DEVICES AND MEDIA

Computer systems use **secondary storage** to save data not currently needed by the system. Commonly used secondary storage devices include magnetic tape and disks, diskettes, and optical disks. Magnetic tape is the most frequently used sequential-access medium; the others are frequently used direct-access media.

Magnetic Tape

Magnetic tape, the oldest secondary storage medium in common use, comes in two forms: reels and cartridges. Both need a tape drive for reading and writing purposes. Magnetic tapes have three advantages: They hold a lot of data, are inexpensive, and take up little storage space. Their disadvantages are their need to be read sequentially and their inability to add, delete, or update records without processing the entire file. Tape cartridges are much faster, store more information, take up less space, and are more convenient to use than reels. Tapes are used for backup purposes, for infrequently needed data, and for data that do not require direct access.

Magnetic Disks

Magnetic disks are the dominant direct-access storage device, providing optimal cost, access time, storage capacity, and flexibility. Those used in mainframes are similar in appearance to a stack of CDs, except for a space between each adjoining pair of disks for one or more read/write heads. The magnetic disk used in PCs and microcomputers is called a **hard disk.** Hard disks are packaged in clean, airtight, sealed boxes that contain one or more disks. This protective

FOCUS 7.2

Massively Parallel Processing (MPP) Computers

Some data processing tasks are so complex and time-consuming that even the most powerful supercomputers "hit the wall" and are overwhelmed. One reason is their use of a single large processor to accomplish tasks sequentially, one at a time. The results are bottlenecks that slow down a system.

A new type of mainframe has been developed that is fast becoming the computer of choice. Called massively parallel processing (MPP) computers, they are composed of scores of inexpensive and very powerful microprocessors linked into a powerful, coordinated whole. They speed up processing by parceling out tasks to scores of microprocessors that work simultaneously. Since MPP computers are based on less expensive PC technology, they are much more economical. They take up half the space and accomplish more work for far less money than traditional mainframes. They use 90% less electricity and quickly pay for themselves; some companies have achieved a 7-to-1 return on their investment. MMP systems are especially useful for accessing data base information because they offer an easy, cost-effective way to process huge volumes of data and images. They are so popular that IBM estimates it will cease to manufacture traditional mainframes early in the next century. Unfortunately, these systems have many of the growing pains of an emerging technology, such as poor systems management, shaky reliability, and a scarcity of reliable software.

Wal-Mart, Kmart, and Hallmark Cards use MPP computers to handle large volumes of POS data for short-term forecasts, to manage ordering and delivery schedules, and to improve marketing analysis. Booz, Allen, & Hamilton, a consulting firm, uses MPP to assist clients in health care fraud investigation and in very large network modeling and analysis. Deloitte & Touche uses MPP computers to eliminate the millions of pages of reports it grinds out every two weeks. Mobil Oil uses them to produce high-quality, three-dimensional seismic images as it explores for oil all over the world. The company's MPP computer can produce seismic images in 10 days that took 29 weeks on their old mainframes. The costs of these images have decreased to $100,000 from $2.8 million. Banks use MPP to track the immense volume of daily banking transactions.

Focus Questions

1. What is the difference between traditional and MPP computers?
2. Why is it that MPP systems can do more work than traditional mainframes for far less money?
3. What other tasks can a company use MPP computers to complete?

---

environment allows hard disks to be operated at high speeds and data to be packed close together.

The advantages of disks are their ease of use, large storage capacity, and direct-access capability. An entire file need not be read to find a record, because the read/write head can move directly to any physical storage location. Thus accessing and updating data can be accomplished more efficiently than if the data were stored on tape. Two disadvantages of disks are their cost and their bulkiness. Magnetic disks take up as much as 10 to 15 times more space than tapes storing the same amount of data. They are also vulnerable to power surges, static electricity, and dirt.

Diskettes

A **diskette,** or **floppy disk,** is a circular piece of flexible magnetic film enclosed in a protective cover. The most common size is 3½ inches, although 5¼ floppies are still used. Its greatest advantages are its ease of use, compactness, and low cost. Diskettes have a much smaller storage capacity and a slower access time than hard disks. The diskette is commonly used as a data entry medium and for secondary storage in smaller computer systems.

Optical Disks

Optical disks use laser technology to store and read data. They store data by burning microscopic holes in their recording surface. Most optical disks are **WORM (write-once, read-many)** devices and are often referred to as **CD ROM (compact disk, read-only memory).** At a minimum, CD-ROMs on a microcomputer should be quadruple spin and have an access speed of less than 350 milliseconds. Some optical disks can be rewritten on, although the process is difficult and the number of rewrites is limited.

Laser optical disks offer significant advantages. First, they can hold a great deal of data. One optical disk can hold over a billion characters, which is roughly the equivalent of 70 floppy disks or 30 four-drawer file cabinets. Groliers has published its 21-volume *Academic American Encyclopedia* on a single optical disk. Second, laser disks can be removed from their drives, so the disk unit can read or write to an almost unlimited number of disks. Third, disks can be mass-produced easily and inexpensively. Fourth, they are much less susceptible to data loss and disk crashes than are hard disks. Disadvantages are that they are more costly and have slower access times than magnetic disks. Also, it is impossible to alter data once it is stored on some CD ROM disks.

Accountants frequently use optical disks. For example, Price Waterhouse provides each office with a CD-ROM resource library containing accounting pronouncements and the firm's policy on accounting issues. In addition, the Research Institute of America sends its tax services via optical disk. Accountants routinely conduct research using these CD-ROM services and then import the results into their word processing programs and include it in letters to clients. Accountants with CD-ROMs on their portable computers can conduct all their research in the field. Alternatively, they can use a modem to access a CD-ROM at their office. Time savings are significant. For example, a 30-minute tax code search using loose-leaf notebooks can be reduced to less than 5 minutes using CD-ROM.

A **videodisk** is an optical disk that stores audio, video, and text data. It can be accessed a frame at a time for motionless viewing or can be played like a videotape for moving action and sound. Any frame of the disk can be accessed in three seconds or less. These disks have many uses, including interactive training and marketing of products, such as cars, real estate, and vacation resorts.

INPUT DEVICES

Business systems have high input and output volumes and simple computations. Because input and output devices are much slower than CPUs, business systems are **input/output-bound.** This characteristic reduces **throughput,** which is the amount of useful work performed during a given period of time. Most approaches to increasing throughput focus on utilizing data-entry methods that minimize human interaction and that maximize the use of high-speed computer input devices. Several data-entry approaches are taken:

1. *Keying data captured on source documents.* This approach is time-consuming, costly, and error-prone. It requires that data first be captured on paper and then transcribed to tape or disk. It involves several steps: data capture, keying onto a magnetic medium, and key verification.
2. *On-line entry.* Terminals and microcomputers can be used to key data directly into the computer. Although this process is time-consuming, costly, and error-prone, it avoids capturing data on paper.
3. *Turnaround documents.* Turnaround documents, such as utility bills, are produced by the AIS, sent to the customer, and returned as inputs. This procedure reduces the input preparation workload and its potential for errors and is faster than keystroke entry. Unfortunately, it is often impossible to use, since much of the data that is input comes from outside the company.
4. *Source data automation.* These devices, such as the scanners used in grocery stores, automate the data capture and entry process. As a result, they decrease the time, effort, and errors associated with the first two approaches.
5. *Electronic data interchange.* This approach involves one company's computer talking to another company's computer, for example, a buyer electronically sending a purchase order to a supplier. This approach is attractive in terms of cost, speed, minimal human effort, and accuracy. Electronic data interchange is discussed in detail in Chapter 9.

The hardware devices used in these five alternatives are discussed next.

Data Preparation Devices

Key-to-tape and **key-to-disk encoders** enter data onto tapes and disks, respectively. A key-to-disk encoder links several keying stations to a minicomputer and accepts data simultaneously from the stations and pools it on a disk. The computer edits, sorts, and stores the data for subsequent processing.

On-Line Entry Devices

A **visual display terminal (VDT)** is an input/output device that can enter and receive data directly from the computer. It uses a keyboard for input and a monitor for output. Although VDTs are still used, microcomputers more often than not perform these input functions. Not only can microcomputers do everything the terminals can, they also function as a PC.

On-line data entry devices have significant advantages. First, editing transaction data for accuracy is facilitated, since the computer can perform various tests on each item. The computer notifies users of errors and requests that they be corrected. Second, they can be placed in remote locations, so transactions can be entered from their place of origin as they occur.

Because keying is slow and tedious, several more user-oriented approaches have been developed. A **mouse** is a small device with push buttons that can be used to point to **icons,** or pictures, on the screen that represent functions. Clicking a button on the mouse causes the activity represented by the icon to take place. **Light pens** use photoelectric circuitry to enter data through the screen. Their principal use is graphics applications; they can draw, fill, or color shapes on the screen and move the cursor and make menu selections. A **joystick** looks like a gearshift lever and is used to move the cursor on the screen. Joysticks are especially popular for controlling video games and for computer-assisted design. **Touch-sensitive screens** allow users to enter data or select menu items by touching the surface of a sensitized video display screen with a finger or a special pointer.

Source Data Automation Devices

Most organizations are moving toward **source data automation (SDA)** devices that collect input in machine-readable form at the time and place the data originate. This technique significantly decreases human involvement, resulting in time and cost savings, greater accuracy, more timely input, and avoids bottlenecks that can occur with slower input methods.

Magnetic ink character recognition (MICR) devices read characters that have been encoded with a special magnetic ink. Its most significant use is in banking, where it is used to encode customer checks and deposit slips. For example, a blank check has the bank, account, and check number encoded on the lower left portion. When a check is processed, the check amount is inscribed in the lower right corner.

Optical character recognition (OCR) devices, which read printed or handwritten characters, are commonly used in business. For example, American Express installed OCR equipment that reads 60% of the handwritten numbers on the 900,000 charge slips that it processes every day. The $10-million system will pay for itself in four years. The IRS uses OCR to read handwritten 1040EZ forms and by the year 2000 hopes to read all tax forms electronically. Other uses include reading turnaround documents such as insurance company premium notices and utility company billings.

Most students have used an **automated teller machine (ATM)** to withdraw cash from their bank accounts. However, ATMs dispense more than cash. Wells Fargo Bank customers use their ATMs to purchase additional shares of mutual funds and move cash between funds. ATMs also cash checks and sell bus passes, postage stamps, airline and event tickets, and travelers checks. ATMs can also be used to make mortgage or credit card payments and to dispense rolls of coins.

ATM cards are accepted by many businesses in lieu of credit and debit cards. In fact, Software Etc.'s stores in California no longer accept checks, preferring instead to be paid using an ATM card. After the card is read by a countertop terminal, the customer enters his or her **personal identification number (PIN)** using a pinpad. The account number, PIN number, and purchase amount are sent over phone lines to the customer's bank. If funds are available, the purchase amount is immediately withdrawn and placed in the store's account. Retail stores favor ATM cards (sometimes called plastic checks) because they eliminate the loss and hassle associated with bad checks and eliminate the float associated with charge cards and checks. Residents in some communities can even pay parking tickets and property taxes using ATM cards. Customers enjoy benefits such as the widespread acceptance of these cards (unlike checks, they can be used out-of-town), ease of use, and convenience.

Most debit, credit, and ID cards have a **magnetic stripe** that contains information such as name, address, and account number. When the card is used, a POS terminal reads the information on the stripe, transmits it to the bank, and verifies its validity. United Airlines has begun placing a magnetic stripe containing the customer's name, flight, and seat number on the back of all airline tickets. The stripe, which is run through an electronic reader at the gate, replaces the gate agent.

A **smart card** contains a microprocessor, memory chips, and software. Smart cards are used extensively in Europe and their use is increasing in the United States. A smart card can function as a credit or an ATM card as well as a storage center for costs and expense records. Since it can store up to three pages of text, it can contain vital personal data such as medical history and employment information. Marines at Parris Island boot camp receive their pay on smart cards that are good anywhere on base. At Loyola University, students can pay for almost everything on campus using smart cards, including books, meals, and traffic tickets. The travel industry is working on a system that will allow customers to make reservations using a smart card. With the reservations encoded on the card, it becomes a boarding pass and room key. Car keys will be obtained by inserting the smart card into a key-dispensing machine. The use of smart cards will partially or totally eliminate waiting in a line to board a plane or obtain car and room keys. They will also facilitate paying for phone calls, highway tolls, and gasoline. When travel is completed, the card will be read by a PC, which will fill out an expense reimbursement and credit the amount due to the traveler's account.

Radio frequency identification tags track data from one location to another by sending and receiving radio signals that identify the objects attached to them. They track products such as Federal Express or UPS packages. Respiratory therapists at the University of California Medical Center use hand-held computers and radio frequency to access the hospital mainframe where patients' records and treatment schedules are stored. After a treatment, therapists update patient records with these devices. This device cuts down on the time and costs associated with paperwork and maximizes the appointment time between therapists and patients.

Radio frequency data communication transmits data through air waves rather than through wires. Costco discount warehouses use hand-held computers and radio frequency to scan bar-coded items on the sales floor. For each scanned item, the system can retrieve information such as weekly sales, profitability, quantity on hand, and a reorder quantity. JC Penney utilizes radio frequency in its distribution centers to help receive and warehouse merchandise from vendors and then ship it to their stores.

An electronic identification, called an **active badge,** is explained in Focus 7.3.

Point-of-sale (POS) recorders, which read price or product code data, are usually built into counters or are used as hand-held wands. One example is the optical scanner used in grocery stores to read the **universal product code (UPC),** one of many types of **bar codes** used to identify products. The scanner emits an intense light, recognizes the pattern of bars and spaces, retrieves the price of the item sold, and transmits it to the cash register. The computer also updates the quantity sold and the inventory balance of the product. For credit sales, after the clerk enters the customer's account number, the system will check the customer's credit, as well as update the accounts receivable record. Figure 7.3 shows a UPC bar code and a terminal that reads the bar code.

FOCUS 7.3

"Active Badges" Keep Silent Tabs on Employees' Whereabouts

George Orwell's Big Brother is watching more keenly than ever at the Olivetti Research Laboratory and the computer laboratory at Cambridge University in Cambridge, England. Employees there are sporting experimental infrared tracking devices called "active badges" that allow a computer network to silently keep tabs on each person's whereabouts. In addition to enhancing physical security in corporate buildings, this automatic tracing system can be used in airports to track objects, ranging from luggage to lost children.

The small clip-on badges hanging from shirt pockets and dangling from belts are equipped with transceivers that emit uniquely coded signals every few seconds. The signals are picked up by infrared sensors located in each room and transferred to workstations and PCs that serve as nodes on a distributed computer network. When telephone calls come in to the facility, the receptionist can call up the system, locate the individual, and transfer the call to the nearest telephone.

The practical benefits of active badge tracing have turned some initial doubters into believers. Users found that the badges had many advantages, such as helping them to not miss phone calls. After a few months many of those who refused to wear the badges reconsidered and asked for one.

One potential stumbling block is that the system responds to the badge, not the individual. Whoever wears that uniquely coded badge can assume the identity of the proper owner. Solving the authentication problem is the target of a related Olivetti/DEC research project.

The introduction of this technology raises a number of legal and ethical issues. Critics argue that the new technology sacrifices individual privacy in favor of convenience and efficiency. Some employees wearing active badges may feel like house arrest victims whose bracelets trigger an alarm when they leave home. Some people feel it is great technology in the right hands, but a bad manager could make an employee's life miserable.

Focus Questions

1. What legal or ethical standards, if any, should society set on the use of this new employee-tracking technology?
2. What safeguards must be developed to make active badge technology more palatable to the public?
3. A year after one company adopted an active badge system a manager was reprimanded for poor communication with his staff. He claimed to have held regular meetings with his employees. An examination of the badge system records showed that he and his subordinates had never been in the same room together. The company faced a dilemma. Should they use this information to confront the manager? Should they ignore it to avoid negative behavioral reactions from their employees? What do you think they should have done? Why?

Bar codes provide the advantages of improved accuracy of data entry, better customer service through faster checkout at the point-of-sale, and greater control and reliability of inventory records. They are used in industries that must count and track inventory, such as retail, medical, libraries, military and other government operations, transportation facilities, and the automotive industry. Because of the savings it provides, the Post Office gives discounts to companies that bar code their mail. Two people can sort 32,000 bar-coded letters in an hour, compared to 17 people using older sorting equipment and 40 people sorting by hand.

Two-dimensional (2D) bar codes, which read the whole bar code rather than just the pattern of lines, have been developed that store the equivalent of

Figure 7.3

Data Collection Terminal Capable of Reading Barcodes and Magnetic Stripes

two text pages in the same amount of space as a traditional UPC. One of the code's first uses was handling barrels of hazardous toxic waste. Now it is commonly used in a variety of industries. For example, every shipping carton sent to one of Wal-Mart's distribution centers must have a 2D bar code. The bar code contains the purchase order, stock numbers, the contents of each box, a product's origin, its destination, and how it should be handled during shipping. These bar codes automate many of the mundane and time-consuming shipping tasks.

A **voice recognition** system understands spoken words and transmits them into a computer at speeds faster than most users can type. Current systems can recognize, with up to 98% accuracy, either a few key words from many people or as many as sixty thousand words from a single person. Single-person systems allow the user to dictate information (at up to 110 words a minute), instantly review it, and correct errors. It also learns from its mistakes. Voice recognition systems can be used to replace the mouse when operating in Windows. They are used to activate applications, call up files, move or erase data, and turn the system on and off. You can record a voice note and attach it to a word processing, spreadsheet, or other similar file. For example, an accountant with a portable computer could research a problem, create a spreadsheet, dictate a fax, and tell the system where to send the fax and spreadsheet while riding in an airplane or a taxi.

The airline and parcel delivery industries use voice input systems to route packages. AT&T replaced six thousand operators with a computer system that understands speech and forwards phone calls. AT&T's word-spotting technology picks out certain words, such as *collect,* and forwards the call. Accents, stammering, stuttering, and even singing do not affect the accuracy of the system. Large hospitals use computers to call patients and confirm appointments. The computer asks a string of questions relating to the time and date of the appointment, to which the person responds yes or no.

Using voice recognition systems, emergency room physicians at Holy Name Hospital in Teaneck, New Jersey, can quickly and accurately fill out emergency room medical charts. The $27,000 system, which paid for itself in four months, consists of a PC and a phone receiver. It factors out emergency room noises and records only what the doctors say. It uses an expert system and a built-in knowledge base that interacts with the doctors to check for symptoms missed. This system strengthened the hospital's cases against malpractice suits.

COMPUTER OUTPUT DEVICES

Visual Display

Computer monitors vary in price and quality. Standard monitors are referred to as VGA. A higher-quality monitor, referred to as super VGA or SVGA, has higher color quality and better resolution. **Resolution** refers to how clear images are on the monitor; with higher resolution the screen will be sharper, diagonal lines will be straighter, filled-in areas will be darker, and graphics will be clearer. The smaller the dot-pitch rating, the sharper the image. For example, a .28 dot-pitch rating is sharper than a .39 rating. In recent years a flat-panel display that uses liquid crystal or gas discharge technology has also been introduced. It is used on most portable systems.

Voice Response Units

Voice response units contain recorded words and phrases that are used to speak to humans. The units determine the words needed to generate the message, select the appropriate words and phrases from its vocabulary, combine them as necessary, and transmit them to the listener. Accounting applications include verifying a customer's credit and answering inquiries about a customer's bank balance. DHL Worldwide Express has an interactive voice response system that allows customers to determine the status of a package. Customers call a toll-free number, enter the air bill number using the telephone keypad, and receive a voice response that tells them when a package arrived and who signed for it or that a package was not delivered because the recipient was unavailable.

Personal computers also have voice response capabilities. Most PC users desire sound capabilities so they can use multimedia (text, sound, and graphics together) software. To do so, they need a sound card, such as Sound-Blaster.

Printers

A **printer** produces paper output, often referred to as hard copy. Printers vary widely in terms of quality, speed, graphics capabilities, and cost, which is directly affected by the first three elements. Color printing is also available. Some color printers are so sophisticated that they can produce photographic-quality images on paper or transparencies.

Impact printers strike an embossed character against an inked ribbon. The most popular is the dot matrix printer, which forms characters by using a group of small wires to form dots. **Nonimpact printers** transfer images without striking the paper. The most common type are laser printers, which are more reliable and expensive than impact printers. They reflect laser beams off a rotating disk that contains the available characters onto paper, where it forms an electrostatic image. The paper is passed through a toner to produce high-quality images. Ink jet printers form letters by spraying ink on paper. Many devices have been developed that perform multiple functions, such as printing, scanning, faxing, and copying.

A **plotter** is a special type of printer that produces a graphical output by moving a writing arm across a paper surface. Modern plotters can produce three-dimensional and multicolored drawings.

Printers are connected to computers by a cable or a data communications line. If the computer sends the data along a single cable one bit at a time, the printer uses a **serial interface.** If the computer sends the bits simultaneously along parallel cables, the printer has a **parallel interface.** Serial transmission is slower but can be used over longer distances.

Computer Output Microfilm

Computer output microfilm (COM) makes use of a photographic process to store noncurrent accounting records, copies of company documents, and other information on microfilm. For example, banks store copies of depositors' checks on microfilm. Microfilm is less expensive than paper and reduces storage requirements by up to 95%.

SECTION B: SOFTWARE

Software is the detailed instructions that control the functions of hardware devices. A set of instructions that tell a computer how to accomplish a particular task is called a **computer program.** The process of writing software programs to accomplish these tasks is called **computer programming.** Software programs are written in a **programming language.**

Software programs can be divided into two categories. **Application software** is written to perform specific functions and to support users. Examples include programs to keep the accounts receivable, accounts payable, inventory, and payroll records up to date. **Systems software** interprets the application program instructions and tells the hardware how to execute them. The diagram shown in Fig. 7.4 illustrates this relationship.

LEVELS OF COMPUTER LANGUAGES

Computer programs can be written in one of over two hundred programming languages, each with its own unique vocabulary, grammar, and rules for usage. Languages are often classified as high- or low-level. The closer the language is to that used by the computer, the lower the language level; the closer the language is to English, the easier it is to use and the higher the level. This section

Figure 7.4

Interfaces Between Users and Hardware

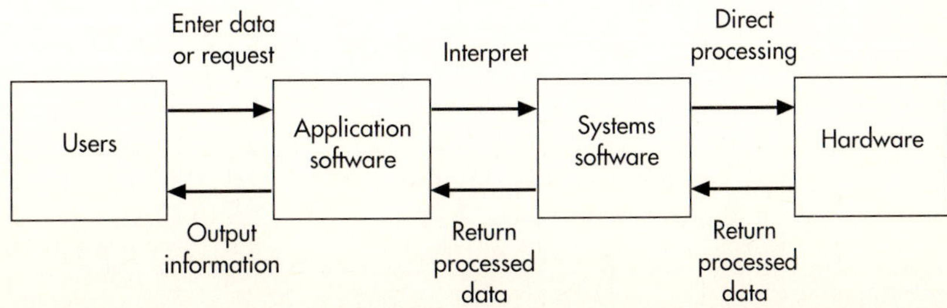

briefly discusses four levels of languages: machine, symbolic, high-level, and fourth-generation. An example of each level is shown in Table 7.2.

Machine and Symbolic Languages

Each computer has its own **machine language,** which is interpreted by the computer's internal circuitry. A **symbolic language** represents machine instructions by symbols and is converted to machine language by an assembler. Machine and symbolic languages are seldom used due to the availability of higher-level languages.

High-Level Languages

High-level languages are **machine-independent languages,** since the same language can be used by many types of computers. As shown in Fig. 7.5, **compilers** convert high-level languages into machine language. The high-level language program, called the **source program,** and the compiler are input to the CPU. The compiler translates the entire source program into a machine language program, called the **object program. Diagnostic messages** inform the programmer of **syntax errors,** or errors in the use of the language. **Logic errors** occur when the instructions given to the computer do not accomplish the desired objective. If there are no significant syntax errors, the object program and the input are read into the computer, the program is executed, and a printed report and a data file are produced. The appendix to Chapter 7 lists some popular high-level languages and their uses.

Some high-level languages are translated by an interpreter. In contrast to a compiler, an **interpreter** translates and executes instructions one at a time. The interpreter does not produce object programs or diagnostics. The BASIC language used in PCs is an example of an interpreted language.

Fourth-Generation Languages

Fourth-generation languages (4GLs) have been developed so that programmers need not tell the computer the exact procedures to follow (multiply this, compare that). With 4GL, users specify the information they want and the 4GL determines the sequence of instructions to follow. The result is a simpler, more efficient programming process that offers cost and time savings. Programs are

Table 7.2 **Typical Instructions in the Four Levels of Programming Languages**

Language	Instruction
Machine language	01011000001000000000100001110000 01011010001000000000100001110001 01010000001000000000100001110010
Symbolic assembly language	L 2,A A 2,B ST 2,C
High-level language	ADD SALARY, COMMISSION, GIVING TOTALPAY
Fourth-generation language	COMPUTE THE TOTALPAY OF ALL EMPLOYEES BY ADDING THEIR SALARY AND COMMISSION

Figure 7.5

Compiling and Executing a High-Level Language Program

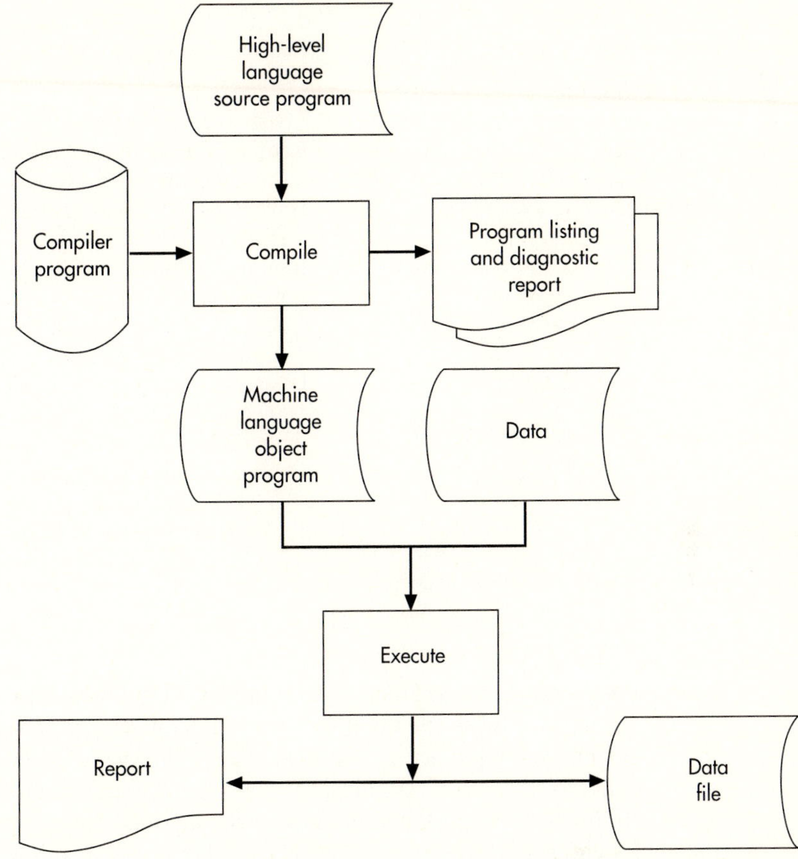

shorter; easier to write, maintain, read, and understand; and more error-free. Some 4GLs so closely resemble English that they are referred to as **natural languages.**

Many 4GLs are simple enough that, with minimal training, end-users can satisfy many of their information needs in just a few minutes. Other 4GLs are so complex and powerful that they are used mainly by professional analysts and programmers. These are full-function, general-purpose languages used to develop application programs. Many users claim tremendous productivity gains; 5 to 10 lines in a 4GL program equal hundreds of lines of COBOL code. Table 7.3 compares 3GLs and 4GLs and summarizes their differences. Two powerful features of 4GL are report and application generators.

Report Generators. To produce reports, a programmer must select and format data, specify titles and page numbers, calculate totals, and specify the number and width of columns. **Report generators** were developed to make customizing reports easier and faster. These programs can access files and data bases, select the data desired, aggregate or manipulate it, and print it in the desired format.

Table 7.3 **Major Differences Between 3GLs and 4GLs**

Third-Generation Languages (3GLs)	Fourth-Generation Languages (4GLs)
Intended for use by professional programmers	May be used by a nonprogramming end-user as well as a professional programmer
Require specification of *how to perform task*	Require specification of *what task* to perform (system determines how to perform the task)
Require that all alternatives be specified	Have default alternatives built in; end-user need not specify these alternatives
Require large number of procedural instructions	Require far fewer instructions (less than one-tenth in most cases)
Code may be difficult to read, understand, and maintain	Code is easy to understand and maintain because of English-like commands
Language developed originally for batch operation	Language developed primarily for on-line use
Can be difficult to learn	Many features can be learned quickly
Difficult to debug	Errors easier to locate because of shorter programs, more structured code, and use of defaults and English-like language
Typically file-oriented	Typically data base–oriented

Source: Adapted from James A. Senn, *Information Systems in Management* (Belmont, Calif.: Wadsworth, 1990), p. 218. Reprinted with permission.

Application Generators. An **application generator** produces a program to accomplish tasks specified by its users. Application generators include a programming language; a code generator; a library of commonly used program code; tools for creating files, data bases, and a data dictionary; a screen-painting feature to develop input and output layouts; a query language; and a graphics and report generator. IBM claims to have achieved a 27:1 improvement in productivity when ADF, its application generating program, was used instead of COBOL to write programs. At another company, a management reporting system that took six months to write was created in half a day using an application generator called FOCUS.

Object-Oriented Languages

With traditional programming approaches, developing a new program means writing entirely new code, one line at a time. The program may be hundreds of thousands of lines long and can take years to complete. Since each program is written from scratch, quality is often poor, productivity of programmers is low, and programs are usually behind schedule. When program modifications are needed, the code must be rewritten and tested. As programs become longer and more complex, achieving a reasonable quality level becomes a formidable task.

One solution to these problems is a new way of developing software using an **object-oriented language (OOL).** An **object** is a predefined set of program code that, after having been written and tested, will always behave the same way so it can be used for other applications. All programs consist of specific tasks such as saving or retrieving data and calculating totals. In object-oriented programming an object is written for each specific task and saved in a library so anyone can use it. Objects can also be items such as a purchasing order or a production schedule.

Using **object-oriented programming (OOP),** objects are combined and the small amount of code necessary for finishing the program is written. Rather than writing a program line by line, programmers select objects by pointing to a representative icon and then linking these objects together. Objects can be modified, reused, copied, or created, just like spreadsheet cells. When an object is updated, all programs using that object can be automatically updated as well.

These objects are then sent messages telling them what to do; the objects complete the task accordingly. For example, selecting an object that looks like a fax machine would mean that data are to be sent by fax. This programmer-machine interface is more natural, powerful, and easy to understand and use than more traditional methods.

The advantages of OOP are its graphical interface, ease of use, faster program development, and enhanced programmer productivity (up to tenfold increases). The programs produced by OOP are more reliable and contain fewer errors, since modules are used that have already been extensively tested. Its disadvantages are its steep initial development costs and a more extensive start-up time. OOP is a new way of thinking, and it can take programmers six months or more to gain proficiency. OOP produces programs that are larger, slower, and use more memory and other computer resources than traditional methods. As a result, it requires powerful PCs and workstations. Investing in OOP is cheaper than hiring additional programming staff, however, and the increase in productivity makes up for the additional costs. Many companies are moving to OOP. For example, Florida Power and Light has seen a fourfold increase in developer productivity since it moved to object-oriented development.

Adherents of OOP claim that the future software market will deal in objects rather than in software packages. In other words, software applications will be sold as collections of objects. Eventually it will result in a do-it-yourself software situation that has users purchasing the necessary objects from a computer store, assembling them, and adding a little coding to tie up loose ends. The most common object-oriented languages are Smalltalk and C ++ .

SYSTEMS SOFTWARE

Systems software controls the use of the hardware, the application software, and other system resources used in executing data processing tasks. It also prepares user programs for execution by translating them into machine language. Three types of systems software are discussed next: operating systems, utility programs, and communications software.

Operating System

The **operating system (OS)** is the most important type of systems software. The OS manages the input, output, processing, and storage devices and operations in order to maximize the system's performance. It performs administrative functions such as scheduling jobs, allocating primary memory space, tracking all application programs and systems software, maintaining operating statistics, and communicating with equipment operators. The OS resides in main memory or in a readily accessible on-line storage device. Most new operating systems can access and manipulate 32 bits at a time. The most popular IBM compatible operating systems (in the order they were introduced) are DOS,

Windows, Windows NT, and Windows 95. Apple computers use the System 7 operating system.

In a **multitasking** environment, as found in Windows 95, several jobs can be processed on the computer simultaneously. The OS can switch back and forth among a number of programs and keep the input/output devices for all the programs working at peak speed. In a **virtual memory** system, the operating system continually moves data back and forth between primary and secondary memory so that the system appears to have a virtually unlimited amount of primary memory.

Some software programs work with the OS and provide desirable enhancements. Microsoft's Windows is an example of a **graphical user interface (GUI)** operating environment in which a mouse is used to point at icons and menu selections. Most GUIs allow the screen to be divided into several windows so that the user can work with several programs. Software with a GUI is so easy to use that workers often get twice as much accomplished than with non-GUI software.

Newer operating systems have a **plug and play** feature that identifies and configures the OS and the hardware so that the PC, peripherals, and software work together with minimal effort on the user's part. This feature minimizes user service and support, especially when a new hardware component or software is added to a system. As a result, it makes PC systems more economical to operate.

Utility Programs

Utility programs handle common file, data manipulation, and housekeeping tasks. Debugging aids help correct programs. On-line users can employ text editors to modify the contents of data files and computer programs. Sort/merge programs sort files into a specific order and merge two or more sorted files into one. Media conversion programs transfer data from one medium to another, such as from tape to disk. Utilities are easy to use, efficient, and inexpensive.

Communications Software

Most EDP users transmit data electronically between computers and between terminals and computers, and they access corporate and public data bases to extract information. **Communications software** controls and supports these activities. The programs connect and disconnect communications links and terminals, automatically poll terminals or other computers for input/output activity, prioritize communication requests, and detect and correct data transmission errors. Communications software is discussed in Chapter 9.

APPLICATION SOFTWARE

Hardware and systems software are not unique—they are available to anyone who can afford them. This isn't the case with application software. It is a scarce commodity, and companies spend millions of dollars to develop application software that will give them a competitive edge. Application software is by far the most important software for accountants because it performs specific data processing and accounting tasks. Application software of interest to accountants can be divided into three categories:

1. *General-purpose programs* handle common tasks such as word processing, spreadsheets, graphics, and data bases. They also include software packages

that some of the major accounting firms, such as Deloitte and Touche and Coopers and Lybrand, have developed to assist in auditing work.

2. *Business programs* update master files and data bases to include the effects of transactions. They also support the various business functions of a company: accounting, marketing, production, finance, human resources, and management.
3. *Intelligent applications* focus on expanding the role of the computer beyond traditional data processing functions. Examples include decision support software, expert systems, and artificial intelligence.

Given the hundreds of types of businesses, each with many unique processing needs, thousands of different application programs are in use. Much of the remainder of this book discusses application software.

SUMMARY AND CASE CONCLUSION

Several weeks after beginning his study of hardware and software, Ashton presented his reports, tables, and diagrams to Scott. Scott was surprised by the technological advancements that had taken place since his college computer course. It is evident to him that companies are demanding more out of their AIS. They want instantaneous access and processing, infinite storage, unlimited communication between computers, and ease of use. Software developers are requiring hardware that is faster, smaller, less expensive, and more powerful. The result has been a technological explosion that won't slacken anytime soon. Scott realizes that keeping abreast of technological advancements will require a lot of effort.

In planning S&S's computer system, Scott and Ashton agree on three guiding principles. First, S&S will grow as fast as is financially feasible. Second, S&S's AIS will make maximum use of technology and eliminate human intervention wherever possible. Third, the system must allow S&S to implement what it can afford and grow into the final design.

It is essential that S&S have good accounting software. Ashton discovered that the Appliance Vendors Association recommends a number of accounting software packages that it has tested and evaluated. They will begin their search using this list. S&S also needs data base, presentation graphics, spreadsheet, and word processing software. They are discussed in Chapter 8.

S&S's current needs can be met with a PC, although at some point it will need more powerful hardware to link future stores together. To forestall the obsolescence that is sure to result with advancing technology, they decide to buy the most recent PC technology, a large amount of primary memory, and a large hard disk. Additional storage can be provided by floppy disks and tape cartridges. They also want each store to have one or more high-speed laser printers. They decide to go with a GUI operating environment such as Windows 95.

Scott suggests they capture as much accounting data and other input as possible using source data automation devices. They plan to use POS devices with audio response units at all their customer checkouts as well as bar coding to capture sales data and perform other tasks, such as taking inventory.

They want customers to use noncash forms of payment such as credit or smart cards. That way they can handle sales payments electronically and avoid the problems of bad checks, credit extensions, cash overages, shortages, and theft. They want to hook the POS devices to their system so that they can have up-to-date inventory records. They want their system to automatically recognize when inventory is needed and order appropriate stock directly from their suppliers.

As S&S expands, Susan wants to print 10–20 separate versions of a customer catalog, each with a different format and product mix. She wants to keep track of every customer purchase so she can select the best catalog for each. She wants to customize the catalog cover by mentioning a previous purchase or the customer's line of business. Furthermore, this data base of customer data will allow her to target particular customers for special discounts.

Scott and Ashton are both excited when they finish their preliminary plan. Scott wants Ashton to investigate further before they make any final decisions. He asks Ashton to conduct an in-depth study of end-user systems and software (see Chapter 8) as well as communication systems (see Chapter 9).

KEY TERMS

computer hardware
peripherals
supercomputers
mainframe computers
data processing center
downsizing
minicomputers
microcomputers
personal computer (PC)
personal digital assistant (PDA)
stylus
software agents
download
upload
central processing unit (CPU)
arithmetic-logic unit
control unit
primary memory
read-only memory (ROM)
random-access memory (RAM)
semiconductor
flash memory chip
on-line devices
off-line devices
bits
byte
kilobyte
megabytes
gigabytes
terabytes
MIPS
BIPS
TIPS
access time
execution time
millisecond
microsecond
nanosecond
picosecond
microprocessor
motherboard
data bus
megahertz
massively parallel processing (MPP)
secondary storage
magnetic tape
magnetic disks
hard disk
diskette
floppy disk
optical disk
WORM (write-once, read-many)
CD ROM (compact-disk, read-only memory)
videodisk
input/output-bound
throughput
key-to-tape encoder
key-to-disk encoder
visual display terminal (VDT)
mouse
icons
light pens
joystick
touch-sensitive screens
source data automation (SDA)
magnetic ink character recognition (MICR)
optical character recognition (OCR)
automated teller machine (ATM)
ATM cards
personal identification number (PIN)
magnetic stripe
smart cards
radio frequency identification tags
radio frequency data communication
active badge
point-of-sale (POS) recorders
universal product code (UPC)
bar codes
voice recognition
resolution
voice response units

printer
impact printers
nonimpact printers
plotter
serial interface
parallel interface
computer output microfilm (COM)
software
computer program
computer programming
programming language
application software
systems software
machine language
symbolic language
machine-independent languages
compilers
source program
object program
diagnostic messages
syntax errors
logic errors
interpreter
fourth-generation languages (4GLs)
natural languages
report generators
application generator
object-oriented language (OOL)
object
object-oriented programming (OOP)
operating system (OS)
multitasking
virtual memory
graphical user interface (GUI)
plug and play
utility programs
communications software

CHAPTER QUIZ

1. When companies downsize their systems, they typically move from
   a. a microcomputer to a network of minicomputers.
   b. a mainframe to a network of mini- and microcomputers.
   c. a minicomputer to a network of mainframes.
   d. a mainframe to a network of supercomputers.

2. Which of the following is *not* one of the three parts of a central processing unit?
   a. Arithmetic-logic unit
   b. Control unit
   c. Graphical user interface
   d. Primary memory

3. One million characters of storage is referred to as a
   a. kilobyte.
   b. megabyte.
   c. gigabyte.
   d. microsecond.
   e. millisecond.

4. The CPU in a microcomputer is called a
   a. semiconductor.
   b. motherboard.
   c. data bus.
   d. microprocessor.

5. Which of the following is *not* a secondary storage device?
   a. Optical disk
   b. Magnetic tape
   c. Magnetic disk
   d. RAM
   e. CD ROM

6. Some gas stations are now equipped with devices that read credit cards at the pump. As a result, you can fill up your tank and pay for your gas without ever entering the store. These stations use which of the following types of data input?
   a. Keying data captured on source documents
   b. On-line entry
   c. Turnaround documents
   d. Source data automation

7. A microprocessor, memory chips, and software are parts of which device?
   a. Bar code
   b. Smart card
   c. Magnetic stripe
   d. Videodisk

8. Which of the following is *not* a computer output device?
   a. Voice recognition
   b. Monitor
   c. Plotter
   d. COM

9. Which of the following is the most English-like computer language?
   a. Machine language
   b. High-level language
   c. Symbolic language
   d. Natural language

10. With traditional programming approaches, developing a new program means writing entirely new code, one line at a time. When program modifications are needed, the code must be rewritten and tested, a very time-consuming process. One solution to these problems is a new way of developing software using

a. language translators.
b. communication software.
c. utility programs.
d. object-oriented programming.

DISCUSSION QUESTIONS

7.1 Service Corp. International, the world's largest operator of funeral homes and cemeteries, retired its IBM mainframe computer and downsized to an IBM minicomputer with 80G of disk storage. The company abandoned all of its custom-written software and replaced it with an integrated business system purchased from Lawson Software in Minneapolis. It also put PCs in all 850 funeral homes and cemeteries and linked them to the minicomputer. The funeral homes and cemeteries use the PCs to fill out the state and federal forms, hospital forms, personal histories, and death certificates that previously were filled out by hand.

If you were Service Corp., what problems would you anticipate in installing the PCs? How can Service Corp. use its new minicomputer and PC network? It cost Service Corp $6.5 million to downsize to the minicomputer. From a financial standpoint, do you think the company made a wise decision?

7.2 Source data automation devices are becoming increasingly popular. Some futurists envision a day when you will not need cash, checks, or credit cards. Rather, you will use a card on which your personal identification number is inscribed. Do you believe this system will help or hinder you? facilitate or complicate business transactions? What are the advantages and disadvantages of moving the data entry process closer to the point at which data originate?

7.3 Accountants use computers in their work both at the office and at the client's location. Clients are also increasingly using computers. Discuss how accountants in each of the functional areas of tax, audit, and consulting use computers and what they need to be aware of in regard to a client's system.

7.4 Researchers at IBM have demonstrated a tiny switch that depends on the motion of a single atom, making it the smallest electronic device in existence. Although any practical application is likely to be more than a decade away, the new "atom switch" raises the possibility that electronic circuits may someday be built with parts measuring only an atom or molecule across. The atom switch is measured in nanometers (billionths of a meter). By comparison, the circuitry in today's top-performance computer chips is measured in microns (millionths of a meter).

Professor Rentzepis of the University of California at Irvine has developed and patented a three-dimensional data storage device the size of a sugar cube that is capable of storing as much as 7.7 terabytes. For storing data a laser is split into two beams, which are aimed at the cube at right angles. The data are stored at the point where the two lasers meet. The cube is inexpensive and fast and has no moving parts, which increases its reliability. The greatest potential use of the technology is in massively parallel computing. A prototype of the technology may be ready within the decade.

It will take several years for these technologies to be refined. But once they are, what are the implications for accounting systems? What will these technologies allow us to do with computer technology?

7.5 Laboratories put bar codes on containers of blood and urine samples for accurate identification. Alamo Rent-a-Car bar-codes its 70,000-car fleet in preparation for a new inventory system. Airlines use standardized bar codes to ensure that luggage gets to the right city. Recently developed bar codes carry more data and will even store computer programs. How will technological developments in bar codes and computers affect an AIS? the way companies do business in the future?

7.6 Tired of going through boxes of disorganized old photos? If so, Eastman Kodak may have the answer for you with a recent product innovation: the photo CD player. Photographers using CD technology continue to take pictures with their regular cameras. When the film is processed, the pictures are stored on a photo compact disk, which is viewed using a special CD player developed to show photographs on a TV screen. As more pictures are taken, they can be added to the CD. In the coming years Kodak plans to add other capabilities, including audio narration features, music, graphics, and text. In what ways could business utilize this photo CD technology? In what ways can business utilize CD-ROM technology?

7.7 In an effort to trim the high cost of cutting trees, Detroit Edison Company is equipping its line clearance group and private tree trimmers with the latest in portable technology. Using a hand-held electronic work pad and pen, inspectors for Detroit Edison fill out electronic work orders as they inspect the company's power lines for overgrown trees. The work orders are stored on memory cards and returned to the main office, which distributes them to independent contractors. The work orders detail the job location, the type of power lines involved, and the branches that the contractor must trim back.

Upon completion, the contractor uses an electronic pen and notepad to record an invoice detailing the work and the total cost of the project. The memory disk with the original work order and the contractor's invoice is returned to the utility company, which processes the invoice and makes payment. Employees at Detroit Edison really like the new technology because it saves time and reduces their paperwork. Although most inspectors had never used PCs, the expected resistance never materialized. Discuss the benefits of portable computer technology. How is recent technology improving user acceptance of new AIS?

7.8 The text mentioned a number of uses for smart cards and voice recognition systems. Discuss at least two additional situations in which this technology could be applied to your everyday activities.

PROBLEMS

7.1 Identify which input, output, or storage medium or device best fits each of the following descriptions.

a. Macy's department stores could use this device to ring up a customer's sales and to post sales information directly to accounts receivable and inventory records.
b. When making a professional graphics presentation, a controller would want to use this device to produce the highest-quality hard copy output.
c. Duke University could store its payroll information on this sequential magnetic medium and then use the medium, in batch processing mode, to update the payroll file and print employee paychecks.
d. When Fleet Bank is closed, a customer uses this device to get $20 for gas and movie money.
e. Credit unions use this device to read their members' checks and accurately deduct the proper amounts from their accounts.
f. When making reservations, Delta employees use this device extensively to access the computer system and get information about the status of a specific flight.
g. Merrill Lynch uses this storage device so a customer's record can be accessed immediately, without processing any other records.
h. Tags such as those used by Federal Express track data from one location to another.
i. This recently developed storage device is used to store historical and other permanent information. Only recently has it been made an erasable medium.
j. Large insurance companies use this device to prepare form letters and hard copies of other computer-generated documents.
k. Your local utility company uses this device to read turnaround documents received from customers.
l. This device is a hand-held computer that helps people organize their schedule and personal affairs.
m. Safeway uses this device to read the UPC of food items. By interpreting the UPC, the system can extract the price of the product from the computer's secondary storage.
n. UPS uses this device to route packages to their appropriate destinations. Background noises need to be controlled so that the device does not become confused.
o. Large industrial corporations use this device to condense historical data by up to 99% for storage on rolls of film.
p. AT&T uses this device to give people the telephone numbers they are seeking when they dial directory assistance.

7.2 The Western Oil Company processes an average of 8500 charge sales documents per business day. To process these transactions, the company is considering two alternatives: an optical character recognition (OCR) system and a shared-processor, key-to-disk system.

The OCR system rents for $1500 per month. It would require an operator who would receive a monthly salary of $1800. It could be expected to read successfully between 97% and 98% of all charge sales documents. For those documents it rejects, the operator would manually enter the correct data from a console. Even considering the time required to deal with rejected documents, this system would have more than enough capacity to handle Western's current and projected volume of charge sales.

If the key-to-disk system were acquired, monthly rent for the shared processor and each keying station would be $1000 and $120 per month, respectively. Each keying station would be operated by a data entry clerk, who would receive a monthly salary of $1700 and could be expected to achieve a net productivity rate of 9700 keystrokes per hour. During each 8-hour day, the clerks would spend approximately 7 hours and 40 minutes working at the keyboard. Each charge sale document has 15 characters that must be keyed.

REQUIRED

a. If the key-to-disk system were acquired, how many keying stations and operators would be required, assuming all work is done on the day shift?
b. From an economic standpoint, which of the two alternatives is most attractive? Show computations.
c. Identify additional factors that should be considered in deciding between the two alternatives?

7.3 Pinta Company is a regional discount department store chain headquartered in Salt Lake City, Utah. Its stores, which are scattered throughout the Southwest, sell general merchandise. The firm is thinking about buying a point-of-sale (POS) system. There are a number of POS systems available, but the type that uses a light pen to scan the universal product code on merchandise seems the most suitable for Pinta's stores.

The company is concerned about a number of potential security problems. It worries that the POS terminals may be a security risk because of the number of devices and their close proximity to customers. It also is concerned that the data collected by the system could be lost or destroyed. A final concern is that there might be unauthorized changes to the prices and other data stored in the computer.

REQUIRED

Pinta's controller has asked you to prepare a report that does the following:
a. Explains the functions and operation of a POS system, including its use in credit checking and electronic transfers of funds.
b. Identifies the advantages and disadvantages of the POS system described in part (a).
c. Identifies controls and security measures that could effectively counteract their security concerns. (CMA Examination, adapted)

7.4 A recent article on bar coding stated that management accountants are under heavy pressure to modernize internal accounting systems and to provide accurate, timely, and relevant reports to users. To alleviate this pressure, many are looking at the key-entry process, which is responsible for many errors and time delays. To achieve better and faster data, accountants are using technologies that capture data at the point of origin in real-time.

REQUIRED

a. Would you agree that bar coding is the most popular and cost effective of these technologies?
b. In what business activities is bar coding most useful? least useful?
c. What benefits does bar coding provide? Even if the benefits of a bar-coded data entry system do not outweigh its costs, why might a company still implement the system?
d. What technical problems might someone using bar coding expect to encounter? What behavioral problems might a company experience in converting to a bar-coded data entry system?
e. Assume that you and the company controller are considering implementing a bar-coded data entry system. In what way should you or your accounting staff be involved in the design and implementation of the system? What concerns might you have about implementing the system?

7.5 Select one of the topics discussed in the chapter (or one assigned by your instructor) and research it to determine what developments have taken place since this textbook was written. There are a number of ways to do this research, including visiting computer stores and reading recent issues of computer magazines (like *PC Week* or *Personal Computing*). Write a report that covers your findings. Alternatively (or in addition), your instructor may ask you to present your findings to the class.

7.6 The Fleming Furniture Company (FFC) in High Point, North Carolina, uses a medium-sized computer to process sales orders. FFC is one of the largest wholesale furniture distributors in the nation. It has purchasing agreements with all the furniture manufacturers in North Carolina. It sells its furniture through mail order catalogs and by displaying its merchandise at quarterly furniture fairs across the country. Its sales force uses WATS lines to contact customers and proceeds to write up orders on company order forms.

Periodically during the day order forms are picked up from the salespeople and taken to the data entry department. There they are batched and entered using a key-to-disk-to-tape system linked to a minicomputer. At the end of the day the orders that have been entered and stored on the disk are sorted and transferred to tape. The tape is then used as input to the order processing program. The output is a sales order containing the data on the order form.

The firm is investigating the possibility of placing terminals on all salespersons' desks and having them enter sales orders directly into the computer. A local company has proposed a hardware configuration that costs $13,000 per month. The proposed system includes all the hardware (terminals, CPU, printer, etc.) needed to process the orders. To determine whether to switch, FFC has asked you, its accountant, to calculate the cost of the current system. You have gathered the following information.

- There are an average of 20 working days in each month.
- An average of 900 sales orders are processed each day: up to double this amount are processed after each quarterly furniture fair.
- Each sales order contains an average of 125 characters of data.
- Each preprinted, multicopy sales order costs $0.20. The order forms cost $0.10 each.
- The internal pricing mechanism used by the company allocates costs for the current medium-sized computer at $250 per hour, which includes the cost of the CPU, the peripherals, and the operator.
- The multiple-station, key-to-disk-to-tape encoder is rented from a local company for $35 per operator-hour. It is used to enter data for several different functions, including order entry.
- The data entry clerks who operate the encoder work 7.5-hour days and are paid $1050 a month.
- Data entry clerks can enter an average of three order forms every two minutes.
- The tape drive reads 70,000 characters per minute.
- It takes the computer 15 minutes per day to read and generate all 900 sales orders.
- It takes the encoder six minutes per day to sort the records.

REQUIRED

a. Compute the monthly costs of the old system according to the following categories:

1. Equipment
2. Labor
3. Materials
4. Total cost

b. Should the company rent the new system or stay with the old one? What factors other than cost should the company consider?

7.7 The basic components of an AIS include the following:

a. Input
b. Storage
c. Processing
d. Output
e. Data communication

REQUIRED

Classify each of the following items into at least one of the five previous categories.

1. Primary memory
2. Keyboard
3. 3½-inch floppy disk
4. CD ROM drive
5. Terminal
6. Math coprocessor
7. Pentium chip
8. Turnaround document
9. Modem
10. Bar code
11. Automated teller machine
12. Personal digital assistant
13. Semiconductor
14. ROM
15. Audio response unit
16. Serial interface

7.8 Selecting the right operating system to handle your desktop applications is easy, right? Not necessarily. Even though your operating system decision boils down to three common operating environments—DOS, OS/2, and Windows 95—the issues surrounding the selection of the right operating system are far more complex. When an organization decides to standardize its operating system, it has to examine not just what would save the most money, but what kind of work each department does and what kind of work it might be doing in the future.

Changing an operating system impacts the organization as a whole and each individual employee. For instance, at Travelers Insurance, managers decided to shift from the current DOS environment to the OS/2 environment, a simple switch considering that Travelers' 15,000 PCs are IBM products. Nevertheless, the shift to OS/2 was a slow one so as to prevent a sudden disruption in the way the company currently operates.

Switching operating systems isn't a simple matter of changing programs. Windows 95 and OS/2 operating systems have distinct differences that a business must consider. For example, the multitasking feature, which is common to both environments, allows for concurrent processing and switching among a number of applications operating simultaneously.

REQUIRED

a. What is an operating system? What role does it play in computer operations?
b. Describe the general features and functions of a standard operating system. Why is the selection of an operating system a complex task?
c. Research the differences between the OS/2 and Windows 95 operating systems. How do these differences affect the selection of an operating system?

7.9 Master's Clothier operates a chain of men's clothing stores in the Seattle, Washington, area. The store offers its own credit card to preferred customers. The store's accounting department is located at corporate headquarters in downtown Seattle and is handled manually by a supervisor and five employees. Three of the employees are full time (40 hours a week) and the other two employees are part time (20 hours a week). The supervisor is paid $30,000 a year, full-time employees are paid $7.50 per hour, and part-time employees are paid $7.00 per hour.

The company has been studying the feasibility of computerizing its accounting. The computer system being considered consists of two Pentium PCs, each with a 450-MB hard disk and a floppy drive, two printers, and all the software needed by the company. This system would provide 30% excess capacity on each machine.

The system would reduce the number of employees needed in the department. The computerized system would require a supervisor, two full-time employees, and two part-time employees working 15 hours a week. Owing to the increased skills needed, salaries for the hourly employees would increase to $10 an hour for full-time employees and $7.50 an hour for part-time employees. The supervisor is a salaried employee, and her salary would not be affected.

The cost for the hardware, which has an estimated useful life of four years, and the software follows:

Computer	$3500 each
Printer	1200 each
Software	600 each
Total	$5300 each

Yearly expenses would also be incurred for the computerized system. These include $300 maintenance contracts for each computer. Software updates would cost $300 per year per machine. Office supplies under the old system run $1500 per year. With the new system office supplies are estimated to be $1100 per year. Money is worth 10% a year to Master's Clothier.

REQUIRED

a. Compare the net present value of the yearly savings generated by the proposed end-user system with the purchase price of the system. Ignore the tax benefits of the purchase in making your calculations. Show your computations.
b. What factors besides the costs shown would influence the acquisition decision for the end-user system?
c. Would you recommend the purchase of the system to Master's Clothier? Would your answer change if the system had a three-year useful life?

CASE 7.1: ANYCOMPANY, INC.—AN ONGOING COMPREHENSIVE CASE

Tour the computer facilities of the business you selected and write a report that discusses the following issues:

1. The kinds of computers the company uses and the size classifications into which they fall.
2. The hardware devices the company uses for input, output, processing, storage, and data communications (if applicable); include items such as equipment, speed of the devices used, storage capacities, and prices (if possible).

3. The systems and application software used by the organization.
4. Your overall impression of the system and the employees who operate and manage it.
5. How the visit helped you gain a better understanding of the key topics covered in the chapter.

CASE 7.2: BUYING A COMPUTER FOR S&S

The summary and case conclusion section of the chapter discussed S&S's decision to buy a PC system. Based on that description and what you know about S&S, visit two or more computer stores, research PC systems, and then recommend a system for S&S. Your recommendation should include the following equipment:

1. A PC (indicate the following about the PC: name, microprocessor chip, megahertz speed, hard disk size, RAM, number of floppy drives, and whether it has a CD-ROM drive).
2. Accounting software and other software, such as word processing, spreadsheets, and so on.
3. An operating system.
4. Printers and other peripherals.
5. Any other items you feel are appropriate.

CASE 7.3: AIS AND THE MANUFACTURING INDUSTRY

The U.S. manufacturing industry has undergone tremendous change in the past 20 years. Once the mainstay of American business, this sector has struggled with aggressive global competition, changing consumer tastes, and a shift in product allegiances. Now after years of mergers, consolidations, and bankruptcies, the survivors are reemerging leaner, stronger, and ready to take on the competition. One reason for this resurgence is the way companies are using advances in information technology.

Ford Motor Company

At Ford Motor Company, the use of information technology has helped it become more efficient and sensitive to customer needs. Their ten mainframes are the lifeblood of their business and are used for mainstream business systems, from order processing to engineering and manufacturing to material logistics.

One of Ford's primary goals is to make technology accessible to every employee. PCs and workstations will play a larger role. PCs provide Ford with access to mainframe computer resources and data, engineering computers, and process control systems, as well as standard automation services. Ford is looking to distributed applications to help employees use information more effectively.

Computer-aided engineering analysis is also boosting Ford's competitive advantage with an improved design process. Previously it took five years from design to the assembly line. Ford has reduced that time frame to three years with process reengineering and tools such as computer modeling and simulation.

Ford's intent is to constantly be ahead of their competition. They use their mainframe and PCs heavily to spot potential problems and to provide employees with a shared library of information that enables them to work as a team to improve quality.

Burroughs Welcome and Company

Data processing at this pharmaceutical concern is decentralized, with systems built on specific needs, including research, regulatory compliance, and environmental control. Burroughs uses a variety of computer hardware, from large systems to PCs to networks, to handle information problems.

For most pharmaceutical manufacturers a product takes at least 10 years to enter the market. During this time Burroughs Welcome uses computers to gather and store critical data, including safety evaluation, development, and manufacturing data. Burroughs has an enormous manufacturing documentation system built to meet government regulations. It requires hundreds of thousands of pages of data a year. Burroughs feels such a system is a vital contribution to their business.

Bio-Met Inc.

Bio-Met prefers small systems. The Indiana-based manufacturer of orthopedic implants uses minicomputers for generalized business processing, controls, and materials planning—with a lot of workstations to collect data.

At Bio-Met the workstations are the backbone of the business. Using computer workstations or PCs, an engineer tests design specifications using CAD/CAM software. Once the design is complete, the software application instructs a numerical-control machine tool to develop the product. Using computer technology eliminates much of the guesswork that goes into designing orthopedic implants for individual patients. Bio-Met feels they have enough computing ability without using mainframes. They are heavily oriented to making their system more efficient, more aligned with their operations. They are central to their business.

Rockwell International Corporation

Most aerospace manufacturers use mainframes to store vast amounts of data used in the design and construction of aircraft and parts. At Rockwell large mainframes support a data center for storing product specifications for millions of parts. For a given airplane, design specifications may include over three hundred thousand parts.

In addition, Rockwell uses workstations in the development of new aerospace products. Currently, researchers are utilizing them in the design of a new high-maneuverability aircraft. Such systems also allow for the exchange of design information with international and domestic partners. In the future Rockwell hopes to shift to a distributed system to make better use of existing computer capacity.

Consider the use of information technology by the four companies in this case, and answer the following questions:

1. Business leaders argue that the decision to acquire an AIS is a business decision, not a systems decision. Do you agree? Why or why not? Use examples from the companies described in this case to support your conclusion.
2. What role does competitive advantage play in the acquisition of an AIS?
3. No one system works for every company. What issues enter into a company's decision to select a particular computer classification (e.g., minicomputer, PCs)? For each classification, discuss its specific advantages and disadvantages.
4. Will information technology alone sustain the manufacturing industry in the years ahead? Discuss.

CASE 7.4: PC PREDICTIONS

In 1991 *Fortune* magazine interviewed a number of PC experts and asked for their predictions for the 1990s. The article is briefly summarized below.

Every once in a while a new product is introduced that changes the way businesses operate. For example, the automobile, the telephone, the fax machine, the copy machine, and the airplane have all had a tremendous impact on business practices. In 1977 the personal computer (PC) was introduced. Little did people realize that this "utilitarian, ivory-colored metal box of chips, wires, and motors" would "reshape organizations, build enormous personal fortunes, and redraw the rules of the computer industry." The PC spawned an industry that now has sales in excess of $100 billion a year. This new invention "rendered the typewriter nearly extinct, turned secretaries into word-processing experts, pulled small businesses into the information age, and inspired man-machine love affairs every bit as passionate as automobiles have." The experts *Fortune* interviewed predicted the following:

- Razzle-dazzle technology will emerge faster than ever. In 1981 a basic IBM PC cost just over $2700. Adjusted for inflation, that purchase price now "buys a computer with 35 times the processing power, 1200 times the disk capacity, a high-quality color monitor, and more." Special chips "manipulate and exchange photographic images, video, and sound, as well as numbers and text." Soon computers will read handwriting and display and edit video images. The makers of semiconductors, the brain of the computer, will "cram practically an entire PC on a single chip no bigger than a dime."
- Data networks will come of age. You will be able to send and receive almost any type of document or image, including still and moving photos, docu-

ments, recordings, and spreadsheets. You will be able to see the person you are conversing with. Employees in offices all over the world will share documents and communicate throughout the day by using a computer rather than a telephone or a fax machine.

• Users could confront a bewildering array of choices. Hundreds of organizations are producing a baffling number of products from which to choose. For example, recently introduced notepads (clipboard-size computers that read handwriting) will put "digital devices in the hands of tens of millions of salespeople, delivery people, construction workers, and even executives who have never before touched a computer." IBM and Apple recently joined forces to develop PCs that electronically send and receive "living documents—fascinating amalgams of images, sounds, numbers, and text that carry with them all the software needed to make them work. The recipient will not only view the material on his or her screen but will be able as well to fiddle with the spreadsheets, edit the text, and dictate comments that the computer will record."

• Japan's electronics companies will become more of a force. They will create entirely new markets with creative devices that combine aspects of computers and inexpensive electronic gadgets. For example, "digital readers" will show up soon in the U.S.—book-size devices that display published material. So will small portable 'personal communicators' that combine a cellular phone, a fax, and a PC that keeps track of phone numbers, memos, and the like."

• Computers will change the nature of organizations and office work. In the past decade there has been little measurable increase in the productivity of office workers. A major reason is that the PC was used to automate old ways of working. The real payoff in using computers is in changing the nature of organizations and in reengineering office work.

• "As computers become a primary means of communication, companies will transport work to the workers instead of transporting workers to the work." This is not in reference to "telecommuting—white-collar workers toiling over keyboards at home—but business travel, everything from flying across America to walking to the conference room down the hall. Computers are evolving into the ultimate communication device—beyond telephones, cellular phones, faxes, even live video hookups. As your computer takes over from such devices, the way you work will change. You'll be less likely to head for the airport, wait on a fax, or even leave your desk for a meeting—unless you want to. That could streamline work and bring a surge in office productivity to greet the new century."

In 1992 *Business Week* made the following predictions:

3 To 5 Years

• Silicon chips containing neural networks able to mimic the human brain's learning and pattern-recognition faculties.

• Computers that double as video conference terminals due to their high-resolution screens and hi-fi audio.

5 To 10 Years

• Palm-top computers that exchange information over radio waves and obey voice and hand-written commands.

• Virtual-reality technology where network users can meet and interact in environments simulated by the computer.

10 To 20 Years

• Neural computers composed of tens of thousands of powerful microprocessors. They will combine optical and electronic circuits and be able to learn and reason.

• Electronic switches based on a single atom.

• Software capable of translating any of the world's languages.

More Than 20 Years

• Biocomputers that, like living creatures, can repair themselves with organic materials.

• Intelligent cities run by electronic control centers. Homes and offices will be wired with fiber optics that send voice, image, and computer data.

How many of these predictions have come true?

Source: Brenton R. Schlender, "The Future of the PC," *Fortune* (August 27, 1991): 40–48; and "What Hitachi's Labs are Hatching," *Business Week* (September 28, 1992).

ANSWERS TO CHAPTER QUIZ

1. b **3.** b **5.** d **7.** b **9.** d
2. c **4.** d **6.** d **8.** a **10.** d

Chapter 7 Appendix High-Level Languages

Name and Original Name	Description and Uses
COBOL (COmmon Business Oriented Language)	Designed specifically for business applications with large amounts of record processing and file updating. Most common programming language for business. English-like and self-documenting.
FORTRAN (FORmula TRANslation)	First high-level language to be widely used and accepted. Designed to solve scientific problems expressed in terms of mathematical formulas. Most common programming language for science and engineering.
BASIC (Beginner's All-Purpose Symbolic Instructions Code)	Designed so that nonprogrammers could easily learn it. Widely used on microcomputers and by on-line time-sharing services.
C^{++} (previous versions were called A and B)	Used extensively in developing software packages, especially for microcomputers. Has the executional efficiency of assembly language, yet has ease of use and machine independence of high-level languages.
ALGOL (ALGOrithmic Language)	Used internationally in place of FORTRAN for scientific and mathematical problems.
PASCAL (named after mathematician Blaise Pascal)	Allows a structured, modular approach to programming. Has a powerful data structuring and data manipulation feature. Very flexible and self-documenting. Used in mainframes and micros.
APL (A Programming Language)	Designed for efficient interactive programming of analytical business and scientific applications. Especially popular for time-sharing.
ADA (Named after Augusta Ada Byron)	Sophisticated multipurpose language designed for Department of Defense. Written to replace COBOL and FORTRAN.
PL/1 (Programming Language 1)	Highly flexible modular language for applications that require many computations and process large amounts of data records.
RPG (Report Program Generator)	Originally designed to produce reports. Has evolved into a powerful, prompt-driven programming language.
LISP (LISt Process)	Designed to manipulate symbols that are grouped into ordered lists. Widely used in artificial intelligence and expert system applications.
PROLOG	Artificial intelligence language especially suited to symbol manipulation. Is nonprocedural. Widely used in Japan for artificial intelligence.

Chapter 8

Personal Information Systems: An End-User Perspective

LEARNING OBJECTIVES

After studying this chapter, you should be able to:

- Explain the importance of end-user computing and appropriate end-user development and use.
- Describe the benefits and risks of end-user computing and how it is best managed and controlled.
- Identify and describe the capabilities, benefits, and uses of the different types of end-user software.

Integrative Case: S&S, Inc.

Scott and Susan have worked hard to establish their new business. S&S had a very successful grand opening a few months ago, and Susan's marketing campaign established them as a force in the appliance business. However, they are not content with a single store, and Susan has developed an aggressive expansion plan for the next three to five years.

With the company on its feet, Scott knows it is time to develop an AIS to provide the information needed to make sound business decisions and achieve the desired growth. Ashton has developed an adequate manual system and has investigated a computerized system. He has also helped Scott better understand current technology. Scott read the computer hardware and software material Ashton gave him (Chapter 6) and accompanied him on several visits to a local computer firm. Scott and Ashton are convinced S&S needs a personal computer-based system.

At their next meeting Scott hands Ashton the following questions and asks him to investigate a PC-based system:

1. Which employees will need access to a PC? How will it enhance their work?
2. How involved should employees be with the system? What are the benefits and risks of their participation? How can the risks be minimized and the benefits maximized?
3. What accounting software is needed? Can we buy a package that meets all our needs?
4. What software is needed? Do we need a spreadsheet? a word processor? a data base system? a graphics package? income tax software? Are there other types of PC software, and will we need any of them?

5. How involved should Ashton and other employees be in developing systems using spreadsheets, data bases, and so on?

INTRODUCTION

During the early days of computers, a company had one or more centralized computers supporting many users. When users wanted a system developed or needed additional information, they submitted a development request to the information systems (IS) department. If the request was approved, systems analysts would meet with users to determine their needs and then develop the new system. Unfortunately, there were a number of problems:

- Up to 80% of IS resources were spent maintaining existing systems. There was never enough computer capacity, staff, or money to meet all user needs on a timely basis. This resulted in a two- to five-year backlog of unfulfilled requests that discouraged additional requests, resulting in a hidden backlog of information needs.
- The development and implementation processes were very lengthy, which meant user needs were not met on a timely basis.
- User needs often changed by the time the development process was completed.
- Systems analysts and users had a hard time communicating. Analysts did not understand user needs and users did not understand computer technology.

As a result it was difficult for analysts to meet the diverse and oftentimes unclear information needs of various users. Users in turn did not get their information on a timely basis or in the form they needed it. In response to these frustrations, IBM of Canada in the late 1970s set up an information center to help employees bypass the normal systems development process and gain access to corporate data. By accessing corporate data themselves, employees were able avoid the long delays and meet their own information needs on a timely basis. Thus was born the process of end-user computing.

END-USER COMPUTING

End-user computing (EUC) is the hands-on development, use, and control of computer-based information systems by end users (EU). In other words, end users use computer technology to meet their information needs rather than rely on IS professionals. For example, a savings and loan in California wanted a system to track loan reserve requirements. The IS department said the system would take 18 months to develop. Rather than wait, the loan department used a PC and a data base program to develop a functional program in a single day. Enhancing the program took several more days. Not only did the loan department cut the development time from 18 months to a few days, it ended up with the exact information it needed because it developed the system.

After the automobile was introduced, a famous sociologist predicted that the automobile market wouldn't exceed 2 million cars because only that many people would be willing to serve as chauffeurs. Instead, tens of millions of cars are sold annually to people who drive themselves. It was also once predicted that the telephone system would collapse because the geometric growth in calls would require everyone to be telephone operators. Instead, equipment was developed that automated many of the functions previously performed by operators.

Since the introduction of the computer, the demand for information systems has grown astronomically. If a company wanted to eliminate all its information backlogs, almost everyone would have to become a programmer. Doesn't this sound similar to the automobile and the telephone examples? The solution? End users meeting their own information needs. As with telephones, technology will be developed to automate much of the process for us. Just as most people learn to drive automobiles, increased computer literacy and easier-to-use programming languages will allow almost everyone to operate powerful computers.

End-user computing and personal computers have revised the way computers are used. Each has made the other a more powerful influence in today's business environment. The trend toward end-user computing was already established when PCs were introduced in the early 1980s. With the advent of inexpensive PCs and a wide variety of powerful and inexpensive software, end-user computing accelerated significantly. Users began to develop their own systems, create and store data, access company data and download it, and share data and computer resources in networks. As end users began to meet their initial needs, two things happened. First, users realized computers could meet more and more existing information needs. Second, increased access to data created many new uses and needs for information. The result has been a tremendous growth in end-user computing, a growth that is expected to continue to accelerate through the next century.

The growth in end-user computing has significantly altered the role of the IS staff. They continue to develop and maintain the transaction processing systems and companywide data bases that end users draw on to meet their information needs. In addition, they provide technical advice and operational support and make as much information available to end users as possible. Although this growth has resulted in more work for the IS staff, it has been counterbalanced by a lessened demand for their traditional services.

If the end-user computing trend continues, it will represent 75% to 95% of all information processing by the turn of the century. Since you will be an end user or have a significant involvement with end-user computing no matter where you go to work, it is essential that you understand end-user computing concepts.

Appropriate End-User Development and Use

End-user development occurs when information users, such as managers, accountants, and internal auditors, develop their own applications using computer specialists as advisers. End-user development is inappropriate for complex systems, such as those that process a large number of transactions or update data base records. Therefore, it is not used for processing payroll, accounts receivable and payable, general ledger, or inventory. End-user development is appropriate for the following tasks:

- Retrieving information from company data bases to produce simple reports or to answer one-time queries. For example, S&S could analyze its sales records to determine which salesperson sold the highest dollar volume of the 10 most profitable products in the store.
- Performing what-if, sensitivity, or statistical analyses. For example, S&S could apply a spreadsheet's what-if capabilities and sales volume estimates to product prices to determine which price produces the greatest contribution margin.
- Developing applications using prewritten software such as a spreadsheet or a data base system. For example, S&S could query its data base and produce a report showing how many units of each inventory item were sold during the week.
- Preparing and processing documents, such as interoffice memos, using word processing and electronic mail.
- Preparing schedules and lists, such as depreciation schedules, accounts receivable aging, and loan amortizations.
- Enhancing presentations using graphics and special fonts. For example, S&S will soon need to approach investors and lenders to obtain the funds necessary for expansion. Showing their sales, revenue, and income growth graphically would improve the quality of their presentations.

Benefits of End-User Computing

One reason end-user computing has increased so significantly is that it offers the following advantages.

- *User creation, control, and implementation.* Accountants and other end users, rather than the IS department, control the development process. They can decide for themselves what information needs are important and whether a system should be developed.
- *Systems that meet user needs.* End users who develop their own systems are more likely to end up with systems that meet their needs. They can also discover flaws in systems that IS people would not catch.
- *Timeliness.* Much of the lengthy delay inherent in the traditional system development process is avoided, such as expensive and time-consuming cost-benefit analyses, detailed requirements definitions, and the inevitable delays and red tape inherent in the approval process.
- *Improved productivity and creativity.* Personal productivity is improved because tedious, time-consuming, and repetitive tasks are reduced or eliminated. This improves the quality of end users' work and allows them to handle more complex tasks. It frees them for more creative, thought-oriented activities and for planning and control activities. It also results in better, faster, and more accurate decisions.
- *Freeing up of IS resources.* The more information needs users can meet, the more time the IS department has to spend on other information and maintenance activities. This reduces both the visible and the invisible backlog of systems development projects.
- *Reduced communication problems.* The user-analyst-programmer communication problems inherent in traditional program development is avoided since the users develop the system.

- *Technological literacy.* Working in an end-user computing environment improves the computer literacy of users. This allows them to make better use of current technology and technological advancements.
- *Versatility and ease of use.* Most end-user computing software is easy to understand and use. Users can change the information they produce or modify their application anytime their requirements change. With portable PCs, work can be completed at home, on a plane, or almost anywhere else.
- *Ownership.* People are more interested in and take better care of things they own. The sense of ownership that comes with end-user development makes users better workers and decision makers.

Risks of End-User Computing

Some significant drawbacks to end-user computing and to eliminating analyst/programmer involvement in the development process are discussed next.

Logic and Development Errors. End users have little experience in systems development and are more likely to make errors and less likely to recognize when they have occurred. The user–developer may solve the wrong problem, poorly define system requirements, apply an inappropriate analytical method, use the wrong software, or use incomplete or outdated information. Often the error is caused by faulty logic or by incorrectly using formulas or software commands.

For example, an oil and gas company developed a complex spreadsheet to analyze a proposed acquisition. Based on the results, the company scheduled a meeting to propose the acquisition to the board of directors. Before making the presentation the company had consultants from its CPA firm test the model to see whether they agreed with its results. Shortly before his speech one of the presenters performed his own tests so he would understand how the model worked and could answer any tough questions the board threw at him. He discovered a few formulas he thought distorted the projections of what the company could attain by selling properties of the acquired company, the restatement of oil and gas reserves, and the consolidated balance sheet of the two combined entities. He called in the group that developed the spreadsheet and several partners of the CPA firm. The formulas were wrong and when they were corrected they showed the acquisition would have led to significant losses. They called off the presentation to the board, the person who developed the spreadsheet was fired, and the CPA firm no longer does any audit or consulting work for the company.

Inadequately Tested Applications. Users are not as likely to test their applications rigorously, either because they don't recognize the need to do so or because of the difficulty or time involved. One result is an application with the types of errors mentioned previously.

Inefficient Systems. Most end users are not programmers and have not been trained in systems development. Although the systems they develop may get the job done, they are not always efficient. For example, a bank clerk spent three weeks developing a program that examined each cell in a spreadsheet and changed its value to zero if it was a negative amount. When the 60-page program began returning a "too many nested ifs" error message, he called in a computer consultant. Within five minutes the consultant developed a finished application using a built-in spreadsheet function.

Poorly Controlled Systems. Many end users fail to implement controls to protect their system. Applications developed without regard to organizational standards or objectives lack sufficient input, output, or processing; data access and manipulation; and security, audit trail, and backup and recovery controls.

System Incompatibilities. Some companies add end-user equipment without considering the technological implications. As a result, they have a diversity of hardware and software that is very hard to support or to network. For example, Aetna Life & Casualty spent more than $1 billion a year on information technology in an attempt to gain a competitive advantage. The result was 50,000 PCs from a few dozen manufacturers, 2000 minicomputers and servers, 108 word processing systems, 19 incompatible E-mail systems, and 36 different communications networks. Aetna finally realized it needed to shift the emphasis from trying to own the latest technology to the effective *use* of technology. The company standardized its systems and now uses only a few types of PCs, Microsoft software products, two electronic mail systems, and one network. The result is compatibility across all systems and significantly less cost.

Poorly Documented Systems. User-created systems are often poorly documented, because the users consider the task boring or unimportant. They fail to realize that without documentation, other users cannot understand their system and how it works.

Duplication of Systems and Data and Wasted Resources. If end users are unaware that other users have similar information needs, duplicate systems occur. Inexperienced users also may take on more than they are able to accomplish, and so they end up wasting time and resources.

Increased Costs. A single PC purchase is inexpensive, but buying them for hundreds or thousands of workers is costly. Updating the hardware and software every few years is also expensive. End-user computing also has a high opportunity cost if it diverts users' attention away from their primary job. In addition, it increases time and data demands on the company mainframe and on IS people for support and assistance.

Dysfunctional Behavior. Some users go overboard in developing end-user systems, and the result is a variety of dysfunctional behaviors. End users may develop an information system to enhance their power, position, or reputation. They may develop information "just in case" they need it. They may get to the point of "analysis paralysis," in which they analyze data to death and are still unable to make a decision. They may develop systems to slant things toward a position they want to support.

As the complexity and sophistication of information systems increase, so do the risks. The risks have to be put into perspective, however, and viewed in light of the benefits to be achieved. A proper balance between maximizing the benefits and minimizing the risks of end-user systems can be achieved by providing systems analysts as advisers and by requiring user-created systems to be reviewed and documented prior to use. In addition, users can be trained in the systems analysis process so they can identify and adequately meet their needs and review the work of other users.

Managing and Controlling End-User Computing

Organizations use several approaches to manage and control end-user computing. Giving the IS department control over end-user computing discourages its growth, denies the organization most of its benefits, and is not in the best long-term interests of a company. If no controls are placed over end users, such as what end-user computing tools are purchased or how they are used, however, chaos is often the result and supporting the system becomes next to impossible. It is best to provide enough guidance and standards to control the system adequately yet allow users the flexibility they need.

One effective approach to managing end-user computing is a **help desk,** to encourage, support, coordinate, and control end-user activities. For example, the 60 help desk analysts and technicians at Schering-Plough, the pharmaceutical manufacturer, handle more than 9000 calls a month. The front-line analysts use expert system software to resolve questions quickly and then provide callers with scripted answers. The second-line technicians handle the more complicated queries. Other companies use multimedia software with animation or videos to help first-line staffers walk callers through a complicated process. The help desk executes the following tasks:

- Provides hot-line assistance to help resolve problems. Serves as a clearinghouse for information, coordination, and assistance.
- Trains end users to use specific hardware and software and provides corresponding technical maintenance and support. Evaluates new end-user hardware and software products.
- Assists with application development.
- Develops and implements standards for (1) hardware and software purchases to ensure compatibility; (2) documentation and application testing; and (3) control of security issues such as fraud, software piracy, and viruses.
- Controls corporate data so that (1) authorized end users can access and share it, (2) it is not duplicated, and (3) access to confidential data is restricted.

END-USER SOFTWARE TOOLS

Much is said in today's world about being computer-literate. However, even more important than knowing about computer hardware and software is knowing what software tool to use and when to use it. End users must be able to determine the problems they face and decide whether computer technology can help solve them. If so, they need to know which end-user software tool is most appropriate. In other words, they need to know how to apply modern technology to their job functions. This section discusses the most frequently used general-purpose software and its most appropriate use. The chapter appendix lists the names of some of the most frequently used software.

Accounting Software

There are two classifications of accounting software: low-end and high-end. Low-end software is an all-in-one product geared toward small and relatively simple organizations. The software contains the basic accounting functions but has limited reporting capabilities. In high-end software each accounting function comes in a separate module, the most popular being the general ledger. Other popular software modules are accounts receivable, accounts payable and cash disbursement, inventory management and control, fixed assets, payroll, order entry, and customer invoicing. Other modules include bill of materials, job costing, materials requirement planning, scheduling, purchasing, point of sale, and sales order. Modules are integrated so they can pass information back and forth. The general ledger is the unifying module and receives summary information from the others.

Each module edits data for correctness and validity, processes it, updates all relevant master files and data bases, and produces reports and documents. The modules are flexible and users can adapt them to their individual needs. They are user-friendly, with simple menus, screen prompts, easy-to-adapt report formats, and easy-to-read documentation. Controls, such as extensive audit trails and forced-balancing features, are included. In addition, modules contain error messages and help features.

Almost all CPAs use accounting software or audit companies that do. PC-based accounting software is especially popular among smaller organizations, because it allows companies to computerize their manual systems and to provide better and more timely information. A number of larger firms are moving their accounting systems from mainframes to networks of PCs. This gives them greater flexibility and lower processing costs and allows those involved in the transactions to process them. One reason companies can process transactions on networks of computers is the power of existing PC-based software. For example, the general ledger module from Armor Systems can generate income statements for over 1200 different departments, handle more than 33,000 employees, and process an almost infinite number of journal entries. And all of this power and flexibility can be purchased for $200 to $1000 per module.

Income Tax

The difficulty in mastering complex and difficult tax laws, combined with the power and flexibility of new tax software, has resulted in significant growth in the use of tax preparation packages. For 1995 an estimated 30 million individual and 3.3 million corporation and partnership returns were prepared using income tax preparation software. About 85% of all returns filed by tax preparers were completed on in-house computers using tax preparation software. Most tax planning is also done using PCs and tax-planning software. Understanding this software is a must for anyone considering a career in taxation.

Over eighty companies sell federal and state tax preparation software. Each package has unique, appealing features, making selection difficult. When selecting income tax software, ensure that the package possesses the following features:

- Handles at least 95% of your federal returns and 90% of your state returns without manual calculations or time-consuming program overrides. It should complete all complex calculations, such as passive losses and the alternative minimum tax.

- Is easy to learn and use, contains all essential tax forms, and prints them at acceptable speeds.
- Allows electronic filing and supports local area networks that link tax preparers together.
- Is integrated with other software, such as client billing, and carries forward information from prior years.
- Comes from a financially sound company that ensures timely delivery so that new features can be learned prior to the tax season.
- Has telephone support lines. Electronic bulletin board, fax, and on-line product support is also desirable.

Audit

Personal computing has revolutionized the auditing profession. It used to take auditors hours to prepare and foot manual trial balances, post adjustments, and prepare financial statements. If additional adjustments or changes were made, the entire footing and preparation process had to be repeated. Trial balance software allows auditors to input the working trial balance, handle all types of adjusting and reclassification entries, and automatically compute the adjusted trial balance. It also facilitates completion of financial statements and their footnotes and tax return information. Audit work papers can also be automated and tied to the trial balance.

Auditors can use a **generalized audit software package (GASP)** to perform auditing tasks. For example, a GASP can access a customer master file, test-foot the balance, select a statistical sample of the accounts, and print a working paper control sheet and confirmation letters. Auditors also use PCs for the following tasks:

- *Analytical reviews.* Ratio analysis (such as comparing the present year to the past 10) pinpoints problems that need investigation.
- *Engagement planning and management.* Comparing budgeted and actual time spent, time management, audit scheduling, and so on.
- *Statistical sampling.* Software can help in the selection and evaluation of audit samples.
- *Clerical tasks.* Time-consuming clerical processes like writing memos and reports, preparing budgets and time reports, and developing audit programs can be automated.
- *Audit tests.* Tests such as depreciation and tax estimates are easily performed.
- *Downloading data.* The PC can access, download, and analyze corporate data.
- *Research.* Accounting, auditing, and tax laws can be investigated.
- *Decision support.* Decisions such as audit scope and the nature and timing of evidence collection are simplified.

Auditors have used PCs to reduce their costs significantly. These savings result from using word processing and spreadsheets to document their work and to revise the documentation when changes occur; improved risk analysis, better planning and control of the audit, better report content and presentation, and enhanced creditability; and from using telecommunications technology to communicate with internal and external employees and clients.

Spreadsheets

An **electronic spreadsheet** is a matrix of columns and rows containing blank cells. It is used like a regular work sheet, except the computer does all the calculating. An impressive spreadsheet feature is its ability to answer what-if questions. Both the reusable nature of the spreadsheet and its what-if capability help managers select among decision alternatives. Users can store a series of keystrokes and activate them with a single command. They can also use macro programming commands to write programs or create menus to customize their templates. Spreadsheets have over 300 financial, engineering, and statistical functions (such as net present value). They also have advanced features such as goal seeking, scenario management, linear and nonlinear solvers, and array functions.

Word Processing

Word processing is the computer-assisted creation, editing, correcting, manipulation, storage, and printing of textual data. Because of its flexibility, ease of use, and time-saving features, a word processor is one of the most popular and indispensable PC software packages. Accountants use word processing to prepare letters, memos, proposals, reports, manuals, product catalogs, price lists, sales literature, newsletters, billings, and financial statements. Most word processors can be integrated with data base, graphics, and spreadsheet software. For example, the user can merge a letter with customer names and addresses in a data base to produce a form letter that looks like a personalized letter. Spreadsheets and graphs can be included in the body of a word processing text.

Data Bases

Data bases were previously available only for mainframe computers, at costs of up to $100,000. Today, there are many quality data base packages for PCs that cost less than $400. Most have security features, network connectivity, and graphics capabilities. Most quality PC-based data base systems allow users to perform the following functions:

- Create, update, and delete records in a file.
- Sort the data base according to one or more key fields.
- Search the data base for specific data.
- Print reports formatted to their specific needs.
- Perform logic operations and use business and scientific functions.
- Transfer information to and from other end-user software.
- Develop a variety of applications using its programming language.

Data bases are discussed in depth in Chapter 5.

Presentation Packages and Graphics Software

Data presented in graphic form is much easier to understand than textual or numerical data. Graphics can be prepared using the graphics capabilities of spreadsheets and data bases or by stand-alone graphics packages. The latter packages are capable of producing some very impressive graphics, including computer-generated presentations using televisions and computer monitors. Graphics can be printed on paper or displayed on color transparencies, slides, and photos. Among the most popular graphics are bar, pie, and line graphs, accompanied by titles, labels, and legends.

Many auditors and managerial accountants are beginning to graph the data in financial statements and other reports. They find that graphics help the reader to better understand trends and changes from prior reporting periods. Graphics presentations provide the following advantages over traditional presentation forums:

- Graphics presentations are more persuasive than verbal presentations or a column of numbers. The right graphics get straight to the point, generating high audience impact.
- Graphics can shorten meetings. The same information can be presented in less time using graphics.
- Graphics can lend decision-making assistance. Graphics help managers spot trends, interrelationships, problems, and opportunities earlier; they assist managers in analyzing and interpreting data.
- Graphics can capture an audience's attention and improve retention. Presenters are perceived as being (1) better prepared; (2) able to make clearer and more interesting presentations; and (3) more effective, credible, and professional.

What-if analysis, which is so popular with spreadsheets, is also possible with graphics packages. By graphically showing the effects of various alternatives, what-if graphing can improve users' productivity and enhance the quality of their analysis and decision making. Some software packages divide the screen into more than one window, allowing graphs to be viewed at the same time as text or spreadsheet data. Thus users can change data in the spreadsheet and see the results of those changes graphically.

Personal Information Managers

Personal information manager software helps end users organize their daily activities. It contains the following components:

- A calendar to keep track of appointments; many use a chime or bell as an alarm clock.
- A calculator for mathematical computations.
- An electronic notepad on which to jot down ideas and notes.
- An electronic name and address system and automatic telephone dialing.
- Features of other programs, such as electronic mail.
- A tickler file, or to-do list.

Many desktop organizers are memory-resident. They remain in a system's memory and are easily called up without disturbing the current application. For example, while working on a spreadsheet you could check your calendar without having to exit and reenter the spreadsheet.

Application Suites

Application suites are end-user software programs, such as spreadsheets, word processors, data bases, graphics, and E-mail, that are packaged and sold together. Their main attraction is price; they are sold at deeply discounted prices, often costing only a little more than the average price of one individual program. The vendors have modified the applications to give them common menu items, icons, and macro commands. When applications have the same look and feel they are easier to use, application development is simplified and more consistent, and training costs and time are reduced. Perhaps even more important, the applications are integrated. For example, a set of financial statements could be prepared using a word processor and all of the financial statements and other spreadsheet material could easily be included in the document. Many companies have purchased the more popular application suites. For example, Coopers and Lybrand bought 40,000 copies of Lotus's SmartSuite because it is integrated with Lotus Notes, its distributed document database technology product.

Desktop Publishing

Desktop publishing (DTP) provides the ability to design, develop, and produce professional quality printed documents containing text, charts, pictures, graphs, spreadsheets, photographs, and illustrations. A DTP package simplifies the complicated and expensive commercial typesetting process and places it all in a desktop computer. Using today's DTP packages, the publishing process is reduced from 6–18 months to as little as a few days.

As shown in Fig. 8.1, DTP involves four steps:

Step 1. Enter the data, usually using a word processor because it often has better text preparation and editing features than DTP. Data can also be entered from data bases, spreadsheets, graphics packages, and other software. Artwork can be entered from a graphics package, clip art (a collection of predrawn images), and scanning pictures, photographs, and drawings using image processing (explained later in the chapter).

Step 2. Format the pages by specifying the number and width of columns and by creating headers, footnotes, captions, borders, backgrounds, and other formatting items. A wide variety of font types and styles are available.

Step 3. Merge the text and illustrations into the page format created. The software will automatically flow the text into the columns and wrap it around the illustrations. The artwork and other images can be edited and scaled to the size desired. The software allows the user to see on the screen an exact image of what the printed page will look like, called WYSIWYG (what you see is what you get).

Step 4. Store and print the finished product. It can be printed on a laser printer or, to obtain the highest-quality copy, a disk copy of the stored document can be taken to a typesetter or professional printer.

Image Processing

Businesses in the United States spend almost $400 billion a year to create, distribute, store, and update paper forms and that figure is growing by up to 25% a year. Research has shown that filing and retrieving a document costs $20 in labor, finding a misfiled document costs $125, and recreating a document costs $350. Many of these costs can be eliminated using document imaging systems.

Image processing captures an electronic image of data so that it can be stored and shared. Imaging systems can capture almost anything, including

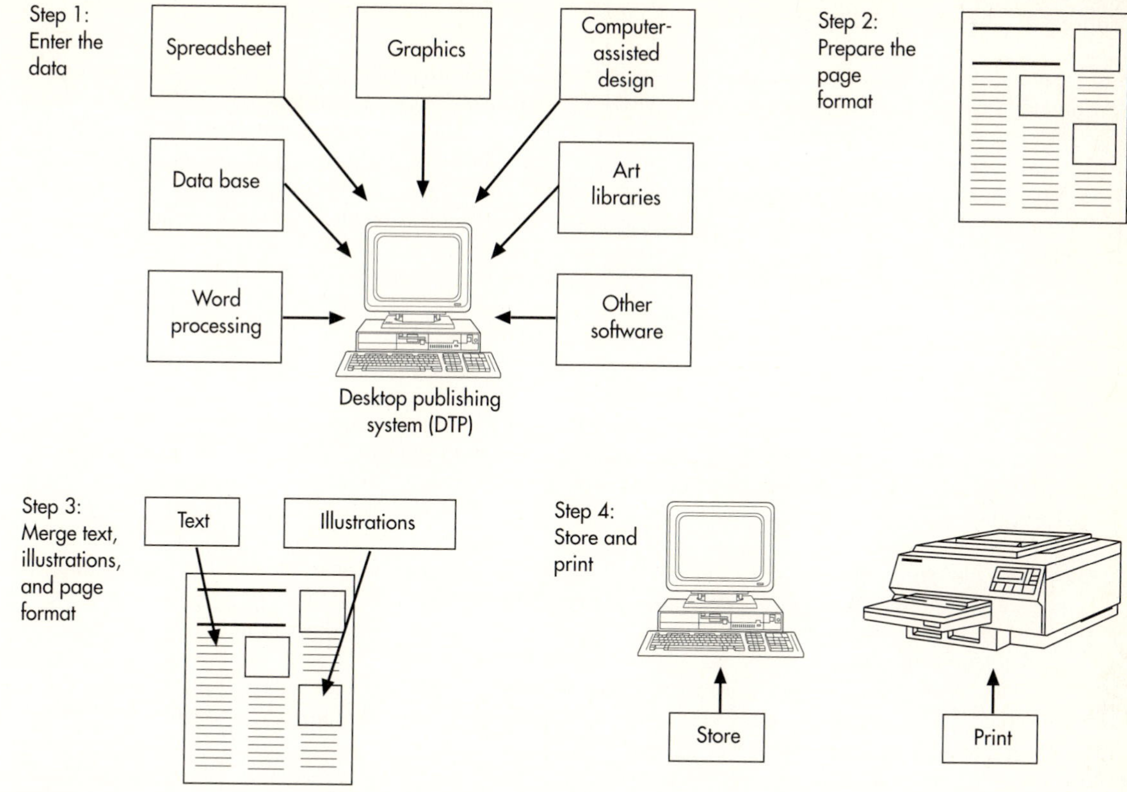

Figure 8.1

Desktop Publishing: The Four-Step Process

keystroked or handwritten documents (such as invoices or tax returns), flowcharts, drawings, and photographs. Many companies that use document imaging are making significant progress toward paperless offices. The benefits that can be derived from document imaging are shown in Table 8.1.

Image processing, which is expected to be a $12 billion a year industry by 1997, is having the impact in the 1990s that word processing had in the 1980s. At the beginning of the decade less than .1% of corporate PCs used document imaging; by the end of the decade this figure is expected to exceed 60%. Part of that growth will come from the major software developers who are working to integrate document imaging in their next-generation, multidocument software.

As shown in Fig. 8.2, there are five distinct steps to document imaging:

- *Step 1: Data capture.* The most common means of converting paper documents into electronic images is to scan them. The scanning device converts the text and pictures into digitized electronic code. This scanner can range from a simple hand-held device to a high-end, high-speed scanner capable of scanning over 2500 pages an hour. Fax modems are also used to receive electronic images of documents.

Table 8.1 **Advantages of Image Processing**

It has been estimated that 90% of the work accountants and others do today is done using paper. It is also estimated that the volume of information required by companies doubles every three or four years. As a result we are faced with being buried by paper. One solution is to make better use of document imaging. More companies are moving to this technology and it is estimated that by 2004 only 30% of our work will be paper-based; 70% will be electronic. The move to document imaging provides the following advantages:

Accessibility. Documents can be accessed and reviewed simultaneously by many people, even from remote locations.

Accuracy. Accuracy is much higher because costly and error-prone manual data-entry processes are eliminated.

Availability. There are no more lost or misfiled documents.

Capacity. Vast amounts of data can be stored in very little space, which significantly reduces storage and office space.

Cost. When large volumes of data are stored and processed, the cost per document is quite inexpensive. As a result, the costs to input, file, retrieve, and refile documents are reduced significantly. For example, while the retail store Carter Hawley Hale was in bankruptcy proceedings the judge allowed it to spend $1.2 million dollars on an imaging system because he was convinced it was going to save rather than cost the company money.

Customer satisfaction. When waiting time is significantly reduced (due to lost or misfiled documents, queue time, etc.), customers can get the information almost immediately.

Security. Various levels of passwords (network, data base, files, etc.) and clearances can be assigned to restrict document access.

Speed. Data can be retrieved at fantastic speeds. Stored documents can be indexed using any number of identifying labels, attributes, or keywords. For example, Norfolk Southern railroad has decreased the time required to retrieve deeds from three days to a few seconds.

Versatility. Handwritten or typed text can be added to an image, as can voice messages. Documents can be added to word processing files; the data can be included in a spreadsheet or data base.

- *Step 2:* *Indexing.* Document images must be stored in a manner that facilitates their retrieval. Therefore important document information, such as purchase order numbers or vendor numbers, is stored in an index.
- *Step 3:* *Storage.* Because images require a large amount of storage space, they are usually stored on an optical disk. One 5¼-inch optical platter can store 1.4 gigabytes, or about 25,000 documents (equivalent to 3 four-drawer filing cabinets). A 12-inch removable optical disk stores up to 60,000 documents, and up to 100 optical disks can be stored in devices called jukeboxes.
- *Step 4:* *Retrieval.* Documents can be retrieved by keying in any information stored in an index. The index tells the system which optical disk to search and the requested information can be quickly retrieved.
- *Step 5:* *Output.* An exact replica of the original document is easily produced on the computer's monitor or on paper or is transmitted electronically to another computer.

Image processing systems have produced significant benefits for many companies. Blue Cross and Blue Shield reduced insurance claims processing from seven to two days and produced annual savings of $10 million. John Hancock

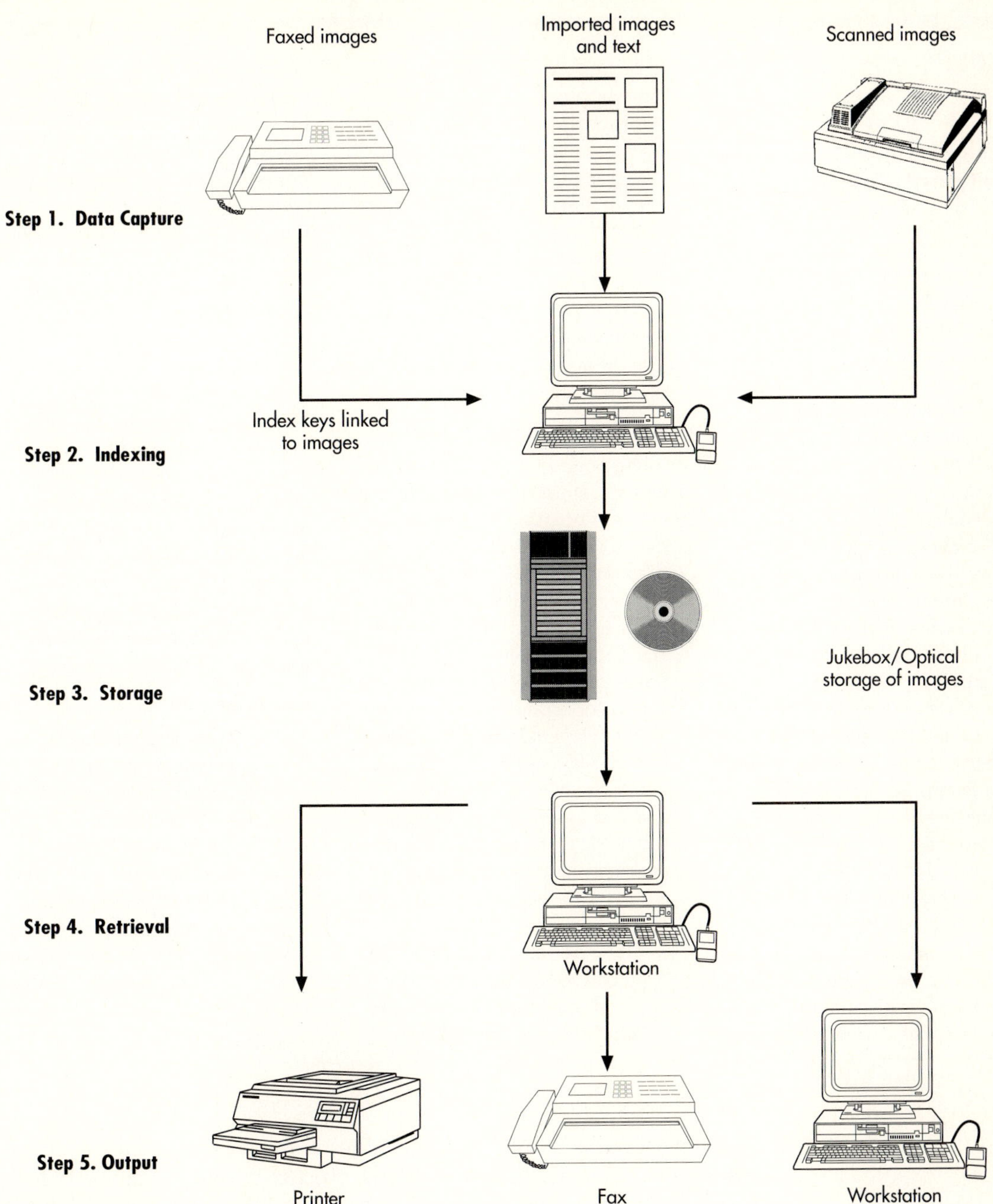

Figure 8.2

Document Image Processing

FOCUS 8.1

Signing Electronically Yields Productivity Benefits

UPS

The old saying "sign on the dotted line" may soon be replaced by "sign electronically." United Parcel Service (UPS) has equipped all 60,000 of its drivers with delivery information acquisition device (DIAD) units. The DIAD units are small computers about the size of a clipboard that contain special image-capturing software. The signer uses a stylus (a penlike rod) to sign on a pressure-sensitive pad. The imaging software displays the signature on the pad and records it electronically. At the end of each day drivers use special hardware and an information network to transmit the delivery data to the UPS Enterprise System/9000 mainframe in Mahwah, New Jersey. The entire system cost UPS about $350 million.

The system has a number of important benefits. Drivers can check out much faster at the end of the day, and a great deal of paperwork is eliminated. In addition, the system labels packages to be tracked more quickly and more accurately. When customer service receives a call requesting package information, an automated retrieval system searches the ES/9000 data base for proof of delivery. The proof of delivery is then printed and sent to the client. Alternatively, UPS clients can dial into a delivery information automated lookup system (DIALS) and search for the package information themselves.

Texas Commerce Bank

In the bank's trust division, each month the mainframe-based transaction processing system produced six copies of every customer's statement. Each copy was filed in a different location and kept on file virtually forever. The paper files filled 23,700 boxes of archive data, a 42,000-square-foot company-owned warehouse, and a 6000-square-foot off-site location. To manage this concern the company decided to use document imaging technology. The technological problems (hardware and software) of the system were the easiest to overcome.

The most difficult challenges to overcome were the company culture and individual behavior, as evidenced by a "paper hierarchy." Positions in the company were defined by paper. For example, managers were supposed to create and review paper reports and secretaries were supposed to type the reports. Eliminating paper documents was a tough sell and met with a great deal of resistance. To overcome this resistance, the bank began an analysis to determine the value of each piece of paper. Rather than dictate what records to keep, the bank informed everyone that it would scan only 2.8 million of the 15 million pages in storage. That meant that the users had to determine what to keep and what to discard. The project, which was begun in 1990, is expected to result in a paperless trust department by 1997.

Focus Questions

1. What advantages and disadvantages do the UPS and Texas Commerce Bank systems provide?
2. Why were the technological problems the easiest and the people problems the hardest to solve at Texas Commerce Bank? Do you think that is true for most new systems? Why or why not?

---

secured new business because of tremendous improvements in customer service. Additional benefits include reduced processing and storage of paper, increased productivity using less manpower, and fewer transcription errors and lost documents. The image processing systems installed at UPS and Texas Commerce Bank are explained in Focus 8.1.

S&S decided to use image processing to automate the selection and purchase of new appliances for its stores. Ashton arranged to receive vendor catalogs as images on an optical disk. Product information and specification images on the disk are accessible for simultaneous review by sales and service

- *What-is.* DSS can be used to answer questions such as: What is S&S's best-selling appliance? Who are the top salespeople? How do the sales of wide-screen TVs compare to last year's? to the sales goal?
- *What-if.* DSS can be used to answer questions such as: What effect would a 10% sales increase have on gross profit? What effect would a new incentive sales program have on net income?
- *Goal seeking.* DSS can be used to determine the tasks involved in accomplishing a specified goal. For example: What sales and expense levels would S&S have to achieve to reach a targeted net income?
- *Simulation.* These packages use different probabilities and expectations to simulate a particular situation.

The following two examples illustrate two types and various uses of DSS. The DSS developed by American Airlines, an Analytical Information Management System, is used by airlines, engine and aircraft manufacturers, consultants, and financial analysts. It supports planning, operations, marketing, and financial functions such as seating capacity and utilization, load factors, aircraft utilization, traffic growth, market share, operating statistics, and revenue and profitability. Citibank developed Managerial Analysis for Profit Planning to help bank managers make decisions about financial planning and budgeting. This DSS also helps them define and identify the costs of providing specific banking products, determine pricing, and allocate resources among products and services.

You have probably worked in groups and are familiar with some of their drawbacks. Some people dominate group discussions or decisions while others are reluctant to contribute or act deferential. Often the discussion bounces around among topics, and by the time it is your turn to speak, the discussion has already shifted to another topic. Some people have axes to grind and return to the same topic repeatedly.

Group decision support software (GDSS) helps overcome these problems by allowing and encouraging everyone to participate in decision making. GDSS brings a group of people together to share information, exchange ideas, explore differing points of views, examine proposed solutions, arrive at a consensus, or vote on a course of action. It also saves time by eliminating or reducing the number of meetings. Research shows that managers spend up to 70% of their time in meetings, leaving them little time to implement or manage their decisions. Another benefit is that people with different experiences, expertise, points of view, areas of responsibility, and backgrounds are brought together. These diverse groups often make better decisions than individuals acting alone.

There are three types of GDSS:

1. A *face-to-face session* in a room equipped with the following: workstations connected to a coordinating computer; a large screen for displaying information such as tables, graphs, and charts; and video and other special equipment for recording the group's ideas. Seating is in a semicircle or a horseshoe so everyone can see one another.
2. A *configuration of two or more decision rooms* linked together so several groups can participate in the decision-making process.

3. A *remote network* of independent workstations. Networking technology and groupware software link individual users with a data base and GDSS tools. All users need not make use of the system at the same time. In fact, the decision-making process may last several days as users respond to comments made by others at their convenience.

Artificial Intelligence and Neural Networks

Susan has an idea for expanding market share and profitability at S&S. She wants to target recent college graduates and young married couples who do not have an established credit rating and cannot afford to pay cash for their appliances. She feels that S&S, by offering credit in-house, can capture much of this untapped market. She has one concern: This is a high-risk group, and if credit is granted to too many poor credit risks, it could end up costing S&S a great deal of money. She asks Ashton whether S&S can use computers to screen applicants in the store as they apply for credit. Ashton responds that artificial intelligence software can assist S&S with this task.

Artificial intelligence (AI) is software that tries to emulate aspects of human behavior, such as reasoning, communicating, seeing, and hearing. AI software can use its accumulated knowledge to reason and, in some instances, learn from experience and thereby modify its subsequent reasoning. There are several types of AI, including natural language, visual recognition, robotics, neural networks, and expert systems; the latter topic is discussed in the next section.

Neural networks are computing systems that imitate the brain's learning process. Like the brain, which uses a network of interconnected neurons, the neural network uses interconnected processors that perform many operations simultaneously and interact dynamically to learn from data as it is processed. They recognize and understand voice, face, and word patterns much more successfully than do regular computer systems and humans. Neural networks can correlate hundreds of variables to make associations and generalize about new situations. In contrast, humans cannot effectively assimilate more than two or three variables at a time.

Like humans, neural networks learn by fine-tuning their accumulated knowledge based on what they learn from each new example and situation they encounter. For example, to teach a computer how to detect a fraudulent credit card transaction, it must be shown examples of both valid and fraudulent transactions until it can tell them apart. Networks do not handle unexpected or one-of-a-kind events very well. However, they are very good at recognizing trends that humans overlook and uncovering emerging trends. They often reach conclusions faster and better than humans do.

There are many business applications of neural networks such as managing big investment funds (and outperforming the S&P 500 stock index), and determining that industrial machinery needs preventive maintenance before it fails. The use of neural networks to detect credit card fraud is discussed in Focus 8.2. Neural networks can also serve as your administrative assistant and make your computer easier to use. For example, they can select newspaper articles you are interested in and store them for you to read. They can also sort your E-mail in order of priority and delete "junk E-mail."

FOCUS 8.2

Neural Networks Detect Credit Card Fraud

Banks and other card issuers lose more than $3 billion a year due to stolen and counterfeit cards. To combat this fraud, Mellon Bank developed an expert system that examines cardholder's spending patterns to detect abrupt and obvious changes, such as purchasing expensive luxury items or large cash withdrawals where none have occurred before. However, keying in on just a few factors, such as the size of the transaction, produced as many as 1000 potential defrauders a day, most of whom had legitimately altered their spending patterns. The unfortunate result is that fraud investigators bothered too many honest customers and wasted limited investigative resources. The limited resources, together with the large number of suspicious transactions, meant that investigators usually didn't get around to checking on a transaction for a couple of days.

Nestor Inc. has developed neural networks that are much more accurate in identifying suspected fraud. The Visa and MasterCard operation at Mellon Bank uses the software to track 1.2 million accounts and produces only one-tenth as many suspicious transactions. Fraud investigators can now investigate cases more effectively and in less than two hours. For example, the neural network spotted illegal use of a credit card and notified the owner only a few hours after it was stolen. The software can also spot trends before bank investigators do. For example, one investigator learned about a new scam from another bank. When he went to the system to have it check for the scam, he noticed that it had already identified the scam and had printed out a list of transactions that fit its pattern. The software cost Mellon Bank less than $1 million and paid for itself in six months.

Focus Questions

1. How do neural networks work?
2. What are some of the differences between expert systems and neural networks? Why are neural networks better able to detect fraudulent credit card transactions than are expert systems?
3. Did Mellon Bank make a wise decision when it purchased the neural network system? What advantages has the system provided? Would other banks and credit card issuers be wise to follow Mellon's example?

Source: Gene Bylinsky, "Computers That Learn by Doing," *Fortune* (September 6, 1993): 96–102.

Expert Systems

An **expert system (ES)** is a computerized information system that allows non-experts to make decisions comparable to those of an expert. Expert systems are used for complex or ill-structured tasks that require experience and specialized knowledge in narrow, specific subject areas. As shown in Fig. 8.3, expert systems typically contain the following components:

1. **Knowledge base.** This includes the data, knowledge, relationships, rules of thumb (heuristics), and decision rules used by experts to solve a particular type of problem. A knowledge base is the computer-equivalent of all the knowledge and insight that a group of experts develop through years of experience in their field.
2. **Inference engine.** This program contains the logic and reasoning mechanisms that simulate the expert logic process and deliver advice. It uses data obtained from both the knowledge base and the user to make associations and inferences, form its conclusions, and recommend a course of action.

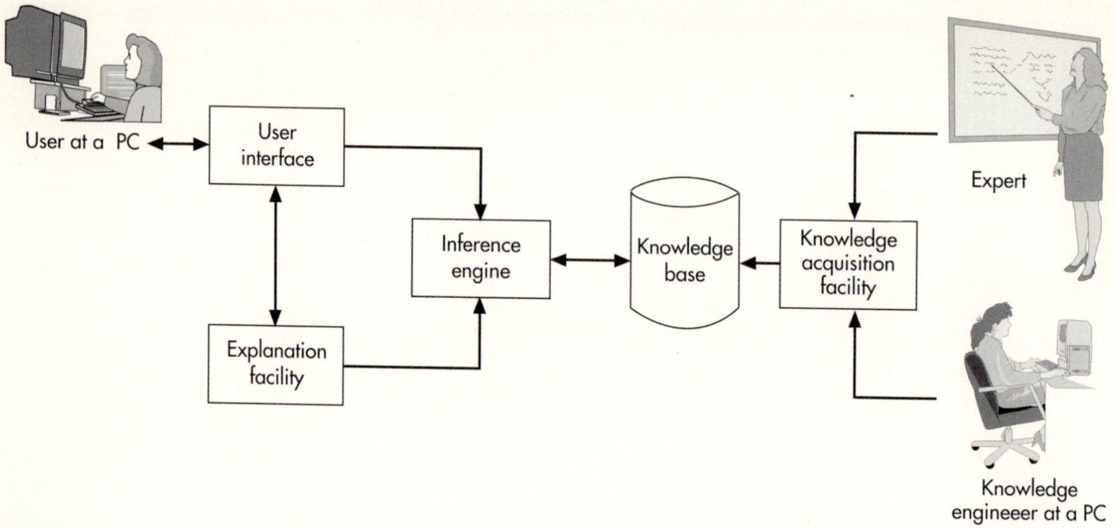

Figure 8.3

Major Components of an Expert System

3. **User interface.** This program allows the user to design, create, update, use, and communicate with the expert system.
4. **Explanation facility.** This facility provides the user with an explanation of the logic the ES used to arrive at its conclusion.
5. **Knowledge acquisition facility.** Building a knowledge base, referred to as **knowledge engineering,** involves both a human expert and a knowledge engineer. The knowledge engineer is responsible for extracting an individual's expertise and using the knowledge acquisition facility to enter it into the knowledge base. Some newer expert system packages are so sophisticated that a knowledge engineer role is removed.

Expert systems can be example-based, rule-based, or frame-based. Using an example-based system, developers enter the case facts and results. Through induction the ES converts the examples to a decision tree that is used to match the case at hand with those previously entered in the knowledge base. Rule-based systems are created by storing data and decision rules as if-then-else rules. The system asks the user questions and applies the if-then-else rules to the answers to draw conclusions and make recommendations. Rule-based systems are appropriate when a history of cases is unavailable or when a body of knowledge can be structured within a set of rules. Frame-based systems organize all the information (data, descriptions, rules, etc.) about a topic into logical units called frames, which are similar to records in data files, that are linked together. Rules are then established about how to assemble or interrelate the frames to meet the user's needs.

Expert systems provide several levels of expertise. Some function as assistants that perform routine analysis and call the user's attention to tasks that require human expertise. Others function as colleagues and the user "discusses" a problem with the system until both agree on a solution. When a user can accept the system's solution without question, the expert system can be referred to as a true expert. Developers of expert systems are still striving to create a true expert; most current systems function at the assistant or colleague level.

Expert systems offer the following benefits:

- They provide a cost-effective alternative to human experts.
- They can often outperform a single expert because their knowledge is representative of numerous experts. They are faster and more consistent and do not get distracted, overworked, or stressed out.
- They produce better-quality and more consistent decisions. Expert systems assist users in identifying potential decision-making problems, which increases the probability that sound decisions will be made.
- They can increase productivity. For example, Westinghouse increased business volume by more than $10 million per year using an expert system. Texas Instruments achieved a 10% increase in semiconductor production.
- They preserve the expertise of an expert leaving the organization.

Although expert systems have many advantages and great promise, they also have a significant number of limitations:

- Development can be costly and time-consuming. Some large systems required up to 15 years and millions of dollars to develop.
- It can be difficult to obtain knowledge from experts who have difficulty specifying exactly how they make decisions.
- Designers have not been able to program "common sense" into current systems. Consequently, rule-based systems break down when presented with situations they are not programmed to handle.
- Until recently, developers encountered skepticism from businesses due to the poor quality of the early expert systems and the high expectations of users.

As technology advances, some of these problems will be overcome and expert systems will play an increasingly important role in accounting information systems. Here are specific examples of companies that have successfully used expert systems:

- The IRS analyzes tax returns to determine which should be passed on to tax fraud investigators.
- IBM designs and evaluates internal controls in both new and existing applications.
- American Express authorizes credit-card purchases to minimize fraud and credit losses. Its ES replaced 700 authorization clerks and saved tens of millions of dollars.
- Coopers and Lybrand's system provides auditors and tax specialists with tax planning and compliance assistance. The system cost more than $1 million, and two dozen of the firm's top tax experts invested over 1000 hours in its development.

- Xerox continually compares actual results against forecasts and updates the financial planning forecast as needed.
- Lockheed Missiles and Space Co. uses expert systems to eliminate procurement errors. For example, an ES examines each on-line request form. If an item has not been properly charged to overhead, the ES advises the requester of the mistake, explains why it is incorrect, and suggests a correction.

SUMMARY AND CASE CONCLUSION

Scott and Ashton met several times to hammer out policies and plans for their new system. They reached three conclusions:

1. Their success depended, in part, on their ability to use technological advancements to increase efficiency and productivity, to improve customer service, and to achieve the growth they desired.
2. The benefits of using end-user computing significantly outweighed the risks. They want all S&S employees to be at least semiskilled and to be significantly involved in end-user development.
3. They should restrict hardware and software purchases to the standards they set to ensure compatibility and connectivity.

With some help from Kimberly Serra, the manager of Computer Applications (CA), S&S acquired several PCs and some software. Ashton and Scott narrowed down the accounting software to three packages that would meet their needs and then bought the one that CA could most easily support. Kimberly trained Ashton and the office staff and helped them install the software and convert all the data to the computer. Ashton knew that using the software the first month or two would be challenging, but Kimberly and the customer support group at CA agreed to help them with any major difficulties.

S&S purchased several copies of a word processing package, a spreadsheet, a graphics package, and a data base system. Ashton and his staff will use the word processing package to handle correspondence, memos, financial statements, and price lists. The spreadsheets will help to develop budgets, forecasts, and a cash flow management template so they can avoid the cash crunch that so often accompanies rapid growth. The graphics package will enable them to make strong presentations using charts and graphs when they try to raise money for expansion. Susan wants to expand sales significantly in the next few months by aggressively granting credit. She wants to use the data base package to keep extensive records on customer's buying preferences. To help manage credit, she wants to buy an expert system to predict creditworthiness.

As mentioned earlier, S&S will use image processing to automate the selection and purchase of new appliances. They decided against audit and income tax software and will hire a local CPA to perform the services they need. They also decided against any specialized decision support or project management software, since they think their spreadsheet can adequately satisfy their current needs.

To improve the computer skills of its employees, S&S started a tuition reimbursement program to pay for seminars or courses at a local community college. S&S also decided to make PC literacy a requirement for all employees regardless of position. Ashton has asked a member of the office staff with significant experience in computers to spend part of her time providing support to the staff.

Scott and Susan are pleased with the progress they have made with computerizing their business. They want to investigate linking S&S's computers internally and with their suppliers. Scott has already begun to make a list of the questions he needs answered before they can decide whether networking and telecommunications software is appropriate for S&S. (See Chapter 9.)

KEY TERMS

end-user computing (EUC)
end-user development
help desk
generalized audit software package (GASP)
electronic spreadsheet
word processing
personal information manager
application suites
desktop publishing (DTP)
image processing
project management software
multimedia
decision support system (DSS)
group decision support software (GDSS)
artificial intelligence (AI)
neural networks
expert system (ES)
knowledge base
inference engine
user interface
explanation facility
knowledge acquisition facility
knowledge engineering

CHAPTER QUIZ

1. Which of the following is a *false* statement?
   a. End-user computing refers to the use of computer technology by IS professionals to meet the information needs of end users.
   b. End-user computing and PCs have revised the way computers are used.
   c. End-user computing was already an established trend, but its growth quickly accelerated with the introduction of PCs.
   d. The growth in end-user computing has altered the role of the IS staff.

2. End-user development is *not* appropriate for
   a. retrieving information from company data bases to produce a list of all employees who speak Spanish.
   b. developing complex systems, such as those that process accounts receivable transactions.
   c. determining what impact a 5% raise for hourly workers would have on yearly budgets.
   d. preparing a business proposal to accompany a bank loan application.

3. Which of the following are benefits of end-user computing (there may be more than one correct answer)?
   a. End users can decide for themselves what their information needs are and whether a system should be developed.
   b. End-user-developed systems are likely to have fewer errors than those developed by the IS department.
   c. Many of the lengthy delays encountered in the traditional system development process are avoided in end-user systems.
   d. Working in an end-user computing environment improves the computer literacy of users.

4. Companies establish help desks to support and coordinate end-user activities. The duties of the help desk typically include which of the following (there may be more than one correct answer)?
   a. Answering employee questions about how PCs can be used to query the company data base

b. Providing training on a newly released version of a spreadsheet package
c. Helping to develop a spreadsheet-based system to combine each department budget into a companywide budget
d. Helping an end-user write a new program to process all purchases, accounts payable, and cash disbursements

5. Which of the following is a *false* statement about accounting software?
a. With low-end accounting software, each accounting function is contained in a separate module.
b. The most popular accounting software module is the general ledger, which receives summary information from the other modules.
c. Each module edits and processes data, updates files and data bases, and produces reports.
d. Most CPAs utilize accounting software or audit companies that do.

6. Auditors are *least* likely to use a generalized audit software package to
a. compare this year's trial balance numbers to those of the last five years.
b. compare actual to budgeted time spent on an audit.
c. process the client's monthly payroll and prepare employee checks.
d. statistically select a sample of 100 sales transactions for testing.

7. Your company needs a professional-looking newsletter to send to its clients. It wants to interweave graphics, rows and columns of numbers, and pictures around the text portion. The best end-user tool for this job is a
a. spreadsheet.
b. word processor.
c. data base.
d. graphics package.
e. desktop publisher.

8. To convert text, documents, and pictures into digitized electronic code and then store it, a company should use a(n)
a. spreadsheet.
b. project management software package.
c. image processing software package.
d. graphics package.
e. desktop publisher.

9. Your local bank wants to grow and expand by increasing its deposit base. It can't decide whether to offer free checking, increase the interest rates it pays, or conduct an intense advertising campaign. The best end-user tool for this job is a(n)
a. desktop organizer.
b. artificial intelligence.
c. project management software package.
d. decision support system.
e. desktop publisher.

10. All of the following are components of an expert system *except*
a. neural network.
b. knowledge base.
c. inference engine.
d. user interface.
e. explanation facility.

DISCUSSION QUESTIONS

8.1 The week before April 15 the IRS receives over 5000 tons of paper and every year it receives over 2.5 billion paper forms. The IRS has to hand-sort, batch, number, and key data from the forms into the computer before any of the income tax documents can be processed. This is a labor-intensive, error-prone, and very slow data-entry process. When a taxpayer has a dispute with the IRS, it can take several weeks just to find the original tax return. What end-user software could the IRS use to improve its data-entry process? to help with the storage and access problems?

8.2 More and more companies are automating their offices. Experts predict that business offices will soon be totally automated and integrated. What advantages and disadvantages do you see coming from this automation?

8.3 PCs have emerged as an efficient source of data processing. However, the uncontrolled proliferation of PC-based end-user systems in an organization creates problems, such as increased maintenance costs and nonstandard documentation. Briefly state three additional problems and describe three steps an organization can take to control these challenges. (CIA Examination, adapted)

8.4 To operate an automobile, you only need to know how to drive. How much do you think accountants need to know about end-user systems? For example, do accountants need to know how to operate and repair them? how all their components work? how to program them? Do you think these needs will change in the future?

8.5 If you were a business owner contemplating a PC and end-user software purchase, what resources might you draw on to assist you with the following challenges: What tasks should your PC-based software accomplish? Which hardware model and what software would best meet your needs?

8.6 Name three specific ways the following types of firms could use PCs and end-user software:

a. The banking industry
b. Manufacturing companies
c. Retail firms
d. Governmental units
e. Universities and colleges
f. Service firms (CPAs, attorneys, etc.)

8.7 Explain the opportunities and risks that skilled end users present to companies. How should these employees be managed?

8.8 One way to maximize the benefits and minimize the risks of end-user development is to establish development standards. What specific issues should end-user development standards cover?

8.9 Assume you have been asked to debate the question, "Are paperless offices possible?" Prepare material to support both the affirmative and the negative sides to this question. Come to class prepared to defend both positions.

8.10 Motivated by a four-year backlog of mainframe application requests, Harley-Davidson, Inc., migrated from mainframes to Applications System/400s minicomputers and PCs. The new computers save as much as 35% in processing costs over the old mainframe system. The smaller systems are easier to develop and 8–10 times cheaper than mainframe systems. Setting up the smaller systems also helps end users to understand the nature of the automated processes they work with and encourages innovation. Why are companies moving from mainframe computing to PC networking? What advantages and disadvantages does end-user computing provide over traditional mainframe applications?

8.11 Bridgestone Tire started a project called Bridgestone Information Network with 14 of its poorest-performing sales representatives. The objective was to empower the field sales force with information to meet the changing needs of customers and to provide direct sales support without delays in information. Software that took advantage of demographic data was developed to improve customer service. Salespeople used the software and laptops to access the company mainframe and provide dealers with information to tailor product lines and promotions to regional buying patterns. The sales representatives had a fairly substantial increase in sales and Bridgestone now has all of its salespeople "on-line." How did Bridgestone's user-oriented system benefit its sales force? How could laptops and user-oriented systems benefit auditors? management accountants? AIS consultants?

8.12 Pizza Hut used to handle 175,000 monthly invoices, with only 75,000 hooked up to an electronic data interchange (EDI) system. The remaining invoices were opened manually, coded, and then keyed into the accounting system. Once Pizza Hut installed an electronic document imaging system to handle the flow of paperwork, incoming invoices arrived in the form of faxes that were fed directly into the image system. The information was coded electronically and referenced to the master supplier data base where the invoice was recorded. Using the imaging strategy, Pizza Hut was able to capture another 50,000 invoices without paper at a 25% improvement in productivity. Payback on the $1.6 million investment is expected in under three years.

How do document imaging systems work? What benefits do document imaging systems provide to businesses? to accountants? How can accountants use document imaging systems?

8.13 Sears, Roebuck and Company installed point-of-sale (POS) terminals in its retail stores. The new terminals aren't typical cash registers but, rather, PCs driven by a microprocessor and linked to the Sears information network. This cut expenses by as much as $50 million a year through improved efficiency. Salespeople can now issue Sears charge cards and gift certificates, access customer information, and ring up orders from the terminals. Training time will be reduced from 3 to 4 hours on old terminals to about 45 minutes on the new PCs. How will PCs change the computing environment at Sears? What advantages will the PC network provide?

8.14 J C Penney uses an expert system in its catalog telemarketing sector. The company employs roughly four thousand operators in 14 centers throughout the United States. When peak calling hours hit, Penney struggles to keep its 800 number open for customers. Using an expert system, Penney reroutes incoming customer phone calls from busy operators to ones who are free. Identify and explain the different components of an expert system. What is the relationship between an expert system and artificial intelligence? In what other ways can expert systems help businesses like J C Penney increase productivity?

PROBLEMS

8.1 Larsen & Larsen is a local CPA firm with about five hundred small clients. The firm's winter work consists of doing individual, partnership, estate, trust, and small-corporation tax returns. During the rest of the year the firm does tax planning, prepares quarterly financial statements and tax returns for clients, and does write-up and consulting work. The firm consists of two partners, two staff accountants, and two secretaries.

REQUIRED

Propose a system that would best serve Larsen & Larsen's needs. Include the following:

a. How an end-user, PC-based system could benefit Larsen & Larsen

b. Some of the drawbacks of an end-user, PC-based system

c. The end-user software Larsen & Larsen would most likely need

d. The hardware needed to make the system effective

8.2 The U-Fix-It auto parts company sells foreign and domestic auto parts in Pasadena, California. Sam Turner started the company six years ago, with his son Bob working as a sales clerk. The company has since blossomed into one of the larger auto parts stores in Pasadena. Sam is now semiretired, and Bob has been promoted to general manager. The company employs a total of 50 people.

Company sales exceeded $1.5 million last year. Of these sales, 30% were at wholesale prices to local garages and mechanics, who have the option of purchasing on credit. When a credit sale takes place, a three-part invoice is prepared. One copy is sent to the customer. A second is used to update the company's inventory records. The third copy is used to help the company keep track of the accounts receivable records of its 500 credit customers. The remaining sales (70%) were made at retail prices to customers who pay with either cash or bank cards.

Because Sam dislikes computers, the company hasn't invested in this technology. Bob does not share his father's views; in fact, he feels computers are necessary if U-Fix-It is to remain competitive. Bob is looking for a computer system that will meet the company's present as well as its future needs.

Bob would like the system to keep track of the company's inventory of 2000 parts. He would like to store information such as part description, quantity on hand, economic order point, retail price, supplier information, and part cost. U-Fix-It purchases its inventory on credit from about a dozen suppliers. When a customer purchases a part, the sales clerk should be able to access relevant inventory status and sales information. If the customer is buying on credit, the system should produce a sales invoice.

Bob also wants to be able to use the computer to spot sales trends and to make sales and cash flow projections. He would like to have reports dealing with sales, accounts receivable, and accounts payable. He feels he could make better decisions if data could be represented graphically. Finally, Bob wants to use the system for all the company's correspondence.

REQUIRED

a. What benefits could a PC-based end-user system offer U-Fix-It? Would there be any disadvantages?

b. List the application software that will be required to meet U-Fix-It's needs.

c. List the hardware and software needed for the system Bob has in mind.

8.3 Federal Express, which has always been a technology leader, recently introduced a new way to mail packages. It installed FedEx On-Line multimedia kiosks in heavy traffic areas to make it convenient for customers to ship packages. Because the kiosks are interactive and are connected directly to FedEx's mainframe computers, they serve as an easy-to-use interface between the company and FedEx customers. Customers communicate with the kiosks using touch-sensitive screens, and the kiosks communicate using a combination of multimedia tools, including audio, images, motion video, graphics, animation, and text. In essence, the kiosks function as mainframe terminals. The kiosk software and data base can be updated remotely from the company's mainframe when changes are needed.

REQUIRED

a. What are the advantages of multimedia kiosks?
b. To get customers to use its kiosks, FedEx has to alleviate customer fears of new technology as well as any resistance to filling out airbill paperwork. What could FedEx do to overcome these challenges? How could multimedia help?
c. How would you design the kiosks to facilitate customer payment of shipping charges?
d. What other features could the kiosks provide other than convenience and a simplified shipping process?

8.4 Rent-A-Fridge (RAF) is a two-year-old company located in Boulder, Colorado. It is owned by two enterprising accounting students who realized there was a need for a company that rented refrigerators to college students. Although the owners started by renting refrigerators, they have now expanded their offerings to stereos, televisions, telephones, VCRs, and microwaves. The company employs three full-time and a dozen part-time employees who work mostly at the beginning and end of the school year. The owners plan to expand their business to other college towns once they graduate.

As accounting students, the owners understand the importance of an efficient and effective information system. To produce the information they need, they have decided to buy a PC. They feel the computer will allow them to process their transactions promptly, keep their files up to date, produce correspondence, assist in planning, and allow them to easily and quickly retrieve large quantities of information.

REQUIRED

a. Diagram the hardware configuration you feel would be most suitable for RAF.
b. List the end-user software packages you feel would be most suitable for RAF's PC system.
c. Suppose RAF grows to four stores and 60 employees. Will a single PC system be sufficient for its needs? If not, what alternative systems might RAF consider?

8.5 The scene is all too typical. You've put off preparation of the earnings analysis report until the last minute. As you search for an available machine to write up the report, you notice most employees are using a Macintosh, while all you would find was an unfamiliar IBM-compatible PC. As you turn on the machine, you're greeted by a strange C$NM prompt. After several failed attempts to call up the word processing program, you pull out a dusty typewriter and begin your work, wondering all along why software can be so daunting to use.

Software designers argue that all this is changing. Current trends in software design and performance reveal that customers are seeking less customer assistance. Graphical user interface (GUI) technology is also making software use easier. Research indicates that users with GUI technology pick up computing concepts faster and are more inclined to improve their existing software skills.

Peripheral technology is also simplifying software applications by removing the keyboard and replacing it with an electronic pen that writes directly on the screen. In the more distant future designers insist users will handle computer operations with vocal commands. Currently, emergency room doctors use voice technology to dictate information into an expert system that assists them in making a quick diagnosis. Such applications don't replace the doctor's judgment but do provide the physician with an additional opinion.

In spite of trends to simplify the use of software, critics argue that designers have a long way to go. Software is frustrating because different applications use entirely separate commands. With each application the user must remember the proper routines while avoiding the dangers of pressing the wrong button. For example, one program may use the F7 key to print a document while another may use the same key to erase data.

An easy-to-use software package can sometimes leave a user frustrated by its limited applications. After taking several hours to learn the program, the user may discover the program does not have sufficient power to handle the desired tasks. Easy-to-use programs also carry a lower price, discouraging manufacturers from developing "simplified" technology.

Computer designers are also to blame for user frustrations. Designers continue to reinforce illogical system designs in upgraded technology to avoid confusing current users. Designers also fail to consider the users' lack of technical education. There is no requirement to "put an idiot in front of the screen" to evaluate his or her responses. Perhaps that's just what the designers need to do.

REQUIRED

a. Why can software technology be so difficult to use?
b. What changes are necessary before software technology can address user frustrations?
c. Describe the recent changes in technology that are making software applications easier to use.

8.6 As computing technology grows more affordable, computer companies are scrambling to provide for a profitable but neglected segment—the small business. According to a survey by the National Federation of Independent Business, computer use among small firms increased 55% over a recent five-year period. Currently, about two-thirds of all small businesses own computer technology. But are computers helping? The final tally is still out, and users are sending in mixed reviews for a number of reasons.

Small companies lack the expertise to operate computer systems as well as the payroll to devote to the task. Companies struggle to find a system that meets their needs and, perhaps the most difficult problem of all, getting competent, affordable help. OCI Inc., a gas distribution company in Connellsville, Pennsylvania, spent $55,000 on computer consultations and software. In the end the advice was ineffective and the software was full of serious flaws. Some business owners have concluded that they almost have to become an expert themselves, which is often a frustrating and time-consuming process.

Training employees is another challenge. Computer training is too expensive for most businesses with a limited budget. All too often they just purchase a computer and assume the employee knows what to do. Many employees know nothing beyond how to turn a computer on and do not feel comfortable with the system. The result is lower productivity and increased errors. If small firms are to survive the information age, business owners can't afford to remain discouraged. Managers must work to integrate computer applications into all areas of their business in order to compete with the bigger players.

REQUIRED

a. Why is computer use growing among small businesses?
b. What challenges are small-business owners facing as they employ computer technology?
c. Assume you are the owner of a small business seeking to purchase a small computer system for your office. Discuss the following issues:

1. What role should you take as the owner in purchasing the system?
2. How can you help your employees adapt to the computer system?
3. Will you seek outside assistance to help with the purchase? Why or why not?

8.7 End-user computing isn't a new idea at Alaska Air Group, Inc., the Seattle-based holding company of Alaska Airlines. In fact, Alaska Air transformed its information system almost 10 years ago to meet the needs of end users and to save money. Most levels of employees and management are linked to the corporate mainframe and to each other through Apple and IBM PCs located throughout the business. By focusing on the skills of end users, the company took the IS group out of the operations cycle, reducing the IS backlog.

Alaska Air hires only competent, skilled computer users as employees and the IS staff has been trimmed dramatically at a significant cost savings to the company. Information is readily available which helps employees participate directly in improving efficiency and frees the IS department to focus on applications development and other strategic projects.

The approach has worked well at Alaska Air, where IS costs have been held to under $10 million, thanks largely to the end-user focus. At the same time, passenger-revenue-miles—the barometer of airline passenger business—has increased by more than 50%. Although IS isn't growing as fast as the airline, it is still installing many new applications which has produced phenomenal productivity.

REQUIRED

a. What benefits does end-user computing provide businesses such as Alaska Air? What threats does end-user computing pose?
b. As the CEO of a major corporation, would you consider end-user computing as a means of controlling IS costs? Why or why not?

8.8 No invention in the past decade has had a more profound effect on business than the PC. The growth of end-user computing is reshaping the structure of organizations, the nature of business transactions, and the scope of information available to the decision maker. Surprisingly enough, the best is yet to come.

REQUIRED

Using your school library, research the following questions:

a. What predictions are futurists making for the next 10 years in the computer industry? Do you agree? Why or why not?

b. How will end-user systems force a complete reorganization of work over the next 10 years?

c. What new or improved hardware devices and software developments will the future bring?

d. What personal predictions do you have for end-user computing in the coming decade?

8.9 With the rise of end-user computing in the workplace, many companies are considering the move to an automated internal audit. The Singer Company, a defense contractor, has pioneered electronic auditing by integrating data processing into virtually all phases of the audit. The result: a paperless internal audit.

Initially, Singer employed the PC for administrative purposes, such as preparing audit risk analysis and time budgets. With encouragement from the internal audit staff the company made the big move to the paperless audit.

Initial problems with automation came from backlogs in the EDP department. Auditors were forced to draw information from mainframe systems that were controlled and administered by the EDP staff. Internal audit needs were always given low priority and were never completed on time. The situation forced auditors to work while technical support was unavailable. In addition, an EDP support person was needed at all times to handle technical problems. Clearly, the audit staff needed its own computer system.

The Internal Audit Department purchased its own integrated minicomputer, which doubled as a file server for a small network. The manufacturer provided training support for the auditors, and the system was operational in three weeks. Problems with implementation included auditors at different levels of end-user training, incompatibilities with the existing mainframe system, and user resistance.

Due to automation, Singer employs only 18 government contract auditors (down from 36) to handle all of Singer's U.S. audits. Access to network information allows auditors at isolated sites to communicate information and ideas, reducing staff travel time. The network allows the immediate transfer of files between audit managers and the field, allowing timely feedback on workpaper reviews and job variances.

REQUIRED

a. What are the benefits of the new paperless audit?

b. Discuss the initial challenges Singer Company had with the mainframe system and the EDP department. Why do these problems occur when centralized data processing systems are used?

c. When Singer introduced end-user technology, several problems developed. List each problem and discuss potential solutions. Should such problems prevent the implementation of the network?

d. Is the systems evolution at Singer Company common in business today? Explain.

CASE 8.1: ANYCOMPANY, INC.—AN ONGOING COMPREHENSIVE CASE

Tour the computer facilities of the business you selected (see Case 1.1) and write a report that discusses the following:

1. The extent to which PCs are used in the company and your perception of how skilled its users are.
2. The benefits they have achieved and the risks they face from end-user computing. Also, explain how they are managing end-user computing to maximize the benefits and minimize the risks they face.
3. The company's end-user software tools and how they are utilized.
4. Your recommendations about how they could make better use of the software discussed in the chapter. Identify any new uses for their existing software, as well as any recommendations for new software purchases.

CASE 8.2: SELECTING A SMALL, BUSINESS-ORIENTED COMPUTER

Cathy Daniels had just returned home to Minneapolis from the annual Retail Hardware Business National Convention. Cathy felt the most impressive session of the conference was Thursday's display on the latest computer technology for small businesses. The conference was clearly worth the cost just to see the opportunities available for today's small-business owners.

Cathy spent the remainder of her ride home thinking about how she could use a computer in her local hardware store. Cathy's first thought was an inventory application. Cathy carried 4200 inventory items from over 50 separate vendors. The information she needed to store for each inventory item consisted of 480 characters of data, each identified by a 12-digit product code. Inventory had been troubling Cathy for some time; she knew that, if she didn't get control of the crisis, she might eventually go bankrupt because of her high carrying costs and the large quantities of slow-moving products. A computer could solve all these problems.

Cathy also recognized the need for some general application software that her employees could use, particularly spreadsheet and word processing programs. Cathy didn't have the cash for a large system, but she felt a budget of $10,000 was reasonable. On her first morning back, Cathy called in Andrew Knight, her accountant. Andrew was just out of college and had a special knack for electronics. Cathy felt confident Andrew could handle the selection and operation of the new system with little direction.

Buying the Hardware

Andrew was elated with the opportunity to select a new system and began with a call to his good friend Anne Larsen, who had just opened a new computer store in town. Over lunch, Andrew discussed the needs of the hardware store with Anne. She had spent two years on the audit staff of a national Big 6 CPA firm and had become intrigued with computers. When a local computer store was put on the market, Anne borrowed $40,000 and opened the store. Recently, Anne attended a four-week school where she learned all about the three lines of computers carried in her store.

A few days after their luncheon Andrew stopped by to ask Anne a few questions. Anne knew exactly what computer hardware the store would need. After some discussion Anne invited Andrew into her office to discuss specific financial terms. They were able to work out a deal that was mutually advantageous. For a reduction in the hardware price Andrew would allow Anne to use the computer system as a showcase of her ability to help clients computerize their businesses. Andrew also got a break on the price of the system, which was on sale. Anne assured Andrew of the 80486 SX model's success over the past four years. Although a new model had replaced the one Andrew was buying, some customers using the newer model were having problems, and Anne thought the manufacturers needed at least six months to work out all its bugs. Andrew was aware that a common mistake among first-time buyers was to purchase equipment that the business would outgrow in a few years. According to Anne, the 80486 SX computer could be expanded by as much as 20% to meet future growth needs.

Installing the Hardware

The next morning at work, Andrew received the following fax copy of the computer system Anne felt would work well for the hardware store:

(4) Model 486SX computers	$6000
(4) Color monitors and VGA graphics adapters	1500
(2) 24 pin dot matrix printers	1000
Showcase discount	(500)
Total price	$8000

Anne also promised Andrew immediate delivery of the computers because she had several in stock. Although the total package cost might exceed the budgeted amount for hardware, Cathy was pleased with Andrew's success in finding a system and encouraged him to accept the proposal promptly.

Anne delivered the computer the following week and helped Andrew install the three machines. Installing the computers was fairly simple, although the installation cost was an additional $500 for extra cables and Anne's time. In the course of two hours the system was ready to go. Cathy and Andrew were pleased with the machines and invited a number of friends in to show them their new PC system. Andrew explained that each computer had 4 MB of internal RAM memory and a 3½-inch drive and a hard drive with 260 MB of storage space. The dot matrix printers were also impressive as state-of-the-art printing technology. Besides, getting the dot matrix printers saved them almost $1000 over the cost of laser printer technology.

Buying the Software

With the hardware in place, Andrew returned to the computer store several days later to discuss software needs. Anne referred him to a friend who offered a broad range of accounting software. Andrew visited the store, Sophisticated Organizational Software (SOS), that afternoon and discussed his needs with the store manager. The manager indicated that in the next week SOS would release its most powerful integrated accounting package ever, Accounting Plus 1.0. Besides handling routine inventory transactions, the program could also handle receivables and payables functions, as well as fixed asset utilization and depreciation. The program also came with financial modeling capabilities and optimization software for decision making. The program even handled routine word processing. The software was perfect for the hardware store's needs because it was designed to operate on solitary PCs. The manager admitted the program was a little more expensive, but for all the extras, it was well worth it.

Andrew spent the remainder of the day testing the demonstration model of the Accounting Plus package. The inventory subprogram was quite versatile, allowing for a 10-digit product number, a 35-digit vendor or customer address, and plenty of additional fields for special codes and balances. The package would also handle up to 600 transactions a day. Besides, if the program didn't meet all of their needs, SOS would easily modify the program. The store manager indicated that after some further testing Andrew could have the software package as early as next week. However, the documentation on the software would still take a few more weeks to complete. As soon as the program was available, SOS would install the program at no additional cost. The package also came with a free training seminar at the SOS headquarters in Milwaukee, Wisconsin. The seminar would last five days and discuss a host of applications for the new software. The hardware store could purchase additional training for a nominal fee. Feeling comfortable with his decision, Andrew paid the modest $3000 price for the software package and signed the vendor's purchase and maintenance contract.

The next day, Andrew reported his progress to Cathy. Including the software and the maintenance package, the total cost was only $11,500. In addition, they could expand the system in the future and add other applications at a minimal cost. To top it all off, Andrew felt confident he could handle the inventory-related items by himself, freeing others to take on additional tasks. Cathy and Andrew were pleased with their progress to date and were looking forward to next week when the software would be available for installation. Installation and start-up would take another day or two, and then the system would be fully operational. In Cathy's opinion, Andrew had done such a good job that she gave him a raise with some of the money she anticipated saving by using the new computer.

Identify and briefly discuss the weaknesses, errors, and misconceptions in both Andrew and Cathy's thinking.

ANSWERS TO CHAPTER QUIZ

1. a	**3.** a, c, d	**5.** a	**7.** e	**9.** d
2. b	**4.** a, b, c	**6.** c	**8.** c	**10.** a

Chapter 8 Appendix Leading End-User Software

Accounting Package	Vendor	Tax Software	Vendor
AccPac Plus	Computer Associates	A-Plus Tax	Arthur Anderson
DacEasy	DacEasy Inc.	GoSystem	CLR Fast-Tax
Great Plains	Great Plains Soft.	Lacerte	Lacerte Software
Macola	Macola Inc.	Pencil Pushers	Pencil Pushers Tax Software
MAS-90	State of the Art		
One-Write Plus	NEBS Software, Inc.	ProSystem fx	CCH Computax
Open Systems	Open Systems	Software 1040	Prentice Hall
Peachtree	Peachtree	Tax Planner	BNA Software
QuickBooks	Microsoft	Turbo Tax	Microsoft
RealWorld	Real World Software		
Solomon	Solomon Software		
DOS/Windows Spreadsheets	**Vendor**	**Macintosh Spreadsheets**	**Vendor**
1-2-3	Lotus/IBM	Clarisworks	Claris
Excel	Microsoft	Excel	Microsoft
Quattro Pro	Borland		
DOS/Windows Data Base	**Vendor**	**Macintosh Data Base**	**Vendor**
Access	Microsoft	4th Dimension	Acius
Alpha Four	Alpha Software	FileMaker Pro	Claris
Approach	Lotus/IBM	FoxPro	Microsoft
dBase	Borland	Helix Express	Helix Technologies
FileMaker Pro	Claris	Omnis	Blyth Software
FoxPro	Microsoft		
Paradox	Borland		
Personal 7	Oracle		
Q&A	Symantec		
R:Base	Microrim		
UltraLite	IBM		
DOS/Windows Word Processors	**Vendor**	**Macintosh Word Processors**	**Vendor**
Ami Pro	Lotus/IBM	MacWrite	Claris
LetterPerfect	Novell	Microsoft Word	Microsoft
Word	Microsoft	WordPerfect	Novell
WordPerfect	Novell		
DOS/Windows Desktop Publishers	**Vendor**	**Macintosh Desktop Publishers**	**Vendor**
Express Publisher	Power Up Powerware	Framemaker	Frame Technology
FrameMaker	Frame Technology	Freehand	Macromedia
PageMaker	Adobe	Illustrator	Adobe
Publisher	Microsoft	PageMaker	Adobe
PagePlus	Serif, Inc.	QuarkXpress	Quark
QuarkXpress	Quark	Publisher	Microsoft
Ventura Publisher	Xerox		

continued

Chapter 8 Appendix **(Continued)**

DOS/Windows Presentation Graphics	Vendor	Macintosh Presentation Graphics	Vendor
CA Cricket	Computer Associates	CA Cricket	Computer Associates
Freelance Graphics	Lotus/IBM	DeltaGraph	DeltaPoint
Harvard Graphics	Software Publishing	Impact	Claris
Persuasion	Adobe	Persuasion	Adobe
PowerPoint	Microsoft	PowerPoint	Microsoft
Presentations	Novell	Quicktime	Apple

Personal Information Managers	Vendor
Ascend	Franklin Quest
Commence	Jensen-Jones
Ecco Professional	Arabesque Software
InfoCentral	Novell
Organizer	Lotus/IBM
Packrat	Polaris Software
Sidekick	Borland International, Inc.

Application Suites	Vendor
ClarisWorks	Claris
Microsoft Office	Microsoft
Perfect Office	Novell
PFS: WindowWorks	Spinnaker
SmartSuite	Lotus/IBM

Project Management Software	Vendor
Superproject	Computer Associates
Project	Microsoft
PS2	Scitor Corp.
Time Line	Symantic

Chapter 9

Data Communications Systems

LEARNING OBJECTIVES

After studying this chapter, you should be able to:

- Explain the fundamental concepts of data communications systems.
- Identify the hardware and software typically found in data communications systems, and explain how they operate.
- Compare and contrast alternative communications channels, communications channel configurations, and data communications carriers.
- Compare and contrast centralized and distributed processing data communications networks.
- Explain the features and uses of local area networks, wide area networks, value-added networks, and telephone networks.
- Describe a number of common data communications applications, and explain how the data communications model elements are combined to meet the user's needs.

Integrative Case: S&S, Inc.

The call from Dominican Electric (DE), one of S&S's suppliers, surprised Scott Parry. Ramon Lantigua, DE's controller, explained that DE is in the process of moving toward a paperless office. DE and many of its customers use electronic data interchange (EDI) to order goods, send invoices, and transfer funds electronically. EDI saved the company over a million dollars last year. DE is offering all non-EDI customers a 5% discount on purchases the first year each customer uses EDI.

Scott's interest in data communications had been sparked the previous week by an article on telecommunications advancements. It stated that it would soon be difficult for businesses to compete without networking capabilities. Scott learned as much as he could about DE's new system over the phone and accepted Lantigua's offer to visit DE's headquarters in Atlanta. Scott and Ashton were intrigued by what they found:

- All of the PCs at DE's three manufacturing sites and six warehouses are part of a local area network (LAN) that can access the site's main computer. Each LAN is part of a wide area network (WAN) and is connected to DE's central computer in Atlanta. Users can communicate electronically with one another on either the LAN or the WAN. The LAN and WAN connections are made using a mixture of telephone lines, cables, satellites, and microwave transmissions.
- Most communication is via electronic and voice mail. Periodic meetings are conducted at different sites using teleconferencing. DE also searches and retrieves crucial accounting data from public data bases.
- Most customers and suppliers are linked electronically to DE's computers. This network allows customer inquiries, purchase orders, and delivery and shipping instructions to be processed electronically, saving time and money.

- DE uses purchase order information to plan and schedule production for the coming month. The system also monitors the supply of parts and raw materials and, based on scheduled production, uses just-in-time inventory techniques to order what is needed for the following week.
- Most cash receipts and disbursements are handled using electronic funds transfer.

The visit to DE helped Scott realize that he wants S&S to be on the cutting edge technologically. He wants PCs at S&S to share data, hardware, and software. He'd like to take advantage of telecommunications capabilities to lower costs and improve customer service and decision making. On the return flight Scott asked Ashton to research certain aspects of data communications. Scott wanted to know what hardware and software are involved, how data are transferred between devices, the types of networks in use, and how organizations use networks. Scott also asked Ashton to investigate the following issues:

1. How should S&S link its PCs so they can talk to one another? What devices should they hook up to their network and share? How should they manage and control this shared data?
2. How should S&S link its internal network to outside networks, such as DE's, so it can use EDI and EFT? How will S&S communicate with the other networks? By telephone? By satellite?
3. What data communication hardware and software should S&S acquire? Will S&S need another computer? Specialized communications equipment? Special communications software?
4. When S&S expands in the future, should the system be centralized or distributed? What does S&S need to consider now, in terms of telecommunications, in its expansion plans?

Ashton was overwhelmed with his assignment and was not sure he had the experience or expertise necessary to lead S&S into the world of networking. His final thought as the airplane taxied up to the terminal was, "Why didn't I learn more about these essential data communications concepts when they were discussed in my AIS class?"

INTRODUCTION

Accountants must make quick and efficient decisions based on timely and accurate information. As businesses become more complex and more geographically dispersed, the problems of data collection, processing, and communication increase, yet the need for information intensifies. As a result, organizations use computers and communications technology to form **data communications networks.** These systems quickly and reliably transmit data between geographically separated points, giving authorized users immediate access to a company's computerized data.

In the early days of computers, organizations consolidated their systems into one large **centralized data processing system.** As they expanded and diversified, centralization often proved inconvenient. Data had to be transported to the data center, entered into the system, processed, and then returned to the user. When minicomputers were introduced, they were placed in remote locations within an organization and linked to a centralized computer to form a **distributed data processing (DDP) system.** DDP systems provide organizations with a great deal of flexibility. Each computer can meet the specific processing needs of the remote location and communicate summary results to the centralized (host) system; or it can be a self-contained system.

PCs have further fueled the trend toward DDP systems. They have also resulted in the development of **local area networks (LAN),** which allow individual users to (1) use a PC to meet their own personal needs; (2) share common resources such as data, printers, and storage; and (3) communicate with everyone else in the LAN and in other networks accessed by the LAN. PCs have also fueled the trend toward wide area networks, value-added networks, and telephone networks, all discussed later in the chapter.

Accountants must understand data communications systems and their networks, for a number of reasons. First, data communications technology is essential to the development and operation of a modern AIS. An AIS cannot exist in isolation; in today's global business environment, it is vital that accounting data be transmitted to the necessary users wherever they may be. The best and fastest way to do so is to use data communication systems.

Second, accountants will use and may manage data communications systems. Therefore they must understand data communications fundamentals, such as the hardware and software used, how the different components of a data communications system interface, the types of data communications systems, and how they are used. This chapter provides a basic understanding of these topics, which are becoming increasingly important to accountants.

Third, accountants will audit and evaluate data communications systems. Since these systems pose special risks, accountants will be called upon to evaluate appropriate controls and security measures. As a result, they need to know how to ensure data reliability and accuracy when data are transferred over a communications system.

Here are a few examples of accounting communication uses:

- Late at night, when phone rates are lowest, PCs in the offices of mortgage brokers nationwide exchange data with a mainframe in Chicago. The PCs receive data on additions or changes to available loan products and a summary of the previous day's transactions. The mainframe also receives data on new loan applications and all accounting transactions processed during the day.
- An auditor working in a client's office wants to double-check a recent accounting pronouncement. Rather than return to her office, she uses her PC to query a data base maintained in New York. Within minutes the pronouncement and the firm interpretation are stored electronically in her PC files.
- A large retail chain transmits data on sales volume and products sold from every store to its headquarters on a daily basis. The data are used to determine what is and isn't selling and to respond quickly to market changes.

Customers at these stores use credit cards issued from banks thousands of miles away to make purchases. Within seconds the retail store's computer is connected electronically with the credit card insurer to perform a credit check.

DATA COMMUNICATIONS SYSTEM MODEL

A data communications system transmits data from one location (the source) to another (the receiver). As shown in Fig. 9.1 a data communications system consists of five major components: 1. the sending device, 2. the communications interface device, 3. the communications channel, 4. the receiving device, and 5. communications software. Consider the example of a remote PC that transmits data to a centralized computer for processing. When the PC is ready to transmit the message or data, a communications interface device (such as a modem) converts the message to signals that are transmitted over a communications channel (such as a telephone line). At its destination another communications interface device converts the message back to internal computer code and forwards it to the receiving computer. When the receiving unit returns a message to the source to verify the message has been received, the communications process is reversed. Communications software controls the system and manages all communication tasks.

In Chapter 7 you learned about the computers that send and receive data (components 1 and 4 in Fig. 9.1). This section discusses the other components of the data communications model: communications interface devices, the

Figure 9.1

Five Components of a Data Communication System

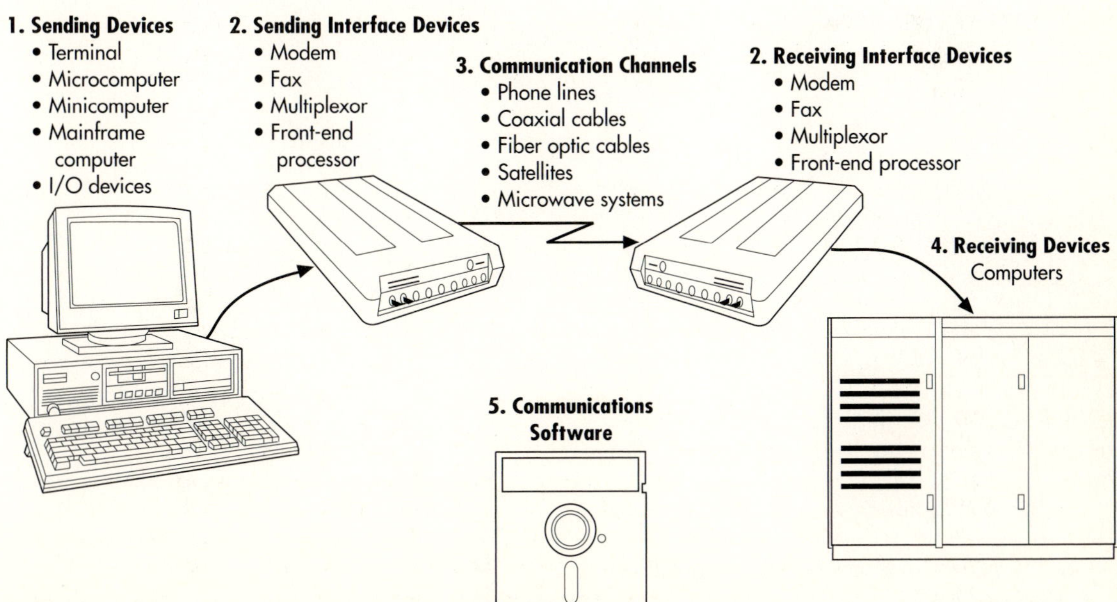

software that controls their activities, and finally the channels that connect sender and receiver.

Data Communications Hardware: Interface Devices

This section discusses four communication interface devices: modems, fax modems, multiplexors, and front-end processors.

Modems. Computers store data internally in discrete, or digital, form as the presence or absence of an electronic pulse. Telephone lines were originally built to carry voice analog transmissions. A **modem** (*mo*dulator/*dem*odulator) converts (modulates) a computer's digital signals to analog signals and then demodulates the signals at the destination. To improve data transmission, telephone companies have developed digital lines that allow data to be transmitted in digital form. Digital transmission is faster and more efficient, is less error-prone, and does not require a modem, since the modulation/demodulation process is unnecessary. However, it will be a number of years before phone companies replace all the analog lines with digital lines. A comparison of analog and digital signals is shown in Fig. 9.2.

Modems can be internal (mounted on an expansion board within the micro) or external (a separate unit connected to the computer). External modems provide greater flexibility, since they can be used with more than one type of com-

Figure 9.2

Digital and Analog Signals

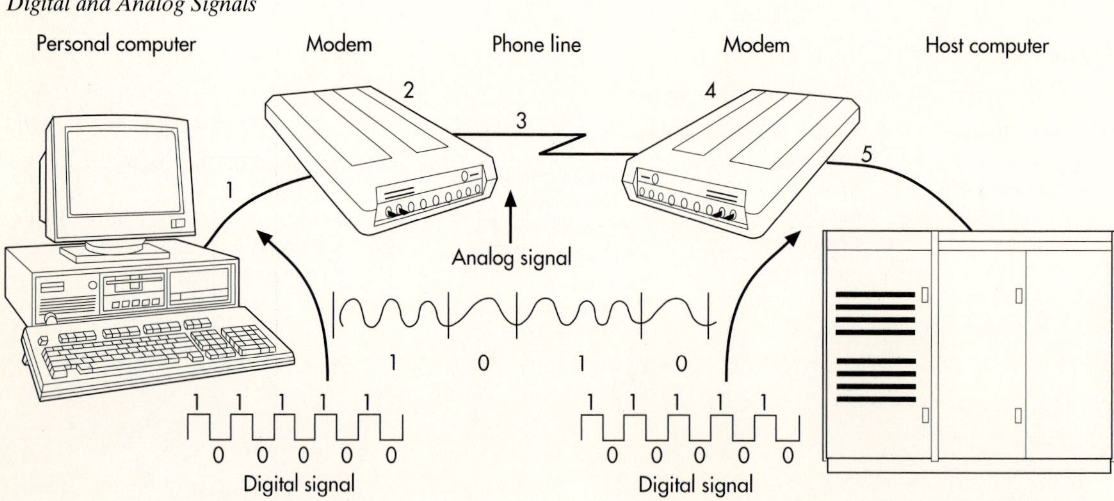

Computers store data in digital form. The steps involved in sending data over a normal phone line follow.

1. The sending device sends a modem a digital signal.
2. The modem translates the digital signal to an analog signal.
3. The analog signal is sent to the receiving modem.
4. The receiving modem translates the analog signal back to a digital signal.
5. The modem sends the digital signal to the receiving device.

Phone companies are currently installing digital lines that do not require modems to make the digital-to-analog-to-digital translation. However, it will take time to replace existing lines with digital lines.

puter. Modems can weigh as little as a pound or less (these lightweight models have become quite popular with travelers). Modem speeds are measured in **bits per second (bps).** The higher the bps, the lower the transmission costs but the higher the modem cost. Currently, four common speeds are available: 2400, 9600, 14,400, and 28,800 bps. Although 28,800 is the current standard, this speed will soon be doubled or quadrupled.

Fax Modems. Most modems now have fax capabilities. With the appropriate **fax modem** and accompanying software, users can send fully formatted documents and data files from their PC to a receiving fax machine or computer without having to print them first. A user merely selects the fax/modem feature, identifies the recipient (or their fax/modem phone number), and selects the print option. The user's software can maintain a listing of the names and phone numbers of frequently faxed people in a pop-up phone book. A user can also establish groups, to do *broadcast faxing,* or sending a fax to every one in a group with one print command or a point and click of a mouse. The software will keep trying if the line is busy and will print a listing of any incomplete destinations or of any problems encountered. The software will also store nonurgent faxes and send them at night when long-distance rates are lowest.

Remote fax retrieval capabilities allow users to retrieve faxes from their office machines while out of town or at home. Users can use optical character recognition capabilities to convert faxes they receive into documents that can be edited and incorporated into word processing files. They can also touch up the visual appearance of the fax with image processing software.

Multiplexors and Front-End Processors. A **multiplexor** combines signals from PCs, terminals, and other devices and transmits them over a high-speed communications channel. A multiplexor on the other end separates the signals back to the individual messages. When data transmission volume is high, a **front-end processor (FEP)** relieves the CPU of time-consuming data communications coordination and control functions. It can handle input and output messages, restrict access to authorized users, edit data, detect and correct errors, and store and process data.

Data Communications Software

Communications software manages data communications activities and may be executed either by the main computer or by a front-end processor. Communications software is written to work with one or more protocols. A **protocol** is a set of rules and procedures governing the exchange of data between systems. An example of a protocol is TCP/IP (Transmission Control Protocol/Internet Protocol). It defines how different computers, running incompatible operating systems, identify themselves, connect, transfer and share data, and handle errors. Communications software performs the following functions:

- *Access control.* Linking and disconnecting the different devices; automatically dialing and answering telephones; restricting access to authorized users; and establishing parameters such as speed, mode, and direction of transmission.

- *Network management.* Polling devices to see whether they are ready to send or receive data; queuing input and output; determining system priorities; routing messages; and logging network activity, use, and errors.
- *Data and file transmission.* Controlling the transfer of data, files, and messages between the various devices.
- *Error detection and control.* Ensuring that the data sent were indeed the data received.
- *Data security.* Protecting data during transmission from unauthorized access.

Communications Channels

A **communications channel** connects the sender and the receiver in the data communications network. This connection can be a line (such as a telephone line) that physically connects the two devices, terrestrial microwaves, satellite, or cellular radios. As shown in Fig. 9.3, a communications network often uses several different transmission media. This figure illustrates how Lantigua's request for Scott's visit to Atlanta was forwarded from his office on the West Coast to the corporate controller in Atlanta.

Characteristics of Channels. This section discusses some of the characteristics of data communications channels.

Serial Versus Parallel. Data transmission is either serial or parallel. With **serial transmission,** bits are transferred one at a time. Transferring an eight-bit byte serially is like having eight cars travel on a single-lane highway. With **parallel transmission,** two or more bits are transferred at the same time over separate communications channels. This is like having eight cars travel abreast down an eight-lane highway. Parallel transmission is used when its increased speed is more important than its added cost. Figure 9.4 illustrates serial and parallel transmission.

Asynchronous Versus Synchronous. When electronic signals are transmitted, both the sending and the receiving unit must be synchronized so that the signals are interpreted properly. As shown in Fig. 9.5, **asynchronous transmission** occurs when each character is sent separately and is preceded by a start bit and followed by a stop bit. These bits tell the software where a character begins and ends. With **synchronous transmission,** a block of characters is transmitted, using only start and stop bits at the beginning and end of each block. Asynchronous transmission is inexpensive and simple and is used for low-speed transmissions. Synchronous transmission is faster and more efficient, but more expensive, and is used for high-speed transmissions. PCs use asynchronous transmission; minicomputers and mainframes use synchronous.

Simplex Versus Duplex. A **simplex channel** can either send or receive signals, but not both. **Half-duplex channels** allow for transmission in both directions, but in only one direction at a time. These channels are sufficient for low-speed data transmission, for telephone service, or when an immediate response is not necessary. **Full-duplex channels** allow the system to transmit data in both directions at the same time. These channels are used for high-speed data transmission between computers or when real-time processing is necessary.

Figure 9.3

Typical Communication Network Using Cables, Telephone Wires, Microwaves, and Satellites

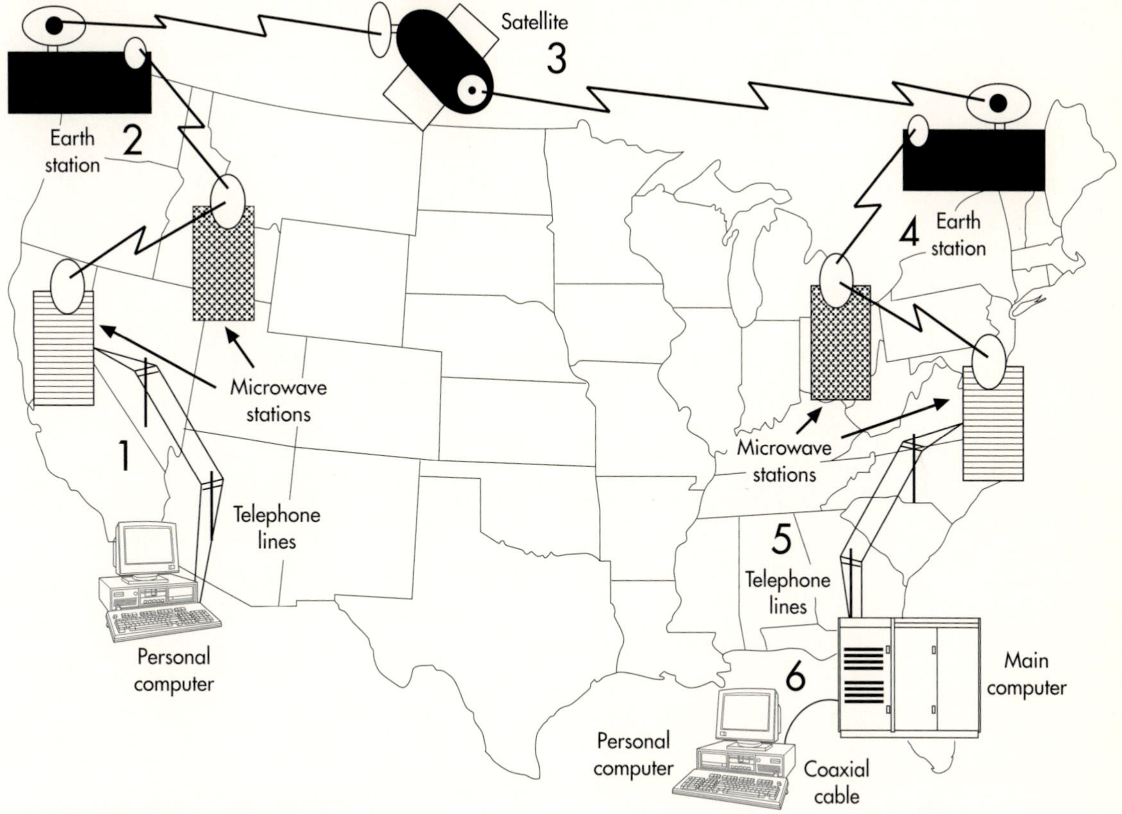

A West Coast corporate accountant for DE uses his PC to send electronic mail to the corporate controller on the East Coast.

1. Lantigua's electronic mail message is sent over phone lines to a microwave transmitter.
2. The message is forwarded by several microwave stations to a satellite earth station.
3. The West Coast earth station forwards the message to a satellite, which relays the message to an earth station on the East Coast.
4. The East Coast earth station forwards the message by microwave stations.
5. The last microwave station forwards the message by telephone wire to DE's main computer in Atlanta.
6. The host forwards the message by coaxial cable to the corporate controller's PC.

Bandwidth. A **bandwidth** is the difference between the highest and lowest frequencies that transmit data. The wider the bandwidth, the more frequencies and the more data capable of being transmitted. **Narrowband lines** are not suitable for transmitting audible or voicelike signals. **Voiceband lines** are used for voice or data communications. Three types of voice-grade telephone service are available: leased lines (dedicated exclusively to the use of a single customer), switched lines (ordinary long-distance telephone lines), and WATS

Figure 9.4

Serial and Parallel Transmissions

Serial Transmission

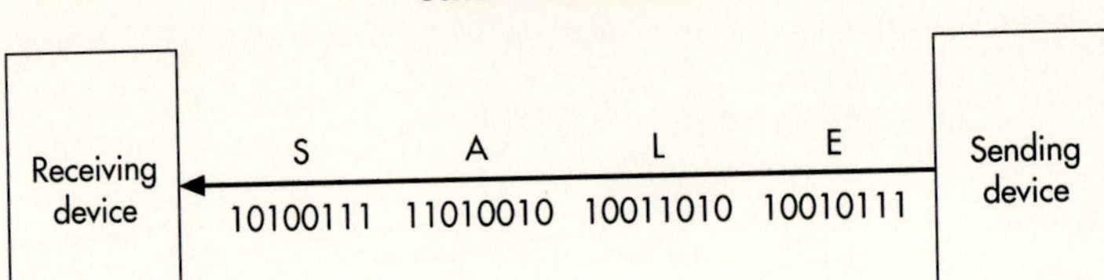

The eight bits representing each character are sent in single file.

Parallel Transmission

Receiving device

S A L E
1 1 1 1
0 1 0 0
1 0 0 0
0 1 1 1
0 0 1 0
1 0 0 1
1 1 1 1
1 0 0 1

Sending device

There are eight separate channels, each carrying one of the eight bits that represent a character.

Figure 9.5

Asynchronous and Synchronous Transmissions

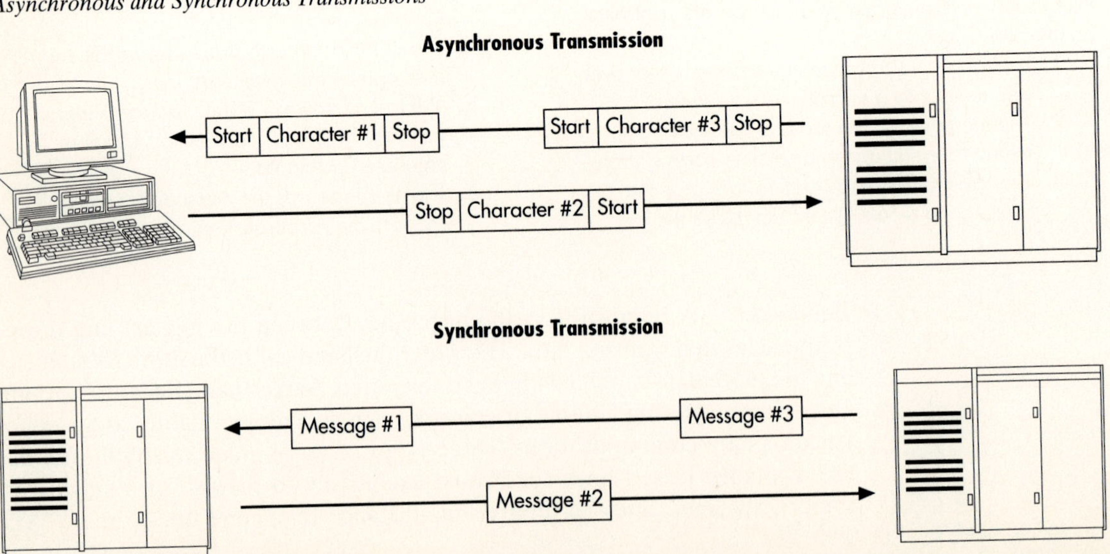

lines (special long-distance telephone service for which users pay a fixed fee for a certain number of hours and a lower charge for additional use). **Broadband lines** are used for high-speed data transmission between computer systems. Coaxial and fiber optics cables, terrestrial microwave systems, and satellites are usually used because of their greater reliability and fewer interferences.

Alternative Communications Channels. Communications channels have a significant impact on system reliability, cost, and security. Therefore accountants should understand the various types of channels and their characteristics, advantages, and disadvantages. Table 9.1 lists some of the more important characteristics of each of these alternatives.

Standard Telephone Lines. Most telephone lines consist of two insulated copper wires, called *twisted pairs*, that are arranged in a spiral pattern. Large numbers of these pairs are bundled together in large cables wrapped in protective sheaths. Telephone lines are the most convenient communications channel because large numbers of them are already installed.

Coaxial Cable. A **coaxial cable** is a group of copper and aluminum wires buried underground or placed on the ocean floor. Used in long-distance telephone networks and LANs, coaxial cable can transmit both analog and digital signals. It can be used at higher frequencies and data rates than twisted pairs because it is less susceptible to interference and distortion.

Fiber Optics. A **fiber optics cable** consists of thousands of tiny filaments of glass or plastic that transmit data using light waves. They are much faster, smaller, lighter, and less expensive than coaxial cables. Optical fibers are practically immune to distortions and therefore have a lower error rate. Fiber optics cables have a very high resistance to wiretaps and offer much higher levels of security. They operate at temperatures that melt copper cables. The new Denver airport used more than one million feet of fiber optic cabling in its air traffic control system.

Microwave Systems. **Terrestrial microwave** is frequently used for long-distance data or voice transmission. Long-distance dish antennas with microwave repeater stations are placed 30 miles apart. Each transmitter station receives a signal, amplifies it, and retransmits it to the next station.

Table 9.1 **Comparison of Communications Channels**

Type of Channel	Cost	Transmission Quality	Relative Speed	Relative Carrying Capacity	Ease of Installation	Ease of Maintenance	Bandwidth
Twisted-pair telephone lines	Low	Poor	1	1	Easy	Easy	Voice
Coaxial cable	Medium	Good	25	1,000	Medium	Medium	Broad
Fiber optics	High	Excellent	2000	1 trillion	Difficult	Easy	Broad
Microwave	Medium	Good	20	10,000	Difficult	Easy	Broad
Satellite	Medium	Good	20	50,000	Difficult	Easy	Broad

Communications Satellites. **Satellite transmission** involves beaming a signal to a satellite in space. The satellite acts as a relay station and sends the transmission back to an earth station. Several dozen of these communications satellites are currently in use. Unlike the costs of most other media, the cost of satellite transmissions is independent of the distance the message must travel. Chevron Oil is one of many oil companies using satellite technology to improve customer service and automate sales data collection. Customers at service stations can now pay for their gasoline without human interaction. Before filling up, motorists insert their credit card into a credit card reader at the pump. This reader passes the information to a satellite dish on top of the service station and that information is beamed by satellite to computers that check the motorist's credit. The approval process takes only five seconds.

Cellular Radio and Telephone. **Cellular radios** and **cellular telephones** use radio frequencies to send and receive messages. A radio frequency can be

Figure 9.6

Four Examples of Wireless Transmission

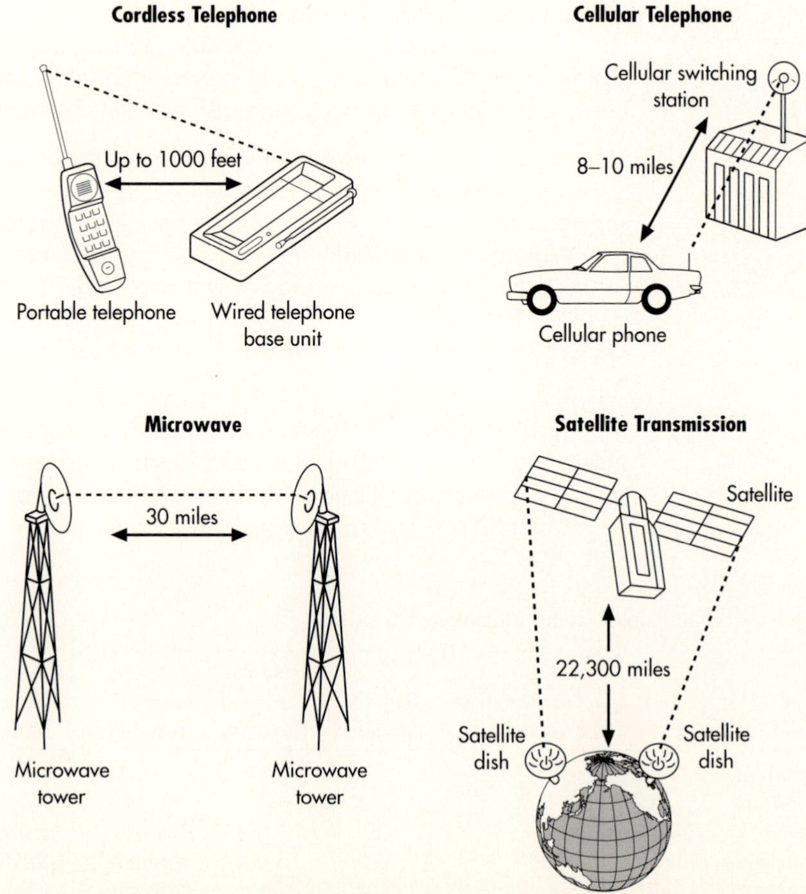

Source: Adapted from Steve Alter, *Information Systems: A Management Perspective,* 2/E, Reading, MA: Addison-Wesley, 1996, p. 475. Reprinted by permission.

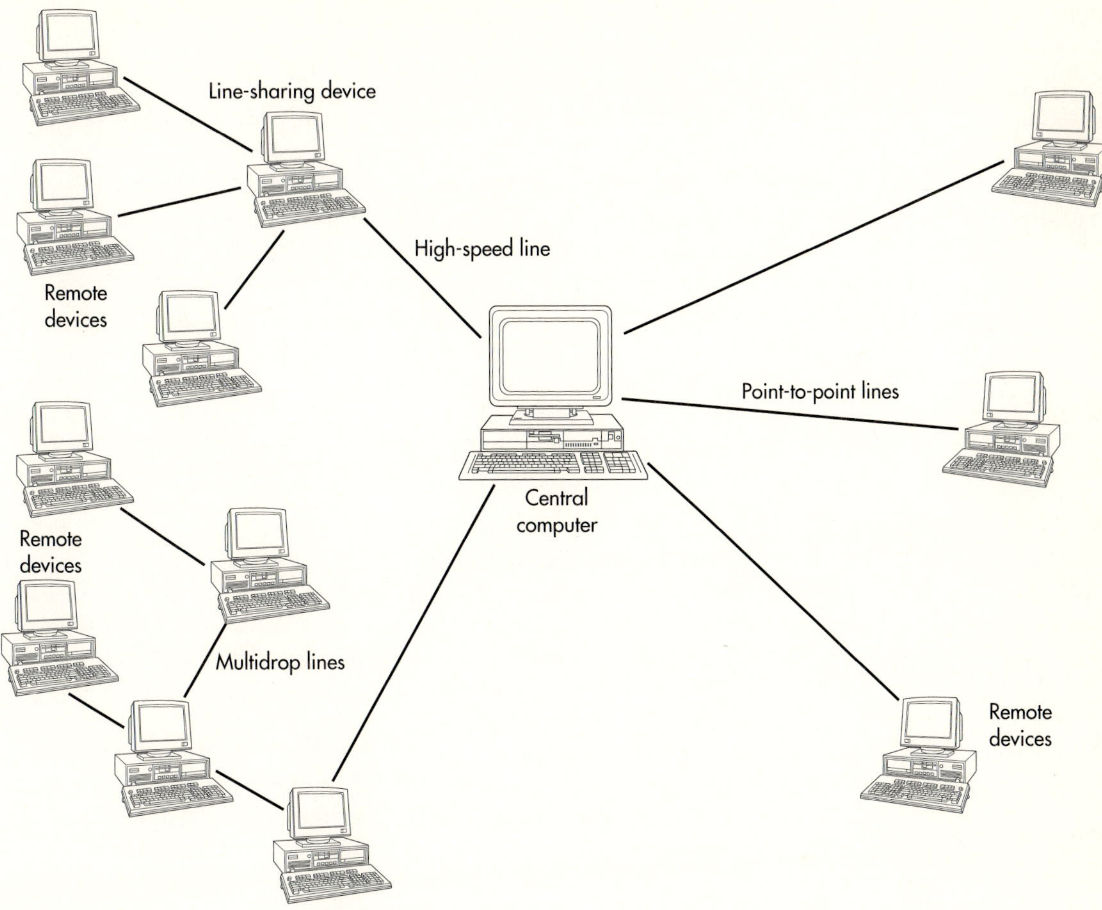

Figure 9.7

Data Communications Network Using Point-to-Point Lines, Multidrop Lines, and a Line-Sharing Device

geographically divided into small sections called **cells** so that users in different locations can all use the same frequency. In this way up to 25 times more people can use the radio frequencies. A powerful central computer and sophisticated interface equipment coordinate and control the transmission between cells. Microwave, satellite, and cellular transmission are compared in Fig. 9.6.

Communications Channel Configurations. As shown in Fig. 9.7, communications channels can be configured using one of three approaches. The simplest configuration uses **point-to-point lines,** or one line from each remote device to the central processor. **Multidrop lines** link the devices to each other, with only one device linked directly to the CPU. A **line-sharing device** allows data from several terminals to be combined for transmission on a single line. A large data communications network often contains a combination of all three approaches, which are contrasted in Table 9.2.

Table 9.2 **Comparison of Point-to-Point, Multidropped, and Line-Sharing Configurations**

	Point-to-Point	Multidrop	Line Sharing
Type of Line	Leased, switched, or WATS	Leased	Leased, switched, or WATS for connecting lines Leased shared line
Advantages	Simple hardware requirements No waiting for tied-up lines Line failure affects only one user	Reduced line mileage Reduced cost	No waiting for tied-up lines Reduced line mileage Reduced line charges
Disadvantages	Maximized line mileage Most costly	Only one terminal can transmit at a time Line failure can affect several users Little flexibility in network	Cost of line-sharing equipment Requires expensive high-speed line Line failure can affect several users

COMMUNICATIONS NETWORK ORGANIZATION

Most information systems consist of one or more computers, a number of other hardware devices, and communications channels that link the devices together to form a **communications network.** This section explains three organizational approaches to networks: centralized, decentralized, and distributed. Figure 9.8 compares these three approaches.

Centralized and Decentralized Data Processing Networks

A **centralized network** processes data at a central location using sophisticated software. User terminals, PCs, and source data automation devices send that data to the host computer for processing and return processed data to the devices as needed. The advantages of a centralized network include economies of scale, better control, more experienced personnel, and unduplicated functions. The disadvantages are greater complexity, higher communications and software costs, significantly less flexibility, and a greater likelihood the system will not meet user needs. Some of these disadvantages are overcome by implementing a **decentralized system,** which has a CPU and data processing manager at each site. Decentralized systems, however, may be lacking in controls, communication between systems, and information availability.

Distributed Data Processing Networks

Distributed data processing (DDP) connects all company locations electronically to form a DDP network. Each location has its own computer, storage, and input/output devices and so can process its own data; thus each location has the advantages of decentralized processing. These local computers can also pass data to a host computer for summarizations and for preparation of top-management reports; this structure provides the benefits of centralized processing. The result is a user-oriented (decentralized) as well as a top-management-oriented (centralized) architecture.

Because each local system is part of the network, both processing tasks and the data base are delegated to different locations and data are transferred electronically as needed. This feature avoids data redundancy but requires more complex data communications to permit other locations to find and access the data they need. Alternatively, the data base is stored at a central location and

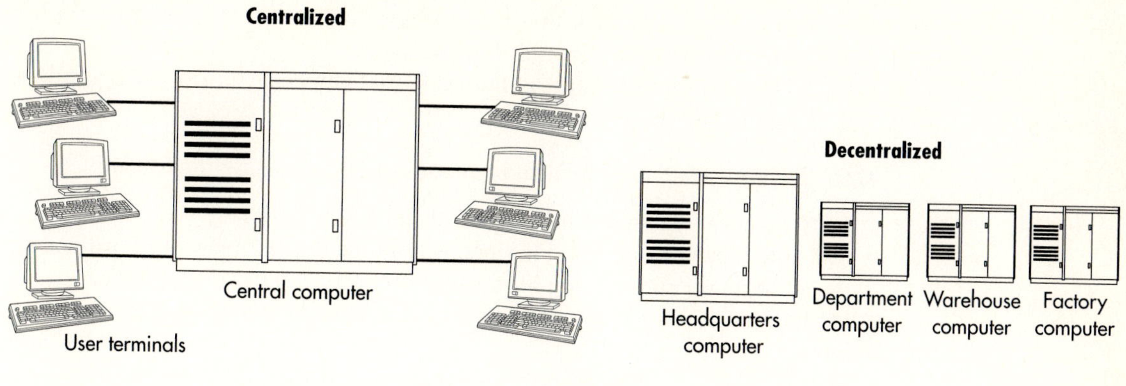

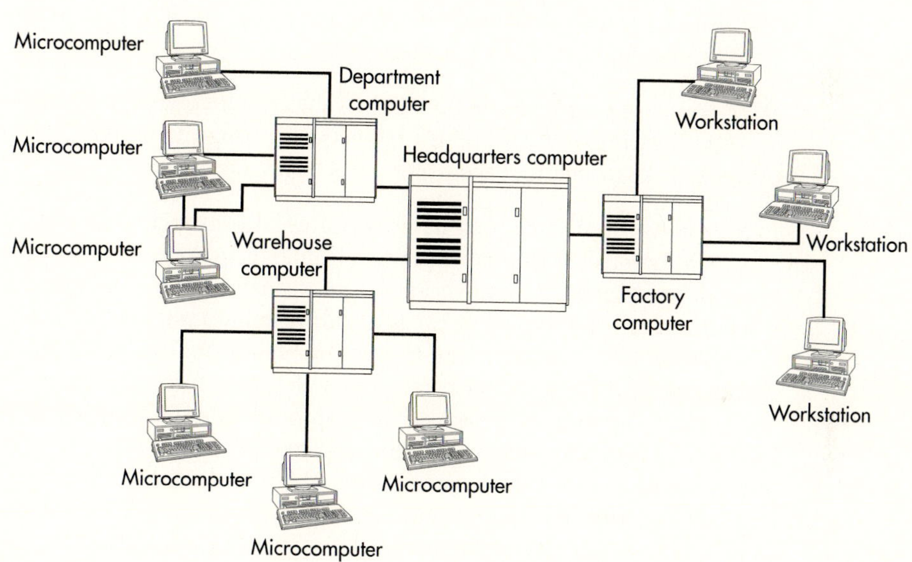

Figure 9.8

Comparison of Centralized, Decentralized, and Distributed Data Processing

copies of the data needed by each location are maintained locally. This feature has the advantage of a centralized data base and simpler data communications but results in data redundancy.

DDP Advantages. DDP has the following advantages:

- Because users control the local system and process their own data, they can tailor the system to their needs and improve the quality of the information generated.
- DDP allows faster, more accurate data entry and correction and provides faster responses.
- Communications costs are lower, since processing is completed locally.

- Network computers back up one another; there is less risk of catastrophic loss, since resources are in multiple locations.
- Each local system is treated as a module that can easily be added, upgraded, or deleted from the system.

DDP Disadvantages. The disadvantages of DDP include the following:

- DDP is more expensive than a centralized system.
- Multiple locations and varying needs complicate the tasks of coordinating the system and maintaining hardware, software, and data consistency.
- Data duplication occurs owing to multiple locations, each with its own data base.
- Standardizing documentation and control is difficult, since authority and responsibility are distributed. Multiple locations and communications channels hinder adequate security controls and separation of duties.
- On-site expertise is reduced because the expertise in a centralized system cannot be duplicated at each site.

DDP Network Configurations. The five ways network devices are linked are illustrated in Fig. 9.9. The nodes labeled A through G stand for computers, printers, disk storage, and the other parts of the network.

1. **Star network.** Distributed devices route data through a central computer, which forwards it to the proper location (this process is referred to as **network switching).** A point-to-point centralized processing system can be changed to a DDP system by substituting computers for the remote terminals and shifting some of the processing responsibilities to them.
2. **Ring network.** Data communications channels form a circular pattern as they link the local processors. Each computer communicates with its neighbor and passes messages on to the appropriate computer.
3. **Hierarchical network.** Several levels of computers are tied to a host computer and look and act like a hierarchical organization chart. For example, a company might have a large computer in the central office, medium-sized computers at each regional office, and small computers in every branch. Each level processes its own data and passes the summary data needed at the higher level upward. Any job too large to be handled is also passed upward.
4. **Bus network.** Devices are attached to a main channel called a bus. Each device reads the address of all messages sent on the bus and selects its own messages. Bus networks are easily expanded, since devices are attached only to the main channel and do not affect other devices. System performance does decrease, however, as the numbers of devices and messages increase.
5. **Hybrid network.** Most organizations have a network that contains a combination of approaches, commonly referred to as a hybrid network. For instance, several large systems might be linked in a ring configuration. Each large system can also serve as the center of a star configuration consisting of smaller systems.

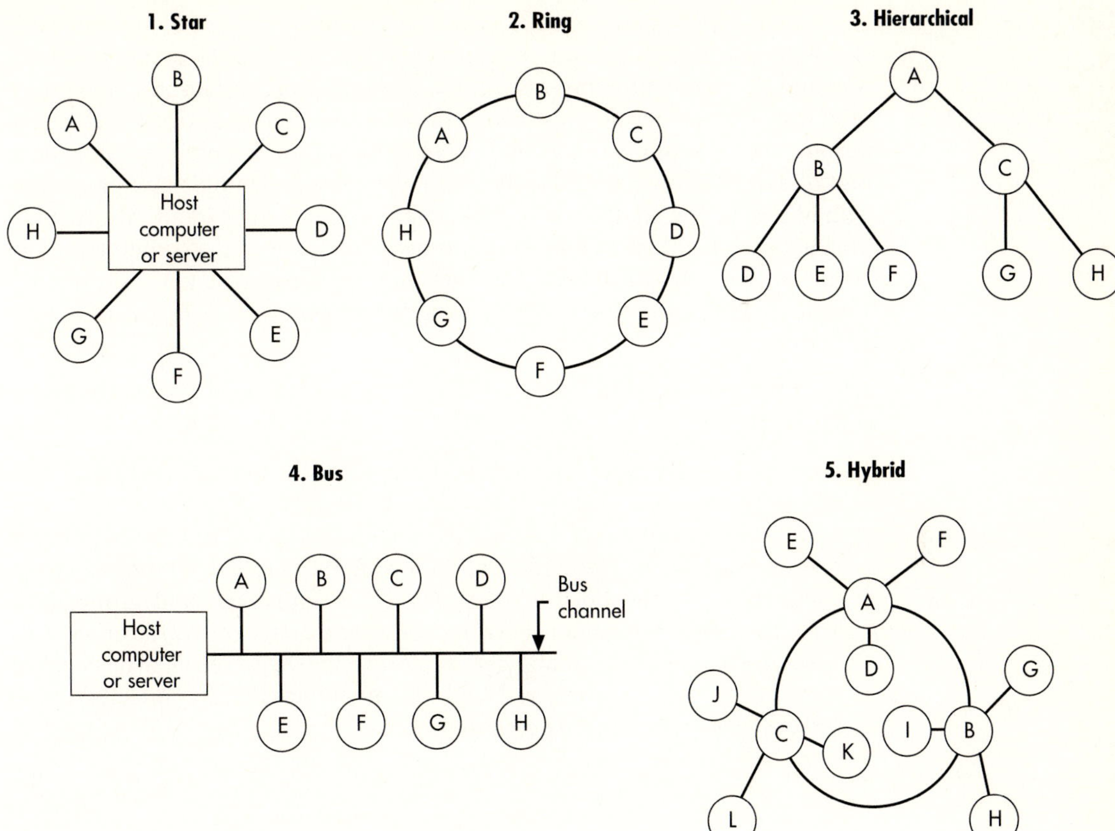

Figure 9.9

DDP Network Configurations

There is no simple answer to the question of which approach is best. That decision is usually based on the distance between the points in the network, the amount of data to be transmitted, the speed with which the message must be communicated, and the ability of each location to handle messages. The decision also depends on the organization's needs and the specific situation.

DATA COMMUNICATIONS NETWORK TYPES

Surveys have shown that as many as 90% of *Fortune* 500 companies have networked systems or plan to downsize mainframe applications to LANs and other smaller platforms linked to a larger wide area network. Companies are moving to smaller platforms because they result in cost reductions, faster application development, empowered users, and increased information access. For example, when Prudential Bank & Trust relied on mainframe systems, it took a week to receive requested reports. After the company developed a networked-based system, reports were processed in minutes and users gained the ability to ask "what-if" queries to discover new trends or correlations in corporate data.

Local Area Networks

One of the best ways to share electronic data is through a local area network (LAN) that connects computers and peripherals of all sizes within a limited proximity, such as a building. The most common LAN configuration is a group of PCs and shared peripherals such as printers and storage devices. LANs have become the most popular corporate computing platform, and increasing numbers of organizations are replacing their mainframe and minicomputer systems with LANs. In one study 98% of the companies surveyed had a LAN. In addition, about 40% of all PCs used in business are connected to a network. The Army National Guard has begun what may be the largest LAN system. By 1998 it plans to install 9000 LANs to serve 60,000 users, at a cost of almost $2 billion.

LAN Components. As shown in Fig. 9.10, a LAN consists of six major components:

1. *Hardware.* LAN hardware includes computers, printers, modems, and disk drives. All data processing in the network is done locally on PCs.
2. *Network server.* A LAN does not have a host computer but instead utilizes one or more specialized, high-capacity computers called **servers.** A server contains the application software as well as individual and group data. Together, the server and the network software manage the traffic on the network and handle the communication, storage, and resource-sharing needs of the other network computers. Network computers can be connected to the server in a star, bus, or ring configuration.

Figure 9.10

Example of a LAN Configuration

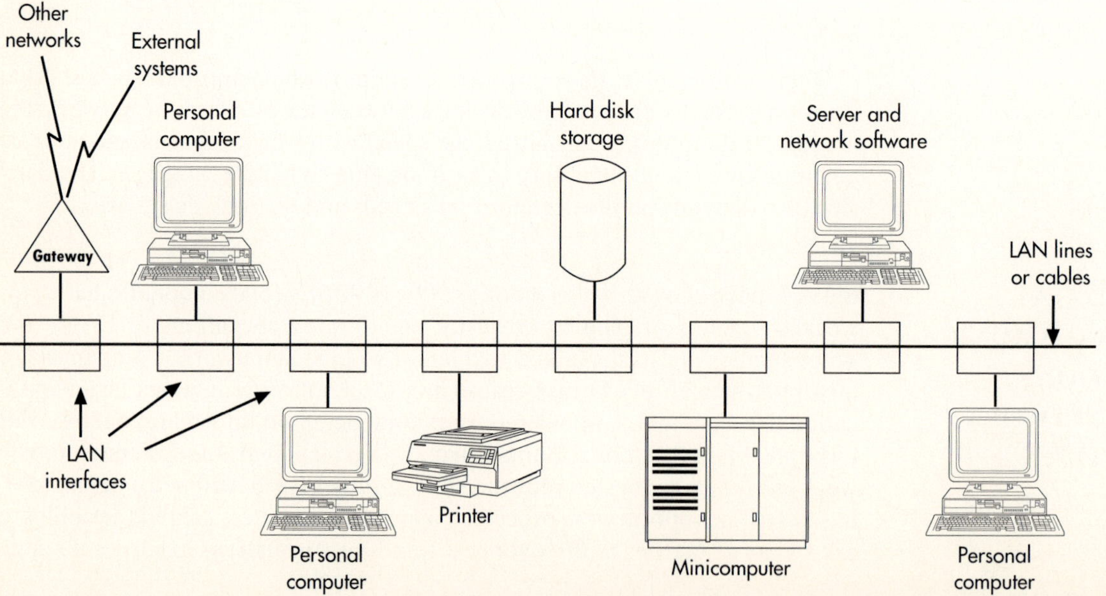

3. *Network software.* The software is the brain or intelligence of the LAN. It acts as a traffic manager to route data between the hardware and to prevent and detect data "collisions."
4. *Cables.* Coaxial cables are the most common way to connect network devices, although fiber optics cables are also used. A LAN generally has a bus or ring topology and a high bandwidth.
5. *LAN interface.* Each device connected to the network cable needs an interface device to send and receive messages.
6. *Communications interface devices.* A **gateway** allows the LAN to be connected to dissimilar networks, such as a wide area network. Gateways allow the LAN to communicate with computers almost anywhere in the world and to draw on the greater computing power and storage capacity of larger systems. A **router** connects two LANs of the same type.

Client and File Servers. Suppose Ashton wanted to know how many of S&S's accounts receivable balances were over $5000 and more than 60 days past due. As shown in Fig. 9.11, a **file server** can be used to send the entire accounts receivable file to Ashton's PC to assist him in finding his answer. The file server simply acts as a repository of data and programs; it sends users what they ask for.

Figure 9.11

Comparison of a File Server and a Client Server at S&S

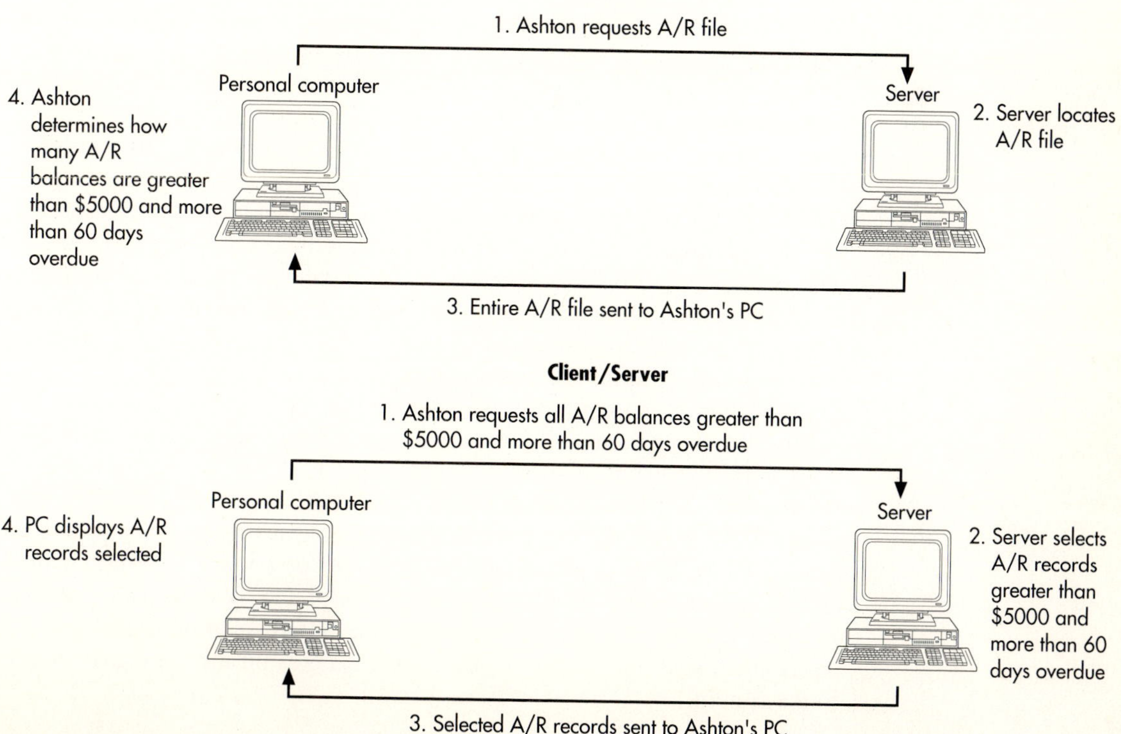
File Server
1. Ashton requests A/R file
Personal computer
Server
2. Server locates A/R file
4. Ashton determines how many A/R balances are greater than $5000 and more than 60 days overdue
3. Entire A/R file sent to Ashton's PC
Client/Server
1. Ashton requests all A/R balances greater than $5000 and more than 60 days overdue
Personal computer
Server
4. PC displays A/R records selected
2. Server selects A/R records greater than $5000 and more than 60 days overdue
3. Selected A/R records sent to Ashton's PC

In a **client/server system,** the server determines which accounts meet the criteria and sends them to Ashton's PC. The clients are the PCs or workstations tied together in the network. The server is the central computer that processes data and responds to user requests.

The client/server approach to LANs is very popular. Price Waterhouse revised its entire technological approach and has moved to a client/server software environment based entirely on a graphical user interface (GUI). United Airlines estimates it saved $4 million when it moved a crew-scheduling application from a mainframe to a Unix-based client/server application. The client/server application doubled available processing capacity and resulted in better performance and more efficient crew scheduling. Canadian utility BC Gas expects to realize annual savings of $1.4 million by moving to a client/server system.

LAN Advantages. A LAN can be used in a number of ways to make organizations more effective and efficient:

- *Electronic messages.* Users can send electronic (rather than paper) mail, messages, documents, and files. For example, Microsoft has a network that links over five thousand employees. All major decisions and changes in company policy are announced on the network, and any employee is free to send Chairman Bill Gates an electronic response.
- *Shared resources.* A LAN allows users to share a high-quality printer, files, and modems. Software can also be shared by buying a software site license. Upgrading software is much easier and cheaper with a site license because only one copy is replaced.
- *Shared data.* Hundreds of users can be linked in a network and can access common data bases. Motorola abandoned its two mainframes in favor of three LANs with over 1000 computers and workstations connected to 30 minicomputer servers.
- *Remote access.* LAN users can use wide area networks to access other data bases and networks.
- *Flexibility.* A LAN allows users to coordinate, control, and share resources, yet individuals are free to meet their own needs. LANs can accommodate multiple operating systems (such as DOS, Windows, Macintosh, and Unix) and communicate with other networks, whether they are similar or not.
- *Low cost.* A LAN is less expensive than other systems, since it does not require a central computer system and can easily share equipment. Niagara Mohawk Power estimates it saves $2000 annually for every mainframe user switched to a networked PC. Motorola cut information systems costs by a third, from 3.7% of sales to 1.2%, by moving to LANs.
- *Installation, modification, and development.* LANs are easily installed anywhere they are needed, and hardware devices can be added to or deleted from a LAN. LAN applications are easier to develop and program than mainframes. General Electric has hundreds of LANs that are constantly being modified as needs change. Sprint completed software enhancements on its client/server system in half the time it takes on the company's mainframe system.

- *Reliability.* Breakdowns in a PC attached to the network have no effect on other system devices.
- *Capacity and speed.* A LAN handles large volumes of data at very high transmission speeds. Niagara Mohawk estimates users can access data 10%–25% faster from a network data base than from a mainframe data base.
- *Backup.* A LAN can create backup files easily and regularly, a task that many users shy away from on their individual PCs.

Financial Guaranty Insurance Company (FGIC), a municipal bond insurer with $1.2 billion in assets, was one of the first companies to downsize completely from a mainframe to a PC-based network, beginning in 1987. It took the firm 18 months to install Compaq PCs on a Novell network, write all new applications using Foxbase, and eliminate its mainframe. The improvements were marked. Instead of spending about $6 million per year on a mainframe system that was not adequately serving the growing company, FGIC now has a budget of $2.5 million. The IS staff shrunk from 70 to 20. Development backlog, once a "generation" behind, has been shortened so that the information in requested reports is still timely and relevant when received.

LAN Disadvantages. As popular and useful as LANs are, they do have disadvantages:

- *Lack of standards.* Because the technology is so young, uniform standards for LANs are not very well developed. Many products still do not communicate well with each other.
- *Security.* Computer security methods are also not as well developed as they are with larger systems. The Army National Guard is connecting diskless workstations to their network to reduce the problems of stolen data and viruses being introduced into the network.
- *Specialized staff.* LANs are complex and require specially trained staff to install, manage, and support them. A **network administrator** is often needed to control access to the system and to maintain the shared software and data. For example, St. Paul Company, an international insurance agency, has 26 LANs, each with an administrator and an assistant. Each must understand application software, LAN software, how to troubleshoot, and how to deal with frustrated users.
- *Reliability.* If a server fails, all or part of the network can crash and leave users without computer power. A survey of over 100 large companies showed that each year LAN failures cost an average $7.5 million in lost productivity and revenue. These losses increased sixfold over a four-year period.
- *Cost.* Despite being less expensive than a mainframe system, a LAN system still represents a significant investment. Converting to a LAN is expensive, especially when training, conversion, PC troubleshooting problems, and other such expenses are included.

Wide Area Networks

A **wide area network (WAN)** is a telecommunications network that uses a combination of communication channels to connect a wide variety of hardware devices in many locations. It can cover an area as small as a few cities or as large as the globe. WANs are usually developed so that a company's scattered offices and sites can communicate with one another or with other organizations. They are also developed to assist with activities such as distributed data processing, electronic mail, electronic data interchange, electronic funds transfer, order or reservation servicing, inventory shipment or overnight package tracking, and corporate data consolidation. Many users design their own systems by selecting from services offered by common carriers. **Common carriers** are organizations such as AT&T, Western Union, MCI, Sprint, and GTE that are authorized by the Federal Communications Commission or state agencies to provide public communications services.

Many large organizations have developed extensive WANs. Texas Instruments' extensive WAN now includes 23 mainframes, over 2000 minicomputers, and almost 70,000 terminals and PCs at 50 sites. Engineers in 18 countries use this network for product development. CIGNA insurance spends over $75 million a year (3% of its revenues) running its own network. CIGNA believes its network provides it with higher reliability and lower transaction costs than its competitors have. Merrill Lynch has an extensive network linking over 650 offices all over the world.

Value-Added Networks

One hindrance to interorganizational communication results from different hardware and software utilization. The various hardware and software are often incompatible and require special interfaces to make computer-to-computer communication possible. One solution to this problem is a **value-added network (VAN).** A VAN is designed and maintained by an independent company and offers specialized hardware, software, and data-handling techniques to improve transmission effectiveness and decrease costs. Ford, for example, sends purchase orders electronically to all its vendors by way of a VAN. Ford's only concern is about linking its system to one other system, the VAN—not to hundreds of vendors—and the VAN handles the difficult task of interfacing all of the hardware and software used by the various vendors.

Public Data Bases

Public data bases are electronic libraries containing millions of data items that can be reviewed, retrieved, and analyzed. Over 300 vendors supply more than 2000 data bases to over 30 million people. The advantage to public data bases is instant access to almost any piece of information a user might need. The main disadvantage is the difficulty of learning how to access and effectively search them. The costs of the searches are reasonable given the information retrieved.

A typical search takes 8 to 18 minutes and costs between $5 and $20. For example, an internal auditor with AMRE could easily find operating ratios for siding manufacturers, download them into his PC, and compare them to AMRE's. A CPA firm considering taking on a new client could access past financial statements, check out the company's credit rating, examine industry trends and projections, and accomplish many similar tasks. It might take hours of research to find the same information in a nonelectronic library. Popular services include America Online, CompuServe, Compustat, Dow-Jones News/Retrieval, LEXIS, NEXIS, NAARS, Prodigy, and Value Line. Some companies are using these services to sell their goods. UPS, for example, has opened electronic storefronts on CompuServe, Prodigy, and America Online. Users arrange for the shipment of goods by entering orders into these electronic storefronts.

Bulletin Board Systems

A **bulletin board system (BBS)** is an information-sharing service that allows computer users to meet and share ideas and information. Except for long-distance telephone charges, most of the fifty thousand BBSs are free and cater to a specialized interest such as accounting, education, or investing. Users are free to read the comments posted by others on the BBS and to add their own. Businesses use a BBS to provide information to its employees and customers, download and transfer files, send and receive messages, and participate in on-line conferences. For example, Andrews Records Management uses BBS to store 300,000 boxes of paper documents and 250,000 reels of tape. Customer transactions are handled through the BBS, it serves as the company's E-mail system, and it is used to share audit information with clients.

Telephone Networks

A **private branch exchange (PBX)** is a special-purpose computer that manages a company's telephone network. It handles both voice and digital data, turning it into a LAN that does not need special wiring. Users plug their PCs into a telephone jack and use a modem to send information to any network accessible by phone line. A PBX is limited to regular telephone lines, which are slower and less capable of handling large volumes of data.

The phone companies have developed a system, called the **integrated services digital network (ISDN),** that uses computers to expand the capacity of regular phone lines from 9600 bits per second to over 1.5 million by sending data over multiple lines at the same time. ISDN has built-in intelligence and transmits all types of data (voice, data, images, facsimile, video) over telephone lines. It will permit the simultaneous transmission of voice and text data, so several people could, for example, both see and discuss the same spreadsheet at the same time. It allows all communications devices to talk with each other directly. ISDN will greatly expand the types of data sent over regular phone lines and the speed with which they are sent. It will reduce equipment costs and make equipment more effective.

The Internet

The **Internet** is an international network of independently owned computers that operate as a giant, seamless computing network. No one owns the Internet, no single organization controls its use, and data are not centrally stored. Instead, the Internet is composed of computers, called **Web servers,** that are scattered worldwide and contain every imaginable type of data. The costs of the Internet are shared by its primary users: nearly every university, government, and research facility in the world as well as foreign governments.

The number of commercial sites has increased rapidly since the restrictions against commercial use was lifted in 1991. Each Web server can have thousands of networks and users attached to it and each network handles the traffic of other networks at no charge to the users. The number of WEB servers doubles every few months and the Internet reached nearly 50 million computer users in 1995. It is expected to reach 100 million by the year 2000. Currently almost

80 countries have full Internet access and another 75 have partial service that allows them to send and receive simple Internet E-mail.

The following are among the many ways that accountants use the Internet:

- *Communications channel.* Using E-mail, accountants can communicate with clients, other professionals, employees, suppliers, and customers almost anywhere in the world. Users can send and receive detailed messages, including entire documents and data files, thus enabling accountants to help prepare written documents and spreadsheets. With the right software users can also conduct voice conversations for the price of a local phone call. AT&T has announced plans to offer telephone access to the Internet, which will allow a computer to read your E-mail messages to you, using speech-recognition software.
- *Research.* Information resources such as libraries (such as those for tax and audit research), on-line data bases (such as those containing financial statements and other accounting data), bulletin boards, newsletters, newspapers, and electronic magazines are easily accessed. For example, the entire library of documents that public companies file with the SEC has been put on the Internet. The IRS maintains all of its tax forms on-line for users to download into their systems. As a result, most accountants consider the Internet to be their best source of information, irrespective of its type.
- *User groups.* Thousands of user groups have been formed to allow people to get to know one another and exchange ideas. For example, these user groups can help accountants keep up with the latest changes in tax laws and regulatory pronouncements. The AICPA has set up an Accountants Forum on the Internet so that accountants can ask questions, receive answers, and share information with other accountants and interested parties.
- *Videoconferencing.* Most of the major accounting firms have developed systems that allow fellow users, such as clients, to communicate with each other via their computer screens.
- *An electronic storefront.* Many accounting firms and accountants are setting up a home page (also called a storefront) on the Internet. A **home page** provides useful and interesting information about a firm or an individual accountant. For example, the home page for accounting professors at Brigham Young University contains their picture, the classes they teach, their course syllabus, a listing of the articles and books they have written, and copies of some of their most recent publications. Many practicing accountants are advertising their audit, tax, or consulting expertise and offering free services, such as a newsletter, as a loss leader.
- *On-line business.* Many companies now advertise their products, conduct business, and send and receive payments on-line. Accountants are also conducting more and more business on-line. For example, an accountant in Nevada with clients throughout the United States could have them send their general ledger transactions directly to her bookkeeping system via E-mail. The accountant could then send financial reports and other key data back to her clients the same day.

One significant disadvantage of the Internet is the small number of privacy and security controls to prevent unauthorized access. Many businesses are understandably wary of trusting the Net with credit card numbers and other data needed for on-line shopping. Businesses are now building **firewalls,** or combinations of security algorithms and router communications protocols that prevent outsiders from tapping into corporate data bases and E-mail systems.

Another disadvantage has been the difficulty of moving around on the Internet and finding information. A number of tools have been developed to partially overcome this problem. The **World Wide Web,** for example, is an advanced navigation system that organizes its contents by subject matter. **MOSIAC** and **Netscape** are GUI programs that use menus to help users navigate the Internet by pointing and clicking a mouse on a highlighted piece of text. As a result, users can jump from one Web server to another effortlessly. A **gopher** is used to quickly move from one place on the Internet to another. Archie, Veronica, Jughead, and **WAIS (Wide Area Information Servers)** are tools for searching the Internet's huge information libraries. This area is expanding so rapidly that within months a number of other advancements about how to better access and use the Internet will be in place.

Users can access the Internet with a modem connection to an on-line service such as America Online or to a company that specializes in Internet services. The Internet also permits access through a direct connection to one of the Web servers, such as those available at universities. An Internet address has three parts: the user ID, the user location preceded by the @ (at) symbol, and a suffix preceded by a period. A Brigham Young University faculty member named John Smith, for example, would have the following address: John_Smith@BYU.edu. The suffix "edu" is used for educational institutions, "gov" is used for governmental bodies, and "com" denotes commercial establishments. The latter category usually has further address requirements to help identify the user's computer network and the Internet service used.

Many companies are conducting business on the Internet. Electronics manufacturers in Silicon Valley (Apple, Hewlett-Packard, IBM, and Intel) are building Commerce-Net, a marketplace for electronics goods and services. Companies that use the network will virtually be able to eliminate all invoices, purchase orders, checks, and other paperwork. Robert Redford's Sundance Catalog Inc., for example, sells American handicrafts on the Internet through an electronic catalog containing color pictures of 230 items. Once shoppers have set up an account, they select items by pointing and clicking on the items they want to purchase. When selections are complete, shoppers verify the order and enter shipping and payment information. Computers at Evergreen CyberMart, which manages the operation, complete the order by checking credit card limits and inventory availability. When a transaction is completed, Sundance's accounting, inventory, and shipping records are updated by Evergreen's computers.

DATA COMMUNICATIONS APPLICATIONS

Data communications systems are used to transmit electronically a wide variety of items, including documents, memos, pictures, graphics, mail, and voice messages. This section discusses a few of the data communications systems you will be exposed to or frequently use as a future accountant.

Computer-Based Message Systems

Fax. **Facsimile (fax) transmission** allows documents, pictures, graphics, and signatures to be sent over a data communications system. A facsimile machine at the sending station translates the different shades of light and dark on a page into signals to be sent over the communications links. A similar machine on the receiving end translates the signals back into the proper images and reproduces them on a piece of paper or a computer screen. Many companies are using remote fax capabilities to improve the quality and lower the cost of customer service. They create menus of retrievable faxes on topics like product descriptions, prices, and announcements; credit terms; and advertised specials. Customers can call in and retrieve the information as they need it.

Electronic Mail. **Electronic mail (E-mail)** systems allow a person to send, receive, or forward a message to or from anyone else who has a "mailbox," or electronic storage location, in the system. As soon as a message is sent, the intended receiver is notified that an E-mail message has arrived and who it is from. If the recipient is unable to respond to the message immediately, it is stored until he or she is ready to "open" and read the mail. If a recipient's computer is off, he or she is notified of the E-mail during a subsequent log-on. In most systems the sender can attach files (such as spreadsheets, documents, or reports) along with a message. The system can be used to send messages internally or, using gateways to public E-mail services, to other organizations. By setting up predefined distribution lists, users can avoid reentering names each time a message is sent to the same group.

There are a number of significant advantages to E-mail.

- It is an ideal way to conduct many forms of communication and can at least partially replace the telephone and the regular mail system.
- Messages are sent instantly, rather than taking days by either external or internal mail systems.
- It eliminates games of "telephone tag," in which people who are unable to reach each other keep leaving messages on their respective answering machines.
- Recipients can easily store, save, print, erase, edit, or forward messages to someone else.

E-mail also has some disadvantages. Perhaps the most significant is that E-mail makes it possible for people to send useless and time-wasting messages with just a few keystrokes. Software has been developed to screen E-mail and discard all unwanted and junk E-mail messages.

The volume and the types of E-mail messages being sent are increasing rapidly. One reason for this increase is that companies are moving from mainframe-based E-mail systems (such as IBM's Profs) to LAN-based systems, which are more flexible and less expensive. In addition, LAN E-mail vendors are expanding their programs by developing a variety of interfaces for their systems. These interfaces include converting the E-mail message into a fax, telex, or telegram for recipients who do not have an E-mail system; integrating voice messages with the E-mail message; sending a hard copy of the message using a mailing system; and using radio frequencies to allow portable computer users to send and retrieve messages.

Voice Mail. **Voice mail (V-mail)** is a computerized method of sending spoken messages that combines the storage feature of an answering machine with the accessing, editing, and forwarding capabilities of E-mail. A V-mail system records a spoken message and stores it in the receiver's electronic mailbox. People can access and listen to their voice mail messages wherever a telephone is available. As with E-mail, a recipient can store, erase, or forward a message to someone else. A V-mail message can also be sent to more than one person at a time. V-mail systems have a variety of storage and forwarding capabilities to notify the recipient that a message is waiting. V-mail is more flexible than E-mail because telephones are more widely available than computers linked to networks. However, V-mail is not the best method for conveying long, complicated, or technical messages or data.

Teleconferencing. **Teleconferencing** uses telecommunications technology to conduct a "meeting" with people in separate locations, saving travel time and costs. There are three types of teleconferencing:

1. **Audio teleconferencing.** This is a conference call that allows people in different locations to hear one another.
2. **Video conferencing.** Participants gather in specially equipped rooms so they can both see and hear one another. Because it requires complex video equipment and high-speed communications channels, video conferencing is much more expensive than audio conferencing. Many organizations have set up formal video conferencing rooms. Mellon Bank estimates video conferencing saves $400,000 a year, and J.C. Penney and Merrill Lynch use it to communicate with their stores and offices nationwide. AT&T rents teleconferencing rooms to those who cannot afford their own.
3. **Computer conferencing.** Conference participants are linked to one another via PCs; they enter comments, questions, and ideas at their convenience. Anyone can join the conference at any time because a transcript of everyone's comments is maintained by the system. Likewise, a participant can leave the conference to attend to other duties and return. Participants can direct their comments to a specific person or edit someone else's ideas or comments. The conference can be extended for an indefinite time so others can input their ideas and think about all the ideas presented. People can say exactly what they want, when they want, instead of having to be recognized to make a comment.

Groupware. **Groupware** is computer software designed to support the work of teams. End users have found groupware ideal for sharing information, deciding when to hold meetings, making a departmental calendar, collectively brainstorming on creative endeavors, managing and designing products, and creating documents. Focus 9.1 details the various ways KPMG Peat Marwick utilizes groupware.

Transportation and Travel Reservations

Airlines and major motel chains were among the first to implement data communications systems to process and confirm customer reservations. These systems utilize data terminals or PCs at each reservation counter or hotel lobby and on-line data bases of available services, such as airline seats and hotel

FOCUS 9.1

Groupware: A Powerful Tool at Peat Marwick

KPMG Peat Marwick has embraced groupware wholeheartedly. The firm now has installed worldwide over 17,000 copies of FirstClass, a groupware system from Soft Arc Inc. This groupware supports Knowledge Manager, Peat Marwick's system containing a vast store of information and experience about almost everything associated with the firm. The system also allows users to send E-mail; access private and public bulletin boards, external data bases, and public networks; and process forms. The firm's goal is to soon have every one of its 75,000 professionals worldwide using it.

Most employees use the system almost daily to gain access to hundreds of gigabytes of information. The information is stored in different "folders" containing client experiences, proposals, resumes, methodologies, best practices, vendors, and demonstrations, among others. One of the most popular folders is Help Wanted. Auditors and consultants can post a request for help on a project and usually get feedback within an hour.

Knowledge Manager is an essential part of KPMG Peat Marwick's business strategy and provides the firm with a tremendous competitive advantage. The system helps KPMG gather the best ideas from all over the world and allows the firm to be available to each individual client. Using the expertise of their entire staff of professionals, KPMG personnel can tailor a proposal to a user's exact needs. With access to all prior proposals created by the firm, the best parts of prior proposals are selected and tailored to individual clients.

For example, Peat Marwick needed to create a proposal to bid on a job that required business planning, real estate, and information technology expertise. The partner in charge of preparing the bid used Knowledge Manager to review similar bids and to assemble a team of experts from Washington, Vancouver, and Chicago. Each team member prepared a portion of the proposal and reviewed and edited the entire draft. The result was a customized proposal for the prospective client. The entire proposal, including firm qualifications, partner resumes, and specific real estate project data, was prepared in just four days. Several team members never met until the day they made a formal in-person pitch to the client.

Auditors and consultants in CPA firms used to be rewarded primarily for their individual projects and contributions. Those with the biggest clients and projects had the most influence and were the most highly compensated. This practice led to information hoarding, a lack of cooperation, and an unwillingness to share expertise and other intellectual resources. That attitude is changing and the emphasis at Peat Marwick is now on cooperation and sharing of resources and expertise. Groupware is facilitating this change, as it is one of the best ways to share data.

Focus Questions

1. What is it about groupware that makes it such a powerful tool for sharing information?
2. Many other CPA firms are using groupware. What do you think will happen to CPA firms over time if they do not begin to use groupware to share information?

Source: Stephanie Stahl, "Hire On One, Get 'em All," *InformationWeek* (March 20, 1995): 120–124.

rooms. Reservations made in person or by phone are entered into the system, and if the requested service is available, the data base is updated and the customer's reservation is immediately confirmed. Airline reservations systems also calculate fares, update sales and accounts receivable records, respond to customer requests for reconfirmation, and process passenger check-ins.

Holiday Inn has a companywide PC network linking its 1600 properties to a centralized reservation system. Within each hotel anywhere from 2 to 20 PCs are connected using IBM networks that run Novell's NetWare. A satellite link connects the LANs to the company's reservation system and transfers marketing research data to corporate headquarters. The system substantially reduces the time it takes to book rooms, determine occupancy levels, and establish rates. System response time is now 1 to 3 seconds, compared with 8 to 15 seconds previously. A reservation transaction costs one-third of the industry standard. The cost-effectiveness aspect of the system led to Holiday Inn's achieving the coveted Excellence in Enterprise Networking award.

Banking Systems

Bank systems use data communications systems to maintain customer balances by posting deposits and withdrawals. Hardware requirements include a data terminal for each teller window, ATMs at various locations, and on-line file storage to maintain a record of each customer's account. By providing up-to-date records of each customer's account to every teller and ATM, these systems provide faster and more convenient customer service. The ATM provides bank customers with banking services 24 hours a day and reduces the number of tellers required to serve customers. All customers have to do is find an ATM, insert their specially coded plastic bank card, and type in a PIN (personal identification number) known only to them and the computer. Using the bank's data communications network, the ATM verifies that the PIN matches the account number on the bank card before a user can withdraw or deposit funds. With the proper ATM and data communications links, the user can also purchase a variety of other items, such as stamps and airline, movie, and theater tickets.

Many banks have since expanded their applications into other areas, such as mortgages, commercial and consumer loans, and credit files. It is now common for one large data communications system to handle all banking transactions. Retail merchants are tied into the banking network through point-of-sale terminals and PCs, and sales transactions are immediately charged to the consumer's bank account and simultaneously credited to the merchant's account. Through **electronic funds transfer (EFT),** cash payments are handled electronically rather than by check. For example, Ford pays its suppliers and deposits employee paychecks using EFT. Using PCs and modems, individuals can also access a bank's system and pay bills electronically.

Most banks have set up home pages on the Internet. Users can check account balances, transfer funds, pay bills, research interest rate data, or apply for a loan. Users can also communicate with financial advisers, loan officers, and bank tellers. The future will bring many more advancements, some that we can't even imagine today.

Retail Sales

Retail organizations such as S&S use data communications systems to collect sales data and perform credit-checking and inventory control functions. Electronic cash registers and point-of-sale recorders capture such information as the item sold, the quantity, and the price. The system, which maintains the price of all items, automatically rings up a customer's amount. Many systems use audio response units to inform the customer of the amount. Also, a customer's credit standing can be checked at the time a credit transaction is initiated. As shown in Fig. 9.12, credit is checked by forwarding the credit card number to the bank's computer, which electronically determines the credit standing and amount of credit granted. To maintain an up-to-date record of all inventory items, the inventory file is accessed and updated for the specific merchandise sold. The system can originate inventory reordering as needed and management can obtain up-to-date sales and inventory totals through on-line data base queries.

Figure 9.12

Credit Approval Process in a Retail Organization

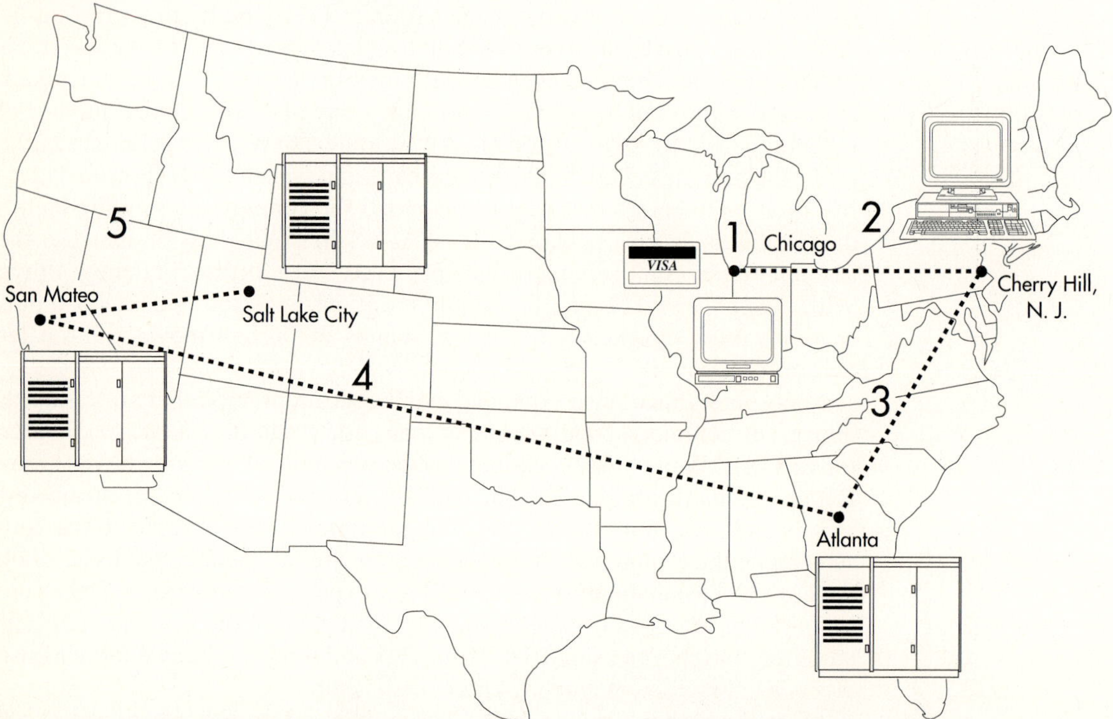

All data in the system travels by satellite, microwave, or telephone lines. The system determines the least expensive route as the approval request is processed.

1. A customer purchases a new $1500 TV in Chicago using a POS device supported by National Data Corporation to read the credit card.
2. The credit request is sent to National Data Corporation's computers in Cherry Hill, New Jersey.
3. NDC's computer in Cherry Hill sends the request to NDC's computer in Atlanta, which, because of the size of the credit approval, turns it over to VISA's minicomputer.
4. VISA's minicomputer forwards the query to VISA's mainframe in San Mateo, California.
5. The San Mateo mainframe forwards the request to the bank in Salt Lake City that issued the VISA card. The Salt Lake City bank verifies that credit is available. The credit approval retraces its path back to Chicago where the purchase is finalized. The credit approval process takes about 15 seconds.

Source: Business Week (October 8, 1990): 144.

FOCUS 9.2

Bell Atlantic Automates Sales Service System

Even though Bell Atlantic has 6500 customer service representatives, it is struggling to meet the needs of its 12.8 million customers. When a customer calls one of its 169 business offices to inquire about a new service, it can take a representative up to 20 minutes to find out what the customer wants, look through huge manuals for pricing information or technical specifications, and log on to one or more unfriendly mainframe systems.

Bell Atlantic is solving the problem by replacing its antiquated and poorly linked service order systems with a new Sales Service Negotiation System (SSNS). The terminals currently used will be replaced with a network of intelligent workstations. Human judgment will give way to artificial intelligence. A new on-line data base will allow Bell Atlantic to replace the 19 million pages of documentation it now sends every year to its order takers with electronic messages and updates. The main objective of the system is to provide better customer service by quickly and efficiently meeting the customers' needs.

Designing and implementing the SSNS will not be an easy task. Several hundred people will work on it for five years at a cost of between $70 and $130 million. It will consist of the following components:

- LANs at all 169 business offices.
- 8000 workstations from Sun Microsystems.
- An IBM 3090 mainframe and multiple Sun servers.
- Support software that prompts the order taker to ask questions based on customer requests and responses.
- An expert knowledge-based sales tool to help order takers match customer profiles with available services and options.
- Data bases of text and product data to replace reference manuals.
- An interface module that translates orders into the formats needed by the various local telephone company order systems.

Focus Questions

1. Why will it take several hundred people at Bell Atlantic five years to install the SSNS system? Why will it be so costly?
2. What benefits will Bell Atlantic derive from the system? Do you think the system will pay for itself? If so, how? If not, why not?

Sales Order Processing

Companies gain significant competitive advantages by using data communications systems to reduce the time between the receipt and delivery of customer orders. Consider the example of a salesperson equipped with a portable computer who enters orders directly from the customer's plant or office. The system confirms the availability of inventory, approves customer credit, enters the order into the system, updates the finished goods inventory file, and posts the invoice to an on-line accounts receivable ledger. The system initiates delivery by electronically transmitting a shipping order to the closest warehouse. With an on-line accounts receivable file, a salesperson can answer customer account inquiries. In addition, a sales analysis master file is updated as orders are placed so marketing executives have up-to-date information on sales trends. As finished goods inventory balances are updated, the system determines whether reordering or additional production is necessary to replenish inventory.

The advantages of this system are the confirmation of sales orders in real time and the complete integration of the accounting function. Data are entered only once, and all accounting records affected by the data and all documents necessary for processing the transaction are updated. Many companies have made their sales order systems more responsive to customer needs. Focus 9.2

discusses the changes Bell Atlantic is making to its system to better meet customer needs.

Electronic Purchasing Systems

Automating the process of purchasing goods and services can bring significant cost and time savings. Coopers and Lybrand developed an electronic purchasing system with the help of IBM. Purchasing officials at Coopers negotiated quantity discounts with suppliers and developed an on-line data base, or catalog, of approved products. To purchase items, Coopers employees access the catalog using their PC and a series of menus and icons to make their selections. The catalog contains product descriptions and pictures, departmental budgets, and the name of the managers that approve the purchases. To comparison shop, the descriptions and prices of competing products can be called up on the screen as well. To order a product, shoppers click on the desired product, enter the quantity, and send the order to a manager for approval with another click of the mouse. Approved orders are sent to vendors using an IBM network. The system tracks the status of each order throughout the process; thus Coopers can find out where the order is at any time. Coopers lowered its purchase order processing costs from a high of $67 to $20 using the on-line system, thereby saving hundreds of thousands of dollars a year.

Electronic Data Interchange

Electronic data interchange (EDI) is the direct, computer-to-computer transmission of business documents. Rather than physically exchanging a purchase order or invoice, users transmit the information found on these documents electronically; the paper flow between organizations is eliminated. EDI is fast becoming the standard means of processing transactions between customers, suppliers, and manufacturers in a number of industries, both domestically and internationally. Tens of thousands of firms are currently using EDI, and the number is expected to double annually for the next several years. In many companies, such as General Motors, K mart, and J.C. Penney, most documents entering their system are electronic output from another system.

EDI has the following advantages:

- *Fast data transmission speed.* EDI eliminates information float, the delay caused by printing information, moving it through the mail system, and reentering it in the recipient's computer. With EDI, a purchase order created today can be received and processed by a supplier that same day.
- *Fewer clerical errors.* Because most human interaction is eliminated, error rates decline.
- *Cost savings.* An estimated 75% of the data involved in an accounting transaction are reentered from another computer. Using EDI to send this redundant data can eliminate rekeying and reduce data entry costs. Inventory levels and carrying costs can also be reduced.
- *Better customer service.* A computer can instantaneously respond to a purchase order, letting a customer know whether the items ordered are in stock.
- *Survival.* Many companies will do business only with vendors and suppliers who use EDI. EDI also protects a company's market share by making it easier for customers to order from the company than from a competitor not using EDI.

Motorola Codex eliminated paper from its business dealings with key suppliers. The communications equipment manufacturer began by using an integrated EDI and EFT system to connect with Texas Instruments (TI), one of its main suppliers. It was one of the first companies to have an electronic "closed loop," from initial production plan to final payment, with EDI transactions integrated into its existing manufacturing, purchasing, and financial applications. Codex transacts about 40% of its purchase orders through EDI, but TI was the first of its EDI-linked suppliers to receive its payments electronically. As soon as Codex receives goods from TI, the system sends an electronic payment authorization to its bank, which sends the payment to TI's collection bank. Codex realized cost savings in reduced product cycle time, supply inventories, paperwork, and filing.

EDI is not without its problems. One difficulty, communicating with the many computer systems of suppliers and vendors, is solved by using a value-added network. Another disadvantage is the lack of standardized product and service codes and transmission protocols. The benefits of EDI seem to far outweigh the disadvantages, however. Given the ability of EDI to address significant problems businesses face in processing transactions with other organizations, its use can only be expected to increase.

SUMMARY AND CASE CONCLUSION

After their visit to DE's headquarters, Scott and Ashton spent as much time as they could spare learning about data communications. They soon realized they needed outside help and hired Data Connections (DC), a firm specializing in data communications systems for small businesses.

After assessing their needs, DC proposed that S&S install a LAN to connect the PCs at each location so users can have E-mail capabilities and share data, printers, and software. As S&S expands, the LANs would be linked in a WAN to provide corporatewide E-mail. The LAN and WAN will provide the advantages of a decentralized and centralized processing system, respectively. To eliminate compatibility problems between S&S's and DE's equipment, the LANs will be connected to DE's VAN. S&S will purchase a client/server to manage the system and store shared software and data. The LAN will also require modems, a LAN interface, and a gateway to connect the LAN to the VAN. S&S will need a LAN operating system, such as NetWare from Novell.

The LAN devices will be connected by coaxial cable. The VAN has a local number S&S can call to avoid long-distance telephone charges while using the EDI system. The VAN uses a combination of leased lines, telephone lines, satellites, and microwave transmission. It has sophisticated software to optimize line use and minimize communications channel costs.

S&S liked DC's proposal and hired the firm to install the system, train employees, and prepare a recent accounting graduate for her role in maintaining and supporting the system. She will take on those duties on a part-time basis until the system requires a full-time position.

S&S Five Years in the Future

Susan and Scott opened warehouse appliance clubs nationwide to sell high-volume and low-markup appliances. Each evening a robot counts inventory in S&S's regional warehouses using a laser to scan the UPC on all merchandise.

The robot enters the data into the warehouse computer, which reconciles the prior day's inventory, the current day's shipments and receipts, and the new inventory count. Discrepancies are sent to a manager's computer for investigation. The computer analyzes inventory on hand, daily usage, historical and seasonal trends, economic order quantities, and delivery times. It automatically orders goods from approved vendors and schedules their just-in-time arrival. All orders are sent to the inventory manager's computer for review. The computer reviews all store orders received and schedules appliance deliveries. Where appropriate, it arranges for goods to be sent directly from the suppliers to the individual stores. A similar system in the stores is linked to the warehouse computer. This is done electronically; there are no paper documents.

S&S encourages customers to pay electronically, to provide instant access to cash and eliminate handling large amounts of currency. When merchandise is delivered, funds are electronically transferred to supplier accounts. Employees and most bills are also paid electronically. For instance, when the utility company sends an electronic notice showing energy consumption, the computer verifies that usage is within acceptable parameters before electronically transferring funds to the utility.

S&S subscribes to a personalized information service that focuses on individual information needs. The service remembers what subscribers like to read, combs information sources, and produces a personalized, electronic newspaper. Periodic feedback allows the system to learn each subscriber's needs and wants. One of the first things Scott and Susan do every day is read their personal newspaper. Articles they want to store are filed by the service, and items they want to act on are transferred to their personal productivity software (a combination spreadsheet, decision support system, graphics package, and word processor).

On a recent business trip, Susan received a message from the Appliance Vendors Association president telling her that Congress was proposing import restrictions on countries that were key appliance suppliers. Based on this information, he asked Susan to produce a report that he could take to a meeting scheduled with his congressman. She used her laptop computer to access her files at S&S and download information. To get data on foreign imports and on pricing differences between their products and comparable U.S. ones, she downloaded data from a public data base. Susan then accessed the association's expert system to determine where appliances could be purchased most inexpensively when cost, freight, import duties, and several similar factors were included.

Susan used a special audiovisual room at the hotel to film a videotape presentation. She electronically sent a copy of her report and presentation to her office computer and directed that the report be printed and placed on her desk and that the presentation be stored on videotape. She sent a message on the S&S LAN scheduling a meeting with her buyers the day after her return. Finally, she sent the report and visual presentation to the association president with a note telling him where she could be reached for the remainder of the trip.

Two days later the hotel clerk told her she had E-mail waiting and transferred it to the computer in her room. She found her report with requests for some minor changes. She made the corrections on the hotel's computer, sent a copy to the president and her office computer, and stored a copy on her laptop.

Does this sound farfetched? It shouldn't. Most of the technology required for such a scenario is already in place. It is just a matter of designing systems to take advantage of the technology. Remember that the personal computer is less than 15 years old. Think of all the progress that has been made since then. If technology advances as fast in the next 20 years as it has in the last 20, there are endless possibilities in store for the information systems of the future.

KEY TERMS

data communications networks
centralized data processing system
distributed data processing (DPP) system
local area network (LAN)
modem
bits per second (bps)
fax modem
multiplexor
front-end processor (FEP)
communications software
protocol
communications channel
serial transmission
parallel transmission
asynchronous transmission
synchronous transmission
simplex channel
half-duplex channels
full-duplex channels
bandwidths
narrowband lines
voiceband lines
broadband lines
coaxial cable
fiber optics cable
terrestrial microwave
satellite transmission
cellular radios
cellular telephones
cells
point-to-point lines
multidrop lines
line-sharing device
communications network
centralized network
decentralized system
distributed data processing (DDP)
star network
network switching
ring network
hierarchical network
bus network
hybrid network
servers
gateway
router
file server
client/server system
network administrator
wide area network (WAN)
common carriers
value-added network (VAN)
public data bases
bulletin board system (BBS)
private branch exchange (PBX)
integrated services digital network (ISDN)
Internet
Web servers
home page
firewalls
World Wide Web
MOSIAC
Netscape
gopher
WAIS (Wide Area Information Servers)
facsimile (fax) transmission
electronic mail (E-mail)
voice mail (V-mail)
teleconferencing
audio teleconferencing
video conferencing
computer conferencing
groupware
electronic funds transfer (EFT)
electronic data interchange (EDI)

CHAPTER QUIZ

1. Which of the following is *not* one of the five major components of a data communications system?
   a. Sending device
   b. Communications interface device
   c. Communications channel
   d. Communications software
   e. Message

2. The communications device that is used to relieve the CPU of time-consuming data communications coordination and control functions is the

a. modem.
b. protocol.
c. multiplexor.
d. front-end processor.
e. PBX.

3. Communications software performs all of the following functions except
a. error detection and control.
b. access control.
c. network management.
d. data and file transmission.
e. It performs all four of the above functions.

4. When two or more bits of data are transferred at the same time over separate communications channels, the process is referred to as
a. serial transmission.
b. parallel transmission.
c. synchronous transmission.
d. asynchronous transmission.

5. Which of the following communications channels consists of thousands of tiny filaments of glass or plastic that transmit data using light waves?
a. Twisted pair cables
b. Coaxial cable
c. Fiber optics cable
d. Glass microwave cables

6. Which of the following statements is false?
a. Data communications networks transmit data between geographically separated points, giving users immediate access to company data.
b. In a decentralized network all data are processed at a central location using sophisticated software.
c. Distributed data processing systems are user-oriented as well as top-management-oriented.
d. In the early days of computers, organizations consolidated their systems into one large, centralized data processing system.

7. In which of the following DDP network configurations are all of the devices in the network linked to a host computer?
a. Ring
b. Star
c. Bus
d. Hierarchical

8. Which of the following is *not* a benefit of a LAN?
a. Electronic messages
b. Shared resources and data
c. Remote access
d. Improved security

9. Assume S&S has expanded to six stores located in different parts of the country. The company wants to develop its own network to link the stores electronically. The best way to do this would be to use a
a. bulletin board system.
b. value-added network.
c. wide area network.
d. public data bases.
e. local area network.

10. S&S has arranged to pay its supplier, Dominican Electric, electronically. The best way to do this is to use
a. electronic data interchange.
b. electronic funds transfer.
c. electronic mail.
d. groupware.
e. a PBX.

DISCUSSION QUESTIONS

9.1 In the future all households and merchants may possess a PC that serves as an on-line terminal to a communitywide data communications computer system. Discuss some of the ways you and your family and friends might use such a system.

9.2 Communication is vital to any organization, especially to a multidivisional company spread over a wide geographic area. Corporate structure is often aligned along communication lines. Discuss the organizational structure that might conform to the star, ring, or hybrid network configuration. If an improper configuration were chosen, what kind of organizational difficulties might arise?

9.3 Public data bases are increasingly popular. They are used by accountants, doctors, lawyers, and other professional and private groups. Public data base systems are changing the way people think about information. Some people feel that data bases will eventually replace books and libraries. To what extent do you feel these predictions are true? Also, discuss the implications of rapid information retrieval.

9.4 Discuss how a data communications system might be usefully applied within the following organizations.
a. A university
b. A life insurance company

c. A hospital
d. A construction company

9.5 Scott is unsure whether to implement a centralized, decentralized, or distributed data processing system at S&S. He has asked you to briefly enumerate the advantages and disadvantages of each approach and to outline the control factors required in a distributed processing system. Prepare a one-page memo to summarize this information. (SMAC Examination, adapted)

9.6 Corporate America is using tools such as electronic mail and computer bulletin boards to improve communications and reduce paperwork. For instance, Motorola has a nationwide service that allows laptop and palmtop computers to receive up to 56 E-mail messages at one time. Radio waves and satellites are used to send the message from the sender's location to the recipient's computer. If the recipient's computer is off, it will store the incoming messages until they can be read. How is the use of E-mail changing corporate business? What advantages will remote E-mail provide? What problems could arise from the use of communication networks?

PROBLEMS

9.1 The management of Cross Country Company is currently considering a change from centralized to decentralized or distributed data processing.

REQUIRED

a. Briefly define centralized, decentralized, and distributed data processing.
b. Each of these approaches has advantages and disadvantages. Match the advantages and disadvantages in the right column with the processing approaches shown in the left. The advantages and disadvantages may be used more than once. (SMAC Examination, adapted)

Approach	Advantages or Disadvantages
1. Centralized	a. Reduces the risk of loss or destruction to hardware and critical data
2. Decentralized	b. Doesn't provide the opportunity for a distributed network
3. Distributed	c. Depends on one computer
	d. Facilitates the data base approach and minimizes the duplication of common data
	e. Makes maintaining overall data security difficult
	f. Provides no method for coordinating or exchanging data during processing

9.2 Colorgraph Printing is reviewing a proposal to acquire Puball Publishers. Puball's operations are located 300 miles from Colorgraph's headquarters. Colorgraph's recent success has been due in large part to its computerized AIS. Puball, however, has used a computer only for financial accounting applications such as payroll and inventory records. In considering the acquisition, Colorgraph's board of directors focused on two options for developing an AIS that would include Puball: a centralized or a distributed system.

REQUIRED

a. Indicate how PCs may be used with a centralized system, a distributed system, or with both.
b. Compare the information likely to be transmitted to headquarters in a centralized and in a distributed system.
c. Explain why Puball's management is more likely to be involved in and concerned with data processing in a distributed rather than a centralized system. Assume Puball is a separate profit center.
d. Explain briefly why a distributed system is less subject to a complete system breakdown. (CIA Examination, adapted)

9.3 The Widget Manufacturing Company is installing a LAN at its San Francisco sales office that will be on-line to its computer center in Los Angeles 400 miles away. One decision that must be made is whether to lease a line, obtain a WATS line, or use switched public lines. The monthly cost of a leased line includes a service charge of $83.50 plus mileage charges based on the following rates.

Mileage	Rate/Mile
0–100	$2.82
101–250	$1.48
251–300	$0.79
Over 300	$0.26

In computing total monthly mileage charges, a separate calculation is needed for each individual mileage segment, with the results then added to obtain a total cost. For example, a 300-mile line includes a fixed cost of $83.50 plus mileage charges of $2.82(100) + $1.48(150) + $0.79(50), for a total of $627.00.

The charge for a WATS line includes $30.50 per month for the service charge plus $18 per hour for the monthly use charge. Public telephone rates are $0.57 for the first minute and $0.34 for each additional minute. Estimated time for entering a transaction over the terminal will average two minutes.

REQUIRED

a. Compute the monthly cost of the leased line.
b. At what average monthly volume of transactions will the total cost of the leased line be equal to the cost of using (1) the WATS line and (2) the switched public lines? (Make each computation separately.)
c. Assume an average volume of 810 transactions per month. Which of the three alternatives is least expensive? Show supporting calculations.
d. If switched public lines are used, assume that the transactions will be entered in groups of three so that the extra rate for the first minute will be avoided for two-thirds of all transactions. How will this factor affect your answer to part (c)?

9.4 The Texas Machinery Distributing Company, a machinery products wholesaler, has its headquarters and a central warehouse in Houston, Texas. Sales offices are in Dallas, Waco, Austin, San Antonio, Laredo, Corpus Christi, and Abilene. The company plans to install a data communications system for processing sales orders. The computer center is located in Houston, and PCs will be located in each sales office. A major concern of the company is the cost of the data communications network. The company is considering four alternative configurations:

1. Voice-grade leased lines from Houston to each sales office.
2. A wideband line from Houston to Austin and a communications processor in Austin to service six voice-grade leased lines from the other six sales offices.
3. Normal telephone dial-up service from each sales office to Houston.
4. A wideband line from Houston to Austin and a communications processor in Austin to service dial-up lines from the other six sales offices.

In addition to a monthly charge of $98.50, monthly cost figures for each voice-grade leased line are as follows:

Mileage	Rate/Mile
0–50	$2.20
51–150	$1.40
Over 150	$1.05

Monthly costs for wideband leased lines are as follows:

Mileage	Rate/Mile
0–50	$2.40
51–150	$1.60
Over 150	$1.20

In addition, there is a $165.20 monthly charge for each wideband line. (*Note:* For an explanation of how these rates are used, see Problem 9.3.)

The following table shows the distance in miles from Houston to the seven sales offices and from Austin to the other six sales offices.

	Houston	Austin
Waco	181	106
Austin	164	—
Dallas	244	198
San Antonio	195	79
Laredo	312	233
Corpus Christi	208	194
Abilene	349	217

The following table shows the cost of a two-minute long-distance call from Houston to the seven sales offices and from Austin to the other six sales offices.

	Houston	Austin
Waco	$0.88	$0.82
Austin	0.85	—
Dallas	0.91	0.88
San Antonio	0.88	0.76
Laredo	0.94	0.91
Corpus Christi	0.88	0.88
Abilene	0.94	0.91

It is assumed that each call will last approximately two minutes.

The following table shows the expected average monthly volume of calls from each of the seven sales offices.

Office	Monthly Volume
Waco	200
Austin	450
Dallas	650
San Antonio	500
Laredo	150
Corpus Christi	350
Abilene	200

If either alternative 2 or 4 is chosen, the communications processor will cost $500 per month.

REQUIRED

Determine the total monthly cost of the data communications network under each of the four alternatives. Based on cost, which alternative should the company select?

9.5 Classy Videos is a chain of eight video rental stores located in Chicago. Classy rents videocassettes of the most popular movies and VCRs. Each store has between 5000 and 6000 videos in stock, as well as 50 to 75 VCRs. Last year, the chain had its best year ever, with rental revenue in excess of $9 million.

Classy Videos only rents to members of its Rental Club. A person can become a member by filling out an application and paying a $10 fee. The company requires the application information and fee because it has experienced problems with movies and machines being stolen by customers.

Each cassette and VCR has its own identification number and checkout card. When club members want to rent a movie or VCR, they select its checkout card from the rental catalog and give the card to a clerk on duty. The clerk then pulls the customer's file and enters the rental information. A club member may also reserve a movie or machine by calling the store and having the clerk pull the identification card. If a store does not have the desired movie in stock, the movie can be acquired on loan from another store.

This system was adequate when Classy Videos consisted of a few stores. Since its expansion two of its biggest problems are lost identification cards and lengthy customer lines during peak hours. Additional problems include an inability to determine which movies and VCRs are available for rent, the wrong movies and VCRs being checked out to customers, reserved movies losing their "hold" status, and inventory inconsistencies.

Classy is in the process of reviewing computer systems that will help solve some of these problems as well as provide for future expansion. The company is trying to decide among (1) stores connected by terminals to a minicomputer at a central store, (2) PCs at each store that can communicate with each other on demand, and (3) PCs at each store and a minicomputer at the headquarters store.

REQUIRED

a. Identify the hardware needed for each approach, and explain the advantages and disadvantages of each of the three alternatives.

b. Select the configuration that you feel will best meet Classy's needs. Be prepared to defend your position to the class.

c. Irrespective of your decision in part (b), draw and label the configuration for option 3.

d. Describe the files that Classy must maintain in order to store the information it needs.

e. Can a computer system solve all of Classy Video's problems? Explain why or why not.

9.6 The Savings Bank of California (SBC) is a large bank headquartered in Los Angeles. One of its selling points is a customer's ability to bank at offices throughout the state. SBC has regional offices in San Diego, Orange County, southern and northern Los Angeles, and San Francisco. Each region consists of between five and eight local banks.

SBC has established its own statewide real-time computer system. Each regional office maintains a data base for its local savings, checking, and loan customers. This data base can be accessed by the banks in that particular region, by other regional offices, and by corporate headquarters. Each local bank has 4 to 12 terminals that tie into a minicomputer. The minicomputers at each local bank are linked directly to computers located at SBC's regional offices. The lines between the local banks and the regional offices have fairly heavy use because of the number of transactions handled each day. Each regional computer is tied to two others, so that if one goes down, information can quickly be rerouted. In addition to being tied to two other regional computers, each one is tied directly to a mainframe computer at corporate headquarters.

Both the regional computers and the headquarters mainframe use front-end processors to help manage the data communications process. The regional computers are used during the day to process checks, bank card payments, and other transactions to customer accounts. During each day, the regional computers periodically update the mainframe data bases based on transactions processed during the last 24 hours. The mainframe computer at corporate headquarters coordinates the activities of the regional computers and maintains SBC's companywide records. The headquarters mainframe also handles all fund transfers with the bank's office in New York. Communication between corporate headquarters and the New York office is through microwave transmission.

Tellers at each local branch use terminals hooked up to the bank's minicomputer to access the regional computer data base. If a customer is from the local region, his or her account is updated for the transaction. If not, the correct regional data base is accessed and updated. Funds from the local region are then transferred from or to the accessed region to cover the transaction.

REQUIRED

a. What type of communications network is SBC using: centralized, decentralized, DDP, LAN, VAN, PBX, or ISDN? What evidence do you have that rules out the other alternatives?
b. Draw the communications network configuration used by SBC. Is this network a star, ring, hybrid, or hierarchical network?
c. What kinds of communications channels can SBC use in its data communications system?
d. The communications channels that connect the local banks and the regional offices can be either point to point, multidrop, or line sharing. When is each most appropriate, and what are the advantages and drawbacks of each?
e. Should the channels that connect the local banks and the regional centers be narrowband, voiceband, or wideband?

9.7 The corporate office of Chancy's Inc., located in Portland, Oregon, handles the company's billings, collections, accounting, and projections. Currently, all computer processing is done on the company's mainframe computer using terminals. Because of the heavy demands placed on the system, it is often overtaxed. Users sometimes have to wait in long queues to gain access. Once the system has been accessed, response time is often slow because of the number of jobs being run on the mainframe. This overloading causes the system to periodically malfunction. The malfunctions and poor response time have had a negative effect on company productivity; for example, billings are often late and the collection process is very slow.

The company has purchased a number of PCs in the past few years in an attempt to improve productivity. The PCs have allowed Chancy's to increase the quality of their projections, forecasts, and other planning tools significantly. The company is currently thinking about installing a LAN to allow users to process and share data locally. It would also allow users to access Chancy's mainframe data base using their PCs.

REQUIRED

a. What are the advantages of installing a LAN?
b. What risks will the company be taking by installing a LAN?
c. What controls should Chancy implement to minimize its risk?

9.8 For each of the cases described in paragraphs a–d, diagram the configuration and then determine the following:

1. Whether the configuration is a centralized, decentralized, or distributed processing system
2. Whether a star, ring, hierarchical, or hybrid configuration is used
3. Whether the lines used in the configuration are point to point, multidrop, or line sharing

a. Mountain West Milk Producers process milk and milk products for consumers in Utah. The association's headquarters is in downtown Salt Lake City. Milk is processed at a plant 10 miles west of downtown, ice cream is made 30 miles south of Salt Lake City, and cheese is cured 60 miles north of Salt Lake City.

Each morning, drivers collect and transport raw milk from the association's milk producers to storage tanks at the processing plant. Information on the amount of milk collected and its fat content is keyed into the processing plant's PC. The types of products produced, their cost, sales data, and transfers are also kept on the micro. The processing plant prints out daily reports to meet its information needs. Similar information is also collected at the ice cream and cheese processing plants.

The information from the three locations is transferred by modem to a front-end processor linked to the mainframe computer at company headquarters. The information gathered is stored on disk and used by headquarters to prepare payroll, invoices, payment checks to milk producers, and financial statements.

b. The Nevada Department of Motor Vehicles (DMV) has an office in the state capital as well as in major cities to register motor vehicles and license drivers. The capital office has a number of PCs that are linked to a front-end processor. Upon receipt of a registration form in the mail, processing clerks at the state office use the vehicle's serial number to update the vehicle record in the DMV's data base. As customers enter to be licensed or to register their vehicles, the clerks use the micro to update the local division data base. At the end of each working day, the capital's mainframe pulls the day's update information from the division minicomputers and updates the state's data bases. Receipts are printed at both the local and state offices and given or mailed to the appropriate people.

Besides being linked to the capital mainframe, the local minicomputers are linked to the computers of two other divisions. As a result, all the division minis are linked together to provide quicker access to local information as well as to provide system backup. Computerization of the system has helped police to quickly obtain driver's license and registration information. These agencies are tied by modem to the local and state data bases.

c. Rollo Community Bank in Rollo, North Dakota, is an independently held and operated bank. The bank makes business, car, farm, and mortgage loans. Because of its close proximity to the Canadian border, the bank handles currency exchanges for a small fee. The bank employs three officers and seven tellers. The tellers operate five terminals that are tied to a minicomputer and handle all monies coming into or going out of the bank. The three officers have access to the minicomputer through the terminals but do not have the authorization to conduct transactions. When the loan officer approves a loan, the debtor presents the loan papers to a teller, who issues a check. The bank also uses the minicomputer to communicate with a currency exchange data base in New York. Up-to-date exchange rate information is vital, especially in times of rapid currency rate fluctuation.

d. Luxury Cars International is an automobile manufacturer headquartered in Kansas City. Its U.S. operations include 4 production plants, 20 regional warehouses, and 300 distributors. The company's production efforts are driven by demand, so accurate distribution information is vital to ensure proper inventory levels.

Dealerships keep their inventory records on a PC. Car orders are generated when a customer makes a special order or when the dealer orders inventory to meet estimated demand. Dealers are tied by modem to a minicomputer at a regional warehouse. When the dealer has a special order, the PC accesses a regional data base containing warehouse and all region dealerships' inventory. If the car is unavailable, the order is sent to a minicomputer in St. Louis that polls the other regional computers. If the car is found, the computer decides whether to have the car transferred or to place a special-order. If transferred, the appropriate regional warehouse is notified.

For special orders, the St. Louis computer calls a computer in Chicago that controls Luxury's production. The production computer forwards the order to the plant that makes the car, and the order is processed. Each of the four plants makes a different line of cars. The plants use a mainframe to process order requests and to control production. A regular order is processed in the same manner, except that dealership inventories are not scanned.

Franchises periodically forward summary data to the regional minicomputer, which summarizes them and produces regional reports. The regions pass summary-level information to a St. Louis computer that produces corporate-level sales and inventory reports. Production plant computers produce managerial information and send summary-level information to the computer in Chicago, which summarizes the data and produces corporate-level production reports. The Chicago and St. Louis computers pass information to the headquarters computer in Kansas City, which prepares corporate financial statements.

9.9 Luana's Clothing Distribution, Inc., has installed a mainframe computer at its headquarters building. All 12 branch offices will be linked to the mainframe and have access to the company's on-line data base. The diagram that follows (p. 312) shows the locations of each branch with respect to the corporate headquarters. The headquarters mainframe is labeled by HQB in the diagram. Branch locations are labeled BR and the branch number.

BR1

BR4

BR2

BR5

BR9

BR12

HQB

BR6

BR11

BR10

BR8

BR3

BR7

REQUIRED

a. Join the various branch locations to form a centralized computer network using point-to-point, multidrop, and line-sharing configurations. Assume that the branch locations are using terminals.
b. Assume that one of the branches in each of the three clusters has a minicomputer and the others have a PC. Each cluster will have its own distributed processing system. Draw this distributed processing system using star, ring, and hybrid configurations.

9.10 The past two decades have witnessed a transition from a centralized mainframe computer environment to a distributed network, where an organization has the ability to share computer processing. One of the fastest-growing segments of the computer industry is LANs, which are viewed as the wave of the future. LANs permit the transfer of information between PCs, word processors, data storage devices, printers, voice devices, and telecommunication devices. Organizational communication has been enhanced by moving from traditional distributed networks to LANs.

REQUIRED

a. Describe the reasons why an organization would choose a distributed network over the traditional centralized computer environment.
b. Compare and contrast the characteristics of a traditional distributed computer network with those of a LAN as they relate to the following.

1. Utilization of computer hardware.
2. User interaction and the sharing of electronic information.

c. Identify and explain three problems that can result from the use of LANs.
d. Explain the hardware characteristics associated with a computer modem as it relates to distributed information processing. (CMA Examination, adapted)

9.11 An integrated services digital network (ISDN) found an experimental home in an unlikely location: Harrah's Casino in Reno, Nevada. Using ISDN technology, Harrah's hoped to speed a customer's hotel check-in so that he or she is free to immediately head to the gambling tables.

The system they installed works as follows: At the Reno airport, customers go to a kiosk and use a screen menu to enter a room request. A hotel clerk appears on a large monitor and converses with the customer; the customer communicates with the clerk using an attached telephone. Payment is made by credit card using a magnetic card reader. A camera in the kiosk takes a picture of the customer and faxes it through the network to the hotel. The doorman, with fax in hand, greets the customer personally, hands him a room key, and takes the customer's bags.

The process rarely worked—but not because of the technology. The system scared people. Each day only about 10 customers used the system. The other 60 to 70 customers were frightened when they attempted to use the kiosk and left when the hotel clerk appeared on the screen. Since the system could not be cost-justified for only 10 people a day, it was removed. However, Harrah's management remains convinced that ISDN technology is still the wave of the future. Sometime in the next few years it expects to try other uses of the technology.

REQUIRED

a. What is ISDN? What do developers hope to accomplish with it?
b. What advantages can ISDN provide over traditional communications devices? What are the drawbacks of ISDN technology? How can users respond to these problems?
c. Discuss three potential applications for ISDN technology in business.

CASE 9.1: ANYCOMPANY, INC.—AN ONGOING COMPREHENSIVE CASE

Visit a local company and obtain permission to study its data communications system. Once you have lined up a company, complete the following tasks:

1. Write a report that summarizes the following information:
   a. What is the general structure of the company's data communications network? Is processing and control centralized, decentralized, or distributed? Why?
   b. Identify the data communications hardware and software the company employs.
   c. Identify the data communications channels the company uses by determining what the principal characteristics of each channel are and what channel configurations are used.
   d. Identify any network systems by determining what LANs the company utilizes, how they are configured, what servers are used to regulate the systems, and what other networks the company employs.
   e. What other data communications applications does the company employ? How do these applications assist the company in its day to day business activities?

2. Develop a comprehensive diagram of the company's data communications system.
   a. Identify the general strengths and weaknesses of this system.
   b. Make at least two recommendations for improving the existing system. Be prepared to discuss your findings with the class.

CASE 9.2: J C PENNEY

J C Penney is on the leading edge with respect to information technology. For the past 20 years Penney has been hard at work innovating and updating computer technology to improve efficiency and create a competitive advantage. It seems that the strategy has paid off. Steady sales growth and the maximization of revenue per employee has made J C Penney a leader in retail sales.

The reasons for Penney's success with technology begins at the top. Management has made the implementation of technology a top priority in order to give the retail chain an edge against the competition. Better end-user technology has reduced the demands upon the IS staff, allowing Penney to reduce both its size and budget. Remaining IS personnel focus their efforts on developing custom applications for Penney and providing technical backup for end-user applications. J C Penney has further developed its information strategy over the past years in the following ways.

• *Network applications.* Penney was one of the earliest adopters of the IBM System Network Architecture (SNA) and remains a firm believer in networks and distributed processing. The network was conceived to operate as a utility so that end users can access the network from virtually anywhere. In a given year the national network handles 350 million credit authorizations and 300 million transactions a year. Custom software secures the network and a built-in, menu-driven interface allows first-time users easy access throughout the system. The network also provides access to a variety of corporate information including stock quote data, office automation software, and development tools.

• *POS systems.* Using optical character recognition (OCR) devices, Penney monitors every piece of inventory from purchase to final sale. On a given day a store's transactions are stored on a computer for nightly transmission to a host processor in one of Penney's six major data centers, where the information is assimilated and returned within 24 hours. This information is invaluable in helping Penney discern changing consumer trends in regional areas. With such information Penney can respond instantly by redirecting warehouse merchandise to profitable regions and by directing the efforts of corporate buyers.

• *EDI.* Penney relies on electronic data interchange (EDI) to handle transactions with over two hundred suppliers. On a daily basis suppliers can dial into the

Penney system and access orders for delivery the following morning. Use of EDI saves Penney time and money by eliminating a host of manual procedures.

• *Corporate TV.* Using corporate teleconferencing, Penney maintains the largest business TV network of any U.S. retailer. Prior to the start of a new buying season, corporate buyers select their seasonal lines. Using corporate TV, these buyers then display their products for store buyers, who choose merchandise for their local store using a corporate computer program.

• *Strategic applications.* Penney uses expert systems in its catalog telemarketing sector. Penney employs 4000 operators in 14 centers to handle telephone orders. During peak hours the pace is intense. An expert system assists operators by redirecting telephone calls from busy operators to those who are free.

• *Software development.* With routine tasks handled by end users the IS staff is free to devote time to custom applications and software development. The IS staff reports that they've never had to spend millions of dollars to implement and then scrap a project.

• *Productivity center.* A final key to Penney's success is a center designed for the benefit of all end users. The productivity center is a place where employees can come to address end-user problems and tinker with new software. Staffers assist end users by answering questions and addressing specific user problems.

Given the foregoing information, answer the following questions:

1. Why is an information strategy important? How can an effective information strategy create competitive advantage for a store such as J C Penney? Why do you think Penney has been so successful in implementing its strategy?
2. Discuss the various information system strategies employed by Penney in terms of the information provided and how the strategy contributes to the success of the business.
3. What role does the IS staff play in the strategy? What are the advantages of such a strategy?

CASE 9.3: A MOVE TO COOPERATIVE COMPUTING

TO:	All Department Heads
FROM:	Jim Brady, Network Applications Division
DATE:	January 7, 1997
SUBJECT:	Unification of Department Servers

Recent trends toward centralizing network applications are changing the way networks are employed in meeting business needs. Network operating systems are becoming more powerful, allowing a single server to accommodate more users. Managing a LAN is now a full-time responsibility as additional services become essential. Finally, as networks are employed in more serious applications, organizationwide standards are needed to regulate data integrity, security, and reliability.

The Role of the Student Affairs Division

As you know, the student affairs division provides a number of student services through several departments, including career planning, job placement, student employment, counseling, and testing. When networks were introduced in 1989, each department established an autonomous network to handle its information. As time has passed, these individual networks have expanded to the point where they do not operate very efficiently. To handle the problem, we propose the use of a single server for all of the network applications in the division.

A Single-Server System

Our recommendation is to install a single-client/server system to meet the needs of the entire division. Such a system will provide several advantages, including the following:

• End users will see improved performance with the use of more advanced server technology.

• A single server will allow the LAN administrator to focus efforts on improving network applications and developing new network services.

• The switch will bring significant cost savings in the long run, with a greater variety of applications.

Implementation

• Implementing the plan will require the cooperation of all department heads as well as a number of support organizations.

• We want to get rid of your old servers ASAP so that we can install the new server immediately.
• Implementation of the single-server system will begin in September, with installation scheduled for completion in two weeks.

Conclusion

Our division's evolution from mainframes to minis to PCs to networks represents a shift from centralized to decentralized to cooperative computing. Implementing the single server for our division is a step in the right direction and will require your full support. Thank you.

Answer the following questions, in view of this memo:

1. As a department head, how would you evaluate Jim Brady's suggestion to integrate department servers into one server?
   a. What are the risks of such an approach?
   b. What are the advantages of a single server?
   c. What concerns do you have over the implementation of the new server?
   d. Do you support this idea? Why?
2. Discuss the evolution of computing from centralized systems to cooperative systems. Is this consistent with national trends? Which approach do you think is best? Why?
3. Why is network computing considered by many as "cooperative computing"? Why are network systems increasing in popularity?
4. How do network configurations fit in with general changes in organizational structure and management style?

ANSWERS TO CHAPTER QUIZ

1. e	**3.** e	**5.** c	**7.** b	**9.** c
2. d	**4.** b	**6.** b	**8.** d	**10.** b

P A R T   T H R E E

Chapter 10

Systems Analysis

LEARNING OBJECTIVES

After studying this chapter, you should be able to:

- Explain the five phases of the systems development life cycle.
- Discuss the key issues and steps in systems analysis.
- Discuss the various types of feasibility analysis, and calculate economic feasibility.
- Explain the principles and challenges of business process reengineering.
- Explain why systems change triggers behavioral reactions, what form this resistance to change takes, and how to avoid or minimize the resulting problems.

Integrative Case: Shoppers Mart

Several months ago Ann Christy, a successful accountant, was promoted to controller of Shoppers Mart (SM), a small but rapidly growing regional chain of discount stores. Since her promotion she has been assessing how the accounting function could better serve Shoppers Mart. She has held meetings with the president and CEO and with other key managers at headquarters. She has also spent several weeks visiting various SM stores, talking one on one with store managers and employees. Here are her findings:

- Store managers cannot obtain information other than what is contained on SM's periodic, preformatted reports. As soon as information is needed from several functional areas, the system bogs down.
- Purchasing cannot get timely information about what products are or are not selling well. As a result, stores are often out of popular items and overstocked with ones that customers aren't buying.
- Top management is concerned that SM is losing market share to larger rivals with better prices and selection. The current system cannot provide management with the information it needs to analyze and solve this problem.

After analyzing the situation, Ann is convinced that Shoppers Mart needs a new information system—one that is flexible, efficient, and responsive to user needs. Ann knows that a new system will never be successful unless it has the complete support of top management. Before she asks for approval and funding for the new system, Ann schedules a meeting with the head of systems development. She has the following questions:

1. What process must the company go through to design and implement a new system?

2. What types of planning are necessary to ensure the system's success? Who will be involved, and how? Do any special committees need to be formed? What resources need to be planned for? How should all of the planning be documented?
3. How will employees react to a new system? What problems might this changeover cause, and how can they be minimized?
4. How should the new system be justified and sold to top management? How can expected costs and benefits be quantified to determine whether the new system will indeed be cost-effective?

INTRODUCTION

Because we live in a highly competitive and ever-changing world, organizations continually face the need for new, faster, and more reliable ways of obtaining information. To meet this need, an AIS must continually undergo changes, ranging from minor adjustments to major overhauls. Occasionally, the changes are so drastic that the old AIS is scrapped and replaced by an entirely new one. Change is so constant and frequent that at any given time most organizations are involved in some system improvement or change. Companies usually change their AIS for one of the following reasons:

- *Changes in user or business needs.* Increased competition, business growth or consolidation, mergers and divestitures, new regulations, or changes in regional and global relationships can alter an organization's structure and purpose. To remain responsive to company needs, the system must change as well.
- *Technological changes.* As technology advances and becomes less costly, an organization can obtain a system more responsive to the needs of its information users.
- *Improved business processes.* Many companies have inefficient business processes that need to be updated. For example, the ordering system at Nashua, an office supply manufacturer, caused customer frustration and dissatisfaction. When a customer called, a clerk would take his or her information and promise to return the call. Before calling the customer back the clerk had to access two separate systems: a mainframe system to verify customer information and perform a credit check and a PC-based system to calculate pricing. If the customer was still interested, the clerk accessed another centralized system to determine inventory availability. When the system was redesigned it took three minutes to process a telephone order instead of two days.
- *Competitive advantage.* Increased quality, quantity, and speed of information can result in an improved product or service and may help lower costs. For example, Wal-Mart invests heavily in technology to provide information about customers and their purchases in order to increase sales. Bell Atlantic hopes to increase revenues by investing $2.1 billion in the development of a new system. This represents a shift in management focus, since previously 90% of new systems were for the purposes of automating labor and reducing expenses.

- *Productivity gains.* Computers automate many clerical and repetitive tasks. Expert systems place the knowledge of experts at the disposal of many others, while system improvements can significantly decrease the performance time of certain tasks. Carolina Power and Light was able to eliminate 27% of its IS staff when it installed a new system that significantly outperformed the old one.
- *Growth.* Companies outgrow their systems and need to either upgrade or replace them entirely.
- *Downsizing.* Companies often move from centralized mainframes to networked PCs in order to take advantage of their plunging price/performance ratios. This places decision making and its corresponding information as far down the organization chart as possible. For example, Consolidated Edison of New York downsized from a mainframe-based system to a client/server system and eliminated 100 clerical positions. The new system does much more than the old one, including handling work-flow management, user contact, data base queries, automatic cash processing, and voice/data integration.
- *Quality improvements.* It is difficult to improve quality without improving the system that generates the data needed to measure and evaluate quality. For example, Carrier Corporation faced eroding market share due to difficulties in servicing customers effectively. Its manual order entry system had a 70% error rate. Carrier started a total quality management (TQM) program and today an expert system coordinates everything from manufacturing to sales, resulting in fewer errors, lower costs, and more satisfied customers.

SYSTEMS DEVELOPMENT: AN OVERVIEW

AIS changes can range from minor corrections to developing and installing whole new systems. Whether the changes are major or minor, most companies go through a systems development life cycle. Steps in that cycle, the players, and planning for systems development are discussed in this section.

The Systems Development Life Cycle

Ann Christy asked the manager of systems development to explain the process Shoppers Mart would go through to design and implement a new AIS. This five-step process, known as the **systems development life cycle (SDLC),** is shown in Fig. 10.1 and briefly explained next.

Systems Analysis. During **systems analysis,** information needed to purchase or develop a new system is gathered. Requests for systems development are prioritized to maximize limited development resources. If a project passes the initial screening, the current system is surveyed to define the nature and scope of the project and understand its strengths and weaknesses. Then, an in-depth study of the proposed system is conducted to determine its feasibility. If feasible, the information needs of system users and managers are identified and documented. These needs are used to develop and document system requirements. System requirements are used to select a prewritten system or develop a new one. A systems analysis report is prepared and submitted to management.

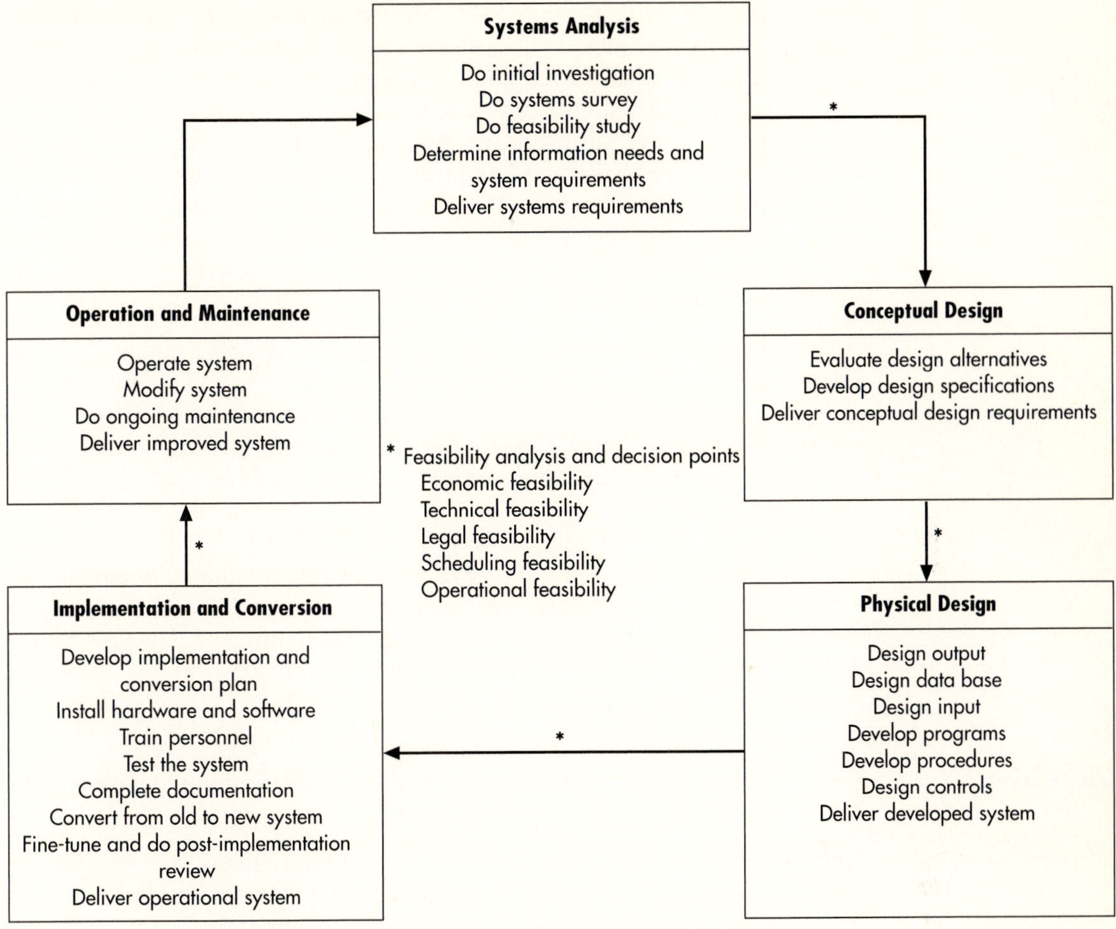

Figure 10.1

The Systems Development Life Cycle

Conceptual Design. During **conceptual systems design** the company decides how to meet user needs. The first task is to identify and evaluate appropriate design alternatives. Once a design alternative has been selected, detailed specifications outlining what the system is to accomplish and how it is to be controlled are developed. This phase is complete when conceptual system design requirements are communicated to management.

Physical Design. During **physical design,** the company translates the broad, user-oriented requirements of the conceptual design into detailed specifications that are used to code and test the computer programs. Input and output documents are designed, computer programs are written, files are created, procedures are developed, and controls are built into the new system.

Implementation and Conversion. The **implementation and conversion** phase is the capstone phase where all the elements and activities of the system come together. Because of the phase's complexity and importance, an implementation and conversion plan is developed and followed. As part of implementation, any new hardware or software is installed and tested. New employees may need to be hired and trained, or existing employees relocated. New processing procedures must be tested and perhaps modified. Standards and controls for the new system must be established and system documentation completed. The final step in this phase is dismantling the old system and converting to the new one.

Operations and Maintenance. After the system is up and running, it is studied to detect and correct any design deficiencies. During its life, the system is periodically reviewed. Minor modifications are made as problems arise or as new needs become evident. This is referred to as **operations and maintenance.** Eventually a major modification or system replacement is necessary and the SDLC begins again.

In addition to these five phases, three activities (planning, managing the behavioral reactions to change, and assessing the ongoing feasibility of the project) are performed throughout the life cycle. These three activities, as well as systems analysis, are discussed in this chapter. The other four SDLC phases are explained in Chapter 11.

The Players

Many people must cooperate to successfully develop and implement an AIS. This section discusses those involved and their roles.

Management. Nothing is as effective in generating systems development support as a clear signal from top management that involvement is important. Top management's most important roles are providing support and encouragement for development projects and aligning information systems with corporate strategies. Other key roles include establishing system goals and objectives, reviewing IS department performance and leadership, establishing project selection and organizational structure policies, and participating in important IS decisions. The principal roles of user management are to determine information requirements for departmental projects, assist systems analysts with project cost and benefit estimations, assign key staff members to development projects, and allocate appropriate funds to support systems development and operation.

Accountants. Accountants must play three roles during systems design. First, as AIS users they need to determine their information needs and system requirements and communicate them to system developers. Second, they must be members of the project development team and the IS steering committee and help manage systems development. Third, accountants must take an active role in designing system controls and periodically monitoring and testing the system to verify that the controls are implemented and functioning properly. All systems should contain sufficient controls to ensure the accurate and complete processing of data. The system should also be easy to audit. If addressed at the start of development, auditability and control concerns can be maximized; trying to achieve them after a system has been designed is inefficient, time-consuming, and costly. Control and audit issues are discussed in depth in Chapters 13–16.

Information Systems Steering Committee. Because AIS development spans functional and divisional boundaries, organizations establish an executive-level **steering committee** to plan and oversee the IS function. The committee consists of the controller as well as IS and user department management. The steering committee sets policies that govern the AIS; ensures top-management participation, guidance, and control; and facilitates the coordination and integration of IS activities to increase goal congruence and reduce goal conflict.

Project Development Team. Each development project has a team of systems specialists, managers, accountants and auditors, and users that guides its development. They plan each project, monitor it to ensure timely and cost-effective completion, make sure proper consideration is given to the human element, and communicate project status to top management and the steering committee. Team members should communicate frequently with users and hold regular meetings to consider ideas and discuss progress so there are no surprises upon project completion. A team approach produces more effective results and facilitates user acceptance of the system, once it is finally implemented.

Systems Analysts and Programmers. **Systems analysts** study existing systems, design new ones, and prepare specifications for computer programmers. The analyst interacts with employees throughout the organization and systems technology in order to successfully bridge the gap between the user and technology. It is their responsibility to ensure that the system meets user needs. **Computer programmers** write computer programs using the specifications developed by the analysts. They also modify and maintain existing computer programs.

Planning Systems Development

Imagine that you built a two-bedroom house for your first home. Several years later you add a bedroom, then another bedroom and a bathroom. Over the years you add a family room, recreation room, deck, and two-car garage; in addition, you expand the kitchen and the dining area. Without prior thought to what you eventually want in a home, your house will end up as a poorly organized patchwork of rooms surrounding the original structure. In addition, the cost of the house can end up greatly exceeding its value. This scenario also applies to an AIS that is not properly planned. The result is a costly and poorly integrated system that is difficult to operate and maintain.

Systems development planning is an important step for a number of key reasons:

- *Consistency.* The system's goals and objectives must correspond to the overall strategic plan of the organization.
- *Efficiency.* Systems are more efficient, subsystems are coordinated, and there is a sound basis for selecting new applications for development.

- *Cutting edge.* The company remains abreast of the ever-present changes in information technology.
- *Lower costs.* Duplication, wasted efforts, and cost and time overruns are avoided. The system is less costly and easier to maintain.
- *Adaptability.* Management is better prepared for future resource needs and employees are better prepared for the changes that will occur.

When development efforts are poorly planned, a company must often return to a prior phase and correct errors and design flaws, as shown in Fig. 10.2. This process is very costly and it also results in delays, frustration, and low morale. Two types of systems development plans are needed: individual project plans prepared by project teams and a master plan developed by the information system steering committee:

1. *Project development plan.* The basic building block of IS planning is the **project development plan.** Each project development plan contains a cost/benefit analysis; developmental and operational requirements, including human resource, hardware, software, and financial resource requirements; and a schedule of the activities required to develop and operate the new application.
2. *The master plan.* A **master plan** is a long-range planning document that specifies what the system will consist of, how it will be developed, who will develop it, how needed resources will be acquired, and where the AIS is headed. The master plan should also provide the status of projects in

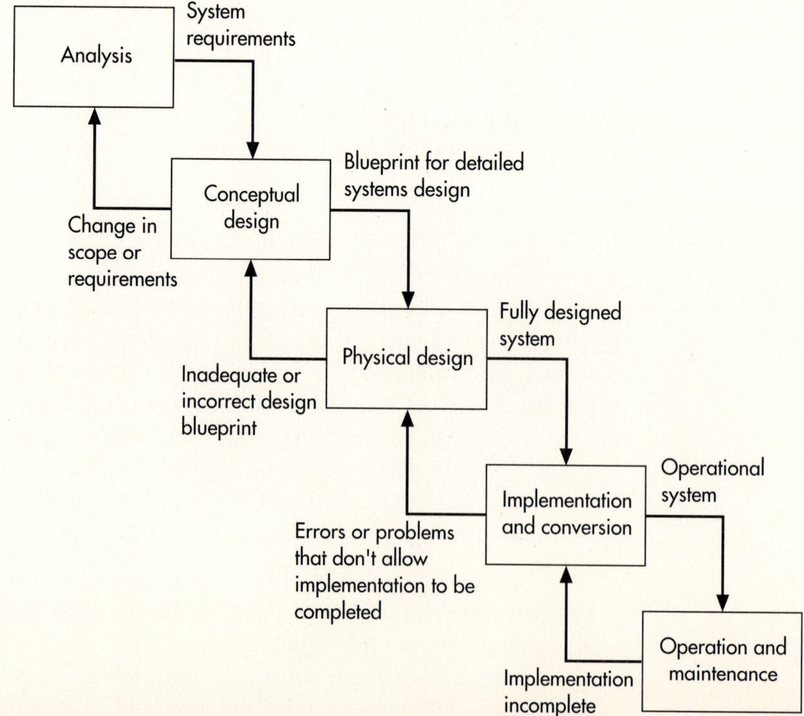

Figure 10.2

Reasons for Returning to a Prior Systems Development Life Cycle Phase

Table 10.1 **Components of Systems Master Plan at Shoppers Mart**

Organizational goals and objectives	Status of systems being developed
Company mission statement and goals	Proposed systems priorities
IS strategic plan and goals	Approved systems development
Organizational constraints	Proposals under consideration
Organizational approach to AIS	Development timetables and schedules
Organizational and AIS priorities	Forecast of future developments
Inventory and assessments	Forecasts of information needs
Current systems	Technological forecasts
Approved systems	Environmental/regulatory forecasts
Current hardware	Audit and control requirements
Current software	External user needs
Current AIS staff	
Assessment of current strengths and weakness	

process, prioritize planned projects, describe the criteria used for prioritization, and provide time tables for development. The projects with the highest priority should be the first to be developed. The importance of this decision dictates that it be made by top management and not by computer specialists. A planning horizon of approximately five years is reasonable for any master plan. The plan should be updated at least once each year. MCI, which uses a five-year plan, updates parts of its plan as often as biweekly. The table of contents of the master plan used at Shoppers Mart is shown in Table 10.1.

Systems planning at MCI has been an important factor in their success, as explained in Focus 10.1.

SYSTEMS ANALYSIS

When a new or improved system is needed, a written **request for systems development** is prepared. The request describes the current system's problems, why the change is needed, and the proposed system's goals and objectives as well as its anticipated benefits and costs. The analysis is conducted by the project development team. The five steps in the analysis phase and their objectives are shown in Fig. 10.3 and discussed in this section.

Initial Investigation

An **initial investigation** is conducted to screen projects. An accountant conducting an initial investigation must gain a clear picture of the problem or need, determine the project's viability and expected costs and payoffs, make an initial evaluation of the extent of the project and the nature of the new AIS, and recommend whether the development project should be initiated as proposed, modified, or abandoned.

During the initial investigation the exact nature of the problem must be determined. In some instances what is thought to be the cause is not the real source of the problem. For example, a governmental accountant once asked a consultant to develop an AIS to produce the information he needed on fund expenditures and available funds. Further investigation showed that the agency's system already provided the information; the accountant simply did not understand the reports he was receiving.

FOCUS 10.1

Planning Helps MCI Cope with Popular New Service

When MCI's Friends & Family service was introduced, order entry transaction volume soared 70% in three months. Fortunately, MCI was able to keep response times for the order entry system within acceptable bounds. One reason MCI was prepared was due to planning. Computer capacity planning and performance management are vital activities at MCI, where double-digit annual growth is the norm and computing does not just support the business—it *is* the business. Five-year plans are updated annually, annual plans are revised quarterly, and quarterly plans may change biweekly. MCI's capacity planning staff has such a good track record that top management will accept, with little question, a recommendation to spend millions on a system.

The planning process takes input from three sources. Sales projections go into a computer model developed by MCI, as do service-level objectives such as response time. Out of the model flows capacity requirements for each of MCI's five data centers, indicating the need for hardware resources such as off-line and on-line storage and main memory and processor power. Capacity planners also factor in advance notice of new software coming from MCI's applications developers and forecasts of new technology from industry research firms and vendors.

Once applications are in production, MCI uses a variety of automated tools to spot abnormal patterns, looming bottlenecks, and other troublespots. When they are found, the consulting group works with users and software developers to fine-tune applications or to smooth work loads.

Focus Questions

1. What made it possible for MCI to handle the tremendous increase in transaction volume when their Friends & Family program was introduced?
2. MCI has a five-year plan, an annual plan, and a quarterly plan. According to the chapter what kinds of plans are these?

The scope of a project (what it should and should not accomplish) should also be determined. A new AIS is useful when problems are a result of lack of information, inaccessibility of data, and inefficient data processing. However, a new AIS is *not* the answer to organizational problems, such as the controller managing too many employees. Likewise, if a manager lacks organization skills or if control problems are caused by a failure to enforce existing procedures, a new AIS is not the answer.

If a project is approved, a **proposal to conduct systems analysis** is prepared, it is assigned a priority and added to the master plan, and the development team begins the survey of the existing AIS. As the investigation progresses, the proposal will be modified as more information becomes available. The table of contents for the Shoppers Mart proposal (see Table 10.7, p. 344) is representative of the information in a proposal to conduct systems analysis.

Systems Survey

During the **systems survey** an extensive study of the current AIS is undertaken. This survey may take weeks or months, depending on the complexity and scope of the system. The objectives of a systems survey are as follows:

- Gain a thorough understanding of company operations, policies, and procedures; data and information flow; AIS strengths and weaknesses; and available hardware, software, and personnel.
- Make preliminary assessments of current and future processing needs and determine the extent and nature of the changes needed.

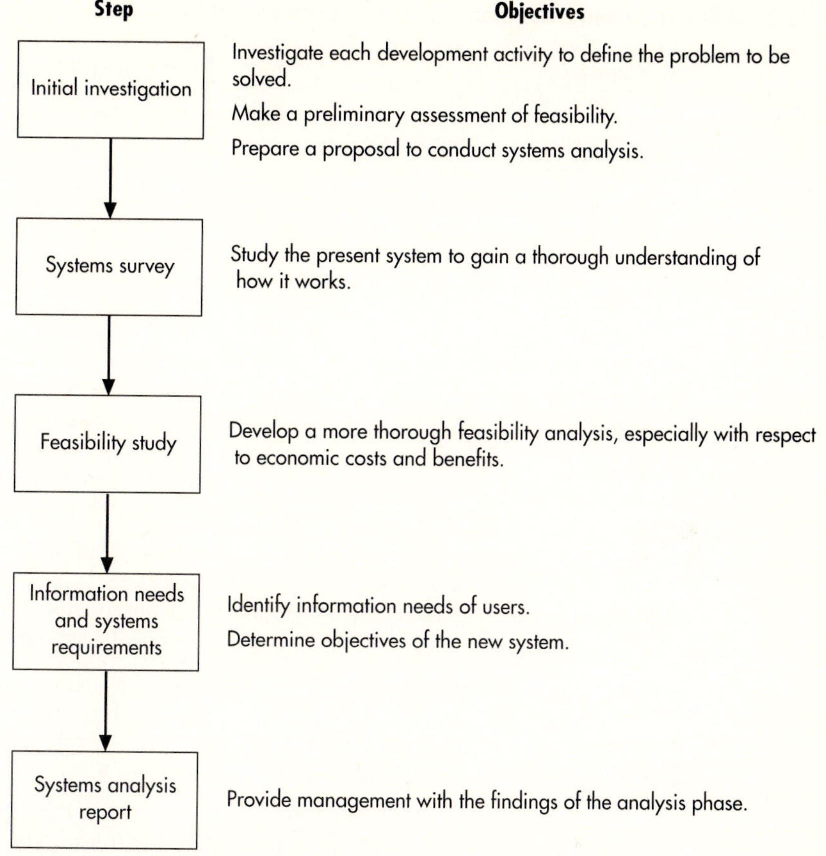

Step
Objectives
Initial investigation
Investigate each development activity to define the problem to be solved.
Make a preliminary assessment of feasibility.
Prepare a proposal to conduct systems analysis.
Systems survey
Study the present system to gain a thorough understanding of how it works.
Feasibility study
Develop a more thorough feasibility analysis, especially with respect to economic costs and benefits.
Information needs and systems requirements
Identify information needs of users.
Determine objectives of the new system.
Systems analysis report
Provide management with the findings of the analysis phase.

Figure 10.3

Steps in Systems Analysis

- Develop working relationships with users and build support for the AIS.
- Collect data that identify user needs, conduct a feasibility analysis, and make recommendations to management.

Data Sources. Data about the current AIS can be gathered internally from both employees and documentation, such as organization charts and procedures manuals. External sources include consultants, customers and suppliers, industry associations, and government agencies. The advantages and disadvantages of four common methods of gathering data are summarized here and in Table 10.2.

An *interview* helps gather answers to "why" questions: Why is there a problem? Why does the AIS work this way? Why is this information important? Care must be taken, however, to ensure that an interviewee's personal biases, self-interests, or desire to say what he thinks the interviewer wants to hear does not produce inaccurate information.

Ann Christy's interviews at Shoppers Mart were successful because of her approach and preparation. For each interview, she made an appointment, explained the purpose beforehand, indicated the amount of time needed, and arrived on time. Before each session she studied the interviewee's responsibilities and listed the points she wanted to cover. She put each interviewee at ease

Table 10.2 Advantages and Disadvantages of Data Gathering Methods

	Advantages	Disadvantages
Interviews	Can answer "why" questions Interviewer can probe and follow up Questions can be clarified Builds positive relationships with interviewee Builds acceptance and support for new system	Time-consuming Expensive Personal biases or self-interest may produce inaccurate information
Questionnaires	Can be anonymous Not time-consuming Inexpensive Allows more time to think about responses	Doesn't allow in-depth questions or answers Can't probe or follow up on responses Questions can't be clarified Impersonal; doesn't build relationships Difficult to develop Often ignored or completed superficially
Observation	Can verify how system *actually* works, rather than how it *should* work Results in greater understanding of system	Time-consuming Expensive Difficult to interpret properly Observed people may alter behavior
System Documentation	Describes how system should work Written form facilitates review, analysis	Time-consuming May not be available or easy to find

by being friendly, courteous, and tactful. Her questions dealt with the person's responsibilities, how the person interacted with the AIS, how the system might be improved, and the person's information needs. She let the interviewee do most of the talking and paid special attention to nonverbal communication, since subtle overtones and body language can be as significant as direct responses to questions. She took notes and augmented them with detailed impressions shortly after the interview. She asked permission to tape especially important interviews.

Questionnaires are used when the amount of information to be gathered is small and well defined, is obtained from many people or from those who are physically removed, or is intended to verify data from other sources. Questionnaires take relatively little time to administer, but developing a quality questionnaire can be challenging and require significant amounts of time.

Observation is used to verify information gathered using other approaches and to determine how a system actually works, rather than how it should work. It can be difficult to interpret observations properly because observed people may change their normal behavior or make mistakes. Observation effectiveness is maximized by identifying what is to be observed, estimating how long it will take, obtaining permission, and explaining what will be done and why. The observer should not make value judgments, and notes and impressions should be formally documented as soon afterward as possible.

System documentation describes how the AIS is intended to work. Throughout the systems survey, the project team should be alert to differences between intended and actual system operation. These differences provide important insights into problems and weaknesses. If documentation is unavailable or incomplete, it may be worthwhile to develop it.

Document Findings and Model the Existing System. The information gathered during the analysis phase must be documented so it can be used throughout the systems development project. Documentation consists of questionnaire copies, interview notes, memos, and document copies. Another way of documenting a system is to model it. **Physical models** illustrate *how* a system functions by describing the flow of documents, the computer processes performed and the people performing them, the equipment used, and any other physical elements of the system. **Logical models** illustrate *what* is being done, irrespective of how that flow is actually accomplished. The logical model focuses on the essential activities and the flow of information, not on the physical processes of transforming and storing data. Table 10.3 contains a list of the analysis and design tools and techniques used by accountants and system developers to create these models and identifies the chapter where each is discussed in this text.

Analyze the Existing System. Once data gathering is complete, the survey team evaluates the AIS's strengths and weaknesses to develop ideas for how to design and structure the new AIS. Where appropriate, strengths should be retained and weaknesses corrected. For example, if output is being duplicated, consolidating reports might produce cost savings. Sometimes, however, revolutionary rather than evolutionary change is needed and an entirely new system is developed. This process, called *reengineering,* is discussed later in the chapter.

Prepare Systems Survey Report. The systems survey culminates with a **systems survey report.** Table 10.7, on page 344, shows the table of contents for the Shoppers Mart systems survey report. The report is supported by documentation such as memos, interview and observation notes, questionnaire data, file and record layouts and descriptions, input and output descriptions, copies of documents, flowcharts, and data flow diagrams.

Feasibility Study

The information gathered during the systems survey is used to conduct a more thorough **feasibility study** (also called a business case) than the cursory analysis completed during the initial investigation. The extent of these studies varies, depending on the size and nature of the system. For example, the study for a large-scale system is generally quite extensive whereas one for a desktop

Table 10.3 **Systems Analysis and Design Tools and Techniques**

CASE (Chapter 11)	Organization charts (Chapter 2)
Coding (Chapter 2)	Program flowcharts (Chapter 3)
Data flow diagrams (Chapter 3)	Prototyping (Chapter 12)
Data modeling (Chapter 6)	Record layouts (Chapter 4)
Decision tables (Chapter 3)	Report layouts (Chapter 11)
Document flowcharts (Chapter 3)	System flowcharts (Chapter 3)
Forms design checklist (Chapter 2)	

system might be conducted informally. The feasibility team should include management, accountants skilled in controls and auditing, systems personnel, and users.

The steering committee uses the study to decide whether to terminate the project, proceed unconditionally, or proceed if specific problems are resolved. Although it can be terminated later, this go/no go decision represents a pivotal point in the process because subsequent SDLC steps require major time and money commitments. As the project proceeds, the study is updated and the project's viability is reassessed. The further into a development project, the less likely it is to be canceled if a proper feasibility study has been prepared and updated.

Although uncommon, systems have been scrapped after they were implemented because they didn't work or did not meet an organization's needs. For example, Bank America hired a software firm to replace a 20-year-old batch system used to manage billions of dollars in institutional trust accounts. After two years of development, it was implemented despite warnings that it was not adequately tested. Ten months later the system was scrapped, the bank's top systems and trust executives had resigned, and the company had taken a $60 million write-off to cover expenses related to the system. During the 10 months the system was in place the company lost 100 institutional accounts with $4 billion in assets. As another example, Focus 10.2 describes a project at Blue Cross and Blue Shield that was scrapped after six years of work and a $120-million investment.

Five important aspects need to be considered during a feasibility study:

1. **Technical feasibility.** Can the planned system be developed and implemented using existing technology?
2. **Operational feasibility.** Does the organization have access to people who can design, implement, and operate the proposed system? Can and will the system be used by those it is intended to serve?
3. **Legal feasibility.** Will the system comply with all applicable federal and state laws and statutes, administrative agency regulations, and the company's contractual obligations?
4. **Scheduling feasibility.** Can the system be developed and implemented in the time allotted? If not, it will have to be modified, postponed, or replaced by an alternative selection.
5. **Economic feasibility.** Will system benefits justify the time, money, and other resources required to implement it?

Economic feasibility, the most important and frequently analyzed of the five aspects, is now discussed in greater depth.

Calculating Economic Feasibility Costs and Benefits. Determining economic feasibility requires a careful investigation of the costs and benefits of a proposed system. Because accountants are familiar with cost concepts, they provide a significant contribution to this evaluation. The basic framework for feasibility analysis is the **capital budgeting model** in which cost savings and other benefits, as well as initial outlay costs, operating costs, and other cash outflows, are translated into dollar estimates. The estimated benefits are compared

FOCUS 10.2

Blue Cross Abandons Runaway

Blue Cross and Blue Shield of Massachusetts hoped that its new information system would usher in a new era. After six years and $120 million, however, the System 21 project was behind schedule and significantly over budget. The project was canceled, and Blue Cross turned its computer operation over to Electronic Data Systems Corporation, an outside contractor.

Although information system failures of this magnitude are rare, they happen more often than one would expect. According to a KPMG Peat Marwick survey, 35% of all major information system projects become a *runaway*—a project that is millions of dollars over budget and months or years behind schedule. Other surveys show that almost every *Fortune* 200 company has had at least one runaway.

One major reason for the development problems was Blue Cross's failure to properly supervise the project. Blue Cross hired an independent contractor to develop the software but neglected to appoint someone to coordinate and manage the project in-house. Top management did not establish a firm set of priorities regarding essential features and the sequence of application development.

When the developers presented the claims processing software to Blue Cross, they thought it was a finished product. The managers and users at Blue Cross had other ideas. They were not happy with the software and requested numerous changes. As a result, the whole project was delayed. This led to ever-increasing cost overruns. By the time System 21 was launched, Blue Cross had fallen far behind its competitors in its ability to process an ever-swelling load of paperwork. In fact, between 1985 and 1991 it lost a million subscribers and came close to bankruptcy. It also had a poorly integrated system—nine different claims processing systems running on hardware dating back to the early 1970s.

The lesson that Blue Cross learned with System 21 was a painful one. The system it spent six years working on was abandoned, and it turned its hardware over to EDS. Fortunately, although the system died, the patient survived.

Focus Questions

1. Why did the Blue Cross and Blue Shield project turn into a runaway?
2. What did Blue Cross learn from the experience?

---

with the costs to determine whether the system is cost beneficial. Where possible, benefits and costs that are not easily quantifiable should be estimated and included in the feasibility analysis. If they cannot be accurately estimated, they should be listed and the likelihood of their occurring and the expected impact on the organization evaluated.

Some of the tangible and intangible benefits a company might obtain from a new system are cost savings; improved customer service, productivity, decision making, and data processing; better management control; and increased job satisfaction and employee morale.

Equipment costs are an initial outlay cost if the system is purchased and an operating cost if rented or leased. Equipment costs vary from $2000 for PC systems to millions for enormous mainframes. Equipment costs are usually less than the cost of acquiring software and maintaining, supporting, and operating the system. Software acquisition costs include the purchase price of prewritten software as well as the time and effort required to design, program, test, and document application software. The human resource costs associated with hiring, training, and relocating staff can be substantial. Site preparation costs may also be incurred for large computer systems. In addition, there are costs involved in installing the new system and converting files to the appropriate storage media.

The primary operating cost is maintaining the system. Studies show that between 65% and 75% of an organization's systems efforts are spent in maintaining current information systems. In addition, there may be significant annual cash outflows for equipment replacement and expansion and software updates. Human resource costs include the salaries of systems analysts, programmers, operators, data entry operators, and management. Costs are also incurred for supplies, overhead, and financial charges. Initial outlay and operating costs are summarized in Table 10.4.

Capital Budgeting. During systems design several alternative approaches to meeting system requirements are developed. Various feasibility measures are then used to narrow the list of alternatives. After this initial culling, capital budgeting techniques are used to evaluate the economic merits of the remaining alternatives. Three capital budgeting techniques are commonly used:

1. **Payback period.** This figure represents the number of years required for the net savings to equal the initial cost of the investment. The project with the shortest payback period is usually selected.

Table 10.4 **Initial Outlay and Operating Costs**

Hardware	Maintenance/backup
Central processing unit	Hardware/software maintenance
Peripherals	Backup and recovery operations
Communications hardware	Power supply protection
Special input/output devices	Documentation
Upgrade and expansion costs	Systems documentation
Software	Training program documentation
Application, system, general-purpose, utility, and communications software	Operating standards and procedures
Updated versions of software	Site preparation
Application software design, programming, modification, and testing	Air-conditioning, humidity, dust controls
Staff	Physical security (access)
Supervisors	Fire and water protection
Analysts and programmers	Cabling, wiring, and outlets
Computer operators	Furnishing and fixtures
Input (data conversion) personnel	Installation
Recruitment and staff training	Freight and delivery charges
Consultants	Set-up and connection fees
Supplies and overhead	Conversion
Preprinted forms	Systems testing
Data storage devices	File and data conversions
Supplies (paper, ribbons, toner)	Parallel operations
Utilities and power	Financial
	Finance charge
	Legal fees
	Insurance

2. **Net present value (NPV).** With the NPV method all estimated future cash flows are discounted back to the present, using a discount rate that reflects the time value of money. The initial outlay costs are deducted from the discounted cash flows to obtain the net present value. A positive NPV indicates the alternative is economically feasible. When comparing projects, the one with the highest positive NPV is usually accepted.
3. **Internal rate of return (IRR).** IRR is the effective interest rate that results in an NPV of zero. A project's IRR is compared with a minimum acceptable rate to determine acceptance or rejection. When comparing projects, the proposal with the highest IRR is usually selected.

Payback, NPV, and IRR are illustrated in Table 10.8, on page 345.

Information Needs and Systems Requirements

Once a project is deemed to be feasible, the company identifies the information needs of AIS users and documents system requirements. Determining information needs can be a challenging process due to the sheer quantity and variety of information that must be specified, even for a relatively simple AIS. In addition, it may be difficult for employees to articulate their information needs or they may identify them incorrectly. Figure 10.4 somewhat humorously illustrates the types of communication associated with this process.

To illustrate the importance of accurately determining system requirements, consider the example of Corning Corporation. When the company began investigating the quality of the ophthalmic pressings it manufactures and sells to the makers of prescription lenses, it found that 35% of its drafting

Figure 10.4

Communications Problems in Systems Analysis and Design

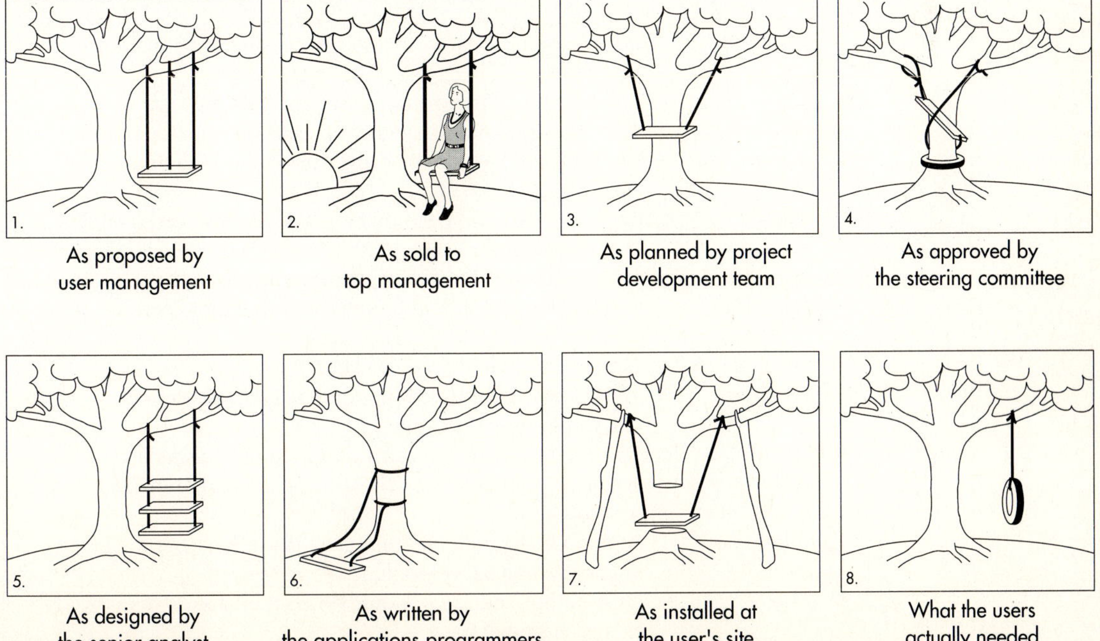
1.
As proposed by user management
2.
As sold to top management
3.
As planned by project development team
4.
As approved by the steering committee
5.
As designed by the senior analyst
6.
As written by the applications programmers
7.
As installed at the user's site
8.
What the users actually needed

documents contained errors. Corning also found that the drafting errors became increasingly expensive to correct at each subsequent stage of the manufacturing process. It cost $250 if discovered before the toolmakers cut the tools, $20,000 if discovered before the assembly line began production, and up to $100,000 after it was sent to the customer. As a result of the study, a number of corrective actions were undertaken that reduced the error rates from 35% to 0.2%. The same type of cost relationship exists in IS development; the cost to correct an error increases as development proceeds through the SDLC phases.

Systems Objectives and Constraints. Determining information needs and system requirements requires that organizations take a **systems approach.** This approach recognizes that every system must have an objective, a set of components, and a set of component interrelationships. These objectives form a framework for the analysis of problems and opportunities. With the systems approach, problems and alternatives are viewed from the standpoint of the entire organization, rather than from any single department or interest group.

It is important to determine system objectives so that analysts and users can focus on those elements most vital to the AIS's success (see Table 10.5). However, it is difficult for a system to satisfy every objective. For example, designing adequate internal controls must be viewed as a trade-off between the objectives of economy and reliability. Similarly, cutting clerical costs must balance the objectives of capacity, flexibility, and customer service.

Organizational constraints usually make it impossible to develop all parts of a new AIS simultaneously. Therefore, the system is divided into smaller sub-

Table 10.5 **AIS Objectives**

Usefulness	Information produced by the system should help management and users in decision making.
Economy	The benefits of the system should exceed the cost.
Reliability	The system should process data accurately and completely.
Availability	Users should be able to access the system at their convenience.
Timeliness	Crucial information should be produced first and then less important items as time permits.
Customer service	Courteous and efficient customer service should be provided.
Capacity	System capacity should be sufficient to handle periods of peak operation and future growth.
Ease of use	The system should be user-friendly.
Flexibility	The system should accommodate reasonable operating or system requirements changes.
Tractability	The system should be easily understood by users and designers and facilitate problem solving and future systems development.
Auditability	Auditability should be built into the system from the beginning of systems development.
Security	Only authorized users should be granted access or allowed to change system data.

systems, or modules, that are analyzed, developed, and installed independently. When changes are made to the system, only the affected module needs to be changed. Great care should be taken to ensure that the modules are properly integrated into a workable system.

A system's success often depends on the project team's ability to cope with the constraints under which the organization is operating. Common constraints include governmental agency requirements, management policies and guidelines, lack of sufficiently qualified staff, the capabilities and attitudes of system users, available technology, and limited financial resources. To maximize system performance, the effects of these constraints on system design must be minimized.

Strategies for Determining Requirements. One or more of the following four strategies are used to determine AIS requirements:

1. *Ask users what they need.* Though this is the simplest and fastest strategy, many people do not realize or understand their true needs. Although they may know how to do their job, they may not be able to break it down into the individual information elements they use. It is sometimes better to ask users questions pertaining to what decisions they make and what processes they are involved in and then help them design a system to address their answers.

2. *Analyze existing systems.* Both internal and external systems should be analyzed. A partial solution may already exist, thus eliminating the problem of "reinventing the wheel."

3. *Examine existing system utilization.* This strategy differs from the previous one by taking into account that users may not use the existing AIS as intended. Certain modules may not be used as intended, may be augmented by manual tasks, or may be avoided altogether. This approach helps determine whether a system can be modified or must indeed be replaced.

4. *Prototyping.* When it is difficult to identify a usable set of requirements, a developer can quickly rough out a system for users to critique. Once users see something on the screen, they can begin to identify what they like and dislike and request changes. This iterative process of looking at what is developed and then improving it continues until users agree on their needs. Prototyping is discussed in Chapter 12.

Documentation and Approval of User Requirements. Detailed requirements (see Table 10.6) for the new AIS that explain exactly what the system must produce should be created. The "how to produce" is determined during the design phase of the SDLC. The requirements list should be supported by sample record layouts and outputs as well as graphs to make it easier for readers to conceptualize the system. A nontechnical summary is often prepared for management that captures important user requirements and development efforts to date.

Once user requirements have been determined and documented, the project team meets with the users, explains the requirements, and obtains their agreement and approval. When an agreement is reached, user management

Table 10.6 **Possible Contents of Systems Requirements**

Processes	A description of all processes in the new system, including what is to be done and by whom
Data elements	A description of the data elements needed, including their name, size, format, source, and significance
Data structure	A preliminary data structure, showing how the data elements will be organized into logical records
Outputs	A copy of system outputs and a description of their purpose, frequency, and distribution
Inputs	A copy of system inputs and a description of their contents, source, and who is responsible for them
Documentation	A description of how the new system and each subsystem will operate
Constraints	A description of constraints such as deadlines, schedules, security requirements, staffing limitations, and statutory or regulatory requirements
Controls	Controls to ensure the accuracy and reliability of inputs, outputs, and processing
Reorganizations	Organizational reorganization needed to meet the users' information needs, such as increasing staff levels, adding new job functions, restructuring, or terminating existing positions or jobs

should sign the appropriate system requirements documents to indicate approval.

Systems Analysis Report

Systems analysis is concluded by preparing a **systems analysis report,** which summarizes and documents the analysis activities and serves as a repository of data from which systems designers can draw. The Shoppers Mart report, shown in Table 10.7, on page 344, shows the information typically contained in the report.

A go/no go decision is generally made three times during systems analysis: (1) during the initial investigation, to determine whether to conduct a systems survey; (2) at the end of the feasibility study, to determine whether to proceed to the information requirements phase; and (3) at the completion of the analysis phase, to decide whether to proceed to the design phase.

After systems analysis is completed, projects developed using the SDLC approach move to the conceptual design phase and then to physical design, implementation and conversion, and operation and maintenance. These topics are discussed in the next chapter. More and more frequently, however, companies are desiring more than an improved system for their existing business processes. They want to reengineer their current business processes completely and find much more effective ways to operate. Once these business processes are reengineered, an AIS is designed and implemented to support the new approach. This procedure is called business process engineering and is discussed in the next section of the chapter.

REENGINEERING BUSINESS PROCESSES

Despite the trillion plus dollars spent on information technology in the past decade, productivity has not increased significantly. One reason is that many "modern" business processes are in fact relics from precomputer days when work was based on economies of scale and specialization of labor. Work was organized as a sequence of narrowly defined tasks, flowing between specialists devoid of thinking or reasoning responsibilities. Workers simply had to carry out their assigned tasks as efficiently as possible. When computers came along, they were used to speed up their manual and paper flow processes and procedures.

In recent years the work environment has changed drastically. Current AIS systems are not designed to handle the flood of new information available today. Nor can they take advantage of the steady stream of new technological advancements that make it possible to do things much differently than previous generations. With powerful data bases and almost unlimited storage, we have access to more and better information than ever before. In summary, an approach is needed that, instead of "paving cow-paths," blazes new trails.

Many management gurus now advocate radical change, or what they refer to as **business process reengineering (BPR). Reengineering** is the thorough analysis and complete redesign of business processes and information systems to achieve dramatic performance improvements. It is a revolutionary process that challenges traditional organization structures, rules, assumptions, work flows, job descriptions, management procedures, controls, and organizational values and cultures associated with underperformance.

BPR reduces a company to its essential business processes and focuses on *why* they are done rather than on the details of *how* they are done. It then completely reshapes organizational work practices and information flows to take advantage of technological advancements. This is done to simplify the system, to make it more effective, and to improve a company's quality and service.

CSC Index, a consulting firm, measured the cost and time savings and the reduction in defects before and after helping 15 clients complete reengineering efforts. CSC found that fundamentally changing business processes produced an average improvement of 48% in cost, 80% in time, and 60% in defects. After Citibank reengineered a credit analysis system, employees spent 43% of their time (instead of 9%) recruiting new business instead of completing paperwork on closed deals. Profits increased by over 750% over a two-year period. By reengineering its customer service operations, Datacard Corporation increased its sales by sevenfold. A process that took a full day and five phone calls was replaced with one that took one hour.

The Principles of Reengineering

What are the secrets to reengineering? How can a company minimize the costs and maximize the benefits received? Michael Hammer, a leading proponent of reengineering, set forth seven principles that help organizations successfully reengineer business processes.[1]

---

[1]Much of this section is after Michael Hammer, "Reengineering Work: Don't Automate, Obliterate," *Harvard Business Review* (July–August 1990): 104–112.

Organize Around Outcomes, Not Tasks. In a reengineered system, the traditional approach of assigning different parts of a business process to many people is not appropriate. This approach, with its numerous handoffs, results in delays and errors. Instead, wherever possible, one person is given responsibility for the entire process. Each person's job is designed around an objective or an outcome, such as a finished component or a completed process, rather than one of many tasks necessary to produce the finished component or complete the process.

At Mutual Benefit Life (MBL), an insurance company, approving an insurance application previously included 30 steps performed by 19 people in five departments. Because paperwork had to be transferred among so many people, an approval took anywhere from 5 to 25 days. When MBL reengineered its business processes, it eliminated existing job descriptions and departmental boundaries. It created the position of case manager and gave each one the authority to perform all application approval tasks. Case managers are supported by a number of information systems, including an expert system, and can call on specialists for help with any particularly difficult application. Because one person is in charge of the entire process, there is no handing off of files. This has resulted in fewer errors, decreased costs, and a dramatically improved turnaround time. Case managers now handle more than twice the volume of new applications, allowing the company to eliminate 100 field positions. A new application can now be processed in as little as four hours, with an average turnaround of only two to five days.

Have Output Users Perform the Process. Owners and managers often organize their company into separate departments, each specializing in a separate task. Because each department passes its completed "product" off to someone else, departments are customers of one another. This strategy may work well for specialized projects, but it can hurt a company's performance when it comes to less significant tasks. For example, consider the problem when accounting wants to order nonstrategic or inexpensive goods such as office supplies. It must requisition the supplies from purchasing, which is responsible for selecting suppliers and ordering goods. This system is slow, cumbersome, and can actually cost the company more, in terms of time and money, than the supplies are worth.

One large manufacturer had this exact problem before reengineering its business processes. The manufacturer took advantage of information technology and set up a computerized data base of approved vendors (maintained by purchasing), developed an expert system for purchasing nonstrategic items, and linked all departments in a network. The new process enables users, with the help of the expert system and the data base, to order their own supplies. The purchasing process is now much faster, simpler, and less costly because the department that orders the supplies is the one that actually uses them.

Have Those Who Produce Information Process It. Most organizations process their acquisition/payment information the way Ford Motor used to. Previously, Ford's purchasing department prepared a multicopy purchase order, sending one copy to the vendor and another to accounts payable and keeping one itself. When goods were received, the receiving department prepared a multicopy receiving report and sent one copy to accounts payable and kept the other. The vendor prepared a multicopy invoice and sent one copy to accounts payable. Accounts payable processed all three documents and matched 14 different data items on the three documents before a payment could be processed. Accounts payable spent most of its time trying to reconcile all of the mismatches. Payments were delayed, vendors were unhappy, and the process was time-consuming and frustrating. It took more than 500 employees to process Ford's accounts payable.

In Ford's reengineered system, the people who produce the information also process it. Purchasing agents create and process their purchase orders by entering them into an on-line data base. Vendors ship goods but do not send an invoice. When the goods arrive, the receiving clerk enters three items of data into the system: part number, unit of measure, and supplier code. The computer compares the receiving information with the outstanding purchase order data. If they do not match, the goods are returned. If they do match, the goods are accepted and the computer prepares the vendor's check, which is sent by accounts payable. The reengineered system saves a significant amount of money, much of it achieved through a 75% reduction of accounts payable staff.

Centralize and Disperse Data. To achieve economies of scale and to eliminate bureaucracy and redundant resources, companies centralize operations. To be more responsive to their customers and to provide better service, they decentralize operations. With current technology, companies no longer have to choose between these two approaches. Corporatewide data bases can centralize data, and telecommunications technology can then disburse it to the necessary locations. In effect, companies can have the advantages of both approaches.

Hewlett-Packard (HP) had a decentralized purchasing system that successfully served the needs of its 50 manufacturing units. However, HP could not take advantage of its extensive buying power to negotiate quantity discounts. HP reengineered its system and introduced a corporatewide purchasing department that developed and maintained a shared data base of approved vendors. Each plant continued to meet its unique needs by making its own purchases from the approved vendors. The corporate office tracked the purchases of all 50 plants, negotiated quantity discounts and other vendor concessions, and resolved disputes with vendors. The result was a significantly lower cost of goods purchased, a 50% reduction in lead times, a 75% reduction in failure rates, and a 150% improvement in on-time deliveries.

Integrate Parallel Activities. Certain processes, such as product development, are performed in parallel and then integrated at the end. For example, Chrysler had departments that worked exclusively on designing engines, another on transmissions, another on frames, and so on. Unfortunately, the departments often did not communicate as well as they should. At the integration and testing phase they often found that the components did not fit together properly. As a result, they had to be redesigned at considerable expense.

Chrysler reengineered its product development process to place at least one person from each department area on a team. Each team was put in charge of a particular automobile. As a result, Chrysler was able to reduce its product development time significantly and reduce costly redesigns.

Empower Workers, Use Built-In Controls, and Flatten the Organizational Chart. Most organizations have a layer of employees who do the work and several layers who record, manage, audit, or control the efforts of the former group. The logic behind this organization is that the workers are not able either to make correct decisions, to monitor and control the process themselves, or both. In a reengineered system, the people who do the work are empowered with this type of decision-making responsibility. It results in a faster response time to problems and increases the quality of the task performed. Information technology, such as expert systems, can help workers make correct decisions and avoid mistakes. This same principle also states that controls should be built into the process itself. For example, the system could be programmed with preventive controls so that it would proceed only when all relevant data have been entered and edited by the system for validity, correctness, and reasonableness. Controls could also be placed in the system to detect and correct any controls that might make their way into the system.

When Mutual Benefit Life empowered its case managers with decision-making ability, it was able to eliminate several layers of managers. Those who were retained changed their focus from supervision and control to support and facilitation.

Capture Data Once, at Its Source. Historically, each functional area has designed and built its own AIS. As a result, information was entered into several different applications. For example, a vendor number was entered in the accounts payable system as well as the purchasing system. Each application had to collect the same piece of information (usually on different forms), enter it into their system, and store it. This is both inefficient and expensive. In addition, there were discrepancies between the individual systems as a result of data capture and data entry errors. EDI and source data automation devices such as bar coding now allow data in a reengineered system to be captured electronically at its source. The data can be entered once in an on-line data base and made available to all who need it. This approach reduces errors, eliminates data processing delays, and reduces clerical and other costs.

A few years ago management at Sun Microsystems decided to solve the problem of its information systems not being able to easily communicate with each other. In addition, certain data needed to be entered as many as ten times into incompatible systems. The system was reengineered and now data that is entered into any system worldwide is entered only once and made available to whomever needs it.

Underlying each of these seven principles is the efficient and effective use of the latest information systems technology. Future advances will allow even more powerful reengineering efforts. Radio and satellite-based communication technology, coupled with very powerful hand-held computers, will have a significant impact on the way companies do business. With image processing, a document can be used by multiple users simultaneously. "Active documents" that automatically know where to go will also have an impact. For example, suppose you are ordering a mail-order computer. After the sales clerk creates the "active order," it will automatically be sent to shipping, inventory control, sales and marketing, the credit card company, and your customer record. With an active document, the decision about where the information on the document is to go need only be made once. From then on, all orders will automatically be sent to the appropriate location.

Challenges Faced by Reengineering Efforts

Business process reengineering is a very difficult venture. Not only must a company be rethought and completely reorganized, but people must abandon the old ways of doing things and learn new jobs and new ways of operating. As a result, many reengineering efforts fail or do not accomplish all they set out to do. Companies that successfully complete the reengineering process must face and overcome the following obstacles:

- *Tradition.* The inefficient business processes that are being reengineered oftentimes are decades old. Traditional ways of doing things do not often die easily, especially practices associated with the culture of an organization. Successful reengineering requires changes in employee culture and beliefs.
- *Resistance.* Change, especially radical change, is always met with a great deal of resistance. Throughout the process, managers must continually reassure, persuade, and provide support to those affected so that the necessary changes will work.
- *Time requirements.* Reengineering is a lengthy process, almost always taking two or more years to complete.
- *Cost.* It is costly to thoroughly examine and question a company's business processes in order to find a faster and more efficient way of operating.
- *Lack of management support.* Reengineering is still in its infancy and, since few companies have completed full-blown reengineering projects, many top managers have not yet been converted to its benefits. Many are afraid of the "big hype, few results" syndrome. Without top management support, reengineering has little chance of succeeding. IS management does not have enough power and influence to push a reengineering project successfully.
- *Reengineering is risky.* Information systems management is aware that pushing a reengineering project can be a risky career move. If it is a success, they will be looked upon with great favor in the organization. If it does not, they may very well be looking for new jobs.
- *Skepticism.* Some in the IS community are skeptical about reengineering. Some view it as traditional systems development, but in a brand new wrapper with a fancy name. One of the biggest obstacles to reengineering is outlasting the "nonbelievers" and the cynics who say it cannot be done.
- *Retraining.* Many reengineering efforts dramatically change the way work is done. That means employees have to be retrained, which is time-consuming and expensive.

BEHAVIORAL ASPECTS OF CHANGE

Individuals involved in systems development are agents of change who are continually confronted by people's reaction and resistance to change. The **behavioral aspects of change** are crucial because the best system will fail without the support of the people it serves. Niccolo Machiavelli discussed resistance to change some four hundred years ago:[2]

> *It must be considered that there is nothing more difficult to carry out, nor more doubtful of success, not more dangerous to handle, than to initiate a new order of things. For the reformer has enemies in all those who could profit by the old order, and only lukewarm defenders in all those who could profit by the new order. This lukewarmness arises partly from fear of their adversaries, who have the laws in their favor, and partly from the incredulity of mankind, who do not truly believe in anything new until they have had an actual experience of it.*

Organizations must be sensitive to and consider the feelings and reactions of persons affected by change. They should also be aware of the type of behavioral problems that can result from change, as discussed in this section.

Why Behavioral Problems Occur

Individuals will usually view change as good or bad depending on how they are personally affected by it. For example, management views change positively if it increases profits or performance or reduces costs. An employee, on the other hand, will view the same change as bad if his or her job is terminated or adversely affected.

To minimize adverse behavioral reactions, one must first understand why resistance takes place. Some of the more important factors include the following:

- *Personal characteristics and background.* Generally speaking, the younger and more highly educated people are, the more likely they are to accept change. Likewise, the more comfortable people are with technology, the less likely they are to oppose changes in an AIS.
- *Manner in which change is introduced.* Resistance is often a reaction to the methods of instituting change rather than to change itself. For example, the rationale used to sell the system to top management may not be appropriate for lower-level employees. The elimination of menial tasks and the ability to advance and grow are often more important to users than are increasing profits and reducing costs.
- *Experience with prior changes.* Employees who had a bad experience with prior changes are more reluctant to cooperate when future changes occur.
- *Top-management support.* Employees who sense a lack of top-management support for change wonder why they themselves should endorse it.
- *Communication.* Employees are unlikely to support a change unless the reasons behind it are personally explained.
- *Biases and natural resistance to change.* People with emotional attachments to their duties or co-workers may not want to change if those elements are affected.

---

[2]Nicollo Machiavelli, *The Prince,* translated by Luigi Rice, revised by E.R.P. Vincent (New York: New American Library, 1952).

- *Disruptive nature of the change process.* Requests for information and interviews are distracting and place additional burdens on people. These disturbances can create negative feelings toward the change that prompted them to occur.
- *Fear.* Many people fear the unknown and the uncertainty accompanying change. They also fear loss of their jobs, loss of respect or status, failure, technology, and automation.

How People Resist AIS Changes

Behavioral problems may begin as soon as people find out that a system change is being made. Initial resistance is often subtle, manifested by tardiness, sub-par performance, or failure to provide developers with information. Major behavioral problems often occur after the new system has been implemented and the change has become a reality. Major resistance often takes one of three forms: aggression, projection, or avoidance.

Aggression. **Aggression** is behavior that is usually intended to destroy, cripple, or weaken the effectiveness of a system. It may take the form of increased error rates, disruptions, or deliberate sabotage. One organization introduced an on-line AIS, only to discover soon thereafter that the data input devices were inoperable; some had honey poured into them, others had been mysteriously run over by forklifts, and still others had paper clips inserted in them. Employees had also entered erroneous data into the system. More subtle forms of aggression can also undermine the system's intended use. In another organization disgruntled workers used the new system to gang up on an unpopular foreman. Instead of clocking in and out as they moved from one station to another, they punched in at the foreman's department for the entire day while they proceeded to work in different areas. This adversely affected the foreman's performance, as he was charged for hours that did not belong to his operation.

Projection. **Projection** involves blaming the new system for any and every unpleasant occurrence. For example, missing and incorrect data, which were present but undetected in a manual system, are blamed on the fact that there is a new automated system until the actual cause is determined. In essence, the system becomes the scapegoat for all real and imagined problems and errors. If these criticisms are not controlled or answered, the integrity of the system can be damaged or destroyed.

Avoidance. Dealing with problems through **avoidance** is a common human trait. For example, a person who cannot decide between two job offers may delay a decision until one company withdraws its offer and the decision is made for him. Likewise, one way for employees to avoid a new AIS is to hope that the problem (the system) will either go away or resolve itself.

Preventing Behavioral Problems

The human element is often thought to be the most significant problem a company encounters in designing, developing, and implementing a system. Although there is no one best way to overcome behavioral problems, people's reactions can be improved by observing the following guidelines:

- *Meet the needs of the users.* It is essential that the form, content, and volume of system output be designed to satisfy user needs.
- *Keep communication lines open.* Managers and users should be fully informed of system changes as soon as possible. They should be told what changes are being made and why, and they should be shown how the new system will benefit them. The objective is to help employees identify with the company's efforts to improve the system. This helps ensure that employees feel they are indeed key players in the company's future goals and plans. Open communication also helps prevent the spread of damaging and inaccurate rumors and misunderstandings.
- *Maintain a "safe" atmosphere.* It is vital that everyone affected by systems development have an attitude of trust and cooperation. If employees become hostile, it will be very difficult to change their attitude or to implement the system successfully.
- *Obtain management support.* Where possible, a powerful champion, who can provide resources for the system and motivate others to assist and cooperate with systems development, should be utilized.
- *Allay fears.* The organization should provide assurances (to the extent possible) that no major job losses or responsibility shifts will occur. These goals can be achieved through relocation, attrition, and early retirement. If employees are terminated, severance pay and outplacement services should be provided.
- *Solicit user participation.* Those who will use or be affected by the system should participate in its development by providing data, making suggestions, and helping make decisions. Participation is ego enhancing, challenging, and intrinsically satisfying. Users who participate in development are more knowledgeable, better trained, and more committed to using the system.
- *Provide honest feedback.* To avoid misunderstandings, users should be told which suggestions are being used and how, which suggestions are not being used and why, and which ones will be incorporated at a later date.
- *Make sure users understand the system.* Effective use or support cannot be obtained if users are confused about or do not understand the system. Generally, those who have a working knowledge of computers often underestimate user training needs.
- *Humanize the system.* System acceptance is unlikely if individuals believe the computer is controlling them or has usurped their positions.
- *Describe new challenges and opportunities.* System developers should emphasize important and challenging tasks that can be performed with the new system. It should also be emphasized that the system may provide greater job satisfaction and increased opportunities for advancement.
- *Reexamine performance evaluation.* Users' performance standards and criteria should be reevaluated to ensure that they are satisfactory in lieu of changes brought on by the new system.
- *Test the system's integrity.* The system should be properly tested prior to implementation to minimize initial bad impressions.
- *Avoid emotionalism.* When logic vies with emotion, it doesn't stand a chance. Emotional issues related to change should be sidestepped, allowed to cool, or handled in a nonconfrontational manner.

- *Present the system in the proper context.* Users are vitally interested in how system changes affect them personally. Relevant explanations should be presented that address their concerns, rather than the concerns of managers or developers.
- *Control the users' expectations.* A system is sold too well if users have unrealistic expectations of its capabilities and performance. Be realistic when describing the merits of the system.
- *Keep the system simple.* Avoid complex systems that cause radical changes. Make the change seem as simple as possible by conforming to existing organizational procedures.

Observing these guidelines is both time-consuming and expensive. As a result, there is a tendency to skip the more difficult steps in order to speed up systems development and installation. However, the problems caused by not following these guidelines are usually more expensive and time-consuming to fix than preventing behavioral problems in the first place.

SUMMARY AND CASE CONCLUSION

An extensive analysis of Shoppers Mart's current system and core business processes was conducted (see Table 10.7 for the table of contents of the systems analysis reports mentioned in the chapter). After the analysis Ann Christy, in consultation with the IS steering committee, decided to reengineer the AIS at Shoppers Mart. They decided to have the corporate office use satellite technology to gather daily sales data from each store. Analyzing the prior day's sales will help Shoppers Mart adapt quickly to customer needs. Providing sales data to suppliers will help avoid stockouts and overstocking.

Coordinating buying at the corporate office will help Shoppers Mart to minimize inventory levels and negotiate lower wholesale prices. Stores will send orders electronically the day they are prepared. Based on store orders, previous day sales figures, and warehouse inventory, Shoppers Mart will send purchase orders to suppliers via EDI. Suppliers will process orders and ship goods to regional warehouses or directly to the stores the day orders are received. Each store will have the flexibility to respond to local sales trends and conditions by placing local orders. Accounts payable will be centralized so the firm can make payments electronically.

Ann reviewed the system with the legal department and the AIS staff and was assured that it complied with all legal considerations and was technologically feasible. Top management and the IS steering committee will decide how to allocate time and resources for this massive project and will communicate all staff assignments to systems management and personnel. An economic feasibility study shows this project makes excellent use of funds. The new system will cost $5 million and will be depreciated over its expected six-year life. Shoppers Mart has a 34% tax rate and a 10% cost of capital. Payback is in the fourth year, NPV is over $3 million, and the IRR is 25%. Details of Ann's study are shown in Table 10.8.

Ann presented the system to top management and described its objectives. Challenges to her estimates were plugged into the spreadsheet model so that management could see the effect of the changed assumptions. Even the stiffest

Table 10.7 **Table of Contents for Reports Prepared During Systems Analysis at Shoppers Mart**

Shoppers Mart Proposal to Conduct Systems Analysis	Shoppers Mart Systems Survey Report	Shoppers Mart Systems Analysis Report
Table of Contents I. Executive Summary II. System Problems and Opportunities III. Goals and Objectives of Proposed System IV. Project Scope V. Anticipated Costs and Benefits VI. Participants in Development Project VII. Proposed Systems Development Tasks and Work Plan VIII. Recommendations	Table of Contents I. Executive Summary II. System Goals and Objectives III. System Problems and Opportunities IV. Current System Operations A. Policies, Procedures, and Practices Affecting System B. Systems Design and Operation (Intended and Actual) C. System Users and Their Responsibilities D. System Outputs, Inputs, and Data Storage E. System Controls F. System Strengths, Weaknesses, and Constraints G. Costs to Operate System V. User Requirements Identified During Survey	Table of Contents I. Executive Summary II. System Goals and Objectives III. System Problems and Opportunities IV. Project Scope V. Relationship of Project to Overall Strategic Information Systems Plan VI. Current System Operations VII. User Requirements VIII. Feasibility Analysis IX. System Constraints X. Recommendations for New System XI. Proposed Project Participants and Work Plan XII. Summary XIII. Approvals XIV. Appendix of Documents, Tables, Charts, Glossary of Terms

challenges to Ann's numbers showed a positive return. As a result of the meeting, top management was very supportive of the new system. They requested a number of changes and gave Ann approval to proceed.

Ann soon found the enthusiastic support of management to be crucial to the system's success. Several employees with vested interests in the current system felt it was adequate and were critical of her ideas. Some employees remembered the problems Shoppers Mart had when the current system was implemented a few years ago. Ann concluded that those who were resistant to the new system were afraid of the change and its effect on them personally. To counter the negative behavioral reactions, Ann took great pains to explain to all employees how the new system would benefit them individually and the company as a whole. With management's approval, she assured employees they

Table 10.8 **Economic Feasibility Study for Shoppers Mart's New Information System**

	Initial Outlay	Year 1	Year 2	Year 3	Year 4	Year 5	Year 6
Initial outlay costs							
Hardware	$2,000,000						
Software	400,000						
Training	200,000						
Site preparation	200,000						
Initial systems design	2,000,000						
Conversion	200,000						
Total initial outlays	$5,000,000						
Recurring costs							
Hardware expansion			$260,000	$300,000	$340,000	$380,000	$400,000
Software			150,000	200,000	225,000	250,000	250,000
Systems maintenance		$ 60,000	120,000	130,000	140,000	150,000	160,000
Personnel costs		500,000	800,000	900,000	1,000,000	1,100,000	1,300,000
Communication charges		100,000	160,000	180,000	200,000	220,000	250,000
Overhead		300,000	420,000	490,000	560,000	600,000	640,000
Total costs		$960,000	$1,910,000	$2,200,000	$2,465,000	$2,700,000	$3,000,000
Savings							
Clerical cost savings		$600,000	$1,200,000	$1,400,000	$1,600,000	$1,800,000	$2,000,000
Working capital savings		900,000	1,200,000	1,500,000	1,500,000	1,500,000	1,500,000
Profits from sales increases			500,000	900,000	1,200,000	1,500,000	1,800,000
Warehousing efficiencies			400,000	800,000	1,200,000	1,600,000	2,000,000
Total savings		$1,500,000	$3,300,000	$4,600,000	$5,500,000	$6,400,000	$7,300,000
Net savings (costs)		540,000	1,390,000	2,400,000	3,035,000	3,700,000	4,300,000
Less income taxes (34% rate)		(183,600)	(472,600)	(816,000)	(1,031,900)	(1,258,000)	(1,462,000)
Cash savings (net of tax)		$356,400	$917,400	$1,584,000	$2,003,100	$2,442,000	$2,838,000
Savings on taxes due to depreciation deduction		340,000	544,000	326,400	195,500	195,500	98,600
Net savings	($5,000,000)	696,400	1,461,400	1,910,400	2,198,600	2,637,500	2,936,600

Payback occurs in the fourth year when the savings net of taxes of $6,266,800 exceed the costs of $5,000,000

Net present value (interest rate of 10%):

(5,000,000)		(5,000,000)
696,400	× 0.9091 =	633,097
1,461,400	× 0.8265 =	1,207,847
1,910,400	× 0.7513 =	1,435,284
2,198,600	× 0.6830 =	1,501,644
2,637,500	× 0.6209 =	1,637,624
2,936,600	× 0.5645 =	1,657,711
Net present value		3,073,206

Internal rate of return is 25.04%

Depreciation on initial investment of $5,000,000

Tax rate 34%

Year	MACRS rate	Depreciation	Tax savings
1	20.00%	1,000,000	340,000
2	32.00%	1,600,000	544,000
3	19.20%	960,000	326,400
4	11.50%	575,000	195,500
5	11.50%	575,000	195,500
6	5.80%	290,000	98,600

would not lose their jobs and that all affected employees would be retrained. She involved the two most vocal opponents to the system change in planning activities, and soon they became two of its biggest advocates.

Ann set up a steering committee and was granted approval to put the managers of all affected departments on the committee. A master plan for developing the system was formulated, and the system was broken down into manageable projects. The projects were prioritized and project teams were formed to begin work on the highest-priority projects. Documentation standards were developed and approved.

KEY TERMS

systems development life cycle (SDLC)
systems analysis
conceptual systems design
physical design
implementation and conversion
operations and maintenance
steering committee
systems analysts
computer programmers
project development plan
master plan
request for systems development
initial investigation
proposal to conduct systems analysis
systems survey
physical models
logical models
systems survey report
feasibility study
technical feasibility
operational feasibility
legal feasibility
scheduling feasibility
economic feasibility
capital budgeting model
payback period
net present value (NPV)
internal rate of return (IRR)
systems approach
systems analysis report
business process reengineering (BPR)
reengineering
behavioral aspects of change
aggression
projection
avoidance

CHAPTER QUIZ

1. Which of the following is *not* one of the reasons why companies make changes to their AIS?
   a. To gain a competitive advantage
   b. To increase productivity
   c. To keep up with company growth
   d. To downsize
   e. All of the above are reasons why companies change an AIS

2. Which of the following is *not* one of the seven principles of reengineering?
   a. Organize around tasks, not outcomes.
   b. Have output users perform the process.
   c. Have those who produce information process it.
   d. Integrate parallel activities.
   e. Capture data once, at its source.

3. The purchasing department is designing a new AIS. The person or group best able to determine departmental information requirements is
   a. the steering committee.
   b. the controller.
   c. top management.
   d. the purchasing department.

4. Which of the following is the correct order of the steps in systems analysis?
   a. Initial investigation, determination of information needs and system requirements, feasibility study, system survey
   b. Determination of information needs and system requirements, system survey, feasibility study, initial investigation
   c. System survey, initial investigation, determination of information needs and system requirements, feasibility study
   d. Initial investigation, system survey, feasibility study, determination of information needs and system requirements

5. The long-range planning document that specifies what the system will consist of, how it will be

developed, who will develop it, how needed resources will be acquired, and its overall vision is referred to as the
a. steering committee agenda.
b. master plan.
c. systems development life cycle.
d. project development plan.

6. Resistance is often a reaction to the methods of instituting change rather than to change itself.
a. True
b. False

7. Increased error rates, disruptions, and sabotage are examples of
a. aggression.
b. avoidance.
c. projection.
d. payback period.

8. The most significant problem a company encounters in designing, developing, and implementing a system is
a. the human element.
b. technology.
c. legal challenges.
d. planning for the new system.

9. Determining whether the organization has access to people who can design, implement, and operate the proposed system is referred to as
a. technical feasibility.
b. operational feasibility.
c. legal feasibility.
d. scheduling feasibility.
e. economic feasibility.

10. Which of the following is *not* one of the tangible or intangible benefits a company might obtain from a new system?
a. Cost savings
b. Improved customer service and productivity
c. Improved decision making
d. Improved data processing
e. All are benefits of a new system

DISCUSSION QUESTIONS

10.1 The approach to long-range AIS planning described in this chapter is important for large organizations with extensive investments in computer facilities. Should small organizations with far fewer IS employees attempt to implement planning programs? Why or why not? Be prepared to defend your position to the class.

10.2 Assume you are a consultant advising a firm on the design and implementation of a new system. Management has decided to let several employees go after the system is implemented. Some have many years of company service. How would you advise management to communicate this decision to the affected employees? to the entire staff?

10.3 While reviewing a list of benefits from a computer vendor's proposal, you note an item that reads "improvements in management decision making—$50,000 per year." How would you interpret this item? What influence should it have on the economic feasibility and the computer acquisition decision?

10.4 This chapter suggests that an organization should make special efforts to ease fears among its employees about potential job or seniority loss. One advantage of mechanizing a system, however, is a reduction of clerical costs, which often results in job losses. Are these two concepts inconsistent? What policies should be consistent with both concepts?

10.5 The president of Monteer Signature Homes is perplexed by requests for computers from three different areas of the firm. The EDP manager wants $4.5 million to upgrade the mainframe computer. The vice president of engineering wants $450,000 to replace a minicomputer. The vice president of finance wants $200,000 to purchase microcomputers. Rapid growth is putting a strain on computer resources, keeping profits down. Payroll, accounting, inventory, and engineering functions are computerized; other tasks are manual. The firm is organized by business functions, with vice presidents for manufacturing, marketing, engineering, finance, and human resources. The president wonders whether a steering committee is needed. Discuss the objectives, responsibilities, and composition of an information systems steering committee. Justify your recommendations concerning its membership and the selection of a chairperson. (CIA Examination, adapted)

10.6 Clint Grace is the owner of a chain of regional department stores and has been in the business for over 30 years. He has definite ideas about how department stores should be run. He is financially conservative and is reluctant to make expenditures that do not have a clear financial payoff.

In recent years the stores' profitability has declined sharply, and customer dissatisfaction is at an all-time high. Store managers never know exactly how much inventory is on hand and when purchases are needed until a shelf is empty. Grace asks you to study the reason for the profitability decline and to recommend a solution. During your research you find that the current AIS is inefficient and unreliable and that the company's processes and procedures are old and out of date.

You believe that the solution is to reengineer the business processes at the department stores and in the central office. What are some of the challenges you might face in reengineering Grace's stores? Knowing what you do about Grace's personality, how will you present your recommendation?

10.7 Describe some examples of systems analysis decisions that involve a trade-off between each of the following pairs of objectives:

a. Economy and usefulness
b. Economy and reliability
c. Economy and customer service
d. Simplicity and usefulness
e. Simplicity and reliability
f. Economy and capacity
g. Economy and flexibility

10.8 For years Jerry Jingle's dairy production facilities led the state in total sales volume. However, recent declines left Jerry wondering what his company was doing wrong. When he asked several customers to rate his products, they seemed satisfied but did note several areas of concern. First on the list was the dairy company's record of late deliveries and incomplete orders. Further discussion with some of the company's production employees (not the cows) revealed several problems, including bottlenecks in milk pasteurization and homogenization due to a lack of coordination in job scheduling; mixups in customers orders; and improperly labeled products. How would you suggest Jerry begin addressing the company's problems? What types of data gathering techniques would be helpful at this early stage?

10.9 The following problem situations could arise in any manufacturing firm. What questions should you ask to understand the problem?

- Customer complaints about product quality have increased.
- Accounting sees an increase in the number and dollar value of bad debt write-offs.
- Operating margins have risen the past four years due to higher-than-expected production costs from idle time, overtime, and reworking of products.

10.10 For each case, discuss which data gathering method(s) are most appropriate and why.

a. Surveying the adequacy of internal controls in the purchase requisition procedure
b. Identifying the controller's information needs
c. Determining how cash disbursement procedures are actually performed
d. Surveying the opinions of employees concerning the move to a total quality management program
e. Investigating an increase in uncollectible accounts

PROBLEMS

10.1 Yuping Chai has seen the future, and so far she wants no part of it. The offices at Sierra Manufacturing Company, where Chai is vice president, have just been automated. Sitting at her desk in Sacramento, Chai can push buttons on the keyboard of a computer terminal and staff memos will appear on the screen. She can respond with her own memos, which will instantly be sent to colleagues, either for immediate viewing or for storage and later retrieval. By pressing a few other buttons, she can view company financial data stored in the corporate computer. Chai can do all that and more, but instead she has unplugged the terminal. "I think most managers, including me, are talkers," she states. "I would much rather talk than push buttons." Chai's resistance exemplifies the reaction of many professionals and executives who are being forced to make major psychological and behavioral adjustments as they begin to move into a paperless world.

REQUIRED

a. What do you believe is the real cause of Chai's resistance to the computer system?
b. As a colleague of Chai, how could you help her realize the benefits of computerization and overcome her computer phobia?

10.2 Mary Smith is the bookkeeper for Dave's Distributing Company, a distributor of soft drinks and juices. Because the company is rather small, Mary performed all the daily accounting tasks by herself. Dave, the president and owner of the company, supervises the warehouse/delivery and front office staff, but he also spends much of his time jogging and skiing.

For several years profits were good and sales grew faster than industry averages. Although the accounting system was working well, Dave was being pressured by bottlers to computerize. With a little guidance from a CPA friend and with no mention to Mary, Dave bought a new microcomputer and some accounting software. Only one day was required to set up the hardware, install the software, and convert the files. The morning the vendor installed the computer, Mary's job performance changed dramatically. Although the software company provided two full days of training, she had trouble learning the new system. As a result, Dave decided she should run both the manual and computer systems for a month to verify the accuracy of the new system.

Mary continually complained that she lacked the time and expertise to run both systems by herself. She also complained that she did not understand how to run the new computer system. To keep accounts up to date, Dave spent two to three hours a day running the new system himself. Dave found that much of the time spent running the system was devoted to identifying discrepancies between the computer and manual results. When the error was located, it was almost always in the manual system. This significantly increased Dave's confidence in the new system.

At the end of the month Dave was ready to scrap the manual system, but Mary said she was not ready. Dave went back to skiing and jogging, and Mary went on with the manual system. When the computer system fell behind, Dave again spent time catching it up. He also worked with Mary to make sure she understood how to operate the computer system.

Months later Dave was still keeping the computer system up to date and training Mary. He was at the height of frustration. "I know Mary knows *how* to run the system, but she doesn't seem to *want* to. I can do all the accounting work on the computer in two or three hours a day, but she can't even do it in her normal eight-hour workday. What should I do?"

REQUIRED

a. What actions and lack of actions may have contributed to the new system's failure?

b. In retrospect, how should Dave have handled the computerization of the accounting system?

c. At what point in the decision-making process should Mary have been informed? Should she have had some say in whether the computer was purchased? If so, what should have been the nature of her input? If Mary had not agreed with his decision to acquire the computer, what should Dave have done?

d. A hard decision needs to be made about what to do with Mary. Significant efforts have been made to train her, but they have been unsuccessful. What would you recommend at this point? Should she be fired? Threatened with the loss of her job? Moved somewhere else in the business? Given additional training?

10.3 Wright Company employs a computer-based data processing system to maintain company records. The present system was developed in stages over the past five years and has been fully operational for the past two. During the design process, department heads were asked to specify the types of information and reports they would need. Company management also asked for a number of reports. By the time the development stage began, there were several staff changes and the new department heads requested additional reports. AIS complied with these changes, and reports were discontinued only upon the request of a department head. Few reports were actually discontinued and a large number of reports are generated each period.

Company management is concerned about the quantity of information produced by the system. Internal auditing was asked to evaluate the effectiveness of the system and determined that more information was being generated than could be used effectively. They noted the following reactions to this information overload.

- Many department heads did not act on certain reports during periods of peak activity. They let them accumulate in the hope of catching up later.
- Some department heads had so many reports they did not act at all, or misused the information.
- Frequently, no action was taken until another manager needed a decision made. Department heads did not develop a priority system for acting on the information.
- Department heads often developed information from alternative, independent sources. This was easier than searching the reports for the needed data.

REQUIRED

a. Indicate whether each of the observed reactions is a functional or dysfunctional behavioral response. Explain your answer in each case.
b. Recommend procedures to eliminate any dysfunctional behavior and prevent its recurrence. (CMA Examination, adapted)

10.4 The controller of Tim's Travel (TT), a rapidly growing travel corporation, is deciding between upgrading the company's existing computer system or replacing it with a new MANTIS XIT-470. The present system is eight years old. Upgrading will cost $97,500 and will extend its useful life for another seven years. The book value is $19,500, although it would sell for $24,000. Upgrading will eliminate one employee at a salary of $19,400; the MANTIS will eliminate two employees. Annual operating costs are estimated at $15,950 per year. Upgrading is expected to increase profits 3.5% above last year's level of $553,000.

The BetaTech Company has quoted a price of $224,800 for the new MANTIS, which has a useful life of seven years. Annual operating costs are estimated to be $14,260. The average processing speed of the MANTIS is 12% faster than that of other systems in its price range, which would increase TT's profits by 4.5%.

Tim's present tax rate is 35% and money is worth 11%. Also assume that after seven years the salvage value, net of tax, would be $12,000 for the MANTIS and $7500 for the present system. For tax purposes, computers are depreciated over five years and the cost recovery percentages are as follows:

Year	Percent
1	20.00
2	32.00
3	19.20
4	11.52
5	11.52
6	5.76

REQUIRED

Use a spreadsheet package to perform an economic feasibility analysis to determine whether TT should rehabilitate the old system or purchase the MANTIS. As part of the analysis, compute the after-tax cash flows for years 1 through 7 and the Payback, NPV, and IRR of each alternative.

10.5 Rossco Incorporated is considering purchasing a new Z-660 computer to maximize office efficiency. The proposal estimates that initial systems design would cost $54,000; hardware, $74,000; and new software, $35,000. One-time initial training costs are expected to be $11,000, an additional $20,000 will be required to install the system, and $12,000 will be required to convert the files. A net reduction of four employees, whose average salaries are $40,000 per year, is expected if the new machine is acquired. A special study was just completed that found that computerization could decrease average yearly inventory by $150,000. Annual operating costs, other than employee wages, are expected to be $20,000 per year higher than those for the current manual system.

The expected life of the machine is four years, with an estimated salvage value of zero. The effective tax rate is 40%. For purposes of the feasibility study assume that all costs associated with the computer purchase will be depreciated equally over the four-year life using the straight line method. Assume that Rossco can invest money made available from the reduction in inventory at 11% annually. Also, assume that all cash flows, except for the initial investment and start-up costs, are at the end of the year. Assume 365 days in a year.

REQUIRED

Use a spreadsheet to perform a feasibility analysis to determine whether Rossco should purchase the computer. Compute the following as part of the analysis:
a. Initial investment
b. After-tax cash flows for years 1–4
c. Payback period
d. Net present value
e. Internal rate of return

10.6 XYZ Conglomerate Company has completed a feasibility study to upgrade its computer system. Management received the information in Table 10.9, which shows the benefits of the new system.

REQUIRED

As a board member, which of the benefits would you accept as relevant to the cost justification of the system? Defend your answer. (SMAC Examination, adapted)

10.7 The Alkin Chemical Company manufactures and sells chemicals for agricultural and industrial use. The company has grown significantly over the past five years. However, the company's accounting information system is the original one developed and installed by the former president's son while he was

Table 10.9 **Benefits to be Derived from the New System**

1. Production		
a. Marketing forecasting is presently in dollars per product line. Calculation of units by product line takes an estimated two man-days, a total of $80. This saving would be repeated each time the market forecast was updated, presumably monthly. The program to calculate the forecast in units would be more accurate than the present method of applying factors to dollar value.	$ 960	
b. More effective inventory control would permit an overall reduction in inventory. The ability to quickly establish total requirements would help to overcome parts stockout situations. For this calculation we estimate a 10% inventory reduction. The cost of capital at XYZ Conglomerate Company approximates 20%, and the benefit then approximates 20% of $100,000.	$20,000	
c. Evaluation of changes to plans will be possible in detail. This is not so under our manual system. Parts explosions are time-consuming and can only be done monthly. The impact here would be increased production flexibility and the reduction of sales losses due to finished goods stockouts. We estimate that this can be valued as the equivalent of hiring two clerks.	$15,000	$35,960
2. Engineering		
a. Use of the computer in filing and updating bills of material would save 40% of the industrial engineer's time.	$ 4,000	
b. The improved updating of files, which includes the bills of material and product structure files, which affect many areas, should save a minimum 25% of one clerk (if we took all areas, this would probably be closer to 50%).	$ 1,500	
c. Estimated clerical savings in labor calculations, rates, and bonus detail is two days per week, or 40% of one person.	$ 2,000	$ 7,500
3. Sales		
a. Improved reporting will enable sales staff and sales management to react more quickly to prevailing conditions. The implied benefit would be sales increases, especially during promotions, and a better sales/expense ratio. We are assuming an improvement in sales of only $1000 per person, for a total of $5000.		$ 5,000
4. Marketing		
a. Revised reports and an improved forecasting system will help in establishing sales trends and will help the production department in flexibility and inventory control.		
5. Accounting		
a. Standard costing of all bills of material, and in fact, the side effect of being able to cost new products quickly, can be expressed as the equivalent of saving 30%–40% of the plant accountant's time.	$ 3,000	
b. A revised incentive earnings and payroll system installed on the computer should reduce the payroll department clerical labor from three days to one day—possible benefit of 40% of one clerk.	$ 2,400	$ 5,400
Total		$53,860

in college. Much of the information generated by the system is irrelevant and more appropriate and timely information is needed.

The controller is concerned that actual monthly cost data for most production processes are compared with actual costs of the same processes for the previous year. However, the production supervisors contend that the system is adequate because it accounts for discrepancies. The current year's costs seldom vary from the previous year's costs when adjusted for inflation. Thus they feel that costs are under control.

The vice president of manufacturing has found that preparing even the simplest of cost analyses requires that she spend days compiling information generated by the current system. She feels that the system should be flexible enough for each manager to develop quickly his or her own recurring reports.

As a result of these concerns, the new president has appointed a committee to review the system. It will determine management's information needs for cost control and decision purposes and ensure that the behavioral needs of the company and its employees are met. The committee is chaired by the vice president of finance and administration.

Shortly after announcing the formation of this committee, the VP of finance overheard a cost accountant say, "I've been doing it this way since the company began and now this committee plans to make my job redundant." Several employees in the general accounting department also felt that their positions would be eliminated or changed significantly. Several days later, the vice president of finance and administration overheard one of the production managers state that he believed the system was in need of revision because the most meaningful information that he was receiving came from a junior salesperson.

REQUIRED

a. Identify the behavioral implications of utilizing an AIS that does not appear to meet management's needs.
b. Identify and explain the problems that employees have with the AIS.
c. Identify policies or practices the company could follow during systems implementation that would reduce costs without laying off employees. (SMAC Examination, adapted)

10.8 Recent years have brought an explosive growth in electronic communication. Computers, photocopiers, fax machines, word processors, electronic mail, teleconferencing, and sophisticated management information systems have changed and altered the way information is received, processed, and transmitted. With the decreasing costs of computer equipment and the increasing power of automation, the full impact of computerization has not yet been felt. Although the development of computer applications is directed at being user-friendly or user-oriented, the integration of computers into the organization has had both positive and negative effects on employees.

REQUIRED

a. Describe the benefits that companies and their employees can receive from electronic communication.
b. Discuss the organizational impact of introducing new electronic communication systems.
c. Explain (1) why an employee might resist the introduction of electronic communication systems and (2) the steps an organization can take to alleviate this resistance. (CMA Examination, adapted)

10.9 PWR Instruments is a manufacturer of precision nozzles for fire hoses. The company was started by the president, Ronald Paige, an engineer. This closely held corporation has been very successful and has experienced steady growth. Reporting to Paige are six vice presidents representing the company's major functions—marketing, production, research and development, information services, finance, and human resources. The information services department was just established during the past fiscal year, when PWR began developing a new computer-based information system. The new data base system employs a minicomputer as a central processing unit and, connected to it, several terminals and microcomputers in each of the six departments. The microcomputers are capable of both downloading data from and uploading data to the main computer. For example, financial analysts can access the data stored on the main computer through the microcomputers and use the latter as smart terminals on a stand-alone basis. PWR is still in the process of designing and developing new applications for its computer system.

Paige has recently received the management letter prepared by the company's external audit firm, and he has called a meeting with his vice presidents to review the recommendations. One major item that Paige wants to discuss is the recommendation that PWR form an IS steering committee.

REQUIRED

a. Explain why the external auditor would recommend that PWR establish an IS steering committee, and discuss its specific responsibilities. What advantages can an IS steering committee offer PWR?
b. Identify the PWR managers who would be most likely to serve on the committee. (CMA Examination, adapted)

10.10 Over four hundred years ago, Machiavelli wrote in *The Prince,* "It must be considered that there is nothing more difficult to carry out, nor more doubtful of success, nor more dangerous to handle, than to initiate a new order of things." This statement is as applicable today as it was in 1520.

Implementing organizational change is one of the most demanding assignments faced by any executive. It has been suggested that every change requires three steps: "unfreezing" the current situation, implementing the change, and finally "refreezing" the effected change. This view, however, lacks the specific details needed by an operating manager who must initiate the change.

REQUIRED

a. Identify and describe the specific steps a manager must take to implement an organizational change.
b. Suppose an organization does make a change that affects employees directly or affects how they conduct their operations.

1. Explain why employees generally resist change.
2. Outline and describe the ways a manager can reduce the resistance to change. (CMA Examination, adapted)

10.11 Don Richardson, vice president of marketing for the JEM Corporation, has just emerged from another strategic planning session aimed at developing a new line of business. The company's management team has been discussing these plans for several months, since major organizational changes will be required to implement the strategic plan. Rumors about the plans have been circulating the office for months, and Richardson has already been confronted by several employees who are anxious about the expected changes. His only response has been to tell them that an official announcement of this new business plan is expected shortly.

When he returns to his office, Richardson is met by an ad hoc committee composed of his department managers. The sales manager, Susan Williams, has been the most vocal of the group and, as expected, is acting as spokesperson. "Mr. Richardson, it is imperative that we speak to you right away. The employees are becoming very apprehensive about the proposed changes, and lately their job performance has slacked off."

"That's right," adds George Sussman, accounting manager. "My subordinates are asking me all sorts of questions concerning this new line of business, and I don't have any answers for them. They're not buying the 'official announcement' line any longer. I suspect that some of them are already looking for jobs in the event that department 'changes' phase out their positions."

REQUIRED

a. Describe the general steps in the decision-making process that a company should follow before choosing to implement a major organizational change.
b. Explain why employees generally resist organizational change.
c. Discuss ways JEM Corporation can alleviate employee resistance to change. (CMA Examination, adapted)

10.12 Remnants, Inc., is a large company that manufactures and markets designer clothing throughout the United States. From its St. Louis headquarters, Remnants has developed a regional system for marketing and servicing its products. Each region functions as a profit center because of the authority given to regional managers within their territories.

Each regional organization consists of an accounting and a budget department, a human resources and training department, and several area offices to market and service the products. Each area office consists of sales, service, and administrative departments, whose managers ultimately report to one area manager.

The New York area office departed from the standard organizational structure by establishing a branch office to market and service the firm's products in the Boston area. The local office is headed by a branch manager who reports directly to the area manager.

In recent years the Boston branch manager has encouraged the area manager to consider a new information system to handle the local branch's growing information needs. The New York area manager and the eastern regional manager have concluded that they should establish a project team with employees from the regional office, the area office, and the branch office to (1) assess the information needs at the Boston branch office and (2) develop system recommendations, if necessary. The following employees have been appointed to the project team, with Keith Nash acting as chairperson:

Eastern Region Office

Kurt Johnson, Budget Supervisor
Sally Brown, Training Director

New York Office

Keith Nash, Administrative Director

Boston Branch

Heidi Meyer, Branch Manager and Sales Manager
Bobby Roos, Assistant Branch Manager and Service Manager
Matthew Knight, Salesperson
Tara Jolly, Serviceperson

REQUIRED

a. A project team, similar to the one organized at Remnants, Inc., is organized to contribute their skills to accomplish a given objective. Characteristics of group members can influence the functioning and effectiveness of a project team. Identify some of these characteristics.
b. Due to the team's composition, what sources of conflict can you see arising among its members? Do you think the group will succeed in its objective to develop an information system for the Boston branch office? Why or why not?
c. What contribution would a person who holds a position as budget supervisor make in a project team such as this one?

10.13 Managers face a continual crisis in the systems development process: IS departments develop systems that businesses can't use. At the heart of the problem is a proverbial "great divide" that separates the world of business from the world of information systems. Few departments seem able or ready to cross this gap.

A major reason for the resulting information systems development crisis is that many large systems currently handling corporate information needs are seriously out of date. As a result, companies are looking for ways to improve existing systems or to build new ones.

Another reason for the crisis is the widespread use of PC-based systems that have spawned a high level of user expectation that is not being met by IS departments. As computer education increases, users are seeking more powerful applications that are not available on many older systems.

The costs of the "great divide" can be devastating for unprepared companies. An East Coast chemical company spent more than $1 million on a budgeting and control system that was never used. The systems department created an administrative budgeting system; the company's expertise was technical excellence, not budgets. As a result, the new system completely missed the mark when it came to meeting business needs.

Another example of poor systems development comes from a midwestern bank. It used an expensive computer-aided software engineering (CASE) tool to develop a system that users ignored because there had been no design planning. According to Michael Miller, a senior analyst for Franklin Savings Association, "They built the system right; but, unfortunately, they didn't build the right system."

So what is the solution? The first step in effective systems design is a thorough business analysis, not a systems analysis. A business analysis includes a thorough review of how a business operates and how the functions of the business relate. Only with this understanding can systems professionals and business managers communicate effectively when developing an integrated system.

In addition, businesses are seeking managers that have a systems background, because they provide a liaison between the systems department and the finance and accounting departments, helping business managers to clearly communicate their needs.

What's still missing is more involvement between systems staff and end users. Systems designers must take more time to interact with end users. In addition, business managers must provide their employees with the training time required to make the system work right.

REQUIRED

a. What is the "great divide" in the systems development process? What are the reasons for the gap?
b. What are the suggested solutions to the information crisis? How will the systems approach to development help?
c. Discuss the role that a systems designer, a business manager, and an end user can take to narrow the "great divide."
d. Who plays the most vital role in the effective development of the system?

10.14 The following list outlines the activities a company may perform in the process of reengineering its business.

Reengineering Activities

a. One person processes an employment application from beginning to end.
b. The department manager using the yearly budget is also the one who prepared it.
c. The purchasing manager has the authority to handle every aspect of purchase making.
d. Each plant issues its own purchase orders, and a new corporate department coordinates purchasing across all the plants.
e. All customer service representatives share a corporatewide data base that contains customer sales data.
f. A salesclerk enters a customer's order into a computer terminal. The order is then automatically sent over the LAN to shipping, inventory control, and the credit manager. In addition, the master file is updated immediately.

Match each activity on the list with one of the following seven principles of reengineering.

Seven Principles of Reengineering

1. Organize the business and information system around outcomes, not individual tasks.
2. Individuals who need to use the output from a process should be the ones performing it.
3. Individuals who produce information should process it as well.
4. Use information technology to achieve the benefits of both centralization and decentralization of data.
5. Integrate parallel processes instead of performing them separately and trying to integrate them at the end of the process.
6. Flatten the organizational chart by giving workers the power to make decisions and utilizing built-in controls.
7. Capture data only once, at its source, using source data automation.

10.15 The management of Quickfix would like to decrease costs and increase customer service by reengineering its computer repair procedures. Currently, when a defective or broken computer needs servicing, the customer calls one of five regional customer service centers. A customer service representative manually logs in the relevant customer information and then searches through a list to find the closest qualified technician. That technician is then contacted by phone to see whether the repair fits into his or her schedule. If not, the representative finds the next closest technician. When a technician who can perform the service is located, the customer and repair information is provided over the phone. The technician then calls the customer and makes arrangements to pick up the broken computer and replace it with a loaner. Making these arrangements takes one to two days and sometimes more if technicians are not available or do not promptly return calls.

The broken computer is sent to a repair depot. Typically, the entire repair process takes another four to seven days. Overall, it can take up to three weeks for an item to be repaired. When a customer calls to see whether their computer is ready, the customer service representative must then call the technician, find out the status of the item, and call the customer back. Throughout the entire repair process, usually five phone calls take place between the customer, the customer service representative, and the technician.

There are three main problems with this process: (1) it is time consuming; (2) it is an inconvenience for customers to have their computer removed, a new one installed, and then the old one reinstalled; and (3) customer service representatives do not have immediate access to information about items currently being repaired.

REQUIRED

a. Identify the most basic activities that occur when an item is repaired and around which the reengineered process should be developed.
b. Describe how the current repair process can be reengineered to achieve the goal of more timely repair and increased customer service.
c. What will be the specific benefits of reengineering the repair process?

10.16 Joanne Grey, a senior consultant, and David Young, a junior consultant, were assigned by their firm to conduct a systems analysis for a client. The objective of the study was to consider the feasibility of integrating and automating certain clerical functions. Grey had previously worked on jobs for this client, but Young had been hired only recently.

On the morning of their first day on the job, Grey directed Young to interview a departmental supervisor and learn as much as he could about the operations of the department. Young went to the supervisor's office, introduced himself, and made the following statement: "Your company has hired my firm to study the way your department works and to make recommendations as to how its efficiency could be improved and its cost lowered. I would like to interview you to determine what goes on in your department."

Young questioned the supervisor for about thirty minutes but found him to be uncooperative. He then gave Grey an oral report on how the interview had gone and what he had learned about the department.

REQUIRED

Describe several flaws in the approach taken to obtain information about the operation of the department under study. How should this task have been performed?

10.17 Business organizations are required to modify or replace a portion or all of their financial information system in order to keep pace with their growth and take advantage of improved information technology. The process involved in modifying or replacing an AIS requires a substantial commitment of time and resources. When an organization undertakes a change in its AIS, a systems analysis takes place.

REQUIRED

a. Explain the purpose and reasons for surveying an organization's existing system during a systems study.
b. Identify and explain the general activities and techniques that are commonly used during the systems analysis.
c. Systems analysis is often carried out by a project team composed of a systems analyst, a management accountant, and other persons in the company who would be knowledgeable and helpful in the systems study. What would be the role of the management accountant in systems analysis? (CMA Examination)

CASE 10.1: ANYCOMPANY, INC.—AN ONGOING COMPREHENSIVE CASE

Identify a local company (you may use the same company that you identified to complete Case 1.1) and perform the following steps:

1. Schedule a visit with a member of the AIS staff. With help, identify the most significant revision in the company's AIS (for some, this may mean the initial design and implementation). Discuss the following issues.
   a. What groups were organized to oversee systems design/revision and implementation? How was the implementation strategy developed?
   b. What problems did the company run into when it was developing/revising its system? How did the company handle the problems?
   c. Which staff members were affected by the change in the AIS? In general terms, how did employees react to the changes? What did the project development team do to minimize potential negative effects of the system change?
   d. If the company was starting the project over again, what would it do differently? Why?
2. Review the documentation that covers system design/revision and implementation. Take a few moments to review any project development plans and the master plan, if available.
3. If appropriate, ask to review the feasibility analysis surrounding the implementation of the AIS.
4. From your interview and your observations, write a brief report summarizing your findings. Consider the following issues:
   a. How well did the company organize the design/revision and implementation of the AIS?
   b. What suggestions do you have for improving the company's development and implementation procedures?

CASE 10.2: AUDIO VISUAL CORPORATION

Audio Visual Corporation (AVC) manufactures and sells visual display equipment. The company is headquartered outside of Boston. The majority of sales are made through seven geographical sales offices located in Los Angeles, Seattle, Minneapolis, Cleveland, Dallas, Boston, and Atlanta. Each sales office has a warehouse located nearby that carries an inventory of new equipment and replacement parts. The remainder of the sales are made through manufacturers' representatives.

AVC's manufacturing operations are conducted in a single plant, which is highly departmentalized. In addition to the assembly department, there are several departments responsible for various components used in the visual display equipment. The plant also has maintenance, engineering, scheduling, and cost accounting departments.

Early in 1993 management decided that its AIS needed upgrading. As a result, the company installed a mainframe at corporate headquarters and local area networks at each of the seven sales offices.

The integration of the new computer and the LANs into the AVC AIS was carried out by the IS staff. The IS manager and the four systems analysts who had the major responsibility for the integration were hired by the company in the spring of 1994. The department's other employees—programmers, machine operators, and keypunch operators—have been with the company for several years.

During its early years AVC had a centralized decision-making organization. Top management formulated all plans and directed all operations. As the company expanded, some of the decision making was decentralized, although the information processing was still highly centralized. Departments had to coordinate their plans with the corporate office, but they had more freedom in developing their sales programs. However, information problems developed, and the IS department was assigned the task of improving the company's information processing system once the new equipment was installed.

The IS analysts reviewed the current AIS prior to the acquisition of the new computer and identified its weaknesses. They then designed new applications to overcome these problems. During the 18 months since the acquisition of the new equipment the following applications have been redesigned or developed and are now operational: payroll, production scheduling, financial statement preparation, customer billing, raw material use in production, and finished goods inventory by warehouse. The operating departments of Audio Visual affected by the systems changes were rarely consulted or contacted until the system was operational and the new reports were distributed to the operating departments.

AVC's president is very pleased with the work of the IS department. During a recent conversation with an individual who was interested in AVC's new system, the president stated, "The IS people are doing a good job and I have full confidence in their work. I touch base with them frequently, and they have encountered no difficulties in doing their work. We paid a lot of money for the new equipment and the IS people certainly cost enough, but the combination of the new equipment and new IS staff should solve all of our problems."

Recently, two additional conversations regarding the computer and the AIS have taken place. One was between Jerry Adams, plant manager, and Bill Taylor, the IS manager; the other was between Adams and Terry Williams, the new human resources manager.

Taylor–Adams Conversation

Adams: Bill, you're trying to run my plant for me. I'm supposed to be the manager, yet you keep interfering. I wish you would mind your own business.

Taylor: You've got a job to do, but so does my department. As we analyzed the information needed for production scheduling and by top management, we saw where improvements could be made in the work flow. Now that the system is operational, you can't reroute work and change procedures, because that would destroy the value of the information we're processing. And while I'm on that subject, it's getting to the point where we can't trust the information we're getting from production. The documents we receive from production contain a lot of errors.

Adams: I'm responsible for the efficient operation of production. Quite frankly, I think I'm the best judge of production efficiency. The system you installed has reduced my work force and increased the work load of the remaining employees, but I don't see that this has improved anything. In fact, it might explain the high error rate in the documents.

Taylor: This new computer cost a lot of money, and I'm trying to ensure that the company gets its money's worth.

Adams–Williams Conversation

Adams: My best production assistant, the one I'm grooming to be a supervisor when the next opening occurs, came to me today and said he was thinking of quitting. When I asked him why, he said he didn't enjoy the work anymore. He's not the only one who is unhappy. The supervisors and department heads no longer have a voice in establishing production schedules. This new computer system has taken away the contribution we used to make to company planning and direction. We seem to be going way back to the days when top management made all the decisions. I have more production problems now than I used to. I think it boils down to a lack of interest on the part of my management team. I know the problem is within my area, but I thought you might be able to help me.

Williams: I have no recommendations for you now, but I've had similar complaints from purchasing and shipping. I think we should explore your concerns during tomorrow's plant management meeting.

Evaluate the preceding information, and answer the following questions:

1. Apparently the development of and transition to the new computer-based system has created problems among AVC's staff. Identify and briefly discuss the apparent causes of these problems.
2. How could the company have avoided these problems in the first place? How could they prevent them from happening in the future? (CMA Examination, adapted)

ANSWERS TO CHAPTER QUIZ

1. e	**3.** d	**5.** b	**7.** a	**9.** b
2. a	**4.** d	**6.** a	**8.** a	**10.** e

Chapter 11

Systems Design, Implementation, and Operation

LEARNING OBJECTIVES

After studying this chapter, you should be able to:

- Discuss the conceptual systems design processes and the activities undertaken in this phase.
- Discuss the physical systems design processes and the activities undertaken in this phase.
- Discuss the systems implementation and conversion process and the activities undertaken in this phase.
- Discuss the systems operation and maintenance process and the activities undertaken in this phase.

Integrative Case: Shoppers Mart

Ann Christy, the controller at Shoppers Mart, presented the results of her systems analysis to top management and received permission to develop a new AIS (Chapter 10 conclusion). The following day she sat in her office planning the rest of the project. Ann is concerned because many development projects bog down during the design and implementation phases. She certainly does not want to have a runaway project on her hands—one that she cannot control. She feels that her staff has adequately determined the requirements for the new system and wants to make sure that the rest of the development process is completed correctly. She decides to schedule another meeting with the head of systems development to discuss the following questions:

1. She has to determine what type of system will best meet Shoppers Mart's needs and to make a proposal to management. Should her team develop what they consider to be the best approach to meeting Shoppers Mart's needs, or should they develop several?
2. What can be done to ensure that system output will meet user needs? When and how should input, such as accounting transactions, be captured and who should capture it? Where should AIS data be stored and how should it be organized and accessed?
3. Is software available that can automate or make the system development process more effective?
4. How should Shoppers Mart convert from its current to its new AIS? How much time and effort will be needed to maintain the new AIS? How should Ann's accounting staff be involved?

INTRODUCTION

Developing quality, error-free software is a very difficult and time-consuming task. However, most companies that want to implement a new system want their new system immediately. As developers feel the pressure to perform system miracles, they begin skipping the basics of systems analysis and design and begin writing code. Omitting systems analysis steps only leads to disaster, as they develop nice, well-structured systems that do not meet user needs and have nothing to do with the business problems they were trying to solve. An American Management Systems study revealed that 75% of all large systems either are not used, are not used as intended, or generate meaningless reports.

In a recent survey Peat Marwick found that 35% of all major IS projects were classified as "runaways"—hopelessly incomplete and over budget. Although not the only cause of runaways, skipping or skimping on systems analysis and design steps is a major factor in their occurrence. Runaways can consume a great deal of time and money and in the end produce no usable results, as illustrated by the following examples:

- Pacific Gas & Electric (PG&E) recently pulled the plug on a client/server information system for all of its residential and commercial customers. The system, five years in development, was labeled a financial disaster with no end product by people in and out of the utility. In an effort to fix the problem PG&E used several consulting firms, including 3 of the Big 6 CPA firms.
- California's Department of Motor Vehicles decided to overhaul its system, which was originally developed in 1965. The system was so difficult to maintain that it took the equivalent of 18 programmers working for an entire year to add a social security number file to the drivers license and vehicle registration file. After seven years, $44 million, and not a single usable application, the state canceled the project.

Many of these problems can be attributed to ineffective or incomplete systems analysis and design efforts. Effective systems analysis and design can ensure that developers correctly define the business problem and design the appropriate solution. As discussed in Chapter 10, systems analysis is a crucial phase in the systems development life cycle (SDLC). It begins with problem recognition, feasibility analysis, and a study and documentation of the existing system. The goal is to define the new system's requirements so it will take the organization where it needs to go. This chapter discusses the other four steps (see Fig. 10.1) in the systems development life cycle: conceptual systems design, physical systems design, systems implementation and conversion, and operation and maintenance. Chapter 12 discusses how some of the steps in the SDLC can be shortened or made more effective.

Accountants must understand the development process. They are involved in this process in several ways, as users helping to specify their needs, as members of the development team, and as auditors after the system is complete. Accountants should help keep the project on track by evaluating and measuring benefits, monitoring costs, and ensuring that the project is on schedule.

CONCEPTUAL SYSTEMS DESIGN

In the **conceptual systems design** phase, a general framework is developed for implementing user requirements and solving problems identified in the analysis phase. As shown in Fig. 11.1, there are three main steps in conceptual design: evaluate design alternatives, prepare design specifications, and prepare the conceptual systems design report. We will discuss these steps in the following subsections.

At some point during conceptual systems design the organization must decide whether to develop or to buy AIS software. The decision should be made after AIS requirements have been determined in systems analysis. A company can't evaluate packages until they know what requirements the package must meet. Systems acquisition is discussed in more depth in Chapter 12.

Step 1: Evaluate Design Alternatives

There are many ways to design an AIS, so accountants and others involved in systems design must continually make design decisions. For example: Should the company mail hard copy purchase orders or use EDI? Should the company have a large centralized mainframe and data base, or distribute computer

Figure 11.1

Steps in Conceptual Systems Design

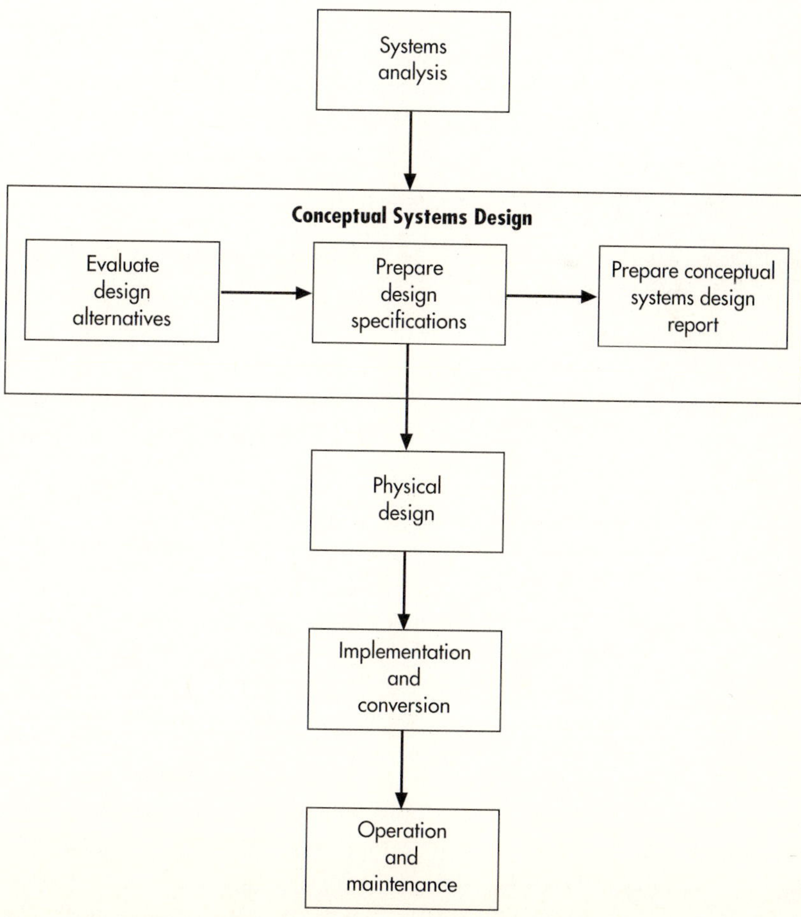

power to the stores using minis, PCs, distributed data bases, LANs, and WANs? Should data entry be through keyboard, OCR, POS, or some combination?

The design team should identify a variety of design alternatives and evaluate each with respect to the following standards: (1) how well it meets organizational and system objectives, (2) how well it meets users' needs, (3) whether it is economically feasible, and (4) its advantages and disadvantages. The steering committee evaluates the alternatives and selects the one that best meets the organization's needs. Table 11.1 shows some examples of conceptual and physical design considerations and their corresponding design alternatives.

Step 2: Prepare Design Specifications

Once a design alternative has been selected, the project team develops the **conceptual design specifications** for the following elements:

1. *Output.* Because the system is designed to meet users' information needs, output specifications *must* be prepared first. For example, to evaluate store sales using a sales analysis report, Shoppers Mart must decide: (a) how often to produce the report (daily or weekly), (b) what it should contain (store number, sales volume, etc.), (c) what it will look like, and (d) whether users will need a hard copy or screen (or both) output.
2. *Data storage.* Development decisions for Shoppers Mart include which data elements must be stored to produce the sales report, whether the data should be stored in sequential or random order, what type of file or data base to use, and which field size is appropriate for the data items.

Table 11.1 **Design Considerations and Alternatives**

Design Consideration	Design Alternatives
Communications channel configuration	Point to point, multidrop, or line sharing
Communications channels	Telephone lines, coaxial cable, fiber optics, microwave, or satellite
Communications network	Centralized, decentralized, distributed, or local area
Data storage medium	Tape, floppy disk, hard disk, or hard copy
Data storage structure	Files or data base
File organization and access	Random or sequential
Input medium	Keying, OCR, MICR, POS, EDI, or voice
Operations	In-house or outsourcing
Output frequency	Instantaneous, hourly, daily, weekly, or monthly
Output medium	CRT, hard copy, voice, or turnaround document
Output scheduling	Predetermined times or on demand
Printed output	Preprinted forms or system-generated forms
Processing	Manual, batch, or real-time
Processor	Micro, mini, or mainframe
Software acquisition	Canned, custom, or modified
Transaction processing	Batch or on-line
Update frequency	Instantaneous, hourly, daily, weekly, or monthly

3. *Input.* Design considerations for Shoppers Mart include which sales data to enter, sale location and amount, and where, when, and how to collect data. Inputs are considered only after the desired output is identified. Considering inputs before outputs is like opening the refrigerator and mixing food items (inputs) with no thought as to what you are fixing (output).
4. *Processing procedures and operations.* Design considerations for Shoppers Mart include how to process the input and stored data in order to produce the sales report, and also the sequence in which the processes must be performed.

Step 3: Prepare the Conceptual Systems Design Report

At the end of the conceptual design phase, the project development team prepares and submits a **conceptual systems design report.** The purpose of this report is to (1) guide physical systems design activities, (2) communicate how management and user information needs will be met, and (3) help the steering committee assess system feasibility. The main component is a description of one or more recommended system designs. This description contains the contents of each output, data base, and input; processing flows and the relationships among the programs, files, inputs, and outputs; hardware, software, and resource requirements; and audit, control, and security processes and procedures. Any assumptions or unresolved problems that may affect the final systems design should be discussed. The table of contents of the Shoppers Mart report is shown in Table 11.3, on page 381.

PHYSICAL SYSTEMS DESIGN

During the **physical systems design** phase, the company determines *how* the conceptual AIS design is to be implemented. Physical design translates the broad, user-oriented AIS requirements of conceptual design into detailed specifications that are used to code and test the computer programs. As shown in Fig. 11.2, the steps that occur during this phase include designing output and input, creating files and data bases, writing computer programs, developing procedures, and building controls into the new AIS. The following subsections describe these activities in detail.

Output Design

The objective of output design is to determine the nature, format, content, and timing of printed reports, documents, and screen displays. Tailoring the output to user needs requires cooperation between users and designers. Some important output design considerations include the following:

- *Use.* Who will use the output, why do they need it, and what decisions will they need to make based upon it?
- *Medium.* Should output be on paper, screen, voice response, diskette, microfilm, or some combination?
- *Format.* The format that clearly conveys the most information should be selected (table, narrative, graphic). For example, large volumes of data can be easily condensed into graphs that are easy to read and interpret.
- *Preprinted.* Should paper output be on a preprinted form, such as a check or purchase order?
- *Location.* Where should AIS output be sent?
- *Access.* Who should have access to hard copy and computer screen output?

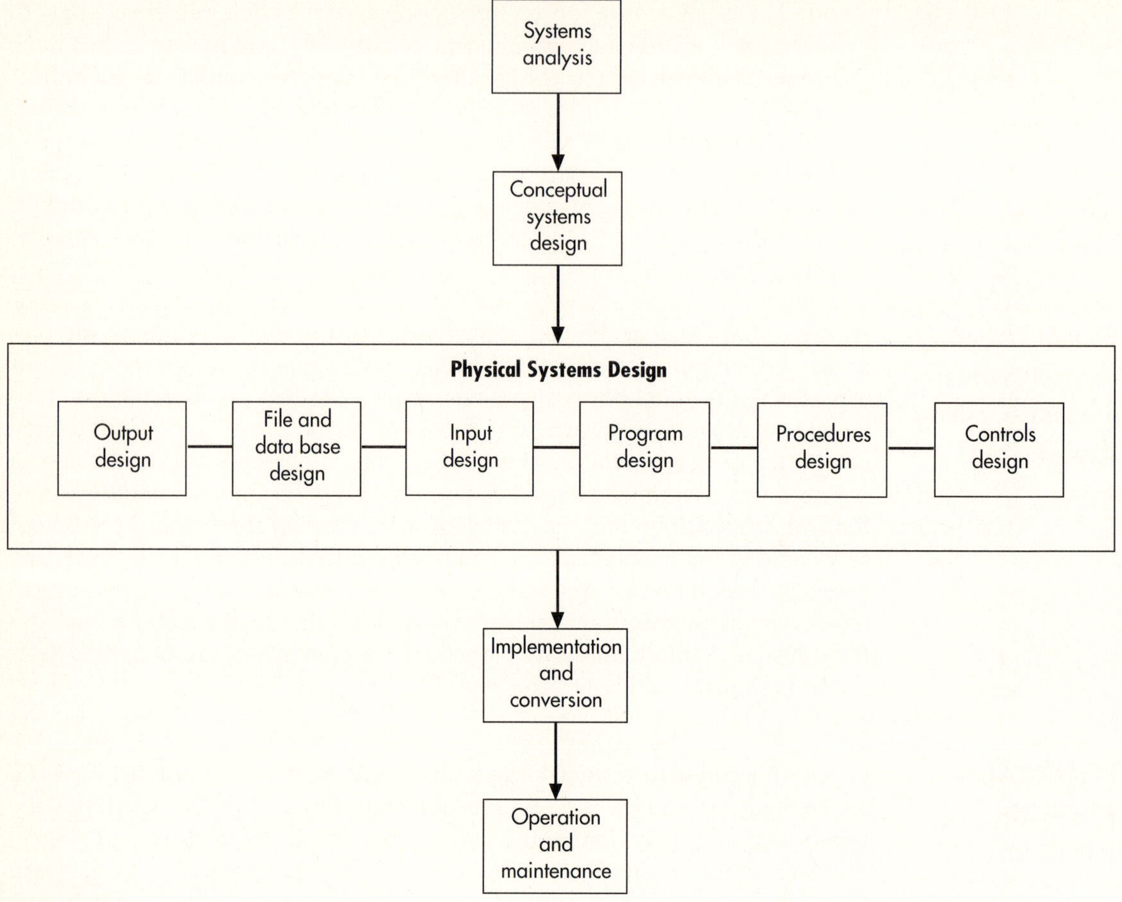

Figure 11.2

Physical Systems Design

- *Detail.* Lengthy output should be preceded by an executive summary and a table of contents. Headings and legends organize data and highlight important items. Detailed information is placed in an appendix.
- *Timeliness.* How often should AIS output be produced?

Output usually fit into one of the following four categories:

1. **Scheduled reports** have a prespecified content and format and are prepared on a regular basis. Examples include monthly performance reports, weekly sales analyses, and annual financial statements.
2. **Special-purpose analyses** have no prespecified content or format and are not prepared on a regular schedule. They are prepared in response to a management request to evaluate an issue, such as which of three new products would provide the highest profits.
3. **Triggered exception reports** have a prespecified content and format but are prepared only in response to abnormal conditions. Excessive absenteeism,

cost overruns, inventory shortages, and situations requiring immediate corrective action trigger such reports.

4. **Demand reports** have a prespecified content and format but are prepared only upon request. Both triggered exception reports and demand reports can be used effectively to facilitate the management process.

The AIS developers prepare an output sample, and users evaluate it to ensure that it is complete, relevant, and useful. Unacceptable output is modified and reviewed as many times as necessary to make it acceptable. To avoid the expense and time delays resulting from changes made later in the SDLC, many organizations require users to sign a document stating that the form and content are acceptable.

File and Data Base Design

In Chapters 4 through 6 you learned about files and data bases and how to design them. Here are some important considerations to remember about file and data base design and data storage and retrieval:

- *Medium.* Should data be stored on disk, diskettes, optical disk, or tape?
- *Organization and access.* Should sequential, indexed-sequential, or random-access methods be used?
- *Processing mode.* Should batch or real-time processing be used?
- *Maintenance.* What procedures are needed to maintain data effectively?
- *Size.* How many records will be stored in the data base and how large are they? How fast is the number of AIS records expected to grow?
- *Activity level.* What percentage of the records will be added or deleted each year? What percentage will need to be updated?

It is advantageous that all of the various divisions or departments of a company store data in a compatible format. This measure can help companies avoid the problem currently facing AT&T: 23 business units and a jumble of incompatible systems. Some of these units find it difficult to share E-mail with other units. Perhaps more importantly, the business units don't maintain customer records in formats that allow them to be easily shared. AT&T has undertaken a five-year project to create a "single view" of each customer so that customer data can be shared across all business units.

Input Design

When evaluating input design, the design team must identify types of data input and optimal input methods.

Considerations in input design include the following:

- *Medium.* Should AIS data be entered using key-to-disk methods; a keyboard; an OCR, MICR, or POS terminal; or voice input?
- *Source.* Where does data originate (a computer, customer, remote location, etc.), and how does that affect data entry?
- *Format.* What format (source or turnaround document, screen) efficiently captures the data with the least effort and cost?
- *Type.* What is the nature of AIS data?
- *Volume.* How much data are to be entered?
- *Personnel.* What are the data entry operators' abilities, functions, and expertise? Is additional training necessary?

- *Frequency.* How often does AIS data need to be entered?
- *Cost.* How can costs be minimized without adversely affecting efficiency and accuracy?
- *Error detection and correction.* What errors are possible, and how can they be detected and corrected?

Forms Design. Many information systems still capture input data on paper and later transfer that data to a computer medium. Although more and more systems are moving away from the use of paper documents and toward source data automation techniques, forms design is still a very important topic. Forms design was discussed in detail in Chapter 2, and a number of important forms design principles are summarized in Table 2.3. This checklist is a useful tool for evaluating existing forms and designing new ones.

Designing Computer Screens. When data must be keyed into a system, it is more efficient to enter it directly on a computer screen than to put it on paper for subsequent entry. As a result, it is important to understand how to design computer screens for input as well as for output. Computer screens can be utilized most effectively when the following principles are followed:

- Organize the screen in such a way that data can be entered quickly, accurately, and completely. Minimize data input by displaying as much information as possible on the screen or have it retrieved by the system. For example, entering a customer number could automatically cause the system to retrieve the customer's name, address, and other important information.
- Enter data in the same order it is displayed on paper forms used to capture the data.
- Fill the screen out from left to right and top to bottom. Group logically related data together.
- Design the screen so that users either can jump from one data entry location to another using a single key or can go directly to screen locations.
- Make it easy to correct mistakes. Clear and explicit error messages that are consistent across all screens are essential. There should be a Help feature to provide on-line assistance.
- Restrict the amount of data on a screen to avoid clutter. Limit the number of menu options on a single screen.

Program Design

Program development is one of the most time-consuming activities in the entire SDLC. Here are some procedures for improving program development:

- *Modules.* Subdivide programs into small, well-defined modules to reduce complexity and enhance reliability and modifiability. Modular programming is referred to as **structured programming.** Modules should interact with a control module rather than with each other. Each module should have only one entry and exit point, to facilitate testing and modification.
- *Common routines.* Use a set of basic coding structures for common routines such as input, output, and file maintenance.

- *Standards.* Develop programming standards (rules for writing programs). They contribute to consistency among programs, making them easier to read and maintain.
- *Walk-through.* Conduct a structured program walk-through to find incorrect logic, errors, omissions, or other problems.
- *Team approach.* Use a team consisting of a chief programmer, assistant programmers, and a programming secretary. The chief and the assistants work together to produce code. The secretary performs clerical functions and prepares program documentation.

Procedures Design

Everyone who interacts with the newly designed AIS should follow procedures that answer the who, what, when, where, why, and how questions related to all AIS activities. Procedures should cover input preparation, transaction processing, error detection and correction, controls, reconciliation of balances, data base access, output preparation and distribution, and computer operator instructions. Procedures may take the form of system manuals, user instruction classes, training materials, or on-line Help screens. They may be written by development teams, users, or teams representing both groups.

Controls Design

An often-heard saying in the computer industry is, "Garbage in, garbage out." This adage emphasizes that improperly controlled input, processing, and data base functions produce information of little value. Controls must be built into an AIS to ensure its effectiveness, efficiency, and accuracy. They should prevent errors and detect and correct them when they do occur. Accountants play a vital role in this area. Some of the more important control concerns that must be addressed are briefly listed here. Controls are discussed in greater detail in Chapters 13–15.

- *Validity.* Are all system interactions valid? For example, how can the AIS ensure that cash disbursements are made only to legitimate vendors?
- *Authorization.* Are input, processing, storage, and output activities authorized by the appropriate managers? For example, how can the AIS ensure that payroll additions have been authorized?
- *Accuracy.* Is input verified to ensure accuracy? What controls are in place to ensure that data passed between processing activities isn't lost?
- *Access.* Is access to data adequately controlled? For example, how are hackers denied access to data files?
- *Numerical control.* Are documents prenumbered to prevent errors or intentional misuse and to detect when documents are missing or stolen?
- *Audit trail.* Can transaction data be traced from source documents to final output (and vice versa)? For example, if a customer calls with a question, can transaction details be easily accessed?

Physical Systems Design Report

At the end of the physical design phase, the team prepares a **physical systems design report.** (Table 11.3, on page 381, shows a table of contents for the report prepared at Shoppers Mart.) This report becomes the basis for management's decision whether to proceed to the implementation phase.

SYSTEMS IMPLEMENTATION

Systems implementation is the process of installing hardware and software and getting the AIS up and running. This process generally consists of developing a plan, developing and testing software, preparing the site, selecting and training personnel, developing documentation, and testing the system. These activities are shown in Fig. 11.3 and are discussed in this section.

The state of Virginia has been especially successful in designing and implementing its AIS. In fact, it serves as a model for other governmental agencies. Focus 11.1 describes the improvements the state has made to its AIS.

Figure 11.3

Systems Implementation

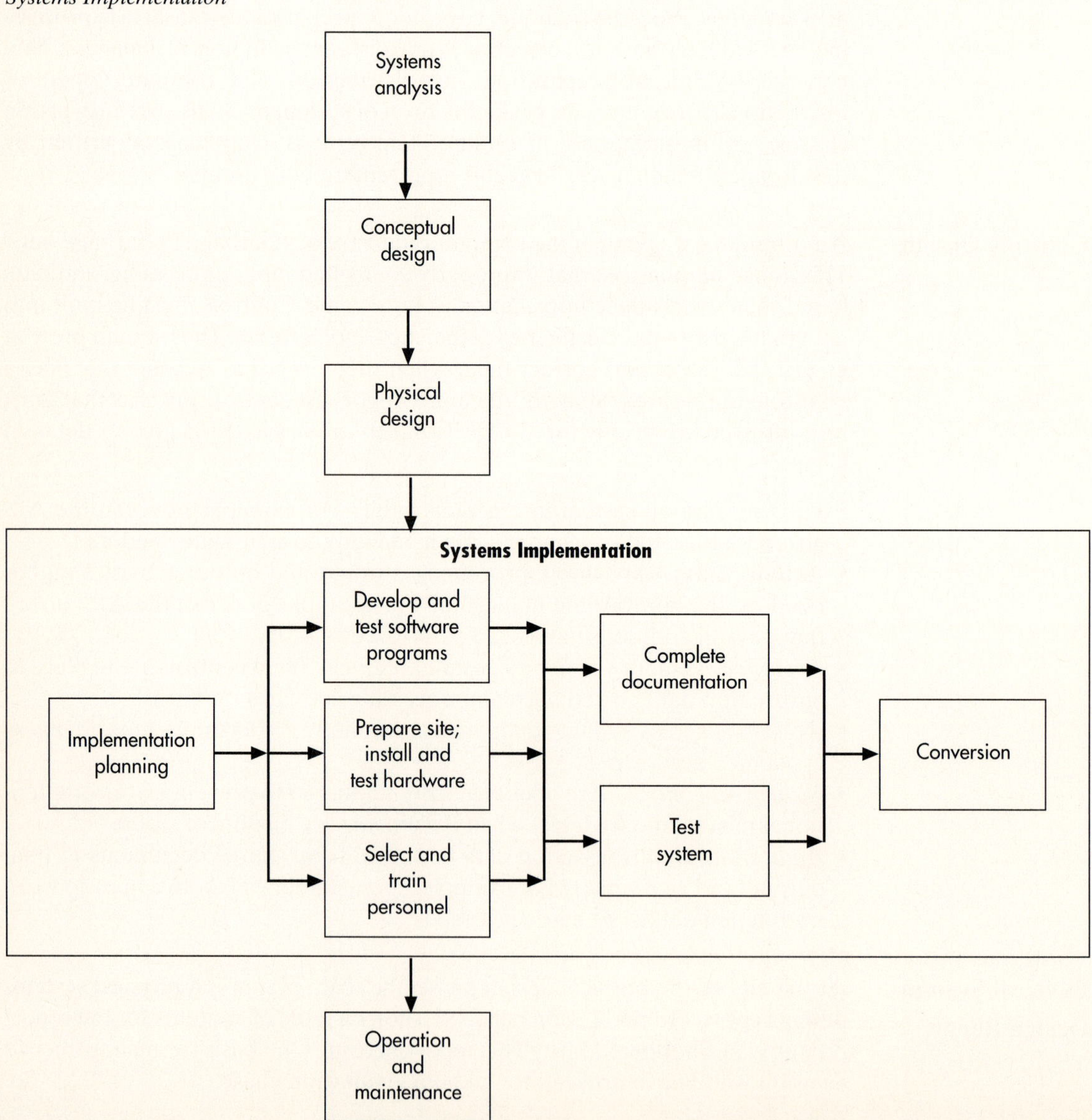

FOCUS 11.1

Stars Saves Virginia $80 Million

Hundreds of thousands of Virginia taxpayers now receive tax refunds within a week of filing instead of the two to three months it previously took. They owe the quick turnaround to Jane Bailey, director of AIS at the Department of Taxation. Bailey managed the development of the State Tax Accounting and Reporting System (STARS), a multisystem project requiring nine years for completion. STARS has been so successful that the IRS, 27 states, and a Canadian province have sent teams to Richmond to see whether a little magic might rub off on their own systems development and implementation efforts.

The state's central information technology group strongly recommended that the department engage outside contractors for the job, saying Bailey's six-person staff was far too small and unsophisticated to overhaul the vast and motley collection of manual and batch systems formerly in place. But Bailey insisted on going with an inside job. She was able to convince management by letting them know that once it was developed, the system would be maintained by her and that she would be able to respond quickly to tax law changes.

Bailey's staff eventually swelled to 45 people. She insisted that these employees be first-rate; if she could not hire the experts and specialists she needed, she retained them as consultants and then used them to train her existing staff. In addition, she recruited five management analysts to redesign business processes, write user documentation, and train users. Ten people from her staff are management analysts who work full-time on user procedures and issues. Seeing user involvement as crucial, Bailey succeeded in getting six managers from user areas assigned full-time to the project.

Over the years STARS' scope has expanded to encompass more functions and more users, and its budget climbed from its original $3 million to $11 million. A major new piece of software was installed every three to six months. Users had to adapt, often getting 15 new screens at a time. The megaproject eventually involved putting together 1500 COBOL programs, 40 IBM IMS data bases, and 350 on-line screens in 25 applications for 1800 users.

The state, which asked for a Chevrolet, got a Cadillac and the payoff has been impressive. STARS' users estimate that it saved the state $80 million over five years, most of it from added collections from would-be tax cheats.

Focus Questions

1. What do you think would have occurred if Bailey had not been successful? had been only marginally successful?
2. Why was Bailey so successful? What were some of the secrets of her success?
3. Do you think other states should try to do what Bailey and Virginia did? Why or why not?

Implementation Planning

An **implementation plan** consists of implementation tasks, expected completion dates, cost estimates, and the person or persons responsible for each task. The plan specifies when the project should be complete and the AIS operational. The implementation team should identify risk factors that decrease the likelihood of successful implementation, and the plan should contain a strategy for coping with each one.

Planning Techniques. Two techniques for scheduling and monitoring implementation activities are PERT and the Gantt chart. **PERT (program evaluation and review technique)** requires that all activities and the precedent and subsequent relationships among them be identified. They are used to draw a PERT diagram, or a network of arrows and nodes representing, respectively, project activities that require an expenditure of time and resources and the completion and initiation of activities. Completion time estimates are made and the critical path—the path requiring the greatest amount of time—is determined. A PERT diagram is illustrated in Fig. 11.4. Its critical path is activities B, C, F, H, I, J, K, and M. Project completion time is 83 weeks. If any of the activities on the critical path are delayed, the whole project is delayed. If possible, resources are shifted to critical path activities to reduce project completion time.

A **Gantt chart** (Fig. 11.5) is a bar chart with project activities listed on the left-hand side and units of time (days or weeks) across the top. For each activity a bar is drawn from the scheduled starting date to the ending date, thereby defining expected project completion time. As activities are completed they are recorded on the Gantt chart by filling in the bar. Thus at any time it is possible to determine quickly which activities are on schedule and which are behind. The capacity to show, in graphic form, the entire schedule for a large, complex project, including progress to date and current status, is the primary advantage of the Gantt chart. Gantt charts do not show, however, the relationships among various project activities.

Plan for Organizational Changes. AIS changes may require adjustments to a company's existing organizational structure. New departments may be created and existing ones eliminated or reduced in size. The structure and status of the data processing department itself may change. For example, Blue Cross and Blue Shield of Wisconsin contracted for a new $200-million system. The system—initiated by technical staff who did not understand the company's

Figure 11.4

PERT Network of the AIS Implementation Process

Activity	Time (weeks)	Predecessor Activities	Activity Description
A	36	None	Physical preparation (including vendor lead time)
B	4	None	Organizational planning
C	2	B	Personnel selection
D	2	A	Equipment installation
E	10	C	Personnel training
F	15	C	Detailed systems design
G	9	F	File conversion
H	4	F	Standards and controls development
I	9	H	Program preparation
J	9	I	Program testing
K	20	D,E,G,J	Parallel operations
L	8	I	System documentation completion
M	20	K,L	Follow-up

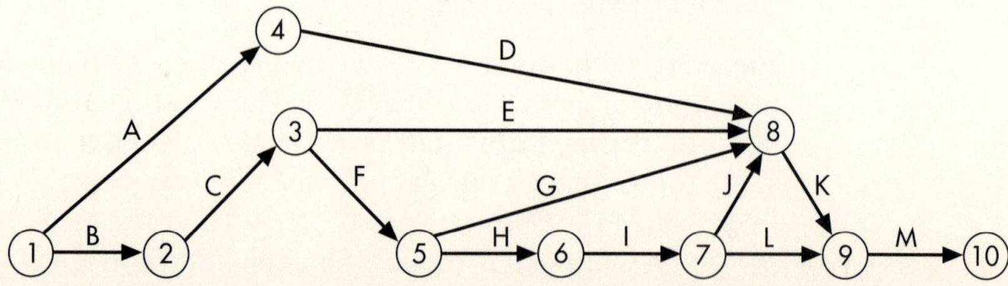

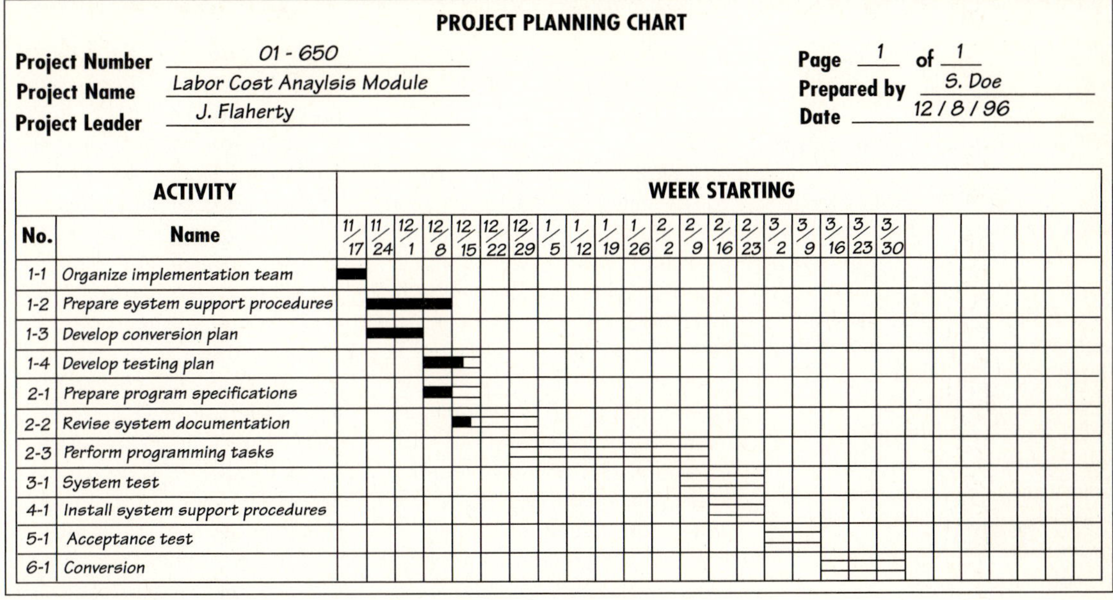

Figure 11.5

Sample Gantt Chart

business or vision—did not work properly. It sent hundreds of checks to a nonexistent town, made $60 million in overpayments, and resulted in the loss of 35,000 clients. One reason the system failed was that its implementation should have included an organizational restructuring.

Development and Test Software Programs

Although accountants need not be computer programmers, they should understand how software is created. Program preparation time may range from a few days to a few years, depending on program complexity. Seven steps are followed when developing software:

1. *Determine user needs.* The team should consult with users and draw up an agreement about software requirements.
2. *Develop a plan.* A development plan should be developed and documented.
3. *Write program instructions (code).* The overall program approach and major processing tasks should be identified first, before each program step is planned in greater detail. Designing a program from the top down to more detailed levels is referred to as **hierarchical program design.**
4. *Test the program.* **Debugging** is the process of discovering and eliminating program errors. The process begins after a program is coded, when a visual and mental review, referred to as **desk checking,** is conducted to discover keying or programming errors. During program compilation, syntax errors are uncovered. A program is tested for logic errors using test data that simulate as many real processing situations or input data combinations as possible. Test data should include all valid transactions and all possible error

FOCUS 11.2

Software Bugs Take Their Toll

An $18.5-million rocket explodes seconds after lift-off. Telephone networks mysteriously crash in three cities, leaving 10 million customers without service. A nuclear plant releases hundreds of gallons of radioactive water near Lake Huron. These three events have one disturbing fact in common: They were caused by tiny errors (bugs) buried in computer programs. The term *bug* was coined during World War II when a researcher, puzzled by a computer shutdown, removed a moth stuck between two electric relays. Lately, these electronics pests have been on a rampage.

- Without warning, Washington, D.C., Los Angeles, and Pittsburgh residents lost local phone service at almost the same time each morning. The culprit? Three missing digits in several million lines of programming that controls the phone companies' call-switching computers.
- During the Persian Gulf War, a software error prevented a Patriot missile from destroying an incoming Iraqi Scud missile that killed 28 people.
- American Airlines' reservations system shut down for almost 12 hours, crippling 14,000 travel agencies nationwide and forcing American's agents to write tickets by hand.
- A bug in a linear accelerator—a device that uses X rays to treat cancer victims—caused the accelerator to deliver a radiation overdose, killing one patient and leaving two others deeply burned and partly paralyzed.
- Ashton-Tate, a powerhouse in PC software, never recovered after it shipped bug-filled software.

Where do these bugs come from? To create software, a programmer writes millions of lines of code. One incorrect letter or punctuation mark in a line of code—even a missing period—can cause a computer to issue an incorrect command or no command at all. For instance, a flaw in DSC's call-switching computers sent hundreds of erroneous messages to other DSC computers, asking for assistance in rerouting calls when no help was necessary. The flood of messages shut down the computers and gave callers busy signals for hours.

Bugs exist in most software and are almost impossible to get rid of. A program containing bugs can work just fine for quite some time until suddenly with no warning—zap—the bug triggers something and the computer suddenly goes haywire.

Programmers go to great pains to detect and eliminate bugs before software is shipped.

---

conditions. Large programs are often tested in three stages: individual program modules, the linkages between modules and a control module, and interfaces between the program being tested and other application programs.

Focus 11.2 discusses the difficulty of testing software and the consequences of releasing software with undetected errors. Many software developers state that 20% to 30% of software development costs should be allocated to testing, debugging, and rewriting software.

5. *Document the program.* Because documentation explains how the program works, it can assist in correcting and resolving errors. Flowcharts, record layouts, decision tables, and related items should be retained as part of program documentation and organized into a meaningful documentation manual.
6. *Train program users.* Training begins during the later portion of the test phase. Program documentation is often used to train users.
7. *Install and use the system.* The process of revising an existing program is referred to as **program maintenance.** Factors that necessitate this type of change include requests for new or revised reports; input changes, file

But no one has the time or money to find every bug—or to simulate the exact situations the computer program will encounter in the real world. It would take 3000 years to completely test a program with several hundred instructions if one performed 1000 tests a second. Instead, software is tested with assumptions about how it will be used. Only a certain amount of information—for instance, the number of paychecks to be sent out each Friday—is used to test the program. No one can predict that a few enterprising customers will add more information than the software can handle.

A former Lotus Development product manager estimated that Lotus often found 5000 bugs in each product. The company would fix serious flaws before shipping the product and ignore minor or cosmetic flaws and those that were highly unlikely to ever cause a problem. If software developers took the time to find every one of these flaws, they would miss getting their product out to market on a timely basis and they would lose the market share to competitors able to get their products out on time.

Software developers also can't predict whether computer users will work faster than the software itself. The linear accelerators that killed and maimed cancer patients were controlled by an operator who typed extremely fast. She accidentally selected the X-ray mode and then switched to the electron beam. The software wasn't quick enough to recognize the change and the machine beamed radiation at full power to a tiny spot on the patients' bodies. The bug was so subtle it took programmers a year to detect and eliminate it.

The sheer volume of software code needed in a complex program makes finding bugs difficult. There are over 2.5 million lines of code in systems that check for cracks in the engine wheel of a space shuttle and 12 million in a phone company's call-switching computer. Finding a flaw in this code is as difficult as looking for one misspelled name in the New York City phone book.

Focus Questions

1. Why is testing new software so crucial to reducing the incidence of programming errors (bugs)?
2. Can effective software testing eliminate the threat of bugs altogether?
3. How are the risks associated with bugs minimized during the software development process?

Source: John Schneidawind, "Getting the Bugs Out," *USA Today* (August 29, 1991): 1–2. Copyright 1991, *USA Today*. Reprinted with permission.

content, or values such as tax rates; error detection; and conversion to new hardware.

Site Preparation

A PC, or minicomputer, requires little site preparation. A large system may require extensive changes, such as additional electrical outlets, data communications facilities, raised floors, humidity controls, special lighting, and air-conditioning. Security measures, such as fire protection and an emergency power supply, may also be necessary. Space is needed for equipment, storage, and offices. Site preparation is a lengthy process and should begin well in advance of the installation date.

Select and Train Personnel

Employees can be hired from outside the company or transferred internally. Hiring from within the company is the less costly and more effective alternative, since employees already understand the firm's business and operations. Transferring employees who are displaced as a result of the new system would also boost employee loyalty and morale.

Studies of large companies show that over 90% of employees have computers but more than a third don't feel they have the skills to use them adequately. Employees lack computer skills for a number of reasons. First, because effective training is time-consuming and expensive, companies take shortcuts. Second, those who understand the system are so busy trying to maintain and update it that they lack the time to provide training. When users are not adequately trained, the company is unable to achieve the expected benefits and return on their investment. The hidden cost of inadequate training is that users turn to co-workers who have mastered the system for help, resulting in less productive co-workers and increased company costs.

Effective AIS training must consist of more than just the hardware and software skills needed to use the new AIS. Employees must be oriented to new policies and operations, and training should be planned and scheduled so it occurs just before systems testing and conversion. Many types of training programs are available to companies: technical training from vendors, self-study manuals, computer-assisted instruction, videotape presentations, role playing, case studies, and experimenting with the AIS under the guidance of experienced users.

Boots the Chemists, a London-based international pharmacy chain with over a thousand stores, came up with a novel approach to training. Store employees, nervous about a forthcoming computer system, were invited to a party at a store where a new POS system had been installed. They were asked to try to harm the system by pushing the wrong buttons or fouling up a transaction. Employees quickly found they could not harm the system and that it was easy to use.

Complete Documentation

Three types of documentation must be prepared for new systems:

1. *Development documentation* describes the new AIS. It includes a system description; copies of output, input, and file and data base layouts; program flowcharts; test results; and user acceptance forms.
2. *Operations documentation* includes operating schedules; files and data bases accessed; and equipment, security, and file retention requirements.
3. *User documentation* teaches users to operate the AIS. It includes a procedures manual and training materials.

Test the System

One reason for the Blue Cross and Blue Shield system failure, described earlier, was inadequate system testing. The developers underestimated the complexity of the system and promised an overly optimistic delivery time of 18 months. One of the shortcuts they took to meet that deadline was to deliver an untested system.

Documents and reports, user inputs, operating and control procedures, processing procedures, and computer programs should all be given a trial run in realistic circumstances. In addition, capacity limits and backup and recovery procedures should be tested. There are three common forms of testing:

1. **Walk-throughs** are step-by-step reviews of procedures or program logic. Walk-throughs early in system design are attended by the development team and system users. The focus is on the inputs, files, outputs, and data

flows of the organization. Subsequent walk-throughs, attended by programmers, address logical and structural aspects of program code.

2. **Processing of test transactions** determines whether a program operates as designed. Valid and erroneous data are processed to determine whether transactions are handled properly and errors are detected and handled appropriately. To evaluate test results, the correct system response for each test transaction must be specified in advance.
3. **Acceptance tests** use copies of real transaction and file records rather than hypothetical ones. Users develop the acceptance criteria and make the final decision whether to accept the AIS.

Chemical Bank suffered the consequences of not adequately testing an upgrade to its ATM system. Shortly after its installation, New York customers who withdrew cash from one of Chemical's 900 ATMs found their accounts were debited twice. Before the problem could be corrected, 150,000 withdrawals with a total value of $8 million were posted twice to customer accounts. Thousands of small accounts were overdrawn or emptied, which annoyed and angered customers. Chemical lost a great deal of credibility with its customers as a result of the glitch.

Even software purchased from an outside vendor must be tested thoroughly before being installed. Kane Carpets learned this lesson after it installed an AIS custom-tailored to the floor covering industry. No sooner was the software up and running when Kane began experiencing serious problems. For example, its inventory control system told its salespersons that orders could not be filled when the product was in fact available and vice versa. Kane destroyed almost all of its credibility and lost many of its customers.

SYSTEMS CONVERSION

Conversion is the process of changing from the old AIS to the new. Many elements must be converted: hardware, software, data files, and procedures. The process is complete when the new AIS has become a routine, ongoing part of the system.

Conversion Approaches

As shown in Fig. 11.6, four conversion approaches are used to change from an old to a new system.

Direct conversion is an immediate discontinuance of the old AIS when the new one is introduced. For example, Shoppers Mart could discontinue its old system on Saturday night and use its new AIS on Monday morning. Direct conversion is appropriate when the old AIS has no value or the new one is so different that comparisons between the two are meaningless. The approach is inexpensive, but it provides no backup AIS. Unless a system has been carefully developed and tested, therefore, direct conversion carries a high risk of failure.

Parallel conversion operates the old and new systems simultaneously for a period of time. For example, Shoppers Mart could process transactions with both systems, compare the outputs, reconcile the differences, and correct problems with the new AIS. After the new system proves itself, Shoppers Mart could discontinue the old one. Parallel processing protects companies from errors, but it is costly and stressful for employees to process all transactions twice.

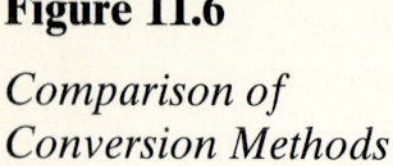

Figure 11.6

Comparison of Conversion Methods

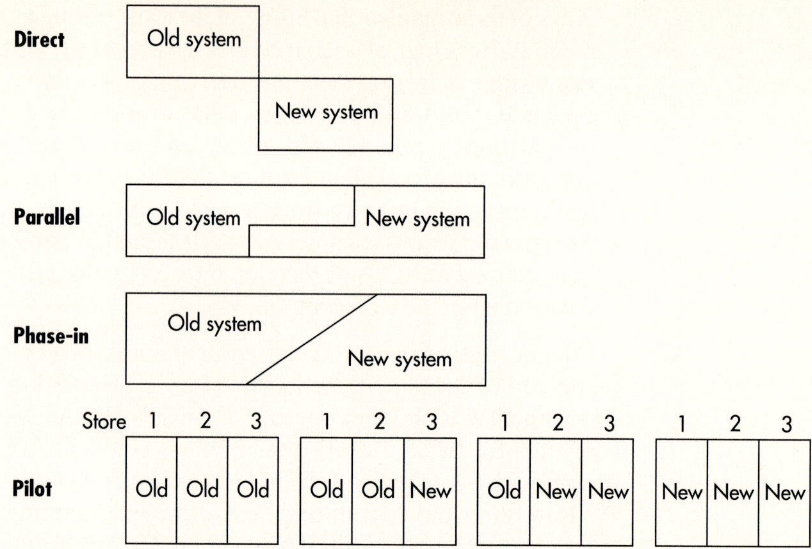

However, because companies often experience problems during conversion, parallel processing has gained widespread popularity.

Phase-in conversion gradually replaces elements of the old AIS with the new one. For example, Shoppers Mart could implement its inventory system, then disbursements, followed by sales collection, and so forth, until the whole system is functional. These gradual changes mean that data processing resources can be acquired over time. The disadvantages are the cost of creating the temporary interfaces between the old and the new AIS and the time required to make the gradual changeover.

Pilot conversion implements a system in just one part of the organization, such as a branch location. For example, Shoppers Mart could install its new POS system at one of its stores using a direct, parallel, or phase-in approach. When problems with the system are resolved, the new system could be implemented at the remaining locations. This approach localizes conversion problems and allows training in a live environment. The disadvantages are the long conversion time and the need for interfaces between the old and the new systems, which coexist until all locations have been converted. Owens-Corning Fiberglass implemented its accounts payable, travel and expense, and payroll systems by getting the system up and running in one plant and then moving it to all the others one by one.

Data Conversion

Data conversion can be time consuming, tedious, and expensive. The difficulty and magnitude of the task can be easily underestimated. Data files may need to be modified in three ways:

1. *Medium.* Files may be moved to a different storage medium, from tapes to disks, for example.
2. *Content.* Data content may be changed; for example, fields and records may be added or deleted.
3. *Format.* File format may be changed.

The first step in the data conversion process is to decide which data files need to be converted. They then must be checked for completeness and any data inaccuracies and inconsistencies removed. Actual data conversion is next. Validating the new files, to ensure data were not lost during conversion, follows. If the file conversion is lengthy, the new files must be updated with the transactions that occurred during data conversion. Once the files and data bases have been converted and tested for accuracy, the new AIS is functionable. The system should be monitored for a time to make sure it runs smoothly and accurately. The final activity is to document the conversion activities.

OPERATION AND MAINTENANCE

The final step in the SDLC is to operate and maintain the new system. A **postimplementation review** should be conducted on a newly installed AIS to ensure that it meets its planned objectives. Some important factors to consider and questions to answer during the postimplementation review are listed in Table 11.2. Any problems uncovered during the review should be brought to the attention of management and the necessary adjustments made. When the review has been completed, a **postimplementation review report** is prepared. The table of contents in Table 11.3 (page 381) illustrates what this report

Table 11.2 **Factors to Investigate During Postimplementation Review**

Factors	Questions
Goals and objectives	Does the system help the organization meet its goals, objectives, and overall mission?
Satisfaction	Are the users satisfied with the system? What would they like changed or improved?
Benefits	How have users benefited from the system? Were the expected benefits achieved?
Costs	Are actual costs in line with expected costs?
Reliability	Is the system reliable? Has the system failed and, if so, what caused its failure?
Accuracy	Does the system produce accurate and complete data?
Timeliness	Does the system produce information on a timely basis?
Compatibility	Are the hardware, software, data, and procedures compatible with existing systems?
Controls and security	Is the system safeguarded against unintentional errors, fraud, and unauthorized intrusion?
Errors	Do error-handling procedures exist, and are they adequate?
Training	Are systems personnel and users adequately trained to support and use the system?
Communications	Is the communications system adequate?
Organization changes	Are any organizational changes brought about by the system beneficial or harmful? If harmful, how can they be resolved?
Documentation	Is system documentation complete and accurate?

should contain. User acceptance of the postimplementation review report is the concluding activity in the systems development process. Control of the AIS is passed to the data processing department. Work on the new system is not finished, however. Studies show that, over the life of a system, only 20%–30% of the work takes place during development; the other 70%–80% is spent maintaining the system. Most maintenance costs relate to software modifications and updates.

The experience of the Hartford Insurance Group illustrates the cost of maintenance. Approximately 70% of its personnel resources are devoted to maintaining existing systems. Hartford must maintain an inventory of 34,000 program modules containing 24 million lines of COBOL code. The job is even more difficult because recent changes in insurance regulations and business strategies have reduced the structure of the code and increased its complexity.

COMPUTER-AIDED SOFTWARE ENGINEERING (CASE)

Software developers have been compared to the shoemaker's children who had to go barefoot; they develop software for others, yet fail to create software to simplify their own work. That has changed with the development of powerful **computer-aided software (or systems) engineering (CASE)** tools, an integrated package of computer-based tools that automate important aspects of the software development process. CASE tools are used to plan, analyze, design, program, and maintain an AIS. They are also used to enhance the efforts of managers, users, and programmers in understanding information needs.

Many companies are currently using CASE tools. For example, Florida Power's new $86 million customer information system was created using a CASE tool sold by Andersen Consulting. The system has been so successful that Andersen Consulting is packaging it for other utility companies. America West Airlines has more than half of its 90 programmers developing applications using a PC-based CASE tool. Its employees use the tool to model data and business processes, then the tool uses this information to design and construct a system.

Front-end (or upper) CASE tools support the early stages of the SDLC, such as analysis and design. For example, CASE is used to help developers produce complete and consistent specifications and develop graphic models of systems. **Back-end (or lower) CASE** tools support the later SDLC phases. For example, programmers generate structured program code from data base specifications and from screen and report layouts.

A **data repository** or **CASE encyclopedia** stores and manages project data dictionaries. It contains information about the system and is cross-referenced to other system components such as data bases, programs, files, and input and output screens. Stored data can be reused, providing developers with increased flexibility and productivity.

Upper and lower CASE tools are combined into an **integrated CASE** package that is linked by the data repository. In future years it is entirely possible that accountants will simply enter system specifications, the desired output, and the input and output forms. The CASE tool will do the rest.

CASE Tools

CASE tools do not replace skilled designers; instead they provide a host of well-integrated tools that give developers effective support for all SDLC phases. An integrated CASE product has the following components:

- *Strategic planning tools* help identify business information needs as well as which projects should receive priority treatment.
- *Project management tools* help managers plan, schedule, organize, manage, control, and report the progress of the SDLC.
- *Data base design tools* use data descriptions in the data repository to generate a data base, a data dictionary to support the data base, and Entity–Relationship diagrams to show relationships between data tables.
- *Diagraming tools* are used to prepare data flow and Entity–Relationship diagrams, flowcharts, and organizational charts.
- *Screen and report layout tools* are used to design input and output screen displays and printed outputs.
- *Automatic code generators* use system specifications to write between 50% and 75% of an application program's source code.
- *System management tools* are used to configure controls over programs and data base structures and to correct errors.

Advantages and Disadvantages of CASE Technology

CASE tools provide several important advantages:

- *Improved productivity.* Sony and Dupont reported that CASE tools increased productivity by over 600%. CASE can generate bug-free code from system specifications as well as automate repetitive tasks, such as drawing diagrams and charts, creating models, and converting models into an efficient data base. A programmer at Baptist Medical System, using an integrated CASE tool, developed a system in one week that was estimated to take four months!
- *Improved program quality.* CASE tools simplify the enforcement of structured development standards, thus improving the quality of development and reducing the threat of serious design errors. CASE tools also can check the internal accuracy of the design and detect inconsistencies. Storing design data in the data repository makes it easier for developers to share design details and review and modify the work of others.
- *Cost savings.* Savings of 80%–90% are possible. At Dupont, an application estimated to require 27 months at a cost of $270,000 was finished in 4 months for $30,000. Over 90% of the code was generated by a CASE package directly from design specifications.
- *Improved control procedures.* CASE tools encourage the development of system controls, security measures, and system auditability and error handling procedures early in the design process.
- *Simplified documentation.* CASE tools automatically document the system as the development process progresses.

Some of the more serious problems with CASE technology include the following:

- *Incompatibility.* CASE tools lack programming standards that allow different CASE tools to interact effectively.

- *Cost.* CASE technology is relatively expensive, with some packages in excess of $300,000. Additional costs are incurred to develop CASE standards and methodologies and to train developers. As a result, most small companies can't afford integrated CASE tools.
- *Limited capabilities.* CASE technology is still a new concept; progress is needed to make CASE tools more powerful and versatile.
- *Unmet expectations.* According to a recent Deloitte & Touche survey, only 37% of the chief information officers using CASE believe they achieved the expected benefits.

The steps in the SDLC are followed by most organizations that develop an AIS. However, the process can be a lengthy and difficult one. A number of approaches have been developed to speed up the SDLC or to partially replace some of its steps. You will learn about these methods in the next chapter.

SUMMARY AND CASE CONCLUSION

Ann tackled the sales processing portion of the AIS first. She gave the project development team her system analysis report and accompanying data. During conceptual systems design, the team visited stores with similar operations and identified ways to meet AIS requirements. Alternative approaches were discussed with users, management, and the steering committee and were narrowed down to Ann's original approach. The team developed conceptual design specifications for the output, input, processing, and data storage elements.

The company decided to utilize screen-based output as much as possible and to capture data electronically using POS devices. Data that can't be captured electronically will be entered using PCs. Each store will have a LAN that connects their PCs to a local data base. POS cash registers will be used to capture and feed sales data electronically to this data base. Each store will be linked electronically to the central office using a WAN. All sales data, store orders, and other summary-level information will be uploaded to the corporate data base daily. The corporate data base will download the information needed to manage the store. The central office will use EDI to order goods and pay suppliers. The table of contents for the conceptual systems design report is shown in Table 11.3.

During physical design, the development team designed each report identified during conceptual design in screen or hard copy format. The reports were shown to users and reworked until everyone involved was satisfied. The team then designed all files, data bases, and input screens. Next came the detailed design of the software programs needed to collect and process data and produce the output. The team also developed new procedures for handling data and operating the AIS. The accountants and the internal audit staff were especially helpful during the design of the controls needed to protect the system against errors and fraud. The physical systems design report table of contents is shown in Table 11.3.

Ann and her staff started implementation planning early. A location for the new mainframe was identified, and site preparation began during the design phase. First the hardware and then the software were installed and tested, fol-

Table 11.3 **Table of Contents for Shoppers Mart Documentation Reports**

Shoppers Mart Conceptual Systems Design Report	Shoppers Mart Physical Systems Design Report	Shoppers Mart Postimplementation Review Report
Table of Contents	Table of Contents	Table of Contents
I. Executive Summary of Conceptual Systems Design II. Overview of Project Purpose and Summary of Findings to Date III. Recommended Conceptual Design(s) of Proposed System A. Overview of Recommended Design(s) B. Objectives to Be Achieved by Design(s) C. Impact of Design(s) on Information System and Organization D. Expected Costs and Benefits of Design(s) E. Audit, Control, and Security Processes and Procedures F. Hardware, Software, and Other Resource Requirements G. Processing Flows: Relationships of Programs, Data Bases, Inputs, and Outputs H. Description of System Components (Programs, Data Bases, Inputs, and Outputs) IV. Assumptions and Unresolved Problems V. Summary VI. Appendixes, Glossary	I. Executive Summary of Physical Systems Design II. Overview of Project Purpose and Summary of Findings to Date III. Major Physical Design Recommendations A. Output Design B. Input Design C. Data Base Design D. Software (Processing) Design E. Hardware Design F. Controls Design G. Procedures Design IV. Assumptions and Unresolved Problems V. Summary VI. Appendixes, Glossary	I. Executive Summary of Postimplementation Review II. Overview of Project Development Project III. Evaluation of the Development Project A. Degree to Which System Objectives Were Met B. Analysis of Actual Versus Expected Costs and Benefits C. User Reactions and Satisfaction IV. Evaluation of Project Development Team V. Recommendations A. Recommendations for Improving the New System B. Recommendations for Improving the System Development Process VI. Summary

lowed by testing of the entire AIS. The new AIS was staffed almost exclusively with existing employees trained as the system was tested. System documentation was completed before data from the old AIS were converted to the new one.

Ann and her staff used a variety of conversion approaches. Because corporate-wide mainframe data were vitally important, Ann used a parallel conversion strategy. The new and old systems were operated together for a month, and the results were compared. When the bugs in the new AIS were ironed out, the old AIS was discontinued. A modular approach was used for the store AIS. The AIS was installed at several stores and all problems were resolved before implementing the system at the remaining Shoppers Marts. Conversion was not easy and required a fair amount of overtime and duplicate processing. After a few months Ann and her staff conducted a postimplementation review and made some adjustments to enhance the already high user acceptance and satisfaction of the new AIS.

Ann made a final presentation to top management after the AIS was installed and operating. She was widely congratulated and even heard the president mention to an executive vice president that she "was worth keeping an eye on" for even more responsibility in the firm.

KEY TERMS

conceptual systems design
conceptual design specifications
conceptual systems design report
physical systems design
scheduled reports
special-purpose analyses
triggered exception reports
demand reports
structured programming
physical systems design report
systems implementation
implementation plan
PERT (program evaluation and review technique)
Gantt chart
hierarchical program design
debugging
desk checking
program maintenance
walk-throughs
processing of test transactions
acceptance tests
conversion
direct conversion
parallel conversion
phase-in conversion
pilot conversion
postimplementation review
postimplementation review report
computer-aided software (or systems) engineering (CASE)
front-end (or upper) CASE
back-end (or lower) CASE
data repository or CASE encyclopedia
integrated CASE

CHAPTER QUIZ

1. The developers of your new system have proposed two different AIS designs and have asked you to evaluate them. This evaluation process is *most* likely to be a part of which SDLC step?
   a. Systems analysis
   b. Conceptual design
   c. Physical design
   d. Implementation and conversion
   e. Operation and maintenance

2. The purpose of the conceptual systems design report is to
   a. guide physical systems design activities.
   b. communicate how management and user information needs are met.
   c. help the steering committee assess system feasibility.
   d. a and b
   e. All of the above

3. Which of the following is the correct order of the steps in physical systems design?
   a. Input, file and data base, output, controls, procedures, and program
   b. File and data base, output, input, procedures, program, and controls
   c. Output, input, file and data base, procedures, program, and controls
   d. Output, file and data base, input, program, procedures, and controls

4. A monthly payroll register showing all hourly employees, the number of hours they worked, their deductions, and their net pay is *most* likely a
   a. scheduled report.
   b. special-purpose analyses.
   c. triggered exception report.
   d. demand report.

5. Considerations in input design include all of the following *except*
   a. which errors are possible and how they can be detected and corrected.
   b. how data are entered (key-to-disk, keyboards, OCR, MICR, or POS terminal).
   c. which format efficiently captures the input data with the least effort and cost.
   d. how often the system should produce reports and forms.

6. Which of the following procedures is most likely to help improve program development?
   a. Gantt chart
   b. Strategic plan
   c. Walk-through
   d. Record layout

7. A planning technique that identifies implementation activities and their relationships, constructs a network of arrows and nodes, and then determines the critical path through the network is referred to as a
   a. Gantt chart.
   b. PERT diagram.
   c. physical model.
   d. data flow diagram.

8. The systems testing approach that uses real transaction and file records rather than hypothetical ones is called
   a. a walk-through.
   b. processing of test transactions.
   c. an acceptance test.
   d. a parallel conversion test.

9. The process of discontinuing an old system when a new one is introduced is called
   a. direct conversion.
   b. parallel conversion.
   c. phase-in conversion.
   d. pilot conversion.

10. Which of the following are advantages of CASE tools? (There may be more than one correct answer.)
   a. Improved productivity
   b. Inexpensive to buy and use
   c. Improved control procedures
   d. Automation of repetitive tasks

DISCUSSION QUESTIONS

11.1 Prism Glass Company is currently in the process of converting from a manual data processing system to a computerized one. To expedite the implementation of the system, the CEO has asked your consulting team to postpone establishing standards and controls until after the system is fully operational. How should you respond to the president's request?

11.2 When a company converts from one system to another, many areas within the organization are affected. Explain how conversion to a new system will affect the following groups, both individually and collectively.
   a. Personnel
   b. Data storage
   c. Operations
   d. Policies and procedures
   e. Physical facilities

11.3 The following notice was posted in the employee cafeteria on Monday morning.

TO:	All Accounting and Clerical Employees
FROM:	I.M. Krewel, President
SUBJECT:	Termination of Employee Positions

Effective this Friday, all accounting and clerical employees not otherwise contacted will be terminated. Our new computer system eliminates the need for most of these jobs. We're grateful for the loyal service you've rendered as employees and wish you success. You may wish to pick up your final checks on Friday before you go.

Discuss the president's approach to human resource management. What are the possible repercussions of this episode? Assuming that job termination is the best alternative available, how would you approach the situation?

11.4 In which phase of the systems development cycle would each of the following positions be most actively involved? Justify your answers.

a. Managerial accountant
b. Programmer
c. Systems analyst
d. Financial vice president
e. Information systems manager
f. Auditor

11.5 During which of the five SDLC stages is each task labeled a–m performed? More than one answer may apply for each activity.

SDLC Stages

1. Systems analysis
2. Conceptual systems design
3. Physical systems design
4. Implementation and conversion
5. Operation and maintenance

Tasks

a. Write operating procedures manuals
b. Develop program and process controls
c. Identify alternative systems designs
d. Develop a conceptual model of the system
e. Identify external and administrative controls
f. Test the system
g. Train personnel
h. Evaluate the existing system
i. Analyze the achievement of systems benefits
j. Modify and alter programs
k. Analyze TQM performance measures
l. Conduct a feasibility analysis
m. Align AIS development plans with business objectives

PROBLEMS

11.1 The Glass Jewelry Company manufactures costume jewelry. You have just been hired as the management accountant in charge of the accounting and control functions. During your introductory meeting with the president, he outlined your first project: the design and implementation of a new AIS for the company. He stated that the new system must be fully implemented within six months. Total company sales for the past year were $10 million. Sales are expected to double within the next eighteen months.

REQUIRED

a. Outline the procedures you would follow to complete your assigned project. Your response should include a description of the following:

1. The various sources of information
2. The methods of documenting information collected
3. The methods of verifying the information collected

b. One of the subsystems that you plan to design is the accounts payable system. This system will contain a number of programs, two of which include "ENTER INVOICES" and "PRINT PAYABLE CHECKS." For each of these programs, describe its purpose and outline the application control considerations. (SMAC Examination, adapted)

11.2 Selling goods to a manufacturer that employs a just-in-time (JIT) inventory system requires immediate and reliable information from a company's AIS—just ask Sony Corporation of America. The need for faster information is partially a result of Sony's shift in business strategies. Over the past decade Sony has increased market penetration by supplying electronic parts to computer manufacturers. However, the AIS, originally built for the consumer market, was simply not prepared to handle this shift in information needs.

The problems with the system are readily apparent. One of Sony's biggest obstacles is that it does not get the information it needs, when it needs it, from its factories. As a result, it can't provide good delivery information to its customers. And that causes a big problem—if Sony isn't responsive to its customers' needs, it will probably lose them.

To speed system development, the IS organization at Sony is employing a computer-aided software engineering (CASE) tool from Texas Instruments. The tool lets systems designers use local workstations linked to a mainframe and uses artificial intelligence features to develop program code.

To use the CASE tool, the designer enters statements that describe the data the company will use and the relationships between the data files that will store the data. The CASE tool checks the data relationships to ensure that they are consistent. After any inconsistencies have been corrected, the CASE tool produces code that describes the relationships. The information is then stored in a global encyclopedia of corporate information. This process continues until a model of how the company operates is developed. The CASE tool allows this model to be updated and altered as relationships change.

Sony is finding several advantages to using CASE technology. For instance, use of CASE technology requires that developers possess a certain business expertise; this expertise makes designers more effective in translating business problems into systems solutions. The CASE system has also provided a significant productivity boost. Recent smaller development projects at Sony have seen sixfold increases in programming productivity. CASE tools also require significant planning long before any source code is written. Such planning minimizes wasted programming time and the possibility of a "runaway" system.

REQUIRED

a. What are the benefits of CASE technology? How does CASE technology improve the systems development process?

b. Discuss why CASE technology may not be used in systems development.

11.3 The following list denotes specific project activities and their scheduled starting and completion times:

Activity	Starting Date	Ending Date
A	Jan. 5	Feb. 9
B	Jan. 5	Jan. 19
C	Jan. 26	Feb. 23
D	Mar. 2	Mar. 23
E	Mar. 2	Mar. 16
F	Feb. 2	Mar. 16
G	Mar. 30	Apr. 20
H	Mar. 23	Apr. 27

REQUIRED

a. Using a format similar to that illustrated in Fig. 11.5, prepare a Gantt chart for this project. Assume that each activity starts on a Monday and ends on a Friday.

b. Assume today is February 16 and activities A and B have been completed, C is half completed, F is a quarter completed, and the other activities have not yet commenced. Record this information on your Gantt chart. Is the project behind schedule, on schedule, or ahead of schedule? Explain.

c. Discuss the relative merits of the Gantt chart and PERT as tools for project planning and control.

11.4 Refer to the PERT network of the computer implementation process shown in Fig. 11.4. Using months as the basic unit of time, prepare a Gantt chart for the project represented in Fig. 11.4. Assume that each activity is scheduled to begin immediately following the scheduled completion of any preceding activities. To simplify your analysis, you may assume that four weeks equal one month.

11.5 Chaotic order processing at Wang Laboratories had long been accepted by its customers as the cost of doing business with the computer giant. The tremendous growth of Wang throughout the 1970s left the company with a serious revenue tracking problem: Customers would often wait months for Wang to fill orders and process invoices. Repeated attempts by Wang's understaffed AIS department to solve these problems always met with failure.

Finally, Wang Laboratories hired a small consulting organization in 1980 to solve its revenue tracking problems and expedite prompt receipt of payments. The 18-month project turned into a three-year nightmare. After three years and $10 million, the consultants were dismissed from the unfinished project.

The reasons for the project failure were clear. First, the project was too large and far too complex for the appointed consulting team. According to one consultant, the systems development process was so dynamic that the failure to complete the project quickly was self-defeating, as modifications took over the original design.

Second, management had no clear vision of the new AIS system and lacked a strong support staff. As a result, a number of incompatible tracking systems sprung up throughout the company's distributed computer system.

Third, the consulting firm had little experience with the desired technology: a complex data base that represented the heart of the new system.

Finally, the project had too many applications. Interdependencies among subprograms and subroutines left consultants with few completed programs. Every program was linked to several subprograms, which in turn were linked to several other programs. Programmers would begin an initial program only to find that several subroutines were necessary. They eventually found themselves lost in a myriad of subroutines with no completed program.

Wang's ultimate solution to the crisis came from the internal AIS department. However, the revenue tracking system that the internal staff developed suffered quality problems for years.

REQUIRED

The president of Wang Laboratories has asked you, as a member of the AIS staff, to write a memo explaining the failure of the systems development project.

a. Outline the specific reasons for the development failure. What role did the consultants play in the project's failure?

b. Identify the organizational issues that management must address in the future.

c. Recommend any future steps the company could take to guarantee the quality of consulting services.

11.6 Tiny Toddlers Company, a large multinational manufacturer of children's toys and furniture, is planning the design and implementation of a distributed data processing system to assist its sales force. The company has 10 sales offices in Canada and 20 sales offices in the United States. The company's sales departments have been set up in a regional structure: Each sales office maintains its own customers and is responsible for granting credit and collecting receivables.

The proposed system will not only permit inquiries but also allow entry of daily sales and maintenance of the customer master file. Forms used by each sales office to maintain the customer master file and to enter the daily sales orders are shown in Figs. 11.7 and 11.8.

Figure 11.7

Customer Maintenance Form for Tiny Toddlers

CUSTOMER MAINTENANCE FORM

New Customer?	☐ Yes ________
	☑ No 24671
Name	The Little Ones Furniture Store
New Address	5 St. Antoine Street N. Quebec City
Old Address	305 St. Antoine Street S. Quebec City
Salesperson #	02
Requested Credit Limit	50,000
Sales Office	Eastern Canada
Pricing Code	25
Estimated Sales	300,000
Credit Limit	10,000
Currency	U.S.A. ☐, Canada ☐
Bank	Canadian Credit Bank 50 St. Antoine Street Quebec City
Bank Line	________
Rating	Satisfactory

____
Sales Manager

____
Credit Manager

Figure 11.8

Sales Order Form for Tiny Toddlers

SALES ORDER FORM

Customer: 24671 Date:
The Little Ones Furniture Store
5 St. Antoine Street N.
Quebec City

Product Code	Description	Quantity
24571	Crib	4
M0002	Mattress	102
HG730	High chair – white	32
HG223	High chair – natural wood	22
CT200	Change table	300
D0025	Desk – modern design	2
C9925	Chair – modern design	5
BP809	Bumper pads	1200

Salesperson No.:

Entered by:

REQUIRED

Evaluate the reports shown in Figs. 11.7 and 11.8 using the following format: (SMAC Examination, adapted)

Form Weakness	Explanation	Recommendation(s)

11.7 Mickie Louderman is the new assistant controller of Pickens Publishers, a growing company with sales of $35 million. She was formerly the controller of a smaller company in a similar industry, where she was in charge of accounting and data processing and had considerable influence over the entire computer center operation. Prior to Louderman's arrival at Pickens, the company revamped its entire computer operations center, placing increased emphasis on decentralized data access, microcomputers with mainframe access, and on-line systems.

John Richards, the controller of Pickens, has been with the company for 28 years and is near retirement. He has given Louderman managerial authority over both the implementation of the new system and the integration of the company's accounting-related functions. Her promotion to controller will be dependent on the success of the new AIS.

Louderman began to develop the new system by using the same design characteristics and reporting format that she had used at her former company. She sent details of the new AIS to the departments that interfaced with accounting, including inventory control, purchasing, human resources, production control, and marketing. If they did not respond with suggestions by a prescribed date, she would continue the development process. Louderman and Richards determined a new schedule for many of the reports, changing the frequency from weekly to monthly. After a meeting with the director of computer operations, she selected a programmer to help her with the details of the new reporting formats.

Most of the control features of the old system were maintained to decrease the initial installation time, while a few new ones were added for unusual situations; however, the procedures for maintaining the controls were substantially changed. Louderman appointed herself the decisive authority for all control changes and program testing that related to the AIS, including screening the control features that related to batch totals for payroll, inventory control, accounts receivable, cash deposits, and accounts payable.

As each module was completed, Louderman told the corresponding department to implement the change immediately, in order to take advantage of the labor savings. However, incomplete instructions accompanied these changes, and specific implementation responsibility was not assigned to departmental personnel. Louderman believes that operations people should "learn as they go," reporting errors as they occur.

Accounts payable and inventory control were the initial areas of the AIS to be implemented; several problems arose in both of these areas. Louderman was disturbed that the semimonthly runs of payroll, which were weekly under the old system, had abundant errors and, consequently, required numerous manual paychecks. Frequently, the control totals of a payroll run would take hours to reconcile with the computer printout. To expedite matters, Louderman authorized the payroll clerk to prepare journal entries for payroll processing.

The new inventory control system failed to improve the carrying level of many stock items, causing several critical raw material stock-outs that resulted in expensive rush orders. The primary control procedure under the new system was the availability of ordering and use information. It was available by direct-access terminals to both inventory control and purchasing personnel so that both departments could issue purchase orders on a timely basis. The inventory levels were updated daily, so the previous weekly report was discontinued by Louderman.

Because of these problems, system documentation is behind schedule, and proper backup procedures have not been implemented in many areas. Louderman has requested budget approval to hire two systems analysts, an accountant, and an administrative assistant to help her implement the new system. Richards is disturbed by her request, since her predecessor had only one part-time employee as his assistant.

REQUIRED

a. List the steps Louderman should have taken during the design of the AIS to ensure that end-user needs were satisfied.

b. Identify and describe three areas where Louderman has violated the basic principles of internal control during the implementation of the new AIS.

c. Refer to Louderman's approach to implementing the new AIS.

1. Identify and describe its weaknesses.
2. What recommendations do you have that would improve the situation and allow development to continue on the remaining areas of the AIS. (CMA Examination, adapted)

11.8 Columbia Corporation is a medium-sized, diversified manufacturing company. Ryon Pulsipher has been promoted recently to manager of the company's property accounting division. Pulsipher has had difficulty responding to requests from other departments for information about the company's fixed assets. Five of the requests and problems Pulsipher has been involved with follow:

1. The controller has requested schedules of individual fixed assets to support the balance in the general ledger. Although Pulsipher has furnished the necessary information, it has always been late. The manner in which the records are organized makes it difficult to obtain information easily.
2. The maintenance manager wishes to verify the existence of a punch press that he thinks was repaired twice. He has asked Pulsipher to confirm the asset number and location of the press.
3. The insurance department wants data on the cost and book values of assets to include in its review of current insurance coverage.
4. The tax department has requested data that can be used to determine when Columbia should switch depreciation methods for tax purposes.
5. The company's internal auditors have spent a significant amount of time in the property accounting division in a recent attempt to confirm the annual depreciation expense.

The property account records that are at Pulsipher's disposal consist of a set of manual books. These records show the date the asset was acquired, the account number to which the asset applies, the dollar amount capitalized, and the estimated useful life of the asset for depreciation purposes.

After many frustrations Pulsipher realized that his records are inadequate and that he cannot supply the data easily when they are requested. He has decided to discuss his problems with the controller, Gig Griffith.

Pulsipher: Gig, something has to give. My people are working overtime and can't keep up. You worked in property accounting before you became controller. You know that I can't tell the tax, insurance, and maintenance people everything they need to know from my records. Also, the internal auditing team is living in my area and that slows down the work pace. The requests of these people are reasonable, and we should be able to answer their questions and provide the needed data. I think we need an automated property accounting system. I would like to talk with the AIS people to see if they can help me.

Griffith: Ryon, I think you have a great idea. Just be sure you are personally involved in the design of any system so that you get all the information you need. Keep me posted on the project's progress.

REQUIRED

a. Identify and justify four major objectives Columbia Corporation's automated property accounting system should possess in order to respond to departmental requests for information.
b. Identify the data that should be included in the computer record for each asset included in the property account. (CMA Examination, adapted)

11.9 A savings and loan association has decided to develop a new AIS. The internal auditors have suggested planning the systems development process in accordance with the SDLC concept. The following nine items have been identified as major systems development activities that will have to be undertaken:

1. System test
2. User specifications
3. Conversion
4. System planning study
5. Technical specifications
6. Postimplementation planning
7. Implementation planning
8. User procedures and training
9. Programming

REQUIRED

a. Arrange the nine items in the sequence in which they should logically occur.
b. One major subactivity that will occur during system implementation is the conversion of data files from the old system to the new one. Indicate three types of documentation for a file conversion work plan that would be of particular interest to an auditor. (CMA Examination, adapted)

CASE 11.1: ANYCOMPANY, INC.—AN ONGOING COMPREHENSIVE CASE

Visit a local company and obtain permission to study its systems development approach. Once you have lined up a company, do the following:

1. With a member of the IS staff, discuss the procedures the company follows in designing and implementing AIS changes.
   a. When a decision is made to change an existing system, how does the company approach conceptual systems design? Who determines which design alternatives are selected? What are the outputs from conceptual systems design?
   b. How does the company handle the physical design procedures involved in the development of the system? If available, view any documentation or flowcharts used in the development of a prior system.
   c. What implementation strategy does the company employ? What conversion procedures does the company find most effective in making the transition from an old system to a new one?

2. Obtain the documentation manual for one of the company's software programs. Evaluate the effectiveness of the documentation and identify its strengths and weaknesses. What suggestions do you have for improvement?

3. Summarize the results of your findings in a memo report.
   a. How effective are the company's conceptual and physical design procedures?
   b. How effective are the company's implementation, conversion, operation, and maintenance procedures?
   c. What recommendations do you have for improving the company's AIS development procedures?

CASE 11.2: CITIZEN'S GAS COMPANY

Citizen's Gas Company is a medium-size gas distribution company that provides natural gas service to approximately 200,000 customers. The customer base is divided into three revenue classes. Data by customer class is as follows:

Class	Customers	Sales in Cubic Feet	Revenues
Residential	160,000	80 billion	$160 million
Commercial	38,000	15 billion	25 million
Industrial	2,000	50 billion	65 million
		145 billion	$250 million

Residential customer gas use is primarily for residential heating purposes and so is highly correlated to the weather. Commercial and industrial customers, on the other hand, may or may not use gas for heating purposes, so consumption does not necessarily depend on the weather.

The largest 25 out of the company's 2000 industrial customers account for $30 million of the industrial revenues. Each of these 25 customers uses gas for both heating and industrial purposes and has a consumption pattern governed almost entirely by business factors.

The company obtains its gas supply from ten major pipeline companies. The pipeline companies provide gas in amounts specified in contracts that extend over periods ranging from 5 to 15 years. For some contracts the supply is in equal monthly increments, whereas for others the supply varies in accordance with the heating season. Supply over and above the contract amounts is not available, and some contracts contain take-or-pay clauses—that is, the company must pay for the volumes specified in the contract, whether or not it uses that amount of gas.

To assist in matching customer demand with supply, the company maintains a gas storage field. Gas can be pumped into the storage field when supply exceeds customer demand; likewise, gas can be obtained when demand exceeds supply. There are no restrictions on the use of the gas storage field except that the field must be filled to capacity at the beginning of each gas year (September 1). Consequently, whenever the contractual supply for the remainder of the gas year is less than that required to satisfy projected demand and replenish the storage field, the company must curtail service to the industrial customers (except for quantities that are used for heating). The curtailments must be carefully controlled so that an oversupply does not occur at year-end. Similarly, care must be taken to ensure that curtailments are adequate during the year to protect against the need to curtail commercial or residential customers in order to replenish the storage field at year-end.

In recent years the company's planning efforts have not provided a firm basis for the establishment of long-term contracts. The current year has been no different. Planning efforts have not been adequate to control the supply during the current gas year. Customer demand has been projected only as a function of the total number of customers. Commercial and industrial customers' demand for gas has been curtailed. This has resulted in lost sales and caused an excess of supply at the end of the gas year.

In an attempt to correct the problems of Citizen's Gas, the president has hired a new director of corporate planning. The director has been presented with a conceptual design of a system to assist him in the analysis of the supply and demand of natural gas. The system should provide a monthly gas plan for each year for the next five years, with particular emphasis on the first year. The plan should provide a set of reports that assists in the decision-making process and that contains all necessary supporting schedules. The system must provide for the use of actual data during the course of the first year to project demand for the rest of the year and the year in total. The president has indicated to the director that he will base his decisions on the effect alternative plans have had on operating income.

1. Discuss the criteria that must be considered in specifying the basic structure and features of Citizen's Gas Company's new system to assist in planning its natural gas needs.
2. Identify the major data items that should be incorporated into Citizen's Gas Company's new system to provide adequate planning capability. For each item identified, explain why the data item is important and describe the level of detail that would be necessary for the data to be useful. (CMA Examination, adapted)

ANSWERS TO CHAPTER QUIZ

1. b	**3.** d	**5.** d	**7.** b	**9.** a
2. e	**4.** a	**6.** c	**8.** c	**10.** a, c, d

Chapter 12

Systems Acquisition, Outsourcing, and Prototyping

LEARNING OBJECTIVES

After studying the chapter, you should be able to:

- Describe how organizations acquire application software, vendor services, and hardware.
- Explain why organizations outsource their information systems, and evaluate the benefits and risks of this strategy.
- Describe how prototypes are used to develop an AIS, and discuss the advantages and disadvantages of doing so.

Integrative Case: Shoppers Mart

Several months after the new AIS for Shoppers Mart was completed, Ann Christy was summoned to the office of Scott Miles, the president of Shoppers Mart. Scott informed Ann that Shoppers Mart was acquiring Home Improvement Center (HIC), a chain of home improvement stores. HIC, once a market leader, had fallen on hard times and could be acquired at a good price.

The board of directors feels there are two reasons for HIC's problems. First, it grew faster and larger than the company could manage and is overstaffed and inefficiently operated. Once HIC is acquired, the board will close unprofitable stores, reduce staff, and dramatically improve operational efficiency. Second, HIC's computer system does not provide the information needed to judge customer demands or respond quickly when customer preferences change. The board wants to develop an AIS that captures and anticipates customer tastes and preferences so that HIC can respond to changes more rapidly than its competitors. The board wants to use the expertise of Ann and her staff to design a new AIS for HIC. Speed is important, because competition in the home improvement market is intensifying and the window of opportunity to increase market share is closing fast.

Ann accepts the challenge but is concerned about developing a quality AIS on such a tight deadline. She decides to explore three ways to speed up or replace the traditional development process: purchasing software, outsourcing the system, or using prototyping. She has the following questions about these approaches:

1. Can she buy the needed software from an outside vendor? If not, can development time be reduced by adapting Shoppers Mart software?

2. Can she hire an outside company to process HIC's nonstrategic data so her staff could concentrate on systems that provide a competitive advantage?
3. Can her staff quickly put together a prototype, or working model, of the new AIS that users can evaluate as a way of speeding up the traditional development process?

INTRODUCTION

Traditionally, accountants have experienced a number of difficulties in developing an AIS:

- Demands for development resources are so numerous that AIS projects can be backlogged for several years.
- The newly designed AIS does not always meet user needs. The problem is often not discovered until after a lengthy development process. Only when AIS users begin to use the final product do they realize it is inadequate. This happens even when users are involved in the design and approval process. One reason for this problem is the inability of users to visualize how the AIS will look or how it will operate strictly by reviewing design documentation. In addition, systems developers do not understand the company's business needs and as a result are unable to grasp user needs or make meaningful suggestions for improvement.
- The development process can take so long that the system no longer meets company needs. For example, Fannie Mae spent eight years and $100 million developing the largest loan-accounting system in the world. Unfortunately, when it was finally completed it no longer met most of Fannie Mae's business needs.
- Users are unable to specify their needs adequately. Often they do not know exactly what they need; and when they do, they sometimes cannot communicate these ideas to systems developers.
- Changes to the AIS cannot be made after requirements have been "frozen." If users were able to keep changing the requirements, the AIS would never be finished, and costs would skyrocket each time the AIS was reworked.

In today's fast-changing world many accountants and AIS developers find themselves in Ann Christy's position. They must meet user information needs quickly and efficiently. In this chapter you will learn about three ways to accomplish this goal: purchasing prewritten software, hiring an outside company (outsourcing) to operate the system, and prototyping.

SYSTEMS ACQUISITION

AIS software can be developed internally, bought as a prewritten (or "canned") package, or purchased and modified. The advantages and disadvantages of each approach are discussed in this section and summarized in Table 12.1.

Custom Software

In the past most organizations developed **custom software** because prewritten software that fit their specific needs was not available. Despite the availability of many good prewritten packages today, many organizations still develop

Table 12.1 **Advantages and Disadvantages of Custom, Canned, and Modified Software**

	Advantages	Disadvantages
Custom Software Approach	Programs can be tailored to exact needs. There are no limitations, as with canned programs. Software is better integrated with current programs. The program development process can be managed and controlled. Employees have greater loyalty to systems they help develop. A competitive advantage is possible by building a unique AIS.	This approach is costly and labor intensive. It may take months, or years, to develop. Most new programs contain bugs. It is is hard for users to specify needs and for developers to understand them. Significant management time and stringent controls are required. Programming, development, and documentation standards must be developed. Employee concerns: availability, salary, promotion, supervision. The development process is frustrating: analyze needs, develop system, revise, test, debug, revise, etc. Most companies lack experienced in-house staff.
Canned Software Approach	These highly specialized packages are difficult or expensive to duplicate. Minimal downtime results, since software is ready to run. Users can "test drive" software, or talk to other users to reduce risk. Users can select package that best meets their needs. These high-quality programs are more likely to be bug-free. Updates are inexpensive. This is the least costly approach. Better user documentation.	Canned software may not fit company needs. Changes to use software may not be in the company's best interests. The software is not as efficient as custom or modified software. In-house expertise is not available to solve software problems. The developer may go out of business or cease to maintain and update software. Software evaluation is time-consuming and costly.
Modified Software Approach	There are no limitations, as with canned programs. Company needs are better met than with canned software. This approach is less costly and time-consuming than the custom program approach. It can achieve best mix of custom and canned benefits.	Modification is difficult; it may introduce errors, control problems. Documentation of changes may be nonexistent or incomplete. Significant modifications can cost as much as a custom program. The vendor may not allow the program to be modified. Unauthorized modification is not supported or updated.

their own software because their requirements are unique or their size and complexity necessitate a custom package.

Developing custom software is difficult and error-prone and consumes a great deal of time and resources. After end users define their requirements, analysts work with them to determine the format of paper and screen outputs. The analysts then identify the data required for each input and the data to be retained in the files. Analysts also develop detailed program specifications to be interpreted and coded by a programmer. Because of the many and varied development tasks, the process requires a significant amount of discipline and management supervision. Management accountants are heavily involved in developing custom AIS software, either as project supervisors, users, or members of the development team.

Custom software is usually developed and written in-house. Alternatively, organizations may engage an outside company, such as Andersen Consulting or EDS, to develop a package or assemble it from their inventory of program modules. These modules are adapted, combined, and organized to form a customized product that meets a company's specific requirements. When contracting with an outside organization, a company should maintain control over the development process. The following guidelines are recommended:

- *Carefully select a developer.* The outside developer should have experience in the company's industry, have a good understanding of business in general, and have an in-depth understanding of how the company conducts its business.
- *Sign a contract.* The contract should place responsibility for meeting the company's requirements on the developer and allow the company to discontinue the project if certain conditions are not met.
- *Plan and monitor each step.* All aspects of the project should be designed in detail, and there should be frequent checkpoints for monitoring the project.
- *Maintain effective communication.* The relationship between the company and the developer should be rigorously defined: frequent communication should be expected.
- *Control all costs.* Costs should be tightly controlled and cash outflows minimized until the project has been completed and accepted.

Canned Software

One of the most popular alternatives to developing AIS software in-house is to purchase software. Many software developers specialize in a particular industry. For example, a number of systems are geared to doctors, dentists, and others in the medical fields; others to automobile repair and service, full-service restaurants, fast-food outlets, video rentals, and other retail stores.

Written by computer manufacturers or software development companies, **canned software** is sold on the open market to a broad range of users with similar requirements. Some developers combine their software with hardware and sell them as a package, called a **turnkey system** because the vendor installs the entire system and the user need only "turn on the key." Because of their advantages (see Table 12.1), an estimated 80% of companies currently installing computers are either using or considering canned software packages.

By the year 2000 it is likely that application systems will be developed in-house only by very large organizations or companies with unique requirements. However, even today many large organizations purchase software from outside suppliers. For example, Pacific Gas & Electric Company signed a $750,000 contract that calls for the license and installation of

Dun & Bradstreet's General Ledger software to replace the in-house-developed general ledger system. Lockheed Aeromod Center, an aircraft maintenance services company, also signed a $1-million contract to acquire the Dun & Bradstreet General Ledger system and related professional services. The software will be used to track direct and indirect expenses and determine project-specific revenue figures. A recent Deloitte & Touche survey found that most chief information officers expect to replace their current systems with commercially available packages rather than custom-developed systems.

Companies that buy rather than develop AIS software still go through the SDLC process:

- *Systems analysis.* Companies must conduct an initial investigation, system survey, and feasibility study. They must also determine AIS requirements.
- *Conceptual systems design.* An important part of conceptual design is determining whether software that meets AIS requirements is already available. If it is, a make-or-buy decision must be made.
- *Physical design.* If software is purchased, some of the physical design phase, such as designing and coding the program, can be omitted. However, it may be necessary to modify the purchased software to better meet company needs. Even when software is purchased, companies still have to design output, input, and files as well as design procedures and controls.
- *Implementation and conversion.* Companies must plan implementation and conversion activities, select and train personnel, install and test the hardware and software, document their procedures, and convert from the old to the new AIS. However, they do not have to develop and test software modules or document the computer program.
- *Operation and maintenance.* The AIS has to be operated just like any other software. The software is maintained by the vendor.

Modified Canned Software

The best of both worlds can sometimes be achieved with **modified canned software.** Changes to canned packages can be made by the software vendors or internal programmers in order to meet the specific requirements of users. For example, about 90% of Dow Chemical's software are canned packages that have been modified to match their businesses processes; the rest is custom software written in-house. However, any modifications not authorized by the vendor will not be supported and may make the program unreliable and unstable.

Which Approach Is Best?

As a general rule, canned software is best when a package adequately meets an organization's needs or when a company can adapt its requirements to the package's capabilities. As the size and complexity of the AIS or its requirements increase, there is less likelihood that the company will find canned software that meets, or can be adapted to meet, its needs. Many systems experts believe that a company should not write custom software unless experienced, in-house programming personnel are available and the job can be done less expensively on the inside. Arthur D. Little and other consulting firms tell clients to develop custom software only if it provides a significant competitive advantage. For example, there is usually no measurable benefit to having a custom-written payroll or accounts receivable system. On the other hand, there may be significant benefits to sophisticated, just-in-time inventory management or product manufacturing software. If a software application will not provide a competitive advantage, Little advises its clients to buy software from an outside supplier.

In the final analysis, an organization has to look at its specific needs, investigate available software, analyze the pros and cons of each approach, and decide what is best. Gillette used to develop its own software but recently decided to move from proprietary systems to off-the-shelf software wherever possible. Its rationale is that the firm gains a greater competitive advantage from deciding *how* software should be used than from determining *what* software should be used and then creating it. If the canned software does not meet all of Gillette's needs, it is modified using high-level development tools. Pepsi Cola has moved in the opposite direction. It used to buy most of its mainframe software but, after moving to a client/server architecture, it could not find software sophisticated enough to meet its needs. Although Pepsi still buys software when it can find it, it has had to create most of its newly installed software.

The decision to make or purchase software can be made independently of the decision to acquire hardware, service, maintenance, and other AIS resources. Likewise, these resources can be purchased independently of the software, although the hardware and vendor decisions are often dependent upon the software decision. The flowchart in Fig. 12.1 summarizes the process of acquiring software, hardware, and vendor services.

Selecting a Vendor

The computer industry is replete with vendor types. They can be found by looking in the phone book, obtaining referrals, scanning computer or trade magazines, attending conferences, or using search organizations. An organization considering computer acquisition should evaluate the services of many types of vendors, such as turnkey suppliers or peripheral equipment manufacturers.

A number of organizations evaluate hardware and software products in addition to vendors. Some—for example, Datapro, Computerworld Buyers Guide, and Auerbach—offer subscription services for an annual fee. Monthly magazines such as *PC World* and *PC Magazine* and weekly newspapers such as *InfoWorld* and *PC Week* also evaluate computer products and services and publish the results.

The computer industry is very competitive. Many hardware and software vendors have flourished for a while and then gone out of business. For example, Ashton-Tate was once the supplier of the best-selling data base package, until product development problems and economic hardships forced the firm to sell out to Borland. Osborne Computers produced the first portable PC, but it, too, went out of business. Additionally, many companies offer computer services but have little experience or capital. When vendors go out of business, they often leave the companies that use their products high and dry. As a result, it is important to be very selective when choosing a vendor.

Acquiring Hardware and Software

Once AIS requirements have been defined, an organization is ready to purchase software and hardware. Companies requiring only a PC, a word processor, and a spreadsheet can usually complete their own research and make a selection. Companies buying large and complex systems, however, send

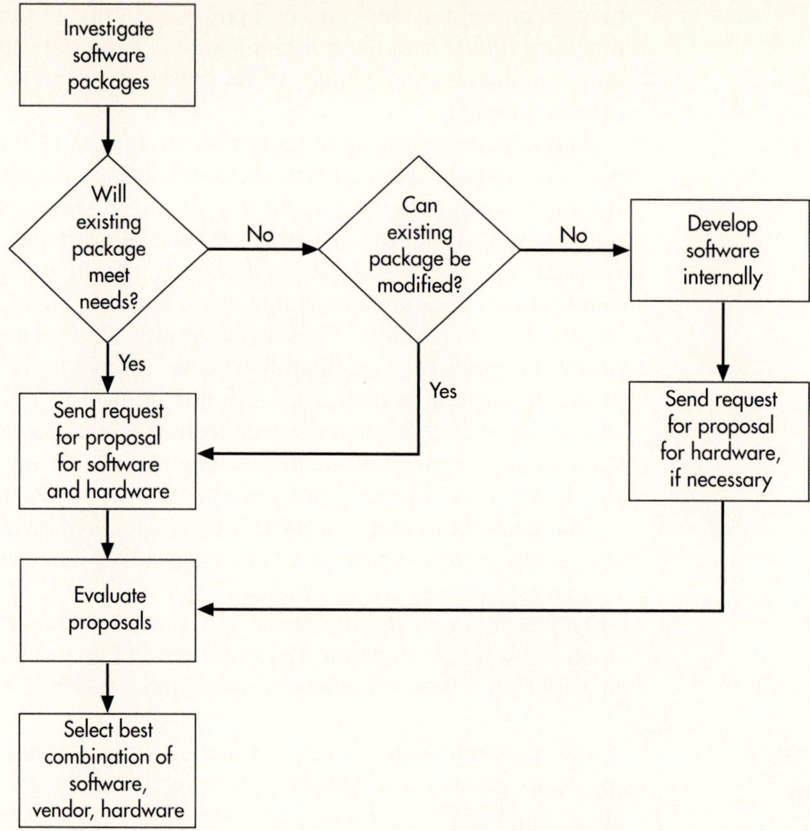

Figure 12.1

Systems Acquisition Process

vendors a **request for a proposal (RFP),** an invitation to propose a system by a specified date. Each proposal is evaluated, with the best systems investigated in-depth to verify that company requirements can be met. A formal approach to acquiring system resources, such as an RFP, is important for the following reasons:

1. *Saves time.* The same information is provided to all vendors, eliminating repetitive interviews and questions.
2. *Simplifies the decision-making process.* All responses are written in the same format and based on the same information.
3. *Reduces errors.* The chances of overlooking important factors are reduced.
4. *Avoids potential for disagreement.* Both parties possess the same expectations and all pertinent information is captured in writing.

When an RFP is solicited based on exact hardware and software specifications, total costs are usually lower and less time is required for vendor preparation and company evaluation. However, this RFP does not permit the vendor to recommend alternative technology. In contrast, a generalized RFP contains a problem definition and requests a system that meets specific performance objectives and requirements. This RFP allows the requesting company to leave the technical issues to the vendor. Disadvantages include a greater difficulty in evaluating proposals and the potential for more costly bids.

Generally speaking, the more information a company provides to a vendor, the better the chances of receiving a system that meets its requirements. Vendors need detailed specifications for the new AIS, including the required applications, inputs and outputs, files and data bases, frequency and methods of file updating and inquiry, and unique characteristics or requirements. It is also essential to distinguish between mandatory and desirable requirements.

Evaluating Proposals and Selecting a System

Vendor proposals should be evaluated as they are received. Proposals that are missing key requested information, fail to meet certain minimum requirements, or are ambiguous should be eliminated. The proposals that pass this preliminary screening should be carefully compared against the proposed AIS requirements to determine (1) whether they meet all mandatory requirements and (2) how many of the desirable requirements they do indeed meet. The top one or two vendors should be invited to demonstrate their system using company-supplied data to measure the system's performance and validate the vendor's claims. If the AIS cannot handle the company's data, the system should be eliminated from consideration and another selected. Table 12.2 presents a list of criteria that can be used to evaluate hardware, software, and vendors.

One way to compare system performance is to use a **benchmark problem**—a data processing task with input, processing, and output jobs typical of those the new AIS will be required to perform. Processing times are calculated and compared; the AIS with the lowest time is judged the most efficient.

Another approach is **point scoring.** The point-scoring approach Ann and her team used at HIC is shown in Table 12.3. For each criterion, Ann assigned a weighting factor based on its relative importance. Then each vendor was assigned a score for each criterion based on how well its proposal measured up to the standard. The total of the weighted scores gave Ann a basis for comparing and contrasting the various systems. Based on the point-scoring approach in this example, vendor 3 offers the best AIS. Its system scored 190 points more than vendor 2, the second place candidate.

Point scoring focuses on key selection factors by converting them into a common unit, a weighted score. The outcome should not be overemphasized, however, because point scoring does not recognize that these factors can interact in ways not taken into account. Nor does it evaluate the effects of a particular weakness on other factors or assess compensating strengths. In addition, since both the weights and the points are assigned subjectively, the margin for error is sizable.

Requirements costing estimates the cost of purchasing or developing features that are not present in a particular AIS. The total cost for each AIS is computed by adding the acquisition cost and the purchasing or developing costs. The resulting sums represent the costs of systems with all required features and provides an equitable basis for comparison.

Neither point scoring nor requirements costing is totally objective. Point scoring does not incorporate dollar estimates of costs and benefits. Requirements costing partially overcomes this problem, but it overlooks intangible factors such as reliability and vendor support. In any event, the final choice

Table 12.2 **Hardware, Software, and Vendor Evaluation Criteria**

Hardware Evaluation	Is the cost of the hardware reasonable based on its capabilities and features? Can the hardware run the desired software? Are the CPU's processing speed and capabilities adequate for the intended use? Are the secondary storage capabilities adequate? Are the input and output speeds and capabilities adequate? Does the system have adequate communication capabilities? Is the system expandable? Is the hardware based on the most recent technology, or on technology that is old or soon to be out of date? Is the hardware available now? If not, when? Is the system under consideration compatible with existing hardware, software, and peripherals? How do evaluations of the system's performance compare to those of its competitors? What is the availability and cost of support and maintenance? What guarantees and warranties come with the system? Are financing arrangements available? (if applicable)
Software Evaluation	Does the package meet all mandatory specifications? How well does the package meet desirable specifications? Will program modifications be required to meet company needs? Does the software contain adequate controls? Is the performance (speed, accuracy, reliability, etc.) adequate? How many other companies use the software? Are other users satisfied with the package? Is the package well documented? Is the software compatible with existing corporate software? Is the software user-friendly? Can the software be demonstrated and test driven? Does it have an adequate warranty? Is is flexible and easily maintained? Is on-line inquiry of files and records possible? Will the vendor keep the package up to date?
Vendor Evaluation	How long has the vendor been in business? How large is the vendor? Is the vendor financially stable and secure? How much experience does the vendor have with a product? How well does the vendor stand behind its products? How good is its guarantee? Does the vendor regularly update its products? Does the vendor have financing? Will the vendor put promises in a contract? Will the vendor supply a list of customers as references? Does the vendor have a reputation for reliability and dependability? Does the vendor provide hardware and software support and maintenance? Does the vendor provide implementation and installation support? Does the vendor have high-quality, responsive, and experienced personnel? Does the vendor provide training? How responsive and timely is vendor support?

Table 12.3 **Home Improvement Center: Point Scoring Evaluation of Vendor Proposals**

		Vendor 1		Vendor 2		Vendor 3	
Criterion	**Weight**	**Score**	**Weighted Score**	**Score**	**Weighted Score**	**Score**	**Weighted Score**
Hardware compatibility	60	6	360	7	420	8	480
Hardware speed	30	6	180	10	300	5	150
Memory expansion	60	5	300	7	420	8	480
Hardware current	30	9	270	9	270	6	180
Software compatibility	90	7	630	7	630	9	810
On-line inquiry capabilities	40	9	360	10	400	8	320
Controls	50	7	350	6	300	9	450
Positive references	40	10	400	8	320	6	240
Documentation	30	9	270	8	240	7	210
Easily maintained; updated regularly	50	7	350	8	400	9	450
LAN and WAN capabilities	50	8	400	7	350	8	400
Vendor support	70	6	420	9	630	10	700
Totals	600		4,290		4,680		4,870

among vendor proposals is not likely to be a clear-cut decision, because it must rely to some extent on subjective factors and cost considerations.

Once the best AIS has been selected, the software should be thoroughly test-driven, other users contacted, vendor personnel evaluated, and proposal details confirmed. In essence, the company wants to verify that the AIS that appears to be the best on paper actually is the best in practice. The lessons that Geophysical Systems Corporation learned from its vendor selection process highlights the importance of a thorough vendor evaluation (see Focus 12.1). When the best system has been identified, the contract can be negotiated, financing arranged, and the system acquired.

Financing Systems Acquisition

Once an AIS has been selected, it must be purchased, rented, or leased. Rental payments are higher than lease payments because a rental contract can be terminated with a few months' notice, whereas a lease can run from two to ten years. Lease contracts usually allow the user to purchase the AIS at a specified price at the conclusion of the lease term. Both plans provide for manufacturer-maintained equipment and include the charge for this service in the monthly payment. Maintenance for purchased equipment is handled by a separate contract payable on a monthly basis. The advantages and disadvantages of these three approaches are listed in Table 12.4. (p. 403)

It used to be that companies assumed that a new computer system was a necessity, so its expected return on investment was not scrutinized as closely as other capital investments. This is no longer the case. In recent years an AIS has

FOCUS 12.1

A Software Purchase That Went Awry

Geophysical Systems Corporation (GSC), which specializes in developing drilling equipment, developed a device that uses sonar to analyze the production potential of oil and gas discoveries. The company needed a software program to analyze the data generated by its sonar device. GSC hired Seismograph Service Corporation and paid it $20 million to write the computer system. To its dismay, Geophysical found that the Seismograph system could not accurately process the massive volume of data and perform the complex computations needed. When this failing became apparent, Geophysical's clients canceled their contracts. As a result, the company went from yearly sales of $40 million and profits of $6 million to filing for bankruptcy two years later.

Geophysical sued Seismograph, claiming that the supplier's system failed to perform as promised. In addition, it claimed that Seismograph knew the system would not be able to perform as desired before it began the development project. The jury agreed, awarding Geophysical over $48 million as compensation for lost profits and the cost of the computer system. (Seismograph has appealed on the basis that its system did work and that Geophysical's sales decline resulted from a slump in oil prices.)

Geophysical's experience is not uncommon; there are many systems development projects that do not produce the intended results.

Focus Questions

1. How could GSC have avoided the problems with the failed software?
2. What factors should companies consider when evaluating software vendors?

had to compete with other acquisitions for scarce financial resources. If a proposed AIS does not provide a greater return than other investments, it does not get funded. That is one reason organizations have begun to hire outside companies to operate their AIS and process their data.

OUTSOURCING

Another way to acquire an information system is to outsource. **Outsourcing** is the practice of hiring an outside company to handle all or part of an organization's data processing activities. In a mainframe outsourcing agreement, the outsourcers buy their client's computers and hire all or most of the client's employees. They then operate and manage the entire system on the client's site, or they migrate the system to the outsourcer's computers. For example, natural gas producer Enron signed a $750-million agreement with EDS to outsource its entire information system. EDS bought Enron's computers, software, and transmission network. It also hired all 550 of Enron's information systems staff at comparable wages and benefits. Most mainframe outsourcing contracts are for ten years or more and cost from hundreds of thousands to millions of dollars a year. Enron pays EDS a fixed annual fee, plus additional fees based on processing volume. During the 10-year life of the contract Enron expects to save $200 million, which is almost 25% of its computing costs.

In a client/server or a desktop outsourcing agreement, an organization outsources a particular service, a segment of its business, a particular function, or PC support. For example, Taco Bell has outsourced its PC help desk services to Coopers & Lybrand. Royal Dutch Shell, the international oil company, has 80,000 PCs worldwide, for which most of the installation, maintenance, train-

Table 12.4 **Advantages and Disadvantages of Purchasing, Leasing, and Renting an AIS**

	Advantages	Disadvantages
Purchasing	The cumulative cash outflow is the lowest. The computer often has residual value at disposal date. There are ownership advantages, such as total user control. The computer can be sold at any time.	Purchase costs tie up company capital. Ownership has risks and responsibilities. Equipment can become obsolete or be outgrown. Maintenance service charges are extra. There are expenses such as taxes and insurance.
Leasing	There are no upfront cost to purchase. It is less expensive than renting. There is no risk of technological obsolescence. An option to purchase equipment is available. It is more flexible than purchasing.	Longer time commitment is involved than with renting. There is no ownership interest. The cumulative cash outflow is higher than with purchasing. It is less flexible than renting. A fee is required if the lease is terminated early.
Renting	There is no purchase cost or long-term investment. There is no risk of obsolescence. It minimizes risks; it is especially good for inexperienced buyers. Maintenance charges are included in the rent. It is more flexible than leasing or purchasing.	The cumulative cash outflow is highest. There is no ownership interest. Extra charges are incurred if the computer is used more than a predetermined number of hours.

ing, help desk, and technical support are outsourced. Outsourcing is not unusual, as surveys have found that most *Fortune* 2000 companies outsource anywhere from 10% to 80% of their PC support functions.

Client/server outsourcing gives a company a very active management role over the system and the IS function. The IS department is retained and is responsible for the hardware, while the outsourcer focuses on end-user support and training. The outsourcer also refreshes the technology at regular intervals to ensure that the hardware and software remain current. Client/server outsourcing agreements rarely last for more than five years.

The Growth in Outsourcing Applications

Outsourcing was initially used for standardized applications such as payroll, accounting, and purchasing or by companies that were struggling to survive and wanted a quick infusion of cash from selling their hardware. However, in 1989 Eastman Kodak surprised the business world by hiring three different companies to operate its computer systems. Kodak outsourced its data processing operations and sold its mainframes to IBM. It also outsourced its telecommunications functions to DEC and its PC operations to Businessland (and later Entek Information Services). When the performance of DEC and Entek began to slip in 1994, Kodak opened those services to new bids. Kodak continues to perform its own information systems strategic planning and systems development, but system implementation and operation are the responsibility of the three outsourcers. The results have been dramatic. Capital expenditures for computers fell 90% while operating expenses decreased between 10% and 20%. Kodak expects the annual information systems savings to reach approximately $130 million over the 10-year period of the agreement.

In 1994 Xerox signed what was then the largest outsourcing deal in history: a $3.2-billion, 10-year contract with EDS to outsource its computing, telecommunications, and software management in 19 countries. The company moved to outsourcing to cut costs, to speed up the move from a mainframe architecture to client/server computing, and to free management to focus on strategic management issues rather than on day-to-day concerns. However, Xerox did retain control over its IS functions, such as IS strategic planning and new application development, in order to support its reengineering efforts.

The decisions by Kodak and Xerox have motivated other organizations to consider outsourcing their information systems. For example, 10 of the top 25 *Fortune* 500 companies outsource some or all of their information systems. AIS consultants estimate that half their clients are interested in investigating outsourcing for all or part of their information systems operations. The president of IBM's outsourcing subsidiary stated that IBM expects outsourcing to grow faster than any other part of the data processing industry.

The largest outsourcers in the world, sometimes referred to as the Big Five, have captured roughly 50% of the worldwide outsourcing market. The Big Five are EDS, IBM, Andersen Consulting, Digital Equipment, and Computer Sciences Corporation. Most major computer manufacturers, computer consultants, and accounting firms also provide outsourcing services to clients.

The Benefits of Outsourcing

You've already seen two successful examples of outsourcing. This section discusses the benefits of outsourcing in depth. The disadvantages of outsourcing will be discussed in the next section.

A Business Solution. Outsourcing is a plausible business solution, rather than just an IS solution. Kodak and Enron believe outsourcing is a viable approach, strategically and economically, because it allows them to concentrate on their core competencies. Kodak believes in focusing its efforts on what it does best—selling film and cameras—and leaving data processing to more qualified computer companies. Kodak treats outsourcers as partners and works closely with them to meet their strategic and operational data processing objectives.

Some organizations, because they are reluctant to outsource their entire information system, downsize them to core activities and outsource the nonessential and maintenance activities. For example, Copperweld Corporation, a tube maker in Pittsburgh, turned over its routine data processing to Genis Enterprises. Outsourcing reduced its information systems budget from $9 million to $4 million and its staff from 100 to 20. The remaining 20 employees were then free to concentrate on developing strategic information systems that will provide the firm with a competitive advantage.

Asset Utilization. Many organizations have millions of dollars tied up in information technology. They can improve their cash position by selling those assets to an outsourcer, thereby reducing their annual expenses. For example, when General Dynamics outsourced its information systems, it sold its data centers and other facilities to Computer Sciences Corporation for $200 million. In addition, with technology changing so rapidly, the AIS function can drain a company's cash reserves as it tries to keep up with the latest advancements. To stem this cash flow, some companies choose outsourcing. For example, Health Dimensions, a hospital management company, outsourced the data processing functions of its four hospitals so it could use its limited monetary resources for revenue-generating purchases.

Access to Greater Expertise and More Advanced Technology. As systems technology becomes more complex and confusing, businesses are seeking the expertise and special services provided by outsourcers. Many companies cannot afford to retain a staff to manage and develop the increasingly complex networks required in today's businesses. Business changes, such as downsizing and reorganization, as well as growth, also lead companies to outsource. Continental Bank and Del Monte Foods turned to outsourcing because the cost and time involved in staying at the cutting edge of technology were rising significantly. Washington Water Power Company began outsourcing when the prospect of upgrading and replacing its obsolete computer system seemed too daunting a task.

Lower Costs. Outsourcing is cost-effective for many firms, especially those utilizing their AIS resources inefficiently. Outsourcers can pass along some of the savings achieved from standardizing users' applications, buying hardware at bulk prices, splitting development and maintenance costs between projects, and operating at higher volumes. Companies that outsource save on average 15%–30% of their AIS costs. For example, Continental Bank will save $100 million (20% of information technology costs) during the life of its 10-year contract. However, many companies, such as Occidental Petroleum and USX, have rejected outsourcing as costing more than internal AIS development and operation.

Improved Development Time. When development projects are outsourced, a company may benefit from the skills of experienced industry specialists who can develop and implement a system faster and more efficiently than can its in-house staff. Outsourcers can also help a company cut through much of the internal politics surrounding systems development.

Elimination of Use Peaks and Valleys. Many companies have seasonal businesses that require heavy computer power during the peak periods but very little the remainder of the year. These heavy fixed costs can erode company profits. For example, from January to March, W. Atlee Burpee & Company processes mail-order and wholesale requests for its seeds and gardening products. During this period its IBM mainframe operates at 80% capacity; it functions at 20% the rest of the time. Yet, the company previously incurred the same monthly leasing cost for the busy months as for the lean ones. In addition, it paid the salary of five operators and managers for the whole year, even though they were underutilized most of the time. Burpee turned to outsourcing and now pays Computer Sciences Corporation according to how much the system is used. In doing so, Burpee cut its processing costs in half.

Facilitation of Downsizing. Companies that downsize are often left with an unnecessarily large AIS function. General Dynamics downsized dramatically in the early 1990s due to reduced spending in the defense industry. When cutting a thousand IS jobs did nothing to alleviate its system problems, the company decided to outsource. General Dynamics sold all of its data centers to Computer Sciences Corporation (CSC) for $200 million and transferred 2600 employees to CSC. It signed a $3-billion, 10-year outsourcing contract even though its IS function was rated number one in the aerospace industry in 1989 and 1990.

The Risks of Outsourcing

Companies that outsource often experience one or more of the following drawbacks.

Inflexibility. Most outsourcing contracts are signed for 10 years. If problems arise during this time, if the company is dissatisfied, or if the company goes through extensive structural changes, the contract is difficult to break. In such cases companies may find themselves in the equivalent of a technological strait-jacket. For example, before they merged Integra Financial Corp. and Equimark Corp., two banking organizations, had outsourcing contracts with different outsourcers. After the merger one of the contracts had to be eliminated at a cost of $4.5 million.

In addition, outsourcing contracts sometimes contain vague language regarding dispute resolution. An outsourcing agreement should clearly define both partners' requirements, specify how disagreements are to be resolved, allow the contract to be broken if certain conditions are not met, and tie cost increases to improved company performance. The latter provision often instills in the outsourcer additional incentive and motivation.

Loss of Control. A company that outsources a significant portion of its AIS runs the risk of losing control of its system and its data. In addition, when an external party processes its business data, the company is exposed to possible abuse. An outsourcer that handles the systems for rival companies, for example, has the potential to share confidential data, unintentionally or intentionally. For that reason, Ford's outsourcing agreement with Computer Sciences Corporation excludes CSC from taking on other automobile manufacturers as clients.

Reduced Competitive Advantage. Over the long run a company can lose a fundamental understanding of its own AIS needs and how the system can provide it with competitive advantages. A system that does not evolve and improve cannot add value and help achieve corporate objectives. In addition, outsourcers cannot be expected to be as motivated as their clients in trying to meet a particular industry's competitive challenges.

Locked-In System. Once a company outsources its entire AIS and sells its data processing centers, it is very expensive and difficult to reverse the process. If the company is unable to buy back the data processing facilities, it will have to buy new buildings and equipment as well as hire a new data processing staff, often at prohibitive costs. For example, Blue Shield of California decided that the performance of its outsourcer, EDS, was so poor that it would end their agreement. However, when Blue Cross started to initiate the change, it realized it knew virtually nothing about its AIS and ultimately could not afford to discharge EDS.

Unfulfilled Goals. Outsourcing in itself does not guarantee that a company's goals or expectations will be achieved. For example, if an outsourcer hires a company's employees without assigning additional staff to help operate or improve the system, the company does not have access to additional expertise. Moreover, if an outsourcer knows little about how the company or their industry operates, such inexperience can prove costly. Critics of outsourcing point out that many outsourcing benefits are never realized. At least one study has shown that some alleged benefits, such as increased efficiency, are a myth. USF&G Corporation, an insurance company, canceled its $100-million contract with Cigna Information Services and brought its system back in-house after just 18 months. USF&G stated that Cigna was unable to implement the changes needed to make the system work properly. Texas State Bank sued EDS for $300 million for lost business opportunities resulting from faulty computer operations.

PROTOTYPING

Prototyping is an approach to systems design in which a simplified working model, or **prototype,** of an information system is developed. This scaled-down, experimental "first draft" is quickly and inexpensively built and provided to users for testing. Experimenting with the prototype allows users to determine what they like and don't like about the system. Based upon their reactions and feedback, the developers modify the system and again present it to the users. This iterative process of trial usage and modification continues until the users are satisfied that the system adequately meets their needs.

The basic premise of prototyping is that it is easier for people to express what they like or dislike about an existing system (the prototype) than to imagine what they would like in a system. In other words, if users can try out an actual application, they can provide feedback as to what they do and do not like about it. Even a simple system that is not fully functional demonstrates features far better than diagrams, drawings, verbal explanations, or volumes of documentation.

UNUM Life Insurance, the world's largest disability insurance carrier, used prototyping to show how a new system using image processing would work. UNUM realized that the systems it developed in the 1970s and 1980s merely automated its manual and paper processes. The company wanted to use new technologies, such as image processing, to link its system with all external and internal systems and their users. However, top management had a hard time getting middle managers to envision how they wanted to use image processing and to understand the issues involved in the change. After viewing a prototype, the managers caught on to the possibilities and issues associated with image processing. Up until that point, all image processing meant to these managers was replacing file cabinets; only after viewing the prototype did they realize its business potential.

Steps in Developing a Prototype

As shown in Fig. 12.2, four steps are involved in developing a prototype. The first step is to identify basic system requirements by meeting with the user to agree on the size and scope of the system and to decide what the system should include and exclude. The developer and user also determine decision-making and transaction processing outputs, as well as the inputs and data needed to produce these outputs. The emphasis is on *what* output should be produced rather than *how* it should be produced. The developer must ensure that user expectations are realistic and that the user's basic information requirements can be met. The designer uses the information requirements to develop cost, time, and feasibility estimates for alternative AIS solutions. Because only general requirements are identified, determining requirements for the prototype is less formal and time-consuming than in the traditional SDLC approach.

Figure 12.2

Steps to Developing a System from a Prototype

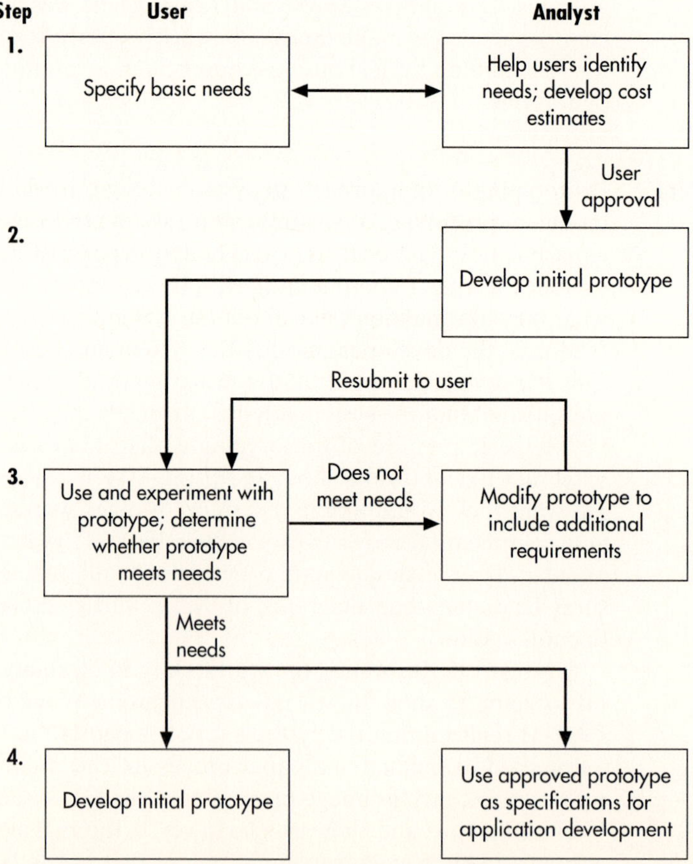

Detailed system requirements are developed by users as they interact with the prototype.

In the second step the analyst develops an initial prototype that meets the agreed-upon requirements. In prototyping, the emphasis is on speed and low cost rather than efficiency of operation. The goal is to implement the prototype within a short time period, perhaps days or weeks. Because of these time limitations, some aspects of the system are sacrificed in the interests of simplicity, flexibility, and ease of use. Therefore, nonessential functions, system controls, exception handling, validation of input data, processing speed, and efficiency considerations are often ignored at this point. It is crucial, however, that users see and use tentative versions of data entry display screens, menus, input prompts, and source documents. They must also respond to prompts, query the system, judge response times, and issue commands.

A number of tools help designers develop prototypes. These tools are efficient, are easy to use, and can create files, screens, reports, and program code much faster and with much less effort than conventional programming languages. They include fourth-generation languages, CASE tools, data bases, high-level query languages, generalized report writers, and various application software packages.

When the prototype is finished, the developer returns to the user and demonstrates the system. The user is instructed to experiment with the system and comment on what he or she does and doesn't like about its content and performance. The results are communicated to the developer, who implements the changes.

The third step is an iterative process in which users identify changes, developers make changes, and the system is again turned over to the user for evaluation and experimental use. This iterative process continues until the users are satisfied with the system. A typical prototype will go through four to six iterations.

The fourth step is to use the system approved by the users. As shown in Fig. 12.2 an approved prototype is typically used in one of two ways. Half of all prototypes are turned into fully functional systems referred to as **operational prototypes.** To make the prototype operational, the developer must incorporate needed controls, improve operational efficiency, provide backup and recovery, and integrate the prototype with the systems with which it interfaces. Changes may be necessary in order to allow the program to accept real input, access real data files, process data, make the necessary computations and calculations, and produce real output.

In many instances it is not practical to modify the prototype to make it a fully functional system. These **nonoperational** or **throwaway prototypes** can be used in several ways. The prototype may be discarded, and the system requirements identified during the prototyping process can be used to develop a new system. The system development life cycle is followed to develop the system, with the prototype as the model for development. The prototype can also be used as the initial prototype for an expanded system designed to meet the needs of many different users. Finally, if the user and the developer decide that the system under consideration is unsalvageable, the prototype can be discarded completely. In this instance, the company has saved itself years of development work and a lot of wasted money by avoiding the much more costly traditional SDLC process.

When to Use Prototyping

In most cases prototyping supports rather than replaces the SDLC. Prototyping is appropriate when there is a high level of uncertainty about the AIS, when it is unclear what questions to ask, when the final AIS cannot be clearly visualized because the decision process is still unclear, when speed is an issue, or when there is a high likelihood of failure. Systems that are especially good candidates for prototyping are decision support systems, executive information systems, expert systems, and information retrieval systems. Prototyping is also appropriate for systems that involve experimentation and trial-and-error development or where the requirements evolve as the system is used. Prototyping is not usually appropriate for large or complex systems that serve major organizational components or cross a number of organizational boundaries. Nor are they commonly used for developing standard AIS components such as accounts receivable and payable, or inventory management. A summary of the conditions that make prototyping an appropriate design methodology is presented in Table 12.5.

Advantages of Prototyping

The advantages of prototyping are discussed in the following subsections.

Better Definition of User Needs. Because of intensive end-user involvement, prototyping usually results in a good definition of user needs. It produces clear and concise specifications when users find it difficult to generate requirements before development starts and when requirements change significantly during development. Many users find that systems developed using prototypes do not have to be modified for quite some time because they were done "right" the first time. When significant changes are needed, it is usually because business requirements have changed.

Table 12.5 **Conditions That Favor the Use of Prototyping**

Users do not understand their needs very well, or their needs change rapidly.
System requirements are hard to define.
System inputs and outputs are not known.
The task to be performed is unstructured or semistructured.
Designers are uncertain about what technology to use.
The system to be developed is crucial and needed quickly.
The risk associated with developing the wrong system is high.
The users' reactions to the new system are important development considerations.
Many design strategies must be tested.
The development staff is experienced with 4GL and other prototyping tools.
The design staff has little experience developing the system or application under consideration.
The system will be used infrequently (and therefore processing efficiency is not a major concern).

FOCUS 12.2

Prototyping: The Third Dimension

An architect develops two-dimensional blueprints that show how a custom home will look. But that is not the same as walking through a model of the proposed home. That third dimension, walking through the home, lets you actually see the rooms and get a feel for the layout. Creating customized software provides a similar challenge. Users must try to visualize the look and feel of their software from written specifications. Prototypes are very helpful to users who have ideas or plans but do not know how to turn them into reality as well as to users who have a problem but don't know how to begin solving it. A prototype lets them "walk through" the proposed system and experiment with its look and feel before committing to the expense of application development.

John Hancock Mutual Life Insurance Company was dissatisfied with the traditional development process: determining user specifications (getting information from high-level executives was especially difficult), writing them up, developing the system, and presenting it to the end users. The typical reaction from a user was, "I may have said that this is what I wanted, but it isn't."

To counter these problems, Hancock used a prototyping approach to develop an executive information system (EIS). The EIS was needed because the company was dissatisfied with its inability to obtain data quickly and easily from the existing system.

A team was formed that included systems development consultants from IBM, user representatives, systems analysts, and programmers. The prototyping process was very interactive, and the continual involvement of the end users eliminated a great deal of misunderstanding. The programmers on the team started programming almost immediately. They prepared sample screens for the first interview session with users. The development staff sat down with users and showed them how the system would work. Users were then given a chance to try the screens. Almost immediately, users could determine whether what they said they wanted was really what they needed.

The result was a prototype for an EIS that took only one month to build. The prototype allows top management at Hancock to access and query current and historical financial data and measurements. Top managers who had been skeptical when the project began were impressed by how much the team was able to accomplish in one short month.

Focus Questions

1. Why are users unable to accurately describe what they need? How do prototypes help them with these determinations?
2. How does developing a prototype significantly cut down on the time required to develop a system?

Higher User Involvement and Satisfaction. Because a prototyped AIS better meets user requirements, it results in greater user satisfaction. User acceptance reduces the risk that the AIS will not be used. It also improves the productivity of the users and the designers, since they are better able to communicate with each other. Early user involvement also helps to build a climate of acceptance rather than skepticism and criticism about the new AIS.

Faster Development Time. It only takes a few days or weeks to get a prototype system up and running. For instance, John Hancock Mutual Life Insurance developed the prototype of an executive information system in only one month, as described in Focus 12.2. Such short development time allows users to immediately evaluate significant changes in the way business is transacted, because they can see the results at once. In contrast, it may take a year or more under the traditional approach before the new system can be evaluated.

During that time the system may no longer be useful, and enough time has passed for user resistance to build.

Fewer Errors. Because the user experiments with and uses each version of the prototype, errors are detected and eliminated early in the development process. As a result, the systems are more reliable and less costly to develop. In addition, it is much easier to identify and terminate an infeasible AIS before a great deal of time and expense are incurred.

More Opportunity for Changes. Under the traditional SDLC approach, the design team is responsible for identifying AIS requirements the first time around. These requirements are then "frozen" so that the team can complete the AIS. With prototyping, however, users can continue to suggest changes until the system is exactly what they want. It is much easier and less expensive to change a prototype than the real AIS once it is in place.

Less Costly. Several studies have shown that some prototype systems can be developed for 10% to 20% of the cost of systems developed using the traditional approach. For example, one utility company claimed a 13-to-1 improvement in development time over traditional methods using COBOL when prototyping was used to develop 10 major applications.

Disadvantages of Prototyping

Despite its significant advantages, prototyping is not necessarily the best systems development approach in all cases. The disadvantages to prototyping are discussed in the following subsections.

Significant User Time. Prototyping can be successful only if users are willing to devote a significant amount of time to working with the AIS and providing the developer with feedback and suggestions. Prototyping may require a greater involvement and commitment than busy users are willing to give.

Less Efficient Use of System Resources. The same shortcuts that make rapid prototyping iterations possible do not always allow for efficient use of computer resources. As a result, poor performance and reliability and high maintenance and support costs may be incurred. As systems become less expensive and faster, however, this limitation is reduced.

Incomplete Systems Development. In large or complex systems with many users, prototyping may not lead to a comprehensive and thorough requirements analysis.

Inadequately Tested and Documented Systems. Because prototypes are used heavily before acceptance, developers are often tempted to shortchange the testing and documentation process. In this case, a poorly documented AIS that is error-prone and hard to maintain can result.

Negative Behavioral Reactions. If a prototype is a throwaway, users may react negatively to learning the system and then not being able to use it. They may also become dissatisfied if all their demands for improvements are not met or if they have to go through too many iterations.

Never-Ending Development. If prototyping is not managed properly, the prototype may never be completed. Unending iterations and revisions may be proposed because changes are so easy to make.

SUMMARY AND CASE CONCLUSION

A number of development approaches can help speed up the traditional SDLC or overcome some of its problems. One alternative to developing custom software is to purchase or modify canned software. Another alternative is to hire an outsourcing company to handle data processing activities. A third alternative is to develop a prototype, a scaled-down version of a system, that users can experiment with to determine what they do and don't like about it.

Ann wasted no time in getting started on the new AIS for Home Improvement Center. She immediately assigned members of her staff to analyze the requirements of the company and investigate prototyping, outsourcing, and the acquisition of software and hardware. The findings of the development team supported the beliefs of the board; the existing AIS at HIC was antiquated and out of date. Ann recommended that the AIS be replaced and the board gave her the approval to proceed.

Ann had team members interview the users to determine their requirements. Based upon the interviews, Ann prepared and sent an RFP to vendors asking them to propose a system to meet the specified needs. After evaluating the responses, she decided against buying existing software; the proposed packages did not give her the information she felt was needed to give HIC a competitive advantage. She did use the RFP responses, however, to select the hardware she needed for the system that was developed.

Ann also considered outsourcing a portion of the AIS. She ultimately decided against it because she did not feel that option would provide HIC with the type of system the board was looking for. She also believed her team could do a better and faster job developing the system than an outsourcer.

From the data gathered in the interviews and during systems analysis, the team developed a prototype of the AIS. The iterative process of presenting the prototype to the users, soliciting their feedback, and making revisions was followed until the AIS met the needs of users. The prototype then served as the systems requirements for that part of the AIS.

As Ann and her team developed the system, they were able to use many components of the Shoppers Mart AIS. They found that modifying the software written for Shoppers Mart was a big timesaver. As a result, Ann and her team were able to develop the AIS at HIC and still meet their deadlines.

In developing the AIS, Ann made use of the latest technological advancements. She required vendors to bar-code all merchandise. Bar codes and POS devices are used to capture sales data. Company service representatives were instructed to enter into the computer all customer requested items that are out of stock or that HIC does not carry. The sales and stock-out data are fed into a centralized data base, and a program tracks and anticipates buying trends. When a buying trend is detected either at an individual store or at the regional or national level, the stores are notified so they can respond quickly. Each store is free to order goods electronically from the central warehouse or directly from approved buyers. When the goods are received, they are matched with an approved purchase order, and an electronic payment is sent to the vendor. Corporate buyers monitor individual store purchases and negotiate quantity discounts.

As time passes, the wisdom of the board became evident. The AIS that Ann and her team designed did indeed provide the company with a competitive edge. It was not long before HIC was not only the market leader but also very profitable. Nor did it take long for the company to decide to acquire other retail businesses and repeat their successes.

KEY TERMS

custom software
canned software
turnkey system
modified canned software
request for a proposal (RFP)
benchmark problem
point scoring
requirements costing
outsourcing
prototyping
prototype
operational prototypes
nonoperational or throwaway prototypes

CHAPTER QUIZ

1. Which of the following is *not* one of the difficulties accountants have experienced using the traditional systems development life cycle?
  a. AIS development projects are backlogged for years.
  b. Changes are not possible after requirements have been frozen.
  c. The AIS that is developed does not meet their needs.
  d. All of the above are difficulties with the SDLC.

2. Companies that buy rather than develop an AIS must still go through the systems development life cycle.
  a. True
  b. False

3. Which of the following statements is false?
  a. As a general rule, companies should buy rather than develop software if they can find a package that meets their needs.
  b. As an AIS increases in size and complexity, there is a greater likelihood that canned software can be found that meets user needs.
  c. A company should not attempt to develop its own custom software unless experienced, in-house programming personnel are available and the job can be completed less expensively on the inside.
  d. As a general rule, a company should develop custom software only when it will provide a significant competitive advantage.

4. When buying large and complex systems, vendors are invited to submit systems for consideration. These solicitations are referred to as a
  a. request for a quotation.
  b. request for a system.
  c. request for a proposal.
  d. good faith estimate.

5. To compare system performance, a company can create a data processing task with input, processing, and output jobs. This task is performed on the system under consideration and the processing times are compared. The AIS with the lowest time is the most efficient. This process is referred to as
  a. benchmarking.
  b. requirements costing.
  c. point scoring.
  d. performance testing.

6. Which of the following statements is true?
  a. Because the AIS is so crucial, companies never outsource the entire AIS.
  b. Most mainframe outsourcing contracts are for one to two years and cost a few thousand dollars a year.

c. In elaborate agreements outsourcers often buy their clients' computers and hire all or most of their employees.
d. Outsourcing is used only by companies struggling to survive and wanting a quick infusion of cash from selling their hardware.

7. Which of the following is a benefit of outsourcing? There may be more than one correct answer.
a. It offers a great deal of flexibility because it is relatively easy to change outsourcers.
b. It may provide access to the expertise and special services provided by outsourcers.
c. It may allow companies to move to a more sophisticated level of computing at a reasonable cost.
d. It is a cost effective way to handle the peaks and valleys found in seasonal businesses.

8. Which of the following is a true statement with respect to prototyping?
a. In the early stages of prototyping, system controls and exception handling may be sacrificed in the interests of simplicity, flexibility, and ease of use.
b. A prototype is a scaled-down, first-draft model that is quickly and inexpensively built and given to users to evaluate.
c. The first step in prototyping is to identify system requirements.
d. All of the statements are true.

9. All of the following are advantages of prototyping *except*
a. better definition of user needs.
b. adequately tested and documented systems.
c. higher user involvement and satisfaction.
d. faster development time.

10. It is most appropriate to use prototyping when
a. there is a little uncertainty about the AIS.
b. it is clear what user needs are.
c. the final AIS cannot be clearly visualized because the decision process is still unclear.
d. there is a low likelihood of failure.

DISCUSSION QUESTIONS

12.1 What is the role of the accountant in the computer acquisition process? Should the accountant play an active role, or should all the work be left to computer experts? In what aspects of computer acquisition might an accountant provide a useful contribution?

12.2 A city in the Midwest, with a population of 45,000, purchased a computer and began developing application programs with in-house programmers. Four years later, only one major application had been developed and it was neither complete nor functioning properly. Moreover, none of the application software running on the system met the users' minimum requirements. Both the hardware and the software frequently failed. A similarly configured system, fully programmed with canned software, would have saved the city nearly half a million dollars. Moreover, the city's annual DP costs exceeded the annual costs of a brand-new turnkey system with packaged software.

Why do you think the city was unable to produce quality, workable systems? Would the city have been better off purchasing canned software? Do you think the city would have been able to find software to adequately meet their needs? Why or why not?

12.3 Custom, canned, and modified canned software all have advantages and disadvantages. In this age of increasing computerization, which do you feel will become predominant? Will any of the methods be phased out? How does your response vary depending on the type and size of user organizations?

12.4 You are a systems consultant for Cooper, Price, and Arthur, CPAs. During your country club's annual golf tournament, your partner is Frank Fender, owner of an automobile dealership. He describes a proposal he received from Turnkey Systems and asks for your opinion. The system will handle inventories, receivables, payroll, accounts payable, and general ledger accounting. Turnkey personnel would install the $70,000 system and train Fender's employees. Identify the major themes you would touch upon in responding to Fender. Identify the advantages and disadvantages of using a turnkey system to operate the organization's accounting system.

12.5 Sara Jones is the owner of a rapidly growing department store and faces stiff competition. The store is using an out-of-date AIS, resulting in poor customer service, late or error-prone billing, and inefficient accounting of inventory. If the store is to continue growing, its AIS must be upgraded. However, the company is not exactly sure what it wants the AIS to accomplish. Sara has heard about prototyping, but she doesn't know what it is and whether it would help her. What would you tell Sara if she asked you to define and explain prototyping? Include an explanation of the advantages and disadvantages of prototyping and the circumstances in which it would be most appropriate.

PROBLEMS

12.1 Don Otno is confused. He has been researching software options but cannot decide between three alternatives. He has come to you for help.

Otno started his search at Computers Made Easy (CME), a computer store in his office complex. He almost wished he hadn't looked any further. Steve Young, the manager of CME, appeared to be knowledgeable and listened attentively as Otno explained his problems, needs, and concerns. Young stated that he had a series of software packages that would, with a few exceptions, come close to meeting Otno's needs. He could fix Otno up with both hardware and software, and Otno could start implementing the package almost immediately. The system's price was unexpectedly reasonable.

Impressed but wanting to shop around, Otno visited Custom Designed Software (CDS). After three hours, he left convinced that CDS could produce a program that was exactly what he needed. Cost and time estimates hadn't been established, but CDS assured him that the cost would be reasonable and that the programs would only take a few months to complete.

Seeking a third opinion, Otno visited Modified Software Unlimited (MSU). The MSU representative said customized packages were very good but expensive, whereas canned software was inexpensive, but rarely met more than a few needs. The best of both worlds could be achieved by having MSU modify the package that came closest to meeting Otno's needs.

On his way back to his office Otno stopped by CME and asked Young about customized and modified software. Steve expressed enough concerns about both that Otno came full circle; he began thinking canned software was best. Late that night Otno realized that he wasn't able to make an objective decision. He was swayed by whichever vendor he was talking to at the time. The next morning he called you for help.

REQUIRED

a. At Otno's request you agree to conduct a study and submit a report showing the advantages and disadvantages of each vendor's approach. Outline the report's contents, identifying the advantages and disadvantages of each approach.

b. Recommend the course of action that you feel would be best for Otno, and support your decision.

12.2 One unhappy federal agency spent almost $1 million on a development contract for an integrated human resources/payroll system that produced no usable software. The original contract was for $445,158 and 15 months; the agency terminated the contract after 28 months and $970,000. The agency had not fully developed user requirements or system specifications for the proposed software when it issued the RFP. There were a number of problems:

- The contractor did not understand the desired software systems.
- User requirements were never adequately defined and frozen. Changes delayed completion schedules and caused disagreements about whether new requirements were included in the original scope of work.
- The contract did not specify systems requirements or performance criteria and the terminology was vague. The contract was amended 13 times to add or delete requirements and to reimburse the contractor for the extra costs resulting from agency-caused delays. The amendments increased the cost of the contract to $1,037,448.
- The contractor complained of inexcusable agency delays, such as taking too much time to review items submitted for approval. The agency blamed the delays on the poor quality of the documentation under review.
- The agency did not require each separate development phase to be approved before work continued. When the agency rejected the general system design, the contractor had to scrap work already completed.

The agency eventually became convinced that the contractor could not deliver at an acceptable time and cost, canceled the contract, and tried to withhold payment for poor performance. A negotiated settlement price of $970,000 was agreed upon. None of the software was ever used by the agency.

REQUIRED

a. Who is to blame for the agency's problems? How could the agency have done a better job of managing the systems development project? What about the contractor?
b. Can we generalize from this case that organizations and governmental agencies should not try to have custom software written for them? Why or why not?
12.3 Wong Engineering Corporation (WEC) operates in 25 states and three countries. WEC faced a crucial decision: choosing a network operating system that would maximize functionality, manageability, and acceptance of the system by end users. WEC developed and followed a four-step approach:

Step 1: Develop the evaluation criteria. WEC organized a committee to develop proper evaluation criteria. Committee members interviewed users and developed the following criteria:

Menu or graphical user interface
Ease of use
Scope of vendor support
Ease of LAN management and administration
Cost, speed, and performance
Wide area communications abilities
Ability to access other computing platforms
Security
Fault tolerance and recovery abilities
Ability to connect workstations to the LAN
Global naming services
Printing capabilities
Upgrade and enhancement options
Stability of vendor

WEC organized the criteria into the following four categories and prioritized them.

1. *Business criteria* refer to overall business, economic, and competitive issues.
2. *Operational criteria* refer to tactical issues and operating characteristics.
3. *Organizational criteria* refer to people issues such as the LAN's impact on the AIS structure.
4. *Technical criteria* refer to hardware, software, and communications issues.

The evaluation committee used a weighting scale of 1 to 5, with 5 as the highest, to select the top three evaluation criteria for each category. Criteria vital to short-term and long-term business goals were given a 5. "Wish list" criteria were weighted a 3. Inapplicable criteria were given a 1.

Step 2: Define the operating environment. A number of data-gathering techniques were used to collect information from which an IS model was developed. The model revealed the need to share accounting, sales, marketing, and engineering data at three organizational levels: the district, division, and home office. In addition, district offices needed access to centralized financial information to handle payroll. WEC decided it needed a distributed LAN that allows users throughout the organization access to company data.

Step 3: Identify the operating alternatives. Using the criteria developed in step 1, WEC evaluated each package identified. Each committee member established personal matrixes for each product, then members compared notes during a roundtable discussion.

Step 4: Test and prototype products. The highest-scoring products were tested further using prototypes. Finally, WEC selected the product that "fit" the organization's needs most completely.

REQUIRED

a. Discuss the role of the evaluation committee in the selection process. How should members of the committee be selected? What advantages and problems result from using a committee to make the selection?
b. What data-gathering techniques could WEC use to assess user needs? to select a vendor?
c. What is the benefit of analyzing the operating environment before selecting a LAN operating system? What data-gathering techniques should a company employ in understanding the operating environment?
d. In selecting a system using the point-scoring method, how should the committee resolve scoring disputes? List at least two methods.
e. Assume the point-scoring approach narrowed the process to three candidates. Should a purchase decision be made on the point-scoring process alone? What other procedure(s) should the committee employ in making the final selection?
12.4 Mark Mitton is the accountant acting as liaison to the IS department for a medium-sized retail firm in Salem, Oregon. Mark has been investigating several computer systems and has narrowed the

selection to three turnkey systems. Mark developed a shopping list of features the system needs. He carefully reviewed each system, talked to other users, and interviewed appropriate system representatives. Using a point-scoring system, Mark assigned weights to each factor to coincide with his evaluation. Mark developed Table 12.6 to help him select the best turnkey system.

REQUIRED

a. Use a spreadsheet program to develop a point-scoring matrix and determine which of the three systems Mark should select.

b. Mark's co-worker, Susan Shelton, didn't agree with Mark's weightings. Susan suggested the following changes:

Flexibility	60
Reputation and reliability	50
Quality of support utilities	10
Graphics capability	10

On the basis of the changes, which vendor should Mark recommend?

c. Mark's manager suggested the following changes to Susan's weightings:

Reputation and reliability	90
Training assistance	65
Experience with similar systems	40
Internal memory size	10
Installation assistance	40

Will the manager's changes affect the decision about which system to buy?

d. What can you conclude about point scoring from the changes made by Susan and Mark's manager? Develop your own weighting scale to evaluate the selection of the three software packages. Be prepared to discuss your results with the class.

e. What are the weaknesses of the point-scoring method?

12.5 Nielsen Marketing Research USA (NMR), with operations in 29 countries, is the recognized world leader in the production and dissemination of marketing information. Nielsen was a pioneer in the development of the decision support information

Table 12.6 **An Alternative Evaluation Matrix**

Selection Criteria	Weight	System 1	System 2	System 3
Software				
Fulfillment of business needs	100	6	8	9
Acceptance in marketplace	30	6	7	6
Quality of documentation	50	7	9	8
Quality of warranty	50	4	8	7
Ease of use	80	7	6	5
Control features	50	9	7	9
Flexibility	20	4	5	9
Security features	30	4	4	8
Modularity	30	8	5	4
Integration with other software	30	8	9	6
Quality of support utilities	50	9	8	5
Vendor				
Reputation and reliability	10	3	9	6
Experience with similar systems	20	5	5	6
Installation assistance	70	9	4	6
Training assistance	35	4	8	6
Timeliness of maintenance	35	5	4	4
Hardware				
Internal memory size (RAM)	70	5	6	8
Diskette capacity	40	9	9	5
Graphics capabilities	50	7	7	8
Processing speed	30	8	8	5
Overall performance	40	9	4	4
Expandability	50	7	2	5
Support for LAN technology	30	3	4	7

business and has been the primary supplier for over 70 years. NMR's most recognizable product is the Nielsen television ratings.

Nielsen is one of the largest users of computer capacity in the United States. Its information system has consistently ranked above average in efficiency for its industry. However, it commissioned IBM's Integrated Systems Solutions Corporation (ISSC) to evaluate outsourcing NMR's information processing. NMR wants to know whether outsourcing will allow it to concentrate on giving its customers value-added services and insights and whether outsourcing can increase its flexibility, promote rapid growth, and provide it with more real-time information.

REQUIRED

What are the benefits and risks of outsourcing for NMR? Do you think the benefits of outsourcing outweigh the risks? Why or why not?

12.6 The Pedaler, one of the largest bicycle manufacturers in the world, has grown significantly in the 20 years since it was formed. Eighteen years ago the company began using a computer to handle its data processing needs. Since then, several million dollars have been spent on hardware and software.

For the past several years the DP department has effectively handled company needs. During the slow season DP employees have light schedules, work on special projects, and spend one to two weeks at training seminars. During the peak season employees average five hours of overtime per week. Recently, the Pedaler has grown so fast that DP is having a hard time keeping up. Management realizes the benefit DP provides and is thinking of expanding the department at a cost of $1 million over the next three years. Due to their rapid expansion, the Pedaler would have to borrow the money for this project. Investing in a new system, however, may slow the company's growth or, worse, add significantly to debt.

At the last board of directors meeting outsourcing was suggested as a possible solution. Brian Cycle, the president, has asked you, an independent consultant specializing in AIS strategies, for your advice.

REQUIRED

Write a one-page memo explaining outsourcing and summarizing the benefits and drawbacks of outsourcing the Pedaler's DP functions. Address the issues of whether outsourcing fits the Pedaler's situation, whether it can save the Pedaler money, and whether it can effectively meet the needs of a growing company.

12.7 Meredith Corporation publishes books and magazines, owns and operates television stations, and provides a real estate marketing and franchising service. Meredith is dissatisfied with its ability to retrieve correct and timely inventory information from its AIS. Each division either developed its own inventory system or already had one in place when it was acquired by Meredith. As a result, Meredith has 11 different inventory systems that are unable to communicate with each other. Management wants to tie the systems together and have one consistent inventory pool from which to extract the information needed for making good business decisions. Meredith has decided to use prototyping to develop the system.

REQUIRED

a. What three key questions would you ask when interviewing Meredith's personnel to determine system requirements? What type of information are you attempting to elicit from each question?

b. What do you think Meredith's basic information needs are?

c. Explain how the prototyping process would work for Meredith. What would the system developer do during the iterative process step? Why would you want the fewest iterations possible?

d. What tools will you use to design your prototype? Why would you use them instead of conventional programming languages?

e. Would you want this prototype to be operational or nonoperational? Why? If it were an operational prototype, what would have to happen? If it were a nonoperational prototype, how would the prototype be used?

f. Suppose the company decides the prototyped system is not practical, abandons the system, and takes some other approach to solving its inventory problem. Does that mean prototyping is not a valid systems development approach? Why or why not?

CASE 12.1: ANYCOMPANY, INC.—AN ONGOING COMPREHENSIVE CASE

Visit a local company and obtain permission to study its systems development approach. Once you have lined up a company, do the following:

1. With a member of the information systems staff, discuss the following issues:
   a. What procedures does the company follow in determining its hardware and software needs? How does the company select software, hardware, and vendors?
   b. Does the company outsource any of its data processing activities? If so, what benefits is it now deriving, and what risks is it exposed to? Does the company think the decision was a good one? If it does not outsource, has it considered the option? If so, why was it rejected?
   c. Has the company used prototyping? If so, what benefits did it derive? What were the disadvantages? Does the company continue to use prototypes, or has it discontinued their use? If it hasn't used prototypes, was it the approach considered? If so, why was it rejected?
2. Summarize your findings in a written report and be prepared to share your findings with the class.

CASE 12.2: WIDGET MANUFACTURING COMPANY

The Widget Manufacturing Company is a major producer of widgets, with total sales of $50 million annually. Its AIS department currently has an ABC Model 115 computer, which operates 12 hours per day, five days a week. It processes payroll, general accounting, inventory control, and accounts receivable using a batch mode. This equipment also supports an on-line order entry system with four workstations located in the sales department. This application processes an average of 240,000 transactions per year.

The company prepared a two-year information systems plan. D. MacTavish, Widget's AIS director, determined that the present computer could absorb any additional work load caused by rapidly increasing sales. This increase could be handled by scheduling a full second shift and possibly a third shift. The present computer would not have sufficient memory or be fast enough, however, to handle a new production scheduling system that was planned and that would require more workstations be added in the production planning department and at several locations throughout the plant. This new system would increase the number of workstation transactions by approximately 720,000 per year but would require approximately one year to develop and implement following the availability of a new system.

After a presentation to the president and executive committee, MacTavish was authorized to prepare the hardware and software specifications for a system that would meet the needs of Widget for the next two years. Also, because the company was expanding so quickly, the president asked MacTavish to include the cost of renting space in a nearby office building in which the entire AIS department could be relocated. This would provide space in the Widget head office building for additional staff that were needed by other company departments. The AIS department currently occupies approximately 3300 square feet of space in the basement of the Widget head office building. MacTavish was asked to prepare a financial summary showing the cost of the present and proposed systems for presentation to the company's board of directors.

MacTavish prepared the specifications for the new systems and sent them to the ABC Computer Company, the supplier of the present computer. He also invited the PQR Company to submit a proposal for its equipment and software, and he decided to ask XYZ, an outsourcing company, to respond with the prices it would charge to process Widget's information. Included in the specifications were all processing volumes and transaction rates for existing and proposed applications. Also included was the fact that Widget uses 75 magnetic tapes for backup storage of important disk files. This figure was expected to increase to 100 tapes with the implementation of the production scheduling system.

The important facts from each of the three proposals MacTavish received are as follows.

The ABC proposal. The ABC representative recommended a Model 138 computer that leased for $273,478 per year. This system would have sufficient memory and speed to handle all current applications plus the new system. Because it is also a member of the same "family" of computers as Widget's Model 115, it would use the same software as the 115 and therefore require the same amount of training as was needed on the present equipment. He pointed out, however, that the larger 138 could use a new series of workstations that ABC had recently announced and would enable Widget to acquire the additional workstations it needed to replace its present terminals at a total cost of $14,100 per year for the two years. This new system would require the same space as the present Model 115.

The PQR proposal. The PQR Company recommended a Model 906 system. The equipment that would be located in the Widget computer center would cost $213,660 per year, and all of the necessary workstations would be supplied at a cost of $9468. PQR's marketing policy differed from that of ABC in that all software and staff training costs were included in the price of the equipment. It also was willing to provide a discount of $66,000 during the second year if Widget would sign a two-year lease for the equipment. The PQR proposal indicated that its equipment would fit into an area equivalent to that occupied by the present computer.

The XYZ proposal. The XYZ outsourcing proposal involved the installation of a minicomputer at the Widget computer center that would be used for editing and balancing all batch input. The data would be sent over a telephone line several times a day to a large computer located at the outsourcing company, where it would be processed. Output would be returned to Widget over the same communications line to the minicomputer, where it would be stored on a disk until it could be printed out and distributed. The on-line order entry system and the new production scheduling system would use workstations connected to the large computer at XYZ, and any printed output from these systems would be sent by telephone line to the minicomputer for printing and distribution. The cost to Widget for leasing the minicomputer would be $32,724 per year, and workstations would be leased for $11,000 annually. The cost of the communications line between the minicomputer at the Widget offices and the large system at XYZ would be $21,420 each year, with an installation charge of $4020 the first year.

On the basis of benchmark tests using existing Widget programs, XYZ estimated that the cost of running all batch programs would be $132,000 per year. The cost of storing the backup tapes for Widget would be $1 per tape per year.

XYZ used a price schedule for on-line applications based on the number of transactions entered through the workstations. Its price was quoted at 10¢ per transaction, which included software charges. As an incentive to Widget, XYZ offered a volume discount of $109,800 during the second year and agreed to provide all necessary training of Widget staff during the first year of the agreement at no cost. Widget would have to pay for training during the second year. Since XYZ used an ABC computer, Widget's staff could take the same courses at the same cost as the ones required for the larger ABC machine.

In the opinion of XYZ, the installation of a minicomputer by Widget would reduce the computer center space requirements by 450 square feet.

During negotiations for a nearby office building MacTavish was able to negotiate the lease of space for his department at a rate of $10 per square foot per year, the amount of space dependent on the alternative selected by Widget's board of directors.

Present computer costs are as follows:

Central site hardware (monthly)	$16,764.00
Software (monthly)	1,516.00
Workstations (monthly)	1,292.50
Training costs (annually)	7,000.00

Note: All hardware and software is leased. The company follows the policy of capitalizing lease payments for financial statement purposes.

As MacTavish, write a report to the board of directors recommending which proposal to accept. Include the quantitative and qualitative aspects of each proposal. Indicate what impact, if any, the decision regarding the development of the proposed production scheduling system would have on your recommendation. (SMAC Examination, adapted)

CASE 12.3: PROFESSIONAL SALON CONCEPTS

Steve Fleming is the owner of Professional Salon Concepts (PSC), a distribution company for hair salon products in Mesa, Arizona. Steve started working for his father, a distributor of barber and beauty salon products, at age 16 and a decade later decided to start his own business. He rented a small warehouse, hired four people, and began selling products carrying the name of famous hairstylist Paul Mitchell. Unfortunately, hairstylists ignored the products and did not buy them. Steve eventually had to let his people go and move his products to an inexpensive basement location.

The tables turned for Steve when he put on a free two-hour seminar at a local hair salon demonstrating how hairstylists could successfully use his products. He left with a $1000 order and the realization that he had found his niche. He decided to sell only to salons that allowed him to put on a seminar and demonstrate his products.

PSC has done very well using Steve's strategy. Sales took off, reaching $7 million in 1993, as PSC grew to 45 employees and 3000 salon customers. Warehouse operations ran smoothly due to Paul Mitchell's specialized product line, which was 75% of PSC's business. PSC carried 1000 products, compared to 10,000 for the average salon distributor. This more focused product line enabled PSC to achieve a 24-hour turnaround on orders, in contrast to more than two days for the competition. To achieve this quick turnaround, Steve sometimes worked late packing orders so he could drive them to the UPS hub a few towns away by the 2 A.M. deadline.

In 1985 Steve bought PSC's first computer, a $2000 IBM PC-XT. He soon installed a $3000 accounting package, which served his accounting needs very well. In fact, Steve thought everything was going great until Terri Olivero, a consultant from PSC's second largest supplier, stopped by. Terri asked Steve some questions designed to reveal how well he knew his business:

- Do you know exactly to whom you ship each month?
- Do you know how much each customer bought, by supplier?
- Can you rank your customer sales?
- Can you break your sales down by product?
- Do you know how the profit per client breaks down into product lines?
- Do you know how revenues per salesperson vary over the days of the week?

Steve's answer was an uncomfortable no to each question. Terri told him that people who can't answer these questions are losing money. That upset Steve and he terminated the session, politely dismissing Terri. Steve and Terri got married shortly afterward, however, and she joined the company.

Steve realized that Terri's skills could be used either to help PSC's business grow or to help PSC internally. Believing it was more important to grow the business, he asked Terri to help make the salons more profitable. She developed a template to break down and, with PSC's help, analyze every aspect of their business. The template helped salon owners determine such statistics as how much each hairstylist brings in per client, whether enough clients receive extra services, and how many clients, and which ones, buy hair products. The Cowans soon became more like partners to their customers than trainers and educators. If a salon had employee problems, the Cowans would help settle the issues. If a salon fell behind in a grand opening, the Cowans lent a hand. The only catch was the salons had to buy PSC's products. The better the customer, the more time the Cowans gave.

PSC began selling turnkey systems and support services at cost to help salons answer questions like those Terri posed to Steve. Unfortunately, PSC's computer couldn't answer those same questions. Steve asked Mike Kruger, a consultant with Arthur Andersen, for help and sent Mike as much raw data as could be extracted from his PC-based accounting system. Mike entered it into a database and wrote programs to produce the information Steve wanted. The system worked, but it was very slow—so slow that accounts payable and purchasing information was handled manually. Nor did the system answer all of Terri's questions, and her list was getting longer. To make matters worse, only a few months of detailed information was available at any time. To partially alleviate some of these problems, Steve hired Mike, who had married Steve's sister, as the company's controller.

After reading a special industry report, Steve realized that his company was well positioned in every aspect, except investment in technology. Steve and Mike realized it was time to purchase a new system. They considered outside consultants but felt they would take too much time trying to understand PSC's special needs. In addition, Mike believed consultants knew little about the detailed workings of the software they recommend. They decided to evaluate and select the software themselves and rely on the vendor for installation help.

Steve and Mike spent months researching software and attending demonstrations before settling on a generic AIS software program. They paid the $20,000 price tag and the vendor began installing the system and training PSC personnel. Three days prior to conversion, Steve met a distributor from North Dakota at a social gathering. The distributor described how his system not only provided all the detailed accounting and customer reporting features but also met his distributorship's inventory management and order-fulfillment needs. Steve was so impressed that he excused himself and called Mike, telling him to halt the conversion. They immediately went to North Dakota to check out the system, then flew to Minneapolis to visit DSM, the software developer.

DSM did a great job of demonstrating the software and provided Steve and Mike with several great references. The only hitch was DSM's inability to demonstrate two features that were particularly important to Steve. The first was the ability to adjust orders automatically to reflect outstanding customer credits and back orders. The second was the ability to determine the least expensive way to pack and ship each order. DSM's salespeople assured Steve and Mike that those features would be up and running on the package by the time it was delivered to PSC.

Before committing to the system, Steve and Mike sat down to determine whether it was economically feasible. They estimated $234,000 in yearly savings:

$144,000 Most of PSC's orders consisted of several boxes, 95% of which were sent COD. PSC's old system had no way of writing orders for shipments of more than one box; in other words, an order shipped in five boxes had required five sales invoices and five separate COD tickets. The new system would allow PSC to generate one sales order and ship one box COD. The other four would be shipped by regular delivery, which was much less costly than COD delivery. Eliminating the need to ship every box COD would save the company $144,000 a year.

$50,000 PSC paid outside accountants $40,000 a year to prepare their financial statements. The new software would prepare most of those statements automatically.

$40,000 Because the old system did not have credit-managing capabilities, it was hard to detect past-due accounts. Steve believed earlier detection of past-due accounts would result in faster collections, fewer lost customers, and fewer write-offs.

Unknown The major reason for acquiring the system was to improve customer service by making more detailed customer information available.

Steve and Mike estimated annual maintenance costs of $10,000 and an annual return on investment of $224,000. Since the system would pay for itself in less than a year, Steve bought it and wrote off his $20,000 investment in the other system.

At the end of 1993 DSM technicians arrived at PSC to install the software. To Steve's dismay, the promised features weren't part of the package and there was no immediate plan to add them. Although Steve and Mike were upset, they realized they had to shoulder some of the blame for not insisting on seeing the two features before signing the deal. A subsequent search found a program that automatically determined the cheapest way to pack and ship an order. DSM agreed to pay half of the $10,000 cost to integrate it into the program. DSM also offered to create the module to reflect customer credits and back orders for another $20,000, but Steve declined. These problems pushed the conversion date back several months.

PSC spent the first three months of 1994 preparing to implement the new system. Training PSC employees to use the new system was particularly important. For example, adding a customer to the data base required only one screen with the old system; the new software required six screens. Employees were taught to shout "Fire!" if they came upon a problem they couldn't handle. Mike, or one of the DSM programmers, would come to their assistance and explain what they had done wrong and how to fix the problem. During implementation the new system was tested for glitches by processing real data. Looking back, Mike admits three months wasn't nearly long enough for the training and testing; they should have used twice as much time to identify and eliminate glitches.

PSC dismantled the old system and converted over to the new one on April 20, 1994. Before long, telephone operators grew confused and forgot how to move from one part of the system to another. They began bumping up against unfamiliar error messages and getting themselves into situations they hadn't been trained to handle. Soon everyone was yelling

"Fire" at the same time. In less than an hour so many people were waiting for help that the programmers stopped explaining the correct procedures and simply ran from operator to operator correcting problems. Mistakes were repeated over and over again, and the situation intensified. Some employees, feeling embarrassed and ashamed at their inability to work the new system, broke down and cried openly.

Steve was running the warehouse area and wasn't having much fun either. On a normal day PSC has 200 to 300 boxes ready for 3:30 P.M. shipment. On conversion day only one box was ready to go. Facing the first default on his 24-hour turnaround promise since he started PSC, Steve, along with Terri, Mike, and a few others, stayed long after midnight packing boxes and loading them on trucks. They just barely made it to the nearest UPS hub on time.

The next day, order entry and shipping ran much smoother. However, when Steve sat down to retrieve the data he needed to monitor sales, he couldn't get the system to work. It wasn't that the system didn't have the information, Steve just didn't know how to get it. Needless to say, he wasn't feeling too kindly toward his $200,000 system or the company who sold it to him.

It took Steve several weeks to figure out how to get the data he needed to monitor sales. When he did, he was horrified that sales had dropped nearly 15%. They had focused so hard at getting the system up and running, that they had taken their eyes off the customers. To make matters worse, Steve couldn't get information on sales by customer, salesperson, or product, and he couldn't figure out why or where sales were falling.

However, things quickly improved after "Hell Week." Orders are now entered just as quickly as before, and printed copies aren't needed for filing purposes. Warehouse operations are improved thanks to the integrated add-in program. The new system provides pickers with the most efficient path to follow when picking orders. It also tells them which items to pack in which boxes based on destination and weight. The system selects a carrier and prints out labels for the boxes. Order turnaround time was shaved to 20 minutes from 5 hours.

Months after the system was installed, it still doesn't do everything Steve needs it to do, including some things the old system did. Nor does it answer all of Terri's questions. However, Steve is confident that the system will eventually provide PSC with a distinct competitive advantage. He is negotiating with DSM to write the credit and back-order module.

With all that has happened, Steve believes that the step up to the new system was necessary, even the right move, for his growing company. With the exceptions of taking the DSM salesperson's word and not taking enough time to practice with the system, Steve feels PSC did as good a job as they could have in selecting, installing, and implementing a new system.

Write a memo to address the following questions. Be prepared to defend your position to the class.

1. Do you agree with Steve's assessment that PSC did a good job selecting, installing, and implementing the new system considering the exceptions he noted? If so, why? Or, do you feel PSC could have done a better job? If so, what did they do wrong and what should they have done differently?
2. How could PSC have avoided the problem of the missing features?
3. Based on what you read about systems conversion in Chapter 11, how could PSC have avoided some of the conversion and reporting problems they faced?
4. Based on what you read about economic feasibility in Chapter 10, evaluate Steve's analysis. Do you agree with his numbers and his conclusions? Why or why not?
5. How could PSC's customers use the new multibox shipping approach to defraud PSC?
6. On a scale of 1 to 5, with 1 being the best, how would you rate the service that PSC received from DSM? Could it have been improved? If so, how?

Source: David H. Freedman, "Computer Upgrade: To Hell and Back," *INC. Technology:* 46–53.

ANSWERS TO CHAPTER QUIZ

1. d	**3.** b	**5.** a	**7.** b, c, d	**9.** b
2. a	**4.** c	**6.** c	**8.** d	**10.** c

PART FOUR

Chapter 13

Control and Accounting Information Systems

LEARNING OBJECTIVES

After studying this chapter, you should be able to:

- Explain the basic concepts of control as applied to business organizations.
- Describe the major elements in the control environment of a business organization.
- Describe control policies and procedures commonly used in business organizations.
- Evaluate a system of internal accounting control, identify its deficiencies, and prescribe modifications to remedy those deficiencies.
- Conduct cost-benefit analyses for particular threats, exposures, risks, and controls.

Integrative Case: Springer's Northwest Lumber & Supply

After completing his bachelor's degree in accounting at Idaho State, Jason Scott has been hired as an internal auditor for Northwest Industries, a diversified forest products company. He is assigned to audit Springer's Lumber & Supply, Northwest's building materials outlet in Bozeman, Montana. His supervisor, Maria Pilier, has asked him to trace a sample of purchase transactions from purchase requisition to cash disbursement to verify that proper control procedures were followed. By midafternoon Jason is frustrated with this task, and for good reasons:

- The purchasing system is poorly documented.
- He keeps finding transactions that have not been processed as Ed Yates, the accounts payable manager, said they should be.
- Purchase requisitions are missing for several items that had been personally authorized by Bill Springer, the purchasing vice president.
- Some vendor invoices have been paid without supporting documents, such as purchase orders or receiving reports.
- Prices charged for some items seem unusually high and there are a few discrepancies in item prices between the vendor invoice and the corresponding purchase order.

Yates seemed to have a logical answer for every question Jason raised. Yates ended the discussion by advising Jason that the real world is not always as tidy as the world portrayed in college textbooks. When Jason discussed his findings with Maria, he learned that she also has some concerns:

- Springer's is the largest supplier in the area and has a near monopoly.
- Management authority is concentrated in the company president, Joe Springer, and his two sons Bill (the purchasing VP) and Ted (the

controller). Several relatives and friends are on the payroll. Together the Springers own 10% of the company.

- Lines of authority and responsibility within the company are loosely defined and hard to understand.
- Maria feels that Ted Springer may have engaged in "creative accounting" to make Springer's one of Northwest's best-performing retail outlets.

After talking to Maria, Jason ponders the following issues:

1. Since Ed Yates had a logical explanation for every unusual transaction, should Jason describe these transactions in his report?
2. Is a violation of proper control procedures acceptable if it has been authorized by management?
3. Maria's concerns about Springer's loosely defined lines of authority and possible use of "creative accounting" are matters of management policy. Regarding Jason's control procedures assignment, does he have a responsibility to get involved? What about ethically?

INTRODUCTION

Our society has become increasingly dependent upon accounting information systems, which have grown increasingly more complex to meet our escalating needs for information. As the complexity and importance of these systems increase, companies face the growing risk that the security of these systems is being compromised. As a result, ensuring that our AIS are adequately controlled has become an extremely important issue.

In an abstract sense, **control** is the process of exercising a restraining or directing influence over the activities of an object, organism, or system. Assisting management in the control of a business organization is one of the primary objectives of an AIS. The accountant can help achieve this objective by designing effective control systems and by auditing (or reviewing) control systems already in place to assure that they are operating effectively. The four chapters in Part IV of this text focus on the control and audit of an AIS.

The goal of control is to prevent losses to the organization arising from several possible hazards:

- Wasteful and inefficient use of resources.
- Poor management decisions.
- Unintentional errors in recording or processing data.
- Accidental loss or destruction of records or other system resources.
- Loss of assets through employees' carelessness or pilferage.
- Lack of compliance by employees with management policies or government regulations.
- Unauthorized changes to an AIS or one of its components.
- **Embezzlement,** the theft or misappropriation of assets by employees, accompanied by the falsification of records in order to conceal the theft.
- Other illegal acts by employees, such as accepting a bribe.
- Penalties or damages arising from failure to comply with regulatory or contractual requirements.

Any potential adverse occurrence or unwanted event that could be injurious to either the AIS or the organization, such as one or more of these elements, is referred to as a **threat.** The potential dollar loss should a particular threat become a reality is referred to as the **exposure** from the threat, and the likelihood that the threat will actually come to pass is referred to as the **risk** associated with the threat.

As a future accountant, you must understand how to protect systems from threats. Management expects accountants to be their "control consultants." That is, it's the accountant's job to (1) take a proactive approach to eliminating system threats and (2) detect, correct, and recover from threats if and when they occur. The four chapters in Part IV focus on control concepts. This chapter explains general principles of control in business organizations and describes key control procedures most suitable for a typical AIS. Chapter 14 describes how these general control principles apply to a computer-based AIS and explains the control procedures most applicable to them. Chapter 15 provides an in-depth examination of the causes and remedies for fraud, one of the most substantial threats faced by an AIS. Chapter 16 examines the processes and procedures used in auditing a computer-based AIS.

Accounting systems generally consist of several accounting subsystems, each designed to process transactions of a particular type. Although they differ with respect to the type of transactions processed, all accounting subsystems follow the same sequence of procedures. These procedures are referred to as *accounting cycles.* The five major accounting cycles and their related control objectives and procedures are described in detail in Chapters 17–21.

OVERVIEW OF CONTROL CONCEPTS

A brief overview of the historical development of internal control concepts is presented in Table 13.1. It is interesting to note how this concept of control has evolved from its origins as a way of helping external auditors determine the most efficient method of planning an independent audit to a central principle of good management. As is discussed later in the chapter, the importance of internal controls is underscored by a federal statute requiring that U.S. corporations maintain a system of internal accounting control.

Internal control is the plan of organization and the methods a business uses to safeguard assets, provide accurate and reliable information, promote and improve operational efficiency, and encourage adherence to prescribed managerial policies. These internal control purposes are sometimes at odds with each other. For example, many people are pushing for radical business process reengineering so they can have better and faster information and improve operational efficiency. Others resist those changes because they impede the safeguarding of company assets and require significant changes to managerial policies.

Management control is broader than internal accounting control and encompasses the following three features. (1) It is an integral part of management responsibilities, (2) it is designed to reduce errors and irregularities and achieve organizational goals, and (3) it is personnel-oriented and seeks to help employees attain company goals by following organizational policies.

Table 13.1 Overview of the Historical Development of Internal Control Concepts

Year	Source	Contribution
1949	American Institute of Accountants (now AICPA) monograph on internal control	Promulgates first definition of internal control as having four objectives: to safeguard assets, check the accuracy and integrity of accounting data, promote operational efficiency, and encourage adherence to prescribed managerial policies.
1958	AICPA, *Statement on Auditing Procedure No. 29*	Introduces the distinction between accounting controls, or controls concerned mainly with safeguarding assets and the reliability of financial records, and administrative controls.
1972	AICPA, *Statement on Auditing Procedure No. 54*	Further clarifies the distinction between accounting controls and administrative controls, and specifies four objectives of accounting controls.
1977	U.S. Congress, Foreign Corrupt Practices Act	Codifies the AICPA's 1977 definition of internal accounting control as a legal requirement for public corporations subject to the Securities Exchange Act of 1934.
1981	Research Foundation of the Financial Executives Institute (FEI)	Introduces a definition of management control and draws a distinction between internal accounting control and management control.
1988	AICPA, *Statement on Auditing Standards No. 55*	Introduces the concept of internal control structure, consisting of the control environment, accounting system, and control procedures.
1992	Committee of Sponsoring Organizations of the Treadway Commission (includes AICPA and FEI)	Proposes a broad definition of internal control as a process designed to achieve objectives relating to operating effectiveness and efficiency, reliability of financial reporting, and compliance with laws and regulations. Five interrelated components of internal control are identified, encompassing both management control and accounting control considerations.

Administrative controls help ensure operational efficiency and adherence to managerial policies. In contrast, **accounting controls** help safeguard assets and ensure the reliability of financial records.

The **internal control structure** is the policies and procedures established to provide reasonable assurance that the organization's specific objectives will be achieved. It has three elements: a control environment, an accounting system, and control procedures. These three elements are defined and summarized in Table 13.2.

Internal Control Classifications

The concepts of internal control, administrative and accounting control, and management control are broad in scope, aimed at describing entire control systems. The specific control procedures used in these systems may be classified

Table 13.2 **Elements of the Internal Control Structure**

Control Environment	Accounting System	Control Procedures
The control environment represents the collective effect of various factors on establishing, enhancing, or mitigating the effectiveness of specific policies and procedures. Such factors include the following. Management's philosophy and operating style The organization structure The functioning of the board of directors and its committees, particularly the audit committee Methods of assigning authority and responsibility Management's control methods for monitoring and following up on performance, including internal auditing Human resources policies and practices Various external influences that affect an organization's operations and practices, such as examinations by bank regulatory agencies	The accounting system consists of the methods and records established to identify, assemble, analyze, classify, record, and report an organization's transactions and to maintain accountability for the related assets and liabilities. An effective accounting system gives appropriate consideration to establishing methods and records that will function as follows. Identify and record all valid transactions Describe on a timely basis the transactions in sufficient detail to permit proper classification of transactions for financial reporting Measure the value of transactions in a manner that permits recording their proper monetary value in the financial statements Determine the time period in which transactions occurred to permit recording of transactions in the proper accounting period Present properly the transactions and related disclosures in the financial statements	Control procedures are those policies and procedures in addition to the control environment and accounting system that management has established to provide reasonable assurance that specific organizational objectives will be achieved. Generally, they may be categorized as procedures that pertain to the following. Proper authorization of transactions and activities Segregation of duties that reduce the opportunities to allow any person to be in a position to both perpetrate and conceal errors or irregularities in the normal course of duties — assigning different people the responsibilities of authorizing transactions, recording transactions, and maintaining custody of assets Design and use of adequate documents and records to help ensure the proper recording of transactions and events Adequate safeguards over access to and use of assets and records Independent checks on performance and proper valuation of recorded amounts

Source: Adapted from Auditing Standards Board, AICPA, *Statement on Auditing Standards No. 55,* (New York:AICPA, 1988), paragraphs 9–11.

in a number of ways. This section discusses four common internal control classifications.

Preventive, Detective, and Corrective. **Preventive controls** are intended to deter problems before they arise. Hiring highly qualified accounting personnel, appropriately segregating employee duties, and effectively controlling physical access to assets, facilities, and information are effective preventive controls.

Because not all potential control problems can be prevented, **detective controls** are needed to discover control problems soon after they arise. Examples of detective controls are duplicate checking of calculations and preparing bank reconciliations and monthly trial balances. **Corrective controls** remedy problems discovered with detective controls. They include procedures taken to (1) identify the cause of a problem, (2) correct resulting errors or difficulties, and (3) modify the system so that future problems are minimized or eliminated. Examples include maintaining backup copies of key transaction and master files and adhering to procedures for correcting data entry errors as well as those for resubmitting transactions for subsequent processing.

Feedback and Feedforward. Some preventive controls are referred to as **feedforward controls** because they monitor a process and its inputs in order to predict potential problems. If problems can be identified *before* they arise, adjustments can be made to prevent their occurrence. For example, a cash budgeting system is used to monitor a company's cash flow so steps can be taken to arrange for a line of credit to cover any projected cash deficiencies. Another example is an inventory control system that predicts when inventory items will be out of stock and initiates reorders to replenish the stock. Some detective controls are referred to as **feedback controls** because they measure a process and adjust it when it deviates from plan. For example, a responsibility accounting system measures the cost of a business process and sends management a performance report when the cost is substantially in excess of a budget or standard amount.

General and Application. **General controls** are designed to ensure that an organization's control environment is stable and well managed to enhance the effectiveness of application controls. **Application controls** are used to prevent, detect, and correct errors and irregularities in transactions as they are processed. These control classifications are discussed in Chapter 14.

Input, Processing, and Output. Controls can also be classified according to where they are implemented in the data processing cycle. **Input controls** are designed to ensure that only accurate, valid, and authorized data are entered into the system. For example, the computer could be programmed to reject payroll input for employees unless they are included on a list of authorized employees. **Processing controls** are designed to ensure that all transactions are processed accurately and completely and that all files and records are properly updated. An example is the batch totals described later in the chapter. **Output controls** are designed to ensure that system output is properly controlled. For example, unauthorized employees should be prevented from obtaining a copy of the report documenting top management's salaries.

The nature of a particular control procedure is less important than whether it effectively accomplishes its objective, which is to prevent losses to the organization resulting from a particular threat or hazard. In analyzing controls, it is important first to define an organization's control objectives. The next step is to determine whether effective control procedures (of any type) are in place to accomplish these control objectives.

The Foreign Corrupt Practices Act

In 1977 shock waves reverberated through the accounting profession when Congress incorporated language from an AICPA pronouncement into the Foreign Corrupt Practices Act. Specifically, all publicly owned corporations subject to the Securities Exchange Act of 1934 are now legally required to keep records that accurately and fairly reflect their transactions and assets in reasonable detail. They must also devise and maintain an internal accounting control system sufficient to provide reasonable assurances that

> *i. transactions are executed in accordance with management's general or specific authorization;*
> *ii. transactions are recorded as necessary (1) to permit preparation of financial statements in conformity with generally accepted accounting principles or any other criteria applicable to such statements, and (2) to maintain accountability for assets;*
> *iii. access to assets is permitted only in accordance with management's general or specific authorization; and*
> *iv. the recorded accountability for assets is compared with the existing assets at reasonable intervals and appropriate action is taken with respect to any differences.*[1]

The primary purpose of the act was to prevent the bribery of foreign officials in order to obtain business. A significant effect of the act, however, was to require corporations to maintain good systems of internal accounting control! Needless to say, this requirement has generated tremendous interest among management, accountants, and auditors in the design and evaluation of internal control systems. It is important to recognize that it is much easier to build controls into a system at the initial design stage than to add them after the system has been designed or built. For that reason, accountants and other control experts should be important members of the team that develops or modifies an AIS.

Study by the Committee of Sponsoring Organizations

The Committee of Sponsoring Organizations (COSO) is a private sector group consisting of the American Accounting Association, the AICPA, the Institute of Internal Auditors, the Institute of Management Accountants, and the Financial Executives Institute. In 1992 COSO issued the results of a study to develop a definition of internal controls and guidance for evaluating a system of internal controls. The report has been widely accepted as the authority on internal controls by management, accountants, auditors, and users of financial statements.

The study took three years and involved tens of thousands of hours of research, discussion, analysis, and due process. It involved hundreds of people, including members of the five COSO organizations, corporate chief executives

---

[1]*Foreign Corrupt Practices Act of 1977, U.S. Code,* 1976 edition, Supplement II, Volume One (Washington, D.C.: U.S. Government Printing Office, 1979), p. 862.

and board members, legislators and regulators, lawyers, consultants, auditors, and academics. The report spells out employees' responsibilities for the proper functioning of controls and describes the external auditor's role in assessing controls. The report goes well beyond financial controls to incorporate the controls that management uses in running the company.

The COSO study defines internal control as the process implemented by the board of directors, management, and those under their direction to provide reasonable assurance that control objectives are achieved with regard to the following:

1. Effectiveness and efficiency of operations.
2. Reliability of financial reporting.
3. Compliance with applicable laws and regulations.

Internal control is referred to as a *process* because it permeates an organization's operating activities and is an integral part of the basic management activities of planning, executing, and monitoring. Internal control provides reasonable, rather than absolute, assurance, because the possibilities of human failure, collusion, and management override of controls make this process an imperfect one.

The preceding explanation represents a significant move away from an internal control definition that is confined to accounting controls to one that addresses a wide range of board and management objectives. COSO's control model is integrated with the management process and is, in fact, derived from the way management runs a business. COSO states that an internal control system has five crucial components. These five components are summarized in Table 13.3 and are discussed in greater depth in the remainder of the chapter.

THE CONTROL ENVIRONMENT

The AICPA identified seven factors that are important to a control environment (see Table 13.2). All but monitoring performance are discussed in detail in this section. Monitoring is one of the five crucial components of internal control identified by the COSO report and is the topic of a later section of the chapter.

Management's Philosophy and Operating Style

The central component of an organization's control environment is management's philosophy and operating style. If management shows little concern for internal control and ethical behavior, employees are not likely to be diligent or effective in achieving specific control objectives. For example, Maria Pilier found that lines of authority and responsibility at Springer's were loosely defined and she suspected that management may have engaged in "creative accounting" to show its performance in the best light. Meanwhile, Jason Scott found evidence of poor internal control practices in the purchasing and accounts payable functions. It is quite possible that these two conditions are related—that is, that management's loose attitude contributed to purchasing's inattentiveness to good internal control practices.

Management's philosophy and operating style can be assessed by answering questions such as the following:

Table 13.3 **Five Interrelated Components of COSO's Internal Control Model**

Component	Description
Control environment	The core of any business is its people—their individual attributes, including integrity, ethical values and competence—and the environment in which they operate. They are the engine that drives the organization and the foundation on which everything rests.
Control activities	Control policies and procedures must be established and executed to help ensure that the actions identified by management as necessary to address risks to achievement of the organization's objectives are effectively carried out.
Risk assessment	The organization must be aware of and deal with the risks it faces. It must set objectives, integrated with the sales, production, marketing, financial and other activities so that the organization is operating in concert. It must also establish mechanisms to identify, analyze, and manage the related risks.
Information and communication	Surrounding the control activities are information and communication systems. They enable the organization's people to capture and exchange the information needed to conduct, manage, and control its operations.
Monitoring	The entire process must be monitored, and modifications made as necessary. In this way the system can react dynamically, changing as conditions warrant.

- Does management take undue business risks to achieve its objectives, or does it assess potential risks and rewards prior to acting?
- Does management attempt to manipulate such performance measures as net income so that its performance can be seen in a more favorable light?
- Does management pressure employees to achieve results regardless of the methods required, or do they demand ethical behavior? In other words, do they believe the ends justify the means?

The answers to questions such as these reflect management's philosophy and operating style. The more responsible management's philosophy and operating style is, the more likely it is that employees will also behave responsibly in working to achieve the organization's objectives.

Organizational Structure

A company's organizational structure defines its lines of authority and responsibility and provides the overall framework for planning, directing, and controlling its operations. Important aspects of organizational structure include the centralization or decentralization of authority, the assignment of responsibility for specific tasks to departments and individuals, the way allocation of responsibilities affects management's information requirements, and the organization of the accounting and IS functions. An overly complex or unclear organizational structure may be indicative of more serious problems. ESM, a brokerage company dealing in government securities, used a multilayered organizational structure to hide a $300 million fraud. Company officers funneled cash to themselves and hid it by reporting a fictitious receivable from a related company in their financial statements.

In today's business world, drastic changes are occurring in management practices and in the organization of companies. Hierarchical organizational structures based on command and control are giving way to flat organizations. Layers of autocratic managers and supervisors are being replaced by self-directed work teams composed of employees formerly assigned to separate and segregated departments. Team members are empowered to make decisions and no longer seek multiple layers of approvals to complete their work. In addition, there is an emphasis on continuous improvement rather than the periodic reviews and appraisals characteristic of earlier evaluations. All of these changes have and will continue to have an enormous impact on management's philosophy and operating style as well as a company's organizational structure.

The Audit Committee of the Board of Directors

All corporations listed on the New York Stock Exchange must have an audit committee composed entirely of outside (nonemployee) directors. The audit committee is responsible for overseeing the corporation's internal control structure, its financial reporting process, and its compliance with related laws, regulations, and standards. The committee works closely with the corporation's external as well as its internal auditors. One of its goals is to provide an independent review of the actions of corporate managers on behalf of the company's shareholders. This review serves as a check on the integrity of management and increases the confidence of the investing public in the propriety of financial reporting.

Methods of Assigning Authority and Responsibility

Authority and responsibility may be assigned through formal job descriptions, employee training, and operating plans, schedules, and budgets. Of particular importance is a formal company code of conduct addressing such matters as standards of ethical behavior, acceptable business practices, regulatory requirements, and conflicts of interest. A written policy and procedures manual is an important tool for assigning authority and responsibility in many organizations. The manual spells out management policy with respect to handling specific transactions. In addition, it documents the systems and procedures employed to process those transactions. It includes a detailed listing of the organization's chart of accounts, along with sample copies of forms and documents. A policy and procedures manual encompassing these elements serves as a helpful on-the-job reference for employees and a useful tool in training new employees.

Human Resources Policies and Practices

Policies and practices dealing with hiring, training, evaluating, compensating, and promoting employees have an important effect on an organization's ability to minimize internal control risks and exposures. Employees should be hired and promoted based on how well they meet written job requirements. Resumes, reference letters, and background checks are important means of evaluating the qualifications of job applicants. Training programs should be implemented to familiarize new employees with their responsibilities as well as organization policies and procedures. Finally, policies with respect to working conditions, compensation, job incentives, and career advancement can be a powerful force in encouraging efficiency and loyal service.

The importance of thorough background checks is underscored by the case of Philip Crosby Associates (PCA), a consulting and training firm. PCA undertook an exhaustive search to select a financial director. The person hired was John C. Nelson, an MBA and CPA with a glowing reference from his former employer. In reality, however, both the CPA and the reference were phony. John C. Nelson was really Robert W. Liszewski, who had recently served an 18-month jail sentence for embezzling $400,000 from a bank in Indiana. By the time PCA discovered his past, Liszewski had embezzled $960,000 using wire transfers to a dummy corporation supported by forged signatures on contracts and authorization documents.

Additional control policies are appropriate for employees with access to cash or other property. They should be required to take an annual vacation, and during this time their job functions should be performed by other staff members. Many employee frauds are discovered when the perpetrator is suddenly forced by illness or accident to take time off. Periodic rotation of duties among key employees can achieve the same results. Of course, the very existence of such policies acts to deter fraud and thus enhance internal control. Finally, fidelity bond insurance coverage of key employees is important. A fidelity bond protects companies against losses arising from deliberate acts of fraud by bonded employees.

External Influences

External influences affect an organization's control environment and heighten management's awareness of the importance of internal control policies and procedures. They include requirements imposed by stock exchanges, by the Financial Accounting Standards Board (FASB), and by the Securities and Exchange Commission (SEC). They also include regulatory agency requirements, such as those for banks, utilities, and insurance companies. Examples include enforcement of the internal control provisions of the Foreign Corrupt Practices Act by the SEC, and audits of financial institutions by the Federal Deposit Insurance Corporation.

While a company's control environment lays the foundation for effective internal control, sound procedures ensure that its internal control objectives are indeed achieved. The next section describes control activities that may be applied at various levels of an organization in order to achieve this success.

CONTROL ACTIVITIES

Control activities are policies and rules that provide reasonable assurance that management's control objectives are achieved. Generally, control procedures fall into one of five categories:

1. Proper authorization of transactions and activities.
2. Segregation of duties.
3. Design and use of adequate documents and records.
4. Adequate safeguards over access to and use of assets and records.
5. Independent checks on performance.

FOCUS 13.1

Control Problems in a School District

The director of finance for a midwestern school district with 42 separate schools hired a CPA firm to audit the school district books. The audit was accompanied by a report that showed that the district's system had a number of serious internal control deficiencies. The director, a former auditor, went to work to improve the control system. The district (1) selected a new software package that all sites would use, (2) standardized accounting and bookkeeping procedures, (3) instituted consistent purchase order procedures, (4) implemented a separation of duties, and (5) created a control system for student vending machine cash and inventory.

As the changes were being made the director noted that book collection fees for the middle school were low. He asked the district's internal auditor to investigate. The auditor contacted the middle school secretary responsible for making daily deposits of all student fees and writing checks to the central office for book fees. The secretary said the low amount was due to the increase in the number of fees waived by the principal for students who qualified for free or reduced lunches.

The principal denied that he was waiving the fee. The principal, the auditor, and the director examined the fee cards for each child. Their investigation showed that the daily deposits into the activity checking account did not agree with the dates stamped paid on the student fee cards. A thorough search of the premises revealed no uncashed checks. So where did the money go and how did the secretary manage to take it when most of the fees were paid with checks made out to the school?

They finally discovered that the secretary was also in charge of the faculty welfare and vending machine receipts fund. The district was not responsible for the fund and so it was never audited or examined. Nor was the fund subject to the newly implemented system of internal controls. Deposits to the welfare fund consisted of checks from the faculty and cash from the vending machines.

An examination of the available records revealed how the $20,000 fraud took place. The secretary stole cash received from the vending machines. She wrote and recorded checks to vendors. However, on some checks she erased the name of the payee and replaced it with her name. She deposited student fees into the faculty welfare to cover up for the stolen funds.

The secretary was immediately discharged due to improper bookkeeping practices. The secretary was bonded, so the district was able to recover all of its missing funds.

The school district made a number of changes to strengthen control. Internal auditors now examine all funds at the schools. The control of faculty welfare funds was transferred to a faculty member. Since the investigation revealed that the secretary had a prior criminal record, a background check was implemented so all future hires could be screened.

Focus Questions

1. How many of the controls mentioned in the chapter were violated in this fraud?
2. What were the major control weaknesses that allowed the fraud to take place?
3. What additional control procedures, if any, should the school district implement to prevent future control problems?

Focus 13.1 discusses how a violation of specific control activities combined with control environment factors resulted in a fraud at a school district in the Midwest.

Authorization

Employees perform tasks and make decisions that affect company assets. For example, a salesclerk at Pep Boys auto parts stores handles cash and approves sales to customers on account. Management does not have the time or resources to supervise all of these activities or approve all related decisions. Instead, they establish general policies for employees to follow and, based on job description, empower them to perform activities and make decisions. This empowerment, called **authorization,** is an important part of an organization's control procedures.

Authorizations are often documented by signing, initializing, or entering an authorization code on the document or record representing the transaction. Computer systems are now capable of recording a **digital signature** (or fingerprint), a means of signing a document with a piece of data that can't be forged. Employees who subsequently process the transaction should verify the presence of the appropriate authorization(s). Auditors review samples of transactions to verify proper authorization, since their absence indicates that a control problem may exist. For example, when reviewing purchase transactions, Jason Scott discovered that some did not have a purchase requisition authorizing the purchase. Instead, they had been "personally authorized" by Bill Springer, the purchasing vice president. In addition, Jason found that some vendor invoice payments had been authorized without proper supporting documents, such as purchase orders and receiving reports. These findings are cause for concern about the adequacy of Springer's internal control procedures.

Certain activities or transactions may be of such consequence that management must grant **specific authorization** for them to occur. For example, management review and approval is often required for sales in excess of $20,000, capital expenditures in excess of $10,000, or uncollectible write-offs in excess of $5000. In contrast, management can authorize employees to handle routine transactions without special approval, a procedure known as **general authorization.** Management should have written policies on both specific and general authorization for each type of transaction the company conducts. Table 13.4 shows some examples of authorization functions.

Separation of Duties

Good internal control demands that no single employee be given too much responsibility. An employee should not be in a position to perpetrate *and* conceal fraud or unintentional errors. Effective segregation of duties requires that the following functions be separated:

- *Authorization,* as previously discussed, involves approving transactions and decisions.
- *Recording* involves preparing source documents; maintaining journals, ledgers, or other files; preparing reconciliations; and preparing performance reports.
- *Custody* may be direct, as in the case of handling cash or maintaining an inventory storeroom, or indirect, as in the case of receiving customer checks via mail or writing checks on the organization's bank account.

If two of these three functions are the responsibility of a single person, problems can arise. For example, the former city treasurer of Fairfax, Virginia, was convicted of embezzling $600,000 from the city treasury. Her scheme worked as follows: When residents used cash to pay their taxes, she would keep the currency. She recorded tax collections on the property tax records but did not report them to the city controller. Eventually, an adjusting journal entry was made to bring her records into agreement with those of the controller. When cash was received to pay for business license fees or court fees, it would be

***Table 13.4* Examples of Authorization Functions**

Transaction Types	Examples of Authorization Functions
Sales orders	Approval of customer credit Approval of shipment Approval of sales returns and allowances
Purchases	Authorization to order goods or services Authorization of capital expenditures Selection of vendors Acceptance of delivered products
Production	Approval of products and quantities to be produced Approval of raw materials issued for use in production Approval of production schedules Approval of completed products
Human resources/payroll	Hiring of new employees Approval of increases in employee compensation Approval of records of time worked Approval of payroll withholdings
Cash receipts	Endorsement of checks for deposit in bank Write-offs of uncollectible accounts
Cash disbursements	Approval of vendor invoices for payment Approval of checks written to settle accounts payable Approval of replenishment of petty cash fund

recorded on a cash register and deposited at the end of each day. She stole portions of this currency but made up discrepancies in the bank deposit by substituting miscellaneous checks received in the mail that would not be missed when they went unrecorded. In this example one person was responsible both for the *custody* of cash receipts and for the *recording* of those receipts. As a result, the controller was able to divert cash receipts and falsify the accounts to conceal the diversion.

Consider another example, this time of an employee who was responsible for *authorizing* transactions and had *custody* of cash. The utilities director of Newport Beach, California, was charged with embezzling $1.2 million from the city. His alleged scheme worked this way. First, he would forge invoices or easement documents (for example, for the rights to put a water line through a person's land) authorizing payments to a real or fictitious city property owner. Finance department officials gave him the checks to deliver to the property owners. He would then forge signatures, endorse the checks to himself, and deposit them in his own accounts. The control weakness in this case was that the utility director was given physical custody of checks relating to transactions that he had also authorized. This enabled him to authorize fictitious transactions and divert the related city payments.

Finally, suppose that an employee is responsible for both *authorization* and *recording* functions. The former payroll director of the Los Angeles Dodgers pleaded guilty to embezzling $330,000 from the team. He would credit employees for hours not worked and then receive a kickback of around 50% of their extra compensation. He also added fictitious names to the Dodgers payroll and cashed their paychecks. The fraud was discovered when the payroll director became ill and another employee took over his duties. Since the perpetrator was responsible for both authorizing the hiring of new employees and for recording employee hours worked, he did not need to prepare or handle the actual paychecks. The club treasurer would simply mail the checks to an address specified by the payroll director.

In modern information systems the computer often can be programmed to perform one or more of the already mentioned functions, in essence, replacing employees. The principle of separating duties remains the same; the only difference is that the computer performs the function rather than a human. For example, many gas stations are now equipped with pumps that allow customers to insert a credit card to pay for their gas. In such cases, the custody of the "cash" and the recording function are both performed by the computer. In addition to improving internal controls, these machines actually improve the process of serving the customer by increasing convenience and eliminating lines to pay for the gas.

In a system that incorporates an effective separation of duties, it should be difficult for any single employee to commit embezzlement successfully. Detecting fraud where two or more people collude to override the controls is more difficult. For example, two women in a credit card company colluded to steal funds. One woman was authorized to set up credit card accounts, the other to write off unpaid accounts of less than $1000. The woman who created the accounts simply created a new account for each of them using fictitious data. When the amount outstanding neared the $1000 limit, the woman in collections wrote them off. The first woman would then create two new cards and the process would be repeated. The women were caught when the jilted boyfriend of one of them sought revenge; he called the credit card company and disclosed the fraudulent scheme.

Documents and Records

The proper design and use of documents and records helps ensure the accurate and complete recording of all relevant data about transactions and events. Their form and content should be kept as simple as possible to facilitate efficient record keeping, minimize recording errors, and facilitate review and verification. Documents that initiate a transaction should contain a space for authorizations. Those used to transfer assets to someone else should have a space for the receiving party's signature. To reduce the likelihood of fraudulent use by dishonest employees documents should be sequentially prenumbered so each can be accounted for. Record keeping should be well coordinated to facilitate tracing individual transactions through the system. A good audit trail facilitates the correction of errors and the verification of system output.

Safeguarding of Assets

When people consider the safeguarding of assets, they most often think of cash and physical assets, such as inventory and equipment. In today's world, however, one of a company's most important assets is its information. Accordingly, steps must be taken to safeguard both information and physical assets. The following procedures are used to safeguard assets from such threats as theft, unauthorized use, and vandalism:

- Effectively supervising and segregating duties.
- Maintaining accurate records of assets, including information.
- Restricting physical access to assets, thereby limiting the chances of loss. Cash registers, safes, lockboxes, and safety deposit boxes are used to limit access to cash, securities, blank checks, and other paper assets. Restricted storage areas are used to protect inventories. For example, over $1 million was embezzled from Perini Corp. because of poor controls (blank checks were kept in an unlocked storeroom). It was easy for employees to take a check, make it out to a fictitious vendor, run it through the check signing machine (also left unlocked), and cash the check.
- Restricting access to physical locations, such as computer rooms.
- Protecting records and documents. Fireproof storage areas and alternative backup locations are effective means of protecting records and documents. Access to vital records can be restricted by locking them in desks or file cabinets. Access to blank checks and documents should be limited to authorized personnel. In Inglewood, California, a janitor was charged with stealing 34 blank checks while cleaning the city finance office. He forged the names of city officials on the checks and cashed them in amounts ranging from $50,000 to $470,000.
- Controlling the environment. Sensitive computer equipment should be located in a room with adequate cooling and special fire protection. The room should be elevated and reinforced to protect the equipment from flooding and falling objects.
- Restricting access to computer files and information using passwords and security codes. Access controls are covered in Chapter 14.

Independent Checks

Internal checks to evaluate the performance of each transaction processing function are another important control element. They should be "independent" because they are generally more effective if performed by someone other than the person responsible for the original operation. Various types of independent checks are now discussed.

Reconciliation of Two Independently Maintained Sets of Records. One way to check the accuracy and completeness of records is to reconcile them with other records that should have the same balance. One example, a bank reconciliation, verifies that company checking accounts agree with bank statements. Another check compares the total of the accounts receivable subsidiary ledgers with that of the accounts receivable general ledger control account.

Comparison of Actual Quantities to Recorded Amounts. Comparing actual quantities with records would include reconciling the cash in a cash register drawer at the end of each operator's shift with the amount recorded on the cash register tape. Inventories should be counted at periodic intervals and the results compared with perpetual inventory records of quantities on hand. Such a check should be done for all inventory items at least once annually and more frequently for high dollar value items, such as jewelry or furs.

Double-Entry Accounting. The maxim that debits must equal credits provides numerous opportunities for internal checks in processing accounting data. For example, debits in a payroll entry are allocated to numerous inventory and/or expense accounts by the cost accounting department. Credits are allocated to several liability accounts for wages and salaries payable, taxes withheld, employee insurance, union dues, and so on, by the payroll department. At the conclusion of these two complex operations, the comparison of total debits to total credits provides a powerful check on the accuracy of both processes. Any discrepancy indicates the presence of one or more errors.

Batch Totals. When records are grouped for processing, **batch totals** (also called control totals) are created by adding a numerical item from each transaction in the batch. In a batch processing application, source documents are assembled in groups and batch totals are manually computed from the source documents before the source data are entered into the system. In an on-line system, batch totals are sometimes computed for all transactions entered within a particular time frame, such as one hour.

In either case, the same control totals should be generated by the computer during each subsequent processing step. An employee who was not involved in preparing the original batch totals should compare the two sets of totals. Otherwise, a person who generated the original control totals *and* reconciled the two sets of totals could easily hide errors or fraudulent transactions.

Any discrepancies between the two totals indicate that an error occurred during the previous processing stage. Examples of errors include lost records, unauthorized records added to the batch, or data transcription or data processing errors. The cause of discrepancies should be identified and the errors corrected before the transactions are processed further. Finding the cause of a discrepancy may require checking each record against its original source document. Limiting batch sizes to 50 records reduces the time required to track down the cause of any individual discrepancy.

Five types of batch totals are commonly used in computer systems:

1. A **financial total** is the sum of a dollar field in a set of records, such as total sales or total cash receipts.
2. A **hash total** is a sum generated from a field that would usually not be added, such as the sum of all customer account numbers or employee identification numbers.
3. A **record count** is the number of documents entered into a process.
4. A **line count** is the number of lines of data entered, such as the number of line items on a sales or purchase order.
5. A **cross-footing balance test** is performed on data that are added horizontally (across several columns) as well as vertically (down each column). This test adds the horizontal and vertical totals and confirms that they are equal.

An example of the use of batch totals to prevent accounting and recording errors is provided by Sarah Robinson. She runs a mail-order business selling imported candies from her home in Salt Lake City, Utah. Sarah's CPA has established an accounting system that includes accounts receivable and general ledger files. Once a week Sarah processes customer payments on account, as illustrated in Fig. 13.1 and by the following procedure:

1. When Sarah receives checks in the mail, she lists customer names and amounts received and computes the total dollar amount of all checks. She notes this batch total on the receipts list she gives to her CPA.
2. She prepares a bank deposit slip and deposits the checks in the bank. To verify the accuracy of the bank deposit, she compares the bank-validated copy of the deposit slip with her original batch total.
3. Using Sarah's receipts list, her CPA posts credits to the appropriate customer accounts and updates each customer's balance. He computes the new

Figure 13.1

Example of the Use of Batch Totals in Processing Cash Receipts

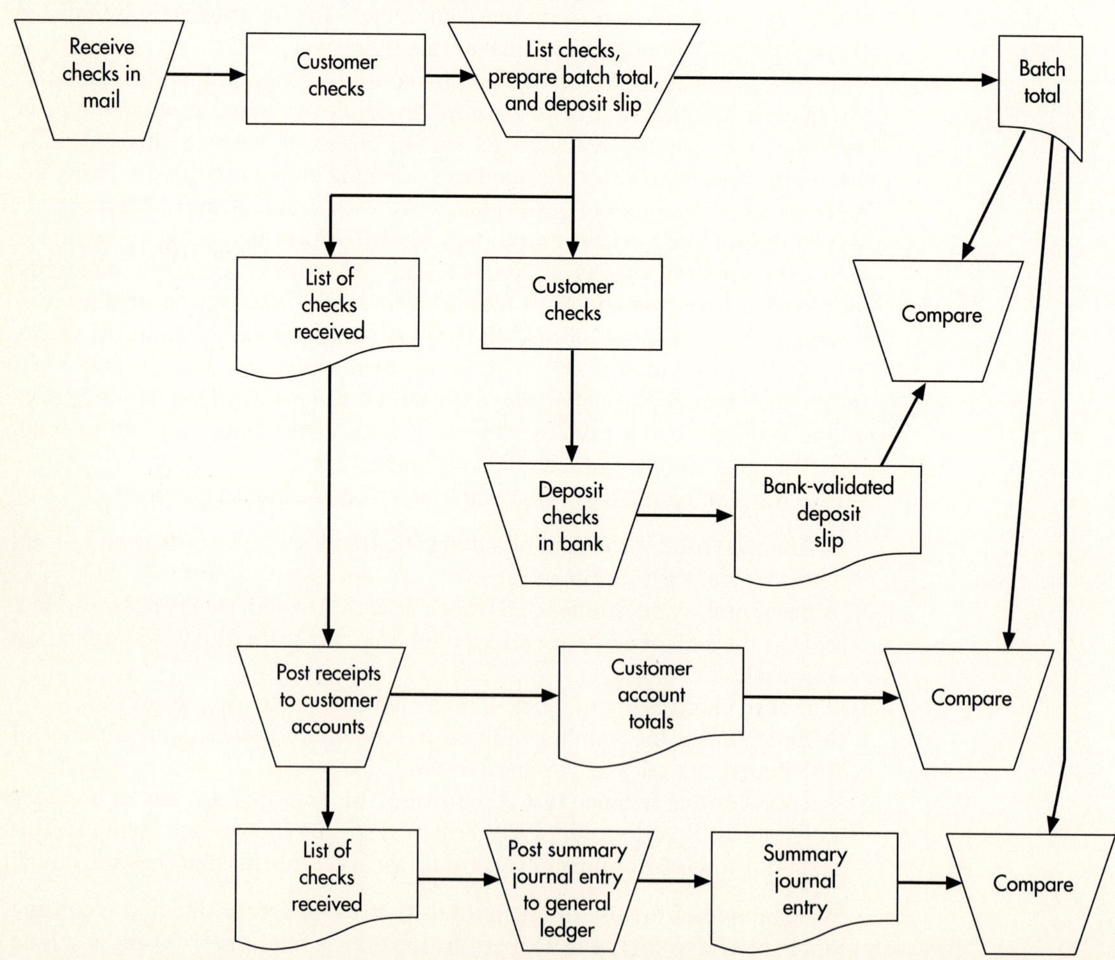

total balance of the accounts receivable file, determines the difference between the old and new file totals, and verifies that this difference agrees with Sarah's batch total. This comparison serves as an independent check on the accuracy of posting receipts to the customer accounts.

4. Her CPA prepares a summary journal entry and posts it to the general ledger, again verifying that the entry amount is equal to Sarah's batch total.

As you can see, the batch total provides an independent check on the accuracy of each processing step. If a discrepancy is discovered, the difference between the batch totals often provides a clue about where the error occurred. For example, if the difference equals a transaction amount, that transaction may have been omitted. If the difference, divided by 2, is equal to a transaction amount, the latter may have been incorrectly debited instead of credited or added instead of subtracted. If it differs by a nonzero digit, there may be a **transcription error,** in which a digit is entered incorrectly during processing (i.e., a 4 in the tens column entered as a 9, causing an error of 50). If it is evenly divisible by 9, the likely cause is a **transposition error,** in which two adjacent digits were inadvertently exchanged (for example, 46 for 64).

Simple errors can have large financial consequences. For example, a single transposition error almost cost the U.S. Treasury $14 million. A clerk at the Federal Reserve Bank of Philadelphia transposed two digits while calculating the interest on newly issued five-year Treasury notes. The operator erroneously entered the interest rate as 8.67% rather than 6.87%. Fortunately, an investor detected the error when he received a notification of the amount to be paid. The bank was able to correct the error before the checks were issued and mailed. The bank quickly implemented new control procedures to make sure the problem did not reoccur.

Independent Review. Generally, segregation of duties results in two or more persons processing a transaction. In such cases the second person should review the work of the first, performing such tasks as the following:

- Checking for proper authorization signatures on source documents.
- Reviewing documents supporting disbursements, loan approvals, and account write-offs.
- Checking the accuracy of crucial data items, including prices, quantities, and extensions on documents such as invoices and purchase orders.

The maintenance of accurate accounting records is not the only benefit derived from the prevention, detection, and correction of errors in accounting data. Records produced by the accounting system are a crucial part of transactions involving employees, customers, vendors, and other important constituents of a business organization. Frequent errors in record keeping may erode the organization's credibility with these groups and thereby undermine management's efforts to achieve its organizational objectives. Internal checks and other related control procedures thus play an important role in the effective management of a business organization.

RISK ASSESSMENT

Helping management control a business is one of the primary objectives of an AIS. Accountants play an important role in this process by designing effective control systems and auditing (or reviewing) those currently in place to ensure that they are operating effectively. One way accountants can design an effective system of internal controls is to follow the risk assessment strategy shown in Fig. 13.2. We will now walk you through the major steps in this strategy. Focus 13.2 discusses how Dow Chemical assesses risk and designs control systems.

Identify Threats

Companies must identify the potential threats they face, such as natural or political disasters, software errors, hardware malfunctions, unintentional errors and accidents, and fraud or abuse. For example, companies built along fault lines are especially susceptible to earthquakes, as companies in the Los Angeles and San Francisco quakes can attest. Companies located near rivers

Figure 13.2

Risk Assessment Approach to Designing Internal Controls

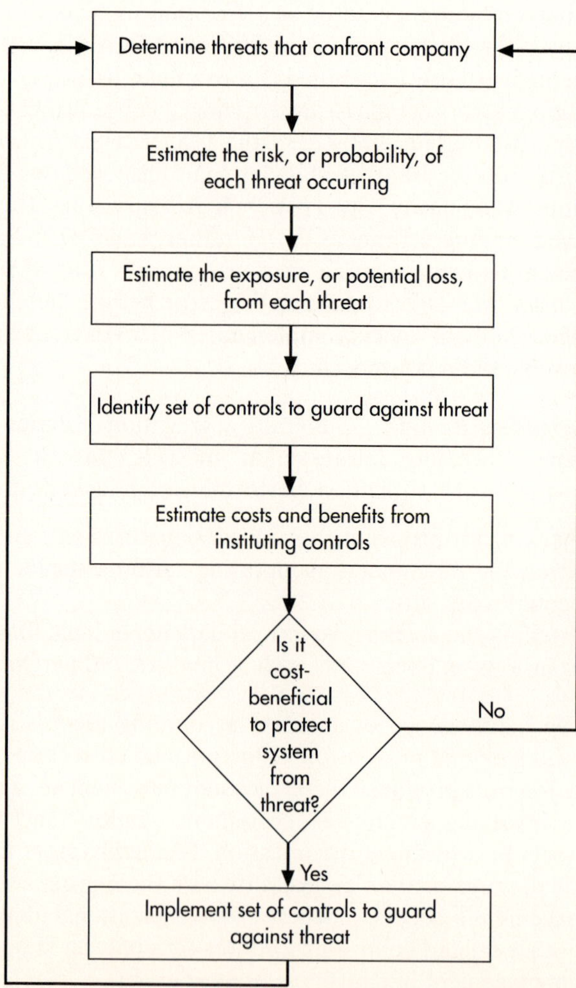

and large bodies of water, such as those along the Mississippi River, are especially susceptible to flood damage. Almost any system can be damaged by terrorist attacks, as the governmental agencies bombed in the Oklahoma City attack can affirm.

Estimate Risk

The likelihood, or probability, that a threat will actually come to pass is referred to as risk. Some threats pose a greater risk because the probability of their occurrence is more likely. For example, it is more realistic to expect that a company will be the victim of a computer fraud rather than of a terrorist attack. Likewise, employees are more likely to make unintentional errors than they are to commit intentional acts of fraud against their companies.

Estimate Exposure

The potential dollar loss should a particular threat become a reality is referred to as exposure. The risk of an earthquake may be very small but the exposure can be enormous; it could completely destroy a company and force it into bankruptcy. The exposure from a fraud is usually not as great, as most frauds do not threaten a company's existence. The exposure from unintentional errors could range from very small to very large, depending on the nature of the error and how long it persists. Risk and exposure must be considered together. As either increases, the materiality of the threat and the need to protect against it also rises.

Identify Controls

Management must identify one or more controls that will protect the company from each threat. In evaluating the benefits of specific internal control procedures, management should consider their effectiveness and timing. All other factors being equal, a preventive control is superior to a detective one. By the time a detective control identifies a problem, a loss may already have been sustained, and additional cost may be required to correct the problem. However, if preventive controls fail and a control problem arises, detective controls are essential to discover the problem and recover from it. Thus preventive and detective controls complement each other, and a good internal control system should employ both.

Estimate Costs and Benefits

No internal control system can ever provide an organization with foolproof protection against all internal control risks. The cost of a foolproof system would be prohibitively high. In addition, since many controls negatively impact operational efficiency, a surfeit of controls would slow down the system and make it inefficient—restricting a company's ability to meet its goals. Therefore the objective in designing an internal control system is to provide "reasonable assurance" that control problems do not take place. Thus the benefit of an internal control procedure must exceed its cost.

The costs of an internal control system are easier to measure than its benefits. A primary cost element is personnel, including the time to perform control procedures, the costs of hiring additional employees to achieve effective segregation of duties, and the costs of programming controls into a computer system.

FOCUS 13.2

Risk Analysis at Dow Chemical

Risk analysis is often perceived as an expensive and lengthy process that outside consultants perform with a minimum of employee contact. Consequently, few end users actually understand or even desire the recommended controls and are reluctant to implement or enforce them. Dow Chemical is out to change this attitude; it has recently developed a simple and quick way to help users evaluate risk.

The key component of the Dow security program is the risk analysis matrix (RAM). The RAM is a grid-based question-and-answer chart that helps users identify potential threats and the associated data and assets that require protection. The first step in using the RAM is to classify undesirable events in terms of their effect. In the grid that follows the vertical axis has three columns related to security objectives: data integrity (unauthorized data modification or destruction), data sensitivity (unauthorized data disclosure), and data availability (unavailability of data or system services).

The horizontal axis pinpoints the accidental acts (such as an error or omission) and the deliberate acts (such as a hacker or employee fraud) from which data must be protected. After undesirable events are identified, employees affected by the system are assembled. For example, if a regional sales office is to have a LAN installed, a salesperson, a LAN technician, and a clerk from the sales office are invited to a special meeting.

The manager of security prepares a visual aid of the matrix and asks each participant to think about the risks associated with each of its squares. For example, they might discuss what could happen if data were accidentally modified by an employee. Each square is considered in turn (reducing data integrity due to deliberate acts, unauthorized data disclosure due to an accident, etc.) until the chart is complete.

The next step is to determine which controls will address each security concern. For example, sensitive documents should be shredded to guard against their falling into the wrong hands. Another example is using a tape backup system to guard against the main server being accidentally destroyed. That is followed by management determining the economic feasibility of the controls. The last step is to assign implementation responsibilities to team members.

Many security managers find security to be a daunting proposition and do not know where to start. Dow Chemical claims that

---

Internal control benefits stem from reduced losses. One way to calculate benefits involves **expected loss,** the mathematical product of risk and exposure:

$$\text{Expected loss} = \text{risk} \times \text{exposure}.$$

The benefit of a control procedure is the difference between the expected loss with the control procedure(s) and the expected loss without it. To determine whether a control is cost beneficial, the cost of the control is subtracted from the benefit.

Determine Cost/Benefit Effectiveness

After estimating the benefits and costs of a particular control, management must determine whether the control is cost beneficial. This can best be illustrated using an example provided by Atlantic Richfield, the oil company. Data errors occasionally require that an entire payroll be reprocessed, at a cost of \$10,000. Management is considering a data validation step that would reduce error risk from 15% to 1%, at a cost of \$600 per pay period. Should this particular validation step be employed? An example of the cost-benefit analysis required to answer this question is shown in Table 13.5. If the proposed payroll validation procedure is not employed, the expected loss to the company is companies can now empower themselves and develop their own system of controls. No longer do they have to count on someone else to do it for them.

Focus Questions

1. What is your opinion of the RAM? Do you think users and others affected by a system can develop an adequate system of controls?
2. Would you be more inclined to implement and follow a system of internal controls that you had been instrumental in designing? Why or why not?

Risk Analysis Matrix

	Data Integrity	**Data Sensitivity**	**Data Availability**
Accidental Acts Errors and Omissions	Major or minor concern	Confidential or nonconfidential	Essential or nonessential
Deliberate Acts Fraud and Misuse	Major or minor concern	Confidential or nonconfidential	Essential or nonessential
	Data Destruction or Modification	**Data Disclosure**	**Data Inaccessibility**

estimated at $1500. Since the expected loss with the validation step is $100, the control provides an expected benefit of $1400. After deducting the control costs of $600, the validation step provides a net benefit of $800 and clearly should be implemented. Although such estimates are difficult to come

Table 13.5 **Cost-Benefit Analysis of Payroll Validation Procedure**

	Without Validation Procedure	With Validation Procedure	Net Expected Difference
Cost to reprocess entire payroll	$10,000	$10,000	
Risk of payroll data errors	15%	1%	
Expected reprocessing cost ($10,000 × risk)	$1500	$100	$1400
Cost of validation procedure	$0	$600	$(600)
Net expected benefit of validation procedure			$800

by and the calculations are subjective and susceptible to error, they are still useful.

In evaluating the costs and benefits of internal control, management must employ good judgment and consider factors other than those reflected in the simple expected benefit calculation. For example, an exposure may be so large that it threatens the organization's continued existence. In such cases, management should be willing to implement internal control procedures having a cost higher than the simple reduction in expected loss. It may be worthwhile to spend more than indicated by the cost-benefit analysis to minimize the possibility that the organization will perish. This extra cost can be viewed as an insurance premium to protect the organization against catastrophic loss.

Compliance with the Foreign Corrupt Practices Act

Cost-benefit analysis provides management with a framework for evaluating and documenting its compliance with the internal control provisions of the Foreign Corrupt Practices Act. Most of the internal control systems established prior to the act are, and continue to be, adequate. However, most executives deem it necessary to take specific steps to demonstrate their compliance. These procedures often include the following:

- Document existing internal control systems. Documentation may include narrative descriptions of internal control objectives and procedures; document and systems flowcharts; data flow diagrams; and organizational charts, job descriptions, and other explanations of assigned responsibilities within the organization. One recommendation for completing documentation is to make each major accounting cycle the focal point of a separate effort.
- Evaluate the quality of the internal control system. Because the law stipulates that the system must provide "reasonable assurances" that certain control objectives are met, this evaluation may be based on a cost-benefit analysis. All significant control threats within each accounting cycle should be identified, and estimates of the exposure and risk associated with each threat should be developed. Any control threats for which expected loss exceeds a minimum threshold (determined by management) represent potential control weaknesses that require further analysis. For example, a company might investigate any threat that has an expected loss greater than $5000.
- Evaluate the costs and benefits of instituting controls to deal with each control weakness identified. Costs include direct expenditures to implement control procedures and indirect effects such as reductions in employee morale or delays in transaction processing. Benefits include overestimations of expected losses and factors such as increased management confidence and prevention of threats having potentially catastrophic effects.
- Weigh costs and benefits and determine whether more control is needed. If the quantitative and subjective benefits of a control procedure outweigh the related costs, the procedure should be implemented. If proposed procedures are not cost beneficial, the existing internal control system should be retained. These careful evaluations demonstrate that management has

obtained "reasonable assurances" in identifying, evaluating, and dealing appropriately with any potential control weaknesses.

Compliance with the internal control requirements of the Foreign Corrupt Practices Act is a continuous process of reviewing and evaluating control systems. The primary responsibility for this process rests with management. However, management must rely on the assistance of accounting systems designers and internal and external auditors. The board of directors and its audit committee are also responsible for ensuring that management adopts compliance policies and processes. Regardless of the legal requirements, a compliance program that continuously monitors the effectiveness of internal accounting controls makes good business sense.

INFORMATION AND COMMUNICATION

The primary purpose of an AIS is to record, process, store, and communicate information about an organization. This means that accountants must understand how (1) transactions are initiated, (2) data are captured in machine-readable form or converted from source documents to machine readable form, (3) computer files are accessed and updated, (4) data are processed to prepare information, and (5) information is reported to internal users and external parties. Accountants must also understand the accounting records and procedures, supporting documents, and specific financial statement accounts involved in processing and reporting transactions.

According to the AICPA, an AIS has five primary objectives:

1. Identify and record all valid transactions. For example, if a company intentionally records a fictitious sale, it can overstate revenues and income. If a company forgets to record some expenses at the end of the year, expenses are understated and net income overstated.
2. Properly classify transactions. For example, improperly classifying an expense as an asset overstates assets and net income.
3. Record transactions at their proper monetary value. For example, an account receivable that becomes uncollectible should be written off.
4. Record transactions in the proper accounting period. Recording 1998 sales in 1997 overstates sales and net income for 1997 and has the opposite effect for 1998.
5. Properly present transactions and related disclosures in the financial statements. Failing to disclose a lawsuit or a contingent liability could mislead the reader of a financial statement.

Accounting systems generally consist of several accounting subsystems, each designed to process transactions of a particular type. Although they differ with respect to the type of transactions processed, all accounting subsystems follow the same sequence of procedures. These procedures are referred to as accounting cycles. The five major accounting cycles and their related control objectives and procedures are described in detail in Chapters 17–21.

MONITORING PERFORMANCE

Key methods of monitoring performance include effective supervision, responsibility reporting, and internal auditing. Effective supervision involves training and assisting employees, monitoring their performance, correcting errors, and safeguarding assets by overseeing employees who have access to them. Supervision is especially important in organizations that cannot afford elaborate responsibility reporting or are too small to have an adequate segregation of duties. Responsibility accounting systems include budgets, quotas, schedules, standard costs, and quality standards; performance reports that compare actual with planned performance and highlight significant variances; and procedures for investigating significant variances and taking timely action to correct the conditions leading to such variances.

Internal auditing involves reviewing the reliability and integrity of financial and operating information and providing an appraisal of internal control effectiveness. It also involves assessing employee compliance with management policies and procedures and applicable laws and regulations, and evaluating the efficiency and effectiveness of management. Unlike external auditors, internal auditors place great emphasis on a company's management controls. Thus, they can detect excess overtime, underused assets, obsolete inventory, padded travel expense reimbursements, excessively loose budgets and quotas, poorly justified capital expenditures, and production bottlenecks. Objectivity and effectiveness require that the internal audit function must be organizationally independent of accounting and operating functions. For example, the head of internal auditing should report to the audit committee of the board of directors rather than to the controller or chief financial officer.

One alert internal auditor noted that a department supervisor took the entire office staff out to lunch in a limousine on her birthday. During the remainder of the audit he noted other evidences of an extravagant lifestyle. Questioning whether her salary could support her lifestyle, he began a more in-depth investigation. He found that she had set up several fictitious vendors, sent the company invoices from these vendors, and then cashed the checks when they were mailed to her.

SUMMARY AND CASE CONCLUSION

After three days in Bozeman, Jason and Maria returned to Northwest's main office and filed their audit report. One week later, they were summoned to the office of Roger Sawyer, Northwest's director of internal auditing, to explain their findings. Shortly thereafter, a high-level internal audit team was dispatched to Bozeman to take a closer look at the situation.

When the audit team returned, Jason and Maria inquired about their findings and were told the situation was still under investigation. Six months later, a company newsletter included an announcement that the Springer family had sold their remaining 10% interest in the Bozeman business to Northwest and had resigned from their management positions. Two Northwest executives were transferred in to replace them. Still, there was no word on the audit findings.

Two years later Jason and Maria were assigned to a job supervised by Frank Ratliff, a member of the high-level internal audit team. After-hours one evening, Ratliff told them the story. Based on Jason and Maria's reports, the investigation team had examined a large sample of purchasing transactions and all employee timekeeping and payroll records for a 12-month period. It had also taken a detailed physical inventory. The team discovered that the problems identified by Jason—including missing purchase requisitions, purchase orders, and receiving reports, as well as excessive prices—were widespread. They found that these problems had occurred almost exclusively in transactions with three large vendors from whom Springer's had purchased several million dollars worth of inventories and supplies. The team discussed the unusually high item prices with the vendors, but did not receive a satisfactory explanation. However, a check of the county business licensing bureau revealed that Bill Springer held a significant ownership interest in each of these three companies. By authorizing excessive prices to companies he partially owned, Springer had earned a share of several hundred thousand dollars of excessive profits, all at the expense of Northwest Industries.

The investigation team had also found evidence that several of Springer's employees were paid for more hours than documented by timekeeping records. Finally, the team had determined Springer's inventory account was materially overstated. The physical inventory revealed that a significant portion of recorded inventory did not exist, and that other portions were obsolete. The adjusting journal entry reflecting Springer's "real" inventory wiped out much of the outlet's profits over the past three years.

When confronted, the Springers vehemently denied any laws had been broken. Northwest considered going to the authorities for a formal fraud investigation, but were concerned their case was not strong enough to prove in court. They were also worried that adverse publicity might damage the company's position in Bozeman. After months of negotiation, the Springers agreed to the settlement reported in the newsletter. Part of the settlement was that no public statement would be made about any alleged fraud or embezzlement involving the Springers. According to Ratliff, this was not unusual. In many cases of fraud, settlements are reached quietly, with no legal action taken, so the company can avoid adverse publicity.

KEY TERMS

control
embezzlement
threat
exposure
risk
internal control
management control
administrative controls
accounting controls
internal control structure
preventive controls
detective controls
corrective controls
feedforward controls
feedback controls
general controls
application controls
input controls
processing controls
output controls
authorization
digital signature
specific authorization
general authorization
batch totals
financial total
hash total
record count
line count
cross-footing balance test
transcription error
transposition error
expected loss

CHAPTER QUIZ

1. Which of the following includes the three essential elements of an internal control structure?
   a. Control environment, administrative controls, and accounting controls
   b. Management, administrative, and accounting controls
   c. Control environment, accounting system, and control procedures
   d. Management controls, administrative controls, and accounting system

2. Which of the following statements is false?
   a. Administrative controls help ensure operational efficiency and adherence to managerial policies.
   b. Accounting controls help safeguard assets and ensure the reliability of financial records.
   c. Internal control encompasses both administrative and accounting controls.
   d. Management control has a narrower, less encompassing definition than internal accounting control.

3. Which of the following statements is true?
   a. The COSO report is narrow in scope and is limited to financial controls.
   b. The COSO report states internal control is a process that should provide reasonable assurance control objectives are achieved.
   c. The Foreign Corrupt Practices Act requires *all* U.S. companies to maintain a good system of internal accounting control.
   d. It is easier to add controls to an already designed system than to include them during the initial design stage.

4. All other things being equal,
   a. detective controls are superior to preventive controls.
   b. corrective controls are superior to preventive controls.
   c. preventive controls are equivalent to detective controls.
   d. preventive controls are superior to detective controls.

5. Which of the following statements about the control environment is false?
   a. Management's attitudes toward internal control and ethical behavior have little impact on employee beliefs or actions.
   b. An overly complex or unclear organizational structure may be indicative of more serious problems.
   c. A written policy and procedures manual is an important tool for assigning authority and responsibility in many organizations.
   d. Supervision is especially important in organizations that cannot afford elaborate responsibility reporting or are too small to have an adequate separation of duties.

6. To achieve effective segregation of duties, certain functions must be separated. Which of the following is the correct listing of the functions that must be segregated?
   a. Control, recording, and monitoring
   b. Authorization, recording, and custody
   c. Control, custody, and authorization
   d. Monitoring, recording, and planning

7. All of the following are independent checks *except*
   a. bank reconciliation.
   b. periodic comparison of subsidiary ledger totals to control accounts.
   c. a trial balance.
   d. re-adding the total of a batch of invoices and comparing it to your first total.

8. Which of the following is a control procedure relating to the design and use of adequate documents and records?
   a. Locking blank checks in a drawer
   b. Reconciling the bank account
   c. Sequentially prenumbering sales invoices
   d. Comparing actual physical quantities to recorded amounts

9. Which of the following is the correct order of the risk assessment steps discussed in the chapter?
   a. Identify threats, estimate risk and exposure, identify controls, estimate costs and benefits
   b. Identify controls, estimate risk and exposure, identify threats, estimate costs and benefits
   c. Estimate risk and exposure, identify controls, identify threats, estimate costs and benefits
   d. Estimate costs and benefits, identify threats, identify controls, estimate risk and exposure

10. Your current system is deemed to be 90% reliable. A major threat has been identified with an exposure of $3,000,000. Two control procedures exist to deal with the threat. Implementation of control A would cost $100,000 and reduce the risk to 6%. Implementation of control B would cost $140,000 and reduce the risk to 4%.

Implementation of both controls would cost \$220,000 and reduce the risk to 2%. Given the data and based solely on an economic analysis of costs and benefits, what should you do?

a. Implement control A only
b. Implement control B only
c. Implement both control A and control B
d. Implement neither control

DISCUSSION QUESTIONS

13.1 Answer the following questions about the audit of Springer's Northwest Lumber & Supply.

a. What deficiencies existed in the control environment at Springer's?
b. Do you agree with the decision to settle with the Springers rather than prosecute them for fraud and embezzlement? Why or why not?
c. Should the company have told Jason and Maria the results of the high-level audit? Why or why not?

13.2 For each of the control activities listed, discuss whether the activity contains elements of a preventive control, a feedback control, and/or a feedforward control. (*Note:* Some may contain elements of two or all three.)

a. Audit of a governmental agency by the General Accounting Office
b. Tabulation and review of customer complaints by a manager
c. Analysis of potential employee resumes by a human resources manager
d. Analysis of accident statistics in a factory

13.3 Effective segregation of duties is sometimes not economically feasible in a small business. What internal control elements do you think can help compensate for this threat?

13.4 Craig Robinson has just purchased a PC and intends to computerize his sister Sarah's manual system (see Fig. 13.1). What effect will this have on the use of batch totals in cash receipts processing?

13.5 Some people feel that, instead of producing tangible benefits, business controls create resentment and loss of company morale. Discuss this position.

13.6 In recent years Supersmurf's external auditors have given clean opinions on its financial statements and favorable evaluations of its internal control systems. Discuss whether it is necessary for this corporation to take any further action to comply with the Foreign Corrupt Practices Act.

13.7 When you go to a movie theater, you buy a prenumbered ticket from the window or counter cashier. This ticket is then handed to another person at the entrance to the movie. What kinds of irregularities is the theater trying to prevent? What controls is it using to prevent these irregularities? What remaining risks or exposures can you identify?

PROBLEMS

13.1 You are an audit supervisor who has recently been assigned to a new client, Go-Go Corporation, that is listed on the New York Stock Exchange. You recently visited Go-Go's corporate headquarters to become acquainted with key personnel and to conduct a preliminary review of the company's accounting policies and systems. During this visit, the following events occurred:

1. You met with Go-Go's audit committee, which consists of the corporate controller, treasurer, financial vice president, and budget director.
2. You recognized the treasurer as a former aide to John Boatsky, who was convicted of fraud in an insider-trading scandal three years ago.
3. Management explained its plans to change its method of accounting for depreciation from the accelerated method to the straight-line method. Management implied that, if your firm does not concur with this change, Go-Go will employ other auditors.
4. You learned that the financial vice president serves as the manager of a staff of five internal auditors.
5. You noted that all management authority seems to reside with three brothers, who serve as chief executive officer, president, and financial vice president.
6. You were told that the performance of divisional and departmental managers is

evaluated on a subjective basis, because Go-Go's management believes that formal performance evaluation procedures are "counterproductive."

7. You learned that the company has reported increases in earnings per share for each of the past 25 quarters. However, earnings during the current quarter have leveled off and may decline.
8. You reviewed the company's policy and procedures manual, which listed policies for dealing with customers, vendors, and employees.
9. Your preliminary assessment is that the accounting systems are well designed and employ effective internal control procedures.

REQUIRED

The information you have obtained suggests potential problems relating to one or more of the elements of Go-Go's internal control structure. Identify these problems, and explain each in relation to internal control structure concepts.

13.2 The first column in Table 13.6 lists source document amounts that have been summed to obtain a batch total. You may assume that these amounts and the batch total are correct. Columns (a)–(d) contain batch totals computed from the same amounts after these source documents were processed in a subsequent processing step. One processing error occurred during each of these four cases.

REQUIRED

For each case, you are to do the following:
a. Compute the difference between the batch total obtained after processing and the correct batch total shown on the left.
b. Explain specifically how this difference is helpful in discovering the processing error.
c. Identify the processing error.

13.3 Explain how the principle of organizational independence is violated in each of the following situations. Also suggest one or more procedures to reduce the risk and exposure highlighted in each example.
a. A payroll clerk recorded a 40-hour workweek for an employee who had quit the previous week. He then prepared a paycheck for this employee, forged her signature, and cashed the check.
b. While opening the mail, a cashier set aside, and subsequently cashed, two checks payable to the company on account.

***Table 13.6* Amounts from Source Documents**

	(a)	(b)	(c)	(d)
$3,630.62	$3,630.62	$3,630.62	$3,630.62	$3,630.62
1,484.86	1,484.86	1,484.86	1,484.86	1,484.86
2,164.67	2,164.67	2,164.67	2,164.67	2,164.67
946.43	946.43	946.43	946.43	946.43
2,626.28	−2,626.28	2,626.28	2,626.28	2,626.28
969.97	969.97	969.97	969.97	969.97
2,772.42	2,772.42	2,772.42	3,772.42	2,772.42
934.25	934.25	934.25	934.25	934.25
1,620.94	1,620.94	1,620.94	1,620.94	1,620.94
4,566.86	4,566.86	4,656.86	4,566.86	4,566.86
1,249.32	1,249.32	1,249.32	1,249.32	1,249.32
1,070.27	1,070.27	1,070.27	1,070.27	1,070.27
2,668.51	2,668.51	2,668.51	2,668.51	2,668.51
1,762.62	1,762.62	1,762.62	1,762.62	873.26
873.26	873.26	873.26	873.26	$27,578.66
$29,341.28	$24,088.72	$29,431.28	$30,341.28	

c. A cashier prepared a fictitious invoice from a company using his brother-in-law's name. He wrote a check in payment of the invoice, which the brother-in-law later cashed.

d. An employee of the finishing department walked off with several parts from the storeroom and recorded the items in the inventory ledger as having been issued to the assembly department.

e. A cashier cashed a check from a customer in payment of an account receivable, pocketed the cash, and concealed the theft by properly posting the receipt to the customer's account in the accounts receivable ledger.

13.4 McClain's Lumberyard uses the following procedures to sell lumber to its customers:

- The customer tells an office clerk the sizes and quantities of lumber he wants to purchase.
- The clerk records the items on a sales document, calculates the total cost, and collects the customer's payment.
- A worker obtains the lumber from the yard and loads it into the customer's car or truck. If the purchase is large and the customer wishes, McClain's will deliver the order.

REQUIRED

Explain several aspects of the design and use of the sales document that will facilitate control of cash receipts and inventories by McClain's.

13.5 The Gardner Company, a client of your firm, has come to you with the following problem: It has three clerical employees who must perform the following functions.

1. Maintain the general ledger.
2. Maintain the accounts payable ledger.
3. Maintain the accounts receivable ledger.
4. Prepare checks for signature.
5. Maintain the disbursements journal.
6. Issue credits on returns and allowances.
7. Reconcile the bank account.
8. Handle and deposit cash receipts.

Assuming equal abilities among the three employees, the company asks you to assign functions 1–8 to them in order to maximize internal control. Assume that these employees will perform no accounting functions other than the ones listed.

REQUIRED

a. List four possible unsatisfactory pairings of the functions.

b. State how you would distribute the functions among the three employees. Assume that with the exception of the nominal jobs of the bank reconciliation and the issuance of credits on returns and allowances, all functions require an equal amount of time. (CPA Examination adapted)

13.6 The Future Corporation is a small manufacturing company located in Aggie, Texas. It operates one plant and employs 50 workers in its manufacturing facility. Employees are paid weekly. Each week the department supervisors supply the payroll clerk with signed time sheets and also with a list of any employees hired or terminated by the supervisor. The payroll clerk compares the time sheets with the time cards and prepares and signs payroll checks. The paychecks are then given in sealed envelopes to the supervisors, who in turn give them to the respective employees.

REQUIRED

Identify several internal control weaknesses in Future's payroll system. For each weakness, describe how internal control could be improved.

13.7 You are auditing the Alaska Branch of Far Distributing Company. This branch has substantial annual sales, which are billed and collected locally. As a part of your audit, you find that the procedures for handling cash receipts are as follows.

Cash collections on over-the-counter sales and COD sales are received from the customer or delivery service by the cashier. Upon receipt of cash, the sales ticket is stamped "paid" and a copy is filed for future reference. The only record of COD sales is a copy of the sales ticket, which is given to the cashier to hold until the cash is received from the delivery service.

Mail is opened by the secretary to the credit manager, and remittances are given to the credit manager for review. The credit manager then places the remittances in a tray on the cashier's desk. At the daily deposit cutoff time the cashier delivers the checks and cash on hand to the assistant credit manager, who prepares remittance lists and makes up the bank deposit that the manager also takes to the bank. The assistant credit manager also posts remittances to the accounts receivable ledger cards and verifies the cash discount allowable.

You also ascertain that the credit manager obtains approval from the executive office at Far Distributing Company, located in Chicago, to write off uncollectible accounts. In addition, the manager has retained in custody, as of the end of the fiscal year, some remittances that were received on various days during the last month.

REQUIRED

a. Describe irregularities that might occur under the current procedures for handling cash collections and remittances.
b. Detail procedures that you would recommend to strengthen internal control over cash collections and remittances. (CPA Examination)

13.8 Your junior accountant has prepared the following description of the accounting and internal control procedures relating to purchases by the Branden Company, a medium-sized manufacturer of special order machinery.

After approval by manufacturing department supervisors, materials purchase requisitions are forwarded to the purchasing department supervisor, who distributes the requisitions to his employees. These employees prepare prenumbered purchase orders in triplicate, account for all numbers, and send the original purchase order to the vendor. One copy of the purchase order is sent to the receiving department, where it is used as a receiving report. The other copy is filed in the purchasing department.

When the materials are received, they are moved directly to the storeroom and issued to the supervisors on an informal request basis. The receiving department sends a receiving report (with its copy of the purchase order attached) to the purchasing department and forwards copies of the receiving report to the storeroom and to the accounting department.

Vendors' invoices for material purchases, received in duplicate in the mail room, are sent to the purchasing department and directed to the employee who placed the related order. He or she then compares (1) the invoice with the copy of the purchase order on file in the purchasing department for price and terms; and (2) the invoice quantity received as reported by the shipping and receiving department on its copy of the purchase order. The purchasing department employees also check discounts, footings, and extensions, after which they initial the invoice to indicate approval for payment. The invoice is then submitted to the voucher section of the accounting department, where it is coded for account distribution, assigned a voucher number, entered in the voucher register, and filed according to payment due date.

REQUIRED

Discuss the weaknesses, if any, in the internal control of Branden's purchasing and subsequent procedures. Suggest supplementary or revised procedures for remedying each weakness with regard to (a) requisition of materials and (b) receipt and storage of materials. (CPA Examination)

13.9 During a recent review ABC Corporation discovered that it has a serious internal control problem. It is estimated that the exposure associated with this problem is $1 million and that the risk is presently 5%. Two internal control procedures have been proposed to deal with this problem. Procedure A would cost $25,000 and would reduce risk to 2%. Procedure B would cost $30,000 and would reduce risk to 1%. If both procedures were implemented, risk would be reduced to a tenth of 1%.

REQUIRED

a. What is the estimated expected loss associated with ABC Corporation's internal control problem before any new internal control procedures are implemented?
b. Compute the revised estimate of expected loss (1) if procedure A were implemented, (2) if procedure B were implemented, and (3) if both procedures were implemented.
c. Compare the estimated costs and benefits of procedure A, of procedure B, and of both procedures combined.
d. Considering only the estimates of cost and benefit, which procedure or procedures should be implemented? What other factors might be relevant to the decision?

CASE 13.1: ANYCOMPANY, INC.—AN ONGOING COMPREHENSIVE CASE

Visit a local company and obtain permission to study its system of internal controls. Once you have lined up a company, do the following:

1. Obtain copies of organizational charts, job descriptions, and related documentation on how authority and responsibility have been assigned

within the organization. Evaluate whether lines of authority and responsibility seem to be clearly defined.

2. Determine whether the company has an internal audit function. If so, visit with an internal audit supervisor or manager and learn (a) to whom in the organization the head of internal auditing reports and (b) what kinds of jobs internal auditing generally performs.

3. If the company is a corporation whose equity securities are publicly traded,

a. determine whether it has taken steps to document its compliance with the internal control provisions of the Foreign Corrupt Practices Act of 1977. If possible, examine and evaluate this documentation.

b. determine whether an audit committee is part of the board of directors. If so, obtain a list of the members of the audit committee and a copy of the committee's charter or bylaws.

4. Interview someone who hires employees for positions in accounting and data processing. Find out the following information:

a. What sort of background checks are performed before these employees are hired?

b. Is fidelity bond coverage normally obtained for them?

c. Does the company require rotation of duties and enforced vacations for these employees?

5. Select any one of the five accounting data processing cycles described in this chapter (e.g., the revenue cycle, the procurement cycle, etc.), and examine your company's internal control procedures within that accounting cycle.

a. Identify the persons responsible for transaction authorization, record keeping, and asset custody functions.

b. Learn how transaction documents and/or records are used to facilitate internal control.

c. Follow the audit trail by tracing one accounting transaction from its original source document through its entry in journals, ledgers, files, and so on, and ultimately the general ledger accounts.

d. Identify some policies and procedures used to safeguard assets and records.

e. Identify several internal check procedures.

CASE 13.2: THE GREATER PROVIDENCE DEPOSIT & TRUST EMBEZZLEMENT

On a Saturday afternoon in the spring of 1988 Nino Moscardi received an anonymous note in his mail. Moscardi, president of Greater Providence Deposit & Trust, was shocked to read the note's allegations: that an employee of the bank was putting through bogus loans. On the following Monday he directed the bank's internal auditors to investigate certain transactions detailed in the note. The investigation led to James Guisti, manager of a North Providence branch office and a trusted 14-year employee who had once worked as one of the bank's auditors. Guisti was later charged with embezzling $1.83 million from the bank through 67 phony loans taken out over a 3-year period.

Court documents revealed numerous details of Guisti's embezzlement scheme. For example, the first bogus loan was written in April 1985 for $10,000. The loans were 90-day notes requiring no collateral and ranged in amount from $10,000 to $63,500. Guisti originated the loans; when each one matured, he would take out a new loan, or rewrite the old one, to pay the principal and interest due. Some loans had been rewritten five or six times.

The 67 loans were taken out in various names, including his wife's maiden name, the name of his father, and the names of two of his friends. These people denied they received any stolen funds or knew anything about the embezzlement. In addition, one loan was in the name of James Vanesse, who police said did not exist. The Social Security number on Vanesse's loan application was issued to a female, and the phone number belonged to a North Providence auto dealer.

Court records also disclosed the details of police interviews with bank employees to determine how the loan money was dispensed. According to Lucy Fraioli, a customer service representative who co-signed checks to the five names to which Guisti had originated loans, Guisti was her supervisor and she thought nothing was wrong with the checks, though she didn't know any of the five people. Marcia Perfetto, head teller at the branch, told police that she had cashed checks for Guisti made out to four of the five persons. Asked if she gave the money to Guisti when he gave her the checks to cash, she answered, "Not all of the time," though she could not recall ever having given the money directly to any of the four, whom she said she didn't know.

According to news reports, Guisti was authorized to make consumer loans up to a certain dollar limit without loan committee approvals, which is a standard industry practice. Guisti's lending limit was $10,000 until January 1987, when it was increased to $15,000. In February 1988 it was increased again to $25,000. However, some of the loans, including the one for $63,500, far exceeded his lending limit. In addition, all loan applications should have been accompanied by a report on the applicant's credit history, purchased from an independent credit rating firm. The loan taken out in a fictitious name would not have had a credit report and should have been flagged by a loan review clerk at the bank's headquarters.

News reports raised several questions about why the fraud was not detected earlier. State regulators had examined the bank's books in September 1986. The bank's own internal auditors also failed to detect the fraud. However, in checking for bad loans, bank auditors do not examine all loans and generally focus on loans much larger than the ones in question. In addition, Greater Providence had recently dropped its computer services arrangement with a local bank in favor of an out-of-state bank, and this changeover may have reduced the effectiveness of the bank's control procedures. Finally, the bank's loan review clerks were frequently rotated, making follow-up of questionable loans more difficult.

Court records indicate that Guisti was a frequent gambler and used the proceeds of the embezzlement to pay gambling debts. The bank's losses totaled $624,000, and its bonding company, Hartford Accident and Indemnity Company, covered the loss. The loss was less than the $1.83 million in bogus loans because Guisti used some of the borrowed money to pay back some loans as they came due.

According to financial reports made available by Greater Providence officials, the bank had assets of $220 million and outstanding loans of $184 million as of the end of 1987, and it earned a record $1.6 million for 1987. It had eight branches in the Providence area.

The bank experienced other adverse publicity during that period. In 1985 it was fined $50,000 after pleading guilty of failure to report a series of cash transactions exceeding $10,000, which is a felony. In 1986 the bank was taken private by its current owners, but only after a lengthy public battle with State Attorney General Arlene Violet. The state charged that the bank had inflated its assets and overestimated its capital surplus to make its balance sheet look stronger. The bank denied this charge.

1. Discuss how Greater Providence Deposit & Trust might improve its control procedures over the disbursement of loan funds to minimize the risk of this type of fraud. In what way, if any, does this case indicate a lack of proper segregation of duties?
2. Discuss how Greater Providence might improve its loan review procedures at bank headquarters to minimize their fraud risk. Was it a good idea to rotate the assignments of loan review clerks? Why or why not?
3. Discuss whether Greater Providence's auditors should have been able to detect this fraud.
4. Are their any indications that the control environment at Greater Providence may have been deficient? If so, could this have contributed in any way to this embezzlement? How?

Source: John Kostrezewa, "Charge: Embezzlement," *Providence Journal-Bulletin* (July 31, 1988): F-1.

ANSWERS TO CHAPTER QUIZ

1. c	**3.** b	**5.** a	**7.** d	**9.** a
2. d	**4.** d	**6.** b	**8.** c	**10.** b

Chapter 14

Computer-Based Information Systems Control

LEARNING OBJECTIVES

After studying this chapter, you should be able to:

- Describe the threats to an AIS and discuss why these threats are growing.
- Identify and explain the general controls that should exist within a computer-based information system.
- Identify and explain the control procedures and techniques that should be incorporated into data processing applications of computer-based information systems.

Integrative Case: Seattle Paper Products (SPP)

During his fifth month at Northwest Industries, Jason Scott is assigned to audit Seattle Paper Products (SPP), a Northwest subsidiary. Jason's first task is to review 50 randomly selected payables transactions, track down all supporting documents, and verify that all the transactions have been properly authorized and correctly processed. Within a short time he locates vendor invoices and disbursement vouchers for all 50 transactions, and he finds purchase orders and receiving reports for 45 of them. After reviewing these documents, Jason is satisfied that these 45 transactions are valid and accurate.

The other five transactions involve the purchase of services, which are processed on the basis of vendor invoices approved by management. One particular invoice, from Pacific Electric Services, lists $450 for maintenance and repair work but does not have an authorization signature. Jason locates five more invoices from Pacific Electric, all for maintenance and repair services in amounts ranging from $300 to $500. These five bear the initials "JLC." JLC is Jack Carlton, the general supervisor of the plant. Much to Jason's surprise, Carlton denies initialing them and claims he has never heard of Pacific Electric. They find no such firm in the phone book.

Jason can't believe he has found another "hidden problem." After brooding over his bad luck, he begins to think about the following questions:

1. Is Jack Carlton telling the truth? If so, where did the Pacific Electric Services invoices come from?
2. If Carlton is not telling the truth, what is he up to?
3. If Pacific Electric Services is a fictitious company, how could SPP's control systems allow its invoices to be processed and approved for payment?

INTRODUCTION

Our society has become increasingly dependent upon computerized information systems, which in turn have grown ever more complex. As system complexity and our dependence on them increase, companies face the growing risk of their systems being compromised. The four types of threats a company faces are discussed in the first part of this chapter. This chapter also examines internal control policies, procedures, and techniques that specifically address the control and security requirements of a computer-based AIS. Computer controls are often classified as either general or application controls. The second part of the chapter discusses general controls, while the third part discusses application controls.

AIS THREATS

Types of Threats

One type of threat to companies is natural and political disasters such as fires, excessive heat, floods, earthquakes, high winds, and war. An unpredictable disaster can completely destroy an information system and cause a company to fail. When a disaster strikes, many companies can be affected at the same time. For example, the 1992 flood in Chicago destroyed or damaged 400 data processing centers. Examples of these types of disasters include the following:

- In July 1993 unrelenting rains caused the Mississippi and Missouri rivers to overflow and flood parts of eight states. Many organizations lost their computer systems, including the city of Des Moines, Iowa, whose computers were buried by 8 feet of water. In 1992 a number of computer facilities in Chicago were also destroyed by floods.
- The January 1994 earthquake in Los Angeles destroyed a number of systems. Others were damaged by falling debris, water from ruptured sprinkler systems, dust, and severed communication lines. Companies in San Francisco suffered a similar fate a few years earlier.
- Terrorist attacks on the World Trade Center in New York City and the Federal Building in Oklahoma City destroyed or disrupted the systems in those buildings.

A second threat to companies is software errors, or bugs, and equipment malfunctions such as hardware failures, power outages and fluctuations, and undetected data transmission errors. For example:

- Bugs in a new tax accounting system were to blame for the state of California's failure to collect $635 million in business taxes.
- At the Bank of New York, a field used to count the number of transactions was too small to handle the volume on a busy day. The error shut the system down and left the bank $23 million short when it tried to close its books. It had to borrow money overnight at a significant cost.

A third threat to companies is unintentional acts such as accidents or innocent errors and omissions. They are usually caused by human carelessness and by failure to follow established procedures. They often occur when employees are tired, overworked, or distracted. They are also caused by incompetent or poorly trained or supervised personnel. End users are especially prone to making errors because they usually receive little or no training in developing and operating systems. Users often lose or misplace data and accidentally erase or alter files, data, and programs. Computer operators and users can enter the wrong input or erroneous input, use the wrong version of a program, use the wrong data files, or misplace files. Systems analysts and programmers often make logic errors, develop systems that do not meet the company's needs, or develop systems incapable of handling the tasks they were designed to do. Examples of these errors include the following:

- A data entry clerk at Giant Food, Inc., mistakenly keyed in a quarterly dividend of $2.50 instead of $0.25. As a result, the company paid over $10 million in excess dividends.
- In a large financial institution a programmer mistakenly calculated interest for each month using 31 days. In the five months before the mistake was discovered, over $100,000 in excess interest was paid out on the savings accounts.
- For years programmers have economized by using only the last two digits of a year (97 for 1997). As the year 2000 nears, problems due to this shortsightedness will increase. The Gartner Group, a consulting firm, estimates that 20% of business software will malfunction in 1996 due to this problem and 90% by the year 2000 if this "millennial bug" is not fixed. They estimate it will take $300 to $600 billion to fix the problem.

A fourth threat that companies face is intentional acts, typically referred to as computer crimes. This threat can take the form of sabotage, whereby the intent is to destroy a system or some of its components. Or it can be a computer fraud, where the intent is to steal something of value such as money, data, or computer time or services. For example:

- A technology enthusiast, John Draper, discovered that the whistle offered as a prize in Cap'n Crunch cereal exactly duplicated the frequency of a WATS line. He used his discovery to defraud the phone companies by making a large number of free telephone calls.
- An AIS manager at a Florida newspaper went to work for a competitor when he was fired. Before long the first employer realized that its reporters were constantly being scooped. The newspaper finally discovered that the AIS manager still had an active account and password and regularly browsed its computer files for information on its exclusive stories.

Each of these four threats represents real risks to information systems. Due to their sensational nature, acts of fraud are considered by many to be the most significant threat companies face. This is not the case, however. The greatest risks to information systems and the greatest dollar losses result from innocent errors and omissions. Carl Jackson, past president of the Information Systems Security Association, estimates that 65% of security problems are caused by human errors and accidents. Approximately 20% are caused by physical threats such as fires, floods, food spills, and electrical surges; 10% by dishonest or disgruntled insiders; and 5% by outsiders.

Why AIS Threats Are Increasing

As a result of these problems, controlling the security and integrity of computer systems has become a very important issue. Most AIS managers indicate that control risks have increased in the last few years. For example, an

Ernst & Young study shows that more than one in four executives surveyed said their companies had a financial loss in the past two years due to fraud, natural disasters, or system malfunctions. Among the many reasons for the increase in security problems are these:

- Increasing numbers of client/server systems means that information is available to an unprecedented number of workers. Computers and servers are everywhere; there are PCs on most desktops and portables accompany people wherever they go. Chevron, for example, has 33,000 PCs.
- Because LANs and client/server systems distribute data to many users, they are harder to control than centralized, mainframe systems. At Chevron, information is distributed among many systems and thousands of employees working locally and remotely as well as nationally and internationally.
- WANs are giving customers and suppliers access to each other's systems and data, making confidentiality a major concern. For example, you learned in Focus 1.2 that Wal-Mart allows Procter & Gamble to have access to certain information in its computers as a condition of their alliance. Imagine the potential confidentiality problems if P&G also formed alliances with Wal-Mart competitors such as Kmart and Target Stores.

Unfortunately, many organizations do not adequately protect their data due to one or more of the following reasons:

- Computer control problems are often underestimated and downplayed, and companies view the loss of crucial information as a distant, unlikely threat. For example, less than 25% of 1250 participants in a 1994 Ernst & Young study thought computer security was an extremely important issue. That figure was down from about 35% in the prior year's survey.
- Control implications of moving from the centralized, host-based computer systems of the past to those of a networked system are not fully understood.
- Many companies do not realize that data security is crucial to their survival. Information is a strategic resource, and protecting it must be a strategic requirement. For example, one company lost millions of dollars over a period of several years because it did not protect its data transmissions. A competitor tapped into its phone lines and obtained faxes of new product designs sent to an offshore plant.
- Productivity and cost pressures motivate management to forgo time-consuming control measures.

Fortunately, companies are increasingly recognizing the problems and are taking positive steps to increase computer control and security. For example, they are becoming proactive in their approach. They are devoting full-time staff to security and control concerns and educating their employees about control measures. Many are establishing and enforcing formal information security policies. They are making controls a part of the applications development process and are moving sensitive data off the unsecured client servers to a more secure environment, such as a mainframe.

As a future accountant, you must understand how to protect systems from the threats they face. You must also have a good understanding of information technology (IT) and its capabilities and risks. This knowledge can help you use IT to achieve an organization's control objectives.

Achieving adequate security and control over the information resources of an organization should be a top management priority. Although internal control objectives remain the same regardless of the data processing method, a computer-based AIS requires different internal control policies and procedures. For example, while computer processing reduces the potential for clerical errors, it may increase the risks of unauthorized access to or modification of data files. In addition, segregating the authorization, recording, and asset custody functions within an AIS must be achieved differently, since computer programs may be responsible for two or all three of these functions. Fortunately, computers also provide opportunities for an organization to enhance its internal controls.

GENERAL CONTROLS

A company designs **general controls** to ensure that its overall computer system is stable and well managed. This portion of the chapter discusses ten categories of general controls: segregation of duties within the systems function, management control of the AIS function, physical access controls, logical access controls, data storage controls, data transmission controls, documentation standards, decreased system downtime, disaster recovery planning, and protection of PCs and client/server networks.

Segregation of Duties Within the Systems Function

In a highly integrated AIS, procedures that used to be performed by separate individuals are combined. Therefore any person who has unrestricted access to the computer, its programs, and live data could have the opportunity to both perpetrate and conceal fraud. To combat this threat, organizations must implement compensating control procedures such as the effective segregation of duties within the AIS function. Authority and responsibility must be clearly divided among the following functions:

1. *Systems analysis.* The analysis and programming functions must be separated from the other functions to prevent unauthorized changes in application programs or data. For example, if a programmer for a credit union were allowed to use actual data to test her program, she could erase her car loan balance while conducting the test.
2. *Programming.* Organizations should require formal authorizations for program changes. A written description of such changes should be submitted to a supervising manager for approval and modifications should be thoroughly tested prior to implementation. The introductory case in Chapter 15 illustrates the importance of this step.
3. *Computer operations.* Computer operators should be rotated among jobs and should not have access to program documentation or logic. When possible, two operators should be in the computer room during processing. A processing log should be maintained and reviewed periodically for evidence of irregularities. For example, without these controls a computer operator processing payroll could alter the program and increase her salary.

FOCUS 14.1

Harnessing Runaway Systems

Westpac Banking Corporation of Sydney, Australia, instigated a five-year systems development project that was supposed to redefine the role of information technology. The project, designated Core System 90 (CS90), was budgeted at $85 million. Its objective was to decentralize Westpac's information systems by equipping branch managers with CASE (computer-aided software engineering) tools and expert systems, in order to generate new financial products. Decentralization would enable Westpac to respond more rapidly to customer needs while downsizing its internal AIS department.

Some three years after it began the project, Westpac took stock of CS90 and concluded that it was out of control. Despite an outlay of nearly $150 million on the project, no usable results had been attained. In addition, bank officials determined that the scheduled completion date could not be realized. Facing serious problems with its loan portfolio and asset management programs, Westpac decided that it could not afford to risk several more million dollars on CS90. So, the bank fired IBM, the systems integrator* and primary software developer, and brought in Andersen Consulting to review the project and develop recommendations for salvaging it.

Westpac's CS90 boondoggle is merely one example of what has become an all-too-frequent story: a computer project that is over budget and behind schedule, often due to a systems integrator that is unable to deliver on lofty promises. Industry experts refer to such projects as runaways. Since 1988 KPMG Peat Marwick has taken over some fifty runaway computer projects, and it estimates that, in about two-thirds of these cases, the problems arose from mismanagement by a systems integrator.

Computer systems built by a third party are subject to the same cost overruns and missed deadlines as systems developed internally. Therefore it makes sense to use the same basic rules of project management and control, including close monitoring of system progress during development. Unfortunately, many companies are not doing this.

Instead, they rely on the integrator's assurance that the project will be completed on time. Too often, the integrator falls behind schedule but doesn't tell the client, figuring that the project can still be completed on time if a big push is made at the last minute. In such cases, the CIO and other AIS executives are as much at fault as the systems inte-

4. *Transaction authorization.* User departments should submit a signed form along with each batch of input to verify that it has been authorized and that the appropriate control totals have been compiled. Data control personnel should verify the signatures and control totals prior to submitting the input for processing. This procedure would prevent a payroll clerk from submitting a form to increase his pay rate.
5. *AIS library.* The AIS librarian maintains custody of data bases, files, and programs in a separate storage area—the AIS library. To separate the custody and operations functions, access to files and programs should be limited to authorized operators at scheduled times or with user authorization. The librarian should keep a record of all data and program file usage but should not hold computer access privileges. The records should be reviewed regularly for evidence of unauthorized access.
6. *Data control.* The data control group ensures that source data have been properly approved, monitors the flow of work through the computer operations department, reconciles input and output, maintains a record of input errors to ensure their correction and resubmission, and distributes systems output. A data control function inhibits

grator, according to experts in salvaging runaway systems.

These experts suggest that a systems integration project should be monitored by a sponsors committee, established by the CIO and chaired by the project's internal champion. Department managers for all units that will use the system should be on this committee. The role of this committee should be to establish formal procedures for measuring and reporting the status of the project. The best approach is to break the project down into manageable tasks, assign responsibility for each task, and then meet on a regular basis (at least monthly) to review progress and assess quality.

Equally important are steps that should be taken at the outset of the project. Before third parties are called in to bid on a project, clear specifications must be developed, including exact descriptions and definitions of the system, explicit deadlines, and precise acceptance criteria for each stage of the project. While specification development may seem expensive, it usually saves money in the long run. For example, Suffolk County, New York, recently spent 12 months and $500,000 preparing detailed specifications for a new $16 million criminal justice information system before accepting bids. The county then hired Unisys Corporation and Grumman Data Systems to develop the system. County officials believe that their diligent upfront efforts helped ensure the success of their new system and saved the county $3 million in hardware costs.

Some systems integrators may object to detailed specifications and rigorous project control methods. For example, after reviewing Suffolk County's specifications, only six integrators out of 22 that had originally expressed interest bid on the project. This should be viewed as a blessing rather than a problem. Those integrators who disdain a company's attempts to rigorously control the cost and quality of its systems projects are most likely the same ones responsible for most of the recent profusion of runaway systems.

Focus Questions

1. Why do so many projects developed by systems integrators fail?
2. What can companies do to ensure that their systems integration projects do not fail?

*A systems integrator is a vendor that takes the responsibility for managing a cooperative systems development effort involving its own development personnel, those of the buyer, and possibly the systems development personnel of one or more other vendors, using common standards as much as possible.

unauthorized access to the computer facility, provides an additional element of supervision, and contributes to more efficient data processing operations.

Management Control of the AIS Function

Examples abound of poorly managed development projects that have wasted large sums of money because certain basic principles of management control were ignored. For example, the Oklahoma State Insurance Fund terminated a development contract with Policy Management Systems for a software system that would issue policies and process and track claims and premiums. The contract was canceled when the project fell several months behind schedule and went $1 million over budget. As explained in Focus 14.1, Westpac Banking Corporation terminated a large-scale systems integration project after spending over $150 million.

To minimize failures, the basic principles of responsibility accounting should be applied to the AIS function. Adherence greatly reduces the potential for cost overruns and project failures while substantially improving the efficiency and effectiveness of the function. Management control includes the following key elements:

- *Long-range master plan.* This plan provides a framework for management control and a standard against which performance can be measured.
- *Project development plan.* A project should be divided into phases, with time and cost estimates for each. The plan should specify **project milestones,** or significant points when progress is reviewed and actual and estimated completion times compared.
- *Data processing schedule.* The schedule should assign each job to a specific time period to maximize equipment utilization.
- *Assignment of responsibility.* Each project should be assigned to a manager and team responsible for its respective success or failure.
- *Periodic performance evaluations.* Each job should be broken down into modules or tasks; performance should be evaluated as each is completed.
- *Postimplementation review.* This review determines whether anticipated benefits were achieved. Unfavorable variances should be investigated and corrected. Reviews help control project development activities and encourage accurate and objective initial cost and benefit estimates.
- *System performance measurements.* This should include throughput (output per unit of time), utilization (percentage of time system is being productively used), and response time.

Physical Access Controls

Both the physical ability to use computer equipment, referred to as **physical access,** and the ability to use the equipment to access company data, called **logical access,** should be restricted. Physical access security can be achieved by the following controls:

- Locating computers and computer devices in locked rooms and restricting access to authorized personnel.
- Having only one or two entrances to the computer room. The entrances should be securely locked and monitored carefully by security guards and closed-circuit television systems.
- Requiring proper employee ID, such as a security badge, for passage through an access point. Modern security badges incorporate photos and magnetic, electric, or optical codes that can be read only by special badge readers. With advanced ID techniques, each employee's entry and exit may be automatically recorded in a log that is maintained on the computer and periodically reviewed by supervisory personnel.
- Requiring that visitors sign a log as they enter and leave the site. They should be briefed on company security policies, assigned visitor's badges, and escorted to their destination.
- Using a security alarm system to detect unauthorized access during off-hours.
- Restricting remote access to private, secured telephone lines or to authorized terminals or PCs.
- Installing locks on PCs and other computer devices.

Logical Access Controls

With respect to logical access security, users should be allowed access only to the data they are authorized to use and then only to perform specific, authorized functions such as reading, copying, and adding to and deleting data. It is also important to protect data from those outside the organization who could benefit from it. For example, a manufacturing company's competitor broke into its system and browsed through its data until it discovered its bid on a billion-dollar project. The competitor narrowly underbid the company and won the contract. The intrusion was discovered by an auditing system the manufacturing company had installed on its network. By the time the intrusion was uncovered, however, it was too late and this particular bid was lost.

Restricting logical access means that a system must have some way to differentiate between authorized and unauthorized users. The most common method of determining user authorization is by what the user knows, what the user possesses, where the user is accessing the system, or by some personal characteristic. Perhaps the most common approach is what a person knows. For example, the computer could ask users a series of personal questions, such as mother's maiden name. Or users could be asked to enter a personal identification number (PIN).

Passwords. The most frequent knowledge identifier is a user identification (ID) and authentication system. When signing on to a system, users identify themselves by entering an employee number, name, or account number. Users then enter a **password,** a series of characters that uniquely identifies the user and is known only to the user and the system. Each password is meant to be known and used by only one system user. If the user-entered ID and password match those in the computer, the system assumes it is a bona fide user who has authority to access and use the system. The downside of passwords is that they can be guessed, lost, or given away, creating the potential for unauthorized, and in some cases, dangerous persons to gain system access. For example, a convicted child rapist working in a Boston hospital used a former employee's password to gain access to confidential patient files. He proceeded to obtain telephone numbers of families that had children.

This risk can be virtually eliminated by a control system that performs the following functions:

1. Requires users to keep their ID number and password confidential. The system should not display ID numbers or passwords on the screen as they are entered. Users should never reveal passwords. At Pacific Bell teenage hackers posed as company employees and persuaded system users to give them the passwords they needed to access the system.
2. Randomly assigns passwords to users, since user-selected passwords are often easily guessed. Passwords should also be changed frequently to maintain their confidentiality. One breach of this confidentiality was committed by Ming Jyh Hsieh, a software company service representative in Palo Alto, California. Two months after she was fired the company discovered she had logged on to its computers late at night to copy and damage files. The police raided her home and seized millions of dollars of company software. The company had invalidated her password, but she had stolen someone else's to access the computer.
3. Assigns electronic ID numbers to each authorized device; only these devices are allowed to interact with the system. In addition, they can only be

used to access certain data. For example, access to payroll records could be restricted to computers and terminals in the payroll department.

4. Disconnects and then deactivates the ID of anyone unable to provide a valid ID number within three attempts. This control prevents hackers from programming a computer to try all combinations of user IDs and passwords.
5. Immediately investigates devices from which repeated attempts to access the system utilizing invalid ID numbers or passwords originate.
6. Requires employees to log off their computers when they are not in use. It is especially important not to leave computers unattended during on-line interactions with confidential corporate data bases.
7. Restricts some user or terminal transactions to specified times, such as normal business hours.
8. Immediately restricts employee access to data when they are transferred to another department. For example, someone leaving the payroll department should no longer have access to payroll data.
9. Immediately deactivates the user ID and password of any employee who is terminated. In a security review conducted by Ernst & Young, 240 ex-employees still retained access to their company's dial-in system.

Physical Possession Identification. People can be identified not only by what they know but by what they physically possess. Perhaps the most common physical possession is the ID card. These cards can record the name, ID number, picture, and other pertinent information about a user. They can be read by the computer and other security devices, such as door locks. Unfortunately, they can also be lost, stolen, or given away. Security can be increased significantly if a user is required to have both an ID card and a password before receiving access to the system. However, even these systems can be compromised. For example, a hacker broke into the Motorola system by calling the help desk and saying he was an employee working at home who had forgotten his ID card (the card generated random passwords that change every few seconds). The help desk believed him and let him into the corporate network. Fortunately, he did no permanent damage to their system.

Active badges transmit a radio signal that is picked up by special receivers. As Focus 7.3 explains, the use of active badges to continuously track a person's whereabouts is controversial.

Biometric Identification. The most effective ID approach bases user recognition on **biometric identifications.** Biometric identification devices identify unique user physical characteristics such as fingerprints, voice patterns, retina prints, facial patterns and features, body odor, signature dynamics, and keyboarding patterns (the way a user types certain groups of characters). When a person desires access to the system, his or her biometric identifications are matched against those stored in the computer. For example, a retina scanner captures and digitizes the pattern of blood vessels produced when light is reflected off a retina. This pattern is more unique and accurate than a fingerprint.

U.S. Immigration has begun to use electronic hand readers to verify a person's identification. The handprint of passport applicants is captured and stored on a wallet-sized card. When a cardholder enters the country, his or her card and hand are placed in a special reading device that matches the two. In airports equipped with hand readers, passports do not have to be shown when a cardholder reenters the country. The eventual goal is to put coded handprint data on machine-readable passports.

The ideal biometric device is one that is precise enough to adapt to slight personal changes, but at the same time will reject unauthorized users. Unfortunately, there are still some problems to work out. For example, voice recognition devices may reject a person with a head cold or whose voice is muffled over a phone line, while retina scanners may reject someone with bloodshot eyes. Another disadvantage to these devices is user resistance. Not all people are comfortable looking into retina scanners or having their fingers scanned. Another disadvantage is that, with the exception of voice scanners, users have to be physically present to use the system.

An important step in restricting access is to define specific access privileges for every company employee. Access privileges are statements that specify and circumscribe what hardware, software, and data an employee can access.

Compatibility Tests. Once an authorized ID and password have been entered, the system should perform a **compatibility check** to determine whether the user is indeed authorized to perform the type of transaction or inquiry being initiated. For example, factory employees would not be authorized to make entries involving accounts payable, and purchasing agents would not be allowed to enter sales orders. This procedure is necessary to prevent both unintentional errors and deliberate attempts to manipulate the system.

Compatibility tests utilize an **access control matrix,** which is a list of authorized user ID numbers and passwords, a list of all files and programs, and the access each user has to them. Figure 14.1 shows an access control matrix with code for four types of access. User 12345-ABC is permitted only to read and display file C and is restricted from any kind of access to other files or programs. User 12389-RST, apparently a programmer, is authorized to make any type of change in program 2 and to read and display records in file B. User 12567-XYZ, probably a supervisor, is authorized to read and display the contents of all files and programs.

Data Storage Controls

Information is generally what gives a company a competitive edge and makes it viable. Because information is such a valuable resource, it must be protected from unauthorized disclosure and destruction. For example, a repairman working late to repair a printing press at Webco Press in Lapeer, Michigan, was trusted to complete his assignment without supervision. The repairman gained access to Webco's mainframe computer and made a printout of the company's customer list, complete with prices. He attempted to sell the customer list to a Webco competitor for $5000 but was apprehended.

A company should identify the types of data maintained and the level of protection required for each. Obviously, the more confidential, important, and valuable the information, the greater the need for protection. A company must also document the steps taken to protect data. A company should keep track of security efforts; maintain records of confidential documents, records, and

Figure 14.1

Access Control Matrix

USER IDENTIFICATION		FILES			PROGRAMS			
Code Number	**Password**	**A**	**B**	**C**	**1**	**2**	**3**	**4**
12345	ABC	0	0	1	0	0	0	0
12346	DEF	0	2	0	0	0	0	0
12354	KLM	1	1	1	0	0	0	0
12359	NOP	3	0	0	0	0	0	0
12389	RST	0	1	0	0	3	0	0
12567	XYZ	1	1	1	1	1	1	1

Codes for type of access:
0 = No access permitted
1 = Read and display only
2 = Read, display, and update
3 = Read, display, update, create, and delete

files; and implement audit trails to track those with access to confidential data. One important step is to have employees sign contracts that require them to maintain the confidentiality of company data.

A properly supervised file library is one essential means of preventing loss of data. The file storage area should also be protected against fire, dust, excess heat or humidity, and other conditions that could harm stored data.

File labels can protect data files from inadvertent misuse. An **external label,** a gummed paper label attached to a storage device (i.e., diskette), contains information such as the file name, contents, and date processed. **Internal labels** are written in machine-readable form on the data recording media. There are three different internal labels. A **volume label** identifies the contents of each separate data recording medium, such as a hard disk, diskette, or tape reel. A **header label,** located at the beginning of the file, contains the file name, expiration date, and other identification data. A **trailer label,** located at the end of the file, contains file control totals, which are checked against those accumulated during processing.

Tape rings and disk write protection mechanisms protect against users' accidentally writing over or erasing data files. A **tape file protection ring** is a plastic ring that, when removed, prevents a tape file from being written upon. Many diskettes have on/off switches or removable strips of plastic that perform the same function. Unfortunately, these write protection mechanisms can easily be circumvented.

Data base systems use data base administrators, data dictionaries, and concurrent update controls to provide data protection. The administrator establishes and enforces procedures for accessing and updating the data base. The data dictionary ensures that data items are defined and used consistently. **Concurrent update controls** protect records from errors that occur when two or more users attempt to update the same record simultaneously. This is accomplished by "locking out" one user until the system has finished processing the update entered by the other.

Data Transmission Controls

To reduce the risk of data transmission failures, companies should monitor the network to detect weak points, maintain backup components, and design networks so that capacity is sufficient to handle peak-processing periods. They should also establish multiple communication paths between crucial network nodes so the system can function if one of the paths fails. Checkpoint and rollback procedures will facilitate recovery from system failures. By way of preventive maintenance, companies can upgrade to conditioned telecommunications lines that are faster and more efficient, have fewer problems with static, and are less likely to fail.

Data transmission errors are minimized using data encryption, routing verification, parity checking, and message acknowledgment procedures.

Data Encryption (Cryptography). **Data encryption (cryptography)** can be used to prevent competitors from electronically monitoring confidential data transmissions. Data are converted into a scrambled format prior to data transmission and converted back into meaningful form once transmission is completed. Encrypted data can be read only by someone with a matching decryption key. Encryption is now so common and inexpensive that many companies are encrypting all E-mail messages on WANs and LANs. Secure encryption schemes are especially valuable to companies that buy and sell goods over the Internet.

Routing Verification Procedures. Several **routing verification procedures** can ensure that messages are not routed to the wrong system address. For example:

- Transmitted data can be given a header label that identifies its destination. Before and after transmission, the system verifies that the destination is valid and authorized to receive it.
- **Mutual authentication schemes** require both computers to exchange their passwords before communication can take place.
- With **dial-back systems**, the computer disconnects the modem when a modem user requests access to the system, then calls it back to verify the user's identity and password(s). In addition, once a user is recognized as authorized, the computer can automatically disconnect that person, search its directory for the authorized location, and call him or her back.

Parity Checking. Computers use a combination of bits to represent a single character. For example, the digits 5 and 7 might be represented by 0101 and 0111, respectively. When data are transmitted, bits may be lost or received incorrectly. To detect these errors, a **parity bit** is added to every character. In even parity, each bit has an even number of 1s. The parity bit for 5 is 0 (0101 0), since 5 already has an even number of 1s. The parity bit for 7 is a 1 (0111 1) so there are an even number of 1s. In odd parity there are an odd number of 1s.

Parity checking—verifying that there are an even (or odd) number of 1s—is performed by devices that receive data. Two-dimensional parity checking tests parity both vertically and horizontally. Dual checking is important in telecommunications because noise bursts frequently cause two or more adjacent bits to be lost. A one-dimensional parity check will not detect all such errors.

Message Acknowledgment Techniques. It is important for the sender of an electronic message to receive verification that his or her message was indeed received and confirmation that this message was actually the one that was originally transmitted. A number of message acknowledgment techniques are used for this purpose:

- ***Echo check.*** When data are transmitted, the system calculates a summary statistic such as the number of bits in the message. The receiving unit performs the same calculation and sends the result back to the sending unit. If the two counts agree, the data transmission is presumed to be accurate.
- *Trailer label.* The receiving unit can check the trailer label to verify that the entire message was received.
- *Numbered batches.* If a large message or a set of transactions is transmitted in a batch, each transaction or message segment can be numbered sequentially. The receiving unit can assemble all the parts in the correct sequence.

Whenever a data transmission error is detected, the receiving unit will signal the sending unit and the data will be retransmitted. Generally, the system will do this automatically and the user is unaware that it has occurred. Occasionally, the system may not be able to accomplish automatic retransmissions and will request that the user at the sending end manually retransmit the data.

Data Transmission Controls for EDI and EFT. Data transmission controls take on added importance in organizations that utilize electronic data interchange (EDI) or electronic funds transfer (EFT) because of the risk of unauthorized access to proprietary data. EFT systems are also vulnerable to fraudulent fund transfers. In these types of environments sound internal control is achieved using the following control procedures:

- Physical access to network facilities should be strictly controlled. Electronic identification should be required for all authorized network terminals.
- Strict logical access control procedures are essential, with passwords and dial-in phone numbers changed on a regular basis.
- Encryption should be used to secure stored data as well as data being transmitted.
- Details of all transactions should be recorded in a log that is periodically reviewed for evidence of invalid transactions.

Documentation Standards

Another important general control is documentation procedures and standards. Well-planned and enforced documentation standards offer the following benefits:

- Facilitating communication and regular progress reviews during systems development.

- Using the documentation as a reference and training tool for system users, machine operators, and newly hired employees within the systems function.
- Simplifying program maintenance. Maintaining and updating applications written by someone else is extremely difficult without adequate documentation.
- Easing the problems related to job turnover. For example, if a programmer quits in the middle of a major project, much time can be wasted trying to continue the work if up-to-date documentation has not been maintained.

Documentation may be classified into three basic categories:

1. **Administrative documentation** describes the standards and procedures for the data processing facility, including the justification and authorization of new system and systems changes; standards for systems analysis, design, and programming; and procedures for file handling and file library activities.
2. **Systems documentation** describes each application system. It includes narrative material, flowcharts, and program listings. It shows an application's inputs, processing steps, outputs, and error-handling procedures.
3. **Operating documentation** includes all information needed to run a program, including the equipment configuration, program and data files, procedures to set up and execute the job, conditions that may interrupt program execution, and corrective actions for program interruptions.

Minimizing System Downtime

If hardware or software malfunctions cause an AIS to fail, a company's primary operating activities could come to a halt and significant financial losses could be incurred. Among the methods to minimize system downtime are the following:

- **Preventive maintenance** involves regular testing of system components and replacement of those in poor condition. This greatly reduces the likelihood of system failure during regular operations.
- **Uninterruptible power system (UPS)** is an auxiliary power supply that smooths the flow of power to the computer, preventing loss of data due to momentary surges or dips in power. In the event of a complete power failure, a UPS provides a backup power supply to keep the computer operating without interruption until regular power is restored.
- **Fault tolerance** is the system's ability to continue operating even though some of its components have failed. Fault tolerance is achieved using redundant components that take over in the event of failure. For example, in a real-time system where service is essential, system components (such as PCs, terminals, data transmission lines, and disk drives) may be duplicated so the system can switch to the backup component if necessary.

Disaster Recovery Planning

Every organization should be prepared to respond to a major disaster such as a fire, flood, earthquake, hurricane, or an act of sabotage. A **disaster recovery plan** is essential so that data processing capacity can be recovered as smoothly and quickly as possible. Being without an AIS can be very costly; some companies have reported losses as high as $500,000 per hour of downtime. John Alden Life Insurance estimates that without its disaster recovery plan when

FOCUS 14.2

A Model for Disaster Recovery Planning

The value of a disaster recovery plan is underscored by numerous case histories. Perhaps the best known is the story of the worst bank fire in history and how the bank recovered by following a plan that has since become a disaster recovery planning model.

On Thanksgiving Day a huge fire swept through the offices of Northwest National Bank of Minneapolis, destroying bank transaction records and data processing facilities. It was described as one of the worst fires in the city's history. Yet the following Monday bank employees were back on the job in new quarters—handling deposits, withdrawals, investments, loans, and other routine bank transactions. The fire could have threatened the bank's ability to remain in business, but it did not, thanks to a detailed disaster recovery plan. Because a record of nearly every bank transaction was stored elsewhere in computers or on microfilm, the bank lost few, if any, important records. The day after the fire, computers at a local service bureau were hard at work making new copies of the destroyed records. The recovery plan provided bank executives with a detailed blueprint for lining up new office space, replacing computer equipment and supplies, procuring new office equipment, and making other arrangements essential to the continuation of Northwest's banking operations.

An early morning fire struck the Bank of the Sierra in Porterville, California, destroying its corporate offices and melting its mainframe computer. Though the facility was seemingly well protected by a sprinkler system and a halon gas fire-extinguishing system, this fire burned through the building's roof, which collapsed, crushing the sprinkler system and releasing the halon gas into the air. The bank's central data bases and related records, including all personal and mortgage loan records, credit card records, and unprocessed checks, were lost.

Using a 150-page disaster recovery plan grounded in Northwest National Bank's experience, Bank of the Sierra officials quickly identified team members, crucial tasks, and required equipment, and began an overnight effort to restore bank services. By 10:00 A.M. the following morning, nine hours after the fire started, backup files were on-line and tellers were conducting business at branch windows as if nothing had happened. For processing of the bank's 25,000 to 40,000 daily transactions, a data processing hot site in nearby San Ramon was utilized. Updated files were downloaded from the hot site to a mainframe computer provided by a Denver company, from which printouts were flown back to Porterville daily. Within six days after the fire, the bank had cleaned up its transaction processing backlog and its customer accounts were current.

Focus Questions

1. What made the disaster plan of Northwest National Bank so effective that other companies modeled their plan after it?
2. Why do most companies not have a disaster recovery plan as good as Northwest National Bank's?

Hurricane Andrew hit, the company would have been out of business in three days. Many of the 350 companies that had their information systems destroyed in the World Trade Center bombing were unprepared; 150 of them went out of business.

A recent survey of 200 large U.S. businesses showed that only a third have a disaster recovery plan with off-site data storage for their client/server applications. Those that have them are well rewarded for their planning and foresight when disaster strikes. As Focus 14.2 illustrates, sound disaster recovery plans have enabled many organizations to recover from unexpected catastrophes that might have been devastating, if not fatal.

The objectives of a recovery plan are to (1) minimize the extent of the disruption, damage, and loss; (2) temporarily establish an alternative means of processing information; (3) resume normal operations as soon as possible; and (4) train and familiarize personnel with emergency operations. A sound disaster recovery plan should contain the following elements.

1. *Priorities for the recovery process.* It should identify the applications most important to keeping the organization running, the hardware and software requirements necessary to sustain them, and the sequence and timing of activities that each recovery team should perform.

2. *Backup data and program files.* Because no set of preventive controls is foolproof, procedures should exist for recovering lost or destroyed data files. All program and data files should be backed up on a frequent schedule and stored at a secure site some distance from the main computer. The offices of the Federal Employees Credit Union were destroyed and 18 of its 33 employees killed in the April 1995 bombing of the Federal Building in Oklahoma City. Even though all its records and computers were destroyed, the agency reopened its doors two days after the blast in a new location with new computer and phone systems. It was able to do so because duplicate copies of all crucial information had been stored offsite. Backup files may be transported to the remote site physically or electronically using **electronic vaulting,** which permits prompt on-line access to backup data when necessary.

Batch processing files are backed up using the **grandfather-father-son** concept. When a master file (the father) is updated with a set of transactions, a new master file (the son) is created. If the father and son files are damaged or destroyed during the update, the father file can be reconstructed using the grandfather file and a copy of the prior transaction file. Each time an update is completed, a new generation of files is created and the prior grandfather file can be discarded. For example, when an accounts receivable file is updated on Monday night, the newly created file is the son. On Tuesday night the accounts receivable file becomes the father and is updated with Tuesday's transactions. On Wednesday night it is the grandfather and is not used unless the father (Tuesday night) file is damaged. When the update is complete on Thursday night, the file is no longer needed and the disk or tape can be reused.

A similar procedure is employed to ensure that on-line master files can be reconstructed. Periodically during processing a **checkpoint** is created when the system generates a copy of the master file and the information needed to restart the system. The checkpoint is stored on a separate disk or tape file. The system can be restarted by reading the last checkpoint and then reprocessing all subsequent transactions. Using a procedure called **rollback,** a preupdated copy of each record is created prior to processing a transaction. If a hardware failure occurs, the records are "rolled back" to the preupdate values and the transaction is reprocessed from the beginning.

PC hard disks are often backed up on diskettes and tape files. However, if the backup copies are stored next to the PC, they can also be destroyed by a disaster that wipes out the PC. That is exactly what happened when First Interstate Bancorp suffered a fire in its headquarters building in Los Angeles.

First Interstate now repeatedly reminds employees to back up their files and take them home at the end of each day. Salomon, a large brokerage firm, has a system that creates weekly backup copies of all files on its 3000 workstations worldwide. They also have a copy of all application programs on a duplicate computer system.

It is important to document the backup procedures and periodically practice restoring a system from the backup data. This way employees know how to expeditiously restart the system in the event of a failure.

3. *Specific assignments.* A disaster recovery coordinator who is responsible for implementing the plan should be appointed. The plan should assign responsibility for recovery activities to specific individuals and teams. These activities should include arranging for new facilities, operating the computer, installing software, establishing data communications facilities, recovering vital records, and arranging for forms and supplies.

4. *Complete documentation.* The disaster recovery plan should be fully documented, with copies stored securely at multiple locations.

5. *Backup computer and telecommunications facilities.* Backup facilities can be arranged in several ways:

- Establish a reciprocal agreement with an organization that has compatible facilities so each party can temporarily use the other's data processing facilities in the event of an emergency. For example, four banks whose computers and data were damaged or destroyed in the World Trade Center bombing were able to use the New York Clearing House Association backup facilities to complete $90 billion of transactions on the day of the bombing.
- Contract with a vendor to provide contingent sites for emergency use. A **hot site** is a facility configured to meet the user's requirements. A **cold site** provides everything necessary to quickly install computer equipment (power, air conditioning, and support systems, etc.) but doesn't have the computers installed. A cold site user must contract with its vendor to ensure prompt delivery of equipment and software in the event of an emergency. For example, Brody White & Co., a brokerage, rerouted its distributed operations to a disaster recovery facility in New Jersey after the World Trade Center bombing.
- In a multilocation organization, distribute processing capacity so that other facilities can take over if one location becomes damaged or destroyed.
- In some cases a system may be so important that a company invests in on-site or off-site duplicate hardware, software, or data storage devices. For example, the AIS at Caesar's Palace in Las Vegas is so vital that an exact duplicate of the entire system, including an up-to-the-minute copy of the data base, is maintained 500 feet from the main system.

Four other aspects of disaster recovery planning deserve mention:

1. The plan is incomplete until it has been satisfactorily tested by simulating a disaster and having each disaster recovery team carry out its prescribed recovery activities. The plan should be retested twice a year. Most plans fail their initial test and even tested plans rarely anticipate and deal with all problems that crop when a disaster strikes.

2. The plan must be continuously reviewed and revised to ensure that it reflects the organization's current computer applications, equipment configuration, and personnel assignments.
3. The disaster recovery plan for data processing should be part of an overall business interruption plan for the organization. It is important to make sure that these two plans are properly integrated.
4. A disaster plan should include insurance coverage to defer costs of equipment replacement, recovery activities, and business interruption.

Protection of Personal Computers and Client/Server Networks

Internal Controls. In the rush to move from mainframe to client/server networks, many companies have failed to develop adequate systems of internal controls. They are now forced to go back and retrofit those applications with security features as substantial as those found on corporate mainframes. Other companies have built mission critical client/server applications that cannot be used because they lack adequate security features. PCs and networks of PCs are more vulnerable to security risks than are mainframes for several reasons:

1. PCs are everywhere, which means that it is difficult to restrict physical access to them. Each of these network PCs becomes a device that must be controlled. The more legitimate users there are, each possessing one or more PCs, the greater the risk of an attack on the network. For example, Chevron distributes information to tens of thousands of employees using 33,000 PCs in different systems worldwide.
2. PC users are less conscious of the importance of security and control because they have not been taught the importance of controls. They do not see the need for controls because they perceive that they are the only users of the system or the data.
3. Many more people are familiar with the operation of PCs and are proficient at using them, either legitimately or illegitimately. This increases the number of locations where security breaches could occur.
4. Adequate segregation of duties is often impossible because PCs are located in user departments, and one person may be responsible for both programming and operations.
5. Networks are now being accessed from remote locations using modems, EDI, and other communication systems. The sheer number and variety of these access points significantly increases the risks networks face.
6. PCs are portable and the most elaborate security system in the world cannot protect the data a PC contains if it is lost, stolen, or misplaced.

Most of the policies and procedures for mainframe control are applicable to PCs and networks. The following controls are also important:

- Train users in PC-related control concepts and their importance. Security should be an essential part of the application development process. Users who develop their own application programs should be taught how to test and document them.
- Restrict access by using locks and keys on PCs and, where appropriate, on the disk drives. Equipment should be clearly labeled with unremovable tags.

- Establish policies and procedures to (1) control the data that can be stored in the system or downloaded to PCs and (2) minimize the potential that PCs removed from company premises are stolen. In addition, users should not be allowed to load personal software onto company PCs, to copy company software for personal uses, or to make unauthorized use of the system. It was a lack of these controls (or the failure to enforce them) that allowed employees at a major stock brokerage in San Francisco to use the company's computer system to buy and sell cocaine.
- Portable PCs should not be stored in cars and should be carried onto airplanes rather than checked.
- Keep sensitive data in the most secure environment possible, such as storing it on a mainframe as opposed to a portable PC. Alternatively, sensitive data can be placed on removable diskettes and stored in a locked safe.
- Use a super erase utility program that actually wipes the disk clean when confidential data are deleted. The delete command on most PCs merely erases the index to the data rather than the data itself. Deleted (rather than erased) data can be retrieved by most common utility programs.
- Build protective walls around operating systems to keep users from altering crucial system files.
- Since PCs are most vulnerable when they are turned on, they should be booted up within a security system. Users should not be able to boot from a diskette, nor should they be able to use any part of the system until they have been properly authorized. Any attempt to remove security software from the system should render the keyboard inoperable.
- Use specialists or security programs to detect holes in a network. Security programs mimic an intruder and provide valuable information about how secure the network is and where improvements should be made. Care should be exercised to make sure these programs are not used improperly. For example, SATAN (System Administrator Tool for Analyzing Networks), a free security program offered on the Internet, actually helps open networks to outsiders in certain situations.
- Audit and record what users do and when they do it so security breaches can be traced and corrected.
- Educate users about the risks of computer viruses and how they can be minimized (see Chapter 15).

In most organizations PCs are electronically linked using local and wide area networks. One advantage of PC networks is improved security and control procedures and enforcement through the central network controller. In particular, password controls can be required, PC utilization can be centrally monitored, virus protection procedures can be enforced, and backup procedures can be performed automatically.

The development of an internal control strategy for PCs begins by inventorying all PCs and identifying their uses. Then each PC should be classified according to the risks and exposures associated with its applications. For example, a PC used to maintain accounts payable records and prepare cash disbursements is subject to more risk and exposure than one used for word processing. Next, a security program should be tailored to each PC according to the degree of risk and exposure and the nature of the system applications. Perhaps the most sensitive PC applications are accounting systems under the control of one individual, which implies an inadequate segregation of duties. In such cases sound human resource practices must be followed such as background checks prior to hiring, fidelity bond coverage, enforced vacations, and periodic rotation of duties.

Internet Controls. Organizations and individuals should use caution when doing business on the Internet. Before an Internet message arrives at its destination, it can easily pass through six to ten computers. Therefore sending an Internet message is like sending a message on a postcard. Anyone of the postal workers that handles the postcard before it is delivered can read what it says. Likewise, anyone at one of the computers that handles an Internet message could read or make an electronic copy of it. It is more difficult to read a message if data encryption is used. However, even encrypted messages are not totally secure.

Another challenge to security is protecting computers attached to the Internet from hackers. For example, six young people, all under the age of 23, were arrested in Denmark for using the Internet to break into the National Weather Service computers. Fortunately, the hackers did not bring the system to its knees, which could have grounded all commercial airline flights that depend on the center's weather forecasts. The hackers were discovered when obsolete employee passwords began appearing in the system. In another case, a 16-year-old hacker used his home computer and the Internet to break into more than 100 international networks. Although they have no proof, some investigators fear that the hacker was able to steal secret nuclear data.

One approach to protecting the system from hackers is installation of a **firewall,** a collection of components (computers, software, communication lines, etc.) between the Internet and company networks and computers. All communications to and from the Internet have to pass though the firewall. Control efforts can then be focused on constructing an impenetrable firewall to prevent unauthorized system access. It is much easier to have strong access controls at a single point of entry than to try controlling numerous points of entry. Digital Equipment Corp. installed a firewall, called SEAL (screening external access link), between its internal corporate network and the Internet. SEAL has not allowed a single intruder in 11 years. To create secure Internet links between users of its Quicken software and banks, Intuit purchased 20 of Sun Microsystems' SunScreen firewall systems. However, other companies have not been so lucky. Over the Thanksgiving holiday in 1994 a hacker was able to bore through the firewall at General Electric and access the company's proprietary information. GE had to shut down its Internet access for 72 hours to assess the damage and correct the problem.

Some companies have taken a different tact in dealing with hackers on the Internet. They have set up an Internet server that is not connected to their other computer systems in any way. The only items stored on the server are data that the company wants to make available to Internet users and is not afraid to lose. If hackers manage to bring the system to its knees, the company simply restarts the system and reloads the data stored in the system. Other

Table 14.1 **Controlling AIS Threat Using General Controls**

Category of Controls	Threats/Risks	Description and Examples
Segregation of duties	Leaving one individual in a position to both perpetrate and conceal computer fraud	Separation of the applications programming function from the computer operations function, and, where possible, both of these from the systems programming, transaction authorization, file library, and data control functions.
Management controls	Systems development projects that consume excessive resources	A timetable for each systems development project that includes a master plan and milestones for formal progress review; a policy of terminating projects that are not progressing toward a satisfactory conclusion; periodic performance evaluations; postimplementation reviews; adherence to a schedule for data processing work.
Physical access controls	Damage to computer equipment and files; unauthorized access to confidential data	Limited points of physical access to the computer site; employees required to show personal identification before passing through each access point; security guards and alarms; access control procedures using passwords.
Logical access controls	Unauthorized access to systems software, application programs, data files, and other system resources	User authentication by means of passwords; protect confidentiality of passwords; change passwords frequently; compatibility test of all user requests using access control matrix; electronic identification of terminals; record and follow up attempted system access by unauthorized users.
Data storage controls	Unauthorized disclosure or destruction of stored computer data	File library; file labels; write protection mechanisms; concurrent update controls; data encryption; virus protection; file backup and recovery procedures; checkpoint and rollback procedures.

companies take the opposite approach. They have a one-way, outgoing Internet connection only, so employees can get into the Internet to do research. There is no access into the system from the outside. Some companies use both approaches simultaneously to protect their systems. Doing so, however, limits the effectiveness of the Internet. For example, people could not use this type of system to send and receive E-mail.

Internet security has a long way to go before it can be considered secure. As soon as a company introduces a new security program, a hacker will most likely find a way to compromise it. For example, the security locks on Netscape Communications' Navigator Webbrowser were broken twice within a couple

Table 14.1 **Continued**

Category of Controls	Threats/Risks	Description and Examples
Data transmission controls	Unauthorized access to data being transmitted or to the system itself; system failures; errors in data transmission	Site access controls for data communications equipment; data encryption; access control procedures using passwords; redundant equipment components; checkpoint and rollback procedures; routing verification procedures; message acknowledgment procedures; parity checking.
Documentation standards	Ineffective design, operation, review, audit, and modification of applications systems	Development and enforcement of standards relating to administrative documentation covering overall data processing standards and procedures; both systems documentation and operating documentation for all computer applications.
Decreased system downtime	Temporary system failure leading to interruption of critical business operations	Regular preventive maintenance on key system components; uninterruptible power system; fault-tolerant systems design incorporating duplicate system components.
Disaster recovery planning	Prolonged interruption of data processing and business operations due to fire, natural disaster, sabotage, or vandalism	Disaster recovery planning that identifies crucial system applications and related hardware, software, and data files; specifies all necessary disaster recovery activities and assigns responsibility for them; arranges the availability of backup facilities in the event of emergency.
Protection of personal computers	Damage to computer equipment and files; unauthorized access to confidential data; users who are not security-conscious	End-user training; site access controls; online access control procedures using passwords; backup procedures for data and program files; virus protection; firewalls; application of sound personnel practices in areas of greatest risk and exposure.

of months of the software's release. To motivate hackers to inform the company about future security problems, Netscape began offering prizes to anyone who finds new loopholes in its software.

Table 14.1 summarizes the key aspects of general controls that you have learned in this section.

APPLICATION CONTROLS

The primary objective of **application controls** is to ensure the accuracy of a specific application's inputs, files, programs, and outputs, rather than control the computer system in general. As you learned in the opening case, Jason Scott discovered several fictitious invoices at SPP that may have been processed by the accounts payable and cash disbursements system. If so, this represents a failure in the system's application controls. However, inadequate general controls also may have contributed to this control breakdown. General controls and application controls are important and necessary, because application controls will be much more effective in the presence of strong general controls.

If application controls are weak, AIS output is likely to contain errors. Erroneous data can lead to poor management decision making and can negatively affect a company's relationships with customers, suppliers, and other external parties. For example, TRW Information Services, a large credit reporting bureau, was sued by several states for reporting inaccurate credit information and violating consumer privacy. These lawsuits were reportedly triggered by thousands of consumer complaints about inaccurate and negative information surfacing on their credit reports.

This section will discuss six categories of application controls: batch totals, source data controls, input validation routines, on-line data entry controls, file maintenance controls, and output controls.

Batch Totals

Batch totals are easily implemented in a computerized data processing environment, since the computer can be programmed to calculate and check the totals. It occurred to Jason Scott that batch total checks should have detected the fictitious invoices inserted into SPP's accounts payable system. He discovered that vendor invoices were approved for payment by an accounts payable clerk, who would assemble the invoices and supporting documents into batches of 50 items. The clerk computed a record count and financial total for each batch, then entered them on a batch control sheet. The batches, with their corresponding control sheets, were taken to the data entry department. Data entry personnel keyed the batch control record into the system, then entered all the transaction data. The batch totals were reconciled at the end of the data entry process and at each subsequent processing stage. The source documents were stored alphabetically in a manual file, and the batch control sheets were discarded.

Jason realized that there were at least two flaws in this system. First, the person who created the batch totals also approved the invoices for payment. If that person submitted a fictitious invoice, he or she would be able to include the fictitious invoice data in the batch totals. Second, the batch control sheet was discarded by the data entry clerk at the end of the data entry process. Thus the data entry clerk would be able to submit a fictitious invoice and alter the batch totals, since this could only be detected by reference to the discarded batch control sheet. Jason concluded that although SPP's batch control procedures appeared to be strong on the surface, in reality they were not at all effective, at least not in minimizing the risk of fraud.

Source Data Controls

Source data controls regulate the accuracy, validity, and completeness of input. There are a number of source data controls:

- *Data control function.* When data are received for processing, data control personnel check for user authorizations and record the name, transaction source, and control totals in a control log. They monitor the data as it is processed, reconcile control totals after each processing step, and initiate data corrections. Corrected input should be resubmitted to validation routines, because the error rate on corrections is higher than that on any other type of transaction. User departments should be notified of any incorrect input that subsequently resulted in errors.

- *Key verification.* **Key verification** is an expensive form of source data control and is used only for crucial input such as customer numbers and amounts and quantities ordered. It consists of an additional employee rekeying data into the computer, which compares the two sets of keystrokes and highlights any discrepancies for correction.
- *Check digit verification.* All authorized ID numbers (such as an account number) contain a **check digit** that is computed from the other digits. The data entry device is programmed to test the check digit each time an ID number is entered. **Check digit verification** will probably (but not certainly) detect errors in ID numbers and signal the operator. For example, in a five-digit number the last digit could be the sum of the first four subtracted from the next highest number ending in zero. The number 90614 would pass this check, since $20 - 16 = 4$. However, 90615 would fail, since $20 - 16 \neq 5$.
- *Prenumbered forms sequence test.* When sequentially prenumbered forms are employed, the system identifies and reports missing or duplicate form numbers.
- *Turnaround documents.* Because turnaround documents are system output that comes back as a machine-readable input record, they are much more accurate than input records prepared by manual keying.

Jason Scott discovered that prenumbered forms were not used at SPP. However, sequentially prenumbered vouchers could have been used, with a separate voucher attached to each vendor invoice and its supporting documents. In addition, supplier numbers were not controlled using self-checking digits. In fact, there was no formal process of approving additions to the supplier (accounts payable) file. If a supplier's invoice was approved for payment, that supplier became an approved creditor. Jason noted in his report that the proper use of either sequentially prenumbered vouchers or check digit verification of supplier numbers could have helped prevent SPP from paying fictitious invoices.

Input Validation Routines

Input validation routines are programs or subroutines that check the validity and accuracy of input data after they have been entered and recorded on a machine-readable file. These programs are also called **edit programs,** and the specific types of accuracy checks they perform are called **edit checks.** In on-line processing, edit checks are performed during the source data entry process. As shown in Fig. 14.2, input validation in batch processing is performed by a separate program prior to regular processing. Errors identified by edit programs should be corrected without delay. In on-line processing, the system will not accept the data until it has been corrected. In batch processing, the corrected data should be resubmitted with the next batch of transactions and re-edited using the same input validation routine.

Figure 14.2

Edit Program

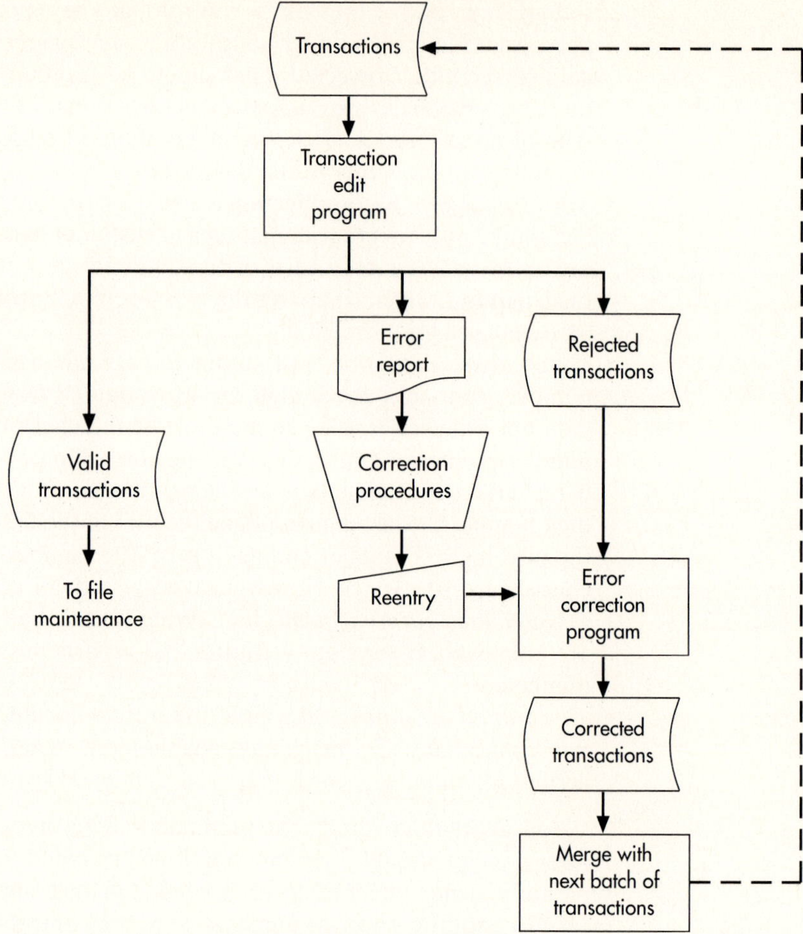

Several edit checks are used in input validation routines:

- A **field check** determines whether the characters in a field are of the proper type. For example, a check on a numerical field would indicate an error if it contained blanks or alphabetic characters.
- A **limit check** tests a numerical amount to ensure that it does not exceed a set predetermined limit. For example, the hours worked field in weekly payroll input can be compared to a maximum amount, such as 60 hours.
- A **range check** is similar to a limit check except that it has both upper and lower limits. Range checks are used on transaction date fields, since a date should be within, but not in excess of, a few days of the current date.
- A **reasonableness test** determines the logical correctness of input and master file data. For example, a \$1000 monthly salary increase is reasonable for an executive with a current salary of \$15,000 per month but not for a data entry clerk making \$1500 per month. Similarly, inventory receipts can be tested by checking whether they exceed twice the value of the quantity ordered.

- A **redundant data check** uses two identifiers in each transaction record to confirm that the correct master file record has been updated. For example, the customer account number and the first five letters of the customer's name can be used to retrieve the correct customer master record from the accounts receivable file. The system retrieves the master record based upon the customer account record and compares the first five letters from both records. If they do not match, the input data must be in error.
- A **sequence check** tests whether a batch of input data is in the proper numerical or alphabetical sequence.
- A **sign check** determines whether the data in a field have the appropriate arithmetic sign. For example, data in an inventory balance field should never possess a negative sign.
- A **validity check** compares ID numbers or transaction codes with those already authorized. For example, if a sale to customer 65432 is entered, the computer must locate customer 65432 in the customer master file to confirm that the sale was indeed made to a valid customer.

On-Line Data Entry Controls

The goal of on-line data entry controls is to ensure the accuracy and integrity of transaction data entered from on-line terminals and PCs. On-line data entry controls include the following:

- Field, limit, range, reasonableness, sign, validity, and redundant data checks, as described in the previous section.
- User ID numbers and passwords that limit data entry to authorized personnel.
- **Compatibility tests** to help ensure that employees entering or accessing data are actually authorized to make those particular entries or view the data.
- **Prompting,** in which the system requests each input data item and waits for an acceptable response.
- **Preformatting,** in which the system displays a document with highlighted blank spaces and waits for the data to be entered.
- A **completeness check** on each input record to determine whether all required data items have been entered.
- Assignment of a specific **default value.** For example, the default value for the transaction date field can be set as the current date.
- Where possible, the system should automatically enter transaction data, which saves keying time and reduces errors. For example, the system can determine the next available document number and enter it into the transaction record. The system can also generate new ID numbers that satisfy the check digit algorithm and do not duplicate existing numbers, then enter them into the input record.
- **Closed-loop verification** can be used to help data entry personnel check the accuracy of input data. Suppose one of the data items being entered is an account number. The system could retrieve the account name and display it on the operator's terminal. This would help the operator know that the correct account number had been entered. Closed-loop verification can be used instead of a redundant data check to protect against entry of a valid but incorrect identification number.

- A **transaction log** that includes a detailed record of all transaction data, the date and time of entry, the terminal and operator identification, and the sequence in which the transaction was entered. If an on-line file is damaged, the log can be used for reconstruction purposes. If a malfunction temporarily shuts down the system, the internal sequence number of the last successful transaction can be displayed once service is restored. This ensures that transactions are not lost or inadvertently entered twice.
- Clear messages that indicate when an error has occurred, which item is in error, and what the operator should do to correct it. The system should recheck the operator's response to the error message prior to accepting further transaction input.

File Maintenance Controls

File maintenance controls are designed to help preserve the accuracy and completeness of stored data. Some of the more common controls include the following:

- *Data currency checks.* Stored data often become out of date. For example, suppliers or customers may move or go out of business and employees may retire or quit. To help identify such conditions, records should contain a "date of last transaction" field. Periodically, files should be scanned to identify and investigate records that are more than one year old.
- *Exception reporting.* While searching for noncurrent records, the system can also check for other unusual conditions and list them on an exception report. Virtually all of the edit checks described earlier can be used, but the sign check and the completeness test should always be performed. The sign check detects conditions such as a negative inventory or customer account balance. The completeness test detects data that may have been lost while the file was being copied or updated.
- *External data reconciliation.* Master file totals can often be reconciled with data maintained outside the system. For example, each time the payroll file is processed, the computer can report the number of employee records, and this amount can be compared with the total maintained by the human resources department. This external data reconciliation process should detect attempts to add fictitious employees to the payroll master file.
- *Control account reconciliation.* A general ledger system affords numerous reconciliation opportunities. For example, the inventory control account balance in the general ledger should always be equal to the sum of the item balances in the inventory master file. This should hold true for the accounts receivable, capital assets, and the accounts payable control accounts as well. General ledger control account balances should be reconciled to the corresponding master file totals on a regular basis.
- *File security.* These procedures include a file library, a librarian that logs files in and out, internal and external labels, write protection mechanisms, and backup copies of files stored at a secure off-site location.
- *File conversion controls.* Sound controls over the file conversion process are needed to ensure that the new files are error-free. Edit checks and batch control totals should check all significant fields. The old and new systems should be run in parallel at least once and the results compared to identify discrep-

ancies. File conversion should be carefully supervised. It should also be reviewed by an internal audit.

- *Error logs.* All errors should be entered in a log. As they are corrected and the corresponding data successfully resubmitted to the system, the status of the error record in the log is changed from open to closed. A notation of the resubmission date and the cause of the error should be recorded.
- *Error reporting.* Periodically, the error log should be used to prepare management reports summarizing errors by record type, error type, and cause. Reports listing all outstanding errors should be provided to operations supervisors. They should follow up on uncorrected errors and ensure that they are corrected as quickly as possible.

Output Controls

The data control function should review all output for reasonableness and proper format and should reconcile corresponding output and input control totals. Data control is also responsible for distributing computer output to the appropriate user departments. Special care should be taken in handling checks and other sensitive documents and reports. Users are responsible for carefully reviewing the completeness and accuracy of all computer output that they receive. A shredder can be used to destroy highly confidential data such as obsolete customer listings, research data, and payroll registers.

Table 14.2 summarizes the key application controls discussed in this section.

Application Controls: A Batch Processing Example

Many of the application controls described in the chapter can be illustrated using a credit sales transaction example. The following transaction data are used: sales order number, customer account number, inventory item number, quantity sold, sale price, and delivery date. If the customer purchases more than one product, the inventory item number, quantity sold, and price fields will occur more than once in each sales transaction record. Processing these transactions includes the following steps:

1. Preparing batch totals.
2. Keying the source data into the system.
3. Editing the transaction file.
4. Accessing each inventory record to subtract the quantity sold from the quantity on hand.
5. Accessing each customer record to add the total sale amount to the customer's account balance.
6. Preparing and distributing shipping and/or billing documents.

Figure 14.3 (pp. 489-490) illustrates this process and identifies the application controls that should be employed at each stage.

Preparing Batch Totals. Employees who assemble batches of sales order documents prepare the following four batch totals:

1. A record count of the number of customer transactions.
2. A line count of the number of inventory transactions.
3. Hash totals showing the total quantity of all items sold and the total of all price fields.
4. A financial total of total dollar sales (price × quantity).

Table 14.2 **Summary of Key Application Control Procedures**

Category of Controls	Threats/Risk	Description and Examples
Batch totals	Lost input records; bogus input records; errors in data entry or data processing	Totals should be manually prepared prior to processing and checked after each subsequent stage of processing; examples include financial totals, hash totals, record counts, line counts, and the cross-footing balance test.
Source data controls	Invalid, incomplete, or inaccurate source data input	Examples include key verification; check-digit verification; sequentially prenumbered forms; turnaround documents; review of source data input for appropriate authorization; control log; and monitoring and expediting data entry process by data control personnel.
Input validation routines	Invalid or inaccurate data in computer-processed transaction files	Transaction files are processed by edit programs that perform edit checks on key data fields, including sequence checks, field checks, sign checks, validity checks, limit checks, range checks, reasonableness tests, and redundant data checks.
On-line data entry controls	Invalid or inaccurate transaction input entered through on-line terminals	Examples include edit checks; prompting operators during the data entry process; preformatting; completeness test; automatic system data entry; closed-loop verification; and a transaction log maintained by the system.
File maintenance controls	Inaccurate or incomplete data in computer-processed master files	Examples include checks on currency of master file data; reporting exceptions identified by edit checks; reconciliation of master file totals with externally maintained totals; storage of files in secure file library; use of file labels and write protection mechanisms; backup file copies stored in secure off-site location; and file conversion controls.
Output controls	Inaccurate or incomplete computer output	Data control personnel should perform visual review of computer output, reconciliation of batch totals, and proper distribution of output; users should also review computer output for completeness and accuracy.

These totals are recorded on batch control forms appended to each group of sales documents. The batches are delivered to data control, where each batch is checked for proper authorization and recorded in a control log.

Data Entry. Several controls are used when transaction data are keyed into the system and entered into a transaction file:

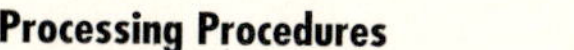

Figure 14.3

Flowchart of Sales Order Processing and Related Control Procedures

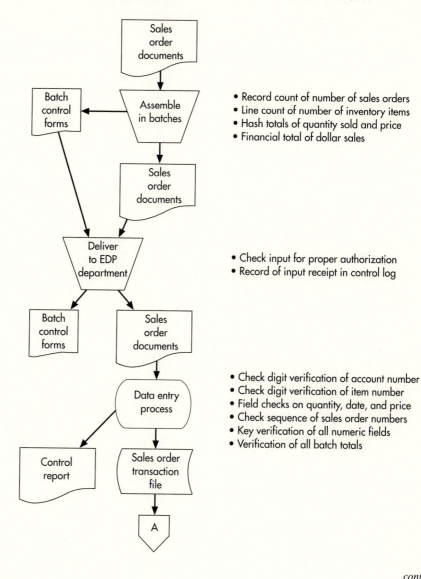

Processing Procedures	Control Procedures
Sales order documents → Assemble in batches → Batch control forms; Sales order documents	• Record count of number of sales orders • Line count of number of inventory items • Hash totals of quantity sold and price • Financial total of dollar sales
Batch control forms, Sales order documents → Deliver to EDP department → Batch control forms; Sales order documents	• Check input for proper authorization • Record of input receipt in control log
Sales order documents → Data entry process → Control report; Sales order transaction file → A	• Check digit verification of account number • Check digit verification of item number • Field checks on quantity, date, and price • Check sequence of sales order numbers • Key verification of all numeric fields • Verification of all batch totals

continued

- Check digit verification, to verify the customer account number and the inventory item number.
- Field checks, to confirm the presence of numeric characters in the quantity, date, and price fields.
- Accounting for the numerical sequence of sales orders, to ensure that each has been accounted for.
- Calculation of relevant batch totals for comparison with the original control totals.

Figure 14.3

Continued

Processing Procedures	Control Procedures
A → Sort and edit process → Control report; Sales order transaction file	• Sequence check on account number • Limit checks on quantity and price • Range check on delivery date • Completeness test on entire record • Reconciliation of batch totals • Review errors identified by edit checks • Investigation and correction of erroneous input
File update ↔ A/R and inventory master files → Shipping/billing documents; Control report	• Security of master files in file library • Protection of master files with file labels • Maintenance of backup copies of master files • Validity check of customer account number • Validity check of inventory item number • Sign check of inventory quantity on hand • Limit check of sale amount versus credit limit • Range check on sale price • Reasonableness test of quantity ordered • Redundant data check on customer data • Redundant data check on inventory data
Review and distribute → Shipping/billing documents	• Reconciliation of batch totals • Review of errors identified by edit checks • Investigation and correction of erroneous input • Distribution of billing and shipping documents • Recording of output distribution in control log • Return of master files to file library
User review	• Visual inspection of output • Reconciliation of batch totals

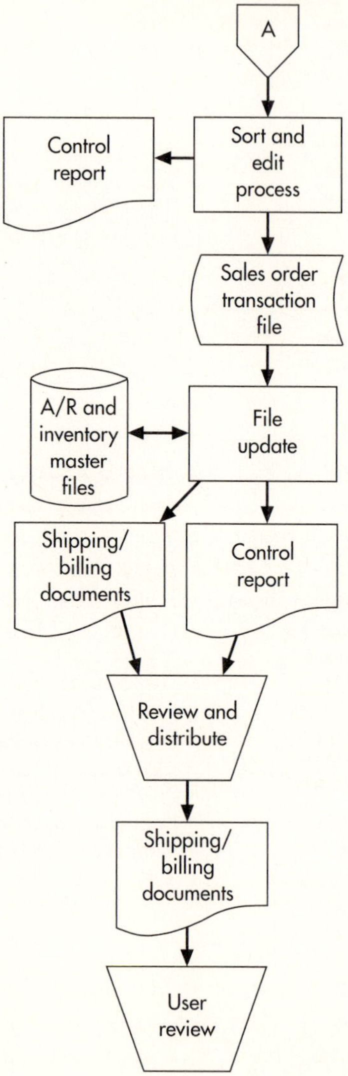

Source data entry errors generally fall into one of two types. Operator errors arise when an operator reads a source document incorrectly or accidentally strikes the wrong key. These errors are generally benign and can be corrected immediately. Incorrect source data, such as an unauthorized sales transaction or an invalid account number, is more problematic and should be corrected before the sales transaction data are processed any further.

Editing the Transaction File. After the sales transaction file is sorted into customer number sequence, an edit program performs the following checks:

1. A sequence check on the customer account number field.
2. Limit checks on the quantity and price fields.
3. A range check on the requested delivery date.
4. A completeness test to verify that all input record fields contain data.

Rejected transactions are listed on a control report along with the computed batch totals. Data control reconciles the batch totals, investigates and corrects any errors, and submits the corrected transactions.

File Updating. The sales transaction file is processed against customer (accounts receivable) and inventory master files. Care must be taken to ensure that the correct file copies are retrieved from the file library and loaded onto the system. The operator must check the file name and processing date on the external labels before loading the files. The file-update program checks the internal header label before processing begins. Each file has a trailer label containing a record count and other file totals; these are checked and updated during the file-updating run. Backup copies of the transaction file and both master files are created and conveyed to a secure off-site location for storage purposes.

Because the file update program accesses the customer and inventory master file records, it performs additional input validation tests by comparing data on each transaction record with data on the corresponding master file record. These tests include the following:

- Validity checks on the customer and inventory item numbers.
- Sign checks on inventory-on-hand balances (after subtracting sales quantities).
- Limit checks that compare each customer's total amount due to their credit limit.
- Range checks on the sale price of each item sold relative to the permissible range of prices for that item.
- Reasonableness tests on the quantity sold of each item relative to normal sales quantities for that item.

To prevent the entry of valid but incorrect customer or inventory item numbers, redundant data (customer name and item description) are entered for each transaction. The data are cross-checked against the corresponding values in the master files. This step prevents the posting of a credit sale to the wrong accounts receivable record or an inventory reduction to the wrong inventory record.

Preparing and Distributing Output. Outputs include billing and/or shipping documents and a control report. The control report contains batch totals accumulated during the file update run and a list of transactions rejected by the update program. Data control reconciles batch totals, investigates rejected transactions and discrepancies in batch totals, and corrects any errors. Data control also distributes the documents, updates their control log, and returns the updated master files to the file library. Users in the shipping and billing departments perform a limited review of the documents by visually inspecting them for misaligned or incomplete data or other obvious deficiencies.

Application Controls: An On-Line Processing Example

When a user accesses an on-line system, logical access controls confirm the identity of the terminal and validity of the user's ID number and password. A compatibility test is performed on all user interactions to ensure that only authorized tasks are performed. To assist authorized personnel in entering sales data, the system asks for customer and item numbers as well as other required input. After each prompt the system waits for a valid response. As data are entered the system performs validity, field, limit, range, and sign checks as well as check digit verification, reasonableness tests, and completeness tests. A significant advantage of on-line systems is the immediate correction of any detected errors.

After the data entry operator enters the customer and inventory item numbers, the system retrieves the corresponding customer name and item descriptions from the master files and displays them on the terminal. The terminal operator visually examines the customer name and item descriptions displayed. If they match the sales order document, the operator signals the system to proceed with the transaction. If they do not match, the operator rechecks the account or item number and enters the correct value.

For adequate control, all significant transaction data are checked at least once. Generally, tests performed by the computer, such as edit checks, are less costly and more effective than tests performed by people, such as key verification and visual inspection. The earlier in the process a data entry error is caught, the easier and less costly it is to correct.

SUMMARY AND CASE CONCLUSION

Jason Scott and his supervisor were unable to identify the source of the fictitious invoices. They asked the police to identify the owner of the Pacific Electric Services bank account. The police discovered that Patricia Simpson, a data entry clerk at SPP, was the owner of the account. Under questioning by police fraud investigators, Patricia admitted to an embezzlement scheme in which she created fictitious invoices, inserted them into batches of invoices submitted to her for data entry, modified the batch control totals, and destroyed the original batch control sheet. According to Patricia, the scheme had been initiated only three months previously, and no one else at SPP was involved. She also claimed that all fictitious invoices were in the name of Pacific Electric Services.

Jason examined SPP's cash disbursement records to corroborate Patricia's story. He wrote a program that reads cash disbursements transaction files and identifies disbursements to Pacific Electric Services. Then he undertook the daunting task of retrieving several hundred tape files containing disbursement transactions over the past two years from SPP's archives. He identified 40 fraudulent transactions totaling over $20,000. Contrary to Patricia's account, the earliest of these transactions occurred 18 months earlier, although there was a two-month gap, ending three months earlier, that contains no fraudulent transactions.

Since Patricia had not been truthful about the duration of her scheme, Jason wondered whether she might also have used other fictitious company names. By this time, however, she wasn't supplying any further information, on the advice of her lawyer. So Jason wrote another computer program to scan the cash disbursement records and retrieve the supplier account number, name, address, and authorization code for every vendor invoice processed without a supporting purchase order or receiving report. This check eventually yielded a file containing 175 supplier records; payment authorization for which have been granted by 23 different employees at SPP. Jason sorted this file by authorization code and prepared 23 printouts containing data about the suppliers each of these employees contracted with. Each printout was sent to the corresponding employee, with a request to confirm the authenticity of every supplier on his or her list. After having received all of these printouts, Jason concluded that the embezzlement scheme was indeed confined to Pacific Electric Services.

SPP implemented several changes in its accounts payable and cash disbursements system in response to the auditors' recommendations:

1. There must be an approved purchase order for every disbursement, including those solely for service purposes.
2. Disbursements can be made only to approved suppliers, and every supplier must be approved by a purchasing agent who is not involved in the cash disbursements process. Approved suppliers are assigned an account number that contains a check digit. That account number must be included in every cash disbursement record. The purchasing department now maintains a count of the number of approved suppliers. This list is regularly compared with a computer-generated count of the number of supplier records on the accounts payable file.
3. When payment of vendor invoices is approved, a voucher record is prepared to document the approval. This voucher accompanies the invoice and any supporting documents through all subsequent processing steps. These vouchers are sequentially prenumbered, and all outstanding voucher numbers are accounted for on a regular basis.
4. Batch totals for the daily batch of cash disbursement transactions are prepared by an employee other than the person who approves the payments. The accounts payable department retains a copy of the batch control sheet for comparison to the final batch control report generated by the cash disbursement system.

As he learned about the changes SPP made to improve its internal control system, Jason reflected on how management rejected similar changes suggested by Northwest's internal audit staff, including those made by his supervisor, just one year ago. Jason realized he has learned an important truth about internal control: There are many companies and managers who do not realize the importance of internal control until they have been burned.

KEY TERMS

general controls
project milestones
physical access
logical access
password
biometric identifications
compatibility check
access control matrix
external label
internal labels
volume label
header label
trailer label
tape file protection ring
concurrent update controls

data encryption
cryptography
routing verification procedures
mutual authentication schemes
dial-back systems
parity bit
parity checking
echo check
administrative documentation
systems documentation
operating documentation
preventive maintenance
uninterruptible power system (UPS)
fault tolerance
disaster recovery plan
electronic vaulting
grandfather-father-son
checkpoint
rollback
hot site
cold site
firewall
application controls
key verification
check digit
check digit verification
input validation routines
edit programs
edit checks
field check
limit check
range check
reasonableness test
redundant data check
sequence check
sign check
validity check
compatibility test
prompting
preformatting
completeness test
default value
closed-loop verification
transaction log

CHAPTER QUIZ

1. Controls that are designed to ensure that an organization's computer-based control environment is stable and well managed are called
   a. general controls.
   b. application controls.
   c. detective controls.
   d. preventive controls.

2. All of the following are effective control procedures to ensure that operators do not make unauthorized changes to programs and files except
   a. rotating duties.
   b. having multiple operators in the computer room during processing.
   c. requiring formal written authorization and documentation of program changes.
   d. maintaining and reviewing a log of all operator activity and interventions.

3. Password effectiveness is enhanced by all of the following except
   a. frequent changes.
   b. user selection of passwords.
   c. not displaying the password on the screen.
   d. automatic disconnection after several failed attempts.

4. The best method to reduce the risk of electronic eavesdropping is
   a. the use of parity bits.
   b. compatibility tests.
   c. data encryption.
   d. checkpoints and roll-back procedures.

5. Descriptions of each application program, including narratives, flowcharts and code, are called
   a. administrative documentation.
   b. accounting documentation.
   c. operating documentation.
   d. systems documentation.

6. Controls that are designed to prevent, detect, or correct errors in transactions as they flow through the various stages of a specific data processing program are referred to as
   a. general controls.
   b. application controls.
   c. administrative controls.
   d. data processing controls.

7. A batch total that equals the sum of all part numbers ordered is called a
   a. financial total.
   b. hash total.
   c. record count.
   d. line count.

8. The computer sums the first four digits of a customer number to calculate the value of the fifth digit and then compares that calculation to the number typed in data entry. This is an example of a
   a. field check.
   b. parity check.

c. check digit.
d. batch total.

9. The edit check that would detect the entry of a customer number that does not exist is called a
a. check digit.
b. limit check.
c. sequence check.
d. validity check.

10. In an on-line system, the user enters the customer number and the system responds by displaying the customer name and asking the user for verification. This is called a
a. closed-loop verification test.
b. redundant data check.
c. compatibility test.
d. completeness test.

DISCUSSION QUESTIONS

14.1 A computer implementation project is often performed in a state of crisis, with the implementation group working feverishly to keep pace with the implementation schedule. In this atmosphere corners are often cut with respect to documentation and application controls. What arguments do you feel would be effective to prevent these types of shortcuts?

14.2 Theoretically, a control procedure should be adopted if its benefit exceeds its cost. Explain how the benefits and costs of the following controls can be estimated.
a. Separation of functions
b. Data protection procedures
c. Logical access controls
d. Input validation routines

14.3 Prudential-Bache Securities in New York contracted with Comdisco Computing Service Corporation in New Jersey to back up its data (over 500,000 securities transactions per day) by transmitting it on a real-time basis to an electronic vaulting service. The service includes use of a high-speed data transmission line and an automated tape library. Comdisco also agreed to make a hot site available to Prudential-Bache in the event that a disaster shuts down their central data center. The hot site has a direct link to the vaulting system, ensuring that all but the last 15 minutes of trading data would be recovered.

Though terms of the contract were not disclosed, this arrangement is certainly a very expensive proposition for Prudential-Bache. Discuss how this contract could have been justified on a cost-benefit basis. In addition, name at least three steps that Prudential-Bache should take to prevent unauthorized access to its backup data.

14.4 For control purposes, the function of transaction authorization should be performed by employees outside the systems department. However, computers are increasingly being programmed to initiate transactions, such as issuing a purchase order when an inventory balance is low. Discuss whether such automatic transaction generation represents a violation of good internal control principles.

14.5 The Foster Corporation recently fired its AIS director after experiencing several years of budget overruns in systems development and computer operations. You have been appointed as interim director and are charged with investigating the problems the department has experienced. There is little written information about the activities of the department or the policies under which it was managed. The previous director communicated assignments, standards, and performance evaluations verbally. This management style was popular with some employees but unpopular with many others, some of whom have left the company.

The major systems project under development is an MIS. Objectives for the project are loosely defined, although a good deal of analysis, design, and programming has been completed. The project director estimates the project is half-finished. The computer operations department runs jobs on an as-received basis. The operations supervisor suggests that a more reliable system is needed to satisfy demand during peak periods and cope with expected processing growth.

Identify and briefly describe several elements of control that appear to be lacking in this situation and that you feel should be implemented in the information systems department.

PROBLEMS

14.1 Your company has purchased a number of microcomputers. One has been installed in the stores department, which is responsible for disbursing stock items and maintaining stores records. In your audit you find that one employee, trained in computer applications, receives the requisitions for stores, reviews them for completeness and approvals, disburses the stock, maintains the records, operates the computer, and authorizes adjustments to the total amounts of stock accumulated by the computer.

When you discuss the applicable controls with the department manager, you are told that the microcomputer is assigned exclusively to that department. Therefore it does not require the same types of controls that are applicable to large computer systems.

REQUIRED

Comment on the manager's contentions, discussing briefly five types of control that would apply to this microcomputer application. (CIA Examination, adapted)

14.2 You are the general manager of a manufacturing company in Woodbridge, Virginia. During the past six months your company has consistently lost bids to a competitor whose bids always seem to be slightly lower. On a hunch that this could not keep happening by chance, you hire a private detective. She reports that one of your employees with access to the computer is stealing your bid data and selling it to the competitor for $25,000 per bid.

REQUIRED

a. Identify the likely deficiencies in internal control over your company's computer systems that could have allowed this fraud to occur.
b. How else could bids have been stolen and sold?
c. How would you guard against each of these methods?

14.3 Consider the set of numeric computer input data in Table 14.3.

REQUIRED

a. From the data in Table 14.3, calculate and show one specific example of the following:

Hash Total: Financial Total:
Record Count:

b. For each of the following controls, give a specific example from the four records in Table 14.3 of an error or probable error that would be caught by the control (list the error—don't merely describe it):

Field Check: Reasonableness Test:
Sequence Check: Crossfooting Balance Test:
Limit Check:

14.4 You are the data security administrator for a small company. Its system uses two programs: a payroll system and an inventory processing system. It maintains three files: a payroll master file, an inventory master file, and a transaction log. The following users should have the indicated access to the system:

User	Access Needed
Salesperson	Read and display records in the inventory file
Inventory control analyst	Read, display, update, create, and delete records in the inventory file
Payroll analyst	Read, display, and update records in the payroll file

Table 14.3 **Computer Input Data, Problem 14.3**

Employee Number Col. 1–3	Pay Rate Col. 4–6	Hours Worked Col. 7–8	Gross Pay Col. 9–13	Deductions Col. 14–18	Net Pay Col. 19–23
121	250	38	$9500	01050	08450
123	275	40	11000	01250	09750
125	200	90	16000	02000	12000
122	280	40	11200	11000	00200

Human resources manager	Read, display, update, create, and delete records in the payroll file
Payroll programmer	Perform all payroll system operations. Read and display payroll file records and transaction log records
Inventory programmer	Perform all operations on the inventory system. Read and display inventory file records and transaction log records
Data processing manager	Read and display all programs and files
Yourself	Perform all operations on all programs and files

REQUIRED

a. Create an access control matrix that allows the users to have the indicated levels of access. For each user, assign a six-character user code and select access authority codes. Use the following access authority coding system.

0 = no access permitted
1 = read and display only
2 = read, display, and update
3 = read, display, update, create, and delete

b. What changes would you make to the access privileges of the employees mentioned earlier?

14.5 What control or controls would you recommend to prevent the following situations from occurring?

a. The "time worked" field for salaried employees is supposed to contain a 01 for one week. One employee's field contained the number 40, and a check for $6872.51 was accidentally prepared and mailed.

b. A programmer obtained the master payroll file, loaded it into the system, and changed his monthly salary from $1400 to $2000 through the computer console.

c. The accounts receivable file on disk was inadvertently destroyed and could not be reconstructed after being substituted for the accounts payable file in a processing run.

d. A company lost almost all of its vital business data in a fire that destroyed the room in which it stored its magnetic disks and tapes.

e. A programmer quit the firm in the middle of an assignment. Because no other programmers could make sense of the work already completed, the project was started over from scratch.

f. A bank programmer obtained the disks containing the program that calculates interest on customer accounts. She loaded the program into the computer and modified it so the fractions of a cent from each interest calculation, which would otherwise be rounded off, were added to her account.

g. During keying of customer payment records, the digit 0 in a payment of $102.34 was mistakenly typed as the letter O. As a result, the transaction was not processed correctly, and the customer received an incorrect statement.

h. After the inventory master file maintained on magnetic tape was updated, the old master tape was removed for use in other applications. The updated master was then accidentally mislabeled, and its contents were subsequently erased. Considerable difficulty was encountered in reconstructing the master inventory file.

14.6 What control or controls would you recommend in an on-line computer system to prevent the following situations from occurring?

a. A teenager gained unauthorized access to the system by programming a PC to enter repeated user numbers until a correct one was found.

b. An employee gained unauthorized access to the system by observing her supervisor's user number and then correctly guessing the password after 12 attempts.

c. A salesperson for a PC manufacturer, keying in a customer order from a remote laptop computer, entered an incorrect stock number. As a result, an order for 50 monitors was placed for a customer who wanted to order 50 PCs.

d. A salesperson received a laptop computer to enter sales orders while calling on customers. She used it to increase her own monthly salary by $500.

e. A salesperson keying in a customer order from a remote computer inadvertently omitted the delivery address from the order.

f. A company's research and development center utilizes remote PCs tied into its computer center 100 miles away. Through a wiretap the company's largest competitor stole secret plans for a major product innovation.

g. A $400 multiplexor at a bank served terminals at eight drive-in windows. When the multiplexor failed, the bank was forced to shut down the windows for two hours during a busy Friday afternoon.

h. A 20-minute power failure that shut down a firm's computer system resulted in loss of data for several transactions that were being entered into the system from remote terminals.

14.7 The headquarters of Gleicken Corporation, a private company with $3.5 million in annual sales, is located in California. For its 150 clients Gleicken provides an on-line legal software service that includes data storage and administrative activities for law offices. The company has grown rapidly since its inception three years ago, and its data processing department has mushroomed to accommodate this growth. Because Gleicken's president and sales staff spend a great deal of time out of the office soliciting new clients, planning the EDP facilities has been left to the data processing professionals.

Gleicken recently moved its headquarters into a remodeled warehouse on the outskirts of the city. While remodeling the warehouse, the architects retained much of the original structure, including the wooden-shingled exterior and exposed wooden beams throughout the interior. The minicomputer distributive processing hardware is situated in a large open area with high ceilings and skylights. This openness makes the data processing area accessible to the rest of the staff and encourages a team approach to problem solving. Before Gleicken began to occupy its new facility, city inspectors declared the building safe (i.e., adequate fire extinguishers, sufficient exits, etc.).

Gleicken wanted to provide further protection for its large data base of client information. Therefore it instituted a tape backup procedure that automatically backs up the data base every Sunday evening to avoid interrupting daily operations and procedures. All the tapes are labeled and carefully stored on shelves in the data processing department reserved for this purpose. The departmental operator's manual has instructions on how to use these tapes to restore the data base should the need arise. In the event of an emergency there is a home phone list of the individuals in the data processing department. Gleicken has recently increased its liability insurance for data loss from $50,000 to $100,000.

This past Saturday the Gleicken headquarters building was completely ruined by fire. The company must now inform its clients that all their information has been destroyed.

REQUIRED

a. Describe the computer security weaknesses present at Gleicken Corporation that made it possible for a disastrous data loss to occur.

b. List the components that should have been included in the disaster recovery plan at Gleicken Corporation in order to ensure computer recovery within 72 hours.

c. What factors, other than those included in the plan itself, should a company consider when formulating a disaster recovery plan?

d. What threats, other than the fire, should Gleicken have protected itself from? (CMA Examination, adapted)

14.8 The Moose Wings Cooperative Flight Club owns a number of airplanes and gliders. It serves less than 2000 members, who are numbered sequentially from the founder, Tom Eagle (0001), to the newest member, Jacques Noveau (1368). Members rent the flying machines by the hour, and all planes must be returned on the same day. The club uses a CRT terminal on its premises and a dial-up line to send the billing data to a computer utility. The utility bills its members monthly.

The following six records were among those entered for the flights taken on November 1, 1996.

Member #	Flight Date DDMMYY	Plane Used*	Takeoff Time	Landing Time
1234	011196	G	0625	0846
4111	011196	C	0849	1023
1210	011196	P	0342	0542
0023	011196	X	0159	1243
012A	011196	P	1229	1532
0999	011196	L	1551	1387

*G = glider; C = Cessna; P = Piper Cub; L = Lear Jet

REQUIRED

a. For each of the five data fields, suggest one or more edit controls that could be included in the program for detecting possible errors.

b. Identify and describe any errors in the records.

c. Suggest other controls to prevent input errors if on-line entry were employed. (SMAC Examination, adapted)

14.9 Talbert Corporation hired an independent computer programmer to develop a simplified payroll application for its newly purchased computer. The programmer developed an on-line data entry system that minimized the level of knowledge required by the operator. It was based upon typing answers to input cues that appeared on the terminal's viewing screen. Examples of the cues follow.

- a. Access routine:
  1. Operator access number to payroll file?
  2. Are there new employees?
- b. New employees routine:
  1. Employee name?
  2. Employee number?
  3. Social Security number?
  4. Rate per hour?
  5. Single or married?
  6. Number of dependents?
  7. Account distribution?
- c. Current payroll routine:
  1. Employee number?
  2. Regular hours worked?
  3. Overtime hours worked?
  4. Total employees this payroll period?

The independent auditor is attempting to verify that certain input validation (edit) checks exist. The checks should ensure that errors resulting from omissions, invalid entries, or other inaccuracies are detected as soon as the answers to the input cues are entered.

REQUIRED

Identify the various types of input validation (edit) checks the independent auditor would expect to find in the EDP system. Describe the assurances provided by each identified validation check. Do not discuss the review and evaluation of these controls. (CPA Examination)

14.10 Babbington-Bowles is an advertising agency that employs 625 salespersons who travel and entertain extensively. Each month salespersons are paid both salary and commissions. The nature of their job is such that expenses of several hundred dollars a day might be incurred. In the past these expenses were included in each monthly paycheck. Salespersons were required to submit their expense reports, with supporting receipts, by the twentieth of each month. These reports would be reviewed and then sent to data entry in a batch. Suitable controls were incorporated on each batch during input, processing, and output. This system worked well from a company viewpoint, and the internal auditor was convinced that while minor padding of expense accounts might occur, no major losses had been encountered.

As interest rates began to climb, the salespersons became unhappy. They pointed out that they were often forced to carry several thousand dollars for an entire month. If they were out of town around the twentieth, they might not be reimbursed for their expenses for two months. They requested that Babbington-Bowles provide a service whereby a salesperson or his or her representative could submit receipts and expense reports to the accounting department and receive a check almost immediately.

The data processing manager said that this procedure could be done. A CRT terminal would be set up in the accounting office, along with a small printer. The salesperson's name would be entered along with the required expense amount broken down into the standard categories. A program would process these data and post them to the proper accounts and, if everything checked out suitably, print the check on presigned check blank stock in the printer.

REQUIRED

Identify five important controls, and explain why they might be incorporated in the system. These controls may be physical, they may relate to jobs and responsibilities, or they may be part of the program. (SMAC Examination)

CASE 14.1: ANYCOMPANY, INC.—AN ONGOING COMPREHENSIVE CASE

Visit a local company and obtain permission to study its system of internal controls. Once you have lined up a company, do the following:

1. Obtain copies of organization charts, job descriptions, and related documentation on how authority and responsibility have been assigned within the information systems function. Evaluate whether lines of authority and responsibility seem to be clearly defined and whether incompatible duties have been appropriately segregated.

2. Determine how the company evaluates the progress of systems development projects during the design and implementation stages.
3. Observe how the company controls physical access to its mainframe computer site, as well as to its microcomputers and on-line terminals. Evaluate whether the company's site access controls seem to be effective.
4. Determine the procedures used by the company to protect its stored program and data files from loss or destruction, including procedures for recovery of any program or data files that may be lost. Evaluate whether these procedures appear to be sound.
5. Examine the company's policies and procedures relating to the use of passwords to control logical access to its system resources. Evaluate these policies and procedures.
6. Briefly examine copies of the company's administrative, systems, and operating documentation. Evaluate the quality and completeness of this material.
7. Determine the techniques used by the company to minimize the risk of system downtime.
8. Ask whether the company has a written disaster recovery plan for its computer facilities. If so, examine a copy of the plan, and assess its strengths and weaknesses.

CASE 14.2: THE STATE DEPARTMENT OF TAXATION

The Department of Taxation in your state is developing a new computer system for processing individual and corporate income tax returns. The new system features direct data input and inquiry capabilities. Identification of taxpayers is provided by using the Social Security number for individuals and federal identification number for corporations. The new system should be fully implemented in time for the next tax season.

The new system will serve three primary purposes.

1. Data will be input directly into the system from tax returns through CRT terminals located at central headquarters.
2. The returns will be processed using the main computer facilities at central headquarters. Processing will include four steps.
   a. Verifying mathematical accuracy.
   b. Auditing the reasonableness of deductions, tax due, etc., through the use of edit routines, which also include a comparison of current and prior years' data.
   c. Identifying returns that should be considered for audit by department revenue agents.
   d. Issuing refund checks to taxpayers.
3. Inquiry service will be provided to taxpayers upon request through the assistance of tax department personnel at five regional offices. A total of 50 CRT terminals will be placed at each regional office. A taxpayer will be allowed to determine the status of his or her return or get information from the last three years' returns by calling or visiting one of the department's regional offices.

The state commissioner of taxation is concerned about data security during input and processing, over and above protection against natural hazards such as fire and flood. This includes protection against the loss or damage of data during data input and processing as well as the improper input or processing of data. In addition, the tax commissioner and the state attorney general have discussed the general problem of data confidentiality that may arise from the nature and operation of the new system. Both individuals want to have all potential problems identified before the system is fully developed and implemented so that the proper controls can be incorporated into the new system.

1. Describe the potential confidentiality problems that could arise in each of the following three areas of processing, and recommend the corrective action(s) to solve the problem.
   a. Data input
   b. Processing of returns
   c. Data inquiry
2. The state tax commission wants to incorporate controls to provide data security against the loss, damage, improper input, or use of data during data input and processing. Identify the potential problems (outside of natural hazards such as fire or floods) for which the Department of Taxation should develop controls, and recommend the possible controls for each problem identified. (CMA Examination)

ANSWERS TO CHAPTER QUIZ

1. a	**3.** b	**5.** d	**7.** b	**9.** d
2. c	**4.** c	**6.** b	**8.** c	**10.** a

Chapter 15

Fraud and Computers

LEARNING OBJECTIVES

After reading the chapter, you should be able to:

- Understand what fraud is, including the difference between fraudulent financial reporting and employee fraud and the process that constitutes a fraud.
- Discuss why fraud occurs, including the pressures, opportunities, and rationalizations that are present in most frauds.
- Compare and contrast the approaches and techniques that are used to commit computer fraud.
- Describe how to deter and detect computer fraud.

Integrative Case: Northwest Industries

It was late on the last Sunday of March when Jason Scott finished his tax return. Before sealing the envelope, he reviewed his return for a final time. Jason quickly compared the documents used to prepare his return with the actual numbers. Everything was in order except his withholding amount. For some reason the federal income tax withholdings on his final paycheck was $5 higher than on his W-2 form. He decided to use the W-2 amount and made a note to check with payroll to find out what happened to the other $5. The next day was a typical Monday at Northwest Industries and Jason was swamped. After reviewing his "To Do" list, he decided to dismiss the $5 difference because the amount was immaterial.

At lunch on April 16 several people were joking about their last-minute attempts to complete their tax returns. In the course of the conversation one of Jason's co-workers grumbled about the company taking out $5 more from his check than he was given credit for on his W-2. No one followed up on the comment and it was not until after lunch that the coincidence hit Jason: He was not the only one to have a $5 discrepancy between his withholdings and his W-2 statement. After obtaining the appropriate clearances, it was once again time to investigate. By the end of the following day Jason was worried. Most of the 1500 company employees had a $5 discrepancy between their reported withholdings and the actual amount withheld. Interestingly enough the W-2 of Don Hawkins, one of the programmers in charge of the payroll system, showed that thousands of dollars more in withholdings had been reported to the IRS than had been withheld from his paycheck.

It certainly looked to Jason like Northwest had a serious problem. He knew that when he reported the situation, management would ask a lot of questions. For example:

1. What constitutes a fraud, and is the withholding problem a fraud?
2. If this is indeed a fraud, how was it perpetrated? What motivated Don to commit it?
3. Why didn't the company catch these mistakes earlier? Was there a breakdown in controls?
4. What can the company do to detect fraud? to prevent fraud?
5. Just how vulnerable are computer systems to fraud?

INTRODUCTION

Fraud is any and all means a person uses to gain an unfair advantage over another person. Fraudulent acts include lies, suppressions of the truth, tricks, and cunning, and they often involve a violation of a trust or confidence. The economic losses to fraud each year are staggering; the Justice Department estimated that fraud costs the United States $200 billion a year.

A fraud can be committed by someone within an organization or by an external party. The controls most organizations use to protect corporate assets make it difficult for an outsider to steal from a company. Instead, theft is most often accomplished by an insider with an understanding of the company's policies and procedures. Using this knowledge, an insider can violate a trust, evade control procedures, and commit and conceal a crime. The National Center for Computer Crime Data studied 75 cases of computer fraud that were prosecuted over an eight-year period. It found that 80% of the frauds were the work of insiders. The frauds in this study were carried out most frequently by programmers, data entry clerks, and bank tellers.

Internal fraud can be broken down into two categories: employee fraud and fraudulent financial reporting. **Employee fraud** is committed by a person or group of persons for personal financial gain. The type of fraud discovered by Jason Scott at Northwest Industries is an example of employee fraud.

The National Commission on Fraudulent Financial Reporting (the Treadway Commission) defines **fraudulent financial reporting** as intentional or reckless conduct, whether by act or omission, that results in materially misleading financial statements. Fraudulent financial reporting is of special concern to independent auditors; the Treadway Commission studied 450 lawsuits against auditors and found undetected fraud to be a factor in half of them. Financial statements can be falsified to deceive investors and creditors, to cause a company's stock price to rise, to meet cash flow needs, or to hide company losses and problems. The perpetrators receive indirect benefits: They keep their jobs, their stock rises, and they receive pay raises and promotions they do not deserve. They can also gain more power and influence than they should.

The Treadway Commission recommended four actions to reduce the possibility of fraudulent financial reporting.

1. Establish an organizational environment that contributes to the integrity of the financial reporting process.
2. Identify and understand the factors that lead to fraudulent financial reporting.

3. Assess the risk of fraudulent financial reporting within the company.
4. Design and implement internal controls to provide reasonable assurance that fraudulent financial reporting is prevented.

This chapter discusses fraud in four main sections. The first section describes the fraud process. Then the reasons why fraud occurs are explored. The third section describes the approaches to computer fraud and the specific techniques used to commit it. Finally, several methods that companies can use to deter and detect computer fraud are analyzed.

THE FRAUD PROCESS

Most frauds involve three steps.

1. The *theft* of something of value, such as cash, inventory, tools, supplies, equipment, or data. Most employee fraud involves the theft of assets. Most fraudulent financial reporting involves the overstatement of assets or revenues. Few employees or companies are motivated to steal or overstate liabilities. Likewise, few frauds involve the theft or direct overstatement of equities.
2. The *conversion* of the stolen assets into cash. For example, stolen inventory and equipment must be sold or otherwise converted into cash.
3. The *concealment* of the crime in order to avoid detection. When assets are stolen or overstated, the only way to balance the basic accounting equation is to inflate other assets or to decrease liabilities or equity. Unless perpetrators find some way to keep the accounting equation in balance, their theft or misrepresentation can be discovered. Concealment often takes more effort and time and leaves behind more evidence than the actual theft. For example, taking cash requires only a few seconds, whereas altering records to hide the theft can be more challenging and time-consuming.

A common and effective way to hide a theft is to charge the stolen item to an expense account. For example, one employee stole $10,000 and charged it to miscellaneous expense. Assets were reduced by $10,000 but so was equity, since expense accounts decrease net income as they are closed out, which in turn lowers the retained earnings amount. As another example, an enterprising payroll clerk added a fictitious name to his company's payroll records, intercepted the paycheck, and cashed it. Although the company was missing funds, its books were balanced because there was a debit to a wages expense and a credit to cash. In both cases the perpetrator's exposure is limited to a year or less, because the expense accounts are zeroed out at the end of the year. On the other hand, perpetrators who hide a theft by affecting another balance sheet account must continue the concealment. Hence one of the most popular ways to cover up a fraud is to hide the theft in an income statement account.

Another way to hide a decrease in assets is by lapping. In a **lapping** scheme the perpetrator steals cash received from customer A to pay its accounts receivable. Funds received at a later date from customer B are used to pay off customer A's balance. Funds from customer C are used to pay off B, and so forth. The cover-up must continue indefinitely unless the money is replaced, since the theft will be uncovered if the scheme is stopped.

In a **kiting** scheme the perpetrator covers up a theft by creating cash through the transfer of money between banks. For example, the perpetrator creates cash by depositing a check from bank A into bank B and then withdraws the money. Since there are insufficient funds in bank A to cover the check, the perpetrator deposits a check from bank C to bank A before his check to bank B clears. Since bank C also has insufficient funds, money must be deposited to bank C before the bank A check clears. The check to bank C is written from bank A, B, or D, which also has insufficient funds. The scheme continues, with checks and deposits occurring as needed to keep the checks from bouncing.

WHY FRAUD OCCURS

An understanding of why fraud occurs can be gleaned by examining the profile of a fraud perpetrator. Fraud perpetrators are often referred to as **white-collar criminals,** to distinguish them from criminals who commit violent crimes. Researchers have compared the psychological and demographic characteristics of three groups of people: white-collar criminals, violent criminals, and the general public. Although they found significant differences between violent and white-collar criminals, they found few differences between white-collar criminals and the general public. White-collar criminals tend to mirror the general public in terms of education, age, religion, marriage, length of employment, and psychological makeup.

Fraud perpetrators share a number of common characteristics. Most spend their illegal income rather than invest or save it. Once they begin the fraud, it is very hard for them to stop. They usually begin to rely on the extra income. If the perpetrators are not caught shortly after they begin, they typically become brazen and their desire for even more money can cause them to increase the amount they take. As time passes many perpetrators grow careless, overconfident, or greedy. Those who do usually make a mistake that leads to their apprehension.

A few key differences have been found between computer fraud perpetrators and other white-collar criminals. Perpetrators of computer fraud tend to be younger and possess more computer knowledge, experience, and skills. Some computer fraud perpetrators are more motivated by the challenge of "beating the system" than by the actual gain and view their actions as a game rather than as dishonest behavior. A study performed by the National Center for Computer Crime Data shows computer crime to be an equal opportunity employer: 32% of the perpetrators were women and 43% were minorities. Not surprisingly, former and current employees are much more likely to perpetrate a computer fraud than are nonemployees. Because employees understand the company's system and its weaknesses, they are better able to commit a fraud, evade detection, and cover their tracks.

Some fraud perpetrators are disgruntled and unhappy with their job and are seeking to get even with their employer. Others are regarded as ideal employees who are dedicated, hard working, and in a position of trust. Most have no previous criminal record. Prior to their committing fraud they were honest and upright citizens who were valued and respected members of their communities. Why, then, would they risk everything by committing a fraud? Fraud research shows that three conditions are necessary for fraud to occur: a pressure or motive, an opportunity, and a rationalization.

Pressures

A **pressure** is a person's motivation for committing a fraud. Three types of motivation that often lead to fraud are described next and are summarized in Table 15.1. Pressures can be financial, such as living beyond one's means or having heavy debts or unusually high bills. Often times this pressure cannot be shared, and the perpetrator feels it must be kept secret.

An illustration of how financial losses can create enormous pressures is the case of Raymond Keller, the owner of a grain elevator in Stockport, Iowa. Raymond was a local boy who worked his way up from driving a coal truck to owning a local grain company. He made money by trading on commodities and built a lavish house overlooking the Des Moines River. No one knows why his financial situation declined. Some say he lost a lot of money speculating on the commodities markets; others say it was a grain embargo that virtually halted the buying and selling of grain. Whatever the reason, Raymond had a severe cash shortage and went deeply into debt. He asked some farmers to wait for their money, and he gave others bad checks. Finally, the seven banks to which he owed over $3 million began to call in their loans. So Raymond began to embezzle the grain to cover his losses—until a state auditor showed up at his door unexpectedly. Rather than face the consequences that he surely knew would follow, Raymond chose to end it all by taking his life.

Pressures can also be work related. Some employees turn to fraud because they have strong feelings of resentment or believe they have been treated unfairly. They may feel that their pay is too low, that their contributions to the company are not appreciated sufficiently, or that the company is taking advantage of them. Some fear losing their job and commit a fraud hoping to preserve their position by making themselves or their company look better. In one case an accountant in California, passed over for a raise, increased his salary by 10%, the amount of an average raise. When apprehended, he defended his

Table 15.1 **Pressures That Can Lead to Fraud**

Financial	Work-Related	Other
Living beyond means	Low salary	Challenge
Too much debt	Nonrecognition of performance	Family/peer pressure
"Inadequate" income	Job dissatisfaction	Emotional instability
Poor credit ratings	Fear of losing job	
Financial losses		
Bad investments		
Health care expenditures		
Large gambling debts		
Need to support a drug or alcohol addiction		

actions as being honest; he was only taking what was rightfully his. When asked how he would have felt if he had increased his salary by 11%, he responded that that would have been stealing 1%.

Other motivations that lead to fraudulent actions include family or peer pressure, emotional instability, and the challenge of "beating the system." Many computer hackers commit fraud for the challenge of subverting the controls and breaking into a system. In one case a company boasted in its advertisements that its new information system was so secure that outsiders would not be able to break into it. Within 24 hours of its implementation, a team of individuals had broken into the system and left a message that the impenetrable system had just been compromised.

Opportunities

An **opportunity** is the condition or situation that allows a person to commit and conceal a dishonest act. The list of opportunities that make fraud easy to commit and conceal is almost endless. Table 15.2 notes some of the more frequently mentioned opportunities noted in fraud research studies.

Opportunities often stem from a lack of internal controls. For example, a company might lack proper procedures for authorizations, clear lines of authority, or independent checks on performance. Likewise, there may not be a separation of duties among the authorization, custodial, and record-keeping functions. However, the most prevalent opportunity for fraud results from a company's failure to *enforce* its system of internal controls.

One control feature that many companies lack is a background check on all potential employees. A background check would have saved one company from the "phantom controller." In that case the company president stopped by

Table 15.2 **Perceived Opportunities**

Internal Control Factors	Other Factors
Failure to enforce internal controls	Too much trust in key employees
Lack of proper procedures for authorizations	Close association with suppliers/customers
No separation of transaction authority from custody	Incompetent personnel
No independent checks on performance	Operating on a crisis basis
No separation of accounting duties	Failure to discipline violators
Lack of clear lines of authority	Confusion about ethics
Lack of frequent reviews	Lack of explicit conflict-of-interest statements
Inadequate documentation	Inadequate physical security
No background checks	Inadequate staffing
	Poor management philosophy
	Lack of employee loyalty
	Inadequate training
	Apathy
	Inattention to details

the office one night, saw a light on in the controller's office, and went over to see why he was working so late. He was surprised to find a complete stranger at work. An investigation showed the controller was not an accountant and had been fired from three of his previous five jobs in the last eight years. Because he was unable to do the accounting work, he had hired someone to come in at night to do his work for him. Before his scam was discovered, the "controller" had defrauded the company of several million dollars.

A number of other situations make it easy for someone to commit a fraud: excessive trust in key employees, incompetent supervisory personnel, inattention to details, inadequate staffing, lack of training, and unclear company policies. Also, many frauds arise when employees build mutually beneficial personal relationships with customers or suppliers. For example, a buyer could agree to purchase goods at an inflated price in exchange for a kickback from the vendor. Frauds can also occur when a crisis arises and the company disregards its normal control procedures. For instance, one *Fortune* 500 company was hit with three multimillion-dollar frauds in the same year. All three took place when the company was trying to resolve a series of crises and failed to follow the standard internal control procedures.

Rationalizations

Most fraud perpetrators have an excuse or a **rationalization** that allows them to justify their illegal behavior. Perpetrators rationalize either that they are not actually being dishonest or that their reasons for committing fraud are more compelling than honesty and integrity. Perhaps the most frequently used rationalization is that the perpetrator is just "borrowing" the stolen assets. He just needs a little money to tide him over a rough spot for a time. Therefore he is not really being dishonest, since he has every intention of paying it back.

Some perpetrators rationalize that they are not hurting a real person. It is just a faceless and nameless computer system that will be affected or a large, impersonal company that won't miss the money. For example, one perpetrator took pains to steal no more than $20,000, which was the maximum that the insurance company would reimburse the company for losses.

The list of rationalizations people use is lengthy. Here are some of the most frequently used.

- You would understand if you knew how badly I needed it.
- What I did was not that serious.
- It was for a good cause. (This is the Robin Hood syndrome, robbing from the rich to give to the poor.)
- I occupy a very important position of trust. I am above the rules.
- Everyone else is doing it, so it can't be that wrong.
- No one will ever know.
- The company owes it to me, and I am taking no more than is rightfully mine.

COMPUTER FRAUD

The U.S. Department of Justice defines **computer fraud** as any illegal act for which knowledge of computer technology is essential for its perpetration, investigation, or prosecution. More specifically, computer fraud includes the following:

- Unauthorized use, access, modification, copying, and destruction of software or data.
- Theft of money by altering computer records or the theft of computer time.
- Theft or destruction of computer hardware.
- Use or the conspiracy to use computer resources to commit a felony.
- Intent to illegally obtain information or tangible property through the use of computers.

Using a computer, fraud perpetrators are able to steal more, in much less time, and with much less effort. For instance, they can steal millions of dollars in less than a second. Perpetrators are able to commit a fraud and leave little or no evidence. Therefore computer fraud is often much more difficult to detect than other types of fraud.

The Rise in Computer Fraud

Organizations that track computer fraud estimate that it nets perpetrators $300 million to $9 billion per year. However, no one knows for sure exactly how much companies lose to computer fraud, for several reasons:

1. Not everyone agrees on what constitutes computer fraud. For example, some people restrict the definition to a crime that takes place inside a computer or is directed at one. For others it is any crime where the perpetrator uses the computer as a tool. Many people do not believe that making an unlicensed copy of software constitutes computer fraud. Software publishers think otherwise, however, and prosecute those who make illegal copies. Similarly, some people do not think it is a crime to browse through someone else's computer if they don't have any intentions of harming the organization or its data.
2. Many computer frauds go undetected. The FBI estimates that only 1% of all computer crime is detected; other estimates are between 5% and 25%.
3. An estimated 80%–90% of the frauds that are uncovered are not reported. Only the banking industry is required by law to report all frauds. The most commonly cited reason for failure to report computer fraud is a company's fear that adverse publicity would cost more than the fraud itself. As a result, fraud estimates are based on the limited number of frauds that are both detected and reported.

What is known is that computer fraud is large and growing. The National Center for Computer Crime Data concluded that the costs of computer crime exceeded $555 million and that the average computer fraud loss is $109,000. According to an Ernst and Whinney study, between 50% and 90% of companies have lost money to a computer fraud. The Bank Administration Institute has calculated that U.S. banks lose over $1 billion a year because of information system abuse.

As early as 1979 *Time* magazine labeled computer fraud as a "growth industry." Some of the reasons attributed to the steady growth of fraud include (1) a growing number of competent computer users; (2) easier access to remote computers through both public and private data networks; and (3) the belief of many companies that "it won't happen to us."

Approaches to Computer Fraud

Various studies have examined fraud to determine the types of assets stolen and the approaches used. Figure 15.1 breaks down the major categories of computer crime and indicates the frequency of each. As this figure indicates, there are many types of fraud and many ways the computer can be used to commit or be the object of fraud. One way to categorize computer fraud is to use the data processing model: input, processor, computer instructions, stored data, and output.

Input. The simplest and most common way to commit a fraud is to alter computer input. It requires little, if any, computer skills. Instead, perpetrators need only to understand how the system operates so they can cover their tracks.

Paul Sjiem-Fat used desktop publishing technology to perpetrate one of the first cases of computer forgery. Sjiem-Fat created bogus cashier's checks from various banks such as Chase Manhattan. He then used the checks to buy computer equipment, which he subsequently sold in the Caribbean. He was caught while trying to steal $20,000 from Bank of Boston. When the bank checked his credit card application, it found that he had lied about being an employee of a Dutch consulate. The bank called in the Secret Service, who raided his apartment and found nine bogus checks totaling almost $150,000. Sjiem-Fat was prosecuted and sent to prison.

Another perpetrator opened an account at a New York bank, then had a printer prepare blank deposit slips. The slips were similar to those available in bank lobbies, except that his account number was encoded on them. Early one morning he replaced all the deposit slips in the bank lobby with his forged ones. For three days all bank deposits using the forged slips went directly into the perpetrator's account. After three days the perpetrator withdrew the money, then disappeared. He used an alias; his identity was never uncovered nor was he ever found.

Figure 15.1

Breakdown of the Major Types of Computer Crime

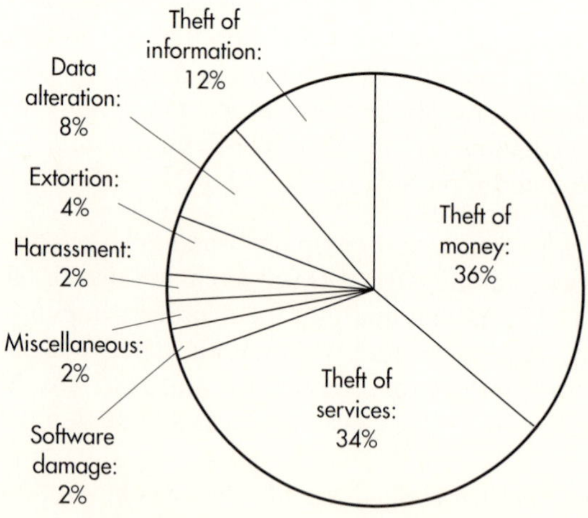

Source: Michael Alexander, "Computer Crime: Ugly Secret for Business," *Computerworld* (March 12, 1990): 104.

In disbursement frauds, the perpetrator causes a company either to pay too much for ordered goods or to pay for goods never ordered. One perpetrator used a desktop publishing package to prepare fraudulent bills for office supplies that were never ordered, then mailed those bills to companies across the country. The perpetrator kept the dollar amount low enough so that most companies did not bother to require purchase orders or approvals. An amazingly high percentage of the companies paid the bills without question.

To commit inventory fraud, a perpetrator can enter data into the system to show that stolen inventory has been scrapped. For example, several employees at an East Coast railroad entered data into the company's system to show that over 200 railroad cars were scrapped or destroyed. They next removed the cars from the railway system, then repainted and sold them.

To commit payroll frauds, perpetrators can enter data to increase their salary, create a fictitious employee, or retain a terminated employee on the records. Under the latter two approaches, the perpetrator proceeds to intercept and cash the "illegal" checks.

In a cash receipts fraud the perpetrator hides the theft by falsifying system input. For example, an employee at the Arizona Veteran's Memorial Coliseum sold customers full-price tickets, entered the sale as a half-price ticket, and pocketed the difference.

Processor. Computer fraud can be committed through unauthorized system use, including theft of computer time and services as well as use of a system for purposes outside an employee's job description. For example, some companies do not permit employees to use company computers to keep personal or outside business records. Violating this policy would constitute a fraud.

Computer Instructions. Computer fraud can be accomplished by tampering with the software that processes company data. This may involve modifying the software, making illegal copies, or using it in an unauthorized manner. It might also involve developing a software program or module to carry out an unauthorized activity. This approach to computer fraud is one of the least common because it requires a specialized knowledge about computer programming that is beyond the scope of most users.

Data. Computer fraud can be perpetrated by altering or damaging a company's data files or by copying, using, or searching them without authorization. There have been numerous instances of data files being scrambled, altered, or destroyed by disgruntled employees. In one instance an employee removed all the external labels from hundreds of tape files. In another case an employee used a powerful magnet to scramble all the data on magnetic tape files.

Company data can also be stolen. In one case the office manager of a Wall Street law firm found information about prospective mergers and acquisitions in the firm's word processing files. He sold the information to friends and relatives, who made several million dollars by illegally trading securities. In another case, in Europe, a disgruntled employee removed all of a company's data files from the computer room. He then drove to the off-site storage location and removed the company's backup files. He demanded half a million dollars in return for the files, but he was arrested while trying to exchange the tapes for the ransom.

Output. Computer fraud can be carried out by stealing or misusing system output. System output is usually displayed on monitors or printed on paper. Unless properly safeguarded, monitor and printer output is subject to prying eyes and unauthorized copying. A study by a Dutch engineer has shown that many computer monitors emit a televisionlike signal that can be picked up, restructured with the help of some very inexpensive electronic gear, and displayed on a standard TV screen. Under ideal conditions these signals can be picked up from terminals as far away as two miles. During one experiment the engineer was able to set up his equipment in the basement of an apartment building and read the screen on a terminal on the eighth floor of the building.

Computer Fraud Techniques

Over the years, perpetrators have devised many methods to commit computer fraud. This section discusses some of the more common techniques.

A **Trojan horse** is a set of unauthorized computer instructions in an authorized and otherwise properly functioning program. It performs some illegal act at a preappointed time or under a predetermined set of conditions. For example, a computer programmer for a Minneapolis bank instructed the computer to ignore an overdraft on his account. He was caught when the computer broke down and the bank was forced to operate manually.

The **round-down technique** is used most frequently in financial institutions that pay interest. In the typical scenario the programmer instructs the computer to round down all interest calculations to two decimal places. The fraction of a cent that is rounded down on each calculation is put into the programmer's account or one that he or she controls. No one is the wiser, since all the books balance. Over time these fractions of a cent can add up to a significant amount, especially when interest is calculated daily.

With the **salami technique** tiny slices of money are stolen over a period of time. For example, a disgruntled chief accountant for a produce-growing company in California used the salami technique to get even with his employer. He used the company's computer system to falsify and systematically increase all the company's production costs by a fraction of a percent. These tiny increments were put into the accounts of dummy customers and then pocketed by the accountant. Every few months the fraudulent costs were raised another fraction of a percent. Because all expenses were rising together, no single account or expense would call attention to the fraud. The accountant eventually was caught when an alert bank teller brought to his manager's attention a check the perpetrator was trying to cash because he didn't recognize the name of the company it was made out to.

A **trap door** is a set of computer instructions that allows a user to bypass the system's normal controls. Programmers use trap doors to modify programs during systems development and normally remove them before the system is put into operation. When a trap door is not removed before the program is implemented, anyone who discovers it can enter the program and commit a fraud.

Superzapping is the unauthorized use of special system programs to bypass regular system controls and perform illegal acts. The name of this technique is derived from a software utility, called Superzap, developed by IBM to handle emergencies, such as restoring a system that has crashed.

Software piracy is the unauthorized copying of software. It is estimated that for every legal copy of software, between one and five illegal ones have been made. The software industry estimates the economic losses of piracy at between $2 and $4 billion a year. Piracy is such a serious problem that the Software Publishers Association (which represents over 500 software publishers) has begun filing lawsuits against companies. One lawsuit claimed that the University of Oregon's Continuing Education Center violated copyright law by making illegal and unauthorized copies of programs and training manuals. The university settled the case by agreeing to (1) pay a $130,000 fine; (2) launch a campaign to educate its faculty, staff, and students on the lawful use of software; and (3) host a national conference on copyright law and software use.

Data diddling is changing data before, during, or after it is entered into the system. The change can be made to delete, alter, or add key system data. For example, a clerk for a Denver brokerage altered a transaction to record 1700 shares of Loren Industries stock worth about $2500 as shares in Long Island Lighting worth more than $25,000.

Data leakage refers to the unauthorized copying of company data. The Encyclopedia Britannica company claimed losses in the millions of dollars when several of its employees made a copy of its customer list and began selling it to other companies.

Piggybacking is tapping into a telecommunications line and latching on to a legitimate user before the user logs into a system. The legitimate user then unknowingly carries the perpetrator into the system. In **masquerading** or **impersonation** the perpetrator gains access to the system by pretending to be an authorized user. This approach requires a perpetrator to know the legitimate user's ID number and password. Once inside the system, the perpetrator enjoys the same privileges as the legitimate user being impersonated.

A **logic time bomb** is a program that lies idle until some specified circumstance or a particular time triggers it. Once triggered, the bomb sabotages the system by destroying programs, data, or both. Most bombs are written by disgruntled programmers who want to get even with their company. In one case Donald Burleson, a former security officer at USPA & IRA Company, allegedly broke into his former employer's system two days after he was fired. Because he knew everyone's password, he was able to break into the system and erase 168,000 sales commissions records. As a result, company paychecks were held up for a month. The program, which was attached to a legitimate one, was designed to go off periodically and erase more records. The bomb was discovered before it could go off again by a fellow programmer who was testing a new employee bonus system. The company's computers were shut down for two days while the bomb was located and diffused.

Hacking is the unauthorized access to and use of computer systems, usually by means of a personal computer and a telecommunication network. There have been numerous cases of students tapping into their school's computers and changing their grades. Many hackers do not intend to cause any damage. They are usually motivated by the challenge of breaking and entering and are just browsing or looking for things to copy and keep. In addition, hackers have broken into the computers of governmental agencies such as the U.S. Department of Defense, NASA, and the Los Alamos National Laboratory. One 17-year-old hacker, nicknamed "Shadow Hawk," was convicted of electronically penetrating the Bell Laboratories national network, destroying files valued at $174,000, and copying 52 proprietary software programs worth $1.2 million. He published confidential information, such as telephone numbers, passwords, and instructions on how to breach AT&T's computer security system, on underground bulletin boards. He was sentenced to nine months in prison and given a $10,000 fine. Like Shadow Hawk, many hackers are fairly young, some as young as 12 and 13.

Scavenging is gaining access to confidential information by searching corporate records. Scavenging methods range from searching trash cans for printouts or carbon copies of confidential information to scanning the contents of computer memory. In one of the most famous cases Jerry Schneider, a high school student, noticed a trash can full of papers on his way home from school. Rummaging through them, he discovered operating guides for Pacific Telephone computers. Over time his scavenging activities resulted in a technical library that later allowed him to steal a million dollars worth of electronic equipment.

Eavesdropping enables perpetrators to observe private transmissions. One way to intercept signals is by setting up a **wiretap.** The equipment needed to wiretap an unprotected communications line is readily available at local electronics stores. One alleged wiretapping fraud involved Mark Koenig, a 28-year-old consultant to GTE, and four associates. Federal agents say they pulled personal identification numbers and other crucial information about Bank of America customers from GTE telephone lines. They used this data to make 5500 fake ATM cards. They allegedly intended to use the cards over one weekend to withdraw money from banks all over the country. However, authorities were tipped off and they were apprehended before they were able to use the cards.

Computer Viruses

One of the most serious problems facing today's systems is the threat of a computer virus. A **computer virus** is a segment of executable code that attaches itself to an application program or some other executable system component. It is intended to damage the systems of others, to spread a particular message, or to serve as a prank. Viruses are contagious and are easily spread from one system to another. A virus creates copies of itself and inserts them into other programs or data files. To spread rapidly, a virus must be introduced into a network with a large number of computers. In a relatively short period of time the virus can spread to thousands of systems. When the virus is confined to a single machine or to a small LAN, it will soon run out of computers to infect. A virus also spreads when users share programs or diskettes or when they access and use programs from external sources such as bulletin boards and suppliers of free software.

Many viruses lie dormant for extended periods of time without causing any specific damage, except to propagate themselves. Triggering the hidden program, which leaves no external signs of infection, unleashes unauthorized alterations to the way a system operates and causes widespread damage. For example, a virus may destroy or alter data or programs. It can take control of the computer, destroy the hard disk's file allocation table, or keep users from booting the system or accessing data on a hard disk. It can intercept and change transmissions, print disruptive images or messages on the screen, or cause the screen image to disappear. As the virus spreads, it takes up space, clogs communications, and hinders system performance.

Many computer viruses have long lives because they can create copies of themselves faster than they can be destroyed. A number of viruses, such as Stone and Jerusalem-B, have spread so furiously that they have become epidemics. According to a survey conducted by Dataquest, 63% of the 600,000 microcomputer users surveyed had experienced a virus and 38% of those affected had lost data.

A **worm** is like a virus, except that it is a program rather than a code segment hidden in a host program. A worm also copies and actively transmits itself directly to other systems. It usually does not live very long, but it is quite destructive while it is alive. One of the more destructive worms, written by Robert T. Morris, affected 6000 computers in a very short time. Focus 15.1 details the impact of this worm on systems across the country.

DETERRING AND DETECTING COMPUTER FRAUD

Because fraud is such a serious problem, organizations must take every precaution to protect their information systems. A number of measures can significantly decrease the potential for fraud and any resulting losses. For example, a company can create a climate that makes fraud less likely, increase the difficulty of committing a fraud, reduce the amount of loss if a fraud occurs, increase the likelihood of detecting fraud, prosecute fraud perpetrators, and increase the penalty for committing fraud.

Make Fraud Less Likely to Occur

Some computer consultants claim that the most effective method of obtaining adequate system security is to rely on the integrity of company employees. At the same time, research shows that most fraud is committed by current and former employees. Thus employees are both the greatest control strength and weakness. Organizations can take steps to increase employee integrity and reduce the likelihood of employees' committing a fraud, as described in the following sections.

Hiring and Firing Practices. As discussed in Chapter 13, one of a manager's most important responsibilities is to hire and retain honest people. Similarly, a company should be very careful when firing employees. Dismissed employees should be removed from sensitive jobs immediately and denied access to the computer system to prevent sabotage or copying of confidential data before they leave.

FOCUS 15.1

A Worm Run Amok

Scientists at Berkeley's Experimental Computing Facility noticed a rash of unknown users trying to log into their system. The break-in attempts increased in frequency until they could no longer be monitored. Within minutes the program invaded computer processing space and brought Berkeley's mammoth system to a halt. At this point they realized a program was trying to access the system.

Within a half hour it was clear that the program was not limited to the Berkeley system; it was invading the *entire* Internet. Within hours computer experts discovered the existence of a powerful "worm" in the Internet. While scientists attempted to stop the worm, law enforcement officials and the press were beginning their own investigations of the unauthorized entry. Information on a possible suspect was scarce until an unidentified phone caller tipped a *New York Times* writer by inadvertently referring to the criminal programmer as RTM.

Robert Tappan Morris loved computers and challenges. He acquired a passion for computer security issues while working with his father, a scientist at Bell Labs. At Harvard he received extensive recognition for problem-solving work using the school's main computer facility, which was linked to the Internet. Robert's most successful projects centered on improving the Bell systems Internet operations and its operating system, UNIX. By the age of 20 Robert's skills in UNIX security issues were so extensive that his father had him address a computer security conference at the National Security Agency. The next day he delivered the same address to the Naval Research Laboratory.

While Robert was attending graduate school at Cornell University, the first computer viruses were receiving national media attention. This sparked Robert's interest in developing an undetectable worm that would invade the Internet. His goal was to reach as many computers as possible. With Robert's background in UNIX security issues and his unlimited access to the Cornell computer, developing a

Managing Disgruntled Employees. Many employees who commit fraud are seeking revenge or "justice" for some wrong they perceive has been done to them. Hence companies should have procedures for identifying these individuals and either helping them resolve their feelings or removing them from jobs that allow them access to the system. One way to avoid disgruntled employees and to maintain high company morale is to provide grievance channels and employee counseling. Employees need someone outside the normal chain of command to talk with about their grievances and problems with the company. Having someone who will listen to them and help them resolve their problems can significantly decrease the number of dissatisfied employees. This is often not easy to accomplish, since most employees fear that airing their feelings could have negative consequences on their career.

Employee Training. Fraud is much less likely to occur in an environment where employees believe security is everyone's business. An ideal corporate culture for fraud deterrence exists when employees are proud of their company and are protective of its assets. They believe they have a responsibility to report fraud because what harms the company harms them. This culture does not just happen; it has to be created, taught, and practiced. To develop this type of culture, a company should educate and train employees in the following areas:

worm was easy. Robert had discovered three programming flaws in the UNIX operating system that allowed him unauthorized access to any computer on the Internet. Robert developed a worm capable of entering a given system without authorization using a bug in the Sendmail subprogram. The worm used Sendmail to enter related systems entirely undetected and replicate itself.

When the worm was finished, Robert illegally logged on to the artificial intelligence lab computer at MIT from his system at Cornell and released his creation. After dinner Robert attempted to log on, but the computer didn't respond. He immediately knew something was wrong and after several unsuccessful attempts to remedy the problem, the significance of the damage was clear. Robert had made a fatal programming error that allowed the worm to replicate out of control throughout the Internet.

Cleaning out the Internet system and recreating the files destroyed by the worm took several months. On final tally the worm had infected more than six thousand computers, and the estimated costs to resolve the problem ranged from \$150,000 to almost \$200 million.

Robert was arrested and charged with a felony violation of the 1986 Counterfeit Access Device and Computer Fraud and Abuse Act, which prohibits unauthorized computer access. The case was brought to a jury trial.

Focus Questions

1. What motivated Robert to create the worm program? What rationale did he use to justify his actions?
2. What program feature in the UNIX operating system allowed Robert to send his worm through the Internet system undetected? What could have been done to prevent such a opportunity?
3. In your opinion, did Robert commit a crime? Why or why not? If so, what sentence would you give Robert for his crimes? Explain your position.

Source: Katie Hafner and John Markoff, *Cyberpunk* (New York: Simon and Schuster, 1991; and Jeff Goldberg, "Computerized Breaking and Entering," *OMNI* (September 1990): 18.

- *Security measures.* Employees should be well schooled in security measures, taught why they are important, and motivated to take them very seriously. Security should be monitored and enforced as a way of reinforcing this training.
- *Fraud awareness.* Employees should be made aware of fraud, its prevalence, and its dangers. They should be taught why people commit fraud and how to deter and detect it.
- *Ethical considerations.* The company should promote its ethical standards in its practices and through company literature such as employee handouts. Acceptable and unacceptable behavior should be defined so that employees are aware of a company's ethical position should a problem arise. Many business practices fall into a gray area between right or wrong, and this problem is especially prevalent throughout the computer industry. For example, many professionals see nothing wrong with utilizing corporate computer resources for personal use. Likewise, gaining unauthorized access to another company's data bases and browsing through them isn't an uncommon practice. One programmer, when arrested for unauthorized browsing, was shocked to find out that he was going to be prosecuted for his "crime"; he felt his activities were a common industry practice.
- *Punishment for unethical behavior.* Employees should be informed of the consequences of unethical behavior (reprimands, dismissal, prosecution, etc.). This information should be disseminated not as a threat but as the

consequence of choosing to act unethically. For example, employees should be informed that using a computer to steal or commit fraud is a federal crime and anyone so doing faces immediate dismissal and/or prosecution. Likewise, the company should display notices of program and data ownership and inform employees of the penalties of misuse.

As simple as it sounds, educating employees in security issues, fraud awareness, ethical considerations, and the consequences of choosing to act unethically can make a tremendous difference. This education can be accomplished by conducting informal discussions and formal meetings, issuing periodic departmental memos, distributing written guidelines and codes of professional ethics, circulating reports of securities violations and their consequences, and promoting security and fraud training programs.

Increase the Difficulty of Committing Fraud

One way to deter fraud is to design a system with sufficient controls to make fraud difficult to perpetrate. These controls help ensure the accuracy, integrity, and safety of system resources. This section discusses how companies can develop a strong system of internal controls and details some of the more important fraud prevention techniques.

Develop a Strong System of Internal Controls. The overall responsibility for a secure and adequately controlled system lies with top management. Managers typically delegate the design of adequate control systems to systems analysts, designers, and end users. The corporate information security officer and the operations staff are typically responsible for ensuring that control procedures are followed.

To develop efficient and cost-effective controls, designers should follow the risk assessment strategy shown in Fig. 13.2. These controls are much more effective when placed in the system as it is built, rather than as an afterthought. Management must also establish a set of procedures to ensure that the controls are complied with and enforced. Some of the more important controls are discussed next.

Segregate Duties. As discussed in Chapter 13, there must be an adequate separation of duties to prevent individuals from stealing assets and covering up their tracks.

Enforced Vacations and Rotation of Duties. Many fraud schemes, such as lapping and kiting, require the ongoing attention of the perpetrator. If mandatory vacations were coupled with a temporary rotation of duties, as explained in Chapter 14, these types of ongoing fraud schemes would fall apart. For example, when federal investigators raided an illegal gambling establishment, they found that Roswell Steffen, who earned $11,000 a year, was betting up to $30,000 a day at the racetrack. Investigators at Union Dime Savings Bank discovered he had embezzled and gambled away $1.5 million of their money over a three-year period. A compulsive gambler, Steffen started out by borrowing $5000 to place a bet on a "sure thing" that did not pan out. He embezzled ever increasing amounts trying to win back the original money he had "borrowed."

Steffen committed his fraud by transferring money from inactive accounts to his own account. If the owner of an inactive account complained, Steffen, who as the chief teller had the power to resolve these types of problems, replaced the money by taking it from some other inactive account. After being caught and asked how the fraud could have been prevented, he said the bank could have coupled a two-week vacation period with several weeks of rotation to another job function. That would have made his embezzlement, which required his physical presence at the bank and his constant attention, almost impossible to cover up.

Restrict Access. Computer fraud can be reduced significantly if access to computer equipment and data files is restricted. As explained in Chapter 13, both physical and logical access to computer equipment should be restricted. Unfortunately, companies often fail to delete or change ID codes and passwords when employees leave or are transferred to another department.

Encrypt Data and Programs. Another way to protect data is to translate it into a secret code, thereby making it meaningless to anyone without the means to decipher it. Data encryption is explained in Chapter 14.

Protect Telephone Lines. Computer hackers use telephone lines to transmit viruses and to access, steal, and destroy data. They also use lines to steal telephone services. One way to protect telephone lines is to attach an electronic lock and key to them. When one such device was tested, researchers concluded that it would take a hacker 188 days working nonstop to break the more than 1 trillion combinations. Few hackers would make the attempt; if they did, they would most likely be detected before they were successful.

Protect the System from Viruses. There are hundreds of thousands of virus attacks every year and an estimated 90% of the PCs that suffer a virus attack are reinfected within 30 days. A system can also be protected from viruses by following the guidelines listed in Focus 15.2.

Fortunately, some very good virus protection programs are available. Virus *protection* programs are designed to remain in computer memory and search for viruses trying to infiltrate the system. The intrusion is usually detected when there is an unauthorized attempt to access an executable program. When an infection attempt is detected, the software freezes the system and flashes a message to the user. The user can then instruct the program to remove the virus. Virus *detection* programs, which spot an infection soon after it starts, are more reliable than virus protection programs. Virus *identification* programs scan all executable programs to find and remove all known viruses from the system. These programs work by scanning the system for specific characteristics of known virus strains.

Control Sensitive Data. To protect its sensitive data, a company should shred discarded paper documents. Controls can be placed over data files to prevent or discourage copying. Employees should be informed of the consequences of using illegal copies of software, and the company should institute controls to see that illegal copies are not in use. Sensitive and confidential information

FOCUS 15.2

Keeping Your Microcomputers Virus-Free

While there is no technological reason why a virus cannot attack a mainframe or a minicomputer (some have), viruses have traditionally targeted the microcomputer and micro-based networks, especially local area networks (LANs). Why? Because they are so much more accessible and because there are so many more of them. Here are some practical suggestions for protecting microcomputers.

- Vaccinate machines with software that prevents virus execution. Vaccination programs are different from virus detectors, which uncover viruses. A vaccination can keep a virus out, but it may not alert you to its presence; a virus detector will tell you when a virus is there.
- Don't put your diskettes in strange machines; your diskette may become infected. Don't let others put their diskettes in your disk drives; your machine may become infected. Scan strange diskettes with antiviral software before any data or programs are copied to your machine.
- Use write-protect tabs that prohibit writing to diskettes; a virus cannot spread to a write-protected diskette.
- Obtain software and diskettes only from known and trusted sources. While the likelihood of contracting a virus in this manner is small, even purchased software may be infected.
- Be wary of software or diskettes from unknown sources. They may be virus bait, especially if their prices or functionality sound too good to be true.
- Deal with software retailers you trust. Some dealers rewrap and sell used software as if it were new.
- Some software suppliers use electronic techniques to make tampering evident. Ask whether the software you are purchasing has such protection.
- Write-protect new software diskettes before installing them. This will prevent infection and provide you with backup.
- Check new software on an isolated machine with virus detection software.
- If you can, use the B: drive for data entry. Because of PC design, it is marginally more difficult for a virus to execute from the B: drive.
- Contrary to popular belief, importing software through LANs and modems is safer; most infection originates from diskettes.
- When you restart, use the "power-off–power-on" to clear and reset the system. It is possible for a virus to survive a warm start-up using Ctrl-Alt-Del or Reset keys.
- It's safer to start up or "boot" the machine from a write-protected diskette than from a hard disk. This type of start-up will resist viruses that obtain control via the "boot sector" of the hard disk.
- Back up your data. Data files should be backed up separately from programs; this resists the contamination of backup data. Keep write-protected copies of the original disks and restore from them.
- Restrict the use of public bulletin boards. All outside software should be certified as virus-free before loading it into the system.

Source: Information Protection Review 2 (1) Deloitte & Touche: 6.

should be locked up at night and should not be left out on desks. Local area networks can use dedicated servers that allow data to be downloaded but never uploaded to avoid infection by a network computer. Closed-circuit televisions can be used to monitor areas where sensitive data or easily stolen assets are handled.

Some organizations with particularly sensitive data are installing diskless PCs or workstations. All data are stored centrally in a network, and users download the data they need to work on each day. At the end of the day all data to be saved must be stored in the network, thereby controlling the problem of unguarded information created and stored in desktop computers. Since users are able to delete or destroy only the data on their screens, the company's data is secure; the system is virtually immune to disasters a user might intentionally or unintentionally cause. In addition, without disk drives, users cannot introduce viruses into the system with contaminated diskettes. Nor does the company lose valuable data, because employees cannot copy company data on diskettes and remove them from the premises.

Improve Detection Methods

Many companies are currently being defrauded and do not know it. The following steps can be taken to detect fraud as soon as possible.

Conduct Frequent Audits. One way to increase the likelihood of detecting fraud is to conduct periodic external and internal audits. Auditors should regularly test system controls and periodically "browse" data files looking for suspicious activities. However, care must be exercised to make sure employees' privacy rights are not violated. Informing employees that auditors will conduct a **random surveillance** not only helps resolve the privacy issue but also has a significant deterrent effect on computer crime. One large financial institution that implemented this strategy uncovered a number of abuses, including some that resulted in the termination of one employee and the reprimand of another. Systems auditing is addressed in depth in Chapter 16.

Use a Computer Security Officer. Most frauds are not detected by internal or external auditors. In a study published in the *Sloan Management Review*, only 4.5% of 259 cases of fraud were uncovered by auditors. Normal system controls uncovered 45%, accidental discovery uncovered 32%, and computer security officers found 8%. The study shows that assigning responsibility for fraud deterrence and detection to a **computer security officer** has a significant deterrent effect on computer frauds. The security officer can monitor the system and disseminate information about improper system uses and their consequences.

Set Up a Fraud Hot Line. People witnessing fraudulent behavior are often torn between two conflicting feelings. They feel an obligation to protect company assets and turn in fraud perpetrators, yet they are uncomfortable in the "whistleblower" role and find it easier to remain silent. This reluctance is even stronger if they are aware of whistleblowers who in the past have been ostracized or persecuted by their co-workers or superiors, or have had their career damaged.

Enabling employees to report someone anonymously often allows them to resolve this conflict. Therefore anonymous fraud hot lines are an effective way to uncover fraud. This is supported by research conducted at Brigham Young University. Researchers there studied 212 frauds and found that 33% of them were uncovered by anonymous tips.

Hot lines have been very effective. The insurance industry set up a hot line in an attempt to control an estimated $17 billion a year in fraudulent claims. In the first month they received in excess of 2250 calls, almost 15% of which resulted in investigative action. The downside of hot lines is that many of the calls are not worthy of investigation. Some are made seeking revenge, others are vague reports of wrongdoing, and others have no merit.

A potential problem with a hot line is that those who operate the hot line may report to people who are involved in top-management fraud. This threat can be avoided by using a fraud hot line set up by a trade organization or commercial company. Reports of management fraud can be passed by this company directly to the board of directors.

Use Computer Consultants. Many companies hire computer consultants to find weaknesses in their current systems. Each means of breaching the system is closely evaluated, and corresponding protective measures are incorporated. Some companies dislike this approach because they do not want their weaknesses exposed nor do they want their employees to know that the system can indeed be broken into.

Monitor System Activities. All system transactions and activities should be recorded in a log. The log should indicate who accessed what data, when, and from which terminal. These logs are used to monitor system activity and trace any problems to their source.

Prosecute and Incarcerate Fraud Perpetrators

Most fraud cases go unreported and unprosecuted for several reasons. First, many cases of fraud are as yet undetected. Second, companies are reluctant to report computer crimes because a highly visible fraud is a public relations disaster. A company stands to lose business from any type of adverse publicity. Fraud also reveals system vulnerability, possibly attracting more acts of fraud. One study found that less than 10% of computer abuses were reported to law enforcement officials. Unreported fraud creates a false sense of security; people think systems are more secure than they really are.

Third, law enforcement officials and the courts are so busy with violent crimes that they have little time for fraud cases where no physical harm is present. A fourth reason fraud goes unreported is that it is difficult, costly, and time-consuming to investigate. Successfully prosecuting computer fraud cases is also extremely difficult. Until 1986 law enforcement officials did not have a law that dealt specifically with computer crimes. As a result, they had to prosecute using laws written for other purposes. This problem was partially resolved when the U.S. Congress passed the Computer Fraud and Abuse Act of 1986. The law covers computers used by the federal government, financial institutions, and certain medical organizations. It also covers computers used in interstate or foreign commerce. The law makes it illegal to knowingly gain access to computers with intent to defraud. Trafficking in computer access passwords is also prohibited. The crime is a felony if more than $1000 worth of software is damaged or if money, goods, or services are stolen. The penalties are severe: 1–5 years for the first offense, 10 for the second, and 20 for three or more. Fines can be up to $250,000 or twice the value of the stolen data. Although the law has resulted in increased prosecutions, many say it is vague and unclear and an easy target for defense attorneys. The laws are supplemented by computer fraud statutes in all 50 states.

A fifth reason for unreported fraud is that many law enforcement officials, lawyers, and judges lack the computer skills needed to investigate, prosecute, and evaluate computer crimes. Increased training, which is time-consuming and costly, is necessary in order for officials to understand and detect computer fraud.

Finally, when fraud cases are prosecuted and a conviction is obtained, the sentences received are often very light. For example, Judge John Lord, when sentencing convicted white-collar criminals, stated that the perpetrators were God-fearing, highly civic minded men, who had spent their lifetimes in sincere and honest dedication and service to their families, churches, country, and communities. He said he could never send them to jail. One investigator noted that the average sentence for a fraud perpetrator was one year in jail for every $10 million stolen.

One of the most famous cases of a light sentence involved C. Arnoldt Smith, former owner of the San Diego Padres baseball team who was named Mr. San Diego of the Century. Smith was very involved in the community and made large political contributions. When investigations showed that he had stolen $200 million from his bank, he pleaded nolo contendere (no contest). He was given a sentence of four years probation and a fine of $30,000. The fine was to be paid at the rate of $100 a month for the following 25 years, with no interest. Mr. Smith was 71 at the time. The embezzled money was never recovered.

Use Forensic Accountants

Forensic accountants specialize in fraud auditing and investigation. In the past few years it has been the fastest-growing area in accounting. Many forensic accountants have degrees in accounting and have received specialized training with the FBI, the IRS, or other law enforcement agencies. A new professional designation has also been created to recognize this field. The Association of Certified Fraud Examiners in Austin, Texas, has developed a Certified Fraud Examiner certification program. To become a CFE, candidates must pass a two-day exam. Today there are approximately 14,000 CFEs scattered all over the world. There are few CFE firms; most CPEs work for CPA or law firms and private and public companies.

Reduce Fraud Losses

No matter how hard a company tries to prevent fraud, chances are that it will occur. Therefore the best strategy is to do everything possible to prepare for it in order to minimize potential losses. Some of these methods include the following:

- Maintain adequate insurance.
- Keep a current backup copy of all program and data files in a secure off-site location.
- Develop a contingency plan for fraud occurrences and other disasters that might occur.
- Use special software designed to monitor system activity and help companies recover from frauds and malicious actions. One such software utility helped a company recover from a rampage that resulted after a disgruntled employee received a negative performance evaluation. The perpetrator ripped cards and cables out of PCs, changed the inventory control files, and edited the password file to stop people from logging onto the LAN. Shortly

after the incident the software identified the corrupted files and flashed an alert to company headquarters. The damage was undone by issuing simple commands to the utility software, which restored the corrupted file to its original status.

SUMMARY AND CASE CONCLUSION

Jason Scott believed Don Hawkins had committed a fraud, but he needed more details to support that conclusion. In preparation for his meeting with management, he expanded the scope of his investigation. A week later Jason presented his findings to the president of Northwest. To introduce the problem and to make it hit a little closer to home, Jason presented the president with a copy of his own withholding report filed with the IRS and pointed out the president's withholdings. Then he showed him a printout of withholdings from the payroll records and pointed out the $5 difference, as well as the difference of several thousand dollars in Don Hawkins' withholdings. This immediately got the president's attention, and Jason proceeded to tell him how he believed a fraud had been perpetrated.

During the latter part of the prior year the payroll system had undergone some minor modifications. Don had been in charge of the project. Due to pressing problems with several other projects, the payroll project had been completed without the usual review by other systems personnel. Jason arranged for a member of the audit staff, who was a former programmer, to review the code changes. She found a few lines of unusual code in the program for generating the withholdings report for the IRS. The code subtracted $5 from most employee's withholdings and added it to Don's. Don got his hands on the money when the IRS sent him a huge refund check.

It appeared that Don intended to use the scheme every year, since he had not removed the incriminating code. He must have been fairly confident of his scheme, because he had not tried to modify the company's copy of the withholdings report. Somehow he knew there was no reconciliation of withholdings from the payroll records with the IRS report. It was a simple plan, and it could have gone undetected for years if Jason had not overheard someone in the cafeteria talk about a $5 difference.

Jason quietly investigated Don and found he had a reputation of being hard to work with. He had been passed over last year for a managerial position in the programming department and had been unhappy ever since. He made numerous comments to co-workers about favoritism and unfair treatment. He even mentioned getting even with the company somehow. Don had also recently purchased a fairly expensive sports car. No one knew where he got the money, but did mention to a co-worker that he had made a sizable down payment when he bought the car in April.

When the president asked the inevitable question of how the company could prevent this type of thing from happening again, Jason suggested the following guidelines:

1. A review of the company's internal controls should be conducted to analyze their effectiveness in preventing fraud. One control that already existed, reviewing program changes, could have prevented Don's scheme had it

been followed. As a result, Jason suggested a stricter enforcement of the existing controls.

2. New controls should be put into place to detect fraud. For example, he suggested a reconciliation of the withholdings on the IRS report with those on the payroll records.
3. Employees should be trained in fraud awareness, security measures, and ethical issues.

Jason also urged the president to prosecute the case. The president was reluctant to do so because of the adverse publicity and the problems it would cause for Don's wife and children. Jason's supervisor tactfully suggested that if other employees found out that Don was not prosecuted, it would send the wrong message to the rest of the company. The president finally conceded to prosecute if the company could prove that Don was guilty. The president agreed to hire a forensic accountant to build a stronger case against Don and try to get him to confess.

KEY TERMS

fraud
employee fraud
fraudulent financial reporting
lapping
kiting
white-collar criminals
pressure
opportunity
rationalization
computer fraud
Trojan horse
round-down technique
salami technique
trap door
superzapping
software piracy
data diddling
data leakage
piggybacking
masquerading
impersonation
logic time bomb
hacking
scavenging
eavesdropping
wiretap
computer virus
worm
random surveillance
computer security officer
forensic accountants

CHAPTER QUIZ

1. A fraud in which later payments on accounts receivable are used to pay off earlier payments that were stolen is called
   a. lapping.
   b. kiting.
   c. a Ponzi scheme.
   d. the salami technique.

2. Which type of fraud is associated with as many as 50% of all lawsuits against auditors?
   a. Kiting
   b. Fraudulent financial reporting
   c. Ponzi schemes
   d. Lapping

3. Which of the following statements is false?
   a. The psychological profiles of white-collar criminals differ from those of violent criminals.
   b. The psychological profiles of white-collar criminals differ from those of the general public.
   c. Computer fraud perpetrators are different from other types of white-collar criminals.
   d. Computer fraud perpetrators often do not view themselves as criminals.

4. Which of the following conditions are usually necessary in order for a fraud to occur? (There may be more than one right answer.)
   a. Pressures
   b. Opportunities

c. Explanations
d. Rationalizations

5. All of the following are examples of computer fraud except
a. theft of money and altering computer records.
b. intent to obtain information illegally through use of a computer.
c. failure to perform preventive maintenance on a computer.
d. unauthorized modification of a software program.

6. A set of instructions to increase a programmer's pay rate by 10% is hidden inside an authorized program. It changes and updates payroll files. This computer fraud technique is called a
a. virus.
b. worm.
c. trap door.
d. Trojan horse.

7. A set of instructions hidden inside a calendar utility that copies itself until memory is filled and the system crashes is a computer fraud technique called a
a. logic bomb.
b. worm.
c. virus.
d. Trojan horse.

8. Which of the following control procedures is most likely to deter lapping?
a. Encryption
b. Continual update of the access control matrix
c. A background check on employees
d. Periodic rotation of duties

9. Which of the following is the most important, basic, and effective control to deter fraud?
a. Enforced vacations
b. Logical access control
c. Segregation of duties
d. Virus protection controls

10. Which of the following are methods of reducing fraud losses? (There may be more than one right answer.)
a. Insurance
b. Regular backup of data and programs
c. A fraud recovery program
d. Segregation of duties

DISCUSSION QUESTIONS

15.1 Do you agree that the most effective method of obtaining adequate system security is to rely on the integrity of company employees? Why or why not? Does this seem ironic? What measures should a company take to ensure the integrity of its employees?

15.2 You are the president of a multinational company. One of your senior executives confessed to kiting $100,000. Explain what kiting is and what your company can do to prevent it. How would you respond to your employee's confession? What issues must you consider before pressing formal charges?

15.3 One December morning the computers at U.S. Leasing Company began acting sluggish. Computer operators were relieved when a software troubleshooter from Digital Equipment called several hours later. They were more than happy to let him help correct the problem they were having with the Digital software. The troubleshooter asked for a phone number for the computers as well as a log-on number and passwords—a common procedure employed by Digital in handling software problems.

The next morning the computers were worse. A call to Digital confirmed U.S. Leasing's suspicion: Someone had impersonated a Digital repairman to gain unauthorized access to the system and destroy the entire computer data base. U.S. Leasing was also concerned that the intruder had devised a program that would let him get back into the system even after all the passwords were changed.

What techniques could the imposter have employed to breach U.S. Leasing's internal security? What could U.S. Leasing do to avoid these types of incidents in the future?

15.4 To address the need for tighter data controls and lower support costs, Manufacturers Hanover has adopted a new diskless PC. It is little more than a mutilated personal computer described as a "gutless wonder." The concept behind the diskless PC is simple: A LAN server-based file system of high-powered diskless workstations is assembled throughout an organization and connected with a central repository or mainframe. The network improves control by limiting user access to company data previously stored on desktop hard disks. Since the user can destroy or delete only the information currently on the screen, a company's financial data is protected from user-instigated catastrophes. The diskless computer also saves money in user support costs by distributing applications and upgrades automatically, as well as by offering on-line help.

What threats to the information processing and storage system does the diskless PC minimize? Do the security advantages of the new system outweigh potential limitations?

15.5 Biometric security systems are becoming a cost-effective solution to the troubling problem of computer security. Biometric security devices measure our unique physical traits, such as speech patterns, eye and finger physiology, and written signature dynamics. The ideal system must be reliable and yet flexible enough to handle minor changes in physical characteristics such as a cut finger or a hoarse voice. The system also requires that the user be physically present to gain access to the system. Hertz and Security Pacific Bank are two companies seeking to use the new technology. For both companies the security devices will aid in ensuring that only authorized individuals have access to computer systems and its related operations.

Why are biometric security devices increasing in popularity? What are the advantages and disadvantages of these systems in comparison to traditional security measures (e.g., passwords, locked doors, etc.)?

15.6 A few days after the inventory control system for Revlon, the cosmetics giant, went down, officials discovered that the downtime was caused by Logisticon, a software developer. Seven months earlier Revlon had signed an agreement to have Logisticon install a real-time invoice and inventory processing system. Prior to completing phase I of the project, Revlon discovered a series of programming bugs. Revlon proceeded to withhold any additional payment on the contract to Logisticon. Logisticon contended that the software was fine but that the computer hardware was faulty. When Revlon refused payment, Logisticon sought repossession: It used a telephone dial-in feature in the software to make a disabling phone call and render the system unusable.

After a three-day standoff Logisticon reactivated Revlon's inventory system. Revlon filed suit in California Superior Court charging Logisticon with trespassing, breach of contract, and misappropriation of trade secrets (use of Revlon passwords). Logisticon filed a countersuit for contract breach. Revlon and Logisticon later settled out of court.

Would Logisticon's actions be classified as sabotage or repossession? Why? Would you find the company guilty of committing a computer crime? Be prepared to defend your position to the class.

15.7 Improved computer security measures create their own set of problems: user antagonism, sluggish response time, and hampered performance. Many professionals feel that the most effective way to promote computer security is to educate users about good moral conduct. According to Richard Stallman, president of the Free Software Foundation, MIT programmer, and computer activist, software licensing is antisocial because it prohibits the growth of the technology by keeping information away from your neighbors. He believes high school and college students should have unlimited access to computers without security measures in order to teach constructive and civilized behavior. He states that a protected system is a puzzle and, since it is human nature to solve puzzles, eliminating computer security so that there is no temptation to break in would reduce hacking.

Do you agree with Stallman's statements? Do you agree that software licensing is antisocial? Is ethical teaching the solution to computer security problems? Would the removal of computer security measures reduce the incidence of computer fraud? Why or why not?

15.8 Discuss the following statement by Roswell Steffen, a convicted embezzler: "For every foolproof system, there is a method for beating it." Do you believe a completely secure computer system is possible? Explain. If internal controls are less than 100% effective, why should they be employed at all?

15.9 What motives do people have for hacking? Why has hacking become so popular in recent years? Do you regard it as a crime? Explain your position.

PROBLEMS

15.1 An experienced senior auditor was assigned to investigate a possible fraudulent situation characterized by extremely high, unexplained merchandise shortages at one location of the company's department store chain. During the course of the investigation the auditor determined the following.

1. The supervisor of the receiving department was the owner and operator of a small boutique carry-

ing many of the same labels as the chain store. The chain store's general manager was unaware of the ownership interest.

2. The receiving supervisor signed receiving reports showing that the total quantity shipped by a vendor had been received. A total of 5% to 10% of each shipment was diverted to the boutique.
3. The chain's buyers were unaware of the short shipments because the receiving supervisor would enter the correct quantity on the move ticket accompanying the merchandise to the sales areas.
4. The chain's accounts payable department paid vendors for the total quantity shown on the receiving report.
5. Based on the supervisor's instructions, quantities on the move tickets were not compared with those on the receiving report.

REQUIRED

Classify each of the five situations as a fraudulent act, an indicator of fraud, or an event unrelated to the investigation. Justify your answers. (CIA Examination, adapted)

15.2 A small but growing firm has recently hired you to investigate a potential fraud. The company heard through its hot line that the purchases journal clerk periodically enters fictitious acquisitions. The nonexistent vendor's address is given as a post office box, which is rented by the clerk. He forwards notification of the fictitious purchases for recording in the accounts payable ledger. Payment is ultimately mailed to the post office box. He then deposits the check in an account established in the name of the nonexistent vendor.

REQUIRED

a. Define fraud, fraud deterrence, fraud detection, and fraud investigation.
b. List four red-flag indicators (personal as opposed to organizational) that might point to the existence of fraud in this example.
c. List two procedures you could follow to uncover the fraudulent behavior of the purchases journal clerk in this situation. (CIA Examination, adapted)

15.3 Most experts maintain that the number of computer frauds publicly revealed represent only the tip of the iceberg. Although the major threat to computer security is perceived by many to be external, the more dangerous threats come from insiders. Management must recognize these problems and develop and enforce security programs to deal with the many types of computer fraud.

REQUIRED

Explain how each of the following six types of fraud is committed. Also, identify a different method of protection for each and describe how it works. Use the following format.

Type of Fraud	Explanation	Identification and Description of Protection Methods

a. Input manipulation
b. Program alteration
c. File alteration
d. Data theft
e. Sabotage
f. Theft of computer time
(CMA Examination, adapted)

15.4 The Treadway Commission study shows that fraudulent financial reporting usually occurs as the result of environmental, institutional, or individual influences and opportune situations. These influences and opportunities, present to some degree in all companies, motivate individuals and companies to engage in fraudulent financial reporting. The prevention and detection of fraudulent financial reporting requires that these influences and opportunities be identified and evaluated in terms of the risks they pose to a company. These risk factors include internal ethical and control factors as well as external environmental conditions.

REQUIRED

a. Identify two company situational pressures that would increase the likelihood of fraud.
b. Identify three corporate opportunities that make fraud easier to commit and detection less likely.
c. For each of the following, identify the external environmental factors that should be considered in assessing the risk of fraudulent financial reporting.

1. The company's industry.
2. The company's business environment.
3. The company's legal and regulatory environment.

d. According to the Treadway Commission, what can top management do to reduce the possibility of fraudulent financial reporting? (CMA Examination, adapted)

15.5 The impact of employee and management fraud is staggering both in terms of dollar costs and effect on the victims. For each of the following independent cases of employee fraud, describe the recommendations internal auditors should make to prevent similar problems from occurring in the future.

a. A retail store that was part of a national chain experienced an abnormal inventory shrinkage in its audiovisual department. The internal auditors, noting this shrinkage, included an in-depth evaluation of the department in the scope of their store audit. During their review the auditors were "tipped off" by an employee that a particular customer bought a large number of small electronic components and that the customer always went to a certain cashier's checkout line. The auditors' work revealed that the cashier and the customer had colluded to steal a number of electronic components. The cashier did not record the sale of several items the customer took from the store.

b. During an unannounced visit to a large hospital, internal auditors discovered a payroll fraud when they observed the distribution of paychecks. The supervisors of each department distributed paychecks to employees and were supposed to return unclaimed checks to the payroll department. When the auditors took control of, and followed up on, an unclaimed paycheck for an employee in the food service department, they discovered that the employee had quit four months previously. The employee and the supervisor had had an argument, and the employee had simply left and never returned. The supervisor had continued to turn in a time card for the employee and had taken the unclaimed checks and cashed them.

c. While performing an audit of cash disbursements at a manufacturing firm, internal auditors discovered a fraud committed by an accounts payable clerk. She made copies of supporting documents and used them to support duplicate payments to a vendor of manufacturing materials. The clerk, who had opened a bank account in a name similar to that of the vendor, took the duplicate checks and deposited them in her bank account. (CMA Examination, adapted)

15.6 Rent-A-Wreck's policy requires a "sealed bid" to sell motor vehicles that are no longer efficient. In reviewing the sale of some vehicles that had been declared obsolete, the auditor found that management had not always complied with the stated policy. Records indicated that several vehicles on which major repairs had recently been performed were sold at "negotiated prices." The auditor was assured by management that by performing limited repairs and negotiating with knowledgeable buyers, better prices had been obtained for the salvaged vehicles than had the required sealed-bid procedures been followed. The auditor suspected that there might be more involved than management indicated. Further investigation revealed that the vehicles had been sold to employees at "negotiated prices" well below market value. The auditor's work eventually resulted in three managers' and five other employees' pleading guilty to criminal charges and making restitution to the organization.

REQUIRED

a. Based on this scenario, outline the symptoms or indications of possible fraud that should have aroused the auditor's suspicion.

b. Suggest audit procedures that the auditor might have employed to establish the fact that fraud had in fact occurred. (CIA Examination, adapted)

15.7 On March 6, 1992, the computer world braced for a shock. News began circulating months before about a computer virus named Michelangelo that was set to "ignite" on the birthday of the famous Italian artist. The virus itself was spread via floppy disks used with IBM compatible PCs. When a software package containing the virus was introduced to the computer system, the virus would attach to the computer's operating system boot sector. On the magical date the virus would release itself, freezing the system's boot function and destroying all of its data.

When March 6 arrived, the virus did minimal damage. Preventive techniques limited the damage to isolated personal and business computers. Though the excitement surrounding the virus was largely illusory, Michelangelo helped the computer-using public realize their own system's vulnerability to outside attack.

REQUIRED

a. What is a computer virus? Cite at least three reasons why no system is completely safe from a computer virus.

b. Why do viruses represent a serious threat to information systems? What damage can a virus do to a computer system?

c. Why is a virus often classified as a Trojan horse?
d. What steps can individuals and companies take to prevent the spread or propagation of a computer virus?

15.8 The auditor of a bank is called to a meeting with a senior operations manager because of a customer's report that an auto loan payment was not credited. According to the customer, the payment was made at a teller's window using a check drawn on an account in that bank. The payment was made on its due date, May 5. On May 10 the customer decided to sell the car and called the bank for a payoff on the loan. The payment had not been credited to the loan. The customer came to the bank on May 12 to inquire about the payment and meet with the manager. The manager found that the payment had been credited the night before the meeting (as of May 11); the customer was satisfied, since no late charge would be assessed until May 15. The manager asked whether the auditor was comfortable with this situation.

The auditor located the customer's paid check in the deposit department and found that it had cleared as of May 5. The auditor traced the item back through the computer entry records and found that the check had been processed by the teller as a cashed check. The auditor traced the payment through the entry records of May 11 and found that the payment had been made with cash instead of a check.

REQUIRED

What type of embezzlement scheme does this appear to be, and how does that scheme operate? (CIA Examination, adapted)

15.9 It was a typical Wednesday on the UCLA campus when everything began going wrong in the student computer lab. The computer lab was filled to capacity as the end of the semester neared. Nearly 70 students were logged into the UCLA computer network, run by Netware software, when the system came to a halt. Students tried running software without success, and many students couldn't even log in without getting a frustrating ABORT RETRY message from the Netware operating system.

System directors initially expected a cable break or an operating system failure as the culprit, but diagnostics revealed nothing. After several frustrating hours a staff member began running the SCAN virus detection program and uncovered a Jerusalem virus on the lab's main server. The virus was eventually traced to floppy disks used by unsuspecting UCLA students. When staff workers used the infected computers to gain supervisor access to the operating system, the virus spread.

The virus cost UCLA about 25 person-hours and disrupted the lives of frantic students preparing for finals. Later that evening the system was brought back on-line after infected files were replaced with backup copies.

REQUIRED

a. What conditions made the UCLA system a potential "breeding ground" for the Jerusalem virus?
b. What symptoms indicated that a virus was present?
c. What advice would you give UCLA's director of computing to prevent the same incident from reoccurring?

CASE 15.1: KEVIN MITNICK: THE DARK-SIDE HACKER

No one is entirely certain when Kevin Mitnick's "professional" hacking career began. During his mid-teens, Kevin was a part of the "phone phreak" subculture in California. By their own definition, phone phreaks were telephone hobbyists more expert at understanding the workings of the Bell system than most Bell employees. Using their knowledge of the phone system and computers, phreaks would often arrange free phone service, long-distance calling, and airline tickets for friends.

In spite of his unique talents Kevin never sought pay for his efforts. His reward came in defeating the computer system and gaining power and control over others in the process. The phone phreak logo said it all: If it could be done, it was legal. When Kevin's telecommunications hobby culminated in one of the boldest acts of computer piracy, no one was the least bit surprised.

As the manager of research and development for the University of California's (USC) computer services, Mark Brown was all too familiar with the threat of unauthorized break-ins. Most of the hackers were harmless, many just wanting to take a look around. One day Mark began a low-key investigation of some intruders and discovered that they were accessing the USC system through a modification in the Gatekeeper subprogram of the computer's VMS operating system.

A few days later Mark's amusement turned to concern as he noted that storage space was disappearing from the computer system at an alarming rate. After a more thorough investigation Mark discovered that the intruders were storing vast amounts of information in bogus system index files. When Mark opened the files, he was alarmed to find a source code copy of the newest version of the Digital VMS operating system.

Source code represents the lifeblood of software development. Computer programs are written in a user-friendly source code language such as FORTRAN or C and then converted into unreadable binary code for distribution. Such a process allowed software developers to protect the integrity of their programs from alterations and modifications from outside sources. Digital's source code had clearly been compromised.

Mark immediately called Digital Equipment to inform them of his discovery. He was surprised by the guarded reception he received from Digital representatives. Digital asked Mark to continue monitoring the intruders and keep careful logs of all suspicious activities.

Kevin and his friend Lenny DiCicco had years of experience with computers, networks, and VMS operating systems. They used that knowledge, the computer at Voluntary Plan Administrators (VPA), Lenny's workplace, and a list of stolen MCI long-distance accounts to exploit Digital's Easynet network. They gained access through an operating system bug in Easynet and sent a copy of the VMS operating system to the USC computer. With help from a friend the data was retrieved from the USC computer and stored on magnetic disk. From their viewpoint their actions were harmless; they weren't really stealing because they never tried marketing the software.

However, Kevin was not satisfied with a copy of the VMS source code. He also wanted a copy of the source code for Doom, a lucrative game developed by Digital. When Lenny refused to help, Kevin became angry and began harassing him at work. When Lenny's boss called him into his office to discuss these problems, he came unglued. His boss, Ralph Hurley, was stunned when Lenny confessed to using VPA's computer to exploit Digital Equipment. Ralph convinced Lenny to call Digital and relate a similar confession to a Digital security team.

A Digital security expert, accompanied by an FBI agent, arrived the following morning to verify Lenny's claims and to compare them with the statements made by Mark Brown from USC. With Lenny's help the police spent the evening monitoring Kevin as he logged onto Digital's Easynet system with the VPA computer system.

Kevin kept much of his pirated software in a duffel bag in his car. Hoping to catch Kevin with stolen software and data, the FBI had Lenny ask if he could make copies of some of Kevin's pirated software. When Kevin went to the car and retrieved the duffel bag, the police made the arrest.

Kevin was charged with four felony counts, including unauthorized computer entry, theft of data, and software piracy. Hoping to avoid additional publicity, Digital sought a plea-bargain arrangement. Although the judge initially rejected the plea bargain, the arrangement was eventually made and Kevin was sentenced to one year in prison and six months in a rehabilitation program working to overcome his obsession with computer piracy. For his role in the crime Lenny received five years probation after pleading guilty to one felony count.

1. What is source code and what role does it play in software design and maintenance? What is the danger of having source code exposed to unauthorized users?
2. In what ways do Kevin and Lenny represent typical white-collar computer criminals? How are they different?
3. What were the hackers' motives for entering Digital's Easynet network without authorization? What rationale did Kevin and Lenny use to justify their invasion of the Easynet network?
4. How were the hackers so readily able to gain access to the USC computers as well as Digital's Easynet? What steps should Digital take to minimize the impact of computer crime on its operations in the future?
5. Discuss whether or not Digital Equipment should press charges against Kevin and Lenny for their piracy of Digital's VMS operating system source code.
   a. What charges should be brought against the hackers?
   b. What impact could publicity have upon Digital Equipment?

Source: Katie Hafner and John Markoff, *Cyberpunk* (New York: Simon and Schuster, 1991).

CASE 15.2: DAVID L. MILLER: PORTRAIT OF A WHITE-COLLAR CRIMINAL

There is an old saying in crime-fighting circles: Crime doesn't pay. However, for David Miller crime has paid rich dividends. It paid for two Mercedes-Benz sedans, a $280,000 suburban house, a condominium at Myrtle Beach, South Carolina, $500 suits, and $75 tailored, monogrammed shirts. It also paid for diamond, sapphire, ruby, and emerald rings for his wife and a new car for his father-in-law. Though he has confessed to embezzling funds from six different employers over a 20-year period, he has never been prosecuted and has never been incarcerated. In large part Miller's freedom is the result of the fear that companies have about turning in employees who defraud them.

Miller's first employer was also his first victim. In 1965, after ten months of selling insurance in Wheeling, West Virginia, he was fired for stealing about $200. After an assortment of odd jobs he moved to Ohio and worked as an accountant for a local baker. Miller was caught embezzling funds and paid back the $1000 he had stolen. Again, he was not reported to the authorities and was quietly dismissed.

Miller returned to Wheeling and went to work for Wheeling Bronze, Inc., a bronze-castings maker. In December 1971 the president of Wheeling Bronze discovered that several returned checks were missing and that there was a $30,000 cash shortfall. After an extensive search workers uncovered a number of canceled checks with forged signatures in an outdoor sandpile. Miller was questioned and confessed to the scheme. He was given the choice of paying back the stolen amount or going to jail. Miller's parents took out a mortgage on their home to pay back the stolen money. No charges were ever filed and Miller was dismissed.

Several months later Miller found a job in Pennsylvania working for Robinson Pipe Cleaning. When Miller was caught embezzling funds, he again avoided prosecution by promising to repay the $20,000 he had stolen.

In 1974 Crest Industries hired Miller as an accountant. Miller proved to be the ideal employee and was quickly promoted to the position of office manager. He was very dedicated, worked long hours, and did outstanding work. Soon after his promotion he purchased a new home, a new car, and a new wardrobe.

In 1976 Miller's world unraveled again when Crest's auditors discovered that $31,000 was missing. Once again there was a tearful confession and a promise to repay all money stolen. Miller confessed that he'd written several checks to himself and had then recorded payments to vendors on the carbon copies of the checks. To cover his tracks, he intercepted and altered the company's monthly bank statements. He had used the money he had stolen to finance his life-style and to repay Wheeling Bronze and Robinson Pipe Cleaning.

Miller claimed in his confession that he had never before embezzled funds. He showed a great deal of remorse, so much so that Crest even hired a lawyer for him. He gave Crest a lien on his house, and he was quietly dismissed. Because the president of Crest did not want the publicity to harm Miller's wife and three children, Crest never pressed charges against him.

Miller next took a job as an accountant in Steubenville, Ohio, with Rustcraft Broadcasting Company, a chain of radio and TV stations. Rustcraft was acquired in 1979 by Associated Communications, and Miller moved to Pittsburgh to become Associated's new controller.

Miller immediately began dipping into Associated's accounts. Over a six-year period he embezzled approximately $1.36 million, $445,000 of that in 1984 when Miller was promoted to CFO. Miller used various methods to embezzle the money. One approach to circumvent the need for two signatures on every check was to ask another executive who was leaving on vacation to sign several checks "just in case" the company needed additional cash while he was gone. Miller used most of these checks to siphon funds off to his personal account. To cover the theft, Miller retrieved the canceled check from the bank reconciliation and destroyed it. The amount stolen was then charged to an expense account of one of the units to balance the company's books.

While working at Associated, Miller was able to lead a very comfortable life-style. He bought a new house and several expensive cars. He bought vacation property and a very expensive wardrobe, and he was very generous with tips and gifts. The life-style could not have been supported by his $130,000 salary, yet no one at Associated ever questioned the source of his conspicuous consumption.

Miller's life-style came crashing down in December 1984 while he was on vacation. A bank officer called to inquire about a check written to Mr. Miller. An investigation ensued and Miller confessed to embezzling funds. As part of the 1985 out-of-court settlement with Miller, Associated Communications received most of Miller's personal property.

Miller can't explain why he was never prosecuted. He always insisted that he was going to pay the company back. Such statements would usually satisfy his employers and get him off the hook. He believes that these agreements actually contributed to his subsequent thefts. For example, one rationale for starting to steal from a new employer was to pay back the former one.

After leaving Associated, Miller was hired by a former colleague. Miller underwent therapy and believed he had resolved his problem with compulsive embezzlement.

When interviewed about his past activities, Miller said that he felt his problem with theft was an illness, just like alcoholism or compulsive gambling. The illness was driven by a subconscious need to be admired and liked by others. He thought that by spending money, others would like him. Ironically, he was universally well liked and admired at each job, and it had nothing to do with money. In fact, one associate at Associated was so surprised at the news of the thefts that he said that it was like finding out that your brother was an ax murderer. In the interview Miller also claimed that he is not a bad person. He says he never intended to hurt anyone, but once he got started, he just could not stop.

As a forensic accountant, you've been asked to address a conference of top business leaders concerning the David Miller case and the prevention of fraud.

1. How does Miller fit the profile of the average fraud perpetrator? How does he differ? How did these characteristics make him difficult to detect?
2. Discuss the threefold fraud process (theft, conversion, concealment) Miller followed in embezzling funds from Associated Communications. What specific concealment techniques did Miller use?
3. What pressures motivated Miller to embezzle? What opportunities allowed him to steal and cover up his theft? How did Miller rationalize his actions?
4. Miller had a framed T-shirt in his office that said, "He who dies with the most toys wins." What does this tell you about Miller? What life-style red flags could have tipped off the company to the possibility of fraud?
5. Identify several reasons why companies hesitate in prosecuting white-collar criminals. What are the problems with such rationalizations? What could law enforcement officials do to encourage more rigorous prosecution of white-collar criminals?
6. Identify the primary action each of the victimized companies could have done to prevent Miller's embezzlement. What other controls could help in preventing future fraud?

Source: Bryan Burrough, "David L. Miller Stole from His Employer and Isn't in Prison," *Wall Street Journal* (September 19, 1986): 1.

CASE 15.3: LEXSTEEL CORPORATION

Lexsteel Corporation is a leading manufacturer of steel furniture. While the company has manufacturing plants and distribution facilities throughout the United States, the purchasing, accounting, and treasury functions are centralized at corporate headquarters in Fresno, California.

While discussing a recent management letter with the external auditors, Ray Landsdown, controller of Lexsteel, became aware of potential problems with the accounts payable system. The auditors had to perform additional audit procedures to attest to the validity of accounts payable and cutoff procedures. The auditors have recommended a detailed systems study of the current procedures to assess the company's exposure to potential embezzlement and fraud and to identify ways to improve management controls.

Landsdown has assigned the study task to Dolores Smith, a relatively new accountant in the department. Because Smith could not find adequate documentation of the accounts payable procedures, she interviewed those employees involved and constructed a flowchart of the current system. This flowchart is shown in Fig. 15.2, and descriptions of the current procedures follow.

Computer Resources

The host computer mainframe is located at corporate headquarters with interactive, remote job-entry terminals at each branch location. In general, data entry

Figure 15.2

Accounts Payable Procedures at Lexsteel

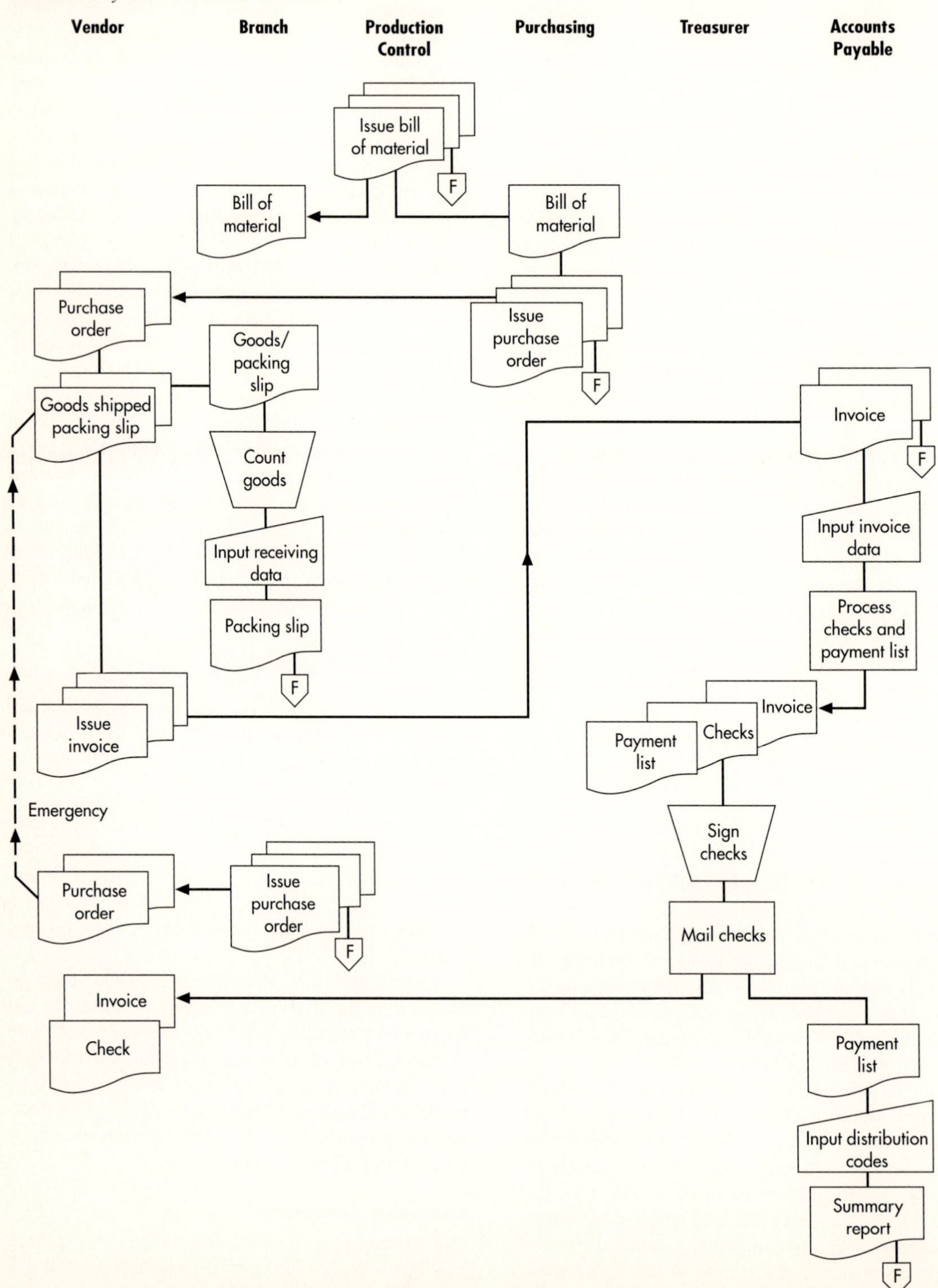

occurs at the source and is transmitted to an integrated data base maintained on the host computer. Data transmission occurs over leased telephone lines between the branch offices and the host computer. The software allows flexibility for managing user access and editing data input.

Procedures for Purchasing Raw Materials

Production orders and appropriate bills of material are generated by the host computer at corporate headquarters. From these bills of material, purchase orders for raw materials are generated by the centralized purchasing function and mailed directly to the vendors. Each purchase order instructs the vendor to ship the materials directly to the appropriate manufacturing plant. Assuming that the necessary purchase orders have been issued, the manufacturing plants proceed with the production orders received from corporate headquarters.

Upon receipt of goods, the manufacturing plant examines and verifies the count against the packing slip and transmits the receiving data to accounts payable at corporate headquarters. In the event that raw material deliveries fall behind production, each branch manager is given the authority to order materials and issue emergency purchase orders directly to the vendors. Data about the emergency orders and verification of materials receipt are transmitted via computer to accounts payable at corporate headquarters. Since the company employs a cost-effective computerized perpetual inventory system, physical counts of raw materials are not performed.

Accounts Payable Procedures

Vendor invoices are mailed directly to corporate headquarters and entered by accounts payable personnel when received. This often occurs before the receiving data are transmitted from the branch offices. The final day of the invoice term for payment is entered as the payment due date. This due date must often be calculated by the data entry person using information listed on the invoice.

Once a week invoices due the following week are printed in chronological entry order on a payment listing, and the corresponding checks are drawn. The checks and the payment listing are sent to the treasurer's office for signature and mailing to the payee. The check number is printed by the computer, displayed on the check and the payment listing, and validated as the checks are signed. After the checks are mailed, the payment listing is returned to accounts payable for filing. When there is insufficient cash to pay all the invoices, certain checks and the payment listing are retained by the treasurer until all checks can be paid. When the remaining checks are mailed, the listing is then returned to accounts payable. Often weekly check mailings include a few checks from the previous week, but rarely are there more than two weekly listings involved.

When accounts payable receives the payment listing back from the treasurer's office, the expenses are distributed, coded, and posted to the appropriate plant/cost center accounts. Weekly summary performance reports are processed by accounts payable for each cost center and branch location reflecting all data entry to that point.

1. Identify and discuss three areas where Lexsteel Corporation may be exposed to fraud or embezzlement due to weaknesses in the procedures described. Recommend improvements to correct these weaknesses.
2. Describe three areas where management information could be distorted due to weaknesses in the Lexsteel's procedures. Recommend improvements to correct these weaknesses.
3. Identify three strengths in Lexsteel's procedures, and explain why they are strengths. (CMA Examination, adapted)

CASE 15.4: WARD CORPORATION

Ward Corporation is a manufacturer of cleaning products with three wholly owned subsidiaries that are operated as separate divisions. Ward's corporate headquarters are located in an industrial park in a Chicago suburb. The industrial products division is located in the same industrial park but in its own building. The other two divisions are located in Milwaukee and Indianapolis.

The operating and financial records are maintained on a mainframe computer at corporate headquarters. Each division has a small accounting department that submits operating and financial data to corporate headquarters on a regular basis.

The profit planning department at corporate headquarters is responsible for preparing special analyses and reports for Ward. To facilitate its work, the profit planning department has linked a microcomputer to the mainframe to download data. The special analyses are prepared using these data and a purchased spreadsheet software package.

Beth Simons recently joined the industrial products division as an accounting analyst. Simons is proficient in the use of microcomputers and spreadsheet software. She has been assigned to work with Doug Laird, marketing manager of the industrial products division, to develop analyses and reports. One week into the assignment she suggested that the microcomputers used in the marketing department for word processing could be valuable analytical tools if spreadsheet software were acquired. Laird knows little about computers, but he has received some of the special analyses prepared by the profit planning department at corporate headquarters. Laird wants Simons to try her idea, but he has suggested that she first borrow the software from the profit planning department.

Simons approached Tom Field, manager of profit planning, regarding the use of the software package. Field was very sympathetic to Simons's request, but he did not want to loan the original system disk since the software is used extensively in his department and was copy-protected. However, Field did have a utility program that allowed him to make backup copies of most copy-protected software. Since there was no backup of the spreadsheet software, Field decided to make a copy and give it to Simons for her use during regular business hours. His instructions were as follows: "This is my only copy, but you may borrow it for your use only. Don't give it to anyone else. Once you have tried the software for your assignment, you must return it to me. Industrial product's accounting or marketing department will have to purchase its own copy."

Field did not give Simons a copy of the licensing agreement that accompanied the original software package. The license agreement that follows was affixed to the original sealed disk package. Although Simons was not aware of the specific provisions of the licensing agreement that pertained to the borrowed software, she knew that licensing agreements accompanied computer software packages.

Software License Agreement

IMPORTANT: Please read this agreement before opening the envelope.

Opening the disk envelope indicates the user's acceptance of the agreement to abide by these terms.

1. *The software may be used on any compatible hardware that the purchaser owns or uses.*
2. *Backup copies of the software can be made provided that these copies are for exclusive use of the purchaser and only one copy of the software is in use at any one time.*
3. *No alterations to the software or the documentation are permitted.*
4. *The software may not be distributed on a permanent or temporary basis.*
5. *This license and the software may be transferred to another party provided that all copies of the software and documentation are transferred and the original party ceases to use the software after the transfer.*

Consider the stipulations set forth in the license agreement for the spreadsheet software.

1. Did Field violate the agreement when he made a copy of the software disk using the utility program?
2. Did Field violate the agreement when he gave Simons the copy of the software disk he had made?
3. Without prejudice to your preceding answers, assume that Field did violate the license agreement when he copied the software disk and gave it to Simons. Identify Field's alternatives in determining whether the spreadsheet software meets the needs of the industrial products division's marketing department without violating the license agreement. (CMA Examination, adapted)

ANSWERS TO CHAPTER QUIZ

1. a **2.** b **3.** b **4.** a,b,d **5.** c **6.** d **7.** c **8.** d **9.** c **10.** a,b,c

Chapter 16

Auditing of Computer-Based Information Systems

LEARNING OBJECTIVES

After studying this chapter, you should be able to:

- Describe the scope and objectives of audit work, and identify the major steps in the audit process.
- Identify the objectives of an IS audit, and describe the four-step approach necessary for meeting these objectives.
- Design a plan for the study and evaluation of internal control in an AIS.
- Describe computer audit software, and explain how it is used in the audit of an AIS.
- Describe the nature and scope of an operational audit.

Integrative Case: Seattle Paper Products

Shortly after learning how to use a computer audit software package, Jason Scott was assigned to a project at Seattle Paper Products (SPP). SPP is modifying its sales department payroll system to change the way it calculates sales commissions. Under the old system commissions were a fixed percentage of dollar sales. The new system is considerably more complex, with commission rates varying according to the product sold and the total dollar volume of sales.

Jason's assignment is to use the audit software to write a "parallel simulation test" program to calculate sales commissions and compare them with those generated by the new system. Jason obtained the necessary payroll system documentation and the details on the new sales commission policy. After a few days his program was ready to run.

Jason obtained the file containing sales transaction data from the last payroll period and used it to run his program. To his surprise, his calculations were $5000 less than those produced by SPP's new program; in fact, individual differences existed for about half of the company's salespeople. Jason double-checked his program code but couldn't locate any errors. He selected a salesperson for whom there was a discrepancy and recalculated the commission by hand. The result agreed with his program. He reviewed the new commission policy with the sales manager, line by line, and concluded that he understood the new policy completely. Jason is now convinced that his program is correct and that the error lies with the new program. Based on this conclusion, he ponders the following questions:

1. How could a programming error of this significance be overlooked by experienced programmers who thoroughly reviewed and tested the new system?

2. Is this an inadvertent error, or could it be another attempted fraud?
3. What can be done to find the error in the program?

INTRODUCTION

This chapter focuses on the concepts and techniques used in auditing an AIS. Auditors are employed by many different organizations for a wide range of tasks and responsibilities. Many organizations employ internal auditors to evaluate company operations. The General Accounting Office and state governments employ auditors to evaluate management performance and compliance with legislative intent in government departments. The Department of Defense employs auditors to review the financial records of companies with defense contracts. Publicly held companies hire external auditors to provide an independent review of their financial statements.

This chapter is written primarily from the perspective of the internal auditor. Internal auditors are directly responsible for helping management improve organizational effectiveness and efficiency, including assisting in the design and implementation of an AIS that contributes to the organization's goals. In contrast, external auditors are primarily responsible to corporate shareholders and investors and are only indirectly concerned with the effectiveness of a corporate AIS. Despite this distinction, many of the internal audit concepts and techniques discussed in this chapter are applicable to external audits.

The first section of this chapter provides an overview of auditing, the scope and objectives of internal audit work, and the steps in the auditing process. Then a methodology and a set of techniques for evaluating internal controls in an AIS are described. The third section discusses techniques for evaluating the reliability and integrity of information in an AIS. Finally, operational audits of an AIS are reviewed.

THE NATURE OF AUDITING

The American Accounting Association has formulated the following general definition of **auditing:**

> *Auditing is a systematic process of objectively obtaining and evaluating evidence regarding assertions about economic actions and events to ascertain the degree of correspondence between those assertions and established criteria and communicating the results to interested users.*[1]

Auditing requires a step-by-step approach characterized by careful planning and judicious selection and execution of appropriate techniques. Auditing involves the collection, review, and documentation of audit evidence. In developing recommendations, the auditor uses established criteria, such as the principles of management and control described in earlier chapters, as a basis for evaluation.

While the auditing principles have changed little in recent years, auditing methods and techniques have changed substantially. Auditors used to ignore

---

[1]Committee on Basic Auditing Concepts, *A Statement of Basic Auditing Concepts* (Sarasota, Fla.: American Accounting Association, 1973), 2.

the computer and its programs and merely examine the system's printed records and output. The assumption underlying auditing "around" the computer was: If output was correctly obtained from system input, then processing must be reliable. However, the technique of auditing around the computer was abandoned as better methods of auditing an AIS were developed. In addition, this approach was almost impossible to apply to a disappearing audit trail. The current approach, auditing "through" the computer, uses the computer to check the adequacy of system controls, data, and output. Most auditing techniques discussed in this chapter involve auditing through the computer.

Internal Auditing Standards

According to the Institute of Internal Auditors (IIA) the purpose of an internal audit is to evaluate the adequacy and effectiveness of a company's internal control system and determine the extent to which assigned responsibilities are actually carried out. The IIA's five audit scope standards outline the internal auditor's responsibilities:

1. Review the reliability and integrity of operating and financial information and how it is identified, measured, classified, and reported.
2. Determine whether the systems designed to comply with operating and reporting policies, plans, procedures, laws, and regulations are actually being followed.
3. Review how assets are safeguarded and verify the existence of assets as appropriate.
4. Examine company resources to determine how effectively and efficiently they are utilized.
5. Review company operations and programs to determine whether they are being carried out as planned and whether they are meeting their objectives.

Today's organizations use a computerized AIS to process, store, and control company information. To achieve the preceding five objectives, an internal auditor must be qualified to (1) examine all elements of the computerized AIS and (2) use the computer as a tool to accomplish these auditing objectives. In other words, computer expertise is essential to conducting an internal audit.

Types of Internal Auditing Work

Three different types of audits are commonly performed:

1. The **financial audit** examines the reliability and integrity of accounting records (both financial and operating information) and therefore correlates with the first of the five scope standards.
2. The **information systems (IS) audit** reviews the general and application controls of an AIS to assess its compliance with internal control policies and procedures and its effectiveness in safeguarding assets. Its scope roughly corresponds to the IIA's second and third standards.
3. The **operational,** or **management, audit** is concerned with the economical and efficient use of resources and the accomplishment of established goals and objectives. Its scope corresponds to the fourth and fifth standards. Operational audits are discussed in greater depth later in this chapter.

An Overview of the Auditing Process

All audits follow a very similar sequence of activities and may be divided into four stages: planning, collecting evidence, evaluating evidence, and communicating the results of the audit. Figure 16.1 depicts an overview of the auditing process, specifying many of the procedures typically performed within each of these stages. This section discusses the four auditing stages and activities in greater detail.

Audit Planning. The purpose of audit planning is to determine why, how, when, and by whom the audit will be performed. The first step in audit planning is to establish the scope and objectives of the audit. For example, the audit scope of a publicly held corporation extends to its corporate stockholders with the purpose of evaluating the fairness of financial statement

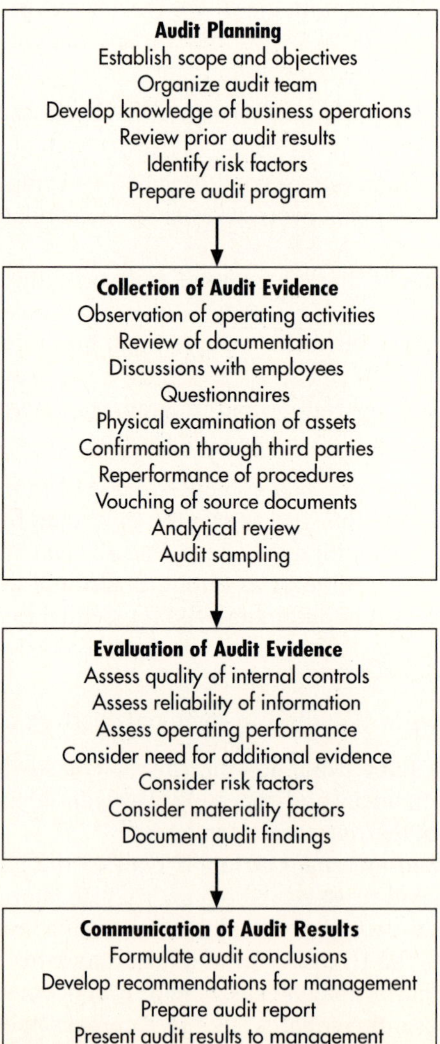

Audit Planning
Establish scope and objectives
Organize audit team
Develop knowledge of business operations
Review prior audit results
Identify risk factors
Prepare audit program
Collection of Audit Evidence
Observation of operating activities
Review of documentation
Discussions with employees
Questionnaires
Physical examination of assets
Confirmation through third parties
Reperformance of procedures
Vouching of source documents
Analytical review
Audit sampling
Evaluation of Audit Evidence
Assess quality of internal controls
Assess reliability of information
Assess operating performance
Consider need for additional evidence
Consider risk factors
Consider materiality factors
Document audit findings
Communication of Audit Results
Formulate audit conclusions
Develop recommendations for management
Prepare audit report
Present audit results to management

Figure 16.1

Overview of the Auditing Process

presentation. In contrast, an internal audit may examine an entire division, a specific department, or a computer application. It may focus on internal controls, financial information, operating performance, or some combination of the three.

An audit team with the necessary experience and expertise is formed. Team members become familiar with the auditee by conferring with supervisory and operating personnel, reviewing system documentation, and reviewing the findings of prior audits.

An audit should be planned so that the greatest amount of audit work focuses on the areas with the highest risk factors. There are three types of risk when conducting an audit:

1. **Inherent risk** is the susceptibility to material risk in the absence of controls. For example, a system that employs on-line processing, networks, data base software, telecommunications, and other forms of advanced technology has more inherent risk than a traditional batch processing system.
2. **Control risk** is the risk that a material misstatement will get through the internal control structure and into the financial statements. A company with weak internal controls has a higher control risk than one with strong controls. Control risk can be determined by reviewing the control environment and considering control weaknesses identified in prior audits and evaluating how they have been rectified.
3. **Detection risk** is the risk that auditors and their audit procedures will *not* detect a material error or misstatement.

To conclude the planning stage, a preliminary audit program is prepared. It shows the nature, extent, and timing of the procedures necessary for achieving audit objectives and minimizing audit risks. A time budget is prepared, and staff members are assigned to perform specific audit steps.

Evidence Collection. Most audit effort is spent collecting evidence. The following are among the most commonly used methods of collecting audit evidence:

- *Observation* of the activities being audited. Examples include watching how employees enter the computer site or how data control personnel handle data processing work as it is received.
- *Review of documentation* to understand how a particular AIS or internal control system is supposed to function.
- *Discussions* with employees about their jobs and how they carry out certain procedures.
- *Questionnaires* that gather data about the system.
- *Physical examination* of the quantity and/or condition of tangible assets such as equipment, inventory, or cash.
- *Confirmation* of the accuracy of certain information, such as customer account balances, through communication with independent third parties.
- *Reperformance* of selected calculations in order to verify quantitative information on records and reports. For example, the auditor could recompute a batch total or recalculate the annual depreciation charge.

- *Vouching* for the validity of a transaction by examining all supporting documents, such as the purchase order, receiving report, and vendor invoice supporting an accounts payable transaction.
- *Analytical review* of relationships and trends among information to detect items that should be further investigated. For example, an auditor for a chain of dress shops discovered that at one shop the ratio of accounts receivable to sales was far too high. An investigation revealed that the manager had diverted funds from collections to her personal use.

Because many audit tests and procedures cannot feasibly be performed on the entire set of activities, records, assets, or documents under review, they are often performed on a sample basis. A typical audit will usually consist of a mix of audit procedures, depending on the audit objectives. For example, an audit designed to evaluate AIS internal controls would make greater use of observation, review of documentation, discussions with employees, and reperformance of control procedures. An audit of financial information would focus on physical examination, confirmation, vouching, analytical review, and reperformance of account balance calculations.

Evaluation of Audit Evidence. The auditor evaluates the evidence gathered in light of the specific audit objective and decides whether it supports a favorable or unfavorable conclusion. If inconclusive, the auditor plans and executes additional procedures until sufficient evidence is obtained to reach a definitive conclusion.

Materiality and reasonable assurance are important when deciding how much audit work is necessary and when evaluating evidence. Since errors are bound to exist in any system, auditors focus on detecting and reporting those that have a significant impact on management's interpretation of the audit findings. Determining **materiality,** what is and is not important in a given set of circumstances, is primarily a matter of judgment. Materiality is generally more important to external audits, where the overall emphasis is on the fairness of financial statement presentation than to internal audits, where the focus is on determining adherence to management's policies.

The auditor seeks **reasonable assurance** that no material error exists in the information or process audited. Since it is prohibitively expensive to seek complete assurance, the auditor must be willing to accept some risk that the audit conclusion is incorrect. It is important to realize that when inherent or control risk is high, the auditor must obtain greater assurance to offset the greater uncertainty.

At all stages of the audit, findings and conclusions are carefully documented in audit working papers. Documentation is especially important at the evaluation stage, when final conclusions must be reached and supported.

Communication of Audit Results. The auditor prepares a written (and sometimes oral) report summarizing the audit findings and recommendations, with references to supporting evidence in the working papers. This report is presented to management, the audit committee, the board of directors, and other appropriate parties. After the audit results are communicated, auditors often perform a follow-up study to ascertain whether or not recommendations have been implemented.

The Risk-Based Audit Approach

The following four-step approach to internal control evaluation, referred to as the "risk-based" audit approach, provides a logical framework for carrying out an audit:

1. Determine the threats (errors and irregularities) facing the AIS.
2. Identify the control procedures that should be in place to minimize each threat by preventing or detecting the errors and irregularities.
3. Evaluate the control procedures. Reviewing system documentation and interviewing appropriate personnel to determine whether the necessary procedures are in place is called a **systems review. Tests of controls** are conducted to determine whether these procedures are satisfactorily followed. These tests include activities such as observing system operations; inspecting documents, records, and reports; checking samples of system inputs and outputs; and tracing transactions through the system.
4. Evaluate weaknesses (errors and irregularities not covered by control procedures) to determine their effect on the nature, timing, or extent of auditing procedures and client suggestions. This step focuses on the control risks and whether the control system as a whole adequately addresses them. If a control deficiency is identified, the auditor asks whether there are **compensating controls,** or procedures that compensate for the deficiency. Control weaknesses in one area may be acceptable if they are compensated for by control strengths in other areas.

The risk-based approach to auditing provides auditors with a clear understanding of the errors and irregularities that can occur and the related risks and exposures. This understanding provides a sound basis for developing recommendations to management on how the AIS control system should be improved.

INFORMATION SYSTEMS AUDITS

The purpose of an AIS audit is to review and evaluate the internal controls that protect the system. When performing an IS audit, auditors should ascertain that the following objectives are met:

1. Security provisions protect computer equipment, programs, and data from unauthorized access, modification, or destruction.
2. Program development is performed in accordance with management's general and specific authorization.
3. Program modifications have the authorization and approval of management.
4. Processing of transactions, files, reports, and other computer records is accurate and complete.
5. Source data that are inaccurate or improperly authorized are identified and handled according to prescribed managerial policies.
6. Computer data files are accurate, complete, and confidential.

Figure 16.2 depicts the relationship between these six objectives and IS components. Each of these objectives is now discussed in detail. Each description includes an audit plan to accomplish each objective, as well as the techniques and procedures necessary for carrying out the plan.

Objective 1: Security

Table 16.1 contains a framework for auditing computer security. It shows the following:

1. *Types of security errors and irregularities* faced by companies. They include accidental or intentional damage to system assets; unauthorized access, disclosure, or modification of data and programs; theft; and interruption of crucial business activities.
2. *Control procedures* to minimize security errors and irregularities. They include restricting physical and logical access, encrypting data, protecting against viruses, and preventing and recovering from system failures or disasters.

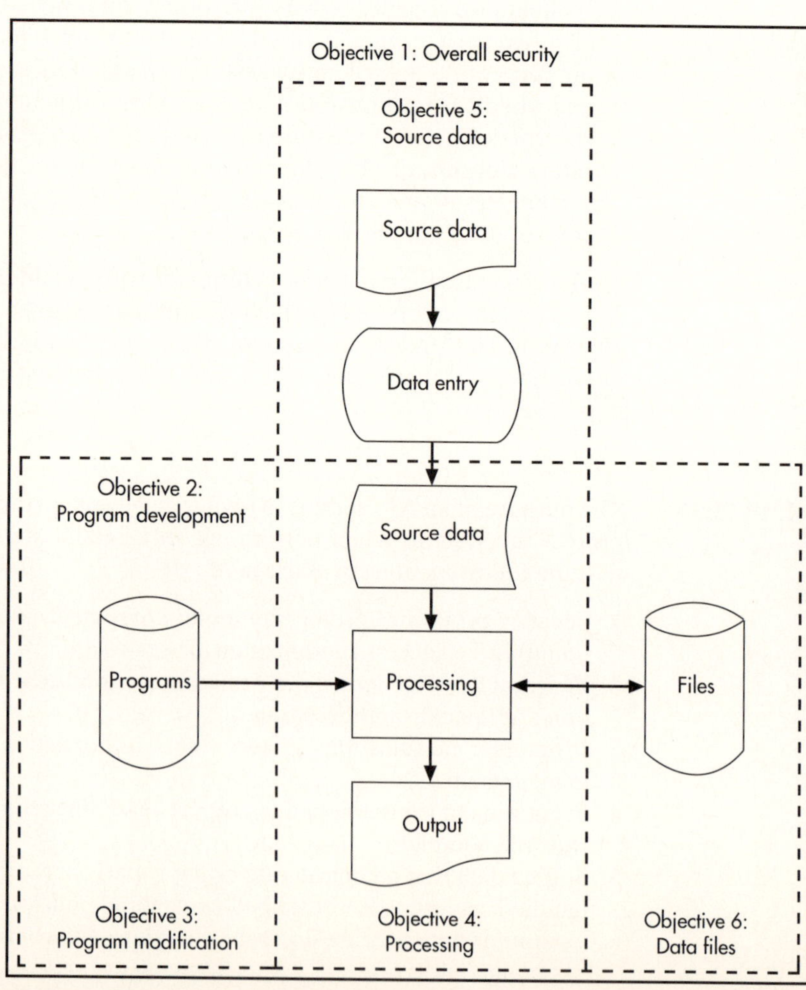

Figure 16.2

Information Systems Components and Related IS Audit Objectives

Table 16.1 Framework for Audit of Computer Security

Types of Errors and Irregularities	
• Accidental or intentional damage to hardware and files • Unauthorized access to programs, data files, and other system resources	• Unauthorized disclosure of confidential data • Theft or unauthorized modification of programs and data files • Interruption of crucial business activities
Control Procedures	
• Restrictions on physical access to computer equipment • Logical access controls based on password protection • Encryption of data during storage and transmission	• Virus protection procedures • File backup and recovery procedures • Fault-tolerant systems design • Disaster recovery planning
Audit Procedures: System Review	
• Inspect computer sites • Interview IS personnel about security procedures • Review written documentation about physical access policies and procedures • Review logical access policies and procedures • Review file backup and recovery policies and procedures	• Review procedures employed to minimize system downtime • Examine system access logs • Examine disaster recovery plan • Examine casualty insurance policies
Audit Procedures: Tests of Controls	
• Observe computer site access procedures • Observe the preparation and off-site storage of backup files • Review records of password assignment and modification • Investigate how unauthorized access attempts were dealt with • Verify the extent of data encryption use	• Verify the effective use of virus protection procedures • Verify the use of preventive maintenance and uninterruptible power • Verify amounts and limitations on insurance coverage • Examine results of test simulations of disaster recovery plan
Compensating Controls	
• Sound personnel policies • Effective user controls	• Segregation of incompatible duties

3. *System review audit procedures.* They include inspecting computer sites; interviewing personnel; reviewing policies and procedures; and examining access logs, insurance policies, and the disaster recovery plan.
4. *Tests of controls audit procedures.* Auditors test security controls by observing procedures, verifying that controls are in place and work, investigating errors or problems to ensure they were handled correctly, and examining any tests previously performed. For example, one way to test logical access controls is to try to break into a system. During a U.S. government agency security audit, auditors used agency terminals to gain unauthorized access to its computer system, disable its security-checking procedures, and control the system from the terminal. The security breakdown was possible because of poor administrative controls and inadequate security software.

5. *Compensating controls.* If security controls are seriously deficient, the organization faces substantial risks. Sound personnel policies and effective segregation of incompatible duties can partially compensate for poor computer security. Good user controls will also help, if user personnel can recognize unusual system output. However, it is unlikely these controls can continue to compensate indefinitely for poor computer security. Hence auditors should strongly recommend that steps be taken to correct security weaknesses.

Objective 2: Program Development

Table 16.2 provides a framework for reviewing and evaluating the second objective, the program development process. Two things could go wrong in program development: (1) inadvertent errors due to misunderstanding system specifications or careless programming and (2) unauthorized instructions deliberately inserted into the programs. These problems can be controlled by requiring both management and user authorization and approval, thorough testing, and proper documentation.

The auditor's role in systems development should be limited to an independent review of systems development activities. To maintain the objectivity necessary for performing an independent evaluation function, auditors should not be involved in developing the system. During the system review, auditors should gain an understanding of development procedures by discussing them

Table 16.2 **Framework for Audit of Program Development**

Types of Errors and Irregularities
- Inadvertent programming errors
- Unauthorized program code

Control Procedures
- Management approval of programming specifications
- User approval of programming specifications
- Thorough testing of new programs
- User acceptance testing
- Complete systems documentation, including approvals

Audit Procedures: System Review
- Independent and concurrent review of systems development process
- Review systems development policies and procedures
- Review systems authorization and approval procedures
- Review programming evaluation standards
- Review program documentation standards
- Review program testing and test approval procedures
- Discuss systems development procedures with management, system users, and IS personnel
- Review final application system documentation

Audit Procedures: Tests of Controls
- Interview users about involvement in systems design and implementation
- Review minutes of development team meetings for evidence of involvement
- Verify user sign-off at milestone points in the development process
- Review test specifications, test data, and results of systems tests

Compensating Controls
- Strong processing controls
- Independent processing of test data by auditor

with management, system users, and IS personnel. They should also review the policies, procedures, standards, and documentation listed in Table 16.2.

To test systems development controls, auditors should interview managers and system users, examine development approvals, and review the minutes of development team meetings. The auditor should review thoroughly all documentation relating to the testing process and ascertain that all program changes were tested. The auditor should examine the test specifications, review the test data, and evaluate the test results. If unexpected test results were obtained, the auditor should ascertain how the problem was resolved.

Strong processing controls (see objective 4) sometimes can compensate for inadequate development controls. If compensatory processing controls are relied on, the auditor should obtain persuasive evidence of compliance, using techniques such as independent processing of test data. If this type of evidence cannot be obtained, the auditor may have to conclude that a material weakness in internal control exists and that the risk of significant errors or irregularities in application programs is unacceptably high.

Objective 3: Program Modification

Table 16.3 presents a framework for auditing application program and system software changes. The same errors and irregularities that can take place during program changes can happen during program development. For example, one programmer assigned to modify his company's payroll system inserted a command to erase all company files if a termination notice was ever entered into his own payroll record. When the programmer was fired, his termination notice caused the system to crash and erase key files.

When a program change is submitted for approval, a list of all required updates should be compiled and then approved by management and program users. All program changes should be thoroughly tested and documented. During the change process, the development version of the program must be kept separate from the production version. After the amended program has received final approval, the change is implemented by replacing the production version with the development version.

During system review, auditors should gain an understanding of the change process by discussing it with management and user personnel. The policies, procedures, and standards for approving, modifying, testing, and documenting the changes should be examined. A complete set of final documentation materials for recent program changes, including test procedures and results, should be reviewed. Finally, the auditor should review the procedures used to restrict logical access to the development version of the program.

An important part of an auditor's tests of controls is to verify that program changes were identified, listed, approved, tested, and documented. This step requires that the auditor observe how changes are implemented in order to verify that separate development and production programs are maintained and that changes are implemented by someone independent of the user and programming functions. The auditor should review the development program's access control table to verify that only those users assigned to carry out the modification had access to the system.

To test for unauthorized program changes, auditors can use a source code comparison program. After auditors thoroughly test a newly developed

Table 16.3 Framework for Audit of Program Modification Procedures

Types of Errors and Irregularities
- Inadvertent programming errors
- Unauthorized program code

Control Procedures
- Listing of program components that are to be modified
- Management authorization and approval of program modifications
- User approval of program change specifications
- Thorough testing of program changes, including user acceptance test
- Complete program change documentation, including approvals
- Separate development, test, and production versions of program
- Changes implemented by personnel independent of users and programmers
- Logical access controls

Audit Procedures: System Review
- Review program modification policies, standards, and procedures
- Review documentation standards for program modification
- Review program modification testing and test approval procedures
- Discuss program modification policies and procedures with management, system users, and IS personnel
- Review final documentation for some typical program modifications
- Review test specifications, test data, and results of systems tests
- Review logical access control policies and procedures

Audit Procedures: Tests of Controls
- Verify user and IS management approval for program changes
- Verify that program components to be modified are identified and listed
- Verify that program change test procedures comply with standards
- Verify that program change documentation complies with standards
- Verify that logical access controls are in effect for program changes
- Observe program change implementation and verify that:
  - Separate development, test, and production versions are maintained
  - Changes are not implemented by either user or programming personnel
- To test for unauthorized or erroneous program changes, use:
  - Source code comparison program
  - Reprocessing
  - Parallel simulation

Compensating Controls
- Independent audit tests for unauthorized or erroneous program changes
- Strong processing controls

program (objective 2), they keep a copy of its source code. At any subsequent time the auditor may use the comparison program to compare the current version of the program with the original source code. If no changes have been authorized, these two versions should be identical. Therefore any unauthorized differences should result in an investigation. If the difference represents an authorized change, the auditor can refer to the program change specifications to ensure that the changes were authorized and correctly incorporated.

Two additional techniques detect unauthorized program changes. The **reprocessing** technique also uses a verified copy of the source code. On a surprise basis, the auditor uses the program to reprocess data and compare that output to the company's data. Discrepancies in the two sets of output are investigated to ascertain their cause. **Parallel simulation** is similar to reprocessing except that the auditor writes a program instead of saving a verified copy of the source code. The auditor's results are compared to the company's and any differences are investigated. Parallel simulation can be used to test a program during the implementation process. For example, Jason used this technique to test a portion of SPP's new sales department payroll system.

Auditors should observe the testing and implementation, review related authorizations and documents, and, if necessary, perform independent tests for each major program change. If this step is skipped and program change controls are subsequently determined to be inadequate, it may not be possible to rely on program outputs. In addition, auditors should always test programs on a surprise basis as a precaution against unauthorized program changes being inserted after the examination is completed and then removed just prior to the next scheduled audit.

If internal controls over program changes are deficient, a compensating control is source code comparison, reprocessing, or parallel simulation performed by the auditor. In addition, the presence of sound processing controls, independently tested by the auditor, can partially compensate for such deficiencies. However, if the deficiencies are caused by inadequate restrictions on program file access, the auditor should strongly recommend actions that will strengthen the organization's logical access controls.

Objective 4: Computer Processing

Table 16.4 provides a framework for auditing computer processing controls. The focus of the fourth objective is processing transactions, files, and related computer records to update files and data bases and to generate reports.

During computer processing the system might fail to detect erroneous input, improperly correct input errors, process erroneous input, or improperly distribute or disclose output. The control procedures to detect and prevent these errors and the system review and tests of control procedures the auditor employs are shown in Table 16.4. The purpose of these audit procedures is to gain an understanding of the controls, evaluate their adequacy, and observe operations for evidence that the controls are actually being followed.

Auditors must periodically reevaluate processing controls to ensure their continued reliability. If processing controls are unsatisfactory, user and source data controls may be strong enough to compensate. If not, a material weakness exists and steps should be taken to eliminate the control deficiencies.

Several specialized techniques allow the auditor to use the computer to test processing controls. They include processing test data, using concurrent audit techniques, and analyzing program logic. Each of these procedures is explained next.

Test Data Processing. One way to test a program is to process a hypothetical series of valid and invalid transactions. The program should process all of the valid transactions correctly and identify and reject all of the invalid ones. All logic paths should be checked for proper functioning by one or more of the test transactions. Examples of invalid data include records with missing data, fields

Table 16.4 **Framework for Audit of Computer Processing Controls**

Types of Errors and Irregularities
- Failure to detect incorrect, incomplete, or unauthorized input data
- Failure to properly correct errors flagged by data editing procedures
- Introduction of errors into master files during file updating
- Improper distribution or disclosure of computer output

Control Procedures
- Computer data editing routines
- Proper use of internal and external file labels
- Reconciliation of batch totals
- Effective error correction procedures
- Understandable operating documentation and run manuals
- Competent supervision of computer operations
- Effective handling of data input and output by data control personnel
- File change listings and summaries prepared for user department review
- Maintenance of proper environmental conditions in computer facility

Audit Procedures: System Review
- Review administrative documentation for processing control standards
- Review systems documentation for data editing and other processing controls
- Review operating documentation for completeness and clarity
- Review copies of error listings, batch total reports, and file change lists
- Observe computer operations and data control functions
- Discuss processing controls with operators and IS supervisory personnel

Audit Procedures: Tests of Controls
- Evaluate adequacy of processing control standards and procedures
- Evaluate adequacy and completeness of data editing controls
- Verify adherence to processing control procedures by observing computer operations and the data control function
- Verify that selected application system output is properly distributed
- Reconcile a sample of batch totals, and follow up on discrepancies
- Trace disposition of a sample of errors flagged by data edit routines to ensure proper handling
- Verify processing accuracy for a sample of sensitive transactions
- Verify processing accuracy for selected computer-generated transactions
- Search for erroneous or unauthorized code via analysis of program logic
- Check accuracy and completeness of processing controls using test data
- Monitor on-line processing systems using concurrent audit techniques

Compensating Controls
- Strong user controls
- Effective source data controls

containing unreasonably large amounts, invalid account numbers or processing codes, nonnumeric data in numeric fields, and records out of sequence.

Several resources are available when preparing test data. For example:

- A listing of actual transactions.
- The test transactions the programmer used to test the program.
- A **test data generator program,** which automatically prepares test data based on program specifications.

In a batch processing system, the company's program and a copy of relevant files are used to process the test data. The results are compared to the predetermined correct output; discrepancies indicate processing errors or control deficiencies that should be thoroughly investigated.

In an on-line system, auditors enter test data using a data entry terminal and observe and log the system's response. If the system accepts erroneous or invalid test transactions, the auditor reverses the effects of the transactions, investigates the problem, and corrects the deficiency.

Although processing of test transactions is usually effective, it does have the following disadvantages:

1. The auditor must spend considerable time developing an understanding of the system and preparing an adequate set of test transactions.
2. Care must be taken to ensure that test data do not affect the company's master file. The auditor can reverse the effects of the test transactions or process the transactions in a separate run using a master file copy. However, a separate run removes some of the authenticity obtained from processing test data with regular transactions. Also, since the reversal procedures may reveal the existence and nature of the auditor's test to key personnel, it can be less effective than a concealed test.

Concurrent Audit Techniques. Millions of dollars of transactions can be processed in an on-line system without leaving a satisfactory audit trail. In such cases, evidence gathered after data processing is insufficient for audit purposes. In addition, since many on-line systems process transactions on a continuous basis, it is difficult or impossible to stop the system in order to perform audit tests. Thus the auditor uses **concurrent audit techniques** to continuously monitor the system and collect audit evidence while live data are processed during regular operating hours. Concurrent audit techniques use **embedded audit modules,** which are program code that performs audit functions. They also report test results to the auditor and store the evidence collected for the auditor's review. Concurrent audit techniques are time-consuming and difficult to use, but are less so if incorporated when programs are developed.

Auditors commonly use five concurrent audit techniques. An **integrated test facility (ITF)** technique places a small set of fictitious records in the master files. The records might represent a fictitious division, department, or branch office or a customer or supplier. Processing test transactions to update these dummy records will not affect the actual records. Because fictitious and actual records are processed together, company employees usually remain unaware that this testing is taking place. The system must distinguish ITF records from actual records, collect information on the effects of the test transactions, and report the results. The auditor compares processing and expected results in order to verify that the system and its controls are operating correctly.

In a batch processing system the ITF technique eliminates the need to reverse test transactions and is easily concealed from operating employees. ITF is well suited to testing on-line processing systems because test transactions can be submitted on a frequent basis, processed with actual transactions, and traced throughout every processing stage. All this can be accomplished without disrupting regular processing operations. However, care must be taken not to combine dummy and actual records during the reporting process.

The **snapshot technique** examines the way transactions are processed. Selected transactions are marked with a special code that triggers the snapshot process. Audit modules in the program record these transactions and their master file records before and after processing. Snapshot data are recorded in a special file and reviewed by the auditor to verify that all processing steps have been properly executed.

SCARF (system control audit review file) uses embedded audit modules to continuously monitor transaction activity and collect data on transactions with special audit significance. The data are recorded in a SCARF file or **audit log.** Transactions that might be recorded in a SCARF file include those which exceed a specified dollar limit, involve inactive accounts, deviate from company policy, or contain write-downs of asset values. Periodically the auditor receives a printout of the SCARF file, examines the information to identify any questionable transactions, and performs any necessary follow-up investigation.

Audit hooks are audit routines that flag suspicious transactions. For example, internal auditors at State Farm Life Insurance determined that their policyholder system was vulnerable to fraud every time a policyholder changed his or her name or address and then subsequently withdrew funds from the policy. They devised a system of audit hooks to tag records with a name or address change. The internal audit department is now notified when a tagged record is associated with a withdrawal and can appropriately investigate the transaction for fraud. When audit hooks are employed, auditors can be informed of questionable transactions as soon as they occur. This approach, known as **real-time notification,** displays a message on the auditor's terminal. Additional information about State Farm's use of audit hooks, including how a major fraud was detected, is contained in Focus 16.1.

Continuous and intermittent simulation (CIS) embeds an audit module in a data base management system. The CIS module examines all transactions that update the DBMS using criteria similar to those of SCARF. If a transaction has special audit significance, the module independently processes the data (in a manner similar to parallel simulation), records the results, and compares them with those obtained by the DBMS. If any discrepancies exist, the details are written onto an audit log for subsequent investigation. If serious discrepancies are discovered, the CIS may prevent the DBMS from executing the update process.

Analysis of Program Logic. If an auditor suspects that a particular application program contains unauthorized code or serious errors, a detailed analysis of the program logic may be necessary. Since this process is time-consuming and requires programming language proficiency, it should be used only as a last resort. To perform the analysis, auditors refer to systems and program flowcharts, program documentation, and a listing of the program source code. The following software packages serve as aids in this analysis:

- **Automated flowcharting programs,** which interpret program source code and generate a corresponding program flowchart.

FOCUS 16.1

Using Audit Hooks at State Farm Life

At State Farm Life Insurance Company the computer system consists of a host computer located in Bloomington, Illinois, and 26 minicomputers in the regional offices. More than fifteen hundred CRT input devices located in the regional offices are used to update the 3.9 million individual policyholder master records that reside in the host computer. The system handles more than 30 million transactions a year.

Since the system is an on-line, real-time one, all master record updating and transaction processing take place almost instantly. Paper audit trails have virtually vanished. Documents in support of changes to the policyholder master record have been all but eliminated or are only held a short time before disposition. Sitting in the 3.9 million asset records are policyholder funds valued at more than $6.7 billion. Anyone with access and a working knowledge of the system could potentially commit fraud.

The challenge facing the internal audit staff was to identify the key life insurance transactions in which the potential for fraud existed. The internal auditors brainstormed ways to defraud the system. Various system users were interviewed, and they provided the internal auditors with extremely valuable insights.

Auditors currently have 33 embedded audit hooks monitoring 42 different transactions. One hook is designed to monitor unusual transactions in transfer accounts, which are clearing accounts for temporarily holding funds that are to be credited to multiple accounts.

The audit hooks have been very successful. One employee obtained cash by processing a fraudulent loan for $250 on her brother's life insurance policy, forging her brother's endorsement on the check, and cashing it at a liquor store. To cover up the fraud, the employee needed to repay the $250 loan before the annual status report was sent to her brother. She did so by using a series of fictitious transactions involving a transfer account. However, this fraud was uncovered almost immediately when the transfer account audit hook, in response to the first of these fictitious transactions, generated a computer output notification (CON) that was sent to the auditor. Within one month after the CON was received, the case had been investigated and the employee terminated.

Focus Questions

1. What characteristics of audit hooks make them useful to auditors?
2. When should audit hooks be designed and implemented?

Linda Marie Leinicke, W. Max Rexroad, and John D. Ward, "Computer Fraud Auditing: It Works." Reprinted with permission from August 1990 issue of *Internal Auditor,* published by The Institute of Internal Auditors, Inc.

- **Automated decision table programs,** which generate a decision table representing the program logic.
- **Scanning routines,** which search a program for occurrences of a specified variable name or other character combinations.
- **Mapping programs,** which identify unexecuted program code. This software could have uncovered the program code the unscrupulous programmer inserted to erase all computer files when he was terminated as detailed in an earlier example.
- **Program tracing,** which sequentially prints all application program steps (line numbers or paragraph names) executed during a program run. This list is intermingled with regular output so auditors can observe the precise sequence of events that unfold during program execution. Program tracing helps auditors detect unauthorized program instructions, incorrect logic paths, and unexecuted program code.

Objective 5: Source Data

Table 16.5 shows the internal controls that prevent, detect, and correct inaccurate or unauthorized source data. It also shows the system review and tests of

Table 16.5 **Framework for Audit of Source Data Controls**

Types of Errors and Irregularities
- Inaccurate source data
- Unauthorized source data

Control Procedures
- Effective handling of source data input by data control personnel
- User authorization of source data input
- Preparation and reconciliation of batch control totals
- Logging of the receipt, movement, and disposition of source data input
- Check digit verification
- Key verification
- Use of turnaround documents
- Computer data editing routines
- File change listings and summaries prepared for user department review
- Effective procedures for correcting and resubmitting erroneous data

Audit Procedures: System Review
- Review documentation about responsibilities of data control function
- Review administrative documentation for source data control standards
- Review methods of authorization and examine authorization signatures
- Review accounting systems documentation to identify source data content and processing steps and specific source data controls used
- Document accounting source data controls using input control matrix
- Discuss source data control procedures with data control personnel, IS management, and system users

Audit Procedures: Tests of Controls
- Observe and evaluate data control department operations and specific data control procedures
- Verify proper maintenance and use of data control log
- Evaluate how items recorded in the error log are dealt with
- Examine samples of accounting source data for proper authorization
- Reconcile a sample of batch totals, and follow up on discrepancies
- Trace disposition of a sample of errors flagged by data edit routines

Compensating Controls
- Strong user controls
- Strong processing controls

control procedures that auditors use for evaluation. In an on-line system the source data entry and processing functions are one operation. Therefore source data controls such as proper authorization and editing data input are integrated with processing controls.

Auditors use an **input controls matrix,** such as the one depicted in Fig. 16.3, to document the review of source data controls. The matrix shows the control procedures applied to each field of an input record.

Auditors should make sure that the data control function is independent of other functions, maintains a data control log, handles errors, and ensures the overall efficiency of operations. It is usually not economically feasible for small businesses and PC installations to have an independent data control function. To compensate, user department controls over data preparation, batch control totals, edit programs, restrictions on physical and logical access to the system, and error-handling procedures must be stronger. These procedures should be

Figure 16.3

Input Controls Matrix

Record Name: Employer Weekly Time Report / **Input Controls**	**Field Names:** Employee number	Last name	Department number	Transaction code	Week ending (date)	Regular hours	Overtime hours		Comments
Batch totals						✓	✓		
Hash totals	✓								
Record counts									Yes
Cross-footing balance									No
Key verification	✓					✓	✓		
Visual inspection									All fields
Check digit verification	✓								
Prenumbered forms									No
Turnaround document									No
Edit program									Yes
Sequence check	✓								
Field check	✓		✓			✓	✓		
Sign check									
Validity check	✓		✓	✓	✓				
Limit check						✓	✓		
Reasonableness test						✓	✓		
Redundant data check	✓	✓	✓						
Completeness test				✓	✓	✓	✓		
Overflow procedure									
Other:									

the focus of the auditor's system review and tests of controls whenever the presence of an independent data control function is absent.

Although source data controls may not change often, the strictness with which they are applied may. Therefore auditors should test them on a regular basis. The auditor tests the system by evaluating samples of source data for proper authorization. A sample of batch controls should be reconciled. A sample of data edit errors should be evaluated to check that they were resolved and resubmitted into the system.

If source data controls are inadequate, user department and computer processing controls may compensate. If not, the auditor should strongly recommend steps to correct the source data control deficiencies.

Objective 6: Data Files

Objective 6 is concerned with the accuracy, integrity, and security of data stored in machine-readable files. Data storage risks include the unauthorized modification, destruction, or disclosure of data. Many of the controls discussed in Chapter 14 are used to protect the system against these risks. If file controls are seriously deficient, especially with respect to physical or logical access or to backup and recovery procedures, the auditor should strongly recommend they be rectified. Table 16.6 summarizes the errors, controls, and audit procedures for this objective.

The auditing-by-objectives approach is a comprehensive, systematic, and effective means of evaluating internal controls in an AIS. It can be implemented using an audit procedures checklist for each objective. The checklist

Table 16.6 **Framework for Audit of Data File Controls**

Types of Errors and Irregularities

- Destruction of stored data due to inadvertent errors, hardware or software malfunctions, and intentional acts of sabotage of vandalism
- Unauthorized modification or disclosure of stored data

Control Procedures

- Secure file library and restrictions on physical access to data files
- Logical access controls using passwords and access control matrix
- Proper use of file labels and write-protection mechanisms
- Concurrent update controls
- Use of data encryption for highly confidential data
- Use of virus protection software
- Maintenance of backup copies of all data files in an off-site location
- Use of checkpoint and rollback to facilitate system recovery

Audit Procedures: System Review

- Review documentation for functions of file library operation
- Review logical access policies and procedures
- Review operating documentation to determine prescribed standards for
  - Use of file labels and write-protection mechanisms
  - Use of virus protection software
  - Use of backup data storage
  - System recovery, including checkpoint and rollback procedures
- Review systems documentation to examine prescribed procedures for
  - Use of concurrent update controls and data encryption
  - Control of file conversions
  - Reconciling master file totals with independent control totals
- Examine disaster recovery plan
- Discuss data file control procedures with IS managers and operators

Audit Procedures: Tests of Controls

- Observe and evaluate file library operations
- Review records of password assignment and modification
- Observe and evaluate file-handling procedures by operations personnel
- Observe the preparation and off-site storage of backup files
- Verify the effective use of virus protection procedures
- Verify the use of concurrent update controls and data encryption
- Verify completeness, currency, and testing of disaster recovery plan
- Reconcile master file totals with separately maintained control totals
- Observe the procedures used to control file conversion

Compensating Controls

- Strong user controls
- Effective computer security controls
- Strong processing controls

FOCUS 16.2

Battling Federal Budget Deficits with Audit Software

The U.S. government is finding that computer audit software is a valuable tool in its attempts to reduce massive federal budget deficits. Audit software is being used to identify fraudulent Medicare claims, pinpoint excessive charges by defense contractors, and in many other ways.

A computer audit by the General Accounting Office (GAO) cross-checked figures with the IRS and discovered that thousands of veterans lied about their income to qualify for pension benefits. The audit revealed that 116,000 veterans receiving pensions on the basis of need failed to disclose $338 million in income from savings accounts, stock dividends, or rents. Over 13,600 veterans underreported their income by at least $4000, 5500 by $10,000 or more, and one didn't report over $300,000.

Before the computer check was instituted, the VA relied on the vets for accurate income reports. Once the VA notified beneficiaries that their income would be verified with the IRS and the Social Security Administration, the pension rolls dropped by more than 13,000, at a savings of $9 million a month, the GAO reported.

The VA plans to use the same system for checking income levels of those applying for medical care. If their income is found to be above a certain level, patients will be required to make copayments.

Focus Questions

1. What is it about computer audit software that makes it so useful to government auditors?
2. In what other ways could the government use computer audit software?

should help the auditor reach a separate conclusion for each objective and suggest compensating controls when an objective is not fully achieved. A separate version of the checklist should be completed for each significant application.

Auditors should review system designs while there is still time to adopt their suggestions for control and audit features. Techniques like ITF, snapshot, SCARF, audit hooks, and real-time notification should be incorporated into a system during the design process, rather than as an afterthought. Similarly, most application control techniques are easier to design into the system than to add after the system is developed.

FINANCIAL AUDITS AND COMPUTER SOFTWARE

A number of computer programs, called **computer audit software (CAS)** or **generalized audit software (GAS),** have been written especially for auditors. They are available from software vendors and the larger public accounting firms. In essence, CAS is a computer program that, based on the auditor's specifications, generates programs that perform the audit functions. CAS is ideally suited for examination of large data files to identify records needing further audit scrutiny. For example, Focus 16.2 describes how the U.S. government uses CAS to battle the federal budget. Table 16.7 contains a list of CAS functions and one or more audit examples for each function.

Figure 16.4 shows how CAS is used. The auditor's first step is to decide on audit objectives, learn about the files to be audited, design the audit reports, and determine how to produce them. This information is recorded on reformatted specification sheets and entered into the system via a data entry program. This program creates specification records that the CAS uses to produce one or more auditing programs. The auditing programs process the source

Table 16.7 **General Functions of Computer Audit Software**

Function	Explanation	Examples
Reformatting	Read data in different formats and data structures, and convert to a common format and structure	Read inventory records from purchasing data base and convert to an inventory file usable by the GAS program
File manipulation	Sort records into sequential order; merge files sequenced on the same sort key	Sort inventory records by location; merge customer transaction files with receivables master file
Calculation	Perform the four basic arithmetic operations: add, subtract, multiply, and divide	Foot client accounts receivable file; recalculate client inventory valuation; recalculate client depreciation; sum employee payroll by department
Data selection	Review data files to retrieve records meeting specified criteria	Identify customer accounts having a balance exceeding the credit limit; select all purchase transactions in excess of a specified dollar amount
Data analysis	Examine records for errors or missing values; compare fields in related records for inconsistencies	Perform data editing of client files; compare personnel and payroll files to verify consistency
File processing	Provide programming capability for file creation, updating, and downloading to a personal computer	Use parallel simulation to verify that client gross pay calculations are correct; download sample of client inventory records to personal computer for further analysis to support inventory test counts
Statistics	Stratify file records by item valuation; select statistical samples; analyze statistical sampling results	Stratify customer accounts by size of account balance and select a stratified sample of accounts for audit confirmation
Report generation	Format and print reports and documents	Prepare analysis of financial statement ratios and trends; prepare accounts receivable aging schedule; prepare audit confirmations

files and perform the auditing operations needed to produce the specified audit reports. Frequently, an initial CAS computer run is performed to extract key auditing information and place it in an audit work file. Additional audit reports and analyses are generated by subsequent computer runs that use the audit work file as input.

The following case illustrates the value of audit software. In a small New England town a new tax collector was elected, defeating the incumbent. The new tax collector requested an audit of the city's tax collection records. Using CAS, the auditor accessed the tax collection records for the past four years, sorted them by collection date, summed the amount of taxes collected monthly, and prepared a four-year summary report of monthly tax collections. The analysis revealed that tax collections during January and July, the two busiest months, had declined by 58% and 72%, respectively. Auditors used the CAS to compare the tax collection records, one by one, with the city's property records.

Figure 16.4

Overview of GAS Processing

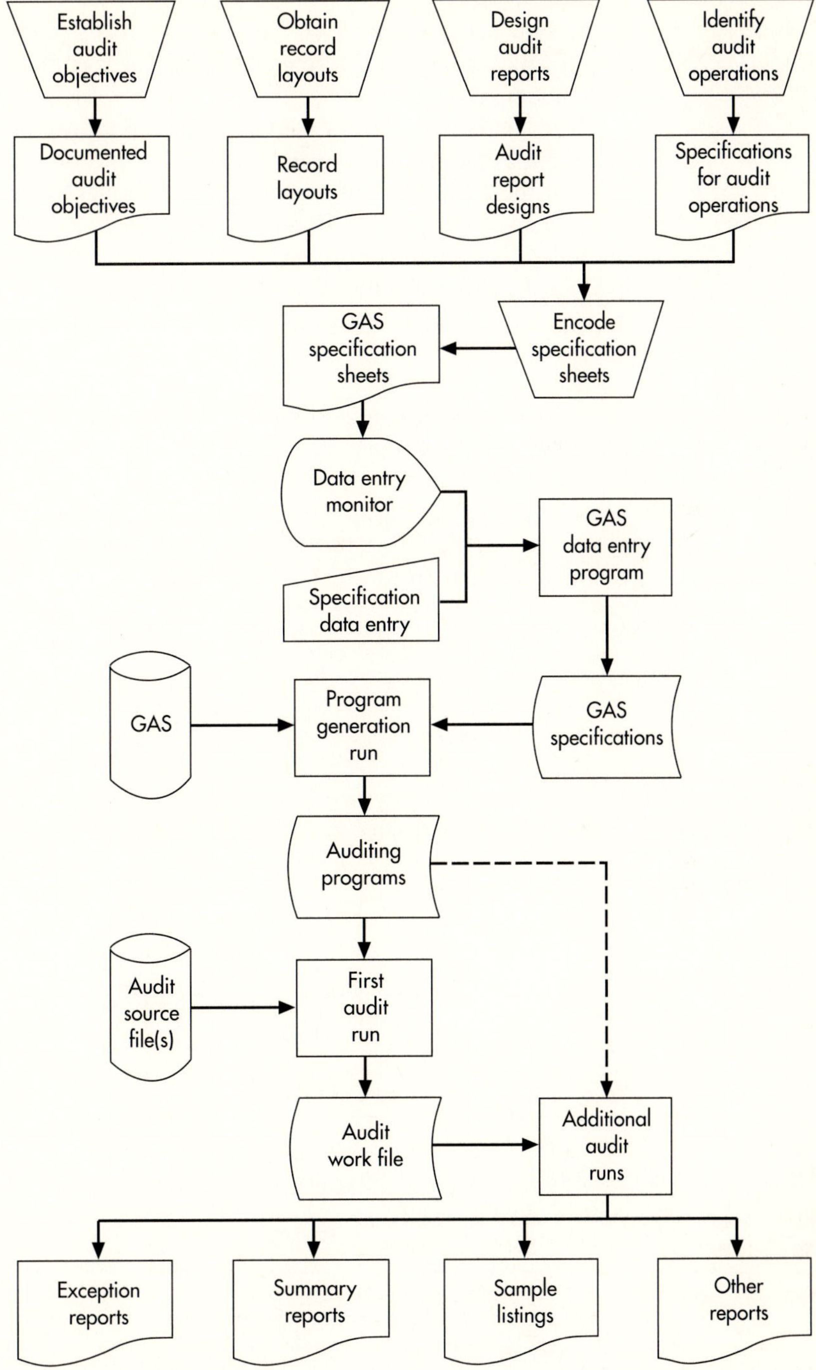

The ensuing report identified several discrepancies, including one case where the former tax collector used another taxpayer's payment to cover her own delinquent tax bills. The former tax collector was arrested and charged with embezzlement.

The primary purpose of CAS is to assist the auditor in reviewing and retrieving information in computer files. When the auditor receives the CAS reports, most of the audit work still remains to be done. Items on exception reports must be investigated, file totals must be verified against other sources of information such as the general ledger, and audit samples must be examined and evaluated. Although the advantages of using CAS are numerous and compelling, CAS cannot replace the auditor's judgment or free her from other phases of the audit.

An Example of an Audit Software Application

Jason Scott was assigned to audit the accounts receivable information produced by the AIS at Northwest Builders Supply (NBS) in Tacoma, Washington. The system has an accounts receivable master file and transaction detail files for sales on account, cash collections, and credit memos. Copies of record layouts for these files are reproduced in Fig. 16.5. Jason's supervisor specified the following objectives for the CAS application:

Figure 16.5

Record Layouts for Accounts Receivable System

Record Name: Accounts Receivable Master

Field Name	Account number	Name	Address				Credit code	Credit limit	Previous balance	Current balance
			Street	City	State	Zip				
Position	1 – 6	7 – 31	32 – 56	57 – 74	75 – 76	77 – 81	82 – 83	84 – 91	92 – 99	100 – 107

Record Name: Sales Detail

Field Name	Account number	Transaction code	Transaction date	Invoice number	Amount	
Position	1 – 6	7	8 – 13	14 – 18	19 – 26	

Record Name: Cash Collections Detail

Field Name	Account number	Transaction code	Transaction date	Reference number	Amount	
Position	1 – 6	7	8 – 13	14 – 18	19 – 26	

Record Name: Credit Memo Detail

Field Name	Account number	Transaction code	Transaction date	Credit memo number	Amount	
Position	1 – 6	7	8 – 13	14 – 18	19 – 26	

1. Recalculate the current balance of every customer master record using the previous balance and the intervening transactions. Identify all accounts with an incorrect current balance.
2. Sum the current balance, credit sales, cash collections, and credit memo amounts. They will be verified using independently maintained information.
3. Perform edit checks on selected fields in each file to confirm the reliability of data editing procedures.
4. Check transaction files for records that do not match a master record.
5. Prepare an accounts receivable aging schedule and an analysis of accounts having current balances in excess of their credit limit. These reports will be used to evaluate the sufficiency of NBS's allowance for uncollectible accounts and assess the performance of NBS's credit department.
6. Select a sample of accounts for confirmation. This will be used to verify the existence and accuracy of the receivables in NBS's customer master file.
7. Analyze cash collections and credit memos subsequent to the test date for those customers who do not respond to confirmation requests.

Figure 16.6 shows the sequence of computer operations Jason used to achieve the first six objectives. RUN 1 sorted the four source files into account number sequence and merged them into a combined master and transaction file. Details about the two transaction records lacking a matching master record were listed on the unmatched transaction report. Jason discovered that keying errors had caused invalid account numbers to be entered into these transaction records. Corrections were promptly recorded in NBS's records and in Jason's merged file.

During RUN 2 Jason completed the following functions:

- Extracted the records he needed from the merged file and placed them in sequential order on an audit work file.
- Created an audit record for each customer containing the account number, name, address, credit limit, current balance, last invoice (sale) date and amount, last credit payment or credit memo date, and last credit amount on the audit work file.
- Edited information on the merged master and transaction file and printed the exceptions on an exception report.
- Added sales to the previous balance and subtracted cash collections and credit memo amounts. If any results were not equal to the customer's current balance, all data pertaining to the account were printed on an exception report.
- Edited selected data fields and printed all erroneous records on the exception report. The edits included a validity check on the transaction codes and dates, a completeness test for each record, a sign test of the current balance, field checks of all numeric fields, and a sequence check based on account number. He investigated the errors and concluded that they were caused by inadvertent mistakes in data entry. Luckily, they had a negligible effect on NBS's accounts and did not affect the overall reliability of their accounts receivable information.
- Footed the amount fields for cash collections, sales, credit memos, and account balances and printed the totals on the edit exceptions report. He

Figure 16.6

Application of Computer Audit Software to Accounts Receivable

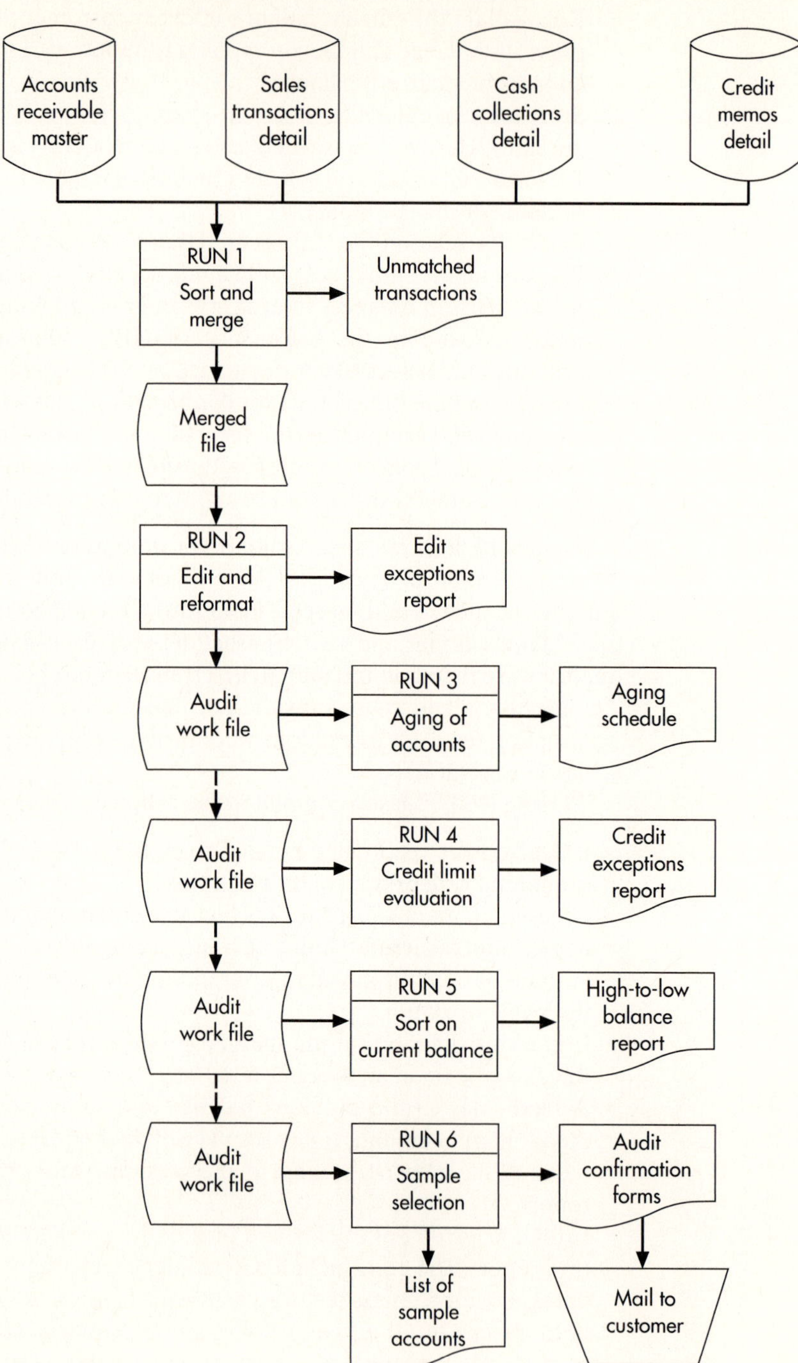

compared these totals with corresponding totals from NBS's sales and cash receipts journals and general ledger accounts.

RUN 3 processed the audit work file to generate an aging schedule for receivables. RUN 4 compared the current balance against the credit limit for each customer. If a limit was exceeded, the account was printed on the credit exceptions report. Jason gave the aging schedule and the exceptions report to his supervisor, who used them to evaluate the allowance for uncollectible accounts and the credit department's effectiveness in administering credit policies.

In RUN 5 the audit work file was sorted into sequence from high to low current balance and classified into a dollar range ($0 to $500, $501 to $1000, and so on to all accounts over $20,000). A summary report was printed listing the number of accounts and the cumulative dollar amount for each range. Jason used this report to select an accounts receivable confirmation sample. He selected all customer accounts above $15,000, 10% of accounts between $5001 and $15,000, 1% of those $5000 or less. This **stratified sampling** plan allows auditors to include a high percentage of the total dollars in the population, even though the sample may include a low percentage of the total number of accounts. The high-to-low-balance summary report helps the auditor decide how many sample strata (or ranges) to use and what their boundaries should be.

RUN 6 randomly selected and printed the accounts for the smaller strata and printed all of the confirmations as well. Although Jason mailed the confirmation forms to all of NBS's customers, several chose not to respond. Jason used the CAS to examine subsequent collections from these particular customers and verify that they paid off the amounts they owed NBS.

Once Jason obtained and examined confirmation responses and other related evidence, he would use the audit software to evaluate the results of the sample. Northwest's audit software program is capable of statistically evaluating sample results by computing means, variances, confidence intervals, and sampling risks.

The CAS allowed Jason to gather and evaluate evidence quickly and inexpensively. Note that Jason was able to perform these functions independently of NBS's IS personnel. The results Jason obtained from the CAS represented only the first step in the audit. Jason still had to investigate exceptions, audit sample items, independently verify file totals, evaluate the significance of summary reports, and perform other audit procedures.

OPERATIONAL AUDITS OF AN AIS

The techniques and procedures used in operational audits are similar to those of IS and financial audits. The basic difference is that the IS audit scope is confined to internal controls whereas the financial audit scope is limited to IS output. In contrast, the operational audit scope is much broader, encompassing all aspects of IS management. In addition, operational audit objectives include evaluating such factors as effectiveness, efficiency, and goal achievement.

The first step in an operational audit is audit planning, during which the scope and objectives of the audit are established, a preliminary review of the system is performed, and a tentative audit program is prepared.

Evidence collection includes the following activities:

- Reviewing operating policies and documentation.
- Confirming procedures with management and operating personnel.
- Observing operating functions and activities.
- Examining financial and operating plans and reports.
- Testing the accuracy of operating information.
- Testing controls.

At the evidence evaluation stage the auditor measures the actual system against an ideal one, a system that follows all the best principles of systems management. One important consideration is that the *results* of management policies and practices are more significant than the policies and practices themselves. That is, if good results are achieved through policies and practices that are theoretically deficient, then the auditor must carefully consider whether recommended improvements would substantially improve results. In any event, the auditor should thoroughly document the findings and conclusions and communicate the audit results to management.

Being a good operational auditor requires some degree of management experience. Those with strong auditing backgrounds but weak or no management experience often lack the perspective necessary to understand the management process. Thus the ideal operational auditor is a person with auditing training and experience and a few years' experience in a managerial position.

SUMMARY AND CASE CONCLUSION

Jason was trying to figure out how his parallel simulation program generated sales commission figures that differed from those of SPP's program. When he studied the figures, he noticed that in all the differences the sales commission was higher than average. This meant there might have been a systematic error in one of the programs. After verifying that his program was correct, he asked to review a copy of SPP's program.

The program was very lengthy, so Jason used the "scanning" technique to search the code for a specified set of characters. Under the new commission policy the commission rate changes when sales for the period exceed $40,000. Jason searched the code for occurrences of "40000," which directed him to the place where the commission rate structure resides. To his astonishment, he discovered a commission rate of 0.085 for sales in excess of $40,000, while the policy called for only 0.075. Some quick calculations confirmed this was the source of the differences between the two programs.

Jason reported his findings to his supervisor, who called in the audit manager. A meeting was arranged between the audit manager and the head of the systems development team. The meeting was quite embarrassing for the team head and her staff, but the coding error was acknowledged and corrected.

The audit manager called Jason to congratulate him and informed him that if the programming error had gone undetected, Seattle Paper would have paid over $100,000 per year in excess sales commissions. While Jason was grateful to receive the manager's praise, he also took the opportunity to point out deficiencies in the programming practices employed by the development team. First, the commission rate table had been embedded in the program code; good programming practice would require that it be stored in a separate table to be called by the program when needed. Second, he suggested that the incident called into question the quality of SPP's program development and testing practices. Jason asked whether a more extensive operational audit of those practices might be appropriate. The audit manager agreed that this might be worth looking into, and he promised to raise the issue at his next meeting with Northwest's director of internal auditing.

KEY TERMS

auditing
financial audit
information systems (IS) audit
operational audit
management audit
inherent risk
control risk
detection risk
materiality
reasonable assurance
systems review
tests of control
compensating controls
reprocessing
parallel simulation
test data generator program
concurrent audit techniques
embedded audit modules
integrated test facility (ITF)
snapshot technique
SCARF
audit log
audit hooks
real-time notification
continuous and intermittent simulation (CIS)
automated flowcharting programs
automated decision table programs
scanning routines
mapping programs
program tracing
input controls matrix
computer audit software (CAS)
generalized audit software (GAS)
stratified sampling

CHAPTER QUIZ

1. Which of the following is a characteristic of auditing?
  a. Auditing is a systematic, step-by-step process.
  b. Auditing involves the collection and review of evidence.
  c. Auditing involves the use of established criteria to evaluate evidence.
  d. All of the above are characteristic of auditing.

2. Which of the following is *not* one reason why an internal auditor should participate in internal control reviews during the design of new systems?
  a. It is more economical to design controls during the design stage than to do so later.
  b. It eliminates the need for testing controls during regular audits.
  c. It minimizes the need for expensive postimplementation modifications.
  d. It permits the design of audit trails while they are economical.

3. Which type of audit involves a review of general and application controls, with a focus on determining whether there is compliance with policies and adequate safeguarding of assets?
  a. Information systems audits
  b. Financial audits
  c. Operational audits
  d. Compliance audits

4. At what step in the audit process do the concepts of reasonable assurance and materiality enter into the auditor's decision process?
  a. Planning
  b. Evidence collection
  c. Evidence evaluation
  d. *Materiality* is important in *all* 3 steps.

5. Examining whether the necessary controls have been designed into the system is called
  a. risk analysis.
  b. systems review.

c. tests of controls.
d. the risk-based approach to auditing.

6. Which of the following procedures is not used to detect unauthorized program changes?
a. Source code comparison
b. Parallel simulation
c. Reprocessing
d. Reprogramming code

7. The concurrent audit technique that monitors all transactions and collects data on those that meet certain characteristics specified by the auditor is called
a. an integrated test facility.
b. snapshot techniques.
c. SCARF.
d. audit hooks.

8. A computer technique that assists an auditor in understanding program logic by identifying all occurrences of specific variables is called
a. a mapping program.
b. program tracing.
c. automated flowcharting.
d. a scanning routine.

9. A computer program written especially for audit use is called
a. GAS
b. SCARF
c. ITF
d. CIS

10. The focus of an operational audit is on
a. the reliability and integrity of the financial information.
b. the efficient use of resources.
c. internal controls.
d. safeguarding assets.

DISCUSSION QUESTIONS

16.1 Auditing an AIS effectively requires that an auditor have some knowledge of computers and their accounting applications. However, it may not be feasible for every auditor to be a "computer expert." Discuss the extent to which auditors should possess computer expertise in order to be effective auditors.

16.2 Should internal auditors be members of systems development teams that design and implement an AIS? Why or why not?

16.3 Berwick Industries is a fast-growing corporation that manufactures industrial containers. The company has a very sophisticated AIS utilizing advanced technology. Berwick's executives have decided to pursue listing the company's securities on a national stock exchange, but they have been advised that their listing application would be stronger if they were to create an internal audit department.

At present, Berwick doesn't have any employees with audit experience. To staff its new internal audit function, Berwick could (a) train some of its computer specialists in auditing, (b) hire experienced auditors and train them to understand Berwick's IS, (c) use a combination of the first two approaches, or (d) try a different approach. Which approach would you support, and why?

16.4 In 1985 the assistant finance director for the city of Tustin, California, was fired after city officials discovered that she had used her access to city computers to cancel her daughter's $300 water bill. An investigation revealed that she had embezzled a large sum of money from the city in this manner over a long period. She was able to conceal the embezzlement for so long because the amount embezzled always fell within a 2% error factor used by the city's internal auditors. Should Tustin's internal auditors have discovered this fraud earlier? Discuss.

PROBLEMS

16.1 You are the director of internal auditing at a university. Recently, you met with Issa Arnita, the manager of administrative data processing and expressed the desire to establish a more effective interface between the two departments. Arnita wants your help with a new computerized accounts payable system currently in development. He recommends that your department assume line responsibility for auditing suppliers' invoices prior to payment. He also wants internal auditing to make suggestions during system development, assist in its installation, and approve the completed system after making a final review.

REQUIRED

Would you accept or reject each of the following? Why?

a. The recommendation that your department be responsible for the preaudit of suppliers' invoices.

b. The request that you make suggestions during development of the system.

c. The request that you assist in the installation of the system and approve the system after making a final review. (CIA Examination, adapted)

16.2 As an internal auditor for the Quick Manufacturing Company, you are participating in the audit of the company's AIS. You have been reviewing the internal controls of the computer system that processes most of its accounting applications. You have studied the company's extensive documentation of its systems and have interviewed the MIS manager, operations supervisor, and other employees in order to complete your standardized computer internal control questionnaire.

You report to your supervisor that the company has designed a successful set of comprehensive internal controls into its computer systems. He thanks you for your efforts and asks for a summary report of your findings for inclusion in a final overall report on accounting internal controls.

REQUIRED

Have you forgotten an important audit step? Explain. List five examples of specific audit procedures that you might recommend before reaching a final conclusion.

16.3 As an internal auditor, you have been assigned to evaluate the controls and operation of a computer payroll system. To test the computer systems and programs, you will be submitting independently created test transactions with regular data in a normal production run.

REQUIRED

a. List four advantages of this technique.

b. List two disadvantages of this technique. (CIA Examination, adapted)

16.4 You are involved in the internal audit of accounts receivable, which represent a significant portion of the assets of a large retail corporation. Your audit plan requires the use of the computer, but you encounter the following reactions.

a. The computer operations manager says that all time on the computer is booked for the foreseeable future and that it won't be available to help the auditor with his work.

b. The computer scheduling manager suggests that your computer program be cataloged into the computer program library (on disk storage) so that it can be run when computer time becomes available.

c. You are refused admission to the computer room.

d. The systems manager tells you that it will take too much time to adapt the computer audit program to the EDP operating system and that the computer installation programmers would write the programs needed for the audit.

REQUIRED

For each of the four situations described, state the action the auditor should take to proceed with the accounts receivable audit. (CIA Examination)

16.5 You are a manager for the regional CPA firm of Dewey, Cheatem, and Howe (DC&H). You are reviewing your staff's working papers of an audit of the state welfare agency. You find that the test data concept was used to test the agency's computer program that maintains accounting records. Specifically, your staff obtained a duplicate copy of the program and of the welfare accounting data file from the manager of computer operations and borrowed the test transaction data file used by the welfare agency's programmers when the program was written. These were processed on DC&H's home office computer. A copy of the edit summary report that listed no errors was included in the working papers, along with a notation by the audit senior that the test indicates good application controls.

You note that the quality of the audit conclusions obtained from this test is flawed in several respects, and you decide to ask your subordinates to repeat the test.

REQUIRED

Identify three existing or potential problems with the way this test was performed. For each problem, suggest one or more procedures that might be performed during the revised test to avoid flaws in the audit conclusions.

16.6 You are auditing the financial statements of Aardvark Wholesalers, Inc. (AW), a wholesaler with operations in 12 western states and total revenues of about $125 million. AW uses a computer system in several of its major accounting applications. Accordingly, you are carrying out an IS audit to evaluate internal controls in their computer system.

You have obtained a manual containing job descriptions for key personnel in AW's IS division. Excerpts from these job descriptions follow.

Director of IS: Reports to administrative vice president. Responsible for defining the mission of the IS division and for planning, staffing, and managing a department that optimally executes this mission.

Manager of systems and programming: Reports to director of IS. Responsible for managing a staff of systems analysts and programmers whose mission is to design, program, test, implement, and maintain cost-effective data processing systems. Also responsible for establishing and monitoring documentation standards.

Manager of operations: Reports to director of IS. Responsible for cost-effective management of computer center operations, for enforcement of processing standards, and for systems programming, including implementation of operating system vendor upgrades.

Data entry shift supervisor: Reports to manager of operations. Responsible for supervision of data entry operators and monitoring of data preparation standards.

Operations shift supervisor: Reports to manager of operations. Responsible for supervision of computer operations staff and monitoring of processing standards.

Data control clerk: Reports to manager of operations. Responsible for logging and distributing computer input and output, monitoring source data control procedures, and custody of program and data files.

REQUIRED

a. Prepare an organization chart for AW's IS division.

b. Name two positive and two negative aspects (from an internal control standpoint) of this organization structure.

c. What additional information, if any, would you require before you could make a final judgment on the adequacy of AW's separation of functions in the IS division?

16.7 Robinson's Plastic Pipe Corporation uses a computerized inventory data processing system. The basic input record to this system has the format shown in Table 16.8. You are performing an audit of source data controls for this system, and you have decided to use an input controls matrix for this purpose.

REQUIRED

Prepare an input controls matrix using the same format and listing the same input controls as the one in Fig. 16.3. However, replace the field names shown in Fig. 16.3 with those of the inventory transaction file shown in Table 16.8. Place checks in the cells of the matrix that represent input controls you might expect to find for each field.

16.8 As an internal auditor for the state auditor's office, you have been assigned to review the implementation of a new computer system in the state welfare agency. The agency is installing an on-line

Table 16.8 **Parts Inventory Transaction File**

Field Name	Field Type	Positions
Item number	Numeric	1–6
Description	Alphanumeric	7–31
Transaction date	Date	32–37
Transaction type	Alphanumeric	38
Document number	Alphanumeric	39–46
Quantity	Numeric	47–51
Unit cost	Monetary	52–58

computer system to maintain the state's data base of welfare recipients. Under the old system, state residents applying for welfare assistance completed a form giving their name, address, and other personal data, plus details about their income, assets, dependents, and other data needed to establish their eligibility. The data on these forms are checked by welfare examiners to verify their authenticity. The welfare examiners then certify the applicant's eligibility for assistance and determine the form and amount of aid.

Under the new system welfare applicants will provide their case data to clerks, who will simultaneously enter the data into the system using on-line terminals. Each applicant record will be assigned a "pending" status until a welfare examiner can verify the authenticity of the crucial data used in determining eligibility for assistance. When this verification process has been completed, the welfare examiner will enter a change in the status code from "pending" to "approved," then the system will execute a program to calculate the appropriate amount of aid.

Periodically, the circumstances (income, assets, dependents, etc.) of welfare recipients change and the data base needs to be updated accordingly. Welfare examiners will enter these change transactions into the system as soon as their accuracy has been verified. The system will then immediately recalculate the recipient's welfare benefit. At the end of each month checks are generated and mailed to all eligible welfare recipients.

Welfare assistance in your state amounts to several hundred million dollars annually. You are concerned about the possibilities of fraud and abuse.

REQUIRED

a. Describe how you could employ concurrent audit techniques within this system to reduce the risks of fraud and abuse.

b. Describe how computer audit software could be used to review the work of welfare examiners in verifying applicant eligibility data. For this purpose you may assume that the state auditor's office has access to computerized data bases maintained by other state and local government agencies.

16.9 You are an internal auditor for the Military Industrial Company. You are presently preparing test transactions for the company's weekly payroll processing program. Each input record to this program contains the following data items.

Spaces	Data Item
1–9	Social Security number
10	Pay code (1 = hourly; 2 = salaried)
11–16	Wage rate or salary
17–19	Hours worked, in tenths
20–21	Number of exemptions claimed
22–29	Year-to-date gross pay, including cents
30–80	Employee name and address

The program performs the following edit checks on each input record.

- Field checks to identify any records that do not have numeric characters in the fields for wage rate/salary, hours, exemptions, and year-to-date gross pay.
- A validity check of the pay code.
- A limit check to identify any hourly employee records with a wage rate higher than $20.00.
- A limit check to identify any hourly employee records with hours worked greater than 70.0.
- A limit check to identify any salaried employee records with a weekly salary greater than $2000.00 or less than $100.00.

Records that do not pass these edit checks are listed on an error report. For those that pass the edit checks, the program performs a series of calculations. First, the employee's gross pay is determined. Gross pay for a salaried employee is equal to the salary amount contained within spaces 11–16 of the input record. Gross pay for an hourly employee is equal to the wage rate times the number of hours up to 40, plus 1.5 times the wage rate times the number of hours in excess of 40.

The program computes federal withholding tax for each employee by multiplying gross pay times a tax rate determined from Table 16.9. The program next computes state withholding tax for each employee by multiplying gross pay times a tax rate determined from Table 16.10.

The program next computes the employee's pension contribution, which is 3% of gross pay for hourly employees and 4% of gross pay for salaried employees. Finally, the program computes the employee's net pay, which is gross pay minus tax withholdings and pension contribution. Once all these calculations have been completed for one employee record, the program prints that employee's paycheck and summary earnings statement and then proceeds to the next employee input record to perform edit checks and payroll calculations, continuing this cycle until all input records have been processed.

Table 16.9 **Computation of Federal Withholding Tax**

Number of Exemptions	Gross Pay Range $0–$99.99	$100–$249.99	$250–$499.99	Over $500
0–1	0.06	0.12	0.18	0.24
2–3	0.04	0.10	0.16	0.22
4–5	0.02	0.08	0.14	0.20
Over 5	0.00	0.06	0.12	0.18

Table 16.10 **Computation of State Withholding Tax**

Number of Exemptions	Gross Pay Range $0–$249.99	Over $500
0–3	0.03	0.05
Over 3	0.01	0.03

Your short-term goal is to prepare a set of test transactions containing one of each possible type of error and another set of test transactions that will test each of the computational alternatives one at a time. Transactions to test for multiple errors in one record, or to test for multiple combinations of logic paths, are to be developed later.

The test transactions you prepare need not include a Social Security number or an employee name and address (your assistant will add those after reviewing a file printout). Accordingly, each of your test transactions will consist of a series of 20 characters representing data in spaces 10–29 of an input record. For example, for an hourly employee who has a wage rate of $9.50, worked 40.5 hours, claims two exemptions, and has a year-to-date gross pay of exactly $12,000, the test transaction would be 10009504050201200000.

REQUIRED

Prepare a set of test transactions, each of which:

a. Contains one of the errors tested for by the edit checks. Determine the expected results of processing for each of these test transactions.

b. Tests one of the ways in which gross pay may be determined. Determine the expected gross pay for each of these transactions.

c. Tests one of the ways in which federal withholding tax may be computed. Determine the expected value of federal withholding tax for each of these test transactions.

d. Tests one of the ways in which state withholding tax may be computed. Determine the expected value of state withholding tax for each of these test transactions.

e. Tests one of the ways in which the pension contribution may be computed. Determine the expected value of the pension contribution for each of these test transactions.

16.10 The internal audit department of Sachem Manufacturing Company is considering the purchase of computer software that will aid the auditing process. Sachem's financial and manufacturing control systems are completely automated on a large mainframe computer. Melinda Robinson, the director of internal auditing, believes that Sachem should acquire computer audit software to assist in the financial and procedural audits that her department conducts. Robinson is considering the following types of software packages:

- A generalized audit software package that assists in basic audit work such as the retrieval of live data from large computer files. The department would review this information using conventional audit investigation techniques. More specifically, the department could perform criteria selection, sampling, basic computations for quantitative analysis, record handling, graphical analysis, and the printing of output (i.e., confirmations).

• An integrated test facility (ITF) package that uses, monitors, and controls "dummy" test data through existing programs. It also checks the programs and the existence and adequacy of program data entry and processing controls.
• A flowcharting package that graphically presents the flow of information through a system and pinpoints control strengths and weaknesses.
• A parallel simulation and modeling package that uses actual data to conduct the same systemized process by using another program, a computer logic program developed by the auditor. The package can also be used to seek answers to difficult audit problems (involving many comparisons) within statistically acceptable confidence limits.

REQUIRED

a. Without regard to any specific computer audit software, identify the general advantages of using computer audit software to assist with audits.
b. Describe the audit purpose facilitated and the procedural steps to be followed by the internal auditor in using the following:

1. Generalized audit software package.
2. Integrated test facility package.
3. Control flowcharting package.
4. Program (parallel) simulation and modeling package. (CMA Examination)

16.11 The Thermo-Bond Manufacturing Company maintains its fixed asset records on its computer. The fixed asset master file includes the data items listed in Table 16.11.

REQUIRED

Refer to Table 16.7, which describes the general functions of computer audit software. Then explain several ways it could be used by an auditor in performing a financial audit of Thermo-Bond's fixed asset account.

16.12 An auditor is conducting an examination of the financial statements of a wholesale cosmetics distributor with an inventory consisting of thousands of individual items. The distributor keeps its inventory in its own distribution center and in two public warehouses. An inventory computer file is maintained on a computer disk, and at the end of each business day the file is updated. Each record of the inventory file contains the following data.

Item number	Location of item
Description of item	Cost per item
Quantity on hand	Date of last purchase
	Date of last sale
	Quantity sold during year

The auditor will have a CAS and a computer tape containing inventory data as of the date of the

Table 16.11 **Fixed Asset Master File**

Item Number	Location	Description
1	1–6	Asset number
2	7–30	Description
3	31	Type code
4	32–34	Location code
5	35–40	Date of acquisition
6	41–50	Original cost
7	51–56	Date of retirement*
8	57	Depreciation method code
9	58–61	Depreciation rate
10	62–63	Useful life (years)
11	64–73	Accumulated depreciation at beginning of year
12	74-83	Year-to-date depreciation

*For assets still in service the retirement date is assigned the value 99/99/99.

distributor's physical inventory count. The auditor will perform the following audit procedures.

1. Observe the distributor's physical count of inventories as of a given date, and test a sample for accuracy.
2. Compare the auditor's test counts with the inventory records.
3. Compare physical count data with the inventory records.
4. Test the mathematical accuracy of the distributor's final inventory valuation.
5. Test inventory pricing by obtaining item costs from buyers, vendors, or other sources.
6. Examine inventory purchase and sale transactions on or near the year-end date to verify that all such transactions were recorded in the proper accounting period.
7. Ascertain the propriety of inventory items located in public warehouses.
8. Analyze inventory for evidence of possible obsolescence.
9. Analyze inventory for evidence of possible overstocking or slow-moving items.
10. Test the accuracy of individual data items listed in the distributor's inventory master file.

REQUIRED

Describe how the use of the general-purpose software package and the tape of the inventory file data might be helpful to the auditor in performing each of these auditing procedures. (CPA Examination, adapted)

CASE 16.1: ANYCOMPANY, INC.—AN ONGOING COMPREHENSIVE CASE

Select a local company with an internal auditing department, and obtain permission to study its internal auditing policies and procedures.

Then complete the following steps and prepare a report describing your findings and conclusions:

1. Determine to whom internal auditing reports. Does this reporting arrangement provide the internal audit function with sufficient independence?

2. Does the internal audit function perform IS, financial, and operational audits? Does it perform other kinds of audits? About what percentage of its total audit work falls into each of these categories?

3. Determine how the internal auditors perform IS audits. If possible, obtain copies of audit programs, checklists, and/or questionnaires used in performing IS audits. Comment on the company's approach to IS auditing.

4. In performing IS audits, do the internal auditors use methods of auditing through the computer, such as reprocessing, parallel simulation, program tracing, test data processing, on-line testing, and concurrent audit techniques? Describe how the internal auditors use these methods.

5. In carrying out financial audits, does the internal audit function employ computer audit software? If so, obtain a copy of the documentation and describe the functions it can perform. If possible, observe how the audit software is used to carry out a financial audit, and examine copies of the output.

6. Ask the internal auditors to tell you about some specific audit jobs where they discovered something unusual and/or were able to recommend improvements in controls or operating procedures that saved the company substantial amounts of time or money.

CASE 16.2: PRESTON MANUFACTURING COMPANY

You are performing a financial audit of the general ledger accounts of the Preston Manufacturing Company. At the beginning of the current fiscal year the company converted its general ledger accounting from a manual to a computer-based system. The new system uses two computer files, whose contents are specified as follows:

Each day as detailed transactions are processed by Preston's other computerized accounting systems, summary journal entries are accumulated; at the end

General Journal		
Field Name	**Field Type**	**Size**
Account number	Numeric	6
Amount	Monetary	9.2
Debit/credit code	Alphanumeric	1
Date (MM/DD/YY)	Date	6
Reference document type	Alphanumeric	4
Reference document number	Numeric	6

General Ledger Control		
Field Name	**Field Type**	**Size**
Account number	Numeric	6
Account name	Alphanumeric	20
Beginning balance/ year	Monetary	9.2
Beg-bal-debit/credit code	Alphanumeric	1
Current balance	Monetary	9.2
Cur-bal-debit/credit code	Alphanumeric	1

of the day they are added to the general ledger file. At the end of each week and each month the general journal file is processed against the general ledger control file to compute a new current balance for each account and to print a trial balance.

The following resources are available as you complete the audit:

- Your firm's generalized computer audit software package, which can perform the general functions listed in Table 16.7.
- A complete copy of the general journal file for the entire year.
- A copy of the general ledger file as of the fiscal year-end (i.e., current balance = year-end balance).
- A printout of Preston's year-end trial balance listing the account number, account name, and balance of each account on the general ledger control file.

Design a series of procedures utilizing the CAS to analyze the data in these files, and prepare the reports needed to carry out your financial audit. Your application design should include the following:

1. A description of the data content of each output report, preferably in the form of a tabular layout chart of the report format.
2. A description of the auditing objectives of each report and how the report would be used in subsequent auditing procedures to achieve those objectives.
3. A detailed system flowchart showing each of the processing steps in the computer audit software application.

ANSWERS TO CHAPTER QUIZ

1. d **3.** a **5.** b **7.** c **9.** c
2. b **4.** d **6.** d **8.** d **10.** b

PART FIVE

Chapter 17

The Revenue Cycle: Sales and Cash Collections

LEARNING OBJECTIVES

After studying this chapter, you should be able to:

- Describe the major business activities and related data processing operations performed in the revenue cycle.
- Assess how developments in information technology affect the performance of revenue cycle activities.
- Document your understanding of the revenue cycle.
- Identify major threats in the revenue cycle and evaluate the adequacy of various control procedures for dealing with those threats.
- Discuss the key decisions that need to be made in the revenue cycle and identify the information needed to make those decisions.
- Read and understand a data model (E–R diagram) of the revenue cycle.

Integrative Case: Alpha Omega Electronics

Alpha Omega Electronics (AOE) is a manufacturer of a variety of inexpensive consumer electronic products, including calculators, digital clocks, radios, pagers, toys, games, and small kitchen appliances. AOE's primary customers are discount retail stores, but the company has recently begun selling in bulk to mail order firms that advertise in catalogs and magazines. Figure 17.1 shows a partial organization chart for AOE.

Over the past three years, AOE has been steadily losing market share. At the last executive meeting, Trevor Whitman, vice president of marketing, explained that one reason for AOE's declining market share is its competitors' ability to provide better customer service. Currently, it takes AOE 24 *hours* to notify customers whether the items they ordered are in stock or need to be back-ordered. It also takes at least a full day to approve credit for new customers or to increase an existing customer's credit limit. Moreover, the sales staff estimates that they spend at least 10% of their time revisiting customers to collect data missing or erroneous on the original order.

Trevor suggested redesigning AOE's entire sales order entry system. He recommended supplying the sales force with portable computers so that they can check inventory availability from the field, thereby providing customers with more accurate delivery estimates. He also suggested increasing AOE's focus on the mail order business, which he perceived as being more lucrative and less volatile than the retail trade.

Linda Spurgeon, president of AOE, was skeptical of both proposals. She asked Elizabeth Venko, the controller, to investigate the costs and benefits of redesigning the sales order entry system around Trevor's suggestions and of increasing AOE's focus on the mail order market.

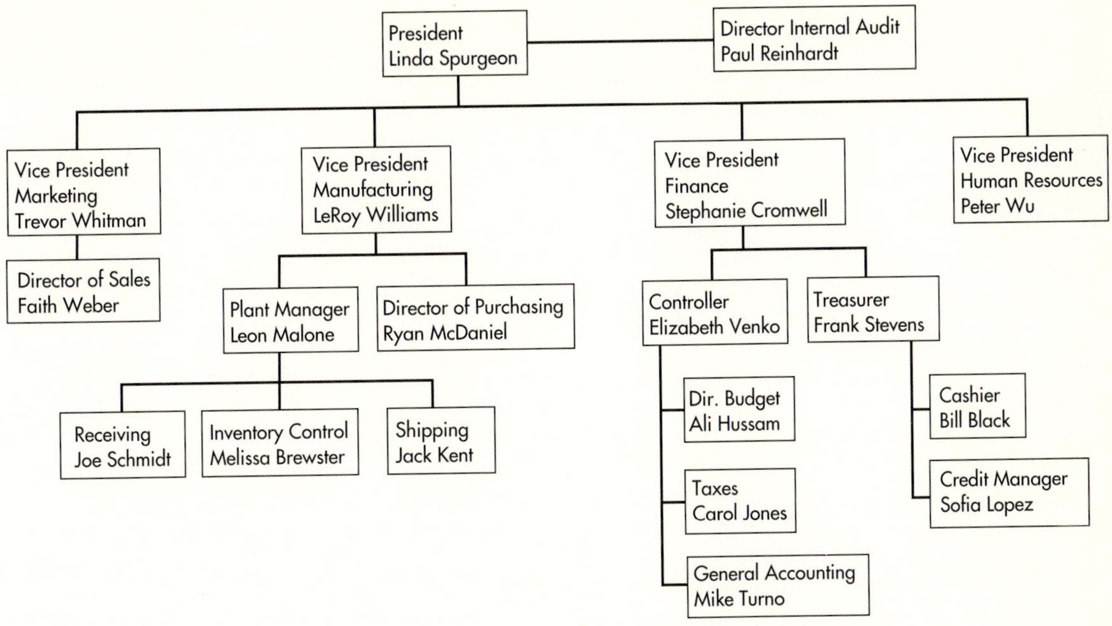

Figure 17.1

Partial Organization Chart for AOE

Linda was also concerned about AOE's cash flow and asked Elizabeth to review the company's current cash collection procedures. The most recent accounts receivable aging schedule indicated a significant increase in the number of past due customer accounts. Consequently, AOE has had to increase its short-term borrowing because of delays in collecting customer payments. In addition, the Best Value Company, a retail chain that has been one of AOE's major customers, recently went bankrupt. Elizabeth admitted that she is not sure whether AOE will be able to collect the large balance due from Best Value.

Elizabeth began her assignment by listing the questions for which she needs answers:

1. How could AOE's sales order entry system be redesigned so as to provide better information to sales staff and reduce the time to fill customer orders? to improve customer service?
2. What opportunities exist in mail order sales? What is the likely effect of the Internet and other technological advances on the mail order industry?
3. How can AOE improve its monitoring of credit accounts? How would any changes in credit policy affect both sales and uncollectible accounts?
4. How could information technology (IT) be used to improve cash collection procedures?
5. How could AOE identify its most profitable customers and markets?

As the AOE case indicates, deficiencies in the information system used to support revenue cycle activities can create significant problems for an organization. Accurate and timely information about inventory availability and customer credit status is essential. As you read this chapter, think about how AOE's information system can be redesigned to provide more efficient and effective support of its revenue cycle activities.

INTRODUCTION

The **revenue cycle** is a recurring set of business activities and related information processing operations associated with providing goods and services to customers and collecting cash in payment for those sales (see Fig. 17.2). As shown in Fig. 17.2, the primary external exchange of information is with customers. In addition, internal information flows between the revenue cycle and the other accounting cycles. For example, sales transaction data flow to the following cycles:

- The expenditure and production cycles to initiate the purchase or production of additional inventory to meet demand.
- The human resource management/payroll cycle to calculate sales commissions and bonuses.
- The general ledger and reporting cycle to prepare financial statements and performance reports.

This chapter is organized around the three basic functions of the AIS in the revenue cycle. The first section describes the basic business activities performed in the revenue cycle and how data about those activities are captured and processed by the AIS. The second section discusses the major control objectives in the revenue cycle and explains how the AIS can be designed to mitigate the threats associated with revenue cycle activities. The final section presents a data model that shows how the AIS can effectively and efficiently store and organize the information needed to make key revenue cycle decisions.

Figure 17.2 *Context Diagram of the Revenue Cycle*

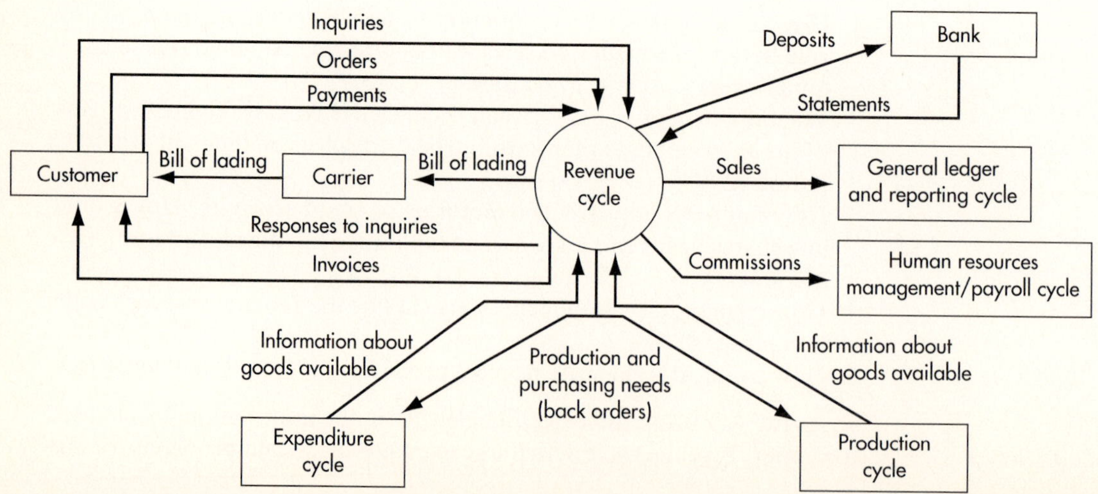

REVENUE CYCLE BUSINESS ACTIVITIES

One objective of the AIS in the revenue cycle is to support the performance of the organization's business activities by efficiently processing transaction data. Figure 17.3 shows the four basic revenue cycle business activities: sales order entry, shipping, billing, and cash collections. Although the remainder of this section discusses each of these activities separately, keep in mind that advances in IT often enable several of them to be performed simultaneously.

Sales Order Entry

The first step in the revenue cycle is sales order entry (circle 1.0 in Fig. 17.3). This function includes all the activities involved in soliciting and processing customer orders. These activities are performed by the sales order department, which reports to the vice president of marketing (refer back to Fig. 17.1).

Key Decisions and Information Needs. The sales order entry function obtains needed information about inventory availability and customer credit status from the inventory control and accounting functions, respectively. Decisions concerning credit policies, including the approval of credit for new customers and increasing the credit limits of existing customers, however, are made by the credit manager, who reports to the treasurer and ultimately to the vice president of finance. This arrangement effectively segregates the duties of authorization and recording.

As shown in Fig. 17.4, the sales order entry function involves three main activities: responding to customer inquiries, checking and approving customer credit, and checking inventory availability.

Responding to Customer Inquiries. Customer inquiries may be handled directly by the sales order department or by a customer service department,

Figure 17.3

Level 0 Data Flow Diagram of the Revenue Cycle

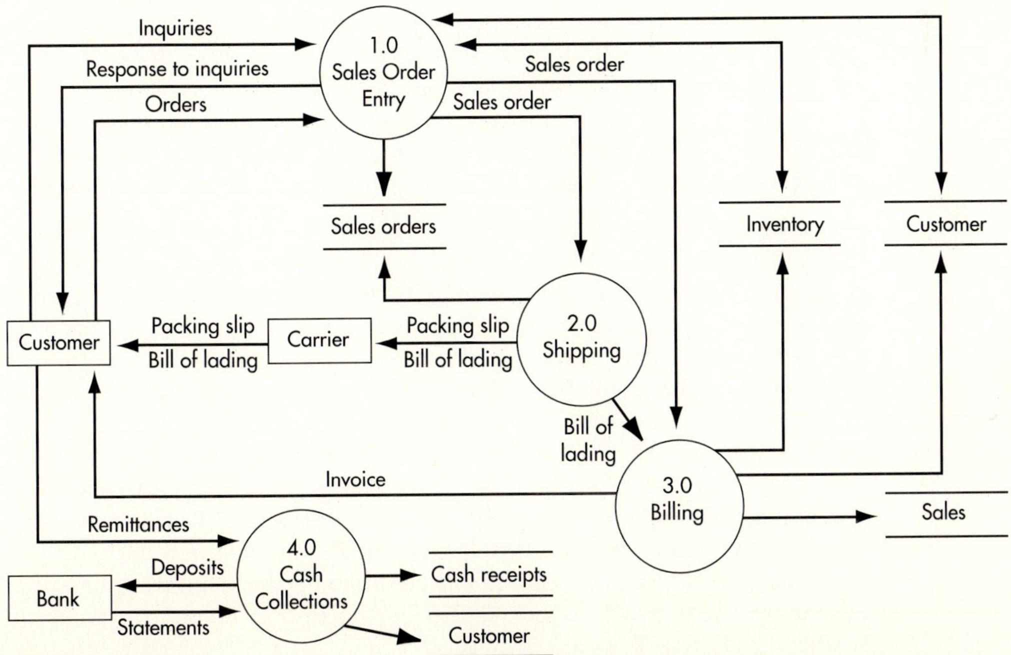

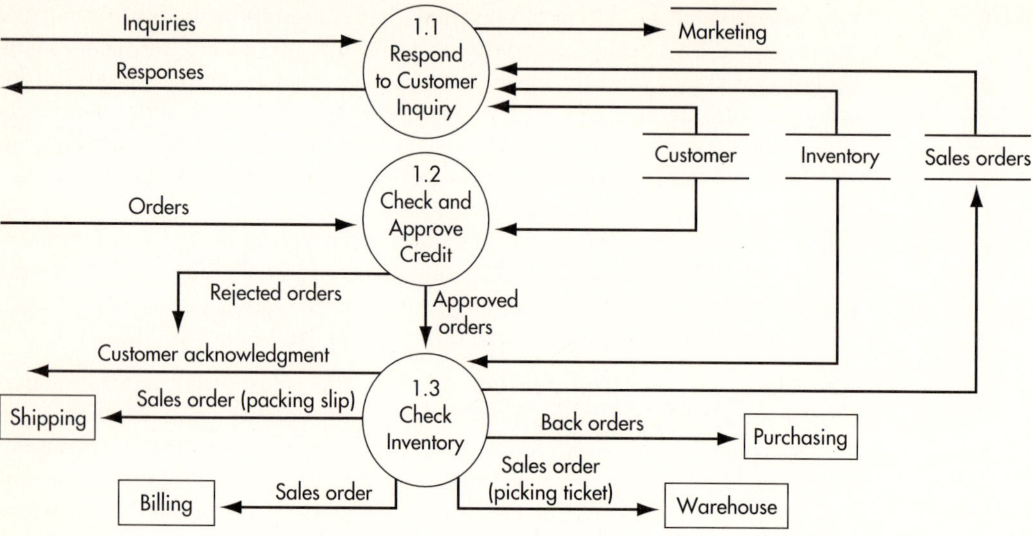

Figure 17.4

Level 1 Data Flow Diagram: Sales Order Entry

which also reports to the vice president of marketing. Inquiries about current account balances or the status of orders are answered by retrieving information from the customer and sales orders files. Customer inquiries and comments should be analyzed because they can provide insights for improving customer service. For example, NEC noted that in one month about 3% of its 50,000 customer service calls were complaints that its new CD-ROM reader was defective. Customer service representatives soon found, however, that most of the problems occurred because customers had failed to put disks into the drives! NEC used this information to redesign its product by adding an LCD panel to the drive. Now, if a user tries to access an empty drive, the panel lights up and prompts the user to first put a disk into the drive.

New developments in IT provide companies with additional opportunities to improve customer service. Focus 17.1 describes how some companies are using the Internet to monitor customer satisfaction and do market research.

Credit Approval. Credit sales should be approved before they are processed. For existing customers with well-established payment histories, a formal credit check for each sale is usually unnecessary. Instead, order takers have general authorization to approve orders from "customers in good standing," meaning those without past due balances. This usually is accomplished by establishing a **credit limit** (maximum allowable account balance) for each customer based on past credit history and ability to pay. In such cases, approving customer credit involves checking the customer master file to verify the account exists, identifying the customer's credit limit, and verifying that the amount of the order plus any current account balance does not exceed this limit. Thus the customer master file should be accurate and current at all times. For new customers, or when the order exceeds the customer's credit limit, or when the customer has outstanding, past due balances, specific authorization for approving credit should be made by the credit manager.

FOCUS 17.1

Surfing the Internet for Market Research

Market research may never be the same. The days of mail and telephone surveys may be a thing of the past. Today, Dell Computer Corporation and many other companies are surfing the Internet and commercial networks such as CompuServe, America Online, and Prodigy to find out what customers think about their products. Gathering data from such networks is less expensive than traditional telephone and mail surveys. Moreover, according to Mal Ransom, marketing vice president for Packard Bell Electronics, Inc., responses from electronic surveys are more candid.

Companies can also find out useful information about their competitors by joining newsgroups that focus on specific products. For example, there are Internet newsgroups devoted solely to specific computer vendors such as Dell and Gateway 2000, Inc. Marketing executives at rival companies, such as Compaq Computer Corporation, admit that such newsgroups are useful for learning about bugs, product delays, and their competitors' new products.

A number of computer manufacturers and software companies, including International Business Machines Corporation, Apple Computer, Inc., Dell, and Microsoft Corporation, have established "home pages" on the Internet's World Wide Web to enhance customer service. The home pages contain product information that customers can either browse on-line or download to their personal computers.

A few companies, including Dell and Gateway, even dedicate full-time staff to monitor the Internet and respond to customer questions. Dell receives thousands of inquiries each week, some of which point out bugs in its products that its own engineers had not yet discovered. Moreover, it is less expensive to respond to customer questions via the Internet than to staff a 24-hour toll-free telephone number. Dell has even used the Internet to poll its customers about a proposed product change involving the color of its product, thereby obtaining information for free that in the past it would have had to pay a market research firm to collect.

Focus Questions

1. In what ways could networks like the Internet be used in the revenue cycle? Could they be used for sales order entry? shipping? billing? cash collections? Why or why not?
2. Although many companies are doing so, is it ethical to join product-specific newsgroups to gain information about bugs in competitors' products or to learn about their new product ideas?
3. Do you agree or disagree with Mal Ransom's belief that people are more candid when responding to electronic, as opposed to paper or telephone, surveys? Why?

Source: Scott McCartney, "Companies Go On-Line to Chat, Spy, and Rebut," *Wall Street Journal* (September 15, 1994): B1, B6.

Checking Inventory Availability. Inventory quantities on hand must also be checked, so that customers can be informed about availability and expected delivery dates. This function is important because if inventory records are not accurate and up-to-date, customers may become justifiably upset when unexpected delays occur in filling their orders.

If sufficient inventory is on hand to fill the order, the sales order is completed and the shipping, inventory control, and billing departments are notified of the sale. An acknowledgment may also be sent to the customer. If there is not sufficient inventory on hand to fill the order, a **back order** for those items must be created. In manufacturing companies, this task involves notifying the production department to initiate the production of the requested items. In retail companies the purchasing department would be notified about the need to order the required items.

Documents, Records, and Procedures. The receipt of a customer's order triggers the sales order entry process and produces several internal documents. To assist you in following the flow and purpose of these documents, Fig. 17.5 depicts a typical batch-oriented sales order entry process such as the one currently used at a typical manufacturing company like AOE.

Figure 17.5

Sales Order Entry: Batch Processing

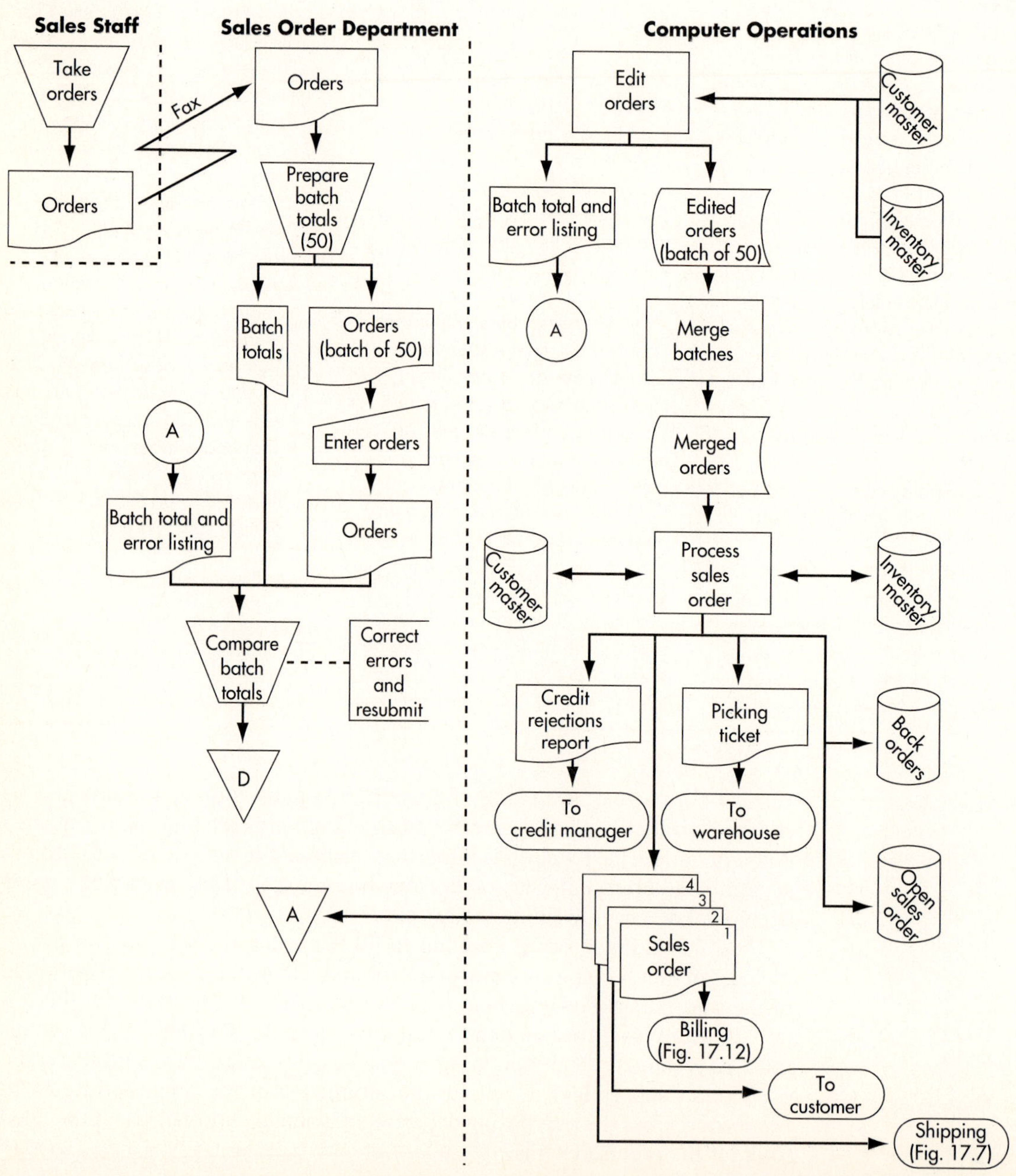

As they complete calls, sales representatives write up orders on preprinted forms. These forms are faxed nightly to the sales order department, where they are assembled in batches of approximately 50 transactions for data entry. Before proceeding with data entry, batch totals (a record count and a hash total of quantities ordered) are manually calculated for each group of 50 transactions. Sales order clerks then enter only the following items for each transaction: customer account number, salesperson number, product numbers and quantities, and requested delivery date. The customer number is used to access the appropriate record in the customer file. The system then retrieves the customer's name and address to complete the sales order. Similarly, the product number is used to access the appropriate record in the inventory file and to retrieve the item description and price.

At this point a number of edit checks are performed to ensure input accuracy, including the following:

- Validity checks of the customer account and inventory item numbers are performed by matching them to information in the customer and inventory master files, respectively.
- Redundant data checks of customer account numbers and names and item numbers and descriptions are made to detect cases where a valid but incorrect account or item number was entered.
- Field checks are made to ensure that only numeric data are entered in all other numeric fields and to avoid subsequent processing errors.
- A reasonableness test is performed to verify the accuracy of the quantity ordered. The test compares the quantity ordered to the standard amounts normally ordered as indicated in the corresponding master inventory item record.
- Range checks on the order and delivery date are made to verify feasibility.
- A completeness test is run to verify that each transaction record contains all appropriate data items.

Transaction records that pass all these edit tests represent accurate and valid sales orders. Those that fail one or more tests are listed in an error and exception report for investigation and correction.

As the orders are entered, the system also automatically calculates batch totals. After processing, these system-generated batch totals are compared with those calculated manually to ensure that all transactions have been entered. Any discrepancies are investigated and corrected. The use of small batches facilitates identifying error sources.

The batches of valid sales orders are then merged into one large transaction file in order to process the orders and update the various master files. The system first calculates the sales amount and compares it to the customer's available credit (credit limit less any outstanding unpaid purchases). Orders that fail this credit check are printed on a *credit rejections report.* The credit manager evaluates this report and determines whether to increase the customer's credit limit or reject the order. Accepted orders are reentered with the next batch of orders; customers who are denied credit are notified that their order must be prepaid (these last two steps are not shown in Fig. 17.5).

Next, the system checks whether the inventory is sufficient to fill accepted orders. If it is, the customer's account balance is debited for the amount of the sale and the "quantity available" field in the inventory file is reduced for the amount of the order. Otherwise, a back-order record is generated for the needed items.

At this point several documents are printed. The primary internally generated document produced by sales order entry is the **sales order,** which lists the item numbers, quantities, prices, and terms of the sale (see Fig. 17.6). One copy of the sales order is filed in the sales order department where it can be referenced to respond to customer inquiries, such as the status of open orders. Another copy is sent to the customer to acknowledge acceptance of the order. Copies of the sales order are also sent to the billing and shipping departments, to notify them of a pending shipment. The copy sent to the shipping department is often attached to the package, serving as a **packing slip** that identifies the contents of the shipment (note the columns for recording quantity shipped and quantity back-ordered).

The other document produced by sales order entry is the **picking ticket,** which authorizes the release of merchandise to the shipping department. The

Figure 17.6

Sample AOE Sales Order

12345

SALES ORDER
Alpha Omega Electronics
2431 Bradford Lane
St. Louis, MO 63105–2311

Sold To: **Ship To:**

Date:	Customer Purchase Order No.	Salesperson	Shipping Instructions:

Quantity Ordered	Quantity Shipped	Quantity Back Ordered	Item Number	Description	Unit Price	Amount

Thank You!

picking ticket is often printed so that the item numbers and quantities are listed in the sequence in which they can be most efficiently retrieved from the warehouse.

Opportunities for Using Information Technology. At this point, you have probably noticed several inefficiencies with the batch processing of sales orders. For example, errors in customer orders are not caught until after they have been entered into the system, so the customer will have to be recontacted to obtain the correct information. The credit approval process also requires considerable time.

To correct these inefficiencies, most organizations are switching to on-line processing of sales orders. For example, sales staff can be equipped with portable computers and modems so they can enter and edit customer orders from the field. Direct entry would enable them to catch and correct any mistakes in data entry as they occur, instead of having to revisit the customer. Sales representatives would also be able to inform the customer immediately whether the order had been approved and whether the items being ordered were in stock or had to be back-ordered.

Elizabeth Venko's research revealed that alternative types of portable computers could be used by AOE's sales force. The Gillette Company, for example, provides its sales force with pen-based computers, instead of laptops with keyboards. Gillette claims that the pen-based computers are more useful because sales representatives can use the pen to check off items that need to be ordered and write short notes while walking down store aisles with the customer's purchasing agent. On the other hand, Ingersoll-Rand Corporation gives its sales representatives portable computers equipped with CD-ROM drives so that they can make multimedia presentations of technical products. The representatives can carry portable computers around more easily than lugging flip charts or boxes of slides. Moreover, their presentations are interactive because the multimedia software facilitates jumping to any topic raised by the customer simply by clicking on the appropriate icons. Presentations are further enhanced by including video clips of "live" customer testimonials and demonstrations of how technical products work. Elizabeth decided to meet with Faith Weber, AOE's director of sales, to discuss which type of portable computer would be most appropriate for AOE's sales force.

Adding E-mail to the dial-in sales order entry system can further improve the effectiveness of the sales force. For example, Owens-Corning uses E-mail to provide sales representatives with detailed up-to-date data about each of the customers they are scheduled to call on that day and about any new promotions or marketing strategies. Thus E-mail reduces the need for salespeople to return to the home office and enables them to spend more time with customers. E-mail also speeds up the approval of special deals for customers. For example, AT&T sales representatives use E-mail to simultaneously send proposals to all appropriate managers, thereby reducing overall approval time. Finally, E-mail streamlines the management of the sales force. For example, one E-mail message can inform the entire sales staff of last-minute price changes.

Elizabeth also learned that another way to improve the sales order entry process involves using electronic data interchange (EDI) to link directly with

FOCUS 17.2

Scotch Maid: Managing Your Customer's Inventory to Increase Your Sales

Scotch Maid is a manufacturer of stretchy women's garments known as bodywear. It is the largest private-label supplier of bodywear in the United States, supplying such retail giants as Kmart, Wal-Mart, Sears, and J.C. Penney. Scotch Maid's annual revenues have grown from $3 million to more than $70 million in the five-year period 1989–1993.

Ivars Eichvalds, the chief information officer of the company, attributes this growth to the philosophy that Scotch Maid does not just sell clothing, it sells both clothing and service, the service being information. Wal-Mart, Kmart, and other major retailers have pressured suppliers to use EDI to help better manage inventory. Scotch Maid has taken that system one step further. It provides value to its customers by performing sales analyses for them. For example, Scotch Maid downloads Kmart's current and historical sales figures for each of the approximately 140 items that it supplies and performs detailed sales analyses of each item. The company studies sales trends to spot any deviations from Kmart's projections. It uses that information to adjust its own production schedules so that it is able to meet Kmart's needs. This system has enabled Scotch Maid to almost always fill at least 99% of Kmart's weekly orders. That level of performance is not extraordinary, but expected. When the order fill rate once slipped to 97%, a Kmart buyer sent a fax asking what was going wrong.

Scotch Maid's success has led Kmart to include it in the selective vendor-managed inventory system. The system completely eliminates the need for ordering inventory. Kmart simply specifies the inventory levels that it wants to maintain. Scotch Maid will monitor sales at each Kmart store and inventories at Kmart's regional distribution centers and then automatically decide when it is time to replenish those inventories. Eichvalds believes that, although Scotch Maid's use of information technology currently provides it with a competitive advantage, in a few years such a capability will be necessary for all suppliers.

Focus Questions

1. The arrangement between Scotch Maid and Kmart is an example of an interorganizational system (IOS). What are the internal control ramifications of establishing such an IOS?
2. Do you think such an IOS can be established in all industries, or are they most likely to be limited to retail stores and supermarket chains? Why?

Source: David H. Freedman, "Why Big Retailers Love Little Scotch Maid," *Forbes ASAP* (February 28, 1994): 106–109.

customers. With EDI, retail stores would send their orders directly to AOE's sales order system in a format that would eliminate the need for data entry. EDI would cut costs, eliminate errors, and reduce order processing time.

Linking EDI with customers' point-of-sale (POS) systems can provide additional service improvements. For example, Focus 17.2 describes how one manufacturer uses POS data from large retailers like Kmart for monitoring inventories of its products and for automatically replenishing stocks when they run low. Perhaps AOE could explore a similar arrangement with some of its major customers.

Sales order entry efficiency can also be improved by allowing customers to enter sales order data themselves. One way involves the use of optical character recognition (OCR) devices. For example, retail stores such as Service Merchandise and many mail order firms have customers mark item numbers and quantities on preprinted order forms that can be read by an OCR reader. The Internet provides another method for direct customer order entry. For example, Hello Direct, a supplier of high-end telephone gear, has an electronic catalog on the Internet. Not only can customers place their order but Hello Direct can monitor what parts of the catalog get the most attention, thereby improving its sales projections and product line offerings.

Finally, Elizabeth learned that information technology can also be used to improve customer service and response to inquiries. For example, Norfolk Southern Corporation needed to provide its customers with current status reports about the location of over 100,000 freight cars. It implemented a new information system that enabled customer service representatives to access a customer's file as soon as the telephone call was answered. The system uses automatic number identification and ISDN lines to identify a caller's telephone number as the call arrives. That number is then used to search the customer data base to retrieve the appropriate customer's file and display it on the service representative's computer screen. The entire process takes less time than asking for the customer's name or account number. It also eliminates errors associated with manually entering that data.

Shipping

The second step in the revenue cycle involves filling customer orders and shipping the desired merchandise (circle 2.0 in Fig. 17.3). Warehouse workers are responsible for filling customer orders by removing items from inventory according to the instructions on the picking ticket. The shipping department is responsible for the actual delivery of the merchandise to customers. As shown in Fig. 17.1, both of these functions, which involve the custody of inventory, report ultimately to the vice president of manufacturing.

Key Decisions and Information Needs. One major decision that needs to be made when filling and shipping customer orders concerns the choice of delivery method. Traditionally, many companies have maintained their own truck fleets for deliveries. Large companies such as GM have even assigned entire departments to this function. Increasingly, however, manufacturers are outsourcing this function to commercial carriers such as Ryder System, Inc., Roadway Services, Inc., and Schneider National Company. Outsourcing deliveries reduces costs and allows manufacturers to concentrate on their core business activity (the production of goods). Selecting the proper carrier, however, requires collecting and maintaining information about carrier performance (i.e., percentage of on-time deliveries, damage claims) and integrating that information in the AIS.

Whichever delivery method is used, the shipping department needs accurate information about what to ship and where to send the merchandise. This information is provided on the documents that it receives from the sales order and warehouse departments.

Documents, Records, and Procedures. The picking ticket printed by sales order entry triggers the shipping process. Warehouse workers use the picking ticket to identify which products to remove from inventory. The quantities picked are marked on the picking ticket and then the inventory, along with the completed picking ticket, is brought to the shipping department.

Figure 17.7 illustrates the flow of documents in the shipping process. The shipping department compares the physical count of inventory with the quantities indicated on the picking ticket and with the quantities indicated on the packing slip (copy 3 of the sales order) that was sent directly to shipping from sales order entry. Discrepancies can arise either because the items were not stored in the location indicated on the picking ticket or because the perpetual inventory records are inaccurate due to the loss of inventory. In such cases, the shipping department needs to initiate the back ordering of the missing items and enter the correct quantities shipped on the packing slip (these steps are not shown in Fig. 17.7).

After the shipping clerk counts the goods delivered from the warehouse, the sales order number, item number(s), and quantities are entered using on-line terminals. A variety of edit checks similar to those described earlier for sales order entry are used to ensure that the shipping data are valid, accurate, and complete. This process updates the quantity on hand field in the inventory master file and produces multiple copies of the bill of lading. The **bill of lading** is a legal contract that defines responsibility for the goods that are in transit. It identifies the carrier, source, destination, and any special shipping instructions, and it indicates who (customer or vendor) must pay the carrier (see Fig. 17.8).

Figure 17.7

Shipping Procedures

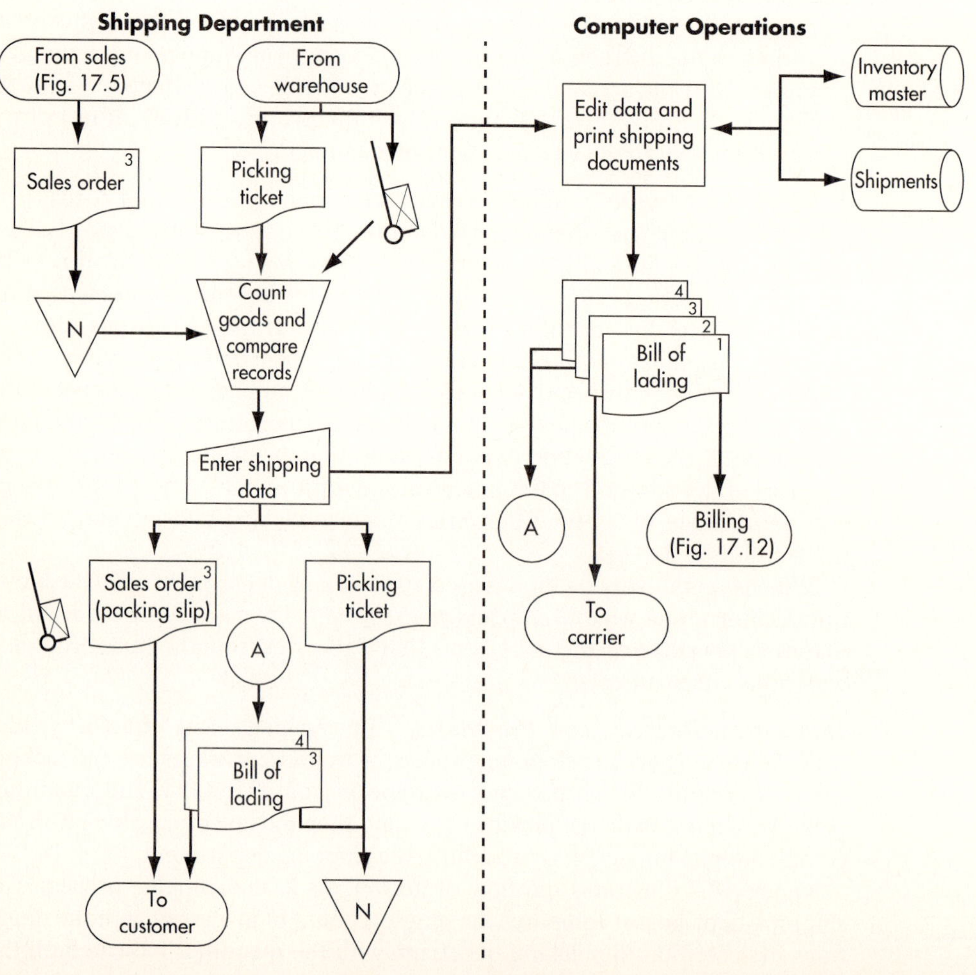

Figure 17.8

Sample Bill of Lading

STRAIGHT BILL OF LADING—SHORT FORM **Not Negotiable.**

Shipper's No.

Carrier **Carrier's No.**

RECEIVED, subject to the classifications and tariffs in effect on the date of the issue of this Bill of Lading.

at ______________________ 19______ **from** ______________________

the property described below, in apparent good order, except as noted (contents and condition of contents of packages unknown), marked, consigned, and destined as indicated below, which said carrier (the word carrier being understood throughout this contract as meaning any person or corporation in possession of the property under the contract) agrees to carry to its usual place of delivery at said destination, if on its route, otherwise to deliver to another carrier on the route to said destination. It is mutually agreed, as to each carrier of all or any of said property over all or any portion of said route to destination, and as to each party at any time interested in any or all of said property, that every service to be performed hereunder shall be subject to all terms and conditions of the Uniform Domestic Straight Bill of Lading set forth (1) in Uniform Freight Classification in effect on the date hereof, if this is a rail or a rail-water shipment, or (2) in the applicable motor carrier classification or tariff if this is a motor carrier shipment.

Shipper hereby certifies that he is familiar with all the terms and conditions of the said bill of lading, including those on the back thereof, set forth in the classification or tariff which governs the transportation of this shipment, and the said terms and conditions are hereby agreed to by the shipper and accepted for himself and his assigns.

Consigned to ______________________

(Mail or street address of consignee—For purposes of notification only.)

Destination ______________________ State ________ Zip Code ______ County ______________

Delivery Address ★ ______________________

(★ To be filled in only when shipper desires and governing tariffs provide for delivery thereat.)

Route ______________________

Delivering Carrier Car or Vehicle Initials No.

No. Packages	Kind of Package, Description of Articles, Special Marks, and Exceptions	*Weight (Sub. to Cor.)	Class or Rate	Check Column

Subject to Section 7 of Conditions of applicable bill of lading, if this shipment is to be delivered to the consignee without recourse on the consignor, the consignor shall sign the following statement.

The carrier shall not make delivery of this shipment without payment of freight and all other lawful charges.

(Signature of Consignor.)

If charges are to be prepaid, write or stamp here, "To Be Prepaid."

Received $ ____________ to apply in prepayment of the charges on the property described hereon.

Agent or Cashier

Per ______________________

(This signature here acknowledges only the amount prepaid.)

Charges advanced:

$

*If the shipment moves between two ports by a carrier by water, the law requires that the bill of lading shall state whether it is "carrier's or shipper's weight."

NOTE—Where the rate is dependent on value, shippers are required to state specifically in writing the agreed or declared value of the property.

The agreed or declared value of the property is hereby specifically stated by the shipper to be not exceeding

per

†"The fibre boxes used for this shipment conform to the specifications set forth in the box maker's certificate thereon, and all other requirements of Uniform Freight Classification."

†Shipper's imprint in lieu of stamp; not a part of bill of lading approved by the Interstate Commerce Commission.

______________________ Shipper, per ______________________ Agent, Per ______________

Permanent post office address of shipper, ______________________

Figure 17.7 shows that one copy of the bill of lading, along with the packing slip, accompanies the shipment. If the customer is to pay the shipping charges, this copy of the bill of lading sometimes serves as a **freight bill,** to indicate the amount the customer should pay to the carrier; in other cases, the freight bill is a separate document.

Another copy of the bill of lading is kept by the shipping department to track and confirm the transfer of goods to the carrier. A copy of the bill of lading is also sent to the billing department to indicate that the goods have been shipped and that an invoice should be prepared and mailed. The carrier also retains a copy of the bill of lading for its records.

Opportunities for Using Information Technology. Elizabeth's research suggested a number of ways that information technology could be used to streamline AOE's shipping and warehousing procedures. Automated warehouse systems consisting of computers, bar-code scanners, conveyer belts, and forklifts can reduce the time and cost of moving inventory into and out of the warehouse. For example, J.C. Penney equips its forklifts with radio frequency data communication (RFDC) terminals to provide drivers with information about which items to pick next and where they are located. Drivers no longer need to return to a central printer to receive instructions. Once picked, items are run through a bar-code scanner; this provides real-time and accurate recording of all inventory movements into and out of the warehouse, which is essential for perpetual inventory systems.

Automated warehouse systems not only cut costs and improve efficiency in handling inventory but can also enable more customer-responsive shipments. For example, Levi Strauss & Company's advanced warehouse system uses bar-code scanners on conveyor belts to route jeans and shirts so that they can be packed and shipped to customers in matched sets. Customers are also sent an electronic packing slip indicating the size, style, and colors of clothing in a pending shipment. The cartons are then bar-coded so retailers can quickly check in the merchandise and move it to the floor. All these services not only save retailers time and money but also help improve turnover of Levi Strauss products, thereby increasing the manufacturer's sales.

Elizabeth decided to talk to Jack Kent, head of the shipping department, and Melissa Brewster, head of inventory control, about the possibility of applying some of these techniques at AOE.

Billing and Accounts Receivable

The third step in the revenue cycle is billing (circle 3.0 in Fig. 17.3). Two activities are performed at this stage of the revenue cycle: invoicing customers and maintaining customer accounts. These processes are performed by the billing/accounts receivable department, which reports to the director of accounting and, ultimately, to the controller (see Fig. 17.1).

Key Decisions and Information Needs. Accurate billing for shipped merchandise is crucial, of course. It requires information from the shipping department identifying the items and quantities shipped, and information about prices and any special sales terms from the sales department. The **sales invoice** (see Fig. 17.9) notifies customers of the amount to be paid and where to send payment. The **monthly statement** summarizes all transactions that occurred during the past month and informs customers of their current account balance (see Fig. 17.10).

Sometimes adjustments to a customer's account are necessary. For example, customer accounts may be credited to reflect either the return of items or allowances granted for damaged goods. To credit a customer's account for returned goods, the credit manager must obtain information from the receiving dock that the goods were actually returned and replaced into inventory. Upon notification from the receiving department that the goods have been returned, the credit manager issues a **credit memo** (see Fig. 17.11), which authorizes the billing department to credit the customer's account. If the damage to the goods is minimal, the customer may agree to keep them for a price reduction. In such cases the credit manager issues a credit memo to reflect the amount that should be credited to the customer's account. One copy of the credit memo is sent to accounts receivable, to authorize an adjustment to the customer's account balance; the other copy is sent to the customer.

Figure 17.9

Sample AOE Sales Invoice

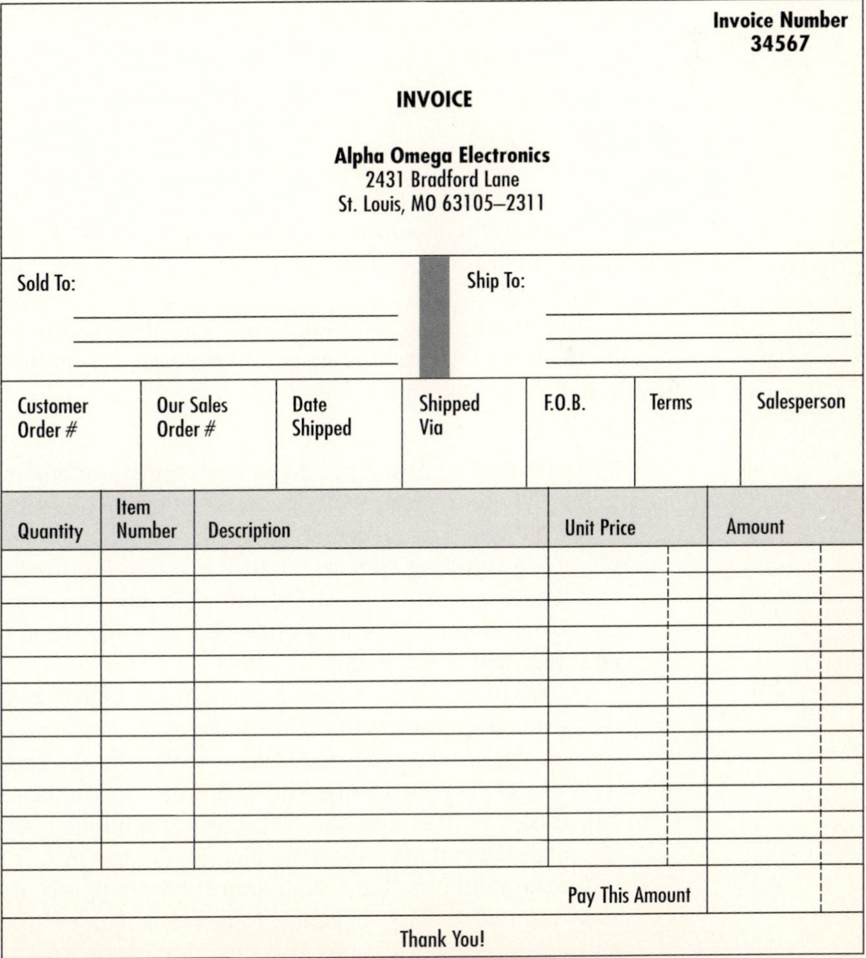

Invoice Number
34567

INVOICE

Alpha Omega Electronics
2431 Bradford Lane
St. Louis, MO 63105–2311

Sold To: | Ship To:

Customer Order #	Our Sales Order #	Date Shipped	Shipped Via	F.O.B.	Terms	Salesperson

Quantity	Item Number	Description	Unit Price	Amount
			Pay This Amount	

Thank You!

Figure 17.10

Sample AOE Monthly Statement

MONTHLY STATEMENT
Alpha Omega Electronics
2431 Bradford Lane
St. Louis, MO 63105–2311

November 1996

Invoice Number	Date	Current	Past Due 1–30	Past Due 31–60	Past Due 61–90	Past Due Over 90
	Totals					
			Total Amount Due			

Occasionally, after all attempts to collect payment have failed, it may be necessary to write off a customer's account as uncollectible. The credit manager issues a credit memo to authorize the write-off. Unlike the cases involving damaged or returned goods, however, a copy of the credit memo is not sent to the customer.

To prevent fraud, decisions leading to the issuance of credit memos should be made by the credit manager. Otherwise, an employee with access to cash could steal a significant amount and then issue a fake credit memo to conceal the theft.

Types of Billing Systems. Most companies use either a prebilling or a postbilling system to generate invoices. At AOE, invoices are prepared after a copy of the bill of lading is received from the shipping department. This is an example of a **postbilling system,** because invoices are prepared *after* confirmation that the items were shipped. Postbilling systems are common in manufacturing companies, where there may often be a delay between the receipt of the order and shipment of the goods.

In contrast, mail order catalog companies, such as L.L. Bean and Spiegel, may use a **prebilling system,** in which invoices are prepared (but not sent) as soon as the order is approved (i.e., after credit has been approved and inventory availability checked). The inventory, accounts receivable, and general ledger files are also updated at this time. Prebilling systems eliminate the need for some documents—for example, the invoice also fills the role of the sales order. Prebilling systems do require extremely accurate inventory records, since all prebilled merchandise found to be out of stock requires accounting entries and file corrections and the addition of information about the back-

Figure 17.11

Sample AOE Credit Memo

11121

CREDIT MEMORANDUM

Alpha Omega Electronics
2431 Bradford Lane
St. Louis, MO 63105–2311

Credit To:	Date Salesperson

Apply To Invoice Number	Date	Customer's Order No.

Quantity	Item Number	Description	Price	Amount

Reason Credit Issued:

Received By: | Authorized By:

We Credit Your Account For This Amount

ordered items to the invoice. In addition, customers are likely to be unhappy if their merchandise is not delivered when originally promised.

Figure 17.12 depicts a typical batch-oriented postbilling system such as the one used by AOE. When a copy of the bill of lading is received from the shipping department, the billing clerk matches it up with the corresponding copy of the sales order sent from sales order entry. The billing clerk then generates invoices by entering information about the item numbers and quantities shipped. The system performs a number of edit checks on the data entered, such as testing the validity of the item numbers entered and comparing the quantities to those listed in the open sales order file.

After these preliminary edit checks, the following operations are performed:

1. New records are created in the sales invoice file, and multiple copies of the sales invoice are printed.
2. The customer master file is accessed and the customer's account is debited for the amount of the sale.

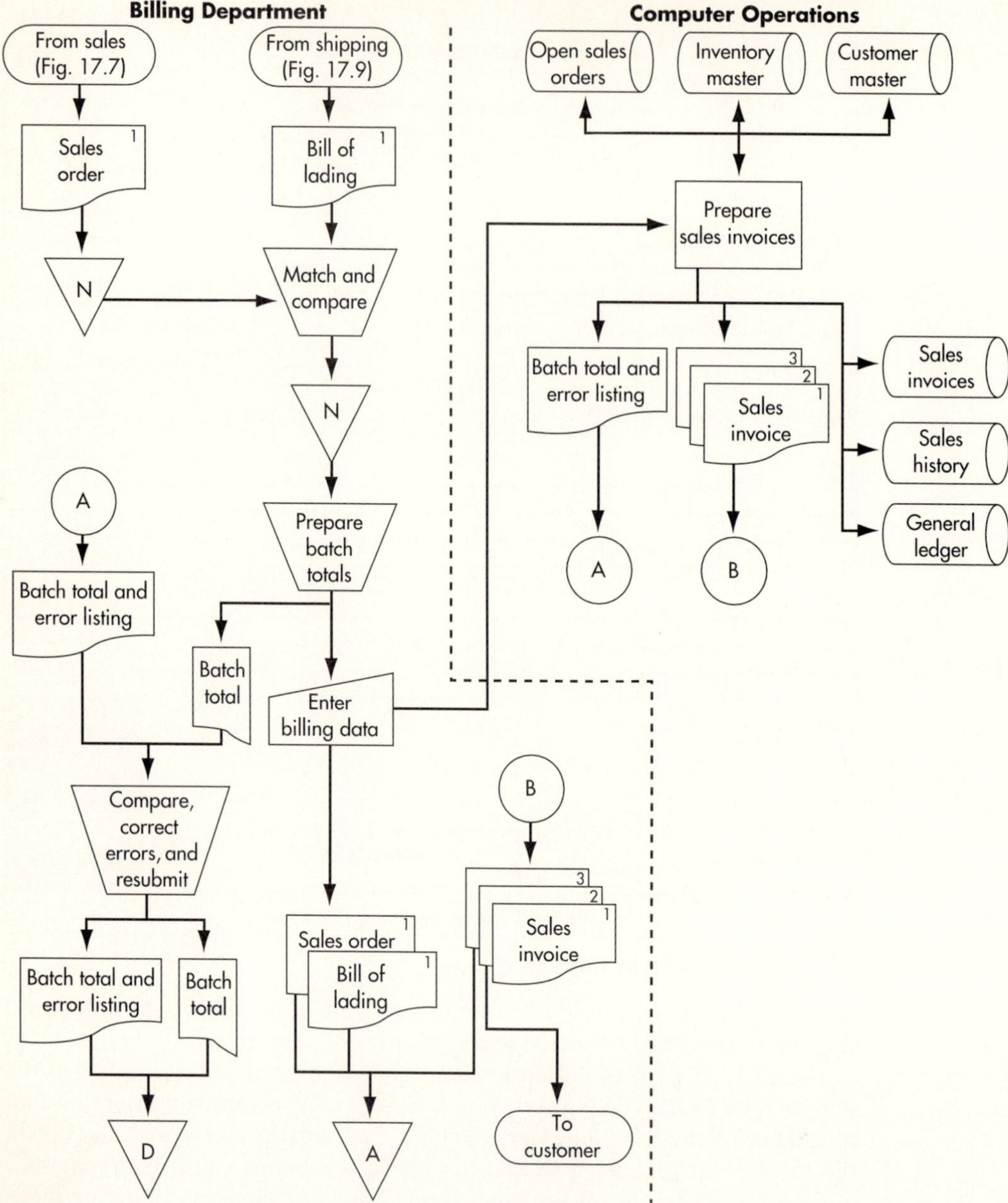

Figure 17.12

Post Billing System

3. The open sales orders are closed to the sales order history file.
4. Finally, after all invoices have been processed, the system generates a summary journal entry reflecting the total amounts to be posted to the sales and accounts receivable accounts in the general ledger.

Methods for Maintaining Accounts Receivable. Most companies use either the open-invoice or the balance-forward method for maintaining accounts receivable. The two methods differ in terms of when customers remit payments, how those payments are applied to update the accounts receivable master file, and in the format of the monthly statement sent to customers.

Under the **open-invoice method,** customers typically pay according to each invoice. Usually, as shown in Fig. 17.12, two copies of the invoice are mailed to the customer, who is requested to return one copy along with the payment. This copy is a turnaround document called the **remittance advice.** Customer payments are then applied against specific invoices. The monthly statement produced under the open-invoice method lists all outstanding invoices and ages them individually (see Fig. 17.10).

In contrast, under the **balance-forward method,** customers typically pay according to the amount shown on a monthly statement, rather than by individual invoices. Remittances are applied against the total account balance, rather than against specific invoices. The monthly statement usually shows the beginning balance, all current charges, and the current balance due, but it does not age individual invoices.

One advantage of the open-invoice method is that it is conducive to offering discounts for prompt payment, since invoices are individually tracked and aged. It also results in a more uniform flow of cash collections throughout the month. A disadvantage of the open-invoice method is the added complexity required to maintain information about the status of each individual invoice for each customer.

Companies with large numbers of customers who make many small purchases each month, such as credit card companies like Visa and Master Card or national retail chains like Sears and J.C. Penney, typically use the balance-forward method. For them, this method is more efficient and reduces costs by avoiding the need to process cash collections for each individual sale. It is also more convenient for the customer to make one monthly remittance.

To obtain a more uniform flow of cash receipts, many of these companies use a process called cycle billing to prepare and mail monthly statements to their customers. Under **cycle billing,** monthly statements are prepared for subsets of customers at different times. For example, the customer master file might be divided into four parts, and each week monthly statements would be prepared for one-fourth of the customers. Cycle billing not only produces a more uniform flow of cash collections throughout the month but also reduces the time that the computer system is dedicated to printing monthly statements. To appreciate this benefit, note that if a credit card company like Visa or Master Card prepared monthly statements for all its customers at the same time, its computer system would be tied up for several days.

Opportunities for Using Information Technology. Batch processing of invoices, as shown in Fig. 17.12, can create cash flow problems for two reasons. First, there is a delay between the time the goods are shipped and when the invoices are printed. Second, there is an additional delay of several days while the invoices are processed through the regular mail system. Switching to online processing of invoices can eliminate the first problem, by printing invoices as soon as notification is received from the shipping department that the order has been shipped. The second problem can be eliminated by using electronic data interchange (EDI) to bill customers. Not only does EDI result in quicker billing of customers, but it also cuts costs by reducing paper handling and processing. For example, Sonoco Products Company estimates that EDI saves it $0.70 to $0.80 per invoice over processing of paper invoices. Depending upon how many invoices are processed in a year, the savings can be significant. EDI invoices would also benefit customers by reducing their time and costs associated with processing paperwork.

Another information technology that can improve the billing and accounts receivable function uses imaging to create and store digital versions of all paper relating to a customer's account. The digital images can then be stored on an optical disk connected to a LAN, where they can be easily retrieved, manipulated, and integrated with other images and data to produce various types of output.

Image processing provides a number of advantages in managing customer accounts. First, employees have fast access to all documents relating to a customer—no more wasted time searching through file cabinets for lost paperwork. If a customer needs a duplicate copy of a monthly statement or an invoice to replace a lost original, it can be retrieved, printed, and faxed while talking to the customer on the phone. Second, image processing helps with resolving customer complaints, since the same image can be viewed simultaneously by more than one person. Thus a customer account representative and his credit manager could both review an image of a document in question while discussing the problem with the customer on the telephone. Finally, image processing reduces the space and cost associated with storing paper documents. The savings in this area can be substantial; one optical disk can store up to 20,000 documents, in a fraction of the space.

Cash Collections

The fourth step in the revenue cycle is cash collections (circle 4.0 in Fig. 17.3). Two departments are involved in this activity. The cashier, who reports to the treasurer (see Fig. 17.1), handles the remittances and deposits them in the bank; the accounts receivable function, which reports to the controller, credits customer accounts for the payments received. This arrangement effectively segregates the custody and recording functions, thereby reducing the risk of theft.

Key Decisions and Information Needs. Because cash can be stolen so easily, it is important to take appropriate preventative measures to safeguard its value. The next section discusses in more detail one means of safeguarding cash collections: preventing the billing/accounts receivable function, which is responsible for recording customer remittances, from having physical access to cash or checks.

Nevertheless, cash collections must be accurately recorded and customer accounts must be properly credited for all remittances. To do this, the accounts receivable function must be able to identify the source of any remittances and the applicable invoices that should be credited. One such method has already been discussed: mailing the customer two copies of the invoice and requesting that one be returned with the remittance. If this copy also contains a space for the customer to indicate the amount being remitted, the remittance data can be input by an OCR machine, thereby eliminating the potential for mistakes during data entry. An alternative solution is to have mail room personnel prepare a detailed listing of the names and amounts of all customer remittances, or photocopy those remittances, and send that information to accounts receivable.

Documents, Records, and Procedures. Figure 17.13 depicts a typical batch-oriented approach to processing cash collections, which is used by AOE. The cash collections process begins when two mail room clerks open the mail. One clerk restrictively endorses the checks received for deposit to one of the company's bank accounts. The other clerk prepares a **remittance list,** a document listing all checks received. The checks and one copy of the remittance list are then sent to the cashier, who prepares them for deposit. The second copy of the remittance list is sent to the internal audit department, where it is later used to reconcile the bank statements. The third copy of the remittance list and the remittance advices are sent to accounts receivable for use in updating customer accounts.

Figure 17.13

Cash Receipts Processing

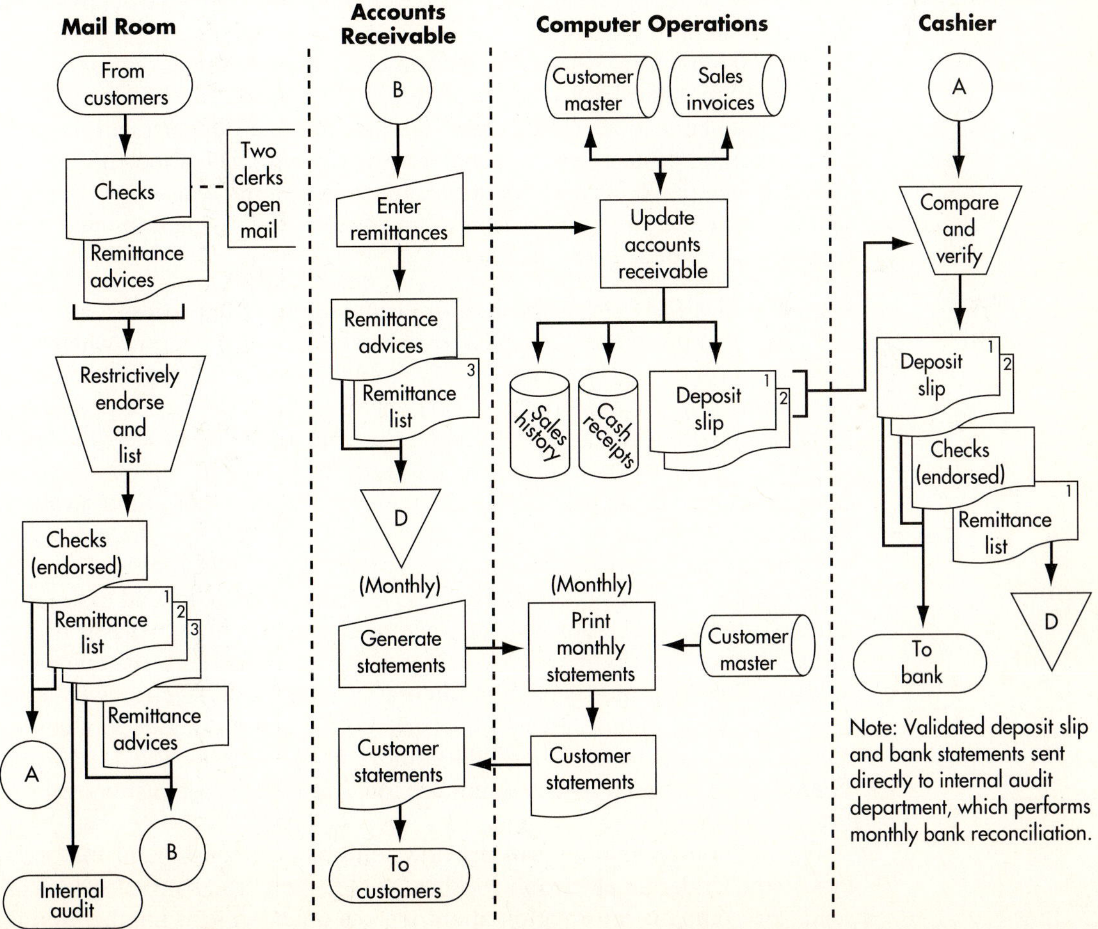

An accounts receivable clerk uses an on-line terminal to enter the sum of the remittance list as a batch total, the customer and invoice numbers, and the amount of each payment. The system performs a number of on-line edit checks to verify the accuracy of data entry, including the following:

1. Validity checks on the customer and invoice numbers.
2. Closed-loop verification to ensure that the proper account is credited. After the clerk enters the customer account number, the system displays the customer name corresponding to that account number and asks for confirmation that this is the correct person.
3. A field check to ensure that only numeric values are entered for payment amounts.
4. Summation of all amounts entered and a comparison of this total to the batch total entered by the clerk; if the two numbers agree, the batch is accepted and the respective files are then updated.

After these edit checks are performed, each customer's account in the customer master file is credited for the amount remitted, open sales invoices are marked paid and closed to the sales history file, and the total cash received is recorded in the cash receipts file. The system then prints two-part deposit slips and sends them to the cashier. The cashier compares the deposit slips with the checks and remittance list and, after verifying that all customer remittances are accounted for, sends the deposit to the bank. Someone not involved in processing cash collections (in this case, the internal audit department) receives the monthly bank statement and prepares the bank reconciliation, thereby providing an independent check on the accuracy and completeness of all deposits. Finally, once a month, the accounts receivable clerk generates and mails monthly statements to all customers.

Opportunities for Using Information Technology. The process depicted in Fig. 17.13 contains three steps that create a delay between the time when a sale is made and the time when the company obtains use of the funds remitted to pay for that sale. The first source of delay involves the time the customer's payment is in the mail system. The second is the time it takes to process the remittance once it has been received. A third source of delay is the time between when the checks are deposited and when the bank makes those funds available to the company.

Companies can reduce these time lags by setting up a lockbox arrangement with a bank. A **lockbox** is a postal address to which customers send their remittances. This post office box is maintained by the participating bank by picking up the checks several times each day and depositing them to the company's account. The bank then sends the remittance advices, an electronic list of all remittances, and photocopies of all checks to the company. Typically, companies select several banks around the country to maintain lockboxes; the locations would be chosen so as to minimize the time it takes for customer checks to arrive by mail.

Information technology can provide additional efficiencies in the use of lockboxes. Under an **electronic lockbox** arrangement, the bank electronically sends the company information about the customer account number and the

FOCUS 17.3

EDI and EFT at Cummins Engine

In the mid-1980s Cummins Engine decided to pursue the productivity benefits of electronic data interchange (EDI) as an important element of its business strategy. Cummins is a major producer of diesel engines, components, and power systems for heavy-duty trucks and industrial machinery. Its primary U.S. customers are truck and equipment manufacturers and a nationwide network of distributors. Cummins found it relatively easy to implement EDI, since the majority of its business is conducted with relatively few (a hundred or so) trading partners.

By mid-1989 Cummins was ready to start tackling implementation with its 32 distributors, all of whom were already exchanging data, in private formats, with Cummins's main computer. Because the distributors already had access to its computer, Cummins decided to have them transmit the remittance detail information directly to its accounts receivable system, rather than send it via a bank. Funds, however, would be transferred separately, as an automated clearinghouse (ACH) payment, through existing bank procedures.

Over a 14-month period Cummins Engine's credit group went from "novice" to "expert" in receiving electronic remittance advice and payment orders from outside customers, distributors, and banks. Cummins reaped three key benefits from this use of EDI: reduced cost, improved accuracy, and increased timeliness of information. A major source of these benefits was eliminating the need to reenter data generated by another computer system. Indeed, it is generally accepted that approximately 70% of all computer input is output from another computer.

Focus Questions

1. How do you think a company can authenticate the validity of EDI transactions (e.g., establish the identity of the sender and the time it was sent)? *Hint:* Think about what information is used to authenticate paper-based transactions.
2. What additional control procedures need to be added when a company adopts the use of EDI and EFT?

Source: Martha M. Heidkamp, "Reaping the Benefits of Financial EDI," *Management Accounting* (May 1991): 39–43. Reprinted with permission of the Institute of Management Accountants.

amount remitted as soon as it receives and scans those checks. This method enables the company to begin applying remittances to customer accounts before the photocopies of the checks arrive.

Lockbox arrangements only eliminate the delays associated with internal processing of remittances mailed directly to the company, however. Electronic funds transfer provides the opportunity to reduce the other two causes of delay in obtaining access to customer funds. With **electronic funds transfer (EFT),** customers send their remittances electronically to the company's bank. This arrangement eliminates the delay associated with the time the remittance is in the mail system. It also reduces the time lag before the bank makes the deposited funds available to the company by eliminating the time it takes the checks to clear the banking system. Focus 17.3 describes one company's experience in using both EDI and EFT to improve its cash collections processing.

Lockbox arrangements not only improve the efficiency of processing cash collections, but also increase control by eliminating employee handling of customer remittances. In the next section, we discuss additional control procedures that can be used to ensure that revenue cycle activities are performed in accordance with management's policies and in a manner that safeguards the organization's assets.

CONTROL: OBJECTIVES, THREATS, AND PROCEDURES

A second function of a well-designed AIS is to provide adequate controls to ensure that the following objectives are met:

1. All transactions are properly authorized.
2. All recorded transactions are valid (actually occurred).
3. All valid, authorized transactions are recorded.
4. All transactions are recorded accurately.
5. Assets (cash, inventory, and data) are safeguarded from loss or theft.
6. Business activities are performed efficiently and effectively.

The documents and records described in the previous section play an important role in achieving these objectives. Simple, easy-to-complete documents with clear instructions facilitate the accurate and efficient recording of transaction data. The inclusion of appropriate application controls, such as validity checks and field (format) checks, further increases the accuracy of data entry when using electronic documents. Providing space on paper and electronic documents to record who completed and who reviewed the form provides evidence that the transaction was properly authorized. Finally, prenumbering the documents facilitates checking that all transactions have been recorded.

Table 17.1 lists the major threats and exposures in the revenue cycle and the additional control procedures, besides adequate documents and records, that should be in place to mitigate them. Every company, regardless of its line of business, faces these threats. Therefore, it is important to understand how the AIS can be designed to counter them. Our discussion will be organized around the four stages of the revenue cycle: sales order entry, shipping, billing, and cash collections.

Sales Order Entry

The primary objective of sales order entry is the efficient processing of customer orders. Threat 1 in Table 17.1 relates to this objective.

Threat 1: Sales to Customers with Poor Credit. The principal threat in sales order entry is the possibility of making sales that later turn out to be uncollectible. This threat is diminished by requiring proper authorization for each credit sale. For cases requiring specific authorization, such as new customers or the extension of additional credit to existing customers, approval should be granted by someone other than the sales representative, especially if the sales staff are paid on commission. The organization chart for AOE (see Fig. 17.1) shows this segregation of duties: the credit manager, who sets credit policies and approves the extension of credit to new customers and the raising of credit limits for existing customers, is independent of the marketing function.

Maintaining accurate and current records of customer account balances and credit limits further diminishes the risk of making uncollectible sales. Indeed, the concept of general authorization of credit sales cannot work effectively if the information about customer account balances and credit limits is inaccurate. Therefore edit checks and input validation routines must be in place to ensure the accuracy of sales transaction data used to update customer master files.

Table 17.1 **Threats, Exposures, and Control Procedures in the Revenue Cycle**

Threat	Exposure	Applicable Control Procedures
1. Credit sales to customers with poor credit	Uncollectible sales and losses due to bad debts	Credit approval by credit manager, not by sales function Accurate records of customer account balances
2. Shipping errors: Wrong merchandise Wrong quantities Wrong address	Customer dissatisfaction	Reconciliation of sales order with picking ticket and packing slip Bar-code scanners Data entry application controls
3. Theft of inventory	Loss of assets Overstated inventory	Restrict physical access to inventory Documentation of all internal transfers of inventory Periodic physical counts of inventory and reconciliation of counts to recorded amounts
4. Failure to bill customers	Loss of inventory Loss of revenue (not collected) Overstated inventory and understated accounts receivable	Separation of shipping and billing functions Prenumbering of all shipping documents and periodic reconciliation of all bills of lading to invoices
5. Billing errors	Customer dissatisfaction Incorrect records and poor decision making	Reconciliation of picking tickets and bills of lading with sales orders Data entry edit controls Price lists
6. Theft of cash	Loss of assets Overstated accounts receivable	Segregation of duties Minimization of cash handling Lockbox arrangements Prompt endorsement and deposit of all receipts Periodic reconciliation of bank statement with records by someone not involved in cash receipts processing
7. Posting errors in updating accounts receivable	Customer dissatisfaction Incorrect records and poor decision making	Reconciliation of subsidiary accounts receivable ledger with general ledger Monthly statements to customers
8. Loss of data	Incorrect data for decision making Loss of confidential information	Backup and disaster recovery procedures Access controls (physical and logical)
9. Poor performance	Inefficient or ineffective processes	Preparation and review of performance reports

Shipping

The primary objective of the shipping function is the efficient and accurate delivery of goods to customers. Threats 2 and 3 in Table 17.1 relate to this objective.

Threat 2: Shipping Errors. Shipping the wrong items or quantities of merchandise and shipping to the wrong location are serious errors because they can significantly reduce customer satisfaction and thus future sales. Shipping mistakes can be caught by reconciling the copy of the sales order sent to the shipping department with the information on the picking ticket received from the warehouse. The use of bar-code scanners to record the picking and shipping of inventory can virtually eliminate data entry errors. At companies where data entry is still performed manually the use of application controls, such as field checks, completeness tests, and the like, can significantly reduce errors.

Threat 3: Theft of Inventory. Another threat in the shipping stage of the revenue cycle involves the theft of inventory. Theft not only represents a loss of assets, but it also results in inaccurate inventory records, which can lead to problems in filling customer orders. Several control procedures can reduce the risk of inventory theft. First, inventory should be kept in a secure location to which physical access is restricted. Second, all inventory transfers within the company should be documented. Inventory should be released to shipping employees based only on approved sales orders. In addition, both warehouse and shipping employees should sign the document accompanying the goods (or make the appropriate acknowledgment of the transfer on-line) at the time the goods are transferred from inventory to shipping. This procedure facilitates tracking the cause of any inventory shortages. In addition, such accountability encourages employees to prepare and maintain accurate records. Finally, recorded amounts of inventory should be periodically reconciled with physical counts of inventory on hand, and the employees responsible for inventory custody should be held accountable for any shortages.

Billing

The primary objective of the billing function is to generate prompt and accurate bills for all sales. Accordingly, threats 4 and 5 in Table 17.1 relate to this objective.

Threat 4: Failure to Bill Customers. The first major threat in the billing function is failure to bill customers for items shipped. Unbilled items result in the loss of assets and erroneous data about sales, inventory, and accounts receivable. This threat is diminished by segregating the shipping and billing functions. Otherwise, an employee performing both functions could ship merchandise to friends without billing them. Additional control is provided by prenumbering and periodically accounting for all documents (sales orders, bills of lading, and invoices). Any sales orders or bills of lading that cannot be matched to a sales invoice represent shipments that have not been billed, and corrective action should then be taken.

Threat 5: Billing Errors. A second threat includes errors such as pricing mistakes and billing customers for items not shipped or back-ordered. Overbilling can result in customer dissatisfaction; underbilling results in a loss of assets to the company. Pricing mistakes can be avoided by having the computer retrieve the appropriate data from the inventory master file. Mistakes involving quantities shipped can be caught by reconciling the quantities listed on the bill of lading with those on the sales order.

Cash Collections

The primary objectives of the cash collections function are to safeguard customer remittances and properly credit customer accounts. Threats 6 and 7 in Table 17.1 relate to these objectives.

Threat 6: Theft of Cash. As mentioned previously, special control procedures are needed to safeguard cash. Segregation of duties is the most effective control procedure for reducing the threat of the loss of cash. Employees who have physical access to cash should not have responsibility for recording or authorizing any transactions involving its receipt. Specifically, the following pairs of duties should be segregated:

1. *Handling cash or checks and posting remittances to customer accounts.* A person performing both of these duties could commit a type of embezzlement called *lapping.*
2. *Handling cash or checks and authorizing credit memos.* A person performing both of these duties could conceal theft of cash by creating a credit memo equal to the amount stolen.
3. *Issuing credit memos and maintaining customer accounts.* A person performing both of these duties could write off amounts owed by friends as uncollectible.

In general, the handling of money and checks within the organization should be minimized. The optimal methods are a bank lockbox arrangement or the use of EFT for customer payments. Of course, the costs of these arrangements must be weighed against the benefits of reduced internal processing costs and faster access to customer payments.

If customer payments must be processed internally, prompt documentation of remittances is crucial because the risk of loss is greatest at the time of first receipt. Thus, as shown in Fig. 17.13, a list of all checks received should be prepared immediately after opening the mail. The checks should also be restrictively endorsed at that time. In addition, two people should open all incoming mail, to minimize the risk of misappropriating any cash or checks received.

Several additional procedures that minimize the risk of lapping are also depicted in Fig. 17.13. The accounts receivable department has access to remittance advices rather than customer checks. The cashier receives customer checks but doesn't have access to the customer (accounts receivable) master file; therefore, the cashier has no means of altering the records to conceal the theft of checks. In addition, the copy of the remittance list that is sent to the internal audit department can be compared to the validated deposit slips and bank statements to verify that all checks received by the organization were deposited. Finally, the monthly statements mailed to customers provide another layer of control, since customers would notice the failure to properly credit their accounts for payments remitted.

Retail stores and organizations that receive cash directly from customers should use cash registers that automatically produce a written record of all cash received. In these situations, customers can also play a role in controlling cash collections. For example, many stores use signs to inform customers that their purchase is free if they fail to get a receipt or that receipts marked with a red star entitle them to a discount. Such policies encourage customers to watch that employees actually do ring up the cash sale, and do so correctly.

All customer remittances should be deposited, intact, in the bank each day. Daily deposits reduce the amount of cash and checks at risk of theft. Depositing all remittances intact, and not using any of them for miscellaneous expenditures, facilitates reconciliation of the bank statement with the records of sales, accounts receivable, and cash collections.

Finally, the employee who reconciles the bank statements should be independent of any of the other activities involved in handling or recording the receipt of cash. This separation of duties provides an independent check on the cashier and prevents manipulating the bank statement to conceal the theft of cash.

Threat 7: Posting Errors in Updating Accounts Receivable. The other threat related to the cash collections step of the revenue cycle involves errors in maintaining customer accounts. Posting errors can be detected by reconciling the results of processing with both internal and external data. For example, after processing customer payments, the sum of all individual customer account balances (the accounts receivable subsidiary file) should equal the total balance of the accounts receivable control account in the general ledger. If the two are not equal, an error in posting has probably occurred and all transactions just entered should be reexamined.

To ensure that all remittances were processed, the number of customer accounts updated should be compared with the number of checks received. These reconciliations should be performed by someone other than the individual involved in processing the original transactions, because (1) it is easier to catch someone else's mistakes than your own and (2) it provides a means to identify irregularities. Finally, mailing monthly account statements provides an additional independent review of the accuracy of all postings to customer accounts because customers will complain if their accounts have not been properly credited for payments remitted.

General Control Issues

Threats 8 and 9 in Table 17.1 are general threats that affect all phases of the expenditure cycle.

Threat 8: Loss of Data. Another threat in the revenue cycle is loss of data about customer accounts. Accurate customer account and inventory records are important not only for external and internal reporting purposes, but also for responding to customer inquiries. Moreover, loss of all accounts receivable data could threaten a company's continued existence. Therefore, those records must be protected from loss or damage.

The master accounts receivable, sales, and cash receipts files must all be backed up regularly. Two backup copies of key files, such as the accounts receivable master file, should be made; one should be kept on-site, the other stored off-site. Moreover, the grandfather-father-son technique should be used to store several generations of the master file and the intervening transaction files. All disks and tapes should have both external and internal file labels to reduce the possibility of accidentally erasing important files.

Access controls are also important. Leakage of customer information to competitors can hurt sales and may even subject the company to legal liability. Unauthorized access also increases the risk of damage to important data files. A system of passwords and user IDs should be used to limit employees' access to and allowable operations on files. For example, only sales staff should be allowed to create sales orders. Moreover, sales staff should have read-only access to customer credit limits and current account balances. Access controls should also exist for individual terminals. For example, the system should be programmed to reject any attempts to enter sales orders from a terminal located at the shipping dock. Finally, logs of all activities, especially any actions involving managerial approval (e.g., extending credit limits) should be recorded and maintained for later review as part of the audit trail.

Threat 9: Poor Performance. In addition to ensuring accuracy and safeguarding assets, another objective of internal controls is to encourage efficient and effective performance of duties. The preparation and review of reports provides a basis for assessing the efficiency and effectiveness of revenue cycle activities and for diminishing the threat of substandard performance. The potential number of such reports is limited only by management's choice about what activities are important to monitor and control. For example, sales order entry efficiency can be monitored by preparing periodic reports of sales orders processed per individual in a given time period. The efficiency and effectiveness of the sales force can be assessed by **sales analyses,** a breakdown of sales by salesperson, region, or product (see Table 17.2). Further insights about overall marketing performance can be provided by preparing a **profitability analysis,** which breaks down the marginal profit contribution made by each territory, customer, distribution channel, salesperson, product, or other basis (see Table 17.3).

Table 17.2 **Sample Sales Analysis Report**

Period Ending: October 31, 1997						**Territory: East Texas**
Salesperson	**Period**	**Actual Sales**	**Prior Year Sales**	**Percent Change**	**Sales Quota**	**Percent Variance from Quota**
Benjamin, H.L.	This month	$ 50,000	$ 40,000	+25	$ 48,000	+4
	Year to date	120,000	115,000	+4	125,000	−4
Carlton, J.C.	This month	40,000	38,000	+5	45,000	−11
	Year to date	105,000	110,000	−5	130,000	−19
.	.	.	.	.	.	.
.	.	.	.	.	.	.
.	.	.	.	.	.	.
.	.	.	.	.	.	.
.	.	.	.	.	.	.
Territory totals	This month	$300,000	285,500	+5	$350,000	−14
	Year to date	850,000	840,000	+1	950,000	−11

Table 17.3 Sample Profitability Analysis by Product

	A	B	C	D	E	F	G
1							
2				For the Month of January 1998			
3							
4			Unit	Total	Variable	Contribution	Margin
5	Product Class		Volume	Revenue	Cost	Margin	Percent
6	Calculators		164500	$ 259,750	$ 184,500	$ 75,250	28.97
7	Digital clocks		109750	$ 318,500	$ 220,500	$ 98,000	30.76
8	Radios		128750	$ 335,400	$ 230,200	$105,200	31.36
9	Small appliances		142200	$ 382,900	$ 251,500	$131,400	34.31
10	Pagers		56800	$ 246,700	$ 144,800	$101,900	41.3
11	Toys and games		124500	$ 253,200	$ 121,400	$131,800	52.05
12	Totals		726500	$1,796,450	$1,152,900	$643,550	35.82

Reports on the frequency and size of back orders provide insight about the effectiveness of inventory management policies in satisfying customer demands. Similarly, reports that identify slow-moving products help to avoid excessive stockpiling. An **accounts receivable aging schedule** lists customer account balances by length of time outstanding; it provides useful information for evaluating current credit policies and for deciding whether to increase the credit limit for specific customers. It also provides information for estimating bad debts.

A cash budget provides precise estimates of cash inflows (projected collections from sales) and outflows (outstanding payables). This information is essential for effective cash management. For example, an organization that foresees a pending short-term cash shortage can plan ahead to secure short-term loans at the best possible rates. Conversely, an organization that knows a surplus of cash is pending can take steps to invest those excess funds to earn the best possible returns. A cash budget could have helped AOE better manage its short-term borrowing needs.

In the next section we discuss in more detail how the AIS can be designed to provide these various reports and other information useful for effectively managing revenue cycle activities.

REVENUE CYCLE INFORMATION NEEDS AND DATA MODEL

The third function of the AIS is to provide information useful for decision making. As related to the revenue cycle, the AIS should provide the operational information needed to perform the following functions:

- Respond to customer inquiries about account balances and order status.
- Decide whether to extend credit to a particular customer.
- Determine inventory availability.

- Decide what types of credit terms to offer.
- Set prices for products and services.
- Set policies regarding sales returns and warranties.
- Select methods for delivering merchandise.

In addition, the AIS should provide the following kinds of strategic and performance evaluation information:

- Response time to customer inquiries.
- Time required to fill and deliver orders.
- Percentage of sales that required back orders.
- Customer satisfaction.
- Analyses of market share and sales trends.
- Profitability analyses by product, customer, and sales region.
- Sales volume in both dollars and number of customers.
- Effectiveness of advertising and promotions.
- Sales staff performance.
- Bad debt expenses and credit policies.
- Expected cash collections and short-term borrowing needs.

Notice that both financial and operating information is needed to manage and evaluate revenue cycle activities. For example, evaluating the efficiency and effectiveness of sales order entry requires data not only about sales volumes but also about order processing time. In addition, information from external sources, such as measures of customer satisfaction, is also needed. Traditionally, the AIS has provided the internally generated financial measures of performance and managers have turned to other sources for the internal operating and external information they need. This situation is both costly and inefficient. It is also no longer necessary. With the use of data base systems, it is now possible to redesign the AIS to capture and store both financial and operating data about revenue cycle transactions and to integrate that internally generated data with information from external sources.

Revenue Cycle Data Model

As explained in Chapter 6, the REA data model provides one method for designing a data base that efficiently integrates both financial and operating data. Figure 17.14 shows a simplified REA data model for the revenue cycle of a manufacturing company such as AOE. It includes the following information:

- The two major resources (cash and inventory) used in the revenue cycle.
- The four major business events in the revenue cycle (orders, shipments, sales [billing], and cash collections).
- The primary external agent (customers) as well as the various internal agents involved in revenue cycle activities.

If the data model depicted in Fig. 17.14 were implemented in a relational data base, there would be a table for each entity and for each many-to-many relationship. The bottom half of Fig. 17.14 lists many of the attributes that would be found in those tables.

As you recall, each box in an E–R diagram represents either a resource, an event, or an agent entity about which information is collected. The labeled

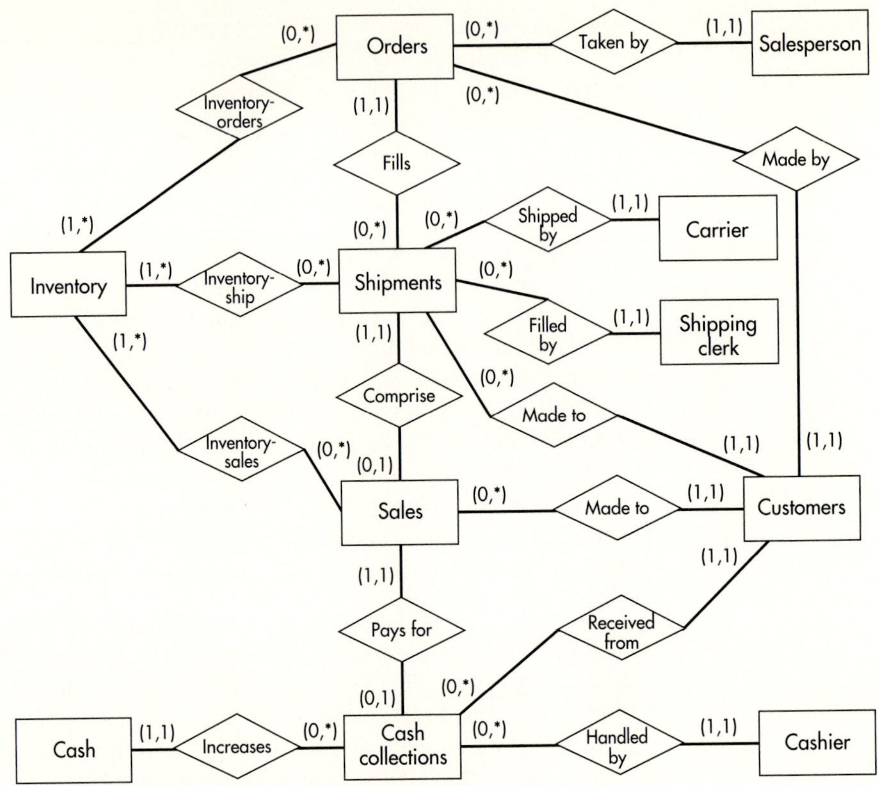

Figure 17.14

Partial E–R Diagram for the Revenue Cycle

Attributes for Relational Tables Based on Fig. 17.14

Table Name	Contents (primary key, foreign key)
Inventory	**Product-Number,** Description, Cost, Price, Quantity-on-Hand, Quantity-Available, Weight, ...
Cash	**Bank-Account-Number,** Balance, Interest-Rate, . . .
Orders	**Sales-Order-Number,** Date, *Customer-Number, Salesperson-Number,* Terms, Ship-to-Address, . . .
Shipments	**Bill-of-Lading-Number,** *Carrier-Number, Sales-Order-Number, Shipping-Clerk-Number,* Date, Terms, . . .
Sales	**Invoice-Number,** Date, Time, Amount, *Customer-Number, Bill-of-Lading-Number,* . . .
Cash Collections	**Remittance-Advice-Number,** Date, Amount, *Customer-Number, Invoice-Number, Bank-Account-Number, Cashier-Number* . . .
Inventory-Order	**Product-Number, Sales-Order-Number,** Quantity
Inventory-Ship	**Product-Number, Bill-of-Lading-Number,** Quantity
Inventory-Sales	**Product-Number, Invoice-Number,** Quantity
Salesperson	**Employee-Number,** Name, Salary, Date-of-Hire, Commission-Rate, Region, *Manager-Number,* Date of Birth, . . .
Customers	**Customer-Number,** Name, Bill-to-Address, Ship-to-Address, Balance, Credit-Limit, . . .
Cashier	**Employee-Number,** Name, Pay-Rate, Date-of-Hire, *Manager-Number,* Date-of-Birth, . . .
Shipping Clerk	**Employee-Number,** Name, Pay-Rate, Date-of-Hire, *Manager-Number,* Date-of-Birth, . . .
Carrier	**Carrier-Number,** Name, Address, Performance-Rating, . . .

diamonds between these entities represent the relationships of interest. Finally, the cardinalities of those relationships, which are shown in parentheses on the E–R diagram, reflect important information about the organization's policies and the nature of its business.

For example, the one-to-many relationship in Fig. 17.14 between the customer order and shipment events indicates that sometimes it takes AOE several shipments to fill a customer order. Moreover, the minimum cardinality of zero associated with the shipment event indicates that customer orders are not always filled immediately. In turn, the one-to-one relationship between the shipment and the sales events indicates that AOE bills customers for each shipment separately. The minimum cardinality of zero associated with the sales event, however, indicates that invoices are not always generated at the time the shipment is made. The one-to-one relationship between the sales and cash collections events indicates that AOE expects its customers to pay by the invoice, rather than by a monthly statement. The minimum cardinality of zero associated with the cash collections event indicates that AOE does sell on credit. The one-to-many relationships between the various agent and event entities represent the fact that every event must involve both an internal and an external agent. Finally, the many-to-many relationships between inventory and the customer order, shipment, and sales events represent the fact that AOE sells mass-produced items.

But where are data about accounts receivable stored? Accounts receivable represents sales for which payment has not yet been received. Therefore, recall from Chapter 6 that accounts receivable can be calculated by taking the difference between the total amount of sales and the amount of cash collections linked to those sales events.

Benefits of the Data Model

Notice how the data model depicted in Fig. 17.14 effectively integrates both traditional accounting transaction data (for example, the date and amount of the sale) with other operational data (for example, information about the time the sale was made) that have not traditionally been captured by the AIS. Moreover, the system can capture some of this additional information, like the time of the sale, automatically without any extra data entry. It also dramatically increases the types of analyses that are possible. For example, sales can be analyzed by time of day to better plan for staffing needs.

It would also be easy to link this internal data with various types of external information. For example, credit rating data about current and potential customers could be downloaded from a commercial data base and stored in additional columns in the customer table. Similarly, information about customer satisfaction collected from surveys could also be stored in additional columns in the customer table.

Most importantly, decision makers can easily retrieve all this information by using query languages like SQL (Table 17.4). Thus implementing the REA data model in a relational data base significantly improves the ability of the AIS to provide management with the information necessary for effectively managing revenue cycle activities.

In addition to providing decision makers with quick and easy access to information, a well-designed data base can provide strategic benefits to a company's

Table 17.4 SQL Query of Revenue Cycle Data Base

Query: Which customers have outstanding unpaid invoices, and how much do they owe?

```
SELECT   Customer-Number, Amount, Invoice-Number
FROM     Sales
WHERE    Invoice-Number NOT IN
         (SELECT   Invoice-Number
         FROM      Cash Collections)
```

Sales

Invoice-Number	Date	Amount	Customer-Number	Bill-of-Lading-Number
1232	06/30/97	6595	1255	1134
1233	07/01/97	8500	2344	1135
1234	07/01/97	15000	2165	1136
1235	07/02/97	3500	1255	1137
1236	07/03/97	4290	1842	1138

Cash Collections

Remittance-Advice-Number	Date	Amount	Customer-Number	Invoice-Number	Bank-Account-Number	Cashier-Number
1566	07/13/97	7200	1163	1230	1011	211
1567	07/13/97	6595	1255	1232	1011	211
1568	07/13/97	3500	1255	1235	1011	212
1569	07/15/97	4290	1842	1236	1012	212

The second SELECT clause retrieves the invoice numbers in the Cash Collections table. The first SELECT clause then identifies the rows in the Sales table where the Invoice-Number is not found in the list returned by the second SELECT clause.

Response to Query

Customer-Number	Amount	Invoice-Number
2344	8500	1233
2165	15000	1234

marketing efforts. For example, the 1990s have witnessed the emergence of what is called *precision marketing.* This strategy involves tailoring advertising and sales promotions to the needs and desires of specific customers. Instead of sending mass "junk mail" promotions to every potential customer in a geographic area, precision marketing sends specific messages to targeted groups of people.

For example, General Motors Corporation uses data collected from its affinity program with Master Card and its own sales records to determine the type of vehicle information—makes, models, colors, and so on—it should send to specific customers. Similarly, Blockbuster Entertainment Corporation tracks a customer's rental history and mails promotions that suggest titles that may appeal to that customer. Kraft General Foods, Inc. uses information collected from surveys to prepare customized mailings that offer nutrition information and recipes featuring the very same Kraft products that a customer has purchased in the past. Siemens Rolm Communications Company tracks customer requests for moving, adding, or changing communications network switches. It uses this information to predict when a customer is approaching capacity limits and would therefore be receptive to a sales call recommending the purchase of additional capacity.

These examples illustrate how companies can use information about their customers to generate increased sales. The success of these strategies depends on two factors. First, data from both internal and external data sources must be integrated effectively, possibly by using the REA data model as the basis for redesigning the AIS. Second, adequate control procedures must also be built into the system to ensure that the data stored therein are accurate.

Internal Control Considerations

Data accuracy is vital when using a DBMS. Fortunately, the relational data model provides some built-in controls to ensure data accuracy and consistency. One of the more important of these controls is support for foreign keys and referential integrity. It ensures, for example, that, when a new row is added to the orders table, the system will verify that the customer number (which appears as a foreign key in that table) actually exists as primary key in the customer table (that there really is such a customer).

The use of DBMS also increases the importance of having effective access controls. Most relational DBMS provide a means to control access by letting different users see only a portion of the data base (called a view). For example, sales order entry clerks would see only the portion of Fig. 17.14, such as the tables for inventory, customers, and orders, relevant to their job duties. In addition, sales order entry clerks would be permitted to perform only certain operations on those tables. For example, they would have read-only rights to the customer table, to prevent any unauthorized changes to the customer account balances or credit limits.

Our discussion of the threats listed in Table 17.1 stressed the importance of properly segregating incompatible duties. E–R diagrams are useful in evaluating the extent to which incompatible duties are segregated, because they indicate which internal agents participate in each event. Moreover, if the REA model is implemented in a DBMS, the computer can be programmed to enforce segregation of duties by rejecting any employee attempts to perform incompatible functions. Conversely, the system can also be programmed to list all cases of an employee performing multiple roles, so that the auditors can investigate whether adequate compensating controls exist. Finally, the use of a DBMS makes adequate backup and disaster recovery procedures vital components of the system.

SUMMARY AND CASE CONCLUSION

The four basic functions in the revenue cycle are sales order entry, shipping, billing, and cash collections. The AIS should be designed to maximize the efficiency with which each of these functions is performed. The AIS must also incorporate adequate internal control procedures to mitigate threats such as uncollectible sales, billing errors, and lost or misappropriated inventory and cash. Control procedures are also needed to ensure that the information provided for decision making is both accurate and complete. Finally, to facilitate strategic decision making, the AIS should be designed to accommodate the integration of internally generated data with data from external sources.

Figure 17.15 depicts the new AIS that Elizabeth Venko has proposed for AOE. The proposal includes the following key points:

1. *On-line sales order entry.* Each salesperson will be equipped with a pen-based portable computer and a modem. As they walk down store aisles, sales representatives can check off the items that need to be restocked and then write in the appropriate quantities. When the order is complete, they can plug

Figure 17.15

Proposed Revenue Cycle System for AOE. (a) Sales order entry, (b) Cash receipts

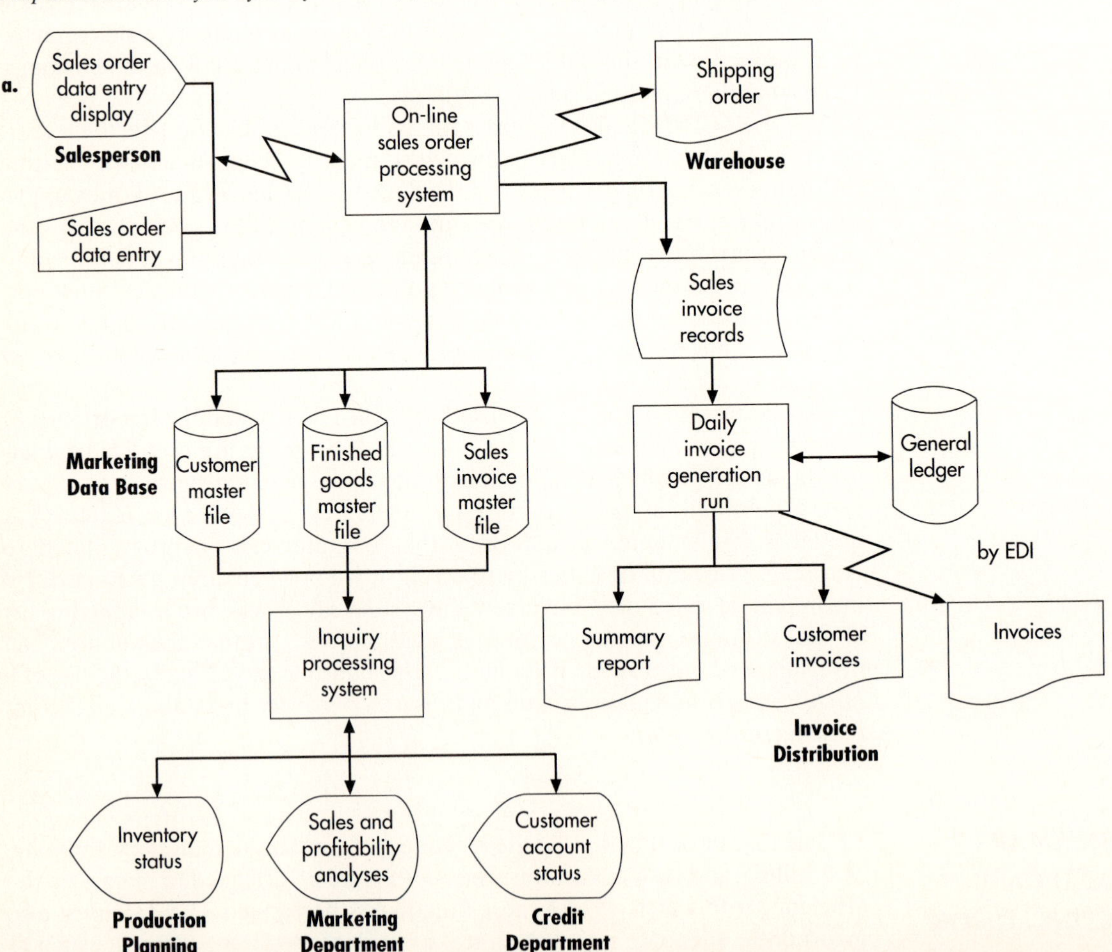

Figure 17.15

Continued

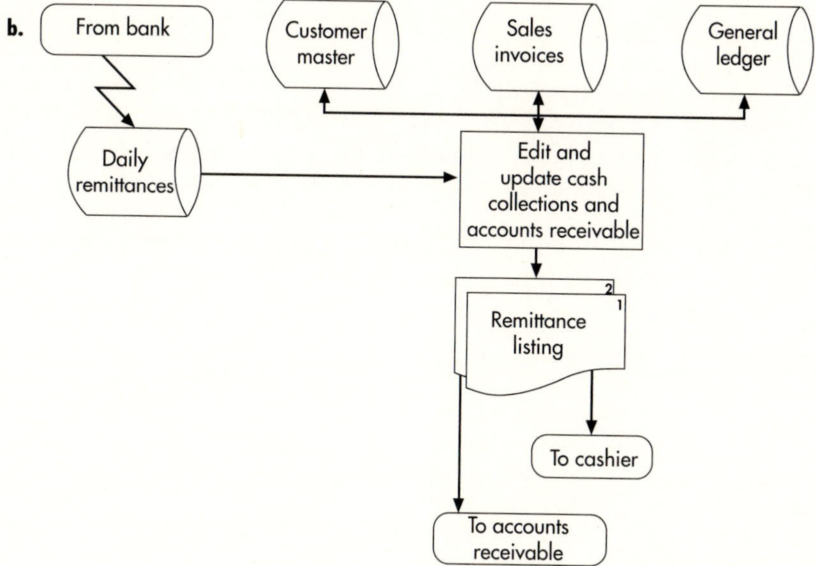

in their modem and transmit the order back to headquarters. The new system checks the customer's credit status and inventory availability and confirms orders within minutes, including an estimated delivery date. After the customer approves the order, the system immediately updates all affected files, so that current information about inventory status is available to other sales representatives.

Once this system is implemented and smoothly functioning, Elizabeth plans to open a Home Page on the Internet so that customers can deal directly with AOE. This will not eliminate the need for a field sales force, however. Trevor Whitman, vice president of marketing, believes that AOE will still need its sales staff to visit existing customers to help identify which additional products can be profitably carried. Sales staff will also continue to make "cold calls" on prospective customers to try to convince them to carry AOE's products.

2. *EDI invoicing.* EDI will be used to bill customers, although paper invoices will still be printed nightly for those customers not yet ready for EDI. EDI will speed up the billing process and improve AOE's cash flow. Moreover, once EDI links have been established with major customers, Elizabeth intends to obtain access to their POS data so that AOE can help them better manage their inventory of AOE products.

3. *Electronic lockboxes.* Electronic lockbox arrangements have also been established with six regional banks. Customers will be encouraged to use EFT for their remittances. This will further improve AOE's cash flow.

4. *Implementation of a relational data base.* A relational data base designed along the lines of the data model presented in Fig. 17.14 will pull together

the internal and external information that Elizabeth Venko and other decision makers need to manage revenue cycle activities effectively. Moreover, SQL will give AOE's decision makers easy access to the information they require.

Linda Spurgeon, president of AOE, approved Elizabeth's proposal. She is impressed with the move to EDI and EFT for invoicing and cash collections and asked Elizabeth to begin thinking about whether these techniques can also be used to streamline some of AOE's expenditure cycle activities.

KEY TERMS

revenue cycle
credit limit
back order
sales order
packing slip
picking ticket
bill of lading
freight bill
sales invoice
monthly statement
credit memo
postbilling system
prebilling system
open-invoice method
remittance advice
balance-forward method
cycle billing
remittance list
lockbox
electronic lockbox
electronic funds transfer (EFT)
sales analyses
profitability analysis
accounts receivable aging schedule

CHAPTER QUIZ

1. Which activity is part of the sales order entry process?
   a. Setting customer credit limits
   b. Preparing a bill of lading
   c. Checking customer credit
   d. Approving sales returns

2. Which document often accompanies merchandise shipped to a customer?
   a. Picking list
   b. Packing slip
   c. Credit memo
   d. Sales order

3. Which approach to billing customers prepares invoices *after* merchandise has been shipped?
   a. Open-invoice method
   b. Prebilling system
   c. Postbilling system
   d. Cycle billing

4. Having customers send checks directly to a postal address, rather than to the company, is an example of
   a. an EFT system.
   b. an EDI system.
   c. image processing.
   d. a bank lockbox arrangement.

5. Which of the following is *not* likely to be included in a data model of the revenue cycle?
   a. Cash collections
   b. Sales
   c. Orders
   d. Purchases

6. A(n) ______ would be most useful for determining which sales region needs to receive additional attention to improve sales.
   a. accounts receivable aging schedule
   b. profitability analysis
   c. sales analysis
   d. cash budget

7. The document used to authorize the release of merchandise from the inventory control (warehouse) to shipping is the
   a. picking list.
   b. packing slip.
   c. shipping order.
   d. sales invoice.

8. For a retail store like Wal-Mart, the relationship between sales and inventory items is most likely to be represented as being
   a. one-to-one.
   b. one-to-many.
   c. many-to-one.
   d. many-to-many.

9. For good internal control, credit memos should be approved by the
   a. credit manager.
   b. sales manager.
   c. billing manager.
   d. controller.

10. For good internal control over customer remittances, the mail room should separate the checks from the remittance advices and send the checks to

a. billing.
b. accounts receivable.
c. the cashier.
d. the controller.

DISCUSSION QUESTIONS

17.1 The marketing department of the RSC Company maintains a computerized customer file that contains information on each customer, including the products in which the customer is interested, recent requests for information, recent contacts with sales personnel, recent order and delivery activity, reports on customer satisfaction, and customer service requirements. The accounting department currently maintains a separate customer file that contains accounting information on recent sales transactions and payments from customers, including the customer's current account balance.

The RSC Company has recently acquired a data base management system. The systems department has proposed building the new data base using the REA data model. One consequence of this approach is that a chart of accounts would no longer be used to record and store data. The controller is concerned about this change and argues that she will not be able to generate financial statements without a chart of accounts. Comment on the controller's concerns, and discuss the advantages and disadvantages of using the REA model, instead of a chart of accounts, as the basis for storing data about revenue cycle activities.

17.2 Compaq Computer Corporation provides an example of how information technology is changing the nature of the sales process. In April 1993 it cut one-third of its sales force and shifted the remaining staff out of the office to work from their homes, using portable computers and networks to keep in touch with customers and the corporate data base. Discuss the implications of this move. What are some of the human resource issues that such a work design raises? What new control considerations, if any, need to be addressed?

17.3 What types of external information are needed for effectively managing the revenue cycle? How does the use of a data model similar to the one depicted in Fig. 17.14 facilitate the integration of the external data with internally generated data about revenue cycle business activities?

17.4 Compare the relative advantages and disadvantages of using a prebilling versus a postbilling system.

17.5 Advances in information technology are creating new ways to perform sales activities. For example, customers can order directly from a company's Home Page on the Internet. CD-ROMs can be mailed to customers to demonstrate new products. Do you think that these and other developments will eliminate the need for an external sales force? Why or why not?

17.6 Dell Computer Corporation recently contracted with Roadway Services, Inc. to perform all its shipping and receiving functions. Its objective was to cut costs; prior to signing the contract, approximately 40% of the cost of a Dell product consisted of the logistics costs of receiving raw materials and shipping finished goods. The move will also avoid the need to hire as many as 2000 additional workers. Discuss the advantages and disadvantages of outsourcing functions such as shipping. What control issues are raised by such an arrangement?

PROBLEMS

17.1 Kids Choice Corporation is a manufacturer and distributor of children's toys. Over the past three years the company's sales volume has declined as several important distributors have dropped the Kids Choice product line. In response, the company's top management has just ordered every department within the company to reevaluate its operations, identify potential problems that may be contributing to the company's loss of business, and prepare recommendations for improvement.

You have been asked to evaluate the revenue cycle activities.

At present, customers are sent catalogs, price lists, and order forms each quarter, and they mail completed order forms to a central data processing facility. There the orders are keyed into the computer system and processed in batches. Shipping documents are printed for approved orders and routed to the Kids Choice distribution center closest to the customer, where the merchandise is picked, packaged, and shipped to the customer. The process typically takes two to three weeks from time of receipt of the customer order to delivery.

The billing department prepares and mails invoices to customers after receiving notification from the shipping department that the order has been filled and shipped. Customers mail their remittances to the central Kids Choice office. Cash collections are processed and customer accounts are updated weekly. Several customers have complained that their account balances are incorrect and do not reflect recent payments.

REQUIRED

Could Kids Choice Corporation's AIS be one of the factors contributing to the company's recent decline? Describe several ways to use information technology to improve the sales and cash collections procedures used by Kids Choice.

17.2 What internal control procedure(s) would provide protection against the following threats? If more than one control procedure could be used to solve a problem, rank the alternatives in terms of their effectiveness.

a. Theft of goods by the shipping dock workers, who claim that the inventory shortages reflect errors in the inventory records.
b. The posting of the amount of a sale to the wrong customer account, because a customer account number was incorrectly keyed into the system.
c. A credit sale to a customer who is already four months behind in making payments on his account.
d. Authorization of a credit memo for a sales return when the goods were never actually returned.
e. Writing off a customer's accounts receivable balance as uncollectible in order to conceal the theft of subsequent collections.
f. Billing customers for the quantity ordered when the quantity shipped was actually less due to back ordering of some items.
g. Theft of checks by the mail room clerk, who then endorsed the checks for deposit into the account of a fictitious company.
h. Theft of funds by the cashier, who cashed several checks and did not record their receipt.
i. Theft of cash by a waiter who destroyed the customer sales ticket for customers who paid cash.

17.3 Refer to Fig. 17.14 to answer the following questions:

a. If the relationship between billing and cash collections were one-to-many, what would that reveal about the company's sales policy? What if the relationship were many-to-one? What if it was many-to-many? Think of real company examples that reflect each of these options.
b. What does the one-to-many relationship between orders and shipments mean? Provide examples of real companies for which other relationships between orders and shipments exist.
c. What would a one-to-one relationship between inventory and sales imply about the types of products sold by the company?
d. Can the relationship between sales and customers ever be one-to-many or many-to-many? Why or why not?

17.4 Your company has just acquired a data base management system and wants to develop an REA data model for its revenue cycle activities.

REQUIRED

a. Use the following facts, plus the generic description of the revenue cycle included in the chapter, to modify Fig. 17.14:

1. The company uses the balance-forward method to bill its customers.
2. The company carries its own credit; customers may pay all or only a portion of their bill each month.
3. There are no back orders or deliveries.
4. The company wants to track the performance of its customer service representatives in terms of responding to customer inquiries.

b. In addition to modifying the E–R diagram, list the attributes that should be stored about the customer service event. Indicate which of these attributes should be the primary key and which, if any, are foreign keys.

17.5 Table 17.5 shows some of the relational tables used to implement an REA model of a company's revenue cycle.

Table 17.5
Relational Tables for Problem 17.5

Inventory

Part Number	Description	Cost	Price
101	Monitor	899	1295
102	CPU	2150	2599
103	CD-ROM drive	95	199
104	Printer	345	499
105	Tape unit	195	259

Inventory-Sales

Part Number	Invoice Number	Quantity
101	25	1
102	25	1
103	25	1
104	26	2

Cash Collections

Remittance Number	Amount	Invoice Number	Customer Number
120	499	23	1001
121	4851	24	1003
122	4851	27	1001

Sales

Invoice Number	Date	Customer Number	Salesperson Number
23	11/05	1001	12
24	11/05	1003	10
25	11/06	1002	8
26	11/07	1003	12
27	11/07	1001	8
28	11/07	1003	12

Salesperson

Salesperson Number	Name
8	Jones
10	Brown
12	Alawi

Customer

Customer Number	Name	Address
1001	Agrawal	Chicago
1002	Chen	Memphis
1003	Finney	St. Louis

REQUIRED

a. Identify the primary key of each table.
b. Identify the foreign key(s), if any, of each table.
c. Which tables represent resources? events? agents?
d. Draw an E–R diagram of the system. List any assumptions you made in assigning cardinalities to relationships.
e. Write the SQL queries required to display all the information (date, items sold, prices, customer name and address, salesperson, etc.) that would normally be found on invoice number 25.
f. Write the SQL query, or queries, needed to show the current account balance for Charles Finney.
g. Write the SQL query to determine the item with the largest markup.
h. Write the SQL query, or queries, to calculate total accounts receivable.

17.6 The Quality Building Supplies Company operates six wholesale outlets that sell roofing materials, electrical and plumbing supplies, lumber, and other building materials to general contractors in a large metropolitan area. The company is studying the feasibility of introducing a guaranteed same-day delivery plan, under which it would guarantee delivery within four hours for orders received from approved customers by noon of that day. For orders received in the afternoon, delivery would be guaranteed by

8 A.M. the next day. The company believes that this system would give it a substantial competitive advantage relative to other regional building wholesalers, because it would enable contractors to maintain smaller inventories yet still be assured of having building supplies when needed.

You have been asked to assist in designing the proposed system. It will be designed to receive customer orders by phone, so that contractors can call from the construction site. Customers will be billed monthly for all purchases. You want to streamline the processing of cash collections and minimize the time it takes to deposit those funds in the company's bank account.

REQUIRED

a. Specify not only the credit-related, but the other factors that should be used to qualify customers for this new service.
b. Identify the input transactions that this system must process and the output documents (excluding reports) that it should produce.
c. Draw an E–R diagram based on the REA data model to describe the information that must be captured and maintained by the new system.
d. Describe several reports that would be useful to management's implementation of the new credit sales policy. What data need to be collected to produce these reports? What application controls should be in place to ensure that these reports contain complete, accurate, and valid information?
e. Draw a systems flowchart of your proposed system.
f. Describe the threats that need to be protected against and the control procedures that should be included in the new system to address those threats.

17.7 O'Brien Corporation is a medium-sized, privately owned industrial instrument manufacturer supplying precision equipment manufacturers in the Midwest. The corporation is 10 years old and operates a centralized AIS. The administrative offices are located in a downtown building, and the production, shipping, and receiving departments are housed in a renovated warehouse a few blocks away. The shipping and receiving areas share one end of the warehouse.

The marketing department consists of four sales representatives. Upon obtaining an order, usually over the telephone, a salesperson manually prepares a prenumbered, two-part sales order. One copy of the order is filed by date and the second copy is sent to the shipping department. All sales are on credit, FOB destination. Because of the recent increase in sales, the sales representatives have not had time to check credit histories. As a result, 15% of credit sales are either late collections or uncollectible.

The shipping department receives the sales orders and packages the goods from the warehouse, noting any items that are out of stock. The terminal in the shipping department is used to update the perpetual inventory records of each item as it is removed from the shelf. The packages are placed near the loading dock door in alphabetical order by customer name. The sales order is signed by a shipping clerk indicating that the order is filled and ready to send.

The sales order is forwarded to the billing department, where a two-part sales invoice is prepared. The sales invoice is prepared only upon receipt of the sales order from the shipping department, so that the customer is billed just for the items that were sent, not for back orders. Billing sends the customer's copy of the invoice back to shipping; shipping then inserts it into a special envelope on the package in order to save postage.

The carrier of the customer's choice is then contacted to pick up the goods. In the past, goods were shipped within two working days of the receipt of the customer's order; however, shipping dates now average six working days. One reason for this slippage is that two new shipping clerks are still undergoing training. Because they have fallen behind, the two clerks in the receiving department, who are experienced, have been assisting them.

The receiving department is located adjacent to the shipping dock, and merchandise is received daily by many different carriers. The clerks share a computer terminal with the shipping department. The date, vendor, and number of items received are entered upon receipt in order to keep the perpetual inventory records current.

Hard copies of the changes in inventory (additions and shipments) are printed once a month. The receiving supervisor makes sure that the additions are reasonable and forwards the printout to the shipping supervisor, who is responsible for checking the reasonableness of the deductions from inventory (shipments). The inventory printout is stored in the shipping department by date. A complete inventory list is printed only once a year, when the entire inventory is counted.

The diagram in Fig. 17.16 presents the document flows employed by O'Brien Corporation.

Figure 17.16

Revenue Cycle Activities for O'Brien Corporation

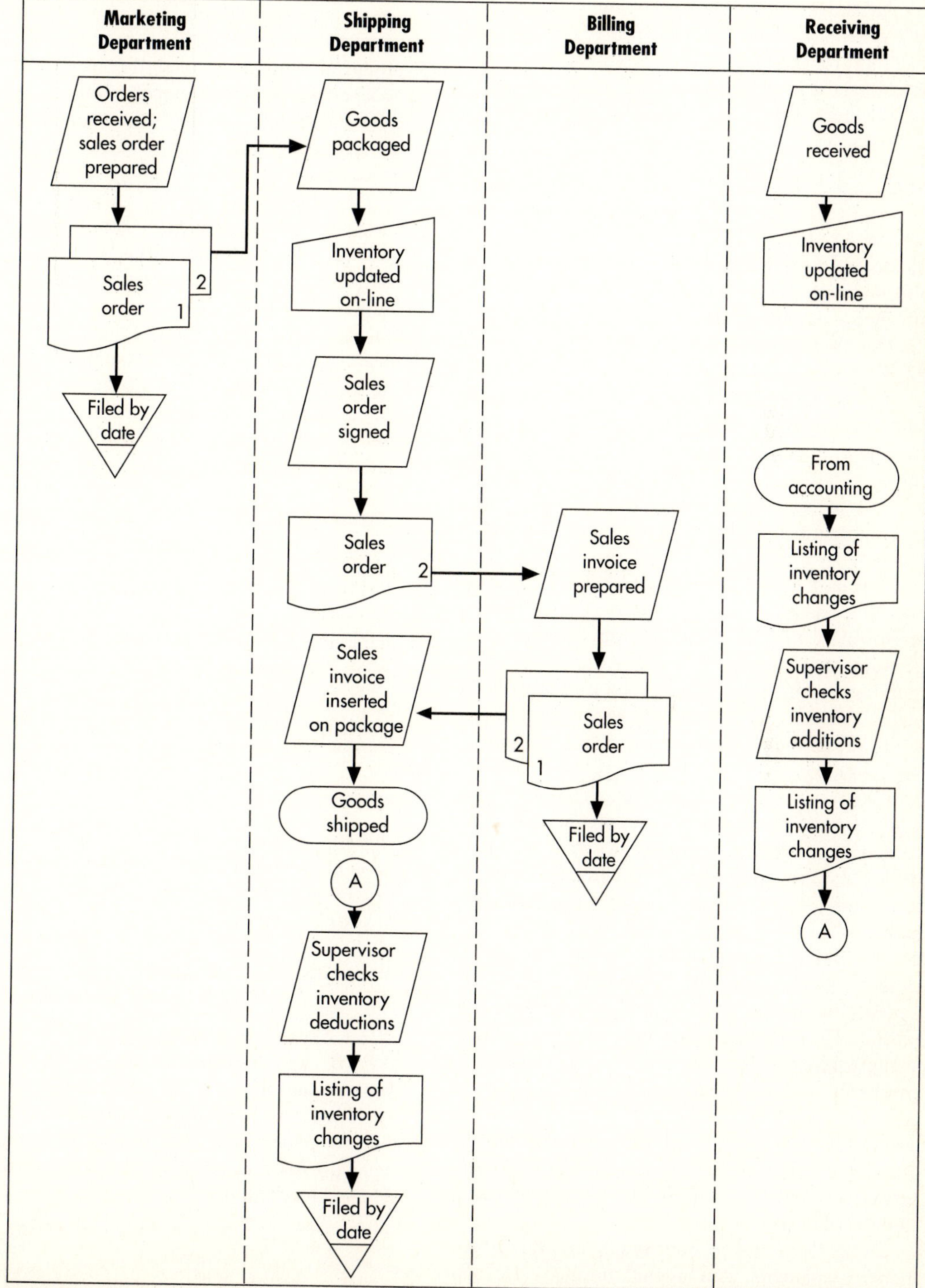

REQUIRED

a. Identify at least five weaknesses in O'Brien Corporation's marketing, shipping, billing, and receiving information system. Describe the exposure resulting from each weakness. Recommend control procedures that should be added to the system to correct each weakness. Format your answer as follows:

Weakness	Exposure	Recommended Control Procedure(s)

b. Discuss how O'Brien Corporation could use information technology to improve both control and efficiency during sales order processing. (CMA Examination, adapted)

17.8 Parktown Medical Center, Inc. is a small health care provider that is owned by a publicly held corporation. It employs seven salaried physicians, ten nurses, three support staff, and three clerical workers. The clerical workers perform such tasks as reception, correspondence, cash receipts, billing, and appointment scheduling. All are adequately bonded.

Most patients pay for services by cash or check at the time services are rendered. Credit is not approved by the clerical staff. The physician who is to perform the respective services approves credit based on an interview. When credit is approved, the physician files a memo with the billing clerk (clerk #2) to set up the receivable from data generated by the physician.

The servicing physician prepares a charge slip that is given to clerk #1 for pricing and preparation of the patient's bill. Clerk #1 transmits a copy of the bill to clerk #2 for preparation of the revenue summary and for posting in the accounts receivable subsidiary ledger.

The cash receipts functions are performed by clerk #1, who receives cash and checks directly from patients and gives each patient a prenumbered cash receipt. Clerk #1 opens the mail and immediately stamps all checks "for deposit only" and lists cash and checks for deposit. The cash and checks are deposited daily by the office manager. The list of cash and checks together with the related remittance advices are forwarded by clerk #1 to clerk #2. Clerk #1 also serves as the office receptionist with general correspondence duties.

Clerk #2 prepares and sends monthly statements to patients with unpaid balances. He also prepares the cash receipts journal and is responsible for the accounts receivable subsidiary ledger. No other clerical employee is permitted access to the accounts receivable subsidiary ledger. Uncollectible accounts are written off by clerk #2 only after the physician who performed the respective services believes the account is uncollectible and communicates the write-off to the office manager. The office manager then issues a write-off memo that clerk #2 processes.

The office manager supervises the clerks, issues write-off memos, schedules appointments for the doctors, makes bank deposits, reconciles bank statements, and performs general correspondence duties.

Additional services are performed monthly by a local accountant who posts summaries prepared by the clerks to the general ledger, prepares income statements, and files the appropriate payroll forms and tax returns. The accountant reports directly to the parent corporation.

REQUIRED

Identify at least four control weaknesses at Parktown. Describe the potential threat and exposure associated with each weakness. Also recommend how to best correct each weakness.
(CPA Examination, adapted)

17.9 Figure 17.17 on page 620 depicts the activities performed in the revenue cycle by the Newton Hardware Company.

REQUIRED

Identify the weaknesses in Newton Hardware's revenue cycle. Explain the resulting exposure and suggest methods to correct the weakness. Organize your answer as follows:

Weakness	Exposure	Recommended Improvement

(CPA Examination, adapted)

17.10 Complete the cell entries in Table 17.6, which lists the various activities performed in the revenue cycle and the journal entries, documents, data, and control issues associated with them (adapted from teaching materials developed by Dr. Martha Eining, University of Utah).

Table 17.6 **Overview of Revenue Cycle Business Activities**

	Revenue Cycle							
	Contact Customer	**Customer Agrees to Sale**	**Approve Credit**	**Transfer Goods**	**Bill Customer**	**Receive Remittance**	**Credit Accounts Receivable**	**Deposit Cash**
Accounting transaction				Sale				
Journal entry							Dr. Cash Cr. A/R	
Documents		Purchase order from customer						
Data collected	Name Address Contact person							
Department					Accounting			
Control issues			Only approved customer get credit					
Information required								
Information generated								
Effect of automation								

Source: Adapted from teaching materials developed by Martha Eining, University of Utah. Reprinted with permission.

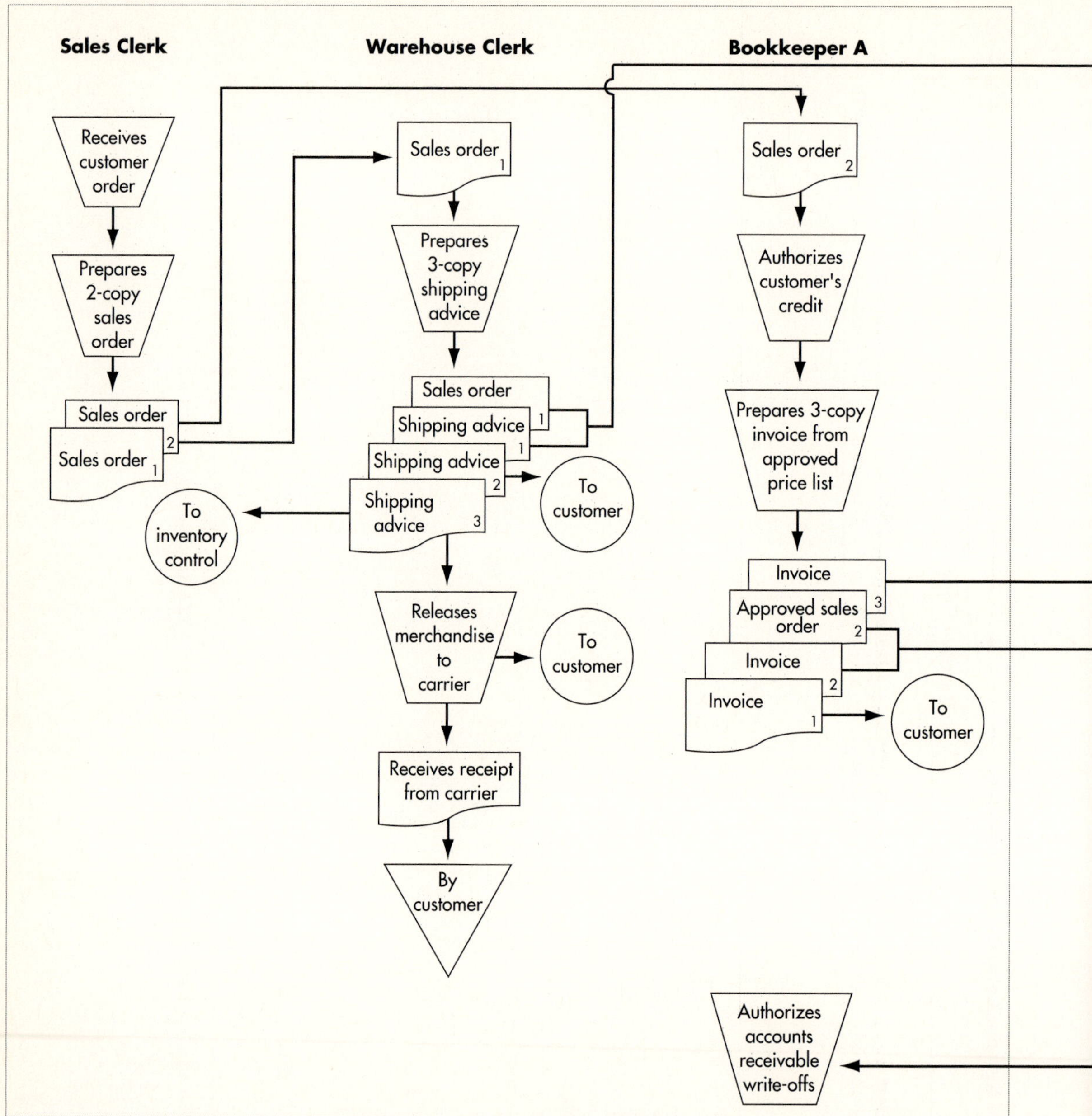

Figure 17.17

Newton Hardware Company: Revenue Cycle Procedures

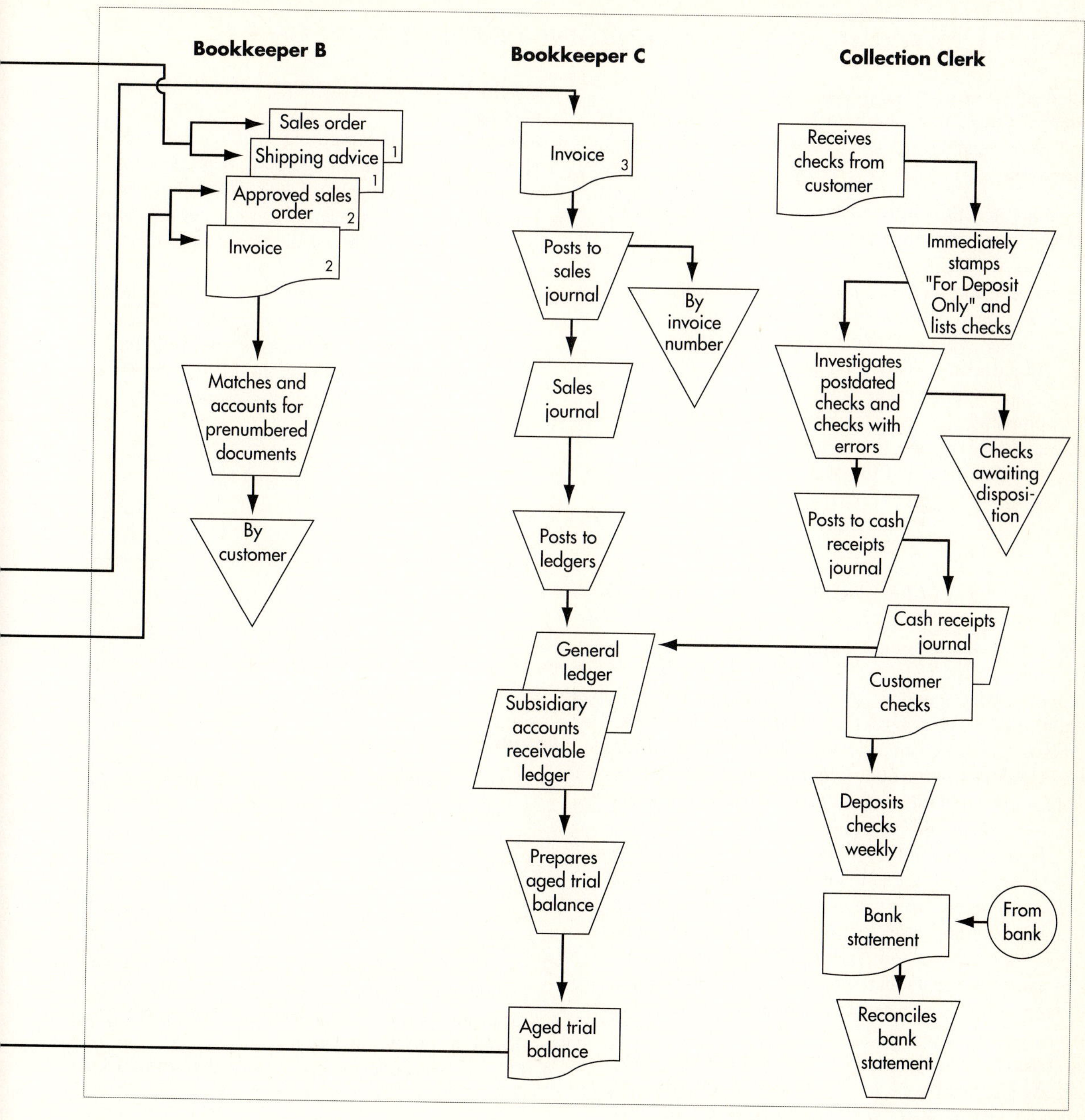
Bookkeeper B
Bookkeeper C
Collection Clerk
Sales order
Shipping advice 1
1
Approved sales order 2
Invoice 2
Matches and accounts for prenumbered documents
By customer
Invoice 3
Posts to sales journal
By invoice number
Sales journal
Posts to ledgers
General ledger
Subsidiary accounts receivable ledger
Prepares aged trial balance
Aged trial balance
Receives checks from customer
Immediately stamps "For Deposit Only" and lists checks
Investigates postdated checks and checks with errors
Checks awaiting disposition
Posts to cash receipts journal
Cash receipts journal
Customer checks
Deposits checks weekly
Bank statement
From bank
Reconciles bank statement

CASE 17.1: ANYCOMPANY, INC.—AN ONGOING COMPREHENSIVE CASE

Identify a local company (you may use the same company that you identified to complete this case in prior chapters), and answer the following questions:

1. Who are the individuals responsible for sales order preparation, credit checks, safeguarding of physical inventories, shipping, billing, maintaining accounts receivable, and handling cash collections? How are these duties segregated to diminish the threat of errors or irregularities?
2. What documents are used in the system? Are they designed in a manner that makes them easy to complete? Do they collect all the information needed to manage the various revenue cycle business activities? Do the reports generated by the system provide adequate information for decision making?
3. Are data stored in separate files or in a data base? How is this information updated? What process is used to update the general ledger? What application controls are in place to ensure accuracy, completeness, and validity of data entry, processing, and output?
4. Document your understanding of the system using flowcharts, data flow diagrams, and E–R diagrams. Discuss how current developments in information technology could be used to improve the efficiency and effectiveness of existing procedures.

CASE 17.2: ELITE PUBLISHING COMPANY

Elite Publishing Company has established Business Book Club, Inc. (BBC), a subsidiary that operates as follows: BBC's editors select from among recently published business books those they feel will be most interesting to businesspeople. BBC will purchase these books in large quantities at approximately 40% of list price and then sell them to their club members at approximately 75% of list price.

Both direct mail and advertisements in selected publications are used to solicit new customers. The advertisements offer an introductory membership bonus whereby new members who purchase one book will receive four free titles. Each month club members are sent a list of new selections and a book order form. For every four books they purchase, members earn one free book.

You have been called upon to design a computerized billing and book inventory system for BBC. The advertising manager wants to know which advertising media are most effective, the credit manager wants to know which accounts are more than 90 days past due, and the editors want to know which books are best-sellers for the club.

REQUIRED

1. Draw an E–R diagram of the system, and prepare a list of attributes that should be stored in the system.
2. Identify the input transactions that this system must process and the output documents and reports that the system should be designed to produce.
3. Describe how information technology can be used to maximize efficiency of sales order entry, shipping, billing, and cash collections. Draw a systems flowchart of your proposal.
4. Describe the control procedures that should be included in this system.

ANSWERS TO CHAPTER QUIZ

1. c	**3.** c	**5.** d	**7.** a	**9.** a
2. b	**4.** d	**6.** c	**8.** d	**10.** c

Chapter 18

The Expenditure Cycle: Purchasing and Cash Disbursements

LEARNING OBJECTIVES

After studying this chapter, you should be able to:

- Describe the major business activities and related data processing operations performed in the expenditure cycle.
- Assess the relative benefits of alternative methods for using information technology (IT) to improve the efficiency of expenditure cycle activities.
- Document your understanding of expenditure cycle activities.
- Identify the major threats in the expenditure cycle and evaluate the adequacy of various control procedures for dealing with them.
- Discuss the key decisions that need to be made in the expenditure cycle and identify the information needed to make those decisions.
- Read and understand a data model (E–R diagram) of the expenditure cycle.

Integrative Case: Alpha Omega Electronics

Sales volume for Alpha Omega Electronics (AOE) has leveled off the past two years after a period of strong growth. Surveys indicate that product pricing and quality are significant concerns among AOE's customers.

LeRoy Williams, vice president of manufacturing for AOE, is disappointed with the second quarter financial results. He is especially distressed with escalating production costs at both the Dayton and Wichita plants. Several production runs were delayed at the Wichita plant because components that, according to inventory records, should have been in stock, were unavailable. The problems at the Dayton plant arose because of numerous instances when suppliers either did not deliver components on a timely basis or delivered substandard products. LeRoy is also concerned about AOE's failure to take advantage of the discounts offered by its suppliers for prompt payment of invoices. The combined effect of these problems was a 15% drop in AOE's gross margin, compared to the previous year.

LeRoy asked Elizabeth Venko, the controller, for some recommendations on how AOE's information system could be used to solve these problems. Specifically, he asked Elizabeth to address the following issues:

1. What must be done to ensure that AOE's inventory records are current and accurate? to prevent unexpected components shortages like those experienced at the Wichita plant?
2. How could the problems at the Dayton plant be avoided in the future? What can be done to ensure timely delivery of quality components?
3. Is it possible to reduce AOE's investment in materials inventories?

4. What must be done to ensure that available vendor discounts are taken?
5. How could the information system provide better information to guide planning and production?
6. How could IT be used to reengineer expenditure cycle activities?

As this case suggests, deficiencies in the information system used to support expenditure cycle activities can create significant financial problems for an organization. The availability of current and accurate information about inventories, vendors, and the status of outstanding purchase orders is crucial for effective management of the expenditure cycle. As you read this chapter, think about how changes in AOE's information system could improve the effectiveness and efficiency of its expenditure cycle activities.

INTRODUCTION

The **expenditure cycle** is a recurring set of business activities and related data processing operations associated with the purchase of and payment for goods and services (see Fig. 18.1). This chapter focuses on the acquisition of raw materials, finished goods, supplies, and services. Chapters 19 and 20 address two other special types of expenditures: the acquisition of fixed assets and labor services, respectively.

In the expenditure cycle, the primary external exchange of information is with vendors. Internally, the expenditure cycle receives notification from the revenue and production cycles about the need to purchase goods and materials; it then notifies those cycles when those goods have been received. The expenditure cycle also sends expense data to the general ledger and reporting cycle for inclusion in financial statements and performance reports.

This chapter is organized around the three basic objectives of the AIS in the expenditure cycle. The first section describes the basic business activities performed in the expenditure cycle and explains how data about those activities are captured and processed by the AIS. Opportunities for using information technology (IT) to improve the effectiveness and efficiency of those activities are also discussed. The second section discusses the major control objectives in the expenditure cycle and explains how the AIS can be designed to mitigate the threats associated with each expenditure cycle business activity. The final sec-

Figure 18.1

Context Diagram of the Expenditure Cycle

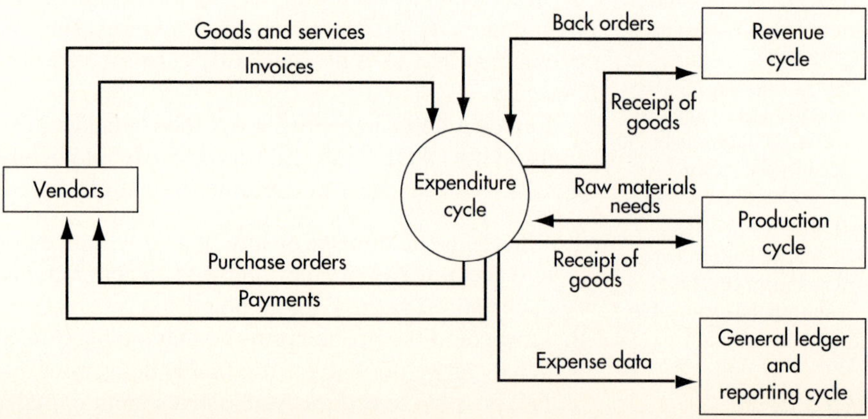

tion discusses the key decisions that need to be made and presents a data model that shows how the AIS can effectively and efficiently store and organize the information needed to make those decisions.

EXPENDITURE CYCLE BUSINESS ACTIVITIES

One function of the AIS is to support the effective performance of the organization's business activities by efficiently processing transaction data. Figure 18.2 shows the five basic business activities in the expenditure cycle:

1. Requesting the purchase of needed goods.
2. Ordering goods to be purchased.
3. Receiving ordered goods.
4. Approving vendor invoices for payment.
5. Paying for goods purchased.

Figure 18.2

Level 0 DFD for Expenditure Cycle

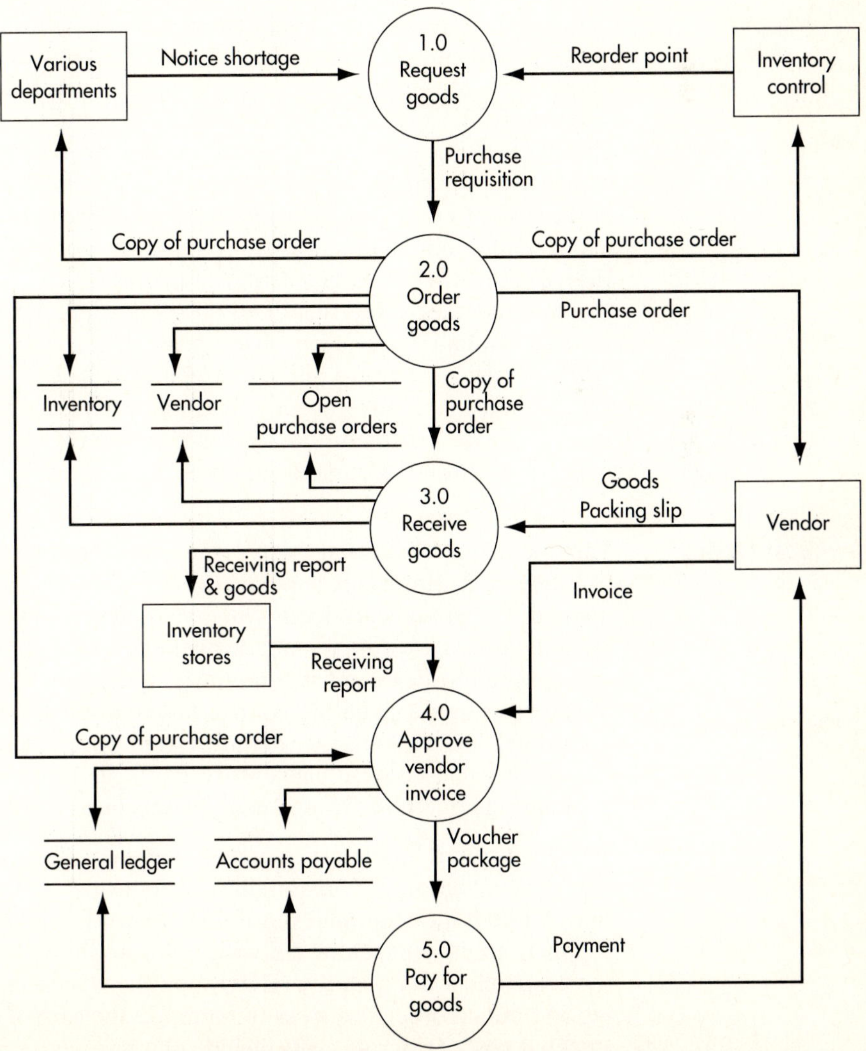

Notice that the last four activities in the expenditure cycle are mirror images of the basic activities performed in the revenue cycle:

- The order goods activity (circle 2.0 in Fig. 18.2) generates the purchase order that serves as the customer input to the sales order entry process (circle 1.0 in Fig. 17.3).
- The receive goods activity (circle 3.0 in Fig. 18.2) handles the goods sent by the vendor's shipping function (circle 2.0 in Fig. 17.3).
- The approve vendor invoice for payment activity (circle 4.0 in Fig. 18.2) processes the invoices generated by the vendor's bill customer activity (circle 3.0 in Fig. 17.3).
- The pay for goods activity (circle 5.0 in Fig. 18.2) generates the payments that are processed by the vendor's cash collection activity (circle 4.0 in Fig. 17.3).

As we will see later in the chapter, these close linkages between the buyer's expenditure cycle activities and the seller's revenue cycle activities have important implications for the design of an AIS. Specifically, by applying new IT developments to reengineer expenditure cycle activities, companies create the opportunity for their suppliers to reengineer their revenue cycle activities. Conversely, the use of IT to redesign a company's revenue cycle can create opportunities for customers to modify their own expenditure cycles. Indeed, in many cases the changes in one company's operations may *necessitate* changes in the AIS of other companies with which it does business. For example, the major automobile manufacturers require that suppliers transmit invoices via EDI, or they will not do business with them.

The remainder of this section discusses how the AIS captures and processes transaction data about each of the basic activities in the expenditure cycle. Although each activity is discussed separately, keep in mind that IT developments often enable several activities to be performed simultaneously. In addition, the same key data about transactions must still be collected, whether paper or electronic documents are used.

Request Goods

The first major business activity in the expenditure cycle involves the request to purchase inventory or supplies (circle 1.0 in Fig. 18.2). The key decisions made in this process are identifying what, when, and how much to purchase. These decisions are normally made by the **inventory control** function, although the need to reorder items is sometimes noticed by various user departments. Weaknesses in the inventory control function can create significant problems, as the introductory AOE case demonstrated. Specifically, inaccuracies in inventory records caused AOE's inventory shortages at the Wichita plant and led to the failure to purchase needed components in a timely manner.

The Traditional Inventory Control Method. The traditional approach to managing inventory is to maintain sufficient stock so that production can continue without interruption even if inventory use is greater than expected or if suppliers are late in making deliveries. This traditional approach is often called the **economic order quantity (EOQ)** approach because it is based on calculating an optimal order size so as to minimize the sum of ordering, carrying, and stockout costs. **Ordering costs** include all expenses associated with processing purchase transactions. **Carrying costs** are the costs associated with holding inventory. **Stockout costs** represent costs that result from inventory shortages, such as lost sales or production delays.

Actual application of the EOQ approach varies depending on the type of item. For high-cost or high-use items, such as the computer chips and displays used by AOE, all three types of costs are included in the formula. For low-cost or low-usage items, such as the screws and springs used by AOE to assemble its products, ordering and carrying costs are usually ignored and the sole objective is to maintain sufficient inventory levels.

The EOQ formula is used to calculate how much to order. The **reorder point** specifies when to order. Companies typically set the reorder point based on considerations involving delivery time and desired levels of safety stock to handle unexpected fluctuations in demand.

Alternative Inventory Control Methods. The traditional EOQ approach to inventory control often results in carrying significant amounts of inventory. In recent years many large U.S. manufacturing companies, including Xerox, Ford, Motorola, NCR, Intel, McDonnell Douglas, and Delco Electronics, have adopted alternative methods of inventory control that seek to minimize or even eliminate the amount of inventory that must be carried.

One alternative approach to managing inventory is called **materials requirements planning (MRP).** MRP seeks to reduce required inventory levels by *scheduling* production, rather than *estimating* needs. For example, the production planning department of a company using MRP would prepare a detailed schedule specifying the quantities of each finished product that it wants to manufacture in a specified time period, such as the next three months. Using this schedule and the engineering specifications for each product, the quantities of raw materials, parts, and supplies that will be needed in production, and the point in time when they will be needed, can be determined. Thus MRP systems reduce uncertainties about when raw materials are needed and therefore require less inventory to be carried.

A **just-in-time (JIT) inventory system** is another alternative approach to managing inventory. JIT systems attempt to minimize, if not totally eliminate, both carrying and stockout costs. JIT systems are characterized by frequent deliveries of small amounts of materials, parts, and supplies directly to the specific locations that require them, when they are needed, rather than by infrequent bulk deliveries to a central receiving and storage facility. Thus a factory utilizing a JIT system will have multiple receiving docks, each assigned to accept deliveries of items needed at nearby work centers.

A major difference between MRP and JIT systems involves the scheduling of production. MRP systems schedule production to meet *estimated sales needs,* thereby creating a stock of finished goods inventory. JIT systems, in contrast, schedule production to meet *customer demands,* thereby virtually eliminating finished goods inventory.

Documents and Procedures. The request to purchase goods or supplies is triggered either by the inventory control function or by employees noticing a shortage of materials. The advanced inventory control systems used in large manufacturing companies, such as IBM and Ford, automatically generate purchase requisitions whenever the quantity of an item on hand falls below its reorder point. In contrast, in smaller companies employees who use the items note when stock is running low and request that it be reordered. For example, your neighborhood hair stylist is usually responsible for replacing shampoos, hairbrushes, and other supplies. Moreover, even in large companies, office supplies such as copier paper and pencils are often ordered by the employees who use those items whenever they notice that stock is running low.

Regardless of its source, the need to purchase goods or supplies usually results in the creation of a purchase requisition. The **purchase requisition** (Fig. 18.3) is a document that identifies the requisitioner; specifies the delivery location and date needed; identifies the item numbers, descriptions, quantity, and price of each item requested; and may suggest a vendor. The person approving the purchase requisition indicates the department number and account number to which the purchase should be charged.

Opportunities for Using Information Technology. One way to improve the efficiency of the purchase requisition process involves the use of on-line data entry instead of paper documents. Electronic documentation reduces the time required to process purchase requisitions, as well as the costs of storing the data. The incorporation of appropriate edit controls can also increase accuracy.

The use of on-line processing systems and integrated data bases linking sales, purchasing, and production information is necessary for implementing alternative methods of inventory control, such as JIT or MRP systems. Both systems require accurate perpetual inventory records so that the computer can be programmed to monitor inventory levels and automatically generate purchase requisitions whenever quantities on hand fall below the reorder point.

Bar-code technology facilitates the maintenance of accurate perpetual inventory records. The printed lines in a bar code contain information such as

Figure 18.3

Sample AOE Purchase Requisition (items in boldface are preprinted)

ALPHA OMEGA ELECTRONICS

PURCHASE REQUISITION **No. 89010**

Date Prepared:	**Prepared by:**	**Suggested Vendor:**
07/02/97	Harold Brown HB	Best Office Supply

Deliver To: Copy Center	**Attention:** Harold Brown	**Date Needed:** 7/15/97

Item Number	**Quantity**	**Description**	**Price/Unit**
32047	15 boxes	Xerox 4200 paper, 20 wt., 10 ream box	$33.99
80170	5 boxes	Moore 2600 continuous form, 20 lb	$31.99
81756	20 boxes	Dysan 100 HD diskettes, box of 10	$ 6.49
10407	10	IBM 4207 Proprinter ribbon, black	$ 8.99

Approved by:	**Department:**	**Date Approved:**	**Account No.:**
Susan Chen	Admin. Services	07/02/97	91887

the item's number, location, cost, and price. This information is read by an optical scanner, thereby eliminating the need for human data entry. Bar coding not only reduces the time and cost associated with taking inventory, but it also virtually eliminates data entry errors. The effect on accuracy can be dramatic: Studies have found that even expert typists make one mistake for every 300 keystrokes.

Bar coding is not a panacea, however. Errors can still occur due to human mistakes, most likely when bar-code scanning is used to record the sale of assorted varieties of a product. For example, if you purchase 24 cans of store-brand soda at a grocery store, the clerk may scan only one can and then manually enter the number purchased. Since the flavors are all priced the same, the amount of the sale is correctly calculated. The perpetual inventory records will be incorrect, however, because the exact count of the flavors sold is not correctly recorded. Consequently, the grocery store may not be able to use POS data to maintain its perpetual inventory records, but must still rely on counting what is actually on the shelves. Nevertheless, because bar coding makes it easier and faster to count inventory, such counts can be more frequent, thereby reducing the risk of running out of stock. For example, employees at Costco, a chain of discount warehouses, use portable bar-code scanners to track inventory status on the floor and to initiate the replenishment process.

Order Goods

The second major business activity in the expenditure cycle involves the ordering of supplies and materials (circle 2.0 in Fig. 18.2). The purchasing activity is usually performed by purchasing agents (sometimes called buyers) within the purchasing department. In manufacturing companies, such as Alpha Omega Electronics, the purchasing function is closely related to the production cycle. Consequently, Ryan McDaniel, the head of the purchasing department at AOE, reports directly to LeRoy Williams, the vice president of manufacturing (see Fig. 17.1, page 575).

Key Decision: Vendor Selection. The crucial decision in the purchasing activity involves the selection of vendors for inventory items. Several factors should be considered in making this decision:

- Price.
- Quality of materials.
- Dependability in making deliveries.

In terms of quality and dependability vendor reliability is very important, especially to JIT systems, because a late delivery or defective parts can bring the entire system to a halt. Consequently, vendor certification is a key component of most JIT systems, and many companies require that their suppliers meet ISO 9000 quality standards. Focus 18.1 introduces the concept of vendor certification and explains what ISO 9000 does, and does not, imply about vendor quality.

Once a vendor has been selected for a product, that company's identity should normally become part of the product inventory master record. This avoids having to repeat the vendor selection process for every subsequent order. (In some cases, however, such as for the purchase of high-cost and

FOCUS 18.1

ISO 9000 Certification

In 1987 the International Organization for Standardization issued a set of five standards, referred to as ISO 9000, for assessing potential suppliers' quality control systems. These standards set guidelines for the procedures that should be included in a company's quality control systems. They cover such matters as documentation, inspection, and complaint resolution. The specific requirements vary across companies, with different standards for companies that merely purchase and resell products as opposed to companies that design and manufacture goods. To obtain ISO certification, companies must document their quality control process and hire an accredited company to inspect and evaluate their quality control system.

The continuing globalization of business makes ISO 9000 standards increasingly important. For example, the European Community requires suppliers of certain products to have ISO 9000 certification. So does the U.S. Department of Defense and many large American companies, including Ford, IBM, and Motorola. Thus it is not surprising to learn that the number of U.S. manufacturing plants meeting those standards skyrocketed from 400 in 1992 to almost 1500 in 1993.

Meeting ISO 9000 standards may help improve a company's effectiveness and efficiency. For example, the defect rate at one DuPont manufacturing plant fell from 30% to 8%. Similarly, a Rockwell International plant reported that complying with ISO 9000 standards resulted in a productivity increase of 21% while reducing product defect rates by 32% and cycle times by 18%.

Nevertheless, it is important to note that ISO 9000 addresses *process,* not product quality standards. Therefore ISO 9000 certification does not say anything about product quality. It only means that a company has a total quality control system in place, that the system is adequately documented, and that the system functions as documented. Thus it is possible for a company with poor product quality, but with a good customer complaint resolution system, to obtain ISO 9000 certification.

Focus Questions

1. Given that ISO 9000 certification does not ensure product quality, how important should it be as a criterion for selecting vendors?
2. What role should the management accountant play in seeking and meeting ISO 9000 certification?

Sources: Peter C. Brewer and Tina Y. Mills, "ISO 9000 Standards: An Emerging CPA Service Area," *Journal of Accountancy* (February 1994): 63–67; and "Focus On: ISO 9000," *Journal of Accountancy* (February 1994): 60–61.

low-usage items, management may explicitly want to reevaluate all potential vendors each time that product is ordered.) A list of potential alternative vendors for each item should also be maintained, in case the primary vendor is ever out of stock of a needed item.

Vendor performance should also be tracked and periodically evaluated to determine whether there is a need to switch suppliers. The AIS can be designed to capture and track the information needed for this purpose. For example, AOE could measure the quality of a vendor's products by tracking how often its items fail to pass inspection in the receiving department. Data on the amount of production that had to be reworked or scrapped because of substandard materials could also be collected. AOE could also measure vendor dependability by matching and tracking actual delivery dates versus those promised.

Documents and Procedures. As shown in Fig. 18.2, the receipt of a purchase requisition triggers the process of ordering goods and supplies. The principal document produced by this process is the purchase order. A **purchase order** is a document that formally requests a vendor to sell and deliver specified products at designated prices. It is also a promise to pay and becomes a contract once it is accepted by the vendor. The purchase order includes the names of the vendor and purchasing agent; the order and requested delivery dates; the delivery location and method of shipment; and information about the items ordered (see Fig. 18.4). Frequently, several purchase orders are generated to fill one purchase requisition because different vendors may be the preferred suppliers for the various items requested.

Figure 18.5 shows a typical on-line purchasing system, like that used by AOE. Approved purchase requisitions arrive daily from inventory control and various user departments. The purchasing agent uses an on-line terminal to enter the requisition data and create a purchase order. After the item number is entered, the system searches the inventory master file to identify the preferred vendor for that item. The system then proceeds to create a purchase order record by retrieving data from the inventory and vendor master files and prompting the purchase agent to enter the remaining data, such as quantity

Figure 18.4

Sample AOE Purchase Order (items in boldface are preprinted)

Alpha Omega Electronics **No. 2463**

Billing Address: **2431 Bradford Lane**
St. Louis, MO 63105–2311
(314) 467-2341

Reference the above number on all invoices and shipping documents

PURCHASE ORDER

To: Best Office Supply
4567 Olive Blvd.
St. Louis, MO 63112–2345

Ship To: AOE, Inc.
1735 Sandy Dr.
Dayton, OH 33421–2243

Vendor Number:	**Order Date:**	**Requisition Number:**	**Buyer:**	**Terms:**
121	07/03/97	89010	Fred Mozart	1/10, n/30
F.O.B. Destination	**Ship Via:** Your choice	**Delivery Date:** 07/15/97	**Remarks:**	

Item	**Item Number**	**Quantity**	**Description**	**Unit Price**
1	32047	15 boxes	Xerox 4200 paper, 20 wt., 10 ream box	$33.99
2	80170	5 boxes	Moore 2600 continuous form, 20 lb.	$31.99
3	81756	20 boxes	Dysan 100 HD Diskettes, box of 10	$6.49
4	10407	10	IBM 4207 Proprinter ribbon, black	$8.99

Approved by: *Susan Beethoven*

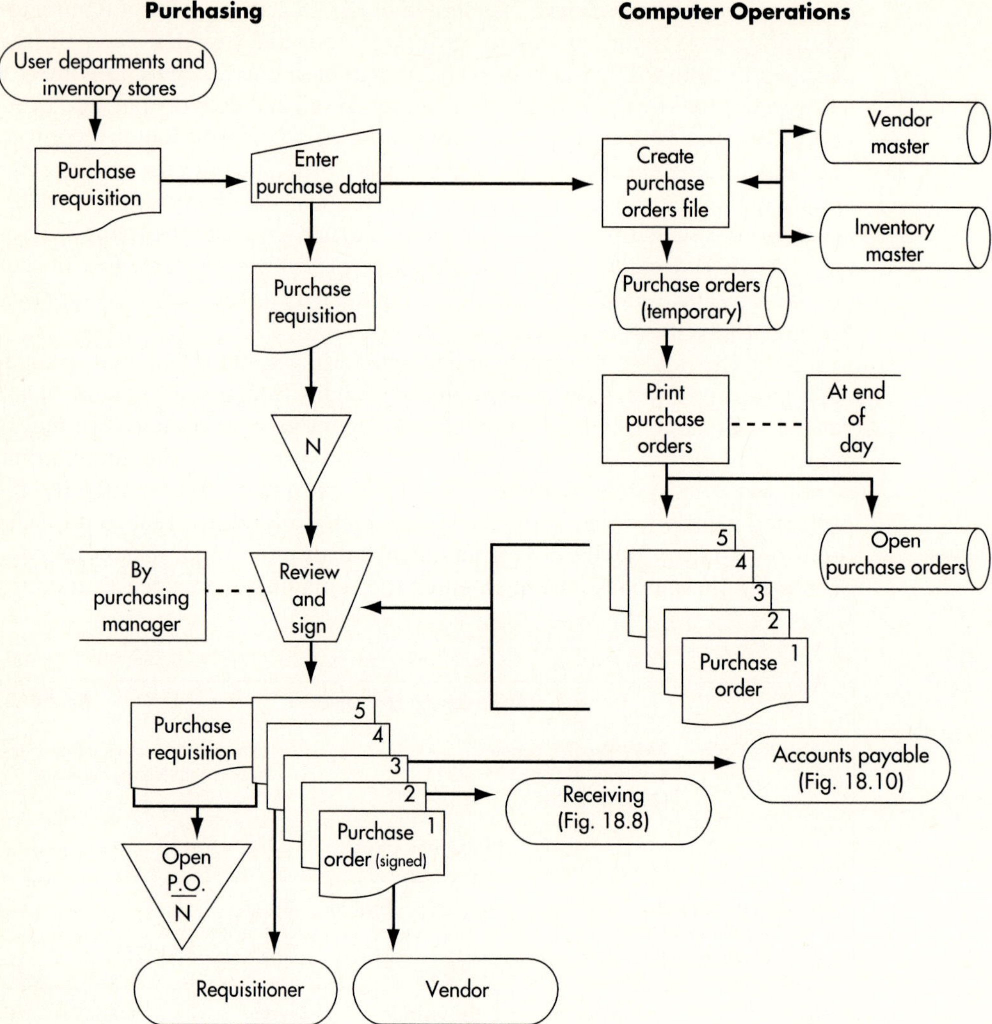

Figure 18.5

Flowchart of Purchasing System

needed and desired delivery date. The purchase requisition is then temporarily filed in numerical order.

The system stores the completed purchase order record in a temporary disk file. At the end of the day, all items to be ordered from the same vendor are consolidated into a single purchase order record. Each of these records is assigned a purchase order number and added to the open purchase order file, and five copies of the purchase order are printed.

The five copies of the purchase order are sent to the purchasing manager for review and approval. After the purchase orders have been signed, the original is sent to the vendor. Copy two goes to the receiving department to inform them of anticipated deliveries. Copy three goes to accounts payable to notify them of a pending financial commitment. A fourth copy of the purchase order goes to the department that generated the purchase requisition, to let them know their request has been acted on. The final copy is retained in purchasing, where it is attached to the purchase requisition and filed numerically, by purchase order number, in the open purchase order file.

Many companies maintain special purchasing arrangements with important vendors. One such arrangement involves the use of blanket orders. A **blanket order** is a commitment to purchase specified items at designated prices from a particular supplier for a set time period, often one year. The use of blanket orders reduces the buyer's uncertainty about reliable sources of raw materials and provides the vendor with a better basis for planning its capacity and operations. For example, Steelcase Company has an agreement with Cannon Mills to purchase large volumes of fabrics for upholstered furniture. Steelcase provides detailed weekly reports to Cannon listing the quantities of various fabrics that it will need for the next several weeks. Steelcase can make these commitments only because it has a reliable purchasing and inventory control information system.

Opportunities for Using Information Technology. One way to improve the purchasing process involves the use of EDI. Transmitting purchase orders via EDI reduces costs by eliminating the clerical work associated with printing and mailing paper documents. It also reduces the time between recognizing the need to reorder an item and subsequently receiving it. Consequently, the risk of running out of stock is lessened, which can significantly increase profitability. For example, the J.C. Penney Company credits its rebound from the recession of the early 1990s to its ability to reduce merchandise replenishment cycle time through the linkage of EDI with its POS systems. Other companies, such as K mart, have gone even further in their use of EDI to streamline the inventory control and purchasing process by letting suppliers manage and automatically replenish inventory (refer back to Focus 17.2, on page 584).

It is also important to improve the efficiency of the purchasing process for miscellaneous supplies. These purchases usually involve such small dollar amounts that the cost of processing the orders through the same system used to purchase inventory can exceed the cost of the supplies themselves. Moreover, the quantities involved are often too small to justify using a JIT system. Therefore many companies are exploring alternative methods for processing purchases of miscellaneous supplies. Focus 18.2 describes one such alternative that is used by ITT Automotive: procurement cards.

Procurement cards not only reduce costs and improve efficiency, but they can also help combat employee fraud. For example, one New Jersey service company used procurement cards provided by Portland, Maine-based Wright Express to detect and stop hundreds of thousands of dollars of theft by its union drivers. The magnetic strip on the back of the cards identified the vehicle for which fuel was being purchased. To get a purchase authorized, drivers had to enter their personal identification number and odometer reading. The system then automatically recorded the location of the filling station, the amount and type of fuel purchased, and the time of the transaction. All this information was used to document numerous cases in which union drivers purchased more gas than the tank of the truck could hold. In these cases, drivers had convinced gas station attendants to pad the amount purchased and had

FOCUS 18.2

Using Procurement Cards to Streamline Purchasing at ITT Automotive

In 1993 ITT Automotive conducted a detailed study of its accounts payable function. The results indicated that 59% of the manufacturing unit's invoices were for noninventory items, such as office and shop supplies. Moreover, 91% of those purchases totaled less than $1000. Nevertheless, ITT Automotive, like many companies, applied the same set of stringent controls to all purchases, regardless of size. Consequently, the average cost to requisition, order, receive, and pay for each invoice was $142, even though almost 34% of all purchases cost less than $100! Clearly, something needed to be done to streamline these procedures.

ITT Automotive's solution was to use procurement cards for all noninventory purchases below $1000. Procurement cards are like credit cards in that employees can use them to charge purchases up to a set dollar limit. Unlike credit cards, however, ITT Automotive receives just one monthly bill summarizing all employee purchases. Moreover, unique monthly and per-transaction limits can be assigned to each employee. Card usage can even be restricted to vendors in specific SIC industry codes.

The use of procurement cards creates savings in a number of ways. For example, the purchasing department is no longer involved in negotiating and ordering miscellaneous supplies. A single electronic funds transfer exchange replaces the writing of tens of thousands of monthly checks. Postage costs decrease as less checks are mailed. Overall, less paper is processed internally. Indeed, ITT Automotive anticipates that procurement cards could eliminate up to 75% of all noninventory purchase orders and 81% of related invoices. In effect, ITT Automotive is outsourcing its paperwork to the banks that issue the procurement cards!

In addition to cost savings, procurement cards have had a positive effect on employee morale and business practices. Employees are empowered to make small-dollar purchases as they see fit. In addition, the time lag between recognition of supply need and its acquisition is reduced.

Focus Questions

1. The use of procurement cards, while cutting costs and streamlining processing, also reduces control. Explain how control is reduced, and evaluate the magnitude of the increased risk.
2. In this example, procurement cards were used for noninventory purchases, such as supplies. Could they also be used for regular inventory purchases? Why or why not? What about using procurement cards to purchase services, such as cleaning?

Source: Richard J. Palmer, "Reengineering Payables at ITT Automotive," *Management Accounting* (July 1994): 38–42.

---

split the excess with them. The procurement card data gave the company the evidence it needed to fire those union drivers. It also deterred future thefts of that nature.

Receive and Store Goods

The third major business activity in the expenditure cycle involves the receipt and storage of ordered items (circle 3.0 in Fig. 18.2). The receiving department is responsible for accepting vendor deliveries; it usually reports to the warehouse manager, who in turn reports to the vice president of manufacturing (see Fig. 17.1, page 575). The inventory stores department, which also reports to the warehouse manager, is responsible for storage of the goods. Information about the receipt of ordered merchandise must also be communicated to the inventory control function, to update the inventory records.

Key Decisions and Information Needs. Figure 18.6 shows that the receiving department has two major responsibilities: deciding whether to accept a deliv-

Figure 18.6

Level 1 DFD of Receiving Function

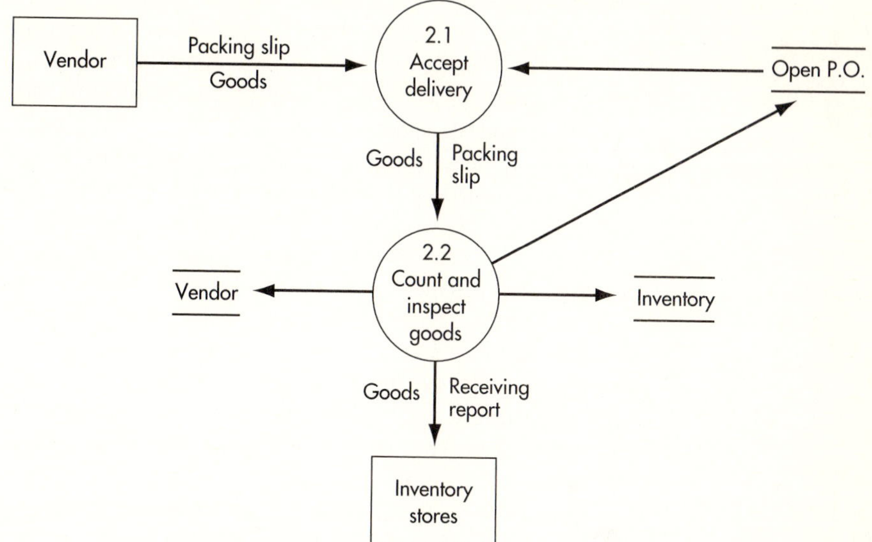

ery, and verifying the quantity and quality of the goods delivered. The first decision is made based on information provided by the purchasing function: The existence of a valid purchase order indicates that the delivery should be accepted. This decision is important, because the acceptance of unordered goods would result in wasted time and space in handling and storing those items until they can be returned.

Verifying the quantity of goods delivered is extremely important to ensure that the company pays only for goods actually received and that inventory records are accurately updated. To encourage the receiving clerk to accurately count what was delivered, many companies black out the quantity ordered field on the receiving department's copy of the purchase order. Nevertheless, the receiving clerk still knows the expected quantity of goods because vendors usually include a packing slip with each order. Consequently, there is a temptation to do just a quick visual comparison of quantities received with those indicated on the packing slip, in order to quickly route the goods to where they are needed. Therefore, companies must clearly communicate to receiving clerks the importance of carefully and accurately counting all deliveries. An effective means of communication is to require the receiving clerk not only to record the quantity received, but also to sign the receiving report. Signing a document indicates an assumption of responsibility, which usually results in more diligent work.

The receiving clerk should also carefully examine each delivery for signs of obvious damage, before routing the inventory to the warehouse. Information about the delivery time and condition of the goods is added to the vendor file, the inventory file is updated to reflect the quantity of goods received, and the receipt of goods is noted on the purchase order. Upon transfer of the goods to the warehouse, the inventory stores department verifies the count of the items placed into inventory.

Documents and Procedures. The primary document used in the receiving subsystem of the expenditure cycle is the receiving report. A **receiving report** documents details about each delivery, including the date received, shipper, vendor, and purchase order number (Fig. 18.7). For each item received, it shows the item number, description, unit of measure, and count of the quantity received. It also contains space to identify the persons who received and inspected the goods as well as for remarks concerning the quality of the items received.

A receiving report is typically not used to document the receipt of services, such as advertising and cleaning. Instead, receipt of such services is usually documented by supervisory approval of the vendor's invoice.

Figure 18.8 depicts an on-line receiving process used by a manufacturing company such as AOE. The copy of the purchase order sent from the purchasing department is filed alphabetically, by vendor. When a delivery arrives, a receiving clerk verifies that the goods were indeed ordered by comparing the purchase order number referenced on the vendor's packing slip with the copy of the purchase order from the purchasing department. The receiving clerk then counts and inspects the goods and uses an on-line terminal to enter the inventory item numbers, count, and purchase order number. The system checks that data against the open purchase order file; any discrepancies are immediately displayed on the screen and must be resolved.

Once the goods are accepted, the system updates the quantity on order and quantity on hand fields in the inventory master file, records the date of receipt in the vendor master file, and notes the quantity received in the open purchase order file. Two copies of a prenumbered receiving report are also printed in the

Figure 18.7

Sample AOE Receiving Report (items in boldface are preprinted)

Alpha Omega Electronics

RECEIVING REPORT **No. 3113**

Vendor: Best Office Supply	**Date Received:** 07/13/97
Shipped via: UPS	**Purchase Order Number:** 2463

Item Number	**Quantity**	**Description**
32047	15	Xerox 4200 paper, 20 wt., 10 ream box
80170	5	Moore 2600 continuous form, 20 lb.
81756	20	Dysan 100 HD diskettes, box of 10
10407	10	IBM 4207 Proprinter ribbons, black

Remarks:
Two boxes of Moore 2600 paper received with water damage on outside, but the paper appears to be okay

Received by:	**Inspected by:**	**Delivered to:**
Nathan Hale	*Nathan Hale*	*Harold Brown*

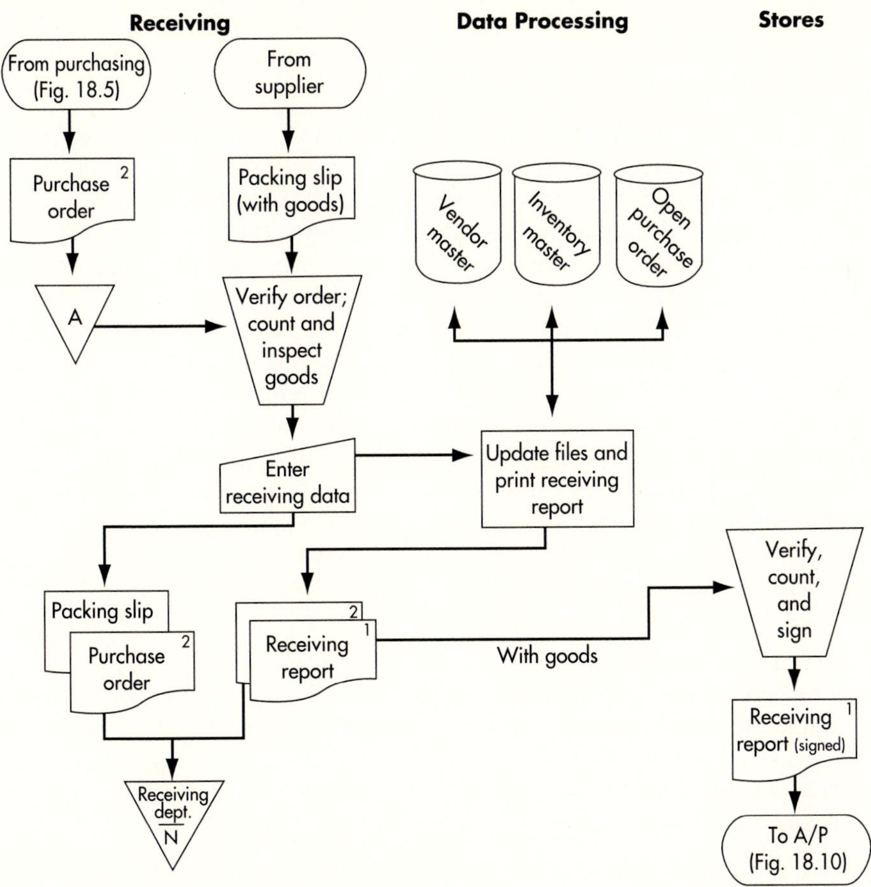

Figure 18.8 *Flowchart of Receiving System*

receiving department. One of these accompanies the goods to the inventory stores department, where a clerk signs off to acknowledge transfer of the goods into inventory. This signed copy of the receiving report is then sent to accounts payable, where it is used to approve the vendor invoice. The other copy of the receiving report is filed in the receiving department, along with the related purchase order and packing slip.

Three possible exceptions to this process are not shown in Fig. 18.8: (1) receiving a quantity of goods different from the amount ordered, (2) receiving damaged goods, or (3) receiving goods of inferior quality that fail inspection. In all three cases, the purchasing department must resolve the situation with the vendor. Usually, the vendor will give the buyer permission to correct the invoice for any discrepancies in quantity. In the case of damaged or poor-quality goods, a document called a debit memo is prepared after the vendor agrees to take back the goods or to grant a price reduction. The **debit memo** records the adjustment being requested. One copy of the debit memo is sent to the vendor, who subsequently creates and returns a credit memo in acknowledgment. Another copy of the debit memo goes to accounts payable, where it is used to adjust the account balance owed to that vendor. A third copy of the debit memo accompanies the goods to the shipping department to authorize their return to the vendor.

Opportunities for Using Information Technology. Counting and recording inventory deliveries is a labor-intensive task. One way for companies like AOE to improve the efficiency of this process is to require vendors to bar-code all of their products. Bar coding would enable receiving clerks to scan in the product number, description, and quantity of all items received, thereby virtually eliminating data entry errors. Moreover, although the goods would still have to be manually inspected to ensure they meet quality standards, the use of bar-code scanners can significantly reduce delivery processing time. For example, Sea-Land Service, Inc. uses hand-held bar scanners to enter data about the quantities and conditions of cargo containers at its Charleston, South Carolina, port. The data are then sent over a radio-based communications system to a SQL Server data base. Previously, it took 50 to 55 minutes to inspect containers moving through the shipyard; with the new system, most containers are inspected in 30 minutes. J. C. Penney uses a similar system of radio-transmission bar-code scanners in its warehouses and claims to have increased productivity by 23%.

Approve Vendor Invoices

The fourth activity in the expenditure cycle entails approving vendor invoices for payment (circle 4.0 in Fig. 18.2). This process is performed by the accounts payable department, which reports to the controller (see Fig. 17.1, page 575). This is an example of an important segregation of duties. The purchase transaction was *authorized* when the purchase order was issued; the accounts payable department *records* the obligation to pay the vendor.

Key Decision and Information Needs. Legally, an obligation to pay vendors arises at the time goods are received. For practical reasons, however, most companies record accounts payable only after receipt and approval of the vendor's invoice (as shown in Fig. 18.2). This timing difference is usually not important for daily decision making, but it does require making appropriate adjusting entries to prepare accurate financial statements at the end of a fiscal period.

Approval of vendor invoices is based on internally generated information from both the purchasing and receiving functions. The copy of the purchase order sent from purchasing confirms that the goods or services listed on the vendor invoice were actually ordered. The copy of the receiving report that came from inventory stores confirms the quantity and condition of the goods received and also documents that they were either placed into inventory or released to production.

Documents and Procedures. There are two basic ways to process vendor invoices, referred to as nonvoucher or voucher systems. In a **nonvoucher system,** each approved invoice is posted to individual vendor records in the accounts payable file and is then stored in an open invoice file. When a check is written to pay for an invoice, the invoice is removed from the open-invoice file, marked paid, and then stored in the paid-invoice file.

In a **voucher system,** a document called a disbursement voucher is also prepared. The **disbursement voucher** identifies the vendor, lists the outstanding invoices, and indicates the net amount to be paid after deducting any applicable discounts and allowances (see Fig. 18.9). Thus a disbursement voucher summarizes the information contained in a set of vendor invoices. It also specifies the general ledger accounts to be debited.

The use of disbursement vouchers offers three advantages. First, it reduces the number of checks that need to be written, because several invoices may be included on one voucher. Second, because the disbursement voucher is an internally generated document, it can be prenumbered to simplify tracking all payables. Third, because the voucher provides an explicit record that a vendor invoice has been approved for payment, it facilitates separating the time of invoice approval from the time of invoice payment. This makes it easier to schedule both activities to maximize efficiency.

Figure 18.10 depicts the accounts payable process used at AOE, which is typical of traditional voucher systems. When an invoice is received from a vendor, it is compared with the information contained in copies of the purchase order and receiving report to ensure accuracy and validity. For purchases of supplies or services, which do not usually involve purchase orders and receiving reports, the invoice is sent to the appropriate supervisor for approval. The vendor invoice itself is also checked for mathematical accuracy.

The accounts payable clerk then enters the approved invoice data and creates an open-invoice file. At this time the system also updates the open-purchase order file to reflect the receipt of the vendor invoice. At the end of each day, the system uses the open-invoice file to update the balances due to each vendor in the vendor master (accounts payable) file. At this time disbursement vouchers are printed and the accounts payable control account in the general ledger is updated.

Figure 18.9

Sample AOE Disbursement Voucher (items in boldface are preprinted)

Alpha Omega Electronics

DISBURSEMENT VOUCHER — **No. 16123**

Date Entered: 07/22/97	**Debit Distribution**	
Prepared by: BC	**Account No.**	**Amount**
Vendor Number: 109	22-140 22-145 20-699 20-799	$868.33 629.01 30.56 98.45
Remit To: Avalon Electronics 1401 East Grand St. Louis, MO 63106–2211		

Vendor Invoice					
Number	**Date**	**Amount**	**Returns & Allowances**	**Purchase Discount**	**Net Remittance**
5386	07/15/97	$984.50	$98.45	$17.72	$868.33
5389	07/20/97	641.85	0.00	12.84	629.01
Voucher Totals:		$1626.35	$98.45	$30.56	$1497.34

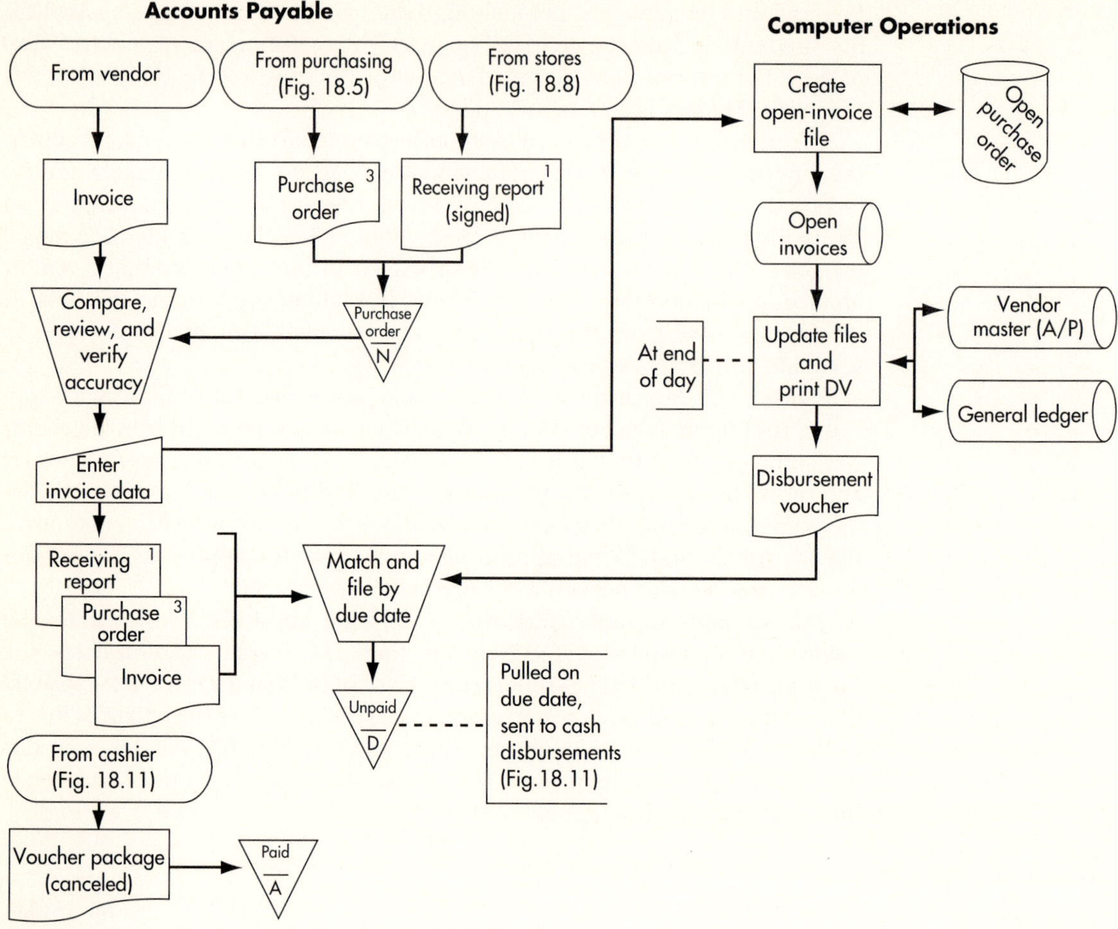

Figure 18.10

Flowchart of Accounts Payable System

The accounts payable clerk compares the disbursement vouchers with the supporting documents (vendor invoice, purchase order, and receiving report) and files them by due date in an unpaid vouchers file. Prior to the due date, the disbursement voucher and supporting documents, which are often referred to as a **voucher package,** are sent to the cashier for payment.

Opportunities for Using Information Technology. The vouching process, which matches invoices to purchase orders and receiving reports, is a prime candidate for automation. Companies like AOE can improve the efficiency of their accounts payable system by requiring vendors to send invoices by EDI. EDI eliminates the need to enter invoice data manually, saving time and the associated clerical costs while also removing the chance for errors. Additional time and cost savings can be realized by having the system automatically match the EDI invoice to the computer files of purchase orders and receiving reports. Together, these steps would enable companies to approve vendor invoices more quickly, allowing them to take advantage of any vendor discounts offered for prompt payment.

Another option is to eliminate vendor invoices entirely. One company that has done so is the Industrial Products division of the Lord Corporation in Erie, Pennsylvania. Lord wrote a vouchering program that automatically generates a disbursement voucher upon receipt of goods. The program matches information about quantities received with price information on the purchase order. This system requires 100% accuracy from the receiving department in counting and inspecting goods received and relies on the purchasing department's ability to negotiate firm prices upon issuance of the purchase order. These requirements, however, have produced amazing results for Lord: Paper flow was reduced by 80% and the time and cost associated with processing invoices was cut in half.

For companies that still use paper invoices, image processing and optical character recognition provide yet another method for improving the efficiency and effectiveness of the accounts payable function. Image processing works similarly to a fax machine. The paper document (in this case, the vendor invoice) is scanned into the system and converted into a binary representation, thereby creating an electronic image of the original document. The image is then run through an OCR program to capture individual data elements, such as item numbers, prices, and quantities, for further processing. Image processing can reduce costs and improve access to information. As Focus 18.3 shows, however, reaping the benefits of image processing requires both careful planning and good data base design.

Pay for Goods

The final activity in the expenditure cycle is the payment of approved invoices (circle 5.0 in Fig. 18.2). This activity, referred to as the cash disbursements function, is performed by the cashier, who reports to the treasurer (see Fig. 17.1, page 575). This segregates the *custody* function, performed by the cashier, from the *authorization* and *recording* functions, performed by the purchasing and accounts payable departments, respectively.

Key Decision: Taking Vendor Discounts. A key decision in the cash disbursement process is determining whether to take advantage of any vendor discounts offered for prompt payment. A short-term cash flow budget is useful for making this decision. This report lists projected inflows and outflows of cash for a period of time, up to a year in advance. The information in this budget comes from a number of sources. Accounts receivable provides projections of future cash collections. The accounts payable and open–purchase order files indicate the amount of current and pending commitments to vendors, while the human resources function provides information about payroll needs. If the cash flow budget indicates that sufficient cash is available, vendor discounts for prompt payment should be taken because they provide substantial savings. For example, a 1% discount for paying within 10 days, instead of 30, represents a savings of 18% annually.

Documents and Procedures. Figure 18.11 depicts the cash disbursements process used by AOE, which reflects a typical batch-oriented accounts payable system. The cashier receives the voucher package, which consists of the vendor

FOCUS 18.3

Image Processing: Creating a Paperless Office

Chaparral Steel Company, a subsidiary of Texas Industries, Inc., uses a document imaging system to reduce costs and improve access to information. The system has two input workstations, each equipped with scanners that can be set to different resolution levels, depending upon the type of document being scanned. Large 19-inch color monitors are used so that clerks can clearly check image quality; if an image is not readable, the documents need to be scanned at another time. All documents related to a transaction (purchase orders, receiving reports, and vendor invoices) are grouped together and scanned consecutively. Related reports produced by the accounting system, such as journal listings, are electronically merged into the scanned data base. The documents are indexed as they are scanned; the accounting reports are stored as text and can be searched just like any other word processing document. The images are stored on optical disks; the index, however, which is already 400 MB and growing, is stored on a hard drive because it provides faster access. To retrieve a document, the data base server searches the index, finds the access keys, and sends them to the jukebox server, which retrieves the document from the appropriate optical drive.

Chaparral learned by experience that proper design of the index scheme is as crucial to the success of a document imaging system as the design of the chart of accounts is to an effective accounting system. When the document imaging system was first implemented, documents were scanned and indexed by department, since that was the traditional way they had always been processed. The result was chaos: Some documents that crossed departmental boundaries, such as purchase orders, were "lost" in the system. Linking related documents was almost impossible. After carefully working through the problems, the current approach of grouping documents by transaction, rather than department, was developed.

Two years after initial implementation, the system is saving the company an estimated $18,500 annually by reducing the time and costs associated with processing paper documents. In addition, productivity has greatly increased because the accounting staff can now easily locate and examine copies of any document needed to resolve a question with either suppliers or customers.

Focus Questions

1. Do you think that document imaging systems will totally eliminate the use of paper documents? Why or why not?
2. Scanned images, when processed by an optical character recognition (OCR) program, can be manipulated like any other document. What control risk implications does this capability raise?

Source: James E. Hunton, "Setting up a Paperless Office," *Journal of Accountancy* (November 1994): 77–85.

invoice, purchase order, receiving report, and disbursements voucher, from the accounts payable department. The cashier reviews each voucher package, computes a batch total of the amounts to be paid, and enters the disbursement data.

The system then uses the disbursement voucher file to update the accounts payable, open-invoice, and the general ledger files. For each vendor, the totals of all vouchers are summed and that amount is subtracted from the balance field in that vendor's master file record. The invoices being paid are then deleted from the open-invoice file. A remittance advice is prepared for each vendor, listing each invoice being paid and the amounts of any discounts or allowances taken. The checks and remittance advices are then printed. After all disbursement transactions have been processed, the cash disbursements register is printed and sent to the controller. At the same time, the system generates a summary journal entry debiting accounts payable and crediting cash and posts that entry to the general ledger.

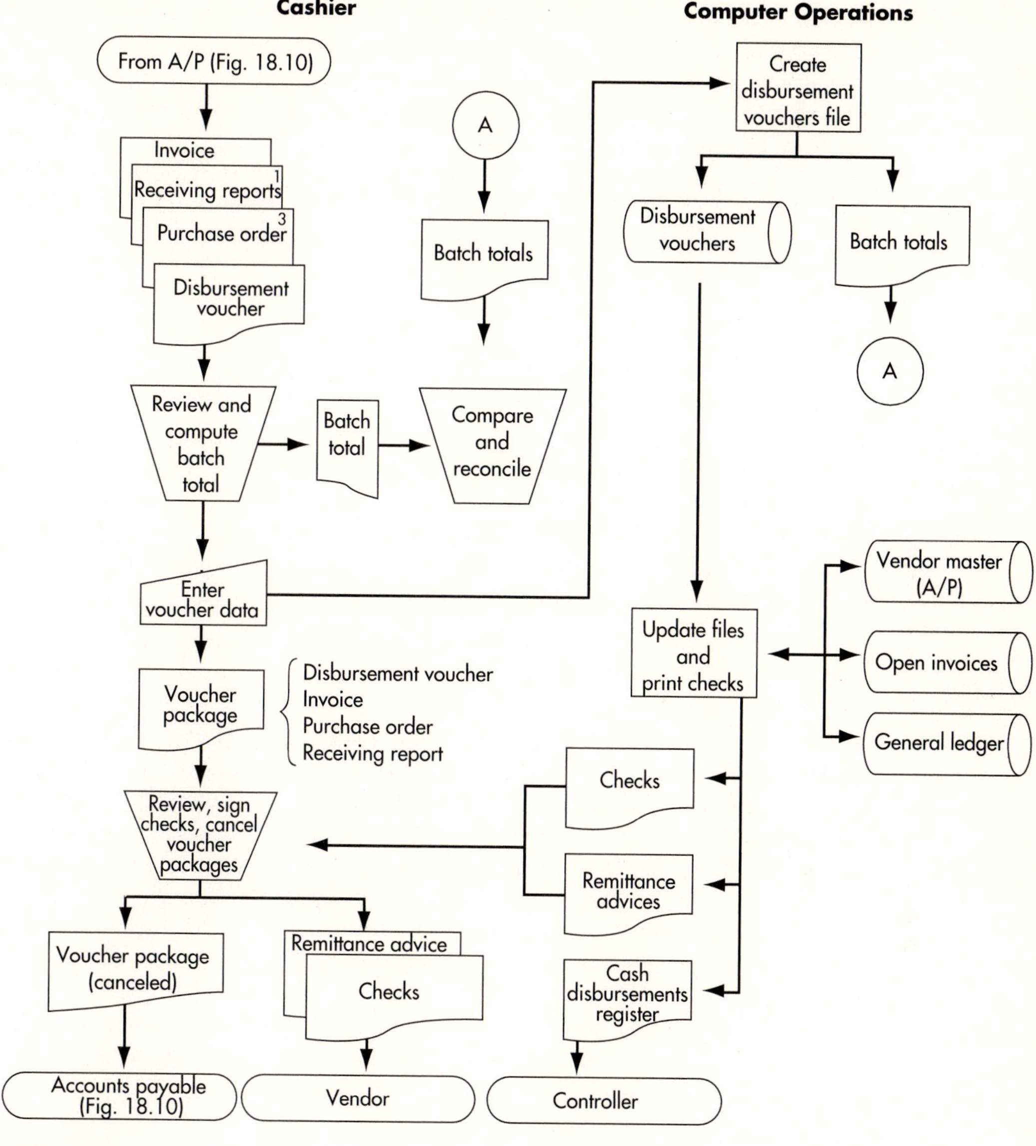

Figure 18.11

Flowchart of Cash Disbursements System

The checks and remittance advices are then returned to the cashier for signing. After reviewing the checks against the voucher package, the cashier signs the checks. (Checks above a specified amount may also require the treasurer's signature.) The cashier then mails the checks and remittance advices to the vendors, and cancels supporting documents before returning them to accounts payable, where they are filed alphabetically by vendor.

Opportunities for Using Information Technology. IT can be used to improve the cash disbursement process by paying vendors through electronic funds transfer instead of by check. With EFT, companies provide instructions to their bank about transferring funds out of their bank account and into the vendor's account. EFT can generate considerable cost savings because the time and expenses associated with preparing, signing, and mailing checks, as well as storing canceled checks, are eliminated. Indeed, many large companies, such as Chevron, Mobil, and DuPont, have begun to use EFT for remittances, which is a natural extension of using EDI for purchase orders and invoices.

EFT does create new exposures, however, which in turn require additional control procedures. The topic of designing control procedures to deal with all the expenditure cycle threats, including those arising from the use of EFT, is covered in the next section of this chapter.

CONTROL OBJECTIVES, THREATS, AND PROCEDURES

A second function of a well-designed AIS is to provide adequate controls to ensure meeting the following objectives:

1. All transactions are properly authorized.
2. All recorded transactions are valid (actually occurred).
3. All valid, authorized transactions are recorded.
4. All transactions are recorded accurately.
5. Assets (cash, inventory, and data) are safeguarded from loss or theft.
6. Business activities are performed efficiently and effectively.

The documents and records described in the previous section play an important role in achieving these objectives. Simple, easy-to-complete documents with clear instructions facilitate the accurate and efficient recording of transaction data. The inclusion of appropriate application controls, such as validity checks and field (format) checks, further increases the accuracy of data entry when using electronic documents. Providing space on paper and electronic documents to record who completed and who reviewed the form provides evidence that the transaction was properly authorized. Finally, prenumbering the documents facilitates checking that all transactions have been recorded.

Table 18.1 lists the major threats and exposures in the expenditure cycle and the additional control procedures, besides adequate documents and records, that should be in place to mitigate them. Every company, regardless of its line of business, faces these threats. Therefore it is important to understand how the AIS can be designed to counter them. Our discussion will be organized around the stages of the expenditure cycle.

Request Goods

The primary objective of the purchase requisition process is to maintain an adequate supply of all needed materials. The first two threats listed in Table 18.1 pertain to this objective.

Threat 1: Stockouts. To guard against the threat of stockouts, companies need to establish an accurate inventory control system. The perpetual inventory method should be used to ensure that information about inventory stocks is always current. Companies should select vendors that are known to meet their delivery commitments. The AIS should prepare a **vendor performance report** that highlights deviations in product quality, prices, and delivery commitments. As explained earlier in the chapter, this report should be reviewed periodically and new vendors selected whenever a supplier's performance falls below acceptable levels.

Threat 2: Requesting Goods Not Needed. Companies must also beware of purchasing items that are not currently needed. Accurate perpetual inventory records ensure the validity of purchase requisitions generated automatically by the inventory control system. Purchase requisitions initiated by individual employees should be reviewed and approved by appropriate supervisors. Access to blank purchase requisitions should be restricted. In addition, purchase requisitions should be prenumbered and accounted for periodically.

Table 18.1 **Threats, Exposures, and Control Procedures in the Expenditure Cycle**

Threat	Exposure	Applicable Control Procedures
1. Stockouts	Production delays lost sales	Inventory control system Vendor performance analysis
2. Purchasing unnecessary goods or in too great a quantity	Increased inventory costs	Accurate perpetual inventory Approved purchase requisitions Restricted access to blank purchase requisitions Prenumbered purchase requisitions
3. Purchasing goods at inflated prices	Cost overruns	Price list consultation Solicitation of written bids Approved purchase orders Budgetary controls
4. Purchasing goods of inferior quality	Production delays Cost overruns	Use of approved vendor lists Review of purchase orders Vendor performance analyses
5. Purchasing from unauthorized vendors	Inferior quality of purchased goods Inflated prices Violation of laws or import quotas	Approval of purchase orders Restricted access to approved vendor list and approval of any changes made to that list Prenumbered purchase orders
6. Kickbacks	Inferior quality of purchased goods Inflated prices Violation of law	Prohibition of gifts from vendors Requirement that purchasing agents disclose financial interest in suppliers Vendor audits
7. Receiving unordered goods	Increased inventory costs	Approved purchase order for all deliveries
8. Errors in counting goods received	Payment for items not received Inaccurate inventory records	Blank quantity field on copy of the purchase order sent to receiving Incentives to count all deliveries
9. Theft of inventory	Loss of assets Inaccurate records	Physical access controls Documentation of all internal transfers of inventory Periodic physical counts of inventory and reconciliation with recorded amounts
10. Errors in vendor invoices	Inaccurate records Inaccurate payment	Recheck of invoice accuracy Comparison of invoice to purchase order and receiving report

continued

***Table 18.1* Continued**

Threat	Exposure	Applicable Control Procedures
11. Paying for goods not received	Loss of cash Overstated costs	Requirement of voucher package to support payment of invoices
12. Failure to take available purchase discounts	Increased expenses	Procedures to track invoice due dates Cash flow budgets
13. Paying the same invoice twice	Cash flow problems Erroneous records (overstated expenses)	Approval of invoices for payment only when accompanied by complete voucher package Payment of only original invoices that are accompanied by original copies of supporting documents Cancellation of voucher package once checks are signed
14. Errors in recording and posting purchases and payments	Incorrect financial statements Erroneous decisions	Data entry controls Periodic reconciliation of subsidiary accounts payable with general ledger
15. Misappropriation of cash by a) Payments to fictitious vendors b) Alteration of checks	Loss of assets	Restricted access to cash, blank checks, and check signing machine Prenumbered checks Imprinted amounts on checks Bank check protection services (Positive Pay) All purchases paid by check Imprest petty cash fund Segregation of duties Independent bank account reconciliation
16. Theft associated with use of EFT		Strict access controls Frequent changing of user IDs and passwords Encryption of transmissions
17. Loss of data	Incorrect data for decision making Loss of confidential information	Backup and disaster recovery procedures Access controls (logical and physical)
18. Poor performance	Inefficient or ineffective processes	Preparation and review of performance reports

Order Goods

The primary objective of the purchasing activity is to secure the most reasonable prices for ordered items while satisfying quality standards. Threats 3–6 in Table 18.1 relate to this objective.

Threat 3: Purchasing Goods at Inflated Prices. Companies strive to secure the best prices for raw materials and inventory. Price lists for frequently purchased items should be stored in the computer and consulted when ordering. The prices of many low-cost items can be readily determined from catalogs. Competitive, written bids should be solicited for high-cost and specialized items. Purchase orders should be reviewed to assure that these policies have been followed.

Budgetary controls are also helpful in controlling expenses. Purchases should be charged to an account that is the responsibility of the person or department approving the requisition. Actual costs should be compared periodically to budget allowances. To facilitate control, these reports should highlight any significant deviations from budgeted amounts for further investigation (the principle of management by exception).

Threat 4: Purchasing Goods of Inferior Quality. In their quest to obtain the lowest possible prices, companies must beware of purchasing inferior-quality products. Substandard products can result in costly production delays; moreover, the costs of scrap and rework often result in higher total production costs than if better-quality materials, at higher prices, had been initially purchased.

Buyers, through experience, often learn which vendors provide the best-quality goods at competitive prices. Such informal knowledge should be incorporated into formal control procedures so that it is not lost when a particular employee leaves the company. Establishing lists of approved vendors known to provide goods of acceptable quality will achieve this goal. Purchase orders should be reviewed to ensure that only these approved vendors are being used. In addition, vendor performance data should be collected and periodically reviewed to maintain the accuracy of these approved vendor lists.

Threat 5: Purchasing from Unauthorized Vendors. Purchasing from unauthorized vendors can result in a number of problems. Items may be of inferior quality or may be excessively priced. The purchase may even cause legal problems, such as violating import quotas. Consequently, all purchase orders should be reviewed to ensure that only approved vendors are used. Access to the approved vendor list must also be restricted, and the list should be reviewed periodically for any unauthorized changes. Purchase orders should also be prenumbered and accounted for periodically.

Threat 6: Kickbacks. **Kickbacks** are gifts from vendors to purchasing agents for the purpose of influencing their choice of suppliers. Kickbacks may result in the purchase of goods at inflated prices or of inferior quality. Even if neither of these problems occurs, kickbacks impair the objectivity of buyers. Moreover, employees should not profit from performing their regular business duties.

To prevent kickbacks, companies should prohibit purchasing agents from accepting any gifts from potential or existing suppliers. (Trinkets that are clearly of inconsequential value, such as pens or calendars, may be allowed.) In addition, purchasing agents should also be required to sign annual conflict of interest statements, disclosing any financial interests they may have in current or potential suppliers. Admittedly, kickbacks are difficult to prevent. Consequently, detective controls are also needed. Focus 18.4 discusses one particularly effective detection control: the vendor audit.

Effect of EDI. The use of EDI for purchase orders requires additional control procedures. Access to the EDI system should be controlled and limited to authorized personnel through the use of passwords, user IDs, access control matrices, and physical access controls. Procedures to verify and authenticate EDI transactions are also needed. Most EDI systems are programmed to send

FOCUS 18.4

Vendor Audits: A Means to Control Purchasing

B. Ray Mize, a consulting auditor in Kenner, Louisiana, believes that vendor audits may be one of the most effective tools for assessing the effectiveness of expenditure cycle controls. A vendor audit entails visiting a supplier's office to check its records. It is designed to answer a number of questions. Who determines the business requirements for a good or service? How is the good or service consumed, and how is this documented? What is the procurement process, and how is the company assured that the best-quality goods or services were obtained at the best price? Were any gifts or favors provided to purchasing agents?

After doing a number of vendor audits, Mize developed a list of "red flags" that identify vendors likely to represent potential problems:

1. A large percentage of the vendor's gross sales was to one company.
2. The vendor's pricing methods differ from standard industry practice.
3. The vendor does not own the equipment it rents to customers, but is itself renting that equipment from a third party.
4. Entertainment expenses are high in terms of a percentage of the vendor's gross sales.
5. Third-party invoices submitted by the vendor are altered or fictitious.
6. The vendor's addresses on their invoices are fictitious.

Vendor audits can yield substantial returns. Mize reports that the first six vendor audits he performed helped his former employer recover more than $250,000 for such failures as duplicate billings. Audits also uncovered a major violation of the company's conflict of interest policy. Interestingly, Mize notes that virtually all of the suppliers he has audited support the idea of vendor audits because the process gives them a "good excuse" for not offering purchasing agents gifts or entertainment. This reduces the vendor's costs and results in better procurement terms for the buyer.

Focus Questions

1. Do you agree with Mize's opinion that suppliers support the idea of vendor audits? Why or why not?
2. What should the internal auditor do if management does not support the idea of vendor audits? What if they support the general idea, but want the internal auditor to exclude certain vendors from the program?

Source: B. Ray Mize, Jr., "Vendor Audits," *The CPA Journal* (February 1994): 18–22.

an acknowledgment for each transaction, which provides a rudimentary accuracy check. Further protection against transmission problems, which can result in the loss of orders, is provided by time-stamping and numbering all EDI transactions. Companies should maintain and periodically review a log of all EDI transactions to ensure that all have been processed and that established policies are being followed. Encryption can be used to ensure the privacy of EDI transactions, which is especially important for competitive bids.

Purchase of Services. Thus far, the discussion has centered on the purchase of inventory items. Different procedures are needed to control the purchase of services, such as painting or maintenance work. The major challenge in this area is establishing that the services were actually performed. This is not always easy to do. For example, visual inspection can indicate whether a room has been painted. It does not, however, reveal whether the walls were appropriately primed, unless the inspection was done during the painting process, which may not always be feasible.

One way to control the purchase of services is to hold the appropriate supervisor responsible for all such costs incurred by that department. The supervisor is required to acknowledge receipt of the services, and the related expenses are then charged to accounts for which he or she is responsible. Actual versus budgeted expenses should then be routinely compared, and any discrepancies investigated.

Receive and Store Goods

The primary objectives of the receiving and storage function are to verify the receipt of ordered inventory and to safeguard it against loss or theft. Threats 7–9 in Table 18.1 apply to the receipt and storage of inventory.

Threat 7: Receiving Unordered Goods. Accepting delivery of unordered goods results in costs associated with storing, and later returning, those items. The best control procedure to mitigate this threat is to instruct the receiving department to accept only deliveries for which it has an approved copy of the purchase order. Effective control requires that a copy of every purchase order be sent to the receiving department upon issuance and that these copies be filed in a manner that facilitates their subsequent retrieval.

Threat 8: Errors in Counting Goods Received. Accurate counting of goods received is crucial for maintaining accurate perpetual inventory records. It also ensures that the company pays only for goods actually received. This threat is best dealt with by the procedures discussed earlier for encouraging receiving clerks to count all deliveries accurately: blacking out the quantities ordered on their copy of the purchase order and requiring them to sign each receiving report. Some companies also offer bonuses to receiving clerks for catching discrepancies between the packing slip and actual quantity received before the delivery person leaves. Additional control is provided by requiring inventory stores, or the appropriate user department, to count the items transferred from receiving and then hold that department responsible for any subsequent shortages.

Threat 9: Theft of Inventory. Several control procedures can be used to safeguard inventory against loss. First, inventories should be stored in secure locations to which access is restricted. Second, all transfers of inventory within the company should be documented. For example, both the receiving department and the inventory stores department should acknowledge the transfer of goods from the receiving dock into inventory. Similarly, the release of inventory into production should be acknowledged by both the inventory stores and the production departments. This documentation provides the necessary information for establishing responsibility for any shortages, thereby encouraging employees to take special care to record all inventory movements accurately. Finally, it is important to take periodic physical counts of inventory on hand and to reconcile those counts with the inventory records.

One annual physical inventory count will generally *not* be sufficient to maintain accurate inventory records, especially for MRP and JIT systems. Instead, an ABC cost analysis should be used to classify items according to their importance: The most critical items (A items) should be counted most frequently, and the least critical items (C items) can be counted less often. Note that use of this approach might have alerted management at AOE's Wichita plant about shortages of key components early enough to avoid production delays.

Approve Vendor Invoices

The objective of this activity is to ensure that the company pays only for goods that were ordered and received. Threats 10–14 in Table 18.1 apply to this objective.

Threat 10: Errors in Vendor Invoices. Vendor invoices may contain various errors, such as discrepancies between quoted and actual prices charged or miscalculations of the total amount due. Consequently, the mathematical accuracy of vendor invoices must be verified and the prices and quantities listed thereon compared to those indicated on the purchase order and receiving report.

Threat 11: Paying for Goods Not Received. The best control to prevent paying for goods not received is to compare the quantities indicated on the vendor invoice with the quantities indicated on the copy of the receiving report that was signed by the person accepting the transfer of those goods from the receiving department.

Threat 12: Failure to Take Available Purchase Discounts. Failure to take advantage of purchase discounts can cost a company money. Proper filing can significantly reduce the risk of this threat. Approved invoices should be filed by due date, and the system should be designed to track invoice due dates and to print a periodic list of all outstanding invoices. A cash flow budget, indicating expected cash inflows as well as outstanding commitments, can also help companies plan to take advantage of any available purchase discounts.

Threat 13: Paying the Same Invoice Twice. The same invoice can be submitted for payment more than once for a variety of reasons. It may be a duplicate invoice that was sent after the company's check was already in the mail, or it may have become separated from the other documents in the voucher package. Although paying invoices a second time is usually detected by the vendor and results in a credit to the company's account, it can affect a company's cash flow needs. In addition, the financial records will be incorrect, at least until the duplicate payment is detected.

Three control procedures can mitigate this threat. First, invoices should be approved for payment only when accompanied by a complete voucher package (purchase order and receiving report). Second, only the original copy of an invoice should be paid. Most duplicate invoices sent by vendors clearly indicate that they are not originals; therefore payment should never be authorized for a photocopy of an invoice. Third, when the check to pay for an invoice is signed, the invoice and the voucher package should be canceled (marked "paid") in a manner that would prevent their resubmission. If paper documents are not used, the computer records of accounts payable should be marked with a code indicating that the invoice has been paid.

Threat 14: Recording and Posting Errors. Errors in recording and posting payments to vendors will result in errors in financial and performance reports that, in turn, can contribute to poor decision making. Appropriate data entry and processing controls are necessary to prevent these types of problems. One such control involves comparing the difference in vendor account balances before and after processing checks to the total amount of invoices processed. The total of all individual vendor account balances (or unpaid vouchers, whichever exists) should also be reconciled periodically with the amount of the accounts payable control account in the general ledger.

Pay for Goods

The primary objective of this activity is to safeguard cash by ensuring that all disbursements are legitimate. Thus threats 15 and 16 in Table 18.1 apply to the cash disbursement function.

Threat 15: Misappropriation of Cash. Cash is the easiest asset to steal; consequently access to cash and blank checks should be restricted. Checks should be sequentially numbered and periodically accounted for by the cashier. If a check signing machine is used, access to it should be restricted as well.

Check alteration and forgery are major problems. Check-protection machines can reduce the risk of this threat by imprinting the amount in distinctive colors, typically using a combination of red and blue ink. Using special inks that change colors if altered, and printing checks on special papers that contain watermarks, can further reduce the probability of alteration. Many banks also provide special services to help protect companies against fraudulent checks. One such service, called Positive Pay, involves sending a daily list of all legitimate checks to the bank; the bank will then clear only checks appearing on that list.

Whenever possible, expenditures should be made by check. Nevertheless, it is often more convenient to pay for minor purchases, such as coffee or pencils, in cash. A petty cash fund, managed by an employee who has no other cash-handling or accounting responsibilities, should be established to handle such expenditures. The petty cash fund should be set up as an imprest fund. An **imprest fund** has two characteristics: (1) It is set at a fixed amount, such as $100, and (2) it requires vouchers for every disbursement. At all times, the sum of cash plus vouchers should equal the preset fund balance. When the fund balance gets low, the vouchers are presented to accounts payable for replenishment. After accounts payable authorizes this transaction, the cashier then writes a check to restore the petty cash fund to its designated level. As with the supporting documents used for regular purchases, the vouchers used to support replenishment of the petty cash fund should be canceled at the time the fund is restored to its preset level.

The operation of an imprest petty cash fund technically violates the principle of segregation of duties, because the same person has custody of the cash, authorizes disbursements from the fund, and maintains a record of the fund balance. The threat of misappropriation is more than offset, however, by the convenience of not having to process small miscellaneous purchases through the normal expenditure cycle. Moreover, the risk of misappropriation can be mitigated by having the internal auditor make periodic unannounced counts of the fund balance and vouchers and by holding the person in charge of the petty cash fund responsible for any shortages discovered during those counts.

Proper segregation of duties is crucial for minimizing the risk of cash misappropriations by check issuances to fictitious vendors. First, access to the approved vendor list should be restricted and any changes to that list should be carefully reviewed and approved. Second, the authorization of payment, including the assembling of a voucher package, should be performed by the accounts payable function; checks should be signed, however, only by the treasurer or cashier. Moreover, checks in excess of a certain amount, such as $5,000–$10,000, should require two signatures, thereby providing yet another independent review of the expenditure.

Once signed, the checks should be mailed by the cashier and not returned to accounts payable, to ensure that they are indeed sent to the intended payee. The cashier should also cancel all documents in the voucher package to prevent their being resubmitted to support another disbursement. Finally, all bank accounts should be reconciled by someone who did not participate in processing either cash collections or disbursements. This control provides an independent check on accuracy and prevents someone from misappropriating cash and then concealing the theft by adjusting the bank statement.

Threat 16: Theft Associated with the Use of EFT. The use of EFT requires additional control procedures. Because EFT involves the movement of funds, strict access controls are needed. Passwords and user IDs should be used and changed regularly. The user as well as the location of the originating terminal should be recorded so that the adequacy of access controls can be monitored. All EFT transmissions should be encrypted, to prevent alteration. In addition, all EFT transactions should be time-stamped and numbered, to facilitate subsequent reconciliation. A control group should also be established and given responsibility for monitoring EFT transactions for validity and accuracy and maintaining the adequacy of the controls outlined here.

General Control Issues

Threats 17 and 18 in Table 18.1 are general threats that affect all phases of the expenditure cycle.

Threat 17: Loss of Data. Data about pending cash disbursement obligations and open orders must be safeguarded from loss or corruption. Both external and internal file labels should be used to reduce the possibility of accidentally erasing important files and to ensure that the most recent version of the master file is being updated. In addition, the purchases, receipts, master accounts payable, and cash disbursements files should be backed up regularly. Two backup copies should be made: one to be stored on-site and the other off-site. Moreover, the grandfather-father-son technique should be used to store several generations of the master file and intervening transaction files.

Access controls are also important. A system of passwords and user IDs should be used to limit employee access to various files. For example, only the cashier should be able to alter the field indicating whether an invoice has been paid. Access controls should also exist for individual terminals. For example, the system should be programmed to accept approval of invoices only from terminals located in the accounts payable department.

Threat 18: Poor Performance. In addition to ensuring accuracy and safeguarding assets, another objective of internal controls in the expenditure cycle is to encourage efficient and effective performance of business activities. The preparation and review of performance reports is effective in achieving this objective. Several have already been discussed in this chapter, such as reports on vendor performance and lists of outstanding invoices. Another useful report that provides one measure of operating efficiency gives the number of purchase orders processed per employee per time period. Data about average order sizes and error rates provide measures of effectiveness, as well. Reports indicating the percentage, and dollar amount, of purchase discounts taken provide another measure of the efficiency and effectiveness of expenditure cycle activities.

The number of additional performance reports that can be developed is limited only by the ingenuity of the controller and by management's decisions about what factors are important to monitor and control. The ease with which such reports can be produced, however, is affected by the methods used to store and maintain expenditure cycle data.

EXPENDITURE CYCLE INFORMATION NEEDS AND DATA MODEL

A third function of the AIS is to provide information useful for decision making. Usefulness in the expenditure cycle means that the AIS must provide the operational information needed to perform the following functions:

- Determine when and how much additional inventory to order.
- Select the appropriate vendors from whom to order.
- Verify the accuracy of vendor invoices.
- Decide whether purchase discounts should be taken.
- Monitor cash flow needs to pay outstanding obligations.

In addition, the AIS needs to provide the following kinds of strategic and performance evaluation information:

- Efficiency and effectiveness of the purchasing department.
- Analyses of vendor performance such as on-time delivery, quality, and so on.
- Time taken to move goods from the receiving dock into production.
- Percentage of purchase discounts taken.

Notice that these decisions require both financial and operating data. For example, vendor selection should take into consideration not only price, but also information about vendor performance in meeting delivery dates and quality of goods. Traditionally, the AIS has provided the financial information needed to make expenditure cycle decisions, and other information systems have generated the operating data about expenditure cycle activities. One problem with using separate information systems, however, is that the two sets of resulting data may be inconsistent. Moreover, the existence of multiple, overlapping systems increases costs and reduces efficiency. Fortunately, the advent of relational DBMS makes the need to maintain separate information systems for financial and operating data obsolete.

Many expenditure cycle decisions also require externally generated information. For example, data about vendor financial characteristics may be useful in selecting vendors that are stable and likely to be able to meet future commitments. A well-designed data model facilitates the integration of such externally generated information with internally generated financial and operating data about expenditure cycle activities.

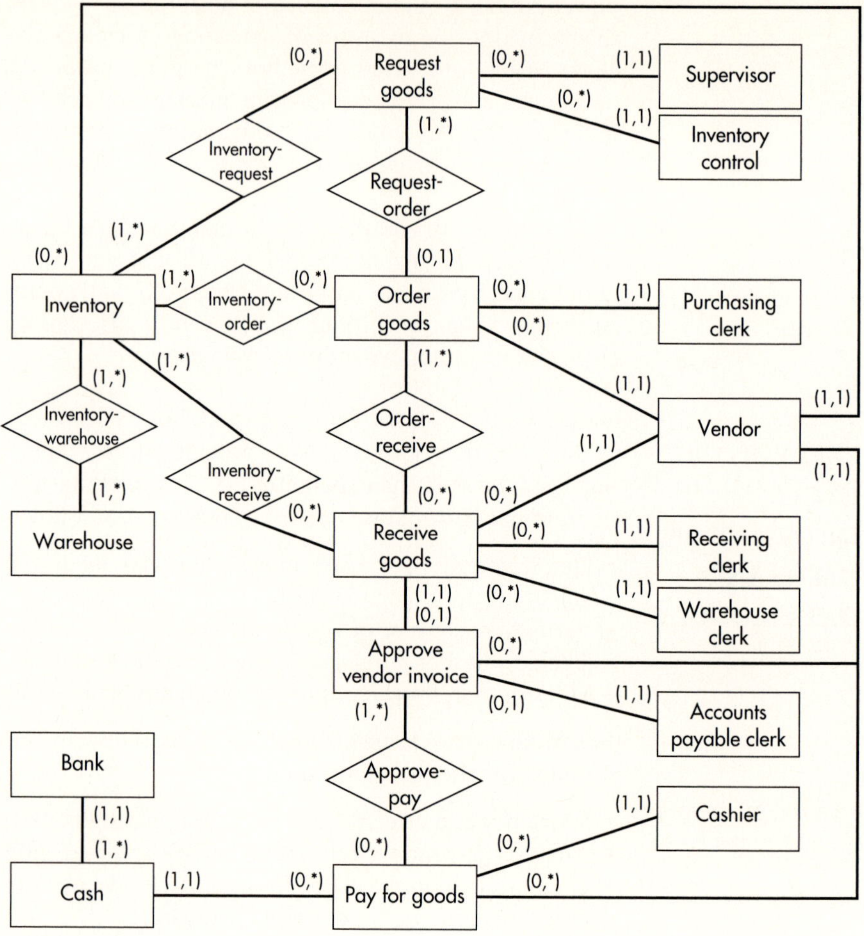

Figure 18.12

E–R Diagram of Expenditure Cycle for AOE (only relationships implemented as tables are shown, to simplify the figure)

Expenditure Cycle Data Model

Figure 18.12 shows a simplified example of an REA data model for the expenditure cycle of a manufacturing company such as AOE. It includes information about the following activities:

- The two major resources (cash and inventory) used in the expenditure cycle and the location in which they are stored (bank and warehouse).
- The five major business events in the expenditure cycle (request goods, order goods, receive goods, approve vendor invoices,[1] and pay for goods).
- The primary external agent (vendors) as well as the various internal agents involved in expenditure cycle activities.

---

[1]Some REA data modelers would argue that the activity of approving vendor invoices should not be modeled as a separate event. We choose to do so for the following reasons. First, it facilitates modeling the use of a vouchering system; indeed, the primary key of this event is the voucher number. Second, it allows us to store information explicitly about the person(s) responsible for approving vendor invoices, thereby increasing the utility of using the E–R diagram to evaluate internal controls. Third, certain attributes, such as the date an invoice is due, are more logically stored as attributes of the approved invoice event than as properties of other events.

Figure 18.12 *Continued*

Table Attributes for Fig. 18.12

Table Name	Contents (**primary key,** *foreign key*)
Inventory	**Item_Number,** Description, Selling_Price, Reorder_Point, *Preferred_Vendor_Number,* Quantity on Hand, Quantity_Available, Standard_Cost, . . .
Cash	**Bank_Account_Number,** Balance, Interest_Rate, *Bank_Number*
Warehouse	**Warehouse_Number,** Location, *Manager_Number,* Phone_Number, Number_of_Employees, . . .
Bank	**Bank_Number,** Name, Address, Phone_Number
Request Goods	**Requisition_Number,** *Supervisor_Number, Inventory_Control_Clerk_Number,* Date, Date_Needed, . . .
Order Goods	**Purchase_Order_Number,** Date, *Vendor_Number, Purchasing_Agent_Number,* Amount, . . .
Receive Goods	**Receiving_Report_Number,** Remarks, Date_Received, *Vendor_Number, Receiving_Clerk_Number, Warehouse_Clerk_Number*
Approve Vendor Invoice	**Voucher_Number,** Vendor_Invoice_Number, Date_Approved, Date_Due, Amount_*Purchase_Order_Number,* Receiving_ *Report_Number, Accounts_Payable_Clerk_Number,* Discount_Available
Pay for Goods	**Check_Number,** Date, Amount, *Vendor_Number, Cashier_Number, Bank_Account_Number,* . . .
Vendors	**Vendor_Number,** Name, Rating, Address, Telephone_Number
Supervisor[1]	**Employee_Number,** Name, Date_Hired, Date_of_Birth, Salary, ...
Inventory-Warehouse	**Warehouse_Number, Item_Number,** Quantity_on_Hand
Inventory-Request	**Item_Number, Requisition_Number,** Quantity_Requested
Inventory-Order	**Item_Number, Purchase_Order_Number,** Quantity_Ordered, Cost
Inventory-Receive	**Item_Number, Receiving_Report_Number,** Quantity_Received, Condition
Request-Order	**Requisition_Number, Purchase_Order_Number**
Order-Receive	**Purchase_Order_Number, Receiving_Report_Number,** Complete
Approve-Pay	**Voucher_Number, Check_Number,** Amount_Applied_to_Invoice, Discount_Taken

[1]Similar tables would exist for all other employee types shown in the E–R diagram; because each table would have identical columns, only the supervisor table is shown here to save space.

If the data model depicted in Fig. 18.12 were implemented in a relational data base, there would be a table for each entity (box) and for each many-to-many relationship. Figure 18.12 lists many of the attributes that would be found in those relational tables. Most of these attributes and their placement in specific tables should be self-explanatory. The placement of standard and actual costs, however, deserves some explanation.

Standard cost is stored as an attribute of the inventory table because it is the same for all units of a given inventory item. In contrast, the actual cost of inventory is stored in the inventory-order table. This reflects the fact that purchase prices can vary over time. By storing the cost of each order along with the quantity purchased, the system can easily calculate the actual cost of ending inventory and the cost of goods sold according to any accepted inventory valuation method (LIFO, FIFO, weighted-average, or specific identification). If, on the other hand, actual cost were stored as an attribute of the inventory table, it would necessitate the use of the weighted-average method because all units of a given inventory item would be assigned the same cost. In addition, cost data would be available only in this format; it would be impossible to compute alternative values for inventory because the detailed data about the cost associated with each purchase would not be stored in the data base.

Reading the E–R Diagram

Figure 18.12 provides a great deal of information about AOE's business policies. The figure models the relationship between the request goods and order goods events as being many-to-one. This reflects the fact that AOE sometimes issues purchase orders for individual purchase requests, but at other times it takes advantage of volume discounts by issuing one purchase order for a set of requests.

Figure 18.12 depicts a many-to-many relationship between the order goods and receive goods events. This reflects the fact that vendors sometimes make several separate deliveries to fill one purchase order, at other times fill several purchase orders with one delivery, and sometimes make a delivery to fill a single purchase order in full.

The relationship between the receive goods and approve vendor invoice events is depicted as being one-to-one because vendors bill AOE for each delivery. The relationship between the approve invoice and pay for goods events, however, is modeled as being many-to-many. This reflects the fact that AOE sometimes pays vendor invoices individually, that at other times it writes one check to pay for several invoices, and that it also occasionally makes installment payments for purchases. Finally, there is always some amount of time lag between events, as depicted in Fig. 18.12 by the minimum cardinality of zero associated with the later of the two events linked in a relationship.

Events must always involve internal or external agents; consequently, Fig. 18.12 shows that both the minimum and maximum cardinalities associated with the various agent entities is 1. Each agent, however, can potentially be involved in zero or many instances of an event; this is depicted by the (O,*) cardinality attached to the event entity in each event-agent relationship.

AOE manufactures and sells mass-produced items from a limited set of component parts; consequently, each component part (represented by a row in the inventory table) can be linked to many different request, order, and receipt events. At the same time, each of those events can involve many different component parts. Thus the relationships between inventory and those three events are all depicted in Fig. 18.12 as being many-to-many. Notice, however, that the minimum cardinality for the inventory entity is 1, but the minimum cardinality for each event entity is zero. This reflects the fact that each event (request, order, or receipt of inventory) must involve at least one component part, but a specific component part, if used infrequently, may not be linked to any of those events.

AOE has several warehouses; consequently, a given inventory item can be stored at more than one warehouse, and each warehouse can store many different inventory items. This is reflected in the many-to-many relationship between the inventory and warehouse entities. Note, however, that the minimum cardinality associated with each entity in that relationship is 1; this reflects the fact that a given inventory item must be stored somewhere, and each warehouse must contain at least one kind of component part.

AOE uses one bank account to pay for its purchases; this is reflected in the one-to-many relationship in Fig. 18.12 between the cash resource entity and the pay for goods event. AOE does, however, have several different bank accounts and sometimes has more than one account at a given bank. This is reflected in Fig. 18.12 by the many-to-one relationship between the cash and bank entities. Notice, moreover, that the minimum cardinality for both entities is 1; AOE maintains information only about banks at which it has accounts, and each account must be associated with one and only one particular bank. Figure 18.12 also includes a relationship between the inventory resource entity and the vendor agent entities. This relationship represents the fact that AOE has developed a list of preferred vendors for each component part that it purchases.

Where are the data about accounts payable stored? Accounts payable represents those purchases that have not yet been paid for. Therefore, as explained in Chapter 6, accounts payable can be calculated by computing the difference between total purchases and the cash disbursements linked to those purchase events.

Benefits of the Data Model

Notice that the data model in Fig. 18.12 effectively integrates both traditional accounting transaction data (for example, the date and amount of each purchase) with other operational data (for example, information about where that item is stored and vendor performance measures, such as delivery date). It would also be easy to link this internally generated data with various types of external information. For example, information about the financial position and credit rating of vendors could be downloaded from a commercial data base, appended as additional columns in the vendor table, and used in the vendor selection process. Most importantly, implementing the data model shown in Fig. 18.12 in a relational DBMS would enable LeRoy Williams and other decision makers at AOE to directly access and manipulate the information they need by using powerful but easy-to-use query languages such as SQL (see Table 18.2).

Internal Control Considerations

Our discussion of the threats listed in Table 18.1 stressed the importance of properly segregating incompatible duties. E–R diagrams are useful for this task because they indicate which internal agents participate in each event. In addition, if the REA model is implemented in a DBMS, the computer can be programmed to enforce segregation of duties by preventing the same person from performing incompatible functions. Conversely, the system can be programmed to list all cases of an employee performing multiple roles, so that the auditors can investigate whether adequate compensating controls exist.

The use of DBMS also increases the importance of having effective access controls. Most relational DBMS provide a means to control access by letting users see only a portion of the data base (called a view). For example, purchasing agents should see only the portion of Fig. 18.12 relevant to their job duties, such as the tables for inventory, vendors, and purchases. Moreover, purchasing agents should be allowed to perform only a restricted set of operations on those tables. For example, they should have read-only rights to the vendor

Table 18.2 **Sample SQL Queries of Fig. 18.12 Data Model**

Query 1: List the vendors and purchase orders for which some goods were back-ordered.

```
SELECT  Vendor_Number, Purchase_Order_Number
FROM    Order Goods, Order-Receive
WHERE   Order Goods.Purchase_Order_Number=Order-Receive.Purchase_Order_Number
        AND   Complete = 'No'
```

Order Goods

Purchase_Order Number	Date	Vendor-Number	Purchasing Agent_Number	Amount
2471	06/25/97	101	1	2500
2472	06/26/97	105	3	3300
2473	06/26/97	103	2	2200
2474	06/30/97	101	1	3400
2475	07/03/97	104	4	2700

Order-Receive

Purchase_ Order_Number	Receiving_ Report_Number	Complete
2471	2832	Yes
2472	2833	No
2473	2834	Yes
2475	2835	No
2472	2836	Yes

Response to Query 1

Vendor_ Number	Purchase_ Order_Number
105	2472
104	2475

Query 2: List the amount of purchase discounts available and the amount taken.

```
SELECT  Sum(Discount_Available), Sum(Discount_Taken)
FROM    Approve-Pay, Approve_Vendor_Invoice
WHERE   Approve-Pay.Voucher_Number = Approve_Vendor_Invoice.Voucher_Number
```

Approve-Pay

Voucher_ Number	Check_ Number	Amount Applied_to_ Invoice	Discount_ Taken
2812	1876	3450	125
2813	1877	2235	–0–
2814	1878	4265	–0–
2815	1879	2795	–0–
2816	1880	3360	140
2817	1881	2000	–0–

Approve_Vendor_Invoice (partial table)

Voucher_ Number	Vendor_ Invoice_ Number	Discount_ Available	Other Columns -------
2812	34224	125	.....
2813	10338	100	.....
2814	3876	300	.....
2815	21992	–0–	.....
2816	6329	140	.....
2817	42945	50	.....

Response to Query 2

Sum (Discount_ Available)	Sum (Discount_ Taken)
715	265

table, to prevent them from making any unauthorized changes to the list of approved vendors.

Data accuracy is vital when using a DBMS. Fortunately, the relational data model provides some built-in controls to ensure data accuracy and consistency. One of the more important of these controls is support for foreign keys and referential integrity. For example, when a new row is added to the approve vendor invoice table, the system should automatically verify that the vendor number (which appears as a foreign key in that table) actually exists as a primary key in the vendor table. This control ensures that there really is such a vendor. Finally, the use of a DBMS makes adequate backup and disaster recovery procedures crucial.

SUMMARY AND CASE CONCLUSION

Activities performed in the expenditure cycle include the following:

- Requesting the purchase of needed goods.
- Ordering goods from vendors.
- Receiving goods from vendors.
- Approving vendor invoices for payment.
- Disbursing cash to pay for purchases.

The efficiency and effectiveness of these activities can significantly affect a company's overall performance. For example, deficiencies in requesting and ordering necessary inventory and supplies can create production bottlenecks and result in lost sales due to stockouts of popular items. Problems in the procedures related to receiving and storing inventory can result in a company's paying for items it never received, accepting delivery and incurring storage costs for unordered items, and experiencing a theft of inventory. Problems in approving vendor invoices for payment can result in overpaying vendors or failing to take available discounts for prompt payment. Weaknesses in the cash disbursement process can result in the misappropriation of cash.

IT can help improve the efficiency and effectiveness with which expenditure cycle activities are performed. In particular, the use of EDI, bar coding, and EFT can significantly reduce the time and costs associated with ordering, receiving, and paying for goods. In addition, the use of a well-designed data model can allow for the integration of internally generated financial and operating data with externally generated information so that all three types of data can be considered when making important operating and strategic decisions. Finally, proper control procedures, especially segregation of duties, are needed to mitigate the various threats, such as errors in performing expenditure cycle activities and the theft of inventory or cash.

Figure 18.13 depicts the new system recommended by Elizabeth Venko to help solve AOE's expenditure cycle problems. This proposed system is typical of the systems used by many large manufacturing companies such as Ford, IBM, and McDonnell Douglas.

The proposed system puts on-line terminals in each of AOE's departments. A JIT inventory control system will be implemented, to minimize inventory

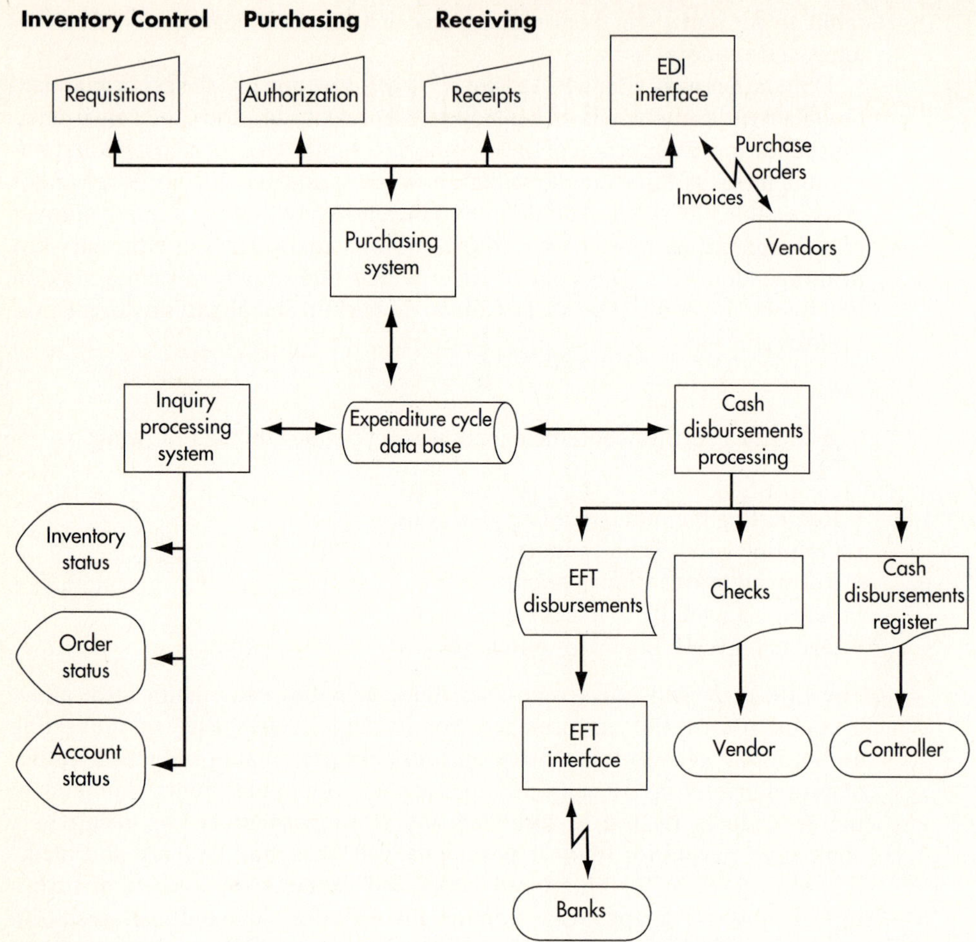

Figure 18.13

Flowchart of AOE's Proposed New Expenditure Cycle

carrying costs. EDI will be used to send purchase orders to vendors, thereby improving the efficiency of the ordering process and also reducing the lead time between ordering and receiving goods. On-line data entry by receiving dock workers and by the warehouse clerk will improve the accuracy and timeliness of AOE's perpetual inventory records. Vendors will be asked to bar-code their shipments so that the use of hand-held bar-code scanners can further improve the speed and accuracy of recording inventory receipts and movements. Vendors will also be asked to send invoices via EDI, which should improve the efficiency and accuracy of processing invoices and also reduce the costs associated with handling and storing paper invoices. The system will automatically match the EDI invoices with the related purchase orders and receiving reports. It will also track invoice due dates so that AOE will not miss out on any available discounts for prompt payment. Finally, EFT will be used as much as possible to streamline the cash disbursements process and reduce the costs associated with processing payments by check.

The proposed system will also use a relational data base built on a data model similar to that shown in Fig. 18.12. The availability of SQL will make it easy for LeRoy Williams, Elizabeth Venko, and other AOE managers to retrieve the information needed to make purchasing and payment decisions. Appropriate access controls will be used to limit the tables that individual employees can see and the operations that they can perform on those tables.

KEY TERMS

expenditure cycle
inventory control
economic order quantity (EOQ)
ordering costs
carrying costs
stockout costs
reorder point
materials requirement planning (MRP)
just-in-time (JIT) inventory system
purchase requisition
purchase order
blanket order
receiving report
debit memo
nonvoucher system
voucher system
disbursement voucher
voucher package
vendor performance report
kickbacks
imprest fund

CHAPTER QUIZ

1. Which of the following inventory control methods is least likely to require maintenance of perpetual inventory records?
a. JIT
b. Economic order quantity
c. MRP
d. ABC

2. Who should prepare purchase orders?
a. Factory personnel who notice the need for items
b. Purchasing agents
c. Accounts payable
d. Supervisors of any department needing items

3. Which of the following documents is not always a part of the voucher package?
a. Purchase order
b. Receiving report
c. Vendor invoice
d. Disbursement voucher

4. Which document is used to establish a contract for the purchase of goods or services from a vendor?
a. Vendor invoice
b. Purchase requisition
c. Purchase order
d. Disbursement voucher

5. Which method would provide the greatest efficiency improvements for cash disbursements?
a. Bar coding
b. EDI
c. EFT
d. Vendor certification

6. Which of the following is *not* one of the events that would be included in the REA data model of the expenditure cycle?
a. Purchasing
b. Cash receipts
c. Receiving
d. Cash disbursements

7. The best control procedure to prevent paying the same invoice twice is
a. segregation of check-preparation and check-signing functions.
b. preparing checks only for invoices that have been matched to receiving reports and purchase orders.
c. requiring two signatures on all checks above a certain limit.
d. canceling all supporting documents when the check is signed.

8. Who should sign checks?
a. Cashier
b. Accounts payable
c. Purchasing
d. Controller

9. Which of the following procedures is least effective in preventing the purchasing agent from receiving kickbacks?
a. Maintaining a list of approved vendors and requiring all purchases to be made from vendors on that list
b. Requiring purchasing agents to disclose any financial investments in potential suppliers
c. Requiring approval of all purchase orders

d. Prenumbering and periodically accounting for all purchase orders

10. Which document is used to record adjustments to accounts payable based on the return of unacceptable inventory to the vendor?

a. Receiving report
b. Credit memo
c. Debit memo
d. Purchase order

DISCUSSION QUESTIONS

18.1 In both Chapters 17 and 18, the controller of AOE played a major role in evaluating and recommending ways to use IT to improve efficiency and effectiveness. Shouldn't these decisions be made by the company's chief information officer instead? Should the controller be involved in making these types of decisions? Why or why not?

18.2 Some companies, like IBM and Ingersoll-Rand, have moved beyond JIT to JIT-II systems. In JIT-II systems, vendor sales representatives work on site so that they can monitor inventory levels and have access to current sales data and forecasts. The vendor representatives use this information to reorder goods automatically and meet production needs. Discuss the potential advantages and disadvantages of this arrangement. What special controls, if any, need to be developed to monitor JIT-II systems?

18.3 A standard control procedure that ensures an organization pays only for inventory actually received is to require that all vendor invoices be matched with purchase orders and receiving reports. How can an organization verify that services, such as cleaning and painting, for which no receiving report is prepared, were actually performed?

18.4 Will the use of EFT reduce the opportunity for fraud by eliminating the problems associated with the use of checks, such as forgery? Why or why not?

18.5 Some people argue that if total quality control principles are followed, there should be little or no "shrinkage" of inventory and therefore little need for periodic inventory counts. Comment on this argument.

18.6 In what ways can you apply the control procedures discussed in this chapter to paying your own personal debts (e.g., credit card bills)?

PROBLEMS

18.1 Which internal control procedure would be most cost effective in dealing with the following expenditure cycle threats?

a. A purchasing agent orders materials from a vendor that he partially owns.

b. Inventory was stolen by receiving dock personnel; they claim the inventory was sent to the warehouse.

c. An unordered supply of laser printer paper was delivered to the office; it was accepted and paid for because the "price was right." After jamming all of the laser printers, however, it became obvious that the "bargain" paper was of inferior quality.

d. A vendor's invoice overcharged for items ordered and delivered.

e. A company was late in paying a particular invoice. Consequently, a second invoice that crossed the first invoice's payment in the mail was sent. The second invoice was submitted for processing and also paid.

f. Inventory records showed that an adequate supply of copy paper was supposed to be in stock, but none was available on the supply shelf.

g. The inventory records were incorrectly updated when a receiving dock employee entered the wrong product number at the terminal.

h. A clerical employee obtained a blank check and wrote a large amount payable to a fictitious company.

i. A fictitious invoice was received and used to pay for goods that were never ordered or delivered.

j. The petty cash custodian confessed to having "borrowed" $12,000 over the last five years.

18.2 The data models for both the revenue and expenditure cycles (Chapters 17 and 18) contain some common elements, such as inventory and cash. Discuss how the two cycles interact with each other. Sketch out a combined E–R diagram to cover both cycles.

18.3 Figure 18.12 lists the attributes that would be included in each table of a relational data base for AOE's expenditure cycle. Table 18.2 shows some sample tables from that data base. Refer to this figure and table to write SQL queries that answer the following questions:

a. What is the total amount of purchases made by each purchasing agent?

b. What is the name of the vendor from which the most purchases were made?

c. How much of each component is stored in the Dayton warehouse?

d. What is the total cost of circuit boards purchased in May?

e. What is the total amount of accounts payable?

f. What is the total amount of accounts payable for each vendor?

18.4 Refer to Fig. 18.12 to answer the following questions:

a. If the relationship between cash disbursements and approve vendor invoices was one-to-many, what would that reveal about the company's payment policy?

b. Why is the relationship between inventory and purchases many-to-many? What other possible cardinalities can exist between inventory and purchases? What would those other possibilities indicate about the company's business practices?

c. Why is the relationship between purchases and receive goods many-to-many?

d. If a company regularly bought inventory on an installment payment plan, how would that be reflected in Fig. 18.12?

e. Accounts payable is not explicitly shown in Fig. 18.12. Why not? How can this information be retrieved?

18.5 The following documents are used in the expenditure cycle:

- Vendor invoice
- Purchase order
- Disbursement voucher
- Purchase requisition
- Packing slip
- Receiving report
- Check

REQUIRED

a. Identify which of these documents are internally generated and which are externally generated.

b. For each internally generated document, how many copies are needed? What is the purpose of each copy? Where does each copy go?

c. Describe the application controls that should be in place if each of these paper documents were replaced by electronic forms.

18.6 The receiving department at Culp Electronics Company processes inventory deliveries upon arrival by means of on-line data terminals located on the receiving dock. Each inventory receipt entered into the system is processed to update both the inventory master file and the open-purchase order file. The system then automatically generates a voucher to authorize a cash disbursement for each receipt.

REQUIRED

a. What items of data should be entered by receiving department employees?

b. Describe several application controls that should be programmed into the system to check the accuracy and validity of the data entered by the receiving department employees. Relate your answer specifically to the data items mentioned in part (a).

18.7 This problem consists of two parts.

Part I. What is the purpose of each of the following control procedures?

a. Cancellation of the voucher package by the cashier after signing the check

b. Separation of duties of approving invoices for payment and signing checks

c. Prenumbering and periodically accounting for all purchase orders

d. Periodic physical count of inventory

e. Requiring two signatures on checks for large amounts

f. Requiring that a copy of the receiving report be routed through the inventory stores department prior to going to accounts payable

g. Requiring a regular reconciliation of the bank account by someone other than the person responsible for writing checks

h. Maintaining an approved vendor list and checking that all purchase orders are issued only to vendors on that list

Part II. How can the objectives of the control procedures listed in part I be accomplished in an automated AIS?

18.8 The systems flowchart presented in Fig. 18.14 and the following description summarizes ConSport Corporation's cash disbursements system:

1. The accounts payable department approves all invoices for payment by matching them with the related purchase requisitions, purchase orders, and receiving reports. The accounts payable clerks focus on matching the vendor names on all documents and skim the remaining information.
2. The vendor file is searched daily for the disbursement vouchers of invoices due to be paid. Both copies of these vouchers are sent to the treasury department, along with the other supporting documents. The cashier prepares and signs a check for each vendor and records the check in the check register.
3. The cashier receives the monthly bank statement with canceled checks and prepares the bank reconciliation. If an adjustment is required as a consequence of the bank reconciliation, a two-copy journal voucher is prepared. A copy of the bank reconciliation is sent to the internal audit department.

REQUIRED

a. Identify weaknesses in ConSport's cash disbursements system. Use the reference numbers that appear to the left of each symbol in Fig. 18.14 to label each weakness.
b. Describe the nature of each weakness (i.e., what exposures are likely to result).
c. Recommend a control procedure to correct each weakness.
(CMA examination, adapted)

18.9 In 1995, the Diamond Manufacturing Company purchased over $10 million worth of office equipment under its "special" ordering system, with individual orders ranging from $5000 to $30,000. "Special" orders entail low-volume items that have been included in an authorized user's budget. As part of their annual budgets, department heads request equipment and specify estimated costs. The budget, which limits the types and dollar amounts of office equipment a department head can requisition, is approved at the beginning of the year by the board of directors. A purchase requisition form for all approved equipment purchases must be prepared and forwarded to the purchasing department. The "special" ordering system functions as follows.

Purchasing. Upon receiving a purchase requisition, one of the five purchasing agents (buyers) verifies that the requester is indeed a department head. The buyer next selects the appropriate vendor by searching the various catalogs on file. The buyer then phones the vendor, requests a price quote, and places a verbal order. A prenumbered purchase order is then processed, with the original sent to the vendor and copies to the department head, receiving, and accounts payable. One copy is also filed in the open requisition file. When the buyer is verbally informed by the receiving department that the item has been received, the purchase order is transferred from the open to the filled file. Once a month, the buyer reviews the unfilled file to follow up on open orders.

Receiving. The receiving department is sent a copy of each purchase order. When equipment is received, that copy of the purchase order is stamped with the date and, if applicable, any differences between the quantity ordered and the quantity received are noted in red ink. The receiving clerk then forwards the stamped purchase order and equipment to the requisitioning department head and verbally notifies the purchasing department that the goods were received.

Accounts Payable. Upon receipt of a purchase order the accounts payable clerk files it in the open-purchase order file. When a vendor invoice is received, it is matched with the applicable purchase order, and a payable is created by debiting the equipment account of the requisitioning department. Unpaid invoices are filed by due date. On the due date, a check is prepared and forwarded to the treasurer for signature. The invoice and purchase order are then filed by purchase order number in the paid invoice file.

Treasurer. Checks received daily from the accounts payable department are sorted into two groups: those over and under $10,000. Checks for less than $10,000 are machine signed. The cashier maintains the check signature machine's key and signature plate and monitors its use. All checks over $10,000 are signed by both the cashier and the treasurer.

REQUIRED

a. Describe the weaknesses relating to purchases and payments of "special" orders by the Diamond Manufacturing Company.
b. Recommend control procedures that need to be added to overcome weaknesses identified in (a).

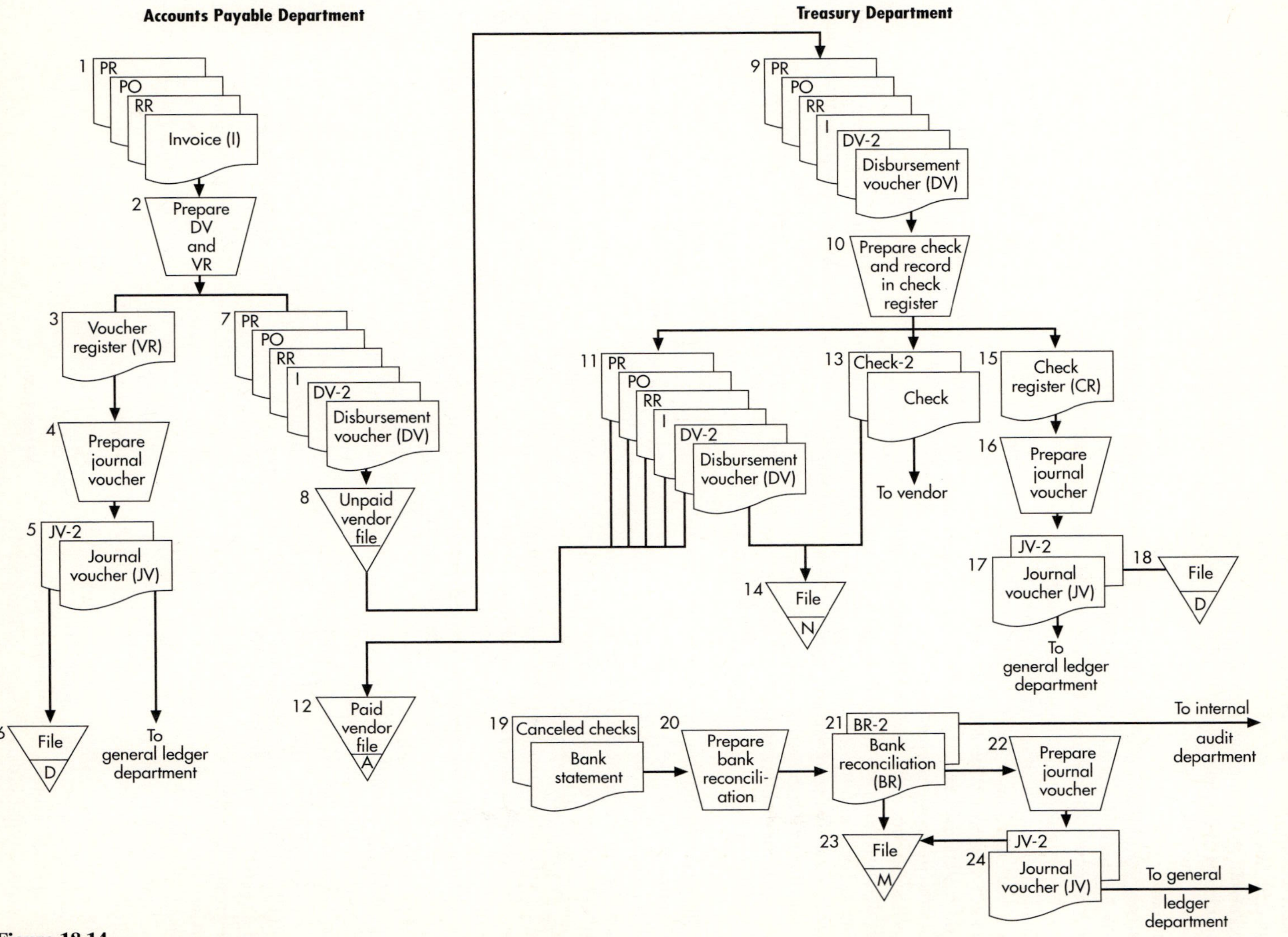

Figure 18.14
Cash Disbursements System for ConSport Corporation

c. Describe how the control procedures you recommended in step (b) should be modified if Diamond reengineered its expenditure cycle activities to make maximum use of current IT (e.g., EDI, EFT, bar-code scanning, and electronic forms in place of paper documents).
(CPA examination, adapted).

18.10 Lecimore Company has a centralized purchasing department managed by Tawanda Mason. Mason has established policies and procedures to guide the clerical staff and purchasing agents in daily department operations. She is satisfied that these guidelines conform with company objectives and that no major problems exist in the regular operations of the purchasing department.

Lecimore's internal audit department recently performed a routine operational audit of the purchasing department. Mason's policies and procedures that were first reviewed are described here:

- All significant purchases are made on a competitive basis. The probability of timely delivery and vendor reliability is taken into account on a subjective basis.
- Quality acceptability requirements are provided to all potential vendors.
- Vendor adherence to quality specifications is checked by the materials manager of the inventory stores department, not by the purchasing department. The materials manager inspects the goods upon arrival and ensures that only goods meeting minimum quality standards are transferred to the storeroom.
- All purchase requests are prepared by the materials manager and are based on the production schedule for the next four months.

The internal audit staff then observed the purchasing department's operations and noted the following:

- One vendor provides 90% of the crucial raw materials used by Lecimore. This vendor has a good reliable delivery record and has been the low bidder for several years.
- As production plans change, rush and expedite orders are made by production directly to the purchasing department. Materials ordered for canceled production runs are stored for future use. The purchasing department absorbs the costs associated with both types of changes because Mason believes this is a way of being a "good team player."
- As soon as the production department announces changes, purchasing orders the appropriate materials. Mason is very proud of her staff's quick response time to such orders. Materials on hand are not reviewed before these orders are placed, however.
- Partial and advance shipments are accepted by the materials manager, who notifies the purchasing department of the receipt of the goods. The purchasing department is responsible for following up on partial shipments; no action is taken to discourage advance shipments.

REQUIRED

a. Identify weaknesses and inefficiencies in the purchasing procedures that Mason developed for Lecimore.
b. Suggest ways to overcome those weaknesses or inefficiencies.
(CMA Examination, adapted).

18.11 You have been hired by the management of Alden, Inc., to review its internal controls over the purchase, receipt, storage, and issuance of raw materials. You observed the following:

- Raw materials, which consist mainly of high-cost electronic components, are kept in a locked storeroom. Storeroom personnel include a supervisor and four clerks. All are well trained, competent, and adequately bonded. Raw materials are removed from the storeroom only upon written or oral authorization by a production supervisor.
- No perpetual inventory records are kept; hence the storeroom clerks do not keep records for goods received or issued. To compensate, a physical inventory count is performed monthly by the storeroom clerks. The clerks are supervised during this count, and other appropriate procedures are followed.
- After the physical count, the storeroom supervisor matches the quantities on hand against a predetermined reorder level. If the count is below the reorder level, the supervisor enters the part number on a materials requisition list that is sent to the accounts payable clerk. The accounts payable clerk prepares a purchase order for each item on the list and mails it to the vendor from whom the part was last purchased.
- When ordered materials arrive, they are received by the storeroom clerks. The clerks count all items and verify that the counts agree with the quantities on the bill of lading. The bill of lading is then initialed, dated, and filed in the storeroom, to serve as a receiving report.

REQUIRED

a. Describe the weaknesses that exist in Alden's expenditure cycle.

b. Suggest control procedures to overcome the weaknesses noted in step (a).

c. Discuss how those control procedures would be best implemented in an automated AIS utilizing the latest developments in IT.

(CPA Examination, adapted)

18.12 Table 18.3 lists the various activities performed in the expenditure cycle and the journal entries, documents, data, and control issues associated with them. Complete each of the cell entries in this table. (Adapted from teaching materials developed by Martha Eining at the University of Utah)

18.13 The purchasing procedures followed by the Branden Company, a medium-sized manufacturer of specialized machinery, are as follows:

- Materials purchase requisitions are approved by manufacturing supervisors and then forwarded to the purchasing department.
- Purchasing clerks prepare prenumbered purchase orders in triplicate. The original copy is sent to the vendor. The second copy is sent to the receiving department to notify them of an incoming shipment. The third copy is filed in the purchasing department.
- When materials are delivered, they are moved directly to the storeroom, along with a copy of the receiving report. The receiving department sends another copy of the receiving report, along with its copy of the purchase order, to the purchasing department. The third copy of the receiving report is sent to the accounting department.
- Vendor invoices are sent to the purchasing department and directed to the employee who placed that order. He or she checks the invoice for accuracy in terms of discounts, extensions, and footings. The purchasing clerk then compares the invoice with (1) the copy of the purchase order and (2) the copy of the receiving report to verify the quantities ordered and received. He or she then approves the invoice for payment.

Table 18.3 **Overview of Expenditure Cycle Business Activities**

	Expenditure Cycle						
	Request Purchase of Goods	**Approve Purchase**	**Receive Goods**	**Receive Invoice**	**Approve Vendor Invoice**	**Prepare Check**	**Pay Vendor**
Accounting transaction							
Journal entry					Dr. Purchases Cr. A/P		
Documents		Purchase order					
Data collected	• Name • Item #						
Department					Accounting		
Control issues	Order only what is needed						
Information required							
Information generated							
Effect of automation							

Adapted from teaching materials developed by Martha Eining, University of Utah. Reprinted with permission.

- The approved invoice is then sent to the accounting department, where it is coded for account distribution, assigned a voucher number, entered in the voucher register, and filed according to payment due date.

REQUIRED

Identify weaknesses in Branden's expenditure cycle activities and recommend methods to correct them. (CPA Examination, adapted)

CASE 18.1: ANYCOMPANY, INC.—AN ONGOING COMPREHENSIVE CASE

Identify a local company (you may use the some company you identified to complete this case in previous chapters) and do the following:

1. List who is responsible for decisions involving (a) requisitioning, ordering, and receiving inventories; (b) authorizing cash disbursements; and (c) making cash disbursements. Assess whether there is adequate segregation of duties regarding these activities.
2. Describe the paper documents and electronic forms used by the company. Evaluate the design of each document or electronic form, and assess its appropriateness for its intended use.
3. Draw a data model, in the form of an E–R diagram, of all the information stored in the system.
4. Describe how the system updates the master files (or data base) after each type of transaction (purchase, receipt, cash disbursement). Draw a systems flowchart of these processes.
5. List and evaluate the adequacy of the control procedures used to ensure accuracy and validity of all transaction processing.
6. Examine copies of the reports produced by the system. Identify the major decisions that must be made in the expenditure cycle. Evaluate the adequacy of existing reports in assisting good decision making.

CASE 18.2: BLACKWELL INDUSTRIES

Blackwell Industries manufactures sporting goods. You have been asked to evaluate the proposed redesign of Blackwell's purchasing system. The new system will utilize a materials inventory master file, an open–purchase order master file, and a vendor history file, all organized and stored in a relational data base system. System inputs will include materials inventory receipts and issue transactions, which will be keyed in as they occur from on-line terminals located in the appropriate departments. System outputs will include batches of purchase orders and periodic reports of overdue deliveries, vendor performance, and cash flow commitments. These reports will be generated by programs that are separate from the main update program and also by on-line queries.

The main update program will begin by reading a transaction record and determining whether it is a receipt or issue transaction. Then it will update the appropriate inventory master record. As each issue transaction is processed, the program will also check the quantity on hand in master inventory record; if it falls below the reorder point, a reorder record will be written to a temporary file on a separate disk. This file will be processed at the end of each day, to prepare purchase orders. For each inventory receipt transaction, the program will update not only the quantity on hand in the inventory master record but also the corresponding open purchase order and vendor history records.

The purchase order preparation program will process the temporary reorder file by first sequencing it by vendor code number. All reorder records for the same vendor will be consolidated into one purchase order. When all reorder records for a vendor have been processed, a purchase order will be generated and transmitted by EDI. The order will also be added to the open purchase order file.

At the end of each day, the open purchase order file will be processed to identify any purchase orders for which delivery is past due, and an overdue deliveries report will be generated. At the end of each month, the vendor history and open purchase order files will be processed to generate vendor performance and cash flow commitments reports.

1. Prepare a systems flowchart of the main update program.
2. Prepare a systems flowchart of the purchase order preparation program.
3. Draw an E–R diagram of the data included in the proposed system.
4. Suggest potential ways that IT could be used to further improve the efficiency of the proposed system.
5. Identify the data that will be input on each transaction record. Suggest appropriate application controls to ensure accurate and reliable input.
6. Identify potential threats relating to the proposed system and suggest appropriate internal control procedures for mitigating them.

ANSWERS TO CHAPTER QUIZ

1. b	**3.** d	**5.** c	**7.** d	**9.** d
2. b	**4.** c	**6.** b	**8.** a	**10.** c

Chapter 19

The Production Cycle

LEARNING OBJECTIVES

After studying this chapter, you should be able to:

- Describe the major business activities and related data processing operations performed in the production cycle.
- Document your understanding of production cycle activities.
- Explain how a company's cost accounting system can help it achieve its manufacturing goals.
- Identify major threats in the production cycle and evaluate the adequacy of various control procedures for dealing with those threats.
- Discuss the key decisions that need to be made in the production cycle and identify the information needed to make those decisions.
- Read and understand a data model (E–R diagram) of the production cycle.

Integrative Case: Alpha Omega Electronics

LeRoy Williams, vice president for manufacturing at Alpha Omega Electronics (AOE), is concerned about problems associated with AOE's change in strategic mission. Two years ago, AOE's top management decided to shift the company from its traditional position as a low-cost producer of consumer electronic products (see Chapters 16 and 17). Under the new strategy, AOE is positioning itself as a producer of top-quality products sold at moderate prices. As part of this strategy, AOE increased the variety of sizes, styles, and features within each of its product lines.

To support its shift in strategic focus, AOE has invested heavily in factory automation. AOE's cost accounting system has not been changed, however. For example, manufacturing overhead is still allocated on the basis of direct labor hours, even though automation has drastically reduced the amount of direct labor used to manufacture a product. Consequently, investments in new equipment and machinery have resulted in dramatic increases in manufacturing overhead rates. This situation has created a number of problems:

1. Production supervisors complain that the accounting system "does not make sense" and that they are being "penalized" for making investments that improve overall efficiency. Indeed, some products now "cost" *more* to produce using state-of-the-art equipment than they did before the new equipment was purchased. Yet, use of the new equipment has increased production quantity while reducing defects.
2. The marketing and product design executives have all but dismissed the system's product cost figures as useless for setting prices or determining the potential profitability of new products. Indeed, some competitors have begun to price their products below AOE's reported cost to produce that item!
3. Although a number of steps have been taken to improve quality, the cost accounting system does not provide adequate measures to evaluate

the effect of those steps and to indicate areas that need further improvement.

4. Performance reports continue to focus primarily on financial measures. Line managers in the factory, however, need accurate information on physical activities, such as units produced, defect rates, and production time.

LeRoy has expressed these concerns to Linda Spurgeon, AOE's president, who agrees that these problems are serious. Linda then called a meeting with LeRoy; Stephanie Cromwell, AOE's vice president of finance; and Elizabeth Venko, AOE's controller. At the meeting, Elizabeth agreed to undertake a study of how to modify the cost accounting system to more accurately reflect AOE's new production processes. To begin this project, LeRoy agreed to take Elizabeth on a tour of the factory so that she could see and understand how the new technology has affected production cycle activities.

As this case suggests, deficiencies in the information system used to support production cycle activities can create significant problems for an organization. The availability of current and accurate information about product costs is crucial for effective management of the production cycle. As you read this chapter, think about how the introduction of new technology in the production cycle may require corresponding changes in a company's cost accounting system.

INTRODUCTION

The **production cycle** is a recurring set of business activities and related data processing operations associated with the manufacture of products. Figure 19.1 shows how the production cycle is linked to the other subsystems in a company's AIS. The revenue cycle information system (see Chapter 17) provides the information (customer orders and sales forecasts) used to plan production and inventory levels. In return, the production cycle information system sends the revenue cycle information about finished goods that have been produced and are available for sale. Information about raw materials needs is sent to the expenditure cycle information system (see Chapter 18) in the form of purchase requisitions. In exchange, the expenditure cycle system provides information about raw material acquisitions and also about other expenditures included in manufacturing overhead. Information about labor needs is sent to the human resources cycle (see Chapter 20), which in return provides data about labor costs and availability. Finally, information about the cost of goods manufactured is sent to the general ledger and reporting cycle information system (see Chapter 21).

A company's AIS plays a vital role in the production cycle. Accurate and timely cost accounting information is essential input to decisions about the following:

- Product mix (what to produce).
- Product pricing.
- Resource allocation and planning (e.g., whether to make or buy a product, relative profitability of different products).

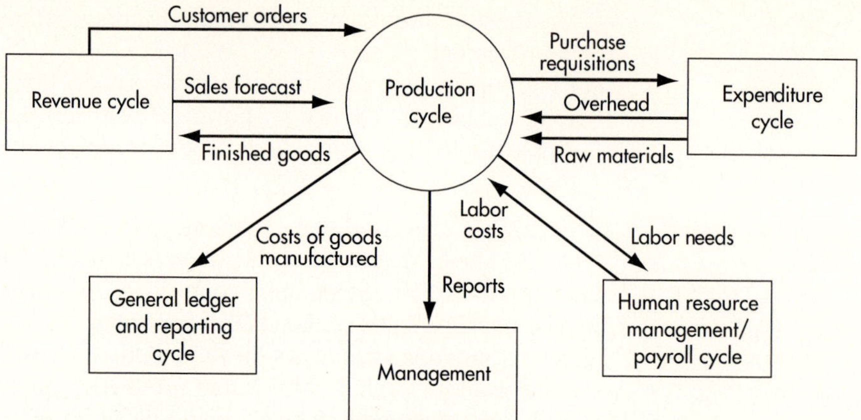

Figure 19.1

Context Diagram of the Production Cycle

- Cost management (planning and controlling manufacturing costs, evaluating performance).

These decisions require much more detailed information about costs than the data needed to prepare financial statements in accordance with GAAP. Thus the design of a company's production cycle AIS must go beyond merely meeting external financial reporting requirements.

This chapter is organized around the three major functions of the AIS in the production cycle. The first section describes production cycle activities and discusses how data about their costs are collected and processed. The second section discusses the major control objectives in the production cycle and explains how the AIS can be designed to achieve them. The final section discusses the key production cycle decisions and presents a data model that shows how the AIS can effectively and efficiently store and organize the information needed to make those decisions.

PRODUCTION CYCLE ACTIVITIES

Figure 19.2 shows the four basic activities in the production cycle: product design, planning and scheduling, production operations, and cost accounting. Figure 19.2 also depicts the principal information flows between each of those activities and the other AIS cycles. Although accountants are primarily involved in the fourth step, cost accounting, they need to understand the processes and information needs of the other steps as well. It is the accountant's role to ensure that the AIS is capable of providing the information needed to manage the four activities of the production cycle.

Product Design

The first step in the production cycle is product design (circle 1.0 in Fig. 19.2). The objective of this activity is to design a product that meets customer requirements in terms of quality, durability, and functionality while simultaneously minimizing production costs. Some of these criteria conflict with one another, making the product design task a challenging one.

Documents and Procedures. The product design activity creates two main documents. The first, a **bill of materials,** specifies the part number, description, and quantity of each component used in a product. The second

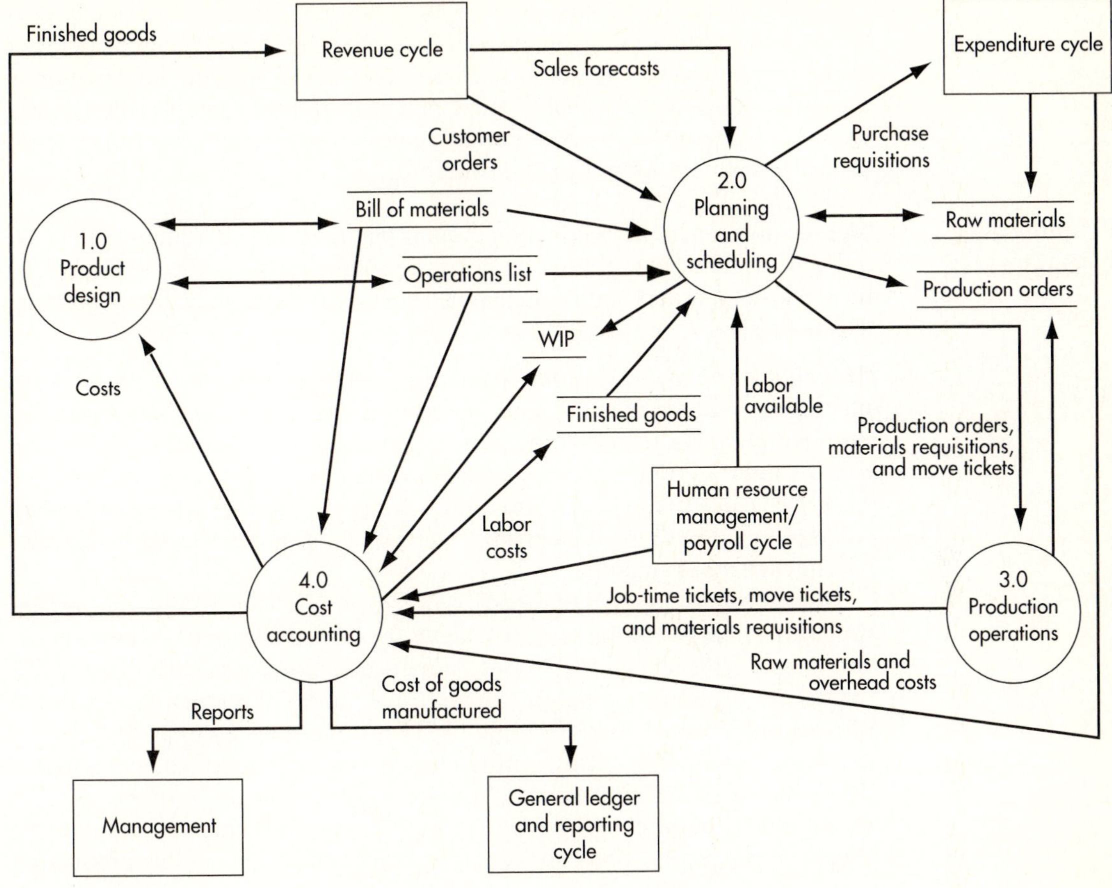

Figure 19.2

Level 0 DFD of the Production Cycle

is an **operations list,** which specifies the labor and machine requirements needed to manufacture the product. The operations list is also referred to as a **routing sheet** because it indicates how a product moves through the factory, specifying what is done at each step and how much time each operation should take.

Role of the Accountant. Accountants should play an important role in product design because 65% to 80% of product costs are determined at this stage of the production process. Accountants can become involved in product design by showing how various design trade-offs affect production costs and thereby profitability. For example, the costs of producing a line of related products can be significantly reduced by increasing the number of common components used in each product. The AIS should be able to provide data about current component usage in various products and the projected costs of using alternative components. Similarly, aspects of product complexity, such as the number of different components and manner of assembly, can significantly affect production time and costs. Again, the AIS should be designed so that it can provide information about the machine setup and materials handling costs associated with alternative product designs.

Finally, data about repair and warranty costs associated with existing products can be useful for designing better products. This data should be collected in the revenue cycle; the key is to design the AIS so that the information is accessible to product designers. Notice that in all of these examples the accountant adds value not by merely measuring costs, but by using cost information proactively to improve long-run profitability.

Planning and Scheduling

The second step in the production cycle is planning and scheduling (circle 2.0 in Fig. 19.2). The objective of this step is a production plan efficient enough to meet existing orders and anticipated short-term demand without creating excess finished goods inventories.

Planning Methods. Two common methods of production planning are manufacturing resource planning and just-in-time manufacturing. **Manufacturing resource planning (MRP-II)** is an extension of materials resource planning (see Chapter 18) that seeks to balance existing production capacity and raw materials needs to meet forecasted sales demands. MRP-II systems are often referred to as "push manufacturing," because goods are produced in expectation of customer demand.

Just as MRP-II is an extension of MRP inventory control systems, **just-in-time (JIT) manufacturing** systems extend the principles of just-in-time inventory systems (see Chapter 18) to the entire production process. The goal of JIT manufacturing is to minimize or eliminate inventories of raw materials, work in process, and finished goods. The use of JIT is often referred to as "pull manufacturing," because goods are produced in response to customer demand. Theoretically, JIT manufacturing systems produce only in response to customer orders. In practice, however, most JIT manufacturing systems develop short-run production plans. For example, Toyota develops monthly production plans so that it can provide a stable schedule to its suppliers. This strategy enables the suppliers to plan their production schedules so that they can deliver their products to Toyota at the exact time they are needed for production. Otherwise, production will come to a halt. Thus both MRP-II and JIT manufacturing systems plan production in advance; they differ, however, in the length of the planning horizon. MRP-II systems may develop production plans for up to 12 months in advance, whereas JIT manufacturing systems use much shorter planning horizons.

Documents and Procedures. The **master production schedule (MPS)** specifies how much of each product is to be produced during the planning period and when that production should occur (see Fig. 19.3). Information about customer orders, sales forecasts, and finished goods inventory levels is used to determine production levels. Although the long-range part of the MPS may be modified in response to changes in market conditions, production plans must be frozen a few weeks in advance in order to provide sufficient time to procure the necessary raw materials, supplies, and labor resources.

The MPS is used to develop a detailed timetable that specifies daily production. It is also used to determine whether any raw materials need to be purchased, by "exploding" the bill of materials to determine the immediate raw materials requirements for meeting the production goals listed in the MPS (see

Figure 19.3

Sample Master Production Schedule (MPS)

MASTER PRODUCTION SCHEDULE								
Product Number 120				**Description:** VCR				
Lead time[a]:	**Week Number**							
1 week	**1**	**2**	**3**	**4**	**5**	**6**	**7**	**8**
Quantity on hand	500	350[b]	350	300	350	300	450	300
Scheduled production	150[c]	300	250	300	250	400	250	300
Forecasted sales	300	300	300	250	300	250	400	250
Net available	350[d]	350	300	350	300	450	300	350

[a]Time to manufacture product (1 week for VCR).
[b]Ending quantity on hand (net available) from prior week.
[c]Calculated by subtracting quantity on hand from sum of this week's and next week's forecasted sales, plus a 50 unit buffer stock. For example, begin week 1 with 500 units. Projected sales for weeks 1 and 2 total 600 units. Add 50 unit desired buffer inventory yields 650 units needed by end of week 1. Subtracting beginning inventory of 500 units results in planned production of 150 units during week 1.
[d]Beginning quantity on hand plus scheduled production less forecasted sales.

Table 19.1). These requirements are compared to current inventory levels; purchase requisitions are generated and sent to the purchasing department (see Chapter 18) to initiate the acquisition of any required items.

Figure 19.2 shows that three other documents are produced by the planning and scheduling step: production orders, materials requisitions, and move tickets. A **production order** authorizes the manufacture of a specified quantity of a particular product. It lists the operations that need to be performed, the quantity to be produced, and the location where the finished product should be delivered (see Fig. 19.4).

A **materials requisition** authorizes the removal of the necessary quantity of raw materials from the storeroom to the factory location where production operations are to begin. This document contains the production order number, date of issue, and, based on the bill of materials, the part numbers and quantities of all necessary raw materials (see Fig. 19.5). Subsequent transfers of raw materials throughout the factory are documented on **move tickets,** which identify the parts being transferred, the location to which they are transferred, and the time of the transfer (see Fig. 19.6 on page 678).

Role of the Accountant. The accountant must ensure that the AIS collects and reports costs in a manner consistent with the production planning techniques used by the company. This may require making changes to the AIS whenever new planning techniques are adopted. For example, AOE is thinking about adopting the JIT approach to manufacturing. JIT manufacturing emphasizes working in teams and seeks to maximize the efficiency and synergy of all teams involved in making a particular product. Consequently, Elizabeth Venko realizes that collecting and reporting labor variances at the individual or team level may create dysfunctional incentives to maximize local performance at the

Table 19.1 Example of "Exploding" a Bill of Materials

Step 1: Multiply the component requirements for ONE product by the number of products to be produced next period (from the MPS).

Components in Each VCR				
Part No.	**Description**	**Quantity**	**Number of VCRs**	**Total Requirements**
105	Control Unit	1	2000	2,000
125	Back Panel	1	2000	2,000
148	Side Panel	4	2000	8,000
173	Timer	1	2000	2,000
195	Front Panel	1	2000	2,000
199	Screw	6	2000	12,000

Components in Each CD Player				
Part No.	**Description**	**Quantity**	**Number of CD Players**	**Total Requirements**
103	Control Unit	1	3000	3,000
120	Front Panel	1	3000	3,000
121	Back Panel	1	3000	3,000
173	Timer	1	3000	3,000
190	Side Panel	4	3000	12,000
199	Screw	4	3000	12,000

Step 2: Calculate total component requirements by summing products.

Part No.	VCR	CD Player	Total
103	0	3,000	3,000
105	2,000	0	2,000
120	0	3,000	3,000
121	0	3,000	3,000
125	2,000	0	2,000
148	8,000	0	8,000
173	2,000	3,000	5,000
190	0	12,000	12,000
195	2,000	0	2,000
199	12,000	12,000	24,000

Step 3: Repeat steps 1 and 2 for each week during planning horizon.

Part No.	Week 1	Week 2	Week 3	Week 4	Week 5	Week 6
103	3,000	2,000	2,500	3,000	2,500	3,000
105	2,000	2,000	2,500	2,500	2,000	3,000
120	3,000	2,000	2,500	3,000	2,500	3,000
121	3,000	2,000	2,500	3,000	2,500	3,000
125	2,000	2,000	2,500	2,500	2,000	3,000
148	8,000	8,000	10,000	10,000	8,000	12,000
173	5,000	4,000	5,000	5,500	4,500	6,000
190	12,000	12,000	10,000	12,000	10,000	12,000
195	2,000	2,000	2,500	2,500	2,000	3,000
199	24,000	20,000	25,000	27,000	22,000	30,000

Figure 19.4

Sample Production Order for AOE

								4587
Alpha Omega Engineering								
PRODUCTION ORDER								
Order No. 2289	**Product No.** 4430	**Description:** Cabinet Side Panel		**Production Quantity** 1000				
Approved by: *PJS*	**Release Date:** 02/24/97	**Issue Date:** 02/25/97	**Completion Date:** 03/09/97	**Deliver to:** Assembly Department				
Work Station No.	**Product Operation No.**	**Quantity**	**Operation Description**	**Start Date & Time**		**Finish Date & Time**		
MH25	100	1003	Transfer from stock	02/28	0700	02/28	0800	
ML15-12	105	1003	Cut to shape	02/28	0800	02/28	1000	
ML15-9	106	1002	Corner cut	02/28	1030	02/28	1200	
S28-17	124	1002	Turn & Shape	02/28	1300	02/28	1700	
F54-5	142	1001	Finish	03/01	0800	03/01	1100	
P89-1	155	1001	Paint	03/01	1300	03/02	1300	
QC94	194	1001	Inspect	03/02	1400	03/02	1600	
MH25	101	1000	Transfer to assembly	03/02	1600	03/02	1700	

Explanation of numbers in Quantity column:

1. Total of 1003 sheets of raw material used to produce 1000 good panels and 3 rejected panels.
2. One panel not cut to proper shape, thus only 1002 units had operations 106 and 124 performed on them.
3. One panel not properly turned and shaped; hence only 1001 panels finished, painted, and received final inspection.
4. One panel rejected during final inspection; thus only 1000 good panels transferred to assembly department.

Figure 19.5

Sample Materials Requisition for AOE

				No. 2345
MATERIALS REQUISITION				
Issued To: Assembly		**Issue Date:** 08/15/96	**Production Order Number:** 62913	
Part Number	**Description**	**Quantity**	**Unit Cost**	**Total Cost**
115	Calculator Unit	2000	2.95	5900.00
135	Lower Casing	2000	.45	900.00
198	Screw	16000	.02	320.00
178	Battery	2000	.75	1500.00
136	Upper Casing	2000	.80	1600.00
199	Screw	12000	.02	240.00
Issued by: *AKL*				10,460.00
Received by: *GWS*		**Costed by:** *ZBD*		

Note: Cost information is entered when the materials requisition is turned in to the cost accounting department. Other information, except for signatures, is printed by the system when the document is prepared.

Figure 19.6

Sample Move Ticket for AOE

MOVE TICKET			No. 8753
Production Order Number: 2345	**Date Transferred:** 08/18/96		
From: Assembly *KLS*	**To:** Finishing *NRC*		
Operation To Perform	**Completed**	**Date**	**Time**
Clean	X	08/19/96	0900
Polish	____		
Package	____		
Comments:			

expense of plantwide performance. Therefore she plans to redesign AOE's AIS so that it collects and reports costs in a manner that highlights the joint contributions of all teams involved in making a particular product. Focus 19.1 describes similar changes that Harley-Davidson made to its cost accounting system when it implemented a JIT manufacturing system.

Production Operations

The third step in the production cycle is the actual manufacture of products (circle 3.0 in Fig. 19.2). The manner in which this activity is accomplished varies greatly across companies, differing according to the type of product being manufactured and the degree of automation used in the production process.

The use of various forms of information technology (IT) in the production process, such as robots and computer-controlled machinery, is referred to as **computer integrated manufacturing (CIM).** CIM can significantly reduce production costs. For example, Northrop Corporation used to collect 16,000 sheets of paper containing shop-floor work instructions related to the manufacture of plane fuselages. When on-line terminals were installed at each assembly station, the elimination in paper flow and improved efficiency reduced costs by 30%!

Accountants do not need to be experts on every facet of CIM, but they do need to understand how it affects the AIS. One effect of CIM is a shift from mass production to custom order manufacturing. For example, every Northrop Grumman product is assembled to order. Each product, however, can use any of about 256,000 separate components. Thus, to minimize inventory carrying costs, Northrop's AIS must maintain accurate perpetual inventory records.

Levi Strauss is another company experimenting with a shift from mass to custom manufacturing. In 1994 sales clerks at selected stores began to collect the customer's measurements in order to create tailor-made blue jeans. The data are entered in on-line terminals and electronically sent to a factory, where robots cut the denim bolts to customer measurements. In a week or two, customers receive custom-made jeans, for only about $10 more than the cost of mass-produced ones. As with Northrop, this new system requires that the AIS keep accurate perpetual inventory records. In addition, it will require that Levi Strauss improve its logistics function before the service can be offered nation-

FOCUS 19.1

JIT + A New Cost Accounting System = Success for Harley-Davidson

The adoption of a JIT manufacturing system saved Harley-Davidson over $22 million in less than one year by reducing its work-in-process inventory. After it switched to JIT, however, Harley-Davidson did not initially modify its cost accounting system to reflect the changes in the production process. This created several problems. Overhead, for example, continued to be allocated on the basis of direct labor. This meant that the overhead rate increased even though the amount of labor required to make a product decreased. Consequently, products with small differences in labor content had large differences in total costs.

Another problem involved the practice of measuring plant performance based on period-end inventory absorption. This measure implied that as long as monthly goals were met, daily production goals were not that important. In a JIT environment, however, period-end performance measures are of little value for controlling operations. For example, failure to meet daily goals could cause an entire assembly line to shut down. Consequently, plant managers wanted continuous performance measures.

By the end of the second year following implementation of the JIT system, Harley-Davidson's accountants realized that the cost accounting system needed a major overhaul. They toured the factory to observe firsthand how the new production processes worked. This led to the following changes in the cost accounting system:

1. Detailed accounting for direct labor was eliminated. Direct labor now represented only 10% of product costs, so it was combined with overhead into one account called conversion costs. Conversion costs were then applied to cost products according to process hours. This change not only simplified the accounting system, but reduced administrative costs dramatically (almost 62% of administrative costs under the old system related to collecting and reporting on direct labor!). In place of direct labor costs, plant managers received reports about the number of employees at work each day and daily overtime hours. This information was easy to collect and report on a daily basis; it also represented the most important controllable aspects of labor use in a JIT manufacturing system.
2. A "backflush" costing system was adopted. Backflush costing begins with the outputs of production and works backward to apply production costs to finished goods inventory and cost of goods sold. Costs are applied upon completion of production. In contrast, conventional cost accounting tracks costs through a work-in-process account as they are incurred. Thus backflush costing essentially eliminates the use of a separate WIP inventory account.

Together, these two changes greatly simplified Harley-Davidson's cost accounting system. They reduced the administrative costs of the system and made it possible to provide timely information to plant managers.

Focus Questions

1. What advantages and disadvantages are realized when labor and overhead costs are combined into one category called conversion costs?
2. How does a JIT manufacturing system encourage the use of backflush costing?

Source: William T. Turk, "Management Accounting Revitalized: The Harley-Davidson Experience," in *Readings in Management Accounting* (edited by S. Mark Young) (Englewood Cliffs, NJ: Prentice-Hall), 1995, pp. 135–144.

---

wide. In 1994 it only took about eight minutes to stitch a pair of Levi's 501 jeans; but 61 days were required to move those jeans from the factory to the stonewashing plant, then to the distribution warehouse, and out to the retail store! Such a delay is not feasible for custom-made jeans. Consequently, Levi Strauss is investing heavily in warehouse automation with the objective of reducing this average lead time to a matter of days. Its AIS will also have to be revised to track the status of all orders and inventory more accurately.

Although both the nature of the production process and the extent of CIM vary across companies, every firm needs to collect data about the following three facets of its production operations: raw materials used, labor hours expended, and machine operations performed and other manufacturing overhead costs incurred. In the next section, we discuss the methods used to collect and process this data.

Cost Accounting

The final step in the production cycle is cost accounting (circle 4.0 in Fig. 19.2). The two principal objectives of the cost accounting system are (1) to provide information for planning, controlling, and evaluating the performance of production operations; and (2) to provide accurate cost data about products for use in pricing and product mix decisions. In addition, the cost accounting system provides the information used to calculate the inventory and cost of goods sold values that appear in the company's financial statements.

To accomplish these objectives, the AIS collects costs by various categories and then assigns those costs to specific products and organizational units. Careful coding of cost data during collection is important, because often the same costs may be allocated in multiple ways, for several different purposes. For example, factory supervisory costs may be assigned to departments for performance evaluation purposes, but to specific products for pricing and product mix decisions.

Types of Cost Accounting Systems. Most cost systems use either job-order or process costing to assign production costs. **Job-order costing** assigns costs to specific production batches, or jobs; it is used whenever the product or service being sold can be distinctly identified. For example, construction companies use job-order costing for each house being built. Similarly, public accounting and law firms use job-order costing to account for the costs of individual audits or cases, respectively. AOE currently uses job-order costing.

In contrast, **process costing** assigns costs to each process, or work center, in the production cycle, then calculates the average cost for all units produced. Process costing is used whenever similar goods or services are produced in mass quantities. For example, breweries accumulate the costs associated with the various steps (e.g., mashing, primary fermentation, filtering, bottling) in producing a batch of a particular kind of beer, then compute the average total unit cost for that product. Similarly, mutual funds accumulate the costs associated with handling customer deposits and withdrawals, then compute the per unit costs of those transactions.

Data Processing. Figure 19.7 depicts a typical on-line AIS for the production cycle, such as the one used by AOE. Engineering department specifications for new products result in the creation of new records in both the bill of materials and operations list files. To develop those specifications, engineering accesses both files to examine the design of similar products. It also accesses the general ledger and inventory files for information about the costs of alternative product designs. Sales forecasts and customer special order information are entered by the sales department. That information, and data about current inventory levels, is used by the production planning department to develop the master production schedule. New records are then added to the production order file to authorize the production of specific goods. At the same time, new records are added to the work-in-process file, to accumulate cost data. The list of operations to be performed is displayed at the appropriate work station. Corresponding instructions are also sent to the CIM interface to guide the operation of computerized machinery and robots. Finally, materials requisitions are sent to the inventory stores department to authorize the release of raw materials to production.

The system shown in Fig. 19.7 could be used to implement either a job-order or process costing system. Both systems require accumulating data about three basic kinds of costs: raw materials, direct labor, and manufacturing overhead. The choice of job-order or process costing affects only the method used to assign those costs to products, not the methods used for data collection. Let us now examine how these three types of cost data are collected.

Figure 19.7

On-Line Production Cycle Information System

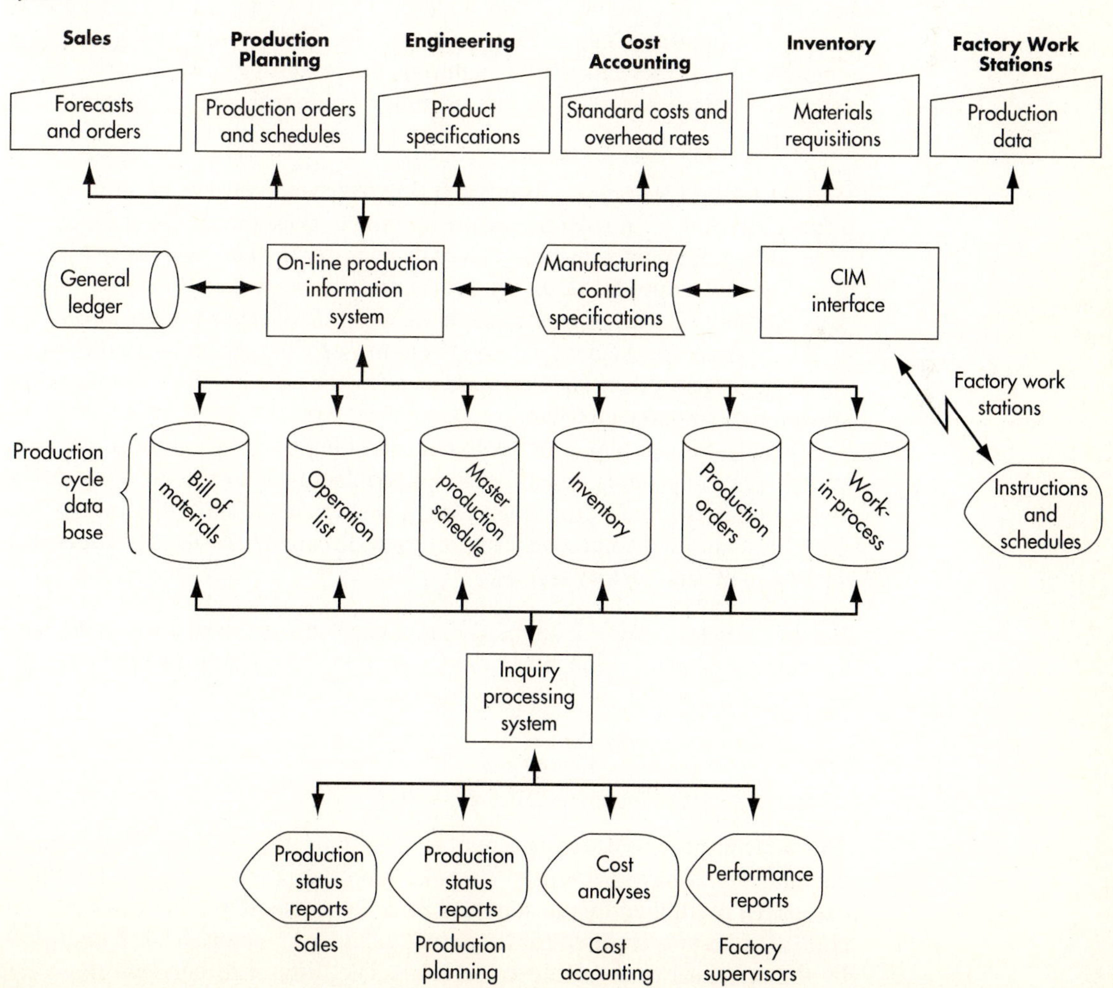

Raw Materials. When production is initiated, the issuance of a materials requisition triggers a debit to work-in-process for the raw materials sent to production. If additional materials are needed, another debit is made to work-in-process; conversely, work-in-process is credited for any materials not used and returned to inventory. Most raw materials are bar-coded; this enables usage data to be collected by scanning the products when they are released from, or returned to, inventory. Inventory clerks use on-line terminals to enter usage data for those items that are not bar-coded.

Direct Labor. In the past, AOE used a paper document called a **job-time ticket** to collect data about labor activity. This document recorded the amount of time a worker spent on each specific job task. Now, as shown in Fig. 19.7, workers enter this data using on-line terminals at each factory work station. To further improve the efficiency of this process, AOE is considering switching to coded identification cards, which workers would run through a badge reader or bar-code scanner when they start and finish any task. The time savings associated with using bar coding to automate data collection can be significant. For example, Consolidated Diesel Company, a joint venture between Cummins Engine Company and J.I. Case, found using bar-code scanners to capture data about materials usage and labor operations saved about 12 seconds per work station, resulting in a permanent 15% increase in productivity.

Manufacturing Overhead. **Manufacturing overhead** consists of all manufacturing costs that are not economically feasible to trace directly to specific jobs, or processes. Examples include the costs of water, power, and other utilities; miscellaneous supplies; rent, insurance, and property taxes for the factory plant; and the salaries of factory supervisors. Most of these costs are collected by the expenditure cycle information system (see Chapter 18), with the exception of supervisory salaries, which are processed by the human resources cycle information system (see Chapter 20).

Accountants can play a key role in controlling costs by carefully assessing how changes in product mix affect total manufacturing overhead. They should go beyond merely collecting such data, however, and identify the factors that drive the changes in total costs. This information can then be used to adjust production plans and factory layout.

Journal Entries. AOE, like many companies, uses standard costs as the basis for making its production cycle journal entries. Thus, when raw materials are issued to production, the following journal entry is made:

Work-in-Process Control	xxx	
Raw Materials Control		xxx
Raw Materials Efficiency Variance		xxx

The work-in-process control account is debited for the quantity of raw materials that *should* have been used to make a product (as specified in the bill of materials) multiplied by the standard price for those items. The raw materials control account is credited for the actual quantity of materials used multiplied by the standard price of those materials. The difference between these two amounts is the raw materials efficiency variance; a debit (credit) to this account reflects an unfavorable (favorable) variance.

A similar entry is made to record the use of direct labor:

Work-in-Process Control	yyy	
Labor Price Variance	yyy	
Accounts Payable		yyy
Labor Efficiency Variance		yyy

The work-in-process control account is debited for the standard amount of labor that *should have been used to produce actual output* (as specified in the operations list) multiplied by the standard labor rate. Wages payable is credited for the actual amount of labor used, multiplied by the actual labor rates. The difference between these two amounts is recorded in the labor price and efficiency variance accounts. The former is calculated by multiplying the actual direct labor hours by the difference between standard and actual wage rates; the latter is computed by multiplying the standard wage rate by the difference between standard and actual labor hours used.

When manufacturing overhead costs are incurred, the following journal entry is made:

Manufacturing Overhead Control	zzz	
Accounts Payable		zzz
Supplies Expense		zzz
Wages Payable (indirect labor)		zzz

The manufacturing overhead control account is debited for the actual amount of those costs and the appropriate accounts (e.g., accounts payable, supplies, etc.) are credited. As mentioned in the chapter opening case, AOE, like many companies, allocates manufacturing overhead on the basis of direct labor hours. Thus, when direct labor usage is recorded, manufacturing overhead is allocated to production as follows:

Work-in-Process Control	xxx	
Manufacturing Overhead Allocated		xxx

The work-in-process control account is debited for the number of hours used times the standard overhead rate per hour; the manufacturing overhead allocated account is credited for the same amount. At the end of the accounting period, an adjusting entry is made to dispose of any under (over) allocated overhead, as well as to close out the raw materials and direct labor variance accounts.[1]

Once production is completed, the items are transferred to the finished goods stockroom (if produced to meet anticipated demand) or to the shipping department (if produced to fill a specific customer order). This transfer is documented on the final move ticket. The status of the production order record is then changed from "open" to "completed" and a journal entry is made debiting finished goods inventory and crediting work-in-process:

---

[1]See any cost accounting textbook for details about the nature of these journal entries.

Finished Goods Inventory	yyy	
Work-in-Process Control		yyy

Accounting for Fixed Assets. Thus far we have focused on accounting for the costs associated with the production of inventory. The AIS also needs to collect and process information about investments in the property, plant, and equipment used in the production cycle. Indeed, such fixed assets represent a significant portion of total assets for a *Fortune* 500 company. Thus it is important to monitor this investment.

Fixed assets should be bar-coded. Bar coding enables quick and accurate periodic updating of the fixed asset data base. At a minimum, every organization should maintain the following information about each of its fixed assets: identifying number, serial number, location, cost, date of acquisition, vendor name and address, expected life, expected salvage value, depreciation method, depreciation charges to date, improvements, and maintenance services performed.

The procedures involved in authorizing the purchase of fixed assets vary, depending on the size of the purchase request. Large capital expenditures are first recommended by a supervisor or manager, who provides details about expected cash flows and other costs and benefits of the proposed expenditure. All such recommendations are reviewed by a senior executive or by an executive committee, and the various projects are ranked in order of priority. Smaller capital expenditures (e.g., those costing $10,000 or less) can usually be purchased directly out of departmental budgets, which avoids a formal approval process. In either case, the output of this process is a document that provides formal authorization to acquire a particular fixed asset.

Due to the size of fixed asset purchases, most companies invite several competing vendors to provide bids. A document called a *request for proposal (RFP)*, which specifies the desired properties of the asset, is sent to each vendor. The capital investments committee reviews vendor responses and selects the best one.

Once a vendor has been selected, the acquisition of the asset may be handled through the regular expenditure cycle process, as described in Chapter 18. Specifically, a formal purchase order is prepared, receipt of the asset is formally documented using a receiving report, and a disbursement voucher is used to authorize payment to the vendor. The same set of processing controls and edit checks employed for other purchases should also be used for fixed asset acquisitions (for details, refer back to the discussion in Chapter 18). In the next section we will discuss the controls that should be in place for transactions involving the disposal of fixed assets.

CONTROL OBJECTIVES, THREATS, AND PROCEDURES

A second function of a well-designed AIS is to provide adequate controls in order to meet the following production cycle objectives:

1. All production and fixed asset acquisitions are properly authorized.
2. Work-in-process inventories and fixed assets are safeguarded.
3. All valid, authorized production cycle transactions are recorded.
4. All production cycle transactions are recorded accurately.

5. Accurate records are maintained and protected from loss.
6. Production cycle activities are performed efficiently and effectively.

The documents and records described in the previous section play an important role in achieving these objectives. Simple, easy-to-complete documents with clear instructions facilitate the accurate and efficient recording of transaction data. The inclusion of appropriate application controls, such as validity checks and field (format) checks, further increases the accuracy of data entry when using electronic documents. Providing space on paper and electronic documents to record who completed and who reviewed the form provides evidence that the transaction was properly authorized. Finally, prenumbering the documents facilitates checking that all transactions have been recorded.

Table 19.2 lists five major threats and exposures in the production cycle and the additional control procedures, besides adequate documents and records, that should be in place to mitigate them. As you will see in the following discussion, every company, regardless of its line of business, faces these threats. Therefore it is important to understand how the AIS can be designed to counter them.

Threat 1: Unauthorized Transactions

Unauthorized production can result in a supply of goods in excess of short-run demands, thereby creating potential cash flow problems because resources are tied up in inventory. Overproduction also increases the risk of carrying inventory that becomes obsolete. In addition, the associated costs of storing and handling inventory increase expenses and reduce profitability. These problems can have significant negative effects on a company's finances. For example, in the early 1990s Herman's Sporting Goods, Inc. was turning over its inventory only four times a year; one of its competitors, Sports Authority, boasted turnover rates ranging from 8 to 12 times annually at each of its stores. The result? Herman's lost $18.5 million on $580 million in sales in 1993, whereas Sports Authority earned $10 million on only $412 million in sales.

A related threat is failing to produce enough goods to meet demand. This can result in lost sales and customer dissatisfaction. For example, Apple underestimated demand for its new Power Mac computers in 1995. Consequently, it could not follow its planned strategy of reducing prices to increase market share. Indeed, Apple's market share plummeted drastically due to the shortage of its new machines.

Over- and underproduction can be prevented by more accurate production planning. Improvement requires accurate and current sales forecasts and data about inventory stocks, information that can be provided by the revenue and expenditure cycle systems. In addition, information about production performance, particularly concerning trends in total time to manufacture each product, should be regularly collected. All of these sources of data should be periodically used to review and adjust the master production schedule.

Proper approval and authorization of production orders is another control to prevent overproduction of specific items. One means is to restrict access to the production scheduling program using passwords and an access control matrix. It is also important to ensure that the correct production orders are

Table 19.2 **Threats, Exposures, and Control Procedures in the Production Cycle**

Threat	Exposure	Applicable Control Procedures
1. Unauthorized transactions	Overproduction and excess inventories Obsolescence Underproduction, stockouts, and lost sales Excess investment in fixed assets	Accurate sales forecasts Accurate inventory records Authorization of production Restricted access to production planning program and to blank production order documents Review and approval of capital asset expenditures
2. Theft or destruction of inventories and fixed assets	Loss of assets Overstated inventory records	Restricted physical access Documentation of all internal movements of inventory Proper segregation of duties Periodic physical counts of inventory, reconciled to records Assignment of accountability and responsibility for fixed assets Proper approval and documentation of all disposals of fixed assets Insurance
3. Recording and posting errors	Ineffective scheduling and planning Decision errors (product mix, product pricing, over/under-production) Increased expenses and taxes on fixed assets that are incorrectly valued	Source data automation On-line data entry edit controls Periodic physical counts of inventory and fixed assets, and reconciliation of those counts to corresponding records
4. Loss of data	Loss of assets Ineffective decision making	Backup and disaster recovery procedures File labels Access controls Creation and review of logs of all computer activity
5. Inefficiencies and quality control problems	Increased expenses (scrap, rework, warranty repairs, sales returns and allowances) Loss of customer goodwill and future sales	Regular performance reports Exception reports highlighting variances from budget plan Measure throughput Measure cost of quality control

released. Closed loop verification can accomplish this control: The production planner enters the product number and the system retrieves the description, order quantity, and other relevant data, and requests the user to verify that the correct production order is being released. Finally, if blank production order documents are used, access to them should be restricted. These documents should also be prenumbered and periodically accounted for to ensure that all production is authorized.

Unauthorized acquisition of fixed assets can result in overinvestment and reduced profitability. The procedures discussed earlier for reviewing, approving, and documenting fixed asset purchases can prevent this threat. Holding managers accountable for their department's return on the fixed assets provides additional incentive to control such expenditures.

Threat 2: Theft or Destruction of Inventories and Fixed Assets

The theft of inventories and fixed assets is a major threat to manufacturing companies. In addition to the loss of assets, thefts also result in overstated asset balances, which can lead to erroneous analyses of financial performance and, in the case of inventory, underproduction.

To reduce the risk of inventory loss, physical access to inventories should be restricted and all internal movements of inventory should be documented. Thus materials requisitions should be used to authorize the release of raw materials to production. Both parties involved should sign the requisition to acknowledge release of the goods to production. Requests for additional materials in excess of the amounts specified in the bill of materials should be documented and authorized by supervisory personnel. Move tickets should then be used to document subsequent movement of inventory through various stages of the production process. The return of any materials not used in production should also be documented.

Proper segregation of duties is also important to safeguard inventory. Maintaining physical custody of the raw materials and finished goods inventories is the responsibility of the inventory stores department; department or factory supervisors have primary responsibility for work-in-process inventories. The authorization function, represented by the preparation of production orders, materials requisitions, and move tickets, is the responsibility of the production planners or, increasingly, of the production information system itself. Bar-code scanners and on-line terminals are used to record movement of inventory, thereby maintaining accurate perpetual inventory records. Consequently, proper access controls and compatibility tests are important, to ensure that only authorized personnel have access to those records. Finally, inventory on hand should be periodically counted by an employee without any custodial responsibility. Any discrepancies between these physical counts and recorded amounts should be investigated.

Similar controls are needed to safeguard fixed assets. All fixed assets should be identified and recorded. Managers should be assigned responsibility and accountability for fixed assets under their control. Security measures should be in place to control physical access to fixed assets. Their disposal should be properly authorized and documented. A report of all fixed asset transactions should be printed periodically and sent to the controller, who should verify that each transaction was properly authorized and executed.

Finally, inventories and fixed assets are also subject to loss due to fire or other disasters. Therefore adequate insurance should be maintained to cover such losses and provide for replacement of those assets.

Threat 3: Recording and Posting Errors

Inaccurate recording and posting of production activity data can diminish the effectiveness of production scheduling and undermine management's ability to monitor and control manufacturing operations. For example, inaccurate cost data can result in inappropriate decisions about which products to make and how to set current selling prices. Errors in inventory records can lead to either over- or underproduction of goods. Inaccuracies in financial statements and managerial reports can distort analyses of past performance and the desirability of future investments or changes in operations.

The best control procedure to ensure that data entry is accurate is to automate data collection using bar-code scanners, badge readers, and other devices. When this is not feasible, on-line terminals should be used for data entry. Passwords and user IDs should be used to restrict access to authorized employees. In addition, an access control matrix should be used to limit access to only those portions of the data base that a particular employee needs to perform his or her job. Check-digits and closed-loop verification should be used to ensure that information about the raw materials used, operations performed, and employee number are entered correctly. Validity checks, such as comparing raw materials part numbers to those listed in the bill of materials file, provide further assurance. Finally, to verify the accuracy of data base records, periodic physical counts of inventories should be made and compared to recorded quantities.

As with inventory, periodic inspections and counts of all fixed assets should be made, and those figures should be reconciled to recorded amounts. Overstated fixed assets increase expenses, through extra depreciation and higher property taxes. Understated fixed assets can also cause problems. For example, inaccurate counts of the number of personal computers in use can cause a company to unknowingly violate software license requirements.

Threat 4: Loss of Data

Loss of production data hinders the monitoring of inventory and fixed assets and makes it difficult to ensure that manufacturing activities are being performed efficiently and effectively. Therefore inventory and work-in-process records must be protected from loss or damage, both intentional and accidental. Regular backup of all data files is imperative. Additional copies of key master files, such as open production orders and raw materials inventory, should be stored off-site. All disks and tapes should have both external and internal file labels, to reduce the possibility of accidentally erasing important files.

Access controls are also important. The loss of production trade secrets can destroy a company. That is what happened to Recon Optical of Barrington, Illinois. One of its customers obtained access to its production data base, stole the company's trade secrets, and used that information to become a competitor of Recon. As a result, Recon Optical was forced to lay off 800 of its 1000 employees and is now locked in a court battle to recover damages from its former customer.

Unauthorized access also increases the risk of damage to important data files. A system of passwords and user IDs should be used to limit access to sensitive files. Moreover, access controls should also apply to terminals. For example, the system should be programmed to reject any attempts to alter inventory records from a terminal located in the engineering department. Finally, logs of all activities, especially any actions involving managerial approval, such as requests for additional raw materials or overtime, should be recorded and maintained for later review as part of the audit trail.

Threat 5: Inefficiencies and Quality Control Problems

Inefficiencies in production operations result in increased expenses. Quality control problems also increase expenses and may even reduce future sales. Thus manufacturing activities must be closely monitored and prompt action taken to correct any deviations from standards. It is sometimes possible to enlist customers as part of the quality control process. For example, after Netscape corrected a security weakness in its Internet access software, it offered rewards to any customer who found additional problems.

The AIS can help control efficiency and quality by preparing appropriate performance reports. In addition to traditional comparisons of actual to budgeted performance, measures of throughput and quality control should also be produced by the AIS.

Throughput: A Measure of Production Effectiveness. **Throughput** represents the number of "good" units produced in a given period of time. It consists of three factors, each of which can be separately controlled, as shown in the following formula:[2]

$$\text{Throughput} = (\text{total units produced/processing time}) \times (\text{processing time/total time}) \times (\text{good units/total units}).$$

Productive capacity, the first term in the formula, shows the maximum number of units that can be produced using current technology. Productive capacity can be increased in a number of ways, such as by improving labor or machine efficiency, by rearranging the factory floor layout to smooth the flow of materials, or by simplifying product design specifications.

Productive processing time, the second term in the equation, indicates the percentage of total production time used to manufacture the product. Productive processing time can be improved in a number of ways, such as by improving maintenance to reduce machine downtime or by better scheduling of material and supply deliveries to reduce wait time.

Yield, the third term in the formula, represents the percentage of undefective units produced. Yield can be improved by such actions as using better quality raw materials or improving worker skills.

Information About Quality Control. Information about quality costs can help companies determine the effects of actions taken to improve yield and identify areas for further improvement. Quality control costs can be divided into four areas:

---

[2] This formula is developed by Carole Cheatham, "Measuring and Improving Throughput," *Journal of Accountancy* (March 1990): 89–91.

1. *Prevention costs* are incurred to ensure that products are created without defects the first time.
2. *Inspection costs* are associated with testing to ensure that products do indeed meet quality standards.
3. *Internal failure costs* represent testing to identify defective units before they are ready for sale.
4. *External failure costs* result when defective products were sold to customers, such as product liability, loss of customer satisfaction, and damage to the company's reputation.

The ultimate objective of quality control is to minimize the sum of these four types of costs. This objective recognizes the fact that there are trade-offs between categories. For example, increasing prevention costs can lower inspection costs as well as internal and external failure costs.

Elizabeth Venko agreed with LeRoy Williams that production managers at AOE should receive both throughput and cost of quality reports. She also discussed with him the behavioral effects of performance reporting. For example, measuring total production may encourage the buildup of inventories. Similarly, reimbursing departments for scrap and rework may be less effective in promoting quality control efforts than measuring and rewarding departments on the basis of yield. As a result of this discussion, LeRoy realized that he and Elizabeth will probably need to closely monitor the effects of any new performance reports and make appropriate modifications to them.

PRODUCTION CYCLE INFORMATION NEEDS AND DATA MODEL

A third function of the AIS is to provide information useful for decision making. In the production cycle, cost information is needed by internal and external users. Internally, management uses information about costs to make decisions about product pricing and product mix and to evaluate performance. Externally, costs must be properly matched with revenues when preparing financial statements. Traditionally, most cost accounting systems have been designed primarily to meet financial reporting requirements and have given only secondary attention to meeting the needs of production management. Consequently, in recent years traditional cost systems have been criticized for not providing adequate information to manage production operations in a CIM environment.

Criticisms of Traditional Cost Systems

The two major criticisms of traditional cost accounting systems are reflected in the issues raised in the chapter opening case for AOE: Overhead costs are inappropriately allocated to products, and performance measures do not accurately reflect the effects of factory automation.

Inappropriate Allocation of Overhead Costs. Traditional cost systems use volume-driven bases, such as direct labor or machine hours, to apply overhead to products. Many overhead costs, however, do not vary directly with production volume. Purchasing and receiving costs, for example, vary with the number of purchase orders processed and the number of shipments received from suppliers. Setup and materials handling costs vary with the number of different batches that are run, not with the total number of units that are produced. Thus allocating these types of overhead costs to products on the basis of output volume overstates the costs of products manufactured in large quantities. It also understates the costs of products manufactured in small batches.

In addition, allocating overhead on the basis of direct labor input can distort costs across products. As investments in factory automation increase, the amount of direct labor used in production decreases. Consequently, the amount of overhead charged per unit of labor increases dramatically. As a result, small differences in the amount of labor used to produce two products can result in significant differences in product costs.

Inaccurate Performance Measures. In the modern manufacturing environment, the focus is on total quality management. Thus managers need more than information about the standard costs of inventory and variances. They also need information about how well the production process is functioning, including defect rates, breakdown frequency, percentage of finished goods completed without any rework, and percentage of defects discovered by customers. Although much of this information is collected in the production cycle information system, it is not integrated with cost data. Therefore operational performance measures are not directly linked with their financial consequences.

Indeed, in many companies the cost accounting system has been separate from the production operations information system. The former collects data about the costs of production, storing that information in the work-in-process file; the latter collects data about the physical aspects of manufacturing operations, storing that information in the open production order file. Both types of data are closely related, however, and both are needed for effectively managing the production process. For example, real-time information about production quality enables defects to be spotted and corrected immediately, before additional labor and materials are used. Therefore both cost and operational data should be integrated into one system.

The next two sections discuss two potential solutions to these criticisms. The first topic, activity-based costing, addresses the criticisms about the allocation of overhead costs. The second topic, an integrated data model, addresses the criticisms about the lack of integration of financial and operational measures of production cycle activities.

Activity-Based Costing[3]

Both job-order and process cost systems can be refined and improved by adopting activity-based costing. **Activity-based costing** is so named because it attempts to trace costs to the activities, such as grinding or polishing, that create them and only subsequently allocates those costs to products or departments. An underlying objective of activity-based costing is to link costs to corporate strategy. Corporate strategy results in decisions about what goods and services to produce. Activities must be performed to produce these goods and services, which in turn incur costs. Thus corporate strategy determines costs. Consequently, by measuring the costs of basic activities, such as

[3] In this section, we provide an overview of activity-based costing, its effects on the AIS, and its benefits. For additional details on the mechanics of activity-based costing, see any leading cost accounting textbook.

materials handling or processing purchase orders, activity-based costing provides information for evaluating the consequences of strategic decisions.

Activity-Based Costing Versus Traditional Cost Systems. There are three significant differences between activity-based costing and traditional approaches to product costing:

1. Activity-based costing (ABC) systems attempt to directly trace a larger proportion of costs to products. Advances in information technology make this feasible. For example, bar coding facilitates tracking miscellaneous parts used in each product or process stage. ABC systems accountants observe production operations and interview factory workers and supervisors to obtain a better understanding of how costs relate to production.
2. ABC systems use a greater number of cost pools to accumulate indirect costs (manufacturing overhead). Whereas most traditional cost systems lump all overhead costs together, ABC systems distinguish three separate categories of overhead:
   - *Batch-related overhead.* Examples include setup costs, inspections, and materials handling. ABC systems accumulate these costs for a batch and then allocate them to the units produced in that batch. Thus products produced in large quantities have lower batch-related overhead costs per unit than do products produced in small quantities.
   - *Product-related overhead.* These costs are related to the diversity of the company's product line. Examples include research and development, expediting, shipping and receiving, environmental regulations, and purchasing. ABC systems try to link these costs to specific products whenever possible. For example, if a company produces three products, one of which generates hazardous waste, an ABC system would charge only the latter product for all the costs of complying with environmental regulations. Other costs, such as purchasing raw materials, might be allocated across products on the basis of the relative number of purchase orders required to make each end-product.
   - *Companywide overhead.* This category includes such costs as rent or depreciation. These costs apply to all products; thus ABC systems typically allocate them using departmental or plant rates.
3. The bases used to allocate manufacturing overhead in ABC systems are more likely to be cost drivers. A **cost driver** is anything that has a cause-and-effect relationship on costs. For example, the number of purchase orders processed is one cost driver of purchasing department costs. That is, the total costs of processing purchase orders (e.g., purchasing department salaries, postage, etc.) vary with the amount that are processed. As in this example, cost drivers in ABC systems are often nonfinancial variables. In contrast, traditional costing systems often use financial variables, such as dollar volume of purchases, as the bases for allocating manufacturing overhead.

Benefits of ABC Systems. ABC systems cost more to run than traditional cost systems because they require the collection of more production-related data, and in greater detail. ABC systems are also more complex, in part because more bases are used to allocate manufacturing overhead. Proponents of ABC systems argue that the increased costs and complexity provide two important benefits: (1) more accurate cost data results in better product mix and pricing decisions, and (2) more detailed cost data improves management's ability to control and manage total costs.

Better Decisions. Traditional cost systems tend to apply too much overhead to some products and too little to others, because too few cost pools are used. This leads to two types of problems, both of which AOE experienced. First, companies may accept sales contracts for some products at prices below their true cost of production. Consequently, although sales increase, profits decline. Second, companies may overprice other products, thereby inviting new competitors to enter the market. Ironically, if more accurate cost data were available, companies would find that they could cut prices to keep competitors out of the market and still make a profit on each sale. ABC systems avoid these problems because overhead is divided into three categories and applied using cost drivers that are causally related to production. Therefore product cost data is more accurate.

ABC data can also be used to improve product design. For example, Elizabeth Venko discovered that the costs associated with processing purchase orders can be used to calculate the purchasing-related overhead associated with each component used in a finished product. Engineering can then use this information, along with data on relative usage of components across products, to identify unique components that could be replaced by lower-cost, more commonly used parts.

Improved Cost Management. Proponents argue that another advantage of ABC is that it clearly measures the results of managerial actions on overall profitability. Whereas traditional cost systems only measure spending to acquire resources, ABC systems measure both the amount spent to acquire resources and the consumption of those resources. This distinction is reflected in the following formula:

Cost of activity capability = cost of activity used +
cost of unused capacity.

To illustrate, consider the receiving function at a manufacturing firm like AOE. The total monthly employee cost in the receiving department, including salaries and benefits, represents the cost of providing this function—receiving shipments from suppliers. Assume that the salary expense of the receiving department is $100,000. Further, assume that the number of employees is sufficient to handle 500 shipments. The cost per shipment then would be $200. Finally, assume that 400 shipments are actually received. The ABC system would report that the cost of the receiving activity used is $80,000 ($200 times 400 shipments) and that the remaining $20,000 in salary expense represents the cost of unused capacity.

In this way, performance reports generated by ABC systems help direct managerial attention to how policy decisions made in one area affect costs in another area. For example, a purchasing department manager may decide to increase the minimum size of orders to obtain larger discounts for bulk purchases. This would also reduce the number of incoming shipments that must

FOCUS 19.2

Adapting the General Ledger to ABC

The Original Bradford Soap Works Company manufactures private label bar soap. It makes more than 20 different bases, which can then be combined with various additives and colors to produce about 5000 types of soap each year. Until 1989 this complex manufacturing process was run on the expertise and "gut-feel" of key employees. As the number of new products grew, however, Bradford began to experience wide swings in profitability even as total sales volume increased. In addition, management lost confidence in its ability to accurately estimate the profitability of new products.

These problems were solved by using a relational DBMS to support an ABC system. It took more than three years for Bradford to implement a successful ABC management system. One crucial and time-consuming step involved recasting the general ledger to match the ABC system's cost pool structure. This led to an almost 30% increase in the number of general ledger accounts. For example, instead of a single account for salaries, separate accounts were created for each major soap-making activity, such as milling and perfuming, as well as for indirect activities such as machine setup. Moreover, mapping ABC cost pools to general ledger accounts was not always a straightforward process, but involved many judgment calls and compromises. For example, there was no logical way to set up direct accounts linking utility use, such as electricity, to individual machines. Consequently, a single general ledger account was retained and a formula in the ABC system was created to allocate those costs to various machine pools.

Eventually, Bradford succeeded in mapping its ABC system to its general ledger. Twice each year, the ABC numbers are closed to the general ledger accounts. This allows Bradford to update its estimating data base (used to bid on new business) with the actual financial results of prior periods. In this way, Bradford is able to continuously learn from experience and refine the accuracy of its bidding process.

Although pleased with these results, Bradford's accounting staff plans to continuously improve and change its ABC management system. Specifically, they recognize that the accounting system must always reflect the production processes used on the shop floor. Otherwise, even the best ABC system will eventually become obsolete and useless.

Focus Questions

1. Is it important to integrate the ABC system with the general ledger? Why not maintain two accounting systems: one for financial reporting, and one for internal decision making?
2. If considerable "judgment" is required to map ABC activities and cost pools to general ledger accounts, how accurate can the resulting system be?

Source: Francis Gammell and C.J. McNair, "Jumping the Growth Threshold Through Activity-Based Cost Management," *Management Accounting* (September 1994): 37–46.

be handled by the receiving department, thereby increasing its unused capacity. Similarly, actions taken to improve the efficiency of operations, such as requiring vendors to send products in bar-coded containers, increase practical capacity and also create additional unused capacity. In either case, ABC performance reports highlight this excess capacity for managerial attention. Management can then try to improve profitability either by applying that unused capacity to other revenue-generating activities or by eliminating it.

AIS Design Requirements for ABC Systems. Elizabeth Venko's research indicates that ABC systems impose several requirements on the AIS. First, the general ledger must be redesigned to fit the additional cost categories used by ABC. As shown in Focus 19.2, this task is not necessarily easy to accomplish. Second, ABC systems require extensive use of information technology in order to accumulate more precise data about cost drivers. Third, and perhaps most important, ABC systems require that both financial and nonfinancial measures of production activity be stored in an integrated manner. In the next section we discuss how the REA data model can be used to accomplish this integration.

Production Cycle Data Model

Figure 19.8 presents a simplified example of a data model for the production cycle of a manufacturing company, such as AOE. Four types of resources are shown: equipment and inventory accounts for raw materials, work-in-process, and finished goods. Two event entities are depicted: assembly and finishing (note that there could be many additional production events depending upon the nature of the production process and the type of good being produced). There are also two agent entities: factory workers and their supervisors. Finally, at the bottom of the figure are two abstract entities—production orders and operation type—that we will explain shortly.

Reading the E–R Diagram. To maximize its usefulness for cost management and decision making, production cycle data must be collected at the lowest possible level of aggregation. Therefore the event entities depicted in Fig. 19.8 do not correspond with the processes depicted in the level 0 DFD for the production cycle presented earlier. Rather, they represent the detailed activities that occur during the production operations stage (circle 3.0 in Fig. 19.2).

Let us now examine Fig. 19.8 more closely, to see what it reveals about the nature of this production cycle. The two relationships labeled "bill of materials" and "operations list" represent the outputs of product design. Bill of materials is a many-to-many relationship between raw materials and finished goods. Each finished good consists of one or more raw materials; each raw material must be used to manufacture at least one finished product. Operations list is also a many-to-many relationship: Each finished good is produced as a result of one or more factory operations, and a particular factory operation may be performed in the manufacture of one or more different products.

The relationship between raw materials and assembly is also modeled as a many-to-many relationship. This reflects the fact that at least one raw material item is used to assemble a given product and, conversely, the same item of raw material may be used in many different assembly operations. Note that this relationship records data about *actual* raw materials usage, which is usually recorded on a materials requisition; data about standard usage are recorded in the bill of materials relationship.

The relationship between assembly and work-in-process is modeled as being one to one. This reflects the fact that AOE produces distinctly identifiable products. Therefore each assembly event is linked to a specific work-in-process batch or product. Conversely, each unit of work-in-process can be linked to a specific assembly operation. For similar reasons, the relationships between work-in-process and finishing, and between finishing and finished goods, are also depicted as being one-to-one. Note, however, that the finishing event has a zero minimum cardinality in its relationship to work-in-process; this reflects the fact that this operation may not have been performed yet for some work-in-process.

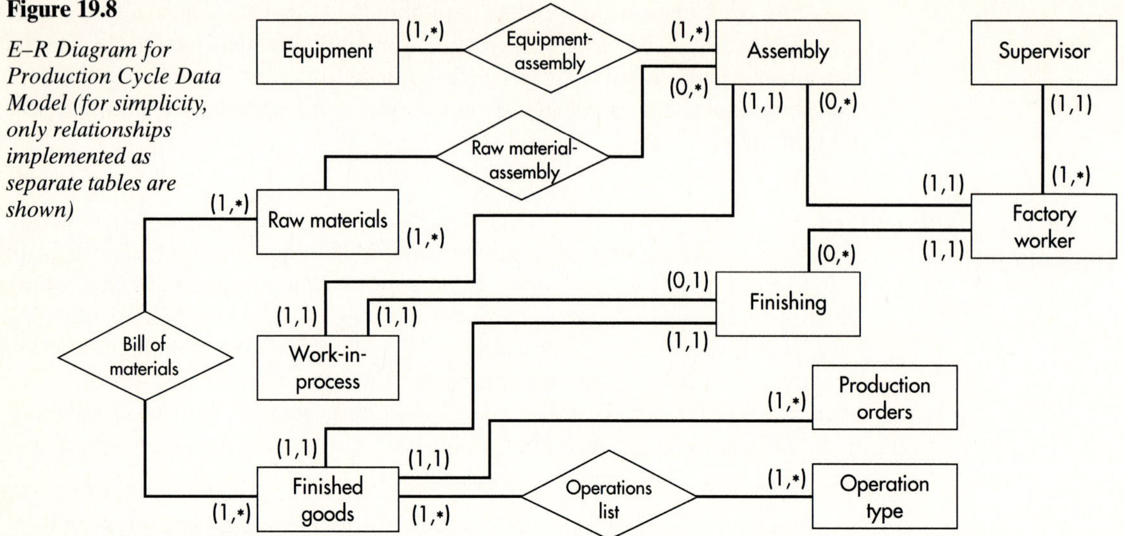

Figure 19.8

E–R Diagram for Production Cycle Data Model (for simplicity, only relationships implemented as separate tables are shown)

Table Attributes for Figure 19.8

Table Name	Attributes (**Primary Key,** *Foreign Keys,* Other Attributes)
Equipment	**Idnumber,** Description, Cost, Date_Acquired, Depreciation_Method, Accumulated Depreciation, Salvage Value, . . .
Raw Materials	**Part_Number,** Description, Standard Cost, Reorder Point, . . .
Work-in-Process	**Job_Number,** *Item Number, Assembly Number,* Quantity, Date, . . .
Finished Goods	**Item_Number,** Description, Quantity on Hand, . . .
Assembly	**Assembly_Number,** *Production_Order_Number, Item_Number, Employee_Number, Operation_Type Number,* Start Time, Stop Time, Units Produced, . . .
Finishing	**Finishing_Number,** *Production_Order_Number, Job_Number, Item_Number, Employee_Number, Operation_Type_Number,* Start Time, Stop Time, Units Finished, . . .
Operation Type	**Operation_Type_Number,** Description, . . .
Production Order	**Production_Order_Number,** *Item Number,* Date, Quantity to Produce, . . .
Factory Worker	**Employee_Number,** *Supervisor Number,* Name, Date Hired, Date of Birth, Pay Rate, . . .
Supervisor	**Employee_Number,** Name, Date Hired, Date of Birth, Salary, . . .
Bill-of-Materials	**Part_Number, Item_Number,** Standard Quantity
Equipment-Assembly	**Idnumber, Assembly_Number,** Actual Hours
Raw Materials-Assembly	**Part_Number, Assembly_Number,** Actual Quantity
Operations-List	**Item_Number, Operation_Type_Number,** Standard Hours

The relationship between equipment and assembly is represented as being many-to-many. This reflects the fact that a given assembly operation may involve one or more different pieces of equipment. Conversely, the same machine may be used in many different assembly operations.

The meaning of the relationships between employees and the various operations should be clear: Each employee may perform one or more instances of assembly or finishing, but each event is linked to the specific employee who performed it. Moreover, each employee is assigned to a specific supervisor; each supervisor, however, is responsible for many employees. (Note that if

AOE changes to a matrix style of organization, where each employee reports to several supervisors, the relationship between factory employees and supervisors would be modeled as being many-to-many.)

Finally, let us examine the two abstract entities: production orders and operation type. The former stores data about planned production activity. The relationship between it and the finished goods entity is modeled as being many-to-one, reflecting the fact that over time there are many production runs for each item. The operation type entity stores general data about the nature of each type of production cycle operation (e.g., the name of the operation, its purpose, etc.). Data about the performance of specific operations, such as the time when the operation was started, the time it was completed, and the number of units produced, are stored in the appropriate event entity (assembly or finishing), however.

Benefits of the Data Model. Examination of the table attributes for the data model depicted in Fig. 19.8 shows that it effectively integrates both financial and nonfinancial measures of production cycle activities. Thus it facilitates multifaceted analyses of performance. For example, Table 19.3 shows the queries that would yield the data needed to compute and analyze the raw materials usage variance. It also shows the query needed to identify which components are used in only a few finished products. This information can then be used to explore possible design modifications that would use more commonly used components. Thus the REA data model provides managers with access both to traditional financial cost data that can be used to evaluate performance and to operational data that can be used to plan changes in production methods.

The data model depicted in Fig. 19.8 also supports activity-based costing because it captures performance and cost data by each activity. Moreover, if desired, the assembly and finishing activities can be further decomposed into substeps, to facilitate more detailed cost analysis of production operations.

Finally, remember that if this data model were implemented in a relational data base, the information would be easily accessed through the use of languages like SQL. This would facilitate the sharing of production information across various departments, such as design, engineering, purchasing, and production. This makes it easier for managers to coordinate activities, thereby reducing the total time involved in designing, producing, and delivering products to customers. The benefits of such coordination can be dramatic. For example, Foxboro, a manufacturer of process controls and systems for oil and chemical refineries, cut its production cycle time from 16 to 6 weeks after it implemented an integrated production cycle data base. The new software enabled the design, engineering, purchasing, and manufacturing departments to share a wide range of data, including information about product specifications, the status of purchase orders, and production schedules. With more accurate and timely information, unforeseen delays in production schedules were all but eliminated. It was also easier to adjust the production schedule in response to changes in customer requirements. Moreover, the reduction in cycle time not only improved customer satisfaction, but it also reduced work-in-process inventory levels by 76%.

Table 19.3 Sample SQL Queries of Production Cycle REA Data Model

Task 1: Compute the raw materials usage variance.

Solution: The raw materials usage variance equals the standard cost of the raw materials times the difference between the quantity of raw materials actually used and the quantity that should have been used to produce the number of units of finished goods that were completed. Four SQL queries are needed to retrieve the data to make this calculation. The answers to these four queries can then be input to a spreadsheet program to compute the variance.

Query 1: Calculate quantity of raw materials used during period.

```
SELECT      Part_Number, Sum(Actual_Quantity)
FROM        Raw_Materials-Assembly
GROUP BY    Part_Number
```

Raw_Materials-Assembly		
Part_Number	**Assembly_Number**	**Actual_Quantity**
....	......	......
1255	254411	250
1284	254412	300
1255	254413	400
....	......	.....

Response to Query	
Part Number	**Sum(Actual_ Quantity)**
....	....
1255	650
....	....
1284	300
....	....

Query 2: Calculate the quantity of items produced in the period.

```
SELECT      Item_Number, Sum(Units_Produced)
FROM        Assembly
GROUP BY    Item_Number
```

Assembly				
Assembly_ Number	**Other Columns**	**Item_ Number**	**Other Cols.**	**Units_ Produced**
....	....	...	...	....
254411	....	125	...	600
254412	....	134	...	700
254413	....	134	...	500
....	....	...	...	....

Response to Query	
Item_ Number	**Sum(Units_ Produced)**
....	....
125	600
....	....
134	1200
....	....

Query 3: Show the standard quantity of raw materials that should be used to produce each finished product.

```
SELECT   *
FROM     Bill_of_Materials
```

Bill_of_Materials		
Part_Number	**Item_Number**	**Standard_Quantity**
....	....	.....
1255	125	6
1273	125	3
1284	125	5
....	....	.....

continued

Table 19.3 **Continued**

Query 4: Retrieve the standard cost for each raw material component.

```
SELECT  Part_Number, Standard_Cost
FROM    Raw_Materials
```

Raw_Materials			
Part_ Number	**Description**	**Standard_ Cost**	**Reorder_ Point**
....	....	....	....
1255	Panel, Side	15.50	50
1273	Control unit	103.75	25
1284	Facing	62.45	30
....	....	....	....

Response to Query	
Part_ Number	**Standard_ Cost**
....	....
1255	15.50
1273	103.75
1284	62.45
....	....

Task 2: Identify the number of finished products using a given part as a component.

```
SELECT    Part_Number, Count(Item_Number)
FROM      Bill_of_Materials
GROUP BY  Part_Number
```

Bill_of_Materials		
Part_Number	**Item_Number**	**Standard_ Quantity**
....	....	....
1255	124	5
1284	124	4
1255	125	6
1273	125	3
1284	125	5
1255	126	4
1284	126	5
....	....	....

Response to Query	
Part_Number	**Count (Item_Number)**
....	....
1255	3
1273	1
1284	2
....	....

Realization of such benefits, however, depends upon the accuracy of the information in the data model. In a data base environment, this means that data entry edit and data base update controls are extremely important. Indeed, accuracy, or the lack thereof, can be costly. For example, Elizabeth Venko recalled reading that Red Devil, a manufacturer of tools and supplies for the do-it-yourself home remodeler, routinely overstocked inventory because it did not trust the accuracy of its inventory figures. After implementing a new integrated data base system that accurately tracked inventory, Red Devil was able to reduce its inventory by $2 million. Elizabeth wondered whether improving the accuracy of AOE's production cycle data base could yield similar savings.

SUMMARY AND CASE CONCLUSION

The production cycle consists of four basic activities: product design, production planning and scheduling, production operations, and cost accounting. Companies are continually investing in information technology to improve the efficiency of the first three activities. However, for a business to reap the full benefit of these changes, corresponding modifications must be made to the cost accounting portion of the AIS.

Indeed, upon completing her tour of the factory, Elizabeth Venko was convinced that some major changes were required in AOE's cost accounting system. For example, although AOE's production operations were highly automated, manufacturing overhead was still being allocated on the basis of direct labor hours. This resulted in distorted product costs due to small differences in the amount of direct labor used to assemble each item. Elizabeth decided that the solution was to do more than merely change the allocation base. Instead, AOE would implement activity-based costing. A number of different pools would be used to accumulate overhead costs, and the appropriate cost drivers would be identified for use in assigning those costs to specific products. Based on her research, and conversations with a controller at another company that had recently implemented an ABC system, Elizabeth believed that these changes would solve AOE's problems with product pricing and mix decisions. In addition, reports prepared by the ABC system would more fairly represent factory supervisor actions.

Elizabeth also decided that two major changes were needed in the reports produced by the AIS. First, data about all the costs associated with quality control, not just those involving rework and scrap, should be collected and reported. Second, performance reports should include nonfinancial as well as financial measures. Elizabeth realized that both of these changes would necessitate a redesign of AOE's production cycle data base. Based on her previous experience with redesigning AOE's revenue and expenditure cycle information systems, she decided that the best way to implement the required modifications would be to adopt a data model similar to the one depicted in Fig. 19.8.

Elizabeth discussed her plans in an executive meeting. LeRoy Williams was satisfied that the changes would indeed address his complaints with AOE's current production cycle information system. Stephanie Cromwell, vice president of finance, stated that resources were available to assign Elizabeth to carry out this project. Linda Spurgeon, AOE's president, supported the proposal and agreed to fund the necessary changes. Peter Wu, the vice president of human resources, was also impressed with Elizabeth's plans. In fact, he left the meeting resolved to secure Elizabeth's cooperation in revamping AOE's human resource management/payroll cycle information system, as soon as she completed her work on the production cycle.

KEY TERMS

production cycle
bill of materials
operations list
routing sheet
manufacturing resource planning (MRP-II)
just-in-time (JIT) manufacturing
master production schedule (MPS)
production order
materials requisition
move tickets
computer-integrated manufacturing (CIM)
job-order costing
process costing
job-time ticket
manufacturing overhead
throughput
productive capacity
productive processing time
yield
activity-based costing
cost driver

CHAPTER QUIZ

1. Most costs are locked in at which stage in the production cycle?
   a. Product design
   b. Production planning
   c. Production operations
   d. Cost accounting

2. Which report provides the most information about production efficiency?
   a. Cost of quality report
   b. Activity-based cost reports
   c. Throughout
   d. MPS

3. What is the best way to ensure accurate collection and recording of materials usage data in a CIM environment?
   a. Turn-around documents
   b. On-line edit checks
   c. Bar-code scanners
   d. Periodic physical counts of inventory

4. The use of move tickets mitigates which threat?
   a. Loss of data
   b. Theft of inventory
   c. Inefficient performance
   d. Overproduction of inventory

5. In a CIM environment, which category usually represents the smallest percentage of product costs?
   a. Raw materials
   b. Direct labor
   c. Distribution costs
   d. Factory overhead

6. Activity-based costing can be used to refine
   a. job-order costing.
   b. process costing.
   c. both job-order and process costing.
   d. neither job-order nor process costing.

7. Which system is most likely to be used by a company that mass produces large batches of standard items in anticipation of customer demand?
   a. Job-order costing
   b. Standard costing
   c. Activity-based costing
   d. Process costing

8. The development of an MPS would be *most* effective in preventing which of the following threats?
   a. Recording and posting errors
   b. Loss of inventory
   c. Production of poor quality goods
   d. Excess production

9. Which control procedure is probably *least* effective in reducing the threat of inventory loss?
   a. Limiting physical access to inventory
   b. Documenting all transfers of inventory within the company
   c. Regular materials usage reports that highlight variances from standards
   d. Periodic physical inventory counts and investigation of any discrepancies between those counts and recorded amounts

10. Which control procedure would be *most* effective in reducing the risk of theft of fixed assets?
   a. Bar-coded identification of all fixed assets
   b. Periodic counts of fixed assets and reconciliation of those counts to recorded amounts
   c. Requirement for proper authorization of the disposal of fixed assets
   d. Physical access controls

DISCUSSION QUESTIONS

19.1 When ABC reports indicate that excess capacity exists, management should either find alternative revenue-enhancing uses for that capacity or eliminate it through downsizing. What factors influence management's decision? What are the likely behavioral side effects of each choice? What implications do those side effects have for the long-run usefulness of ABC systems?

19.2 How might some financial reporting requirements mandated by GAAP, such as absorption accounting, lead to undesirable behaviors by line managers?

19.3 American manufacturing efficiency is improving. Part of the credit is due to a form of CIM called *soft manufacturing* that increases production. Soft manufacturing entails the use of software and computer networks, rather than robots, to improve efficiency. Indeed, one of its tenets is that there can be *too much* automation of the manufacturing process. An often-cited example is that of a robot repeatedly trying to jam a bolt into an opening that is obviously too small. Do you think that soft manufacturing, with its emphasis on augmenting human workers with software, is a viable long-term strategy? Or, do you see it as only a short-term solution until further research in artificial intelligence improves robot performance? Give reasons to support your opinion.

19.4 Some companies have eliminated the collection and reporting of detailed analyses on direct labor costs broken down by various activities. Instead, first-line supervisors are responsible for controlling the total costs of direct labor. The justification for this argument is that labor costs represent only a small fraction of the total costs of producing a product and are therefore not worth the time and effort to trace to individual activities. Do you agree or disagree with this argument? Why?

19.5 Typically, McDonald's produces menu items in advance of customer orders, based on anticipated demand. In contrast, Burger King produces menu items only in response to customer orders. Which system (MRP-II or JIT) does each company utilize? What are the relative advantages and disadvantages of each system?

19.6 Describe some of the trade-offs likely to arise when attempting to reduce the quality control costs associated with prevention, inspection, internal failure, and external failure.

PROBLEMS

19.1 Write a memo discussing the relationships and trade-offs between the concepts of accuracy, precision, and fairness in terms of allocating manufacturing overhead costs.

19.2 What internal control procedure(s) would best prevent or detect the following problems?

a. A production order was initiated for a product that was already overstocked in the company's warehouse.

b. Items of work-in-process inventory were stolen by a production employee.

c. The "rush order" tag on a partially completed production job became detached from the materials and lost, resulting in a costly delay.

d. A production employee prepared a materials requisition and used the document to steal $300 worth of parts from the raw materials storeroom.

e. A production worker entering job time data using an on-line terminal mistakenly entered 3000 instead of 300 in the "quantity completed" field.

f. A production worker entering job-time data using an on-line terminal mistakenly posted the completion of operation 562 to production order 7569 instead of production order 7596.

g. A parts storeroom clerk issued parts in quantities 10% lower than those indicated on several materials requisitions and stole the excess quantities.

h. A parts storeroom clerk stole electronics components and covered up the loss by submitting a form to the accounting department indicating that the missing parts were obsolete and should be written off as worthless.

i. The quantity-on-hand balance for a key component shows a negative balance.

j. Materials requisitions are used to authorize the release of the standard quantities of raw materials needed to manufacture a product. At times, production employees use a lesser amount of materials to finish the product and steal the remaining parts.

k. A factory supervisor accesses the operations list file and inflates the standards for work completed in his department. Consequently, future performance reports show favorable budget variances for that department.

19.3 Refer to Fig. 19.8 to answer the following questions:

a. Why doesn't a direct link exist between finished goods and work-in-process? What SQL queries could retrieve information about the status of production orders for specific end-products?

b. You want to simplify Fig. 19.8 to show only one event entity for factory operations (i.e., you want to combine the assembly and finishing event entities). What other changes in the E–R diagram would also be required? What are the advantages and disadvantages of simplifying the figure in this manner?

c. The relationship between employees and activities is one-to-many. Is any other type of relationship cardinality possible? For which types of companies?

d. Adopting a product life cycle approach to product costing would include linking marketing and sales costs to specific products. Expand Fig. 19.8 to show how this approach could be accomplished.

e. Modify the E–R diagram to include information about equipment repairs and maintenance.

f. Specify the set of on-line application controls that should be used to control updates to the assembly event table.

g. Write SQL queries to determine the standard and actual number of labor hours used on production order 2410.

h. Write SQL queries to calculate the average time spent by each employee on each activity.

i. Specify the access controls that should be designed into a system based on this data model. Specifically, which employees should be allowed to access each table, and what operations (read, write, update, delete) should they be permitted to perform?

19.4 You have been hired to design a production information system for a new company that will manufacture custom automobile wheels. List all the documents (paper and electronic) that should be included in the system and specify the purposes they serve.

19.5 You are a management consultant for a large public accounting firm. One of your firm's clients is the Willard Corporation, a medium-sized manufacturer of karaoke machines and other audio equipment. You have been hired to advise on the following problems:

- Customer order fulfillment has declined from 90% to 50% during the past year.
- Production costs have risen dramatically because of increased charges for overtime and rework. In addition, idle time due to materials shortages and machine downtime has increased.

REQUIRED

What questions would you ask the controller in order to obtain a better understanding of these problems and their potential causes?

19.6 You have recently been hired as the controller for a small manufacturing firm. One of your first tasks is to develop a report measuring throughput for each of the company's three production departments.

REQUIRED

Describe what data you will need to collect and how you could most efficiently and accurately collect it.

19.7 Table 19.4 on page 704 represents the first draft of a report on quality control costs developed by one of your assistants.

REQUIRED

a. Based on the data sources used for this report, what are the most efficient and effective ways to collect the key information needed?

b. Suggest improvements in the design of this report.

19.8 What is the purpose of each of the following control activities?

a. Periodic reconciliation of the work-in-process subsidiary ledger to the work-in-process control account.

b. Documentation of the return of any scrapped products to inventory stores.

c. Use of an MPS to schedule production.

d. Periodic counts of fixed assets and reconciliation of those counts to the fixed asset subsidiary ledger.

e. The use of move tickets to document transfers of work-in-process between factory departments.

f. The prenumbering and periodic accounting of all materials requisitions.

g. Access to the system that generates production orders is controlled by the use of passwords.

h. A list of all transactions involving the acquisition or disposal of fixed assets is printed monthly and reviewed by the controller.

CASE 19.1: ANYCOMPANY, INC.—AN ONGOING COMPREHENSIVE CASE

Visit a local company and obtain permission to study its production information system (you may use the same company you identified to complete this case in previous chapters). Write a report that includes the following:

1. DFDs of each of the four major steps in the production cycle (design, planning, operations, and cost accounting).
2. A list of all paper and electronic documents used by the company, with copies of possible. Evaluate the design of each document.
3. A data model, in the form of an E–R diagram, of all the information stored in the system.
4. A description of how the system updates the master files (or data base) after each type of transaction occurs (materials requisition, machine

Table 19.4 **Quality Cost Report for Problem 19.7**

Quality Cost Report **June 1996**				
Cost Type	**June 1996**	**June 1995**	**YTD 1996**	**YTD 1995**
Prevention:				
QC Admin.	350	450	1800	1700
QC Services	400	550	2100	2200
Training	750	900	4300	4000
Work Safety	400	200	2500	1000
Total Prevent	1900	2100	10,700	8900
Appraisal:				
Inspection	900	1200	5000	5300
Analysis	600	800	4000	4900
Supplier	800	400	4200	2500
Total Appraise	2300	2400	13,200	12,700
Internal Failure:				
Rework	700	1000	3000	4000
Scrap	800	1100	6000	6500
Work. Comp.	500	800	2800	3500
Overtime	600	200	3400	1000
Overruns	500	900	4500	5300
Total Internal	3100	4000	19,700	20,300
External Failure:				
Complaints	800	1200	5600	6500
Returns	900	1300	6300	9000
Freight on returns	500	750	3400	5400
Total External	2200	3250	15,300	20,900

operation, etc.). Draw a systems flowchart for each step in the production cycle.

5. A list and evaluation of the adequacy of the control procedures used to ensure transaction processing accuracy and validity.
6. Your opinion of whether the cost accounting reports produced by the system help managers make good decisions. Suggest changes to improve the use of cost accounting data to help the company attain its strategic objectives.

CASE 19.2: THE CONTROLLER AND CIM

Examine the issues of the *Journal of Accountancy* and *Management Accounting* for the last two years. Write a brief report on one current development in factory automation and its effects on the AIS. Be sure to describe the controller's role in either initiating or responding to the change. In addition, discuss its effect on the risk of the various production cycle threats.

CASE 19.3: DOCUMENTATION AND ANALYSIS OF A PRODUCTION CYCLE INFORMATION SYSTEM

The Joseph Brant Manufacturing Company makes athletic footwear. Processing of production orders is as follows: At the end of each week, the production planning department prepares a list of shoes and quantities to be produced during the next week. Using this list as a source, data entry clerks key in production order release records onto a temporary disk file. Once data entry has been completed, a production order preparation program accesses the operations list (stored on a permanent disk file) and prepares a production order for each shoe to be manufactured. For each new production order, the program (1) prints three copies of a production order document, (2) writes the production order to the open production order master file stored on disk, and (3) prints an operations card identifying each operation that needs to be performed to manufacture that style of shoe.

The operations cards are used as turnaround documents. Each card is sent to the factory department where the operation will be performed. After completing an operation, factory employees mark the elapsed time, quantity completed, and other pertinent data on the card and return it to computer operations. A scanner is then used to read and write the operations data onto a temporary disk file. At the end of each day, this file is processed to update the open production order master file. Once this update has been completed, the program generates departmental production schedules for the next day.

1. Prepare both a data flow diagram and a systems flowchart of all operations described.
2. Describe a comprehensive set of control procedures that should be included in each system. Organize your answer by listing the potential threats and specifying the control procedures that would best address them.

ANSWERS TO CHAPTER QUIZ

1. a	**3.** c	**5.** b	**7.** a	**9.** c
2. c	**4.** b	**6.** c	**8.** d	**10.** d

Chapter 20

The Human Resources Management/Payroll Cycle

LEARNING OBJECTIVES

After studying this chapter, you should be able to:

- Describe the major business activities and related data processing operations performed in the human resources management (HRM)/payroll cycle.
- Assess the relative benefits of using new developments in information technology to improve the efficiency of HRM/payroll cycle activities.
- Document HRM/payroll cycle activities.
- Describe basic governmental reporting requirements relating to HRM and payroll activities and explain what information must be collected to meet those requirements.
- Identify the major threats in the HRM/payroll cycle and evaluate the adequacy of various internal control procedures for dealing with them.
- Explain the key decisions that need to be made in the HRM/payroll cycle and identify the information required to make those decisions.
- Read a data model (E–R diagram of the HRM/payroll cycle.

Integrative Case: Alpha Omega Electronics

Peter Wu has just been hired as the new vice president for human resources at Alpha Omega Electronics (AOE). When hired, Peter was told that his first priority was to correct two weaknesses in AOE's existing human resources management (HRM)/payroll system. First, payroll processing costs have been rising steadily for years, yet the current system does not provide adequate service. For example, employees are unhappy with the lengthy delays required to obtain information about their benefits and retirement plans. Moreover, Linda Spurgeon, AOE's president, wants to provide employees with an expanded flexible benefits plan. Doing so, however, will further increase the demands on the existing system. Thus Peter must find a way to improve the efficiency and responsiveness of AOE's payroll system.

A second weakness with AOE's current HRM/payroll system is its inability to track employee skill development. Consequently, department managers have tended to hire externally to meet new staffing needs, rather than promoting or transferring existing employees. This practice has negatively affected employee morale. It also impedes evaluating the effectiveness of AOE's investment in training and continuing education. Thus Peter's other task is to find a way to improve the effectiveness of AOE's HRM system.

Peter noted that AOE, like many companies, has separate HRM and payroll systems. The payroll system, which is under the control of the accounting department, produces employee paychecks and maintains the related records required by government regulations. The payroll system uses batch processing: Hourly employees are paid biweekly, and salaried employees and those on commission are paid monthly. The HRM system, which is run by the human resources department, maintains files on employee job history, skills, and benefits; these files are updated weekly. Each system maintains its own separate files, sometimes storing the same data, such as pay rates, in different formats. Thus, Peter was not surprised to learn that it was difficult to prepare reports that combined HRM and payroll data.

Peter decided to begin by examining how to improve the payroll processing system, because it handles the routine transactions affecting human resources. He met with Elizabeth Venko, AOE's controller, to discuss how to improve the efficiency of the payroll system. Elizabeth explained how the new methods being used to collect factory labor time data (see Chapter 19) should streamline the initial stages of payroll processing. She added that it may be possible to use information technology to improve the efficiency of other stages of the payroll process. Peter then inquired about the likelihood of redesigning the payroll data base in order to integrate it with the HRM system. Elizabeth said that is possible and agreed to develop a plan to address the following issues:

1. How can AOE use recent advances in information technology (IT) to process payroll more efficiently, while still meeting all government regulations?
2. How can the payroll system be modified to provide employees with direct access to information about their benefits and retirement plans, without creating new threats to the system's integrity?
3. How can a skills inventory system be implemented to provide operating managers with the information they need to make staffing assignments? Can this skills inventory system be integrated with the payroll system so that AOE can track the costs and benefits of training programs?

As you read this chapter, think about how AOE's HRM and payroll systems could be improved in order to resolve these questions.

INTRODUCTION

The **human resources management (HRM)/payroll cycle** is a recurring set of business activities and related data processing operations associated with effectively managing the employee work force. Some of the more important activities include the following tasks:

1. Recruitment and hiring.
2. Training.
3. Assignment of job responsibilities.
4. Compensating for services provided.
5. Evaluation of employee performance.
6. Discharge.

In addition, as discussed in Chapter 19, payroll costs are also allocated to products and departments, for use in product pricing and mix decisions and to evaluate performance.

Tasks 1 and 6 are performed once for each employee; tasks 2–5 are performed repeatedly for as long as the employee works for the company. Moreover, in most companies these six activities are split between two separate systems. Task 4, compensating employees, is performed by the payroll system, which is part of the AIS. The other five steps are performed by the HRM system. In many companies, these two systems are also organizationally separate: The HRM system is usually the responsibility of the director of human resources, and the payroll system is managed by the controller.

This chapter focuses primarily on the payroll system, because it is one of the largest and most important components of the AIS. Moreover, the payroll system must be designed to meet government regulations as well as management's information needs. Indeed, incomplete or erroneous payroll records not only impair decision making but can also result in fines and imprisonment! Thus the design of an efficient and effective payroll system is vital. Figure 20.1 presents a context diagram of the payroll system, depicting its relationships with the HRM system and with the other parts of the AIS. This figure shows five major sources of inputs to the payroll system. The HRM department provides information about hirings, terminations, and pay-rate changes due to raises and promotions. Employees initiate changes in their discretionary deductions (e.g., contributions to retirement plans). The various departments provide data about actual hours worked by employees. Government agencies provide tax rates and instructions for meeting regulatory requirements. Similarly, insurance companies and other organizations provide instructions about how to calculate and remit various withholdings.

Checks are the principal output of the payroll system. Employees receive individual paychecks in compensation for their services. A payroll check is sent to the bank to transfer funds from the company's regular accounts to its payroll account. Checks are also issued to government agencies, insurance companies, and other organizations to meet company obligations (e.g., taxes, insurance premiums). In addition, a variety of reports, which we discuss later in the chapter, are prepared for internal and external use.

An organization's most valuable asset is its employees. Their knowledge and skills affect the quality of the goods and services provided to customers. Moreover, in professional service organizations, such as accounting and law firms, labor costs represent the major expense incurred in generating revenues. Even in manufacturing firms, where direct labor costs represent only a fraction of total direct costs, employees are a key cost driver in that the quality of their work affects both overall productivity and product defect rates. Thus it is not

Figure 20.1

Context Diagram of Payroll Portion of HRM/Payroll Cycle

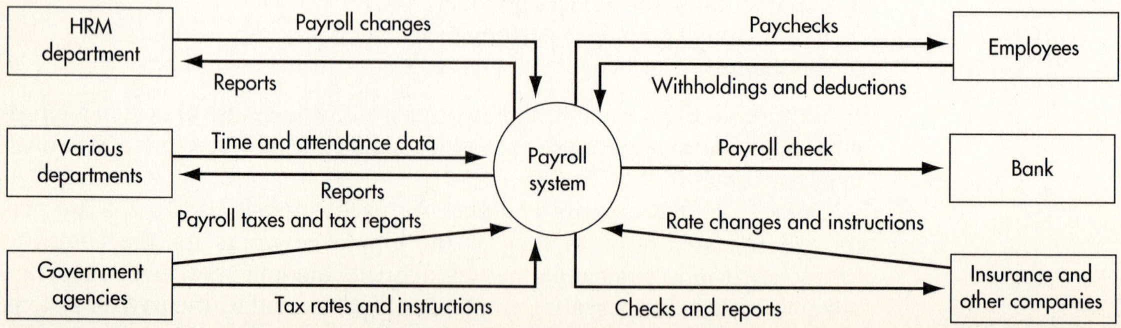

surprising to find that some stock analysts believe that a company's human resources may be worth several times the value of its tangible assets, such as inventory, property, and equipment.

Nevertheless, the AIS has not traditionally been used to measure or report on the status of a company's human resources. One reason is that the assets reported in financial statements represent resources the organization owns but has not yet consumed. Human resources, however, are not "owned" by the company. Consequently, the value of human resources has traditionally been recognized only when they are used, at which time they are either recorded as wages and salary expenses or, in the case of direct labor in manufacturing firms, included as part of the cost of inventory.

This situation is beginning to change. Companies like Dow Chemical have created new executive positions with such titles as director of intellectual assets. Among their responsibilities is the measurement and development of the organization's human resources. Moreover, as Focus 20.1 shows, some companies, like Skandia Group, Scandinavia's largest financial services company, have even begun to include human resources information in their annual reports. Finally, banks, including the Canadian Imperial Bank of Commerce, are beginning to request and use information about a company's employees in making loan decisions. These banks want this data because they believe that such "soft" assets often represent a better credit risk than "hard" assets like office buildings and land.

These examples underscore the importance of designing the payroll system to do more than just record time and attendance data and prepare paychecks. Instead, the payroll system should be integrated with the HRM system in order to provide management with the information it needs to utilize and develop the organization's human resources.

The remainder of this chapter is organized in terms of the three basic functions provided by the AIS: processing transactional data, safeguarding the organization's assets, and providing information for decision making. We begin by describing the basic activities in the payroll cycle. In this section we also explore opportunities for using new developments in information technology (IT) to improve the effectiveness and efficiency of those activities. Next, we discuss the control objectives of the HRM/payroll cycle and describe applicable control procedures for mitigating the major potential threats in this cycle. We conclude this chapter with a discussion of key decisions in the HRM/payroll cycle and identify the information needed to make those decisions. Then we present a data model that effectively integrates payroll data with the information produced by and maintained in the HRM system.

PAYROLL CYCLE ACTIVITIES

Figure 20.2 shows the seven basic activities performed in the payroll cycle. Payroll is one AIS application that continues to be processed in batch mode, because (1) paychecks are prepared periodically (either weekly, biweekly, or monthly) and (2) most employees are paid at the same time. Figure 20.3 on page 712 depicts a typical batch-oriented HRM/payroll system like that used by AOE. We will refer to Fig. 20.3 as we discuss the seven activities depicted in

FOCUS 20.1

Measuring and Reporting "Soft" Capital

Skandia Group, a financial services company, represents what is probably the most innovative and advanced approach to measuring and reporting the value of its human intellectual resources. In 1991 the company hired the corporate world's first director of intellectual capital, and in 1993 it released its first annual report on the value of those assets.

Skandia divides intellectual capital into two categories: human and structural. Human capital is the company's employees and their knowledge, which can be increased and developed through hiring and training. Structural capital represents the organizational resources used to leverage individual human capital so that it can be effectively used throughout the organization. Structural capital includes such assets as information systems, knowledge of market channels and customers, and managerial skills. It is increased by finding ways to institutionalize individual knowledge or by capturing it in the form of expert systems, decision rules, or new procedures. For example, Skandia has captured the basic knowledge required to open an office in a new country and formalized it as a set of standard procedures. This process has allowed it to cut in half the time and costs associated with entering a new country. Skandia's director of intellectual capital believes that structural capital is even more valuable than the human capital because it will not quit or hire on with a competitor and can be used over and over again.

Skandia's director of intellectual capital works closely with the controller to develop multiple measures of intellectual capital. For example, both the number of new products resulting from employee suggestions and the number of suggestions are recorded. The ratio of the former to the latter is then used as one measure of the quality of employee suggestions. A number of measures have been developed to measure the efficiency and effectiveness with which the company's intellectual capital is being used: (1) administrative expenses as a percentage of revenues and compared to the revenue generated per employee, (2) the investment in information technology per employee, and (3) both the number and average size of new accounts. Eventually, Skandia hopes to be able to correlate trends in these measures with changes in traditional measures of financial performance.

Focus Questions

1. Do you think that measuring human capital is useful? accurate? Why or why not?
2. How is the recording of human capital similar to the recording of physical capital? In what ways do the two differ?
3. Do you agree with the distinction that Skandia makes between human and structural intellectual capital? Are there any possible limits to the transformation of the one into the other?
4. How might employees react to knowing that the company's goal is to capture their intellectual knowledge so that it can remain a part of the company even after they leave?
5. What are some of the risks associated with issuing external reports on the value of intellectual capital?

Source: Thomas A. Stewart, "Your Company's Most Valuable Asset: Intellectual Capital," *Fortune* (October 3, 1994): 68–74.

Fig. 20.2, to show the opportunities for using developments in IT to improve the efficiency and effectiveness of payroll processing.

Update Payroll Master File

The first activity in the HRM/payroll cycle involves updating the payroll master file to reflect various types of payroll changes: new hires, terminations, changes in pay rates, or changes in discretionary withholdings (circle 1.0 in Fig. 20.2). This information is provided by the HRM department. Although payroll is processed in batch mode, Fig. 20.3 shows that the HRM department has on-

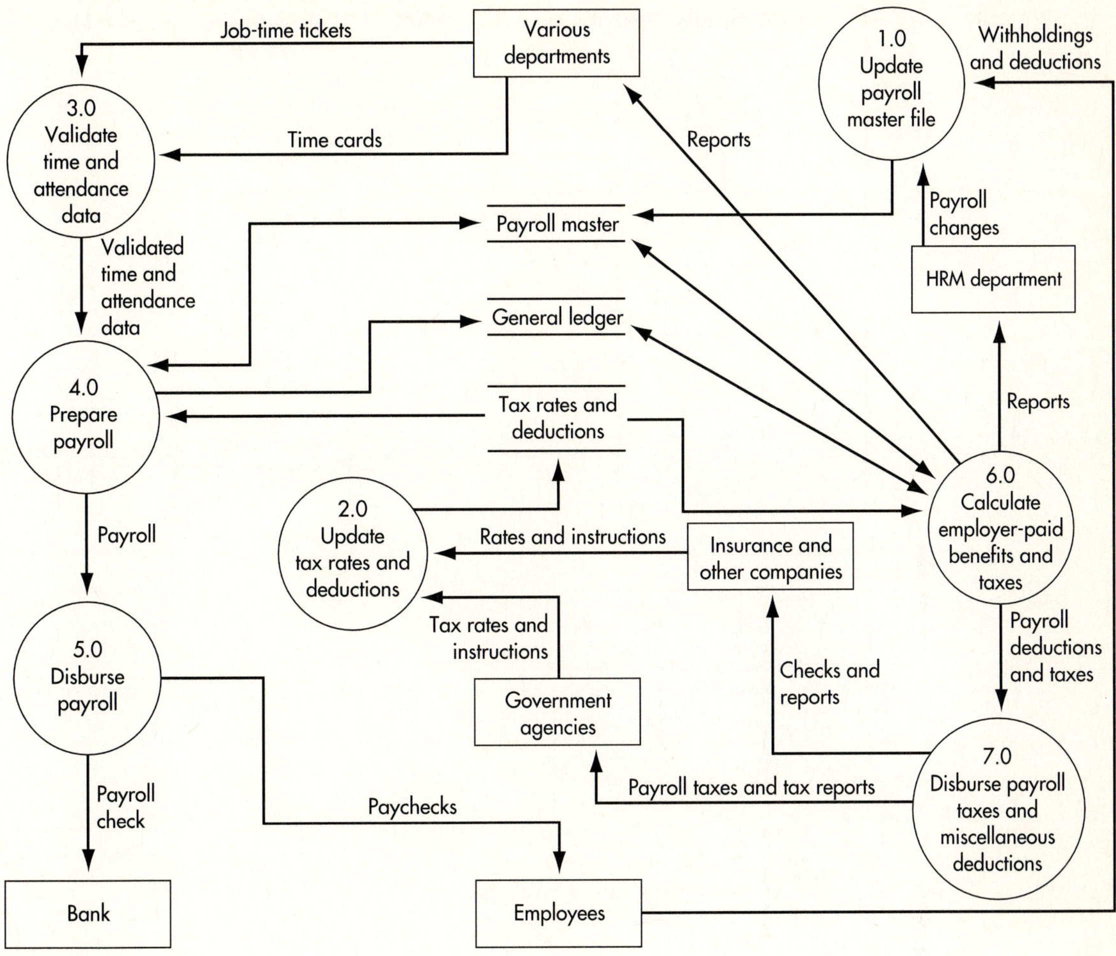

Figure 20.2

Level 0 DFD for Payroll Cycle

line access to make these changes to the payroll master file. Appropriate edit checks, such as validity checks on employee number and reasonableness tests for the changes being made, are applied to all payroll change transactions.

It is important that all payroll changes are entered in a timely manner and are properly reflected in the next pay period. Records of employees who quit or are fired should not be deleted immediately, however, because some year-end reports require data about all employees who worked for the organization at any time during the year.

Update Tax Rates and Deductions

The second activity in the HRM/payroll cycle involves updating information about tax rates and other withholdings (circle 2.0 in Fig. 20.2). These changes are made by the payroll department but are not shown in Fig. 20.3 because they occur infrequently. They happen whenever updates about changes in tax rates and other payroll deductions are received from various government units and insurance companies.

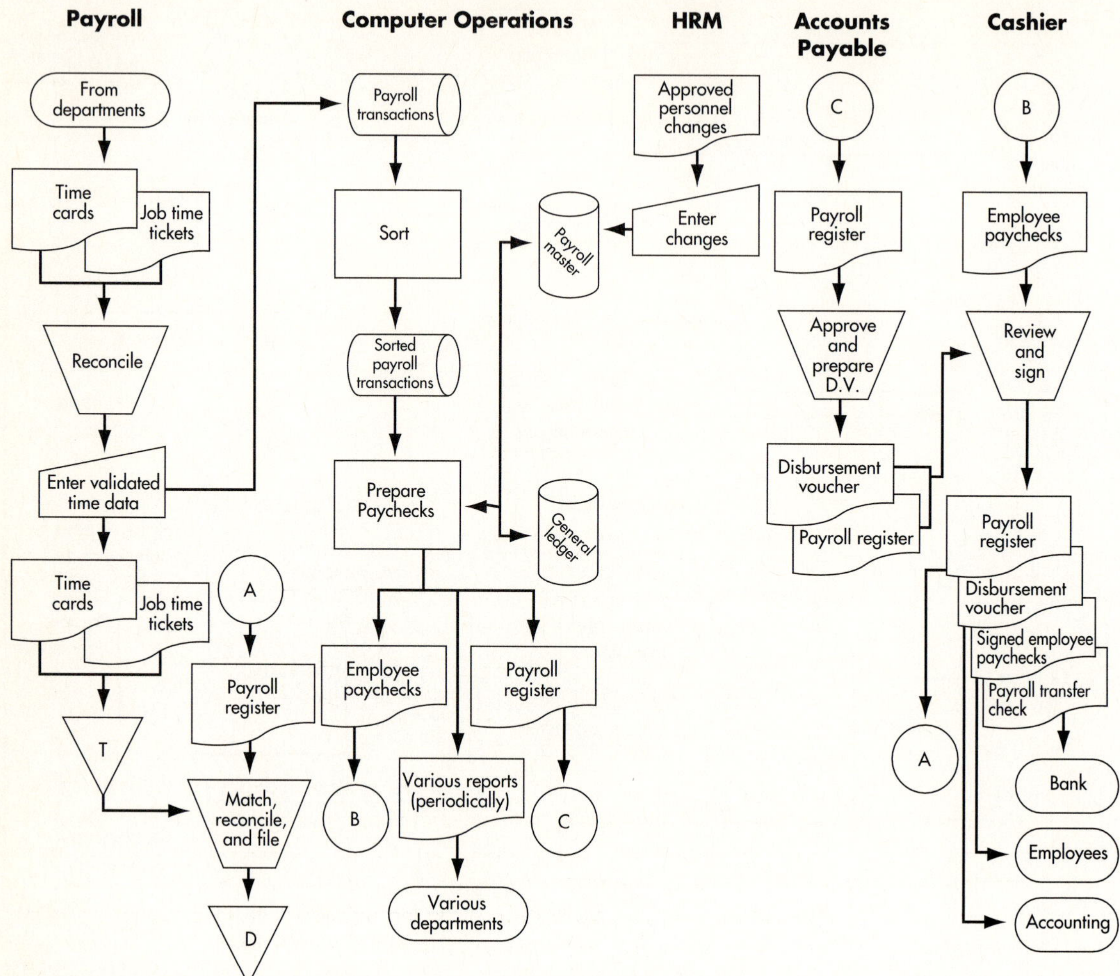

Figure 20.3

Flowchart of Payroll System—Batch Processing at AOE

Validate Time and Attendance Data

The third step in the payroll cycle is to validate each employee's time and attendance data (circle 3.0 in Fig. 20.2). This information comes in various forms, depending upon an employee's pay status.

Pay Schemes. For those paid on an hourly basis, most companies use an employee **time card,** which records the employee's arrival and departure times for each work shift and totals the hours worked during a pay period. As discussed in Chapter 19, manufacturing companies also use job time tickets to record data about the time spent on each job. This data is used to allocate labor costs among various departments, cost centers, and production jobs. The total hours on the job time ticket should equal those on the time card. The reconciliation of these two documents is an important control function performed by the payroll system.

Employees who are paid a fixed salary, such as managers and professional staff, seldom record their labor efforts on time cards. Instead, their presence on the job is usually informally monitored by their supervisors. Professionals in many service organizations, such as accounting, law, and consulting firms, usually self-report the time they spend on each client. This data is the basis for billing clients.

Sales staff often are paid either on a straight commission or on a salary plus commission basis. This requires careful recording of the amount of sales made by each employee. In addition, some sales staff are paid bonuses for exceeding targets. Increasingly, U.S. companies are extending the use of such incentive bonuses to employees other than sales staff, in order to motivate greater productivity and better work quality. For example, Nucor Corporation, one of the largest steel producers in the United States, pays its steel workers an hourly rate set at approximately 60% of the industry average, plus a bonus based on the tons of steel produced and shipped.

The use of incentives and bonuses requires that the payroll system and the information systems of sales and other cycles be linked in order to collect the data used to calculate bonuses. Moreover, as Focus 20.2 shows, if they are to be effective, bonus incentive systems must be carefully designed.

Indeed, poorly designed incentive pay schemes can result in undesirable behavior. For example, when Highland SuperStores, a consumer electronics and appliance chain, adopted a new incentive plan for its sales staff, its salespeople became overly aggressive and alienated many customers. Eventually, the incentive plan had to be drastically changed. Similarly, Sears Automotive experienced unintended negative effects from implementing a new incentive plan. In the early 1990s it instituted an incentive system that paid its repair staff a commission based on the amount of parts sold and labor performed. The intent was to focus employee attention on how their efforts affected the company's bottom line. The result, however, was a scandal in which it was alleged that Sears employees recommended unnecessary repairs in order to boost their own pay. The alleged abuses reduced public trust in Sears Automotive and led to lower revenues. Wisely, Sears finally abandoned this incentive system.

The experiences of Highland and Sears do not mean that all incentive pay plans are problematic. Indeed, as discussed earlier, companies like Nucor have successfully used incentive pay schemes to boost productivity and profits. In designing such plans, however, it is important to think carefully about how the incentive scheme can affect employee behavior.

Procedures. Figure 20.3 shows that the payroll department is responsible for validating employee time records. For factory workers, validation involves comparing the total time worked, as recorded on the time cards, with the time spent on each job, as recorded on the job time tickets. The payroll clerk calculates batch totals, such as record counts and hash totals of hours worked, and enters them along with the time data. The batch totals are recalculated by the computer after subsequent processing steps, to ensure that payroll is processed for all employees.

Payroll transaction data are entered through on-line terminals. This enables errors to be detected at the time the data are being entered. The

FOCUS 20.2

Designing Effective Bonus Pay Schemes

Executive compensation has long included bonuses and incentives linked to corporate performance. Increasingly, companies are beginning to extend such plans to all their employees. In 1988 slightly over half of medium- and large-sized U.S. companies had some form of incentive or bonus pay scheme for their nonsales staff employees; by 1994 this number had jumped to almost 66%. The major objective of extending bonus pay plans beyond the executive level is to motivate *all* employees to increase their productivity and quality.

Incentive pay schemes can be quite effective. For example, after Xel Communications, a Colorado manufacturer of telecommunications equipment, implemented an incentive system that included team-based goals, such as improving on-time delivery, average production time dropped from 30 days to three. Novadyne Computer Company implemented an incentive plan to encourage its service engineers to solicit continuing maintenance contracts while providing on-site repair calls. In its second year, the program brought in over $800,000 of additional revenue. One of the greatest success stories involving the use of incentive plans is Nucor Corporation. The North Carolina–based company, which began making steel in the 1970s, credits its success in becoming the fifth-largest U.S. steel producer to the fact that all of its employees, whether they work in the factory or the office, are covered by some form of incentive pay.

The key to achieving such success, however, depends on how the incentive plan is designed. To be effective, an incentive pay scheme should have the following characteristics:

1. *Attainable goals.* Unrealistic targets can reduce morale and performance.
2. *Controllable goals.* Employees must believe their efforts will influence achievement of the established goal. For example, Monsanto Company faced resistance when it tried to link incentives for factory workers to overall plant financial performance, because that factor was affected by too many things beyond the direct control of the employees.
3. *Goals congruent with corporate objectives.* Incentive plans must be designed to motivate the appropriate behavior. For example, linking bonuses to plant safety measures could encourage employees to cover up any on-site accidents or injuries. Similarly, basing bonuses on individual or work-cell output in a JIT manufacturing plant is counter to the JIT philosophy of maximizing throughput and minimizing work in process. To combat this, Nucor rewards production work cells on the basis of tonnage actually shipped to customers.
4. *Measurable goals.* It can be difficult to quantify productivity for many office tasks. One approach, adopted by companies like American Express and GTE, is to survey customer satisfaction periodically. Although such measures may be subjective, they at least provide some basis for measuring performance.
5. *Periodic review of goals.* In accordance with TQM philosophy, performance goals need periodic increases in order to achieve additional productivity gains. Change must be done in a manner, however, that does not create unrealistic expectations regarding base standards. Otherwise, employees may be motivated to produce at a level near existing standards so that those standards are not raised.

Focus Questions

1. Do you think that bonus incentives can be used to motivate improved productivity for accounting staff? Why or why not?
2. How can the productivity of accounting activities, such as processing purchase orders and expense reimbursements, be measured?
3. What changes will probably need to be made to a company's existing HRM/payroll system to collect and process the data used in incentive plans?

Sources: Howard Gleckman, Sandra Atchison, Tim Smart, and John A. Byrne, "Bonus Pay: Buzzword or Bonanza?" *Business Week* (November 14, 1994): 62–64; Gillian Flynn, "Non-sales Staffs Respond to Incentives," *Personnel Journal* (July 1994): 33–38.

edit checks performed on each time and attendance record include the following:

- *Field checks* for numeric data in the employee number and hours worked fields.
- *Limit checks* on the hours worked field.
- *Range checks* on pay rates.
- *A validity check* of the employee number.

Opportunities for Using Information Technology. Payroll processing can be made more efficient by collecting employee time and attendance data electronically, instead of on paper documents. This can reduce the time, and potential errors, associated with manually recording, verifying, and finally entering employee time and attendance data. For example, badge readers can be used to collect job time data for production employees. Those data are then automatically fed to the payroll processing system. Similarly, electronic timeclocks can transmit time and attendance data directly to the payroll processing program. As discussed in Chapter 19, AOE is planning to implement these techniques to automate collection of time and attendance data for its factory workers.

Similar procedures can be used for professional service staff. For example, AT&T's internal service staff use touch-tone telephones to log in time spent on various tasks, thereby eliminating the use of paper time sheets. The payroll program applies edit checks to verify the accuracy, and reasonableness, of the data at the time it is entered.

Prepare Payroll

The fourth step in the payroll cycle involves preparing payroll (circle 4.0 in Fig. 20.2). Data about the hours worked are provided by the department in which the employee works and usually are confirmed or "signed off" by his or her direct supervisor. Pay rate information is obtained from the payroll master file. As shown in Fig. 20.3, this information can be updated only by the HRM department. Thus file maintenance (updating the payroll master file) is performed by someone other than the person responsible for actual transaction processing (payroll preparation). This separation of duties helps to prevent payments being made to nonexistent workers. Paychecks can be prepared only for employees who are listed in the payroll master file, but the person responsible for preparing paychecks cannot add new records to this file.

Procedures. Figure 20.3 shows that payroll processing is performed in the computer operations department. First, the payroll transaction file is sorted by employee number, so that it is in the same sequence as the payroll master file. If the organization is processing payrolls from several divisions, each of these payroll transaction files must also be merged (this step is not shown in Fig. 20.3).

The sorted time data file is then used to prepare employee paychecks. For each employee, the payroll master file record and corresponding transaction record are read and gross pay is calculated. For hourly employees, this process involves multiplying the number of hours worked by the wage rate and then adding any applicable premiums for overtime or bonuses. For salaried employees, gross pay is a fraction of the annual salary, where the fraction reflects the length of the pay period. For example, a salaried employee paid monthly would receive one-twelfth of his or her annual salary each pay period.

Next, all payroll deductions are summed and the total is subtracted from gross pay to obtain net pay. Payroll deductions fall into two broad categories: payroll tax withholdings and voluntary deductions. The former include federal, state, and local income taxes, as well as Social Security taxes. Voluntary deductions include contributions to a pension plan; premiums for group life, health, and disability insurance; union dues; and contributions to various charities.

At this time the year-to-date fields for gross pay, deductions, and net pay in each employee's record in the payroll master file are updated. Maintaining accurate cumulative earnings records is important for two reasons. First, because Social Security tax withholdings and other deductions have cutoffs, the company must know when to cease deductions for individual employees. Second, this information is needed to ensure that the appropriate amounts of taxes and other deductions are remitted to government agencies, insurance companies, and other organizations (such as the United Way). In addition, this information needs to be included in the various reports that must be filed with those entities.

Finally, the payroll register and employee paychecks are printed. The **payroll register** is a report that lists each employee's gross pay, payroll deductions, and net pay in a multicolumn format; it is often accompanied by a separate **deduction register,** which lists the miscellaneous voluntary deduc-

Figure 20.4

Sample Payroll and Deduction Registers

Alpha Omega Electronics				**PAYROLL REGISTER**				**Period Ended 12/03/97**	
					Deductions				
Employee No.	Name	Hours	Pay Rate	Gross Pay	Fed. Tax	FICA	State Tax	Misc.	Net Pay
37884	Jarvis	40.0	6.25	250.00	35.60	18.75	16.25	27.60	151.80
37885	Burke	43.6	6.50	295.10	42.40	22.13	19.18	40.15	171.24
37886	Lincoln	40.0	6.75	270.00	39.20	20.25	17.55	27.90	165.10
37887	Douglass	44.2	7.00	324.10	46.60	24.31	21.07	29.62	202.50

Alpha Omega Electronics			**DEDUCTION REGISTER**		**Period Ended 12/03/97**	
		Miscellaneous Deductions					
Employee No.	Name	Health Ins.	Life Ins.	Retirement	Union Dues	Savings Bond	Total Misc.
37884	Jarvis	10.40	5.50	7.50	4.20	0.00	27.60
37885	Burke	11.60	5.50	8.85	4.20	10.00	40.15
37886	Lincoln	10.40	5.20	8.10	4.20	0.00	27.90
37887	Douglass	10.20	5.50	9.72	4.20	0.00	29.62

Table 20.1 **Examples of Commonly Generated HRM/Payroll Cycle Reports**

Report Name	Contents	Purpose
Cumulative earnings register	Cumulative year-to-date gross pay, net pay, and deductions for each employee	Used for employee information and annual payroll reports
Work force inventory	List of employees by department	Used in preparing labor-related reports for government agencies
Position control report	List of each authorized position, job qualifications, budgeted salary, and position status (filled or vacant)	Used in planning future work force needs
Skills inventory report	List of employees and current skills	Useful in planning future work force needs and training programs
Form 941	Employer's quarterly federal tax return (showing all wages subject to tax and amounts withheld for income tax and FICA)	Filed quarterly
Form W-2	Report of wages and withholdings for each employee	Sent to each employee for use in preparing their individual tax returns; due by January 31
Form W-3	Summary of all W-2 forms	Sent to federal government along with a copy of all W-2 forms; due by February 28
Form 1099-Misc.	Report of income paid to independent contractors	Sent to recipients of income for use in filing their income tax returns; due by January 31
Various other reports to government agencies	Data on compliance with various regulatory provisions, state and local tax reports, etc.	To document compliance with applicable regulations

tions for each employee. Figure 20.4 provides examples of both reports. The payroll register is also used to authorize the transfer of funds to the company's payroll bank account. Employee paychecks also typically include an earnings statement. The **earnings statement** lists the amount of gross pay, deductions, and net pay for the current period, as well as year-to-date totals for each category.

As each payroll transaction is processed, the system also allocates labor costs to the appropriate general ledger accounts by checking the code on the job-time ticket record. The system maintains a running total of these allocations until all employee payroll records have been processed. These totals, along with the column totals in the payroll register, form the basis for the summary journal entry, which is posted to the general ledger after all paychecks have been printed. Table 20.1 describes some of the additional reports produced by the payroll system.

Opportunities for Using Information Technology. One way to cut costs and improve efficiency is to produce and distribute payroll reports electronically,

FOCUS 20.3

Automating the Human Resources Function at Merck

ATM machines are a familiar sight in many office buildings. At Merck & Company's headquarters in Whitehouse Station, New Jersey, however, there are two similar-looking machines in the lobby. One is an ATM, but the other is actually part of Merck's human resources management function. This second machine currently allows employees to enroll in various fringe benefit plans. Most transactions, such as checking current benefits levels or selecting health care providers, are handled simply by pushing buttons or touching the video screen to select among choices. For those transactions that require signatures, such as changes in withholding allowances, the machine prints a form for the employee to sign.

Merck has installed two dozen of these HRM machines at its various U.S. locations in an effort to control corporate overhead costs. The transition began in 1990, when Merck decided to offer a flexible benefits plan. Merck estimated that enrolling its 15,500 salaried employees in the new plan would have required hiring 20 additional staff to process the related paperwork. Instead, it decided to invest $1 million in writing software and installing machines to automate the task. The plan worked—Merck was able to make the switch in benefits plans and increase service quality to employees without increasing the size of its existing HRM staff.

Merck intends to expand this system even further. It plans to link the machines electronically to the various mutual funds participating in Merck's 401(k) plan, so that employees can directly reallocate their retirement investments. Merck also plans to put internal job postings on the system, thereby eliminating the time and costs associated with paper postings.

Focus Questions

1. What kinds of human resources tasks are best suited for automation? Which human resources tasks will most likely continue to be performed by people?
2. What control threats do such automated employee benefits systems, such as those being used at Merck, create? What control procedures are needed to mitigate those threats?

Source: Carolyn T. Geer, "For a New Job, Press #1," *Forbes* (August 15, 1994): 118–119.

rather than on paper. In addition, IT can also be used to improve employee access to their benefits and earnings records. For example, employees at Sears can use the telephone to find out about their current benefits options and make changes in withholdings, profit sharing, and medical coverage. Employees at Federal Express can make similar changes through on-line terminals. As explained in Focus 20.3, providing such capabilities to employees improves the quality and reduces the costs of HRM services.

Disburse Payroll

The next step is actual disbursement of paychecks to employees (circle 5.0 in Fig. 20.2). Most employees are paid either by check or by direct deposit of the net pay amount into the employee's bank account because, unlike cash payments, both methods provide a means to document the amount of wages paid.

Procedures. Figure 20.3 shows that once paychecks have been prepared, the payroll register is sent to the accounts payable department for review and approval. A disbursement voucher is then prepared to authorize the transfer of funds from the company's general checking account to its payroll bank account. Payroll checks should not be drawn on the organization's regular bank account. Instead, for control purposes, a separate payroll bank account should be used. This limits the company's loss exposure to the amount of cash in the separate payroll account.

The disbursement voucher and payroll register are then sent to the cashier. The cashier reviews the payroll register and disbursement voucher and then prepares and signs a check transferring funds to the company's payroll bank account. The cashier also reviews, signs, and distributes the employee paychecks. Thus the duties of authorizing and recording payroll transactions are segregated from the actual distribution of paychecks. Any unclaimed paychecks are promptly redeposited in the company's bank account by the cashier. As an added control to prevent the creation and distribution of fraudulent paychecks, a list of unclaimed paychecks is sent to the internal audit department for further investigation.

Finally, the payroll register is returned to the payroll department, where it is filed by date along with the time cards and job time tickets. The disbursement voucher is sent to the accounting clerk who uses it to update the general ledger.

Opportunities for Using Information Technology. Direct deposit is one way to improve the efficiency and reduce the costs of payroll processing. Employees who are paid by direct deposit generally receive a copy of the paycheck indicating the amount deposited along with an earnings statement. The payroll system must generate a series of payroll deposit files, one for each bank through which payroll deposits are made. Each file contains a record for each employee whose account is maintained at a particular bank. Each record includes the employee's name, Social Security number, bank account number, and net pay amount. These files are sent electronically, using EDI, to each participating bank. The funds are then electronically transferred from the employer's bank account to the employee's. Thus direct deposit eliminates the need for the cashier to sign individual payroll checks. The cashier does, however, have to authorize the release of funds from the organization's regular checking account.

Direct deposit provides several cost savings to employers. First, the cost of purchasing, processing, and distributing paper checks is eliminated. Second, bank fees and postage expenses are reduced. Third, payroll bank reconciliations can be done more quickly. These savings are partially offset by the loss of "float," which represents the employer's use of the funds between the time the checks are drawn and when they are presented for payment. On balance, however, the savings associated with direct deposit generally exceed its costs; consequently, most companies now offer their employees the option of direct deposit payment and encourage them to elect this form of payment.

Payroll Service Bureaus. Another way to reduce payroll processing costs is by outsourcing this function to a payroll service bureau. A **payroll service bureau** maintains the payroll master file for each of its clients and performs the payroll processing activities described in this section. At the end of each pay period, each client sends time and attendance data to the payroll service bureau, along with information about personnel changes. The payroll service bureau uses that data to prepare employee paychecks, earnings statements, and a payroll register. It also periodically produces employee W-2 forms and other tax-related reports.

Payroll service bureaus are especially attractive to small and medium-sized businesses, for the following reasons:

- *Reduced costs.* Payroll service bureaus benefit from the economies of scale associated with preparing paychecks for a large number of companies. They can charge fees that are typically less than the cost of doing payroll in-house. The use of a payroll service bureau also saves a company money by eliminating the need to develop and maintain the expertise needed to comply with the constantly changing tax laws.
- *Privacy.* To prevent potential morale problems, many companies do not want employees to know the salaries of their co-workers. Use of a payroll service bureau provides increased control over access to payroll data.
- *Freeing up of computer resources.* The use of a payroll service bureau eliminates a major AIS application: payroll. The freed up computing resources can then be used to improve service in other areas, such as sales order entry.

The major drawback associated with the use of a payroll service bureau is the difficulty of fully integrating the payroll system with the HRM system. Thus, as the number of employees grows, the cost and time required to prepare management reports on the utilization of human resources increases. Consequently, many large organizations continue to process payroll in-house.

Calculate Employer-Paid Benefits and Taxes

Some payroll taxes and employee benefits are paid directly by the employer (circle 6.0 in Fig. 20.2). For example, employers must pay Social Security taxes, in addition to the amounts withheld from employee paychecks. Circular E, the Employer's Tax Guide published by the IRS, provides detailed instructions about an employer's obligations for withholding and remitting payroll taxes and for filing various reports.

Federal and state laws also require employers to contribute a specified percentage of each employee's gross pay, up to a maximum annual limit, to federal and state unemployment compensation insurance funds. In addition, employers often contribute some or all of the amounts to pay for their employees' health, disability, and life insurance premiums. Many companies also offer their employees **flexible benefit plans,** under which each employee receives some minimum coverage in medical insurance and pension contributions, plus additional benefit "credits" that can be used to acquire extra vacation time or additional health insurance. These plans are sometimes called cafeteria-style benefit plans because they offer a menu of options. Finally, many employers offer and contribute toward a choice of retirement savings plans.

Providing these additional services and benefits places increased demands on a company's HRM/payroll system. For example, the HRM staff of a large company with thousands of employees can spend a considerable amount of time just responding to 401(k) plan inquiries. Moreover, employees want to be able to make changes in their investment decisions on a timely basis. The use of information technology, such as that discussed in Focus 20.3, provides a means to satisfy employee demands for such service without increasing costs.

Disburse Payroll Taxes and Miscellaneous Deductions

The final activity in the payroll process involves paying the payroll tax liabilities and the other voluntary deductions of each employee (circle 7.0 in Fig. 20.2). An organization must periodically prepare checks or use electronic funds transfer to pay the various tax liabilities incurred. The timing of these payments is specified by the respective government agencies. In addition, the funds voluntarily withheld from each employee's paycheck for various benefits, such as a payroll savings plan, must be disbursed to the appropriate organizations.

CONTROL OBJECTIVES, THREATS, AND PROCEDURES

A second major function of the AIS in the HRM/payroll cycle is to provide adequate internal controls to ensure meeting the following objectives:

1. All payroll transactions are properly authorized.
2. All recorded payroll transactions are valid.
3. All valid, authorized payroll transactions are recorded.
4. All payroll transactions are accurately recorded.
5. Applicable government regulations regarding remittance of taxes and filing of payroll and HRM reports are met.
6. Assets (both cash and data) are safeguarded from loss or theft.
7. HRM/payroll cycle activities are performed efficiently and effectively.

The various documents and records (e.g., time cards, payroll register) described in the previous section play an important role in achieving these objectives. Simple, easy-to-complete documents with clear instructions facilitate the accurate and efficient recording of payroll transactions. The use of appropriate application controls, such as validity checks and field (format) checks, further increases the accuracy of data entry when using electronic documents. Providing space on both paper and electronic documents to record who completed and who reviewed the form provides evidence that the transaction was properly authorized. Finally, prenumbering all documents facilitates checking to verify that all transactions have been recorded.

Table 20.2 lists the major threats in the HRM/payroll cycle and the applicable control procedures for mitigating those threats. Every company, regardless of its line of business, faces these threats. Therefore it is important to understand how the AIS can be best designed to counter them.

Threat 1: Hiring of Unqualified or Larcenous Employees

Hiring unqualified employees can increase production expenses; hiring a larcenous employee can result in the theft of assets. Both threats are best dealt with by appropriate hiring procedures. Skill qualifications for each open position should be stated explicitly in the position control report. Job applicants' skills and references, including possession of college degrees, should be verified. Particular attention should be directed to determining why a job applicant left a previous place of employment.

Threat 2: Violation of Employment Law

The government imposes stiff penalties on firms that violate provisions of employment law. In addition, organizations can also be subject to civil suits by alleged victims of employment discrimination. In this case, the best control procedure is careful documentation of all actions involved in advertising,

Table 20.2 **Threats, Exposures, and Control Procedures in the HRM/Payroll Cycle**

Threat	Exposure	Control Procedures
1. Hiring of unqualified or larcenous employees	Increased expenses Lower productivity Theft	Sound hiring practices, including verification of job applicants' skills, references, and employment history
2. Violation of employment law	Fines Civil suits	Thorough documentation of hiring procedures
3. Unauthorized changes to the master payroll file	Increased expenses Inaccurate records and reports Loss of assets (cash)	Segregation of duties Access controls
4. Inaccurate time data	Incorrect expenses and internal reports Over/underpayment of employees	Automation of data collection Application controls Reconciliation of time card and job time tickets
5. Inaccurate processing of payroll	Inaccurate records and poor decision making Penalties for violation of tax law Reduced morale, if all employees not paid	Batch totals and other application controls Payroll clearing account
6. Theft or fraudulent distribution of paychecks	Increased expenses Loss of assets (cash)	Direct deposit Paycheck distribution by someone independent of payroll process Investigation of all unclaimed paychecks Restricted access to blank paychecks Prenumbering and periodic accounting for all paychecks Separate payroll checking account, run as an imprest fund Independent reconciliation of the payroll bank account
7. Loss or unauthorized disclosure of payroll data	Loss of assets Reduced morale Employee lawsuits	Access controls Backup procedures Encryption

recruiting, and hiring new employees in order to demonstrate compliance with the applicable government regulations.

Threat 3: Unauthorized Changes to the Payroll Master File

Unauthorized changes to the payroll master file can result in increased expenses if wages, salaries, commissions, or other base rates used to determine employee compensation are falsified. These problems also result in inaccurate reports on labor costs, which, in turn, can lead to erroneous decisions.

Proper segregation of duties is the key control procedure for dealing with this threat. As shown in Fig. 20.3, only the HRM department should be able to update the payroll master file for hirings, firings, pay raises, and promotions. This restriction prevents someone with access to paychecks from creating fictitious employees or altering pay rates and then intercepting those fraudulent checks. In addition, all changes to the payroll master file should be reviewed and approved by someone other than the person recommending the change. Traditionally, such approval has involved reading and signing a transaction document. For changes processed through on-line terminals, the system must be designed to verify the identity and authority of the persons making and approving the request. A report documenting these changes should also be sent to each department supervisor for review.

Controlling access to the payroll system is also important. Indeed, in a data base environment, access controls are vital because many previously separate functions are now performed solely by the system. The system should be programmed to compare user IDs and passwords to an access control matrix that (1) defines what actions each employee is allowed to perform and (2) confirms what files he or she is allowed to access. Payroll clerks, for example, should not be permitted to change employee pay rates.

Threat 4: Inaccurate Time Data

Inaccuracies in time and attendance records can result in increased labor expenses and erroneous labor expense reports. Moreover, inaccuracies can either hurt employee morale (if paychecks are incorrect or missing) or result in payments for labor services not rendered. Automation can reduce the risk of unintentional inaccuracies in time data. Badge readers and bar-code scanners can be used to collect data on employee time and attendance in machine-readable form. If their use is not feasible, on-line terminals should be utilized. The data entry program should include a variety of edit checks, including:

- Validity checks on employee numbers.
- Limit checks on hours worked.
- Reasonableness tests of production data, such as comparing the quantity produced with the master production schedule.

Proper segregation of duties can reduce the risk of intentional inaccuracies. Reconciliations are also useful. Job-time ticket data should be reconciled with employee time cards. The total time spent on all tasks, as recorded on the job-time tickets, should not exceed the attendance time indicated on an employee's time card. Conversely, all time spent at work should be accounted for on the job-time tickets. In addition, time cards and job-time tickets should be approved by the employee's supervisor.

Threat 5: Inaccurate Processing of Payroll

The complexity of payroll processing, especially the various tax law requirements, makes it susceptible to errors. In addition to incorrect payroll expense records and reports, processing errors can lead to penalties if the errors result in failure to remit the proper amount of payroll taxes due the government. They can also reduce employee morale if the error results in a late or reduced paycheck.

Three types of control procedures address this threat:

1. *Batch totals.* Even advanced HRM/payroll systems will continue to use batch processing for payroll. Consequently, batch totals should be calculated at the time of data entry and then checked against comparable totals

calculated during each stage of processing. Hash totals of employee numbers, for example, are particularly useful. If the original and subsequent hash totals of employee numbers agree, it means that (1) all payroll records have been processed, (2) data input was accurate, and (3) no bogus time cards were entered during processing.

2. *Cross-footing the payroll register.* The total of the net pay column should equal the total of gross pay less total deductions.
3. *A payroll clearing account.* The **payroll clearing account** is a general ledger account that is used in a two-step process to check the accuracy and completeness of recording payroll costs and their subsequent allocation to appropriate cost centers. First, the payroll control account is debited for the amount of gross pay; cash is credited for the amount of net pay, and the various withholdings are credited to separate liability accounts. Second, the cost accounting process distributes labor costs to various expense categories and credits the payroll control account for the sum of these allocations. The amount credited to the payroll control account should equal the amount it was previously debited when net pay and the various withholdings were recorded. This particular internal check is called a **zero balance check** because the payroll control account should equal zero once both entries have been posted.

The tax status of workers should be properly classified as either employees or independent contractors, because misclassification can cause companies to owe substantial back taxes, interest, and even penalties. This issue often arises when department managers attempt to circumvent a general hiring freeze by using "independent contractors." Any decisions to hire "outside" help should always be reviewed by the HRM department. The IRS provides a checklist of questions that can be used to determine whether a worker should be classified as an employee or an independent contractor.

Threat 6: Theft or Fraudulent Distribution of Paychecks

Another major threat is the theft of paychecks or the issuance of paychecks to fictitious or terminated employees. This can result in increased expenses and the loss of cash. Proper segregation of duties relating to the preparation and distribution of paychecks can reduce the risk of this threat.

Payroll Check Writing Controls. The controls related to other cash disbursements, discussed in Chapter 18, also apply to payroll:

- Access to blank payroll checks and to the check signature machine should be restricted.
- All payroll checks should be sequentially prenumbered and periodically accounted for.
- The cashier should sign all payroll checks only when supported by proper documentation (the payroll register and disbursement voucher).
- The payroll bank account should be reconciled by someone independent of the payroll process.

The use of a separate payroll bank account provides additional protection against forgery or alteration by limiting the total amount of cash at risk. This account should be operated as an imprest fund; that is, the amount of the check written to replenish the fund should equal the amount of net pay for that period. Thus, when all paychecks have been cashed, the payroll account should have a zero balance. The use of a separate payroll checking account also makes it easier to spot any fraudulent checks when the account is reconciled.

Paycheck Distribution Controls. Paychecks should be distributed by someone who is not involved in authorizing or recording payroll. To see why this segregation of duties is so important, assume that the person responsible for hiring and firing employees also distributes paychecks. This combination of duties could enable that person to conveniently "forget" to report the termination of an employee and subsequently keep that employee's future paychecks. Additional control over paycheck distribution is provided by requiring that the person distributing paychecks positively identify each person picking up a paycheck. Furthermore, the paycheck distribution process should be observed periodically by the internal audit department.

Special procedures should be used to handle unclaimed paychecks, because they indicate the possibility of a problem, such as a nonexistent or terminated employee. Unclaimed paychecks should be returned to the treasurer's office for prompt redeposit. They should also be traced back to time records and matched against the employee master payroll file to verify that they are indeed legitimate.

Threat 7: Loss or Unauthorized Disclosure of Data

The HRM/payroll data base is a valuable resource that must be protected from loss or destruction. It is also important to protect the privacy of employee data. For example, morale may suffer if employees learn the salaries of other workers. In addition, unauthorized disclosure of performance evaluation data may subject the organization to lawsuits.

The best control procedure for reducing the risk of unauthorized disclosure of payroll data is the use of passwords and physical security controls to restrict access to authorized persons. Encryption provides additional control by making HRM/payroll information unintelligible to anyone who succeeds in obtaining unauthorized access to the payroll master file. The use of a payroll service bureau also mitigates this threat.

Backup and disaster recovery procedures provide the best controls for reducing the risk of payroll data loss. Both internal and external file labels should be used to ensure that the data base is not inadvertently erased or processed by the wrong program. Backup copies of the payroll master file and recent transaction files should be created; one should be stored on-site, the other off-site.

KEY DECISIONS, INFORMATION NEEDS, AND A DATA MODEL

The previous two sections discussed how the AIS fulfilled the functions of processing payroll transactions and providing controls to safeguard assets. A third function of the AIS in the payroll/HRM cycle is to provide information for managing business activities. The traditional payroll system was designed primarily to meet the needs of external decision makers. Investors, creditors, and various government agencies were generally satisfied with information about a company's periodic salary expenses. As mentioned earlier, however, banks and other external users are beginning to demand additional information about a company's human resources. In response, as Focus 20.1 indicates, some companies are beginning to include more detailed information about their human resources in their annual reports.

Designing the payroll system to satisfy the needs of external users, however, does not ensure the production of all the information management needs to use and develop the company's human resources. Instead, the payroll system must be designed to collect and integrate cost data with other types of information in order to enable management to make the following kinds of decisions:

- *Future work force staffing needs.* How many employees are needed in the next five years to accomplish the organization's strategic plans? Which employees possess the needed skills? Which skills are in short supply? Which skills are in oversupply? How effective are current training programs in maintaining and improving employee skill levels?
- *Employee performance.* Which employees should be promoted or receive pay raises? Which should be discharged? Is overall performance improving or declining? Is turnover excessive? Is tardiness or absenteeism a problem?
- *Employee morale.* What is the overall level of employee morale and job satisfaction? How can the compensation scheme be used to improve morale, satisfaction, and performance? What additional fringe benefits, if any, should be offered?
- *Payroll processing efficiency and effectiveness.* How frequently should employees be paid? Are labor costs being accurately allocated to products and other cost centers? Are all applicable tax reporting requirements being met? How easily can employee requests for information be answered?

Some of the information needed to answer these questions, such as data about labor costs, has traditionally been provided by the payroll system. Other information, such as data about employee skills, has normally been provided and maintained by the HRM system. Still other information, such as data about employee morale, has traditionally not been collected by either the payroll or the HRM system. Finally, note that externally generated information, such as data about tax rates and industry averages for turnover and absenteeism, is also needed to make these decisions. Let us now examine how a well-designed data model facilitates the effective integration of all this information.

Data Model

Figure 20.5 presents a partial REA data model for the HRM/payroll cycle. Notice the importance of the employees entity—it is linked to almost every other entity in the diagram.

If the data model depicted in Fig. 20.5 were implemented in a relational data base, there would be a table for each entity (box) and for each many-to-many relationship. In addition, to improve internal control, there would be a separate table for the relationship between the Services_Provided and Pay_Employees events. (This arrangement ensures that updates to the latter table do not require any additional changes to the former table, as would be the case if the relationship were implemented by including the primary key of the Pay_Employee event as a foreign key in the Services_Provided table.) Figure

Figure 20.5

Partial REA Data Model for the HRM/Payroll Cycle

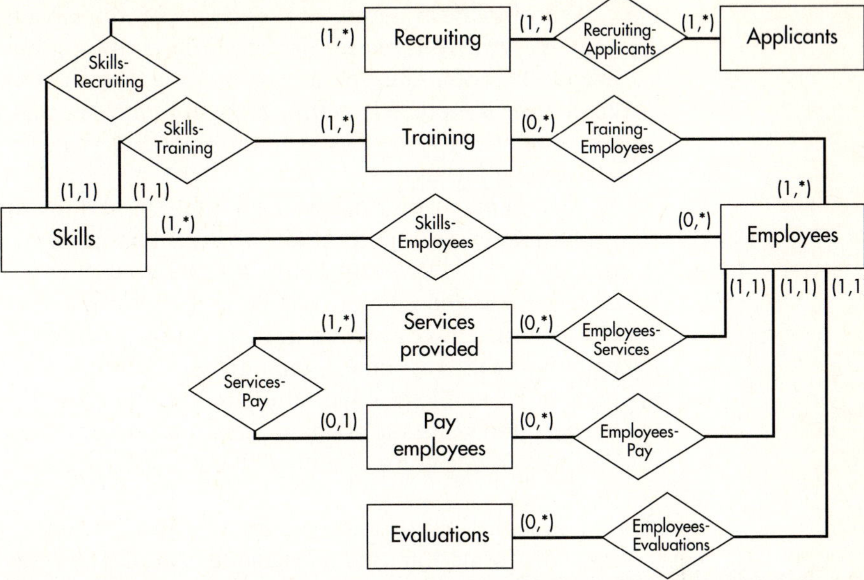

Table Attributes for Figure 20.5

Table Name	Contents (**primary key,** *foreign key*)
Skills	**Skill_Number,** Description, Pay_Rate, . . .
Recruiting	**Event_Number**, Date, Media, *Skillnumber*, . . .
Training	**Course_number,** Date, *Skill_Number*, Location, *Trainer_Number*, Cost, . . .
Services provided	**Pay_Period,** *Employee Number*, Regular_Hours, Overtime_Hours, . . .
Pay_Employees	**Paycheck_Number,** Date, *Employee_Number*, Gross_Pay, Deductions, Net Pay, . . .
Evaluations	**Evaluation_Number,** *Employee_Number*, Date, Comments
Applicants	**Applicant_Number,** Name, Address, . . .
Employees	**Employee_Number,** Name, Title, Date_Hired, Position, Pay_Rate, Marital Status, Number_of_Dependents, Date of Birth, . . .
Recruiting-Applicants	**Event_Number, Applicant_Number**
Training-Employees	**Course_Number, Employee_Number**, Performance, Comments
Skills_Employees	**Skill_Number, Employee_Number**
Services-Pay	**Pay_Period, Paycheck_Number**

20.5 also lists many of the attributes that would be found in each table. Most of these attributes and their placement should be self-explanatory. Nevertheless, we will briefly discuss several points.

The recruiting event entity stores data about activities performed to notify the public of job openings. The data recorded in this entity are useful for documenting compliance with employment laws and also for evaluating the effectiveness of various methods used to announce job opportunities. The one-to-many relationship between skills and recruiting reflects the fact that each advertisement seeks a specific skill and that, over time, there may be several advertisements for a given skill. The relationship between the recruiting event and job applicants is modeled as being many-to-many because many people typically apply for each job opening but a given individual may also apply for several jobs.

The employees entity stores much of the data typically found in the employee (payroll) master file. The skills entity contains data about the different job skills of interest to the organization. The relationship between skills and employees is modeled as being many-to-many because an employee may possess a number of job skills and, conversely, the same skill may be possessed by several employees.

The training event entity represents the various workshops, training programs, and other opportunities provided for employees to develop and maintain their skills. Thus this entity stores data that can be used to evaluate the effectiveness and cost of training and development efforts. The relationship between the employees and training entities is many-to-many because a given employee will, over time, attend numerous training courses and, conversely, a number of employees will attend a specific training class. The relationship between the skills and training entities is one-to-many because each course is designed to develop a specific skill but a specific course may be offered many times.

The services provided event entity stores time and attendance data, providing the information used to calculate payroll. The actual paycheck data (gross pay, deductions, net pay, etc.), however, are stored in the pay employees event entity. Finally, the evaluation event entity stores data about periodic performance evaluations.

Querying the Data Model

If the data model shown in Fig. 20.5 were implemented in a relational data base, managers could use query languages such as SQL for easy retrieval of the data they need to manage their employees. For example, Peter Wu could use the query shown in Table 20.3 to identify which employees at AOE possess a specific skill, such as knowledge of SQL. He could use this type of query to staff special projects or create task forces. The information retrieved by such queries could also be combined with projected future skill needs to plan hiring strategies and to influence the scheduling of future training courses.

Strategic Benefits of the Data Model

Creating a data model for the HRM/payroll cycle like the one depicted in Fig. 20.5 can provide an organization with several strategic benefits. First, as the sample query in Table 20.3 demonstrates, it makes information more easily accessible to managers. This should result in better decisions concerning the use and development of human resources.

A second benefit is that many HRM activities can be performed more efficiently, thereby reducing costs. For example, notice that Fig. 20.5 includes information about job applicants. On-line resume data bases now exist for many professional fields. That information can be downloaded and automatically stored in the job applicant entity, thereby saving considerable time and expense as compared to traditional manual collection and entry of this data. Moreover, once in the system, that information can be quickly distributed. For example, Federal Express now scans all resumes and stores them in an image-processing data base. This system allows managers who are making hiring decisions to access and print out relevant resumes immediately, rather than waiting for days for the paper documents to be routed to them.

Table 20.3 **Sample SQL Query of Payroll Data Base**

Query: List all accounting employees who have attended a seminar on SQL.

```
SELECT  Employee_Number, Name
FROM    Employees, Training-Employees, Training, Skills
WHERE   Employees.Title = 'Accountant' AND
        Employees.Employee_Number = Training-Employees.Employee_Number AND
        Training-Employees.Course_Number = Training. Course_Number AND
        Training.Skill_Number = Skills.Skill_Number AND
        Skills.Description = 'SQL'
```

Employees

Employee_Number	Name	Title	Other
....	....	....	....
1255	Waner	Accountant	....
1256	Speaker	Accountant	....
1257	Cobb	Accountant	....
1258	Ruth	Accountant	....
....	....	....	....

Training-Employees

Course_Number	Employee_Number	Performance	Comments
....	....	....	....
621	1255	Satisfactory	Enjoyed course
621	1256	Excellent	Learned a lot
643	1257	Excellent	Good trainer
675	1258	Satisfactory	....
....	....	....	....

Training

Course_Number	Date	Skill _Number	Other
....	....	....	....
621	June 10	42	....
643	September 15	39	....
675	October 15	42	....
....	....	....	....

Skills

Skill_Number	Description	Pay_Rate	Other
39	Spreadsheets	....	....
40	REA modeling	....	....
41	Word Processing	....	....
42	SQL	....	....
....	....	....	....

Answer

Employee_Number	Name
1255	Waner
1256	Speaker
1258	Ruth...

It is also not uncommon for several related job openings to arise over a short period of time. If data about previous applicants are stored in an easily accessible data base, much of the clerical work associated with processing applications for subsequent job openings can be avoided. National Semiconductor Corporation, for example, typically receives 50,000 resumes each year, many from applicants qualified to fill several different positions. Consequently, National Semiconductor has created a data base containing over 82,000 resumes. It can be easily searched to find candidates with specific characteristics, such as a master's degree in accounting or public accounting experience. As a result, National Semiconductor reports that its hiring cycle has dropped from 110 to 62 days.

A third strategic benefit of a well-designed HRM/payroll data base is that it can help companies more effectively utilize existing employee skills. AT&T, for example, has developed an internal "temporary" professional services staff, called Resource Link. The key to Resource Link is a data base of employee skills. Many of the employees assigned to Resource Link have had their previous positions eliminated due to ongoing restructuring and downsizing efforts. Whenever a department needs temporary help, it first contacts Resource Link to determine whether those needs can be met by existing AT&T employees. AT&T benefits by being able to retain these employees and to avoid paying severance pay.

Similarly, each of the Big 6 public accounting firms are creating data bases of employee expertise. Using these data bases, professional staff can quickly identify and solicit the advice of colleagues who have had prior experience in addressing a given problem. This saves considerable time in developing solutions to client problems and enables geographically dispersed staff to learn from each other. Well-designed and easily accessible data bases are the key to such effective sharing and leverage of knowledge.

Effects on Internal Controls

Our discussion of the threats listed in Table 20.2 stressed the importance of properly segregating incompatible duties. E–R diagrams are particularly useful in assessing these controls because they indicate which internal agents participate in each event. In addition, if the REA model is implemented in a DBMS, the computer can be programmed to enforce segregation of duties by preventing one person from performing incompatible functions. Conversely, the system can also be programmed to list all cases of one employee performing multiple roles, so that the auditors can investigate whether adequate compensating controls exist.

The use of DBMS also increases the importance of effective access controls. Most relational DBMS provide a means to control access by letting users see only a portion of the data base (called a view). For example, the view defined for payroll clerks would probably not include access to the data pertaining to the hiring or performance evaluation events. In addition, they would have read-only access to pay rate data in the employee table; this restriction would enable them to obtain the information needed to prepare payroll but would prevent them from making unauthorized changes to that data.

Data accuracy is vital when using a DBMS. Fortunately, the relational data model provides some built-in controls to ensure data accuracy and consistency.

One of the more important of these controls is support for foreign keys and referential integrity. This ensures, for example, that when a new row is added to the Services_Provided table, the system verifies that the employee number (which appears as a foreign key in that table) actually exists as primary key in the employee table (that is, there really is such an employee). Finally, with a DBMS, adequate backup and disaster recovery procedures become crucial.

SUMMARY AND CASE CONCLUSION

The HRM/payroll cycle information system consists of two related, but separate, subsystems: HRM and payroll. The HRM system records and processes data about the activities of recruiting, hiring, training, assigning, compensating, evaluating, and discharging employees. The payroll system records and processes data used to pay employees for their services.

The HRM/payroll system must be designed to comply with a myriad of government regulations related to both taxes and employment practices. In addition, adequate controls must exist to prevent (1) overpaying employees due to invalid (overstated) time and attendance data and (2) disbursing paychecks to fictitious employees. These two threats can be best minimized by proper segregation of duties, specifically by having the following functions performed by different individuals:

1. Authorizing and making changes to the payroll master file for such events as hirings, firings, and pay raises.
2. Recording and verifying time worked by employees.
3. Preparing paychecks.
4. Distributing paychecks.

Although the HRM and payroll systems have traditionally been separated, many companies, like AOE, are trying to integrate them to manage their human resources more effectively and to provide employees with better benefits and service. Elizabeth Venko explained to Peter Wu that in this regard, the key to success involves designing the payroll data base so that it can be easily linked with the nonpayroll data, such as the employee skills data base, maintained in the HRM system. Working together, Elizabeth and Peter developed a data model for AOE similar to that shown in Fig. 20.5. Elizabeth showed Peter how easily data about employee skills and attendance at training classes could be retrieved from this data base (refer to the query shown in Table 20.3). Peter agreed that this would satisfy the needs of department managers for quick and easy access to such information. He also realized that the HRM staff could similarly use SQL queries for quick response to employee requests for information about their benefits, deductions, or retirement plans. He was even more impressed when Elizabeth explained that the new system would also allow employees to make direct changes in their retirement savings allocations, medical plan choices, and other benefit options. Freeing the HRM staff from these routine clerical tasks would allow his people to devote more time to strategic activities such as planning for future work force needs, career counseling, and employee development.

Elizabeth then described her plans to use IT to improve the efficiency of payroll processing. One source of productivity gains would be achieved through electronic collection and entry of time and attendance data. As discussed in Chapter 19, new time clocks would be installed in the factory that would transmit data directly to the payroll system. Similarly, bar-code scanners would be used to collect job-time ticket data at each factory work station and send it directly to the payroll system. The computer will be programmed to reconcile the timeclock data with the job-time ticket information. This would eliminate the time and expense associated with manually reconciling these two information flows in the payroll department (refer back to Fig. 20.3).

Elizabeth explained that payroll processing itself could continue to be performed in batch mode, because there is no need for on-line processing (employees would continue to be paid only at periodic intervals). Reports, such as the payroll register, however, would be distributed electronically to improve efficiency. Elizabeth also wants to encourage employees to sign up for direct deposit of their paychecks, thereby reducing the number of checks that need to be printed.

Finally, an access control matrix would be created to maintain adequate segregation of duties in the new system and protect the integrity of the HRM/payroll data base. For example, pay rate changes would be entered only by HRM employees from terminals located in the HRM department. Similarly, various department managers would have read-only access to the employee skills and work assignment portions of the HRM/payroll data base. These controls would provide protection against unauthorized changes to payroll data.

KEY TERMS

human resources management (HRM)/payroll cycle
time card
payroll register
deduction register
earnings statement
payroll service bureau
flexible benefits plan
payroll clearing account
zero balance check

CHAPTER QUIZ

1. Which is the best way to validate time worked by employees?
a. Cross-foot the payroll register.
b. Reconcile job-time tickets to time cards.
c. Create batch totals during paycheck preparation.
d. Electronically capture time worked at each factory station.

2. Which is the key entity in an REA data model of the HRM/payroll cycle?
a. Payroll
b. HRM
c. Employees
d. Skills

3. Which document lists the current amount and year-to-date totals of gross pay, deductions, and net pay for one employee?
a. Payroll register
b. Time card
c. Paycheck
d. Earnings statement

4. On-line processing is most useful for which of these tasks?
a. Preparing payroll checks
b. Reconciling job-time tickets and time cards
c. Paying payroll tax obligations
d. Making changes in employee job status and pay rate

5. Use of a payroll service bureau provides all of these benefits *except*
   a. integration of payroll and personnel data, such as job skills.
   b. lower cost of processing payroll.
   c. less need for developing and maintaining payroll tax expertise.
   d. fewer staff needed to process payroll.
6. Which control procedure would be most effective in detecting the failure to prepare a paycheck for a new employee prior to when paychecks are distributed?
   a. Validity checks on the employee number on each time card
   b. Record counts of time cards submitted and time cards processed
   c. A zero balance check
   d. Use of a separate payroll bank account
7. Which department should have responsibility for authorizing pay rate changes?
   a. Timekeeping
   b. Payroll
   c. HRM
   d. Accounting
8. To maximize effectiveness of internal controls over payroll, which of the following persons should be responsible for distributing employee paychecks?
   a. A departmental secretary
   b. The cashier
   c. The controller
   d. A departmental supervisor
9. Unclaimed paychecks should be returned to
   a. the HRM department.
   b. the cashier.
   c. the payroll department.
   d. the absent employee's supervisor.
10. All of the following provide a means to improve the efficiency of payroll processing *except*
    a. direct deposit.
    b. the use of badge readers to collect time worked data.
    c. the use of a payroll clearing account.
    d. the use of a payroll service bureau.

DISCUSSION QUESTIONS

20.1 This chapter noted many of the benefits that can arise by integrating the HRM and payroll data bases. Nevertheless, many companies maintain separate payroll and HRM information systems. Why do you think this is so? (*Hint:* Think about the differences in employee background and the functions performed by the HRM and payroll departments.)

20.2 Focus 20.1 described how some companies are beginning to measure the value of their human resources. Those attempts have generally been separate from the company's financial statements. Some accountants have advocated that a company's human assets be measured and included directly in the financial statements. For example, the costs of hiring and training an employee would be recorded as an asset that is amortized over the employee's expected term of service. What do you think about this proposal? What are some of the benefits and drawbacks of counting human resources as assets in financial statements?

20.3 You are responsible for implementing a new employee performance measurement system that will provide factory supervisors with detailed information about each of their employees on a weekly basis. In conversation with some of these supervisors, you are surprised to learn they do not believe these reports will be useful. They explain that they can already obtain all the information they need to manage their employees simply by observing the shop floor. Comment on that opinion. How could formal reports supplement and enhance what the supervisors learn by direct observation? Why is it difficult to get people to agree to formally document what they think they already know?

20.4 In some aspects, the acquisition and use of employee services is similar to the purchase and use of other resources, such as raw materials and supplies. Discuss the similarities and differences between the way that the purchasing and payroll cycles account for the acquisition of and payment for resources used.

20.5 Direct deposit both reduces the costs of and improves control over payroll distribution. Does this mean that all companies should require their employees to be paid by direct deposit? Why or why not?

PROBLEMS

20.1 What internal control procedure(s) would be *most effective* in preventing the following errors or fraudulent acts?

a. An inadvertent data entry error caused an employee's wage rate to be overstated in the payroll master file.

b. A fictitious employee payroll record was added to the payroll master file.

c. During data entry, the hours worked on an employee's time card for one day were accidentally entered as 80, instead of 8.

d. A computer operator used an on-line terminal to increase her own salary.

e. A factory supervisor failed to notify the HRM department that an employee had been fired. Consequently, paychecks continued to be issued for that employee. The supervisor pocketed and cashed those paychecks.

f. A factory employee punched a friend's time card in at 1:00 P.M. and out at 5:00 P.M. while the friend played golf that afternoon.

g. A programmer obtained the payroll master file and increased his salary.

h. Some time cards were lost during payroll preparation; consequently, when paychecks were distributed, several employees complained about not being paid.

i. A large portion of the payroll master file was destroyed when the disk pack containing the file was used as a scratch file for another application.

20.2 Refer to Fig. 20.5 to answer the following questions:

a. Explain the meaning of the relationship cardinalities that were not discussed in the text.

b. Modify the E–R diagram to include the "interview" event.

c. Explain how to include data about teams of employees assigned to projects.

d. Modify the E–R diagram to include information about supervisors.

20.3 Refer to Fig. 20.5 to write the following SQL queries:

a. How many job applicants are skilled in programming spreadsheet macros?

b. What is the performance evaluation history for Jackson?

c. What is the average performance evaluation rating for all payroll clerks?

d. Which job applicant possesses the same set of skills as Jones?

e. How many employees have attended training sessions to develop new skills in the past year?

f. Is Jackson's pay high or low for his skills?

g. What is the total amount of deductions withheld from the July 10 payroll?

20.4 Assume that the data model depicted in Fig. 20.5 is used to store HRM/payroll data. List the programmed application controls that should be used for adding data to the services provided, performance evaluation, and pay employees tables. Your answer should state which controls should be applied to each data item and the purpose for each control.

20.5 You have been hired to evaluate the payroll system for the Skip-Rope Manufacturing Company. The company processes its payroll in-house. Prepare a list of questions that you would need answered in order to evaluate Skip-Rope's internal control structure as it pertains to payroll processing for its factory employees. Each question should be phrased so that it can be answered with either a yes or a no; all no answers should indicate potential internal control weaknesses. Include a third column listing the potential problem that could arise if that particular control was not in place.

20.6 The internal audit department of the Newberry Manufacturing Company was assigned to review the payroll department of the Galena, Illinois, plant. The internal audit consisted of (1) various tests to verify the numerical accuracy of the payroll department's records and (2) the determination of the procedures used to process payroll.

The internal audit team found that all numerical items were accurate. The proper hourly rates were used and the wages and deductions were calculated correctly. The payroll register was properly footed, totaled, and posted.

Interviews with plant personnel revealed the following information:

- The payroll clerk receives the time cards from the various department supervisors at the end of each pay period, checks the employee's hourly rate against information provided by the HRM department, and records the regular and overtime hours for each employee.
- The payroll clerk sends the time cards to the plant's computer operations department, where the payroll is processed.
- The computer operations department returns the time cards along with the printed checks and payroll register to the payroll clerk. The payroll clerk then

verifies the hourly rate and hours worked for each employee by comparing the detail in the payroll register with the time cards.

• If errors are found, the payroll clerk voids the computer-generated check, prepares another check for the correct amount, and adjusts the payroll register accordingly.

• The payroll clerk obtains the plant's check signature plate from the accounting department and signs the payroll checks.

• An employee of the HRM department picks up and holds the checks until they are delivered to the department supervisors for distribution to employees.

REQUIRED

Identify the shortcomings in the payroll procedures at the Newberry Manufacturing Company and suggest steps to correct those weaknesses.
(CMA Examination)

20.7 Rose Publishing Company devotes the bulk of its work to the development of high school and college textbooks. The printing division has several production departments and employs 400 people. Approximately 95% of the staff is paid hourly rates and can earn overtime pay; the remainder earn fixed salaries. All employees are paid weekly.

A manual time card system is used. Each employee punches in and out when entering or leaving the plant. The timekeeping department audits the time cards daily and prepares input sheets for the computerized functions of the payroll system.

Currently, a daily report of the previous day's clock card information, organized by department, is sent to each supervisor in the printing division for verification and approval. Any changes are made directly on the report, signed by the supervisor, and returned to timekeeping. The altered report serves as the input authorization for changes to the system. Because of the volume and frequency of reports, this procedure is the most expensive process in the system.

Timekeeping submits the corrected hourly data to the general and cost accounting departments. General accounting maintains the payroll system that determines weekly payroll; prepares weekly checks; summarizes data for monthly, quarterly, and annual reports; and generates W-2 forms. The cost accounting department prepares a weekly and monthly payroll distribution report that shows labor costs for each department.

Competition in college textbook publishing has increased steadily in recent years. Although Rose has maintained its sales volume, profits have declined. Direct labor cost is believed to be the basic cause of this decline. Insufficient detail on labor utilization is available, however, to enable management to pinpoint the source of the suspected inefficiencies. Consequently the following proposal to redesign the payroll system was developed:

1. The use of an integrated time and labor attendance (TALC) system would include direct data entry; cost distribution by project as well as by department; on-line access to time and attendance data for verification, correction, and update; and creation and maintenance of individual employee work history files for long-term analysis.
2. The TALC system would incorporate uniquely encoded employee badges that electronically record entry to and exit from the plant directly into the system.
3. Labor cost records would be maintained at the employee level, showing the time worked per project in each department. This would allow labor cost to be fully analyzed. Responsibility for correct and timely entry would reside with the departmental supervisors and be verified daily by project managers.
4. On-line terminals would be available in each department for direct data entry. Access to the system will be limited to authorized users through a password and user ID system. Departmental supervisors will be allowed to inspect, correct, verify, and update only time and attendance data for their employees. Project managers will only be able to access information recorded for their projects. Any corrections they want to make must be certified outside the system and entered by the affected supervisor.
5. Appropriate data will be maintained at the employee level to allow verification of employee personnel files and individual work history by department and project. Access to employee master file data will be restricted to the HRM department. Work history data will be made available for analysis only at the project or department level and only to supervisors and project managers for whom an employee works.

REQUIRED

a. Compared with the existing clock card system, what are the advantages and disadvantages of the recommended system for electronically recording time and attendance data?

b. Identify the items that should be included in the employee master payroll file.

c. The TALC system allows the employee's departmental supervisor and the HRM department to examine the data contained in an individual employee's payroll master record.

1. What information should each supervisor be allowed to examine?
2. What safeguards may be installed to prevent unauthorized access to this data?

d. The recommended system allows both the departmental supervisors and the project managers to obtain current labor cost distribution data on a limited basis. These restrictions might lead to conflicts between the departmental supervisors and project managers.

1. Why are the specific limitations proposed?
2. How would you recommend resolving any disagreements between the departmental supervisors and project managers about labor cost distributions? (CMA Examination)

20.8 The Kowal Manufacturing Company employs about 50 production workers and has the following payroll procedures:

- The factory supervisor interviews and hires all job applicants. The new employee prepares a W-4 form (Employee's Withholding Exemption Certificate) and gives it to the supervisor. The supervisor writes the hourly rate of pay for the new employee in the corner of the W-4 form and then gives the form to the payroll clerk as notice that a new worker has been hired. The supervisor verbally advises the payroll department of any subsequent pay raises.
- A supply of blank time cards is kept in a box near the entrance to the factory. All workers take a time card on Monday morning and fill in their names. During the week they record the time they arrive and leave work by punching their time cards in the time clock located near the main entrance to the factory. At the end of the week the workers drop the time cards in a box near the exit. The completed time cards are retrieved from the box by a payroll clerk on Monday morning. Employees are automatically removed from the payroll master file when they fail to turn in a time card.
- The payroll checks are manually signed by the chief accountant and then given to the factory supervisor, who distributes them to the employees. The factory supervisor arranges for delivery of the paychecks to any employee who is absent on payday.
- The payroll bank account is reconciled by the chief accountant, who also prepares the various quarterly and annual tax reports.

REQUIRED

List your suggestions for improving the Kowal Manufacturing Company's internal controls over hiring and payroll processing.

20.9 Arlington Industries manufactures and sells engine parts for large industrial equipment. The company employs over one thousand workers for three shifts, and most employees work overtime when necessary. Figure 20.6 depicts the procedures followed to process payroll.

Additional information about payroll procedures follows:

- The HRM department determines the wage rates of all employees. The process begins when a form authorizing the addition of a new employee to the payroll master file is sent to the payroll coordinator for review and approval. Once the information about the new employee is entered in the system, the computer automatically calculates the overtime and shift differential rates for that employee.
- A local accounting firm provides Arlington with monthly payroll tax updates. The tape is processed to modify the tax rates used to calculate payroll.
- Employees record time worked on time cards. Every Monday morning the previous week's time cards are collected from a bin next to the time clock, and new time cards are left for employees to use. The payroll department manager reviews the time cards to ensure that hours are correctly totaled; the system automatically determines whether overtime has been worked or a shift differential is required.
- All other activities depicted in Fig. 20.6 are performed by the payroll department manager.
- The system automatically assigns a sequential number to each payroll check. The checks are stored in a box next to the printer for easy access. After the checks are printed, the payroll department manager uses an automatic check-signing machine to sign the checks. The signature plate is kept locked in a safe. After the checks have been signed, the payroll manager distributes the paychecks to all first-shift employees. Paychecks for the other two shifts are given to the shift supervisor for distribution.
- The payroll master file is backed up weekly, after payroll processing is finished.

Figure 20.6

Arlington Industries Flowchart of Payroll Processing

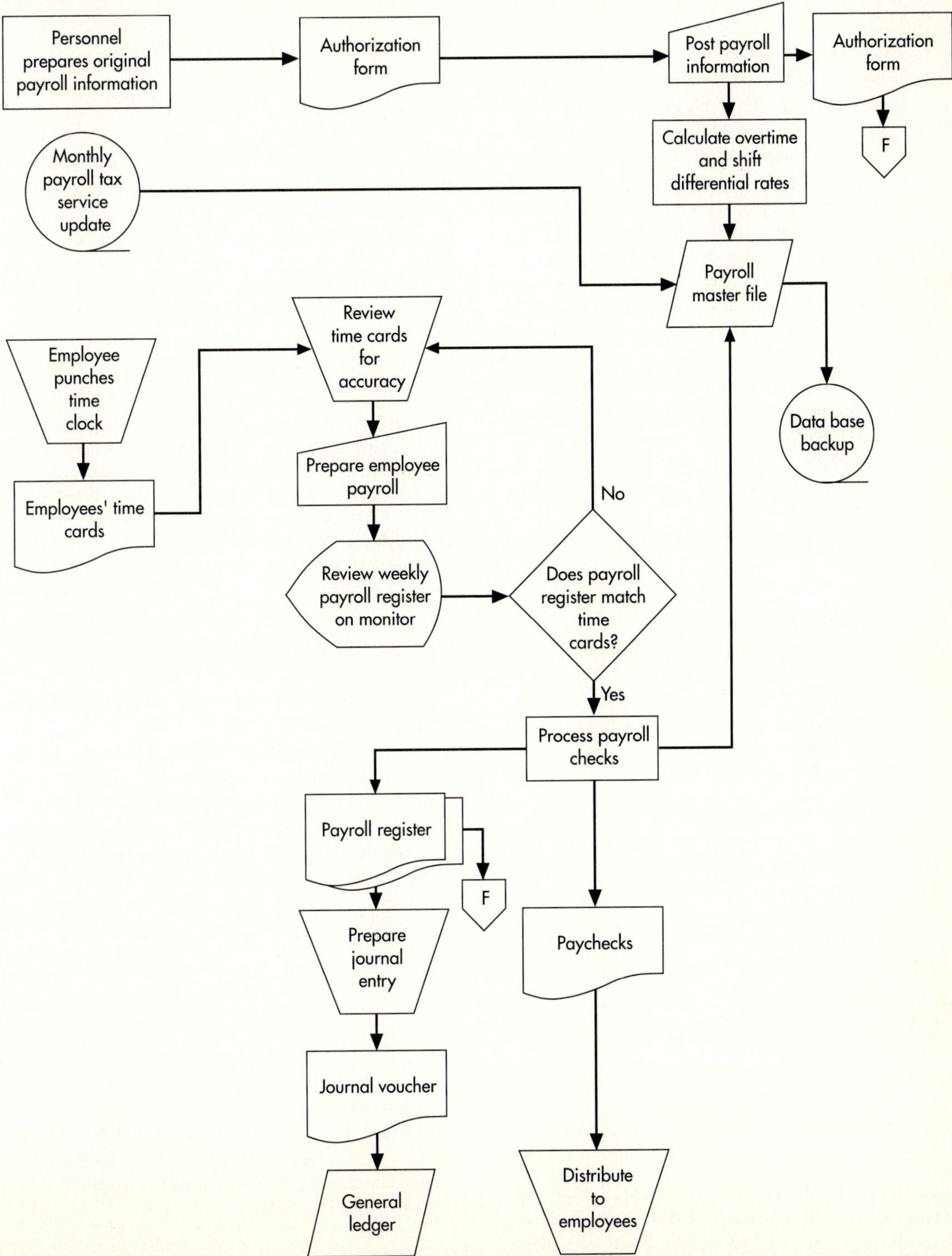

REQUIRED

a. Identify and describe five different areas in Arlington's payroll processing system where controls are inadequate.
b. Identify and describe two different areas in Arlington's payroll processing system where controls are satisfactory. (CMA Examination)

20.10 The local community feels that secondary school education is a necessity in our society and that lack of education leads to a number of social problems. As a result, the local school board has decided to take action to reverse the rising drop-out rate. The board has voted to provide funds to encourage students to remain in school and earn their high school diploma. The idea is to treat secondary education like a job and pay students. The board, however, could not agree on the details for implementing this new plan. Consequently, you have been hired to devise a system to compensate students for staying in school and earning their diploma.

As you devise your compensation scheme, be sure it meets the following general control objectives for the payroll cycle:

- All personnel and payroll transactions are properly authorized.
- All employees are assigned to do productive work, and they do it efficiently and effectively.
- All transactions are accurately recorded and processed.
- Accurate records are maintained.
- All disbursements are proper.

REQUIRED

Your proposal should address these five questions:
a. How should the students be compensated (i.e., attendance, grades, etc.)?
b. How and by whom will the payments be authorized?
c. How will the payments be processed?
d. How should the payments be made (e.g., in cash or other means)?
e. When will the payments be made?

Adapted from "Development of Diversity Awareness and Critical Thinking" by Carol F. Venable, *Proceedings of the Lilly Conference on Excellence in College and University Teaching–West,* Lake Arrowhead, CA, March 1995; and *American Accounting Association Teaching and Curriculum Demonstration Session,* Orlando, FL, August 1995. Reprinted with permission of Dr. Carol Venable.

CASE 20.1: ANYCOMPANY, INC.—AN ONGOING COMPREHENSIVE CASE

Select a local company and study its payroll system (you may use the same company you identified to complete this case in previous chapters). Prepare a report that contains the following:

1. A DFD of the payroll system.
2. A flowchart of the payroll system. Comment on the company's use, or lack thereof, of IT in payroll processing.
3. A list of the various paper and electronic documents used to process payroll. Evaluate the design of each document and assess its appropriateness for its intended use.
4. A list of the various threats and the control procedures employed to mitigate them. Assess the overall adequacy of internal controls.
5. A list of the reports produced by the system. Evaluate how well those reports meet management's information needs.

CASE 20.2: PAYROLL SERVICE BUREAUS

Write a brief report describing the advantages and disadvantages of using a payroll service bureau, rather than processing payroll internally. Perform the following research to collect the data for your report:

1. Contact a local payroll service bureau. Find out what services it provides and how it charges for those services. Ask about the bureau's client base—what size companies does it serve? in what industries?
2. Contact two companies that use a payroll service bureau and two that process their own payroll. Ask them to explain why they do (or do not) use a payroll service bureau.

CASE 20.3: DARWIN DEPARTMENT STORE

The Darwin Department Store pays all of its employees on a salaried basis. Payroll processing is done internally. The payroll master file is maintained on disk. At periodic intervals every month, the HRM department uses on-line terminals to enter batches of payroll file change transactions. After those changes pass the appropriate data entry controls, they are posted to the payroll master file. This run produces a printed report listing all file changes processed.

The payroll run takes place on the last day of each month. Because all employees are paid a fixed salary, there is no transaction input. This run produces printed employee paychecks, earnings registers, a printed summary report, and a payroll register file recorded on disk. The payroll register file is later processed to print a payroll register.

1. What is meant by the term "payroll file change transactions"? Give four examples of these types of transactions.
2. Prepare a flowchart of the processes described.
3. The "summary report" that is generated by the payroll run includes accounting journal entries. Describe the contents of these journal entries. What other information is likely to be found on the summary report?
4. Describe a comprehensive set of internal control procedures and policies for this payroll application. Relate each control procedure to a specific objective and explain what threats it is designed to mitigate.
5. Suppose that Darwin decides to pay commissions to its sales staff. What changes would be required in (a) the payroll master file, (b) the payroll run, and (c) the internal control procedures you developed in step 4?

ANSWERS TO CHAPTER QUIZ

1. b	**3.** d	**5.** a	**7.** c	**9.** b
2. c	**4.** d	**6.** b	**8.** b	**10.** c

Chapter 21

The General Ledger and Reporting Cycle

LEARNING OBJECTIVES

After studying this chapter, you should be able to:

- Describe the information processing operations performed in the general ledger and reporting cycle.
- Discuss methods for improving the efficiency and effectiveness of general ledger processing.
- Identify the major threats in the general ledger and reporting cycle and evaluate the adequacy of various control procedures for dealing with them.
- Explain how to implement a general ledger system in a relational DBMS.

Integrative Case: Alpha Omega Electronics

During the past two years, Elizabeth Venko, AOE's controller, has participated in the successful redesign of the company's various AIS subsystems (see Chapters 17–20). She has now been asked by Stephanie Cromwell, AOE's chief financial officer, to redesign AOE's general ledger and reporting system. She has two primary goals:

1. To speed up the closing process. Currently, it takes two weeks to complete monthly closings and to distribute the financial performance reports to AOE's divisional managers. Last week, Stephanie almost had to postpone her scheduled presentation of AOE's quarterly financial results to Wall Street security analysts because of delays in preparing the interim financial statements.
2. To make financial performance data more accessible to divisional managers. Currently, divisional managers receive printed monthly financial performance reports. Consequently, they have to reenter the data into personal computers in order to do "what if" analyses or to prepare graphical summaries.

As you read this chapter, think about how Elizabeth can utilize recent developments in information technology to improve the efficiency of AOE's general ledger processing and the effectiveness of its reporting systems.

INTRODUCTION

The **general ledger and reporting cycle** consists of the information processing operations involved in updating the general ledger and preparing reports that summarize the results of an organization's activities. As shown in Fig. 21.1, the

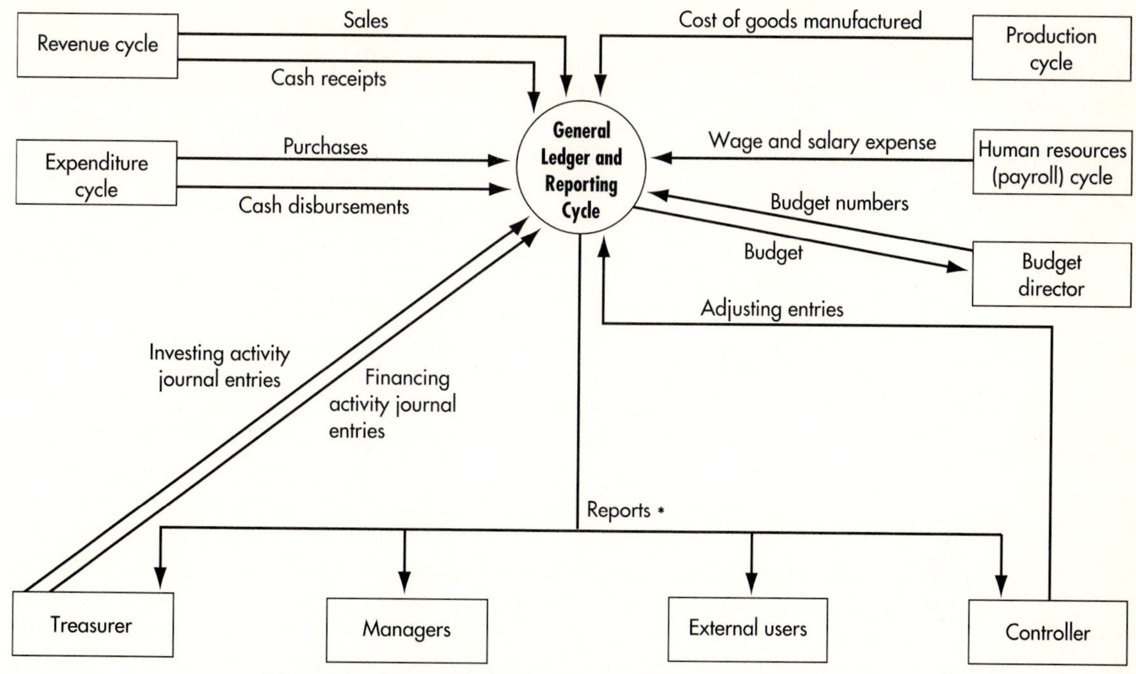

*Financial statements, budget reports, and other performance reports. External users only receive financial statements.

Figure 21.1

Context Diagram of the General Ledger and Reporting Cycle

general ledger and reporting cycle plays a central role in a company's AIS. It collects data from a variety of sources. For example:

- Information about regular transactions is provided by each of the accounting cycle subsystems described in Chapters 17–20. (Only the principal data flows from each subsystem are depicted, to keep the figure uncluttered.)
- Information about financing and investing activities, such as the issuance or retirement of debt instruments and the purchase or sale of investment securities, is provided by the treasurer.
- Budget numbers are provided by the budget department.
- Adjusting entries are provided by the controller.

All of this information is used to produce a variety of reports for internal management and external users. In addition to generating periodic reports, the general ledger and reporting system should also be designed to support inquiry processing by various people in the organization. For example, departmental managers may desire interim reports comparing actual to budgeted performance. These reports should be available on demand, in addition to periodically, so that deviations can be identified early enough to take corrective actions. The treasurer, for example, must closely monitor cash flows so that deviations from forecasts can be identified in time to adjust short-term borrowing plans.

A logical question to ask at this point, however, concerns the need for a general ledger. After all, in Chapters 17–20 we presented REA data models for the various subsystems of the AIS. Theoretically, implementation of these REA data models in each subsystem of the AIS precludes the need for a separate general ledger. Some general ledger accounts, such as inventory and sales, would be represented explicitly as relational tables. Other general ledger accounts, such as accounts receivable and accounts payable, could be derived from data stored in several tables. For example, recall that accounts receivable represents sales for which cash has not yet been received. Thus total accounts receivable can be computed by subtracting cash receipts from sales (the actual queries used to make this calculation would depend upon how the relationship between sales and cash receipts is represented).

Nevertheless, we describe a separate general ledger system in this chapter because the organization you begin to work for after graduation will likely still be using a separate general ledger package. Many organizations have not yet implemented relational data base systems to integrate their operational and financial data. Instead, they continue to use separate files, as illustrated in the flowcharts in Chapters 17–20. Moreover, even companies that have created relational data bases typically continue to maintain a separate general ledger, usually for reasons of tradition and politics. Note that this practice not only creates redundancy, but also continues the separation of financial from nonfinancial operating data. One unfortunate result is that accountants are often tempted to think that the only important data are those representing the financial aspects of operations. As we discussed in Chapters 17–20, such thinking seriously limits the opportunity for accountants to take a proactive value-added role in providing managers with all the information they need to make sound decisions.

What you learned in previous chapters about relational data bases, the REA model, and SQL is still important, however. Indeed, a growing number of general ledger packages are based on the relational data model and support SQL access to financial data. Thus the skills you have developed in earlier chapters can be productively applied to designing and using the general ledger. Moreover, it is likely that over time, as accountants become more comfortable with the concept of producing financial statements directly from a relational data base, the use of separate general ledger packages may eventually disappear.

In the first section of this chapter, we describe the basic information processing operations performed to update the general ledger and to prepare reports for both internal management and external users. Next, we explore opportunities for using information technology to improve the efficiency and effectiveness of those activities. Then we discuss major control threats in the general ledger and reporting cycle and the control procedures that can be used to mitigate them. We conclude the chapter by examining the structure of the general ledger in a data base AIS.

GENERAL LEDGER AND REPORTING CYCLE ACTIVITIES

Figure 21.2 is a level 0 DFD depicting the four basic activities performed in the general ledger and reporting cycle. The first three activities represent the basic steps in the accounting cycle, and they culminate in the production of the traditional set of financial statements. The fourth activity indicates that, in addition to financial reports for external users, the AIS produces reports for internal management as well. We now examine each of these activities in more detail.

Update General Ledger

As shown in Fig. 21.2, the first step in the general ledger cycle (circle 1.0) is to update the general ledger. Updating consists of posting journal entries that originate from two sources:

1. *Accounting subsystems.* Each of the accounting subsystems described in Chapters 17–20 creates a journal entry to update the general ledger. In theory, the general ledger could be updated for each individual transaction. In practice, however, the various accounting subsystems usually update the general ledger by means of summary journal entries that represent the results of all transactions that occurred during a given period of time (day, week, or month). For example, the revenue cycle subsystem would generate a summary journal entry debiting accounts receivable and cash and crediting sales for all sales made during the update period. Similarly, the expenditure cycle would generate summary journal entries to record the purchase of supplies and inventories and to record cash disbursements in payment for those purchases.
2. *The treasurer.* The treasurer's office creates individual journal entries to update the general ledger for nonroutine transactions such as the issuance or retirement of debt, the purchase or sale of investment securities, or the acquisition of treasury stock.

Journal entries to update the general ledger may be documented on a form called a **journal voucher.** Figure 21.2 shows that the individual journal entries used to update the general ledger are then stored in the journal voucher file.

Figure 21.2

Level 0 DFD for the General Ledger and Reporting Cycle

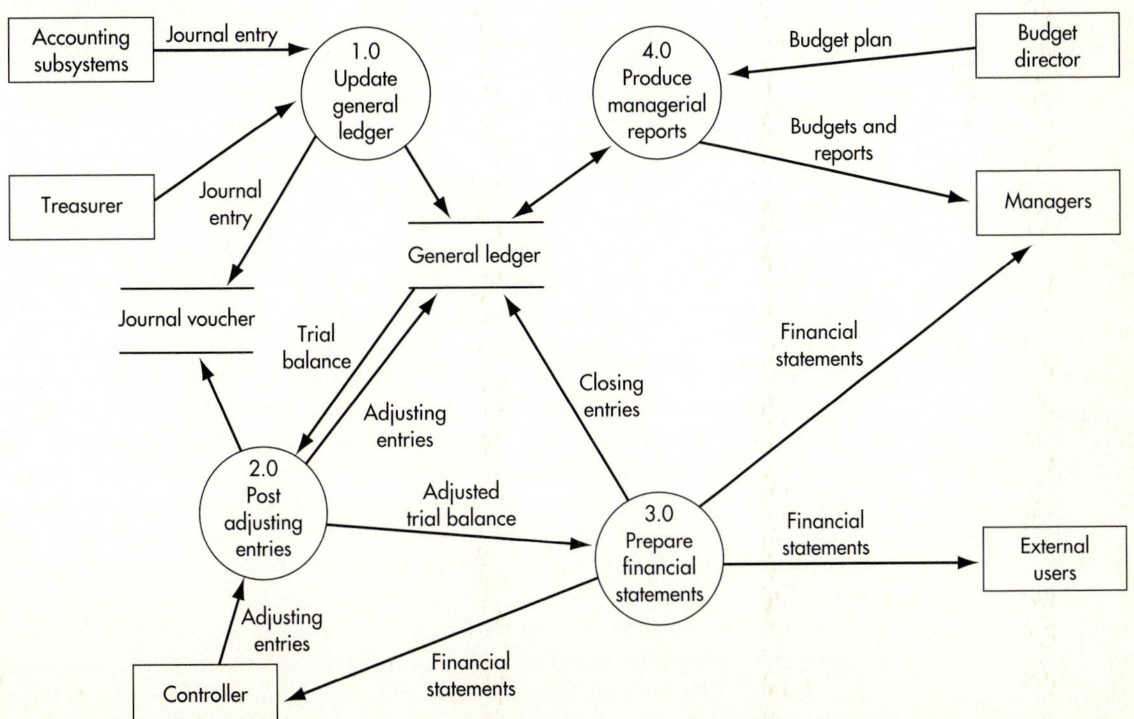

Thus this file contains the information that would be found in the general journal in a manual AIS. Note, however, that the journal voucher file is a by-product of, not an input to, the posting process. As we will explain later in the chapter in our discussion of internal controls, the journal voucher file forms an important part of the audit trail.

Post Adjusting Entries

The second step in the general ledger cycle involves posting various adjusting entries (circle 2.0 in Fig. 21.2). These adjusting entries originate from the controller's office, after the initial trial balance has been prepared. Adjusting entries fall into five basic categories:

1. *Accruals* represent entries made at the end of the accounting period to reflect events that have occurred but for which cash has not yet been received or disbursed. Examples include the recording of interest revenue earned and wages payable.
2. *Deferrals* represent entries made at the end of the accounting period to reflect the exchange of cash prior to performance of the related event. Examples include recognizing the portion of advance payments from customers earned during a specific period and expensing the portion of prepaid assets (e.g., rent, interest, and insurance) used this period.
3. *Estimates* represent entries that reflect a portion of expenses that occur over a number of accounting periods. Examples include depreciation and bad debt expenses.
4. *Revaluations* represent entries made to reflect either differences between the actual and recorded value of an asset or a change in accounting principle. Examples include a change in the method used to value inventory or a writing down of inventory to reflect obsolescence or shrinkage noted during a physical count of inventory.
5. *Corrections* represent entries made to counteract the effects of errors found in the general ledger.

As shown in Fig. 20.2, information about these adjusting entries is stored in the journal voucher file, forming another part of the audit trail. After all adjusting entries have been made, an adjusted trial balance is prepared. It serves as the input to the next step in the general ledger and financial reporting cycle, the preparation of financial statements.

Prepare Financial Statements

The third step in the general ledger and reporting cycle involves the preparation of financial statements (circle 3.0 in Fig. 21.2). The income statement is prepared first, using data from the revenue and expense account balances in the adjusted trial balance. The balance sheet is prepared next. This activity requires closing entries that zero out all revenue and expense accounts and transferring the net income or loss to retained earnings. In manual systems, this was typically performed only once each year. Automated general ledger systems, however, simplify the monthly and annual closing process. The former zeroes out the current month's revenue and expense account balances but leaves the year-to-date totals intact. Thus an income statement generated immediately after a monthly closing would display all zeroes in the current month column but would store cumulative numbers in the year-to-date column. Finally, the statement of cash flows is prepared, using data from both the income statement and balance sheet, plus other information about the organization's investment and financing activities.

Produce Managerial Reports

The final step in the general ledger and reporting cycle (circle 4.0 in Fig. 21.2) involves the production of various managerial reports. They fall into two main categories: general ledger control reports and budgets. The former include lists of journal vouchers by numerical sequence, account number, or date and listings of general ledger account balances. These reports are used to verify the accuracy of the posting process.

A number of budgets are produced for use in planning and evaluating performance. The operating budget depicts planned revenues and expenditures for each organizational unit. The capital expenditures budget shows planned cash inflows and outflows for each project. Cash flow budgets compare estimated cash inflows from operations with planned expenditures and are used to determine borrowing needs.

Budgets and performance reports should be developed on the basis of responsibility accounting. **Responsibility accounting** involves reporting financial results on the basis of managerial responsibilities within an organization. The result is a set of correlated reports that break down the organization's overall performance by specific subunits, as shown in Fig. 21.3. Note that each report shows actual costs and variances from budget for the current month and the year to date, but only for those items that are controllable by the manager of that subunit. Note also the hierarchical nature of the reports: The total cost of each individual subunit is displayed as a single line item on the next higher level report.

The contents of the budgetary performance reports should be tailored to the nature of the unit being evaluated. For example, many production, service, and administrative departments are treated as cost centers. Accordingly, as shown in Fig. 21.3, their performance reports should highlight actual versus budgeted performance in regard to controllable costs (those that can be directly affected by the actions of the unit manager). In contrast, sales departments are often evaluated as revenue centers; consequently, their performance reports should compare actual to forecasted sales, broken down by appropriate product and geographic categories. Some departments, like IT and utilities, charge other units for their services and are evaluated as profit centers; in this case, performance reports should appropriately compare actual revenues, expenses, and profits with their corresponding budgeted amounts. Finally, if plants, divisions, and other autonomous operating units are treated as investment centers, their performance reports should provide data for calculating that unit's return on investment.

No matter which basis is used to prepare a unit's budgetary performance report, the method used to calculate the budget standard is crucial. The easiest approach is to establish fixed targets for each unit, store those figures in the data base, and compare actual performance to those preset values. One major drawback to this approach is that the budget number is static and does not reflect unforeseen changes in the operating environment. Consequently, individual managers may be penalized or rewarded for factors beyond their

Figure 21.3

Sample Set of Reports for a Responsibility Accounting System

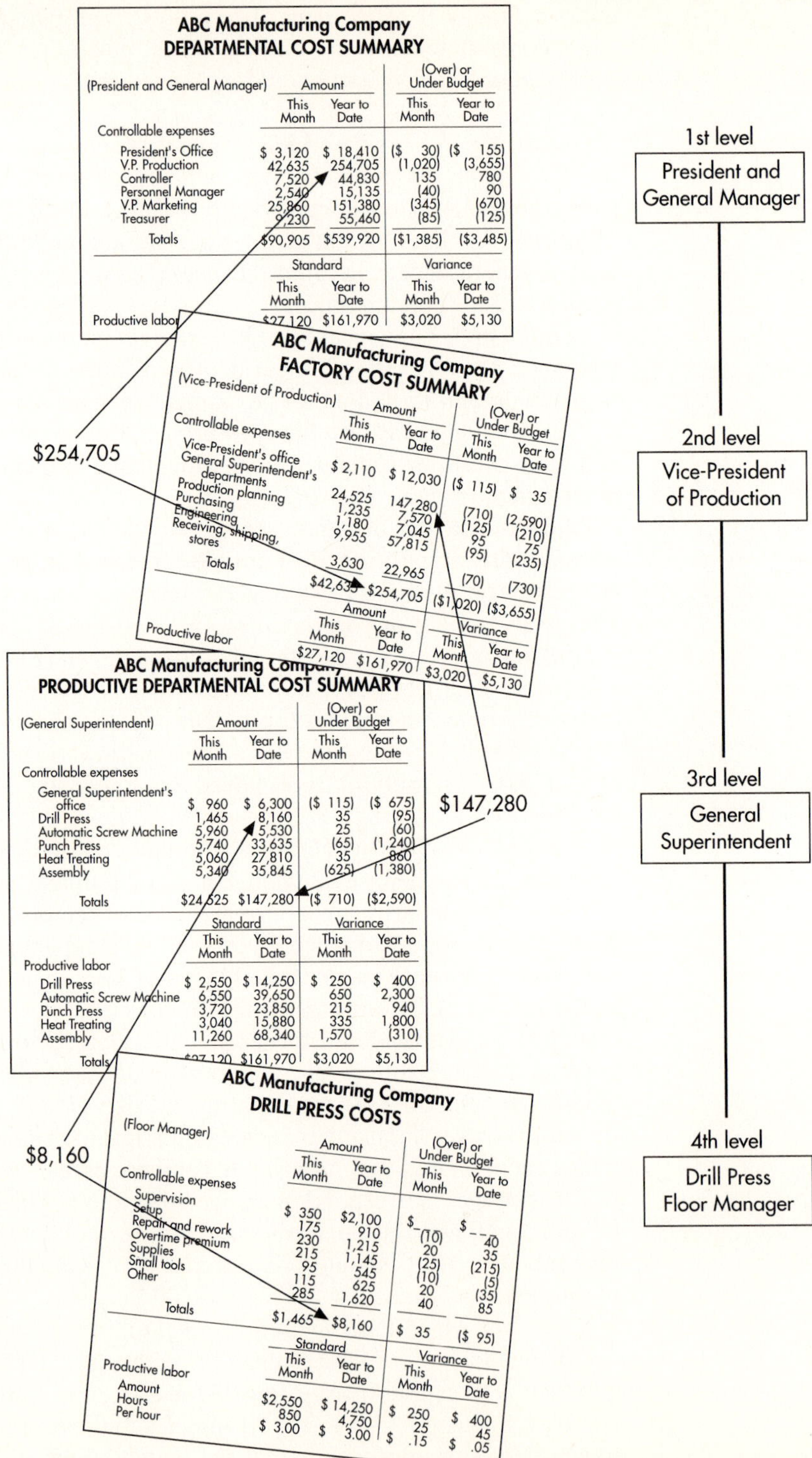

ABC Manufacturing Company
DEPARTMENTAL COST SUMMARY

(President and General Manager)	Amount This Month	Amount Year to Date	(Over) or Under Budget This Month	(Over) or Under Budget Year to Date
Controllable expenses				
President's Office	$ 3,120	$ 18,410	($ 30)	($ 155)
V.P. Production	42,635	254,705	(1,020)	(3,655)
Controller	7,520	44,830	135	780
Personnel Manager	2,540	15,135	(40)	90
V.P. Marketing	25,860	151,380	(345)	(670)
Treasurer	9,230	55,460	(85)	(125)
Totals	$90,905	$539,920	($1,385)	($3,485)
	Standard This Month	**Standard Year to Date**	**Variance This Month**	**Variance Year to Date**
Productive labor	$27,120	$161,970	$3,020	$5,130

ABC Manufacturing Company
FACTORY COST SUMMARY

(Vice-President of Production)	Amount This Month	Amount Year to Date	(Over) or Under Budget This Month	(Over) or Under Budget Year to Date
Controllable expenses				
Vice-President's office	$ 2,110	$ 12,030	($ 115)	$ 35
General Superintendent's departments	24,525	147,280	(710)	(2,590)
Production planning	1,235	7,570	(125)	(210)
Purchasing	1,180	7,045	95	75
Engineering	9,955	57,815	(95)	(235)
Receiving, shipping, stores	3,630	22,965	(70)	(730)
Totals	$42,635	$254,705	($1,020)	($3,655)
	Amount This Month	**Amount Year to Date**	**Variance This Month**	**Variance Year to Date**
Productive labor	$27,120	$161,970	$3,020	$5,130

ABC Manufacturing Company
PRODUCTIVE DEPARTMENTAL COST SUMMARY

(General Superintendent)	Amount This Month	Amount Year to Date	(Over) or Under Budget This Month	(Over) or Under Budget Year to Date
Controllable expenses				
General Superintendent's office	$ 960	$ 6,300	($ 115)	($ 675)
Drill Press	1,465	8,160	35	(95)
Automatic Screw Machine	5,960	5,530	25	(60)
Punch Press	5,740	33,635	(65)	(1,240)
Heat Treating	5,060	27,810	35	860
Assembly	5,340	35,845	(625)	(1,380)
Totals	$24,525	$147,280	($ 710)	($2,590)
	Standard This Month	**Standard Year to Date**	**Variance This Month**	**Variance Year to Date**
Productive labor				
Drill Press	$ 2,550	$ 14,250	$ 250	$ 400
Automatic Screw Machine	6,550	39,650	650	2,300
Punch Press	3,720	23,850	215	940
Heat Treating	3,040	15,880	335	1,800
Assembly	11,260	68,340	1,570	(310)
Totals	$27,120	$161,970	$3,020	$5,130

ABC Manufacturing Company
DRILL PRESS COSTS

(Floor Manager)	Amount This Month	Amount Year to Date	(Over) or Under Budget This Month	(Over) or Under Budget Year to Date
Controllable expenses				
Supervision	$ 350	$2,100	$ —	$ —
Setup	175	910	(10)	40
Repair and rework	230	1,215	20	35
Overtime premium	215	1,145	(25)	(215)
Supplies	95	545	(10)	(5)
Small tools	115	625	20	(35)
Other	285	1,620	40	85
Totals	$1,465	$8,160	$ 35	($ 95)
	Standard This Month	**Standard Year to Date**	**Variance This Month**	**Variance Year to Date**
Productive labor				
Amount	$2,550	$ 14,250	$ 250	$ 400
Hours	850	4,750	25	45
Per hour	$ 3.00	$ 3.00	$ .15	$ .05

control. For example, assume that the budgeted amounts in Fig. 21.3 for the general superintendent are based on planned output of 2000 units. If, however, due to greater than anticipated sales, actual production is 2200 units, then the negative variances for each expense category may not really indicate inefficiency, but merely reflect the increased level of output.

A solution to such problems is to develop a flexible budget, in which the budgeted amounts vary in relation to some measure of organizational activity. In terms of our previous example, flexible budgeting would entail dividing the budget for each line item in the general superintendent's department into its fixed and variable cost components. In this way, budget standards would be automatically adjusted for any unplanned increases (or decreases) in production. Thus any differences between these adjusted standards and actual costs can more appropriately be interpreted.

OPPORTUNITIES FOR USING INFORMATION TECHNOLOGY

Information technology provides opportunities for improving the efficiency and effectiveness of the general ledger and reporting cycle in terms of (1) the timing of general ledger updates, (2) the monthly closing process, and (3) financial reporting.

Timing of General Ledger Update

As described in Chapters 17–20, modern AIS systems often use on-line processing to update the subsidiary ledgers as each transaction occurs. (In an REA data model, subsidiary ledgers take the form of relational tables.) This immediate updating keeps the subsidiary ledger balances current and can improve the quality of subsequent decisions. For example, updating an individual customer's account balance immediately after a sale facilitates subsequent decisions about whether to extend additional credit to that customer.

General ledger account balances, however, traditionally have not been updated immediately because they are not directly used to make operational decisions. For example, decisions about extending credit are based on information about the individual customer's current account balance and credit limit. That information is found in the subsidiary accounts receivable ledger; the general ledger accounts receivable control account only stores information about the total outstanding account balances of all customers.

The information in the general ledger is used to produce periodic performance reports. Traditionally, most organizations have prepared these reports for internal use on a monthly basis, and for external users on a quarterly basis. Consequently, many general ledger systems traditionally have been updated only once a month. Such a policy, however, creates two problems. First, because the general ledger is accurate only immediately after posting the summary monthly journal entries, it cannot be used as a source of data for interim "what if" analyses by management. In the past, the need for such continuous planning was less important. In today's fast-paced global economy, however, management must constantly monitor and reevaluate the organization's financial performance in light of its strategic goals. Firms must be able to alter their plans quickly in response to changes in their environment. A second problem with periodic updates to the general ledger is that any delays or problems

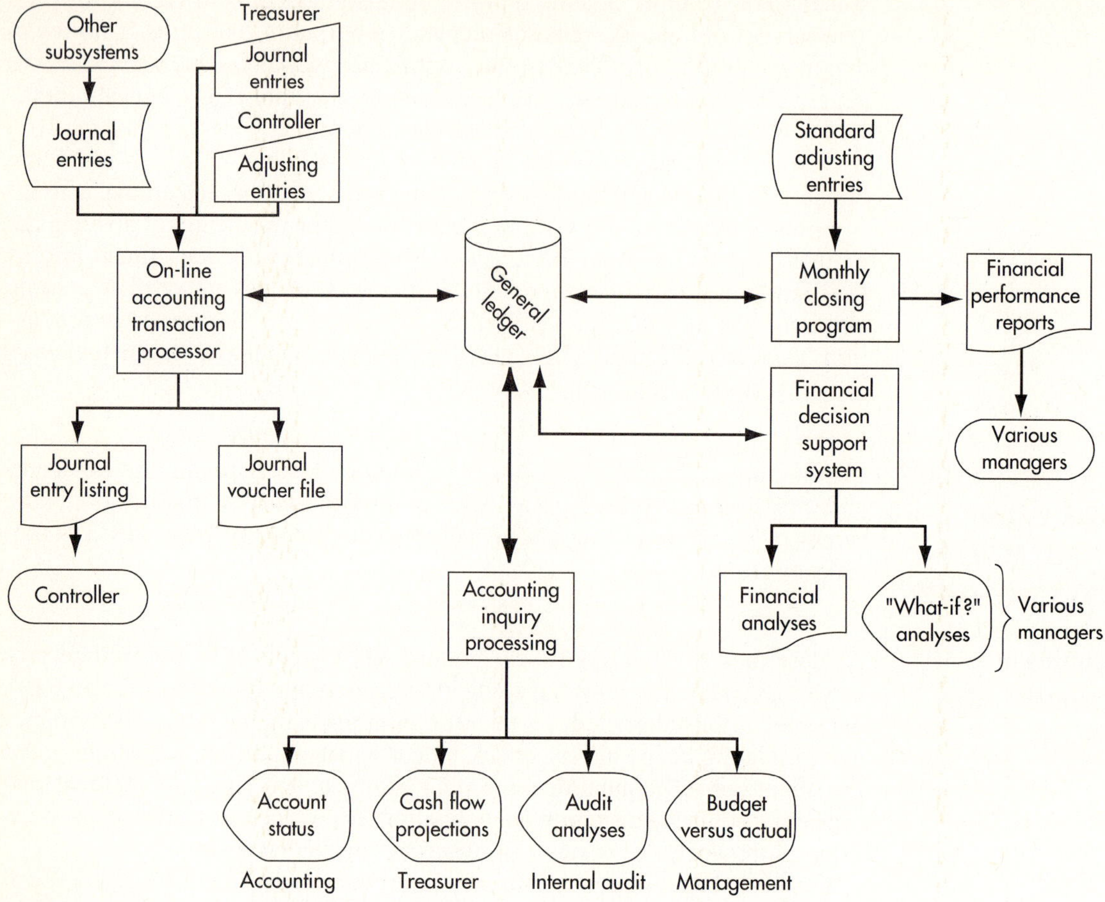

Figure 21.4

Flowchart of On-Line General Ledger and Reporting System

encountered in the monthly update process will cause delays in producing those interim financial statements. This is the situation that arose at AOE, as explained in the introductory case.

Consequently, many organizations are adopting on-line general ledger systems similar to that depicted in Fig. 21.4. Each individual application program in these systems, such as sales order entry or cash receipts, posts summary journal entries to the general ledger at least daily. The treasurer's staff uses on-line terminals to enter data about nonroutine transactions on the day they occur. Thus the general ledger is kept more current, thereby increasing its usefulness as a source of data for managers to perform "what-if" analyses of the effects of policy changes. In addition, the on-line general ledger system supports inquiries by various users, as depicted at the bottom of the figure.

Monthly Closing Process

Many organizations, such as AOE, are interested in finding ways to speed up the monthly closing process. After all, two-week-old monthly income statements are of limited usefulness for taking prompt, corrective actions. In

FOCUS 21.1

How an IT-Savvy Accountant Reengineered Microsoft's General Ledger and Reporting System

Remember the old joke about the shoemaker's children being the last to have shoes? Well, in 1993 when Scott Boggs joined Microsoft as assistant corporate controller, he found that it was using a terribly inefficient and inflexible mainframe-based general ledger and reporting system. It took two weeks to get the monthly profit and loss statements to Microsoft's 60 worldwide subsidiaries. Half of that time was spent in printing, mailing, and faxing the reports because the mainframe-based data could not be distributed electronically.

Boggs worked with the IT group to make several significant improvements to the system. First, the general ledger data was extracted from the mainframe and stored in a client/server relational data base. This made it possible to disseminate the data over Microsoft's Ethernet network. This step alone reduced the monthly closing process to one week. Next, data from 30 order management systems around the world were consolidated into one relational transaction data base built on an SQL server. Now Microsoft divisional managers can easily access subsets of the financial data that are most relevant to their individual needs.

Nevertheless, the amount of data available was overwhelming. The daily revenue data base, for example, was 1.4 gigabytes and contained 1.1 million records. Consequently, Boggs borrowed an idea from the Internet to improve the interface to Microsoft's internal financial network: The accounting department created an internal Home Page. This "Controller's Financial Information" Home Page provides users with graphic-enhanced information about Microsoft's cost centers, accounting policies, and corporate financial planning, thereby helping managers to find the data they need.

Focus Questions

1. What are some of the risks and benefits of creating internal "Home Pages" on an internal LAN to improve management's access to the company's financial data base?
2. If a global organization decides to use the Internet to make its general ledger data base accessible to every division, what control procedures should it implement to protect the integrity and confidentiality of that data base?

Source: Peggy Wallace, "Microsoft's Finance Department Gets Up to Speed," *Infoworld* (June 5, 1995): 58.

---

addition, reducing the closing process frees up more time for the accounting staff to analyze the data and advise operating managers about important trends. The potential time savings can be substantial. For example, in 1987 it took Motorola eight days to perform monthly closings; by 1995 it took just two days.

One way to speed up the monthly closing process is to consolidate overlapping AIS subsystems. Over the years, many organizations have found that their AIS subsystems have proliferated as a result of mergers and acquisitions or internal growth into new markets. For example, IBM once had 315 separate AIS subsystems worldwide. The CFO and the controller worked together to consolidate them into 36 subsystems, which not only sped up the closing process but also substantially reduced costs.

Client/server systems provide another way to improve the closing process and to disseminate financial performance reports more quickly. Focus 21.1 describes the benefits Microsoft derived from putting its general ledger on the corporate LAN and creating internal "Home Pages" to access it.

FOCUS 21.2

Accurately Graphing Financial Data

The following four principles are crucial to designing accurate graphs:

1. *Start the vertical axis at zero.* Failure to do so exaggerates the magnitude of changes because the upper intervals of the graph do not represent the same amount of change as the lower intervals.
2. *Do not extend the vertical scales far beyond the upper limit of the variable being graphed.* This principle is most commonly violated when graphing two variables that differ greatly in their data values, such as income and sales. Although sales and income are related, using one scale to depict both variables on the same graph can hide the actual magnitude of the change in income, because the heights of the columns for income are so small.
3. *Order time series from left to right on the horizontal axis.* Although comparative financial statements may place the most recent year's data on the left, people normally read graphs and text from left to right. Violating this principle can lead to misleading interpretations of trends.
4. *Avoid using three-dimensional column charts.* These type of graphs look dramatic, but they are difficult to interpret correctly. It is hard to note accurate changes in height across columns, because the back of the column is itself higher than the front. Moreover, the change in the volume of each columnar bar is much greater than the change in height.

These principles are easily violated. A detailed study of more than 250 annual reports of *Fortune* 500 companies revealed that 10% contained graphs that violated one or more of these four basic principles of graph design, thereby distorting the

Financial Reporting

Communications technology can also be used to reduce both the time and costs of preparing and disseminating financial statements. For example, controllers can access public financial reporting data bases, such as NAARS and EDGAR, to find examples of how other companies disclose various items. Similarly, tax forms and regulations can be accessed from the IRS on the Internet. Conversely, a company's financial statements can be made available to the public via the Internet. A company can also submit required financial and tax filings electronically to the SEC and the IRS, respectively.

Finally, spreadsheets and graphics packages can improve the financial reporting process by facilitating the creation of graphs to highlight key trends. The utility of graphic analysis, however, depends upon the accuracy with which the graphs are designed. A properly designed graph should lead to the same conclusions as a detailed analysis of the data upon which the graph is based. Focus 21.2 summarizes basic principles for designing accurate graphs and reports the results of a study indicating how often those principles are violated in published financial statements.

CONTROL OBJECTIVES, THREATS, AND PROCEDURES

The control objectives in the general ledger and reporting cycle are similar to those in the other AIS cycles discussed in previous chapters:

1. All updates to the general ledger are properly authorized.
2. All recorded general ledger transactions are valid.

data in a manner favorable to the company.

The most common problem was overstating the magnitude of a change. Specifically, 13 annual reports contained graphs that exaggerated the magnitude of an increase in sales, income, or dividends by 100% or more. In other words, the graph made the amount of change appear to be at least twice as large as it really was. Three other annual reports contained graphs that understated the numerical decline in sales, income, or dividends. On the other hand, the study also found that another 12 annual reports contained graphs that distorted financial results in a manner unfavorable to the company (for example, by understating the magnitude of an increase in sale, income, or dividends).

Interestingly, every annual report that contained a misleading graph also contained other graphs that were indeed accurate. In addition, companies that had experienced a decrease in net income from the prior year were twice as likely to have misleading graphs in their annual reports than were companies that had experienced an increase in net income.

Focus Questions

1. Given that the study found that only a little over 10% of the annual reports contained misleading graphs, how serious is the problem?
2. Are readers of annual reports likely to be misled by improperly designed graphs? Why or why not? What about accountants and other finance professionals?
3. If graphs are included in annual reports or other financial statements presented to external users, should auditors be responsible for evaluating the accuracy of those graphs? Why or why not?

Source: Paul John Steinbart, "The Auditor's Responsibility for the Accuracy of Graphs in Annual Reports: Some Evidence on the Need for Additional Guidance," *Accounting Horizons* (September 1989): 60–70.

3. All valid, authorized general ledger transactions are recorded.
4. All general ledger transactions are accurately recorded.
5. General ledger data are safeguarded from loss or theft.
6. General ledger cycle activities are performed efficiently and effectively.

Well-designed documents and records play an important role in achieving these objectives. If paper journal vouchers are used, they should contain clear instructions about how to complete them. On-line data entry of transactions by the treasurer and the controller, as depicted in Fig. 21.4, facilitates the accurate and efficient recording of general ledger journal entries. In such situations, the use of appropriate application controls, such as validity checks and field (format) checks, enhances the accuracy of data entry. Providing space on both paper and electronic documents to record who completed and reviewed the form provides evidence that the journal entry was properly authorized. Finally, prenumbering all documents facilitates checking to verify that all transactions have been recorded.

Table 21.1 lists the major threats and exposures in the general ledger and financial reporting cycle, along with applicable control procedures for mitigating them. Because the general ledger and reporting cycle involves only information processing activities, there are fewer threats than in the other AIS cycles. Moreover, the threats in the general ledger and reporting cycle primarily relate to the corruption, loss, or destruction of data. Let us now examine the control procedures that can be used to deal with these threats.

Table 21.1 Threats, Exposures, and Control Procedures in the General Ledger and Reporting Cycle

Threat	Exposure	Control Procedures
1. Errors in updating the general ledger: (a) Inaccurate/incomplete journal entries (b) Inaccurate/incomplete posting of journal entries	• Inaccurate records and reports, resulting in bad decisions based on erroneous information	• Input, edit, and processing controls • Reconciliations and control reports • Audit trail
2. Unauthorized access to the general ledger	• Leak of confidential data • Corruption of general ledger • Cover-up of theft	• Access controls • Adequate audit trail
3. Loss or destruction of general ledger data	• Loss of data • Loss of assets	• Proper backup procedures • Disaster recovery plan

Threat 1: Errors in Updating the General Ledger

Errors made in updating the general ledger can lead to poor decision making based on erroneous information in financial performance reports. The control procedures for dealing with this threat fall into three categories: (1) input edit and processing controls, (2) reconciliations and control reports, and (3) maintenance of an adequate audit trail.

Input Edit and Processing Controls. Two types of journal entries are used to update the general ledger shown in Fig. 21.4: (1) summary journal entries from the other AIS cycles and (2) direct entries made by the treasurer or controller. The former are themselves the output of a series of processing steps, each of which was subject to a variety of application control procedures designed to ensure accuracy and completeness. Consequently, the primary input edit control for summary journal entries involves checking their date to ensure that they represent activity for the most recent, unposted time period.

Journal entries made by the treasurer and controller, however, are original data entry. Consequently, the following types of input edit and processing controls are needed to ensure that they are accurate and complete:

1. A *validity check* to ensure that general ledger accounts do exist for each account number referenced in a journal entry.
2. *Field (format) checks* to ensure that the amount field in the journal entry contains only numeric data.
3. *Zero-balance checks* to verify that total debits equals total credits in a journal entry.
4. A *completeness test* to ensure that all pertinent data are entered. It is especially important that the source of the journal entry be identified, because this information forms a key part of the audit trail.
5. A *redundant data check* to match account numbers with account descriptions, to ensure that the correct general ledger account is being accessed. For on-line data entry, this would be referred to as *closed-loop verification.*
6. The *creation of a standard adjusting entry file* for recurring adjusting entries made each period, such as depreciation expense. Input accuracy is improved without repeatedly keying in these entries. The possibility of forgetting to

make a recurring adjusting entry is also reduced, thereby ensuring input completeness.

7. A *sign check* of the general ledger account balance once updating is completed, to verify that the balance is of the appropriate nature (debit or credit).
8. *Calculation of run-to-run totals* can verify the accuracy of journal voucher batch processing. The computer calculates the new balance of the general ledger account, based on its beginning balance and the total debits and credits applied to that account, then compares that to the actual account balance in the updated general ledger. Any discrepancies indicate a processing error that must be investigated.

Reconciliations and Control Reports. The use of reconciliations and control reports can detect whether any errors were made during the process of updating the general ledger. One form of reconciliation used in manual systems is the preparation of a trial balance. It indicates whether the total debit balances in the general ledger equals the total credit balances; if not, an error in posting has occurred. In automated systems, the use of clearing and suspense accounts ensures that the general ledger is always in balance. At the close of a period, all these special accounts should have zero balances; otherwise, an error was made in updating the general ledger.

To illustrate, assume that one clerk is responsible for recording the release of inventory to customers and another is responsible for recording the billing of customers. The first clerk would make the following journal entry:

Unbilled shipments	xxx	
Inventory		xxx

The second clerk would make this entry:

Accounts receivable	yyy	
Unbilled shipments		yyy

Once both entries have been completed, the special clearing account, unbilled shipments, should have a zero balance. If not, an error has been made that needs to be investigated and corrected.

Two other forms of reconciliation are used in both manual and automated systems. One involves comparing the general ledger control account balances to the total balance in the corresponding subsidiary ledger. If these two totals do not agree, the difference must be investigated and corrected. The second involves examining all transactions occurring near the end of an accounting period to verify that they are recorded in the proper time period.

Control reports can help identify the source of any errors that occurred in the general ledger update process. Listing journal vouchers by general account number facilitates identifying the cause of errors affecting a specific general ledger account. Listing the journal vouchers by sequence can indicate the absence of any journal entry postings. Finally, the **general journal listing** shows the details (account number, source reference code, description, and amount debited or credited) of each entry posted to the general ledger. This report indicates whether the total debits equals the total credits posted to the general ledger.

The Audit Trail. In Chapter 2 we explained that the audit trail depicts the path of a transaction through the accounting system. Specifically, it provides the information needed to perform the following tasks:

1. Trace any transaction from its original source document to the general ledger and to any report or other document using that data.
2. Trace any item appearing in a report or other output document back through the general ledger to its original source document.
3. Trace all changes in the general ledger from its beginning balance to its ending balance.

Figure 2.3 (p. 44) illustrated the elements of the audit trail in a manual system. Although the format of the various journals and ledgers may look a little different in a conventional computer-based AIS, the same basic information is preserved and can be displayed on control reports. For example, the general journal listing indicates the source of all entries made to update the general ledger.

Threat 2: Unauthorized Access to the General Ledger

Access to the general ledger by unauthorized persons can result in confidential data "leaks" to competitors or corruption of the general ledger. It can also provide a means for concealing the theft of assets. Consequently, it is important to have adequate controls to prevent unauthorized access to the general ledger.

User IDs and passwords should be used to control access to the general ledger and to enforce the proper segregation of duties by limiting the functions that each legitimate user may perform. For example, employees who have custody of assets or the ability to authorize the release of assets should be prevented from updating the general ledger. Similarly, management should be given read-only access to the general ledger, as depicted in the bottom of Fig. 21.4. The access control matrix should also limit the functions that can be performed at various terminals. Adjusting entries, for example, should be allowed only from terminals in the controller's office.

Controls over the creation of journal voucher records are also important because they authorize changes to general ledger account balances. Thus the system should check for the existence of a valid authorization code for each journal voucher record before posting that transaction to the general ledger. Otherwise, the integrity of the general ledger may be compromised. Note that this authorization code also forms a part of the audit trail. Indeed, inspection of the audit trail provides a means to detect unauthorized access to the general ledger.

Threat 3: Loss or Destruction of the General Ledger

The general ledger is a key component of the organization's accounting information system. Therefore, it is important to provide adequate backup and disaster recovery procedures to protect this asset. Backup controls include the following:

1. The use of internal and external file labels to protect against inadvertent destruction of the current general ledger.

2. Regular backup of the general ledger. At least two backup copies of the general ledger should exist. One copy should be kept on site where it can be immediately accessed. The other copy should be stored elsewhere to provide protection against a major disaster, such as a fire or an earthquake.

Disaster recovery planning is also crucial. Given the increasing reliance on EDI, EFT, and the Internet to conduct daily business activities, no organization can survive for long if its computers go down. As you learned in Chapter 15, organizations need to prepare and periodically practice a plan for dealing with a major disaster that has the potential to shut down their computer systems.

GENERAL LEDGER DATA MODEL

As discussed earlier in the chapter, there is no need for a separate general ledger in an AIS built using a relational data base. Indeed, as we demonstrated in Chapter 6, all the elements of a traditional AIS (journals, ledgers, and financial statements) can be derived by querying the appropriate relational tables. These queries can be made more efficient, however, if the data base contains aggregated values in addition to data about individual transactions. For example, instead of storing the amount of each individual sale and writing a query to sum those amounts to derive total sales for a time period, it is more efficient to create an additional table that contains a running total of all current sales. Similar comments apply to purchases, cash receipts, and other business activities. Although these aggregate tables create some redundancy, they increase the efficiency of report generation. They do not, however, have to take the form of a separate general ledger.

Nevertheless, most companies still maintain a general ledger for storing their financial data. Increasingly, however, many commercial general ledger packages are implemented as a relational data base. Figure 21.5 shows one way to represent the resulting data structure.

Notice that Fig. 21.5 is much simpler than the data models presented in previous chapters. The reason is that the general ledger and reporting cycle consists of information processing activities, rather than basic business activities that involve the transformation or exchange of resources. Indeed, strictly speaking, there are no resources and events, as those terms are defined in the REA data model. The general ledger and general ledger history entities are not resources, rather, they contain data about the organization's resources. Similarly, the journal voucher entity is not an event about which data are collected; it simply contains the data used to update the general ledger.

Reading the Data Model

Each row in the general ledger table stores data about a specific general ledger account. The primary key for this table consists of two attributes: the general ledger account number and the department number. The account number uses block coding to identify the type of account; the department number is used to implement a responsibility accounting system. Other attributes include the account name, beginning date of the current period, account balance at the beginning of the current period, current account balance, whether the account normally has a debit or credit balance, and budget information. The latter may be a specific figure or a formula if a flexible budget is employed.

Figure 21.5

E–R Diagram of General Ledger

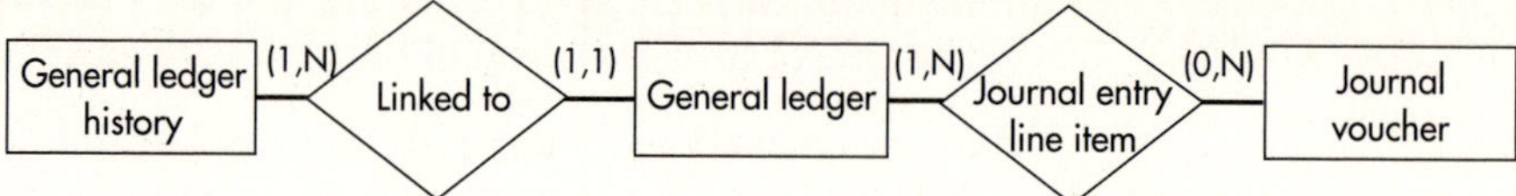

Table Attributes for Fig. 21.5

Table Name	Contents (**Primary Key,** *Foreign Key*)
General ledger	**Account_Number, Department_Number,** Account_Name, Date, Beginning_Balance, Current_Balance, Balance_Code, Budget_Data
General ledger history	**Account_Number, Department_Number, Month, Year,** Account_Name, Beginning_Balance, Ending_Balance, Total_Debits, Total_Credits, Balance_Code, Budget_Data
Journal voucher	**Journal_Voucher_Number,** Date, *Prepared by,* Explanation
Journal entry line item	**Journal_Voucher_Number, Account_Number, Department_Number,** Amount, Balance_Code

Figure 21.5 shows a one-to-many relationship between the general ledger and general ledger history entities. The latter stores data about the general ledger accounts for prior periods. The primary key for the general ledger history entity consists of three attributes: account number, department number, and date. Other attributes include the beginning and ending account balances, total debits and credits during the period, whether the account normally has a debit or credit balance, and budget information.

The data used to update the general ledger accounts are stored in the journal voucher and journal voucher line item entities. Together, these two entities contain the information that would be found in the general journal in manual systems.

Each row in the journal voucher table represents either a special journal entry from the treasurer's or controller's office or a summary entry from one of the subsystems described in Chapters 17–20. The primary key for this entity is the journal voucher number. Other important attributes are the date of the entry, the identification of the person or subsystem generating the journal entry, and an explanation of the nature of the entry.

The summary journal entry amount generated by a subsystem of the AIS may be the result of a query operation on tables in that subsystem. For example, the amount of the credit to the general ledger sales account for July sales may be generated by the following query in the revenue cycle:

```
SELECT    Sum(amount)
FROM      Sales
WHERE     Date BETWEEN 07/01 and 07/31
```

Each journal entry affects at least two general ledger accounts. In addition, each general ledger account can be updated by more than one journal voucher. Consequently, the relationship between the general ledger and journal voucher entities is many-to-many. The primary key for this relationship entity consists of three attributes: general ledger account number, department number, and the journal voucher number. The other attributes record the dollar amount of the journal entry and whether it is a debit or credit.

Benefits of a Relational Data Base General Ledger

A general ledger implemented in a well-designed relational data base can significantly improve the support provided for managerial decision making. To appreciate this fact, consider how the chart of accounts in a traditional general ledger system limits subsequent analyses of expense data. Expenses are typically recorded and stored in an account that reflects either the nature of the expense, such as travel, or its function, such as campus recruiting visits. With the first alternative, it is easy to prepare reports of total travel expenses but difficult to identify how much travel expense is associated with campus recruiting. With the second alternative, it is easy to prepare reports that show the costs associated with campus recruiting but difficult to prepare reports that track total travel costs.

A common response to this problem in file-based general ledger systems is to create more detailed account numbers that identify both the nature and purpose of each expense. Thus there would be separate accounts for campus recruiting travel expenses, sales travel expenses, and so on. The drawback of this approach, however, is that it results in an exponential expansion of the chart of accounts and an increase in the length of each account code. Both of these factors make it more difficult for coding clerks and managers to learn the chart of accounts and apply it correctly. In addition, the ability to further analyze the data remains limited to those categories that were considered when the chart of accounts was designed.

In contrast, a general ledger implemented in a well-designed relational data base avoids these problems and provides greater flexibility for analyzing data. Tables can be created for basic account categories, such as travel expenses. These tables can also include a text attribute for describing the purpose of that expenditure. Managers can then use SQL queries to select all travel expenses associated with campus recruiting:

```
SELECT    Sum(amount)
FROM      Travel_Expenses
WHERE     Purpose = 'campus recruiting'
```

Similar queries can be created for any type of travel. Moreover, these categories can be changed over time in response to different needs simply by changing the condition specified in the WHERE clause of the query. Thus users are not limited to predetermined expense classification schemes. Yet, reports of total travel expenses for all purposes can also be easily generated by eliminating the use of a WHERE clause that restricts the scope of the query.

A second benefit of a well-designed general ledger data model is that it facilitates the integration of financial and nonfinancial information. The importance of this feature is underscored by increasing pressure to expand the scope of the information presented in financial statements. For example, the AICPA Special Committee on Financial Reporting (the Jenkins Committee) recommends that financial reports prepared for external users include nonfinancial information such as measures of customer satisfaction and product cycle times. Similarly, in Chapter 20 we discussed the trend toward including measures of the value of a company's human capital in annual reports. This information can also be easily incorporated in relational data base general ledger.

Internal Control Considerations

One of the major control objectives in the general ledger and reporting cycle is data accuracy. The relational data model provides some built-in controls to ensure data accuracy and consistency. One of the more important of these controls is support for foreign keys and referential integrity. This control ensures that when a new row is added to the journal entry line item table, the system will verify that the general ledger account number (which appears as a foreign key in that table) actually exists as part of the primary key in the general ledger table.

Another control objective is to safeguard access to the general ledger. Most relational DBMS provide a means to control access by letting users see only the portion of a data base (called a view) relevant to their job duties. Finally, the use of a data base general ledger system makes adequate backup and disaster recovery procedures vital.

Does an audit trail exist in a general ledger implemented in a relational data base? Yes, in the form of links between tables. To illustrate, let us examine the process for validating the updates to the sales account in the general ledger. Referring to Fig. 21.5, the first step would involve writing an SQL query linking the general ledger, journal voucher, and journal entry line item tables. This would provide the same information as found in the general journal listing: the dates of each journal entry affecting the sales account, the identity of the person or subsystem generating those entries, and the amounts of each entry.

The next step would be to write SQL queries against the data model for the revenue cycle (refer to Figure 17.14, p. 606). One such query would sum the amount of all sales during the time period of interest. This result should equal the value in the amount column in the journal voucher line item table. Other queries would link the sales, shipments, and orders tables to verify the completeness and validity of all recorded sales. Additional queries could be written to trace sales to specific customers and sales staff. In fact, the number of such cross-table links that can be easily generated is limited only by the investigator's imagination. Thus a data base general ledger system provides for a much richer and more complete audit trail than that typically provided by conventional AIS (whether manual or computer-based).

SUMMARY AND CASE CONCLUSION

The general ledger and financial reporting cycle integrates and summarizes the results of the various accounting subsystems for the revenue, expenditure, production, and human resource cycles. The general ledger is the central master file in the accounting information system. Consequently, it is important to implement control procedures to ensure its accuracy and security. Important controls include edit checks of the journal voucher records posted to the general ledger, access controls, an adequate audit trail, and appropriate backup and disaster recovery procedures.

The reports produced by the general ledger system fall into two primary categories: financial statements and managerial reports. The former are prepared periodically in accordance with GAAP and are distributed to both internal and external users. The latter are prepared for internal use only and therefore often include comparisons between actual and budgeted performance. The usefulness of these reports, whether presented in the form of tables or graphs, is affected by how well they are designed.

In addition to printed reports, the general ledger system should also support inquiry processing by decision makers. This requires adequate controls to limit access to, and permissible operations on, the data in the general ledger. Designing the general ledger in accordance with the relational data model facilitates inquiry processing by making the data more easily accessible to desktop tools found on most personal computers.

Although many organizations have traditionally used batch processing to update their general ledger, there is a movement to switch to on-line systems. Indeed, on-line systems are necessary to provide useful inquiry processing capabilities. They also speed the period-end closing process. Consequently, Stephanie Cromwell and Elizabeth Venko decided that AOE needs to switch to an on-line general ledger system similar to that depicted in Fig. 21.4, set up on a client/server network.

Elizabeth tells Stephanie that her ultimate goal is to eliminate the use of a separate general ledger. She and Stephanie agree, however, that AOE will first acquire a general ledger package that is built on a relational data base, similar to that shown in Fig. 21.5. This will enable the accounting department to gain experience in using a relational data base. It will also provide time to explore the control issues involved with providing managers with increased access to the general ledger.

This chapter concludes our study of accounting information systems. You have learned that accounting information systems have three main objectives: (1) to process transactions for accountability purposes, (2) to maintain adequate controls to ensure the integrity of the organization's data and the safeguarding of its assets, and (3) to provide information to support decision making. We would like to close by reiterating one other theme that appears throughout this book: the need for accountants to move beyond the traditional role of scorekeeper and actively seek to add value to their organization. It is especially important that accountants participate in decisions concerning the adoption of new technology. They have the training to properly evaluate the relative costs and benefits, as well as the economic risks, underlying such investments. Effective evaluation requires that accountants not only keep abreast of current accounting developments, but also stay informed about advances in information technology. Thus you must make a commitment to lifelong learning. We wish you well in this endeavor.

KEY TERMS

general ledger and reporting cycle

responsibility accounting

journal voucher

general journal listing

CHAPTER QUIZ

1. Adjusting entries are normally provided by
  a. the treasurer.
  b. the controller.
  c. the various accounting cycle subsystems, such as sales order entry.
  d. unit managers.

2. Preparing performance reports that contain data only about items that a specific organizational unit controls is an example of
  a. a flexible budget system.
  b. a responsibility accounting system.
  c. closing the books.
  d. management by exception.

3. Which of the following is *not* one of the reasons for continuing to maintain a separate general ledger system?
  a. Because the organization has not yet implemented a relational data base for its various AIS subsystems (e.g., revenue, expenditure, etc.)
  b. Tradition
  c. Because a general ledger system is needed to produce financial statements
  d. Segregation of duties

4. In a relational data base general ledger, such as in Fig. 21.5, which table would contain the amount of the credit to accounts receivable to reflect total cash receipts that period?
  a. General ledger
  b. General ledger history
  c. Journal voucher
  d. Journal entry line item

5. Which control procedure would determine if an entry was posted to the wrong general ledger accounts?
  a. Using passwords to limit access to the general ledger
  b. Preparing and comparing batch totals of journal entries
  c. Review of the general journal listing
  d. Reconciliation of general ledger control accounts with subsidiary account balances

6. Which control procedure would be most effective in preventing a posting error while updating the general ledger?
  a. Passwords and user IDs
  b. Listing all journal vouchers in numerical sequence
  c. A zero-balance check on the equality of debits and credits in the journal entry
  d. Reconciliation of general ledger control account balances with their corresponding subsidiary ledgers

7. Which control procedure would best detect the source of an incomplete update of the general ledger?
  a. Preparation of a trial balance
  b. A general journal listing
  c. A list of all journal vouchers posted, in numerical sequence
  d. Run-to-run batch totals

8. Traditionally, the general ledger is updated
  a. when each transaction occurred.
  b. at year-end.
  c. monthly.
  d. on-demand.

9. Which of the following factors is most likely to result in a graph that distorts the magnitude of a trend in financial numbers?
  a. Not starting the vertical axis at zero
  b. Using 3-D bar charts to illustrate sales growth
  c. Ordering the years from left to right
  d. Failing to include a chart title

10. In performance reports, setting the comparison standards on the basis of the actual level of activity that occurred is an example of
  a. responsibility accounting.
  b. long-range planning.
  c. variance analysis.
  d. flexible budgeting.

DISCUSSION QUESTIONS

21.1 The data model shown in Fig. 21.5 is supposed to accommodate the unified storage of financial and nonfinancial operating data. How can you effectively combine both types of information in one report? For example, how can you compare and relate a 15% reduction in scrap and rework costs with an 8%

increase in customer satisfaction and a 10% increase in sales?

21.2 What effect does the classification of an organizational unit as a cost, revenue, profit, or investment center have on the types of managerial reports produced for that unit?

21.3 It has been proposed that companies should provide users with a computer-readable copy, either on disk or through the Internet, of the organization's general ledger instead of its financial statements. This would permit users to analyze the data in whatever manner they desire. Assuming that this approach is technologically feasible, should it be done? Why or why not?

21.4 Although ATMs print receipts that show the effects of both deposits and withdrawals on account balances, deposits are not immediately credited to accounts. Explain the purpose of such "false updates."

21.5 Many companies are participating in studies to develop "benchmarks" for evaluating the efficiency of their accounting departments. These studies typically report such statistics as the total costs of the accounting department as a percentage of revenues, documents processed per accounting clerk each month, and monthly closing times. Both "best" and "average" figures are usually reported for these categories. Discuss the usefulness and limitations of using such measures to evaluate the accounting department of a specific company.

21.6 Some companies are abandoning the practice of budgeting, because they claim that the costs outweigh the benefits. They argue that instead of comparing actual performance to budgeted standards, closely monitoring trends in actual performance over time would be more effective. Deviations from historical trends would signal the need to take corrective actions. Discuss the advantages and disadvantages of this practice.

PROBLEMS

21.1 Which control procedure would be most effective in addressing the following problems?

a. When entering a nonroutine journal entry, the accounting clerk inadvertently transposes two digits in the debit amount.

b. When entering a nonroutine journal entry, the accounting clerk inadvertently transposes two digits in the account code.

c. Last Tuesday an accounting clerk forgot to mark the source journal voucher as being entered after keying in the data for the issuance of debt. Consequently, another accounting clerk entered that same data on Wednesday.

d. The credit manager makes an entry authorizing the write-off of a friend's account.

e. The general ledger master file is stored on disk. For some reason, the disk is no longer readable. It takes the accounting department a week to reenter the past month's transactions from source documents in order to create a new general ledger master file.

f. An accounting clerk, unsure as to which department to charge for a loss on the disposition of some fixed assets, debited a suspense account in order to make the entry balance. Consequently, performance evaluation reports did not correctly show the results of this transaction.

g. The budget director accessed the payroll file and discovered the salaries of every other financial executive.

h. The treasurer inadvertently omitted the credit portion of the journal entry submitted to account for the repurchase of treasury stock.

i. During data entry, the controller transposed two digits in the debit portion of the adjusting entry for bad debt expense.

j. The treasurer forgot to submit a journal entry to record the accrual of interest on a short-term CD.

k. A nonexistent customer account number is entered during the posting of cash receipts. Consequently, the accounts receivable subsidiary ledger is out of balance with the general ledger control account.

21.2 Refer to the data model in Fig. 21.5. Write SQL queries to accomplish the following:

a. Display the information that would appear in the general journal of a manual system for the month of May.

b. List account balances for a specific department.

c. List all journal entries affecting the accounts payable control account for the entire year.

d. Display total sales by each department.

21.3 Obtain an annual report that contains several graphs and answer the following questions:

a. Which financial and nonfinancial variables are graphed?
b. Do all the graphs satisfy the general principle that the portrayed magnitude of change equal the actual magnitude of change? If not, which of the rules for accurate graphs were violated? Which variables are not graphed correctly?
c. Redraw any graphs identified in part (b) so that they accurately portray the magnitude of change in the variable being graphed.
d. Draw a pie graph, a line graph, and a column graph for data in the annual report that have not already been graphed. Design each graph to communicate *one* essential point about the organization's performance. Defend your choices of graph–variable pairings and your design.

21.4 Give two specific examples of nonroutine transactions that may occur in processing cash receipts and updating accounts receivable. Also specify the control procedures that should be in place to ensure the accuracy, completeness, and validity of those transactions.

21.5 An important control procedure involves the periodic reconciliation of general ledger accounts with their subsidiary ledgers. Explain how this control procedure works in the context of accounts payable. Your answer should specify how to verify the accuracy, completeness, and validity of all entries involving purchases, purchase returns, purchase discounts, and cash disbursements.

21.6 Figure 21.1 is a context diagram for the general ledger and reporting cycle that shows the principal data flows to and from the general ledger.

REQUIRED

a. List the source documents or journals underlying each data flow into the general ledger.
b. Identify at least two additional data flows resulting from the revenue and expenditure cycle systems, and specify the source documents or journals that would support those flows.
c. Write SQL queries to generate the summary data flows in Fig. 21.1 from each subsystem of the AIS. Refer to the data models in Chapters 17–20 when writing those queries.

21.7 Refer to the example of responsibility coding depicted in Fig. 21.3.

REQUIRED

a. Design a coding scheme that will support the production of this set of reports. Make and state any assumptions you believe are necessary.
b. Write a brief (half-page) explanation of how your coding scheme works.
c. Suggest improvements in the set of reports depicted in Fig. 21.3.

CASE 21.1: ANALYSIS OF A LOCAL COMPANY

Select a local company and obtain permission to study its general ledger and financial reporting cycle. Write a report that addresses the following issues:

1. Analyze the structure of its general ledger. How does it reflect the nature of the company's line of business? Is the system file-based or is it organized as a data base?
2. How often is the general ledger updated? Why?
3. Is an operating budget used for performance evaluation purposes? If so, what is the basis for setting the budget?
4. What control procedures are in place to safeguard the integrity of the general ledger?
5. How often do various unit managers receive reports on their unit's financial performance? Do any of those reports combine financial with nonfinancial data? If so, how?
6. Evaluate the tabular reports produced by the system. Are they easy to understand? appropriate for their intended use?
7. Are graphs used to supplement or present performance results? If so, analyze the graphs in light of the principles of graph design discussed in this chapter.

CASE 21.2: EVALUATING A GENERAL LEDGER PACKAGE

Accounting magazines like the *Journal of Accountancy* and *Management Accounting* periodically publish reviews of accounting software. Obtain a copy of a recent software review article and read its comments about a general ledger package to which you have access. Using the software, write a report that indicates whether, and why, you agree or disagree with the review's opinions about the following features of the general ledger package:

1. Ease of installation.
2. Flexibility in the initial setup of the chart of accounts and during subsequent modifications.
3. Frequency of updates from subsystems (sales, cash receipts, etc.).
4. Control procedures available to restrict access.
5. Control procedures to ensure accuracy of input and processing.
6. Report flexibility—how easy it is to design reports, etc.
7. Adequacy of the audit trail. For example, what reference data is automatically provided versus how much of the audit trail has to be manually constructed?

ANSWERS TO CHAPTER QUIZ

1. b	**3.** c	**5.** d	**7.** b	**9.** a
2. b	**4.** d	**6.** c	**8.** c	**10.** d

Appendix: Comprehensive Cases

CASE A.1: F & C CONSTRUCTION[1]

Frank, owner of F & C Construction, has the opportunity to bid on a job that includes remodeling two existing auto dealership offices and constructing a new office. This job would give F & C Construction a chance to move into a new market and expand its customer base. Frank is excited about the possibilities of making this move; however, to operate in this market, Frank will need to prepare formal business reports. Additionally, he is concerned about his ability to bid competitively and track the increased number of jobs this opportunity would provide.

Background

F & C Construction is a small, sole proprietorship. The owner, Frank, started his construction company approximately two years ago. Business is increasing at a steady pace. Currently, jobs range in size from small (kitchen countertop replacements, wooden decks) to large (additions to homes). His customers are individual homeowners.

Advertising is predominantly by word of mouth. The company logo is on both company trucks, and a placard is placed in a high-visibility location at job sites. Business cards are posted on bulletin boards in local stores and handed out at every opportunity. Satisfied customers and suppliers have made many referrals. F & C Construction is known for high standards of workmanship, using quality materials, and a no-surprises billing policy. (If Frank forgets to include a charge in the estimate, it is not added on at a later date. If the customer and Frank negotiate a change in the planned work, the bill is modified accordingly.)

The company currently employs Frank and two construction workers. Frank and his two workers are licensed to do general contracting work only; therefore, any plumbing or electrical work associated with

[1]This case, authored by Martha M. Eining of the University of Utah and Gail Lynn Cook of Syracuse University, appeared in the Spring 1993 issue of the *Journal of Accounting Case Research*. The case requirements have been modified to match the structure and content of this book. Reprinted from the *Journal of Accounting Case Research* with the permission of Captus Press Inc., North York, Ontario, Canada, and the Accounting Education Resource Centre of The University of Lethbridge, Lethbridge, Alberta, Canada.

Note: The purpose of this case is to provide an opportunity to apply the concepts of information systems to a business enterprise that is based on a real-world situation.

F & C Construction is a typical example of a small-business record-keeping system. For many companies this type of system works—at year-end the company has made money. The owner of this company recognizes the benefits to be gained from a formal information system in assisting him with a controlled expansion plan.

Figure 1
Proposal Form

FROM F & C Construction

PROPOSAL

Proposal No.
Sheet No.
Date

Proposal Submitted To | **Work To Be Performed At**

Name ______________________________
Street ______________________________
City ______________________________
State ______________________________
Telephone Number ____________________

We hereby propose to furnish all the materials and perform all the labor necessary for the completion of

All material is guaranteed to be as specified, and the above work to be performed in accordance with the drawings and specifications submitted for above work and completed in a substantial workmanlike manner for the sum of

Dollars ($).

with payments to be made as follows:

____

____

Any alteration or deviation from above specifications involving extra costs, will be executed only upon written orders, and will become an extra charge over and above the estimate. All agreements contingent upon strikes, accidents or delays beyond our control. Owner to carry fire, tornado and other necessary insurance upon above work. Workmen's Compensation and Public Liability Insurance on above work to be taken out by ____________________

Respectfully submitted ____________________

Per ____________________

Note—This proposal may be withdrawn by us if not accepted within days

ACCEPTANCE OF PROPOSAL

The above prices, specifications and conditions are satisfactory and are hereby accepted. You are authorized to do the work as specified. Payment will be made as outlined above.

____

Accepted **Signature**

Date **Signature**

Figure 2

Check Register Form

CHECK REGISTER						
			1	2	3	4
	Date	Paid to/Received from	Check #	Account #	Amount	Total
1						
2						
3						
4						
5						
6						
7						
8						
9						
10						

a job is subcontracted out. Caren, Frank's wife, does the bookkeeping on a part-time basis. A tax accountant is retained as a financial adviser and for filing all necessary tax documents.

F & C Construction is run out of an office in Frank's home. A telephone answering machine takes calls whenever Frank and Caren are both away from the office. F & C Construction's physical assets include two pickup trucks, an assortment of large and small tools, and an inventory of supplies (screws, nuts, bolts, spackle, etc.) that is stored in a shed or on the trucks.

Sales

When a potential customer calls to request a bid on a job, an appointment is scheduled. Frank does all of the bidding for F & C Construction. A formal proposal (Fig. 1, p. A–2) is completed and submitted to the customer. If the customer accepts the proposal, it is signed and becomes a legal contract. The customer keeps one copy, and F & C Construction retains the other copy. The contract also serves as the accounts receivable record, since it includes a schedule of payments and a work schedule. To date, due to the limited size of the business, keeping track of receivables due from customers has not been a problem.

The proposal indicates the customer's name, address, phone number, where the work is to be done, a description of the job, terms of the agreement, and a payment schedule. Payments are required as follows:

- *Large jobs.* Payments are broken down by the following major sections: one-half of the amount owed for the section is due when work begins on that section, and the remainder is due when the work is completed.

1. Subcontractor fees
2. Framing
3. Roofing
4. Siding
5. Sheetrock
6. Trim

- *Small jobs.* One-half of the payment is due up front and the remainder is due at completion.

Cash Receipts

Payments are recorded on the contract or a separate sheet of paper attached to the contract when received. Frank immediately makes out a deposit slip, in duplicate, and brings the deposit to the bank. One copy of the deposit slip is retained, and the other goes to the bank with the cash/check. Caren records all deposits in the check register (Fig. 2). The date the deposit was made, the customer name, the check number, and the amount of the deposit are recorded. Monthly, Caren does the bank reconciliation.

Purchases

As materials, supplies, and tools are needed, they are purchased from local suppliers. Since Frank deals with these suppliers on a regular basis, he mentally compares prices to obtain the best price for the quality products needed. If the purchase is a small dollar amount, Frank usually pays cash. (*Note:* When I asked Frank how he handled receipts for cash purchases, he told me he threw the cash register receipt on the dashboard of whichever truck he was driving, and at month-end he or Caren collected them so Caren could do the bookkeeping.)

If the purchase is for a large dollar amount, Frank charges the purchase. He has a line of credit with all of his major suppliers who bill on a monthly basis.

The charge slips are accumulated along with cash register receipts on the dashboards of the trucks and collected monthly for payment and recording purposes. When an invoice is received, Caren matches it with the charge slip(s).

Occasionally, a special tool is needed to complete a job. In these instances, Frank rents the tool from a local tool rental company. The procedure for rentals is the same as that for credit purchases. If a piece of equipment is rented more than two or three times, it is purchased.

Cash Disbursements

F & C Construction has one checking account that is separate from Frank and Caren's personal checking account. Both Frank and Caren write checks to pay

Figure 3 *Subcontract Agreement Form (front side)*

THIS FORM IS VALID IN ALL 50 STATES — USE THE SECTION BELOW IN STATE OF CALIFORNIA ONLY

"NOTICE TO OWNER"
(Section 7019–Contractors License Law)

Under the Mechanics' Lien Law, any contractor, subcontractor, laborer, materialman or other person who helps to improve your property and is not paid for his labor, services or material, has a right to enforce his claim against your property.

Under the law, you may protect yourself against such claims by filing, before commencing such work or improvement, an original contract for the work of improvement or a modification thereof, in the office of the county recorder of the county where the property is situated and requiring that a contractor's payment bond be recorded in such office. Said bond shall be in an amount not less than fifty percent (50%) of the contract price and shall, in addition to any conditions for the performance of the contract, be conditioned for the payment in full of the claims of all persons furnishing labor, sevices, equipment or materials for the work described in said contract.

STATE OF CALIFORNIA ONLY

Contractors are required by law to be licensed and regulated by the Contractors' State License Board. Any question concerning a contractor may be referred to the Registrar of the Board, whose address is:

Contractors' State License Board
1020 N Street
Sacramento, California 95814

STANDARD SUBCONTRACT AGREEMENT

FOR $ ____________
THE TOTAL CONTRACT AMOUNT
between

____

____

and

____

____

for

____

____

____

Dated ____________________ 19 ___

ARCHITECTS

____

Continued

Figure 3 *Subcontract Agreement Form (Continued)*

SUBCONTRACT AGREEMENT

THIS AGREEMENT, made this ____________________ day of ____________________ A.D. 19 _____,
by and between ____ hereinafter called the
Contractor, and ____ hereinafter called the
Subcontractor.

For the consideration hereinafter named, the Subcontractor agrees with the Contractor, as follows:

ARTICLE 1. WORK: The Subcontractor agrees to furnish all material and perform all work necessary to complete ________

At: ____
ADDRESS CITY COUNTY STATE

For: ____
OWNER OR OWNERS

according to the general conditions of the contract, as per the drawings and specifications, and amendments and/or changes to either (details thereof to be supplied as needed) prepared and identified by ____________________, Architect, and to the full satisfaction of said Architect.

ARTICLE 2. TIME: The Subcontractor agrees to promptly begin work as soon as notified by the Contractor, and to complete the work as follows:

ARTICLE 3. EXTRAS: No deviations from the work specified in the contract will be permitted or paid for unless a written extra work or change order is first agreed upon and signed as required.

ARTICLE 4. ASSIGNMENT: No assignment of this Subcontract agreement is permitted without prior written permission from the Contractor.

ARTICLE 5. INSURANCE: The Subcontractor agrees to obtain and pay for the following insurance coverages: Workmen's Compensation, Public Liability, Property Damage, and any other insurance coverage which may be necessary as required by the Owner, Contractor, or State Law.

ARTICLE 6. TAXES: The Subcontractor agrees to pay any and all Federal, State, or Local Taxes which are, or may be, assessed upon the material and labor which he furnishes under this contract.

IN CONSIDERATION WHEREOF, the Contractor agrees that he will pay the Subcontractor, in ____________ __________ payments, the sum of ____ ____ Dollars ($ __________) for materials and work, said amount to be paid as follows: ____________ percent (______%) of all labor and material which has been fixed in place by the Subcontractor, to be paid on or about the ____________ of the following month, except the final payment, which the Contractor shall pay to the Subcontractor within ____________ days after the Subcontractor shall have completed his work to the full satisfaction of the Architect or Owner.

The Contractor and the Subcontractor for themselves, their successors, executors, administrators and assigns, hereby agree to the full performance of the covenants herein contained.

IN WITNESS WHEREOF, they have executed this agreement the day and year first above written.

____________________ WITNESS	____________________ SUBCONTRACTOR
	____________________ BY
	____________________ STATE LICENSE NO.
	____________________ CONTRACTOR
____________________ WITNESS	____________________ BY
Tops Form No. 3461—Revised Litho in U.S.A.	____________________ STATE LICENSE NO.

SPECIAL CALIFORNIA NOTICE CLAUSE ON REVERSE SIDE

bills, meet payroll, and pay tax obligations. When a check is written, the payee, date, amount, and explanation for the check are recorded on the check stub, which remains in the check register (Fig. 2). All bills are paid by the fifteenth of the month to avoid finance charges. At month-end, Caren updates the check register and ledger book. Cash disbursements are tracked (spread) by category.

Payroll

When a subcontractor is used, jobs are awarded based on bids, and a standard subcontractor agreement (Fig. 3) is executed. Subcontractor fees are collected by F & C Construction according to the payment schedule above. Subcontractors are paid when they have completed their job, unless it is a big job and the subcontractor needs some money up front.

Time cards (Fig. 4) are kept for each of the construction workers. Workers fill out the time card daily to track hours worked. Frank approves the time cards, and workers are paid by check on a weekly basis. Caren uses the time cards to update the payroll register (Fig. 5). Most of this information—name, address, Social Security number, earnings, and withholdings—is necessary for tax purposes.

Frank pays himself a salary on a weekly basis. He writes a check and records the amount on the check stub. This information is then used by Caren to update the ledger book. Caren is not paid.

Quarterly and Yearly Procedures

On a quarterly basis, Caren brings the ledger book up to date and gives it to the accountant, who prepares quarterly financial statements that are used to prepare payroll tax forms. All forms and payments are filed on a timely basis by Caren.

At year-end, a federal tax form 1099 is filed for each subcontractor and construction worker. This form reports the amount paid to subcontractors and workers by federal ID number or Social Security

Figure 4

Weekly Time Card Form

WEEKLY TIME CARD FROM ______________ TO ____________

(This card must be forwarded to Payroll Department before payment is made)

Employee ______________________ Badge No. ____________

Address ______________________ Plant No. ____________

Position ______________ S.S. Acct. No. ______________ Dept. No. ____________

Name of Employer ______________________

	A.M.		P.M.		OVERTIME		EXTRA		TOTAL HOURS		
	In	Out	In	Out	In	Out	In	Out	Regular	Overtime	Extra
MON											
TUE											
WED											
THU											
FRI											
SAT											
SUN											
								TOTAL HOURS			

COMPUTATION OF EARNINGS & DEDUCTIONS		
Regular Time		
Overtime		
Extra Time		
Total Earnings		
S.S.		
Fed.		
State		
Local		
Total Deductions		
Net Pay		

I, the undersigned, certify that the records indicated above were my true and accurate working hours for the payroll period.

Stock Form No. 883

Signature ______________________

The Colonial Co., Brooklyn, NY 11230

Figure 5 *Payroll Register Form*

WEEK ENDING

	NAME	MARRIED SINGLE	EXEMPTIONS	HOURS							TOTAL HOURS	RATE	EARNINGS		
				Sun.	Mon.	Tues.	Wed.	Thurs.	Fri.	Sat.			Regular	Overtime	Other
1											Reg.				
											O.T.				
2											Reg.				
											O.T.				
3											Reg.				
											O.T.				
4											Reg.				
											O.T.				
5											Reg.				
											O.T.				
6											Reg.				
											O.T.				
7											Reg.				
											O.T.				
8											Reg.				
											O.T.				

number. The information needed to file each 1099 is available on the subcontractor agreements or in the payroll account for the workers. The accountant also prepares the income tax return.

Future

Franks expects F & C Construction to continue to grow. The local economy is good, and individual homeowners are investing in home improvements. Frank also wants to expand into the remodeling and office construction areas. This expansion will require competitive bidding and formal reporting, perhaps to meet bonding company requirements. Improvements to the formal information system are needed to support the expected growth and allow Frank to continue doing the actual construction work.

The requirements for this case are divided to coincide with the major sections of the book. In addition, the appropriate chapters are also identified.

Part One: Conceptual Foundations of Accounting Information Systems

1. (Chapter 1) Identify the information system that is currently in place for F & C Construction. What are the major deficiencies in the current information system? In general, what kinds of accounting information would be important to a small construction company?

2. (Chapter 3) Prepare document flowcharts to illustrate the current cycles presented for F & C Construction.

3. (Chapter 4) Explain the transaction processing system that F & C Construction is currently using. Make sure to include a description of the input, storage, processing, and output.

4. (Chapter 5) Discuss how the use of a data base system could improve the information available to Frank and Caren. In this type of small company, what problems would be encountered with the implementation and maintenance of a data base system? What role would (or should) their accountant play in the development of a data base system?

________________ 19 ______

		Deductions						Net Pay	Total Wages	Cumulative Totals						
	Total Wages	Soc. Sec.	U.S. With. Tax	State With. Tax						Soc. Sec.	U.S. With.Tax	State With.Tax				
1																1
2																2
3																3
4																4
5																5
6																6
7																7
8																8

Part Two: The Technology of Information Systems

5. (Chapter 8) Considering the type of company and the number of employees, develop a proposal for the type of computer hardware and software that should be purchased to create a computerized information system. Include a discussion of the concepts of a personal information system for Frank. Determine approximate costs for the items that you propose (you can use information from computer magazines and computer catalogs).

Part Three: The Systems Development Process

6. (Chapter 10) Evaluate the feasibility of computerizing F & C Construction. Since you were given no dollar amount in the case, just consider the items that you would include in this type of analysis (separate them into costs of computerizing and benefits of computerizing). Make sure that you consider items that could be quantified as well as those that are qualitative. From the description of the company, indicate for which of these items you believe you could find information. What would you do about items for which you could find no information?

7. (Chapter 10) Consider the behavioral implications of computerizing F & C Construction. How do you think Frank will react to computerization? Who will actually do the daily computer tasks? Will computerization make Frank and Caren's daily work easier or more complex?

8. (Chapter 10) Develop a plan to determine, in detail, the information needs for F & C Construction. Be sure to take into consideration the fact that Frank wants to expand the business. From the information in the case, indicate the most important information needs for F & C Construction.

9. (Chapter 11) From the information needs discussed in Requirement 8, design one of the reports that would be needed for F & C Construction.

10. (Chapter 11) Design the input forms and screens needed to capture the data for producing the report designed in Requirement 9.

11. (Chapter 12) Assuming that F & C Construction has decided to computerize, discuss the pros and cons of buying off-the-shelf packages versus developing its own software programs.

Part Four: Control and Audit of Accounting Information Systems

12. (Chapter 13) Identify the internal control weaknesses in the current operation of F & C Construction. For each control, offer possible solutions to the weakness. This will be easier if you provide the information by the cycles discussed in the case.

13. (Chapter 14) Assuming that F & C Construction computerizes, set up a system of internal controls over the computer function.

Part Five: Accounting Information Systems Applications

14. (Chapter 19) If you did not complete the document flowcharts for all cycles in Part 1, then you should develop a document flowchart of the production cycle for the current operation of F & C Construction.

15. (Chapter 19) Specifically identify the information needed for the production cycle. Develop documentation to show how this output would be provided.

16. (Chapter 19) Assume that F & C Construction has chosen to implement a relational data base for its production cycle, based on the REA data model. Draw an E–R diagram for this data base.

17. (Chapter 19) Identify the internal control objectives that should be established for F & C Construction's production cycle. Assuming that F & C Construction will computerize its production cycle, describe several internal control policies and procedures that should be established to achieve *each* of these objectives.

18. (Chapter 20) If you did not complete the document flowcharts for all cycles in Part 1, then you should develop a document flowchart of the payroll cycle for the current operation of F & C Construction.

19. (Chapter 20) Specifically identify the information needed for the payroll cycle. Develop documentation to show how this output would be provided.

20. (Chapter 20) Assume that F & C Construction has chosen to implement a relational data base for its payroll cycle, based on the REA data model. Draw an E–R diagram for this data base.

21. (Chapter 20) Identify the internal control objectives that should be established for F & C Construction's payroll cycle. Assuming that F & C Construction will computerize its payroll cycle, describe several internal control policies and procedures that should be established to achieve *each* of these objectives.

CASE A.2: CACTUS SPINE COUNTRY CLUB[1]

Cactus Spine Golf Course is a private country club located outside Las Vegas. It currently provides its members with an 18-hole golf course, driving range, golf shop, and restaurant. Recently a committee was formed to examine the feasibility of expanding member services. In particular, they were interested in developing plans to design and finance a swimming pool complex for the property. Members currently pay for recreational services as they use them. In addition, they pay an initiation fee upon joining the club and an annual fee of $1200 that is due and payable on the anniversary date of membership.

Organization Structure

Figure 1 shows the structure of the Cactus Spine Country Club. The club is governed by a board of directors that is elected from the membership. The board appoints a qualified member to the position of financial secretary for a two-year period. Although the board of directors is not compensated, the financial secretary receives a monthly stipend for services rendered to the club.

John Parr is the new club manager. He was hired two months ago after the retirement of Jerry Putter, who held the position for 10 years. John came to the

[1]This case was prepared by Carol F. Venable, School of Accountancy, San Diego State University, as a basis for classroom discussion rather than to illustrate effective or ineffective handling of an accounting system. Copyright 1993 by Carol F. Venable. Reprinted with permission.

Figure 1 *Cactus Spine Country Club Organization Chart*

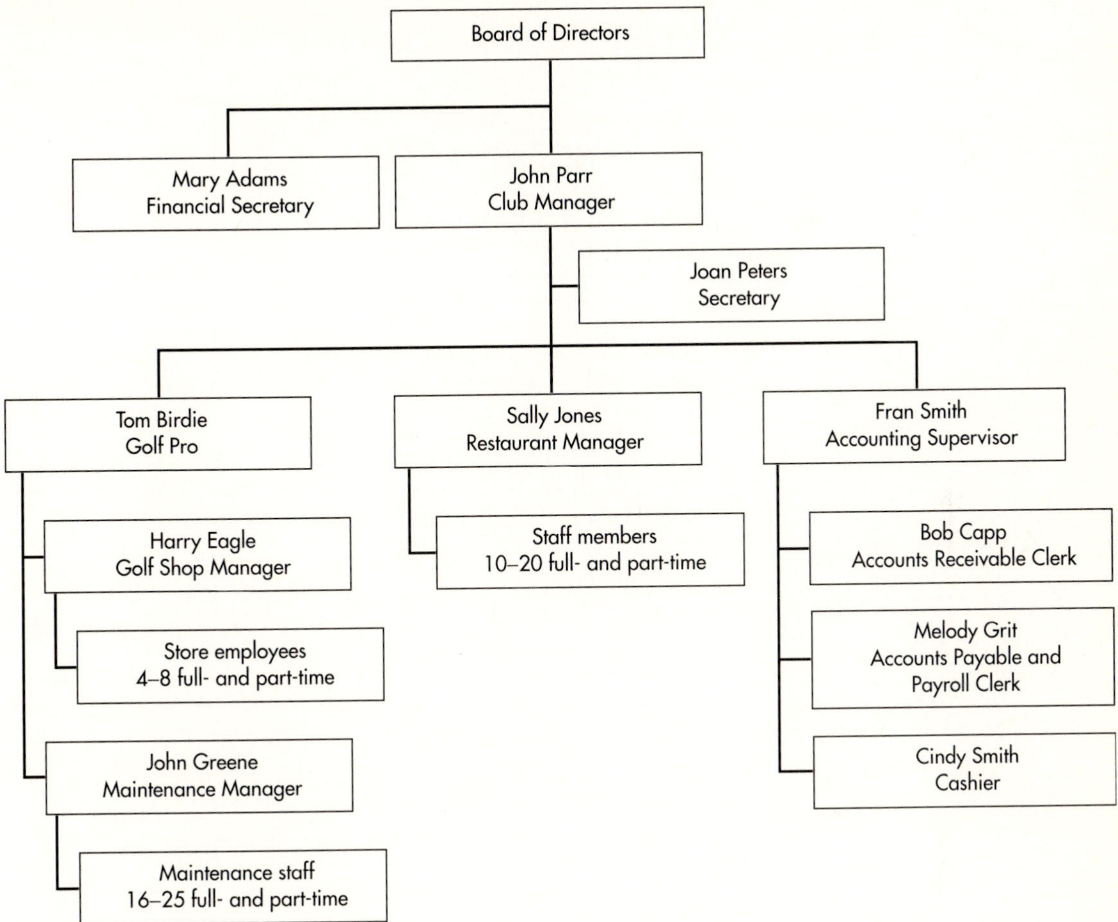

club highly recommended and with considerable experience. John reports to the board of directors. He also works closely with the financial secretary, Mary Adams, and Joan Peters, his personal secretary.

Tom Birdie, golf pro, reports directly to John Parr. Tom oversees the maintenance of the course and the operations of the golf shop. He manages 30–45 full- and part-time employees, including Harry Eagle, golf shop manager, and John Greene, maintenance manager. Sally Jones also reports directly to John Parr. As restaurant manager, she supervises 10–20 full- and part-time staff members. There is a fairly high turnover in these areas since many employees are hired on a temporary basis for peak demand periods.

The accounting department is headed by Fran Smith, a long-time employee. Two accounting clerks and the club cashier report to Fran. In addition, several full-time golf shop employees are cross-trained in cashier and accounting duties. These people are used to maintain the seven-day staffing needs in the cashier and accounting departments and to further fill in during longer summer days.

The Golf Shop

Harry Eagle maintains a small inventory of quality athletic apparel and golf equipment in the golf shop. He and his staff also maintain a supply of related accessories and a cooler with cold beverages and snacks that can be heated in the microwave by golfers waiting to tee off. Golf reservations are made at the golf shop either by phone or in person. They are recorded manually on a daily reservation sheet (Fig. 2) that is preprinted with the available tee times. Up to four people can sign up for one tee time.

Figure 2

Daily Reservation Sheet

Reservation Sheet For ______________________

Time	Name	Signature	ID #	Cart	Guest
0545					
0600					
0615					
0630					
0645					
0700					
0715					
0730					

Members usually sign up in pairs or foursomes. When checking in for their reservation, members sign the daily reservation sheet. The clerk on duty then distributes the key for the mandatory electric cart and records the cart number next to the signature of the party responsible for the key. The members' signatures authorize that the greens fee be charged to their account. Greens fees include the use of one electric cart per two golfers. Fees for a guest can be charged to the member's account or they can be paid in cash. The guest column on the reservation sheet is used to record the few cash payments. These cash payments also are rung into the cash register.

All golf lessons, food, clothing, equipment, and accessory sales are recorded on the cash register whether they are cash or credit purchases. Prenumbered sales invoices also are prepared in triplicate when members charge items at the golf shop (except for the greens fees). Members receive the original invoice. At the end of each day, Harry Eagle takes the daily reservation sheet, cash register tape, duplicate invoices, and cash to the cashier in the accounting department.

Cash Handling and Accounts Receivable Processing for the Golf Shop

When the club cashier receives the daily reservation sheet, cash register tape, invoices, and cash from the golf shop, the amounts from the register tape are compared to the charge invoices and the collected cash. These amounts are recorded by the cashier on the cash drawer summary sheet (Fig. 3). Harry, or his representative, then signs the cash drawer summary sheet to transfer the amounts collected. The cashier combines these funds with those that were collected from the restaurant and prepares a daily bank deposit for all cash sales. This deposit is separate from the one that is prepared to deposit the payments on account that arrive in the mail. All deposits are made by John Parr's secretary. The cashier turns over the daily reservation sheet and one copy of the charge invoices to the accounts receivable clerk, who

Figure 3

Cash Drawer Summary Sheet

GOLF SHOP CASH DRAWER SUMMARY SHEET			Date
	Register Cash Sales	Register Credit Sales	For Office Use
Greens Fees			
Lessons			
Food			
Clothing			
Equipment			
Golf Accessories			
Other			
Totals Per Register Tape			

Plus Beginning Bank ________________ Received by		For Cashier's Use
End of Shift Cash Out Requirement		
Cash Delivered to Cashier ________________ Delivered by		For Cashier's Use ________________ Received by
Cash Over/(Short)		
DR Cash CR Cash Sales Accts CR Other Accts DR/CR Cash Over (Short)	________ ________ ________ ________	For GJ Use ________________ Recorded by

enters the amounts in the accounting system. Posted invoices and the daily reservation sheet are maintained in a file in chronological order in the accounts receivable department. The second copy of the invoice is attached to the cash drawer summary sheet and filed in the cashier's file. At one time, the second copy was sent to the member with the monthly statement, but this procedure was deleted when the accounting records were automated. Members who question an item on their statement can obtain a copy of the invoice from the accounting department.

Restaurant and Catering Services

Sally Jones, restaurant manager, supervises 10–20 full- and part-time individuals who provide breakfast, lunch, and light dinner services. She also arranges for outside catering when the club plans large, formal events or when club members want to utilize the facilities for private parties. Members may charge their daily purchases or pay cash. The daily sales procedures are similar to those that are used in the golf shop. The restaurant opens daily one-half hour before sunrise. It closes at 7 P.M. in the summer and at 4 P.M. in the winter.

Members may rent restaurant and meeting room facilities for private parties. All catering services for private parties must be arranged through Sally Jones. If a private caterer is used in place of or in addition to the regular staff, the club is billed directly and Sally charges the catering fees to the member's account. This is in addition to the rental fee that is charged for using the facilities. The rental fee has remained stable for a number of years. Several private parties are held each month, and the facilities are usually fully booked during holiday and graduation periods. Sally Jones prepares a party charge slip in triplicate for billing members' accounts for room rentals, food, services, and private catering fees. After the event, she mails the original to the member, keeps a copy, and sends another to the accounts receivable clerk.

Incoming Mail and Purchasing

John Parr's secretary, Joan Peters, opens all the mail and prepares a daily cash receipts prelist. She forwards the prelist, the checks, and the remittance advices to the cashier. She also handles all correspondence and prepares purchase orders (Fig. 4) for the approval of John Parr. Department heads must submit purchase requisitions to her before any purchase orders are prepared. When bills arrive, she attaches a copy of the appropriate purchase order and forwards it to the accounts payable clerk after the club manager has reviewed and initialed the bill. Catering bills are handled separately. These are forwarded to Sally Jones, who authorizes payment by initialing the invoice and forwarding it to the accounts payable clerk. The accounts payable clerk inputs all bills to the accounts payable system. The accounting department supervisor reviews the accounts payable listing and authorizes payment. The accounts payable clerk then prints the checks, which must be signed by the financial secretary before being mailed. All accounts payable records are maintained in the accounting department.

The Current Accounting System

Fran Smith is the head of the accounting department. She started with the club 10 years ago as a clerk in the golf shop. After taking several night school courses in accounting, she was promoted to accounts receivable clerk 4 years ago. Fran then was promoted to her current position after the untimely death of the head accountant 3 years ago. Fran carefully has maintained the same procedures that were started before her promotion. However, there is no formal documentation for the current accounting system.

The current accounting system was installed by the former head accountant. It consists of a small IBM personal computer with a simple general ledger package that has accounts payable and accounts receivable modules. The system was designed so that the head accountant made all general journal entries. One clerk is responsible for maintaining the accounts receivable records. Another clerk is responsible for accounts payable records. This second clerk also is responsible for preparing, distributing, collecting, and reviewing time sheets and time cards. Once a week the payroll items are sent to an outside payroll service that prepares the checks and payroll records. The number of employees fluctuates depending on the season of the year. Many temporary employees are hired during summer and holiday periods. Paychecks must be picked up in person from the cashier.

The cashier, Cynthia Smith, is responsible for safeguarding all monies. Incoming receipts are deposited intact with separate bank deposit slips for cash sales, mail receipts, and other cashier-generated monies. Remittance advices are forwarded to the accounts receivable clerk with the prelist. Daily deposits are recorded on a cash receipts report, a copy of which goes to Mary Adams at the end of the month. Since members are provided with check-cashing privileges, Cynthia must replenish the

Figure 4

Purchase Order

Cactus **S**pine **C**ountry **C**lub	SEND INVOICE TO: ACCOUNTING DEPARTMENT 123 Prickly Pear Lane Cacti, NV 12345 (123) 123-1234			PURCHASE ORDER NO. 1332 This number must appear on all documents and packages.	
Vendor			Ship To:		
Date	Ship by Date	Ship Via	Freight Terms	Special Terms	
Quantity	Product Number	Description—Color Code		Unit Cost	Unit

PURCHASE CONDITIONS

1. Acknowledgment required.
2. Vendor is responsible for extra freight on partial shipments.
3. No substitutions without prior approval.
4. Our purchase order number must appear on all documents and packages.

PR File No.	______________________ Purchasing Agent

amount of cash in the club safe twice a week. In addition to her other duties at the end of the day, she prepares the beginning bank for each cash register. The accounting department supervisor acts as cashier when Cynthia Smith is away from the cashier's cage. They each maintain a separate cash drawer. At the end of the day, all paperwork and monies must balance on the reconciliation sheet.

The accounts receivable clerk also is responsible for entering the annual fee into the billing system so that it will be included on the member's bill. Although it is an annual fee, members are allowed to pay it in three monthly installments. The clerk keeps a manual card file which indicates when each member's installment is to be entered into the billing system. The clerk dates and then initials the card when the amount is posted into the automated system.

Responsibilities of the Financial Secretary

Mary Adams is responsible for monitoring the financial position of the club. On a monthly basis, Mary receives a financial report detailing overall income and expenses. She reviews the results and presents the report at the board of directors meeting. Mary spends approximately 5 hours per week working at the club. She signs all checks, and she receives reports which indicate the members who are in arrears. Mary is responsible for monitoring and contacting delinquent members before they are turned over to the board of directors for further action. She also receives copies of the validated bank deposit slips, the monthly bank statement, and a copy of the cash receipts report, which itemizes the daily deposits. She reconciles these records.

Discussion at the Last Board Meeting

At the last board meeting, Mary reported the financial results for the previous month and noted that operating expenses again had exceeded operating revenues. Mary also reported that she and John Parr had reviewed the financial statements for the past year. They both agreed that the club must increase its revenues in the near future. Expenses have risen at a steady pace over the past six months. They recommended that an immediate 10% across-the-board increase in prices be approved by the board. John reported that the club must soon upgrade its maintenance equipment. He currently is working with Tom Birdie and the equipment custodian in inventorying and examining the condition of the maintenance equipment and electric golf carts. He stated that equipment records were incomplete.

During the meeting, John noted that the annual club dues were less than those at comparable facilities, but he refrained from making a recommendation to increase these dues. John also recommended hiring a firm to examine the accounting system and to make recommendations for its improvement. He explained that his requests to the accounting department for departmental reports cannot always be handled by the current system. Although some reports have been manually prepared, the department does not have the time to compile others. He also noted that the accounting department supervisor, Fran Smith, didn't appear to understand all of his concerns about the operations of the accounting system. After considering the reports by John and Mary, the board decided to hire outside consultants. The board wants a review of current operations and recommendations for upgrading the accounting system.

The requirements for this case are divided to coincide with the major sections of the book. In addition, the appropriate chapters are also identified.

Part One: Conceptual Foundations of Accounting Information Systems

1. (Chapter 1) Discuss whether the board of directors should follow the recommendation for an immediate 10% price increase. What effect would a price increase have on demand? What are the external and internal factors that could be negatively affecting the financial operations of the club?

2. (Chapter 2 or 4) Does the current system produce sufficient reports for decision making? Recommend three reports, and explain why they would be useful to management.

3. (Chapter 3) Prepare a flowchart of the purchasing and accounts payable procedures.

4. (Chapter 4 or 5) The company wants to create a new-member master file that can be used for automatic billing when membership fees are due. The club plans to retain the same three-month installment payment plan. Prepare a three-column work sheet that identifies (a) the field names in the new-member master file, (b) the field type (alphabetic, numeric, alphanumeric, date, monetary), and (c) the positions (the number of characters in the field).

5. (Chapter 6) Draw an E–R diagram to represent a relational data base built according to the REA data model, for the expenditure cycle.

Part Two: The Technology of Information Systems

6. (Chapter 7 or 8) Should the club upgrade its computer system? Identify the areas that should be upgraded. Discuss the benefits that would be gained from upgrading the system.

7. (Chapter 9) Design a network configuration for Cactus Spine Country Club. Why did you choose to include certain functions on the network?

Part Three: The Systems Development Process

8. (Chapter 10) Identify the areas within the club where there may be resistance to changing the system. Discuss why there could be resistance, and recommend some ways to avoid potential problems.

9. (Chapter 10) Consider the various strategies for determining information system requirements, and suggest which strategies would be appropriate for this company. What are the factors that affect the level of uncertainty in this company?

10. (Chapter 11) Design a sales invoice for the golf shop.

11. (Chapter 12) Should the club continue to use outsourcing for its payroll? Consider the costs and benefits.

Part Four: Control and Audit of Accounting Information Systems

12. (Chapter 13) Assess the costs and benefits of using part-time and temporary employees. Does the use of these employees increase control risks? Does cross-training of employees benefit the club, and does this increase any risks?

13. (Chapter 14) Assume that a thief broke into the accounting department looking for money. After finding none, he vandalized the department. Records were destroyed, and the computer was stolen. What activities should be listed in a disaster recovery plan to help the department recover from this event?

14. (Chapter 14) Distinguish between fraudulent financial reporting and employee fraud, and identify individuals and/or situations where this could occur within the country club.

15. (Chapter 16) Prepare an input controls matrix using the same format as given in the chapter, but replace the field names with those that would be in the new-member master file (see Requirement 5). Place checks in the cells of the matrix that represent input controls you might expect to find for each field.

Part Five: Accounting Information Systems Applications

16. (Chapter 17) Design a party charge slip that can be used for multiple purposes: (a) to reserve a room and book a party, and (b) to later bill for the party costs.

17. (Chapter 18) Identify the internal control strengths and weaknesses of and recommend improvements to the purchasing and accounts payable functions. Use the following format to prepare your answer.

Item Number	Description	Recommendations to Correct Weaknesses
Strengths Weaknesses		

18. (Chapter 19) Identify the internal control weaknesses of and recommend improvements for the control of fixed assets. Use the following format to prepare your answer.

Item Number	Nature of Weakness	Recommendation to Correct Weakness

19. (Chapter 20) List the activities that the payroll clerk must perform before the completed time sheets and time cards are sent to the outside payroll service. Does anything need to be done after the paychecks are received from the outside payroll service?

CASE A.3: VIDEOS TONITE[1]

Videos Tonite is a family business that is owned and operated by Bob and Mary Smithson. The business consists of two video rental stores in a suburban area of Chicago. Their daughter, Barbara, is a full-time employee who eventually will take over the business when Bob and Mary reach retirement age in a few years. Each store is open for business from 10 A.M. until 8 P.M., Monday through Saturday, and from noon until 5 P.M. on Sunday. There are four part-time employees at each location. The three family members divide their time between the two stores so that new employees are scheduled to work with a family member.

Videos Tonite rents the most popular movies. Each store has approximately 2000 videos in stock, and there are 10 video machines (VCRs) that are available for rent. Bob orders all merchandise, and he has been quite successful in assessing the video rental market. Recently at the urging of his suppliers, Bob added a small line of new videos for sale. The videos seem to be selling well. He has placed two restocking orders since adding this merchandise. Each store also offers bagged popcorn and candy that is restocked on Monday and Friday of each week by the popcorn company supplier. The supplier leaves a delivery slip after each restocking, and the company sends an invoice every two weeks.

Membership Terms

Videos Tonite rents only to members of the Videos Tonite Rental Club. A person becomes a member by filling out an application and paying a $75 deposit. The company requires the application information and deposit because the store originally experienced problems with cassettes and machines being stolen by customers. New customers now receive a

[1]This case was prepared by Carol F. Venable, School of Accountancy, San Diego State University, as a basis for classroom discussion rather than to illustrate effective or ineffective handling of an accounting system. Copyright 1993 by Carol F. Venable. Reprinted with permission.

customer number, which is recorded on their application and used on all subsequent transactions. Once a customer has rented items and promptly returned them six times, the customer can request that the $75 deposit be returned. Refund request forms are kept at the counter. A customer deposit log (Fig. 1) is used to maintain a record of the deposits and refunds. Mary designed the log and had it printed at a local printer, because there was a problem tracking deposit returns when they first initiated the deposit policy. All deposit refunds are made by check. If the original deposit has been returned and a customer does not respond to return requests, Bob will use the services of a collection agency. The collection agency has been successful in tracking down the few customers who move from the area.

Rental Procedures

Each rental cassette and VCR has its own identification number and checkout card. All of the VCRs and rental videos are kept behind the counter. When club members want to check out a movie or VCR, they select its checkout card from the display rack and give the card to a clerk on duty. The clerk selects the video, writes the customer number on the checkout card, and places the checkout card in the video slot. The clerk then pulls the customer card (Fig. 2) from the customer file and enters the rental information. Customers may purchase an optional damage waiver by paying an additional 20 cents on each video rental. If they take this option, the clerk puts a check in the fee waiver column on the customer card. Customers are charged $65 for a damaged or lost video if they have not taken out the separate damage waiver. The customer card is stored in the checkout file box. When a video is returned, the checkout card must be put back on the correct display rack. The customer card is then put back in the customer file after the clerk puts a checkmark next to the item that was returned. When a customer card is full, a new one is prepared and the old one is destroyed. A club member may also reserve a movie or machine by calling the store and having the clerk pull the checkout card, video, and customer card and hold them for the customer behind the counter.

When Videos Tonite first opened, the checkout system was adequate. Now, however, there are approximately 1500 club members at each store. Bob estimates that about 30% are regular customers. Another 40% come in less often, but they still rent videos on a regular basis. Two of the biggest problems are lost or misplaced cards and lengthy lines of customers waiting for service, especially during peak hours. Additional problems include an inability to determine which movies and VCRs are available for rental, movies not being annotated with a checkmark on the member's card after a return, and members' finding out that the movies they reserved have been checked out to someone else. Bob and Barbara go through the checkout box periodically to find overdue rentals and misfiled cards. When the store is busy, cards sometimes get piled up behind the counter before they are filed.

Accounting Procedures

The company only has a few suppliers. When invoices for merchandise are received, Bob checks that the

Figure 1

Customer Deposit Log

"VIDEOS TONITE"
CUSTOMER DEPOSIT LOG

Date Received	Customer Number	Name	Address	Date Returned	Check Number

Figure 2

Customer Card

CUSTOMER CARD			
Number:		Name:	
Phone:		Deposit: Yes No	
Date	Item No.	Description	Fee Waiver

invoice contains only those items that he actually received. Since Bob does all the ordering and unpacking, it is easy for him to keep track of the incoming merchandise. The invoice then goes to Mary, who prepares and signs all the checks. In fact, Mary does all of the bookkeeping. There are no formal financial statements. At the end of the year, Mary takes the records to their tax preparer. She uses columnar paper to maintain the equivalent of a cash receipts journal and an expenditures journal. Mary also prepares and keeps records for the payroll. At the end of each month, she carefully totals her work sheets and reconciles her records to the bank statement. Bob and Mary sit down at the end of each month to review the work sheets and their bank balances. They must manage their cash flows and plan for major purchases and improvements because there are several slow rental seasons during the year.

All sales are recorded on a cash register. In addition, a prenumbered sales invoice is prepared in duplicate when a new member pays a deposit or when a customer pays for a damaged video or VCR. The original is given to the member, and the copy goes in the cash register. At the end of the day, these invoices and the money in the cash register are bagged and put in the floor safe. Before each store opens, Mary opens the bag and prepares the bank deposit. Because the register drawer starts with $35 in change each day, Mary calculates and records the day's sales revenue by subtracting the $35 and the amounts recorded on the invoices. She checks for missing invoices, and she makes sure that the total amount recorded on the register agrees with the amount in the sales drawer. She records the information on a daily sales sheet (Fig. 3) that is later consolidated on columnar paper. There is seldom a shortage or overage. The duplicate invoices for damage deposits are attached to the application form and stored in the application file in alphabetical order. The duplicate invoices for payments of damaged goods are attached to the daily sales sheet.

Expansion Possibilities

Last month one of Bob's old college buddies, Doug Alano, offered to sell Bob his two video stores that are known as Adventures in Video. These stores are located in nearby suburbs and they have done well since they opened. The stores are being offered for sale because Doug's doctor recommended that he take an early retirement due to the onset of a serious illness. Although Doug's two stores have many operating procedures that are similar to Videos Tonite, they cater to several additional market segments with different products and service policies. In

Figure 3
Daily Sales Sheet

VIDEOS TONITE
DAILY SALES SHEET

Location: ______________ Date: ______________

Cash total at end of day:	$
Less beginning bank:	$
Amount deposited to bank:	$
Less damage deposits:	$
Less payments for damaged items:	$
Less other payments (itemize below):	$
Daily sales revenue:	$
Invoice numbers used:	
Description of other payments:	

addition to daily rentals of popular current releases, which are targeted to residents in the immediate vicinity of the stores, there are specialty rental sections for foreign language and classic films. These specialty films target several market segments, and the two stores draw customers from the entire metropolitan area. These customers willingly pay a premium price to rent foreign and classic films, and they expect special services since they travel greater distances. Doug offers a variable rental period rate and variable fees. He has two full-time managers, Janet Wilson and Ricardo Hernandez, who oversee the foreign language and classic film stock and maintain a phone reservation system. Current membership is estimated to be at 12,000. Of the 9500 videos in stock, approximately 1500 are foreign language videos.

Bob, Mary, and Barbara are excited about this expansion opportunity. Mary, however, is worried because she already has her hands full with the records from the two stores. She says that doubling her work load would keep her tied to paperwork all day. They asked their tax accountant for advice. After examining the sales proposal and the tax records of Adventures in Video, he noted that it appeared to be a good financial opportunity to expand in the video business. He suggested, however, that their ability to manage the additional facilities might require some reorganization. He suggested that Bob, Mary, and Barbara speak with a consultant about automating the records and procedures. They agree that they must do something, but they aren't sure what approach to take.

The requirements for this case are divided to coincide with the major sections of the book. In addition, the appropriate chapters are also identified.

Part One: Conceptual Foundations of Accounting Information Systems

1. (Chapter 1) Discuss whether Bob and Mary have adequately monitored their business. Do they need monthly financial statements? How centralized or decentralized are the decision-making processes?
2. (Chapter 2) Develop a coding scheme to identify the items that are rented to customers.
3. (Chapter 3) Prepare flowcharts that describe the new-customer deposit procedures and the video rental procedures.
4. (Chapter 5) Assume that the company will use a relational data base to maintain its rental information. Prepare four relational tables for its rental invoice data. Include a rental invoice table, a member table, a line item table, and an inventory table. Enter three hypothetical entries into each table.
5. (Chapter 6) Draw an E–R diagram representing a relational data base for the revenue cycle, based on the REA data model.

Part Two: The Technology of Information Systems

6. (Chapter 7 or 8) What types of hardware and software could be used in the day-to-day operations of Videos Tonite?

7. (Chapter 9) Could Videos Tonite use a network system in its current stores? Could one be used if it expands? Describe the system you would recommend.

Part Three: The Systems Development Process

8. (Chapter 10) Should Bob and Mary computerize their current operations? What aspects of their business should be computerized? Identify the costs and benefits of computerization. (Dollar values are not necessary.)

9. (Chapter 10) Assume that the company has decided to expand. Identify four systems development projects that should be undertaken now and in the future. Prepare a master plan that specifies what the systems will consist of, how they will be developed, and where the information system is headed. Prioritize the projects, and describe the criteria used for prioritization. Limit your plan to two typewritten pages.

10. (Chapter 10) Consider the various strategies for determining information system requirements, and suggest which strategies would be appropriate for this company. What are the factors that affect the level of uncertainty in this company?

11. (Chapter 11) How could the job responsibilities change for Bob, Mary, and Barbara if they purchase Adventures in Video? What other personnel changes might be necessary? What type of training would be needed?

Part Four: Control and Audit of Accounting Information Systems

12. (Chapter 13) Identify the internal control weaknesses of and recommend improvements in the new-customer deposit procedures. Use the following format to prepare your answer. If you prepared a flowchart for Requirement 3, cross-reference your list to it.

Item Number	Nature of Weakness	Recommendation to Correct Weakness

13. (Chapter 15) Assume that Mary and Bob decide to computerize their customer records and their rental video inventory. Identify four potential threats to this new information system, and make recommendations to minimize these threats.

14. (Chapter 16) Consider the three types of audits discussed in Chapter 16. Select the two that you feel are most needed by this company, and provide the rationale for your decision.

Part Five: Accounting Information Systems Applications

15. (Chapter 17) Identify the internal control weaknesses of and recommend improvements in the video rental procedures. Use the following format to prepare your answer. If you prepared a flowchart for Requirement 3, cross-reference your list to it.

Item Number	Nature of Weakness	Recommendation to Correct Weakness

16. (Chapter 17) Assess the cash-handling procedures and the use of the daily sales sheet. Determine whether the daily sales sheet (a) provides sufficient information for managerial decision making and (b) accurately reflects the company's revenues for external reporting purposes.

17. (Chapter 18) Identify the internal control weaknesses of and recommend improvements in the purchasing of new resale videos and in the purchasing of bagged popcorn and candy. Use the following format to prepare your answer.

Item Number	Nature of Weakness	Recommendation to Correct Weakness

18. (Chapter 20) Mary prepares the payroll manually. Assume that Mary prepares a work schedule one week in advance, although no description of the current timekeeping or payroll system is provided. Design a simple system for timekeeping that meets the internal control objectives for a payroll system. Provide a brief narrative and a copy of any documents that are necessary.

CASE A.4: THE WOODEN NICKEL[1]

Background

The Wooden Nickel is a small retail clothing store located in Stillwater, Oklahoma, across the street from Oklahoma State University. The store was opened in 1976 by K. Cohlmia and is run as a sole proprietorship. The store specializes in casual clothing and caters to the upscale university student market. Stillwater has approximately 35,000 residents, so the 18,000 students at the university have a tremendous impact on all retail stores in town.

The Wooden Nickel divides its inventory into a men's department and a women's department. K. strives to provide the type of clothing that is not found in discount outlets. In fact, the store is the only authorized supplier of Polo products in the city and surrounding area.

At the current time, all accounting is done manually. The store's business can be divided into two cycles: (1) spring and summer and (2) fall and winter. Because of the cyclical nature of the business, it is often necessary to borrow to cover the outlay for purchases. This is then repaid as quickly as the revenue from the sales cycle permits. K. negotiates with local banks to cover this need on a yearly basis. There are currently nine employees (job descriptions are presented in Fig. 1).

The store has a display area which covers the entire front of a renovated older building. One centrally located electronic cash register is used for all sales. The back of the building is divided into a large office and a merchandise storage area. K. uses the office for all of his ownership duties. The bookkeeper also uses this office and the managers use it whenever the need arises. In addition, the safe is located in the office. There is a rear entrance near the storage area where goods can be unloaded.

Owner (K.)
Budgeting and purchasing
Advertising
Writing and controlling checks
Payroll
Bank statement reconciliation
Credit card process

Manager, Women's Department (Melanie)
Supervises salesclerks
Prepares work schedules
Merchandising
Assists with buying for women's department
Sales as needed
Handles alterations

Manager, Men's Department (Jay)
Supervises salesclerks
Prepares work schedules
Merchandising
Assists with buying for men's department
Sales as needed
Handles all vendor returns
Deposits to bank

Bookkeeper (Kim)
Prepares daily deposits
Posts accounts receivables
Prepares statements for customer accounts monthly
Receiving
Makes inventory tags
Filing
Sales as needed

Salesclerks
(5–6)
All sales functions (are not specifically assigned to a department)
Assist with merchandising and inventory tagging
General housekeeping duties

Figure 1 *Job Descriptions*

Revenue Cycle

Regular Sales. The Wooden Nickel has yearly sales of between $700,000 and $800,000. The store generates from 50 to 70 sales tickets each day, with an average of 2 items per ticket. The daily sales process is discussed in detail below. While the majority of the customers pay by cash, check, or credit card, they

[1]This case was prepared by Patrick Dorr, School of Accounting, Oklahoma State University, and by Martha M. Eining, University of Utah, as a basis for classroom discussion rather than to illustrate effective or ineffective handling of an accounting system. Reprinted with permission.

do have approximately 500 charge customers. Historically, K. has allowed only customers he knows personally to open charge accounts. The store has no established policy for charge customers.

When a customer wishes to make a sale, the customer can give the merchandise to any available salesclerk or take it to the cash register station. The salesclerk completes two copies of a prenumbered sales ticket. If a bank card is being used, a three-part bank card receipt is also completed. The transaction is then entered into the cash register by transaction type:

- Cash key. The sales ticket is validated on the back with the date and amount.
- Credit key/charge account. The sales ticket is validated as above.
- Check key. The sales ticket and the check are validated.
- Bank card key. Bank card receipt is validated.

The first copy of the sales ticket (and bank card receipt if applicable) is given to the customer. The second copy is placed in the cash register. The third copy of the bank card receipt is filed by date in the back office. The top copy of the sales ticket is presented in Fig. 2, and the bank card receipt is presented in Fig. 3.

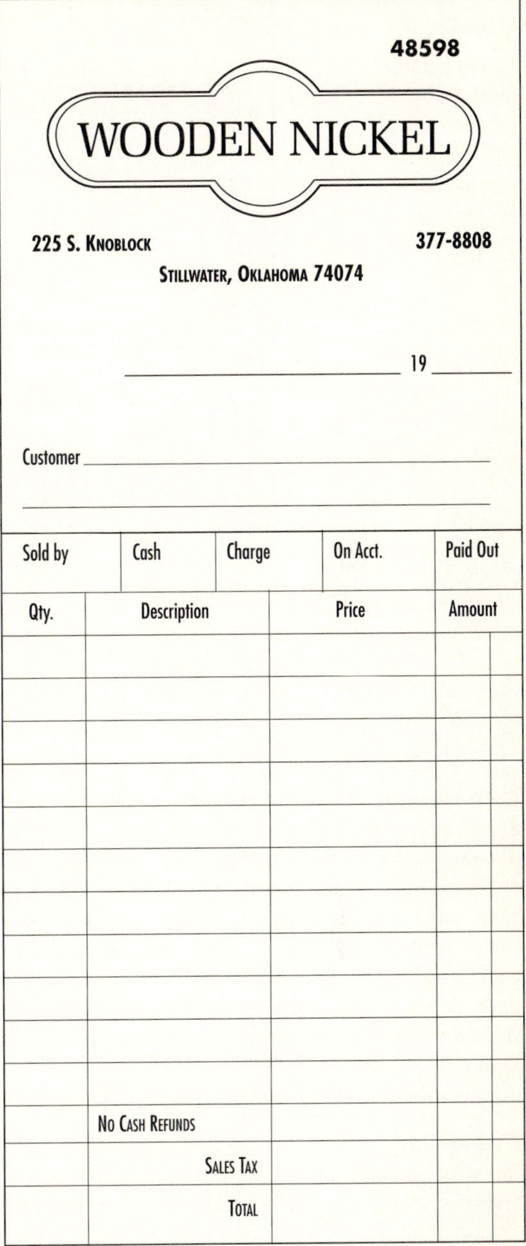

48598

WOODEN NICKEL

225 S. Knoblock 377-8808

Stillwater, Oklahoma 74074

____________ 19 ____

Customer ____________

Sold by	Cash	Charge	On Acct.	Paid Out

Qty.	Description	Price	Amount
	No Cash Refunds		
	Sales Tax		
	Total		

Figure 2 *Example Sales Ticket*

Layaway Sales. When a customer chooses to put an item on layaway, a special layaway form is completed (see Fig. 4). A minimum down payment of 25% is required to hold the merchandise. The balance is due in three equal payments over the next three months. The sale is entered using the layaway key on the register, and the form is validated with the date and amount. The cash deposit is included in the daily sales and handled as described in the sales cycle.

Sales Returns. The store's policy is never to give a cash refund when the item was paid for by cash or check. Instead, it issues a credit for the merchandise that has been returned. A three-part sales ticket is prepared and marked as a return. If the original sale was made on account, only two copies are prepared. If the merchandise was purchased on a credit card, then the refund is made through the credit card. In this case, a bank card credit receipt must also be prepared.

The sales return transaction is entered using the sales return key on the register. After the ticket is validated, the original is given to the customer, the duplicate is placed in the cash register, and the third copy is placed in a credit file which is kept near the cash register. The bookkeeper uses the second copy of credit account returns to post the transaction to the accounts receivable subsidiary cards. Even though the amount of the sales return is actually a credit, it is kept in the accounts receivable card to avoid the necessity of setting up an accounts payable file.

Figure 3

Example Bank Card Receipt

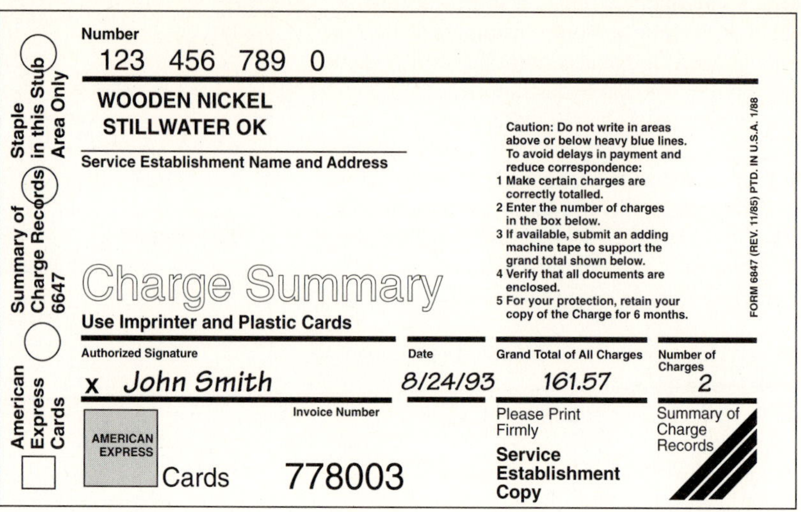

American Express Cards

Summary of Charge Records 6647

Staple in this Stub Area Only

Number

123 456 789 0

WOODEN NICKEL
STILLWATER OK

Service Establishment Name and Address

Charge Summary

Use Imprinter and Plastic Cards

Caution: Do not write in areas above or below heavy blue lines. To avoid delays in payment and reduce correspondence:
1 Make certain charges are correctly totalled.
2 Enter the number of charges in the box below.
3 If available, submit an adding machine tape to support the grand total shown below.
4 Verify that all documents are enclosed.
5 For your protection, retain your copy of the Charge for 6 months.

FORM 6847 (REV. 11/85) PTD. IN U.S.A. 1/88

Authorized Signature	Date	Grand Total of All Charges	Number of Charges
x John Smith	8/24/93	161.57	2

AMERICAN EXPRESS Cards

Invoice Number 778003

Please Print Firmly

Service Establishment Copy

Summary of Charge Records

When the customer returns to use the credit to purchase an item, the credit is verified with the copy which has been placed in the credit file. This copy is then validated and put in the cash register. It is used by the bookkeeper to offset the balance in the accounts receivable subsidiary card.

Cash Receipts. The owner or one of the store managers opens the mail daily and separates the checks or receipts. The manager prepares a sales ticket for each receipt and then enters the checks into the register using the accounts receivable key. The sales ticket is validated with the date and amount. The checks are placed in the drawer and included in the daily deposit. The bookkeeper posts the collections from the information on the sales ticket to the individual accounts receivable cards. The same procedure is used for layaway payments.

End-of-Day Activity. At the end of the day, one of the store managers rings out the register and reconciles the money and bank card receipts in the cash drawer with the total on the register tape. The cash register tape indicates totals by transaction type. Figure 5 presents an example of the cash register tape. The information from the cash register tape is entered into the daily receipts reconciliation (see Fig. 6). One hundred dollars is kept in the cash register drawer and becomes the next day's beginning balance. The manager then places all other money, copies of sales tickets and bank card receipts, the register tape, and the reconciliation in the safe overnight.

The following morning, the bookkeeper retrieves all the items from the safe. The bookkeeper reconciles the register tape with the checks, cash, and bank card receipts from the previous day. A daily deposit is then prepared by the bookkeeper. The manager delivers the deposit to the bank.

Finally, the bookkeeper uses the sales tickets to post credit sales to the accounts receivable subsidiary cards. Daily sales amounts from the daily receipts reconciliation are entered into the sales journal at this time. Figure 7 provides an overview of the daily sales register. All paper documentation is then stored in a file cabinet.

Expenditure Cycle

Purchasing. The owner plans the budget, breaking the total amount down into retail dollars available for each department based on projected sales. He takes 8 to 10 buying trips per year. While on each trip he comes in contact with at least 40 vendors who provide him with their own purchase orders. He uses these purchase orders to make notations on what items he would like to order, constantly trying to maintain a running total so he doesn't exceed the department's budgeted amount. The actual ordering is not done until the owner returns to the store and reviews the purchase orders. He then places the order by sending a copy of the completed purchase order to the vendor. A duplicate copy of the purchase order is filed by vendor.

Receiving. All shipments are sent via UPS. Shipments will typically arrive and be unloaded

Figure 4

Example Layaway Form

LAYAWAY MERCHANDISE IDENTIFICATION TICKET

Date ____________________ No. 1931

Name ______________________________

Address ______________________________

City ______________________________

Telephone ____________________ Clerk No. ____________________

Qty.	Description	Price
	LAYAWAY	

Sub Total	
Tax	
Layaway Fee	
Total	
Deposit	
Balance	

—Agreement—

Payments of $ __________

To Be Made Every ❑ MO. ❑ WK.

Failure to make payment for 30 days will cause merchandise to be replaced in stock and the customer forfeiting all previous payments.

Date ______________

Customer's Signature ____________________

Date	Old Balance	Amount Paid	New Balance
	LAYAWAY		

Location ____________________ No. of Packages ____________________

No Exchanges or Cash Refunds

Customer's Identification Stub

through the back entrance. However, sometimes they will be delivered through the front. The bookkeeper or owner unpacks the goods and compares the units received with the packing list accompanying the shipment. If any discrepancies exist (i.e., errors in amounts shipped), they are noted on the packing list

NET SL W/TAX	0031	2189.33
ITEMS	0065	
NO SLE	0012	
TRAIN	0000	0.00
CASH	0031	330.98
CHECK	0018	1097.03
CHARG	0003	285.82
CARD	0006	410.67
LAYAWY	0002	164.69
GC RED	0000	0.00
LAY RA	0003	69.86
PO	0000	0.00
RA	0001	30.00
MARK	0000	0.00
VOID	0000	0.00
RETURN	0000	0.00
CREDIT	0000	0.00
TAX		128.83

Figure 5

Example Cash Register Tape Totals

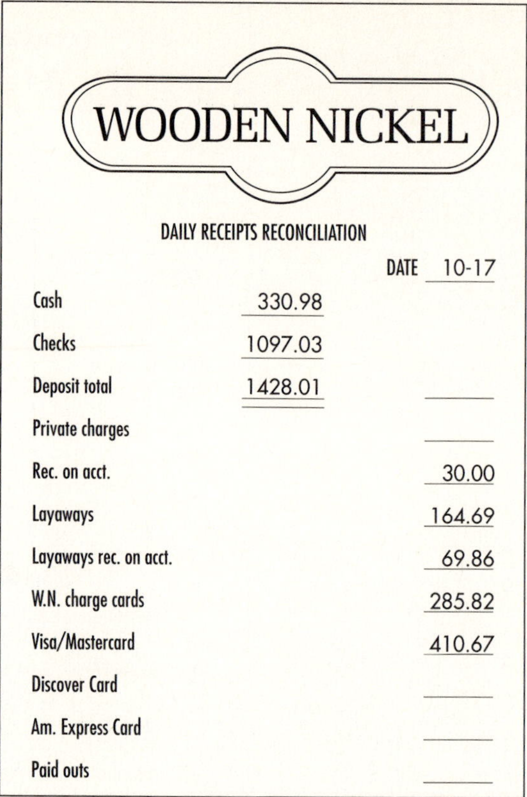

WOODEN NICKEL

DAILY RECEIPTS RECONCILIATION

DATE 10-17

Cash	330.98	
Checks	1097.03	
Deposit total	1428.01	
Private charges		
Rec. on acct.		30.00
Layaways		164.69
Layaways rec. on acct.		69.86
W.N. charge cards		285.82
Visa/Mastercard		410.67
Discover Card		
Am. Express Card		
Paid outs		

Figure 6 *Example Daily Receipts Reconciliation*

and then discussed by phone with the vendor. The same procedure is used if any of the merchandise is damaged. The vendor then issues a return authorization. This must be received before the merchandise is returned.

The packing list is kept in an open file until the invoice is received. Any information about discrepancies and/or damaged goods is transferred to the invoice when it is received and the invoice is adjusted accordingly. The packing list is then used by the bookkeeper to make inventory tags. The salesclerks attach the tags to the merchandise in their spare time.

Cash Disbursements. When the vendor's invoice is received, the packing list is pulled and checked for discrepancies. Any problems are handled by phone; the two documents are stapled together and filed by due date. Most invoices carry a 2/10, net 30 discount. About 10% of the men's clothing vendors and 90% of the women's vendors offer cash discounts of 2%–8%. This cycle is summarized in the flowchart in Fig. 8.

Figure 7 *Daily Sales Register*

Date	Sales *1	Sales Tax	Charges*	Rec/Acct	Layaway*	Layaway Rec/Acct	Cash Refund	Freight	Deposit	Bank Card*
10-17	2189.33	128.83	285.82	30.00	164.69	69.86			1428.01	410.67

* All figures include sales taxes. This is because the information from the cash register tape includes sales taxes.
1. Sales = cash (and check) receipts − receipts on account − layaway receipts + charge sales + layaway sales + bank card sales.

All checks are prenumbered and controlled by the owner. On the tenth of each month he pulls all the invoices, issues the checks, and mails them. All other bills are paid by the owner on the fifteenth of each month. He also keeps track of the payroll, which is paid on the first and sixteenth of the month. He enters all amounts to the check register (see Fig. 9).

Periodic Procedures

The bookkeeper prepares customer statements by making a copy of the accounts receivable subsidiary cards illustrated in Fig. 10 on page A–29. The statements are mailed to customers at the end of each month. At this point there is no real effort to track accounts receivable balances, and no interest is charged on accounts.

The owner reconciles the bank statement and takes care of all bank card activity. A periodic inventory is completed on January 1 and July 1. All available employees assist with the inventory.

An outside accountant is retained to assist with taxes and preparation of any financial reports which may be needed. The store currently maintains a daily sales register, a check register, and a file of accounts receivable subsidiary cards. No other books are being maintained.

The requirements for this case are divided to coincide with the major sections of the book. In addition, the appropriate chapters are also identified.

Part One: Conceptual Foundations of Accounting Information Systems

1. (Chapter 1) Identify the deficiencies in the current information system for the Wooden Nickel. Discuss the information that you think would be most important for internal decision making and for external needs.

2. (Chapter 2) Develop and describe coding schemes for tracking inventory in the Wooden Nickel.

3. (Chapter 3) Develop a data flow diagram for the sales cycle of the Wooden Nickel.

4. (Chapter 3) Prepare document flowcharts to illustrate the current cycles presented for the Wooden Nickel. Use the example presented for the cash disbursements cycle as a guide.

5. (Chapter 5) Discuss how the use of a data base system could improve the information available to the owner and managers of the Wooden Nickel. What problems would be encountered with the implementation of a data base system?

6. (Chapter 6) Draw an E–R diagram to represent a data base for the revenue and expenditure cycles, built according to the REA data model.

Part Two: The Technology of Information Systems

7. (Chapter 7 or 8) To what extent should the Wooden Nickel computerize? What items should be considered in the decision to computerize? Include a

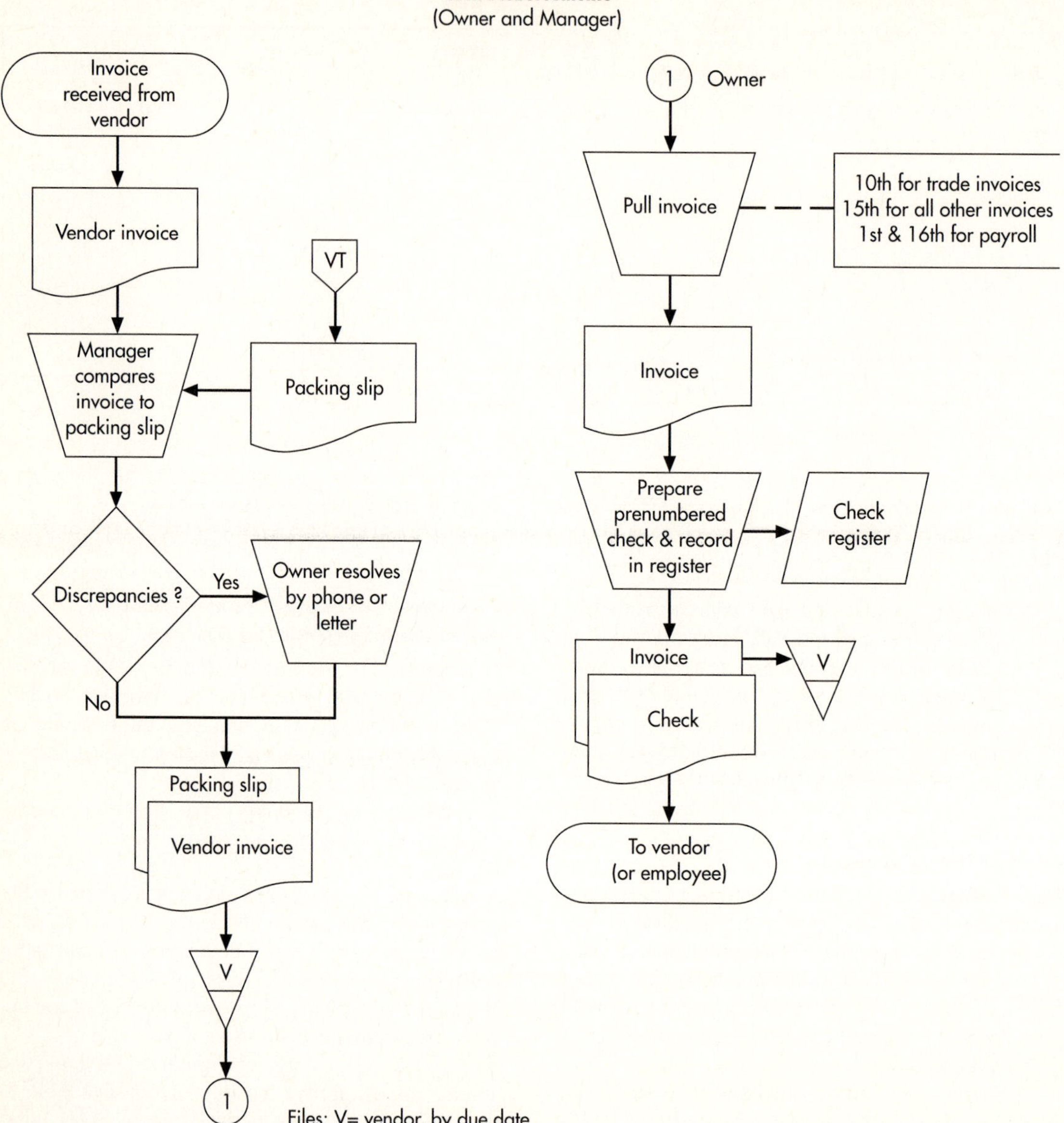

Figure 8 *Flowchart of Cash Disbursement Cycle*

discussion of the type of computer hardware and the type of end-user software that you would suggest to the owner. Make sure that you justify your suggestions.

8. (Chapter 8) Develop a proposal for K. to use microcomputers to support his decision-making process. What should be provided? What would you suggest differently for the two store managers?

9. (Chapter 9) Describe and discuss different possibilities for using data communications at the Wooden Nickel. For example, should it have network? If so, what kind? Should it use a point-of-sale system? In your discussion, include both the positive and negative aspects of each choice.

Date	Chk Number	Description	Purchases	Freight	Advertising	Selling Expense	Repairs	Rent	Wages	Misc Dr	Cr
10-10	2946	Polimer Supply	286.70								
10-10	2947	B. Distributer	1049.21								
10-15	2948	DK Advertising			216.00						

Figure 9 *Check Register*

Part Three: The Systems Development Process

10. (Chapter 10) Prepare a feasibility analysis for the computerization of the Wooden Nickel. Be sure to consider the number of transactions and the needs of the store. You should also include both the quantifiable and the nonquantifiable items.

11. (Chapter 10) Develop a plan to determine, in detail, the information needs for the Wooden Nickel. On the basis of the information in the case, indicate the most important information needs for the Wooden Nickel.

12. (Chapter 10) How could the Wooden Nickel take advantage of reengineering? Consider the sales cycle. How could this cycle be reengineered?

13. (Chapter 11) From the information needs discussed in Requirement 1, design one of the reports that would be needed for the Wooden Nickel.

14. (Chapter 11) Design the input forms and screens needed to capture the information for the report designed in Requirement 13.

15. (Chapter 12) Develop a plan for K. to follow to purchase hardware and software. Include all items that he should consider in choosing vendors.

Part Four: Control and Audit of Accounting Information Systems

16. (Chapter 13) Identify the internal control weaknesses in the current operation of the Wooden Nickel. For each weakness, offer possible solutions. This will be easier if you provide the information by the cycles discussed in the case.

17. (Chapter 13) How can the Wooden Nickel achieve adequate segregation of duties considering the size of the company?

18. (Chapter 14) Assuming that the Wooden Nickel computerizes, set up a system of internal controls over the computer function.

Part Five: Accounting Information Systems Applications

19. (Chapter 17) If you did not complete the document flowcharts for all cycles in Part 1, then you should develop a document flowchart of the sales (revenue) cycle for the current operation of the Wooden Nickel.

20. (Chapter 17) Specifically identify the information needed for the revenue cycle. Develop documentation to show how this output would be provided.

21. (Chapter 17) Identify the internal control objectives that should be established for the Wooden Nickel's revenue cycle. Assuming that the Wooden Nickel will computerize its revenue cycle, describe several internal control policies and procedures that should be established to achieve *each* of these objectives.

22. (Chapter 18) If you did not complete the document flowcharts for all cycles in Part 1, then you should develop a document flowchart of the expenditure cycle for the current operation of the Wooden Nickel.

23. (Chapter 18) Specifically identify the information needed for the expenditure cycle. Develop

Figure 10

Example Accounts Receivable Subsidiary Card

225 SOUTH KNOBLOCK
STILLWATER, OKLAHOMA 74074
405/377-8808

Acct. # 1076

B.B. Customer
Nearby Street
Stillwater, OK 74078

Date	Description	Debit	Credit	Balance
10-1	Purchase	186.16		186.16
10-16	Received on Account		20.00	166.16

documentation to show how this output would be provided.

24. (Chapter 18) Identify the internal control objectives that should be established for the Wooden Nickel's expenditure cycle. Assuming that the Wooden Nickel will computerize its expenditure cycle, describe several internal control policies and procedures that should be established to achieve *each* of these objectives.

CASE A.5: VACATION CARE SERVICES[1]

Until recently, Dom Woods attended college on a golf scholarship. To make extra spending money for essentials, Dom would take temporary jobs during vacation breaks. One day, Dom answered an ad in the college newspaper to house-sit and care for Dr. Whit's cat during a fall-quarter sabbatical to New Zealand. Since Dr. Whit thought Dom did an excellent job caring for his garden and beloved kitten, he recommended Dom to other members of the faculty. Before long, Dom's vacation care services were very popular.

Until January of last year, most requests for Dom's services were fairly straightforward, requiring mail pickup, watering and garden care, and tending of pets and houseplants. One weekend, however, Dr. Evans from the medical school faculty asked whether Dom could also perform some minor cleaning because his regular housecleaners had canceled. When Dr. Evans returned on Monday, he was extremely pleased and stated that he wanted to hire Dom to provide cleaning services on a regular basis. At first, Dom resisted. Dom soon realized, however, that the dream of becoming a famous golf pro probably would not happen. The economy had affected the school's budget and reduced the number of available golf scholarships. Dom was competitively eliminated from the golf scholarship program. Without the scholarship, Dom was forced to think of new ways to finance the last year of school as an English lit. major.

Thus Dom accepted Dr. Evans's offer and began regularly scheduled cleaning and gardening services. The hours were ideal, since the work could be scheduled around class times. After offering this service to several other vacation clients, Dom's workload rapidly expanded. Dom named this new business venture Vacation Care Services. Now, a year later, the company provides weekly, bimonthly, monthly, or one-time cleaning services. In addition, Dom continues to provide vacation care services for established cleaning customers.

Current Operations

Last summer the company grew rapidly. To handle the new business, Dom hired several students to keep up with the demand. Finally, Dom hired another former golfer, Dustie Ramon, as a part-time supervisor. Dom and Dustie now estimate new jobs, train employees, randomly spot-check the work, fill in for absent employees, and respond to complaints. Vacation Care Services employs six to eight part-time cleaners to perform most of the cleaning and gardening care.

The business originally was operated from Dom's apartment, but it moved to a small office space in an industrial park during the summer. The office space is used for storage of equipment and supplies, as well as for the telephone orders and paperwork. Since the business has no "walk-in" customers, Dom or Dustie handles all inquiries regarding the type, availability, and price of services over the telephone. Often, they travel to the homes of potential customers to prepare estimates.

Dom's parents served as cosigners on the 12-month lease of the office space. In addition, they provided an $8000 loan for working capital and the purchase of an old pickup truck and various pieces of cleaning and gardening equipment. Dom signed a promissory note on June 15 that requires monthly interest payments at 6% per annum payable on the first of each month. Twelve equal principal payments are to begin on April 1.

Vacation Care Services recently ran several advertisements in the local paper, but most business has come from customer referrals. On occasion, Dom creates an advertising flyer that the cleaners distribute to neighboring houses. The company does not maintain a formal price list or charge customers for services on a hourly basis. Instead, customers are quoted a fee based upon duration or difficulty of the potential job. Some of the factors that are considered are the size of the home, type and frequency of service, number of people and pets in the home, and number of bedrooms and baths. Occasionally, a cleaner will call to say that the job will take longer than originally planned. In this case, Dom or Dustie will decide whether to charge the customer an additional amount.

Cash-Handling Procedures

Dom maintains a business account at National Security Bank, paying all monthly bills with standard business checks. For credit customers, Dom has

[1]This case was prepared by Carol F. Venable and Alexis Wesbey, School of Accountancy, San Diego State University, as a basis for classroom discussion rather than to illustrate effective or ineffective handling of an accounting system.

Figure 1

Cash Receipts Prelist Form

CASH RECEIPTS PRELIST				
Date Received	Customer	Check No.	Amount	Date Posted
Total Amount Collected				

established a billing cycle of 30 days. Invoices are mailed out at the beginning of each month, with required payment due before the end of the month. No discounts are given. The invoices, purchased at an office supply store, are standardized two-part forms that are prepared by hand. Dom stamps the company name and address on the top of the form. About two-thirds of Dom's customers prefer to pay cash on the day that the cleaning service is provided. Checks or cash are accepted by the cleaning employees and turned over to Dom or Dustie when they return to the office. Each cleaning employee carries a small receipt book, which enables him or her to make out a receipt in duplicate, noting the service and amount received from the customer. The original receipt is left with the customer, and the copy is turned over to Dom or Dustie along with the cash or checks. Vacation Care Services does not accept bank charge cards because Dom does not want to pay the bank service fees.

Invoiced customers mail their payment to the company's post office box. It is Dustie's responsibility to pick up and open the mail. Dustie then records the customer name, check number, and amount on a cash receipts prelist (Fig. 1) that will later be used to update the customer record. These checks are placed with the other cash and checks in a locked box in Dustie's desk until the end of the week. A deposit slip then is made out in duplicate and taken to the bank by either Dom or Dustie. The validated deposit slip is stored in the desk until the bank statement arrives, then it is compared to the statement before being discarded. If a check bounces, Dom requires that the customer pay for future work in cash.

Payroll Services

Dom decided to outsource the payroll and hired a service bureau, Checks-4-U, to handle this service. Checks-4-U charges Vacation Care Services a fee of $30.00 per payroll period for making out the employee payroll checks, withholding all taxes and insurance, and making all deposits with the IRS. Dom simply phones in the gross salary amount to be paid to each employee. Dom determines this amount from employee time slips, which are maintained in a payroll folder. After each day's work, each employee fills out a time slip (Fig. 2), recording the date, customer, total job fee, and number of hours worked on the job. These slips are initialed by Dustie and kept in the file until the employee salary totals are to be phoned to Checks-4-U. Checks-4-U delivers the payroll register with the checks to Dom's office every two weeks.

Dom is pleased with the system, since there are no worries about tax deadlines. Employees have twice complained about being shorted in their paychecks. Dom recognizes that time slips have occasionally been misplaced in the office. Figure 3 is a flowchart of the system that a friend in the business college prepared for Dom as a class project.

Current Hardware and Software

Dom has a personal computer in the office, a Pentium machine with a 1-gigabyte hard disk and 16 MB of RAM. The machine was purchased at a rock-bottom price from his friend, a business school major, who was upgrading. Dom originally purchased the machine to prepare papers for school. The seller provided Dom with a popular word processing program, with which Dom is fairly proficient since English lit. majors do many papers. However, it was difficult learning how to use the word processor, because it came without written documentation. Dom uses the computer to send out various business letters, such as letters to clients who bounce checks. Dom also maintains a customer list using the student version of a popular spreadsheet. This was also installed on the hard disk when Dom got the computer. The person who sold the machine set up the spreadsheet with a very simple file that allows Dom to record the customer's name, address, phone number, job description, fee data, and other pertinent information. A printout of the customer file is kept in the desktop binder for use in scheduling.

Dustie doesn't know how to use the spreadsheet but does all the scheduling on the computer using inexpensive calendar software purchased at a discount software outlet. Scheduling is done as needed. Recurring jobs are entered at the beginning of the month and changes are made for new jobs that occur on short notice. The program records the names of the client and assigned cleaners next to each time slot. A monthly schedule printout is kept in the desktop binder, and additions are made in pencil and updated on the computer when necessary. Each night Dustie uses the schedule and customer file printouts to write out a work order (Fig. 4) for the next day's cleaning employees or vacation services personnel. Employees are given the work order when they check out job supplies. The work orders include the customer's name, address, time estimate, quoted price, job requirements, and special equipment needs. The document is turned in with the time slip at the end of the day and kept in the file cabinet. All other record keeping is done manually. Cleaners may work alone, or in teams for larger jobs. When cleaners pick up the work order, they receive supplies, necessary equipment, and a key for the house if it is unoccupied.

Accounts Receivable and Accounts Payable

Dom has a filing cabinet that contains all of the company's records. Financial details regarding charges

Figure 2

Time Slip Form

VACATION CARE SERVICES TIME SLIP	
Employee	
Customer No.	
Job Fee	
Hours Worked	
Service Date	
Initials	

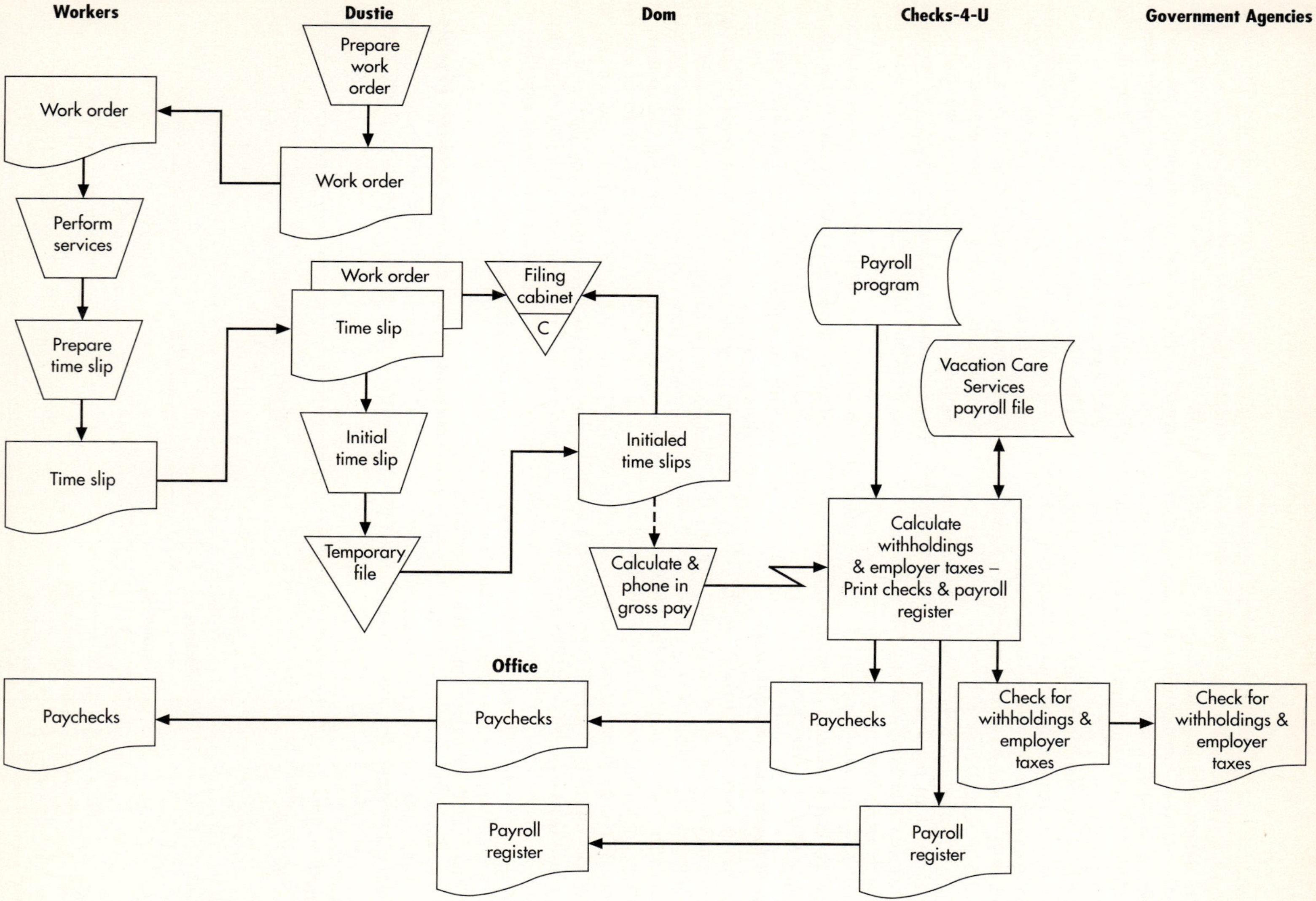

Workers
Dustie
Dom
Checks-4-U
Government Agencies
Prepare work order
Work order
Work order
Perform services
Work order
Time slip
Filing cabinet
C
Payroll program
Prepare time slip
Vacation Care Services payroll file
Initial time slip
Initialed time slips
Time slip
Temporary file
Calculate & phone in gross pay
Calculate withholdings & employer taxes – Print checks & payroll register
Office
Paychecks
Paychecks
Paychecks
Check for withholdings & employer taxes
Check for withholdings & employer taxes
Payroll register
Payroll register

Figure 3 *Payroll Process*

Figure 4

Work Order Form

VACATION CARE SERVICES
WORK ORDER

Assigned to:

Client:	Fee:	Circle One: Cash Charge
Address:	Mileage:	Key Needed: Yes No
Driving Directions:	Time Estimate:	
Description of Assignment:		
Equipment and Supplies Needed:	For Office Use Only	
Key Checkout: ____ Received by:	Key Checkin: ____ Received by:	
Time Out:	For Office Use:	
Time In:		
Total Time on Job:		

and payments to each customer's account are kept on a card (Fig. 5) in a blue binder. Charges are posted from the work orders and are filed chronologically. Payments are posted from the duplicate receipt or the check prelist that Dustie prepares. At the end of the month, Dom totals the record to find out how much to enter on the invoice. Dom uses an accordion file (which has a compartment for each letter of the alphabet) to store a copy of the mailed invoices. All bills received by the company are filed in a separate accordion file (which has a compartment for each day of the month) according to their due date. Once a week, Dom checks the file to see which bills should be paid. When paying a bill, Dom prepares a check, notes the purpose in the check register, writes "paid" on the invoice, and files it in a folder marked "paid bills." The checkbook register contains a space for explaining each outgoing check. Checks-4-U uses the same account to write the employee payroll checks.

After Dom posts the customer payments to the customer record, either Dom or Dustie makes out a deposit slip. The cash, checks, and deposit slips are placed in a bag and taken to the bank. Once a month Dom examines the bank statement to see how well the business did during the month.

Personnel and Salary Policies

The hiring of personnel is handled by both Dom and Dustie. The company regularly advertises for help in the student newspaper. The initial screening interview of employees is handled by Dustie, but the final hiring decision is made by Dom. All cleaning and vacation staff members must qualify for fidelity bonds. Once hired, cleaning employees generally stay with the company for an average of three to six

Figure 5

Customer Record Form

Customer No.

Name:
Address:

Date	Description	Post From	Charge	Payment	Balance

months. The training of new staff members usually is handled by Dustie.

Dom and Dustie receive a salary, but cleaning employees are paid a percentage of the fee received from each cleaning job. Beginning workers are guaranteed to be paid the greater of $4.25 per hour or a fixed percentage (40% during their first six months on the job, 50% thereafter) of the fee received. Cleaners use their own transportation to and from each job and are reimbursed 27 cents per mile. The cleaners are paid for their mileage out of the petty cash box when they return their equipment at the end of the day. Cleaners sign a sheet stored in the cash box that shows the number of miles driven and the amount of cash paid to them. This arrangement has worked well, since most of the cleaning jobs are located within 10 miles of the office.

Vacation services employees, in contrast to cleaning personnel, are treated as short-term contractors. For vacation services, Dom requires a three-day minimum charge at the rate of $15.00 per day. Vacation services are never performed by the cleaners. Rather, Dom and Dustie maintain a list of 15–20 college students who have agreed to work, when available. Generally, they receive two-thirds of the collected fee. Dom does not reimburse these students for mileage, since vacation services are available only to customers in the immediate college area.

Equipment Storage and Usage

Dom tries to maintain tight control over cleaning supplies and equipment. Every morning before class, Dom personally sorts out the supplies and equipment for each job. Either Dom or Dustie distributes the materials. When class schedules conflict, Dom's mother, Patricia Woods, comes in as a relief worker to hand out supplies, answer the phone, and collect the documents and monies that workers submit after each job. She also assists in posting work orders and receipts to the customer record cards. Patricia Woods worked in an accounting department a number of years ago, and she helped design the current documents and records.

Although rushing to sort out supplies and equipment is difficult, Dom feels that it is worth the trouble because some employees have helped themselves to extras in the past. Supplies are kept in a locked cage and are replenished as needed from the local Discount Club. The Discount Club is a local cash and carry warehouse that does not extend credit. Dom does, however, receive a wholesale discount for purchases over $300.00. Major purchases such as vacuums are ordered from local wholesalers.

New Opportunities

Dr. Evans has been very impressed with the growth of Dom's business and has recommended Vacation

Care Services to his associates on staff at the local hospital. Last week, Dr. Evans asked Dom to meet over dinner to discuss the future. He asked about Dom's plans after graduation and learned that Dom was considering applying to grad school because an English lit. B.A. receives few full-time job offers. Dr. Evans then asked whether Dom would be interested in expanding the cleaning business, since the janitorial service contract for Dr. Evans's medical suite would be expiring soon. He stated that he had spoken with another colleague, Dr. Celeste Capp, who also uses Dom's services. They, in turn, had spoken with their investment adviser, Brenda Dillon. Both doctors are prepared to invest in Dom's expansion into the janitorial services field. They know that many fellow physicians are interested in reasonably priced janitorial services. Drs. Evans and Capp also mentioned that they are partners in a new medical office complex that will be built next year. Contracts for the janitorial services in the common areas of this complex would be considerable. Dr. Evans suggested that Dom speak with Brenda Dillon about the proposition.

After the dinner, Dom's parents voiced their support for the business proposal and stated that they also would consider investing in the company. The next day, Dom and Brenda Dillon toured the company's offices. She stated that a full assessment of the company is necessary before she makes a final recommendation to Drs. Evans and Capp. Since the company recently completed its first full year of operations, Dillon has referred Dom to your accounting firm to assess the company's procedures, records, and operations.

The requirements for this case are divided to coincide with the major sections of the book. In addition, the appropriate chapters are also identified.

Part One: Conceptual Foundations of Accounting Information Systems

1. (Chapter 1) Identify the internal and external information requirements at Vacation Care Services.
2. (Chapter 2) Prepare a chart of accounts for the current operations.
3. (Chapter 3) Prepare a flowchart of the cash receipt, cash deposit, and cash reconciliation procedures.
4. (Chapter 5) Prepare a data dictionary for the customer file that is kept on the spreadsheet.

Part Two: The Technology of Information Systems

5. (Chapter 7 or 8) Describe the current hardware and software configuration. Discuss whether the current system is being utilized to its full potential. Should the hardware and software be replaced? Why or why not?

Part Three: The Systems Development Process

6. (Chapter 10) Assuming that the company will expand into janitorial services, identify four systems development projects that could be undertaken. Prepare a master plan that specifies what the systems will consist of, how they will be developed, and where the information system is headed. Prioritize the projects, and describe the criteria used for prioritization. Limit your plan to two typewritten pages.
7. (Chapter 10) Consider the various strategies for determining information system requirements, and suggest which strategies would be appropriate for this company. Which factors affect the level of uncertainty in this company?
8. (Chapter 10) Identify a way to empower the cleaners. Discuss the benefits and risks of empowerment at the company.
9. (Chapter 11) For each project identified in Requirement 6, determine the best method for converting from the old to the new system. Provide reasons for not choosing alternative conversion methods.

Part Four: Control and Audit of Accounting Information Systems

10. (Chapter 13) Identify the internal control weaknesses of and recommend improvements in the cash receipt, deposit, and reconciliation procedures. Use the following format to prepare your answer. If you prepared a flowchart for Requirement 3, cross-reference your list to it.

Item Number	Nature of Weakness	Recommendation to Correct Weakness

11. (Chapter 12 or 15) Examine several software-licensing agreements. Discuss whether the company would be violating a software-licensing agreement.
12. (Chapter 16) Consider the three types of audits discussed in Chapter 16. Select the two that you feel

are most needed by this company, and provide the rationale for your decision.

Part Five: Accounting Information Systems Applications

13. (Chapter 17) Are Dom and Dustie making appropriate pricing decisions? What should be considered in setting pricing policies? What managerial revenue cycle reports could be prepared from the current records?

14. (Chapter 17) Assume that Vacation Care Services wants to implement a relational data base for the revenue cycle, using the REA data model. Draw an E–R diagram to represent the contents of this data base.

15. (Chapter 18) Identify problems in the petty cash system. Prepare the document that is currently being used in the petty cash box. Make recommendations to change the petty cash system.

16. (Chapter 20) Identify the internal control strengths and weaknesses of and recommend improvements in the payroll system. Use the following format to prepare your answer.

Item Number	Description	Recommendations to Correct Weaknesses
Strengths		
Weaknesses		

Glossary

Acceptance Tests. Tests of new systems using specially developed transactions and acceptance criteria. The test results are evaluated to determine whether the system is acceptable.

Access Control Matrix. An internally maintained list that the computer uses to verify that the person attempting to access system resources is authorized to do so. The matrix usually consists of a list of user codes, a list of all files and programs maintained on the system, and a list of the accesses each user is authorized to make.

Access Time. The time required to transfer data to or from a storage device.

Accounting Controls. The plan of organization and the procedures and records concerned with the safeguarding of assets and the reliability of financial records.

Accounting Cycle. The activities corresponding to an organization's major accounting transactions. There are five major accounting cycles: acquisition and cash disbursements, payroll and personnel, sales and collection, capital acquisition and repayment, and inventory and warehousing.

Accounting Information System (AIS). The human and capital resources within an organization that are responsible for (1) the preparation of financial information and (2) the information obtained from collecting and processing company transactions. The AIS is a subset of the management information system.

Accounts Receivable Aging Schedule. A report listing customer account balances by length of time outstanding; it provides useful information for evaluating current credit policies and for deciding whether to increase the credit limit for specific customers. It also provides information for estimating bad debts.

Activity-Based Costing. A cost system that attempts to trace costs to the activities, such as grinding or polishing, that create them, and only subsequently allocates those costs to products or departments.

Ad-Hoc Queries. Nonrepetitive requests for reports or answers to specific questions about the contents of the system's data files.

Adjusted Trial Balance. A trial balance prepared after all adjusting entries have been made. The income statement can be produced from the adjusted trial balance.

Administrative Controls. The plan of organization and all methods and procedures that are concerned with operational efficiency and adherence to managerial policies.

Administrative Documentation. A description of the overall standards and procedures for the data processing facility, including policies relating to justification and authorization of new systems or systems changes; standards for systems analysis, design, and programming; and procedures for file handling and file library activities.

Aggression. A way of resisting change that is intended to destroy, cripple, or lessen the effectiveness of a system. Aggression may take the form of increased error rates, disruptions, or deliberate sabotage.

Application. The problem or data processing task to which a computer's processing power is applied.

Application Controls. Controls that relate to the data inputs, files, programs, and outputs of a specific computer application, rather than the computer system in general. *Contrast with* General controls.

Application Programmer. A person who formulates a logical model, or user view, of the data to be processed and then writes an application program using a programming language.

Application Software. The programs that perform the data or information processing tasks required by the user. Common types of application software in accounting include accounts receivable and payable, inventory control, and payroll.

Application Suites. End-user software programs that are packaged and sold together. They usually include spreadsheets, word processors, data bases, graphics, and E-mail.

Arithmetic-Logic Unit. The portion of the CPU that executes arithmetic calculations and logic comparisons.

Artificial Intelligence (AI). A field of study in which researchers are attempting to develop computers that have the ability to reason, think, and learn like a human being.

Assembler. A special program that converts a symbolic language program to a machine language.

Assembler Language. A programming language in which each machine-level instruction is represented by mnemonic characters that bear some relation to the instruction. It is also referred to as a symbolic language.

Asynchronous Transmission. Data transmission in which each character is transmitted separately. A start bit is required before the character and a stop bit after it, because the interval of time between transmission of characters can vary. *Contrast with* Synchronous transmission.

ATM Card. A bank card that many businesses accept in lieu of credit and debit cards.

Attribute. A characteristic of interest in a file or data base; an individual property of an entity. Examples of attributes are employee number, pay rate, name, and address.

Audio Response Unit. A hardware device that converts computer output into spoken output (e.g., telephone directory assistance).

Audio Teleconferencing. A conference call where several locations are linked together so that they can hear each other.

Audit Hooks. Concurrent audit techniques that embed audit routines into application software to flag certain kinds of transactions that might be indicative of fraud.

Audit Log. A log, kept on magnetic tape or disk, of all computer system transactions that have audit significance.

Auditing. A systematic process of (1) objectively obtaining and evaluating evidence regarding assertions about economic actions and events to ascertain the degree of correspondence between those assertions and established criteria and (2) communicating the results to interested parties.

Audit Trail. A traceable path of a transaction through a data processing system, from source documents to final output.

Authorization. The empowerment of an employee to perform certain functions within an organization, such as to purchase or sell on behalf of the company. Authorization can be either general or specific. With *general* authorization, regular employees are authorized to handle routine transactions without special approval. With *specific* authorization, an employee must get special approval before handling a transaction.

Automated Decision Table Program. A program that interprets the logic used in a computer program and displays the logic in the form of a decision table.

Automated Flowcharting Program. A program that interprets the source code of a program and generates a flowchart of the logic used by the program.

Automated Teller Machine (ATM). A special-purpose, intelligent terminal used by financial institutions to provide remote banking services.

Avoidance. A way of resisting change by not using the new system.

Back-End (or Lower) CASE. CASE tools that support the later SDLC phases. Programmers generate structured program code from data base specifications and from screen and report layouts.

Back Order. A document authorizing the purchase, or production, of items for which sufficient quantity is not available to meet customer orders.

Backup File. Duplicate copy of a current file.

Balance-Forward Method. Method of maintaining accounts receivable in which customers typically pay according to the amount shown on monthly statement, rather than by individual invoices. Remittances are applied against the total account balance, rather than against specific invoices.

Bandwidths. The differences between the highest and the lowest frequency of a communications channel, usually expressed in cycles per second (hertz).

Bar Codes. Special identification labels found on most merchandise. A code includes vertical lines of differing widths that represent binary information that is read by an optical scanner.

Batch Processing. The accumulation of transaction records into groups or batches for processing at some regular interval such as daily or weekly. The records are usually sorted into some sequence (such as numerically or alphabetically) before processing.

Batch Totals. Sums of the instances of numerical items, calculated for a batch of documents. These totals are calculated prior to processing the batch and are compared with machine-generated totals at each subsequent processing step to verify that the data were processed correctly.

Baud Rate. The speed with which data are electronically transferred from one location to another. In many data communications transmissions, it is equal to one bit per second.

Behavioral Aspects of Change. Changes in peoples' behavior that may result from organizational changes due to systems development implementation. Organizations must be sensitive to and consider the feelings and reactions of persons affected by such changes.

Benchmark Problem. A data processing task that is executed by different computer systems. The results are used to measure systems performance and to make comparative evaluations among systems.
Bill of Lading. A legal contract that defines responsibility for goods in transit. It identifies the carrier, source, destination, any special shipping instructions, and which party (customer or vendor) must pay the carrier.
Bill of Materials. A document that specifies the part number, description, and quantity of each component used in a product.
Biometric Identifications. Methods to identify people by using unique physical characteristics such as fingerprints, voice patterns, retina prints, signature dynamics, and the way people type certain groups of characters.
BIPS. Billions of instructions per second; a way of measuring CPU speed.
Bits. Binary digits, which are the smallest storage location in a computer. A bit may be either "on" or "off," or "magnetized" or "nonmagnetized." A combination of bits (usually eight) is used to represent a single character of data.
Bits per Second (BPS). A unit of measurement describing the number of bits of data transmitted electronically in one second.
Blanket Order. A commitment to purchase specified items at designated prices from a particular supplier for a set time period, often one year.
Broadband Lines. Communications channels that are capable of handling high-speed data transmissions, usually in the range of 20,000 to 500,000 bits per second. Their primary use is for high-speed data transmission between computer systems.
Budget. The formal expression of goals in financial terms. Budgets are financial planning tools. *Contrast with* Performance report.
Bulletin Board System (BBS). An information sharing service that allows computer users to meet and share ideas and information. Most BBSs are free and cater to specialized interests.
Bus. The path for moving data, instructions, or other signals between the various components of the CPU. The bus could be in the form of a cable or in the form of the connecting paths within a microcomputer chip.
Business Process Reengineering (BPR). The thorough analysis and complete redesign of business processes and information systems to achieve dramatic performance improvements.
Bus Network. Type of network organization in which all devices are attached to a main channel called a bus. Each network device can access the other devices by sending a message to its address. Each device reads the address of all messages sent on the bus and responds to the messages sent to it.
Byte. A group of adjacent bits that is treated as a single unit by the computer. The most common size for a byte is eight bits. An eight-bit byte can be used to represent an alphabetic, numeric, or special character, or two numeric characters can be "packed" into a single eight-bit byte.
Canned Software. Programs written by computer manufacturers or software development companies for sale on the open market to a broad range of users with similar needs.
Capital Budgeting Model. An estimate of funds to be appropriated for the acquisition of major capital assets and for investment in long-term projects. The estimated benefits are compared with the costs to determine whether the system is cost beneficial.
Cardinality. A property of a data base relationship, indicating the number of occurrences of one entity that may be associated with a single occurrence of the other entity. Three types of cardinalities are one-to-one, one-to-many, and many-to-many.
Carrying Costs. The costs associated with holding inventory.
CASE Encyclopedia (or **Data Repository**). A program that stores and manages project data dictionaries. It contains information about the system and is cross-referenced to other system components.
Cash Budget. A budget that shows projected cash inflows and outflows. A cash budget can provide advance warning of cash flow problems in time to permit corrective action to be taken.
Cathode Ray Tube (CRT). Another name for the monitor on a computer. Sometimes terminals are referred to as CRTs as well.
CD-ROM. A storage device that uses laser optics rather than magnetic storage devices for reading data. Although CD-ROM discs are "read only," the discs are useful for storing large volumes of data (roughly 600 megabytes per disc).
Cells. (1) The intersections of rows and columns in an electronic spreadsheet. (2) Small sections of a larger metropolitan area in which cellular radio is used.
Cellular Radios. A means of making greater use of radio frequencies. A large area is divided into smaller sections called cells,

and each radio frequency is assigned to a different user in each cell. A powerful central computer controls transmission between cells.

Cellular Telephones. Telephones that use radio frequencies to send and receive messages. These radio frequencies are divided into geographic regions called cells so that users in different locations can share the same frequency.

Centralized Data Processing System. The consolidation of all data processing equipment, personnel, and controls are located in the same geographical area.

Centralized Network. A large, centralized computer system that handles a company's data processing needs. Such a system requires complex software and is designed to provide a company with an "economy of scale" advantage in data processing operations.

Centralized System. A centralized processing center that performs data processing. User terminals are linked to the centralized host computer so that users can send data to the host computer for processing and access data as needed.

Central Processing Unit (CPU). The hardware that contains the circuits that control the interpretation and execution of instructions and that serves as the principal data processing device. Its major components are the arithmetic-logic unit, the memory, and the control unit.

Channel. (1) A path that electronic signals follow when traveling between electronic devices. (2) A hardware device that acts as a communication interface between the CPU and input/output devices.

Characters. Letters, numeric digits, or other symbols used for representing data to be processed by a computer.

Chart of Accounts. A listing of all balance sheet and income statement account number codes for a particular company.

Check Digit. A redundant digit in a data field that provides information about the other digits in the data field. It is used to check for errors or loss of characters in the data fields as a result of data transfer operations. If data are lost or erroneously changed, the fact that the check digit does not match the other data in the field will signal that an error has occurred.

Check Digit Verification. The edit check in which a check digit is recalculated to verify that an error has not been made. This calculation can be made only on a data item that has a check digit.

Checkpoint. Any one of a series of points during a long processing run at which an exact copy of all the data values and status indicators of a program is captured. Should a system failure occur, the system could be backed up to the most recent checkpoint and processing could begin again at the checkpoint rather than at the beginning of the program.

Client/Server System. An arrangement of a LAN where information requested by a user is first processed as much as possible by the server and then transmitted to the user. *Contrast with* File server.

Closed-Loop Verification. An input validation method in which data that have just been entered into the system are sent back to the sending device so that the user can verify that the correct data have been entered.

Coaxial Cable. A group of copper or aluminum wires that have been wrapped and shielded to reduce interference. The cables are used to transmit electronic messages between hardware devices.

Coding. (1) The assignment of numbers, letters, or other symbols according to a systematic plan so that a user can determine the classifications to which a particular item belongs. (2) Written program instructions that direct a computer to perform a specific data processing task.

Cold Site. A location that provides everything necessary for quick installation of computer equipment in the event of a disaster-stricken organization.

Common Carriers. Governmentally regulated private organizations that provide telecommunications equipment and services to the public.

Communications Channel. The line, or link, between the sender and the receiver in a data communications network.

Communications Network. An information system consisting of one or more computers, a number of other hardware devices, and communications channels all linked together into a network.

Communications Software. A program that controls the transmission of data electronically over communications lines.

Compatibility Test. A procedure for checking a password to determine whether its user is authorized to initiate the type of transaction or inquiry he or she is attempting to initiate.

Compensating Controls. Control procedures that will compensate for the deficiency in other controls.

Compilers. Programs that convert all high-level language commands (source code) into machine language commands (object code) before any commands are executed. *Contrast with* Interpreter.

Completeness Test. An on-line data-entry control in which the computer checks whether all the data required for a particular transaction have been entered by the user.

Computer-Aided Software (or Systems) Engineering (CASE). This type of software is used by analysts to document and manage a systems development effort.

Computer Audit Software. *See* Generalized audit software.

Computer-Based Information System. Information system in which a computer is used as the data processor. All the equipment, programs, data, and procedures for performing a set of related tasks on a computer.

Computer Conferencing. Personal interaction using computers at remote sites linked through communications facilities.

Computer Configuration Chart. A type of flowchart that shows the different hardware devices in a computer system.

Computer Crime. Any illegal act for which knowledge of a computer is essential for the crime's perpetration, investigation, or prosecution.

Computer Fraud. *See* Computer crime.

Computer Hardware. *See* Hardware.

Computer Integrated Manufacturing (CIM). A manufacturing approach in which much of the manufacturing process is performed and monitored by computerized equipment, in part through the use of robotics and real-time data collection on manufacturing activities.

Computer Output Microfilm (COM). A hardware device that uses a photographic process to record computer output on photosensitive film in microscopic form.

Computer Program. *See* Program.

Computer Programmers. Persons who develop, code, and test computer programs.

Computer Programming. The process of writing software programs to accomplish a specific task or set of tasks.

Computer Security. All of the policies, procedures, tools, and other means of safeguarding information systems from unauthorized access or alteration and from intentional or unintentional damage or theft.

Computer System. The input/output devices, data storage devices, CPU, and other peripheral devices that are connected together. The software necessary to operate the computer is also considered a part of the system.

Computer System Flowchart. A type of flowchart that shows the inputs to a computer system or program, the program modules that process the data, and the output from the system.

Computer Virus. A segment of executable code that attaches itself to an application program or some other executable system component. When the hidden program is triggered, it makes unauthorized alterations to the way a system operates.

Concatenated Key. The combination of two fields in a data base table that together become a unique identifier or key field.

Conceptual Design Specifications. Systems requirements specified for systems output, data storage, input, and processing procedures and operations once a conceptual design alternative has been selected.

Conceptual Level Schema. The organizationwide schema of the entire data base. It lists all data elements in the data base and the relationships between them. *Contrast with* External and Internal level schemas.

Conceptual Systems Design. A phase of the systems development life cycle in which the systems designer proposes a systems design without considering the physical restrictions of particular hardware and software.

Conceptual Systems Design Report. A document specifying the details of the conceptual systems design that is used by physical systems designers to identify the hardware, software, and procedures necessary to deliver the system.

Concurrent Audit Techniques. A software routine that continuously monitors an information system as it processes live data in order to collect, evaluate, and report to the auditor information about the system's reliability.

Concurrent Update Controls. Controls that lock out one user to protect individual records from potential errors that could occur if two users attempted to update the same record simultaneously.

Configuration. For a network, a configuration is the entire interrelated set of hardware. For a microcomputer, the configuration references the complete internal and external components of the computer including peripherals.

Context Diagram. The highest level of a data flow diagram. It provides a summary-level view of a system. It shows the data processing system, the inputs and outputs of the system, and the external entities that are the sources and destinations of the system's inputs and outputs.

Continuous and Intermittent Simulation (CIS). A concurrent audit technique that embeds an audit module into a data base management system rather than into the application software.

Control Account. The general ledger account that summarizes the total amounts recorded in a subsidiary ledger. Thus the accounts payable control account in the general ledger represents the total amount owed to all vendors. The balances in the subsidiary accounts payable ledger indicate the amount owed to each specific vendor.

Control Risk. The risk that a significant control problem will fail to be prevented or detected by the internal control system.

Control Totals. Batch totals used to ensure that all data is processed correctly. Examples are the number of transactions processed and the dollar amount of all updates.

Control Unit. The CPU component that interprets program instructions and controls and coordinates the system's input, output, and storage devices.

Conversion. The process of changing from one form or format to another.

Corrective Controls. Procedures established to remedy problems that are discovered through detective controls.

Cost Driver. Anything that has a cause-and-effect relationship on costs. For example, the number of purchase orders processed is one cost driver of purchasing department costs.

Credit Limit. The maximum allowable account balance for each customer, based on past credit history and ability to pay.

Credit Memo. A document authorizing the billing department to credit the customer's account. Usually issued for sales returns, allowances granted for damaged goods kept by the customer, or to write off uncollectible accounts. Approved by the credit manager.

Cross-Footing Balance Test. A procedure in which worksheet data are totaled both across and down and then the total of the horizontal totals is compared to the total of the vertical totals to make sure the worksheet balances.

Cryptography. *See* Data encryption.

Custom Software. Computer software that is developed and written in-house to meet the unique needs of a particular company.

Cycle Billing. A procedure for producing monthly statements for subsets of customers at different times. For example, the customer master file might be divided into four parts, and each week monthly statements would be prepared for one-fourth of the customers.

Data Administrator (DA). The person responsible for developing general policies and procedures governing all organizational data, not just what is stored in the data base. The DA is ultimately responsible for understanding the information needs of the organization in order to decide what should be included in the data base.

Data. Characters that are accepted as input to an information system for further storage and processing. After processing, the data become information.

Data Base. A set of interrelated, centrally controlled data files that are stored with as little data redundancy as possible. A data base consolidates many records previously stored in separate files into a common pool of data records and serves a variety of users and data processing applications.

Data Base Administrator. The person responsible for coordinating, controlling, and managing the data in the data base.

Data Base Management System (DBMS). The specialized computer program that manages and controls the data and interfaces between the data and the application programs.

Data Base Query Languages. Easy-to-use programming languages that let the user ask questions about the data stored in a data base.

Data Base System. The combination of the data base, the data base management system, and the application programs that access the data base through the data base management system.

Data Bus. The path, or circuitry, that the computer uses to move data and instructions between the different parts of the CPU, and to and from the input/output devices.

Data Communications. The transmission of data from a point of origin to a point of destination.

Data Communications Networks. Communication system that bridges geographical distances, giving users immediate access to a company's computerized data. It also allows multiple companies or computer services to be linked for the purpose of sharing information.

Data Definition Language (DDL). A data base management system language that ties the logical and physical views of the data together. It is used to create the data base, to describe the schema and subschemas, to describe the records and fields in the data base, and to specify any security limitations or constraints imposed on the data base.

Data Destination. A component of data flow diagrams that represents an entity outside of the system that receives data produced by the system.

Data Dictionary. An ordered collection of data elements that is essentially a centralized source of data about data. For each data element used in the organization, the data dictionary has a record that contains data about that data element.

Data Diddling. A change in data before it enters, as it enters, or after it has already been entered into the system. The change can be made to delete data, to change data, or to add data to the system.

Data Encryption. The translation of data into a secret code for storage or data transmission purposes. Encryption is particularly important when confidential data are being transmitted from remote terminals, because data transmission lines can be electronically monitored without the user's knowledge.

Data Flow. A component of a data flow diagram that represents a piece of data flowing into or out of a process.

Data Flow Diagram. A diagram that concentrates on identifying the types of data and their flow through various types of processing. The physical nature of the data (e.g., physical document, electronic) is ignored; the diagram simply identifies the content of the data, the source, and the destination.

Data Independence. A data organization approach in which the data and the application programs that use the data are independent. This means that one may be changed without affecting the other.

Data Leakage. The unauthorized copying of company data, often without leaving any indication that it was copied.

Data Maintenance. The periodic processing of transactions to update stored data. The four types of data maintenance are additions, deletions, updates, and changes.

Data Manipulation Language (DML). A data base management system language that is used to update, replace, store, retrieve, insert, delete, sort, and otherwise manipulate the records and data items in the data base.

Data Model. An abstract representation of the contents of a data base.

Data Modeling. The process of defining a data base so that it faithfully represents all key components of an organization's environment. The objective is to capture and store explicit data about each and every business activity that the organization wishes to plan, control, or evaluate.

Data Processing Center. The room that houses a company's computer system (the hardware, software, and people who operate the system).

Data Processing Cycle. The operations performed on data in computer-based systems in order to generate meaningful and relevant information. The data processing cycle has four stages: data input, data processing, data storage, and information output.

Data Query Language (DQL). A high-level, English-like command language that is used to interrogate a data base. Most DQLs contain a fairly powerful set of commands that are easy to use, yet provide a great deal of flexibility.

Data Redundancy. The storage of the same item of data in two or more files within an organization.

Data Repository (or **CASE Encyclopedia**). A program that stores and manages project data dictionaries. It contains information about the system and is cross-referenced to other system components.

Data Source. A component of a data flow diagram that represents a source of data outside the system being modeled.

Data Store. A component of a data flow diagram that represents the storage of data within a system.

Data Value. The actual value stored in a field. It describes a particular attribute of an entity.

Data Warehouses. Very large data bases.

Debit Memo. A document used to record an adjustment to the balance due a vendor, reflecting a reduction in the amount owed.

Debugging. The process of checking for errors in a computer program and correcting the errors that are discovered.

Decentralized System. An information processing system that has an independent CPU and a data processing manager at each location.

Decision Rule. The vertical columns in a decision table that represent a combination of logical relationships and the actions that should be taken for each of those conditions.

Decision Support Systems (DSS). An interactive computer system designed to help with the decision-making process by providing access to a computer-based data base or decision-making model.

Decision Table. A tabular representation of program logic that indicates the possible combinations of logic conditions and the courses of action taken by the program for each condition.

Deduction Register. A report listing the miscellaneous voluntary deductions for each employee.

Delete Anomaly. A problem that can arise in a poorly designed relational data base, when attributes that are not characteristics of the primary key of a relation are stored in that table. Deleting a row from that table may result in the loss of all information about those attributes that are not characteristics of the primary key. For example, if customer addresses are only stored in the sales invoice table, then deleting the row representing the only sale to a particular customer results in the loss of all information about that customer.

Demand Reports. Reports that have a prespecified content and format but are prepared only in response to a request from a manager or other employee.

Desk Checking. A visual and mental review of a newly coded program to discover keying or program errors.

Desktop Publishing (DTP). Software that provides an end user with the ability to design, develop, and produce professional-quality printed documents containing text, charts, pictures, graphs, spreadsheets, photographs, and illustrations.

Detection Risk. The risk that the auditors and their audit procedures will not detect a material misstatement.

Detective Controls. Controls designed to discover control problems soon after they arise.

Diagnostic Messages. Messages that inform the programmer of syntax errors.

Digital Signature. A piece of data signed on a document by a computer. A digital signature cannot be forged and is useful in tracing authorization.

Direct Access. An access method that allows the computer to access a particular record without reading any other records. Since each storage location on a direct access storage device has a unique address, the computer can find the record needed as long as it has the record's address.

Direct Access Processing. The updating of the master file immediately as transactions occur. With each transaction, the master file is retrieved, updated, and stored.

Direct Access Storage Device (DASD). A storage device (such as a disk drive) that can directly access individual storage locations to store or retrieve data.

Direct Conversion. An approach to converting from one system to another in which the old system is altogether discontinued, after which the new system is started (also known as "burning the bridges" or "crash conversion").

Disaster Recovery Plan. A plan that prepares a company to recover its data processing capacity as smoothly and quickly as possible in response to any emergency that could disable the computer system.

Disbursement Voucher. A document that identifies the vendor, lists the outstanding invoices, and indicates the net amount to be paid after deducting any applicable discounts and allowances.

Diskette. A round piece of flexible magnetic film enclosed within a protective cover. It is a popular storage medium for microcomputers.

Distributed Data Processing (DDP) System. A system in which computers are set up at remote locations and then linked to a centralized mainframe computer.

Documentation. Written material consisting of instructions to operators, descriptions of procedures, and other descriptive material. Documentation may be classified into three basic categories: administrative, systems, and operating.

Document Flowchart. A diagram illustrating the flow of documents through the different departments and functions of an organization.

Documents. Records of transactions or other company data such as checks, invoices, receiving reports, and purchase requisitions.

Downloading. The transmission of data or software maintained on a large host (mainframe) computer to a personal computer for use by an individual working at the personal computer.

Downsizing. The shifting of data processing and problem solving from mainframes to smaller computer systems. Downsizing saves money and allows the end user to be more involved in the processing of the data.

Earnings Statement. A report listing the amount of gross pay, deductions, and net pay for the current period; year-to-date totals for each category are also listed.

Eavesdropping. The act of a computer user observing transmissions intended for someone else. One way unauthorized individuals can intercept signals is by setting up a wiretap.

Echo Check. A hardware control that verifies transmitted data by having the receiving device send the message back to the sending device so that the message received can be compared to the message sent.

Economic Feasibility. The dimension of feasibility concerned with whether the benefits of a proposed system will exceed the costs.

Economic Order Quantity (EOQ). The optimal order size so as to minimize the sum of ordering, carrying, and stockout costs. Ordering costs include all expenses associated with processing purchase transactions. Carrying costs are the costs associated with holding inventory. Stockout costs represent costs, such as lost sales or production delays, that result from inventory shortages.

Edit Checks. Accuracy checks performed by an edit program.

Edit Programs. Computer programs that verify the validity and accuracy of input data.

Electronic Data Interchange (EDI). The use of computerized communication to exchange business data electronically in order to process transactions.

Electronic Data Processing (EDP). The processing of data utilizing a computer system. Little or no human intervention is necessary while data are being processed.

Electronic Funds Transfer (EFT). The transfer of funds between two or more organizations or individuals using computers and other automated technology.

Electronic Lockbox. A lockbox arrangement in which the bank electronically sends the company information about the customer account number and the amount remitted as soon as it receives and scans those checks. This enables the company to begin applying remittances to customer accounts before the photocopies of the checks arrive.

Electronic Mail (E-Mail). A system that allows a person to use a computer to send a message to another person.

Electronic Spreadsheet. An applications program used for analysis, planning, modeling, and decision support. It is a worksheet, or matrix of rows and columns, containing blank cells into which numeric data, alphabetic data, or formulas can be entered.

Electronic Vaulting. Electronically transmitting backup copies of data to a physically different location. Electronic vaulting permits on-line access to backup data when necessary.

Embedded Audit Modules. Special portions of application programs that keep track of items of interest to auditors, such as any unauthorized attempts to access the data files.

Embezzlement. The fraudulent appropriation of business property by an employee to whom it has been entrusted. It is often accompanied by falsification of records.

Employee Fraud. A type of internal fraud where an employee or group of employees use company resources for their own personal gain.

Encapsulation. The bundling together of data and instructions in the object-oriented data model.

End-User Computing (EUC). The creation, control, and implementation by end users of their own information system.

End-User Development. The development of applications by users rather than by the IS department.

End-User System (EUS). Information system developed by the users themselves, rather than professionals in the IS department, to meet their own operational and managerial information needs. An EUS draws upon the information in existing corporate data bases to meet users information needs.

Entity. The item about which information is stored in a record. Examples of an entity include an employee, an inventory item, and a customer account.

Entity Integrity Rule. A design constraint in a relational data base, requiring that the primary key have a nonnull value. This ensures that a specific object exists in the world and can be identified by reference to its primary key value.

Entity–Relationship (E–R) Diagram. A graphical depiction of a data base's contents. It shows the various entities being modeled and the important relationships among them. An entity is any class of objects about which data are collected. Thus the resources, events, and agents that comprise the REA data model are all entities. An E–R diagram represents entities as rectangles; lines and diamonds represent relationships between entities.

Error Message. A message from the computer indicating that it has encountered a mistake or malfunction.

Ethernet. A bus configuration that allows LAN devices to place and retrieve messages on the network. In addition, ethernet regulates "traffic" on the network.

Execution Time. The time required to perform a computer instruction.

Executive Information System (EIS). Information system designed to provide executives with the information necessary to make strategic plans, to control and operate the company, to monitor business conditions in general, and to identify business problems and opportunities.

Expected Loss. A measure of loss based on the potential loss associated with a control problem and the risk, or probability, that the problem will occur.

Expenditure Cycle. A recurring set of business activities and related data processing operations associated with the purchase of and payment for goods and services.

Expert System (ES). A computerized information system that allows nonexperts to make decisions about a particular problem that are comparable to those of experts in the area.

Explanation Facility. A component of an expert system that provides the user with an explanation of the logic that the ES used to arrive at its conclusion.

Exposure. A measure of risk derived by multiplying the potential magnitude of an error, in dollars, by the error's estimated frequency (probability) of occurrence.

External Label. A label on the outside of a magnetic storage medium (e.g., tape, disk) that identifies the data contained on the storage medium.

External Level Schema. An individual user's or application program's view of a subset of the organization's data base. Each of these individual user views is also referred to as a subschema. *Contrast with* Conceptual and Internal level schemas.

Facsimile (Fax) Transmission. The electronic transmission of pictures, contracts, signatures, and so forth over data communications lines.

Fault Tolerance. The capability of a system to continue performing its functions in the presence of a hardware failure.

Fax Modem. A type of modem that, in conjunction with accompanying software, allows users to send fully formatted documents and data files from their PC to a receiving fax machine or computer without having to print them first.

Feasibility Study. An investigation to determine whether the development of a new application or system is practical. This is one of the first steps in the systems evaluation and selection process.

Feedback. Informational output of a process that returns as input to the process, initiating the actions necessary for process control.

Feedback Controls. Controls that measure some aspect of the process being controlled and adjust the process when the measure indicates that the process is deviating from the plan.

Feedforward Controls. Controls that monitor both process operations and inputs in an attempt to predict potential deviations, in order that adjustments can be made to avert problems before they occur.

Femtosecond. One quadrillionth of a second.

Fiber Optics Cable. A data transmission cable consisting of thousands of tiny filaments of glass or plastic.

Field. The part of a data record that contains the data value for a particular attribute. All records of a particular type usually have their fields in the same order. For example, the first field in all accounts receivable records may be reserved for the customer account number.

Field Check. An edit check in which the characters in a field are examined to make sure they are of the correct field type (e.g., numeric data in numeric fields).

File. A set of logically related records, such as the payroll records of all employees.

File Access. The way the computer finds or retrieves each record it has stored.

File Maintenance. The periodic processing of transaction files against a master file. This maintenance, which is the most common task in virtually all data processing systems, includes record additions, deletions, updates, and changes. After file maintenance, the master file will contain all current information.

File Organization. The way data are stored on the physical storage media. File organization may be either sequential or direct (random, nonsequential, or relative).

File Server. An arrangement of a LAN whereby an entire file is sent to the user and then processed by the user, not the server. *Contrast with* Client/server system.

Financial Audit. A review of the reliability and integrity of financial and operating information and the means used to identify, measure, classify, and report such information.

Financial Total. The total of a dollar field, such as total sales, in a set of records. It is usually generated manually from source documents prior to input and compared with machine-generated totals at each subsequent processing step. Any discrepancy may indicate a loss of records or errors in data transcription or processing.

Firewall. A combination of security algorithms and router communications protocols that prevent outsiders from tapping into corporate data bases and E-mail systems.

Flash Memory Chip. A memory chip that does not lose its contents when the power is shut off. Used to replace hard disks in hand-held computers and to store operating systems and application software.

Flat File. A file structure in which every record is identical to every other record in terms of attributes and field lengths.

Flexible Benefit Plans. Plans under which each employee receives some minimum coverage in medical insurance and pension contributions, plus additional benefit "credits" that can be used to acquire extra vacation time or additional health insurance. These plans are sometimes called cafeteria-style benefit plans because they offer a menu of options.

Floppy Disk. A 5¼-inch or 3½-inch diskette.

Flowchart. A diagrammatical representation of the flow of information and the sequence of operations in a process or system.

Flowcharting Symbols. A set of objects that are used in flowcharts to show how and where data move. Each symbol has a special meaning that is easily conveyed by its shape.

Flowcharting Template. A piece of hard, flexible plastic on which the shapes of flowcharting symbols have been cut out.

Foreign Key. An attribute appearing in one table that is itself the primary key of another table.

Forensic Accountants. Accountants who specialize in fraud auditing and investigation. Upon qualification, forensic accountants may receive a certified fraud examiner (CFE) certificate.

Fourth Generation Languages (4GL). High-level, application, or user-oriented languages that are easy to learn and do not require the user to understand the details of the computer.

Fraudulent Financial Reporting. Intentional or reckless conduct, whether by act or omission, that results in materially misleading financial statements.

Freight Bill. A document that indicates the amount the customer should pay to the carrier for delivered goods. May be either a separate document or a copy of the bill of lading.

Front-End Processor (FEP). A dedicated communications computer that is connected to a host CPU. It handles the communications tasks so that the CPU can spend its time processing data.

Front-End (or Upper) CASE. CASE tools that support the early stages of the SDLC, such as analysis and design.

Full-Duplex Channel. A data transmission channel that allows data transmissions in both directions at the same time. *Contrast with* Half-duplex channel and Simplex channel.

Gantt Chart. A bar graph used for project planning and control. Project activities are shown on the left, and units of time are shown across the top. The time period over which each activity is expected to be performed is represented with a horizontal bar on the graph.

Gateway. A communications interface device that allows a local area network to be connected to external networks and to communicate with external mainframes and data bases.

General Authorization. The empowerment of regular employees to handle routine transactions without special approval.

General Controls. Controls that relate to all or many computerized accounting activities, such as those relating to the plan of organization of data processing activities and the separation of incompatible functions. *Contrast with* Application controls.

General Journal. A record of infrequent or nonroutine transactions, such as loan payments and end-of-period adjusting and closing entries.

General Journal Listing. A report showing the details (account number, source reference code, description, and amount debited or credited) of each entry posted to the general ledger.

Generalized Audit Software (GAS). A software package that performs audit tests on the data files of a company.

General Ledger. A record of summary-level data for every asset, liability, equity, revenue, and expense account of the organization.

General Ledger and Reporting Cycle. The information processing operations involved in updating the general ledger and preparing reports that summarize the results of the organization's activities.

Gigabyte. One billion characters of data.

Goal Conflict. Conflict that occurs when decision or action of one subgoal or subsystem is inconsistent with another subgoal or subsystem.

Goal Congruence. The ability of employees to achieve their assigned subgoals while contributing to the achievement of their organization's overall goal.

Gopher. A means of quickly moving from one place on the Internet to another.

Grandfather-Father-Son. A method for maintaining backup copies of files on magnetic tape or disk. The three most current copies of the data are retained, with the son being the most recent.

Graphical User Interface (GUI). Operating environment where the user selects commands, starts programs, or lists files by pointing to pictorial representations (icons) with a mouse. A Macintosh computer, Microsoft's Windows, and IBM's OS/2 are all GUI environments.

Group Decision Support Software (GDSS). Software that encourages and allows everyone in a group to participate in decision making. A GDSS brings a group of people together to share information, exchange ideas, explore differing points of views, examine proposed solutions, arrive at a consensus, or vote on a course of action.

Groupware. Software that combines the power of computer networks with the immediacy and personal touch of the face-to-face brainstorming session. Groupware lets users hold computer conferences, decide when to hold a meeting, make a calendar for a department, collectively brainstorm on creative endeavors, manage projects, and design products.

Hacking. Unauthorized access and use of computer systems, usually by means of a personal computer and telecommunications networks.

Half-Duplex Channel. A data transmission channel that allows two-direction transmissions, but only one direction at a time. *Contrast with* Full-duplex channel and Simplex channel.

Hard Disk. A magnetic storage disk made of rigid material and enclosed in a sealed disk unit to cut down on the chances of the magnetic medium's being damaged by foreign particles. A hard disk has a much faster access time and greater storage capacity than a floppy disk.

Hardware. Physical equipment, or machinery, that is used in a computer system.

Hash Total. A total generated from values for a field that would not usually be totaled, such as customer account numbers. It is usually generated manually from source documents prior to input and compared with machine-generated totals at each subsequent processing step. Any discrepancy may indicate a loss of records or errors in data transcription or processing.

Header Label. Type of internal label that appears at the beginning of each file and contains the file name, expiration date, and other file identification information.

Help Desk. An in-house group of analysts and technicians who answer employees' questions with the purpose of encouraging, supporting, coordinating, and controlling end-user activity.

Hierarchical Network. A variation of the star network. The configuration looks like a hierarchical organization chart.

Hierarchical Program Design. The process of designing a program from the top level down to the detailed level.

History File. A file that contains records of account balances and of past transactions that have already been processed to update appropriate master files. These records are retained for reference purposes.

Home Page. A "store front" or site on the Internet that is set up by individuals and firms to provide useful and interesting information about the individual or firm.

Hot Site. Completely operational data processing facility that is configured to meet the user's requirement and can be made available to a disaster-stricken organization on short notice.

Human Resource Management (HRM)/Payroll Cycle. The recurring set of business activities and related data processing operations associated with effectively managing the employee work force.

Hybrid Network. A combination of both star and ring network configurations.

Icons. Pictures on the screen that represent functions.

Image Processing. Scanning and photographic techniques that capture the exact image of a document. The scanning device converts the text and pictures into a digitized electronic code that can be displayed on a computer monitor and stored on laser optical disks.

Impact Printers. Printers that strike an embossed character against an inked ribbon. Dot matrix printers are the most popular impact printer.

Impersonation. *See* Masquerading.

Implementation. The process of installing a computer. It includes selecting and installing the equipment, training personnel, establishing operating policies, and getting the software onto the system and functioning properly.

Implementation and Conversion. The capstone phase in the SDLC when all elements and activities of the system come together. Implementation includes installing and testing new hardware and software, hiring and training employees, and testing new processing procedures. Standards and controls must be established and documented. The final step, conversion, consists of dismantling the old system and converting it into the new one.

Implementation Plan. A written plan that outlines how the new system will be implemented. The plan includes a timetable for completion, who is responsible for each activity, cost estimates, and task milestones.

Imprest Fund. A cash account with two characteristics: (1) it is set at a fixed amount, such as $100, and (2) it requires vouchers for every disbursement. At all times, the sum of cash plus vouchers should equal the preset fund balance.

Index File. A master file of record identifiers and corresponding storage locations.

Index Sequential Access Method (ISAM). A file organization and access approach in which records are stored in sequential order by their primary key on a direct access storage device. An index file is created, which allows the file to be accessed and updated randomly.

Inference Engine. A component of an expert system that is a program containing the logic and reasoning mechanisms that simulate the expert logic process and deliver advice.

Information. Data that have been processed and organized into output that is meaningful to the person who receives it. Information can be mandatory, essential, or discretionary.

Information Overload. The state in which additional information cannot be used efficiently and has no marginal value.

Information System. An organized way of collecting, processing, managing, and reporting information so that an organization can achieve its objectives and goals. Formal information systems have an explicit responsibility to produce information. In contrast, informal information systems arise out of a need that is not satisfied by a formal channel. They operate without a formal assignment of responsibility.

Information Systems (IS) Audit. A review of the general and application controls of an AIS to assess its compliance with internal control policies and procedures and its effectiveness in safeguarding assets.

Inherent Risk. The susceptibility of a set of accounts or transactions to significant control problems in the absence of internal control.

Initial Investigation. A preliminary investigation to determine whether a proposed system is both needed and possible.

Input. Data entered into the computer system either from an external storage device or from the keyboard of the computer.

Input Controls. A means to ensure that only accurate, valid, and authorized data are entered into the system.

Input Controls Matrix. A matrix that shows the control procedures applied to each field of an input record.

Input Device. Hardware used to enter data into the computer system.

Input/Output Bound. Ability of a system to process data faster than it can receive input and send output. Consequently the processor has to wait on the I/O devices.

Input Validation Routines. Computer programs or routines designed to check the validity or accuracy of input data.

Inquiry Processing. Processing user information queries by searching master files for the desired information and then organizing the information into an appropriate response.

Insert Anomaly. A problem that can arise in a poorly designed relational data base, when attributes that are not characteristics of the primary key of a relation are stored in that table. The problem is that new information about those attributes cannot be entered in the data base without violating the integrity rules. For example, assume that information about vendors is only stored as part of the purchases table. Data about potential new vendors, or about alternative suppliers, could not be added until a purchase from them was made. Otherwise, the purchase order number column, the primary key of the purchases table, would have a null value, violating the entity integrity rule.

Integrated CASE. A software package that combines upper and lower CASE tools, linked by the data repository.

Integrated Services Digital Network (ISDN). An extensive digital network with built-in intelligence to permit all types of data (voice, data, images, facsimile, video, etc.) to be sent over the same line.

Integrated Test Facility. A testing technique in which a dummy company or division is introduced into the company's computer system. Test transactions may then be conducted on these fictitious master records without affecting the real master records. These test transactions may be processed along with the real transactions, and the employees of the computer facility need not be aware that testing is being done.

Integration. The combining of subsystems.

Interface. The common boundary between two pieces of hardware or between two computer systems. It is the point at which the two systems communicate with each other.

Internal Control. A control within a business organization that ensures information is processed correctly.

Internal Control Flowchart. A type of flowchart that shows the internal control structure of a company. Often used by auditors in the planning stage of an audit.

Internal Control Structure. The plan of organization and all the coordinate methods and measures adopted within a business to safeguard its assets, check the accuracy and reliability of its accounting data, promote operational efficiency, and encourage adherence to prescribed managerial policies.

Internal Labels. Labels written in machine-readable form on a magnetic storage medium (e.g., tape, disk) that identifies the data contained on the storage medium. Internal labels include volume, header, and trailer labels.

Internal Level Schema. A low-level view of the entire data base, describing how the data are actually stored and accessed, including information about pointers, indexes, record lengths, and so forth. *Contrast with* External and Conceptual level schemas.

Internal Rate of Return (IRR). The effective interest rate that equates the present value of the total costs to the present value of the total savings.

Internet. An international network of independently owned computers that operate as a giant, seamless computing network. No one owns it and no single organization controls its use. Data are not centrally stored but are stored on computers called Web servers.

Interpreter. A program that, one statement at a time, translates the source language into machine code and then executes it. *Contrast with* Compiler.

Inventory Control. The function of determining what, when, and how much inventory to purchase.

Job-Order Costing. A cost system that assigns costs to specific production batches, or jobs; it is used whenever the product or service being sold can be distinctly identified.

Job Time Ticket. A document used to collect data about labor activity, recording the amount of time a worker spent on each specific job task.

Journal Voucher. A form used to summarize a group of transactions. For example, a group of documents would be gathered and their total entered on the journal voucher.

Joystick. An input device consisting of a stick that can be tilted in any direction to position the cursor on a graphics screen. A joystick is usually used in conjunction with a computer game.

Just-in-Time (JIT) Inventory System. A system that minimizes or virtually eliminates manufacturing inventories by scheduling inventory deliveries at the precise times and locations needed. Instead of making infrequent bulk deliveries to a central receiving and storage facility, suppliers deliver materials in small lots at frequent intervals to the specific locations that require them.

Key. A unique identification code assigned to each data record within a system.

Key-to-Disk Encoder. A device that links several keying stations to a minicomputer that has an attached disk memory. Data may be entered simultaneously from each keying station and pooled on the disk file.

Key-to-Tape Encoder. A device for keying in and recording data on magnetic tape.

Key Verification. A means of checking the accuracy of data entry by having two people enter the same data using a key-operated device. The computer then compares the two sets of keystrokes to determine whether the data were entered correctly.

Kickbacks. Gifts given by vendors to purchasing agents for the purpose of influencing their choice of suppliers.

Kilobyte (K). 1024 bytes of memory capacity. K is usually expressed in terms of 1000 characters of memory; that is, 64K represents approximately 64,000 characters of memory.

Kiting. A fraud scheme in which the perpetrator covers up a theft of cash by creating cash through the transfer of money between banks.

Knowledge Acquisition Facility. A component of an expert system. It is used to enter knowledge and expertise into the knowledge base.

Knowledge Base. A component of an expert system that includes data, knowledge, relationships, rules of thumb (heuristics), and decision rules used by experts to solve a particular type of problem.

Knowledge Engineering. The process of building a knowledge base. It involves both a human expert and a knowledge engineer.

LAN Interface. The hardware device that interfaces between the local area network (LAN) cable and the hardware devices (computers, printers, etc.) connected to the LAN.

Lapping. Concealment of a cash shortage by means of a series of delays in posting collections to accounts.

Legal Feasibility. The dimension of feasibility that determines whether there will be any conflicts between the system under consideration and the organization's ability to discharge its legal obligations.

Light Pens. Pencil-shaped devices that use photoelectric circuitry to enter data through the video display terminal of the computer system. Their principal use is in graphics applications.

Limit Check. An edit check to ensure that a numerical amount in a record does not exceed some predetermined limit.

Line Count. Total number of lines entered during a data processing session.

Line-Sharing Device. A device that combines the data from several terminals or computers and sends the data over a single line to the host computer.

Local Area Network (LAN). A network that links microcomputers, disk drives, word processors, printers, and other equipment within a limited geographical area, such as one building.

Lockbox. A postal address to which customers send their remittances. This post office box is maintained by the participating bank, which picks up the checks several times each day and deposits them to the company's account. The bank then sends the remittance advices, an electronic list of all remittances, and photocopies of all checks to the company.

Logical Access. The ability to use computer equipment to access company data.

Logical Design. The third stage in the data base design process. It entails completing the external level schemas and translating the data requirements of different users and application programs into the conceptual level schema.

Logical Models. Descriptions of a system that focus on the essential activities and flow of information in the system, irrespective of how the flow is actually accomplished.

Logical View. The manner in which users conceptually organize, view, and understand the relationships among data items. *Contrast with* Physical view.

Logic Errors. Errors that occur when the instructions given to the computer do not accomplish the desired objective. *Contrast with* Syntax errors.

Logic Time Bomb. A program that lies idle until some specified circumstance or a particular time triggers it. Once triggered, the bomb sabotages the system by destroying programs or data.

Machine-Independent Languages. A programming language that can be used on many types of computer platforms. The language is not dependent upon the type of computer being used.

Machine Language. Binary code that can be interpreted by the internal circuitry of the computer.

Macro. (1) A series of keystrokes or commands that can be given a name, stored, and activated each time the keystrokes must be repeated. (2) A programming command.

Magnetic Disks. Magnetic storage media consisting of one or more flat round disks with a magnetic surface on which data can be written.

Magnetic Ink Character Recognition (MICR). The recognition of characters printed by a machine that uses a special magnetic ink.

Magnetic Stripe. The area on debit, credit, and ID cards that contains information such as name, address, and account number.

Magnetic Tape. A secondary storage medium that is about ½ inch in width and that has a magnetic surface on which data can be stored. The most popular types are seven- and nine-track tapes.

Mainframe Computers. (1) Same as CPU. (2) Large-size digital computers, typically with a separate stand-alone CPU. They are larger than minicomputers.

Main Memory. The internal memory directly controlled by the CPU, which usually consists of the ROM and RAM of the computer.

Management Audit. A review of how well management is utilizing company resources and how well company operations and programs follow established objectives and are being carried out as planned.

Management by Exception. A method for interpreting variances displayed on performance reports. If the performance report shows actual performance to be at or near budgeted figures, a manager can assume that the item is under control and that no action needs to be taken. On the other hand, significant deviations from budgeted amounts, in *either* direction, signal the need to investigate the cause of the discrepancy and take corrective action.

Management Control. Activities by management designed to motivate, encourage, and assist officers and employees to achieve corporate goals and objectives as effectively and efficiently as possible and observe corporate policies.

Management Information System. The set of human and capital resources within an organization that is responsible for collecting and processing data so that all levels of management have the information they need to plan and control the activities of the organization.

Manual Information System. Information system in which most of the data processing load is completed by people without the use of computers.

Manufacturing Overhead. All manufacturing costs that are not economically feasible to trace directly to specific jobs, or processes.

Manufacturing Resource Planning (MRP-II). A comprehensive, computerized planning and control system for manufacturing operations. It is an enhancement of materials requirements planning that incorporates capacity planning for factory work centers and scheduling of production operations.

Mapping Programs. Programs that are activated during regular processing and provide information as to which portions of the application program were not executed.

Masquerading. A perpetrator's gaining access to a system by pretending to be an authorized user. This approach requires that the perpetrator know the legitimate user's identification numbers and passwords.

Massively Parallel Processing (MPP). The simultaneous performance of multiple processing tasks. MPP is made possible by linking multiple microprocessors.

Master File. A permanent file of records that reflects the current status of relevant business items such as inventory and accounts receivable. The master file is updated with the latest transactions from the current transaction file.

Master Plan. A document specifying the overall information system plan of an organization.

Master Production Schedule (MPS). A plan that specifies how much of each product is to be produced during the planning period, and when that production should occur.

Materiality. The concept that an auditor should focus on detecting and reporting only those errors, deficiencies, and omissions that could possibly have a significant impact on decisions.

Materials Requirements Planning (MRP). An approach to controlling and minimizing the inventory of raw materials. The production planning department prepares a schedule of the quantities of each product to be manufactured during a given time period and then purchases raw materials, parts, and supplies when they are needed.

Materials Requirements Planning (MRP-II). An approach to inventory management that seeks to reduce required inventory levels by *scheduling* production to meet sales forecast demands, rather than *estimating* needs.

Materials Requisition. An authorization to move the necessary quantity of raw materials from the storeroom to the factory location in which production operations are to begin.

Megabyte (M). One million characters of data.

Megahertz (MHz). One million computer cycles per second.

Memory Unit. The part of the CPU where data and instructions are stored internally.

Menu. A list of computer commands or options that is displayed by a program. The user chooses the option that will cause the desired action to take place.

Message. (1) The data transmitted over a data communication system. (2) The instructions that are given to an object in object-oriented languages.

Microcomputers. Small computer systems anywhere from a "computer on a chip" to a system that covers a desktop. Often called a personal or desktop computer, this type of computer usually sells for less than $5000.

Microprocessor. A large-scale or very large scale integrated circuit on a silicon chip. Some of the more common microprocessors in use are the 8088, 8086, 80286, 80386, 80486, Pentium (80586), Z80, 68000, and 8080.

Microsecond. One millionth of a second.

Millisecond. One thousandth of a second.

Minicomputers. Digital computers that usually are larger than microcomputers but smaller than mainframe computers. They have a higher performance, a more powerful instruction set, higher prices, more input/output capability, a greater variety of programming languages, and a more powerful operating system than a microcomputer does. However, they have fewer of these features than a mainframe computer does.

MIPS. Millions of instructions per second; a way of measuring CPU speed.

Modem. Modulator/demodulator, a communications device that converts the computer's digital signals into analog signals that can be sent over phone lines. The modem can be internal (mounted on a board within the computer) or external (a freestanding unit).

Modified Canned Software. Canned software that has been modified to meet the particular needs of the user.

Modular Conversion. An approach for converting from an old to a new system in which parts of the old system are gradually replaced by the new until the old system has been entirely replaced by the new.

Monitor. (1) A video display unit or CRT. (2) Software that controls how a system operates.

Monthly Statement. A document summarizing all transactions that occurred during the past month and informing customers of their current account balance.

Mosaic. A GUI program that uses menus to help users navigate the Internet by pointing and clicking a mouse on a highlighted piece of text, causing a jump from one Web server to another.

Motherboard. The main circuit board of a microcomputer. It usually contains the memory, the CPU, and the input/output circuitry.

Mouse. A small device that is connected to a computer, usually by a cord. When the user moves the mouse, the movement is translated into a movement of the screen's cursor; the user issues a command by pressing a button on the mouse when the cursor is positioned on the desired command.

Move Tickets. Documents that identify the internal transfer of parts, the location to which they are transferred, and the time of the transfer.

MS/DOS. An acronym for MicroSoft/Disk Operating System, the operating system used by IBM and many IBM-compatible microcomputers.

Multidrop Lines. Communications channel configurations in which most terminals are linked together, with only one or a few terminals linked directly to the CPU.

Multimedia. Computer-based applications that combine text, three-dimensional graphics, full-screen video, sound, and animation.

Multiplexor. A communications device that combines signals from several sources and sends them out over a single line. Multiplexors can also split the signals back into the individual messages.

Multiprocessing. The simultaneous execution of two or more tasks, usually by two or more processing units that are part of the same system.

Multitasking. The simultaneous processing of several jobs on a computer. Multitasking is possible in the Windows 95 environment.

Mutual Authentication Scheme. A routing verification procedure that requires two computers to exchange their passwords before communication takes place.

Nanosecond. One billionth of a second.

Narrative Description. Written, step-by-step explanation of the system components and how these components interact.

Narrowband Lines. Phone lines designed to accept data transmissions of up to 300 bits per second. This type of line is not suitable for transmitting audible or voice-like signals.

Natural Languages. Fourth-generation languages that closely resemble English.

Net Present Value (NPV). A value determined by discounting all estimated future cash flows back to the present, using a discount rate that reflects the time value of money to the organization.

Netscape. A GUI program that uses menus to help users navigate the Internet by pointing and clicking a mouse on a highlighted piece of text causing a jump from one Web server to another.

Network. (1) A group of interconnected computers and terminals; a series of locations tied together by communications channels. (2) A data structure involving relationships among multiple record types.

Network Administrator. One who installs, manages, and supports a LAN. The network administrator also controls access to the system and maintains the shared software and data.

Network Switching. The routing of all data and messages through a central computer for forwarding to the correct location.

Neural Networks. Computing systems that imitate the brain's learning process by using a network of interconnected processors that perform multiple operations simultaneously and interact dynamically. Neural networks recognize and understand voice, face, and word patterns much more successfully than do regular computers and humans.

Nonimpact Printers. Printers that transfer images without striking the paper. The most common are laser printers.

Nonoperational (or **Throwaway**) **Prototypes.** Part of a design technique whereby the prototypes are discarded but the system requirements identified from the prototypes are used to develop a new system.

Nonvoucher System. A method for processing accounts payable in which each approved invoice is posted to individual vendor records in the accounts payable file and then stored in an open invoice file. *Contrast with* Voucher system.

Normalization. The process of following the guidelines for properly designing a relational data base that is free from delete, insert, and update anomalies.

Object. An element of data and a set of instructions that specify the actions that are to be performed on the data; used in object-oriented languages.

Object-Oriented Data Model. A data model in which the basic conceptual building blocks are objects, rather than tables. An object is a reusable segment of program code that not only describes a data element but also contains instructions on how to manipulate that data. For example, the sales invoice object would not only store information about a particular sales transaction, but would also include instructions on how to (1) calculate extensions for each line item, (2) add sales tax to arrive at the total, and (3) update the appropriate customer account.

Object-Oriented Languages (OOL). A programming language that allows users to select objects instead of writing procedural code. Each object can then be modified, reused, or copied. The objects are then sent messages telling them what to do.

Object Program. A compiled or assembled machine-level program that can be executed by the computer. The source program and the translator are inputs to the computer translation process, and the output is the machine-executable object program.

Off-line Devices. Devices that are not connected to or controlled by the main CPU. Off-line devices are usually used to prepare data for entry into the computer system (e.g., key-to-tape encoder, keypunch/verification equipment). *Contrast with* On-line devices.

On-line Batch Processing. Electronic capture and storage of data so that it can be processed later.

On-line Devices. Hardware devices that are connected directly to the CPU by cable or telephone line (e.g., CRT terminal, disk drive).

On-line Processing. The processing of individual transactions as they occur and from their point of origin rather than by accumulating them for batch processing. On-line processing requires the use of on-line data entry terminals and direct-access file storage media so that each master record can be accessed directly.

On-line, Real-Time Processing. A processing method whereby the computer system processes data immediately after it is captured and provides updated information to the user on a timely basis. On-line real-time processing usually entails one of two forms of processing: on-line updating and inquiry processing.

Open-Invoice Method. Method for maintaining accounts receivable in which customers typically pay according to each invoice. Usually, two copies of the invoice are mailed to the customer, who is requested to return one copy along with the payment.

Operating Budget. A report that projects an organization's revenues and expenses for a given time period, usually a month or a year. Typically, operating budgets are structured along the lines of financial statements.

Operating Documentation. All information required by a computer operator to run a program, including the equipment configuration used, variable data to be entered on the computer console, and descriptions of conditions leading to program halts and related corrective actions.

Operating Environment. A software program that runs on top of the operating system to provide the system with desirable enhancements. For example, Microsoft's Windows is an operating environment that runs on top of DOS.

Operating System. A software program that controls the overall operation of a computer system. Its functions include controlling the execution of computer programs, scheduling, debugging, assigning storage areas, managing data, and controlling input and output.

Operational Audit. *See* Management Audit.

Operational Document. A document that is generated as an output of transaction processing activities. Examples include purchase orders, customer statements, and employee paychecks. *Contrast with* Source document.

Operational Feasibility. The dimension of feasibility concerned with whether a proposed system will be used by the people in an organization. It also is concerned with how useful the system will be within the operating environment of the organization.

Operational Prototypes. Prototypes that are further developed into fully functional systems.

Operations and Maintenance Phase. The last phase of the system development life cycle where follow-up studies are conducted to detect and correct design deficiencies. Minor modifications will be made as problems arise in the new system.

Operations List. A document that specifies the labor and machine requirements needed to manufacture the product. Also referred to as a routing sheet because it indicates how a product moves through the factory, specifying what is done at each step and how much time each operation should take.

Optical Character Recognition (OCR). The use of light-sensitive hardware devices to convert characters readable by humans into computer input. Since OCR readers can read only certain items, a special machine-readable font must be used.

Optical Disk. A mass storage medium that is capable of storing billions of bits. Lasers are used to write to and read from an optical disk.

Ordering Costs. All expenses associated with processing purchase transactions.

Output. The information produced by a system. Output is typically produced for the use of a particular individual or group of users.

Output Controls. Methods designed to ensure that system output is properly controlled.

Outsourcing. The hiring of an outside company to handle all or part of the data processing activities.

Packing Slip. A document identifying the contents of a shipment.

Parallel Conversion. A systems conversion approach in which the new and old systems are run simultaneously until the organization is assured that the new system is functioning correctly.

Parallel Interface. A way of connecting peripherals (like a printer) to a computer. Data are transferred simultaneously along several parallel cables at the same time.

Parallel Port. A communications interface that allows data to be transmitted a whole character (eight bits) at a time. *Contrast with* Serial port.

Parallel Processing. The processing of two or more tasks simultaneously.

Parallel Simulation. An approach auditors use to detect unauthorized program changes and verify data processing accuracy. The auditor writes his or her own version of a program and then reprocesses data. The outputs of the auditor's program and the client's program are compared to verify that they are the same.

Parallel Transmission. The transmission of data in groups of two or more bits. *Contrast with* Serial transmission.

Parity Bit. An extra bit added to a byte, character, or word. The parity bit is magnetized as needed to ensure that there is always an odd (or even) number of magnetized bits. The computer uses the odd (or even) parity scheme to check the accuracy of each item of data.

Parity Checking. A process whereby a computer reads or receives a set of characters and simultaneously sums the number of 1 bits in each character to verify that it is an even number. If not, the corresponding character must contain an error.

Password. A series of letters, numbers, or both that must be entered in order to access and use system resources. Password use helps prevent unauthorized tampering with hardware, software, and the organization's data.

Payback Period. The number of years required for the net savings to equal the initial cost of the investment.

Payroll Clearing Account. A general ledger account used to check the accuracy and completeness of recording payroll costs and their subsequent allocation to appropriate cost centers.

Payroll Register. A listing of payroll data for each employee for the current payroll period.

Payroll Service Bureau. An organization that maintains the payroll master file for each of its clients and performs their payroll processing activities for a fee.

Performance Report. A record of the budgeted and actual amounts of revenues and expenses and of the variances, or differences, between these two amounts. Used for financial control. *Contrast with* Budget.

Peripherals. The hardware devices (such as those used for input, output, processing, and data communications) that are connected to the CPU.

Personal Computer (PC). *See* Microcomputers.

Personal Digital Assistant (PDA). A new type of handheld computer that is expected to have a significant impact on personal productivity.

Personal Identification Number (PIN). A confidential code, known only to an individual and a financial institution, that allows the individual to conduct banking transactions at automated teller machines.

Personal Information Manager. Software that helps end users organize their daily activities. Components include a calendar, a calculator, an electronic notepad, an electronic name and address system, E-mail, and a to-do list.

PERT (program evaluation and review technique). A commonly used technique for planning, coordinating, controlling, and scheduling complex projects such as systems implementation.

Phase-In Conversion. *See* Modular conversion.

Physical Access. The ability to physically use computer equipment.

Physical Design. (1) A phase of the system development life cycle when broad, user-oriented requirements of the conceptual design are implemented by creating a detailed set of specifications for coding and testing the computer programs. (2) The fourth stage of the data base design process, consisting of taking the conceptual design and converting it into physical storage structures.

Physical Models. The description of physical aspects of a data base (e.g., field and file sizes, storage and access methods, security procedures).

Physical Systems Design. The phase of the systems development life cycle when the designer specifies the hardware, software, and procedures for delivering the conceptual systems design.

Physical Systems Design Report. A description of the system that is prepared at the end of the physical design phase. Management uses this report to decide whether to proceed to the implementation phase.

Physical View. The way data are physically arranged and stored on disks, tapes, and other storage media. EDP personnel use this view to make efficient use of storage and processing resources. *Contrast with* Logical view.

Picking Ticket. A document authorizing the release of merchandise to the shipping department. The picking ticket often lists item numbers and quantities in the sequence in which they can be most efficiently retrieved from the warehouse.

Picosecond. One trillionth of a second.

Piggybacking. A perpetrator's latching onto a legitimate user who is logging into a system. The legitimate user unknowingly carries the perpetrator with him as he is allowed into the system.

Pilot Conversion. The implementation of a system in just one part of the organization such as a branch. This approach localizes conversion problems and allows training in a live environment. Disadvantages are the long conversion times and the need to interface the old and the new systems.

Pixel. The smallest particle of information that appears on a monitor's screen. The greater the number of pixels displayed, the better the monitor's resolution.

Plotter. A hard-copy output device that produces drawings and other graphical output by moving an ink pen across a page.

Plug and Play. A feature, found in newer operating systems, that identifies and configures the OS and the hardware so that the PC, peripherals, and software work together with minimal effort on the user's part.

Point-of-Sale (POS) Recorders. Electronic devices that function as both a terminal and a cash register. They are used commonly in retail stores to record sales information at the time of the sale and to perform other data processing functions.

Point Scoring. An objective procedure in which weighted selection criteria are used to evaluate the overall merits of vendor proposals.

Point-to-Point Lines. Communications channel configurations that use a separate line between each terminal and the central computer.

Postbilling System. A system in which invoices are prepared *after* confirmation that the items were shipped. *Contrast with* Prebilling system.

Postimplementation Review. A review made after a new system has been operating for a brief period. The purpose of this review is to ensure that the new system is meeting its planned objectives, identify the adequacy of system standards, and review system controls.

Postimplementation Review Report. A report that analyzes a newly delivered system to determine whether the system achieved its intended purpose and was completed within budget.

Prebilling System. A system in which an invoice is prepared (but not sent) as soon as an order is approved (i.e., after credit has been approved and inventory availability checked). *Contrast with* Postbilling system.

Preformatting. An on-line data entry control in which the computer displays a form on the screen and the user fills in the blanks in the form as needed.

Preventive Controls. A control system that places restrictions on and requires documentation of employee activities so as to reduce the occurrence of errors and deviations. Because preventive controls operate from within the process being controlled, they are perhaps the type of control most consistent with the original meaning of the term *internal control.*

Preventive Maintenance. A program of regularly examining the hardware components of a computer and replacing any that are found to be weak.

Primary Key. A unique identification code assigned to each record within a system. The primary key is the key used most frequently to distinguish, order, and reference records.

Primary Memory. *See* Memory unit.

Printer. An output device that produces a hard copy of computer output.

Private Branch Exchange (PBX). A special-purpose computer that manages a company's telephone network.

Process Costing. A cost system that assigns costs to each process, or work center, in the production cycle and then calculates the average cost for all units produced. Process costing is used whenever masses of similar goods or services are sold.

Processes. A set of actions, automated or manual, that transforms data into other data or information.

Processing Controls. A means to ensure that all transactions are processed accurately and completely and that all files and records are properly updated.

Processing of Test Transactions. The processing of hypothetical transactions through a new system to test for processing errors.

Production Cycle. The recurring set of business activities and related data processing operations associated with the manufacture of products.

Production Order. A document authorizing the manufacture of a specified quantity of a particular product. It lists the operations that need to be performed, the quantity to be produced, and the location to which the finished product is to be delivered.

Productive Capacity. The maximum number of units that can be produced using current technology.

Productive Processing Time. The percentage of total production time that was actually used to manufacture the product.

Profitability Analyses. Reports used to assess overall marketing performance by breaking down the marginal profit contribution made by each territory, customer, distribution channel, salesperson, product, or other basis. *Contrast with* Sales analyses.

Program. A set of instructions that can be executed by a computer.

Program Flowchart. A diagrammatical representation of the logic and sequence of processes used in a computer program.

Program Generators. Computer programs designed to speed up the process of writing programs. The user specifies certain information, such as what the screen layouts should look like and what processing procedures need to be performed, and the program generates program instructions.

Program Maintenance. The revision of a computer program in order to meet new program instructions, satisfy system demands such as the need for a new report, correct an error, or make changes in file content.

Programming Language. The language a programmer uses to write a computer program (e.g., COBOL, BASIC, PASCAL, LOGO).

Program Tracing. A technique used to obtain detailed knowledge of the logic of an application program, as well as to test the program's compliance with its control specifications.

Project Development Plan. A proposal to develop a particular computer system application. It contains an analysis of the requirements and expectations of the proposed application.

Projection. A way of resisting change by blaming anything and everything on the new system. The system becomes the scapegoat for all real and imagined problems and errors.

Project Management Software. A software program that is used to plan, schedule, track, control, and evaluate projects to ensure they are completed within budget and on time.

Project Milestones. Significant points in a development effort at which a formal review of progress is made.

Prompting. An on-line data entry control that uses the computer to control the data entry process. The system displays a request to the user for each required item of input data and then waits for an acceptable response before requesting the next required item.

Proposal to Conduct Systems Analysis. A document calling for the analysis of either an existing or a proposed system. This document is prepared by a user or department, requesting the information systems function to analyze the feasibility of developing a system to perform a specific function.

Protocol. The set of rules governing the exchange of data between two systems or components of a system.

Prototype. A simplified working model of an information system used in prototyping.

Prototyping. An approach to systems design in which a

simplified working model, or prototype, of an information system is developed. The users experiment with the prototype to determine what they like and don't like about the system. The developers make modifications until the users are satisfied with the system.

Public Data Bases. Electronic libraries containing millions of items of data that can be reviewed, retrieved, analyzed, and saved by the general public.

Purchase Order. A document that formally requests a vendor to sell and deliver specified products at designated prices. It is also a promise to pay and becomes a contract once it is accepted by the vendor.

Purchase Requisition. A document that identifies the requisitioner; specifies the delivery location and date needed; identifies the item numbers, descriptions, quantity, and price of each item requested; and may suggest a vendor.

Query. A request for specific information from a computer. Queries are often used with a data base management system to extract data from the data base.

Query-By-Example (QBE) Languages. Graphical query languages for retrieving information from a relational data base.

Query Languages. Languages used to process data files and to obtain quick responses to questions about those files.

Radio Frequency Data Communication. The transmission of data through air waves rather than through wires.

Radio Frequency Identification. Tags that are used to track data from one location to another by sending and receiving radio signals.

Random-Access Memory (RAM). A temporary storage location for computer instructions and data. RAM may have data both written to it and read from it.

Random Surveillance. A way of detecting fraud by having auditors periodically audit the system and test system controls. Informing employees that the auditors will conduct random surveillance is a deterrent to computer crime.

Range Check. An edit check designed to verify that a data item falls within a certain predetermined range of acceptable values.

REA Data Model. A data model developed explicitly for use in designing AIS data bases. REA is an acronym signifying that the data model contains information about three fundamental types of objects: resources, events, and agents. Resources represent identifiable objects that have economic value to the organization. Events represent all of an organization's business activities. Agents represent the people or organizations about which data are collected.

Read-Only Memory (ROM). Internal CPU memory that can be read but usually may not be changed.

Real-Time Notification. A variation of the embedded audit module in which the auditor is notified of each transaction as it occurs by means of a message printed on the auditor's terminal.

Real-Time System. A system that is able to respond to an inquiry or provide data fast enough to make the information meaningful to the user. Real-time systems are usually designed for very fast response.

Reasonable Assurance. The concept that an auditor cannot seek complete assurance that an item is correct, since to do so would be prohibitively expensive. Instead, the auditor accepts a reasonable degree of risk that the audit conclusion is incorrect.

Reasonableness Test. An edit check of the logical correctness of relationships among the values of data items on an input record and the corresponding file record. For example, a journal entry that debits inventory and credits wages payable is not reasonable.

Receiving Report. A document that records details about each delivery, including the date received, shipper, vendor, and purchase order number.

Record. A set of logically related data items that describe specific attributes of an entity, such as all payroll data relating to a single employee.

Record Count. A total of the number of input documents to a process or the number of records processed in a run.

Record Layout. A document that illustrates the arrangement of items of data in input, output, and file records.

Recovery Procedures. A set of procedures that is followed if the computer quits in the middle of processing a batch of data. The procedures allow the user to recover from hardware or software failures.

Redundant Data Check. An edit check that requires the inclusion of two identifiers in each input record (e.g., the customer's account number and the first five letters of the customer's name). If these input values do not match those on the record, the record will not be updated.

Reengineering. A thorough analysis and complete redesign of all business processes and information systems to achieve dramatic performance improvements. Reengineering seeks to reduce a company to its essential business processes.

Referential Integrity Rule. A constraint in relational data base design requiring that any nonnull value of a foreign key must correspond to a primary key in the referenced table. For example, if vendor number is a foreign key in the inventory table, to indicate the preferred source of that item, then any vendor number appearing in that table must appear as a primary key value in the vendor table. This constraint ensures consistency in the data base. Note, however, that the foreign key can be null if there is no existing relationship between the two tables. For example, a null value for vendor number in any row in the inventory table would indicate that there is no preferred vendor for that inventory item.

Relational Data Base. A data base model in which all data elements are logically viewed as being stored in the form of two-dimensional tables called relations. These tables are, in effect, flat files where each row represents a unique entity or record. Each column represents a field where the record's attributes are stored. The tables serve as the building blocks from which data relationships can be created.

Relations. The tables used to store data in a relational data base.

Remittance Advice. An enclosure included with a customer's payment that indicates the invoices, statements, or other items paid.

Remittance List. A document listing all checks received in the mail.

Remote Batch Processing. The accumulation of transaction records in batches at some remote location before their electronic transmission to a central location for processing.

Reorder Point. The level to which the inventory balance of an item must fall before an order to replenish stock is initiated.

Report File. A temporary file generated as an intermediate step in the preparation of a report.

Report Generators. Computer programs designed to make report writing easier and faster.

Reports. System output organized in a meaningful fashion. Used by employees to control operational activities, by managers to make decisions, and by investors and creditors. Prepared for both internal and external use.

Report Writers. Software that lets a user specify the data elements to be printed. The report writer searches the data base, extracts the desired items, and prints them out in the user-specified format.

Reprocessing. An approach auditors use to detect unauthorized program changes. The auditor verifies the integrity of an application program and then saves it for future use. At subsequent intervals, and on a surprise basis, the auditor uses the previously verified version of the program to reprocess data that have been processed by the version used by the company. The output of the two runs is compared, and discrepancies are investigated.

Request for a Proposal (RFP). A request by an organization or department for vendors to bid on hardware, software, or services specified by the organization or department.

Request for Systems Development. A written request for a new or improved system. The request describes the current system's problems, why the change is needed, and the proposed system's goals and objectives as well as its anticipated benefits and costs.

Requirements Costing. A system evaluation method in which a list is made of all required features of the desired system. If a proposed system does not have a desired feature, the cost of developing or purchasing that feature is added to the basic cost of the system. This method allows different systems to be evaluated based on the costs of providing the required features.

Requirements Definition. The second step in the data base design process. It entails defining the scope of a proposed data base system, determining general hardware and software requirements, and identifying user information needs.

Resolution. A term used to describe the density and overall quality of the video display on a terminal or monitor.

Response Time. The amount of time that elapses between making a query and receiving a response.

Responsibility Accounting. A system of reporting financial results on the basis of managerial responsibilities within an organization.

Revenue Cycle. The recurring set of business activities and related information processing operations associated with providing goods and services to customers and collecting cash in payment for those sales.

Ring Network. A configuration in which the data communications channels form a loop or circular pattern when the local processors are linked. *Contrast with* Star network.

Risk. The likelihood that a threat or hazard will actually come to pass.

Rollback. A process whereby a log of all preupdate values is prepared for each record that is updated within a particular interval. Then if there is a system failure, the records can be restored to the preupdate values and the processing started over.

Rounding-Down Technique. A fraud technique used against financial institutions that pay interest. The programmer instructs the computer to round down all interest calculations to two decimal places. The fraction of a cent that was rounded down on each calculation is put into the programmer's own account.

Router. A communications interface device that connects two LANs of the same type.

Routing Sheet. *See* Operations list.

Routing Verification Procedures. Controls to ensure that messages are not routed to the wrong system address. Examples are header labels, mutual authentication schemes, and dial-back.

Sabotage. An intentional act intended to destroy a system or some of its components.

Salami Technique. A fraud technique where tiny slices of money are stolen from many different accounts.

Sales Analyses. Reports used to assess the efficiency and effectiveness of sales by breaking down sales by salesperson, region, or product. *Contrast with* Profitability analyses.

Sales Invoice. A document notifying customers of the amount to be paid and where to send payment.

Sales Order. The document created during sales order entry, listing the item numbers, quantities, prices, and terms of the sale.

Satellite Transmission. A data transmission system that transmits data from earth stations to satellites and back to earth again.

Scanning Routines. Software routines that search a program for the occurrence of a particular variable name or other combinations of characters.

SCARF (System Control Audit Review File). A concurrent audit technique that embeds audit modules into application software to continuously monitor all transaction activity and collect data on transactions having special audit significance.

Scavenging. The unauthorized access to confidential information by searching corporate records. Scavenging methods range from searching trash cans for printouts or carbon copies of confidential information to scanning the contents of computer memory.

Scheduled Reports. Reports that are generated by a system at specified time intervals.

Scheduling Feasibility. The dimension of feasibility that determines whether the system being developed can be implemented in the time allotted.

Schema. A description of the types of data elements that are in the data base, the relationships among the data elements, and the structure or overall logical model used to organize and describe the data.

Secondary Key. A field that can be used to identify records in a file. Unlike the primary key, it does not provide a unique identification.

Secondary Storage. Storage media, such as magnetic disks or magnetic tape, on which data that are not currently needed by the computer can be stored. Also referred to as auxiliary storage.

Security Measures and Controls. Controls that are built into an information system to ensure that data are accurate and free from errors. Security measures also protect the data from unauthorized access.

Segregation of Duties. The separation of assigned duties and responsibilities in such a way that no single employee can both perpetrate and conceal errors or irregularities.

Semiconductor. A tiny silicon chip upon which a number of miniature circuits have been inscribed.

Sequence Check. An edit check that determines whether a batch of input data is in the proper numerical or alphabetical sequence.

Sequential Access. An access method that requires data items to be accessed in the same order in which they were written.

Sequential File Processing. The processing of a master file sequentially from beginning to end. The master and transaction files are processed in the same predetermined order, such as alphabetically.

Sequential Files. A way of storing numeric or alphabetical records according to a key. For example, customer numbers from 00001 to 99999. To access a sequential file record, the system starts at the beginning of the file and reads each record until the desired record is located.

Serial Interface. A way of connecting peripherals (like a printer) to a computer. Data are transferred along a single cable one bit at a time.

Serial Port. A communications interface that allows data to be sent only one bit at a time. *Contrast with* Parallel port.

Serial Transmission. The transmission of data one bit at a time. *Contrast with* Parallel transmission.
Server. High-capacity computer that contains the network software to handle the communications, storage, and resource sharing needs of other computers in the network. The server also contains the application software and data common to all users.
Sign Check. An edit check that verifies that the data in a field have the appropriate arithmetic sign.
Simplex Channel. A data transmission channel that allows data transmissions in only one direction. *Contrast with* Half-duplex channel and Full-duplex channel.
Smart Cards. Cards that can store up to three pages of text; contain a microprocessor, memory chips, and software. Used in Europe in the function of a credit or ATM card.
Snapshot Technique. An audit technique that records the content of both a transaction record and a related master file record before and after each processing step.
Software. A computer program that gives instructions to the CPU. Also used to refer to programming languages and computer systems documentation.
Software Agents. Computer programs that learn how to do often-performed, tedious, time-consuming, or complex tasks.
Software Piracy. The unauthorized copying of software.
Source Code or Program. A computer program written in a source language such as BASIC, COBOL, or assembly language. The source program is translated into the object (machine language) program by a translation program such as a compiler or assembler.
Source Data Automation (SDA). The collection of transaction data in machine-readable form at the time and place of origin. Examples of SDA devices are optical scanners and automated teller machines.
Source Document. A document containing the initial record of a transaction that takes place. Examples of source documents, which are usually recorded on preprinted forms, include sales invoices, purchase orders, and employee time cards. *Contrast with* Operational document.
Specialized Journals. Specialized journals are used to simplify the process of recording large numbers of repetitive transactions. Specialized journals are most commonly used for the following types of transactions: credit sales, cash receipts, purchases on account, and cash disbursements.
Special-Purpose Analyses. Reports that have no prespecified content or format and are not prepared according to any regular schedule; rather, they are generally prepared in response to a management request to investigate a specific problem or opportunity.
Specific Authorization. Special approval that permits an employee to handle a transaction.
Star Network. A configuration in which there is a centralized real-time computer system to which all other computer systems are linked. *Contrast with* Ring network.
Steering Committee. An executive-level committee to plan and oversee the IS function. The committee typically consists of management from the systems department, the controller, and other management affected by the information systems function.
Stockout Costs. The costs, such as lost sales or production delays, that result from inventory shortages.
Storage. Placement of data in internal memory or on a medium such as magnetic disk or magnetic tape, from which they can later be retrieved.
Stratified Sampling. A sampling approach in which a population is divided into two or more groups to which different selection criteria can be applied.
Structured Programming. A modular approach to programming in which each module performs a specific function, stands alone, and is coordinated by a control module. Also referred to as "GOTOless" programming because modular design makes GOTO statements unnecessary.
Structured Query Language (SQL). The standard text-based query language provided by most, but not all, relational DBMS systems. Powerful queries can be built using three basic keywords: SELECT, FROM, and WHERE.
Structured Walkthrough. A formal review process in program design in which one or more programmers walk through the logic and code of another programmer to detect weaknesses and errors in program design.
Stylus. A penlike device used to write directly on a computer screen.
Subschema. (1) A subset of the schema that includes only those data items used in a particular application program or by a particular user. (2) The way the user defines the data and the data relationships.
Subsidiary Ledger. A record of all the detailed data for any

general ledger account that has many individual subaccounts. Subsidiary ledgers are commonly used for accounts receivable, inventory, fixed assets, and accounts payable.

Subsystem. A smaller system that is a part of the entire information system. Each subsystem performs a specific function that is important to and that supports the system of which it is a part.

Supercomputers. Very large, high-speed computers used by businesses and organizations that have high-volume needs.

Superzapping. The use of a special system program to bypass regular system controls to perform unauthorized acts. A superzap utility was originally written to handle emergencies, such as restoring a system that has crashed.

Suspense File. A file containing records that have been identified as erroneous or are of uncertain status.

Switched Line. A regular dial-up telephone line. The charges for line usage are usually based on the amount of time used and the length of line used.

Symbolic Language. A language in which each machine instruction is represented by symbols that bear some relation to the instruction. For example, the symbol A might represent the Add command.

Synchronous Transmission. Data transmission in which start and stop bits are required only at the beginning and end of a block of characters. *Contrast with* Asynchronous transmission.

Syntax. The rules of grammar and structure that govern the use of a programming language.

Syntax Errors. Errors that result from using the programming language improperly or from incorrectly typing the source program. *Contrast with* Logic errors.

System. (1) An entity consisting of two or more components or subsystems that interact to achieve a goal. (2) The equipment and programs that make up a complete computer installation. (3) The programs and related procedures that perform a single task on a computer.

System Flowchart. A diagrammatical representation that shows the flow of data through a series of operations in an automated data processing system. It shows how data are captured and input into the system, the processes that operate on the data, and system outputs.

System Review. A step in internal control evaluation in which it is determined whether the necessary control procedures have been prescribed.

Systems Analysis. (1) A rigorous and systematic approach to decision making, characterized by a comprehensive definition of available alternatives and an exhaustive analysis of the merits of each alternative as a basis for choosing the best alternative. (2) Examination of the user information requirements within an organization in order to establish objectives and specifications for the design of an information system.

Systems Analysis Report. A comprehensive report prepared at the end of the systems analysis and design phase that summarizes and documents the findings of analysis activities.

Systems Analysts. The people within an organization who are responsible for developing the company's information system. The analyst's job generally involves designing computer applications and preparing specifications for computer programming.

Systems Approach. A way of handling systems change by recognizing that every system must have an objective, a set of components, and a set of interrelationships among the components. The systems approach proceeds step by step, with a thorough exploration of all implications and alternatives at each step.

Systems Concept. A systems analysis principle that states that alternative courses of action within a system must be evaluated from the standpoint of the system as a whole rather than that of any single subsystem or set of subsystems.

Systems Design. The process of preparing detailed specifications for the development of a new information system.

Systems Development Life Cycle. Six procedures and steps that a company goes through when it decides to design and implement a new system. The six steps are systems analysis, systems acquisition, conceptual design, physical design, implementation and conversion, and operation and maintenance.

Systems Documentation. A complete description of all aspects of each systems application, including narrative material, charts, and program listings.

Systems Implementation. The task of delivering a completed system to an organization for use in day-to-day operations.

Systems Software. Software that interfaces between the hardware and the application program. Systems software can be classified as operating systems, data base management systems, utility programs, language translators, and communications software.

Systems Survey. The systematic gathering of facts relating to the existing information system. This task is generally carried out by a systems analyst.
Systems Survey Report. The culmination of the systems survey. It contains documentation such as memos, interview and observation notes, questionnaire data, file and record layouts and descriptions, input and output descriptions, copies of documents, flowcharts, and data flow diagrams.
Table File. A file of reference data (generally numeric) that is retrieved during data processing to facilitate performing calculations or other processing tasks.
Tagging. An audit procedure in which certain records are marked with a special code before processing. During processing all data relating to the marked records are captured and saved so that they can be verified later by the auditors.
Tape Drive. The device that controls the movement of the magnetic tape and that reads and writes on the tape.
Tape File Protection Ring. A circular plastic ring that determines when a tape file can be written on. When the ring is inserted on a reel of magnetic tape, data can be written on the tape. If the ring is removed, the data on the tape cannot be overwritten with new information.
Technical Feasibility. The dimension of feasibility concerned with whether a proposed system can be developed given the available technology.
Telecommunications System. An information system that uses data communications technology.
Teleconferencing. The linking of a number of people in different locations electronically or through telecommunications so that they can confer.
Terabyte. One trillion characters of memory.
Terminal. An input/output device for entering or receiving data directly from the computer. Also referred to as cathode ray tube (CRT) or visual display terminal (VDT).
Terrestrial Microwave. A microwave data transmission system that utilizes transmission facilities located on the earth instead of satellites.
Test Data. Data that have been specially developed to test the accuracy and completeness of a computer program. The results from the test data are compared to hand-calculated results to verify that the program operates properly.
Test Data Generator. A program that takes the specifications describing the logic characteristics of the program to be tested and automatically generates a set of test data that can be used to check the logic of the program.
Tests of Controls. A test whose objective is to determine whether control procedures are being followed correctly.
Threats. Potential losses to an organization arising from hazards such as embezzlement, employee carelessness or theft, or poor management decisions.
Throughput. (1) The total amount of useful work performed by a computer system during a given period of time. (2) A measure of production efficiency representing the number of "good" units produced in a given period of time.
Time Card. A document that records the employee's arrival and departure times for each work shift. The time card records the total hours worked by an employee during a pay period.
TIPS. Trillions of instructions per second. A way of measuring CPU speed.
Touch-Sensitive Screens. Sensitized video display screens that allow users to enter data or select menu items by touching their surface with a finger or a special pointer.
Trailer Label. A type of internal label that appears at the end of each file and serves as an indicator that the end of the file has been reached.
Transaction Cycles. A group of related business activities. For example, the set of business activities consisting of sales order entry, shipping, billing, and cash receipts constitutes the revenue cycle. The five major transaction cycles are revenue, expenditure, production, human resource management/payroll, and general ledger and reporting.
Transaction File. A relatively temporary data file containing transaction data that are typically used to update a master file.
Transaction Log. A detailed record of every transaction entered in a system through data entry.
Transaction Processing. A process that begins with capturing transaction data and ends with an informational output.
Transcription Error. An error occurring during data conversion from a manual to an automated environment in which one digit of a number is written incorrectly during the conversion (e.g., a "4" in the tens position transcribed as a "9," which would cause an error of 50 in the value of the number).
Transposition Error. An error that results when the numbers in two adjacent columns are

inadvertently exchanged (for example, 64 is written as 46).

Trap Door. A set of computer instructions that allows a user to bypass the system's normal controls.

Trial Balance. A report listing the balances of all general ledger accounts. It is so named because one of its purposes is to allow the accountant to verify that the total debit balances in various accounts equal the total credit balances in other accounts.

Triggered Exception Report. A preformatted report, generated only when certain conditions exist (e.g., the amount of raw materials on hand falls below the safety stock amount), that brings this information to the attention of a decision maker.

Trojan Horse. A set of unauthorized computer instructions in an authorized and otherwise properly functioning program. It performs some illegal act at a preappointed time or under a predetermined set of conditions.

Tuple. (rhymes with the word couple). A row in a relation. A tuple contains data about a specific occurrence of the type of entity represented by that data base table. For example, each row in the inventory table contains all the pertinent data about a particular inventory item.

Turnaround Document. A document readable by humans that is prepared by the computer as output, sent outside the system, and then returned as input into the computer. An example is a utility bill.

Turnkey System. A system that is delivered to customers ready (theoretically) to be turned on. A turnkey system supplier buys hardware, writes applications software that is tailored both to that equipment and to the specific needs of its customers, and then markets the entire system.

Uninterruptible Power System. An alternative power supply device that protects against the loss of power and fluctuations in the power level.

Universal Product Code (UPC). A machine-readable code that is read by optical scanners. The code consists of a series of bar codes and is printed on most products sold in grocery stores.

Unix. A flexible and widely used operating system for 16-bit machines.

Update Anomaly. A problem that can arise in a poorly designed relational data base. If attributes that are not characteristics of the primary key of a relation are stored in that table, then that data item is stored in many different rows. For example, if customer addresses are stored in the sales invoice table, then the address for a given customer is stored many times (once for each sale). Consequently, if the value of that data item is not changed in every row in which it is stored, inconsistencies in the data base will result.

Updating. The changing of stored data to reflect more recent events (e.g., changing the accounts receivable balance because of a recent sale or collection).

Uploading. The transmission of data to someone else on the network.

User Interface. A component of an expert system that is a program allowing the user to design, create, update, use, and communicate with the expert system.

Users. All the people that interact with the system. Users are the people that record data, manage the system, and control the system's security. Those who use information from the system are end-users.

Utility Programs. A set of prewritten programs that perform a variety of file and data handling tasks (e.g., sorting or merging files) and other housekeeping chores.

Validity Check. An edit test in which an identification number or transaction code is compared to a table of valid identification numbers or codes maintained in computer memory.

Value-Added Network (VAN). A public network that adds value to the data communications process by handling the difficult task of interfacing with the multiple types of hardware and software used by different companies.

Value Chain. The linking of all the primary and support activities in a business. Value is added as a product passes through the chain.

Value of Information. Value of information = benefit − cost.

Value System. The combination of several value chains into one system. A value system includes the value chains of a company, its suppliers, its distributors, and its customers.

Vendor Performance Report. A report that highlights deviations in product quality, prices, and delivery commitments.

Videodisk. A special type of optical disk that can store audio, video, and text data. The disk can be accessed a frame at a time for motionless viewing or can be played like a video tape for moving action and sound.

Video Teleconferencing. A conference in which people in several locations can both see and hear each other.

Virtual Memory (Storage). On-line secondary storage that is used as an extension of primary memory, thus giving the appearance of a larger, virtually unlimited amount of internal memory. Pages of data or program instructions are swapped back and forth between secondary and primary storage as needed.

Visual Display Terminal (VDT). *See* Terminal.

Voiceband Lines. Phone lines designed to accept data transmissions of between 300 and 9600 bits per second. They can be used for transmitting voice or data communications.

Voice Input. A data input unit that recognizes human voices and converts spoken messages into machine-readable input.

Voice Mail (V-Mail). A service that converts voice messages into computer data and stores them so that they can be retrieved later by the person for whom they were intended.

Voice Recognition. A system that understands spoken words and transmits them into a computer at speeds faster than most users can type.

Voice Response Unit. *See* Audio response unit.

Volume Label. A type of internal label that identifies the contents of each separate data recording medium, such as a tape, diskette, or disk pack.

Voucher. A document that summarizes the data relating to a disbursement and represents final authorization of payment.

Voucher Package. The set of documents, consisting of a purchase order, receiving report, and vendor invoice, used to authorize payment to a vendor.

Voucher System. A method for processing accounts payable in which a document called a disbursement voucher is prepared, instead of posting invoices directly to vendor records in the accounts payable subsidiary ledger. The disbursement voucher identifies the vendor, lists the outstanding invoices, and indicates the net amount to be paid after deducting any applicable discounts and allowances. *Contrast with* Nonvoucher system.

WAIS (Wide Area Information Servers). Tools for searching the Internet's huge information libraries.

Walkthroughs. Meetings, attended by those associated with a project, in which a detailed review of systems procedures and/or program logic is carried out in a step-by-step manner.

WATS Line. An acronym for wide area telephone service line, a phone line for which the customer pays both a fixed charge and an additional charge that varies directly with the amount of extra usage.

Web Servers. Large computers on the Internet that are scattered worldwide and contain every imaginable type of data. Each Web server can have thousands of networks and users attached to it.

White-Collar Criminals. Typically, business people who commit fraud. White-collar criminals usually resort to trickery or cunning and their crimes usually involve a violation of trust or confidence.

Wide Area Network (WAN). A telecommunications network that covers a large geographic area anywhere from a few cities to the whole globe. A WAN uses telephone lines, cables, microwaves, or satellites to connect a wide variety of hardware devices in many locations.

Wiretap. The act of listening (eavesdropping) on an unprotected communications line.

Word Processing. A program that facilitates creating, processing, editing, formatting, and printing text data.

World Wide Web. An advanced Internet navigation system that organizes its contents by subject matter.

WORM. Write once, read many. For example, an optical disk can be written on once, but later read many times.

Yield. The percentage of total units produced that are not defective.

Zero-Balance Check. An internal check that requires the balance of the payroll control account to be zero after all entries to it have been made.

References

Chapter 1

Ackoff, R. L. "Management Misinformation Systems." *Management Science* (December 1, 1967): 147–156.

Appleby, Chuck. "Binding Arbitration." *InformationWeek* (December 20/27, 1993):32–34.

Baker, Stephen, and Gary McWilliams. "Now Comes the Corporate Triathlete." *Business Week* (January 31, 1994):71–72.

Cook, Gail Lynn, and Martha M. Eining. "Will Cross Functional Information Systems Work?" *Management Accounting* (February 1993):53–57.

Deloitte Touche Tohmatsu International. *Leading Trends in Information Services.* Information Technology Consulting Services Seventh Annual Survey of North American Chief Information Executives, 1995.

Eisenstodt, Gale. "Information Power." *Forbes* (June 21, 1993):44–45.

Foust, Dean. "Uncle Sam Can't Keep Track of His Trillions." *Business Week* (September 2, 1991):72–73.

Henko, Ronald; James Anderson; and Alison Sprout. "Make Your Office More Productive." *Fortune* (February 25, 1991):72–84.

Keen, Peter G. W., and Michael S. Scott Morton. *Decision Support Systems: An Organizational Perspective.* Reading, MA: Addison-Wesley, 1978.

Mock, Theodore J.; Barry E. Cushing; Gordon B. Davis; Miklos A. Vasarhelyi; Clinton E. White, Jr.; and Joseph W. Wilkinson. "Report of the AAA Committee on Contemporary Approaches to Teaching Accounting Information Systems." *Journal of Information Systems* (Spring 1987):127–156.

Porter, M. E., and V. E. Millar. "How Information Gives You Competitive Advantage." *Harvard Business Review* (July/August 1985):149–160.

Rothfeder, Jeffrey; Jim Bartimo; Lois Therrien; and Richard Brandt. "How Software Is Making Food Sales a Piece of Cake." *Business Week* (July 2, 1990):54–55.

Scrupski, Susan. "Severe Talent Drought Ahead." *Datamation* (May 15, 1995):30.

Stewart, Thomas A. "Welcome to the Revolution." *Fortune* (December 13, 1993):66–77.

Wexler, Joanie M. "Mobile Pen Computing Greases Way to Faster, Cheaper Repairs." *Computerworld* (June 21, 1993):1, 10.

Wreden, Nick. "Sharpening the Corporate Vision." *Beyond Computing* (March/April 1994):29–32.

Zachary, G. Pascal. "Computer Data Overload Limits Productivity Gains." *Wall Street Journal* (November 11, 1991):B1.

Zarowin, Stanley. "The Future of Finance." *Journal of Accountancy* (August 1995):47–49.

Chapter 2

Curley, John. "How a Clerk Built Up a Brokerage Business by Hook or by Crook." *The Wall Street Journal* (February 7, 1985):A1,A22.

Kaplan, Robert S., and David P. Norton. "The Balanced Scorecard—Measures That Drive Performance." *Harvard Business Review* (January–February 1992):71–79.

______. "Putting the Balanced Scoreboard to Work." *Harvard Business Review* (September–October 1993):134–147.

Keys, E. Theodore, Jr. (Editor of Roundtable column). " 'Free' Maintenance Service." *Internal Auditor* (October 1993):74.

______. (Editor of Roundtable column). "Altered Checks." *Internal Auditor* (October 1993):77.

______. (Editor of Roundtable column). "Return to Sender." *Internal Auditor* (June 1995):64.

______. (Editor of Roundtable column). "Budget-Busting Leases." *Internal Auditor* (June 1995):66.

Labrack, Bonnie D. "Small Business Controller." *Management Accounting* (November 1994): 38–41.

Rehnberg, Stephen M. "Keep Your Head Out of the Cockpit." *Management Accounting* (July 1995):34–37.

Chapter 3

Aktas, A. Ziya. *Structured Analysis and Design of Information Systems.* Englewood Cliffs, NJ: Prentice-Hall, 1987.

American National Standard Institute. *Flowchart Symbols and Their Usage in Information Processing.* Publication No. ANSI X3.5. New York: American National Standards Institute, 1970.

DeMarco, Tom. *Structured Analysis and System Specification.* Englewood Cliffs, NJ: Prentice-Hall, 1979.

Faye, David, and Theodore J. Mock. "How to Prepare Better Accounting Systems Flowcharts." *Practical Accountant* (November 1986):106–118.

Kievet, K., and M. Martin. "Systems Analysis Tools—Who's Using Them?" *Journal of Systems Management* (July 1989):26–30.

McMenamin, Stephen M., and John F. Palmer. *Essential Systems Analysis.* Englewood Cliffs, NJ: Yourdon Press, 1984.

Quinn, Juanita C. "Flow Chart Eases Planning Process for Hospitals." *Health Care Strategic Management* (April 1991):16–18.

Viator, Ralph E., and Robert A. Deutsch. "Computers/Technology." *Journal of Accountancy* (December 1992):117–119.

Chapter 4

Ambrosio, Johanna. "UPS 'Dials' Up Fast Data on Deliveries." *Computerworld* (September 14, 1992):79.

Bartholomew, Doug. "B of A's Data Warehouse." *Information-Week* (July 25, 1994):16.

Baum, David. "Au Bon Pain Gains Quick Access to Sales Data." *InfoWorld* (August 10, 1992):46.

Berry, Jonathan; John Verity; Kathleen Kerwin; and Gail DeGeorge. "Database Marketing: A Potent New Tool for Selling." *Business Week* (September 5, 1994):56–62.

Daly, James. "Insurer Sees Future in Imaging Strategy." *Computerworld* (January 6, 1992):41.

Hackathorn, Richard. "Data Warehousing Energizes Your Enterprise." *Datamation* (February 1, 1995):38–45.

Hamilton, Rosemary. "Chase Banks on 'Info' Access." *Computerworld* (January 27, 1992):6.

Levick, Diane. "A New Weapon for Car Insurers: Database Allows Companies to Check Drivers' Records." *New York Newsday* (February 20, 1990): 49.

Luzi, Andrew D., and R. K. McCabe. "Harnessing the Power of Databases." *Journal of Accountancy* (July 1993): 71–75.

Nolan, Richard L. "Computer Databases: The Future Is Now." *Harvard Business Review* (September/October 1973):98–114.

Wilder, Clinton. "Who'd Eat a Blue Squash?" *Information-Week* (January 10, 1994):31–34.

Chapter 5

Andren, Emily. "Scherer Gets System to Gel." *Information-Week* (March 6, 1995):60–62.

Bozman, Jean S. "Coke Plans to Add Life with Relational Data Base Move." *Computerworld* (January 13, 1992):35.

Cushing, Barry E. "On the Feasibility and the Consequences of a Database Approach to Corporate Financial Reporting." *Journal of Information Systems* (Spring 1989):29–52.

DePompa, Barbara. "Objects Drive a New Market." *InformationWeek* (November 7, 1994):48–52.

Eldred, Eric. "Entering the Realm of Complex Data." *Client/Server Today* (May 1994):47–54.

Elliott, Robert K. "Confronting the Future: Choices for the Attest Function." *Accounting Horizons* (September 1994): 106–124.

Garry, Greg. "How the Object-Oriented World Translates into Reality." *Client/Server Today* (May 1994):56–63.

Levick, Diane. "A New Weapon for Car Insurers: Database Allows Companies to Check Drivers' Records." *New York Newsday* (February 20, 1990):49.

"The Relational World of Chris Date." *Interface: Candle's View on IBM's Database World* (Summer 1993):1–5.

Ricciuti, Mike. "Object Databases Find Their Niche." *Datamation* (September 15, 1993):56–58.

Soat, John. "Forging the Future." *InformationWeek* (February 21, 1994):42–50.

The, Lee. "Wedding Bells Sound for Objects and Relational Data." *Datamation* (March 1, 1994):49–52.

Wilson, Linda. "Bank Systems Earn Credit." *InformationWeek* (May 30, 1994):70–72.

Chapter 6

Andros, David P.; J. Owen Cherrington, and Eric L. Denna. "Reengineering Your Accounting, the IBM Way." *Financial Executive* (July/August 1992):28–31.

Byers, C. Randall, and Lysa Beltz. "Financial Data Modeling at Hewlett-Packard." *Journal of Systems Management* (January 1994):28–33.

Chen, Peter. "The Entity Relationship Model—Toward a Unified View of Data." *Transactions on Database Systems* (March 1976):9–36.

Elliott, Robert K. "The Third Wave Breaks on the Shores of Accounting." *Accounting Horizons* (June 1992):61–85.

Hollander, Anita S.; Eric L. Denna; and J. Owen Cherrington. *Accounting, Information Technology, and Business Solutions.* 1st ed. Chicago: Irwin, 1996.

McCarthy, William E. "An Entity–Relationship View of Accounting Models." *The Accounting Review* (October 1979):667–686.

———. "The REA Accounting Model: A Generalized Framework for Accounting Systems in a Shared Data Environment." *The Accounting Review* (July 1982):554–578.

Zarowin, Stanley. "The Future of Finance." *Journal of Accountancy* (August 1995):47–49.

Chapter 7

Alpert, Mark. "Building a Better Bar Code." *Fortune* (June 15, 1992):101.

Anthes, Gary H. "Postal Service Sorts Through Automation." *Computerworld* (October 4, 1993):1, 26.

Boudette, Neal. "Pen PCs Help Utility Trim Costs." *PC Week* (August 10, 1992):19.

Cohen, Eric E. "Reading Between the Lines." *Journal of Accountancy* (August 1994): 59–64.

Coy, Peter. "Big Brother, Pinned to Your Chest." *Business Week* (August 17, 1992):38.

Dalette, Denise, and John Schneidawind. "Computers That 'Hear' Taking Jobs." *USA Today* (March 6–8, 1992): 1A–2A.

Gillooly, Brian. "Why It May Pay to Plug and Play." *InformationWeek* (January 23, 1995): 32–36.

Hof, Robert D. "Intel: Far Beyond the Pentium." *Business Week* (February 20, 1995): 88–90.

Johnson, Maryfran. "Wherever You Go, They Will Follow." *Computerworld* (July 15, 1991):19.

Keller, John J. "Computers Get Powerful 'Hearing' Aids: Improved Methods of Voice Recognition." *Wall Street Journal* (April 7, 1992):B1.

Kirchner, Jake. "GAO Tells a $970,000 Horror Story." *Computerworld* (December 3, 1979):12.

Lazar, Jerry. "The Object Is Productivity." *Information-Week* (January 3, 1994):36–38.

Port, Otis; Neil Gross; Robert Hof; and Gary McWilliams. "Wonder Chips: How They'll Make Computing Power Ultrafast and Ultracheap." *Business Week* (July 4, 1994): 86–92.

Richman, Dan. "Let Your Agent Handle It." *InformationWeek* (April 17, 1995):44–56.

Sadhwani, Arjan T., and Thomas Tyson. "Does Your Firm Need Bar Coding?" *Management Accounting* (April 1990): 45–48.

Saffo, Paul. "Future Tense." *InfoWorld* (December 9, 1991):66.

Schmit, Julie. "The Ticket to Ride: Smart Cards." *USA Today* (January 11, 1994):B1–B2.

"Teaching Computers to Tell a 'G' from a 'C.'" *Business Week* (December 7, 1992):118.

Thyfault, Mary E., and Stephanie Stahl. "The Power of Voice." *InformationWeek* (May 9, 1994):39–46.

Chapter 8

Appleby, Chuck. "Norfolk Southern Speeds Up Service." *InformationWeek* (September 26, 1994):54.

Booker, Ellis. "Sears Selects Compuadd for $53M POS Project." *Computerworld* (January 13, 1992):7.

———. "Pizza Hut: Making It Great with Imaging, EDI." *Computerworld* (January 27, 1992): 67, 72.

Bulkeley, William F. "Technology, Economics, and Ego Conspire to Make Software Difficult to Use." *Wall Street Journal* (May 20, 1991):R7–R8.

Bylinsky, Gene. "Computers That Learn by Doing." *Fortune* (September 6, 1993):96–102.

Courtney, Harley M., and Cheryl L. Flippen. "A Shopper's Guide to Accounting Software." *Journal of Accountancy* (February 1995):37–59.

DeJager, Peter. "Are We Just Plain Lazy?" *Computerworld* (February 21, 1994):85–86.

Ellis, James E. "Roger Schank Wants Your Child's Mind." *Business Week* (July 18, 1994): 74–75.

Elliston, James. "Image Processing: Bright Picture for the Future." *Management Accounting* (August 1991): 23–26.

Fitzgerald, Michael. "Laptops Make Sales Force Shine." *Computerworld* (August 12, 1991):35.

Hunton, James E. "Setting Up a Paperless Office." *Journal of Accountancy* (November 1994): 77–85.

Keefe, Patricia. "Penney Cashes in on Leading Edge." *Computerworld* (June 20, 1988):1, 62–64.

King, Julia. "Buck Bangers." *Computerworld* (December 23, 1991):16.

———. "Users Help Alaska Air Group Soar." *Computerworld* (December 23, 1991/January 2, 1992):16.

Klein, Paula. "Who Manages the Network?" *InformationWeek* (January 17, 1994):38–41.

Korzeniowski, Paul. "Help Desks to the Rescue." *Information Week* (December 19, 1994): 64–73.

McCullar, Robert L. "Improving the Image of Numbers." *Journal of Accountancy* (August 1995):37–40.

Nash, Kim S. "Signing On-Line Yields Productivity Benefits." *Computerworld* (November 18, 1991):29, 37.

Panettieri, Joseph C. "Electronic Forms Distribution: The End of the Paper Chase?" *InformationWeek* (September 13, 1993): 17.

Pepper, Jon C. "Here Comes Multimedia." *InformationWeek* (February 21, 1994):26–34.

Port, Otis. "Computers That Think Are Almost Here." *Business Week* (July 17, 1995): 68–73.

Rifkin, Glenn. "The Future of the Document." *Forbes ASAP* (October 9, 1995):42–60.

Schiff, Jonathan B. "Towards the Paperless Audit." *Internal Auditor* (June 1989):30–35.

Schlender, Brenton R. "The Future of the PC." *Fortune* (August 26, 1991):40–54.

Schwartz, Evan I. "Software Even a CFO Could Love." *Business Week* (November 2, 1992): 132–137.

Schwartz, Evan I., and James B. Treece. "Smart Programs Go to Work." *Business Week* (March 2, 1992):97–105.

Seymour, Jim. "Left Unchecked, Spreadsheets Can Be a What-If Disaster." *PC Week* (August 21, 1984):37.

———. "Selling Imaging to Top Management: A Good Idea for Bad Times." *Beyond Computing* (January/February 1993): 15–16.

Tong, Hoo-Min D., and Amar Gupta. "The Personal Computer." *Scientific American* (September 1982):87–105.

Waller, Thomas C., and Rebecca A. Gallun. "Microcomputer Literacy Requirements in the Accounting Industry." *Journal of Accounting Education* 3 (Fall 1985):31–40.

Weiss, Mitchell Jay. "The Paperless Office." *Journal of Accountancy* (November 1994):73–76.

Wood, Lamont. "Perfect Harmony." *InformationWeek* (May 8, 1995):42–54.

Chapter 9

Anthes, Gary H. "Army Enlists Client/Server." *Computerworld* (March 29, 1993):12.

"At the Pump: A Special Report." *Wall Street Journal* (May 21, 1992):1.

Booker, Ellis. "Motorola to Provide Remote E-Mail." *Computerworld* (November 4, 1991):18.

Borthick, A. Faye, and Harold P. Roth. "Understanding Client/Server Computing." *Management Accounting* (August 1994):36–41.

Caldwell, Bo. "Gearing Up to Integrate Voice and Data." *InfoWorld* (January 13, 1992): S67–S70.

Flynn, Laurie. "Hotels Speed Reservations with PC Network Linking." *InfoWorld* (November 11, 1991):S72.

Jenks, Andrew. "Groupware Fosters Shared Info, Ideas." *USA Today* (October 21, 1991): 10E.

Johnson, Richard A. "The Facts on PC-Based Faxing and Winfax Pro." *New Accountant* (January 1995):18–20.

"May I Take Your Order?" *Computerworld* (October 7, 1991): 29.

O'Leary, Daniel E. "The Internet and Accountants." *AICPA InfoTech Update* (Summer 1994):10–11.

Sager, Ira. "IBM Swings into the On-Line Fast Lane." *Business Week* (December 5, 1994): 100–102.

Stahl, Stephanie. "Hire on One, Get 'Em All." *InformationWeek* (March 20, 1995):120–124.

Verity, John W.; Peter Coy; and Jeffrey Rothfeder. "Special Report: Taming the Wild Network." *Business Week* (October 8, 1990):142–148.

Wallace, Bob. "National Fuel Gas Migrates SCADA Net to LAN Platform." *Network World* (April 15, 1991):24.

Wilder, Clinton. "Codex Goes Paperless with EDI." *Computerworld* (January 13, 1992):6.

———. "The Internet Pioneers." *InformationWeek* (January 9, 1995):38–48.

Chapter 10

Anthes, Gary H. "Planning Spells Results at MCI." *Computerworld* (January 27, 1992):31.

Booker, Ellis. "IS Trailblazing Puts Retailer on Top." *Computerworld* (February 12, 1990): 69, 73.

Bozman, Jean S. "Red Cross Revamp Slowly Takes Shape." *Computerworld* (June 8, 1992):63.

Coy, Peter, and Chuck Hawkins. "The New Realism in Office Systems." *Business Week* (June 15, 1992):128–132.

Hamilton, Rosemary. "Met Life Finds Dividend in Automation System." *Computerworld* (January 6, 1992):41.

Hammer, Michael. "Making the Quantum Leap." *Beyond Computing* (March/April 1992): 10–14.

Laplante, Alice. "For IS, Quality Is 'Job None.'" *Computerworld* (January 6, 1992):57–59.

Nash, Kim S. "Trucking Firm Seeks Faster Dispatching." *Computerworld* (January 2, 1991):33.

Ryan, Alan J. "Banks Assess IS' Worth." *Computerworld* (October 7, 1991):113–116.

Smith, Geoffrey. "The Computer System That Nearly Hospitalized an Insurer." *Business Week* (June 15, 1992):133.

Wilde, Cande. "Staying Aligned: Five Tales." *Computerworld* (May 25, 1992): 78.

Chapter 11

Anthes, Gary H. "Triumph over a Taxing Project." *Computerworld* (November 4, 1991): 65–69.

Appleby, Chuck. "Power Failure: Five Years into a Client-Server Conversion, Pacific Gas & Electric Backs Up and Starts Over." *InformationWeek* (February 21, 1994):12–13.

______. "Agency's Drive to Nowhere." *InformationWeek* (June 13, 1994):72.

Bartholomew, Doug. "Strategic Bungling." *InformationWeek* (October 4, 1993):12–13.

Bartholomew, Doug, and Frank Hayes. "Utility's Bright Idea." *InformationWeek* (March 13, 1995):28.

Bozman, Jean S. "DMV Disaster: California Kills Failed $44M Project." *Computerworld* (May 9, 1994):1, 16.

Caldwell, Bruce, and Doug Bartholomew. "Glitch Zaps Bank Accounts: Chemical ATMs Have Bad Reaction." *InformationWeek* (February 21, 1994):13–14.

Deloitte Touche Tohmatsu International. *Leading Trends in Information Services.* Information Technology Consulting Services Seventh Annual Survey of North American Chief Information Executives, 1995.

DePompa, Barbara. "Waging War on the Applications Backlog." *Beyond Computing* (July/August 1993):40–44.

Dykman, Charlene A., and Ruth Robbins. "Organizational Success Through Effective Systems Analysis." *Journal of Systems Management* (July 1991):6–8.

Gullo, Karen. "Stopping Runaways in Their Tracks." *InformationWeek* (November 13, 1989): 63–70.

Henry, Jacqueline. "Is Your System Ready?" *InformationWeek* (October 17, 1994):38–46.

Kirchner, Jake. "GAO Tells a $970,000 Horror Story." *Computerworld* (December 3, 1979):12.

Lewyn, Mark. "Flying in Place: The FAA's Air-Control Fiasco." *Business Week* (April 26, 1993):87–90.

McPartlin, John P. "$11M System Development Failure: Arizona Begins the Postmortem." *InformationWeek* (September 6, 1993):13.

Marenghi, Catherine. "Nashua Keeps Quality Flame Burning in Customer Service." *Computerworld* (January 6, 1992): 61.

Rigdon, Joan E. "Frequent Glitches in New Software Bug Users." *Wall Street Journal* (January 18, 1995):B1, B5.

Ross, Philip E. "The Day the Software Crashed." *Forbes* (April 25, 1994):142–156.

Rothfeder, Jeffrey. "Using the Law to Rein in Computer Runaways." *Business Week* (April 3, 1989):70–76.

Ryan, Alan J. "D & B Scores Contracts." *Computerworld* (May 13, 1991):29.

______. "Banks Assess IS' Worth." *Computerworld* (October 7, 1991):113–116.

Schneidawind, John. "Getting the Bugs Out." *USA Today* (August 29, 1991):1–2.

Sumner, Mary, and Jerry Sitek. "Are Structured Methods for Systems Analysis and Design Being Used?" *Journal of Systems Management* (June 1986):18–23.

Thyfault, Mary E. "The AT&T Dream Team." *InformationWeek* (March 6, 1995):26–38.

Wreden, Nick. "Build, Buy or Modify?" *Beyond Computing* (January/February 1995): 47–49.

Chapter 12

Appleby, Chuck; John P. McPartlin; and Linda Wilson. "The Human Face of Outsourcing." *InformationWeek* (January 17, 1994):30–34.

Banker, Rajiv D., and Robert J. Kaufmann. "Reuse and Productivity in Integrated Computer-Aided Software Engineering: An Empirical Study." *MIS Quarterly* (September 1991):375–398.

Black, George. "Simplify End-User Computing: Outsource It." *Datamation* (September 15, 1995):67–69.

Caldwell, Bruce. "Xerox Outsources to EDS: A Case of Dollars and Sense. *InformationWeek* (March 28, 1994):15.

______. "Going Against the Grain: USF&G Takes Network Back from Outsourcer." *InformationWeek* (April 11, 1994):15.

______. "Who Needs Programmers?" *InformationWeek* (April 25, 1994):23–30.

______. "Special Counsel." *InformationWeek* (October 31, 1994):40–48.

______. "Farming Out Client-Server." *InformationWeek* (December 12, 1994):46–56.

Caldwell, Bruce; Mary E. Thyfault; and Mike Fillon. "Moving Out." *InformationWeek* (March 14, 1994):12–13.

Coy, Peter. "The New Realism in Office Systems." *Business Week* (June 15, 1992):128–133.

Foxman, Noah. "Succeeding in Outsourcing." *Information Systems Management* (Winter 1994):77–80.

Halper, Mark. "Weather Drives Burpee to Outsourcing." *Computerworld* (October 12, 1992):77, 80.

Halvey, John. "No Longer a Last Resort." *InformationWeek* (August 1, 1994):84.

Hammer, Michael. "Reengineering Work: Don't Automate, Obliterate." *Harvard Business Review* (July/August 1990): 104–112.

———. "Making the Quantum Leap." *Beyond Computing* (March/April 1992):10–14.

Henkoff, Ronald. "Make Your Office More Productive." *Fortune* (February 25, 1991): 72–84.

Kirkpatrick, David. "Why Not Farm Out Your Computing?" *Fortune* (September 23, 1991): 103–112.

Kleinschrod, Walter A. "Outsourcing: Weighing the Issues." *Beyond Computing* (October/November 1992):44–50.

Lee, Louise. "Rent-a-Techs: Hiring Outside Firms to Run Computers Isn't Always a Bargain." *Wall Street Journal* (May 18, 1995):A1, A13.

Margolis, Nell. "Utilities Partner Way to IS Power." *Computerworld* (September 14, 1992):6.

Platenic, Suzanne. "Should I or Shouldn't I?" *Beyond Computing* (Premiere Issue 1992):25–30.

Port, Otis, et al. "The Software Trap: Automate—Or Else." *Business Week* (May 9, 1988): 142–154.

Ricciuti, Mike. "Outsourcing As a Survival Tactic." *Datamation* (April 15, 1994):48–52.

Scrupski, Susan. "Take My PCs, Please." *Datamation* (February 1, 1995):32.

Wilder, Clinton. "80% Satisfied with Outsourcing, Survey Says." *Computerworld* (January 27, 1992):77.

Chapter 13

American Institute of Certified Public Accountants. *Statement on Auditing Standards No. 1–69.* New York: AICPA, 1992.

Carmichael, Douglas R. "The Auditor's New Guide to Errors, Irregularities and Illegal Acts." *Journal of Accountancy* (September 1988):40–48.

Committee of Sponsoring Organizations of the Treadway Commission. *Internal Control—Integrated Framework.* New York: Committee of Sponsoring Organizations of the Treadway Commission, 1992.

Coughlan, John W. "The Fairfax Embezzlement." *Management Accounting* (May 1983):32–39.

Cushing, Barry E. "A Mathematical Approach to the Analysis and Design of Internal Control Systems." *Accounting Review* (January 1974):24–41.

Daly, James. "The 30-Minute Risk Analysis." *Computerworld* (November 29, 1993):68.

Davia, H. R.; P. C. Coggins; J. C. Wideman; and J. T. Kastantin. *Management Accountant's Guide to Fraud Discovery and Control.* New York: Wiley, 1992.

Dumaine, Brian. "Beating Bolder Corporate Crooks." *Fortune* (April 25, 1988):193–202.

Elliott, Robert K., and John J. Willingham. *Management Fraud: Detection and Deterrence.* New York: Petrocelli Books, 1980.

Foreign Corrupt Practices Act of 1977. U.S. Code, 1976 edition, Supplement II, Title 15, Selection 78. Washington, D.C.: U.S. Government Printing Office, 1979.

Goldstein, Leslie M. "Favorite Frauds." *Internal Auditor* (August 1992):35–39.

Hogg, Joseph D. "How Much Does an Error Cost—And How Much Does It Cost to Prevent It?" *Internal Auditor* (August 1992):67–69.

Mautz, Robert K.; Walter G. Kell; Michael W. Maher; Alan G. Merten; Raymond R. Reilly; Dennis G. Severance; and Bernard J. White. *Internal Control in U.S. Corporations: The State of the Art.* New York: Financial Executives Research Foundation, 1980.

Monk, Harold L., Jr., and Kay W. Tatum. "Applying SAS No. 55 in Audits of Small Business." *Journal of Accountancy* (November 1988):40–56.

Thompson, Courtenay. "Fraud Findings." *Internal Auditor* (October 1995):50–52.

Chapter 14

American Institute of Certified Public Accountants. *Statements on Auditing Standards No. 1–69.* New York: AICPA, 1992.

Baker, Richard H. *Computer Security Handbook.* 2nd ed. Blue Ridge Summit, PA: TAB Books, 1991.

Booker, Ellis. "Data Dowsed in Midwest Floods." *Computerworld* (July 19, 1993):6.

Bozman, Jean S. "Quake Shakes IS, Leaves Networks in Disarray." *Computerworld* (January 24, 1994):1, 14.

Caldwell, Bruce, and Doug Bartholomew. "Glitch Zaps Bank Accounts: Chemical ATMs Have Bad Reaction." *InformationWeek* (February 21, 1994):13–14.

Cerullo, Michael J., and Virginia Cerullo. "Microcomputer Controls." *National Public Accountant* (May 1991):28–33.

Cone, Edward. "Taking No Chances." *InformationWeek* (December 12, 1994):30–40.

DePompa, Barbara. "Date with Disaster." *InformationWeek* (May 2, 1994):48–58.

Doedjak, Tina. "Controlling and Auditing Microcomputer Data Security." *EDPACS* (April 1992):4–9.

Forgione, Dana, and Alan Blankley. "Microcomputer Security and Control." *Journal of Accountancy* (June 1990): 83–90.

Gove, Ronald A. "EDI Security." *EDPACS* (December 1990): 1–8.

Groenfeldt, Tom. "The Online Safety Net." *InformationWeek* (January 30, 1995):74–84.

Guldentops, Eric. "Security and Control in Electronic Funds Transfer: The SWIFT Case." *EDPACS* (April 1991):1–11.

Hanson, James V., and Ned C. Hill. "Control and Audit of Electronic Data Interchange." *MIS Quarterly* (December 1989):403–413.

Hoffman, Thomas. "Explosion Spotlights LAN Vulnerability." *Computerworld* (March 15, 1993):67.

Institute of Internal Auditors Research Foundation. *Systems Auditability and Control Report.* Altamonte Springs, FL: Institute of Internal Auditors Research Foundation, 1991.

Keeton, Laura E. "In the Wake of Bombing, One Business Rises from Its Own Ashes." *Wall Street Journal* (April 26, 1995):A1, A9.

Microcomputer Security. New York: American Institute of Certified Public Accountants (Information Technology Division), 1994.

Murphy, Michael A., and Xenia Ley Parker. *Handbook of EDP Auditing.* 2nd ed. Boston, MA: Warren, Gorham & Lamont, 1989.

Norris, Daniel M., and Elaine Wapples. "Control of Electronic Data Interchange Systems." *Journal of Systems Management* (March 1989):21–25.

Oster, Patrick. "A Better Passport: The Human Hand." *Business Week* (May 2, 1994): 132.

Panettieri, Joseph, and Chuck Appleby. "Survival of the Fittest." *InformationWeek* (January 10, 1994):22–30.

Parker, Robert. "Access Control Software: What It Will and Will Not Do." *EDPACS* (February 1991):1–8.

Phillips, Mark. "Planning Speeds Bank's Recovery from Fire." *Disaster Recovery Journal* (January/February/March 1992):56–58.

Rogers, Michael. "A Data Survival Guide." *Disaster Recovery Journal* (April/May/June 1992): 14–16.

Ross, Philip E. "I Can Read Your Face." *Forbes* (December 19, 1994):304–305.

Storkman, Wayne D. "Before Disaster Strikes: 12 Steps to Minimize Computer Losses." *Technology Alert.* American Institute of Certified Public Accountants (July 1994).

Vahtera, Pauli. "Electronic Data Interchange: The Auditor's Slant." *EDPACS* (November 1991):1–14.

Verity, John W., and Rob Hof. "Bullet-Proofing the Net." *Business Week* (November 13, 1995):98–99.

Wilder, Clinton; Bruce Caldwell; Joseph C. Panettieri; and Marianne Kolbasuk McGee. "Hackers' Break-In at General Electric Raises Questions About the Net's Security." *InformationWeek* (December 12, 1994):13–14.

Wilder, Clinton; Mitch Wagner; and Jason Levitt. "Satan's Surprise." *InformationWeek* (April 24, 1995): 22.

Wright, Benjamin. "Controlling EDI." *Management Accounting* (August 1991):46–49.

Chapter 15

Albrecht, W. Steve; Marshall B. Romney; et al. *How to Detect and Prevent Business Fraud.* Englewood Cliffs, NJ: Prentice-Hall, 1982.

Albrecht, W. Steve; Marshall B. Romney; and Keith Howe. *Deterring Fraud: The Internal Auditor's Perspective.* Altamonte Springs, FL: Institute of Internal Auditors, 1984.

Alexander, Michael. "Prison Term for First U.S. Hacker-Law Convict." *Computerworld* (February 29, 1989):1, 12.

———. "Hacker Stereotypes Changing." *Computerworld* (April 3, 1989):101.

———. "Strong Scruples Can Curb Computer Crime." *Computerworld* (April 3, 1989):100.

———. "Biometric System Use Widening." *Computerworld* (January 8, 1990):16.

———. "Computer Crime: Ugly Secret for Business." *Computerworld* (March 12, 1990):1, 104.

Allen, Brandt. "Embezzler's Guide to the Computer." *Harvard Business Review* (July/August 1975):79–89.

———. "The Biggest Computer Frauds: Lessons for CPAs." *Journal of Accountancy* (May 1977):52–62.

Bloombecker, Buck. "Computer Ethics for Cynics." *Computerworld* (February 29, 1988): 17–18.

———. *Spectacular Computer Crimes.* Homewood, IL: Dow-Jones-Irwin, 1990.

———. "My Three Computer Criminological Sins." *Communications of the ACM* 11 (November 1994):15–16.

Booker, Ellis. "Retinal Scanners Eye-Dentify Inmates." *Computerworld* (March 23, 1992): 28.

Bozman, Jean S. "Bell Tolls for the Shadow Hawk." *Computerworld* (August 15, 1988):104.

———. "Airline Hurt by Faulty Fare Estimation." *Computerworld* (September 19, 1988):2.

Burrough, Bryan. "The Embezzler David L. Miller Stole from His Employers and Isn't in Prison." *Wall Street Journal* (September 19, 1986):1.

Churbuck, David. "Desktop Forgery." *Forbes* (November 27, 1989):246–254.

Cole, Patrick. "Are ATMs Easy Targets for Crooks?" *Business Week* (March 6, 1989):30.

Davis, Fred. "Could the Repo Man Grab Your Invaluable Software?" *PC Week* (November 12, 1990):266.

Elliot, Lance B. "AI Crime Busters." *AI Expert* (January 1992):11.

Enyart, Bob. "Software Security System Thwarts Attack on Data." *PC Week* (April 10, 1989):37–38.

Finch, Peter. "Confessions of a Compulsive High-Roller." *Business Week* (July 29, 1991): 78–79.

Gerber, Barry. "Sometimes 'Abort, Retry' Means 'Network Virus.'" *PC Week* (April 2, 1990):57.

Goldberg, Jeff. "Computerized Breaking and Entering." *OMNI* (September 1990):18.

Hafner, K. M. "Is Your Computer Secure?" *Business Week* (August 1, 1988):65–72.

Hafner, Katie, and John Markoff. *Cyberpunk.* New York: Simon and Schuster, 1991.

Hoffer, Jeffrey A., and Detmar A. Straub, Jr. "The 9 to 5 Underground: Are You Policing Computer Crimes?" *Sloan Management Review* (Summer 1989):35–43.

Honon, Patrick. "Avoiding Virus Hysteria." *Personal Computing* (May 1989):85.

Information Protection Review 2(1) Deloitte & Touche, 1–6.

Keefe, Patricia. "Doing Away with Hard Disks." *Computerworld* (March 12, 1990):39.

McAfee, John. "The Virus Cure." *Datamation* (February 15, 1989):30–31.

Mason, Janet. "Crackdown on Software Pirates." *Computerworld* (February 5, 1990): 107–115.

Menkus, Belden. "Eight Factors Contributing to Computer Fraud." *Internal Auditor* (October 1990):71–74.

Romney, Marshall B.; David Cherrington; and W. Steve Albrecht. "Red-Flagging the White-Collar Criminal." *Management Accounting* (March 1980):51–57.

———. "Auditors and the Detection of Fraud." *Journal of Accountancy* (May 1980): 63–69.

———. "The Role of Management in Reducing Fraud." *Financial Executive* (March 1981):28–34.

Russell, Harold F. *Foozles and Frauds.* Altamonte Springs, FL: Institute of Internal Auditors, 1977.

Savage, J. A. "Computer Time Bomb Defused: Felon Nailed." *Computerworld* (September 26, 1988):2.

"University of Oregon Settles Suit Brought by Software Publishers." *Wall Street Journal* (August 23, 1991):B2.

Wells, J. T. "Six Common Myths About Fraud." *Journal of Accountancy* (February 1990): 82–88.

Whiteside, Thomas. *Computer Capers.* New York: Crowell, 1978.

Chapter 16

American Institute of Certified Public Accountants. *Computer-Assisted Audit Techniques.* New York: AICPA, 1979.

———. *Audit and Control Considerations in an On-Line Environment.* New York: AICPA, 1983.

———. *Statements on Auditing Standards No. 1–69.* New York: AICPA, 1992.

Arens, Alvin A., and James K. Loebbecke. *Auditing: An Integrated Approach.* 6th ed. Englewood Cliffs, NJ: Prentice-Hall, 1994.

Babcock, Charles. "Software Development: A Glimpse Ahead." *Computerworld* (June 20, 1994):6.

Brown, Carol E., and David S. Murphy. "The Use of Auditing Expert Systems in Public Accounting." *Journal of Information Systems* (Fall 1990): 63–72.

Champlain, Jack J. "Demystifying Computer Systems Auditing." *Internal Auditor* (December 1995):28–33.

Chapman, Christy. "Just Wired About Software." *Internal Auditor* (August 1995):24–36.

Coderre, Dave, and Jim Kaplan. "Computers and Auditing: Pulling It All Together."

Internal Auditor (June 1995): 20–22.

Committee on Basic Auditing Concepts. *A Statement of Basic Auditing Concepts.* Sarasota, FL: American Accounting Association, 1973.

Cunninghame, Don. "Using the Application Charge Control Audit as a Management Control." *EDPACS* (September 1992):1–7.

Doediak, Tina. "Controlling and Auditing Microcomputer Data Security." *EDPACS* (April 1992):4–9.

Elliott, Robert K. "The Future of Audits." *Journal of Accountancy* (September 1994):74–82.

Flesher, Dale L., and Roberto De Magalhaes. "Electronic Workpapers." *Internal Auditor* (August 1995):38–43.

Hanson, James V., and Ned C. Hill. "Control and Audit of Electronic Data Interchange." *MIS Quarterly* (December 1989):403–413.

Institute of Internal Auditors Research Foundation. *Systems Auditability and Control Report.* Altamonte Springs, FL: Institute of Internal Auditors Research Foundation, 1991.

Khandeker, Jayawant G., and Maria L. Langer. "Personal Computers: An Audit Perspective." *Internal Auditor* (October 1990):55–61.

Lamond, Bruce J. "An Auditing Approach to Disaster Recovery." *Internal Auditor* (October 1990):33–48.

Leinicke, Linda Marie; W. Max Rexroad; and Jon D. Ward. "Computer Fraud Auditing: It Works." *Internal Auditor* (August 1990):26–33.

Lovata, Linda M. "The Utilization of Generalized Audit Software." *Auditing: A Journal of Practice & Theory* (Fall 1988): 72–86.

Murphy, Michael A., and Xenia Ley Parker. *Handbook of EDP Auditing.* 2nd ed. Boston, MA: Warren, Gorham & Lamont, 1989.

Robertson, Jack C. *Auditing.* 8th ed. Homewood, IL: BPI Irwin, 1996.

Sriram, Ram S., and Glenn E. Sumners. "Understanding Concurrent Audit Techniques." *EDPACS* (July 1992):1–8.

Vahtera, Pauli. "Electronic Data Interchange: The Auditor's Slant." *EDPACS* (November 1991):1–14.

Vasarhelyi, Miklos A., and Fern B. Halper. "The Continuous Audit of Online Systems." *Auditing: A Journal of Practice & Theory* (Spring 1991): 110–125.

———. *EDP Auditing: Conceptual Foundations and Practice.* 2nd ed. New York: McGraw-Hill, 1988.

Zarowin, Stanley. "The Future of Finance." *Journal of Accountancy* (August 1995):47–49.

Chapter 17

Askelson, Kenneth. D. "Automatic Identification Technologies." *AICPA InfoTech Update* (Summer 1994):7–9.

Berry, Jonathan; Kathleen Kerwin; and Gail DeGeorge. "Database Marketing: A Potent New Tool for Selling." *Business Week* (September 5, 1994):56–62.

Bigness, Jon. "In Today's Economy, There Is Big Money to Be Made in Logistics." *The Wall Street Journal* (September 6, 1995):A1, A9.

DeJong, Jennifer. "Smart Marketing." *Computerworld* (February 7, 1994):113–118.

Freedman, David H. "Why Big Retailers Love Little Scotch Maid." *Forbes ASAP* (February 28, 1994):106–109.

Gelinas, Ulric J., Jr., and Allan E. Oram. *Accounting Information Systems.* 3d ed. Cincinnati, OH: South-Western College Publishing, 1996.

Halper, Mark. "JC Penney Warehouses Do Away with Paper." *Computerworld* (September 12, 1994):64.

Harrar, George. "Levi's: Cool Brand, Lousy Distribution, IT to the Rescue." *Forbes ASAP* (February 28, 1994):140–142.

Heidkamp, Martha M. "Reaping the Benefits of Financial EDI." *Management Accounting* (May 1991):39–43.

Hollander, Anita S.; Eric L. Denna; and J. Owen Cherrington. *Accounting, Information Technology, and Business Solutions.* 1st ed. Chicago: Irwin, 1996.

Jenkins, Avery. "Get Connected." *Computerworld Premier 100* (September 19, 1994):26–32.

King, Julia. "Big Brother Mans Help Desk." *Computerworld* (October 17, 1994):1, 28.

McCartney, Scott. "Companies Go On-Line to Chat, Spy and Rebut." *The Wall Street Journal* (September 15, 1994):B1, B6.

Maglitta, Joseph E. "Best Face Forward." *Computerworld* (May 16, 1994):100–107.

Montgomery, M. R. "The Genie of Jeans." *The Boston Globe* (January 4, 1995):52–58.

Seideman, Tony. "Who Needs Managers?" *Sales & Marketing Management—Part 2* (June 1994):14–17.

———. "On the Cutting Edge." *Sales & Marketing Management—Part 2* (June 1994): 18–23.

Trumfio, Ginger. "The Case for E-Mail." *Sales & Marketing Management* (July 1994):94–98.

———. "The Future Is Now." *Sales & Marketing Management* (November 1994):74–80.

Verity, John W. "The Gold Mine of Data in Customer Service." *Business Week* (March 21, 1994):113–114.

______. "Hello Direct, Good-Bye Mail Order?" *Business Week* (November 14, 1994):86.

Wilkinson, Joseph W. *Accounting Information Systems: Essential Concepts and Applications.* 2d ed. New York: John Wiley & Sons, 1993.

Wilson, Linda. "One Leg At a Time." *InformationWeek* (April 18, 1994):52.

Chapter 18

Askelson, Kenneth D. "Automatic Identification Technologies." *AICPA InfoTech Update* (Summer 1994):7–9.

Brewer, Peter C., and Tina Y. Mills. "ISO 9000 Standards: An Emerging CPA Service Area." *Journal of Accountancy* (February 1994):63–67.

Churbuck, David C. "Don't Leave Headquarters Without It." *Forbes* (December 20, 1993):242–243.

Cohen, Eric E. "Reading Between the Lines." *Journal of Accountancy* (August 1994): 59–64.

Gelinas, Ulric J., Jr., and Allan E. Oram. *Accounting Information Systems.* 3d ed. Cincinnati, OH: South-Western College Publishing, 1996.

Halper, Mark. "JC Penney Warehouses Do Away with Paper." *Computerworld* (September 12, 1994):64.

Hoffman, Thomas. "Sea-Land Finds Gateway to Excellence Through Automation." *Computerworld* (August 8, 1994):39–42.

Hollander, Anita S.; Eric L. Denna; and J. Owen Cherrington. *Accounting, Information Technology, and Business Solutions.* 1st ed. Chicago: Irwin, 1996.

Hunton, James E. "Setting Up a Paperless Office." *Journal of Accountancy* (November 1994):77–85.

Kalstrom, David J. "Slaying the Paper Dragon." *Financial Executive* (September/October 1993):37–39.

Mize, B. Ray, Jr. "Vendor Audits." *The CPA Journal* (February 1994):18–22.

Palmer, Richard J. "Reengineering Payables at ITT Automotive." *Management Accounting* (July 1994):38–42.

Pavlinko, Jean L. "Paperless Payables at Lord." *Management Accounting* (July 1993): 32–34.

Vollmann, Thomas E.; William L. Berry; and D. Clay Whybark. *Manufacturing Planning and Control Systems.* 3d ed. Homewood, IL: Irwin, 1992:191–193.

Wilder, Clinton. "A Penney Saved." *InformationWeek* (December 20/27, 1993):24–30.

Wilkinson, Joseph W. *Accounting Information Systems: Essential Concepts and Applications.* 2d ed. New York: John Wiley & Sons, 1993.

Chapter 19

Brinkman, Stephen L., and Mark A. Appelbaum. "The Quality Cost Report: It's Alive and Well at Gilroy Foods." *Management Accounting* (September 1994):61–65.

Cheatham, Carole. "Measuring and Improving Throughput." *Journal of Accountancy* (March 1990):89–91.

Gammell, Frances, and C. J. McNair. "Jumping the Growth Threshold Through Activity-Based Cost Management." *Management Accounting* (September 1994):37–46.

Garner, Rochelle. "Open Insecurities." *Computerworld* (September 12, 1994):121–122.

Gelinas, Ulric J., Jr., and Allan E. Oram. *Accounting Information Systems.* 3d ed. Cincinnati, OH: South-Western College Publishing, 1996.

Harrar, George. "Levi's: Cool Brand, Lousy Distribution, IT to the Rescue." *Forbes ASAP* (February 28, 1994):140–142.

Hollander, Anita S.; Eric L. Denna; and J. Owen Cherrington. *Accounting, Information Technology, and Business Solutions.* 1st ed. Chicago: Irwin, 1996.

Horngren, Charles T.; George Foster; and Srikant M. Datar. *Cost Accounting.* 8th ed. Englewood Cliffs, NJ: Prentice-Hall, 1994.

Keegan, Daniel P., and Robert G. Eiler. "Let's Reengineer Cost Accounting." *Management Accounting* (August 1994): 26–31.

LaPlante, Alice. "New Software = Faster Factories." *Forbes ASAP*:36–41.

Luternow, Bonnie A. "Serving Two Masters with IT." *Financial Executive* (September/October 1994): 39–42.

Marion, Larry. "Product Data Management." *Beyond Computing* (September/October 1994):55–56.

Montgomery, M. R. "The Genie of Jeans." *The Boston Globe* (January 4, 1995):52–58.

"Netscape Awards Bounties to Successful Bug Hunters." *Wall Street Journal* (December 11, 1995):C2.

Turk, William T. "Management Accounting Revitalized: The Harley-Davidson Experience." In *Readings in Management Accounting* (edited by S. Mark

Young). Englewood Cliffs, NJ: Prentice-Hall, 1995, 135–144.

Wilkinson, Joseph W. *Accounting Information Systems: Essential Concepts and Applications.* 2d ed. New York: John Wiley & Sons, 1993.

Wilson, Linda. "Two Outs, Bottom of the Ninth . . . ." *InformationWeek* (October 4, 1993):30–34.

Chapter 20

Flynn, Gillian. "Non-Sales Staffs Respond to Incentives." *Personnel Journal* (July 1994): 33–38.

Geer, Carolyn T. "For a New Job, Press #1." *Forbes* (August 15, 1994):118–119.

Gelinas, Ulric J., Jr., and Allan E. Oram. *Accounting Information Systems.* 3d ed. Cincinnati, OH: South-Western College Publishing, 1996.

Gleckman, Howard; Sandra Atchison; Tim Smart; and John A. Bryne. "Bonus Pay: Buzzword or Bonanza?" *Business Week* (November 14, 1994): 62–64.

Greengard, Samuel. "New Technology Is HR's Route to Reengineering." *Personnel Journal* (July 1994):32c–32o.

Hollander, Anita S.; Eric L. Denna; and J. Owen Cherrington. *Accounting, Information Technology, and Business Solutions.* 1st ed. Chicago: Irwin, 1996.

Imberman, Woodruff. "Is Gainsharing the Wave of the Future?" *Management Accounting* (November 1995):35–39.

Meadows, Jim L. "AT&T Workers Form an Internal Contingent Labor Pool." *Personnel Journal* (December 1994):90.

Patterson, Gregory A. "Distressed Shoppers, Disaffected Workers Prompt Stores to Alter Sales Commissions." *Wall Street Journal* (July 1, 1992):B1, B6.

Stewart, Thomas A. "Your Company's Most Valuable Asset: Intellectual Capital." *Fortune* (October 3, 1994): 68–74.

———. "Taking on the Last Bureaucracy." *Fortune* (January 15, 1996):105–108.

Thornburg, Linda. "Accounting for Knowledge." *HRMagazine* (October 1994):50–56.

Wilkinson, Joseph W. *Accounting Information Systems: Essential Concepts and Applications.* 2d ed. New York: John Wiley & Sons, 1993.

Yin, Tung. "Sears Is Accused of Billing Fraud at Auto Centers." *Wall Street Journal* (June 12, 1992):B1, B5.

Chapter 21

AICPA. *Improving Business Reporting—A Customer Focus Report of the AICPA Special Committee on Financial Reporting,* 1994.

Allen, Kenneth A. "The One-Day Close." *Management Accounting* (November 1995):18.

Andros, David P., J. Owen Cherrington, and Eric L. Denna. "Reengineering Your Accounting, the IBM Way." *Financial Executive* (July/August 1992):28–31.

Brachel, John von. "Interpreting Financial Statements: How One Firm Uses the Language of Graphics." *Journal of Accountancy* (April 1995): 42–43.

Flaherty, Daniel J., Raymond A. Zimmerman, and Mary Ann Murray. "Benchmarking Against the Best." *Journal of Accountancy* (July 1995):85–88.

Gelinas, Ulric J., Jr., and Allan E. Oram. *Accounting Information Systems.* 3d ed. Cincinnati, OH: South-Western College Publishing, 1996.

Heid, Jim. "Graphs That Work." *Macworld* (February 1994): 155–156.

Kabak, Irwin, and Thomas J. Beam. "Two-Dimensional Accounting: A New Management Demand." *Industrial Management* (November/December 1990):25–29.

Karon, Paul. "Hallmark Welcomes Change in Handling Finances." *InfoWorld* (December 19, 1994):6.

Lee, John Y. "How to Make Financial and Nonfinancial Data Add Up." *Journal of Accountancy* (September 1992):62–66.

Ramanathan, Kavasseri V., and Douglas S. Schaffer. "How Am I Doing?" *Journal of Accountancy* (May 1995):79–82.

Shank, John K. "How Safe Is Your Job?" *Journal of Accountancy* (October 1993):72–80.

Steinbart, Paul John. "The Auditor's Responsibility for the Accuracy of Graphs in Annual Reports: Some Evidence on the Need for Additional Guidance." *Accounting Horizons* (September 1989):60–70.

Wallace, Peggy. "Microsoft's Finance Department Gets Up to Speed." *InfoWorld* (June 5, 1995):58.

Wilkinson, Joseph W. *Accounting Information Systems: Essential Concepts and Applications.* 2d ed. New York: John Wiley & Sons, 1993.

Zarowin, Stanley. "Motorola's Financial Closings: 12 'Nonevents' a Year." *Journal of Accountancy* (November 1995):59–63.

Index